This Day In American History

by Ernie Gross

Neal-Schuman Publishers, Inc.
New York London

Published by Neal-Schuman Publishers, Inc.
23 Leonard Street
New York, NY 10013

Printed and bound in the United States of America

ISBN 1-55570-046-2

CONTENTS

Preface v

Listings
- January 1
- February 42
- March 75
- April 110
- May 144
- June 180
- July 213
- August 246
- September 277
- October 310
- November 343
- December 374

Bibliography 406

Index 407

PREFACE

This Day in American History offers the reader unique access to the people and events that shaped our nation. Its 11,000 entries are organized sequentially for each day and then in chapters by month, forming a complete timeline of America's development. Each day's listings begin with the earliest date available—frequently from precolonial times—and conclude with events that took place even as the book went to press. The extensive index lists names and events to provide full access to the entries.

In selecting persons for inclusion, I considered their impact on American life through their positions or actions—U.S. presidents and vice presidents and their wives; Supreme Court justices; key legislators; inventors and pioneers; military and business leaders; scientists and doctors; artists, sports figures, and entertainment personalities. I also attempted to include a broad spectrum of events—scientific inventions and geographical discoveries, landmark government actions, and manmade and natural disasters.

This Day in American History had its beginnings years ago when, as a young radio newswriter, I would seek a topical historical item to use in a newscast. First I would contact the wire services, which frequently provided a feature on the historical events of the day, although often as not their material proved unsatisfactory—overly terse and incomplete. My next step was consulting available almanacs, only to discover that these sources did not fulfill my requirements, either. The items in some almanacs were so skimpy that there wasn't enough data to properly identify the subjects. They either assumed prior knowledge or required digging deeper for complete coverage. At the other extreme were reference works with encyclopedic entries whose length and complexity required time-consuming sifting of the data. In between were almanacs focusing on holidays or on artificial observances such as "Mother-in-Law Day" or "Apple Week."

Moreover, the categories of people listed were narrow, largely military or government officials, along with some educators, clergy, and industrialists. Notably missing were most sports and entertainment personalities, despite their impact on and interest for the American people. In short, there was no single source one could turn to for a good overview of the events of a given day in U.S. history. Nor has there been, until now.

It's my hope that *This Day in American History* will help not only the harried newswriter, but also other print and electronic media professionals, speechwriters, planners of special events, teachers and students, and the general reader who is simply curious about what happened on a particular day in American history.

Ernie Gross

JANUARY 1

1673 First regular mail service was inaugurated on a monthly basis between Boston and New York.

1705 Charles Chauncy, Congregational clergymen, was born in Boston; served Boston's First Church for 60 years; opposed George Whitefield's revival movement, efforts of British bishops to impose Church of England doctrine, practices on the Colonies (died 1787).

1735 First American fire insurance company (The Friendly Society for the Mutual Insurance of Houses Against Fire) began receiving subscriptions in Charleston, S.C.; lasted five years, fire destroyed half the city and company.

1735 Paul Revere, silversmith and express rider, was born in Boston; best remembered as one of trio which alerted New England countryside to the British attack in 1775; designed, printed first Continental money; designed, engraved first official seal of the Colonies, Massachusetts state seal; discovered process for rolling sheet copper (died 1818).

1745 Anthony Wayne, Revolutionary officer, was born in Waynesboro, Pa.; known as "Mad Anthony," served in numerous campaigns (Germantown, Stony Point, Yorktown); represented Georgia in the House (1791-92); led American troops to victory over Indiana at Fallen Timbers, Ohio (near present Toledo) (1794) (died 1796).

1750 Frederick A. Muhlenberg, colonial legislator, was born in Trappe, Pa.; represented Pennsylvania in the House, serving as the first Speaker (1789-91, 1793-95) (died 1801).

1752 Gregorian calendar officially adopted by Great Britain and her colonies.

1752 Betsy Ross, noted flagmaker, was born in Philadelphia; made first American flag, reputedly at the request of George Washington, Robert Morris, and her brother-in-law, George Ross (died 1836).

1772 Thomas Jefferson married Martha Wayles Skelton in Williamsburg, Va.

1776 George Washington announced formation of the Colonial Army and, on Prospect Hill in Cambridge, Mass., raised for first time the flag of the united colonies (13 alternate red and white stripes and crosses of St. Andrew and St. George).

1776 Norfolk, Va. was burned on orders of Governor Dunmore, who earlier had the city evacuated; colonists had refused demands for provisions and the city was set afire, burning for 50 hours.

1779 The Universalist Church of America was organized in Gloucester, Mass.

1780 Settlers led by James Robertson arrived at the site of Nashville.

1781 Pennsylvania troops mutinied at Morristown, N.J., killing several officers; started for Philadelphia to place grievances before Continental Congress; grievances were resolved before they arrived in Philadelphia.

1782 Juan Crespi, Spanish Catholic missionary and explorer, died at 61; he was co-discoverer of San Francisco Bay.

1783 The public debt of the United States was reported at $42 million.

1785 Publication of the *Falmouth Gazette and Weekly Advertiser*, the first newspaper in Maine, was begun by Benjamin Titcomb and Thomas B. Wait.

1788 Etienne Cabet, socialist, was born in Dijon, France; created the utopian settlement of Icarians in Nauvoo, Ill., settlement's president (1849-56) (died 1856).

1800 Constantine Hering, homeopathic physician, was born in Oschatz, Germany; organized first homeopathic school (North American Academy of Homeopathic Healing Art, Philadelphia 1836), the first such medical college (1848), Hahnemann Medical College (1867) (died 1880).

1808 A federal law went into effect which provided a penalty of forfeiture of a ship and its cargo if the vessel was involved in the slave trade; disposition of seized slaves left to state where seizure occurred; however, illicit trade continued with about 250,000 slaves imported between 1808 and 1861.

1810 Charles Ellet, civil engineer, was born in Penn's Manor, Pa.; built various suspension bridges — Schuylkill River, near Philadelphia (1842), the first important American suspension structure, and the world's longest (1900 ft.) over the Ohio, near Wheeling (died 1862).

1813 John Kling, physician, was born in New York City; a founder of eclectic school of medicine; introduced into general use podophyllin, hydrastic, and sanguinaria (died 1893).

1817 Second Bank of the United States began operations as depository for federal funds, with an authorized capitalization of $35 million.

1818 Restored White House was opened for a public reception; had been closed since the British burned it in 1814.

1824 James K. Polk and Sarah Childress were married in Murfreesboro, Tenn.

1827 William C. Cabell, Confederate general, was born in Danville, Va.; active in trans-Mississippi area (died 1911).

1831 William Lloyd Garrison began publication of *The Liberator* in Boston; continued until Dec. 29, 1865; an anti-slavery leader, he set the tone in the first issue, stating: "I am in earnest, I will not equivocate, I will not excuse, I will not retreat a single inch, and I will be heard!"

1833 The *Knickerbocker Magazine* began publication in New York City.

1842 The first illustrated weekly magazine (*Brother Jonathan, a Weekly Compend of Belles Lettres and the Fine Arts, Standard Literature and General Intelligence*) was issued by Benjamin H. Day and Nathaniel Parker Willis.

1843 Thomas J. Foster, educator, was born in Pottsville, Pa.; founder, International Correspondence Schools (1891), helping educate about 1 million persons (died 1936).

1848 Willis S. Paine, lawyer and banker, was born in Rochester, N.Y.; compiled, revised, New York State banking laws; New York banking superintendent (1885-89); president, State Trust Co. (1889-1927) (died 1927).

1855 George H. Bissell and Jonathan J. Eveleth, New York City law partners, formed the first American oil company (Pennsylvania Rock Oil Co.), discovered eight products extractable from oil coming from a spring in Venago County, Pa.

1856 The use of adhesive postage stamps, available since 1847, was made mandatory by Congress.

1857 Tim(othy J.) Keefe, baseball pitcher who won 344 games in 14 years, was born in Cambridge, Mass.; named to Baseball Hall of Fame (died 1933).

1858 Albert Gleaves, World War I naval officer, was born in Nashville; conducted convoy operations in the Atlantic (1917-19); commanded Asiatic station (1920-21) (died 1937).

1859 Michael J. Owens, inventor and manufacturer, was born in Mason County, W.Va.; invented bottle-blowing machine; an organizer and officer of Libby-Owens Glass Co. (1916) (died 1923).

1860 The first state insurance department went into operation in New York; William Barnes was the first superintendent.

1860 Clarence R. Edwards, Army officer, was born in Cleveland; commander, American troops, Canal Zone (1915-17); organized, commanded 26th Division in France (1917-18) (died 1931).

1861 John L. Long, author, was born in Hanover, Pa.; best known for *Madame Butterfly*, which became a play and opera (died 1927).

1862 Federal income tax went into effect, imposing a 3% tax on income over $800; lasted until 1872.

1862 James M. Mason and John Sidell, Confederate diplomats, were released and put aboard a British sloop, *Rinaldo*, at Provincetown, Mass.; sailed to Halifax.

1863 Emancipation Proclamation, which was announced by President Lincoln on Sept. 22, 1862, went into effect; provided that all slaves in areas still in rebellion were "Then, thenceforward, and forever free."

1863 The Homestead Act went into effect, providing that anyone over 21 could get title to 160 acres of public land by living on it for five years, making certain improvements, and paying fees of approximately $18; first homesteader was Daniel Freeman, a Union soldier who staked out a claim near Beatrice, Neb.

1864 Alfred Stieglitz, photographer and editor, was born in Hoboken, N.J.; often called the father of modern photography (died 1946).

1867 Lew(is M.) Fields, entertainer, was born in New York City; half of the Weber & Fields comedy team; managed several theatres (died 1914).

1874 Frank (William F.) Knox, publisher and public official, was born in Boston; publisher, *Chicago Daily News* (1931-40); Republican vice presidential candidate (1936); Secretary of the Navy (1940-44) (died 1944).

1876 The Philadelphia Mummers Parade officially got under way; similar parades had been held sporadically for 100 years.

1878 Edwin Franko Goldman, bandmaster and composer, was born in Louisville; remembered for 38 years of summer band concerts in New York's Central Park (died 1956).

1879 William Fox, pioneer movie executive, was born in Tulchva, Hungary; built multimillion dollar empire, virtually controlling production and distribution of silent film era (died 1952).

1879 Knights of Labor, predecessor of American Federation of Labor, was organized.

1880 Thomas A. Edison demonstrated the first experimental overhead line for lighting incandescent lights.

1883 William J. Donovan, attorney and public official, was born in Buffalo; World War I Congressional Medal of Honor winner, earning name of Wild Bill; organized, directed, Office of Strategic Services

(OSS), predecessor of Central Intelligence Agency (1942-45) (died 1959).

1883 Roy W. Howard, editor and publisher, was born in Gano, Ohio; served with United Press, NEA (Newspaper Enterprise Association, and Scripps-Howard chain (1906-64) as board chairman (1921-36), president (1936-52); editor, president *New York World Telegram* (1931-62) (died 1964).

1886 The first Tournament of Roses parade occurred in Pasadena, Cal., staged by the Valley Hunt Club.

1887 Harry Scherman, Book of the Month Club founder, born in Montreal (died 1969).

1888 John C. Garand, firearms inventor, was born in St. Remy, Canada; ordnance engineer, U.S. Armory, Springfield, Mass. (from 1919); developed 30-caliber MI semiautomatic rifle, the basic World War II shoulder weapon, in 1930 (died 1974).

1892 Ellis Island in New York Harbor became the receiving station for immigrants; operated for 62 years, processing about 20 million persons.

1895 J(ohn) Edgar Hoover, law enforcement officer, was born in Washington, D.C.; headed Federal Bureau of Investigation (FBI) (1924-72) (died 1972).

1897 Catherine Drinker Bowen, author, was born in Haverford, Pa.; best remembered for *Yankee from Olympus* and *The Lion and the Throne* (died 1973).

1898 The City of Greater New York was inaugurated with ceremonies, making it (then) the world's second largest city with a population of 3,438,899.

1900 Xavier Cugat, band leader, was born in Barcelona, Spain.

1902 The first Rose Bowl game was held, with Michigan defeating Stanford 49 to 0; first regular annual game was held in 1916.

1903 Pacific cable went into operation, connecting San Francisco and Hawaii.

1907 The Food and Drug Administration went into operation.

1908 Statewide prohibition went into effect in Georgia.

1909 Barry M. Goldwater, legislator, was born in Phoenix; represented Arizona in the Senate (1952-64, 1968-86); Republican presidential nominee (1964).

1913 U.S. Parcel Post Service began throughout the country, and an estimated 6 million parcels were sent the first week.

1914 Seasonal commercial air passenger service was launched between St. Petersburg and Tampa, with two daily round trips at a cost of $10 each.

1914 Dayton, Ohio became the first large American city to adopt the commission-city manager form of government.

1915 Panama-California Exposition opened in San Diego.

1915 Prohibition went into effect in Arizona and Idaho.

1918 The Federal Government took over operation of the railroads, appointing Treasury Secretary William G. McAdoo director general; returned to private hands Mar. 1, 1920.

1919 J(erome) D. Salinger, author, was born in New York City; best known for *Catcher in the Rye*.

1927 Massachusetts adopted compulsory auto insurance, the first of its kind; required $5000/$10,000 liability coverage.

1929 Larry King, author *The Biggest Little Whorehouse in Texas*, was born in Putnam, Tex.

1934 Dr. Francis E. Townsend of Long Beach, Cal. announced his Old Age Revolving Pension Plan, providing that every unemployed American citizen 60 or older should, on application, receive from the U.S. Treasury an annuity not exceeding $200 a month which had to be spent in the United States within a month.

1936 The National Recovery Administration (NRA) ended after 2-1/2 years when the Supreme Court found parts of the act unconstitutional.

1942 The United Nations declaration was signed in Washington by 26 nations, affirming the principles of the Atlantic Charter.

1947 The Atomic Energy Commission, with David E. Lilienthal as chairman, took over control of the nation's atomic energy program; succeeded (Jan. 19, 1975) by the Nuclear Regulatory Commission.

1961 The merger of the American Lutheran Church, Evangelical Lutheran Church, and United Evangelical Church became effective, creating a church of nearly 2.5 million members.

1966 New York City's first transit strike began; ended Jan. 13.

1970 President Nixon signed a bill creating the Council of Environmental Quality.

1971 Three-day holiday weekends became effective for Washington's Birthday, Memorial Day, Columbus Day, and Veterans Day.

1974 Former Attorney General John N. Mitchell and former presidential aides John D. Ehrlichman and H.R. Halderman were found guilty of Watergate coverup charges.

1974 Supplemental Security Income (SSI) program began as a phase of Social Security.

1975 A new state constitution went into effect in Louisiana.

1976 New minimum wage law went into effect, setting rate at $2.30 an hour.

1978 The first phase of increased minimum wages went into effect, providing for $2.65 an hour; to go to $2.90 on Jan 1, 1979; $3.10 on Jan 1, 1980, and $3.35 on Jan 1, 1981.

1979 China and the United States established full diplomatic relations; simultaneously the United States severed diplomatic relations with Taiwan.

1984 The largest reorganization in American corporate history occurred when the American Telephone & Telegraph Co. (AT&T) divested itself of its 22 wholly-owned local Bell telephone companies as a result of a 1982 consent decree agreement between AT&T and the Justice Department.

1988 The Evangelical Lutheran Church in America began functioning as the nation's fourth largest Protestant denomination; the 5.3 million member body was created by the merger of the Lutheran Church in America, the American Lutheran Church, and the Association of Evangelical Lutheran Churches.

JANUARY 2

1608 Christopher Newport arrived at Jamestown with food and 110 new settlers.

1752 Philip M. Freneau, "poet of the American Revolution," was born in New York City; founder, editor, *National Gazette* (1791-93); poet (*The British Prison Ship, The Wild Honeysuckle, Indian Burying Ground*) (died 1832).

1781 Virginia ceded claimed western lands to Federal Government, thus opening the way for Maryland to ratify the Articles of Confederation (Feb 27); Maryland had held up ratification until all western lands had been ceded.

1788 A Georgia convention unanimously ratified the Constitution, entering the Union as the fourth state.

1830 Henry M. Flagler, oil executive and land developer, was born in Hopewell, N.Y.; with John D. Rockefeller, a founder of Standard Oil, vice president (1870-1908); organized Florida East Coast Railway, developed Florida East Coast resort area (died 1913).

1856 Edward S. Martin, editor and writer, was born near Auburn, N.Y.; a founder, *Harvard Lampoon* (1876); founder, first editor, *Life Magazine* (1883); its editorial writer (1887-1933); author of "Easy Chair" column, *Harper's Magazine* (1920-35) (died 1939).

1857 Frederic B. Opper, pioneer cartoonist, was born in Madison, Ohio; creator of "Happy Hooligan" (died 1937).

1860 Louisiana State University opened.

1861 Helen Herron Taft, wife of President Taft, was born in Cincinnati (died 1943).

1863 Three-day battle of Stone River or Murfreesboro, Tenn. ended without a definite decision.

1865 William Lyon Phelps, educator, was born in New Haven, Conn.; among the first to specialize in teaching modern literature (Yale U. 1893-1933) (died 1943).

1871 Tex (George L.) Rickard, boxing promoter, was born in Kansas City, Mo.; first to promote a million dollar gate (died 1929).

1871 Construction began on the Brooklyn Bridge over the East River in New York City.

1872 Albert C. Barnes, drug manufacturer, was born in Philadelphia; created, manufactured the antiseptic argyrol (died 1951).

1875 David H. Miller, international lawyer, was born in New York City; helped draft the League of Nations Covenant (died 1961).

1876 William M. Jeffers, railroad executive, was born in North Platte, Neb.; rose from office boy to president, Union Pacific Railroad (1937-46); rubber production administrator (1942-43) (died 1953).

1878 Frederic J. Fisher, auto body manufacturer, was born in Sandusky, Ohio; principal founder, head, Fisher Body Co. (1908) (died 1941).

1887 Jewish Theological Seminary of America was founded in New York City by Alexander Kohut and Sabato Morais.

1889 Roger Adams, chemist, was born in Boston; with U. of Illinois (1916-71), head of chemistry department (1926-54); a foremost organic chemist of 20th Century; did important research on composition of many natural substances (died 1971).

1890 Tito Schipa, operatic tenor, was born in Lecce, Italy; sang with Chicago and Metropolitan opera companies for more than 30 years (died 1965).

1892 Artur Rodzinski, musician and conductor, was born in what is now Split, Yugoslavia; conducted various symphonies (Los Angeles 1929-33, Cleveland 1933-42, New York 1943-47, Chicago 1947-48) (died 1958).

1900 Lake Michigan waters were diverted into the Chicago Drainage Canal, a major engineering triumph; canal is 40 miles long, 22 ft. deep; built at cost of $45 million.

1904 Sally Rand, entertainer, was born in Elkton, Mo.; noted for exotic fan dance, a sensation of 1933 Chicago's World Fair (died 1979).

1920 Government agents in 33 cities made simultaneous raids on Industrial Workers of the World (IWW) and Communist Party members; resulted in deporting 516 aliens.

1920 Isaac Asimov, biochemist and author, was born in Petrovichi, Russia; prolific fiction and nonfiction writer (200+ books); produced some of the best science fiction (*Foundation Trilogy, Nightfall*).

1929 Canada and the United States signed a convention to preserve Niagara Falls.

1933 American Marines were withdrawn from Nicaragua, ending forceful intervention in Latin America.

1935 The trial of Bruno Hauptmann, charged with the kidnapping and murder of the son of Charles A. Lindbergh, opened in Flemington, N.J.; found guilty and electrocuted Apr 3, 1936.

1936 Electron tube, enabling man to see in the dark, was invented by Vladimir Zworykin and George A. Morton; device was sensitive to ultraviolet and infrared rays.

1942 Manila and Cavite were captured by Japanese troops; American and Philippine forces strengthened positions on Bataan Peninsula, where they held out until Apr 9.

1949 Puerto Rico inaugurated Luis Munoz-Marin, its first elected governor.

1974 President Nixon signed legislation limiting highway speed to 55 miles per hour.

1988 President Reagan and Canadian Prime Minister Brian Mulroney signed a landmark trade agreement that would eliminate all tariffs and lower other barriers to trade and investment before the end of the century.

1988 The collapse of a new storage tank poured an estimated one million gallons of diesel fuel into the Monongahela River at West Elizabeth, Pa. threatening the drinking water of 750,000 Pittsburgh suburbanites.

JANUARY 3

1711 Richard Gridley, military engineer, was born in Boston; chief engineer, Continental Army; fortified Breed's (Bunker) Hill, Dorchester Heights; wounded at Bunker Hill (died 1796).

1777 George Washington secretively moved his pinned-down troops against a large British force, routing them at Princeton, N.J. before British reinforcements could arrive; this and the Trenton victory restored American morale.

1787 People of Maine, meeting in convention, voted to separate from Massachusetts.

1793 Lucretia C. Mott, women's rights activist, was born in Nantucket, Mass.; a Quaker minister, she worked with her husband, James, in anti-slavery activities; associated with Elizabeth Cady Stanton in calling, directing the first women's rights convention (Seneca Falls, N.Y., 1848); made her home a sanctuary for runaway slaves (died 1880).

1814 President Madison ordered the court martial of Gen. William Hull for surrendering Detroit to the British without resistance; court martial found him guilty.

1825 The first secular utopian society was founded in New Harmony, Ind. by Robert Owen; lasted only a few years.

1831 The first building and loan association (Oxford Provident Building Association) was organized in Thomas Sidebotham's tavern in Frankford, Pa.; first loan was $500.

1834 Stephen Austin, visiting in Mexico City to present resolves against Mexican restrictions to Texas colonization, was arrested and imprisoned for eight months.

1835 Larkin G. Mead, sculptor, was born in Chesterfield, N.H.; executed the Lincoln Monument, Springfield, Ill; Ethan Allen, Montpelier, Vt. (died 1910).

1840 Henry Holt, publisher and author, was born in Baltimore, Md.; founder (1873), head of Henry Holt & Co.; author of several novels (died 1926).

1861 The Delaware legislature unanimously rejected succession from the Union.

1861 Fort Pulaski in Savannah was seized by Georgia troops.

1871 The U.S. Weather Service began; Weather Bureau was organized in 1890.

1872 Hugh K. Moore, chemical engineer, was born in Andover, Mass.; invented the unsubmerged diaphragm cell, a new method for making calcium arsenate, acid-resisting hydraulic cement, etc. (died 1939).

1879 Grace A. Goodhue Coolidge, wife of President Coolidge, was born in Burlington, Vt. (died 1957).

1886 Raymond A. Spruance, World War II admiral, was born in Baltimore; commanded forces in Battle of Midway victory; commander, Fifth Fleet (1944-45); commander-in-chief, Pacific Fleet (1945-46); headed Naval War College (1946-48); ambassador to the Philippines (1952-56) (died 1969).

1909 Victor Borge, entertainer, was born in Copenhagen; noted for his humor and piano artistry.

1911 First American postal savings banks opened in 48 selected second class post offices; system ended in 1966.

1915 Jack Levine, artist, was born in Boston; a protest painter, he sought to depict social and political ills.

1918 U.S. Employment Service was established as a separate unit in the Department of Labor.

1919 Herbert Hoover was named head of an international relief organization to help liberated and enemy countries.

1939 Bobby (Robert M. Jr.) Hull, considered the best left wing in ice hockey, was born in Pointe Anne, Canada; played with the Chicago Blackhawks for 16 seasons (1957-71).

1949 The Supreme Court ruled that states have the right to ban the closed shop.

1953 Lyndon B. Johnson was elected minority leader of the Senate.

1959 President Eisenhower signed a proclamation admitting Alaska to the Union as the 49th state.

1961 President Eisenhower announced that the United States had broken diplomatic relations with Cuba after a long series of harassments.

1967 Jack Ruby, the Dallas night club owner charged with the murder of Lee Harvey Oswald, President Kennedy's alleged assassin, died in Dallas before he could be retried for the murder.

1985 The California Institute of Technology and the University of California announced they would built the world's largest telescope on Mauna Kea on the island of Hawaii; scheduled for service in 1992.

JANUARY 4

1679 Roger Wolcott, an early Connecticut leader, was born in Windsor, Conn.; was deputy governor (1741-50), governor (1751-54) (died 1767).

1789 Benjamin Lundy, abolitionist, was born in Sussex County, N.J.; organized one of the first anti-slavery organizations (Union Humane Society, 1815); traveled, wrote, and spoke widely against slavery (died 1839).

1804 Samuel M. Isaacs, orthodox rabbi, was born in Leeuwarden, Netherlands; served New York City congregations (from 1839); founder, editor, *Jewish Messenger* (1857-78); a founder, Mt. Sinai Hospital, United Hebrew Charities, Hebrew Free School Association (died 1878).

1818 Service on the Black Ball Line, first transatlantic sailing packet line, began from Liverpool, England to New York City.

1831 Edward P. Dutton, publisher, was born in Keene, N.H.; founder (1858), head of family publishing firm; co-publisher, *Everyman's Library*, a series of inexpensive reprints (died 1923).

1836 A convention in Little Rock adopted Arkansas state constitution.

1838 Charles S. Stratton, midget, was born in Bridgeport, Conn.; known as General Tom Thumb, exhibited by P.T. Barnum (died 1883).

1858 Carter Glass, legislator and public official, was born in Lynchburg, Va.; publisher, *Lynchburg News*; represented Virginia in the House (1902-18) and Senate (1920-46); Secretary of Treasury (1918-20) (died 1946).

1859 The Senate moved into its newly-completed chambers in the Capitol.

1861 Alabama troops seized Fort Morgan in Mobile.

1866 Niels E. Hansen, horticulturist, was born near Ribe, Denmark; at South Dakota State College (1895-1937), originated Hansen hybrid plums, hybridization of alfalfa (died 1950).

1874 Thornton W. Burgess, author, was born in Sandwich, Mass.; wrote children's books, created character "Peter Rabbit" (died 1965).

1883 Max Eastman, author and editor, was born in Canandaigua, N.Y.; editor, *New Masses, Liberator*; an influential leader of American liberal opinion (died 1969).

1887 Edwin E. Witte, economist, was born in Jefferson County, Wis.; economics professor, U. of Wisconsin (1920-57); wrote the Social Security Act (1935) (died 1960).

1893 President Benjamin Harrison proclaimed amnesty for past offences against the anti-polygamy law.

1895 Leroy R. Grumann, airplane designer and manufacturer, was born in Huntington, N.Y.; founder, Grumann Aerospace Corp. (1929); a designer of fighter planes (died 1982).

1896 Utah entered the Union as the 45th state.

1896 Everett M. Dirksen, legislator, was born in Pekin, Ill.; represented Illinois in the House (1933-49) and Senate (1951-69), serving as minority leader (1959-69) (died 1969).

1904 Supreme Court held that Puerto Ricans are not aliens and are not subject to immigration restrictions.

1951 United Nations forces in Korea gave up Seoul in their retreat.

1974 President Nixon refused to surrender 500 tapes and documents subpoenaed by the Senate Watergate Committee.

1988 The Secretary of Health & Human Services planned to request $1.1 billion to fight AIDS.

1989 Defense Secretary Frank Carlucci approved recommendations of a special commission to close 86 military installations, partially close five others, and revise 54; Congress must accept or reject entire package.

1989 Two F-14 Tomcats from the Aircraft Carrier *Kennedy* shot down two Libyan jets which threatened them and acted in a hostile manner; action occurred over Mediterranean about 70 miles north of Tobruk.

JANUARY 5

1665 **New Haven** formally submitted to union with Connecticut.

1776 New Hampshire voters in convention in Exeter adopted the first written state constitution.

1779 Stephen Decatur, War of 1812 naval officer, was born in Sinepuxent, Md.; commanded vessels in Tripolitanian and War of 1812 battles; a toast attributed to him was: "Our country! may she always be right; but our country right or wrong;" killed in duel in 1820.

1779 Zebulon M. Pike, Army officer and explorer, was born in Lamberton, N.J.; explored much of the Mississippi River headwaters and Southwest; a mountain is named for him; killed while leading troops at York (now Toronto) Apr 27, 1813.

1781 Benedict Arnold, leading a 2000-man British force into Virginia, occupied Richmond, forcing Gov. Thomas Jefferson to flee.

1794 Edmund Ruffin, agriculturist, was born in Prince George County, Va.; developed system to revitalize Virginia's soil; publisher, *Farmer's Register* (1833-42), devoted to scientific agriculture (died 1865).

1811 Cyrus Hamlin, missionary and educator, was born in Waterford, Me.; missionary to Turkey; founder, first president (1863-77), Robert College, Istanbul (died 1900).

1835 Olympia Brown, first American woman ordained in a regularly-constituted religious organization (Universalist, 1863), was born in Prairie Ronde, Mich.; president, Wisconsin Woman's Suffrage Association (1887-1917) (died 1926).

1838 John C. Moss, photoengraver, was born in Bentleyville, Pa.; established photo-engraving as a commercial enterprise in the United States (died 1892).

1838 President Van Buren issued a neutrality proclamation in the dispute between Great Britain and Canada.

1847 George F. Becker, who headed U.S. Geological Survey for 40 years, was born in New York City (died 1919).

1855 King C. Gillette, inventor and manufacturer, was born in Fond du Lac, Wis.; invented the safety razor, blade; headed company named for him (1901-32) (died 1932).

1871 Frederick S. Converse, composer, was born in Newtown, Mass.; composed the first American opera performed at the Metropolitan; professor, dean, New England Conservatory of Music (died 1940).

1873 Charles F. Burgess, chemical engineer and inventor, was born in Oshkosh, Wis.; invented electrolytic process for purifying iron, various alloys (died 1945).

1874 Joseph Erlanger, physiologist, was born in San Francisco; shared Nobel Physiology/Medicine Prize for discoveries "regarding the highly differentiated functions of single nerve fibers" (died 1965).

1876 William J. Hale, sometimes called the father of chemurgy, was born in Ada, Ohio; patented processes for making phenol, aniline, acetic acid (died 1955).

1877 Henry Sloane Coffin, Presbyterian clergyman, was born in New York City; pastor, Madison Ave. Church, New York City (1905-26); president, Union Theological Seminary (1926-45) (died 1945).

1879 Jack Norworth, vaudevillian/lyricist (*Take Me Out to the Ball Game; Shine On, Harvest Moon*), was born in Philadelphia (died 1959).

1882 Herbert Bayard Swope, journalist and editor, was born in St. Louis, brother of Gerard Swope (12/1/1872); war correspondent (1914-16), executive editor (1920-29), *New York World* (died 1958).

1886 The first "piggy-back" operation began on the Long Island Railroad when a produce train, consisting of eight flat cars for carrying farmers' wagons, eight cars for the horses, and a coach for the drivers, went from Albertson's Station to Long Island City, then by ferry across the East River to New York.

1887 The first American library school opened at Columbia U. through the efforts of Melvil Dewey; moved to Albany (1889), became the New York State Library School.

1887 Courtney H. Hodges, World War II Army general, was born in Perry, Ga.; led 1st Army through most of European campaign (died 1966).

1893 The last spike was driven at the east-west junction of the Great Northern Railroad in the Cascade Mountains, forging another transcontinental link.

1913 Kemmons Wilson, hotel executive, was born in Osceola, Ark.; founder, Holiday Inns in Memphis (1952), board chairman, Holiday Inns Inc. (1953-79)

1914 Ford Motor Co. raised the basic wage rate from $2.40 for a nine-hour day to $5 for an eight-hour day.

1915 Supreme Court sustained a lower court in the Danbury hatters case, holding the unions guilty of restraint of trade; ordered to pay $252,130 in fines against 186 union members.

1920 Supreme Court upheld constitutionality of the Volstead (prohibition) Act.

1925 Mrs. Nellie Tayloe Ross was sworn in as Wyoming governor, the first woman state governor; she was the widow of Gov. William B. Ross, who died three months earlier.

1925 John R. Opel, IBM executive (president 1974-83; CEO 1981-85, chairman 1983-86), was born in Kansas City, Mo.

1928 Walter F. Mondale, Vice President (1977-81), was born in Ceylon, Minn.; represented Minnesota in the Senate (1964-76); 1984 Democratic presidential candidate.

1931 Alvin Ailey, dancer and choreographer, was born in Rogers, Tex.; combined modern, jazz, and classical dance forms; founder, American Dance Theater (1958) (died 1989).

1931 Chuck Noll, football coach (Steelers 1969-   ), was born in Cleveland, Ohio.

1933 Construction began on the Golden Gate Bridge.

1933 Former President Coolidge died in Northampton, Mass. at 60.

1940 Static-less FM (frequency modulation) radio, developed by Edwin H. Armstrong, was introduced.

1943 George Washington Carver, agricultural chemist, died at 79; headed agricultural research department, Tuskegee Institute; led a shift from one-crop (cotton) Southern economy by developing more than 400 peanut and soybean byproducts.

1946 Diane Keaton, screen actress (*Annie Hall*), was born in Santa Ana, Cal.

1948 Mary L.S. Harrison, widow of President Benjamin Harrison, died at 89.

1955 Lyndon B. Johnson was elected Senate majority leader.

1957 President Eisenhower told Congress that the United States would use its military and economic power to protect the Middle East against Communist aggression.

1970 United Mine Workers official Joseph A. Yablonski, his wife, and daughter were found shot to death in their home in Clarksville, Pa.; UMW President W.A. (Tony) Boyle was later convicted of the killing.

1972 President Nixon approved plans for the development of a space shuttle.

1987 An Amtrak train crashed into three locomotives which had slid onto the main track near Baltimore; 15 persons were killed and 176 injured.

JANUARY 6

1702 Jean Baptiste Bienville established the capital of Louisiana on Mobile Bay, the first settlement in what became Alabama.

1730 Thomas Chittenden, colonial leader, was born in East Guilford, Conn.; first governor of Vermont (1778-89, 1791-97) (died 1797).

1736 John and Charles Wesley arrived in Georgia at Gov. James Oglethorpe's invitation for what John Wesley was later to describe as the "second rise of Methodism."

1759 George Washington and the widow Martha Dandridge Custis were married by the Rev. David Mossom, rector of St. Peter's Church, in New Kent County, Va.

1776 The Alexander Hamilton Provincial Company of Artillery of the Colony of New York was founded, marking the beginning of the oldest Army unit (now known as Battery D, 5th Field Artillery).

1779 British troops captured Sunbury, Ga.

1793 James M. Porter, public official and railroad executive, was born in Norristown, Pa.; Secretary of War (1843-44); first president, Lehigh Valley Railroad, a founder of Lafayette College (died 1862).

1799 Jedidiah S. Smith, explorer, was born in Bainbridge, N.Y.; the first white man to cross the Great Salt Lake Desert and Sierra Nevada Mountains; killed by Indians on the Cimarron River (1831) .

1807 Joseph Holt, public official, was born in Breckenridge County, Ky.; Postmaster General (1859-61), Secretary of War (1861), Army Judge Advocate General (1862-75), prosecuted assassins of President Lincoln (died 1894).

1811 Charles Sumner, legislator, was born in Boston; represented Massachusetts in the Senate (1851-74); a violent opponent of slavery, his attacks led to an assault on him by Rep. Preston S. Brooks of South Carolina; a leader in effort to impeach President Andrew Johnson (died 1874).

1842 Clarence King, geologist, was born in Newport, R.I.; first head of Geological Survey (1879-81) (died 1901).

1859 Hugh S. Rodman, World War I admiral, was born in Frankfort, Ky.; commander of American battleships (1918), battle squadron, North Sea (1918-19); commander, Pacific Fleet (1919) (died 1940).

1859 Lucius L. Van Slyke, agricultural chemist, was born in Centerville, N.Y.; known especially for his research of milk (died 1931).

1861 Florida state troops captured the federal arsenal at Apalachicola.

1864 Ban (Byron B.) Johnson, baseball official, was born in Norwalk, Ohio; organized, headed the American League (1900-27); organized the World Series; named to Baseball Hall of Fame (died 1931).

1878 Carl Sandburg, author and poet, was born in Galesburg, Ill.; poetry (*Chicago Poems, Corn Huskers, Smoke and Steel, Good Morning, America*); author of six-volume biography of Abraham Lincoln (died 1967).

1879 Joseph M. Patterson, publisher, was born in Chicago, grandson of Joseph Medill (4/6/1823) and brother of Eleanor M. Patterson (11/7/1884); co-editor, *Chicago Tribune* (1918-25); founder, publisher, *New York Daily News* (1925-46) (died 1946).

1880 Tom Mix, screen actor, was born in El Paso, Tex.; appeared in more than 400 Western films, silent and sound (died 1940).

1882 Sam T. Rayburn, legislator, was born in Roane County, Tex.; represented Texas in the House (1913-61), Speaker (1940-46, 1949-53, 1955-61) (died 1961).

1882 Ferdinand Pecora, jurist, was born in Nicosia, Italy; helped create Securities & Exchange Commission, an original member (1934-35); New York State Supreme Court justice; presiding over racketeering trials (1935-52) (died 1971).

1883 Kahlil Gibran, artist and author, was born in Bsherri, Lebanon; best remembered for *The Prophet* (died 1931).

1886 Russell R. Waesche, Coast Guard officer, was born in Thurmont, Md.; Coast Guard commander (1936-46), the first Coast Guard admiral (died 1946).

1889 Most of Seattle's business district was destroyed by fire.

1892 Ted Lewis, musician, was born in Circleville, Ohio; clarinetist and band leader, remembered for phrase, "Is everybody happy?" and battered tophat (died 1971).

1896 Abram N. Pritzker, founder of Hyatt Hotels, was born in Chicago (died 1986).

1906 Clarence H. Graham, psychophysiologist, was born in Worcester, Mass.; contributed much to understanding various aspects of vision (died 1971).

1911 "Flying Fish," the first successful hydroplane was flown by Glenn Curtiss, its inventor, at San Diego.

1912 New Mexico entered the Union as the 47th state.

1919 Former President Theodore Roosevelt died at Oyster Bay, Long Island at 60.

1920 Early Wynn, baseball pitcher who won 300 games (Senators, Indians, White Sox), was born in Hartford, Ala.; named to Baseball Hall of Fame.

1921 Louis Harris, pollster, was born in New Haven, Conn.; began with Elmo Roper polling organization; developed method useful in political campaigns.

1936 Supreme Court found the Agricultural Adjustment Act of 1933 unconstitutional; ruled against paying cash benefits to farmer from tax money to restrict production.

1941 President Franklin Roosevelt, in his annual message, defined his goals for world peace in the "Four Freedoms" — Freedom of Speech, Freedom of Worship, Freedom from Want, Freedom from Fear.

1942 The first round-the-world commercial flight was completed by Pan American Airways.

1957 Nancy Lopez, champion golfer, was born in Torrance, Cal.

1989 President Reagan approved an independent commission report to increase the pay of top federal officials and Congress by about 50%; will go into effect Feb 8 unless Congress turns down recommendations.

JANUARY 7

1608 Jamestown fort burned.

1658 Theophilus Eaton (colonial) leader, died at 68; an original patentee of the Massachusetts Bay Colony, he established a new colony at New Haven, named governor (1638), re-elected annually until his death; helped draw up law code for Connecticut.

1699 Treaty signed by Massachusetts Bay Colony and Abenaki Indians at Casco Bay, Me., ending French-Indian War on New England border.

1718 Israel Putnam, Revolutionary leader, was born in Danvers, Mass., a cousin of Rufus Putnam (4/9/1738); an active military leader (Bunker Hill, Long Island), helped prepare Bunker Hill fortifications, reputedly warned his troops: "Don't fire until you see the whites of their eyes;" incapacitated by a stroke (1779) (died 1790).

1751 William Penn Academy opened; later became the University of Pennsylvania.

1782 The first American commercial bank (Bank of North America) opened in Philadelphia; organized by Robert Morris; original depositors and stockholders included Thomas Jefferson, Alexander Hamilton, Benjamin Franklin, John Paul Jones, James Monroe, John Jay, and Stephen Decatur.

1789 The first national election for president was held, with electors selected variously by different states; they cast all 69 votes for George Washington on Feb 4; the Senate counted the vote Apr 6.

1795 The Yazoo Land companies fraudulently sold 30 million acres of land at 1-1/2 cents an acre after being revived by the Georgia legislature.

1800 Millard Fillmore, 13th president (1850-52), was born in Locke, N.Y.; represented New York in the House (1833-35, 1837-43); Vice President (1849-50), succeeding to the presidency on the death of President Tyler (7/9/1850); a founder, U. of Buffalo (died 1874).

1817 Second Bank of the United States opened in Philadelphia.

1826 Oliver H. Kelley, farm organization founder, was born in Boston; organizer (1867) of the National Grange of the Patrons of Husbandry (died 1913).

1829 James B. Angell, educator and diplomat, was born near Scituate, R.I.; president, U. of Vermont (1866-71), Michigan (1871-1909); minister to Chile (1880-81), to Turkey (1897-98) (died 1916).

1830 Albert Bierstadt, painter, was born in Solingen, Germany; noted for huge scenes (*Discovery of the Hudson River, Settlement of California*) which hang in the Capitol (died 1902).

1830 Baltimore & Ohio Railroad, the first American railway system, began operations.

1839 Georgia Female College (later Wesleyan) opened in Macon; the first college in the world chartered to give degrees to women.

1849 LeVerne Noyes, inventor, was born in Genoa, N.Y.; among his inventions were a wire dictionary holder, improved steel windmill, tractor wheel, harvester reel, cord knotter for grain binders; organized Aëromotor Co. to build windmills (died 1919).

1851 Bernhard E. Fernow, forester, was born in Posen, Germany; first chief, Forestry Division, Agriculture Department (1886-98); organized, headed first forestry school, Cornell U. (1898-1903) (died 1923).

1867 House passed a resolution by James M. Ashley of Ohio calling for the Judiciary Committee to investigate accusations against President Andrew Johnson.

1872 Trial of "Boss" William M. Tweed of New York began in New York City; defended by David Dudley Field, John Graham, and Elihu Root; first civil suit to recovery millions in graft ended in hung jury, second convicted and sent him to prison; after release, was convicted by the State.

1873 Adolf Zukor, movie executive, was born in Riese, Hungary; president, Paramount Pictures (1916-35), chairman (1935-76) (died 1976).

1879 Melvin Jones, Lions Club founder (1917), was born in Ft. Thomas, Ariz.; insurance agency head; founder, secretary-general, Lions (1917-61) (died 1961).

1881 Gene Carr, cartoonist, was born in New York City; created various comic strip series (Lady Bountiful, All the Comforts of Home, Father, Little Nell) (died 1959).

1890 Maurice E. McLoughlin, early tennis great, was born in Carson City, Nev.; on Davis Cup team (1909-14); style of play started tennis on way to becoming a national sport (died 1957).

1894 The first motion picture, showing 47 successive frames of Fred Ott sneezing, was copyrighted; known as the *Edison Kinetoscope Record of a Sneeze.*

1910 President Taft removed Gifford Pinchot as head of the Forest Service because of a letter from Pinchot to a senator criticizing the Interior Secretary; rules forbade subordinates from writing directly to Congress in such cases.

1910 Orval Faubus, public official, was born in Combs, Ark.; served Arkansas as governor (1954-67), defied Federal Government (1957) by blocking integration of Little Rock Central High School; impasse ended with arrival of federal troops.

1911 Woodrow Wilson was inaugurated as governor of New Jersey.

1913 Johnny Mize, baseball player (Cardinals, Giants, Yankees), was born in Demarest, Ga.; named to Baseball Hall of Fame.

1914 The first passage through the Panama Canal was made by a self-propelled crane boat *Alex La Valley*; canal officially opened Aug 15.

1917 Ulysses S. Kay, composer, was born in Tucson, Ariz.; known for compositions in neoclassical style.

1918 Supreme Court upheld the constitutionality of the Selective Service Act.

1927 Transatlantic commercial telephone service opened between New York and London; first conversation was between Walter S. Gifford, AT&T president, in New York and Sir George Murray, British Post Office Secretary, in London; 31 calls made the first day at a cost of $75 for three minute conversations.

1933 Supreme Court held that a section of the National Industrial Relations Act was an unconstitutional delegation of congressional authority to the Executive Branch; entire act was invalidated May 27.

1941 Office of Production Management was created by executive order to supervise defense production; first heads were William S. Knudsen, General Motors president, and Sidney Hillman, Amalgamated Clothing Workers president.

1942 American and Philippine forces completed withdrawal to the Bataan Peninsula.

1944 Lou H. Hoover, wife of President Hoover, died in New York City at 68.

1949 Drs. Daniel Pease and Richard Baker announced success in photographing the gene during experiments at the U. of Southern California; they magnified tissue sections by 120,000 diameters.

1955 Marian Anderson performed at the Metropolitan Opera as Ulrica in Verdi's *Masked Ball*, the first black to perform at the Met.

1963 The cost of first class postage was increased to five cents an ounce.

1968 The cost of first class postage was increased to six cents.

JANUARY 8

1682 Jonathan Belcher, colonial governor, was born in Cambridge, Mass.; governor of Massachusetts and New Hampshire (1730-41) and New Jersey (1747-57) (died 1757).

1732 The first South Carolina newspaper, *South Carolina Gazette*, was published in Charleston by Thomas Whitmarsh.

1735 John Carroll, Catholic prelate, was born in Upper Marlboro, Md.; first American Catholic bishop (1790), first archbishop of Baltimore (1808-15); accompanied Benjamin Franklin on fruitless mission to Canada seeking its support in the Revolution (died 1815).

1771 Elisha North, physician, was born in Goshen, Conn.; pioneer in smallpox vaccination (died 1843).

1777 The first price regulation law went into effect in Rhode Island "to prevent monopolies and oppression by excessive and unreasonable prices for many of the necessaries and conveniences of life, and for preventing engrossers, and for the better supply of our troops in the army with such necessaries as may be wanted."

1786 Nicholas Biddle, banker, was born in Philadelphia; president, Bank of the United States (1822-39); President Jackson refused to issue new charter and bank became a state bank (1836) (died 1844).

1790 President Washington delivered the first annual message to Congress, the first State of the Union address.

1791 Jacob Collamer, legislator and public official, was born in Troy, N.Y.; Postmaster General (1849), served in the House (1843-49), Senate (1855-65) (died 1865).

1792 Lowell Mason, musician and composer, was born in Medfield, Mass.; introduced, directed musical education in Massachusetts public schools; devised system of musical education for children; founder Boston Academy of Music (1833); composer of hymn, "Nearer, My God, to Thee" (died 1872).

1798 The 11th Amendment, by which judicial powers are construed, was ratified.

1800 Edward M. Robinson, merchant and financier, was born in Philadelphia; a leader in shipping and whaling industries; left fortune to daughter, Hetty Green (11/21/1835) (died 1865).

1802 Commission settled British Revolutionary War claims against the United States at $2,664,000.

1810 John J. Thomas, agriculturist, was born in Ledyard, N.Y.; editor, *Rural Affairs* (1869-81); author of "The American Fruit Culturist," which launched American systematic study of fruit (died 1895).

1815 Gen. Andrew Jackson led 6000 American troops to victory over 12,000 British at New Orleans; neither side knew that a peace settlement had been reached two weeks earlier; British suffered more than 2000 casualties, including Gen. Edward M. Pakenham; Americans had eight killed, 13 wounded.

1821 James Longstreet, Confederate general, was born in Edgefield District, S.C.; took part in many major battles; his delay in carrying out Lee's orders was blamed for defeat at Gettysburg; minister to Turkey (1880-81); U.S. railroad commissioner (1898-1904) (died 1904).

1830 Gouvernour K. Warren, Union general, was born in Cold Spring, N.Y.; chief engineer, Army of the Potomac; saved the day (July 2) at Gettysburg by seizing and holding Little Round Top position, where his statue stands; served in various Virginia battles (died 1882).

1831 Charles H. Morgan, inventor, was born in Rochester, N.Y.; invented automatic bag-making machine, a continuous rolling mill for wire making (died 1911).

1840 House passed a resolution refusing to accept resolutions or petitions concerning the abolition of slavery, the first "gag rule."

1847 Col. Stephen Kearny and his forces defeated rebellious Californians at the battle of San Gabriel River.

1857 Augustus Thomas, playwright, was born in St. Louis; wrote numerous plays (*Alabama, In Mizzoura, The Copperhead*) (died 1934).

1862 Frank N. Doubleday, publisher, was born in Brooklyn; a founder, Doubleday & McClure, book and magazine publishers; ran chain of bookstores; headed several successor companies (died 1934).

1867 Blacks were given the right of suffrage in Washington, D.C. by a bill passed over President Andrew Johnson's veto of the previous day.

1867 Emily G. Balch, economist and pacifist, was born in Jamaica Plain, Mass.; international secretary, Women's International League for Peace (1919-21), shared 1946 Nobel Peace Prize (died 1961).

1870 Burton Holmes, traveler and lecturer, was born in Chicago; famed for his travelogues (died 1958).

1871 Walter T. Swingle, agricultural botanist, was born in Canaan, Pa.; helped make growing of figs, dates, and Egyptian cotton possible in the United States; head of crop physiology and breeding research in Agriculture Department (died 1952).

1872 Charles W. Hawthorne, artist, was born in Lodi, Ill.; remembered for such paintings as *The Trousseau, The Mother,* and *Fisherman's Daughter* (died 1930).

1873 Harvey W. Corbett, architect, was born in San Francisco; collaborated with Raymond Hood in designing Rockefeller Center's Radio City (died 1954).

1881 William T. Piper, aircraft designer, was born in Knapp's Creek, N.Y.; first successful mass producer of small, inexpensive planes; designed the Piper Cub (1931) (died 1970).

1881 John G. Neihardt, editor and author, was born in Sharpsburg, Ill.; literary editor, *St. Louis Post-Dispatch*; poet ("A Cycle of the West," "Black Elk Speaks") (died 1973).

1883 Patrick J. Hurley, public official, was born in Oklahoma; Secretary of War (1929-33); special representative to various countries for President Franklin Roosevelt; ambassador to China (1944-45) (died 1963).

1889 Patent issued for the first tabulating machine, invented by Dr. Herman Hollerith of New York City; used punch cards and electrical counters; first used in 1890 census.

1891 Willard M. Kiplinger, magazine publisher, was born in Bellefontaine, Ohio; publications included *Changing Times,* various newsletters (died 1967).

1904 Peter Arno, cartoonist, was born in New York City; his satire of cafe society appeared mostly in *The New Yorker* (died 1968).

1912 National Monetary Commission, headed by Sen. Nelson W. Aldrich, proposed legislation which ultimately led to creation of the Federal Reserve system.

1912 Jose Ferrer, actor and director, was born in Santurce, Puerto Rico; starred in many hit films (*Cyrano de Bergerac, Caine Mutiny, The Shrike*).

1914 Thomas J. Watson, industrialist and diplomat, was born in Dayton, the son of Thomas J. Watson (2/17/1874); president, IBM (1952-79); ambassador to Russia (1979-81).

1917 Supreme Court upheld prohibiting liquor shipments to dry states.

1918 President Wilson outlined 14-point peace program to Congress; later became basis for peace treaties and the League of Nations.

1919 The first transatlantic flight by a Navy seaplane began at Rockaway, N.Y.; ended May 27 in Lisbon.

1935 Elvis Presley, entertainer, was born in Tupelo, Miss.; popular singer, recording artist, and screen actor ("Love Me Tender," "King Creole") (died 1977).

1947 David Bowie, screen actor and musician, was born in London.

1968 President Lyndon Johnson broke ground for the Joseph H. Hirschhorn Museum and Sculpture Garden in Washington, D.C. to house extensive Hirschhorn collection donated to the Federal Government.

1971 President Nixon signed acts establishing the Voyageurs National Park in Minnesota and the Chesapeake & Ohio National Historic Park along an 184-mile stretch from Washington, D.C. to Cumberland, Md.

1971 Annual pensions of former presidents were raised from $25,000 to $60,000 and for presidential widows from $10,000 to $20,000.

1982 The 13-year-old federal lawsuit against the American Telephone & Telegraph Co. was settled; AT&T agreed to give up the 22 Bell system companies in return for which AT&T was permitted to enter previously prohibited areas, such as data processing, telephone and computer equipment sales, computer communications devices; court gave final approval Aug 5, 1983.

1982 Justice Department dropped its anti-trust case against the International Business Machines Corp.

1985 Rev. Lawrence Jenco, Catholic priest, was abducted in Beirut; released July 26, 1986.

1986 President Reagan by executive order froze all Libyan government assets in the United States and American banks abroad.

1988 The presidential task force investigating the cause of the Oct 1987 Wall Street crash blamed it on the use of two types of computerized stock trading.

1988 Stock prices took their sharpest plunge — 140.58 points — since the Oct 1987 crash because of rising interest rates and computerized program trading.

1988 Arizona Governor Evan Mecham was indicted on six felony counts, including perjury and filing of a false contribution report.

JANUARY 9

1745 Caleb Strong, colonial leader, was born in Northampton, Mass.; member of the Constitutional Convention; one of first two senators from Massachusetts (1789-96) and its governor (1800-07, 1812-16) (died 1819).

1781 Lemuel Shaw, jurist, was born in Barnstable, Mass.; drew up Boston city charter (1822), in effect until 1913; chief justice, Massachusetts Supreme Court (1830-60), during which he handed down more than 2200 decisions (died 1861).

1788 The Connecticut legislature ratified the Constitution by a vote of 128 to 40; became the fifth state in the Union.

1789 Treaty of Ft. Harmar signed by Ohio Indians and Gen. Arthur St. Clair.

1793 The first balloon flight in the United States was made by 39-year-old French pilot, Jean Pierre Blanchard, from the courtyard of the Walnut St. Prison, Philadelphia, to near Woodbury, N.J.; the 15-mile trip took 46 minutes and reached an altitude of 5,812 feet.

1803 Christopher G. Memminger, Confederate financier, was born in Nayhingen, Germany; Confederate Secretary of Treasury (1861-64) (died 1888).

1817 Nathan S. Davis, medical educator and physician, was born in Greene, N.Y.; founder, Lind University medical department (1859), which later became Northwestern U. Medical School; instrumental in founding American Medical Association (died 1904).

1839 John Knowles Paine, composer and organist, was born in Portland, Me.; first professor of music in the United States (Harvard 1862-1906) (died 1906).

1856 James F. Bell, Army officer, was born in Shelbyville, Ky.; served in Spanish-American War in Philippines; Army chief of staff (1906-10); commander, 77th Division (1917) (died 1919).

1859 Carrier Chapman Catt, women's rights leader, was born in Ripon, Wis.; president, National American Women Suffrage Association (1900-04, 1915-47); founder, president, International Woman Suffrage Alliance (1904-23); founder, League of Women Voters (died 1947).

1861 *Star of the West,* an unarmed federal supply ship, was fired on by South Carolina batteries in Charleston Harbor, bringing Civil War closer; ship had been sent to supply and reinforce garrison at Fort Sumter.

1861 Mississippi seceded from the Union by a convention vote of 84 to 15.

1865 Tennessee convention adopted anti-slavery constitution amendments; ratified by popular vote Feb 22.

1870 Joseph B. Strauss, bridge engineer, was born in Cincinnati; designed many long-span bridges (Golden Gate, George Washington, Columbia River at Longview, Wash.) (died 1938).

1878 John B. Watson, psychologist, was born in Greenville, S.C.; professor, Johns Hopkins U. (1908-20); founder, behaviorist school of psychology (died 1958).

1879 Emory S. Land, naval officer and public official, was born in Canon City, Colo.; chief, Naval Bureau of Construction & Repair (1932-37); U.S. Maritime Commission (1937-46), chairman (1938-46) (died 1971).

1900 Richard Halliburton, explorer and author, was born in Brownsville, Tenn.; remembered for several books (*Royal Road to Romance, The Glorious Adventure, The Flying Carpet*); lost in a typhoon while sailing a Chinese junk from Hong Kong to San Francisco (1939).

1901 Chic (Murat B.) Young, cartoonist, was born in Chicago; created "Blondie" (died 1973).

1902 Sir Rudolf Bing, British manager of the Metropolitan opera (1950-72), was born in Vienna; co-founder, Edinburgh Festival.

1903 The Wind Cave (S.D.) National Park was established.

1904 George Balanchine, choreographer, was born in Leningrad; a founder, School of American Ballet (1904), head of New York City Ballet (1948-83); choreographed 100 ballets, musicals (died 1983).

1908 The East River Tunnel from New York City's Battery to Brooklyn was opened.

1913 Richard M. Nixon, 37th president (1969-74), was born in Yorba Linda, Cal.; represented California in the House (1947-50) and Senate (1950-53); Vice President (1953-61); Republican presidential candidate 1960, elected in 1968; became the first president to resign (Aug 9, 1974) after Watergate revelations.

1914 Gypsy Rose Lee, entertainer, was born in Seattle; American burlesque queen in 1940s, famed for "intellectual" striptease; musical, *Gypsy*, based on her life (died 1970).

1922 Har Gobind Khorana, chemist, was born in Raipur, India; shared 1968 Nobel Physiology/Medicine Prize for working out most of the genetic code.

1928 Judith Krantz, author (*Scruples, Mistral's Daughter*), was born in New York City.

1941 Joan Baez, folk singer, was born in New York City (Staten Island); active in 1960s civil rights, anti-war movements; founder, Institute for the Study of Non-violence.

1945 American soldiers fulfilled promise of Gen. Douglas MacArthur, "I shall return," when they invaded Luzon in the Philippines.

1951 Crystal Gayle, country music singer, was born in Paintsville, Ky.

1964 Violence in the Panama Canal Zone resulted in the death of 21 Panamanians and four American soldiers; Panama severed diplomatic relations with the United States and asked for "complete revision" of canal treaties.

1968 Surveyor VII made a soft landing on the moon and began to send back both data and pictures.

1987 The Dow Jones industrial average closed above the 2000 point mark for the first time in its 102-year history, reaching 2002.25.

JANUARY 10

1740 Loammi Baldwin, engineer, was born in North Woburn, Mass.; planned, supervised construction of Middlesex Canal; developed Baldwin apple (died 1807).

1744 Thomas Mifflin, Revolutionary general, was born in Philadelphia; saw action at Trenton, Princeton; served in Continental Congress (1774, 1783-84) and as governor of Pennsylvania (1790-99) (died 1800).

1776 Thomas Paine published his pamphlet, "Common Sense" in Philadelphia, urging the colonies to separate from Great Britain and form own nation; published as an anonymous 2-shilling pamphlet of 47 pages.

1781 Office of Secretary of Foreign Affairs was established by the Continental Congress.

1791 Vermont ratified the Constitution; admitted to the Union as the 14th state on May 4.

1804 Oakes Ames, capitalist and legislator, was born in Easton, Mass.; builder of Union Pacific railroad; censured by House, where he represented Massachusetts (1863-73), for trying to forestall investigation of his role in construction dealings; made original fortune manufacturing shovels (died 1873).

1805 U. of South Carolina, chartered in 1801, opened at Columbia.

1810 Jeremiah S. Black, public official, was born near Stony Creek, Pa.; attorney-General (1857-60, exposed California land title frauds; nominated for Secretary of State but Senate refused to confirm him (Feb 5, 1861) (died 1883).

1835 Harry (William H.) Wright, baseball pioneer, was born in Sheffield, England; organized Cincinnati professional team (1868), first team to go on tour (1869); manager (Braves, Phillies); named to Baseball Hall of Fame (died 1895).

1841 George W. Melville, naval officer and Arctic explorer, was born in New York City; modernized Navy ships, streamlined administration as chief of Bureau of Steam Engineering (died 1912).

1843 Rep. John M. Botts of Virginia introduced resolutions to impeach President Tyler for corruption, malconduct of office, high crimes and misdemeanors; rejected 127 to 83.

1847 Jacob H. Schiff, banker and philanthropist, was born in Frankfurt, Germany; headed Kuhn, Loeb & Co. (1885-1920), made many philanthropic gifts (died 1920)

1847 Col. Stephen Kearny and about 600 troops captured Los Angeles from the Mexicans, concluding hostilities in California.

1850 John W. Root, architect, was born in Lumpkin, Ga.; associated with Daniel H. Burnham in Chicago designing the Montauk Bldg., an early skyscraper, and the Monadnock Bldg., which broke completely with tradition (died 1891).

1855 Albert W. Marquis, founder and publisher of *Who's Who in America* and related publications, was born in Brown County, Ohio (died 1943).

1861 Louisiana state troops seized the arsenal and barracks in Baton Rouge.

1861 The Florida legislature voted 62 to 7 to secede from the Union.

1867 John A. Lejeune, Marine Corps commandant (1920-29), was born in Pointe Coupee Parish, La.; served in Mexico and World War I; superintendent, Virginia Military Institute (1929-37) (died 1942).

1870 Standard Oil Co. was incorporated in Cleveland with a capital of $1 million; original stockholders were John D. Rockefeller (2667 shares), William Rockefeller (1333), Henry M. Flagler (1333), Stephen V. Harkness (1334), O.B. Jennings (1000), and the firm of Rockefeller, Andrews & Flagler (1000).

1873 Howard C. Christy, painter, was born in Morgan County, Ohio; best known for his *Christy Girl* and the *Signing of the Constitution*, which hangs in the Capitol (died 1952).

1877 Frederick G. Cottrell, inventor of the electrostatic precipitator used in air pollution control, was born in Oakland, Cal. (died 1948).

1883 Francis X. Bushman, a leading man in more than 400 silent films (1911-18), was born in Baltimore (died 1966).

1883 Fire destroyed Newhall House in Milwaukee, killing 71 persons.

1887 Robinson Jeffers, author, was born in Pittsburgh; poet ("Tamar," "The Roan Stallion," "Cawdor"); playwright (*The Cretan Woman, The Tower Beyond Tragedy*) (died 1962).

1889 John Held Jr., illustrator, was born in Salt Lake City; leading graphic interpreter of the Jazz Age (died 1958).

1892 Dumas Malone, historian and editor, was born in Goldwater, Miss.; editor-in-chief, *Dictionary of American Biography* (1931-36); director, Harvard U. Press (died 1986).

1898 Katherine B. Blodgett, research scientist who developed non-reflecting "invisible" glass, was born in Schenectady, N.Y. (died 1979).

1901 Texas oil boom began with the successful drilling of the Spindletop well near Beaumont, owned by Anthony F. Lucas; delivered 25,000 barrels a day.

1904 Ray Bolger, actor and dancer, was born in Dorchester, Mass.; numerous stage plays (*Where's Charley?, By Jupiter*); played scarecrow in movie, *Wizard of Oz*. (died 1987).

1911 Garrett Birkhoff, mathematician, was born in Princeton, N.J.; made important contributions to abstract theory of structures, or lattices.

1917 White House was picketed by Congressional Union for Woman Suffrage.

1918 The House passed a resolution 274-136 calling for an amendment to the Constitution to provide woman suffrage.

1920 The League of Nations was established; but despite urging of President Wilson, the United States failed to become a member.

1923 An executive order by President Harding ended American army occupation of the Rhine in Germany.

1927 President Coolidge, in a special message to Congress, outlined the reasons for intervention in Nicaragua, which resulted in sending 5000 Marines.

1936 Robert W. Wilson, physicist, was born in Houston; shared the 1978 Nobel Physics Prize for co-discovery of cosmic radiation background which tends to support the "big bang" theory of the origin of the universe.

1938 Willie McCovey, baseball player (Padres, Giants), was born in Mobile, Ala.; named to Baseball Hall of Fame.

1946 The first man-made contact with the moon occurred when a radar signal from a New Jersey Signal Corps installation echoed back from the moon in 2.4 seconds (477,714 mile round trip).

1946 United Nations General Assembly held its first meeting in London.

1966 Georgia legislature refused to seat Julian Bond, a 25-year-old black pacifist and civil rights leaders; later re-elected and Supreme Court ruled unanimously that he must be seated.

1967 President Lyndon Johnson nominated Alan S. Boyd as the first Secretary of Transportation.

1948 Full diplomatic relations with the Vatican were resumed after 117 years.

JANUARY 11

1755 Alexander Hamilton, first Secretary of the Treasury (1789-95), was born in Nevis, Leeward Islands; served in the Revolution as an aide to George Washington; member of the Continental Congress (1782, 1783, 1787, 1788); killed in a duel with Aaron Burr (1804), who he had blocked from the New York governorship.

1759 The first American life insurance company was incorporated in Philadelphia (Corporation of Poor and Distressed Presbyterian Ministers and of the Poor and Distressed Widows and Children of Presbyterian Ministers).

1760 Oliver Wolcott, colonial leader, was born in Litchfield, Conn., son of Oliver Wolcott (12/1/1726); Comptroller of the Treasury (1791-95), Secretary of the Treasury (1795-1801); governor of Connecticut (1817-27) (died 1833).

1775 The first Jewish person in the New World to be elected to public office was Francis Salvador, a plantation owner, who was named to serve in the South Carolina provincial congress; he also was the first Jew to die for American independence, being killed in a skirmish July 31, 1776.

1785 William W. Seaton, journalist, was born in King William County, Va.; an editor, *National Intelligencer* (1812-64); helped make shorthand reports of congressional debates (1812-56), which were published, as were American state papers (1832-61) (died 1866).

1785 Congress convened in New York City.

1793 Cave Johnson, public official, was born in Springfield, Tenn.; represented Tennessee in the House (1829-37, 1839-45); as Postmaster General (1845-49), introduced the use of stamps (died 1866).

1803 James Monroe was named minister extraordinary to France to help buy Louisiana.

1805 Michigan Territory was created by Congress, effective July 1.

1806 Moses Taylor, financier, was born in New York City; president, City Bank of New York (1855-82), involved in first transatlantic cable attempt (died 1882).

1807 Ezra Cornell, founder of Western Union, was born in Westchester Landing, N.Y.; worked with Samuel

F.B. Morse on method of insulating telegraph wires; organized Western Union (1856); co-founder, benefactor, Cornell U (1868) (died 1874).

1825 Bayard Taylor, travel writer and translator, was born in Kennett Square, Pa.; most widely-known travel writer, lecturer of the time; translated Goethe's *Faust*; minister to Germany (1878) (died 1878).

1836 Alexander H. Wyant, landscape painter, was born in Evans Creek, Ohio; one of the Hudson River School of painters (died 1892).

1842 William James, psychologist and philosopher, was born in New York City, brother of Henry James (4/15/1843); created first psychological research laboratory; author (*The Principles of Psychology, The Varieties of Religious Experience*) (died 1910).

1843 Henry Y. Satterlee, Episcopal prelate, was born in New York City; bishop of Washington, D.C. (1896-1908); planned, began work on National Cathedral (died 1908).

1861 Alabama legislature voted 61 to 39 to secede from the Union.

1863 Ft. Hindman (Arkansas Post), which protected Little Rock, surrendered to Admiral David D. Porter's fleet of Union ironclads.

1864 Thomas Dixon, Baptist clergyman and author, was born in Shelby, N.C.; wrote *The Clansman* and from it the screen play, *The Birth of a Nation* (died 1946).

1870 Alice Hegan Rice, author, was born in Shelbyville, Ky.; best remembered for *Mrs. Wiggs of the Cabbage Patch* (died 1942).

1876 Elmer H. Flick, baseball player (Indians), was born in Bedford, Ohio; named to Baseball Hall of Fame (died 1971).

1880 John W. Greenslade, World War II naval officer, was born in Bellevue, Ohio; commander, Western Sea Frontier (died 1950).

1885 Alice Paul, women's rights leader, was born in Moorestown, N.J.; a founder, National Woman's Party (1917), World Women's Party; an early proponent of equal rights constitutional amendment (died 1977).

1889 Calvin B. Bridges, geneticist, was born in Schuyler Falls, N.Y.; made many contributions to the study of heredity (died 1938).

1890 Max Carey, baseball player/manager (Pirates, Dodgers) was born in Terre Haute, Ind.; named to Baseball Hall of Fame (died 1976).

1895 Laurens Hammond, developer of electric organ, was born in Evanston, Ill.; developed electronic organ, known as Hammond Novachord (died 1973).

1897 Bernard A. DeVoto, writer and editor, was born in Ogden, Utah; wrote the "Easy Chair" column in *Harper's* (1935-55); editor, *Saturday Review* (1936-38); author (*Across the Wide Missouri, Mark Twain's America*) (died 1955).

1899 Eva LeGallienne, stage actress, was born in London; founder, director, Civic Repertory Theater, New York City (1926); co-founder, American Repertory Theater.

1904 President Theodore Roosevelt appointed William Howard Taft as Secretary of War, effective Feb 1.

1905 Frederic Dannay, writer, was born in Brooklyn; with his cousin, Manfred B. Lee (10/20/1905), formed team which was Ellery Queen, mystery writer (died 1982).

1909 National Conservation Commission, headed by Gifford Pinchot, submitted report to President Theodore Roosevelt, attempting for the first time to inventory the nation's natural resources.

1909 Canada and the United States signed a waterways treaty, creating an international joint commission to adjudicate disputes, set limits on water diversion at Niagara Falls.

1911 Hank (Henry B.) Greenberg, baseball player, was born in New York City; with Tigers (1930-46), had a career batting average of .313; named to Baseball Hall of Fame (died 1986).

1912 Strike of 15,000 textile workers began against the American Woolen Co., Lawrence, Mass.; Industrial Workers of the World (IWW) succeeded in obtaining wage gains and improved conditions; strike ended March 14.

1916 Pancho Villa, in effort to discredit the new Mexican government of Venustiano Carranza, stopped a Mexican train, removed 17 Americans, shot and killed 16.

1924 Roger C.L. Guillemin, physiologist, was born in Dijon, France; shared 1977 Nobel Physiology/Medicine Prize for research in the role of hormones in body chemistry.

1926 Grant A. Tinker, television executive, was born in Stamford, Conn.; was chairman, National Broadcasting Co. (1981-87).

1940 American Ballet Theater gave its first performance in New York City.

1944 Strategic Allied air offensive was launched from the British Isles as a prelude to the invasion of continental Europe.

1964 Luther L. Terry, Surgeon General, issued a report that cigarette smoking is a definite health hazard.

JANUARY 12

1588 John Winthrop, first governor of Massachusetts Bay Colony, was born in Suffolk, England; served 12 one-year terms; president at trial which banished Anne Hutchinson; attempted to make colony a theocratic society (died 1649).

1662 Samuel Shute, governor of Massachusetts and New Hampshire (1716-27), was born in London (died 1742).

1682 A new set of Fundamental Constitutions was issued for Carolina.

1687 Sir Edmund Andros dissolved the Rhode Island government, changed it to English county status.

1737 John Hancock, first governor of Massachusetts (1780-85, 1787-93), was born in Braintree, Mass.; signer of Declaration of Independence; member of Continental Congress (1775-80, 1785-86), president (1775, 1777) (died 1793).

1773 First American museum established in Charleston, S.C. by the Library Society.

1777 Hugh Mercer, Revolutionary general, was killed at the Battle of Princeton; Mercer County, N.J. named for him.

1828 Treaty with Mexico established American-Mexican boundary in accord with the Adams-Onis Treaty of 1819; agreement effective in 1832.

1837 Thomas Moran, painter, was born in Bolton, England; landscape painter, etcher, best known for work on the Yellowstone region (died 1926).

1846 Rasmus B. Anderson, author and businessmen, was born in Albion, Wis.; president, Wisconsin Life Insurance Co. (1895-1922) and Wisconsin Rubber Co. (1904-36); his major contribution was work on Scandinavian life, history, and contributions to America (died 1936).

1856 John S. Sargent, artist, was born in Florence, Italy of American parentage; one of the greatest portrait painters; did murals for Boston Public Library (died 1925).

1861 Fort Barrancas and Navy Yard at Pensacola seized by Alabama and Florida troops.

1864 Benjamin G. Lamme, engineer and inventor, was born in Clarke County, Ohio; developed various electrical machines (rotary converter, induction motor, AC generator) (died 1924).

1869 National convention of African-American people held in Washington, D.C., first national attempt to organize.

1876 Jack (John G.) London, author, was born in San Francisco; wrote numerous adventure novels (*The Call of the Wild, White Fang, The Sea Wolf*) (died 1916).

1880 Ellen L. Arthur, wife of President Arthur, died in New York City at 42.

1884 Texas (Mary Louise) Guinan, night club hostess, was born in Waco, Tex.; personified the 1920s flapper, hostess at several speakeasies, greeting customers with "Hello, sucker" (died 1933).

1903 General Education Board, funded by John D. Rockefeller, was incorporated to promote education in the United States, regardless of race, creed, or sex.

1907 Tex (Woodward M.) Ritter, singer and screen actor, was born in Murvaul, Tex.; starred on screen (60 films) and radio (died 1974).

1908 José (A.) Limon, dancer and choreographer, was born in Culiacan, Mexico; exerted strong influence on contemporary dance (died 1972).

1920 President Wilson announced the recall of American troops from Russia.

1920 James L. Farmer, civil rights leader, was born in Marshall, Tex.; co-founder of CORE (Congress of Racial Equality), national director (1961-66).

1921 Judge Kenesaw Mountain Landis began 23 years service as the first baseball commissioner following the "Black Sox" scandal.

1932 Mrs. Hattie W. Caraway of Arkansas became the first woman to be elected to the Senate, serving from 1931 to 1945 (originally appointed, then elected).

1942 National War Labor Board, with William H. Davis as chairman, was created by President Franklin Roosevelt to settle labor disputes by mediation and arbitration; successor to National Defense Mediation Board; terminated Dec 31, 1945.

1955 Secretary of State John Foster Dulles announced policy of "massive retaliation," whereby the United States would "depend primarily upon a great capacity to retaliate instantly by means and at places of our choosing."

1980 United States offered $400 million in aid to Pakistan in the face of the Soviet occupation of neighboring Afghanistan.

JANUARY 13

1630 Plymouth patent granted to William Bradford and others by the Council for New England, defining the limits of the June 1, 1961 patent.

1733 James Edward Oglethorpe, with 130 colonists, arrived at what is now Charleston, S.C. with a charter to establish a settlement in Georgia.

1808 Salmon P. Chase, public official and jurist, was born in Cornish, N.H.; Secretary of the Treasury (1861-64), originated the national banking system; served Ohio as governor (1855-60) and in the Senate (1849-55); chief justice, Supreme Court (1864-73), presiding at the President Andrew Johnson impeachment trial (died 1873).

1832 Horatio Alger, Unitarian clergyman and author, was born in Revere, Mass.; wrote more than 100 boys' books emphasizing pluck, honesty, hard work; most popular writer of his generation (died 1899).

1840 The steamboat Lexington caught fire near Eaton's Neck, N.Y.; 140 died.

1847 Treaty of Cahuenga signed ending the California portion of the Mexican War.

1865 Union forces launched a successful two-day assault on Ft. Fisher, N.C., opening Cape Fear River to Union troops; Confederate General Whiting killed in the battle.

1867 Francis E. Townsend, social reformer, was born in Fairbury, Ill.; developed plan to help elderly, proposing a $200 monthly pension for those over 60 to be financed by a 2% transaction tax (died 1960).

1868 Edwin M. Stanton was reinstated as Secretary of War; President Andrew Johnson dismissed him again Feb 21 but he refused to vacate the office.

1870 Ross G. Harrison, biologist, was born in Germantown, Pa.; developed method of culturing animal tissue, vitally important to biology; headed Yale Biology Department (1907-38) (died 1959).

1874 Police charged a meeting of unemployed laborers, injuring hundreds, in what has been called the Tompkins Square riot in New York City.

1884 Sophie Tucker, entertainer, was born in Russia; the last of the "red hot mammas," she is remembered for her theme song, "Some of These Days" (died 1966).

1884 Roy Cross, chemist, was born in Ellis, Kan.; co-inventor of petroleum cracking process; designer of oil refineries (died 1947).

1885 Alfred C. Fuller, businessman, was born in Kings County, Nova Scotia; founder of brush company which bears his name; invented twisted wire brush, developed door-to-door sales method (died 1973).

1885 Schuyler Colfax, former Vice President (1869-73), died at 61 in Mankato, Minn.

1887 Holger Cahill, director, Federal Art Project (1933-43), was born in Snaefellsnessysla, Iceland (died 1960).

1890 Elmer H. Davis, journalist and public official, was born in Aurora, Ind.; with *The New York Times* (1914-39), radio commentator (1939-42); director, Office of War Information (1942-45) (died 1958).

1905 Secretary of State John Hay proclaimed American policy is "to maintain the integrity of China and the Open Door in the Orient."

1908 More than 100 persons were killed in a fire in Rhoades Opera House in Boyertown, Pa.; fire started by explosion of motion picture projector.

1908 Earle G. Wheeler, World War II Army general, was born in Washington, D.C.; Army chief of staff (1962-64); chairman, Joint Chiefs of Staff (1964-70) (died 1975).

1933 Philippines Independence Act, giving the Philippines the right to establish a constitution and an independent government, was passed over President Hoover's veto.

1978 Hubert H. Humphrey, former Vice President (1964-68), died in Waverly, Minn. at 66.

1982 An Air Florida Boeing 737 crashed into the Potomac River after taking off from Washington, D.C.'s National Airport killing 78 persons.

1988 Supreme Court ruled 5-3 that public school officials have broad powers to censor school newspapers in a case involving a Hazelwood, Mo. school.

1989 Bernhardt Goetz, who shot four black men on a New York subway and was convicted of illegal gun possession, was sentenced to one year in jail and a $5000 fine.

1989 Major charges against Oliver L. North were dismissed because national security might be jeopardized by highly-classified information used in the trial; 12 criminal charges remain.

JANUARY 14

1639 Fundamental Orders of Connecticut were drawn up by the freeman of Hartford, Windsor, and Wethersfield, the first written constitution that created a government.

1730 William Whipple, merchant and jurist, was born in Kitery, Me.; a member of the Continental Congress (1776-79), a signer of the Declaration of Independence (died 1785).

1741 Benedict Arnold, colonial leader turned traitor, was born in Norwich, Conn.; led unsuccessful campaign to capture Quebec (1775); helped force Burgoyne's surrender at Saratoga; court martialled for minor irregularities in command of Philadelphia and reprimanded; commanded West Point (1780) and arranged to surrender it to the British; plot discovered and he fled to British (died 1801).

1745 Gershom M. Seixas, rabbi, was born in New York City; led drive (1783) to amend the Pennsylvania constitution to eliminate clause barring Jews from holding public office (died 1816).

1772 Duncan McArthur, War of 1812 general and public official, was born in Dutchess County, N.Y.; in command at Sackett's Harbor, N.Y. (1813), Northwest (1814); represented Ohio in the House (1823-25) and served as its governor (1830-32) (died 1839).

1778 James Madison was elected a member of Virginia's eight-man Council of State.

1780 Henry Baldwin, legislator and jurist, was born in New Haven, Conn.; represented Pennsylvania in the House (1817-22); associate justice, Supreme Court (1830-44) (died 1844).

1784 The Continental Congress, meeting in Annapolis, Md., ratified the 1783 Treaty of Paris, officially ending the American Revolution.

1790 Treasury Secretary Hamilton issued first report on public credit to Congress.

1799 Senate concluded the impeachment trial of Sen. William Blount of Tennessee (1796-97), the first such trial; dismissed the charges for lack of jurisdiction; he was accused of conspiring with British officers to divert part of Louisiana from Spain and England; later served as president of Tennessee Senate.

1806 Matthew F. Maury, pioneer oceanographer, was born in Fredericksburg, Va.; with Naval Observatory, he produced wind, current chart of North Atlantic; his *Physical Geography of the Sea* was first modern oceanography work (died 1873).

1825 Robert G. Harper, lawyer and legislator, died at 60; represented South Carolina in the House (1794-1801); remembered for a toast he proposed: "Millions for defense, but not a cent for tribute."

1863 Richard F. Outcault, pioneer cartoonist, was born in Lancaster, Ohio; originated the "Yellow Kid" and "Buster Brown" strips (died 1928).

1867 Supreme Court ruled in *Cummings v. Missouri* that a state oath excluding Confederate sympathizers from professions violated the law; same applied to a federal test oath.

1871 Felix M. Warburg, banker, was born in Hamburg, Germany; with Kuhn, Loeb & Co.; renowned philanthropist (died 1937).

1878 Supreme Court in *Hall v. DeCuir* ruled unconstitutional a state law requiring equal accommodations to all passengers, regardless of race and creed, because of its bearing on interstate travel.

1881 Joseph A. Green, World War II general, was born in Cherokee, Ia.; chief, Coast Artillery (from 1940) (died 1963).

1881 Francis G. Pease, astronomer, was born in Cambridge, Mass.; astronomer, Mt. Wilson Observatory, known for direct photographs, spectrograms of nebulae, star clusters, moon, planets; developed method of grinding mirror for 200-inch Caltech telescope (died 1938).

1882 Hendrik Van Loon, journalist and writer, was born in Rotterdam; wrote several popular histories (*Story of Mankind, Geography, The Arts*) (died 1944).

1886 Hugh Lofting, author, was born in Maidenhead, England; best known for his *Dr. Dootlittle* stories (died 1947).

1892 Hal Roach, pioneer movie maker, was born; produced early screen comedies in the 1920s, 1930s.

1893 Pope Leo XIII established apostolic delegation in Washington, D.C., with Archbishop Francisco Satolli as the first delegate.

1896 John Dos Passos, author, was born in Chicago; wrote many popular novels (*Manhattan Transfer, 42nd Parallel, 1919, Big Money*) (died 1970).

1902 Alfred Tarski, mathematician, was born in Warsaw; made important studies in general algebra, mathematical logic, set theory.

1914 Henry Ford revolutionized the automobile industry by inaugurating an assembly line, cutting time of assembling an auto from 12-1/2 hours to 93 minutes.

1914 Jane Wyman, first wife of President Reagan, was born in St. Joseph, Mo.; screen actress (*Johnny Belinda, The Lost Weekend, My Man Godfrey*).

1932 Loretta Lynn, entertainer, was born in Butcher Hollow, Ky.; star of country and western music.

1940 Julian Bond, legislator and civil rights leader, was born in Nashville; a founder, Student Nonviolent Coordinating Committee; served in Georgia legislature (1967-78).

1942 President Franklin Roosevelt ordered registration of all aliens.

1943 President Franklin Roosevelt and Winston Churchill began 10-day conference at Casablanca to plan Allied offensive aimed at unconditional surrender of Axis.

1949 Lawrence E. Kasdan, screen writer and director (*The Empire Strikes Back, Raiders of the Lost Ark*), was born in Miami Beach, Fla.

1949 Justice Department filed anti-trust suit against American Telephone & Telegraph Co.

1951 The Today Show began on National Broadcasting Co.

1986 President Reagan signed compact with Micronesia, giving the Pacific islands region limited autonomy.

1986 Supreme Court ruled 6-3 to upset the 23-year-old murder conviction of a defendant because he was indicted by a grand jury from which members of his own race had been excluded unconstitutionally.

1987 Supreme Court upheld a California law that grants pregnant employees four months leave to have the child and guarantees their job afterward.

JANUARY 15

1716 Philip Livingston, merchant and colonial leader, was born in Albany; brother of William Livingston (11/30/1723); member of Continental Congress (1774-78), signer of the Declaration of Independence; a founder, King's College (later Columbia U.) (died 1778).

1777 Vermont, which had been claimed by both New York and New Hampshire, declared its independence, calling itself New Connecticut.

1780 Congress established the Court of Appeals.

1783 William Alexander (also known as Lord Sterling), Revolutionary general, died at 57; had leading role in battles of Long Island, Trenton, Monmouth; served on the court which judged John André, the British officer involved with Benedict Arnold.

1786 Thomas Nutall, botanist and ornithologist, was born in Settle, England; known for his discoveries of numerous North American plants; published bird manual of North America (1832) (died 1859).

1800 Moses Yale Beach, newspaper pioneer, was born in Wallingford, Conn.; invented rag cutting machine (still in use); joined *New York Sun* (1834), bought it out (1838); originated syndicated news story, first European edition of an American paper (died 1868).

1810 Abigail K. Foster, equal rights leader, was born in Pelham, Mass.; a pioneer in women's suffrage movement; also an ardent abolitionist (died 1887).

1811 Congress authorized the president to take temporary possession of East Florida to prevent its falling into foreign hands.

1815 The American frigate, *President*, was taken by a British squadron off Sandy Hook.

1821 Lafayette McLaws, Confederate general, was born in Augusta, Ga.; saw action at Harpers Ferry and Antietam; in command of Savannah (1864-65) (died 1897).

1831 James B. Thayer, legal educator, was born in Haverhill, Mass.; law professor, Harvard (1874-1902), co-founder of case method of teaching law (died 1902).

1841 Charles A. Briggs, Presbyterian leader, was born in New York City; Old Testament scholar and theologian, espoused "higher criticism;" suspended following a heresy trial; as a result, Union Theological Seminary, where he taught (1874-1913) broke with the church, becoming independent; became Episcopal clergyman (1900) (died 1913).

1845 Ella F. Young, educator, was born in Buffalo; Chicago school superintendent (1909-15); first female president, National Education Assn. (died 1918).

1861 Robert L. Bullard, World War I general, was born in Youngsboro, Ala.; led 2nd Army in Argonne Forest offensive (died 1947).

1870 The donkey as an emblem of the Democratic party first appeared as a cartoon by Thomas Nast in *Harper's Weekly*.

1870 Pierre S. DuPont, industrialist, was born in Wilmington, Del., great grandson of Eleuthere I. DuPont

(6/24/1771); headed, DuPont (1909-20); bought into General Motors, president (1920-24) (died 1954).

1876 Eliza McCardle Johnson, widow of President Andrew Johnson, died in Greenville, Tenn. at 65.

1877 Lewis M. Terman, psychologist, was born in Johnson County, Ind.; known for Stanford revision of Binet-Simon intelligence test; coined term IQ (intelligence quotient) (died 1956).

1897 Stringfellow Barr, educator, was born in Suffolk, Va.; president, St. Johns College, Annapolis; abolished elective course system, required study of great books, with emphasis on science, mathematics (died 1982).

1899 The poem, "The Man with the Hoe," by Edwin Markham, a school teacher, appeared in the *San Francisco Examiner*.

1908 Edward Teller, physicist, was born in Budapest; worked on Manhattan Project; sometimes called the father of the hydrogen bomb; administrator of H-bomb project (1949-52).

1909 Gene Krupa, jazz drummer and orchestra leader, was born in Chicago; with Benny Goodman (1935-38), then formed own band (died 1973).

1915 Alan Lomax, folk song collector, was born in Austin, Tex.; with father, John A. Lomax (9/23/1867), collected, recorded thousands of folk songs.

1918 Robert C. Byrd, Senate majority leader (1977-81, 1987-89), was born in North Wikesboro, N.C.; represented West Virginia in the House (1953-59), Senate (1959-   ).

1926 Chuck (Charles E.A.) Berry, musician, was born in St. Louis; one of the major shapers of popular music in the 1950s, 1960s ("Maybellene"; "Roll Over, Beethoven"; "Memphis").

1929 The Senate ratified the Kellogg-Briand Treaty wherein 49 governments agreed to abolish war as an instrument of national policy.

1929 Martin Luther King Jr., civil rights leader, was born in Atlanta; awarded 1964 Nobel Peace Prize; founder, president, Southern Christian Leadership Conference; assassinated in Memphis 1968.

1936 The Ford Foundation, designed to administer funds for scientific, educational, and charitable purposes, was incorporated.

1943 The Pentagon, home of the Defense Department, was completed.

1960 The United States and Japan signed a mutual cooperation and security treaty in Washington, D.C.; provided for American defense of Japan, American military bases in Japan, and "economic collaboration;" treaty ratified in June.

1967 The first Super Bowl game was played in the Los Angeles Coliseum with the Green Bay Packers winning 35-10 over the Kansas City Chiefs.

1973 President Nixon ordered a halt to military actions against North Vietnam.

1987 The Supreme Court ruled 5-4 that the nation's 3 million tenants of low-income housing projects have the right to sue over alleged housing law violations.

JANUARY 16

1754 George Washington returned from what is now western Pennsylvania with a French refusal to the Virginia demand they leave the area.

1782 Nicholas Longworth, horticulturist, was born in Newark, N.J.; known as the father of American grape culture, experimented with wine grapes and strawberry culture (died 1863).

1786 Virginia adopted a statute for religious freedom, drafted in 1779 by Thomas Jefferson; he ranked its authorship as important as that of the Declaration of Independence and the founding the University of Virginia.

1815 Henry W. Halleck, Union general, was born in Westerville, N.Y.; commander, Union Army (1862-64), chief of staff to Grant; active in California's development (died 1872).

1845 Charles D. Sigsbee, Spanish-American naval officer, was born in Albany; commander of the *Maine* when it was blown up in Havana harbor (2/15/1898); worked with Alexander Agassiz in deep-sea exploration (1875-78), invented special apparatus for this work (died 1923).

1864 Frank Bacon, actor and playwright, was born in Marysville, Cal.; starred in numerous plays (*The Miracle Man, The Fortune Hunter*); co-author, star of long-running (three years) *Lightnin'* (died 1922).

1870 Jimmy (James J.) Collins, baseball player, manager (Red Sox), was born in Buffalo; named to Baseball Hall of Fame (died 1943).

1883 Civil Service Commission (now Office of Personnel Management) was established when Pendleton Act went into effect; Dorman B. Eaton headed three-man commission.

1896 Mathew B. Brady, photographer, died at 74; noted for his Civil War pictures.

1909 Ethel Merman, actress and singer, was born in Astoria, N.Y.; starred in many musicals (*Anything Goes, Call Me Madam, Annie Get Your Gun*) (died 1984).

1911 Dizzy (Jerome) Dean, baseball player, was born in Lucas, Ark.; pitched for St. Louis Cardinals, won 150, lost 83; a baseball broadcaster; named to Baseball Hall of Fame (died 1974).

1919 Nebraska became the 36th state to ratify the 18th Amendment, establishing Prohibition.

1920 The 18th Amendment went into effect, limiting the use and sale of alcoholic beverages; launched an era of bootlegging and speakeasies.

1934 Marilyn B. Horne, mezzosoprano, was born in Bradford, Pa.; noted for roles in *Norma, Carmen,* and *Barber of Seville.*

1935 A(nthony) J. Foyt Jr., automobile race driver, was born in Houston; won Indianapolis 500 four times.

1935 FBI agents and local lawmen conducted a four-hour shootout in Oklawaha, Fla., killing Donnie Clark, known as Ma Barker, and her son, Fred, ending a years-long spree of bank robberies, kidnappings, and 10 murders.

1942 Carole Lombard, screen actress, and her mother were among 22 passengers killed in an air crash near Las Vegas; she had been on a bond sale promotion tour.

1942 War Production Board was established by executive order to run the entire war production effort, with Donald M. Nelson as head; terminated Oct 4, 1945.

1944 Gen. Dwight D. Eisenhower arrived in Great Britain to assume his duties as Supreme Commander, Allied Expeditionary Force.

1968 Two teams of scientists, working independently for Merck Laboratories and Rockefeller University, synthesized an enzyme for the first time.

1975 U.S. District Court in Washington, D.C. awarded $12 million in damages for false arrest and infringement of rights of 1200 protestors who had been jailed in 1971 May Day antiwar demonstration.

JANUARY 17

1524 Giovanni de Verrazano, Italian-born explorer for the French, sailed from Madeira, arriving three months later off the Carolina coast.

1700 Sieur d'Iberville built a fort on the Mississippi River, about 38 miles below present New Orleans and 54 miles above the river delta.

1706 Benjamin Franklin, author, scientist, and diplomat, was born in Boston; author, editor of *Poor Richard's Almanac* for 25 years; scientist known for his work with electricity; publisher, *Pennsylvania Gazette* (1730-48); helped established first American subscription library, volunteer fire department, paid police force; a founder, American Philosophical Society, U. of Pennsylvania; invented, improved heating stove; member, Continental Congress (1775-76), signer of Declaration of Independence (died 1790).

1766 London merchants, hurt by American non-importation policy, petitioned Parliament to repeal the Stamp Act.

1768 Smith Thompson, jurist and public official, was born in Armenia, N.Y.; Secretary of Navy (1819-23), associate justice, Supreme Court (1823-43) (died 1843).

1771 Charles B. Brown, father of the American novel, was born in Philadelphia; first American novelist to gain international reputation, author (*Ormond, Wieland, Edgar Huntly*) (died 1810).

1781 At the battle of Cowpens, S.C., 1150 British cavalry under Col. Banastre Tarleton were defeated by Gen. Daniel Morgan with 800 men; described as "one of the most brilliant tactical operations ever fought on United States soil."

1781 Robert Hare, chemist, was born in Philadelphia; invented oxyhydrogen blowpipe (1801), many pieces of laboratory apparatus; studied electricity (died 1858).

1794 Andrew Jackson and Rachel Donelson Robards were married (their second ceremony) in Nashville.

1796 Thaddeus Fairbanks, inventor of platform scale (1831), was born in Brimfield, Mass.; headed company which made all kinds of scales (died 1886).

1800 Caleb Cushing, legislator and public official, was born in Salisbury, Mass.; special envoy to China (1843-45), getting five ports opened to American trade; senior American counsel in "Alabama" claims arbitration; Attorney General (1853-57); nominated for Supreme Court chief justice but not confirmed by the Senate; minister to Spain (1874-77) (died 1879).

1806 James Madison Randolph, grandson of President Jefferson, was born in the White House, the first child born there.

1821 The American settlement of Texas began when Moses Austin secured a charter from what later became Mexico, granting lands for colonization by 300 American families; Austin died soon after; colonization carried out by son, Stephen Austin.

1832 George H. Babcock, inventor and manufacturer, was born near Otsego, N.Y.; inventor of several printing presses, improved boiler design and headed (1881-93) boiler-making company (Babcock & Wilcox) (died 1893).

1849 Charles R. Miller, newspaper editor, was born in Hanover, N.H.; editor, *New York Times* (1883-1922) (died 1922).

1851 Arthur B. Frost, illustrator, was born in Philadelphia; noted for illustration of Joel Chandler Harris books (*Br'er Rabbit, Uncle Remus*) (died 1928).

1853 Alva E.S. Belmont, women's rights leader, was born in Mobile; president, National Women's Party (1920-33) (died 1933).

1856 Charles V. Chapin, public health officer, was born in Providence; health superintendent, Providence (1884-1932); a leader in public health, applying bacteriological discoveries and establishing administrative methodology (died 1941).

1861 Former President Tyler, in a letter to the *Richmond Enquirer*, recommended that border states meet to try to resolve North-South differences; Virginia legislature enlarged idea to include all states.

1867 Carl Laemmle, pioneer movie maker, was born in Laupheim, Germany; organized, headed, Universal Pictures; made first full length movie (*Traffic in Souls)* 1912; first million dollar movie (*Foolish Wives)* 1922; many other films (*All Quiet on the Western Front*) (died 1939).

1870 Alexander Grossett, publisher, was born in Windsor Mills, Canada; with George T. Dunlap formed publishing company (1900), president (1900-34) (died 1934).

1876 Frank Hague, Democratic leader, mayor of Jersey City (1917-47), was born in Jersey City (died 1956).

1878 Treaty of amity and commerce was signed with the Samoan Islands, giving the United States non-exclusive rights to a naval station at Pago Pago.

1880 Mack Sennett, pioneer movie producer, was born in Richmond, Canada; made early comedies, including the *Keystone Kops* (died 1960).

1886 Glenn L. Martin, pioneer airplane manufacturer, was born in Macksburg, Ia.; built his first plane in 1909, built planes in World War I; a twin-engine bomber (1919) became the "clipper" of the 1920s (died 1955).

1886 Harold O. Rugg, author of a series of high school social science texts, was born in Fitchburg, Mass.; education professor, Columbia U. (died 1960).

1892 James David Zellerbach, president, Crown Zellerbach Corp. (1928-45, 1952-56), was born in San Francisco; ambassador to Italy (1956-61) (died 1963).

1893 Provisional government was created in Hawaii; American minister helped depose Queen Liliuokalani; Hawaii was proclaimed a protectorate.

1893 Former President Hayes died in Fremont, Ohio at 70.

1898 Commodore Edward D. Taussig of the USS *Bennington* raised the American flag over Wake Island, taking formal possession for the United States.

1899 Robert M. Hutchins, president, U. of Chicago (1929-51), was born in Brooklyn; dean, Yale Law School (1927-29); headed Ford Foundation, Fund for the Republic, Center for the Study of Democratic Institutions (died 1977).

1899 Al Capone, gangster, was born in Naples, Italy; well-known "Scarface" of Chicago; imprisoned for income tax evasion (died 1947).

1904 Sidney Waugh, architectural sculptor, was born in Amherst, Mass.; did many well-known works (Pulaski Monument, Philadelphia; Mellon Memorial Fountain, Washington, D.C.); a foremost glass designer (died 1963).

1910 Sidney Catlett, all-time great jazz drummer, was born in Evansville, Ind. (died 1951).

1911 George J. Stigler, economist, was born in Renton, Wash.; with U. of Chicago; awarded 1982 Nobel Economics Prize; author(*The Theory of Prices, Capital, and Rate of Return in Manufacturing Industries; Intellectuals and the Market Place*).

1917 The American purchase of the Virgin Islands from Denmark for $25 million was ratified; the islands were transferred Mar 31, 1917.

1922 Nicholas deB. Katzenbach, public official, was born in Philadelphia; Attorney General (1964-66), Undersecretary of State (1966-69).

1949 The trial of top-ranking American Communists, charged with plotting the overthrow of the government, began before Judge Harold R. Medina in New York City; ran for 169 days; all were found guilty.

1961 Canada and the United States signed the Columbia River Treaty, a 60-year water power and water storage agreement; ratified by the Senate Mar 16.

1966 The Senate confirmed Robert C. Weaver as the first secretary of the Department of Housing & Urban Development; became the first black cabinet member.

1969 President Lyndon Johnson signed an act increasing the salary of the president from $100,000 to $200,000, to begin with his successor; also provided $100,000 travel allowance and $12,000 entertainment allowance.

1977 Convicted murderer Gary M. Gilmore was executed by firing squad in Utah State Prison, the first American executed in nearly ten years.

1986 President Reagan signed a secret order authorizing direct American arms shipments to Iran; order instructed Central Intelligence Agency not to tell Congress of the operation.

1989 A gunman opened fire in a Stockton, Cal. elementary school and playground, killing five students and wounding 30; the gunman then took his own life.

JANUARY 18

1770 British soldiers, who had cut down the Liberty Pole in New York City two days earlier, clashed with the Sons of Liberty on Gold Hill (near William St. above Wall St.); liberty poles were symbols before which the Sons of Liberty assembled and "pledged their fortunes and their sacred honor in the cause of liberty."

1782 Daniel Webster, legislator and public official, was born in Salisbury, N.H.; one of America's greatest orators; represented New Hampshire in the House (1813-17) and Massachusetts in the House (1823-27) and Senate (1827-41, 1845-50); Secretary of State (1841-43, 1850-52) (died 1852).

1803 President Jefferson sent a special secret message to Congress proposing the exploration of the West; subsequently led to the Lewis & Clark Expedition.

1813 Joseph F. Glidden, inventor, was born in Charleston, N.H.; invented barbed wire, which was vital in settlement of the West (died 1906).

1850 Seth Low, merchant, public official and educator, was born in Brooklyn; mayor of Brooklyn (1882-86), reform mayor of New York (1901-03); president, Columbia U. (1890-1901) (died 1916).

1854 Thomas A. Watson, electrical engineer, was born in Salem, Mass.; worked with Alexander Graham Bell, was in the first phone conversation (Mar 10, 1876) when Bell said: "Mr. Watson, come here, I want you;" later went into shipbuilding, manufacture of engines (died 1934).

1858 Daniel Hale Williams, surgeon, was born in Hollidaysburg, Pa.; founder, Provident Hospital, Chicago (1891), to provide opportunity for black women to become nurses; also with Freedman's Hospital, Washington, D.C.; performed first successful open heart surgery, closing a heart wound and pericardium (1893); only black charter member, American College of Surgeons (1913) (died 1931).

1862 Former President Tyler died in Richmond, Va. at 71.

1874 Myron C. Taylor, industrialist, was born in Lyons, N.Y.; board chairman, chief executive, U.S. Steel (1932-38); presidential representative to the Vatican (1939) (died 1959).

1892 Oliver Hardy of the Laurel and Hardy comedy team which turned out more than 200 short films and features was born in Atlanta (died 1957).

1904 Cary Grant, screen actor, was born in Bristol, England; starred in many films (*North by Northwest, The Awful Truth, Philadelphia Story*) (died 1957).

1911 Eugene Ely, a civilian pilot, landed a plane on a platform built on the quarterdeck of the battleship *Pennsylvania* in San Francisco harbor; ropes attached to sandbags served as arresting gear; Ely then took off from the same ship.

1913 Danny Kaye, actor and entertainer, was born in New York City; starred in many stage and screen plays (*Up in Arms, Secret Life of Walter Mitty*) (died 1987).

1919 The Versailles Peace Conference opened with 70 delegates from 27 countries attending, including President Wilson, who addressed the opening session.

1942 Muhammad Ali, boxing champion, was born in Louisville as Cassius Clay; world heavyweight champion three times (1964-67, 1974-78, 1978-79); stripped of title after refusing military induction, reinstated after Supreme Court ruled in his favor.

1942 The Office of Civilian Defense, headed by Fiorello H. LaGuardia, was created.

1943 The Supreme Court ruled that the American Medical Association was guilty of violating anti-trust laws by preventing activities of cooperative health groups.

1969 Peace talks to end the war in Vietnam got under way.

1985 The United States formally announced it would not participate in International Court of Justice proceeding brought against it by Nicaragua.

JANUARY 19

1750 Isaiah Thomas, colonial printer, was born in Boston; founder, *Massachusetts Spy* (1770-75), driven out by British; moved to Worcester (1775-1802); fought at Lexington, Concord; launched printing business, turning out many books noted for beautiful typography, and music; founder, first president, American Antiquarian Society (1812) (died 1831).

1789 Pierre Chouteau, fur trader, was born in St. Louis, son of Jean Pierre Chouteau (10/10/1758); operated along the Missouri River; Pierre, S.D. named for him (died 1865).

1807 Robert E. Lee, Confederate general, was born at Stratford (Westmoreland County), Va., son of Henry Lee (1/29/1756); served in Mexican War; superintendent of West Point (1852); commanded detachment which retook Harpers Ferry and captured John Brown; commander of Virginia forces in Civil War, later all Confederate troops; president, Washington College (1865-70), now known as Washington & Lee (died 1870).

1808 Nathaniel M. Hayward, inventor, was born in Easton, Mass.; invented process of treating rubber with sulphur to create partial vulcanization; assigned patent to Charles Goodyear (died 1865).

1809 Edgar Allan Poe, author, was born in Boston; known for his short stories ("Gold Bug," "Fall of the House of Usher," "Murders in the Rue Morgue"); poetry (*The Raven, Ulalume, Annabel Lee*) (died 1849).

1837 William W. Keen, physician, was born in Philadelphia; he was the first American brain surgeon (died 1932).

1840 Lt. Charles Wilkes and his expedition sighted and thus discovered the Antarctic continent; a portion is named in his honor.

1842 George T. Ladd, psychologist and philosopher, was born in Painesville, Ohio; helped found experimental psychology in the United States; author (*Philosophy of the Mind, Philosophy of Religion*) (died 1921).

1848 Minor C. Keith, railroad executive, was born in Brooklyn; also founder, United Fruit Co. (1899) (died 1929).

1851 David Starr Jordan, biologist, was born in Gainesville, N.Y.; probably the world's outstanding ichthyologist; president, Indiana U. (1885-91); first president, then chancellor, Stanford U. (1891-1916) (died 1931).

1856 Rollo Ogden, journalist, was born in Rensselaer County, N.Y.; editor, *New York Evening Post* (1903-20), *New York Times* (1922-32) (died 1937).

1861 A Georgia convention voted 208 to 89 to secede from the Union.

1862 Union troops under Gen. George H. Thomas defeated a Confederate force at the Battle of Mill Springs, Ky., the first important Union victory in the West; Confederate Gen. Felix K. Zollicoffer was killed.

1864 A convention in Arkansas adopted an anti-slavery constitution; ratified by popular vote Mar 14.

1869 American Equal Rights Assn. met in Washington, D.C. to discuss woman suffrage.

1874 President Grant nominated Morrison R. Waite as chief justice of the Supreme Court; confirmed Jan 21.

1881 Western Union Telegraph Co. was formed by Jay Gould and William H. Vanderbilt by consolidating three companies.

1886 Presidential succession act was signed, providing that in the event of death, resignation, or inability of both the president and vice president, the heads of the executive departments in the order of their creation would succeed to office; remained in effect until 1947.

1887 Alexander Woollcott, author and critic, was born in Phalanx, N.J.; drama critic, author (*Shouts and Murmurs, While Rome Burns*); actor (*The Man Who Came to Dinner*); "Town Crier" on radio (1929-39) (died 1943).

1888 Millard F. Harmon, Jr., Air Forces general, was born in San Francisco; commander, Army Air Forces in Southern Pacific, Pacific Theater (1942-45); died when his plane was lost in the Pacific (1945).

1905 Oveta Culp Hobby, newspaper publisher and public official, was born in Killeen, Tex.; editor, publisher, *Houston Post* (from 1931); director, Women's Army Corps (1942-45); first Secretary of Health, Education and Welfare (1953-55).

1918 John H. Johnson, publisher, was born in Arkansas City, Ark.; founder, publisher of *Negro Digest* (1942), *Ebony* (1945), *Tan* (1950), *Jet* (1951).

1931 Robert MacNeil, television reporter (MacNeil-Lehrer Report) was born in Montreal.

1946 Dolly Parton, singer and screen actress, was born in Sevierville, Tenn.; gained fame in country music, several films (*Nine to Five*).

1949 The salary of the president was raised from $75,000 to $100,000; the vice president from $20,000 to $30,000.

1955 The first filmed (television and newsreel) presidential press conference was held in the State Department Treaty Room; President Eisenhower took questions for half an hour.

1975 The Nuclear Regulatory Commission was established to regulate civilian nuclear facilities, assuming all functions previously assigned to the Atomic Energy Commission.

1982 Brig. Gen. James L. Dozier was found unharmed by anti-terrorist police in Padua, Italy, 42 days after he was abducted by the Red Brigades.

JANUARY 20

1724 Isaac Backus, Baptist clergyman, was born in Norwich, Conn.; organizer, pastor, New Light Church (1748-56), then the Middleburg (Mass.) Baptist Church (1756-1806); champion of religious liberty (died 1806).

1775 William Pitt (the Elder) — Earl of Chatham—proposed to Parliament that British troops be withdrawn from Boston; motion defeated by 3 to 1 vote.

1781 Mutiny of New Jersey troops quelled by Gen. Robert Howe.

1783 Preliminary articles of peace were signed by John Adams and Benjamin Franklin and the commissioners from Great Britain, Spain, and France, ending hostilities in the American Revolution.

1801 President John Adams nominated John Marshall of Virginia to be chief justice of the Supreme Court; took seat Jan 31 and served for 34 years; one of the greatest chief justices, participated in 1106 opinions, writing 519 majority opinions.

1806 Nathaniel P. Willis, writer and publisher, was born in Portland, Me.; one of the most widely-known writers of his time; co-publisher, editor, *New York Home Journal* (1846-65) (died 1867).

1814 David Wilmot, legislator, was born in Bethany, Pa.; remembered for legislation (Wilmot Proviso) which brought the slavery question to a head; a founder, Republican Party; represented Pennsylvania in the House (1845-51) and Senate (1861-63) (died 1868).

1874 Congress in the face of public opposition repealed a portion of the "Salary Grab" Act of 1873, which raised congressional salaries from $5000 to $7500; raise of president's salary to $50,000 was retained.

1877 Ruth St. Denis, dancer, was born in Newark; worked with husband, Ted Shawn, in organizing the Denishawn Dancers (died 1968).

1887 The Hawaiian Reciprocity Treaty was ratified by the Senate; gave United States the exclusive right to establish a fortified naval base at Pearl Harbor.

1891 Mischa Elman, violin virtuoso, was born in Talnoye, Russia; made American debut in 1904, numerous worldwide concert tours (died 1967).

1892 Students at the International YMCA Training School in Springfield, Mass. played the first official basketball game, invented by Dr. James Naismith, a teacher at the school.

1894 Harold L. Gray, cartoonist, was born in Kankakee, Ill.; known for "Little Orphan Annie" (died 1968).

1894 Walter H. Piston, composer and educator, was born in Rockland, Me.; composer ("Symphonic Piece," "The Incredible Flutist," various symphonies); author of several widely-known music texts (died 1976).

1896 George Burns, entertainer and screen actor, was born in New York City; part of Burns and Allen comedy team in vaudeville and radio, later television and screen actor (*The Sunshine Boys, Oh God*).

1902 President Theodore Roosevelt sent the Panama Canal Commission report to Congress; report recommended purchase of land rights for the canal at $40 million.

1937 President Franklin Roosevelt was inaugurated for a second term; he was the first president inaugurated in January under the 20th (Lame Duck) Amendment which called for federal officials to take office in January, rather than March.

1940 Carol Heiss (Jenkins), champion figure skater, was born in New York City; United States champion (1957-60), world (1956-60), and 1960 Olympics gold medalist.

1946 President Truman issued an executive order creating the Central Intelligence Agency (CIA).

1949 President Truman proposed the Point Four program to help the world's backward areas by making "the benefits of our scientific advances and industrial programs available for the improvement and growth of underprivileged areas."

1954 The Senate approved construction of the St. Lawrence Seaway.

1981 Iran released American hostages after a year of captivity.

JANUARY 21

1621 The Mayflower company gathered on shore for the first preaching service.

1738 Ethan Allen, commander of the Green Mountain Boys, was born in Litchfield, Conn.; with Benedict Arnold seized Ft. Ticonderoga; captured at Montreal, held prisoner (1775-78); active in seeking recognition of Vermont (died 1789).

1743 John Fitch, inventor, was born in Windsor, Conn.; worked on steamboat, successfully launched (1787) first vessel on Delaware River (died 1798).

1784 Andrew Stevenson, legislator and diplomat, was born in Culpepper County, Va.; represented Virginia in the House (1821-34), serving as Speaker (1827-34); minister to Great Britain (1836-41) (died 1857).

1785 Wyandot, Chippewa, Delaware, and Ottawa tribes ceded most of what is now Ohio to the United States.

1786 The Virginia legislature invited representatives of all states to meet in Annapolis "to consider how far a uniform system in their commercial regulations may be necessary to their common interest and their permanent harmony."

1813 John C. Fremont, explorer and political leader, was born in Savannah; explored, mapped much of the West, known as "The Pathfinder;" one of California's first senators (1850-51); Republican presidential candidate (1856); governor, Arizona Territory (1878-83) (died 1890).

1815 Horace Wells, pioneer dentist, was born in Hartford, Vt.; pioneer in the use of nitrous oxide (laughing gas) in tooth extraction (died 1848).

1815 Daniel C. McCallum, engineer, was born in Johnson, Scotland; invented an arch-truss bridge (1851); military director and superintendent of railroads for the Union (1862-65) (died 1878).

1821 John C. Breckenridge, Vice President (1857-61), was born in Lexington, Ky.; represented Kentucky in the House (1851-55) and Senate (1861); served as Confederate Secretary of War (1865) after serving in its army (1861-65) (died 1875).

1824 Stonewall (Thomas J.) Jackson, Confederate general, was born in Clarksburg, W.Va.; led Confederate troops in Shenandoah Valley Campaign (1862); accidentally wounded by own men at Chancellorsville (May 1, 1863), died nine days later.

1842 Former President John Quincy Adams, as a congressman, presented a petition from the citizens of Haverhill, Mass., asking for peaceful dissolution of the Union; a resolution censuring him was introduced, later tabled and refused.

1853 Helen H. Gardener, suffragist, was born in Winchester, Va.; associated with Susan B. Anthony and Elizabeth Cady Stanton in women's vote movement; first woman member, Civil Service Commission (1920) (died 1925).

1855 John M. Browning, inventor and manufacturer, was born in Ogden, Utah; invented automatic pistol, machine gun, and automatic rifle (died 1926).

1874 Frederick M. Smith, religious leader, was born in Plano, Ill., son of Joseph Smith (11/6/1832); succeeded father as president, Reorganized Church of Latter Day Saints (1915-46) (died 1946).

1884 Roger N. Baldwin, lawyer and civil rights activist, was born in Wellesley, Mass.; director, American Civil Liberties Union (1917-50), national chairman (1950-55) (died 1981).

1888 Amateur Athletic Union (AAU) was formed.

1889 Pitrim A. Sorokin, sociologist, was born in Turya, Russia; founder, head, Harvard U. sociology department, which became a major center of the social sciences (died 1968).

1901 Carry A. Nation, temperance crusader, first used a hatchet in smashing a saloon in Wichita, Kas.; act soon became widespread.

1903 Tom (Thomas A.) Yawkey, owner/president, Boston Red Sox baseball team, was born in Detroit; named to Baseball Hall of Fame (died 1976).

1908 Smoking by women in public places was made illegal in New York City.

1909 Statewide prohibition was passed by Tennessee legislation over the governor's veto.

1911 The National Progressive Republican League was organized by Robert M. LaFollette.

1912 Konrad Emil Bloch, biochemist, was born in Silesia, Germany; traced construction of cholesterol out of two-carbon compound acetic acid; shared 1964 Nobel Physiology/Medicine Prize.

1915 Kiwanis International was founded in Detroit; there now are 8000 clubs in more than 70 countries.

1930 London Naval Conference opened with the United States, Great Britain, France, Italy, and Japan participating; resulted in a treaty regulating submarine warfare, limiting tonnage and size of submarines and other warships.

1940 Jack Nicklaus, one of world's greatest golfers, was born in Columbus, Ohio; won Master's title six times.

1941 Placido Domingo, opera singer, was born in Madrid, Spain.

1947 President Truman named former President Hoover to study food and economic conditions in Germany and Central Europe; recommended (Feb 27) a $475 million aid program.

1950 Alger Hiss, former State Department official, was found guilty of perjury on two counts and sentenced to five years, bringing to an end a long, spectacular court trial.

1954 The world's first atomic-powered submarine, Nautilus, was launched at Groton, Conn.

1968 The restored Ford's Theater in Washington, D.C. was dedicated.

1977 President Carter pardoned Vietnam war draft resisters.

1985 A Lockheed charter airliner carrying 71 persons crashed on takeoff at the Reno, Nev. airport; all aboard were killed.

JANUARY 22

1758 Elkanah Watson, experimental farmer, was born in Plymouth, Mass.; considered the father of county, state fairs; organized Berkshire Agricultural Society, which sponsored first county fair (about 1810) (died 1842).

1789 The first American novel was published in Boston — *The Power of Sympathy, or The Triumph of Nature Founded in Truth* by Philenia (authorship attributed to Mrs. Sarah Wentworth Morton and William H. Brown).

1797 John Harper, publisher, was born in Newtown, Long Island, N.Y.; with brother, James (4/13/1795), founded family publishing business; firm was first to use steam-run presses, to introduce electrotyping on large scale (died 1875).

1802 Richard Upjohn, architect, was born in Shaftesbury, England; known for his Gothic revival churches (Trinity Episcopal, New York City; St. James, New Haven); a founder, head (1857-76), American Institute of Architects (died 1878).

1804 Charles O'Conor, lawyer, was born in New York City; as special deputy state Attorney General, successfully prosecuted Boss Tweed and associates (1871-75) (died 1884).

1807 President Jefferson officially informed Congress of Burr conspiracy.

1812 A convention in New Orleans adopted the Louisiana state constitution.

1813 Captured American troops were slain by Indians at Frenchtown (now Monroe), Mich. in what is called the Raisin River massacre.

1849 Terence V. Powderly, labor leader, was born in Carbondale, Pa.; head of the Knights of Labor (1883-93), instrumental in getting labor bureaus created in several states; general commissioner, Immigration Services (1897-1902) (died 1924).

1850 Robert S. Brookings, industrialist and philanthropist, was born in Cecil County, Md.; helped rebuild Washington U., St. Louis; successful in wooden ware business; a founder (1926), benefactor, Brookings Institution (died 1932).

1855 Iowa enacted statewide prohibition; nullified in 1858.

1874 Edward S. Harkness, capitalist and philanthropist, was born in Cleveland; benefactor of Metropolitan Museum of Art, Presbyterian Hospital, New York City, and Harvard U. to which he donated about $12 million to start a house system (died 1940).

1875 D(avid) W. Griffith, pioneer movie producer, was born in LaGrange, Ky.; most important developer of moviemaking techniques; produced hundreds of films in 23 years, including *The Birth of a Nation* (died 1948).

1890 Frederick M. Vinson, public official and jurist, was born in Louisa, Ky.; represented Kentucky in the House (1924-29, 1931-38); director, Office of Economic Stabilization (1943-45); Treasury Secretary (1945-46); chief justice, Supreme Court (1946-53) (died 1953).

1891 Franz Alexander, physician, was born in Budapest; often called the father of psychosomatic medicine (died 1964).

1895 National Association of Manufacturers held its first meeting in Cleveland.

1897 Rosa Ponselle, opera soprano, was born in Meriden, Conn.; leading dramatic soprano with the Met for 20 years (died 1981).

1903 Hay-Herran Treaty was signed, allowing the new Panama Canal Co., which held an option on a canal route, to sell land to the United States; also provided that Colombia would lease a strip of land across the Isthmus for a canal.

1917 President Wilson called on World War I belligerents to accept "peace without victory."

1932 Reconstruction Finance Corporation, the first government effort to provide direct credit to business in need, was approved by President Hoover; set up Feb 2, with Charles G. Dawes as president; abolished June 30, 1957.

1935 Pierre S. DuPont IV, Delaware governor (1976-84), was born in Wilmington; represented the state in the House (1970-76).

1944 Allied offensive began in Central Italy with costly amphibious landing on Anzio Beach.

1952 Airliner crashed in Elizabeth, N.J., killing 30 persons.

1973 George Foreman celebrated his 25th birthday by knocking out Joe Frazier in the second round to win world's heavyweight boxing crown in Kingston, Jamaica.

1973 Former President Lyndon Johnson died near Johnson City, Tex. at 64.

1973 Supreme Court ruled 7-2 in *Roe v. Wade* that a state may not prevent a woman from having a abortion during the first six months of pregnancy.

1976 The Seminole Indians accepted $16 million payment for Florida after 25 years of litigation.

JANUARY 23

1730 Joseph Hewes, colonial leader, was born in Princeton, N.J.; member of Continental Congress (1774-77, 1779), a signer of Declaration of Independence (died 1779).

1765 Thomas Todd, jurist, was born in King and Queen County, Va.; associate justice, Supreme Court (1807-26) (died 1826).

1775 London merchants petitioned Parliament for reconciliation with the American colonies as exports from England to the colonies dropped sharply.

1789 Georgetown College, the first Catholic college in the United States, was formed in Washington, D.C.

1845 A uniform election day — the first Tuesday after the first Monday in November — was established by Congress and signed by President Tyler.

1849 Elizabeth Blackwell became the first American woman physician, graduating from Geneva (N.Y.) Medical Institute (now Syracuse U. College of Medicine).

1869 Susan B. Anthony and Elizabeth Cady Stanton spoke for woman's suffrage before a Senate committee, the first congressional hearing on women's rights.

1869 Herbert D. Croly, editor, was born in New York City; founder, editor, *The New Republic* (1914-30) (died 1930).

1881 New York State enacted a law making way for cooperative apartments by permitting tenants to purchase their apartments; the first was the Rembrandt House, 152 West 57th Street.

1884 George McManus, cartoonist, was born in St. Louis; developed "Bringing Up Father" (Maggie and Jiggs) (died 1954).

1884 Ralph DePalma, automobile race driver, was born in Troia, Italy; pioneer American driver, won 2,557 of 2,889 races (1908-34) (died 1956).

1915 Potter Stewart, jurist, was born in Jackson, Mich.; justice, U.S. Court of Appeals (1954-59), associate justice, Supreme Court (1958-81) (died 1985).

1916 David Douglas Duncan, photojournalist, was born in Kansas City, Mo.; with *Life* (1946-56); produced several books (*I Protest, Goodbye Picasso*).

1917 North Dakota granted women limited suffrage.

1918 Gertrude B. Elion, research scientist, was born in New York City; shared 1988 Nobel Physiology/Medicine Prize.

1919 Ernie Kovacs, entertainer, was born in Trenton, N.J.; one of the first major television stars; made several films (died 1962).

1933 The 20th Amendment went into effect, setting the dates for the start of the terms of president and vice president (Jan 20) and congressmen (Jan 3).

1944 Allied forces made a second landing on the Italian coast, south of Rome at Anzio Beach, in an effort to outflank the Germans.

1955 The United States signed a treaty with Panama increasing the canal annuity to $1,930,000; agreed to curtail certain businesses in the Canal Zone which compete with local merchants.

1964 The 24th Amendment was ratified, eliminating the payment of poll tax as a prerequisite for voting.

1968 The American intelligence ship, *Pueblo*, was seized by North Korea; 83 men aboard were held as spies; released 11 months later.

1987 Trading volume on the New York Stock Exchange topped the 300 million share mark when it soared to 302,390,000 shares; the previous record was 253,120,000 set a week earlier.

JANUARY 24

1639 Fundamental Orders, a frame of government, was ratified by Hartford, Windsor, and Wethersfield, Conn.; these Orders, adopted a year earlier (1/14/1638), generally declared that authority should rest upon the free consent of the people.

1733 Benjamin Lincoln, Revolutionary general and public official, was born in Hingham, Mass.; commanded army in Southern Department (1778-79); captured at Charleston (1779), exchanged and served in Yorktown campaign; Secretary of War (1781-83) (died 1810).

1754 Andrew Ellicott, surveyor, was born in Bucks County, Pa.; surveyed continuation of the Mason-Dixon Line, many state boundaries, the plan for Washington, D.C. (died 1820).

1791 President Washington issued the Federal District proclamation, the first presidential proclamation, directing commissioners to lay out the exact location of the 10-mile square District of Columbia.

1811 Henry Barnard, educator, was born in Hartford, Conn.; improved Connecticut, Rhode Island public schools; president, U. of Wisconsin (1858-60), St. John's College, Annapolis (1866-67); the first U.S. commissioner of education (1867-70) (died 1900).

1820 Henry J. Raymond, editor, was born in Lima, N.Y.; a founder, editor, *New York Times* (1851-69); a founder, Republican Party; represented New York in the House (1865-67) (died 1869).

1830 John M. Thayer, legislator, was born in Bellingham, Mass.; one of the first Nebraska senators (1867-71) and its governor (1887-91); governor, Wyoming Territory (1875-79) (died 1906).

1832 Joseph H. Choate, lawyer and diplomat, was born in Salem, Mass.; involved in several major cases — the Tweed Ring prosecution, Standard Oil anti-trust cases; ambassador to Great Britain (1899-1905) (died 1917).

1835 Charles K. Adams, educator, was born in Darby, Vt.; president, Cornell U. (1885-92), founded its law school, and U. of Wisconsin (1892-1901) (died 1902).

1848 Gold was discovered by James W. Marshall, a New Jersey mechanic, employed by John Sutter to build a mill race on the American River near Coloma, Cal.; discovery started a gold rush which brought more than 200,000 persons to California in four years.

1860 Bernard H. Kroger, merchant, was born in Cincinnati; founder of a grocery chain (1876) (died 1938).

1861 Georgia state troops seized the federal arsenal in Augusta.

1862 Edith Wharton, author, was born in New York City; wrote several novels (*Ethan Frome, The Age of Innocence*) (died 1937).

1881 Supreme Court in *Springer v. United States* held that the 1862 federal income tax law was constitutional.

1885 Charles H. Niehaus, sculptor, was born in Cincinnati; did numerous portrait busts, the John Paul Jones monument in Washington, D.C. (died 1935).

1895 Eugene V. Debs and associates were placed on trial in Chicago for interfering in the Pullman strike; new trial ordered Feb 12.

1899 Hoyt S. Vandenberg, Air Forces general, was born in Milwaukee; held various commands in World War II, chief of staff (1948-53) (died 1954).

1903 The Alaska-Canada boundary dispute commission of three Americans, two Canadians, and one Briton was created; Lord Albertson (the Briton) later voted with the Americans, thus deciding in their favor.

1913 Norman Dello Joio, composer, was born in New York City; known for his neoclassical music (*Triumph of St. Joan, Psalm of David*).

1915 Robert Motherwell, painter and art teacher, was born in Aberdeen, Wash.; a founder of abstract expressionism.

1916 Supreme Court upheld the constitutionality of the federal income tax law.

1918 Oral Roberts, evangelist, was born in Ada, Okla.; built up Pentecostal Holiness Church to millions of members through radio, television evangelism; founder, Oral Roberts U., Tulsa, Okla. (1963).

1940 Ronald W. Reagan married Jane Wyman in Glendale, Cal.; ended in divorce (1949).

1941 Neil Diamond, composer, was born in New York City; wrote numerous popular hits ("Sweet Caroline," "Song Sung Blue").

1942 Allied naval forces sank five Japanese transports in three-day engagement in Macassar Straits, severely damaging invasion fleet.

1946 United Nations General Assembly created a commission to study the control of atomic energy.

1957 Angela Morgan, poet, died; wrote numerous poems; best known for "The Unknown Soldier," which was read over the bier of the unknown soldier in the Capital Rotunda.

1968 Mary Lou Retten, gymnast who won the 1984 Olympic gold medal, was born in Fairmont, W. Va.

1977 President Carter restored gasoline price controls.

1980 House passed a resolution endorsing President Carter's call for an international boycott of the Olympic Games in Moscow because of the Russian invasion of Afghanistan; Senate did likewise on Jan 29.

1989 American Episcopal bishops approved the election of the first woman bishop in the 2000 year history of the Anglican/Episcopal church; Barbara Harris was elected Sept 24, 1988 by the Massachusetts diocese to become suffragan bishop of the Boston diocese.

JANUARY 25

1615 Ezekiel Cheever, educator, was born in London; headed various New England schools for 70 years, including the Boston Latin School (1670-1708) (died 1708).

1715 Thomas Walker, explorer, was born in King and Queen County, Va.; discovered the Cumberland Gap (died 1794).

1783 William Colgate, manufacturer and philanthropist, was born in Hollingsbourn, England; founder of soap and toiletries business, which became Colgate-Palmolive (1806); benefactor of Colgate U.; founder, American Bible Society (died 1857).

1787 Daniel Shay, leading 2000 debt-ridden and discontented colonists, marched on the federal arsenal in Springfield, Mass. to overthrow the government in what became known as Shay's Rebellion; effort failed.

1807 William Adams, Presbyterian theologian, was born in Colchester, Conn.; a founder (1836), president, Union Theological Seminary (1873-80) (died 1880).

1812 Charles G. Page, physicist, was born in Salem, Mass.; developed principle of modern induction coil, a small reciprocating electromagnatic engine, an electric locomotive (died 1868).

1813 James M. Sims, physician, was born in Lancaster County, S.C.; an originator of operative gynecology; a founder, Women's Hospital, New York City (1855) (died 1883).

1823 Dan Rice, entertainer, was born in New York City; foremost clown of the mid-19th century (died 1900).

1825 George E. Pickett, Confederate general, was born in Richmond, Va.; in his famed charge, led 4500 men across a half mile of broken ground on Cemetery Ridge at Gettysburg, lost three-fourths of them; fought brilliantly at Battle of Five Forks (1865) (died 1875).

1832 Senate by a 24-23 vote rejected the nomination of Martin Van Buren as minister to England.

1845 The House passed a resolution calling for the annexation of Texas; the Senate voted on Feb 27.

1860 Charles Curtis, Vice President (192-33), was born in North Topeka, Kan.; represented Kansas in the House (1893-1907) and Senate (1907-13, 1925-29); was majority leader (1925-29) (died 1936).

1861 William C. Bobbs, publisher, was born in Montgomery County, Ohio; founder, president, Bobbs Merrill Co. (1895) (died 1926).

1863 Rufus M. Jones, a founder (1917) of American Friends Service Committee, was born in South China, Me.; shared 1947 Nobel Peace Prize (died 1948).

1863 President Lincoln removed Gen. Ambrose E. Burnside as commander of the Army of the Potomac, replacing him with Gen. Joseph Hooker.

1871 Maud Park, women's rights leader, was born in Boston; active suffragist; first president, League of Women Voters (1920-24) (died 1955).

1871 William McKinley married Ida Saxton in Canton, Ohio.

1875 John F. Noll, Catholic bishop of Ft. Wayne, Ind. and founder of *Our Sunday Visitor*, was born in Ft. Wayne (died 1956).

1878 Ernst F.W. Alexanderson, engineer and inventor, was born in Upsala, Sweden; invented high frequency alternator, making transoceanic radio communication possible; pioneer in television, electric ship propulsion, railroad electrification (died 1975).

1882 Charles J. Guiteau was found guilty of assassinating President Garfield in 1881; hanged June 30, 1882.

1885 Roy S. Geiger, World War II general, was born in Middlebury, Fla.; served with the Marine Corps in the South Pacific (died 1947).

1890 The United Mine Workers were organized in Columbus, Ohio by William B. Wilson, who later became the first Secretary of Labor.

1890 Nellie Bly (Elizabeth Seaman), a *New York World* reporter, arrived in New York City, completing her round-the-world trip in 72 days, 6 hours, 11 minutes, beating the record of Phineas Fogg in Jules Verne's *Around the World in 80 Days*.

1900 The House refused by 268 to 50 to seat Rep. Brigham A. Roberts of Utah because of his plural marriages.

1903 Francis M. Flynn, publisher of the *New York Daily News* (1947-73), was born in Mt. Ayr, Ia (died 1974).

1915 The first transcontinental telephone conversation was held by Alexander Graham Bell in New York City and his assistant, Thomas A. Watson, in San Francisco; call cost $20.70 for the first three minutes, $6.75 for each minute thereafter.

1939 Dr. George B. Pegram of Columbia U. helped carry out the first successful American demonstration of nuclear fission; advised President Franklin Roosevelt of this in March.

1946 The United Mine Workers returned to the AFL, which they had left in 1936.

1961 The first live presidential televised news conference was held in the State Department auditorium with President Kennedy answering 31 questions in a half hour.

1988 Justice Department charged that Hertz Co. billed rental car customers and their insurance carriers higher prices to fix vehicles damaged in accidents than it actually paid for repairs.

JANUARY 26

1780 A court martial sentenced Benedict Arnold to public reprimand on two charges—acting without authority in permitting a vessel to come into the port of Philadelphia and of using state wagons to transport private property.

1810 Joseph R. Brown, inventor, was born in Warren, R.I.; devised precision instruments, calipers, protractors; co-founder, Brown & Sharpe (1853) (died 1876).

1826 Julia Dent Grant, wife of President Grant, was born in St. Louis (died 1902).

1831 Mary E.M. Dodge, author and editor, was born in New York City; editor, *St. Nicholas Magazine* (1873-1905); author of children's books, best known for *Hans Brinker; or The Silver Skates* (died 1905).

1832 Rufus H. Gilbert, developer of elevator railway, was born in Guilford, N.Y.; built elevated railway in New York City (1876-78) (died 1885).

1832 George Shiras, jurist, was born in Pittsburgh; associate justice, Supreme Court (1892-1903) (died 1924).

1837 Michigan entered the Union as the 26th state.

1837 Daniel S. Tuttle, Episcopal prelate, was born in Windham, N.Y.; missionary bishop of Montana (1869-86); of Missouri (1886-1923); presiding bishop of church (1903-23) (died 1923).

1846 Benjamin F. Keith, theater operator, was born in Hillsboro Bridge, N.H.; a founder of vaudeville circuit (died 1914).

1847 John B. Clarke, economist, was born in Providence; taught at various schools (1877-1923 — Smith, Amherst, Columbia); editor, *Political Science Quarterly* (1895-1911); author (*Philosophy of Wealth, Distribution of Wealth*) (died 1938).

1861 The Louisiana legislature voted 113-7 to secede from the Union; popular vote ratified the action 20,448 to 17,296.

1870 Virginia was readmitted to the Union by an act of Congress.

1871 Samuel Hopkins Adams, author, was born in Dunkirk, N.Y.; wrote many biographies, novels (*Canal Town, Incredible Era, Night Bus* — which became the movie *It Happened One Night*) (died 1958).

1880 Douglas MacArthur, Army general, was born in Little Rock, Ark., son of Arthur MacArthur (6/2/1845); commanded Rainbow Division, World War I; superintendent, West Point (1919-22); Army chief of staff (1930-35); commander, American forces in Far East (1941), Allied Supreme Commander, Southwest Pacific (1942-45); commander, American forces in Japan (1945-51); supreme commander, UN forces in Korea (1950-51), dismissed when he publicly challenged President Truman's conduct of the war (died 1964).

1881 Walter Krueger, World War II general, was born in

Flatow, Germany (now Poland); commanded 6th Army in Pacific (died 1967).

1884 Roy Chapman Andrews, naturalist and explorer, was born in Beloit, Wis.; headed Asian expeditions (1916-30) of the American Museum of Natural History; known for discoveries of geological strata, dinosaur eggs, remains of largest known land mammals, and evidence of ancient human life; director of Museum (1935-41) (died 1960).

1884 Edward Sapir, anthropologist and linguist, was born in Lauenburg, Germany (now Poland); known for studies on Indians in Pacific Northwest (died 1939).

1887 Marc A. Mitscher, naval officer, was born in Hillsboro, Wis.; headed Task Force 58 in Pacific, the principal carrier strike force (1944-45); headed Atlantic Fleet (1945-47) (died 1947).

1907 Congress enacted a law prohibiting campaign contributions by corporations to candidates for national office.

1911 Polycarp Kusch, physicist, was born in Blankenburg, Germany; shared 1955 Nobel Physics Prize for atomic measurements.

1913 James Van Husen, composer of screen musicals (*Going My Way, Our Town*), was born in Syracuse, N.Y.

1915 Rocky Mountain (Colo.) National Park was established.

1918 Americans were asked to observe wheatless Mondays and Wednesdays, meatless Tuesdays, porkless Thursdays and Saturdays, and use of Victory bread.

1925 Paul Newman, screen actor, was born in Cleveland; starred in many films (*Judge Roy Bean, Exodus, The Sting, Butch Cassidy and the Sundance Kid*)

1936 Samuel C.C. Ting, physicist, was born in Ann Arbor, Mich.; shared 1976 Nobel Physics Prize for codiscovery of the J-(psi) particle.

1942 The first Europe-bound American forces arrived in Northern Ireland.

1961 Wayne Gretzky, one of the greatest hockey players, was born in Brantford, Canada; National Hockey League's most valuable player (1980-86); moved from the Edmonton Oilers to the Los Angeles Kings in 1988.

1979 Former Vice President Nelson A. Rockefeller (1974-76) died in New York City at 70.

JANUARY 27

1785 U. of Georgia chartered; opened in 1801 in Athens.

1788 William Tryon, colonial governor, died at 59; governor of New York (1771-78); commanded Loyalist forces (1778-80), raiding Connecticut towns.

1795 Eli W. Blake, inventor, was born in Westborough, Mass., a nephew of Eli Whitney; invented stone, ore crusher, still being used (died 1886).

1814 William H. Appleton, publisher, was born in Haverhill, Mass., son of Daniel Appleton (12/10/1785); expanded family publishing business; an originator of *Popular Science Monthly,* which disseminated ideas of Darwin, Huxley, and Spencer (died 1899).

1818 Congress fixed its compensation at $8 per day plus mileage; House Speaker and Senate President were to receive $16 per day.

1826 Richard Taylor, Confederate general, was born in Jefferson County, Ky., son of President Tyler; served in Shenandoah Valley campaign, Louisiana, Alabama (died 1879).

1850 Samuel Gompers, labor leader, was born in London; a union cigarmaker, he founded, headed American Federation of Labor (1886-1924, except 1895) (died 1924).

1862 President Lincoln issued General War Order #1, directing that all Union forces advance on Feb 22 — "the day for a general movement of all the land and naval forces of the United States against the insurgent forces."

1872 Learned Hand, jurist, was born in Albany; U.S. district judge (1909-24), U.S. Court of Appeals (1924-51), chief justice (1939-51); considered one of the nation's great judges (died 1961).

1880 A patent for an electric incandescent lamp was granted to Thomas A. Edison.

1885 Jerome D. Kern, composer, was born in New York City; dean of American musical comedy composers (*Sally, Sunny, Show Boat, Roberta, The Cat and the Fiddle*) (died 1945).

1888 The National Geographic Society was founded in Washington, D.C..

1895 Harry Ruby, composer, was born in New York City; remembered for "Three Little Words," various screen and stage musicals (died 1974).

1896 Buddy (George G.) DeSylva, lyricist, was born in New York City; wrote lyrics for hundreds of hits ("Look for the Silver Lining," "April Showers,"

"California Here I Come," "Button Up Your Overcoat") (died 1950).

1900 The first convention of the Social Democratic Party was held in Rochester, N.Y.; Eugene V. Debs was nominated for president.

1900 Hyman G. Rickover, admiral, was born in Makov, Poland; considered the father of atomic-powered naval vessels; retired 1982. (died 1986).

1914 President Wilson signed an executive order establishing a permanent civil government for the Panama Canal Zone, effective Apr 1.

1918 Skitch (Lyle) Henderson, band leader, was born in Halstad, Minn.; a long-time musical director of the *Tonight* television show.

1920 Philip Caldwell, auto manufacturer, was born in Bournsville, Ohio; president, Ford Motor Co. (1978-84).

1922 Two-day snowstorm began in Washington, D.C., resulting in the collapse of the Knickerbocker Theater roof and the death of 100 persons.

1926 Senate approved 76 to 17 American adherence to the Permanent Court of International Justice.

1938 The Honeymoon Bridge over the Niagara River at Niagara Falls collapsed under the strain of a massive ice jam.

1943 The 8th Air Force bombed Wilhelmshaven in the first attack on Germany.

1967 Three Apollo astronauts — Virgil I. Grissom, Edward H. White II, and Roger B. Chaffee — were killed in a spacecraft fire in a simulated launch at Cape Canaveral.

1967 The United States, Great Britain, and Russia signed a treaty limiting the use of outer space for military purposes and outlawing claims for national sovereignty.

1973 Defense Secretary Melvin R. Laird announced the end of the military draft.

1988 The Senate approved a bill to reverse the impact of a 1984 Supreme Court ruling that federal funds should be denied only to programs that practice discrimination and not to entire colleges.

1989 Political cult leader Lyndon H. LaRouche Jr. was sentenced to 15 years in prison for scheming to defraud the IRS and deliberately defaulting on more than $30 million in loans from his supporters.

JANUARY 28

1712 North and South Carolina militia, aided by Indian allies, killed 300 Tuscaroras on the Neuse River.

1754 John Wheelock, president of Dartmouth College (1779-1817), was born in Lebanon, Conn. (died 1817).

1760 Matthew Carey, publisher, was born in Dublin; founder of book publishing company and *Pennsylvania Herald* (1785); helped establish first American Sunday school (died 1839).

1818 George S. Boutwell, legislator and public official, was born in Brookline, Mass.; first commissioner of internal revenue (1862-63), Secretary of Treasury (1869-73); represented Massachusetts in the House (1863-67) and Senate (1873-77) and served as its governor (1851, 1852); a leader in move to impeach President Andrew Johnson (died 1905).

1821 William T.H. Brooks, Union general, was born in New Lisbon, Ohio; served in Mexican War, saw action at Antietam, various Virginia battles (died 1870).

1841 Henry M. Stanley, journalist and explorer, was born in Denbighshire, Wales; with *New York Tribune*, assigned to find missionary David Livingstone in Africa; found him Nov 10, 1871; later in service of King Leopold of Belgium, opening up the Congo; repatriated British subject (1895), member of Parliament (1895) (died 1904).

1855 William S. Burroughs, inventor, was born in Rochester, N.Y.; invented first practical, successfully-marketed adding machine (died 1898).

1861 U. of Washington founded in Seattle.

1864 Charles W. Nash, pioneer automobile manufacturer, was born in DeKalb County, Ill.; president, Buick Motor Co. (1910-16), General Motors (1912-16); founder, head, Nash Motor Co. (later Nash-Kelvinator) (1916-48) (died 1948).

1865 Confederate President Jefferson Davis named three commissioners for informal peace talks.

1866 Charles S. Barrett, organizer of farmers, was born in Pike County, Ga.; a founder, president, National Farmers Union (1906-28) (died 1935).

1878 The first commercial telephone switchboard was installed at New Haven, serving 21 subscribing customers.

1884 Twin atmospheric scientists, Auguste and Jean Piccard, were born in Switzerland; Auguste studied radioactivity, atmospheric electricity in balloon flights, developed airtight gondola; Jean designed new type of balloon for stratospheric flights; Auguste died in 1962, Jean in 1963.

1887 Arthur Rubinstein, pianist, was born in Lodz, Poland; a child prodigy, he made his formal debut at 11; famed for international concerts and interpretation of Chopin (died 1982).

1893 Abba Hillel Silver, rabbi, was born in Neinstadt, Lithuania; chief spokesman for Jewish Agency in UN debate on founding of Israel; rabbi, Cleveland Temple (1917-63) (died 1963).

1902 Carnegie Institution in Washington, D.C. was founded by a $10 million endowment by Andrew Carnegie; designed to promote original research.

1902 Alfred H. Barr, Jr., museum director, was born in Detroit; first director, Museum of Modern Art, New York City (1929-43) (died 1981).

1912 Jackson Pollock, painter, was born in Cody, Wyo.; initiator of pop art movement in 1950s, 1960s; a leading abstract expressionist (died 1956).

1915 President Wilson signed legislation creating the Coast Guard by combining the Life Saving Service (established 1871) and the Revenue Cutter Service (founded 1790).

1915 The American vessel, *William P. Frye*, loaded with wheat for Great Britain, was sunk in the South Atlantic by a German cruiser.

1916 Louis D. Brandeis was named to the Supreme Court by President Wilson, the first Jewish justice; confirmed June 1, serving until 1939.

1922 Robert W. Holley, biochemist, was born in Urbana, Ill.; shared 1968 Nobel Physiology/ Medicine Prize for contributions to understanding genetic mechanism and protein synthesis.

1929 Claes Oldenberg, sculptor, was born in Stockholm; creator of happenings, pop art.

1932 Wisconsin enacted the first unemployment insurance act.

1936 Alan Alda, actor, was born in New York City; starred in television (*M*A*S*H*), screen (*Paper Tiger, Seduction of Joe Tynan*).

1942 Foreign ministers of 21 American republics voted to sever relations with Germany, Italy, and Japan at the conclusion of their Rio de Janeiro conference.

1945 The first truck convey carrying war material over the Ledo (later the Stillwell) and Burma roads reached China; 400 mile Ledo Road ran from Ledo, India to the Burma Road, which ran 717 miles into China.

1948 Mikhail Baryshnikov, ballet dancer and choreographer, was born in Riga, Latvia; with American Ballet Theater (1980-   ); had been member of the Kirov Ballet until he defected in 1974.

1986 Space shuttle Challenger exploded 74 seconds after liftoff at Cape Canaveral, killing its crew of seven.

JANUARY 29

1656 Samuel Andrew, Congregational clergyman, was born in Cambridge; pastor, Milford (Conn.) Church (1685-1738); helped found Yale U., its rector (1707-19) (died 1738).

1677 Three commissioners from London arrived to investigate conditions in Virginia; Gov. Berkeley was recalled Apr 27.

1737 Thomas Paine, pamphleteer, was born in Norfolk, England; issued "Common Sense," a 47-page pamphlet urging immediate declaration of independence; "The Rights of Man" (1791-92), defending the French Revolution; 12 issues of *Crisis,* upholding the American cause during the Revolution; "The Age of Reason," a philosophical discussion of deist beliefs (died 1809).

1751 Joseph B. Barnum, public official, was born in Dracut, Mass.; represented Massachusetts in the House (1795-1811), serving as Speaker (1807-11), and the Senate (1811-17) (died 1821).

1754 Moses Cleaveland, colonial leader, was born in Canterbury, Conn.; served in Revolution; a member of the Connecticut Land Co., led exploring party which founded Cleveland (1796) (died 1806).

1756 Henry Lee, colonial soldier and leader, was born in Leesylvania in Prince William County, Va.; served Virginia as governor (1792-95) and represented it in the House (1799-1801); in his eulogy of George Washington he coined the phrase: "First in war, first in peace, first in the hearts of his countrymen." (died 1818).

1761 Albert Gallatin, legislator, diplomat, and public official, was born in Geneva, Switzerland; Secretary of the Treasury (1801-14); minister to France (1816-23), to England (1826-27); represented Pennsylvania in the House (1795-1801) (died 1849).

1779 British troops captured Augusta, Ga.

1795 The Naturalization Act was passed requiring five years residence and renunciation of allegiance and titles of nobility.

1801 Virginian John Beckley, clerk of the House, was named first librarian of Congress, serving until 1807; library was set up in a Capitol room; salary was not to exceed $2 a day for every day of necessary attendance.

1834 Federal troops were used for the first time to intervene in a labor dispute when President Jackson ordered the War Department to put down "riotous assembly" among Irish laborers building Chesapeake & Ohio Canal near Williamsport, Md.

1838 Edward W. Morley, chemist and physicist, was born in Newark; professor, Western Reserve U. (1869-1906), known for experiments on atmospheric oxygen content, ether drift, thermal expansion of gases; worked with A.A. Michelson (12/19/1852) in light experiments which started modern physics (died 1923).

1840 Henry H. Rogers, financier and oil industry leader, was born in Mattapoisett, Mass.; devised machine for separating naptha from crude oil, originated idea of pipeline transportation; chief executive officer, Standard Oil interests (died 1909).

1843 William McKinley, 25th president (1897-1901), was born in Niles, Ohio; served Ohio as governor (1891-95) and represented it in the House (1877-91); fatally wounded in Buffalo (1901) at the Pan-American Exposition.

1845 "The Raven," a poem by Edgar Allan Poe, appeared in the *New York Evening Mirror* over the pseudonym "Quarles."

1845 Charles F. Crisp, legislator, was born in Sheffield, England of American parentage; represented Georgia in the House (1883-96), serving as Speaker (1891-95) (died 1896).

1850 Henry Clay suggested a series of resolutions to the Senate in an effort to resolve issues of sectional strife; wound up as five separate proposals known as the Compromise of 1850; passed Sept 9 and 18.

1861 Kansas entered the Union as the 34th state.

1864 Whitney Warren, architect, was born in New York City; co-designer of many New York City hotels (Ritz Carlton, Biltmore, Commodore) and Grand Central Terminal (died 1943).

1869 Kenneth McKellar, Tennessee legislator (Senate 1916-53), was born in Richmond, Ala. (died 1958).

1874 John D. Rockefeller Jr., banker and philanthropist, was born in Cleveland, son of John D. Rockefeller (7/8/1839); restored Colonial Williamsburg, planned the Rockefeller Center, donated land for the United Nations in New York City (died 1960).

1874 Owen Davis, playwright, was born in Portland, Me.; wrote many plays, farces, and melodramas; best remembered for *Icebound* (died 1956).

1875 Anton J. Carlson, physiologist, was born in Svarteborg, Sweden; while at U. of Chicago, conducted many experiments on self, providing many contributions to understanding the human body (died 1956).

1877 A commission composed for 5 Senators, 5 Representatives, and 5 Supreme Court justices (8 Republicans, 7 Democrats) was created to judge the presidential election; on Mar 2, awarded 20 electoral votes to Rutherford B. Hayes, giving him the necessary 185 votes to defeat Samuel J. Tilden by one vote.

1878 Walter F. George, legislator, was born near Preston, Ga.; represented Georgia in the Senate (1922-56), ambassador to NATO (1956-57) (died 1957).

1878 Barney (Berna Eli) Oldfield, auto racer, was born in Wauseon, Ohio; first to drive a car 60 miles per hour (1903); by 1910 had reached 131.724 miles per hour (died 1946).

1880 W(illiam) C. Fields, actor, was born in Philadelphia; numerous starring film roles (*David Copperfield, Poppy, Little Chickadee*) (died 1946).

1892 Ernst Lubitsch, movie director, was born in Berlin; directed Mary Pickford in movies, worked with several companies (died 1947).

1895 Adolf A. Berle Jr., public official, was born in Boston; part of New Deal "brain trust;" special counsel, Reconstruction Finance Corp. (1933-38); Assistant Secretary of State (1938-44), helped carry out "good neighbor policy" (died 1971).

1900 Baseball's American League was formed but not recognized by the National League and others until 1903.

1901 Allan B. DuMont, inventor, was born in New York City; pioneer in television development; perfected first commercially-practical cathode ray tube (died 1965).

1919 The 18th (Prohibition) Amendment was ratified; effective Jan 16, 1920.

1923 Paddy Chayefsky, screen writer and playwright, was born in New York City; best remembered for screen plays about urban working life (*Marty, The Bachelor Party*) (died 1981).

1936 Baseball Hall of Fame was established in Cooperstown, N.Y.; the first five named to the Hall were Ty Cobb, Walter Johnson, Christy Mathewson, Babe Ruth, and Honus Wagner.

1945 Tom Selleck, television actor (*Magnum, PI*) was born in Detroit.

1960 Greg Louganis, champion diver of 1984 and 1988 Olympics, was born in San Diego, Cal.

1980 Six Americans who avoided capture by Iranian terrorists were smuggled out of Iran by the Canadian embassy.

JANUARY 30

1649 Virginia announced its allegiance to the House of Stuart after the execution of Charles I, gave refuge to more than 300 prominent Cavaliers; Parliament imposed a blockade and sent two armed vessels to put down the insurrection, which ended Mar 12, 1652.

1672 John Mason, colonial leader, died at about 72; one of the first settlers of Windsor, Conn. (1635); magistrate in Connecticut colony (1642-60), deputy governor (1660-69), assistant governor (1669-72).

1797 Edwin V. Sumner, Union general, was born in Boston; acting governor, New Mexico (1852); saw action at South Mountain, Antietam, and Fredericksburg (died 1863).

1801 Pierre Jean DeSmet, Jesuit missionary, was born in Termonde, Belgium; worked 30 years among the American Indians, who called him "Black Robe" (died 1873).

1815 Library of Congress, which was destroyed by invading British troops, was restored when the government purchased former President Jefferson's library of 7000 volumes for $23,950.

1816 Nathaniel P. Banks, Union general and legislator, was born in Waltham, Mass.; led capture of Port Hudson (1863); represented Massachusetts in the House for nearly 20 years (between 1853 and 1891), Speaker (1855-57), and served state as governor (died 1894).

1835 The first attempt to assassinate a president occurred when Richard Lawrence, a demented painter, shot at President Jackson in the Capitol; fired two pistols, both of which misfired; committed to mental hospital for life.

1836 Joseph W. Kiefer, Army officer and legislator, was born near Springfield, Ohio; served in Civil and Spanish-American wars; represented Ohio in the House (1876-84, 1905-11), serving as Speaker (1881-83) (died 1932).

1840 Father Damien, Catholic missionary, was born in Tremeloo, Belgium as Joseph Damien de Veuster; served leper colony on Molokai Island, Hawaii; died of leprosy in 1888.

1862 Walter J. Damrosch, conductor, was born in Breslau, Germany, son of Leopold Damrosch (10/22/1832); directed New York Symphony (1903-27); founder, conductor of radio concerts for schools; composer (*Cyrano, Man Without a Country*) (died 1950).

1862 The ironclad steamer, *Monitor*, was launched at Greenpoint, Long Island.

1863 Gen. U.S. Grant assumed command of troops besieging Vicksburg, Miss.

1866 (Frank) Gelett Burgess, humorist and illustrator, was born in Boston; author of classic "Purple Cow" jingle; illustrator of many whimsical books (died 1951).

1875 President Grant signed a reciprocity treaty with Hawaii, providing for free access of sugar and other products into American ports.

1882 Franklin D. Roosevelt, 32nd president (1933-45), was born in Hyde Park, N.Y., a distant cousin of President Theodore Roosevelt; Assistant Secretary of Navy (1913-20), served New York as governor (1929-33); died suddenly in Warm Springs, Ga. (1945).

1882 Sosthenes Behn, industrialist, was born in St. Thomas, Virgin Islands; a founder, president, chairman, International Telephone & Telegraph (ITT) (1920-56) (died 1957).

1885 John H. Towers, naval officer, was born in Rome, Ga.; pioneer Navy flier; commander Pacific Fleet air force (1942-44), deputy commander, Pacific area (1944-45) (died 1955).

1891 Walter H. Beech, aircraft manufacturer, was born in Pulaski, Tenn.; founder, president, Beech Aircraft Corp. (1936-50) (died 1950).

1894 New York Legislature named Lexow Committee to investigate alleged New York City corruption.

1899 Max Theiler, epidemiologist, was born in Pretoria, South Africa; awarded 1951 Nobel Physiology/Medicine Prize for discoveries about yellow fever and a vaccine (died 1972).

1905 Supreme Court ruled that the "beef trust" (Swift & Co. et al) was illegal; forbade agreements not to bid against each other, price fixing, blacklists.

1908 Ray Milland, screen actor (*Lost Weekend*), was born in Neath, Wales (died 1986).

1909 Saul D. Alinsky, social reformer, was born in Chicago; developed local leadership to meet local problems through self-help (died 1972).

1928 Mitch (Irwin S.) Leigh, composer, was born in Brooklyn; best remembered for *Man of La Mancha.*

1928 Harold S. Prince, producer-director, was born in New York City; responsible for some of Broadway's greatest hits (*Pajama Game, Damn Yankees, West Side Story, Fiddler on the Roof, Cabaret*).

1934 The Gold Reserve Act was passed, nationalizing all gold; all Federal Reserve banks received gold certificates as reserves against deposits and Federal Reserve notes.

1934 The first balls observing President Franklin Roosevelt's birthday were held; the president accepted $1 million for Georgia's Warm Springs Foundation to combat polio and infantile paralysis.

1939 Supreme Court upheld the Tennessee Valley Authority in competition with private companies.

1942 The price control bill was signed, giving the Office of Price Administration power to fix all prices, except on farm products.

1968 The Tet offensive was launched by Communist forces against numerous Allied centers in Vietnam, including the American embassy in Saigon.

JANUARY 31

1583 Peter Bulkeley, Puritan clergyman, was born in Bedfordshire, England; founder, Concord, N.H., its first minister (1635) (died 1659).

1732 Richard Henry Lee, colonial leader, was born in Stratford, Westmoreland County, Va.; member of Continental Congress (1774-79, 1784-89), introduced resolution (6/7/1776) to make colonies free of England; signer of Declaration of Independence; represented Virginia in the Senate (1789-92) (died 1794).

1734 Robert Morris, financier of American Revolution, was born near Liverpool, England; finance superintendent (1781-84); founder, Bank of North America (1782); signer of Declaration of Independence; delegate to Constitutional Convention; represented Pennsylvania in the Senate (1789-95) (died 1806).

1737 Jacob Duché, Anglican clergyman, was born in Philadelphia; chaplain of Continental Congress (1774); had change of heart, asked George Washington to have Declaration of Independence withdrawn; left with Loyalists, returned in 1792 (died 1798).

1752 The ceremony for the Profession of Sister St. Martha Turpin, the first American-born Catholic nun, was held in the Ursaline convent in New Orleans.

1752 Gouverneur Morris, diplomat and financier, was born in what is now New York City, grandson of Lewis Morris (4/8/1726); helped devise American decimal coinage system; commissioner to England (1790-91), minister to France (1792-94); represented New York in the Senate (1800-03) (died 1816).

1774 Parliament dismissed Benjamin Franklin as colonial deputy postmaster general because of his patriotic sympathies, considered subversive.

1801 John Marshall began his 34 years as chief justice of the Supreme Court.

1812 William H. Russell, express business pioneer, was born in Burlington, Vt.; founder, Pony Express (1860) between St. Joseph, Mo. and Sacramento, Cal. (died 1872).

1817 Massachusetts Peace Society asked Congress to call an international meeting for the settlement of controversies.

1830 James G. Blaine, public official, was born in West Brownsville, Pa.; served Maine in the House (1863-76), was Speaker (1869-75), and in the Senate (1876-81); Secretary of State (1881-82, 1892); 1884 Republican presidential nominee (died 1893).

1831 Rudolph Wurlitzer, musical instrument manufacturer, was born in Schoneck, Germany; began making trumpets, drums (1860), pianos (1868); introduced first automatically-played, electric, coin-operated instruments (1892) (died 1914).

1842 President and Mrs. Tyler's daughter, Elizabeth, was married in the White House to William N. Waller; marked the only public appearance of Mrs. Tyler, who was paralyzed and died eight months later.

1843 The Virginia Minstrels, the first such troupe, made its debut at a benefit in New York City's Chatham Theater; organized by Daniel D. Emmett, who went on to write "Blue Tail Fly," "Old Dan Tucker," and "Dixie."

1846 Stephen D. Field, inventor, was born in Stockbridge, Mass.; among his inventions were a multiple call district telegraph box, stock ticker, and an electric locomotive (died 1913).

1848 John C. Fremont was found guilty by a court martial of mutiny and disobeying orders; charges were brought by Gen. Stephen Kearney; dismissed from the service but punishment was cancelled by President Polk; Fremont resigned Mar 15.

1848 Nathan Straus, merchant, was born in Rhenish, Germany; active in Macy's with brothers (Isidore (2/6/1845) and Oscar (12/23/1850)) until 1914; spearheaded national drive for milk pasteurization (died 1931).

1862 President Lincoln was authorized to take over the railroads and telegraph lines when the public safety was involved.

1862 George W. Perkins, businessman and financier, was born in Chicago; as first vice president, New York Life Insurance Co. revolutionized the insurance and other businesses which depended on direct sales by agents; with J.P. Morgan & Co. (from 1901), where he helped organize various large companies (died 1920).

1866 William W. Atterbury, railway executive, was born in New Albany, Ind.; with Pennsylvania Railroad (1886-1935), president (1925-35); directed construction, operation of American military railroads in France (1917-19) (died 1935).

1868 Theodore W. Richards, chemist, was born in Germantown, Pa.; awarded 1914 Nobel Chemistry Prize for determining the atomic weight of many chemical elements (died 1928).

1872 Rupert Hughes, author of biographies, plays, and about 25 novels, was born in Lancaster, Mo. (died 1956).

1875 Zane Grey, author of romantic Western novels (*Riders of the Purple Sage, Last of the Plainsmen*), was born in Zanesville, Ohio (died 1939).

1881 Irving Langmuir, 1932 Nobel Chemistry Prize winner for work in surface chemistry, was born in Brooklyn; developed cloud-seeding technique, a gas-filled tungsten lamp, a high vacuum pump; with Gilbert N. Lewis developed atomic theory (died 1957).

1881 Alfred Harcourt, publisher, was born in Ulster County, N.Y.; a founder, Harcourt Brace (1919) (died 1954).

1891 Paul R. Hawley, medical director, Veterans Administration, was born in West College Corner, Ind.; chief surgeon, European theater in World War II (died 1965).

1892 Eddie Cantor, entertainer, was born in New York City; starred in vaudeville, burlesque, musicals (*Kid Boots, Whoopee*) (died 1964).

1894 Isham Jones, band leader of 1930s, was born in Coalton, Ohio; composer ("I'll See You in My Dreams," "It Had to be You") (died 1956).

1895 (Samuel) Ward McCallister, social leader, died at 68; coined phrase "the 400" in shortening an invitation list to a New York ball, saying only that number was worthy of an invitation.

1903 Gardner Cowles, editor, publisher, *Des Moines Register, Look Magazine* (1937-41), was born in Algona, Ia. (died 1985).

1903 Tallulah Bankhead, stage actress, was born in Huntsville, Ga., daughter of William Bankhead (4/12/1874); starred in many plays (*The Little Foxes, The Skin of Our Teeth*) (died 1968).

1905 John O'Hara, author, was born in Pottsville, Pa.; wrote many short stories, novels (*Appointment in Samara, Butterfield 8, Pal Joey, A Rage to Live*) (died 1970).

1908 Statewide prohibition was enacted in North Carolina.

1913 Don(ald) Hutson, one of the greatest football ends (Green Bay Packers 1935-45), was born in Pine Bluff, Ark.

1915 Thomas Merton, Trappist monk, was born in Paris; spiritual writer (*The Seven Storey Mountain*) (died 1968).

1919 Jackie Robinson, baseball player, was born in Cairo, Ga.; first black player in major leagues (Dodgers 1947-56); named to Baseball Hall of Fame (died 1972).

1919 Nat(haniel G.) Goodwin, stage star of 1880s, 1890s (*The Gilded Fool, Rivals, Oliver Twist*), died at 62.

1923 Carol Channing, actress (*Hello Dolly, Gentlemen Prefer Blonds*), was born in Seattle.

1923 Norman K. Mailer, author, was born in Long Branch, N.J.; best known for *The Naked and the Dead, An American Dream, The Executioner's Song.*

1925 Benjamin Hooks, first black Securities & Exchange commissioner (1972-76), was born in Memphis; executive director, NAACP (1976-82).

1931 Ernie Banks, baseball player (Cubs 1953-71), was born in Dallas; named to Baseball Hall of Fame.

1934 Federal Farm Mortgage Corporation was created to help refinance farm debts, guarantee principal and interest of bonds exchanged for consolidated loan bonds.

1944 American forces invaded the Marshall Islands; Roi and Namur secured Feb 3, Kwajalein Feb 6, and Eniwetok Feb 22.

1947 Nolan Ryan, baseball pitcher (Giants, Angels, Astros), was born in Refugio, Tex.; all-time leader in strikeouts (4000+), winner of more than 250 games.

1949 United States granted de jure recognition of Israel when it created a permanent government.

1950 President Truman ordered the development of the hydrogen bomb; initial objective reached in Nov 1952.

1958 Army's Jupiter-C rocket fired the first American earth satellite, Explorer 1, into orbit from Cape Canaveral, Fla.; a side benefit was discovery of the Van Allen radiation belt.

1966 United States resumed bombing raids on North Vietnam; 27-day pause ended when North Vietnam and China rejected a peace drive.

FEBRUARY 1

1682 William Penn and 11 other Quakers purchased East New Jersey from the Carteret heirs.

1716 John Bard, pioneer physician, was born in Burlington, N.J.; helped introduce into the United States the practice of dissecting human bodies for instruction (died 1779).

1753 George Washington was named adjutant of the counties of the James River; officially became a major.

1763 Thomas Campbell, church co-founder, was born in Scotland; helped son, Alexander, and Barton W. Stone found the Disciples of Christ Church (died 1854).

1775 A second Massachusetts provincial Congress met in Cambridge, framed measures to prepare colony for war.

1781 Gen. William L. Davidson was killed in the battle at Cowans Ford, N.C.

1790 The Supreme Court met for the first time (in the Royal Exchange Building, Broad St., New York City) but did not organize until Feb 2 when all five appointees were present.

1801 Thomas L. Cole, painter, was born in Bolton-le-Moors, England; a founder of the Hudson River School of landscape painting; best known for allegorical cycles (*The Course of Empire, The Voyage of Life*) (died 1848)

1819 The Supreme Court ruled in *Dartsmouth v Woodard* that a college charter was a contract which could not be altered by the state without the consent of the college trustees.

1828 George F. Edmunds, legislator, was born in Richmond, Vt.; regarded as an authority on constitutional law while representing Vermont in the Senate (1866-91); author of anti-polygamy law, wrote most of the Sherman Anti-Trust Act (died 1919).

1828 Meyer Guggenheim, financier and industrialist, was born in Langnau, Switzerland; founder of world-wide copper industry, controlled American Smelting & Refining Co. (died 1905).

1838 Joseph Kepper, caricaturist and publisher, was born in Vienna; a founder of *Puck* in German (1875), in English (1877) (died 1894).

1839 James A. Herne, author and playwright, was born in Cohoes, N.Y.; numerous successful plays (*Hearts of Oak, Shore Acres, Sag Harbor*) (died 1901).

1840 The Baltimore College of Dental Surgery, first dental school, was incorporated.

1844 G(ranville) Stanley Hall, psychologist and educator, was born in Ashfield, Mass.; established one of the first psychology laboratories and founder American experimental psychology (1883); first president, Clark U. (1888-1920); American Psychological Association (1891) (died 1924).

1859 Victor Herbert, conductor and composer, was born in Dublin; composed light operas (*Babes in Toyland, The Red Mill, Naughty Marietta, Sweethearts*); co-founder, American Society of Composers and Performers (ASCAP) (1914) (died 1924).

1860 Henry J. Miller, actor, was born in London; theater manager and star (*The Great Divide, The Servant in the House, The Faith Healer*) (died 1926).

1861 Texas legislature voted 166-7 to secede from the Union, ratified by popular vote (34,794 to 11,255) on Feb 23.

1861 Mint and customhouse in New Orleans was seized by Confederate troops; $536,000 was taken.

1865 President Lincoln signed the 13th Amendment outlawing slavery; day now observed as National Freedom Day.

1885 Alcan Hirsch, chemical engineer, was born in Corpus Christi, Tex.; a founder, Molybdenum Corp. (1920); started American pyrophonic alloy industry (died 1938).

1887 Charles B. Nordhoff, author, was born in London of American parentage; co-author with James Norman Hall of several books (*Mutiny on the Bounty, Pitcairn Island, Botany Bay*) (died 1947).

1895 John Ford, movie director, was born in Cape Elizabeth, Me.; directed many hits (*Tobacco Road, Stagecoach, Grapes of Wrath, The Informer, The Quiet Man*) (died 1973).

1896 Nat Holman, baseball player, was born in New York City; star of original Celtics team, which won 720 of 795 games (1921-30); coach, CCNY (1950-52, 1955-60).

1901 Clark Gable, screen actor, was born in Cadiz, Ohio; starred in many films (*Gone With the Wind, Mutiny on the Bounty, It Happened One Night*) (died 1960).

1902 Langston Hughes, author, was born in Joplin, Mo.; author (*Not Without Laughter*), known as the poet of Harlem (died 1967).

1904 William Howard Taft became Secretary of War; served until June 30, 1908.

1904 S(idney) J. Perelman, author, was born in New York City; humorist (*Dawn Ginsburgh's Revenge; Parlor, Bedlam, and Bath; Westward Ha!*); movie scriptwriter (for the Marx Brothers, *Around the World in 80 Days*) (died 1979).

1905 President Theodore Roosevelt appointed Gifford Pinchot as first chief of the Forest Service in the Agriculture Department.

1905 Emilio G. Segré, physicist, was born in Tivoli, Italy; shared 1959 Nobel Physics Prize for demonstrating the existence of anti-proton; discovered element 43, technitium, first artificially-produced element (died 1989).

1913 The Senate adopted (47-23) recommendation of President Taft for a constitutional amendment limiting presidency to one six-year term; House did not act.

1917 German submarine assaults against all neutral and belligerent shipping renewed.

1926 Gen. Billy Mitchell, air advocate, resigned from the Army after a court martial found him guilty of insubordination in his outspoken views.

1929 Bok Singing Tower near Lake Wales, Fla. was dedicated by President Coolidge.

1940 Hervé Filion, probably the greatest harness racing driver, was born in Angers, Canada; won his 10,000th race in May 1987; named to Harness Racing Hall of Fame.

1942 The Pacific Fleet attacked Japanese bases on the Marshall and Gilbert Islands.

1944 American forces landed on Kwajalein in the Marshall Islands.

1949 A consolidated city-county (parish) government went into effect in Baton Rouge, La.

1960 Four black students sat in at a lunch counter in Greensboro, N.C., resulting in the organization (April 1961) of the Student Non-violent Coordinating Committee (SNCC) and a wave of sit-ins.

1979 President Carter commuted the sentence of Patricia Hearst, who had been kidnapped by the Symbionese Liberation Army and later joined them in a series of robberies.

1988 The Army and Shell Oil Co. agreed to share the cost of $1 billion toxic waste cleanup at the Rocky Mountain Arsenal.

FEBRUARY 2

1619 A patent was granted to Puritans at Leyden, Holland for a settlement in North America.

1651 Sir William Phips, colonial leader, was born in Maine; first royal governor of Massachusetts (1692-94); knighted after recovering sunken treasurer off Haiti (about 1683) (died 1695).

1653 New Amsterdam was proclaimed a municipality by the director-general of the Dutch West India Co.; municipal officials were appointed.

1800 William Gregg, industrialist, was born near Carmichaels, W.Va.; launched textile industry in the South (died 1867).

1803 Albert S. Johnston, Confederate general, was born in Washington, Ky.; surprised, defeated Union forces under Grant at Shiloh (1862); killed in that action.

1804 George Walton, colonial leader, died at 63; member of Continental Congress from Georgia (1776-81), signer of Declaration of Independence; served Georgia as governor (1779-80; 1789-90).

1827 Supreme Court in *Martin v. Mott* declared the President was the final judge on when to call out the militia.

1843 Knute Nelson, legislator, was born in Evanger, Norway; represented Minnesota in the Senate (1895-1912), served state as governor (1893-95) (died 1923).

1846 Francis M. Smith, prospector and financier, was born in Richmond, Wis.; co-discoverer of metal from which borax is extracted; gained control of area and virtual world monopoly (Pacific Coast Borax Co.) (died 1931).

1848 The Treaty of Guadelupe Hidalgo was signed, ending two-year Mexican War; ratified May 30, 1848; added 1,193,061 sq.mi. to United States (Arizona, Nevada, Canada, Utah, and parts of New Mexico, Colorado, Wyoming).

1854 Stephen H. Horgan, photoengraver, was born in Norfolk, Va.; pioneer in developing photoengraving process for newspapers (died 1941).

1875 Fritz Kreisler, violinist and composer, was born in Vienna; composed, arranged, much music for violin, operetta *Apple Blossoms* (died 1962).

1876 National League (baseball) was formed with teams from Philadelphia, Hartford, Boston, Chicago, Cincinnati, Louisville, St. Louis, and New York.

1881 Christian Endeavor Society was organized in Williston Congregational Church, Portland, Me., by its pastor, Rev. Francis E. Clark.

1882 Knights of Columbus organization was founded in New Haven by the Rev. Joseph M. Givney.

1886 William Rose Benet, poet and novelist, was born in Ft. Hamilton, N.Y., brother of Steven Vincent Benet (7/22/1898); a founder, *Saturday Review* (1924); author (*The Dust Which is God, The First Person Singular*) (died 1950).

1890 Charles J. Correll, entertainer was born in Peoria, Ill.; played Andy in *Amos 'N Andy* radio show (died 1972).

1895 George S. Halas, football player and coach, was born in Chicago; with Chicago Bears as founder, owner, coach (1922-83); a founder, National Football League (died 1983).

1901 Jasche Heifetz, one of the world's greatest violinists, was born in Vilna, Russia. (died 1987).

1905 Ayn Rand, author, was born in Leningrad; produced philosophy of self-interest or objectivism (*The Fountainhead, Atlas Shrugged*) (died 1982).

1912 Burton Lane, composer (*Three's a Crowd, Finian's Rainbow*), was born in New York City.

1914 Renato Dulbeco, molecular biologist, was born in Catanzaro, Italy; shared 1975 Nobel Physiology/Medicine Prize for study of animal viruses.

1917 Desi(derio) Arnaz, musician/television personality, was born in Santiago, Cuba; co-star of *I Love Lucy* show (died 1986).

1923 James Dickey, poet and author (*Deliverance*), was born in Atlanta; poetry consultant to Library of Congress (1966-68).

1925 Diphtheria epidemic in Nome, Alaska broken by arrival of antitoxin brought 650 miles by dogsled.

1927 Stan Getz, tenor saxophonist and orchestra leader, was born in Philadelphia.

1980 Two days of rioting began in New Mexico state prison, resulting in 33 deaths.

1988 The Defense Department ordered the military services to enforce rules against sexual discrimination and harassment more vigorously and to open more positions for women.

FEBRUARY 3

1748 Samuel Osgood, public official, was born in Andover, Mass.; a member of Continental Congress (1781-84); first commissioner, U.S. Treasury (1785-89), Postmaster General (1789-91) (died 1813).

1777 Felipe de Neve, Spanish governor, arrived at Monterey, which he made the capital of California.

1807 Joseph E. Johnston, Confederate general, was born near Farmville, Va.; helped win at first Bull Run; commanded troops at Vicksburg, then with Army of the Tennessee; represented Virginia in the House (1879-81); commissioner of railroads (1887-91) (died 1891).

1811 Horace Greeley, journalist and political leader, was born in Amherst, N.H.; founder, editor, *New York Tribune* (1841-72); an important influence on the North before and during Civil War; Democratic presidential candidate (1872) (died 1872).

1821 Elizabeth Blackwell, pioneer doctor, was born in Bristol, England, sister-in-law of Antoinette L.B. Blackwell (5/20/1825); first woman to receive medical degree in modern times (Geneva (NY) Medical School 1849); started New York Infirmary (1857), women's medical college; returned to England (1869) (died 1910).

1823 Spencer F. Baird, naturalist, was born in Reading, Pa.; secretary, Smithsonian Institution (1878-87); his collection formed nucleus of Smithsonian natural history museum; established marine laboratory at Woods Hole, Mass. (died 1887).

1834 Edwin Adams, actor, was born in Medford, Mass.; one of the most popular American actors of his day; one of his greatest successes was *Enoch Arden* (died 1877).

1836 The Whig Party held its first convention in Albany; nominated William Henry Harrison for president.

1842 Sidney Lanier, poet, was born in Macon, Ga.; a leading Southern poet ("Corn," "Song of the Chattahoochee," "Marshes of Glynn") (died 1881).

1844 Tolbert Lanston, inventor, was born in Troy, Ohio; invented typesetting machine Monotype (died 1913).

1853 Hudson Maxim, inventor and explosives expert, was born in Orneville, Me., brother of Sir Hiram S. Maxim (2/5/1840); developed high power explosives, machine gun ammunition (died 1927).

1855 Michigan enacted a prohibition law; repealed in 1875.

1862 George C. Tilyou, amusement rides inventor, was born in New York City; developed Coney Island, other amusement parks (died 1914).

1862 James C. McReynolds, attorney and jurist, was born in Elkton, Ky.; special government counsel in tobacco antitrust suit; Attorney General (19130-14); associate justice, Supreme Court (1914-46) (died 1946).

1865 Three Confederate commissioners, headed by Vice President Alexander H. Stephens, met with President Lincoln aboard the "River Queen" in Hampton Roads without result because the President demanded union as the basis for peace, Confederates wanted independence.

1869 Giulio Gatti-Casazza, opera manager, was born in Udine, Italy; manager, Metropolitan Opera (1908-35) (died 1940).

1872 Sam H. Harris, theatrical producer, was born in New York City; in business with George M. Cohan (1904-20), alone (1920-40); produced many hits (*Music Box Revue, Rain, Dinner at Eight, Of Mice and Men*) (died 1941).

1874 Gertrude Stein, expatriate author, was born in Allegheny, Pa.; lived in Paris, concerned with words, sounds, rhythm ("A rose is a rose is a rose," "Pigeons in the grass, alas"); author (*Three Lives, Autobiography of Alice B. Toklas*) (died 1946).

1883 Clarence E. Mulford, author, was born in Streator, Ill.; author of Westerns, including the *Bar 20, Hopalong Cassidy* series (died 1956).

1884 Frank M. Andrews, World War II Army general, was born in Nashville; early proponent of air power, organized and commanded Air Forces (1930s); commander, Air Forces in Europe (1943); killed in plane crash in Iceland (1943).

1887 Electoral Count Act was passed to prevent a disputed national election such as the 1876 Tilden-Hayes election; each state was made absolute judge over the appointment of electors and state vote returns.

1890 Larry (Leland S.) MacPhail, baseball executive with various clubs, was born in Cass City, Mich.; named to Baseball Hall of Fame (died 1975).

1894 Norman Rockwell, artist, was born in New York City; did about ten covers a year for the *Saturday Evening Post* (1916-69) (died 1978).

1907 James A. Michener, author, was born in New York City; wrote numerous best selling historical novels (*Hawaii, Iberia, Centennial, Space, Chesapeake, Texas*).

1907 Hodding Carter, editor, was born in Hammond, La.; crusading liberal editor of *The Greenville* (Miss.) *Delta Democrat Times* (died 1972).

1908 The Supreme Court ruled that the antitrust laws cover labor combinations and prohibit boycotts by unions (*Danbury Hatters* case).

1917 United States severed relations with Germany after the latter announced intensified submarine activity; President Wilson said "we do not desire any hostile conflict ... we propose nothing more than the reasonable defense of the undoubted rights of our people."

1920 Henry J. Heimlich, surgeon who invented the "Heimlich maneuver" to save persons from choking, was born in Wilmington, Del.

1924 Former President Wilson died in Washington, D.C. at 67.

1930 Chief Justice William Howard Taft resigned from the Supreme Court for reasons of health; President Hoover nominated Charles Evans Hughes to succeed him; confirmed Feb 13.

1940 Fran Tarkenton, football quarterback with the New York Giants, Minnesota Vikings (1961-79), was born in Richmond, Va.

1941 The Supreme Court in *United States v. Darby* upheld the Fair Labor Standards Act.

1943 Four chaplains aboard the *Dorchester*—Alexander Goode, John P. Washington, George L. Fox, and Clark V. Poling—gave up their life jackets to others and went down with the ship.

1944 United States and Mexico signed an agreement for the use of water from the Rio Grande, Colorado, and Tiajuana rivers.

1959 An airliner crashed into the East River in New York City, killing 65 persons.

1980 The press revealed the existence of an extensive FBI investigation into political corruption, which involved a senator and seven members of the House of Representatives.

1984 Anne Townsend, leading American field hockey player, died in Bryn Mawr, Pa. at 84.

1988 The New Jersey Supreme Court ruled 7-0 that paying a woman to have a baby amounts to illegal baby selling in the landmark *Baby M* case, finding surrogate agreements illegal when arranged for profit.

1988 The Senate unanimously confirmed Anthony M. Kennedy to the Supreme Court to succeed retired Justice Lewis F. Powell; sworn in Feb 18.

1988 National Religious Broadcasters, representing most television and radio evangelists, voted 324-6 in Washington, D.C. for self-regulation by requiring members soliciting tax exempt donations to meet the standards of its Ethics & Financial Accountability Commission.

1989 National League baseball owners named former player Bill (William D.) White as National League president, effective Apr 1, to succeed A. Bartlett Giammati, who will become commissioner.

FEBRUARY 4

1789 With only four absences, 69 electors unanimously voted for George Washington as the first President; John Adams received 34 votes for vice president.

1792 James G. Birney, antislavery leader, was born in Dansville, Ky.; executive secretary, American Anti-Slavery Society (1837-57); presidential candidate, Liberty Party (1840, 1844) (died 1857).

1802 Mark Hopkins, educator and author, was born in Stockbridge, Mass.; president, Williams College (1836-72); inspirational teacher, wrote many books on moral and religious subjects (died 1887).

1848 Francis W. Ayer, pioneer advertising executive, was born in Lee, Mass.; founder, N.W. Ayer (1869); first company to do market research, pioneered in use of trademarks, slogans, ad copy (died 1923).

1860 William L. Rodgers, World War I admiral, was born in Washington, D.C.; served in Atlantic Fleet (1917-18); commander, Asiatic Fleet (1918-19) (died 1944).

1861 Convention of Confederate states opened in Montgomery, Ala.; adopted provisional constitution Feb 8, elected Jefferson Davis president and Alexander H. Stephens vice president (only 6 of 15 slave states represented).

1861 Peace convention of states (13 northern, 7 border), met in Washington, D.C. with former President Tyler serving as chairman; meeting was an effort to avoid war; seven states which had already seceded did not send delegates; conference was unsuccessful because recommendations satisfied no one.

1869 William D. Haywood, Socialist labor leader, was born in Salt Lake City; a founder, Industrial Workers of the World (IWW) (1905); accused of murdering Frank R. Steuenberg, former Idaho governor; acquitted; charged with sedition in 1917, fled to Russia while on bail (1921), died there 1928.

1870 John Mitchell, labor leader, was born in Braidwood, Ill.; president, United Mine Workers (1898-1908); chairman, New York State Industrial Commission (1915-19) (died 1919).

1886 Edward B. Sheldon, playwright, was born in Chicago; wrote numerous hits (*Salvation Nell, Romance, Song of Songs*); co-author (*Lulu Belle*) (died 1946).

1887 The Interstate Commerce Act was signed by President Cleveland, setting up federal regulation of commerce.

1899 Filipino guerilla war began in an effort to get independence from the United States; ended with capture of the leader, Emilio Aguinaldo (1901).

1902 Charles A. Lindberg, aviator, was born in Detroit; known as the "Lone Eagle," he became the first to make solo nonstop flight across the Atlantic Ocean (May 20-21, 1927) (died 1974).

1904 MacKinlay Kantor, author, was born in Webster City, Iowa; screenwriter and author of several best sellers (*The Voice of Bugle Anne, Arouse and Beware, Andersonville, Long Remember*) (died 1977).

1912 Byron Nelson, golfer, was born in Ft. Worth, Tex.; a leading golfer of the 1930s and 1940s, he won 11 consecutive tournaments in 1945.

1912 Erich Leinsdorf, conductor, was born in Vienna; conductor of Metropolitan Opera (1930-43, 1957-61), Rochester Philharmonic (1947-56); musical director, Boston Symphony (1962-68).

1913 National Institute of Arts & Letters incorporated, designed to further literature and fine arts.

1921 Betty Friedan, women's rights activist, was born in Peoria, Ill.; her book, *The Feminine Mystique* accelerated the movement; a founder, president, National Organization of Women (NOW) (1966-70).

1928 President Coolidge dedicated the National Press Club.

1932 The Winter Olympics games opened in Lake Placid, N.Y.

1945 President Franklin Roosevelt, Prime Minister Churchill, and Premier Stalin met in Yalta through Feb 11; reaffirmed the unconditional surrender policy.

1947 J. Danforth Quayle, elected Vice President in 1988, was born in Huntington, Ind.; represented Indiana in the House (1979-83) and Senate (1983-89).

1985 The State Department announced that New Zealand had denied a request that a Navy destroyer be allowed to pay a port call during Anzus exercises because the United States refused to say whether or not the ship carried nuclear arms; resulted in the United States saying it no longer regarded New Zealand "a loyal and faithful ally."

FEBRUARY 5

1631 The *Lyon* from Bristol, England arrived at Massachusetts Bay Colony with 26 passengers, including Roger Williams, and provisions to end long famine; Williams served in the Salem and Plymouth churches; he attacked the validity of the charter, questioned the right of civil authorities to legislate in matters of conscience, and urged Salem Church to separate from the rest; he was later (Sept 13) banished.

1703 Gilbert Tennent, Presbyterian clergyman and evangelist, was born in County Armagh, Ireland; one of the leaders of the "Great Awakening" in the United States (died 1764).

1723 John Witherspoon, Presbyterian leader, was born in Yester, Scotland; an organizer of the Presbyterian Church along national lines; president, College of New Jersey (later Princeton) (1768-94); a signer of the Declaration of Independence, member of the Continental Congress (1776-79, 1780-81, 1782) (died 1794).

1725 James Otis, colonial leader and pamphleteer, was born in West Barnstable, Mass.; brilliant speaker, writer for colonial cause, developed powerful legal rationale for colonial rights (died 1783).

1745 John Jeffries, physician and balloonist, was born in Boston; practiced medicine in Boston, moving to England after the Revolution; conducted first experiments in free air, was with first balloon crossing of English Channel (1785) (died 1819).

1777 Georgia voters ratified their state constitution adopted by convention in 1775.

1783 Sweden recognized the independence of the United States.

1817 The first gas light company was incorporated in Baltimore.

1819 Hannah Hoes Van Buren, wife of President Van Buren, died in Albany at 35.

1826 Millard Fillmore and Abigail Powers were married in Moravia, N.Y.

1837 Dwight L. Moody, foremost evangelist of 19th century, was born in Northfield, Mass.; organized North Market Sabbath School, Chicago (1858); made several American and English evangelistic tours (1873-83); founded Northfield Seminary for girls (1879), Mt. Hermon boys school, Chicago (1881), Chicago (now Moody) Bible Institute (1889) (died 1899).

1840 Sir Hiram S. Maxim, machine gun inventor, was born in Sangerville, Me., brother of Hudson Maxim (2/3/1853); moved to England (1881), invented automatic machine gun, illuminating gas equipment; knighted 1901 (died 1916).

1846 *The Spectator*, the first Oregon newspaper, was published in Oregon City.

1858 Mahlon Pitney, jurist, was born in Morristown, N.J.; represented New Jersey in the House (1895-99); justice, New Jersey Supreme Court (1901-12); associate justice, Supreme Court (1912-22) (died 1924).

1871 Maxine Elliott, actress, was born in Rockland, Me.; starred in Shakespearean repertoire and other plays in the United States and England (died 1940).

1872 Lafayette B. Mendel, psychological chemist, was born in Delhi, N.Y.; discovered Vitamin A (1913), function of Vitamin C; did research in digestion, nutrition (died 1935).

1900 Adlai E. Stevenson, public official, was born in Los Angeles, grandson of Adlai E. Stevenson (10/23/1835); served Illinois as governor (1949-52); delegate to United Nations founding conference (1946); Democratic presidential candidate (1952, 1956); UN ambassador (1961-65) (died 1965).

1900 First Hay-Pauncefort Treaty was signed, provided for joint protectorate by England and United States of any transisthmian canal, would permit American construction and operation of a canal.

1915 Robert Hofstadter, physicist, was born in New York City; shared 1961 Nobel Physics Prize for measurements of protons, neutrons, and atomic nuclei.

1917 American troops were withdrawn from Mexico.

1918 The British ship, *Tuscania,* carrying 2000 American troops, was sunk by a submarine off the Irish coast; 210 lives lost.

1926 Arthur O. Sulzberger, publisher, was born in New York City; publisher, *New York Times* (1963-   ).

1933 Addison Mizner, architect, died at 61; designed many of the Florida mansions.

1934 Hank (Henry L.) Aaron, baseball player, was born in Mobile, Ala.; broke Babe Ruth's homerun record (714) in 1974; reached 755 by retirement after playing with Milwaukee, Atlanta Braves (1954-74); named to Baseball Hall of Fame.

1937 President Franklin Roosevelt sent a special message to Congress recommending judiciary reorganization, increasing the Supreme Court from 9 to 15—the so-called "packing" of the Court; Senate returned bill to its Judiciary Committee, where it died.

1942 Roger Staubach, football player, was born in Cincinnati; star quarterback with U.S. Naval Academy, Dallas Cowboys (1969-80).

1979 Three thousand farmers drove campers, tractors, and trucks into Washington to dramatize their demand for price supports.

1988 General Manuel Noriega, Panama military ruler, was indicated by Miami office of the Justice Department on charges of turning Panama over to drug traffickers and making Panama the capital of international cocaine smuggling.

1988 Arizona's Governor Evan Mecham was impeached by the State House of Representatives; faces trial in the Senate.

FEBRUARY 6

1682 Sieur de LaSalle reached the mouth of the Illinois River in his Mississippi Valley exploration.

1733 James Duane, legislator and jurist, was born in New York City; served in the Continental Congress (1774-84), helped draft the Articles of Confederation; mayor of New York City (1784-89); U.S. district judge (1789-94) (died 1797).

1756 Aaron Burr, Vice President (1801-05), was born in Newark; represented New York in the Senate (1791-97); in 1800 election was tied with Jefferson in electoral vote, Congress voted for Jefferson and Burr became vice president; killed Alexander Hamilton in a duel; tried for treason in trying to form a separate nation, acquitted (died 1836).

1778 Franco-American treaties were signed; one was a treaty of amity and commerce, the other a treaty of alliance, effective if and when war broke out between France and England (which happened June 17); ratified by Congress May 4.

1785 Elizabeth P. Bonaparte, socialite, was born in Baltimore; married to Jerome Bonaparte (1803), brother of Napoleon I; marriage annulled (1805) (died 1879).

1788 Massachusetts legislature ratified the Constitution by a vote of 187-168; entered the Union as the sixth state.

1802 War was declared against Tripoli.

1807 Hiram Sibley, a founder of Western Union, was born in North Adams, Mass.; president, Western Union (1856-69); an incorporator, benefactor, Cornell U. (died 1888).

1811 Samuel McIntire, the "architect of Salem," died at 54; designed, constructed great mansions of Salem shipping merchants, churches, and public buildings.

1813 Joseph R. Anderson, industrialist, was born near Fincastle, Va.; owner, head, Tredegar Iron Works in Richmond, which supplied heavy artillery for the Confederacy (died 1892).

1814 Edward F. Sorin, Catholic leader, was born in Laval, France; founder, president, Notre Dame U. (1844-65); superior general, Congregation of the Holy Cross (1868-93) (died 1893).

1814 James Craik, physician, died at 84; served with George Washington on expedition to Ft. Duquesne; chief physician, surgeon, Continental Army.

1818 William M. Evarts, lawyer, was born in Boston; as Attorney General (1868-69), he was chief counsel for President Andrew Jackson at his impeachment trial; led fight against the Tweed Ring; Secretary of State (1877-81); represented New York in the Senate (1885-1901) (died 1901).

1820 Thomas C. Durant, railroad organizer, was born in Lee, Mass.; helped organize, complete Union Pacific Railroad (1863-67) (died 1885).

1833 J.E.B. (Jeb) Stuart, Confederate general, was born in Patrick County, Va.; engaged in numerous battles (Manassas, Chancellorville, Gettysburg); succeeded Stonewall Jackson as corps commander; wounded in action (May 11, 1864), died the next day.

1845 Isidor Straus, merchant, was born in Otterberg, Germany; with father, Lazarus, founded crockery firm (1866), took over department at Macy's (1874); with brother Nathan (1/31/1848) became Macy partners (1888), sole owners (1896); made store world's largest; also developed Abraham & Straus store; represented New York in the House (1893-95); with his wife, he died in the *Titanic* disaster Apr 15, 1912.

1847 Henry J. Hardenberg, architect, was born in New Brunswick, N.J.; designed many leading hotels (Waldorf and Plaza, New York City; Copley Plaza, Boston; Willard, Washington, D.C.) (died 1918).

1857 Ernest Flagg, architect, was born in Brooklyn; designer of St. Luke's Hospital, Singer Bldg. in New York City; Corcoran Art Gallery, Washington, D.C.; buildings at Naval Academy (died 1947).

1862 General Grant's Union troops, assisted by Andrew H. Foote's gunboats, captured Ft. Henry, Tenn.

1865 Robert E. Lee appointed commander in chief of all Confederate armies.

1867 Eldridge R. Johnson, manufacturer, was born in Wilmington, Del.; inventor, founder, Victor Talking Machine Co. (1901) (died 1945).

1868 George A. Dorsey, anthropologist, was born in Hebron, Ohio; anthropology curator, Field Museum, Chicago; author (*Why We Behave Like Human Beings*) (died 1931).

1878 Walter B. Pitkin, author best remembered for his book, *Life Begins at Forty*, was born in Ypsilanti, Mich. (died 1953).

1887 Ernest Gruening, editor and legislator, was born in New York City; newspaperman who became governor of Alaska (1939-53) and Senator (1959-69) (died 1974).

1892 William P. Murphy, medical researcher, was born in Stoughton, Wis.; shared 1934 Nobel Physiology/Medicine Prize for work on anemia; co-discoverer of liver treatment for pernicious anemia.

1895 Babe (George H.) Ruth, baseball home-run hitter who helped popularize the sport in 1920s and 1930s, was born in Baltimore; with Boston Red Sox (1914-19) and Yankees (1920-34); an original member of Baseball Hall of Fame (died 1948).

1900 President McKinley appointed William Howard Taft chairman of the commission to establish civil government in the Philippines.

1911 Ronald Reagan, 40th president, was born in Tampico, Ill.; screen actor, served as governor of California (1967-74), became president 1981 and served until Jan 20, 1989.

1915 Prohibition law, effective Jan 1, 1916, signed by Arkansas governor.

1919 The first American general strike occurred in Seattle, Wash., when most unions and businesses shut down to protest elimination of the Western cost of living differential by the U.S. Shipping Board; strike lasted six days.

1923 Federal Judge Harold H. Greene, who gave final approval (1983) to the consent decree breaking up AT&T, was born in Frankfurt, Germany.

1940 Tom Brokaw, television news reporter, was born in Webster, S.D.; with *Today* Show, then anchorman, *NBC Nightly News* (1980-).

1951 A commuter train plunged through a temporary overpass in Woodbridge, N.J.; 85 were killed, 500 injured.

1974 The House of Representatives authorized its Judiciary Committee to conduct an impeachment inquiry of President Nixon.

FEBRUARY 7

1688 Cadwallader Golden, colonial administrator, was born in Ireland of Scottish parents; lieutenant governor of New York (1761-76), upheld British policy; a botanist of note (died 1776).

1784 Massachusetts Bank of Boston was chartered.

1794 Sidney E. Morse, journalist and inventor, was born in Charlestown, Mass., son of Jedidiah Morse (8/23/1761) and brother of Samuel F.B. Morse (4/27/1791); a founder, editor, *New York Observer* (1823-58); invented method of making stereotype plates from inscribed wax sheets, a bathometer to explore depths (died 1871).

1795 The 11th Amendment, spelling out judicial powers, went into effect.

1796 Tennessee adopted its state constitution.

1799 Federal marshals arrested John Fries, leader of a taxpayers rebellion, in Bethlehem, Pa.; twice convicted of treason, he was sentenced to death but was pardoned by President John Adams.

1804 John Deere, manufacturer and inventor, was born in Rutland, Vt.; invented steel plow; founder, president, Deere & Co. (1868-86) (died 1886).

1814 George P. Putnam, publisher, was born in Brunswick, Me.; founder (1848), president of family publishing firm (died 1872).

1817 Frederick Douglass, human rights leader, was born in Tuckahoe, Md.; one of the most eminent human rights leaders; editor, *North Star*, an abolitionist newspaper (died 1895).

1821 The first documented landing on the Antarctic continent occurred when men from Capt. John Davis' shallop, *Cecilia*, from New Haven, went ashore.

1827 First ballet (*The Deserter*) in America was presented at Bowery Theater, New York City.

1827 Richard W. Johnson, Union general, was born in Smithland, Ky.; saw action at Murfreesboro, Chickamauga, the march through Georgia (died 1897).

1849 Thomas W. Symons, military engineer, was born in Keeseville, N.Y.; advocated New York State Barge Canal, consulting engineer during its construction (died 1920).

1854 Thomas Fitzpatrick, frontier guide and Indian agent, died at about 55; guide for John C. Fremont, Stephen Kearny; negotiated several Indian treaties.

1864 Union troops occupied Jacksonville, Fla., restoring state to federal status.

1870 The Supreme Court in *Hepburn v. Griswold* ruled that Congress did not have the power to make Treasury notes contracted before the legislation legal tender.

1874 Louis A. Fuertes, illustrator of bird books, was born in Ithaca, N.Y. (died 1927).

1874 William L. Hutcheson, labor leader, was born in Saginaw, Mich.; president, Carpenter's Union (1915-52) (died 1953).

1882 John L. Sullivan beat Paddy Ryan in nine rounds in Mississippi City, Miss. to win the world's heavyweight boxing championship.

1883 Eubie Blake, jazz pianist, was born in Baltimore; composer ("I'm Just Wild About Harry") (died 1983).

1885 Sinclair Lewis, author who was the first American to win the Nobel Literature Prize (1930), was born in Sauk Centre, Minn.; wrote many popular novels (*Main Street, Babbitt, Arrowsmith, Elmer Gantry, Dodsworth*) (died 1951).

1886 A riot occurred in Seattle when a group of extremists tried to deport Chinese workers and volunteer home guards interceded; five persons were hurt, one killed.

1886 George H. Brett, World War II general, was born in Cleveland; deputy supreme commander, South Pacific (1942); head, Caribbean Defense Command (1942-45) (died 1963).

1904 Fire wiped out most of Baltimore's business district; lasted 30 hours, destroyed 2600 buildings and did $125 million damage.

1939 John S. Reed, chief executive officer, Citicorp (1984-), was born in Chicago.

1942 The War Shipping Administration was established by executive order.

1964 The Beatles singing group arrived at Kennedy Airport for their first American tour.

1972 President Nixon signed the Federal Election Campaign Act requiring the reporting of all campaign contributions.

1973 The Senate established the Watergate Select Committee headed by Sen. Sam J. Ervin of North Carolina.

1984 Astronaut Bruce McCandless II, a crew member of the shuttle *Challenger*, became the first person to go into space with no ties to the mother ship, using a powered back pack for motive power.

1986 A federal district court held a key provision of the Gramm-Rudman budget deficit bill unconstitutional because it vested executive power in an official removable by Congress; was upheld by the Supreme Court July 7.

1989 Congress voted overwhelmingly to turn down its 51% pay increase; President Bush signed the measure before midnight when the raises would have gone into effect without action.

FEBRUARY 8

1689 King William and Queen Mary granted a charter to the Rev. James Blair to found a college in Virginia—the College of William & Mary in Williamsburg.

1791 Congress passed a bill establishing a national bank; signed by President Washington Feb 25.

1794 The first fire insurance policy was issued, making the beginning of the insurance business in Hartford.

1802 James W. Webb, editor and diplomat, was born in Claverack, N.Y.; owner, editor, *Morning Courier* and *New York Enquirer* in New York City (1829-61); minister to Brazil (1861-69) (died 1884).

1817 Richard S. Ewell, Confederate general, was born in Washington, D.C.; led Confederate forces through Shenandoah Valley to Pennsylvania, took part in Gettysburg battle and Wilderness campaign; in charge of Richmond defense (died 1872).

1820 William T. Sherman, Union general, was born in Lancaster, Ohio, brother of John Sherman (5/10/1823); led march to the sea after razing Atlanta; credited with two famous quotes – "War is hell" and "If nominated, I will not accept; if elected, I will not serve" (died 1891).

1839 Aroostok "war" broke out between Maine frontiersmen and Canadian trespassers; settled in March without hostilities.

1861 Harry W. Leonard, electrical engineer, was born in Cincinnati; worked with Edison on city central electric stations; invented first electric train lighting system, a system of motor control, electric elevator controls, and many others (died 1915).

1861 Arkansas state troops seized federal arsenal in Little Rock.

1861 Jefferson Davis was elected president of the newly-formed Confederate states government, with Alexander H. Stephens as vice president; inaugurated Feb 18.

1862 Union forces took Roanoke Island, N.C., key to rear defenses of Norfolk, Va.

1866 Moses Gomberg, chemist, was born in Kirovograd, Russia; isolated first free radical, triphenylmethyl (died 1947).

1867 Harcourt A. Morgan, entomologist and educator, was born in Strathroy, Canada; president, U. of Tennessee (1919-33); member, Tennessee Valley Authority (1933-41), chairman (1938-41) (died 1950).

1879 Maude Slye, pathologist, was born in Minneapolis; director of cancer laboratory, U. of Chicago (1919-44); known for extensive cancer research (died 1954).

1887 Dawes Act passed, reforming the treatment of Indians and marking an end of 25 years agitation for reform.

1895 King Vidor, screen director, was born in Galveston; among his many films were *War and Peace* and *The Big Parade* (died 1982).

1906 Chester F. Carlson, inventor, was born in Seattle; invented xerography, which led to development to copying machine (died 1968).

1910 Boy Scouts of America was founded and incorporated.

1918 First issue of *Stars & Stripes*, official American Expeditionary Force weekly, published.

1921 Thornton A. Wilson, president, Boeing Co. (1968-), was born in Sikeston, Mo.

1924 President Coolidge signed a joint resolution charging Interior Secretary Albert B. Fall and Navy Secretary Edwin Denby with fraud and corruption in the handling of the 1922 oil leases.

1925 Jack Lemmon, screen actor, was born in Boston; numerous starring roles (*Mr. Roberts, The Odd Couple, Irma LaDouce*).

1931 James Dean, screen actor, was born in Marion, Ind.; symbol of social rebellion for an entire generation (died 1955).

1936 Former Vice President Charles Curtis (1929-44) died in Washington, D.C. at 76.

1965 President Lyndon Johnson ordered air strikes against North Vietnam in retaliation for Viet Cong attacks.

FEBRUARY 9

1690 French and Indians led by Sieur d'Iberville destroyed Schenectady.

1748 Luther Martin, attorney, was born near New Brunswick, N.J.; member of the Continental Congress (1785) and Constitutional Convention; successfully defended Supreme Court Justice Samuel Chase in impeachment trial; a defense attorney in Aaron Burr treason trial (died 1826).

1768 William King, colonial leader, was born in Scarborough, Me.; advocated a separate state of Maine, was its first governor (1819-21) (died 1852).

1773 William Henry Harrison, ninth president, was born in Charles City County, Va.; died (1841) one month after his inauguration from pneumonia he contracted on Inauguration Day; first president to die in office; served the Indiana Territory as governor (1801-13) and represented Ohio in the House (1816-19) and Senate (1825-28).

1775 British Parliament declared Massachusetts in a state of rebellion.

1802 Horatio Potter, Episcopal prelate, was born in Beekman, N.Y., brother of Alonzo Potter (7/6/1800); bishop of New York (1854-87) (died 1887).

1814 Samuel J. Tilden, philanthropist and politician, was born in New Lebanon, N.Y.; served New York as governor (1875-76); Democratic presidential candidate (1876), received 250,000 more popular votes than Rutherford B. Hayes, led electoral vote by 184 uncontested votes to 163; an electoral commission gave 22 missing electoral votes to Hayes and the election by one vote; bequeathed his fortune to Tilden Trust for establishing public interest in New York City (died 1886).

1818 John Milledge, legislator and public official, died at 61; served Georgia as governor (1802-06) and represented it in the House (1792-93, 1795-99, 1801-02) and Senate (1806-09), serving as president pro tem; donated land on which the U. of Georgia was built; state capital, Milledgeville (1807-67) was named in his honor.

1820 Moses G. Farmer, inventor, was born in Boscawen, N.H.; invented a machine for printing paper window shades; co-inventor of electric fire alarm system; paved way for Edison with numerous inventions (died 1893).

1825 The House decided the 1824 presidential election in which no candidate received a majority of the electoral votes by giving John Quincy Adams the votes of 13 states, Andrew Jackson of 7, and William H. Crawford of 4; this made final electoral vote: Adams 87, Jackson 71, Crawford 54.

1826 John A. Logan, Union general and legislator, was born in Jackson County, Ill.; represented Illinois in the House (1859-62, 1867-71) and the Senate (1871-77, 1879-86); helped establish Memorial Day; Republican vice presidential candidate (1884) (died 1886).

1840 William T. Sampson, Spanish-American War admiral, was born in Palmyra, N.Y.; allegedly claimed credit for victory over Spanish fleet fleeing Santiago, Cuba, when it belonged to W.S. Schley (10/9/1839) (died 1902).

1861 The provisional Confederate Congress declared that all laws of the United States not inconsistent with the Confederate constitution continued in force.

1861 A public referendum in Tennessee turned down a proposal to call a secession convention by a vote of 68,282 to 59,449.

1866 George Ade, playwright and humorist, was born in Kentland, Ind.; remembered for his *Fables in Slang* (died 1944).

1869 George H. Moses, legislator, was born in Lubec, Me.; minister to Greece and Montenegro (1909-12); represented New Hampshire in the Senate (1918-33), serving as president pro tem (1925-33) (died 1944).

1870 Weather Bureau began operations.

1871 Howard T. Ricketts, pathologist, was born in Findley, Ohio; discovered the cause of typhus, Rocky Mountain spotted fever (died 1910).

1874 Amy Lowell, poet and critic, was born in Brookline, Mass.; a leading poet of the Imagist school ("Men, Women and Ghosts;" "Patterns," "The Bronze Horses"); a leading exponent of American modernist movement (died 1925).

1889 President Cleveland signed an act creating the Department of Agriculture as an executive department; first secretary was Norman J. Colman of Missouri, who had been serving as commissioner.

1891 Ronald Colman, screen actor, was born in Richmond, England; starred in many films (*Lost Horizon, Arrowsmith, Random Harvest, A Tale of Two Cities*) (died 1958).

1899 Max Miller, author, was born in Traverse City, Mich; best remembered for *I Cover the Waterfront* (died 1967).

1901 Frederick H. Harvey, restaurateur, died at 66; opened restaurants in railroad stations, later adjacent hotels and began operating railroad dining cars (1890).

1909 Dean Rusk, public official, was born in Cherokee County, Ga.; president, Rockefeller Foundation (1952-60); Secretary of State (1961-69).

1911 Arizona voters ratified their state constitution.

1912 Thomas H. Moorer, admiral, born in Mt. Willing, Ala.; chief of naval operations (1967-70); chairman; Joint Chiefs of Staff (1970-74).

1914 William J. Veeck Jr., baseball executive, was born in Chicago; innovative manager, owner (firecracker scoreboards, using a midget as a pinchhitter) with Cleveland, St. Louis, Milwaukee, White Sox (died 1986).

1917 Indiana governor signed prohibition bill, effective Apr 2, 1918.

1928 Roger Mudd, television newsman, was born in Washington, D.C.; served with both CBS and NBC.

1942 The French liner *Normandie,* being converted for transport service, capsized and burned in its New York City berth.

1943 President Franklin Roosevelt decreed that for the duration of the war, the minimum work week was to be 48 hours.

1955 An agreement to merge was reached by the American Federation of Labor and the Congress of Industrial Organizations.

1971 An earthquake rocked the San Fernando Valley in California with a death toll of 64 and damage of $1 billion.

FEBRUARY 10

1665 Lord John Berkeley and Philp Carteret signed the "Concessions and Agreements of the Lord Proprietors of New Jersey," the first constitution of the colony; Carteret was commissioned governor.

1763 The Treaty of Paris ended the French and Indian (Seven Years) War, with France ceding all land east of the Mississippi River, except New Orleans, and Canada.

1766 Benjamin S. Barton, physician and botanist, was born in Lancaster, Pa.; wrote first elementary botany text in America (1803) (died 1815).

1786 John Cadwallader, Revolutionary general, died at 44; led Pennsylvania troops at Trenton, Princeton, and various Philadelphia area battles.

1807 Coast and Geodetic Survey began as the Coast Survey; became Coast and Geodetic Survey June 20, 1878, transferred to Environmental Science Services Administration July 13, 1965, became part of the National Oceanic and Atmospheric Administration (NOAA) Oct 3, 1970.

1837 Harrison G. Otis, publisher, was born in Marietta, Ohio; owner, publisher, *Los Angeles Times* (1886-1917) (died 1917).

1846 Ira Remsen, chemist and educator, was born in New York City; Johns Hopkins U. (1876-1913), chemistry lab head (1876-1906), president (1901-13); founder, editor, *American Chemical Journal*; co-discoverer of saccharin (died 1927).

1851 Indiana adopted its state constitution, effective Nov 1.

1855 Congress enacted a law guaranteeing citizenship to children born abroad to American citizens and to alien women married to American citizens.

1857 Henry DeL. Clayton, legislator, was born in Barbour County, Ala.; represented Alabama in the House (1897-1915), author of Clayton antitrust act (died 1929).

1858 Millard Fillmore, widowed former president, married Caroline C. McIntosh in Albany.

1865 Frank M. Colby, editor, was born in Washington, D.C.; editor, *International Year Book* (1898-1925) (died 1925).

1867 Charles W. Bryan, Nebraska governor (1923-25, 1931-35), was born in Salem, Ill., brother of William Jennings Bryan (3/19/1860); 1924 Democratic vice presidential candidate (died 1945).

1868 William Allen White, editor, was born in Emporia, Kan.; known as the "Sage of Emporia;" owner, editor, *Emporia Gazette* (1895-1944) (died 1944).

1872 John A. Hartford, merchant, was born in Orange, N.J., son of George H. Hartford (9/5/1833); a developer, executive, A&P food chain (died 1951).

1893 Jimmy Durante, entertainer, was born in New York City; starred on stage, screen, and television (died 1980).

1893 William T. ("Big Bill") Tilden, tennis great, was born in Germantown, Pa.; considered one of the greatest players of all time, world champion in 1920s, 1930s (died 1953).

1894 Herb(ert J.) Pennock, baseball player, was born in Kennett Square, Pa.; pitched for 22 years, mostly with New York Yankees; won 241, lost 162; named to Baseball Hall of Fame (died 1948).

1897 John F. Enders, bacteriologist, was born in West Hartford, Conn.; shared 1954 Nobel Physiology/Medicine Prize for producing polio virus, which led to development of Salk vaccine (died 1985).

1898 Dame Judith Anderson, actress, was born in Adelaide, Australia; starred in many plays on American stage (*Mourning Becomes Electra, Strange Interlude, The Old Maid*).

1899 Herbert C. Hoover married Lou Henry in Monterey, Cal.

1902 Walter H. Brattain, physicist, was born in Amoy, China; co-inventor of transistor, shared 1956 Nobel Physics Prize for that (died 1988).

1915 American note to Germany stated that the United States would hold Germany to strict accountability for acts at sea; note to Great Britain protested use of neutral flags on British vessels.

1916 A German note announced that beginning Mar 1 armed enemy merchant ships would be treated as war vessels.

1927 Leontyne Price, operatic soprano, was born in Laurel, Miss.; appeared as Bess in *Porgy and Bess* (1952-54), starred with Metropolitan Opera (1961-85).

1938 Federal National Mortgage Association (FNMA) was created; after being moved to various agencies, became a government-sponsored private corporation (1968).

1950 Mark Spitz, champion swimmer, was born in Modesto, Cal.; first athlete to win seven gold medals in a single Olympiad (1972); won two in 1968.

1967 The 25th Amendment, which set procedures for presidential succession, went into effect.

1988 U.S. Circuit Court of Appeals in California ruled 2-1 that the Army regulations barring homosexuals from military service violate the constitutional guarantee of equal protection; on June 9, the court reversed itself.

FEBRUARY 11

1766 Northampton County (Va.) Court declared the Stamp Act unconstitutional and therefore not binding on the colonies.

1768 Massachusetts Circular Letter, written by Samuel Adams, outlined the steps taken by the colony's assembly and solicited proposals for united action; British ministry demanded that the Massachusetts General Court rescind the letter; the Court was dissolved when it refused; other colonies endorsed the letter.

1780 Eight thousand British troops under Sir Henry Clinton landed at St. John's Island, south of Charleston, S.C.

1801 A count of electoral votes for the presidency resulted in a tie between Thomas Jefferson and Aaron Burr (73 each); sent to the House, which resolved the issue in Jefferson's favor Feb 17.

1802 Lydia Maria Child, author and social reformer, was born in Medford, Mass.; author of practical books (*The Frugal Housewife*, which went through 21 editions in a decade; *The Mother's Book*); founder, *Juvenile Miscellany*, the first monthly children's magazine; active abolitionist (died 1880).

1812 Alexander H. Stephens, Confederate Vice President (1861-65), was born near Crawfordville, Ga.; represented Georgia in the House (1843-59, 1873-82) and served state as governor (1883) (died 1883).

1812 Massachusetts legislature, during Elbridge Gerry's second term as governor, passed a bill redistricting the state for partisan advantage; this gave rise to term "gerrymandering."

1833 Melville W. Fuller, jurist, was born in Augusta, Me.; chief justice, Supreme Court (1888-1910) (died 1910).

1836 Washington Gladden, Congregational clergyman, was born in Pottsgrove, Pa.; moderator, National Council of Congregational Churches (1904-07); pastor, First Church, Columbus, Ohio (1882-1918); preached practical application of religion to current social problems; called "father of American social gospel" (died 1918).

1839 Josiah Willard Gibbs, physicist and mathematician, was born in New Haven; considered greatest American theoretical scientist; established the basic theory of physical chemistry (died 1903).

1839 U. of Missouri at Columbia was chartered; opened in 1841.

1847 Thomas A. Edison, inventor, was born in Milan, Ohio; patented more than 1000 inventions, including the electric light bulb, phonograph, electric pen, various telegraphic devices, alkaline storage battery; produced talking motion pictures (1913), improved dynamos, motors (died 1931).

1861 President-elect Lincoln left Springfield, Ill. for Washington, D.C., telling his neighbors that he did not know "when or whether I ever may return, with a task before me greater than that which rested upon Washington."

1887 Henry K. Hewitt, World War II naval officer, was born in Hackensack, N.J.; directed amphibious landings at Casablanca, Sicily, southern France (died 1972).

1898 Leo Szilard, physicist, was born in Budapest; helped devise chain reaction system; developed first method of separating isotopes of radioactive elements (died 1964).

1900 Thomas Hitchcock Jr., considered the greatest polo player ever, was born in Aiken, S.C. (died 1944).

1907 William J. Levitt, builder and developer, was born in New York City; mass producer of housing after World War II, building about 140,000 in the Northeast.

1917 Sidney Sheldon, author and playwright, was born in Chicago; also noted for several screen and television plays.

1920 Senate began reconsideration of the League of Nations, the Versailles Treaty

1921 Lloyd Bentsen, represented Texas in the House (1948-54) and Senate (1971-), was born in Mission, Tex.; 1988 Democratic vice presidential candidate.

1946 Burt Reynolds, screen actor, was born in Waycross, Ga.; starred in many films (*Smokey and the Bandit, The Longest Yard*).

1949 President Truman named Dwight D. Eisenhower chairman of the Joint Chiefs of Staff; Eisenhower took leave of absence from Columbia U. presidency.

1952 The third airline crash in Elizabeth, N.J. in less than two months killed 33 persons.

1988 Lyn Nofziger, former President Reagan aide, was found guilty of illegally lobbying former colleagues within a year of leaving the government; was sentenced Apr 8 to 90 days and a $10,000 fine.

1988 A federal appeals court in San Francisco struck down as unconstitutional a requirement that rail workers be tested for drugs or alcohol after being involved in an accident or a rules violation.

1989 Rev. Barbara Clementine Harris, 55-year-old black priest, became the first woman consecrated as a bishop in the Episcopal Church.

FEBRUARY 12

1606 John Winthrop, colonial leader, was born in Suffolk, England, son of John Winthrop (1/12/1588); leader of a group that settled in Ipswich, served as governor of Connecticut (1636, 1657, 1659-76); obtained new liberal charter for Connecticut (died 1676).

1663 Cotton Mather, most famous Puritan cleric, was born in Boston, son of Increase Mather (6/21/1639); assisted father at Second Church (1685-1723), succeeded father as pastor (1723-28); helped establish New England as a cultural center; originally led drive against Salem "witches," then later felt the trials were unfair (died 1728).

1733 Settlers, led by Gen. James E. Oglethorpe, founded Savannah after making a treaty with the Indians.

1746 Thaddeus Kosciuszko, Polish general, was born in Lithuania; fought with the Americans in the Revolution, later fought for Polish freedom (died 1817).

1775 Louise C. Johnson Adams, wife of President John Quicy Adams, was born in London (died 1852).

1781 The *Vermont Gazette*, first newspaper in that state, was published at Westminster.

1785 Alden Partridge, soldier and educator, was born in Norwich, Vt.; founder of elementary and secondary grades military academies (died 1854).

1789 The first newspaper in the District of Columbia, the *Times and Patowmack Packet*, began publication in Georgetown under Charles Fierer.

1791 Peter Cooper, businessman and inventor, was born in New York City; designed, built first American steam locomotive; a leader in iron milling, steel production; promoted, financed first Atlantic cable; founded Cooper Union (1857-59) in New York City for the "advancement of science and art" (died 1883).

1792 William Smallwood, Revolutionary general, died at 60; served at Long Island, White Plains, and Camden; governor of Maryland (1785-88).

1793 The Fugitive Slave Act passed, empowering an owner or agent to bring a fugitive before a magistrate to order his return.

1809 Abraham Lincoln, 16th president (1861-65), was born in Hardin (now Larned) County, Ky.; served as president during Civil War; assassinated while sitting in a box in Ford Theater in Washington, D.C. by John Wilkes Booth, the actor (1865).

1813 James D. Dana, geologist and zoologist, was born in Utica, N.Y.; at Yale U. (1855-92), wrote basic mineralology and geology texts; editor, *American Journal of Science* (1840-90) (died 1895).

1815 Martin B. Anderson, educator, was born in New Brunswick, Me.; first president, U. of Rochester (1853-88) (died 1890).

1822 James P. Anderson, Confederate general, was born in Franklin County, Tenn.; saw action at Corinth, Murfreesboro, Chickamauga (died 1872).

1830 Stephen Wilcox, inventor, was born in Westerly, R.I.; invented safety water-tube boiler and steam generator; helped organize (1867) Babcock, Wilcox & Co. to manufacture inventions (died 1893).

1849 A mass meeting in San Francisco established a temporary government for area.

1852 Frank W. Very, astronomer, was born in Salem, Mass.; confirmed existence of water vapor and oxygen in Mars atmosphere, proved that white nebulae are galaxies (died 1927).

1862 Siege of Ft. Donelson, Tenn. was begun by Union forces under Gen. Grant; attack repulsed Feb 14 but Union troops were successful Feb 16.

1870 A Utah law gave full suffrage to women.

1873 The Coinage Act was passed, demonetizing silver and making gold the sole monetary standard.

1880 John L. Lewis, labor leader, was born in Lucas, Iowa; president, United Mine Workers (1920-60); helped organize CIO, its first president (1935-40) (died 1969).

1893 Omar N. Bradley, World War II general, was born in Clark, Mo.; commanded 12th Army Corps, led American ground forces in Normandy invasion; administrator, Veterans Administration (1945-47); Army chief of staff (1948); first permanent chairman, Joint Chiefs of Staff (1949-53) (died 1979).

1896 Isaac Murphy, successful jockey who rode Kentucky Derby winner three times (1884, 1890, 1891), died at about 35; the first jockey to be named to the Racing Hall of Fame.

1896 Oscar M. Charleston, one of the first great black baseball players was born in Indianapolis; named to Baseball Hall of Fame.

1898 Roy E. Harris, composer, was born in Lincoln County, Okla.; composed numerous works (*Third Symphony, Challenge, Folk Song Symphony, Kentucky Spring*) (died 1979).

1898 David K.E. Bruce, diplomat, was born in Baltimore; ambassador to France (1949-52), to Great Britain (1961-69), to NATO (1974-76); headed American delegation to Paris Vietnam peace talks (1970-71); head, American liaison office in Peking (1973-74) (died 1977).

1903 Chick (Charles J.) Hafey, baseball player (Cards, Reds), was born in Berkeley, Cal.; named to Baseball Hall of Fame.

1909 National Association for the Advancement of Colored People (NAACP) was created.

1914 Tex (Gordon) Beneke, tenor saxophonist and band leader, was born in Ft. Worth, Tex.; leader of Glenn Miller band.

1918 Julian S. Schwinger, physicist, was born in New York City; shared 1965 Nobel Physics Prize for research in quantum electrodynamics.

1934 Bill (William F.) Russell, basketball player and coach, was born in Monroe, La.; starred with San Francisco U. and Boston Celtics; first black to coach a major professional sports team (Celtics); named to Basketball Hall of Fame.

1934 Export-Import Bank was created by executive order to facilitate trade with Russia.

1974 The first Susan B. Anthony dollar was struck at the Philadelphia mint.

1980 The Winter Olympics opened in Lake Placid, N.Y.

FEBRUARY 13

1741 First American magazine, *The American Magazine*, published by John Webbe.

1805 David Dudley Field, attorney, was born in Haddam, Conn.; led in codification of New York laws, worked up code of international law.

1812 Samuel P. Lee, Union admiral, was born in Fairfax County, Va., grandson of Richard Henry Lee (1/31/1732); saw action on the Mississippi River at New Orleans, Vicksburg (died 1897).

1844 *Louisville Courier* was established.

1867 Mississippi repealed many of its restrictions, giving blacks nearly full civil rights.

1870 Joseph C. Lincoln, author, was born in Brewster, Mass.; known for his Cape Cod stories (died 1944).

1877 Sidney Smith, cartoonist, was born in Bloomington, Ill.; on staff of *Chicago Tribune* (1911-35), creator of "The Gumps" (died 1935).

1885 Bess (Elizabeth V.) Wallace Truman, wife of President Truman, was born in Independence, Mo. (died 1982).

1892 Robert H. Jackson, jurist, was born in Spring Creek, Pa.; Attorney General (1940-41); associate justice, Supreme Court (1941-54); served as American prosecutor at Neuremberg Trials (1945-46) (died 1954).

1892 Grant Wood, artist, was born in Anamosa, Iowa; noted for realistic paintings (*American Gothic, Dinner for Threshers, Woman with Plants*); often called America's "painter of the soil" (died 1942).

1904 Erwin D. Canham, editor of *Christian Science Monitor* (1941-74) was born in Auburn, Me. (died 1982).

1910 William B. Shockley, physicist, was born in London; shared 1966 Nobel Physics Prize for co-invention of the transistor (died 1989).

1918 Patty Berg, golfer, was born in Minneapolis; won 83 tournaments in 30+ years.

1919 Tennessee Ernie Ford, entertainer, was born in Bristol, Tenn.; starred on television (1955-61, 1962-65), records; remembered for song, "16 Tons."

1919 Edward G. Robinson, football coach, was born in Baker, La.; became most successful football coach in 1986 when his Grambling College team gave him his 324th win.

1920 President Wilson accepted the resignation of Secretary of Robert Lansing, whom he had accused of attempting to usurp presidential powers by calling meetings of the cabinet during his (Wilson's) illness.

1923 Charles E. Yeager, test pilot who broke the sound barrier for the first time (Oct 14, 1947), was born in Myra, W.Va.

FEBRUARY 14

1760 Richard Allen, church leader, was born in Philadelphia; a founder, bishop of African Methodist Episcopal (AME) Church (1816-31); first black ordained as American Methodist minister; founded first Negro church (died 1831).

1790 Thomas Jefferson accepted appointment as first Secretary of State.

1802 John White, legislator (House 1835-45, Speaker 1841-43), was born near Middlesboro, Ky. (died 1845).

1819 Christopher L. Sholes, inventor, was born in Mooresburg, Pa.; invented, perfected typewriter; sold patent rights to Remington (died 1890).

1824 Winfield S. Hancock, Union general, was born in Montgomery Square, Pa.; held key defense positions at Gettysburg; 1880 Democratic presidential candidate (died 1886).

1834 First newspaper was published in Hawaii by Lorrin Andrews missionary school; Andrews later became first justice of Hawaii's Supreme Court.

1838 Edwin Ginn, publisher, was born in Orland, Me.; founder, Ginn & Co. (1867), which specialized in textbooks (died 1914).

1847 Anna Howard Shaw, women's rights activist, was born in Newcastle-on-Tyne, England; president, National American Woman's Suffrage Assn. (1904-15) (died 1919).

1859 Oregon was admitted to the Union as the 33rd state.

1859 George W. Ferris, engineer, was born in Galesburg, Ill.; built the Ferris wheel for the Columbian Exposition (1893) (died 1896).

1864 Robert E. Park, sociologist, was born in Luzerne County, Pa.; one of world's leading race relations experts; author (*Race and Culture, Human Communities, Society*) (died 1944).

1864 Union troops occupied Meridian, Miss., followed by destruction of railroads and supplies.

1865 Carl T. Anderson, cartoonist, was born in Madison, Wis.; creator of comic strip, "Henry" (died 1948)

1878 Julius A. Nieuwland, chemist and botanist, was born in Hausbeke, Belgium; taught at Notre Dame U. (from 1904); known for synthesis of organic compounds, especially artificial rubber, from acetylene (died 1936).

1882 George Jean Nathan, editor and author, was born in Ft. Wayne, Ind.; most widely read American drama critic of his time; co-editor, *Smart Set* (1914-23); co-founder, editor, *The American Mercury* (1924-30) (died 1958).

1890 William Howard Taft was named Solicitor General by President Benjamin Harrison.

1893 Treaty of annexation of Hawaii was concluded; submitted to Senate but later withdrawn (Dec. 18) by President Cleveland.

1894 Jack Benny, entertainer, was born in Chicago; starred on radio (1932-55), television (1956-65); acted in several movies (died 1974).

1903 Department of Commerce and Labor was created, with George R. Cortelyou as the first secretary; divided into two departments in 1913.

1907 Johnny Longden, jockey, was born in Wakefield, England; rode more than 6000 winners in 40 years, including the "triple crown" with Count Fleet.

1912 Arizona entered the Union as the 48th state.

1913 James R. Hoffa, labor leader, was born in Brazil, Ind.; president, Teamsters Union (1957-71); disappeared mysteriously July 30, 1975.

1919 President Wilson returned from France to seek approval of draft covenant of the League of Nations; returned to France Mar 14 to seek some changes.

1921 Hugh (M.) Downs, radio-television personality, was born in Akron; headed *Today* show (1962-72).

1925 Mickey (Mary Kathryn) Wright, an outstanding golfer of the 1960s, was born in San Diego, Cal.; had 82 career victories including the LPGA (1958, 1960) and U.S. Women's Open (1958-59, 1961, 1964); named to LPGA Hall of Fame.

1929 St. Valentine's Day "massacre" occurred in a Chicago garage when seven gangsters were executed by a rival gang.

1979 Adolph Dubs, American ambassador to Afghanistan, was shot and killed after being kidnapped in Kabul by Muslim extremists.

FEBRUARY 15

1643 Swedish settlers arrived at Ft. Christiana (now Wilmington), Del.

1726 Abraham Clark, surveyor, was born in Roselle, N.J.; member of Continental Congress (1776-78, 1779-83), a signer of Declaration of Independence (died 1794).

FEBRUARY 15

1730 Thomas Bray, English clergyman, died at 74; organized the Anglican Church in Maryland (1699).

1764 St. Louis was formed by Pierre Laclede, a French trader from New Orleans.

1776 The Continental Congress named Benjamin Franklin, Catholic Bishop John Carroll and Samuel Chase to go to Canada to try to enlist its help.

1782 William Miller, clergyman, was born in Pittsfield, Mass.; preached about the Second Coming, which he predicted for 1843 or 1844; though his movement died after the failed predictions, it led to the formation of the Adventist Church (1845) (died 1849).

1797 Henry E. Steinway, piano manufacturer, was born in Wolfshagen, Germany; founded Steinway Co. (1853) in New York City (died 1871).

1802 John A. Sutter, California pioneer, was born in Kandern, Germany; owned area where gold was discovered (1848); during gold rush, his workmen deserted, his sheep and cattle were stolen, his land occupied by squatters; became bankrupt, given $250 monthly pension by California (1864-78) (died 1880).

1804 New Jersey enacted a law calling for the gradual abolition of slavery, granted freedom to all born in the state after July 4.

1809 Cyrus H. McCormick, inventor and manufacturer, was born in Rockbridge County, Va., son of Robert McCormick (6/8/1780); developed first successful reaping machine, founded company which became International Harvester Co. (1848) (died 1884).

1812 Charles L. Tiffany, jeweler, was born in Killingly, Conn.; jewelry manufacturer, co-founder of firm bearing his name (1853) (died 1902).

1820 Susan B. Anthony, suffragist, was born in Adams, Mass.; organized (1869) National Woman Suffrage Association; president, National American Woman Suffrage Association (1892-1900) (died 1906).

1822 Henry B. Whipple, first Episcopal bishop of Minnesota, was born in Adams, N.Y.; led successful fight to reform government handling of Indians (died 1901).

1827 Francis A. Pratt, industrialist, was born in Woodstock, Vt.; co-founder, Pratt & Whitney (1864), pioneered in production of machine tools (died 1902).

1829 S(ilas) Weir Mitchell, physician, was born in Philadelphia; with Philadelphia Orthopedic Hospital 40 years; did much work on nerves, physiology of cerebellum, toxicology (died 1914).

1834 Henry B. Hyde, insurance executive, was born in Catskill, N.Y.; founder, Equitable Life Assurance Society (1859), president (1874-99) (died 1899).

1835 Alexander S. Webb, Union general and educator, was born in New York City, son of James W. Webb (2/8/1802); chiefly responsible for repulse of Pickett's charge at Gettysburg; president, City College of New York (1869-1902) (died 1911).

1842 Adhesive postage stamps were used for first time in New York City.

1843 Russell H. Conwell, educator, was born in South Worthington, Mass.; revived Philadelphia Baptist Church, began night school (1884), which became Temple College, serving as its first president; as lecturer gave his "Acres of Diamonds" speech more than 6000 times (died 1925).

1845 Elihu Root, public official, was born in Clinton, N.Y.; War Secretary (1899-1904), Secretary of State (1905-09); represented New York in the Senate (1909-15); president; Carnegie Endowment for International Peace; awarded 1912 Nobel Peace Prize (died 1937).

1850 Albert B. Cummins, Iowa governor (1902-08) and senator (1908-26), was born in Carmichaels, Pa. (died 1926).

1858 William H. Pickering, astronomer, was born in Boston, great grandson of Timothy Pickering (7/17/1745); discovered a Saturn satellite, predicted existence of and located planet Pluto (1919) (died 1938).

1861 Alfred North Whitehead, philosopher, was born in Ramstage, England; author (*Principia Mathematica, Adventures of Ideas, Science and the Modern World*) (died 1947).

1863 James A. Farrell, steel executive, was born in New Haven; began work at U.S. Steel at 16, rose to president (1911-32) (died 1943).

1869 U. of Nebraska was chartered, opened Sept 7, 1871.

1876 A patent was issued for the manufacture of barbed wire to Joseph F. Glidden (1/18/1813), a significant factor in settling the Great Plains.

1879 President Hayes signed an act permitting women to practice before the Supreme Court.

1882 John Barrymore, actor, was born in Philadelphia, son of Maurice (3/26/1905) and brother of Ethel (8/15/1879) and Lionel (4/28/1878); starred in many stage and screen plays (*Beau Brummel, Don Juan, Grand Hotel, Dinner at Eight*); his *Hamlet* was considered one of the greatest (died 1942).

1884 Alfred C. Gilbert, toymaker, was born in Salem, Ore.; developed Erector set, expanded operations with various kits (died 1961).

1884 Alice H.L. Roosevelt, 23-year-old wife of Theodore Roosevelt, died of Bright's disease in New York City and his mother, Martha B. Roosevelt, died of typhoid fever.

1892 James V. Forrestal, public official, was born in Beacon, N.Y.; president, Dillon, Read & Co. (1937-40); Undersecretary of Navy, Secretary (1940-47); first Secretary of Defense (1947-49) (died 1949).

1893 Walter Donaldson, composer, was born in Brooklyn; wrote many Broadway musicals, hit songs ("My Buddy," "Yes, Sir, That's My Baby," "My Blue Heaven," "Little White Lies") (died 1947).

1897 Earl (Red) Blaik, football coach, was born in Dayton; coached Army (1941-59) (died 1989).

1898 The U.S.S. *Maine* was mysteriously blown up in Havana harbor, with the loss of 260 lives, leading to the Spanish-American War.

1898 Fritz Zwicky, physicist, was born in Varna, Bulgaria; became a Swiss citizen; known for studies of cosmic rays; invented many essentials of jet engines (died 1974).

1905 Harold Arlen, composer, was born in Buffalo; wrote numerous musicals, movie scores (*The Wizard of Oz*); many hit songs ("Stormy Weather," "That Old Black Magic") (died 1986).

1911 Leonard F. Woodcock, labor leader and diplomat, was born in Providence; president, United Auto Workers (1970-77); representative, later ambassador, to China (1977-81).

1916 Ian K. Ballantine, publisher, was born in New York City; head of Bantam Books (1945-52), pioneer in publishing paperbacks; president, Ballantine Books (1952-75).

1917 Wyoming enacted a prohibition law.

1929 James R. Schlesinger, public official, was born in New York City; chairman, Atomic Energy Commission (1971-73); director, CIA (1973); Secretary of Defense (1973-76), Secretary of Energy (1977-79).

1933 An assassination attempt was made on President-elect Franklin Roosevelt in Miami by Giuseppe Zangara; Chicago Mayor Anton J. Cermak was fatally wounded; Zangara was convicted, electrocuted Mar 20 in Raiford, Fla.

1934 Civil Works Emergency Relief Act was signed for a civil works and direct relief program through 1935; about 2.5 million unemployed were assisted before the program was returned to state and local agencies.

1936 President Franklin Roosevelt proposed a conference for Latin America peace-keeping; scheduled for Buenos Aires in December.

1953 Tenley Albright of Newton Centre, Mass. became the first American woman to win the world figure skating title.

1961 Maribel Vinson (Owen), champion American figure skater nine times (1928-33, 1935-37) and U.S. pairs champion (1928-29, 1933, 1935-37), died in a plane crash at 50.

1978 Leon Spinks defeated Muhammad Ali in 15 rounds in Las Vegas to win the world heavyweight boxing championship; Ali reversed the decision in Sept.

FEBRUARY 16

1724 Christopher Gadsden, colonial leader, was born in Charleston; member, Continental Congress (1774-76); general, Continental Army, leading South Carolina troops (1776-78) (died 1805).

1766 James Monroe and Elizabeth Kortright were married in New York City.

1783 The first proposal for a new federal government appeared in "A Dissertation on the Political Union of the 13 United States of North America" by Pelatiah Webster.

1804 Stephen Decatur and 80 officers and men in a daring raid recaptured the *Philadelphia*, which had been held by Tripolitans in Tripoli harbor.

1812 Henry Wilson, Vice President (1873-75), was born in Farmington, N.H.; represented Massachusetts in the Senate (1855-73); a founder, Free Soil (1848) and Republican parties (died 1875).

1825 Crosby S. Noyes, journalist, was born in Minot, Me.; editor, *Washington Star* (1861-1908) (died 1908).

1838 Henry Brooks Adams, historian and educator, was born in Boston; son of Charles Francis Adams (8/18/1807); initiated summer teaching at Harvard; editor, *North American Review* (1870-77); author (*The Education of Henry Adams*) (died 1918).

1840 Henry Watterson, editor, was born in Washington, D.C.; editor, *Louisville Courier-Journal* (1868-1919); considered one of America's greatest editors; represented Kentucky in the House (1876-77) (died 1921).

1843 Henry M. Leland, pioneer automaker, was born in Danville, Vt.; founder, president, Cadillac Motor Co. (1902-17); general manager, president, Lincoln Motor Co. (1917-22); developd first eight-cylinder motor (1914), co-developer of electric starter (1911) (died 1932).

1852 Charles Taze Russell, religious leader, was born in Pittsburgh; founder, International Bible Students Assn., which later became Jehovah's Witnesses; founder, *The Watchtower* (died 1916).

1860 Samuel S. Fels, soap manufacturer, was born in Yanceyville, N.C.; partner in company (Fels Naptha) with brother, Joseph (12/16/1854), president (1914-50) (died 1950).

1861 Texas state trops seized the federal arsenal in San Antonio.

1862 Ft. Donelson (Tenn.) and 14,000 Confederate troops under Gen. Simon Buckner fell to Union forces under Gen. Grant; victory brought Grant to national attention.

1866 Billy (William R.) Hamilton, baseball player (Phillies, Braves) was born in Newark, N.J.; batted .344 in 14 years; named to Baseball Hall of Fame (died 1940).

1880 Charles T. Fisher, an organizer (1908) and administrator (1908-34) of Fisher Body Corp., was born in Sandusky, Ohio (died 1963).

1884 Van Wyck Brooks, author and critic, was born in Plainfield, N.J.; author (*The Flowering of New England, New England Indian Summer*) (died 1963).

1893 Katherine Cornell, actress, was born in Berlin to American parents; starred in many stage plays (*Barretts of Wimpole Street, A Bill of Divorcement, Candide*) (died 1974).

1901 Wayne King, musician and orchestra leader known as the "Waltz King," was born in Savannah, Ill. (died 1985).

1903 Edgar Bergen, entertainer who gained fame as a ventriloquist (Charlie McCarthy), was born in Chicago (died 1978).

1904 George F. Kennan, diplomat, was born in Milwaukee; influential in devising the Russian containment policy; ambassador to Russia (1951).

1915 South Carolina established statewide prohibition.

1938 President Franklin Roosevelt signed the Agricultural Adjustment Administratin Act "for the conservation of national soil resources" and to replace the 1933 Act which had been declared unconstitutional by the Supreme Court.

1959 John McEnroe, tennis star of 1970s and 1980s, was born in New York City; won Wimbledon singles title three times.

1970 Joe Frazier knocked out Jimmy Ellis in the fifth round in New York City to win the vacant world heavyweight boxing championship.

1988 The Firestone Tire & Rubber Co. agreed to sell 75% of its tire operations to the Bridgestone Corp. for $1 billion, said to be the largest Japanese investment in an American manufacturer.

FEBRUARY 17

1621 Miles Standish was made a captain with military authority over Plymouth Colony.

1692 Thomas Neale received a royal patent to establish colonial post offices for 21 years.

1708 William Rittenhouse, Mennonite clergyman and industrialist, died at 64; chosen first pastor of Germantown, Pa. church and first American Mennonite bishop (1703); built first American paper mill (1690).

1718 Matthew Tilghman, member of the Continental Congress (1774-76), was born in Queen Anne County, Md.; did not sign the Declaration of Independence because he was called home to help draft first Maryland constitution (died 1790).

1740 John Sullivan, colonial leader, was born in Somersworth, N.H.; Revolutionary War general (Trenton, Princeton); member, Continental Congress (1774, 1780-81); "president" (governor) of New Hampshire (1786-89) (died 1795).

1801 The House on the 36th ballot elected Thomas Jefferson president, with ten states voting for him, four for Aaron Burr, who became vice president; votes of two states were null because delegations were evenly divided; Jefferson and Burr had each received 73 electoral votes.

1805 New Orleans was incorporated as a city.

1807 William L. Dayton, public official, was born in Basking Ridge, N.J.; represented New Jersey in the Senate (1845-51); was the first Republican vice presidential candidate (1856); ambassador to France (1861-64) (died 1864).

1817 United States formally ratified the Treaty of Ghent ending the War of 1812.

1837 Francis J. Herron, Union general, was born in Pittsburgh; was the youngest major general in the war, awarded Congressional Medal of Honor (died 1902).

1843 (Aaron) Montgomery Ward, merchant, was born in Chatham, N.J.; co-founder with George F. Thorne of mail order dry goods business in Chicago (1827); began with one page catalog of 30 items, capital of $2400 (died 1913).

1845 Charles McBurney, surgeon, was born in Roxbury, Mass.; pioneer in antiseptic surgery, an authority on appendectomy (died 1913).

1855 Congress authorized construction of a telegraph line from the Mississippi River to the Pacific Ocean.

1856 Frederick E. Ives, inventor, was born in Litchfield, Conn.; invented various photographic development processes; his half-tone process (1886) is essentially unchanged (died 1937).

1857 Samuel S. McClure, editor, was born in County Antrim, Ireland; founder (1884) of first American newspaper syndicate; founder (1893), editor, *McClure's Magazine* (died 1949).

1864 The Confederate submarine *R.I. Hunley* sank the Union ship USS *Housatonic* and sank with her; the 35-foot submarine was propelled by a screw worked from the inside by eight men.

1865 Columbia, S.C. was captured by Union forces; city was burned but the cause of the fire was never determined; Charleston was evacuated by the Confederates.

1866 David F. Houston, educator and public official, was born in Monroe, N.C.; headed several universities (1902-16); Secretary of Agriculture (1913-20), of Treasury (1920-21); chairman, Federal Reserve Board (died 1940).

1872 William Duane, biophysicist, was born in Philadelphia; with Harvard U. (1917-35), developed methods, apparatus for using x-rays and radium in medicine (died 1935).

1874 Thomas J. Watson, industrialist, was born in Campbell, N.Y.; president, Computing-Tabulating Recording Co., which became International Business Machines (1924); IBM president, board chairman (1924-49) (died 1956).

1879 Dorothy Canfield Fisher, author, was born in Lawrence, Kan.; wrote several novels (*The Brimming Cut, The Deepening Stream, The Bent Twig*) (died 1958).

1888 Otto Stern, physicist, was born in Sohrau, Germany; awarded 1943 Nobel Physics Prize for detection of magnetic momentum of protons; developed molecular beams as tool for studying the structure of molecules (died 1969).

1889 H(aroldson) H. Hunt, oil and natural gas producer, was born in Vandalia, Ill.; became one of world's richest men (died 1974).

1893 State University of Montana was established.

1895 Charles T. Jay, World War II admiral and Allied naval commander in Korean War, was born in St. Louis (died 1956).

1902 Marian Anderson, opera and concert singer, was born in Philadelphia; one of the world's greatest contraltos; first black to perform in a major opera role.

1906 Three men were arrested in Colorado for the murder of former Idaho governor Frank Steuenberg; one was William D. Haywood, head of the Industrial Workers of the World (IWW).

1906 Alice Lee, daughter of President and Mrs. Theodore Roosevelt, was married in the White House to Nicholas Longworth, Speaker of the House.

1909 Geronimo, Apache chief who led raids against the Americans and Mexicans, died at about 80.

1923 A(lden) W. Clausen, president of the World Bank (1981-86), was born in Hamilton, Ill; chief executive officer, Bank of America (1970-81).

1925 Hal (Harold R.) Holbrook, actor, was born in Cleveland; best known for one-man portrayals (Mark Twain).

1936 Jim Brown, football great, was born in St. Simons, Ga.; starred with Syracuse U., Cleveland Browns (1957-65); rushing record of 12,312 yards stood for 20 years.

1964 The Supreme Court ruled that congressional districts should have equal populations.

1988 Two executives of the Beech-Nut Co. were convicted of violating federal law by intentionally distributing bogus apple juice intended for babies.

1988 Lt. Col. William R. Higgins, an American Marine officer, was kidnapped in Beirut while on temporary duty as chief of a UN international truce observer group.

FEBRUARY 18

1688 Germantown (Pa.) Mennonites adopted resolutions against slavery, the earliest known protests against the practice in America.

1735 *Flora, or Hob in the Well* was performed in Charleston, the first recorded opera performance in America.

1783 James Biddle, naval officer, was born in Philadelphia; served in War of 1812; negotiated first treaty between the United States and China (1846) (died 1848).

1792 Jabez Gorham, silversmith, was born in Providence; founder of Gorham Manufacturing Co. (died 1869).

1793 Supreme Court in *Chisholm v. Georgia* ruled that a state could be sued by citizens of another state; this led to 11th Amendment.

1795 George Peabody, financier, was born in South Danvers, Mass.; endowed Peabody Institutes in Baltimore and Peabody, Mass. (named for him), museums at Harvard and Yale, and Peabody Education Fund to advance education in the South (died 1869).

1797 John Bell, legislator, was born in Nashville; represented Tennessee in the House (1827-41), serving as Speaker (1834-35), and Senate (1848-60); 1860 Constitutional Union Party presidential candidate (won Tennessee, Kentucky, Virginia (died 1869).

1804 Elizur Wright, insurance reformer, was born in South Canaan, Conn.; led fight to require insurance companies to establish adequate untouchable reserves with which to pay claims; called the father of legal reserve life insurance (died 1885).

1805 Louis M. Goldsborough, Union naval officer, was born in Washington, D.C.; commanded fleet that captured Roanoke Island, destroyed Confederate fleet (1862) (died 1877).

1817 Lewis A. Armistead, Confederate general, was born in New Bern, N.C., nephew of George Armistead (4/10/1780); killed in Pickett's charge at Gettysburg, July 3, 1863.

1818 Simon Girty, the "great renegade," died at 77; American who led British and Indian raiding parties along the northern, western frontiers; fled to Canada (1796) when British surrendered Detroit.

1832 Octave Chanute, pioneer aviator; was born in Paris; experimented with gliders, designed a biplane glider; his data of value to Wright brothers (died 1910).

1848 Louis C. Tiffany, painter and designer, was born in New York City, son of Charles L. Tiffany (2/15/1812); developed Tiffany glass (died 1933).

1861 Jefferson Davis was inaugurated as provisional president of the Confederacy in Montgomery, Ala., the first Confederate capital; re-elected in October under the Confederate constitution; inaugurated Feb 22, 1862.

1862 Charles M. Schwab, steel industry leader, was born in Williamsburg, Pa.; president, Carnegie Steel Co. (1897-1901); first president, U.S. Steel (1901-03); organized, headed, Bethlehem Steel Co. (1903-13), board chairman (1913-39); director of ship-building, World War I (died 1939).

1865 Charleston, S.C. was captured by Union troops.

1869 The "Chicago Protest" of the Episcopal Church was launched by Charles E. Cheney, who helped organize, headed Reformed Episcopal Church; brought to trial for heresy, deposed; refused to leave Christ Church, Chicago (where he served 1860-1916); court held that church property belonged to the parish, not the diocese; was Bishop of Chicago for Reformed Church (1878-1916).

1884 O(scar) O. McIntyre, journalist, was born in Plattsburg, Mo.; wrote syndicated column, "New York Day by Day" (died 1938).

1885 Richard S. Edwards, World War II admiral who was vice commander of the American fleet (1942-46), was born in Philadelphia, Pa. (d 1956).

1890 Adolf Menjou, screen actor, was born in Pittsburgh; many supporting roles (*The Front Page, Farewell to Arms, A Star is Born*) (died 1963).

1892 Wendell L. Willkie, lawyer and industrialist, was born in Elwood, Ind.; general counsel, president, Commonwealth & Southern Corp. (1933-40); 1940 Republican presidential candidate; author (*One World*) (died 1944).

1896 Dimitri Mitropoulos, conductor, was born in Athens; conductor (Minneapolis 1937-49); musical director (New York Philharmonic 1950-58) (died 1960).

1898 Luis Munoz-Marin, Puerto Rican leader, was born in San Juan, P.R.; founder of Popular Democratic party; Puerto Rican governor (1948-64) (died 1980).

1915 Oregon enacted statewide prohibition, effective Jan 1, 1916.

1922 Helen Gurley Brown, editor and author, was born in Green Forest, Ark.; editor, *Cosmopolitan* (1965-); author (*Sex and the Single Girl*).

1924 Edwin Denby, Navy Secretary, resigned because of his involvement in the Teapot Dome scandal.

1939 Golden Gate Exposition opened in San Francisco; closed Oct 29.

1954 John Travolta, screen actor, was born in Englewood, N.J.; starred in several films (*Saturday Night Fever, Urban Cowboy*).

1976 Pesticides containing mercury were banned.

1988 President Reagan submitted a proposed budget of $1.09 trillion, the first ever to reach a trillion dollars.

1887 Oregon passed the first law recognizing Labor Day as a holiday; began by Knights of Labor in New York City in 1882.

1908 Statewide prohibition was enacted in Mississippi.

1911 Merle Oberon, screen actress (*Wuhering Heights*), was born in Tasmania (died 1979).

1912 Stan Keaton, musician, was born in Wichita; conducted own band (1941-79) featuring screaming "walls of brass" (died 1979).

1915 American steamer, *Evelyn*, was sunk by a German mine off Borkum Island.

1916 Eddie (George E.) Arcaro, jockey, was born in Cincinnati; rode 4779 winners in 24,000+ races, winning Kentucky Derby five times, Preakness and Belmont six times each; rode two Triple Crown winners (Whirlaway, Citation).

1917 Carson McCullers, author, was born in Columbus, Ga.; wrote several popular novels (*The Heart is a Lonely Hunter, A Member of the Wedding, The Ballad of the Sad Cafe*) (died 1967).

1924 Lee Marvin, screen actor, was born in New York City; starred on television, various films (*Cat Ballou, Ship of Fools*) (died 1987).

1942 President Franklin Roosevelt, by executive order, authorized the War Department to evacuate 112,000 West Coast Japanese, two thirds of them American citizens, to relocation centers; terminated Jan 2, 1945.

1945 Month-long battle for Iwo Jima began.

1986 Senate by a vote of 83 to 11 ratified the 1948 United Nations treaty outlawing genocide.

1988 Pope John Paul II is an encyclical letter condemned the rivalry between the superpowers which subjected poor nations to imperialistic "structures of sin" that deny them freedom and development.

FEBRUARY 19

1674 Treaty of Westminster restored the New York Province to the English from Dutch occupation; Dutch formally surrendered to Sir Edmund Andros.

1766 William Dunlap, painter and playwright, was born in Perth Amboy, N.J.; known as the father of American drama (*Leicester, Andre, Father of an Only Child*); founder, National Academy of Design (died 1839).

1792 John Locke, scientist and inventor, was born in Lempster, N.H.; investigated terrestrial magnetism and electricity, invented a surveyor's pass, level, and orrery; also an electromagnetic chronograph to determine longitude (died 1856).

1802 Leonard Bacon, Congregational clergyman, was born in Detroit; sometimes called the Congregational "pope"; served First Church, New Haven (1825-66) (died 1881).

1807 Aaron Burr was arrested in Alabama on a charge of forming an expedition against Spanish territory; charge later changed to treason.

1819 Lydia E. Pinkham, patent medicine manufacturer, was born in Lynn, Mass.; developed a herb medicine ("Vegetable Compound") to remedy "woman's weakness" (died 1883).

1821 Francis P. Blair Jr., Missouri legislator (House 1857-59, 1860-64; Senate 1871-73), was born in Lexington, Ky.; 1868 Democratic vice presidential candidate (died 1875).

1855 William Crozier, Army officer and inventor; was born in Carrollton, Ohio; co-inventor of disappearing gun carriage; chief of Army ordinance (1901-17) (died 1942).

1866 Thomas J.J. See, astronomer and mathematician, was born in Montgomery City, Mo.; established wave theory of solid bodies and the cosmic ray; headed naval observatories (Flagstaff, Ariz.; Mare Island) (died 1962).

1881 Kansas adopted a prohibition law.

1884 Sixty tornadoes, most of them in the South, killed 800 people.

FEBRUARY 20

1528 Pamphillio de Narvaez, Spanish soldier and explorer, sailed from Havana for Florida; landed at Tampa Bay Apr 14 for overland journey to Mexico.

1620 Thomas Weston, a London ironmonger, and John Peirce, a London clothmaker, received a patent from the Virginia Co. and persuaded the Separatists (who also had a patent) to join with them.

1726 William Prescott, Revolutionary commander, was born in Groton, Mass.; commanded troops at Battle of Bunker Hill (died 1795).

1772 Isaac Chauncey, War of 1812 naval officer, was born in Black Rock, Conn.; commanded naval forces on Lakes Erie and Ontario (1812-15) (died 1840).

1781 Robert Morris was named to head the newly-created Department of Finance, responsible to Congress, in an effort to correct colonies' worsening financial state.

1794 Debates of the Senate were opened to the public.

1803 Henry Stanberry, Attorney General (1866-68), was born in New York City; chief counsel for President Andrew Johnson in his impeachment trial (1868) (died 1881).

1805 Angelina Emily Grimké, social reformer, was born in Charleston; with sister, Sarah M. Grimké (11/26/1792), became Quakers, took active role in abolitionist, women's rights movements (died 1879).

1809 Supreme Court in *United States v. Peters* sustained the power of national over state authority.

1811 Senate refused to recharter the Bank of the United States, leading to creation of many local banks.

1815 U.S. frigate *Constitution* captured two British sloops off Lisbon.

1829 Joseph Jefferson, actor, was born in Philadelphia; best known for his role of Rip van Winkle (died 1905).

1831 Patrick J. Ryan, Catholic prelate, was born in Thurles, Ireland; archbisop of St. Louis (1883-84), of Philadelphia (1884-1911) (died 1911).

1840 Congress outlawed the practice of dueling.

1844 Leonidas Merritt, mining prospector, was born in Chautauqua County, N.Y.; discovered Mesabi iron ore deposits in Minnesota (1890) (died 1926).

1874 Mary Garden, operatic soprano, was born in Aberdeen, Scotland; starred with Chicago Civic Opera (1910-31) (died 1967).

1890 Sam (Edgar C.) Rice, baseball player (Washington), was born in Morocco, Ind.; batted .322 in 20 years; named to Baseball Hall of Fame (died 1974).

1893 Russel Crouse, playwright and librettist, was born in Findley, Ohio; collaborated with Howard Lindsay (*Life With Father, Anything Goes, Call Me Madam*) and with Rogers and Hammerstein (*Sound of Music*) (died 1966).

1901 Rene J. Dubos, microbologist, was born in St. Brice, France; pioneer in study of antibiotics, tuberculosis (died 1982).

1901 Louis I. Kahn, architect, was born in Saaremia, Estonia; influenced late 20th century architecture (Yale Art Gallery; Salk Institute, La Jolla, Cal.) (died 1974).

1902 Ansel Adams, photographer, was born in San Francisco; a foremost photographer, specializing in landscapes, nature (died 1984).

1905 The Supreme Court in *Jackson v. Massachusetts* held that states have the police power to enact a compulsory vaccination law.

1905 A mine disaster in Virginia City, Ala. killed 116 persons.

1907 The Senate by a vote of 42-28 confirmed the election of Reed Smoot of Utah, defeating the proposal to unseat him because of membership in the Mormon Church.

1915 The Panama Pacific International Exposition opened in San Francisco; closed Dec 4.

1926 Bob (Rev. Robert E.) Richards, Olympics (1952-1956) pole vault champion, was born in Champagn, Ill.

1927 Sidney Poitier, screen actor, was born in Miami, Fla.; starred in several films (*Porgy and Bess, The Defiant Ones, Guess Who's Coming to Dinner*).

1942 Phil(ip A.) Esposito, a leading hockey player, was born in Sault Ste. Marie, Canada; National Hockey League most valuable player (1969-74) and the league's leading scorer (1971-74).

1946 Congress passed the 1946 Employment Act which set up a Council of Economic Advisors to study economic trends and to recommend to the President policies to alleviate the negative effect of business cycles.

1962 Lt. Col. John H. Glenn Jr. becomes the first American to orbit the earth, circling it three times in 4 hours and 55 minutes in a *Friendship 7* capsule.

1982 Construction began on the $20 million renovation of Carnegie Hall in New York City.

FEBRUARY 21

1787 The Continental Congress called for a meeting in May in Philadelphia "for the sole and express purpose of revising the Articles of Confederation."

1792 The House passed presidential succession act, which provided that in the case of removal, death, resignation, or disabilty of both the president and vice president, the president pro tempore of the Senate would succeed; if there was no president pro tem, the House Speaker would succeed; this arrangement lasted until 1886; the Senate had previously passed the measure.

1807 Martin Van Buren and Hannah Hoe were married in Catskill, N.Y.

1821 Charles Scribner, publisher, was born in New York City; co-founder of family publishing firm (1846); founder, publisher *Scribner's Monthly* (1870) (died 1871).

1822 Oliver W. Gibbs, chemist, was born in New York City; laid foundation for American chemistry; pioneer in spectroscopy; a founder (1863), president (1895-1900), National Academy of Sciences (died 1908).

1848 John Quincy Adams, former president, suffered a cerebral stroke on the House floor, where he had been representing Massachusetts; died two days later at 80.

1855 Alice F. Palmer, pioneer educator, was born in Colesville, N.Y.; president, Wellesley College (1882-87), dean of women, Chicago U. (1892-95) (died 1902).

1863 Rudolph J. Schaefer, brewery executive, was born in New York City; with family-owned F & M Schaefer Brewing Co. (1882-1923); introduced first bottled beer (1891) (died 1923).

1867 Otto H. Kahn, banker and art patron, was born in Mannheim, Germany; with William K. Vanderbilt bought (1907) financially-troubled Metropolitan Opera; later became sole owner, serving as president or chairman (1911-31); many other benefactions, probably nation's greatest art patron (died 1934).

1868 President Andrew Johnson removed Edwin M. Stanton as Secretary of War, leading to presidential impeachment proceedings; motion to impeach was made by Rep. John Covode of Pennsylvania.

1885 The Washington Monument was dedicated.

1907 W(ystan) H. Auden, poet, was born in York, England; also a playwright, librettist for Stravinsky's *Rake's Progress* (died 1973).

1917 Woman suffrage went into effect in Ohio.

1922 The American dirigible *Roma* exploded over Hampton, Va.; 34 were killed.

1927 Erma Bombeck, author and humorist, was born in Dayton; syndicated columnist, author, and television commentator.

1936 Barbara Jordan, legislator, was born in Houston; the first black woman to serve in the Texas legislature, represented the state in the House (1972-78).

1965 Malcolm X, black leader, was assassinated in New York City by Black Muslims.

1972 President Nixon began a week-long visit to China, the first president to visit a nation not recognized by the United States.

1988 Rev. Jimmy Swaggart, television evangelist, confessed to sins before his congregation of 8000 in Baton Rouge, La. and said he would absent himself from his pulpit for "an indeterminate time."

FEBRUARY 22

1732 George Washington, first president (1789-97), was born in Westmoreland County, Va.; commander of American forces in Revolution (died 1799).

1778 Rembrandt Peale, artist, was born in Bucks County, Pa., son of Charles Wilson Peale (4/15/1741); painter of portraits, historical scenes (died 1860).

1784 *Empress of China* sailed from New York to Canton, opening trade with China.

1819 James Russell Lowell, author and poet, was born in Cambridge; wrote "The Vision of Sir Launfall;" a founder, editor, *Atlantic Monthly* (1857-61); minister to Spain (1877-80), to Great Britain (1880-85) (died 1891).

1819 Under the Adams-Onis Treaty, Spain ceded Florida to the United States after long negotiations, ending with a treaty signed by Secretary of State John Quincy Adams and Spanish Minister Onis; ratifications exchanged Feb 22, 1821.

1820 William F. Channing, inventor, was born in Boston, son of William E. Channing (4/7/1780); co-inventor of electric fire alarm telegraph (died 1901).

1831 William N. Byers, surveyor and pioneer, was born in Madison County, Ohio; founder (1859), editor, *Rocky Mountain News*, first Colorado newspaper; mineral byerite was named for him (died 1903).

1838 Anson P. Stokes, financier, was born in New York City; a partner in Phelps Dodge & Co.; successful in New York City building construction, management; a founder, Metropolitan Museum of Art (died 1913).

1855 Pennsylvania State College was chartered as Farmers' High School.

1857 Frank L. Stanton, lyricist, was born in Charleston; remembered for "Mighty Lak a Rose" and "Going Home" (died 1927).

1865 Union troops captured Wilmington, N.C.

1865 Tennessee ratified its constitution; provided for abolition of slavery.

1871 George O. Smith, geologist, was born in Hodgdon, Me.; with Geological Survey (1896-1930), director (1907-30); chairman, Federal Power Commission (1930-33) (died 1944).

1873 Samuel Seabury, attorney, was born in New York City; conducted investigation of New York City administration (1931-32), led to resignation of Mayor Jimmy Walker (June 19, 1881) (died 1958)..

1874 William J. Klem, baseball umpire, was born in Rochester, N.Y.; the first umpire to be named to Baseball Hall of Fame (died 1951).

1877 Bedloe's (now Liberty) Island in New York Harbor was approved by Congress as the site for the Statue of Liberty.

1879 Frank W. Woolworth opened his first 5-and-10-cents store in Utica, N.Y.

1892 Edna St. Vincent Millay, author, was born in Rockland, Me.; poet ("The Harp Weaver," "Wine from These Grapes," "Huntsman, What Quarry?"), playwright (*The Lamp and the Bell, Aria da Capo*) (died 1950).

1892 David Dubinsky, labor leader, was born in Brest-Litovsk, Poland; president, International Ladies Garment Workers (ILGWU) (1932-66); a founder, American Labor Party (1936), Americans for Democratic Action (1947) (died 1982).

1896 Nacio Herb Brown, composer ("Singing in the Rain," "You Were Meant for Me"), was born in Deming, N.J. (died 1964).

1900 Paul Kollsman, aeronautical engineer, was born in Freudenstadt, Germany; invented the altimeter (died 1982).

1901 Charles E. Whittaker, jurist, was born near Troy, Kan.; associate justice, Supreme Court (1957-62) (died 1973).

1904 Peter Hurd, painter, was born in Roswell, N.M.; did portrait of President Lyndon Johnson, who called it "the ugliest thing I ever saw" (died 1984).

1907 Robert Young, screen and television actor, was born in Chicago; noted for role of Dr. Marcus Welby.

1926 (Nelson) Bunker Hunt, financier, was born in El Dorado, Ark.

1932 Ted (Edward M.) Kennedy, legislator, was born in Brookline, Mass., brother of President Kennedy (5/29/1917) and Robert Kennedy (11/20/1925); represented Massachusetts in the Senate (1963-).

1950 Julius Erving, basketball player, was born in Roosevelt, N.Y.; starred with Massachusetts U., Philadelphia 76ers; known as "Dr. J."

1955 Congress received a special message from President Eisenhower calling for the expenditure of $101 billion over ten years for interstate highways.

1973 China and the United States agreed to set up permanent liaison offices in each other's countries.

1983 United States Government purchased the town of Times Beach, Mo. for $33 million because dioxin level in soil posed a threat to the health of the 2400 residents.

1988 Navy Secretary James H. Webb Jr. resigned citing differences with Defense Secretary Frank C. Carlucci over the Navy's budget and Defense Department management; William L. Ball III was later nominated for the post.

FEBRUARY 23

1665 Col. Richard Nicolls, head of a British commission, confiscated all properties of the Dutch West India Co. in the New York area as a result of the second Anglo-Dutch war, which began in Dec 1664.

1680 Jean Baptiste LeMoyne, Sieur de Bieneville, colonial governor, was born in Longueuil, Canada; governor of Louisiana colony (1701-12, 1718-26, 1733-43); founder of New Orleans (died 1768).

1744 Josiah Quincy, colonial leader, was born in Boston; with John Adams, he defended British soldiers accused in Boston Massacre, winning acquittals for most (died 1775).

1751 Henry Dearborn, soldier and public official, was born in Hampton, N.H.; served in Revolution (Ticonderoga, Saratoga, Yorktown); Secretary of War (1801-09), during which he ordered a fortification at "Chikago," which began as Fort Dearborn; minister to Portugal (1822-24) (died 1829).

1778 Baron Friedrich von Steuben arrived at Valley Forge and began to organize and discipline the troops.

1781 George Taylor, Irish-born colonial leader, died at 65; member Continental Congress from Pennsylvania (1776-77), signer of the Declaration of Independence.

1784 Rhode Island General Assembly authorized freeing of slaves; declared all blacks, mulattoes free who were born in the state after Mar 1.

1787 Emma Willard, educator, was born in Berlin, Conn.; pioneer in higher education for women; founder, Middlebury Seminary (1814) and other New York schools to prepare women for college (died 1870).

1823 James G. Batterson, insurance executive, was born in Bloomfield, Conn; founder, president, Travelers Insurance Co. (1863-1901), first American accident insurance company (died 1901).

1832 John H. Vincent, religious educator, was born in Tuscaloosa, Ala.; helped organize training school for Methodist Sunday school teachers; general agent, Methodist Sunday School Union (1866-86); a founder, Chautauqua Assembly (1874); Methodist bishop (1888-1904) (died 1920).

1835 Thomas W. Phillips, petroleum industry executive, was born near Mt. Jackson, Pa.; an early developer of Pennsylvania oil fields; represented Pennsylvania in the House (1893-97); member, U.S. Industrial Commission (1878-1902) (died 1912).

1836 Siege of the Alamo in San Antonio began with 27-year-old Col. William B. Travis in command of 145 men facing 6000-7000 Mexicans; ended Mar 6.

1844 James F. Babcock, chemist, was born in Boston; Massachusetts assayer of liquors, established 3% limit in defining intoxicating liquors; invented a fire extinguisher (died 1897).

1846 William Horlick, industrialist, was born in Ruardeen, England; originated malted milk, headed company named for him (1883-1936) (died 1936).

1847 Zachary Taylor led 4600 American troops to victory over Mexicans at Buena Vista, ending fighting in northern Mexico; Americans had about 600 casualties, Mexicans under Gen. Antonio Santa Anna 1600 casualties and 1900 missing.

1861 Henry B. Wilson, World War I admiral, was born in Camden, N.J.; commanded Atlantic patrol forces (1917-18), American naval forces in France (1917-18); commander-in-chief, Atlantic Fleet (1919-21); superintendent, Naval Academy (1921-25) (died 1954).

1861 President-elect Lincoln arrived in Washington, D.C. after secret night trip because of a warning of an assassination plot in Baltimore.

1868 William E.B. DuBois, editor and civil rights leader, was born in Great Barrington, Mass.; a founder, National Association for the Advancement of Colored People (NAACP); editor of its journal, *Crisis* (1909-32); later joined Communist Party, moved to China (died 1963).

1870 Mississippi was readmitted to the Union, but continued under a reconstruction government until 1875.

1871 George T. Moore, botanist, was born in Indianapolis; in charge of botany at Woods Hole (Mass.) Marine Laboratory (1909-19); discovered way to prevent water polluton by algae, certain bacteria (died 1956).

1880 Roy D. Chapin, auto manufacturer, was born in Lansing, Mich; president, Hudson Auto Co. (1910-23, 1933-36), board chairman (1923-32); Secretary of Commerce (1932-33) (died 1936).

1881 William S. Farish, oil industry leader, was born in Mayersville, Miss.; founder (1917), president (1922-32), Humble Oil Co. (died 1942).

1882 U. of North Dakota was founded at Grand Forks.

1884 Casimir Funk, biochemist, was born in Warsaw; known for his work in vitamins and hormones (died 1967).

1886 Charles M. Hall, after a year's research for a solvent to purify aluminum, found it in molten cryolite (sodium aluminum fluoride); formed company which became Aluminum Company of America.

1889 John G. Winant, public official and diplomat, was born in New York City; first chairman, Social Security Board (1935-37); director, International Labor Organization (1939-41); ambassador to Great Britain (1941-46) (died 1947).

1902 Ellen Stone, American missionary captured by Turkish brigands in Sept 1901, was released on payment of ransom of $72,500 raised by public subscription.

1904 William L. Shirer, journalist, was born in Chicago; foreign correspondent, author (*Berlin Diary, Rise and Fall of the Third Reich*).

1905 Rotary Club was formed in Chicago; there now are 18,000 clubs in 152 countries with 850,000 members.

1906 Thomas Burns defeated Marvin Hart in 20 rounds in Los Angeles to win the world heavyweight boxing championship.

1915 The American steamer *Carib* was sunk by a mine off Germany in the North Sea.

1927 Federal Radio Commission was created.

1945 The American flag was raised on Mt. Suribachi on Iwo Jima by Marines.

1954 The first mass inoculation of Salk Polio vaccine began in Pittsburgh.

1975 Ten-year embargo on arms trade with Pakistan was lifted.

1988 Texaco Co. agreed to pay $1.25 billion to the government to settle an accusation that it overcharged customers for crude oil and refined oil products between 1973 and 1981.

FEBRUARY 24

1750 Theophilus Parsons, jurist, was born in Byfield, Mass.; chief justice, Massachusetts Supreme Court (1806-13); his decisions led to universal adoption of the English common law tradition (died 1813).

1772 William H. Crawford, legislator and public official, was born in Amherst County, Va.; represented Georgia in the Senate (1807-13); minister to France (1813); Secretary of War (1815-16), Secretary of Treasury (1816-25) (died 1834).

1785 John Adams was named the first minister plenipotentiary to Great Britain.

1803 The Supreme Court in *Marbury v. Madison* overturned a law for the first time, declaring a section of the 1789 Judiciary Act unconstitutional; set precedent of authorizing federal courts to review legislative constitutionality.

1808 John Wise, pioneer aeronaut, was born in Lancaster, Pa.; made first ascent in a balloon of own design (1835), carried mail for first time (1859) (died 1879).

1813 The American sloop *Hornet* sank the British sloop *Peacock*.

1824 George W. Curtis, editor and author, was born in Providence; as editor of *Harper's* and author of its "Easy Chair" column, he strongly influenced opinions of his day (died 1892).

1836 Winslow Homer, artist, was born in Boston; noted for his seascapes (*The Gulf Stream, MaineCoast, Northeaster*) (died 1910).

1843 Miles A. Seed, inventor, was born in Preston, England; perfected process for making photographic dry plates, organized company (1882) to manufacture it; sold out to Kodak (1902) (died 1913).

1855 President Pierce signed an act creating the first Court of Claims; before that citizens had to get congressional approval of claims against the government.

1860 Daniel B. Updike, printer, was born in Providence; founder, Merrymount Press (1893); did much to improve American typography (died 1941).

1860 Alabama legislature resolved that the state would not submit to a "foul sectional party" and called for a convention in the event of the election of a "black Republican" president.

1863 Territory of Arizona was established.

1868 House voted 126-47 to impeach President Andrew Johnson, set up a committee of two to lead impeachment proceedings in the Senate.

1874 Honus (John Peter) Wagner, baseball player, was born in Carnegie, Pa.; called the "Flying Dutchman," he was considered one of the greatest all-around players; with Pirates (1900-17), had 3415 career hits and a .327 batting average; one of original five in Baseball Hall of Fame (died 1955).

1885 Chester W. Nimitz, World War II admiral, was born in Fredericksburg, Tex.; commander-in-chief, Pacific Fleet (1941-45); chief of naval operations (1945-47) (died 1966).

1887 Mary Ellen Chase, educator (Smith College (1918-55), was born in Blue Hills, Me.; author (*Mary Peters*) (died 1973).

1908 Supreme Court in *Miller v. Oregon* upheld the Oregon ten-hour day for women in industry.

1919 War Revenue Act levied taxes on incomes, excess profits, estates, and products of child labor.

1931 Supreme Court upheld the constitutionality of the 18th (Prohibition) Amendment.

1942 National Housing Agency was created by presidential executive order.

1955 Steven P. Jobs, co-founder of Apple Computers, was born in Mountain View, Cal.

1977 Securities & Exchange Commission adopted rules to prevent foreign buyers from secretly gaining control of American companies.

1988 Chairman of the Federal AIDS panel, Admiral James D. Watkins, urged a $2 billion a year national effort to expand drug treatment programs and to improve health care services.

1988 The Supreme Court ruled unanimously that public figures who are victims of a satirical attack — even one that is pornographic and "outrageous — may not sue for damages; decision rejected a $200,000 judgment won by Rev. Jerry Falwell against *Hustler Magazine.*

FEBRUARY 25

1643 Gov. William Kieft of New Netherlands began a war against Indians at Pavonia and Corlaer's Hook because of their refusal to surrender murderer of a colonist.

1673 Charles II granted Virginia to Lords Arlington and Culpeper as a proprietary province for 31 years.

1710 Daniel G. Duluth, French explorer, died at 74; explored Lake Superior region, was responsible for French control of the area; Minnesota city named for him.

1746 Charles C. Pinckney, colonial leader, was born in Charleston, brother of Thomas Pinckney (10/23/1750) and cousin of Charles Pinckney (10/26/1757); minister to France (1796-1800); unsuccessful Federalist candidate for president (1804, 1808); a founder, U. of South Carolina (died 1825).

1779 Col. George Rogers Clark with 127 men captured Vincennes, Ind. from a British-Indian force.

1781 John Adams was named minister plenipotentiary to the Netherlands.

1783 Denmark recognized the independence of the United States.

1791 Bank of the United States incorporated as a national bank, given a 20-year charter with a capital of $10 million; President Washington asked cabinet for its opinion and Jefferson held it to be unconstitutional because such power not granted to Congress, Hamilton held it constitutional as an implied power.

1799 First federal forestry legislation approved to acquire timber for the Navy.

1805 Thomas Pownall, colonial governor, died at 83; governor of Massachusetts (1757-59); served in Parliament (1767-80), tried to prevent Revolution by urging changes in colonial taxation.

1807 George A. Trenholm, Congress official, was born in Charleston; served as Confederate Secretary of Treasury (1861-65) (died 1876).

1809 George A. Collum, Union general, was born in New York City; served in Army from 1833 to 1874; endowed construction of Memorial Hall at West Point (died 1892).

1828 John Adams, son of President and Mrs. John Quincy Adams, was married in the White House, the first and only wedding of a president's son there.

1833 John P. St. John, temperance leader and politician, was born in Brookville, Ind.; governor of Kansas (1879-83); presidential candidate, National Prohibition Party (1884); party drew enough votes in New York to give state to the Democrats, thereby he is sometimes credited with Cleveland's election (died 1916).

1836 Samuel Colt received a patent for his six-shooter, an important link in the development of arms, played an important role in development of the West.

1848 Edward H. Harriman, financier and railroad executive, was born in Hempstead, N.Y.; owner, director, Union Pacific and various other railroads; lost control of Northern Pacific in battle with J.P. Morgan and James J. Hill, which touched off stock market panic of 1901; organized first boys clubs (1876) (died 1909).

1856 Charles L. Freer, industrialist and philanthropist, was born in Kingston, N.Y.; amassed fortune in railroad car manufacturing; retired to art collecting, donating 8000 works to Smithsonian for display in Freer Gallery (1906) (died 1919).

1862 Confederate forces evacuated Nashville after the fall of Ft. Donelson; Union forces occupied the city.

1863 President Lincoln signed the national banking system act, which included creation of the office of Comptroller of the Currency.

1864 Anna T. Harrison, widow of President William Henry Harrison, died in North Bend, Ohio at 88.

1873 Enrico Caruso, opera tenor, was born in Naples; one of world's greatest tenors; top attraction at the Metropolitan (1908-21); first operatic singer to capitalize on phonograph recordings (died 1921).

1881 William Z. Foster, American Communist leader, was born in Taunton, Mass.; secretary-general, U.S. Communist Party (1921-30), chairman (1945-56); Communist Party presidential candidate (1924-1928, 1932) (died 1961).

1883 Clarence A. Dykstra, educator, was born in Cleveland; president, Wisconsin U. (1937-45), provost, California U. (1945-50); director, Selective Service (1940-41) (died 1950).

1888 John Foster Dulles, public official, was born in Washington, D.C., brother of Allen W. Dulles (4/7/1893); Secretary of State (1953-59), prime architect of American policy of Communist containment (died 1959).

1894 Bert (DeBenneville) Bell, football executive, was born in Philadelphia; co-owner, Philadelphia Eagles (1933-45); football commissioner (1946-59) (died 1959).

1896 John L. McClellan, legislator, was born in Sheridan, Ark.; represented Arkansas in the House (1935-39) and Senate (1942-77); conducted televised hearings on labor unions (died 1977).

1900 Jed Harris, theater producer (*Front Page, Our Town*) was born in Vienna (died 1979).

1901 U.S. Steel Co. was incorporated in New Jersey, with capitalization of $1.3 billion.

1904 John J. Bittner, biologist, was born in Meadville, Pa.; his work at Minnesota U. Medical School contributed to theory that cancer is caused by a virus (died 1961).

1907 The first Hudson River tunnel between New York and New Jersey was completed.

1907 Mary C. Chase, playwright, was born in Denver; wrote hit play, *Harvey*, as well as *Mrs. McThing* and *Bernardine* (died 1981).

1913 The 16th Amendment creating the federal income tax went into effect.

1918 President Wilson, ordered the construction of Muscle Shoals Dam on the Tennessee River to produce power for the manufacture of explosives and nitrates.

1919 Monte (Montford M.) Irvin, baseball player (Giants) was born in Columbia, Ala.; named to Baseball Hall of Fame.

1933 First American aircraft carrier, *Ranger*, was launched at Newport News, Va.

1964 Muhammad Ali (then Cassius Clay) won the world heavyweight boxing championship for the first time, knocking out Sonny Liston in seven rounds in Miami Beach.

FEBRUARY 26

1732 The first Catholic church in the colonies was finished in Philadelphia and first mass was celebrated.

1775 Col. Alexander Leslie was ordered to go to Salem to seize American stores and cannon collected there; detained at the bridge while material was moved.

1785 Thomson Mason, colonial leader, died at 53, brother of George Mason (6/12/1776); while serving in Virginia Assembly he wrote nine letters of a "British American," upholding the colonial position.

1795 Francis Marion, Revolutionary commander, died at about 63; known as "The Swamp Fox," he commanded troops in South Carolina.

1832 John G. Nicolay, private secretary to President Lincoln (1860-65), was born in Essingen, Germany; author of Lincoln biography, edited Lincoln works (died 1901).

1833 Supreme Court in *Barron v. Baltimore*, held that the Bill of Rights does not protect against state actions.

1844 Horace H. Lurton, jurist, was born in Newport, Ky.; associate justice, Supreme Court (1910-14) (died 1914).

1846 William F. Cody ("Buffalo Bill"), hunter and showman, was born in Scott County, Iowa; pony express rider and scout; Cody, Wyo. named for him (died 1917).

1852 John H. Kellogg, physician, was born in Battle Creek, Mich., brother of Will K. Kellogg (4/7/1860); founder, director of sanitaria; invented medical instruments and apparatus, helped develop breakfast cereals (died 1943).

1857 Charles M. Sheldon, Congregational clergyman, was born in Wellsville, N.Y.; his religious novel, *In His Steps*, was a best seller; editor, *Christian Herald* (from 1920) (died 1946).

1858 William J. Hammer, electrical engineer and inventor, was born in Cressona, Pa.; associated with Edison, established first central station for incandescent electric lighting (in London), invented luminous radium preparation for watch and clock dials; first suggested, used radium for cancer and tumor treatment (died 1934).

1866 Herbert H. Dow, chemist and industrialist, was born in Belleville, Canada; founder, president, Dow Chemical Co. (1897), developed process for removing bromine from brine; developed, patented 100+ chemical processes (died 1930).

1869 The 15th Amendment was enacted, providing that the right to vote must not be abridged because of "race, color, or previous condition of servitude;" ratified in 1870.

1877 Rudolph Dirks, cartoonist, was born in Heinde, Germany; created the "Katzenjammer Kids" (died 1968).

1887 Grover C. Alexander, baseball pitcher (Phils, Cubs, Cards) for 20 years, winning 374, losing 208; named to Baseball Hall of Fame (died 1950).

1890 Chance M. Vought, airplane designer and manufacturer, was born in New York City; built training planes for British in World War I; formed Lewis & Vought (1917), became Chance Vought, merged with Pratt & Whitney Co. (died 1930).

1896 Evans F. Carlson, Marine Corps general, was born in Sidney, N.Y.; led raids in South Pacific; his force was known as Carlson's Raiders (died 1947).

1905 Panama Canal Engineering Commission recommended a sea-level canal to be constructed in 12 years at a cost of $230 million.

1907 Gen. George W. Goethels was named chief engineer for Panama Canal construction.

1916 Jackie Gleason, entertainer, was born in New York City; starred on television for 20 years, screen actor (*The Hustler, Gigot*) (died 1987).

1917 Mt. McKinley, Alaska National Park was established; renamed the Denali National Park in 1980.

1917 President Wilson asked Congress for emergency powers, including arming American merchant vessels; approved by House (403-13) Mar 1, filibustered in the Senate.

1919 The Grand Canyon (Ariz.) National Park was established.

1920 Tony Randall, entertainer, was born in Tulsa; screen actor (*Mating Game, Pillow Talk*), television (*The Odd Couple, Sidney*).

1929 Grand Teton (Wyo.) National Park was established.

1932 Johnny Cash, country and western singer, was born in Kingsland, Ark.; composed and sang many hit songs ("I Walk the Line," "Folsom Prison Blues").

1972 More than 118 died when a slagpile dam collapsed at Man, W.Va., flooding a 17-mile-long valley.

1984 U.S. Marines were withdrawn from Beirut, Lebanon.

1986 Robert Penn Warren, poet, novelist, and essayist, was named the country's first official poet laureate by Daniel J. Boorstin, Librarian of Congress.

FEBRUARY 27

1659 Henry Dunster, English-born first president of Harvard (1640-54), died at 50; had to resign post because of his views on infant baptism; became Baptist pastor in Scituate, Mass. (1655-59).

1720 Samuel Parris, Salem Village (now Danvers), Mass. clergyman, died at 67; credited with starting witchcraft trials when he supported the accusations brought against his West Indian slave.

1773 Christ Church in Alexandria, Va. was completed after six years construction at the cost of $4070; George Washington purchased his family pew for $100.

1775 Lord North's conciliation plan was adopted by Parliament, exempting any colony from taxation if it contributed to the support of civil officials and troops; at the same time, the New England Restraining Act was passed, forbidding New England from trading with any nation but Great Britain and the British West Indies after July 1; barred New Englanders from North Atlantic fisheries after July 20.

1776 American troops defeated a British force, mostly Loyalists, led by Gen. Donald McDonald, at Moore's Creek Bridge, N.C., near Wilmington.

1782 The House of Commons urged King George III to end the American Revolution.

1801 Congress assumed jurisdiction over the District of Columbia.

1801 Thomas Jefferson's *Manual of Parliamentary Practice* was published; code still substantially governs American deliberative bodies.

1807 Henry Wadsworth Longfellow, author, was born in Portland, Me.; modern languages professor (Bowdoin 1829-35, Harvard 1835-54); wrote many well-known poems (*The Wreck of the Hesperus, Evangeline, Hiawatha, Paul Revere's Ride, The Village Blacksmith*) (died 1882).

1823 William B. Franklin, Union general, was born in York, Pa.; saw action at first Bull Run, Antietam (died 1903).

1830 Henry E. Huntington, railway executive, was born in Oneonta, N.Y.; a noted philanthropist (died 1927).

1836 Russell A. Alger, public official, was born in Lafayette, Ohio; served Michigan as governor (1884-88) and represented it as Senator (1902-07); Secretary of War (1897-99), resigned at the request of President McKinley because of criticism of War Department inefficiency (died 1907).

1860 Abraham Lincoln made his Cooper Union speech in which he defended the rights of the Federal Government to prohibit slavery in the territories.

1867 Irving Fisher, economist, was born in Saugerties, N.Y.; pioneered in monetary economic theory (died 1947).

1869 Alice Hamilton, toxicologist, was born in New York City; investigated occupational poisons, Bureau of Labor Statistics (1911-21), Harvard Medical (1919-35) (died 1970).

1872 Ellery Sedgwick, editor (*Atlantic Monthly* 1908-38), was born in New York City (died 1960).

1873 Congress censured two of its members, Oakes Ames (1/10/1804) and James Brooks, for their role in the Crédit Mobilier affair — Ames for selling Union Pacific stock at low prices to congressmen to influence votes, Brooks for corruption.

1882 Burton K. Wheeler, legislator, was born in Hudson, Mass.; represented Montana in the Senate (1923-47); Progressive party vice presidential candidate (1924) (died 1975).

1886 Hugo L. Black, jurist, was born in Harlan, Ala.; represented Alabama in the Senate (1927-37); associate justice, Supreme Court (1937-71); led activists in Court, wrote opinion forbidding prayer in public schools (died 1971).

1888 Lotte Lehman, soprano, was born in Perleberg, Germany; one of greatest singers of German repertory (died 1976).

1888 Arthur M. Schlesinger, historian, was born in Xenia, Ohio; edited 13-volume series, *A History of American Life* (died 1965).

1891 David Sarnoff, radio and television pioneer, was born in Uzlian, Russia; invented radio set (1915); with RCA (1919-71) as president (1930-47), chairman (1947-71); a founder, National Broadcasting Co. (died 1971).

1896 Arthur W. Radford, World War II admiral, was born in Chicago; chairman, Joint Chiefs of Staff (1953-57) (died 1973).

1901 Gene Sarazen, golfer, was born in Rye, N.Y.; an outstanding golfer of 1920s, 1930s.

1902 John E. Steinbeck, author, was born in Salinas, Cal.; wrote many popular novels (*Grapes of Wrath, Of Mice and Men, East of Eden, Cannery Row*); awarded 1962 Nobel Literature Prize (died 1968).

1904 James T. Farrell, author, was born in Chicago; remembered for *Studs Lonigan, Danny O'Neill* series (died 1979).

1907 Mildred Bailey, singer, was born in Tekoa, Wash.; vocalist with Paul Whiteman orchestra (died 1951).

1910 Joan Bennett, screen actress (*Little Women, Woman in the Window*), was born in Palisades, N.J., daughter of Richard Bennett (5/21/1872) and sister of Constance Bennett (10/22/1914).

1910 Peter DeVries, author, was born in Chicago; short story writer of *The New Yorker*, author (*Tunnel of Love; Reuben, Reuben*).

1913 Irwin Shaw, author, was born in Brooklyn; popular novelist (*The Young Lions; Rich Man, Poor Man; Two Weeks in Another Town*) (died 1984).

1922 Supreme Court upheld constitutionality of women's suffrage (19th amendment).

1926 David H. Hübel, medical scientist, was born in Windsor, Canada of American parents; shared 1981 Nobel Physiology/Medicine Prize for research on brain's function in vision.

1930 Joanne Woodward, screen actress, was born in Thomasville, Ga.; starred in several films (*Three Faces of Eve, Long Hot Summer*).

1932 Elizabeth Taylor, screen actress, was born in London; starred in many films (*National Velvet, Butterfield 8, Cleopatra, Who's Afraid of Virginia Woolf?*)

1934 Ralph Nader, consumer advocate, was born in Winsted, Conn.; work led to passage of National Traffic and Motor Vehicles Safety Act.

1939 Supreme Court in *NLRB v. Fansteel* outlawed sit-down strikes.

1942 Two-day battle of Java Sea and Sunda Strait resulted in the loss of four Allied cruisers and four destroyers.

1950 United States and Canada signed a 50-year treaty for the power output increase of Niagara River, protection of Niagara Falls beauty.

1951 The 22nd Amendment, limiting presidency to two terms, went into effect.

1961 James Worthy, basketball player, was born in Gastonia, N.C.; starred with North Carolina U., Los Angeles Lakers.

1973 Two hundred members of American Indian Movement seized Wounded Knee on the Oglala Sioux Reservations in South Dakota; held town until May 8.

1987 The Tower Commission which studied the Iran-Contra affair issued its report castigating President Reagan and some top aides for making serious mistakes in selling arms to Iran and diverting profits to the Nicaraguan Contras.

FEBRUARY 28

1610 A patent was granted to Lord De la Warre as lord governor and captain general of Virginia; arrived with three ships and provisions (June 10), just as settlers were about to abandon Jamestown.

1787 Pittsburgh Academy was founded, became U. of Pittsburgh in 1908.

1797 Mary M. Lyon, educator, was born in Buckland, Mass.; pioneered in providing advanced education for women; founder, Mt. Holyoke Seminary (later College), first women's college in the United States; president (1837-49) (died 1849).

1799 Samuel S. Schmucker, religious leader, was born in Hagerstown, Md.; founder, first president, Gettysburg (now Lutheran) Seminary (1826-64); founder, first president, Gettysburg College (1832-34); leader of American low-church Lutherans (died 1873).

1822 George Vasey, botanist, was born in Scarborough, England; headed National Herbarium (1872-93); specialized in grasses, Vasey grass named for him (died 1893).

1825 Quincy A. Gillmore, Union general, was born in Lorain County, Ohio; served throughout Civil War; commander, Department of the South (1865); president, Mississippi River Commission (1879) (died 1888).

1827 Baltimore & Ohio Railroad was chartered in Maryland; on Mar 8, in Virginia.

1844 President Tyler, his cabinet, and 350 dignitaries were aboard the frigate, USS *Princeton*, when a bow gun exploded; eight men, including Secretary of State Abel P. Upshur, Navy Secretary Thomas W. Gilmer, and Senator David Gardiner of New York, father of President Tyler's fiance, were killed; the President was below decks at the time of the explosion.

1847 Col. A.W. Doniphan and his troops, on a march from New Mexico to California, defeated Mexicans at the pass of Sacramento.

1849 First band of gold seekers arrived in San Francisco aboard the *California*.

1854 Antislavery forces met in a schoolhouse in Ripon, Wis., recommended formation of a "Republican Party."

1860 Carl G.L. Barth, mechanical engineer, was born in Oslo; pioneer of scientific management in the United States (died 1939).

1860 Victor L. Berger, editor and legislator, was born in Nieder Rehbach, Austria; first Socialist elected to Congress, representing Wisconsin in the House (1911-13, 1923-29) (died 1929).

1861 Congress established the Colorado Territory and President Lincoln appointed William Gilpin as first governor.

1861 Missouri state convention rejected secession 89-1.

1867 U. of Illinois at Urbana was incorporated; opened Mar 2.

1869 William V. Pratt, naval officer, was born in Belfast, Me.; assistant chief of naval operations (1917-19); commander-in-chief, U.S. fleet (1929-30); chief of naval operations (1930-33) (died 1957).

1878 Bland-Allison Act was passed, the first of several government subsidies to silver producers during depressed times; law required that the government purchase monthly $2-4 million in silver bullion to be coined.

1882 Geraldine Farrar, dramatic soprano, was born in Melrose, Mass.; sang at the Met (1906-22) in many roles (Nanon, Mignon, Tosca, Juliet) (died 1967).

1894 Ben Hecht, journalist and author, was born in New York City; author (*Erik Dorn, The Egoist*); co-author of plays with Charles MacArthur (*The Front Page, Twentieth Century*) (died 1964).

1896 Philip S. Hench, physician, was born in Pittsburgh; shared 1950 Nobel Physiology/ Medicine Prize for discoveries about hormones of adrenal cortex (died 1965).

1901 Linus C. Pauling, chemist, was born in Portland, Ore.; first to win two unshared Nobel Prizes — Chemistry (1954) for describing the forces holding together proteins and other molecules; Peace (1962).

1907 Milton A. Caniff, cartoonist, was born in Hillsboro, Ohio; creator of "Terry and the Pirates" and "Steve Canyon" (died 1988).

1915 Zero (Sam) Mostel, actor, was born in Brooklyn; starred in several plays, including *Fiddler on the Roof* (died 1977).

1917 Woman suffrage became effective in Indiana.

1920 Transportation Act was passed by Congress, ending the war-time government operation of the railroads and providing for their return to private ownership.

1923 Gyo Obata, architect, was born in San Francisco; designed the National Air & Space Museum, Dallas-Ft. Worth Airport.

1924 Christopher G. Craft, aeronautical engineer, was born in Phoebus, Va.; flight director of American manned space program (1959-70).

1927 Supreme Court ruled that oil contracts and leases granted to Edward L. Doheny by former Interior Secretary Albert B. Fall were illegal, fraudulent, and corrupt.

1930 Leon N. Cooper, physicist, was born in New York City; shared 1972 Nobel Physics Prize for theory of superconductivity of metals.

1931 Dean Smith, basketball coach, was born in Emporia, Kan.; directed North Carolina U. team (1961-).

1940 Mario G. Andretti, automobile race driver, was born in Trieste, Italy; won numerous championships, including the Indianapolis 500.

1945 President Franklin Roosevelt appointed delegates to the United Nations Conference in San Francisco.

1987 President Reagan appointed former Senator Howard H. Baker Jr. as the White House chief of staff, replacing Donald T. Regan.

FEBRUARY 29

1704 The Deerfield (Mass.) massacre occurred when 50 French soldiers and 200 Indians attacked a sleeping settlement, killing about 50 and taking 111 prisoners (17 of whom died on the march to Canada); 137 escaped.

1736 Ann Lee, religious leader, was born in Manchester, England; founder of American Shakers; began first Shaker colony (1776) at what is now Watervliet, N.Y. (died 1784).

1784 John E. Wool, Mexican War general, was born in Newburgh, N.Y.; second in command at Buena Vista; various commands until Civil War (died 1869).

1820 Lewis A. Sayre, first American orthopedic surgeon, was born in Morris County, N.J.; an organizer, surgeon at Bellevue Hospital Medical College (1861) (died 1900).

1840 John P. Holland, submarine developer, was born in County Clare, Ireland; launched successful submarine (1898), sold it to the Navy (1900) (died 1914).

1844 Colby M. Chester, Union naval officer, was born in New London, Conn.; saw action at Mobile Bay; commandant, Naval Academy (1891-94); commander, South Atlantic squadron (1897-98); superintendent, Naval Observatory (1902-06) (died 1932).

1860 Herman Hollerith, tabulating system inventor, was born in Buffalo; invented punch card tabulating system, used in 1890 census; formed Computing-Tabulating Machine Co. (1896), which became IBM in 1924 (died 1929).

1904 Jimmy Dorsey, musician, was born in Shenandoah, Pa., brother of Tommy Dorsey (11/19/1905); noted saxophone player and an important orchestra leader in Big Band era (died 1957).

MARCH 1

1543 Expedition of Juan Cabrillo, who died Jan 3, 1543, reached the mouth of the Rogue River in Oregon at Cape Mendocino.

1625 John Robinson, Separatist clergyman, died at about 50; led his Pilgrim congregation from England to the Netherlands; built up congregation, planned voyage to America; stayed behind with the majority.

1732 William Cushing, jurist, was born in Scituate, Mass.; chief justice, Massachusetts Supreme Court (1777); first associate justice appointed to the Supreme Court; served from 1789 to his death in 1810.

1780 The Pennsylvania legislature adopted an act calling for the gradual emancipation of slaves.

1781 The Artices of Confederation, before the states since Nov 1777, were formally ratified, with the approval of Maryland; the name United States began to be used the next day.

1784 A bill was presented by Thomas Jefferson to the Continental Congress on governing the western territory; approved Apr 23 but was superseded by the Northwest Ordinance of 1787.

1790 President Washington signed an act providing for the first census.

1794 William J. Worth, Mexican War general, was born in Hudson, N.Y.; involved in most major battles; commander, Department of Texas; commandant of cadets, West Point (1830-38) (died 1849).

1803 Ohio was admitted to the Union as the 17th state.

1805 Associate Supreme Court Justice Samuel Chase, impeached for trial conduct, was acquitted after a two-month trial; impeachment sought because of high-handed conduct in a 1799 trial, the first impeachment proceedings against a Supreme Court justice.

1807 Wilford Woodruff, religious leader, was born in Avon, Conn.; with first Mormons arriving at Salt Lake (1847); president, Mormon Church (1889-1898) (died 1898).

1809 Illinois territory was formed by dividing the Indiana Territory.

1837 The Senate by a 23-9 vote recognized the independence of Texas; approved by President Jackson Mar 3.

1837 President Jackson signed the Judiciary Act, which increased the Supreme Court from seven to nine.

1837 William Dean Howells, author and editor, was born in Martins Ferry, Ohio; an editor, *Atlantic Monthly* (1866-81), *Harper's* (1866-1920), where he wrote the "Easy Chair" column (1900-20); author (*The Rise of Silas Lapham*) (died 1920).

1841 Blanche Kelso Bruce, legislator, was born in Farmville, Va.; the first black to serve full Senate term, representing Mississippi (1875-81) (died 1898).

1845 President Tyler signed a joint resolution of Congress annexing Texas.

1848 Augustus Saint-Gaudens, sculptor, was born in Dublin; among best known works are Adoration of the Cross, Admiral Farragut, General Sherman (all New York City), Abraham Lincoln (Chicago), The Puritan (Springfield, Mass.) (died 1907).

1867 Nebraska was admitted to the Union as the 37th state.

1872 Yellowstone National Park was established in Wyoming, Montana, and Idaho.

1875 Congress passed the Civil Rights Act providing for equal rights for blacks in public places and in jury duty; law invalidated by Supreme Court in 1883.

1880 Supreme Court in *Strander v. West Virginia* held the West Virginia law excluding blacks from jury duty unconstitutional.

1882 Gaston Lachaise, sculptor, was born in Paris; did decorative sculptures for the Rockefeller Center, Chicago World's Fair (died 1935).

1899 Edmund Duffy, editorial cartoonist, was born in Jersey City; with *Baltimore Sun* (1924-62) (died 1962).

1904 Glenn Miller, orchestra leader, was born in Clarinda, Iowa; a leading figure of Big Band era; died when plane he was riding disappeared enroute to France in 1944.

1910 Rockefeller Foundation was established by John D. Rockefeller for the benefit of humanity.

1914 Ralph W. Ellison, author, was born in Oklahoma City; best known for the novel, *Invisible Man.*

1914 Prohibition went into effect in Tennessee under a new law.

1914 Statewide prohbition law was enacted in Idaho; effective Jan 1, 1916.

1917 Robert T.S. Lowell, poet and translator, was born in Boston; poet ("Lord Weary's Castle," "The Dolphin," "Life Studies"), translated Aeschylus, Baudelaire (died 1977).

1920 Railroads and express companies were turned back to private operators after being operated by the government during World War I.

1921 Terence J. Cooke, Catholic prelate, was born in New York City; Archbishop of New York (1968-83), elevated to cardinal 1969 (died 1983).

1921 Dinah Shore, singer, screen and television actress, was born in Winchester, Tenn.

1926 Pete (Alvin R.) Rozelle, professional football commissioner (1960-89), was born in South Gate, Cal.; general manager, Los Angeles Rams (1957-60).

1927 Harry Belafonte, singer and screen actor, was born in New York City; noted for calypso songs; films include *Carmen Jones* and *Island in the Sun*.

1932 The son of Charles and Anne Lindbergh was kidnapped from their New Jersey home; found dead May 12.

1943 Point rationing system set up for processed foods.

1954 Five congressmen were wounded in the House by four Puerto Rican independence supporters firing from the spectators' gallery.

1961 The Peace Corps was created by executive order; put on permanent statutory basis Sept 22; R. Sargent Shriver was named director Mar 4; functions of agency were transferred to ACTION July 1, 1971.

1962 A plane crashed into Jamaica Bay after taking off from Idlewild Airport, N.Y., killing 95 persons.

1967 Rep. Adam Clayton Powell of New York was denied his seat in the House because of charges of misusing government funds; re-elected in 1968, seated but fined $25,000.

1971 The Capitol was bombed by radical Weather Underground; device was planted in a Senate wing restroom; did $300,000 damage, no one was injured.

MARCH 2

1643 Virginia Assembly passed an act denying the governor and council the right to impose taxes without its consent; voted to banish non-conformist clergymen.

1685 Colonial post office was established in New York, with Edward Randolph named postmaster by James II.

1769 DeWitt Clinton, legislator, was born in Little Britian, N.Y., son of James Clinton (8/9/1733); served New York City as mayor(1803-15), except for two one-year terms) and New York State as governor (1817-23, 1824-28), sponsored construction of the Erie Canal (died 1828).

1779 Joel R. Poinsett, legislator and diplomat, was born in Charleston; represented South Carolina in the House (1821-25), first minister to Mexico (1825-29), Secretary of War (1837-41); an amateur botanist, he introduced plants from Mexico, poinsettia was named for him (died 1851).

1780 Massachusetts constitution, adopted by convention, was ratified; a clause prohibited slavery.

1793 Sam Houston, frontiersman and Texas leader, was born in Rockbridge County, Va.; represented Tennessee in the House (1823-27) and served it as governor (1827-29); became a founder of Texas, led its troops against Mexico (1836); president of the Texas Republic (1836-38, 1841-44), one of its first senators (1846-59) and its governor (1859-61); deposed when he refused to take oath of allegiance to the Confederacy (died 1863).

1807 President Jefferson signed an act prohibiting importation of slaves after Jan 1, 1808; passed the House 63-49, agreed to by the Senate.

1819 Arkansas Territory was created from part of the Missouri Territory.

1824 The Supreme Court in *Gibbons v. Ogden* gave Congress the power to regulate commerce with foreign nations and among the states.

1824 Henry B. Carrington, Union general, was born in Wallingford, Conn.; fought in Indian wars on the Plains, negotiated treaties and helped create reservations (died 1912).

1829 William B. Allison, legislator, was born in Perry Township, Ohio; represented Iowa in the House (1862-70) and Senate (1872-1908), where he chaired the Appropriations Committee (1881-1908); a most influential legislator (died 1908).

1829 Carl Schurz, soldier and public official, was born in Liblar, Germany; Union general (Bull Run and Gettysburg); Interior Secretary (1877-81), minister to Spain (1861-62); represented Missouri in the Senate (1869-75); editor, *New York Evening Post* (1881-84) (died 1906).

1829 First school for the blind, the New England Asylum for the Blind, was incorporated in Boston; became the Perkins Institute in 1839.

1833 President Jackson signed a compromise tariff act designed to placate the South and an act authorizing collecting tariffs by force if necessary.

1836 Henry B. Brown, associate justice, Supreme Court (1890-1906), was born in Lee, Mass. (died 1913).

1836 A convention in Washington, Tex. adopted a declaration of independence, drew up a constitution; two days later formed a provisional government, named Sam Houston commander of its army.

1836 John W. Foster, diplomat, was born in Pike County, Ind.; minister to Mexico (1873-80), to Russia (1880-81), to Spain (1883-85); Secretary of State (1892-93); American agent in establishing Alaska-Canada boundary (died 1917).

1847 American forces under Col. Alexander Doniphan occupied Chihuahua, Mexico.

1853 The Territory of Washington was created from the northern part of Oregon.

1861 The territories of Nevada and Dakota were created.

1861 The resolutions of a peace convention promoted by former President Tyler were rejected by the Senate 28-7; House did not vote on them.

1865 A Union cavalry force defeated Confederate troops near Waynesboro, Va.

1867 Congress passed the first Reconstruction Act, divided the South into five military districts subject to martial law; adopted over veto of President Andrew Johnson.

1867 A Louisiana convention completed work on a constitution; ratified Aug 17-18.

1867 Congress created the Department of Education, headed by a commissioner; made an office in the Interior Department July 1, 1889.

1867 Congress passed an act strengthening the international exchange of official publications; Library of Congress was the beneficiary; voted $100,000 for purchase of Peter Force Collection of Americana.

1887 The Hatch Act was passed, providing federal funds for establishing agricultural experiment stations.

1890 Paul de Kruif, bacteriologist, was born in New Zealand, Mich.; author (*Microbe Hunters, Hunger Fighters*) (died 1971).

1899 Mt. Rainier (Wash.) National Park was established.

1900 Kurt Weill, composer, was born in Desau, Germany; wrote several hit musicals (*Threepenny Opera, Lady in the Dark, One Touch of Venue, Street Scene*) (died 1950).

1902 Edward U. Condon, physicist, was born in Almagord, N.M.; director, Bureau of Standards (1945-51); made important contributions to quantum mechanics (died 1974).

1904 Theodore S. Geisel, better known as Dr. Seuss, author, was born in Springfield, Mass.; writer and illustrator of children's books.

1905 Marc Blitzstein, composer, was born in Philadelphia; translated, adapted Brecht-Weill's *Threepenny Opera* (died 1964).

1907 H(aason) I. Romnes, industrialist, was born in Stoughton, Wis.; president, Western Electric Co. (1953-63); chief executive officer, president AT&T (1967-72) (died 1973).

1909 Mel(vin T.) Ott, baseball player, was born in Gretna, La.; with New York Giants (1926-44); first National Leaguer to hit 500 home runs; named to Baseball Hall of Fame (died 1958).

1917 President Wilson signed an act making Puerto Rico an American territory and its inhabitants American citizens.

1937 U.S. Steel Corp., to avoid a strike, recognized the Steelworkers Organizing Committee, predecessor of the United Steelworkers.

1949 An Air Force B-50 Superfortress landed at Ft. Worth, Tex, completing the first non-stop around-the-world flight in 94 hours, one minute.

1955 President Eisenhower signed an act raising the salary of the vice president from $30,000 to $35,000, congressmen from $15,000 to $22,500, Supreme Court chief justice from $25,500 to $35,000, associate justices from $25,000 to $35,000.

1968 The National Advisory Commission on Civil Disorders, chaired by Illinois Gov. Otto Kerner, reported that nationwide riots were due to unemployment, underemployment, and white racism.

1972 *Pioneer 10* was launched, the first spacecraft to explore the asteroid belt, and fly by Jupiter.

1973 Ambassador Cleo A. Noel Jr. and Chargé d'Affaires George C. Moore were killed by Palestinian guerillas in Khartoum, Sudan.

1974 The cost of first class postage was increased to 10 cents.

MARCH 3

1513 (Juan) Ponce de Leon, Spanish conquerer of Puerto Rico, sailed to Florida, landing somewhere between St. Augustine and the St. John's River; after short stay (Apr 2-8), explored most of Florida coastline.

1540 Hernando de Soto, continuing exploration across South, entered what is now Georgia and reached present Talladega County, Ala., July 26.

1636 Massachusetts General Court granted powers of government to freemen of the town; required its consent for establishing new churches.

1768 Francis Fauquier, colonial governor, died at about 64; Virginia lieutenant governor (1758-60), acting governor (1760-68).

1776 Continental Congress voted to send Silas Deane to Europe to purchase war material.

1779 An American force was defeated by British at the Battle of Brier Creek, near Savannah, strengthening British position in South.

1791 Congress established the District of Columbia.

1803 Senate began impeachment hearings of U.S. District Judge John Pickering of New Hampshire ; removed Mar 12, 1804 for drunkenness and profanity on the bench; this was the first impeachment of a federal judge.

1805 Territory of Louisiana-Missouri was created; in 1812, Louisiana became a state, Missouri a separate territory.

1817 President Madison signed an act creating the Alabama Territory.

1819 Congress enacted a law providing a $50 bounty to informers for every illegally imported black person seized in the United States or at sea.

1820 The Missouri Compromise went into effect when Maine was admitted as a free state and Missouri as a slave state; slavery excluded from Louisiana Purchase territory north of the line 36°30'.

1823 Congress passed first National Harbor Improvement Act.

1824 George T. Anderson, Confederate general, was born in Georgia; saw action at Gettysburg, Chattanooga, and Knoxville (died 1901).

1826 Joseph Wharton, industrialist, was born in Philadelphia; developed process for making pure malleable nickel; a founder, Bethlehem Steel Co., Swarthmore College; benefactor of Wharton School of Finance (died 1909).

1831 George M. Pullman, inventor and manufacturer, was born in Brocton, N.Y.; invented (1865) railway sleeping car with folding upper berth; founder/head Pullman Palace Car Co. (1867-97); also developed dining, chair cars (died 1897)

1839 President Van Buren sent Gen. Winfield Scott to take charge of the bloodless Aroostok "War," a dispute between Maine and New Brunswick; Scott arranged truce, finally settled by Webster-Ashburton Treaty (1842).

1842 A Massachusetts law was passed requiring a minimum education for every child, a maximum ten-hour work day for those under 12.

1843 Congress appropriated $30 million to aid Samuel F.B. Morse in building the first telegraph line between Washington and Baltimore.

1845 Florida was admitted to the Union as the 27th state.

1845 Congress for the first time overrode a presidential veto—President Tyler's Feb 20 veto of the construction of revenue cutters, steamers for defense.

1845 Congress reduced postal rates to five cents for a half ounce for up to 300 miles.

1847 Alexander Graham Bell, telephone inventor, was born in Edinburgh; also invented the photophone, which transmitted the first wireless telephone message (1880, a recorder for Edison's phonograph; helped solve problem of balance stability in a flying machine; founded Volta Bureau to increase knowledge about the deaf (died 1922).

1848 Territory of Minnesota was created.

1849 Department of the Interior was created; originally called the Home Department, including the Census, General Land, and Indian Affairs offices; Thomas Ewing of Ohio was the first secretary.

1851 Congress reduced postal rates to three cents for a half ounce for up to 3000 miles.

1853 President Fillmore signed an act increasing the salary of vice president from $5000 to $8000.

1859 The first newspaper in Arizona, the *Weekly Arizonan*, was published in Tubac by William Wrightson.

1860 Monty (John M.) Ward, baseball player, manager (Giants, Dodgers), was born in Bellefonte, Pa.; named to Baseball Hall of Fame (died 1925).

1862 Union troops occupied Columbus, Ky.

1863 The National Academy of Sciences, created by Congress, was incorporated.

1863 Territory of Idaho was created.

1863 The first conscription act was passed, making all men 20 to 45 liable for military service; service could be avoided by payment of $300 or procuring a substitute to enlist for three years.

1863 Congress increased the number of Supreme Court justices from nine to ten.

1865 Freedmen's Bureau was created as part of the War Department to care for war refugees, freedmen, and abandoned lands; Maj. Gen. Oliver O. Howard was named commissioner; went out of existence June 30, 1872.

1865 Congress passed an act requiring the deposit in the Library of Congress of all books and other materials on which a copyright was claimed.

1867 James G. Rogers, architect, was born in Bryants Station, Ky.; designed buildings at Yale U., Columbia-Presbyterian Medical Center, New York City (died 1947).

1868 House completed adoption of the 11 articles of impeachment against President Andrew Johnson.

1871 Congress created the Civil Service Commission; President Grant named George William Curtis as its head; Curtis resigned (1875) when his recommendations were ignored and the commission died.

1872 Willie (William H.) Keeler, baseball player, was born in Brooklyn; star outfielder with Baltimore, Brooklyn, and New York Giants (1894-1910); lifetime batting average of .341; named to Baseball Hall of Fame (died 1923).

1873 President Grant signed an act increasing the salaries of president to $50,000, vice president to $10,000, and congressmen from $5000 to $7500.

1873 William Green, labor leader, was born in Coshocton, Ohio; president, American Federation of Labor (1924-52) (died 1952).

1877 Congress passed the Desert Land Act, under which the government would sell up to 640 acres at $1.25 per acre to anyone who would reclaim the land in three years.

1879 Elmer V. McCollum, biochemist, was born near Ft. Scott, Kan.; played fundamental role in developing knowledge of nutrition as a government consultant, educator (Wisconsin, Johns Hopkins); co-discoverer of Vitamin A, discovered Vitamin D (died 1967).

1879 U.S. Geological Survey was established.

1883 Cost of first class mail was reduced to two cents for a half ounce.

1885 Maximum weight for first class mail was raised to one ounce for two cents.

1891 The Immigration and Naturalization Service was created.

1891 The Forest Reserve Act was approved; authorized the president to set apart forest reserve lands anywhere on public lands.

1893 Free postal delivery was extended to rural communities.

1895 Matthew B. Ridgway, World War II general, was born in Ft. Monroe, Va.; commander, 82nd Airborne, UN troops in Korea (1951-52); supreme commander, Europe (1952-53); Army chief of staff (1953-55).

1899 Alfred M. Gruenther, World War II general, was born in Platte Center, Nebr.; led troops in Italy; supreme Allied commander in Europe (1953-56) (died 1983).

1901 The National Bureau of Standards was established.

1901 Roger F. Turner, American men's champion figure skater (1928-35), was born in Milton, Mass.

1911 Jean Harlow, screen actress, was born in Kansas City, Mo.; starred in many films (*Hell's Angels, Dinner at Eight, Platinum Blonde*) (died 1937).

1915 National Committee for Aeronautics was created; terminated July 29, 1958 when its functions were transferred to National Aeronautics & Space Administration (NASA).

1915 Colorado adopted a prohibition law.

1918 Arthur Kornberg, biochemist, was born in New York City; shared 1959 Nobel Physiology/Medicine Prize for discoveries related to compounds within chromosomes, which play vital role in heredity.

1923 Henry B. Luce, with Britton Hadden, published the first issue of *Time* magazine.

1931 "The Star Spangled Banner" was officially adopted as the national anthem by Congress.

1933 Frances Perkins, the first woman cabinet member, assumed her duties as Secretary of Labor; served until June 30, 1945.

1943 Two-day Battle of Bismark Sea resulted in the destruction of 10 Japanese warships, 60 Japanese planes.

1952 Ronald W. Reagan married Nancy Davis in Los Angeles.

1962 Herschel Walker, football player (Generals, Dallas Cowboys), was born in Wrightsville, Ga.

1963 Two-day protest march was begun by thousands of blacks in Birmingham, Ala.

1987 President Reagan nominated FBI Director William H. Webster to be director of the Central Intelligence Agency to succeed the late William Casey; kept on by President-elect Bush (1989).

1987 The Supreme Court ruled 7-2 that people with contagious diseases are handicapped and are covered under civil rights laws; this was seen as protection for AIDS patients from job discrimination.

MARCH 4

1629 A royal charter was granted to the Massachusetts Bay Co.; territory previously had been granted to the Council of New England; company was able to transform itself into a self-governing commonwealth.

1681 William Penn, in return for a debt of 16,000 pounds owed his father, secured a royal charter to land which became Pennsylvania; began to organize a colony by selling shares to those who wanted to join the enterprise.

1747 Kazmierz (Casimir) Pulaski, nobleman and officer who fought with the Americans, was born in Winiary, Poland; commanded a cavalry unit, mortally wounded at siege of Savannah Oct 9, 1779.

1754 Benjamin Waterhouse, physician, was born in Newport, R.I.; first professor of theory, practice of "physic," Harvard Medical School (1783-1812); pioneer in vaccination (died 1846).

1776 Gen. John Thomas led 2000 troops of the Continental Army to occupy, fortify Dorchester Heights, which overlook Boston; British evacuated Boston (Mar 7-17), sailed to Halifax.

1777 Fourth Continental Congress began meetings in Philadelphia.

1789 The first Congress met in New York City; the House did not have a quorum until Apr 1, the Senate Apr 6.

1791 Vermont entered the Union as the 14th state.

1793 President Washington delivered his second inaugural address—the shortest on record—135 words.

1801 Thomas Jefferson became the first president inaugurated in Washington, D.C., the new capital; called for a government of limited powers, economy in the national administration, support of state governments in all their rights, preservation of civil liberties, and "peace, commerce, and honest friendship with all nations, entangling alliances with none."

1806 Ephraim W. Bull, horticulturist, was born in Boston; developed the Concord grape (died 1895).

1826 John Buford, Union general, was born in Woodford, Ky.; a brilliant cavalry commander, fought at Antietam, Gettysburg (died 1863).

1837 Chicago was incorporated as a city, with William B. Ogden as first mayor.

1849 State of Deseret (Utah) was founded at a convention in Salt Lake City, which became its capital.

1851 University of Minnesota was founded.

1853 Frederick B. Power, chemist, was born in Hudson, N.Y.; organized, dean, U. of Wisconsin Pharmacy School (1883-92); director, Wellcome Labs, London (1896-1914); Department of Agriculture (1916-27); known for research in constituents of plant products (died 1927).

1855 Luther E. Holt, physician, was born in Webster, N.Y.; wrote *The Care and Feeding of Children* (1894), which went into 75 printings; *The Diseases of Infancy and Childhood*, a standard text (died 1924).

1861 A flag of seven stars and three stripes was raised over the Confederate capital in Montgomery, Ala.

1862 President Lincoln appointed Andrew Johnson, Tennessee senator and former governor, as military governor of the state; served until he became vice president in 1865.

1864 David W. Taylor, naval architect, was born in Louisa County, Va.; developed and operated testing basin for ship models; devised "Standard Series," matching engine power to hull design (died 1940).

1867 Charles P. Summerall, World War I general, was born in Blount's Ferry, Fla.; commanded 1st Division (1918), later corps commander; Army chief of staff (1926-30); president, The Citadel (1931-53) (died 1955).

1869 Brand Whitlock, diplomat, was born in Urbana, Ohio; served as minister to Belgium (1913-22), a leader in postwar Belgian relief work (died 1934).

1873 Congress amended an act of the previous day to make their pay increase ($5000 to $7500) retroactive for two years; public outcry resulted in repealing amendment Jan 20, 1874.

1880 Channing Pollock, novelist and playwright, was born in Washington, D.C.; play co-author (*Clothes, The Red Widow, 1915 Ziegfeld Follies*); author (*Behold the Men, Footlights*) (died 1946).

1884 Iowa adopted statewide prohibition; a previous law was in effect 1855-58.

1886 U. of Wyoming in Laramie was chartered; opened in 1887.

1888 Knute Rockne, football coach, was born in Voss, Norway; coached at Notre Dame (1918-31), winning 105, losing 12, and 5 ties; killed in plane crash (died 1931).

1889 Pearl White, silent screen actress, was born in Green Ridge, Mo.; starred in early film series (*Perils of Pauline*) (died 1938).

1891 Dazzy (Clarence A.) Vance, baseball player (Brooklyn), was born in Orient, Iowa; named to Baseball Hall of Fame (died 1961).

1897 Robert A. McClure, Army officer, was born in Mattoon, Ill.; helped plan North Africa and Normandy invasions; first chief of psychological warfare (died 1957).

1901 Charles H. Goren, bridge expert, was born in Philadelphia; his point count bidding system became very popular; won two world, 26 American championships.

1902 American Automobile Association was formed in Chicago by representative of nine auto clubs; Winthrop E. Scarritt of New York was the first president.

1904 George Gamow, physicist, was born in Odessa, Russia; known for research in nuclear physics, its application to stellar evolution; a major formulator of "big bang" theory of the origin of the universe; author (*Mr. Tompkins Explores the Atom*) (died 1968).

1908 School fire in Collinwood, Ohio, near Cleveland, killed 161 children, teachers.

1909 President Theodore Roosevelt signed an act increasing the salary of president from $50,000 to $75,000, with his successor (Taft) as the first recipient; also raised vice presidential salary to $12,000.

1912 W. Willard Wirtz, Labor Secretary (1962-69), was born in DeKalb, Ill.

1913 Department of Commerce and Labor was divided into two separate departments, with William B. Wilson as Labor Secretary, William C. Redfield as Commerce Secretary.

1913 John Garfield, screen actor, was born in New York City; starred in several films (*Humoresque, Body and Soul, Gentleman's Agreement*) (died 1952).

1918 Margaret Osborne duPont, one of the great women tennis players, was born in Joseph, Ore.; won the French singles (1946, 1949), U.S. (1948-50), Wimbledon (1947); with Louise Brough won U.S. doubles 12 times, Wimbledon five times, French three times; named to Tennis Hall of Fame.

1918 Bernard M. Baruch was appointed chairman of the reorganized War Industries Board by President Wilson.

1921 Hot Springs (Ark.) National Park was established.

1921 President Harding appointed Herbert Hoover as Secretary of Commerce.

1922 Bert (Egbert A.) Williams, popular comedian and song writer, died at 48; starred in vaudeville and musical comedy; leading comedian in Ziegfeld Follies.

1923 Interior Secretary Albert B. Fall resigned in the wake of developments in the Teapot Dome scandal.

1925 Executive and legislative salaries were increased, with the vice president, cabinet members, and Speaker going from $12,000 to $15,000; congressmen were raised from $7,500 to $10,000.

1930 The Coolidge Dam in Arizona was dedicated.

1933 In his first inaugural address, President Franklin Roosevelt initiated the term "good neighbor policy."

1940 King's Canyon (Cal.) National Park was established.

1944 The first American air raid was made on Berlin.

1971 President Nixon declared South Vietnamese drive into Laos was successful, promised continued withdrawal of American troops.

1987 President Reagan said he accepted "full responsibility" for the Iran-Contra affair, even though he was "angry" and "disappointed" with the actions of subordinates who carried out the policy.

1987 U.S. District Judge W. Brevard Hand banned 31 textbooks from Alabama public schools, saying they illegally promoted "the religion of secular humanism;" U.S. Circuit Court of Appeals on Aug 27 reversed the decision.

MARCH 5

1707 Abraham Pierson, first rector of Yale, died at about 62; Congregational clergyman, active in founding Yale, named rector in 1701.

1770 An early afternoon fight between a soldier and a citizen resulted in the Boston Massacre at about 9 p.m.; three citizens were killed, eight wounded by Customs House guards.

1788 Guy Johnson, loyalist leader, died at 48; superintendent of Indian affairs in North America (1774-82); tried to organize Indians against the Americans.

1794 Robert G. Grier, jurist, was born in Cumberland County, Pa.; associate justice, Supreme Court (1846-70) (died 1870).

1817 John Quincy Adams was named Secretary of State by President Monroe.

1819 Anna C. Mowatt, playwright and actress, was born in Bordeaux, France of American parents; best known for play, *Fashion*; also wrote books on etiquette, cookbooks, novels (died 1870).

1824 James M. Ives of Currier & Ives prints was born in New York City (died 1870).

1835 William Steinway, piano manufacturer and public official, was born in Seesen, Germany, son of Henry E. Steinway (2/15/1797); headed Steinway & Sons (1876-96); first chairman, Rapid Transit Commission, which planned New York City's first subway; subway tunnel under East River named for him (died 1896).

1853 Howard Pyle, illustrator and author, was born in Wilmington, Del.; best known for children's books, also for illustrations of characters and events of early American history (died 1911).

1860 Sam(uel L.) Thompson, baseball player (Tigers, Phillies), was born in Danville, Ind.; named to Baseball Hall of Fame (died 1922).

1870 Frank Norris, author, was born in Chicago; best remembered for *The Pit* and *The Octopus* (died 1902).

1875 Former President Andrew Johnson took his seat in the Senate representing Tennessee.

1882 Egbert Van Alstyne, composer, was born in Chicago; wrote several well-known popular songs ("In the Shade of the Old Apple Tree," "Goodnight Irene," "Drifting and Dreaming") (died 1951).

1891 Daniel R. Fitzpatrick, editorial cartoonist, was born in Superior, Wis.; with the *St. Louis Post-Dispatch* (from 1913) (died 1969).

1918 James Tobin, economist, was born in Champaign, Ill.; awarded 1981 Nobel Economics Prize for analysis of investments and financial markets.

1946 British Prime Minister Winston Churchill, accompanied by President Truman, made his "iron curtain" speech at Westminster College, Fulton, Mo., calling for Anglo-American association to deter Russian ambitions.

1979 *Voyager I* spacecraft relayed a wealth of information after it came within 172,500 miles of Jupiter.

1984 Supreme Court ruled 5-4 that public financing of a Nativity scene did not of itself violate the doctrine of separation of church and state.

MARCH 6

1724 Henry Laurens, colonial leader, was born in Charleston; president of first Continental Congress (1777-78); captured by the British (1780) while enroute to negotiate a treaty with the Dutch; held in Tower of London until exchanged (1782) for Lord Cornwallis (died 1792).

1797 Gerrit Smith, abolitionist and philanthropist, was born in Utica, N.Y.; founder of the Liberty Party (died 1874).

1809 John Quincy Adams was named minister to Russia by President Madison, serving until 1814.

1812 Aaron L. Dennison, watchmaker, was born in Freeport, Me.; devised machine-made interchangeable parts, thus increasing accuracy, lowering costs; known as the father of American watchmaking (died 1895).

1819 The Supreme Court ruled in *McCulloch v. Maryland* that Congress had the power to charter the Bank of the United States, could set up branches in the states without their consent; Chief Justice Marshall held that the national government, while limited in its powers, is supreme within its sphere of action.

1820 Horatio G. Wright, Union general, was born in Clinton, Conn.; served at Gettysburg, the Wilderness Campaign, Shenandoah Valley; chief of engineers (1879-84) (died 1899).

1829 Martin Van Buren was named Secretary of State by President Jackson, serving until 1831; resigned as New York governor after three months to take post.

1831 Philip H. Sheridan, Union general, was born in Albany; leading Union cavalry commander; headed Army of the Shenandoah Valley, cut off Lee's line of retreat at Appomattox; commander-in-chief, Army (1884) (died 1888).

1833 Abraham Lincoln received a saloon license to dispense liquor in Springfield, Ill. (Berry and Lincoln); never used it.

1836 The Alamo in San Antonio fell after 12 days siege; 187 Americans led by William B. Travis and including Davy Crockett and James Bowie, and 1544 Mexicans were killed; original 145 Americans were reinforced by men who crept through Mexican lines to join the beseiged.

1838 John Stevens, inventor, died at 89; involved in developing steamships; built the *Phoenix* (1808), which made trip (1809) from New York to Philadelphia, becoming the first working steamship.

1844 The Mexican government severed diplomatic relations with the United States following passage of a joint resolution to annex Texas.

1848 The people of Illinois ratified their state constitution, effective Apr 1.

1857 The Supreme Court announced the controversial Dred Scott decision, which sharpened differences over slavery; majority ruled that blacks were not citizens and therefore Scott could not sue in federal court, that residence on free soil did not make him a free man on returning to slave territory, and that the Missouri Compromise of 1820 was unconstitutional.

1861 The provisional Confederate Congress established the Confederate Army (one corps of engineers, one of artillery, five regiments of infantry, one of cavalry, and four staff departments); called for 100,000 men to serve 12 months.

1862 President Lincoln sent a special message to Congress recommending compensated emancipation of slaves in states that adopted gradual abolition; Congress (Apr 10) adopted a joint resolution for federal assistance.

1862 Three-day battle of Pea Ridge (or Elkhorn Tavern), Ark. broke the Confederate hold in Arkansas and Missouri; Confederate Gens. Ben McCulloch and McIntosh were killed.

1871 Benjamin R. Harney, musician, was born in Middleboro, Ky.; pianist and vaudeville headliner, popularized ragtime music (died 1938).

1885 Ring(gold) Lardner, sports writer and humorist, was born in Niles, Mich.; best remembered works are *You Know Me, Al* and *Gullible's Travels* (died 1933).

1886 Nine thousand Knights of Labor members struck the Gould system of railroads; strike ended May 4 with no gain for the strikers.

1897 John D. McArthur, insurance executive, was born in Pittston, Pa.; president, Bankers Life Insurance Co. (1936-78) (died 1978).

1899 Richard L. Simon, publisher, was born in New York City; co-founder (1924), partner, Simon & Schuster; introduced Pocket Books (1939), first inexpensive reprints (died 1960).

1900 Lefty (Robert M.) Grove, baseball pitcher considered one of the greatest left-handers, was born in Lonaconing, Md.; played with Athletics (1925-33) and Red Sox (1934-41); named to Baseball Hall of Fame (died 1975).

1902 A permanent Census Bureau was created, effective July 1.

1908 Lou Costello of the Abbott and Costello comedy team was born in Paterson, N.J.; starred in film and radio (died 1959).

1924 Sarah Caldwell, conductor and opera producer, was born in Marysville, Mo.; founder of the Boston Opera Company.

1926 Alan L. Greenspan, economist, was born in New York City; chairman, Council of Economic Advisors (1974-77); chairman, Federal Reserve Board (1987-).

1933 Chicago Mayor Anton J. Cermak died in Miami at 60, the victim of an assassination attempt on President-elect Franklin D. Roosevelt Feb 15.

1933 Four-day bank holiday was begun by proclamation of President Franklin Roosevelt.

1937 Ivan Boesky, investment banker, was born in Detroit; his illegal insider trading in stocks led to his payment of a $100 million fine and a ban on further Wall St. dealings.

1941 Willie (Wilver D.) Stargell, baseball player (Pirates 1962-82), was born in Earlsboro, Okla.; named to Baseball Hall of Fame.

1945 Inter-American Conference on the Problems of the War adopted the Act of Chapultepec, which in essence agreed that an attack on one was an attack on all.

1984 The Senate by a vote of 81-13 confirmed William A. Wilson as ambassador to the Vatican, thus resuming diplomatic relations after a more than 100-year gap.

1986 The commission investigating the bombing of a violent radical group in May 1985 in Philadelphia in which 11 people died and 61 homes were destroyed found Philadelphia Mayor W. Wilson Goode "grossly negligent."

1989 Thomas F. Foley, legislator (House 1965-), was named House Speaker; House majority leader 1987-89.

MARCH 7

1590 Roger Ludlow, one of Connecticut's early leaders, was baptized in Dinton, England; headed Massachusetts Bay Colony (1635), believed to have been the author of the *Fundamental Orders of Connecticut*; codified Connecticut laws and presided over the first court held there; returned to England (died 1664).

1638 Anne Hutchinson was banished from Massachusetts for her religious opinions; she, William Coddington, and 17 others founded Pocassat, R.I. (later renamed Portsmouth).

1644 Samuel Gorton (1592-1677), founder of a religious sect (the Gortonians), was banished from Massachusetts, settled in Rhode Island, founding Warwick; his sect rejected outward religious ceremonies, held that Christ was both human and divine, that heaven and hell exist only in the mind.

1707 Stephen Hopkins, colonial official, was born in Providence; governor of Rhode Island (1755, 1756, 1758-61, 1763, 1764, 1767); a member of Continental Congress (1774-80), a signer of the Declaration of Independence; wrote *The Rights of the Colonies Examined* (1765) (died 1785).

1766 British Parliament enacted the Declaratory Act a day after repeal of the Stamp Act; declared that any colonial legislature which denied Parliament the right to pass laws affecting the colonies "are hereby declared to be utterly null and void to all intents and purposes whatsoever."

1814 John H. Raymond, educator, was born in New York City; an organizer, professor U. of Rochester (1850-55); first president, Brooklyn Polytechnic Institute (1855-64); president, Vassar College (1865-78) (died 1878).

1832 Orlando M. Poe, Army engineer, was born in Navarre, Ohio; served as chief engineer on Sherman's march to the sea; later had charge of many waterway improvements, building locks at Sault Sainte Marie canals (died 1895).

1837 Henry Draper, physiologist and astronomer, was born in Prince Edward County, Va.; devised methods of photographing the skies, did unique work in the stellar spectroscopy; physiology professor, dean of medical faculty, New York U. (1866-82) (died 1882).

1844 Anthony Comstock, reformer, was born in New Canaan, Conn.; conducted spectacular raids on publishers, vendors; co-founder, New York Society for the Suppression of Vice (died 1915).

1845 Daniel D. Palmer, chiropractor, was born in Toronto; began "magnetic healing," which became chiropractic; opened school in Davenport, Iowa (1898) (died 1913).

1849 Luther Burbank, plant breeder, was born in Lancaster, Mass.; experimented, developed more and better varieties of cultivated plants—plums, berries, tomatoes, corn, squash, lillies, the Burbank rose, poppies, the Shasta daisy (died 1926).

1850 Champ (James Beauchamp) Clark, legislator, was born in Lawrenceburg, Ky.; represented Missouri in the House (1893-95, 1897-1921), serving as minority leader (1907-11) and Speaker (1911-19); led successful fight against arbitrary control of House by Speaker Joseph Cannon (died 1921).

1866 Mark A. Carleton, plant pathologist, was born in Jerusalem, Ohio; introduced Kubanka wheat from Asia, founded durum wheat industry (died 1925).

1876 Alexander Graham Bell was granted a patent on his telephone.

1930 Stanley L. Miller, chemist, was born in Oakland, Cal.; noted for a key experiment related to the chemical origins of life.

1938 David Baltimore, microbiologist, was born in New York City; demonstrated existence of "reverse transcriptase," a vital enzyme that reverses normal DNA-to-RNA process; shared 1975 Nobel Physiology/Medicine Prize for that work.

1945 American forces crossed the Rhine, the first foreign military crossing since Napoleon; the 9th Armored Division seized the Rhine bridge at Remagen.

1965 Marchers from Selma to Montgomery, Ala. were met at the Alabama River Bridge outside Selma by state police and a sheriff's posse; marchers were turned back by force, 50 injured.

1984 Jeremy Levin, television news reporter, and William Buckley, CIA station chief, were kidnapped in Beirut; Levin escaped Feb 14, 1985; Buckley was killed.

MARCH 8

1752 William Bingham, banker and legislator, was born in Philadelphia; founder, director, Bank of North America (1781), the first bank in the country; served in Continental Congress (1786-89), represented Pennsylvania in the Senate (1795-1801); founded Binghamton, N.Y. (died 1804).

1765 Stamp Act was passed by the House of Lords (Commons passed it Feb 27) to go into effect Nov 1; British hoped to raise 60,000 additional pounds in the colonies, with stamps to be put on commercial and legal documents, pamphlets, newspapers, almanacs, playing cards, dice; met by unanimous opposition in the colonies as feeling grew against taxation without representation.

1783 Hannah Hoes Van Buren, wife of President Van Buren, was born in Kinderhook, N.Y. (died 1819).

1796 Supreme Court in *Hylton v. United States* upheld for the first time the constitutionality of a congressional act.

1799 Simon Cameron, public official and diplomat, was born in Lancaster County, Pa.; Secretary of War (1861-62), minister to Russia (1862); represented Pennsylvania in the Senate (1845-49, 1857-61, 1867-77) (died 1889).

1803 James Monroe, named special minister to France to clear up the Mississippi Valley situation, sailed for France.

1804 Alvan Clark, astronomer, was born in Ashfield, Mass.; produced telescope lenses for major observatories with son, Alvan G. (died 1887).

1813 Russia offered to mediate war between the United States and Great Britain; offer turned down by British.

1817 New York Stock Exchange was formally chartered; had been operating informally since 1791 when brokers met in the shade of a buttonwood tree on Wall St.

1821 Morgan L. Smith, Union general, was born in Mexico, N.Y., brother of Giles A. Smith (9/29/1829); served at Ft. Donelson, Shiloh, Vicksburg, Missionary Ridge (died 1874).

1839 James M. Crafts, organic chemist and educator, was born in Boston; did research in France, where he was co-discoverer of Friedel-Crafts reaction, through which hundreds of new carbon compounds became possible; MIT professor (1892-98), president (1898-1900) (died 1917).

1841 Oliver Wendell Holmes Jr., jurist, was born in Boston, son of Oliver Wendell Holmes (8/29/1809); justice, Massachusetts Supreme Court (1883-1902); associate justice, Supreme Court (1902-32); one of its towering figures, known as the "Great Dissenter" (died 1935).

1862 Joseph Lee, social worker, was born in Brookline, Mass.; known as "father of American playgrounds;" president, Playground Association of America (1910-37) (died 1937).

1865 Frederick W. Goudy, printer and type designer, was born in Bloomington, Ill.; designed more than 90 type faces; established Village Press (1903) (died 1947).

1874 Former President Fillmore died in Buffalo at 74.

1886 Edward C. Kendall, biochemist, was born in South Norwalk, Conn.; shared 1950 Nobel Physiology/Medicine Prize for discoveries about hormones of adrenal cortex (died 1972).

1930 Former President Taft died in Washington at 72.

1948 Supreme Court ruled that religious training in public schools is unconstitutional.

1954 United States and Japan signed a mutual defense treaty.

1965 First American combat troops landed in South Vietnam when two battalions of Marines arrived to defend the Danang air base.

MARCH 9

1454 Amerigo Vespucci, Italian explorer, was born in Florence; made several trips to New World (1497-1503); made maps of the area; America named for him (died 1512).

1679 Zabdiel Boylston, physician, was born in Brookline, Mass.; first to use inoculation to combat smallpox epidemic, inoculating his son, Thomas, and two slaves first; many more later (died 1766).

1764 George Grenville, chancellor of the Exchequer, introduced an American Revenue Act (generally known as the Sugar Act), the first law specifically passed to raise money for the Crown in the colonies; in retaliation, colonies began program of nonimportation.

1773 Isaac Hull, War of 1812 Navy officer, was born in Shelton, Conn., nephew of Gen. William Hull (8/6/1812); commander of the *Constitution* ("Old Ironsides") when it defeated the British frigate, *Guerriere*, Aug 19, 1812 (died 1843).

1781 A Spanish fleet of 38 ships began a siege of Pensacola; British surrendered city and all of West Florida.

1791 George Hayward, surgeon, was born in Boston; the first American surgeon to use ether anesthetic in a major operation (1846) (died 1863).

1806 Edwin Forrest, actor, was born in Philadelphia; his feud with fellow actor William C. MacReady led to a riot in Astor Place Opera House, New York City (1849), in which 22 were killed when militia fired on the crowd (died 1872).

1814 John Evans, educator and public official, was born in Waynesville, Ohio; a founder, Northwestern U.; Evanston, Ill. named for him; Colorado territorial governor (1862-65); founder, Colorado Seminary, which became U. of Denver (died 1897).

1815 David Davis, legislator and jurist, was born in Cecil County, Md.; represented Illinois in the Senate (1877-83), serving as president pro tem (1881-83); associate justice, Supreme Court (1862-77) (died 1886).

1820 The daughter of President and Mrs. Monroe, Maria Hester Monroe, was married in the White House, the first presidential daughter married there.

1820 Samuel Blatchford, jurist, was born in New York City; associate justice, Supreme Court (1882-93) (died 1893).

1824 (A.) Leland Stanford, railroad executive, was born in Watervliet, N.Y.; governor of California (1861-63), represented state in the Senate (1885-93); a founder, president, Central Pacific Railroad (1853-83), absorbed by Southern Pacific, of which he was president (1884-90); founder of Stanford U. (1885) in memory of his son (died 1893).

1829 The Postmaster General became a member of the Cabinet.

1830 A charter was issued to New York Life Insurance & Trust Co., the first company to specialize in life insurance.

1834 Henry A. Ward, naturalist, was born in Rochester; sold to colleges, museums, etc., collections of natural history items, known as Ward Cabinets; a major collection was purchased by Marshall Field (1893), formed nucleus of the Field Museum of Natural History (died 1906).

1841 The Supreme Court freed blacks taken from the Spanish ship, *Amistad*, after they had seized the ship; former President John Quincy Adams defended the blacks.

1847 The first large scale amphibious operation in American military history took place when 2595 American troops landed on the beaches south of Vera Cruz, Mexico; occupied the city Mar 29.

1856 Edward G. Acheson, inventor, was born in Washington, Pa.; served as assistant to Thomas A. Edison; discovered silicon carbide (carborundum) (1880-81) (died 1931).

1856 Eddie (Edward F.) Foy, entertainer, was born in New York City; popular song-and-dance man with his children ("the seven little Foys") (died 1928).

1862 Ironclad vessels *Merrimac* and *Monitor* met in Hampton Roads, an epoch-making development in naval warfare; battle was indecisive but considered a Union victory because the *Merrimac* was disabled.

1863 A Confederate raiding party, led by John S. Mosby, captured Union general Edwin H. Stoughton and his staff behind Union lines at Fairfax Court House, Va.

1864 President Lincoln commissioned Ulysses S. Grant a lieutenant general, then highest rank in the Army; assumed command of Union forces.

1867 Lillian D. Wald, social worker, was born in Cincinnati; founder (1893), head, public health nursing in Henry St. Settlement, New York City; suggested the Children's Bureau, which was created in 1908 (died 1940).

1900 Howard H. Aiken, mathematician, was born in Hoboken, N.J.; invented Mark I, forerunner of digital computer (1944), weighed 35 tons, was 51 ft. long, had a memory, but did only arithmetic (died 1973).

1902 Edward Durrell Stone, architect, was born in Fayetteville, Ark.; designed the American Embassy, New Delhi; American Pavilion at Brussells World Fair, Kennedy Center in Washington (died 1978).

1903 Albert G. Meyer, Catholic prelate, was born in Milwaukee; archbishop of Milwaukee (1953-58), of Chicago (1958-65); named cardinal 1959 (died 1965).

1910 Samuel Barber, composer, was born in West Chester, Pa.; wrote ballets (*Medea*), operas (*Vanessa*), and other compositions (died 1981).

1916 A band of 1500 men led by Pancho Villa attacked Columbus, N.M., setting the town afire and killing 19 Americans.

1917 President Wilson announced that American merchant vessels would be armed.

1918 Mickey (Frank M.) Spillane, author, was born in Brooklyn; began as a comic book writer (*Captain*

Marvel); best known for his *Mike Hammer* detective stories.

1933 President Franklin Roosevelt signed the Emergency Banking Relief Act authorizing the Treasury Secretary to call in all gold and gold certificates; banned the hoarding and exporting of gold; the bill was submitted to the opening session of Congress at 1 p.m., passed both houses by 7:30 p.m., was signed at 8:36 p.m.; act also empowered the president to reorganize all insolvent banks, permitted sound banks to reopen.

1957 Congress endorsed the Eisenhower Doctrine, which provided economic aid to any Middle East country threatened by Communist aggression.

1964 The Supreme Court in *New York Times v. Sullivan* provided protection to newspapers against libel suits.

1975 Construction of the Alaska oil pipeline began.

1977 Restrictions were lifted on American travel to Cuba, Vietnam, North Korea, and Cambodia.

1977 Twelve Hanafi Muslim gunmen seized three buildings in Washington and held 139 persons prisoner for 39 hours before surrendering; had demanded release of imprisoned Muslims; one person was killed in the ordeal.

1987 Piedmont Aviation accepted the bid of USAir Group of $1.59 billion to take over the airline.

1987 Chrysler Corporation announced it planned to buy American Motors Corp. for more than $1.5 billion in a deal that would reduce to three the number of American car manufacturers.

1989 The Senate by a 53-47 vote rejected the nomination of former Texas Senator John G. Tower as Defense Secretary; 52 Democrats were joined by Republican Senator Nancy Kassenbaum of Kansas against the nomination.

MARCH 10

1775 Daniel Boone and 30 men began to clear the Wilderness Road for access to Transylvania County land in Kentucky.

1783 The last naval battle of the Revolution was fought in the Gulf of Florida, when an American ship under John Barry beat off three British frigates.

1785 Thomas Jefferson was elected by Congress as minister to France for three years, succeeding Benjamin Franklin.

1804 Upper Louisiana was formally transferred to the United States when Capt. Amos Stoddard took command of the area at St. Louis.

1810 John McCloskey, Catholic prelate, was born in Brooklyn; the first American cardinal (1875), served as archbishop of New York (1864-85) (died 1885).

1818 George W. Randolph, Confederate general, was born in Goochland County, Va., grandson of Thomas Jefferson; served as Confederate Secretary of War (1862) (died 1867).

1824 Thomas J. Churchill, Confederate general, was born in Jefferson County, Ky.; served in Trans-Mississippi theater (died 1905).

1848 Senate by a vote of 38 to 14 ratified a treaty ending the Mexican War.

1851 A convention adopted a new constitution for Ohio.

1865 Union forces occupied Fayetteville, N.C., destroying the arsenal and iron works.

1869 Charles W. Eliot was inaugurated as president of Harvard U.; he affected the structure of all American higher education with the elective system and other reforms.

1876 Alexander Graham Bell transmitted the first intelligible sentence on a telephone to his assistant, Thomas A. Watson, saying, "Mr. Watson, come here, I want you."

1880 Max Thorek, surgeon, was born in Hungary; founder, International College of Surgeons; cofounder, American Hospital, Chicago (died 1960).

1888 Oscar G. Mayer, president of meat packing company named for him (1928-55), was born in Chicago (died 1965).

1900 Pete DeRose, composer, was born in New York City; wrote numerous popular songs ("Deep Purple," "Wagon Wheels") (died 1953).

1902 The first anti-trust suit was filed by the United States against the Northern Securities Co., a railroad holding company organized by James J. Hill.

1903 Bix (Leon B.) Beiderbecke, jazz trumpeter, was born in Davenport, Iowa; influenced later jazz musicians; first white musician considered a major jazz innovator (died 1931).

1913 Harriet Tubman, organizer of the underground railroad, died at about 93.

1915 The German cruiser, *Prinz Eitel Friedrich,* arrived in Newport News, Va. after sinking an American vessel, *William P. Frye*, Jan 28; cruiser interned.

1916 President Wilson ordered American troops into Mexico in an effort to capture Pancho Villa, whose troops raided Columbus, N.M. the day before, killing 19 Americans; 4000 troops under Gen. John J. Pershing entered Mexico Mar 15.

1919 Supreme Court unanimously upheld convicition of Eugene V. Debs under the Espionage Act.

1923 Val L. Fitch, Princeton physicist, was born in Merriman, Neb.; shared 1980 Nobel Physics Prize for research in "big bang" theory of universe formation.

1942 Gen. Joseph Stillwell made chief of staff of Allied armies in China.

1945 American troops landed on Mindanao in the Philippines.

1971 Senate approved constitutional amendment lowering the voting age to 18 by a vote of 94-0; House approved 400-19 on Mar 23; ratified by June 30.

MARCH 11

1731 Robert T. Paine, jurist, was born in Boston; member of Continental Congress (1774-78), signer of Declaration of Independence; Massachusetts attorney general (1777-90), judge (1790-1804) (died 1814).

1779 Continental Congress authorized the creation of a Corps of Engineers; disbanded in 1783, but restored permanently Mar 16, 1802.

1781 Anthony P. Heinrich, composer, was born in Schönbüchel, Austria; known as the Beethoven of America (died 1861).

1785 John McLean, legislator and jurist, was born in Morris County, N.J.; represented Ohio in the House (1813-16); Postmaster General (1823-29); associate justice, Supreme Court (1829-61) (died 1861).

1818 Henry Jacob Bigelow, surgeon, was born in Boston; made many important contributions to surgery; published first account of using ether in a surgical operation (died 1890).

1824 Bureau of Indian Affairs was created in the War Department.

1860 Thomas Hastings, architect, was born in New York City; among his designs were the New York Public Library, Senate Office Building (died 1929).

1861 Representatives of Confederate states met in Montgomery, Ala.; adopted their constitution, closely resembling U.S. Constitution; later ratified by seceding states.

1862 President Lincoln relieved Gen. George B. McClellan of command over all military departments, except the Army of the Potomac.

1868 State convention adopted new Georgia constitution.

1888 A tremendous three-day blizzard began in the Midwest; took 400 lives.

1890 Vannevar Bush, was born in Everett, Mass.; built first analog computer, a machine for solving differential equations; director, Office of Scientific Research and Development, which laid groundwork for uranium research (died 1974).

1890 Eugene F. McDonald Jr., businessman, was born in Syracuse; founder (1923), head, Zenith Radio Corp.; founder, National Association of Broadcasters (died 1958).

1898 Dorothy Gish, screen actress, was born in Massillon, Ohio, sister of Lillian Gish (10/14/1896); starred in many early movies (*Orphans of the Storm, Romola, Nell Gwynn*) (died 1968).

1903 Lawrence Welk, orchestra leader, was born in Strasburg, N.D.; an accordionist, he formed own band in 1927.

1903 Dorothy Schiff, newspaper publisher, was born in New York City; publisher, *New York Post* (1939-77).

1920 Nicolaas Bloembergen, physicist, was born in Dordrecht, Netherlands; shared 1981 Nobel Physics Prize for work in developing laser spectroscopy technique.

1923 (Althea) Louise Brough, famous doubles tennis player, was born in Oklahoma City; with Margaret Osborne duPont, won the American doubles 12 times, Wimbledon five times, French three times; also won Wimbledon singles three times; named to Tennis Hall of Fame.

1926 Ralph D. Abernathy, civil rights leader, was born in Lindon, Ala.; a founder, president (1968-77), Southern Christian Leadership Conference.

1931 Rupert Murdoch, newspaper publisher (New York, London, Australia), was born in Melbourne, Australia.

1936 Antonin Scalia, associate justice, Supreme Court (1986-), was born in Trenton, N.J.

1941 Lend Lease Act was signed, making defense material available to any country vital to the defense of the United States; provided military credit to Great Britain and later to Soviet Russia.

1977 The Brazilian Government, angered by what it called intolerable interference in its internal affairs (criticism of human rights), cancelled the 25-year-old military aid treaty with the U.S.

MARCH 12

1773 The Virginia House of Burgesses named a committee to keep in touch with other colonies on matters of mutual interest; five other colonies did likewise by July.

1790 William Grayson, colonial leader, died at about 54; aide to George Washington (1776), commissioner of Board of War (1779-81); member, Continental Congress (1784-87); represented Virginia in the Senate (1789-90).

1801 Joseph Francis, inventor, was born in Boston; invented wooden and metal lifeboats (died 1893).

1806 Jane M. Appleton Pierce, wife of President Pierce, was born in Hampton, N.H. (died 1863).

1818 John L. Worden, Union naval officer, was born in Westchester County, N.Y.; commander of the *Monitor* in its historic battle with the *Merrimac* (died 1897).

1831 Clement Studebaker, pioneer automaker, was born near Gettysburg, Pa.; co-founder with brothers of wagon company (1852), president (1868-91); company produced 750,000 wagons before switching to automobiles (died 1901).

1835 Simon Newcomb, astronomer, was born in Wallace, Nova Scotia; one of the foremost mathematicians/astronomers; professor of mathematics, Naval Observatory (1861-97), Johns Hopkins U. (1884-1900).

1854 Andrew Furuseth, labor leader, was born in Romedal, Norway; president, International Seaman's Union of America (1903-38); helped raise working standards and conditions for American sailors (died 1938).

1858 Adolph S. Ochs, publisher, was born in Cincinnati; publisher, *Chattanooga Times* (1878-1935), *New York Times* (1896-1935), *Philadelphia Times and Public Ledger* (1902-12); originator, Chattanooga-Lookout Mountain Park (died 1935).

1862 Jane A. Delano, nursing coordinator, was born in Townsend, N.Y.; organized American Red Cross nursing service, making possible the enlistment of 20,000 nurses (1911-18) (died 1919).

1864 Gen. U.S. Grant was named general-in-chief of the Armies of the United States, the first to attain the rank of full general.

1885 U. of Arizona was chartered.

1886 Robert Hallowell, painter and publisher, was born in Denver; illustrator, *Century Magazine* (1910-14); a founder, publisher, *New Republic* (1914-25) (died 1939).

1888 The Great Blizzard struck the Atlantic Seabord, centering on New York City; killed about 400 people and did $25 million damage.

1901 Andrew Carnegie offered New York City $5.2 million for 65 branch libraries, the city to provide the sites.

1907 Russell Sage Foundation was created by Mrs. Margaret Olivia Sage (9/8/1828) with a $10 million endowment "for the improvement of social and living conditions in the United States."

1912 Girl Scouts of the United States (originally Girl Guides) was founded in Savannah by Juliette G. Low.

1917 An executive order authorized the arming of merchant vessels bound for submarine zone.

1922 J. Lane Kirkland, labor leader, was born in Camden, S.C.; secretary-treasurer, AFL-CIO (1969-79), president (1979-).

1922 Jack (Jean-Louis) Kerouac, author, was born in Lowell, Mass.; a leading representative of the Beat Generation; wrote several novels (*On the Road, Big Sur, The Dharma Burns*) (died 1969).

1928 Edward F. Albee, playwright, was born in Washington, D.C.; several hit plays (*Who's Afraid of Virginia Woolf?, A Delicate Balance, Tiny Alice*).

1932 Andrew Young, legislator and public official, was born in New Orleans; represented Georgia in the House (1973-77); United Nations ambassador (1977-79); mayor of Atlanta (1982-).

1933 President Franklin Roosevelt made his first "fireside chat," addressing the nation by radio; urged people to return savings to the banks, which were now safe.

1942 American troops landed on New Caledonia

1946 Liza Minnelli, entertainer and actress, was born in Los Angeles, daughter of Judy Garland (6/10/1922); starred in *Cabaret* and *New York, New York*.

1947 President Truman, in what came to be known as the Truman Doctrine, asked for $400 million in aid for Greece and Turkey against Communism; approved May 22.

1978 Theresa W. Blanchard, leading American competitive figure skater between 1914 and 1927, died in

Brookline, Mass. at 85; won women's title five times (1914, 1920-24) and with Nat Niles, the pairs championship title nine times (1918, 1920-27).

1985 Disarmament talks began between representatives of the United States and Soviet Russia in Geneva.

MARCH 13

1639 The Massachusetts General Court named the new school at New Town for John Harvard, who had left books and money for the school.

1798 Abigail Powers Fillmore, first wife of President Fillmore, was born in Stillwater, N.Y. (died 1853).

1813 Lorenzo Delmonico, restaurateur, was born in Marengo, Switzerland; co-founder, operator of famous New York restaurant (died 1881).

1815 James C. Hepburn, Presbyterian medical missionary, was born in Milton, Pa.; one of first missionaries to Japan; compiled first Japanese-English dictionary, supervised translation of Bible into Japanese (died 1911).

1833 William F. Warren, Methodist clergyman and educator, was born in Williamsburg, Mass.; president, Boston Theological School (1867-73), a co-founder, Boston U., of which Boston Theological became part; first president, Boston U. (1873-1903), instrumental in making it the first university to grant doctoral degree to women (died 1929).

1848 Wisconsin residents ratified the state constitution, which prohibited slavery.

1855 Percival Lowell, astronomer, was born in Boston, brother of Amy Lowell (2/9/1874); created observatory near Flagstaff, Ariz. (1893-94); best known for studies of Mars, for mathematical work predicting discovery of the planet Pluto (died 1916).

1868 The impeachment trial of President Andrew Johnson formally began before Supreme Court Justice Salmon P. Chase, presiding in the Senate.

1872 Oswald G. Villard, editor, was born in Wiesbaden, Germany, son of Henry Villard (4/10/1835) and Helen F.G. Villard (12/16/1844); owner, editor, *New York Post* (1897-1918), *The Nation* (1918-32); champion of minority rights, pacifism (died 1949).

1883 Clifford M. Holland, engineer, was born in Somerset, Mass.; in charge of building tunnels under East and Hudson rivers in New York City (1914-24); one under Hudson named for him (died 1924).

1886 Frank Baker, baseball player, was born in Trappe, Md.; known as "Home Run Baker," with Philadelphia A's, Yankees (1908-22); hit 12 homeruns in 1913; named to Baseball Hall of Fame (died 1963).

1887 Alexander A. Vandegrift, Marine Corps commandant (1944-48), was born in Charlottesville, Va.; led Marine landings at Guadalcanal, Bougainville; first Marine to hold rank of general (died 1973).

1899 John H. Van Vleck, physicist, was born in Middletown, Conn; shared 1977 Nobel Physics Prize for work underlying computer memories and electronic devices (died 1980).

1901 Former President Benjamin Harrison died in Indianapolis at 67.

1908 Walter H. Annenberg, publisher and diplomat, was born in Milwaukee, Wis.; president, Triangle Publications (*Racing Form, TV Guide*); ambassador to Great Britain(1969-76).

1911 L. Ron (Lafayette R.) Hubbard, religious leader, was born in Tilden, Neb.; founder of Scientology, a religious movement based on dianetics, a method of achieving mental and physical health (died 1986).

1913 Sammy Kaye, orchestra leader, was born in Lakewood, Ohio; noted for his "swing and sway" music (died 1987).

1924 A temporary injunction was issued by a Wyoming Federal Court judge against further exploitation of Teapot Dome by Sinclair oil interests; a similar injunction was issued (Mar 17) in California on naval reserves and the Doheny interests.

1928 St. Francis Dam on the Santa Clara River, 40 miles north of Los Angeles, gave way, destroying much property and killing 350 persons.

1930 Astronomers at Lowell Observatory at Flagstaff, Ariz. photographed for the first time the ninth planet (Pluto).

1939 Neil Sedaka, composer and entertainer, was born in New York City; wrote and recorded many hits ("Breakin' Up is Hard to Do," "Laughter in the Rain").

1961 President Kennedy offered a 10-year Alliance for Progress program to raise living standards in Latin America.

1981 President Reagan ordered a grant of $1.5 million to help the city of Atlanta finance an investigation of the murders of black children.

1986 Barber B. Conable Jr., former New York congressman, was nominated as president of the World

Bank; the 64-year-old congressman had served in the House of Representatives from 1964 to 1984.

1988 Gallaudet College (Washington, D.C.) Board of Trustees selected a deaf president, Dean I. King Jordan, to head the only American institution for the hearing-impaired after several days of student protests.

1988 American Conservative Judaism issued its first statement of principle, rejecting fundamentalism in all religions.

1989 The Justice Department settled its racketeering case against the Teamsters Union after it agreed to let members vote directly for national officers and to create a review board to guard against organized crime.

MARCH 14

1761 George Washington inherited Mt. Vernon, when his sister-in-law, the widow of his half brother, Laurence, died.

1782 Thomas Hart Benton, legislator, was born in Hillsboro, N.C.; represented Missouri in the Senate (1821-51) and House (1853-55); defender of sound money (died 1858).

1794 A patent was issued to Eli Whitney for the cotton gin.

1800 James Bogardus, inventor, was born in Catskill, N.Y.; among his inventions were a dry gas meter and a method of manufacturing postage stamps, for which he won a $2000 prize from England (died 1874).

1813 Joseph P. Bradley, jurist, was born in Berne, N.Y.; associate justice, Supreme Court (1870-92) (died 1892).

1837 Charles A. Cutter, librarian, was born in Boston; father of the dictionary catalog for libraries (died 1903).

1840 David B. Henderson, legislator, was born in Old Deer, Scotland; represented Iowa in the House (1883-1903), serving as Speaker (1899-1903) (died 1906).

1854 Thomas R. Marshall, Vice President (1913-21), was born in North Manchester, Ind.; Indiana governor (1909-13); memorable quote attributed to him: "What this country needs is a really good five cent cigar" (died 1925).

1859 William G. Sharp, diplomat, was born in Mt. Gilead, Ohio; ambassador to France (1914-19) (died 1922).

1862 New Madrid, Mo., on the Mississippi River, was abandoned when Union forces under Gen. John Pope maneuvered Confederate troops into a cul-de-sac.

1862 Union land and naval forces captured New Berne, N.C.; threatened advance on Richmond, Va.

1877 Edna W. Chase, editor, was born in Asbury Park, N.J.; editor-in-chief, *Vogue* (1914-54); organized first American fashion show (died 1957).

1879 Albert Einstein, physicist, was born in Ulm, Germany; enunciated theory of relativity and unified field theory, which seeks to include in a single mathematical formula the laws of electromagnetism and gravitation; awarded 1921 Nobel Physics Prize for discovery of the photoelectric law (died 1955).

1880 George V. Strong, World War II general, was born in Chicago; commanded, 8th Army Corps; chief of military intelligence (1942) (died 1946).

1886 Hattie Carnegie, fashion designer, was born in Vienna (died 1956).

1891 A group of New Orleans citizens shot and killed 11 Italians accused of murdering Police Chief David C. Hennessy in Oct 1890; trial of 9 of the 11 resulted in acquittal of four, mistrial of three, and dismissal of charges against two.

1895 Robert F. Loeb, medical researcher, was born in Chicago; his studies of salt metabolism led to control of Addison's disease (died 1973).

1897 Polish National Catholic Church of America was organized in Scranton, Pa.

1898 Reginald Marsh, artist, was born in Paris of American parents; painter of New York City scenes (died 1954).

1898 Richard L. Strout, journalist, was born in Cohoes, N.Y.; wrote "TRB" column for *New Republic* (1943-83).

1900 Gold Standard Act was passed and signed after agitation for free silver died down and an agreement for bimetallism failed; gold dollar became standard of value.

1903 An executive order created pensions for Civil War veterans over 62 years old—a minimum of $6 a month, a maximum of $12 at 70; increased gradually over time.

1918 Lucretia R. Garfield, widow of President Garfield, died at Pasadena, Cal. at 85.

1920 Hank (Henry K.) Ketcham, cartoonist, was born in Seattle; creator of *Dennis the Menace*.

1928 Frank Borman, astronaut, was born in Gary, Ind.; took part in first manned flight around the moon (1968); board chairman, Eastern Air Lines (1976-86).

1933 Quincy Jones, composer and arranger ("Famine Aid Song"), was born in Chicago.

1964 Jack Ruby, Dallas nightclub owner, was found guilty of murdering Lee Harvey Oswald, alleged assassin of President Kennedy; sentenced to death but conviction overturned, new trial ordered; Ruby died before new trial.

MARCH 15

1665 John Endicott, colonial governor, died at 76; acted as first governor of Massachusetts Bay Colony (1628-30), served as assistant, deputy governor, and governor until his death.

1767 Andrew Jackson, seventh president (1829-37), was born in Waxhaw, S.C.; known as "Old Hickory," he represented Tennessee in the House (1796-97) and Senate (1797-98, 1823-25); judge, Tennessee Supreme Court (1798-1804); hero of War of 1812, when he successfully led defense of New Orleans against British; governor of Florida Territory (1821) (died 1845).

1781 In Battle of Guilford Court House, N.C., Gen. Charles Cornwallis claimed a British victory in repulsing the Americans; a British legislator said, "Another such victory would ruin the British army."

1800 James H. Hackett, actor, was born in New York City; noted for his role as Rip van Winkle (died 1871).

1820 Maine was admitted to the Union as the 23rd state.

1827 Michael C. Kerr, public official, was born in Titusville, Pa.; represented Indiana in the House (1864-72, 1874-76), serving as Speaker (1875-76) (died 1876).

1838 Alice C. Flether, anthropologist, was born in Cuba of American parentage; specialized in Plains Indians culture, pioneered in study of Indian music (died 1923).

1858 Liberty H. Bailey, horticulturist, was born in South Haven, Mich.; founder, head, New York State College of Agriculture, Cornell U. (1903-13); organized world's first botanical institution devoted to cultivated plants (died 1954).

1874 Harold L. Ickes, public official, was born in Frankstown Township, Pa.; Secretary of the Interior (1933-46), headed Public Works Administration (died 1952).

1875 Archbishop John McCloskey of New York became the first American cardinal; invested Apr 27 in St. Paul's in Rome.

1875 Lee Schubert, theater manager and producer, was born in Syracuse; with brothers J.J. (8/15/1880) and Sam, controlled 37 theaters at one time (died 1953).

1907 A convention adopted Oklahoma's constitution.

1913 The first regular press conference was held in the White House, with about 125 accredited correspondents in attendance.

1916 Harry James, musician, was born in Albany, Ga.; noted trumpeter and orchestra leader (died 1983).

1916 Gen. John J. Pershing led 4000 American troops across the Mexican border to pursue Pancho Villa, who was responsible for many American deaths in various raids; troops were withdrawn in Jan 1917.

1919 An informal organizational meeting of American war veterans was held in Paris in response to a call from Lt. Col. Theodore Roosevelt Jr. to form the American Legion; formally created May 8-10, 1919.

1930 The USS *Constitution* (Old Ironsides) was reconditioned by public subscription, relaunched in Boston; originally launched in 1797.

1937 The first blood bank was created in the Cook County Hospital in Chicago.

1948 360,000 soft coal miners struck over the demand for $100 monthly pensions at 62; strike ended with agreement on a pension plan Apr 12.

1985 Raymond Donovan, the first sitting cabinet member to be indicted, resigned as Secretary of Labor; replaced by William Brock, American trade representative and former Tennessee senator.

1988 Catholic Bishop Eugene A. Marino was elevated to Archbishop of Atlanta by Pope John Paul II, becoming the first black American archbishop; since 1985, he had been secretary of the National Conference of Catholic Bishops.

1989 Former Illinois Representative Edward J. Derwinski was sworn in as the first Secretary of Veterans Affairs, the 14th cabinet department.

MARCH 16

1641 General Court declared Rhode Island a democracy and a new constitution was adopted granting freedom of religion for all citizens.

1679 John Leverett, colonial leader, died at 63; served Massachusetts as colonial agent in England (1655-62), on General Court (1663-65) and council (1665-70), lieutenant governor (1671-73), governor (1673-79).

1696 William Greene, colonial administrator, was born in Warwick, R.I.; deputy governor, Rhode Island (1740-43), governor (1743-45, 1746-47, 1748-55) (died 1758).

1739 George Clymer, merchant and legislator, was born in Philadelphia; member, Continental Congress (1776-78, 1780-83), a signer of the Declaration of Independence (died 1813).

1750 Thomas Walker was sent by the Virginia Council to survey western public lands; crossed mountains at Cumberland Gap, entering Kentucky; completed first house built in Kentucky (Apr 25), near present Barbourville.

1751 James Madison, fourth president (1809-17), was born in Port Conway, Va.; sometimes called the father of the Constitution; with Alexander Hamilton and John Jay wrote *The Federalist Papers*; served in Continental Congress (1780-83) and represented Virginia in the House (1789-98), Secretary of State (1801-09); rector, U. of Virginia (1826-36) (died 1836).

1802 U.S. Military Academy at West Point was authorized by Congress; opened July 4.

1802 The Corps of Engineers was created.

1822 John Pope, Union general, was born in Louisville; commanded Army of the Mississippi; was defeated at second Bull Run (died 1892).

1827 John B. Russworm and John Cornish published *Freedom's Journal*, the first American black newspaper.

1836 Andrew S. Hallidie, engineer, was born in London; built wire suspension bridges, invented cable railway, first used in San Francisco (1873) (died 1900).

1840 John A. Howell, naval officer and inventor, was born in Bath, N.Y.; served in Civil War, Spanish-American War; invented a gyroscope steering torpedo, a disappearing gun carriage, certain high-explosive shells (died 1918).

1845 Alexander McDougall, inventor and shipbuilder, was born in Islay Island, off Scotland; designed "whaleback" Great Lakes freighter (died 1923).

1855 Nebraska enacted a prohibition law; repealed 1858.

1861 The Confederacy sent a delegation (William L. Yancey, Pierre A. Rost, A. Dudley Mann) to Europe to explain Southern position and seek support.

1878 Henry B. Walthall, pioneer screen actor, was born in Shelby City, Ala.; best remembered for *The Birth of a Nation* and *The Scarlet Letter* (died 1936).

1880 William B. Stout, engineer, was born in Quincy, Ill.; built first all-metal plane in United States (1922), formed company to build planes (sold to Ford), founded passenger airline (sold to United); active in developing stainless steel planes, welded steel aircraft engines (died 1956).

1884 Eric P. Kelly, author, was born in Amesbury, Mass.; best known for children's books (*The Trumpeter of Krakow, The Blacksmith of Vilno*) (died 1960).

1889 Elsie Janis, actress, was born in Columbus, Ohio; starred in various plays, gained fame entertaining American troops in France (1917-18) (died 1956).

1889 A hurricane sank six warships in the Samoan harbor of Apia.

1902 Charles D. Jackson, administrative vice president, Time-Life, was born in New York City; publisher, *Fortune* (1949-54), *Life* (1960-64) (died 1964).

1903 Mike (Michael J.) Mansfield, legislator and diplomat, was born in New York City; represented Montana in the House (1945-53) and Senate (1953-77), serving as majority leader (1961-76); ambassador to Japan (1977-1989).

1903 Roy Bean, legendary frontier lawman, died; known as "the law west of the Pecos."

1906 Lloyd J. Waner, baseball player (Pittsburgh for 18 years), was born in Harrah, Okla., brother of Paul Waner (4/16/1903); lifetime batting average of .316; named to Baseball Hall of Fame.

1912 Pat (Thelma C.) Ryan Nixon, wife of President Nixon, was born in Ely, Nev.

1926 Dr. Robert H. Goddard demonstrated the practicabilty of rockets at Auburn, Mass., with the first liquid fuel rocket traveling 184 ft. in two and a half seconds.

1926 Jerry (Joseph L.) Lewis, entertainer and screen actor, was born in Newark; starred in numerous screen comedies; conducts annual fund raising telethon for the Muscular Dystrophy Association.

1961 Senate ratified the treaty which made the United States a member of the Organization for Economic Cooperation and Development (OECD).

1978 By a vote of 68-32, just one above the required two-thirds, the Senate approved the first two Panama Canal treaties, turning the facility over to Panama by the year 2000.

1985 Terry Anderson, Associated Press correspondent in Lebanon, was abducted on a Beirut street.

1988 A federal grand jury indicted former National Security Advisor John M. Poindexter, Lt. Col. Oliver L. North, retired Air Forces Major Richard V. Secord, and Albert Hakim on charges they conspired to divert to the Nicaraguan Contras profits from arms sales to Iran.

1988 President Reagan vetoed a civil rights bill passed by Congress but the vote was overriden Mar 22 by the Senate (73-24) and House (292-133).

MARCH 17

1725 Lachlan McIntosh, Revolutionary War general, was born in Badenoch, Scotland; at Valley Forge with Washington; captured by British at Charleston (1780); killed Button Gwinnett (May 19, 1977) in a duel (died 1806).

1737 The first American celebration of St. Patrick's Day was staged by the Charitable Irish Society of Boston.

1764 William Pinkney, legislator and diplomat, was born in Annapolis; represented Maryland in the House (1791, 1815-16) and Senate (1819-22); minister to Great Britain (1807-11), to Russia (1816-18); Attorney General (1811-14) (died 1822).

1766 House of Lords passed a law repealing the Stamp Act, effective May 1, following the example of the House of Commons.

1776 Ten thousand British troops accompanied by 1000 Loyalists, evacuated Boston, Mass.; troopships took them to Halifax, Nova Scotia.

1777 Roger B. Taney, jurist, was born in Calvert County, Md.; Attorney General (1831-33); Secretary of the Treasury (1833-34) but the appointment was not confirmed by the Senate; nominated as associate justice, Supreme Court, but Senate again (1835) refused to confirm; confirmed as chief justice, Supreme Court, where he served from 1836 to his death in 1864.

1804 James Bridger, trapper and guide, was born in Richmond, Va.; discovered the Great Salt Lake (1824) (died 1881).

1806 Norbert Rillieux, sugar refiner, was born in New Orleans; developed technical innovations which revolutionized sugar refining, established modern industrial evaporation (died 1894).

1828 Patrick R. Cleburne, Confederate general, was born in County Cork, Ireland; died in a charge at Franklin, Tenn. Nov 30, 1864.

1832 Walter Q. Gresham, public official, was born in Harrison County, Ind.; Postmaster General (1883-84), Secretary of the Treasury (1884), Secretary of State (1893-95) (died 1895).

1837 Republic of Texas adopted a constitution.

1843 Henry W. Lawton, Army general, was born in Manhattan, Ohio; served in Civil War and in Indian frontier fighting; captured Geronimo (1886); commanded troops in Cuba, Philippines (1898-99) (died 1899).

1849 Charles F. Brush, electricity pioneer, was born in Euclid, Ohio; inventor of numerous electrical devices (arc light, storage battery); early investigator of electric lighting methods; installed first electric arc street lighting (Cleveland, 1879), first electric store lighting (Wanamakers, Philadelphia, 1878) (died 1929).

1866 Pierce Butler, jurist, was born in Dakota County, Minn.; associate justice, Supreme Court (1923-39) (died 1939).

1874 Stephen S. Wise, rabbi and Zionist leader, was born in Budapest; founder, Zionist Organization of America; a leader in efforts to make Palestine the Jewish homeland (died 1949).

1884 Frank Buck, animal hunter and collector, was born in Gainesville, Tex.; author (*Bring 'em Back Alive, Wild Cargo*) (died 1950).

1894 Paul E. Green, playwright, was born in Lillington, N.C.; wrote numerous hit plays (*In Abraham's Bosom, The Lost Colony, The Common Glory, Trumpet in the Land*) (died 1981).

1902 Bobby (Robert T.) Jones, golfing great, was born in Atlanta; one of the greatest golfers of all time; dominant force in golf in 1920s; helped found Masters Tournament (died 1971).

1905 Franklin Delano Roosevelt married Eleanor Roosevelt in New York City.

1910 Bayard Rustin, civil rights leader, was born in West Chester, Pa.; helped organize the first freedom rides in the South, the march on Washington (1963) (died 1987).

1914 Sammy Baugh, one of greatest football quarterbacks, was born in Temple, Tex.; starred with Texas Christian U., Washington Redskins (1936-52).

1919 Nat "King" Cole, popular singer, was born in Montgomery, Ala.; pianist and singer, with numerous hit records (died 1965).

1941 President Franklin Roosevelt dedicated the National Gallery of Art.

1942 Gen. Douglas A. MacArthur named commander of Allied forces in Southeast Pacific and Australia; left besieged Bataan for Australia.

1943 American Second Corps began offensive in Tunisia.

1960 A Lockheed Electra on a Chicago-Miami flight exploded over Tell City, Ind., killing 63 persons.

1985 Canadian Prime Minister Brian Mulroney and President Reagan met in Quebec and announced appointment of a joint team to examine the problem of acid rain; signed agreements on security, fishing rights, trade, and law enforcement.

1988 Three thousand American soldiers began arriving in Honduras as a show of support to the Honduran government after ten days of border clashes with Nicaraguan troops; began leaving ten days later.

1988 Federal regulator pledged to provide $1 billion to the First Republic Bank Corp. of Dallas in an effort to halt widespread withdrawals.

1989 Richard B. Cheney, congressman from Wyoming and former White House aide, was sworn in as Secretary of Defense after winning Senate confirmation 92-0.

MARCH 18

1747 William Duer, Revolutionary leader, was born in Devonshire, England; served in Continental Congress (1777-78); Assistant Secretary of Treasury (1789), sued by government for irregularities (land speculation and government contracts); imprisoned and financial panic followed (1792), died in prison 1799.

1782 John C. Calhoun, Vice President (1825-32), was born near Calhoun Mills, S.C.; champion of state's rights; represented South Carolina in the House (1811-17) and Senate (1832-33, 1845-50); Secretary of War (1817-24), Secretary of State (1844-45) (died 1850).

1795 Demetrius A. Gallitzin, Dutch-born priest, was ordained, the first Catholic priest who received all his orders and training in the United States.

1800 Francis Lieber, political philosopher, was born in Berlin; influenced the development of American social sciences; edited first American encyclopedia (*Encyclopedia Americana*) (1829-33) (died 1872).

1813 Joshua B. Lippincott, publisher, was born in Juliustown, N.J.; founder (1836) of company bearing his name (died 1886).

1818 Congress approved a pension bill for veterans of the Revolutionary War—$20 per month for life for officers, $8 for soldiers.

1834 James B. Herreshoff, inventor, was born in Bristol, R.I., brother of Nathanael G. Herreshoff (see 1848 below); invented sliding seat for rowboats (later used in racing shells), a fin keel for racing yachts; improved process for making nitric and hydrochloric acids (died 1930).

1837 (Stephen) Grover Cleveland, 22nd and 24th president (1885-89, 1893-97), was born in in Caldwell, N.J.; practiced law in Buffalo (1859-81), mayor (1881-82), governor of New York (1883-85) (died 1908).

1837 U. of Michigan was organized in Ann Arbor, opened to students Sept 20.

1848 Nathanael G. Herreshoff, boat designer, was born in Bristol, R.I., brother of James B. Herreshoff (see 1834 above); developed first Navy torpedo boats, designed five yachts which successfully defended six America Cup races (died 1938).

1857 Henry Berkowitz, rabbi, was born in Pittsburgh; one of the first rabbis ordained in the United States (1883); served Rodolph Sholem Congregation, Philadelphia (1892-1922) (died 1923).

1861 An Arkansas convention rejected secession from the Union.

1861 The Texas legislature deposed Gov. Sam Houston for his refusal to take the oath to support the Confederacy.

1862 Dorr E. Felt, inventor, was born in Beloit, Wis.; invented first wholly key-operated calculating machine, first practical adding, listing machine (died 1930).

1864 Arkansas constitution, abolishing slavery, was ratified by the people.

1864 John H. Kinealy, mechanical engineer, was born in Hannibal, Mo.; invented air purifying apparatus, damper regulator, thermal valve (died 1928).

1869 Congress passed the Public Credit Act, calling for payment in gold of government obligations.

1892 (Robert P.) Tristram Coffin, author, was born in Brunswick, Me.; poet (*Strange Holiness, Golden Falcon*), biographies, novels (died 1955).

1898 Lawrence J. Shehan, Catholic prelate, was born in Baltimore; archbishop of Baltimore (1961-74), named cardinal 1965 (died 1984).

1911 Roosevelt Dam on Salt River in Arizona was dedicated.

1925 Eight Midwest and Southern tornadoes killed 792 people.

1927 John Kander, composer, (*Cabaret, Chicago, Funny Lady*), was born in Kansas City, Mo.

1932 John H. Updike, author, was born in Shillington, Pa.; novelist (*Rabbit, Run; Rabbit Redux, The Cenataur, Couples, The Coup*).

1937 A natural gas explosion destroyed a school in New London, Tex., killing 294 children and teachers.

1963 Supreme Court ruled that all criminal defendants must have counsel, that illegally acquired evidence is not admissible in state, federal courts.

1970 The strike of nearly 200,000 postal employees began in New York City, the largest strike against the Federal Government; spread throughout nation, except South; ended Mar 24-25.

1974 The ban on oil exports to the United States by Arab oil-producing countries was lifted after five months.

1985 Capital Cities Communications, Inc. purchased ABC (American Broadcasting Co.), the first time that any of the nation's three major networks had changed hands.

1986 President Reagan and Canadian Prime Minister Brian Mulroney began two-day session in Washington, D.C. in which they agreed on a plan to reduce acid rain.

1988 Lt. Col. Oliver L. North, indicted in the Iran-Contra affair, resigned from the Marine Corps.

MARCH 19

1590 William Bradford, Pilgrim leader, was born in Austerfield, England; arrived on the Mayflower, where he was a framer, signer of Mayflower Compact; governor of Plymouth Colony 28 years between 1621 and 1657 (died 1657).

1628 New England Company formed by Rev. John White, a Dorsetshire Nonconformist; given patent to land between the Merrimack and Charles rivers; company succeeded by the Massachusetts Bay Company (Mar 14, 1629).

1687 Sieur de LaSalle, Mississippi Valley explorer, shot and killed during mutiny.

1734 Thomas McKean, jurist and legislator, was born in New London, Pa.; member of Continental Congress (1774-83), president of Continental Congress (1781); signer of Declaration of Independence; Pennsylvania chief justice (1777-99), governor (1799-1808) (died 1817).

1778 General Assembly of South Carolina adopted a state constitution.

1816 The compensation of congressmen was changed from per diem to $1500 annually plus mileage; Senate President and House Speaker $3000; repealed Feb 6, 1817.

1835 James E. Scripps, publisher, was born in London; co-founder of newspaper chain (Scripps-Howard); founder, editor, *Detroit News* (1873) (died 1906).

1847 Albert P. Ryder, artist, was born in New Bedford, Mass.; paintings featured landscapes, seascapes, and allegorical scenes; hang in Metropolitan Museum of Art, National Gallery of Art (died 1917).

1848 Wyatt Earp, legendary frontier lawman, was born in Monmouth, Ill. (died 1929).

1855 David Todd, astronomer, was born in Lake Ridge, N.Y.; designed, erected college observatories at Smith, Amherst; first to photograph solar corona from plane (1925); invented automatic device to photograph eclipses (died 1939).

1860 Elizabeth Cady Stanton spoke on woman suffrage to New York Legislature.

1860 William Jennings Bryan, public official, was born in Salem, Ill.; known as "the Commoner," he was a free silver advocate; Democratic presidential candidate (1896, 1900, 1908); Secretary of State (1913-15); a prosecuting attorney in Scopes "monkey" trial (1925); died day after trial ended.

1871 Joe (Joseph J.) McGinnity, baseball pitcher who won 247 games, mostly with New York Giants, was born in Rock Island, Ill.; named to Baseball Hall of Fame (died 1929).

1883 Joseph W. (Vinegar Joe) Stilwell, World War II general, was born in Palatka, Fla.; commanded American forces in Burma-China theater (1942-46) (died 1946).

1891 Earl Warren, chief justice, Supreme Court (1953-69), was born in Los Angeles; served Canada as Attorney General (1939-43) and governor (1944-53); 1948 Republican vice presidential candidate; headed investigation of Kennedy assassination (died 1974).

1899 Henry I. Hodes, World War II and Korean War Army general, was born in Washington, D.C.; commander-in-chief, U.S. Army in Europe (1956-59) (died 1962).

1901 Jo Mielzner, stage designer for more than 360 Broadway productions, was born in Paris; with Eero Saarinen, designed the Vivian Beaumont Theater in Lincoln Center (died 1976).

1903 Paul J. French, executive director, CARE (1945-55), was born in Philadelphia (died 1960).

1904 John J. Sirica, U.S. District Court judge who presided over the Watergate trials (1972-74), was born in Waterbury, Conn.

1917 The Supreme Court upheld the constitutionality of the Eight Hour Day Act, directed primarily at railroads.

1918 Daylight savings time was established by Congress, to be in effect from Mar 31 to Oct 27.

1920 The Senate by a vote of 49-35 refused to ratify the League of Nations Covenant and the Versailles Treaty; the vote was short of the required two-thirds.

1925 Brent Scowcroft, National Security Council chairman (1975-77) and designated chairman by President-elect Bush (1989), was born in Ogden, Utah.

1933 Philip Roth, author, was born in Newark, N.J.; wrote several successful novels (*Goodbye, Columbus; Portnoy's Complaint, The Breast*).

1941 The National Defense Mediation Board was created by executive order to settle labor disputes affecting defense production.

1988 General Manual Noriega rejected an American offer to leave Panama in return for a promise that the United States would not seek his extradition.

MARCH 20

1702 Streets were laid out by d'Iberville in Mobile, the new capital of the Louisiana Colony.

1760 Boston was swept by a disastrous fire.

1777 Edmund F. Gaines, War of 1812 general, was born in Culpeper County, Va.; distinguished self at Ft. Erie, Canada (died 1849).

1782 With the defeat of Cornwallis at Yorktown, the government of Lord North fell, succeeded by Lord Rockingham two days later; he decided to open negotiations with the American peace commission.

1804 Neal Dow, temperance reformer, was born in Portland, Me.; helped found Maine Temperance Union (1838), responsible for enactment of Maine prohibition law (1851) (died 1897).

1823 Edward Z.C. Judson, author, was born in Stamford, N.Y.; under pseudonym of Ned Buntline he pioneered the dime novel; wrote about 400 such novels and adventure fiction (died 1886).

1830 Eugene A. Carr, Union general, was born in Concord, N.Y.; served at Vicksburg, in Missouri; later led troops in many battles against Indians (died 1910).

1834 Charles W. Eliot, educator and editor, was born in Boston; president, Harvard (1869-1909), organized graduate school of arts and sciences (1890), made divinity school nonsectarian; helped establish Radcliff College (1894); edited "five foot shelf" of the classics (died 1926).

1844 Robert Dollar, shipping magnate, was born in Falkirk, Scotland; founded shipping companies in San Francisco, lumber company (died 1932).

1852 *Uncle Tom's Cabin* by Harriet Beecher Stowe was published; had been serialized earlier in anti-slavery newspaper (*National Era*); by mid-1853, about 1.2 million copies had been published.

1856 Frederick W. Taylor, industrial engineer and inventor, was born in Germantown, Pa.; invented largest steel hammer in the United States (1890); co-developer of heat-treating steel; developed "time and motion" studies; became father of scientific management (died 1915).

1856 David Conner, naval officer, died at 64; served in War of 1812 and Mexican War, where he was in charge of landing Scott's army at Veracruz, Mexico, the first large scale amphibious operation.

1883 Wilfred J. Funk, president of Funk & Wagnalls (1925-40), was born in Brooklyn; editor, *Literary Digest* (1936-37) (died 1965).

1890 Lauritz Melchior, operatic tenor, was born in Copenhagen; starred in Wagnerian roles with Metropolitan Opera (1926-50) (died 1973).

1903 Vinnie (Vincent) Richards, tennis star of the 1920s, was born in New York City (died 1959).

1904 B(urrhus) F. Skinner, behavioral psychologist, was born in Susquehanna, Pa.; invented teaching machine, considered the father of programmed instruction.

1908 Frank N. Stanton, broadcast executive, was born in Muskegon, Mich.; president, Columbia Broadcasting System (1946-71); instrumental in developing CBS television.

1909 Edward F. Knipling, entomologist, was born in Port Lavaca, Tex.; developed new agricultural pest control methods.

1920 Lenore Hershey, editor, was born in New York City; editor, *Ladies Home Journal* (1968-).

1933 The Economy Act was passed, reducing federal salaries and veterans payments.

1948 Bobby (Robert G.) Orr, one of the best hockey defense men, was born in Parry Sound, Canada; played with Boston Bruins; named National Hockey League most valuable player 1970, 1971, 1972.

1987 The Dow Jones industrial average climbed over the 2300 mark for the first time, closing at 2333.52.

1987 American Lutheran Church congregations decisively approved merging with the Lutheran Church in America and Association of Evangelical Lutheran Churches; the new 5.3 million-member Evangelical Lutheran Church in America became effective Jan 1, 1988.

MARCH 21

1699 John Bartram, botanist, was born near Darby, Pa.; America's first important botanist; his park, a favorite resort of Franklin and Washington, is now part of the Philadelphia park system (died 1777).

1713 Francis Lewis, colonial merchant and leader, was born in Llandaff, Wales; a member of Continental Congress (1775-79), a signer of the Declaration of Independence (died 1802).

1843 The first date set by William Miller, sectarian leader, for the second coming of Christ; marked his "first disappointment;" although he was again disappointed, his movement led to the formation of the Adventist Church.

1857 Hunter Liggett, World War I general, was born in Reading, Pa.; commander, First Army (1918-19), Army of Occupation on the Rhine (1919) (died 1935).

1865 George O. Squier, military and electrical engineer, was born in Dryden, Mich.; chief signal officer, Army (1917-23); numerous inventions, including nine-wave system of cable telegraphy and multiplex telephony and telegraphy (died 1934).

1866 James G. Harbord, World War I general, was born in Bloomington, Ill.; served at Belleau Woods, second battle of the Marne; president, board chairman, RCA (1930-47) (died 1947).

1869 Florenz Ziegfeld, theatrical producer, was born in Chicago; introduced the "revue," produced annual Follies, *Show Boat, Rio Rita* (died 1932).

1869 Albert Kahn, architect, was born in Rhaunen, Germany; pioneered in modern factory design (Detroit auto plants; Fisher, GM buildings; Willow Run plant) (died 1942).

1880 Hans Hofmann, painter and art teacher, was born in Weissenburg, Germany; introduced modern European painting styles into the United States (died 1966).

1885 Raoul V.G. Lufbery, World War I aviator, was born in Clermont, France, to an American father and French mother; an ace in the Lafayette Escadrille (17 victories) (1916-18); transferred to American service, killed in combat May 19, 1918.

1885 Joseph Pulitzer, publisher, was born in New York City; the son of Joseph Pulitzer (4/10/1847); published the *St. Louis Post-Dispatch* (1912-55) (died 1955).

1896 Ballington Booth, who had resigned as head of the Salvation Army in America, formed a new organization, Volunteers of America.

1898 A naval court of inquiry ascribed the destruction of the battleship *Maine* to an external cause; a Spanish inquiry blamed an internal explosion.

1905 Phyllis McGinley, author, was born in Ontario, Ore.; popular poet (*A Pocketful of Wry, On the Contrary, One More Manhattan*) (died 1978).

1913 Floods in the Miami Valley of Ohio killed more than 400 persons.

1916 Fire in Paris, Tex burned 1400 buildings, with damage of $11 million.

1917 The American steamer *Heraldton* was sunk by a German submarine off the Netherlands with a loss of 20 lives.

1918 President Wilson signed the Railroad Control Act, which established the compensation to be paid during government operations which would end no later than 21 months after peace treaty ratification.

1928 Gordie (Gordon) Howe, the greatest forward in ice hockey, was born in Floral, Canada; played for the Detroit Red Wings for 26 years (1946-71), named National Hockey League most valuable player six times.

1932 Walter Gilbert, molecular biologist, was born in Boston; shared 1980 Nobel Chemistry Prize for pioneering research in genetic engineering.

1952 Tornadoes hit six Mississippi Valley states, killing 239 and injuring 1200.

1965 The 54-mile march from Selma to Montgomery, Ala., led by Rev. Martin Luther King Jr., began with a federalized Alabama National Guard escort; 3200 marchers started and the crowd grew to 25,000 by the end of the march.

1989 The Supreme Court ruled 7-2 to uphold mandatory blood and urine tests for railroad workers involved in accidents; voted 5-4 to uphold urine tests for Customs Service employees seeking drug enforcement jobs.

MARCH 22

1621 Massassoit, chief of the Wampanoag Indians, came to Plymouth to "treat of peace."

1622 Nearly 350 Virginia colonists were massacred by Indians.

1687 The first Anglican service was held in Boston's South Meeting House on Good Friday; on Easter Sunday, the Anglican service was held from 11 AM to 2 PM; the Congregationalists had to wait until Anglicans finished before they could hold their service.

1765 The Virginia House of Burgesses adopted five of seven resolutions introduced by Patrick Henry, a new member from Louisa County, against the Stamp Act; later the fifth resolution was dropped.

1790 Thomas Jefferson, returning from France, assumed office as the first Secretary of State, to which he had been named Sept 26, 1789.

1794 Congress passed a law prohibiting slave trade by American citizens from one country to another.

1799 Joseph Saxton, inventor, was born in Huntington, Pa.; invented a fountain pen, locomotive differential pulley, deep sea thermometer, self-registering tide gauge; designed, built balances to check weights of government assay and coinage offices; superintendent of weights and measures, U.S. Coast Survey (1843-73) (died 1873).

1813 Thomas Crawford, sculptor, was born in New York City; among his many works was the statue of Liberty atop the Capitol dome (died 1857).

1817 Braxton Bragg, Confederate general, was born in Warrenton, N.C.; led victory at Chickamauga, unsuccessfully besieged Chattanooga; military advisor to Jefferson Davis (1864-65) (died 1876).

1819 William W. Adams, Confederate general, was born in Frankfort, Ky.; served at Shiloh, in Mississippi and Alabama (died 1888).

1820 Commodore Stephen Decatur was killed in a duel with James Barron, who had accused Decatur of leading intrigue to block his promotion and sea duty; Barron had been found guilty of negligence (1807) as commander of the Chesapeake.

1868 Robert A. Millikin, physicist, was born in Morrison, Ill.; at U. of Chicago (1896-1921); credited with being first to isolate the electron, measure its charge; awarded 1923 Nobel Physics Prize for work on elementary charge of electricity and photoelectric phenomenon; coined term cosmic ray (died 1953).

1874 First Young Men's Hebrew Association (YMHA) met in New York City.

1876 Robert Fechner, public official, was born in Chattanooga; director, Civilian Conservation Corps (CCC) (1933-39) (died 1939).

1880 Kent Cooper, Associated Press executive, was born in Columbus, Ind.; general manager (1925-48), executive director (1943-51) (died 1965).

1882 Congress adopted the Anti-Polygamy Act, which imposed penalties for the practice, forbade polygamists from voting, holding public office, serving on juries; placed Utah elections under supervision of a five-man presidential board.

1884 Arthur H. Vandenberg, legislator, was born in Grand Rapids, Mich.; represented Michigan in the Senate (1928-51), serving as president pro tem (1947-49); a leader in bipartisan foreign policy (died 1951).

1896 Joseph Schildkraut, screen actor, was born in Vienna; many roles in silent films, also in *Emile Zola* and *Diary of Anne Frank* (died 1964).

1897 The Supreme Court in Trans-Missouri Freight case held 5-4 that railroads are subject to antitrust law.

1914 William E. Miller, legislator, was born in Lockport, N.Y.; represented New York in the House (1950-65); 1964 Republican vice presidential candidate (died 1983).

1918 Texas enacted a prohibition law, effective June 26.

1924 Allen H. Neuharth, newspaper publisher, was born in Eureka, S.D.; president, (1970-), chief executive officer (1973-), Gannett Newspapers; founder, *USA Today* (1983).

1930 Stephen J. Sondheim, composer and lyricist, was born in New York City; composer (*A Little Night Music, Sweeney Todd, A Funny Thing Happened on the Way to the Forum*); lyricist (*West Side Story, Gypsy*).

1931 Burton Richter, physicist, was born in New York City; co-discoverer of J-(psi) particle (1974); shared 1976 Nobel Physics Prize for that discovery.

1933 President Franklin Roosevelt signed a bill legalizing beer of 3.2% alcoholic content; first beer in 15 years sold beginning Apr 7.

1955 A Navy plane crashed into a cliff near Honolulu, 66 killed

1972 The Senate adopted the Equal Rights Amendment (84-8); requires ratification by 38 states to become effective.

1981 The cost of first class postage was increased to 18 cents.

1984 Bernard F. Law, 54-year-old Catholic bishop, began his duties as the Archbishop of Boston; had been Bishop of Springfield-Cape Girardeau, Mo.

1989 Pete Rozelle resigned as National Football League commissioner after 30 years service; will stay on to help train a successor.

MARCH 23

1662 Virginia passed severe laws against the Quakers.

1713 South Carolinians captured Indian stronghold, Ft. Nohucke, ending Tuscarora War.

1775 Speaking at a Virginia convention in St. John's Church, Richmond, Patrick Henry declared: "Is life so dear, or peace so sweet, as to be purchased at the price of chains and slavery? Forbid it, Almighty God! I know not what course others may take, but as for me, give me liberty or give me death."

1818 Emperor Napoleon ordered the seizure, sale of American ships in French ports.

1823 Schuyler Colfax, Vice President (1869-73), was born in New York City; represented Indiana in the House (1855-69), serving as Speaker (1863-69); his involvement in Crédit Mobilier scandal terminated his career (died 1885).

1823 Aaron French, inventor, was born in Wadsworth, Ohio; invented coil and elliptical railroad car springs, revolutionizing railroad industry (died 1902).

1824 Samuel S. Laws, educator, was born in Ohio County, Va. (now W.Va.); president, Westminster College, Fulton, Mo. (1855-61); imprisoned for Confederate views; president, New York Gold Exchange; invented stock ticker; president, Missouri U. (1876-89) (died 1921).

1831 Edwin Reynolds, engineer, was born in Mansfield, Conn.; developd Corliss-Reynolds engine, first triple expansion pumping engine for water works; improved boilers, air compressors, ore crushers, hoists (died 1909).

1842 Clemens Herschel, hydraulic engineer, was born in Boston; invented Venturi tube for measuring flow of water in pipes (died 1930).

1857 Fannie M. Farmer, cooking expert, was born in Boston; conducted school for housewives rather than teachers; produced cookbook still in use; introduced standard level measurements in recipes (died 1915).

1867 U. of California chartered; had been College of California since 1855.

1868 The Senate, seated as court of impeachment, heard President Andrew Johnson reply to charges, that removal of War Secretary Edwin M. Stanton was legal, that Tenure of Office Act was unconstitutional (Supreme Court agreed in 1926).

1868 U. of California was founded at Berkeley.

1884 Florence E. Allen, jurist, was born in Salt Lake City; served in Ohio courts, became first woman on a state supreme court (1922-34) (died 1966).

1887 Sidney Hillman, labor leader, was born in Zagare, Lithuania; president, Amalgamated Clothing Workers (1914-46); co-director, Office of Production Management (1941-43) (died 1946).

1888 Supreme Court Chief Justice Morrison R. Waite died in Washington, D.C. at 72.

1899 Louis Adamic, author, was born in Blato, Czechoslovakia; author of novels about immigrants' lives in America (*The Native's Return, My America*) (died 1951).

1900 Erich Fromm, psychoanalyst and author, was born in Frankfurt, Germany; works include *The Sane Society* and *The Art of Loving* (died 1980).

1901 Emilio Aguinaldo, leader of independent movement in the Philippines against United States, was captured; freed after taking oath of allegiance to the United States.

1908 Joan Crawford, screen actress, was born in San Antonio; many starring roles (*Mildred Pierce, Humoresque, Our Dancing Daughters*) (died 1977).

1912 Wernher von Braun, rocket scientist, was born in Germany; helped develop V-2 bomb for Germany in World War II; with United States, he served as director of missile research facility at Huntsville, Ala.; deputy NASA administrator (1970-72) (died 1977).

1932 Norris-LaGuardia anti-injunction act was passed; forbade injunctions in labor disputes except under defined conditions.

1982 President Reagan sent Congress a plan to revitalize declining urban areas through the creation of "enterprise zones;" businesses would receive tax relief for investments creating jobs.

1982 Supreme Court upheld Federal Trade Commission order requiring the American Medical Association to permit doctors to advertise, compete for business, and enter into non-traditional arrangements for the practice of medicine.

1988 Smoking on all Northwest Airlines flights in North America was banned by the airline, effective Apr 23.

1989 The largest oil spill in North American history occurred when an Exxon tanker ran aground on a reef off Valdez, Alaska; the spill killed thousands of animals, damaged thousands of miles of beaches, endangered fish.

MARCH 24

1754 Joel Barlow, poet and diplomat, was born in Redding, Conn.; consul to Algeria (1795-96), arranged treaties with Tunis, Algiers, Tripoli; poet (*The Vision of Columbus, Advice to a Raven*) (died 1812).

1755 Rufus King, colonial leader, was born in Scarborough, Me.; member of Continental Congress (1784-87), Constitutional Convention (1787); one of New York's first Senators (1789-96, 1813-25); minister to Great Britain (1796-1803, 1825-26); unsuccessful candidate for vice president (1804-1808), president (1816) (died 1827).

1765 The Quartering Act went into effect in the colonies, requiring that barracks, supplies be made available to British troops.

1771 William Shirley, colonial governor, died at 78; governor of Massachusetts (1741-49, 1753-56), led victorious expedition against Cape Breton Island.

1781 Anson G. Phelps, businessman, was born in Simsbury, Conn.; with two sons-in-law, formed Phelps, Dodge & Co., copper producer (died 1853).

1783 Spain recognized the independence of the United States.

1788 Popular referendum in Rhode Island rejected 2945 to 237 the new federal constitution; not ratified until May 29, 1790.

1820 Fanny (Frances J.) Crosby, hymn writer, was born in Southeast, N.Y.; although blind, she wrote about 6000 hymns ("Soft in the Arms of Jesus," "Blessed Assurance," "Sweet Hour of Prayer," "Jesus is Calling") (died 1915).

1825 Texas, part of a state in the new Mexican republic, was opened to colonization.

1828 Pennsylvania legislature approved financial aid to the Pennsylvania Railroad, the first railroad undertaken by a government anywhere in the world.

1828 Horace Gray, jurist, was born in Boston; justice, Massachusetts Supreme Court (1864-73); associate justice, Supreme Court (1882-1902) (died 1902).

1832 Creek Indians ceded all lands east of the Mississippi to the United States.

1834 John Wesley Powell, explorer and geologist, was born in Mt. Morris, N.Y.; explored Rockies, Colorado River, Grand Canyon; first director, Smithsonian Bureau of American Ethnology (1879-1902); director, U.S. Geological Survey (1881-94) (died 1902).

1853 The oath of office was administered to William R.D. King, elected Vice President with Franklin Pierce, in Cumbre, Cuba because he was too ill to make trip to the inauguration; died Apr 18 without assuming office.

1855 Andrew W. Mellon, banker and diplomat, was born in Pittsburgh, Pa.; had extensive interests in coal, coke, steel; Secretary of Treasury (1931-32); ambassador to Great Britain (1932-33); donated funds, art collection, for National Gallery of Art (died 1937).

1884 Peter J.E. Debye, physical chemist, was born in Maastricht, Netherlands; awarded 1936 Nobel Chemistry Prize for work in dipole movements and x-ray diffraction (died 1966).

1886 Edward Weston, photographer, was born in Highland Park, Ill.; noted for nature studies (died 1958).

1890 John Rock, physician, was born in Marlborough, Mass.; helped develop oral contraceptive—the pill—with Gregory Pincus (Apr 9, 1903) (died 1984).

1893 George Sisler,baseball player, was born in Manchester, Ohio; considered the greatest first baseman (St. Louis Browns, 1915-27); had .340 lifetime batting average; named to Baseball Hall of Fame (died 1973).

1893 Walter Baade, astronomer, was born in Schröttinghausen, Germany; redetermined size and age of the universe (died 1960).

1902 Thomas E. Dewey, public official, was born in Owosso, Mich.; "gangbusting" district attorney, New York City (1935-38); New York governor (1942-54); Republican presidential candidate (1944, 1948) (died 1971).

1907 Lucia Chase, ballet dancer and manager, was born in Waterbury, Conn.; former principal dancer, American Ballet Theatre, later manager; with ABT 40+ years.

1919 Lawrence Ferlinghetti, pot, was born in Yonkers, N.Y.; a founder of "beat" movement.

1924 Two Catholic archbishops were elevated to cardinal by Pope Pius XI—Patrick J. Hayes of New York and George W. Mundelein of Chicago.

1930 Steve McQueen, screen actor, was born in Indianapolis; starred in many films (*Bullet, LeMans, Papillon, The Reivers*) (died 1980).

1935 President Franklin Roosevelt signed the Tydings-McDuffie bill, providing independence for the Philippine Islands.

1976 President Ford proposed an immunization program against swine flu; program halted Dec 16 after 58 persons suffered paralysis from the shots.

1981 Supreme Court ruled that a state may require a doctor to notify the parents of a teenage patient before performing an abortion on her.

1988 The DuPont Co. promised to phase out all production of chemicals suspected of destroying the ozone shield.

MARCH 25

1584 Queen Elizabeth I of England granted a charter to Sir Walter Raleigh to colonize North America; sent out five expeditions to New World, including the "lost colony" on Roanoke Island, N.C.

1634 Leonard Calvert, the colony's first governor, led 200 English colonists to Maryland, landing first at St. Clemens (now Blakiston) Island, then establishing a settlement at St. Mary's two days later.

1687 An Episcopal church was established in the Old South Meeting House in Boston, formerly a Congregational church, by order of Gov. Edmund Andros.

1775 George Washington was selected by the Provincial Congress to be a member of the second Continental Congress.

1797 John Winebrenner, founder of Church of God (1830), was born in Walkerville, Md. (died 1860).

1805 George H. Evans, educator and reformer, was born in Bromyard, England; published first important American labor paper, *Working Man's Advocate* (died 1856).

1825 University of Virginia opened.

1827 Stephen B. Luce, military educator, was born in Albany; founder, president, Navel War College (1884-89), world's first such institution (died 1917).

1837 *Philadelphia Public Ledger* began publication.

1838 Elwell S. Otis, Army officer, was born in Frederick, Md.; served in Civil War, general in Spanish-American War; military governor of Philippines (1898-1900), suppressed insurrection (died 1909).

1839 William B. Wait, pioneer in education of blind, was born in Amsterdam, N.Y.; devised a variation of Braille, machine for its printing (died 1916).

1862 George Sutherland, legislator and jurist, was born in Buckinghamshire, England; represented Utah in the House (1901-03) and Senate (1905-17); associate justice Supreme Court (1922-38) (died 1942).

1863 Simon Flexner, pathologist, was born in Louisville, brother of Abraham Flexner (11/13/1866); isolated dysentery bacillus, developed serum for cerebrospinal meningitis (died 1946).

1867 Arturo Toscanini, orchestra conductor, was born in Parma, Italy; one of world's greatest (La Scala 1898-1905, Metropolitan 1908-15, New York Philharmonic 1928-36) (died 1957).

1871 Gutzon Borglum, sculptor, was born in Bear Lake, Ida.; best known for presidential heads on Mt. Rushmore in the Black Hills, the first federally-authorized national memorial (died 1941).

1879 William S. Knudsen, auto manufacturer, was born in Copenhagen; executive vice president, General Motors (1933-41); co-director, Office of Production Management (1941); production director, War Department (1942-45) (died 1948).

1881 Béla Bartók, composer, was born in Nagyszentmiklos, Hungary (now Rumania); noted for compositions of contemporary Hungarian music (died 1945).

1891 Byron Price, newspaper editor and public official, born; with Associated Press (1912-41), executive editor (1937-41); director of censorship (1941-45); Assistant Secretary General, United Nations (1947-54) (died 1981).

1903 Frankie Carle, musician, was born in Providence; pianist and orchestra leader.

1911 Triangle Shirt-Waist factory fire in New York City resulted in the death of 145 women workers; led to sweeping reforms in building and factory laws.

1914 Norman E. Borlaug, agronomist, was born in Cresco, Ia.; developed new strains of wheat, rice and practices in Mexico and elsewhere to help ease world hunger; awarded 1970 Nobel Peace Prize.

1917 An executive order by President Wilson called up the National Guard of the Eastern states; made nationwide July 3.

1918 The third Liberty Bond sale was conducted with the issuance of $412 billion in 4-1/2% gold convertible bonds.

1920 Howard Cosell, abrasive and controversial sports reporter, was born in Winston-Salem, N.C.; with ABC television network (1956-85).

1934 Gloria Steinem, feminist leader and editor, was born in Toledo; co-founder, editor, *Ms* magazine (1972); co-founder, Women's Political Caucus.

1947 An explosion in a Centralia, Ill. coal mine killed 111 miners.

1982 Wayne Gretzky of Edmonton, Canada, became the first National Hockey League player to surpass 200 points in one season; he later became the first unanimous choice for most valuable player of the year.

1988 Catholic bishops refused to set aside the controversial policy statement on AIDS; voted to hold broad discussions of the subject in June.

MARCH 26

1740 Jonathan Trumbull, legislator and public official, was born in Lebanon, Conn., son of Jonathan Trumbull (10/12/1710); first Comptroller of the Treasury (1778-80); represented Connecticut in the House (1789-95), serving as Speaker (1791-93), and in the Senate (1795-96); governor of Connecticut (1797-1809) (died 1809).

1749 William Blount, legislator, was born in Edgecombe County, N.C.; member of Continental Congress; represented Tennessee as its first Senator (1796-97), expelled (July 8, 1797) on charge of plotting to aid British to get control of Spanish Florida and Louisiana (died 1800).

1753 Benjamin Thompson, engineer, was born in Woburn, Mass.; introduced improvements in home heating, cooking, lighting; a Loyalist in the Revolution, he went to England, became Count Rumford (died 1814).

1773 Nathaniel Bowditch, mathematician and navigator, was born in Salem, Mass.; wrote the seaman's "bible"—*New American Practical Navigator* (died 1838).

1784 John W. Taylor, legislator, was born in Charlton, N.Y.; represented New York in the House (1813-33), serving as Speaker (1820-21, 1825-27) (died 1854).

1788 Slave trade was forbidden in Massachusetts.

1789 William C. Redfield, businessman and meteorologist, was born in Middletown, Conn.; saddler and harness maker and railway developer; made study of gales and hurricanes; a founder, first president (1848), American Association for the Advancement of Science (died 1857).

1804 District of Orleans was created; became Territory in 1805 and State of Louisiana in 1812.

1814 A court martial sentenced Brig. Gen. William Hull to death for surrendering Detroit to the British without resistance; sentence remitted because of his Revolutionary War record.

1820 Geroge H. Williams, legislator and jurist, was born in New Lebanon, N.Y.; a framer of Oregon's constitution, one of its first Senators (1865-71); Attorney General (1871-75); nominated for Supreme Court chief justice but rejected by Senate because of apparent involvement in an Oregon vote fraud (died 1910).

1850 Edward Bellamy, author, was born in Chicopee Falls, Mass.; founder of movement to nationalize industry; author of utopian romance, *Looking Backward 2000-1887* (died 1898).

1863 Amended West Virginia constitution was ratified by popular vote; provided for gradual emancipation of slaves.

1874 Robert L. Frost, poet, was born in San Francisco; noted for New England poems (*North of Boston, A Further Range, A Witness Tree*) (died 1963).

1874 Condé Nast, publisher, was born in New York City; publisher of magazines (*Vanity Fair, House and Garden, Vogue*) (died 1942).

1878 William P. Hobby, Texas governor (1917-20), was born in Moscow, Tex.; lieutenant governor (1915-17); owner/publisher, *Houston Post* (1924-64) (died 1964).

1879 Othmar H. Ammann, bridge designer, was born in Schaffhausen, Switzerland; among his bridge designs were the George Washington and Verrazano, New York City; Golden Gate, San Francisco (died 1965).

1880 Duncan Hines, food critic and writer, was born in Bowling Green, Ky.; among his works was *Adventures in Good Eating* (died 1959).

1893 James Bryant Conant, chemist and educator, was born in Dorchester, Mass.; president, Harvard (1933-53); high commissioner; later ambassador, to West Germany (1953-57) (died 1978).

1905 Maurice Barrymore, noted actor, died at 58; starred with Modjeska, Lillie Langtry, Mrs. Minnie Maddern Fiske.

1911 Tennessee (Thomas L.) Williams, playwright, was born in Columbus, Miss.; wrote many hit plays (*The Glass Menagerie, Cat on a Hot Tin Roof, Streetcar Named Desire, Night of the Iguana, Sweet Bird of Youth*) (died 1983).

1914 William C. Westmoreland, Army general, was born in Spartanburg County, S.C.; commanding general, Vietnam (1964-68), Army chief of staff (1868-72).

1916 Christian B. Anfinsen, biochemist, was born in Monessen, Pa.; shared 1972 Nobel Chemistry Prize for pioneering studies in enzymes.

1917 Texas gave women the right to vote in primary elections.

1918 An Allied conference named French General Ferdinand Foch as the supreme commander of Allied forces.

1930 Sandra Day O'Connor, jurist, was born in El Paso, Tex.; first woman to be named to the U.S. Supreme Court.

1944 Diana Ross, singer and screen actress, was born in Detroit; sang with The Supremes; screen actress (*Lady Sings the Blues*).

1961 President Kennedy conferred with British Prime Minister Harold Macmillan at Key West, Fla. about the Laos crisis.

1962 Supreme Court backed the one-man, one-vote apportionment of seats in state legislatures in the case of *Baker v. Carr*.

1972 SALT I (Strategic Arms Limitation Talks) agreement was signed in Moscow by American and Soviet representatives.

1979 Egyptian President Anwar Sadat and Israeli Prime Minister Menachem Begin signed a peace treaty on the White House lawn after the historic Camp David accord which was managed by President Carter.

1988 Donald J. Trump bought New York City's Plaza Hotel for $390 million, saying he planned to convert it to "the most luxurious hotel in the world."

MARCH 27

1797 John D. Fisher, physician, was born in Needham, Mass.; launched American movement for educating the blind, responsible for establishng the Perkins Institution and Massachusetts School for the Blind (1829) (died 1850).

1813 Nathaniel Currier, of Currier & Ives fame, was born in Roxbury, Mass.; founded firm in 1835, joined by Ives in 1857 (died 1888).

1814 The most important engagement of the Creek War occurred at Horseshoe Bend, Ala.; Andrew Jackson's victory there was a major step in his military career.

1840 George F. Baker, banker, was born in Troy, N.Y.; a founder (1863), First National City Bank, New York City, chief operating officer (1865-77), president (1877-1909), board chairman (1909-31); benefactor, Harvard School of Business Administration (died 1931).

1844 Adolphus W. Greely, Army officer and explorer, was born in Newburyport, Mass.; chief, Army Signal Service (1887-1907); in charge of establishing (1881) a chain of circumpolar stations and San Francisco earthquake relief (died 1935).

1848 Frederick C. Beach, editor, was born in Brooklyn, son of Alfred E. Beach (9/1/1826); founder, editor, *American Photography*; editor-in-chief, Encyclopedia Americana (1902-81) (died 1918).

1861 Benjamin Purnell, organizer, was born in Mayville, Ky.; organized (c 1903), headed, communistic religious colony, House of David, at Benton Harbor, Mich. (died 1927).

1865 Gen. Philip Sheridan and 10,000 cavalrymen arrived before besieged Petersburg, Va. after successful raid throughout the Shenandoah Valley.

1865 William S. Graves, World War I general, was born in Mount Calm, Tex.; commanded American expeditionary force to Siberia (1918-20) (died 1940).

1866 A civil rights bill was vetoed by president Andrew Johnson because it conferred citizenship on blacks when 11 of 36 states were not represented in the legislation; act passed over his veto Apr 9.

1879 Edward Steichen, photographer, was born in Luxembourg; pioneer in photography as an art form (died 1973).

1879 Miller Huggins, baseball manager, was born in Cincinnati; with New York Yankees (1918-29); named to Baseball Hall of Fame (died 1929).

1886 Ludwig Mies van der Rohe, architect, was born in Aachen, Germany; developed first glass and steel skyscraper; head, Illinois Institute Architecture School (1938-58); also designed chairs (died 1969).

1892 Ferde Grofé, composer and arranger, was born in New York City; best known for his *Mississippi Suite* and *Grand Canyon Suite* (died 1972).

1896 William Lescaze, architect, was born in Geneva; designed various office buildings in New York City, Philadelphia; Swiss Embassy in Washington, D.C. (died 1969).

1899 Gloria Swanson, screen actress, was born in Chicago; many starring roles (*Sadie Thompson, Sunset Boulevard*) (died 1983).

1905 Hal (James Harold) Kemp, bandleader of 1930s, was born in Marion, Ala. (died 1940).

1910 John R. Pierce, engineer, was born in Des Moines, Ia.; with Bell Laboratories, considered the father of the communications satellite.

1912 The wife of President Taft and Viscountess Chinda, wife of the Japanese ambassador, planted the first of 3000 cherry trees at the Tidal Basin in Washington, D.C., inaugurating the annual cherry blossom festival; trees given by city of Tokyo.

1914 Budd Schulberg, author and film producer; was born in New York City; author (*What Makes Sammy Run?, The Disenchanted*).

1917 Cyrus R. Vance, public official, was born in Clarksburg, W.Va.; Army Secretary (1962-64), Deputy Secretary of Defense (1964-67), Secretary of State (1977-80).

1924 Sarah Vaughan, singer, was born in Newark; vocalist with Earl "Fathah" Hines and Billy Eckstine bands.

1939 Cale(b) Yarborough, a winning stock car race driver, was born in Timmonsville, S.C.; grand national NASCAR (National Association for Stock Car Auto Racing) champion (1976-78); won the Daytona and Southern 500s each four times.

1952 President and Mrs. Truman moved from Blair House back to the White House, which had been undergoing extensive renovation since Nov 1948.

1964 The Good Friday earthquake 80 miles east of Anchorage, Alaska killed 131 persons and did $500-$700 million damage.

1986 The Augustine Volcano in Cook Inlet, Alaska began erupting for the first time in ten years.

MARCH 28

1638 Willem Kieft, new governor of New Netherlands colony, arrived in New Amsterdam; recalled after launching a war against the Indians; died in shipwreck on the way to the Netherlands.

1652 Samuel Sewall, jurist, was born in Bishopstoke, England; presided at the Salem witchcraft trials, condemning 19 persons to death; later (1697) confessed the error of his decisions; justice, Massachusetts Superior Court (1692-1728), chief justice (1718-28) (died 1730).

1674 William Byrd II, colonial leader, was born in Westover, Va.; a member of the Virginia council of state (1709-44), president (1743-44); known for his diaries (died 1744).

1706 Andrew Oliver, colonial official, was born in Boston; secretary of Massachusetts Bay Company (1756-71); appointed stamp officer after Stamp Act passed (1765), lieutenant governor (1771-74), unpopular in both posts (died 1774).

1811 John N. Neumann, Catholic prelate and saint, was born in Prahatice, Bohemia; bishop of Philadelphia (1852-60), built schools and seminaries, helped establish Sisters of Notre Dame (1877) and Sisters of the Third Order of St. Francis (1855); beatified 1963, canonized 1977, the first American prelate so honored (died 1860).

1814 USS *Essex* was captured by British ships in Valparaiso, Chile port.

1818 Wade Hampton, Confederate general, was born in Charleston; cavalry commander, associated with Jeb Stuart; served South Carolina as governor (1877-79) and represented it in the Senate (1879-81) (died 1902).

1834 Senate censured President Jackson for removing federal funds from Second Bank of the United States; censure expunged from record Jan 16, 1837.

1836 Roger B. Taney of Maryland became chief justice of the Supreme Court, succeeding John Marshall; served until 1864.

1845 Mexico broke off relations with the United States over Texas annexation.

1878 Arthur B. Spingarn, civil rights leader, was born in New York City; brother of Joel E. Spingarn (5/17/1875); president, NAACP (1940-65) (died 1971).

1878 Herbert H. Lehman, banker and public official, was born in New York City; served New York as governor (1932-42), represented it in the Senate (1949-56); headed UNRRA (United Nations Relief and Rehabilitation Administration) (1942-46) (died 1963).

1890 State College of Washington was founded in Pullman.

1891 Paul Whiteman, orchestra leader known as the "King of Jazz," was born in Denver (died 1967).

1893 Spyros P. Skouras, movies executive, was born in Skourchourian, Greece; founder, 20th Century Fox (1935), president (1942-62) (died 1971).

1895 Christian A. Herter, Secretary of State (1959-61), was born in Paris of American parents (died 1966).

1897 Frank M. Hawks, aviator, was born in Marshalltown, Ia.; pioneer flyer, set transcontinental speed records (1930) and nonstop transcontinental record of 13 hours, 27 minutes, 15 seconds (1933) (died 1938).

1903 Rudolf Serkin, pianist, was born in Eger, Austria; concert pianist of world renown; with Curtis Institute of Music, Philadelphia.

1905 Marlin Perkins, zoo director, was born in Carthage, Mo.; headed zoos in Buffalo, Chicago, St. Louis; best known for television show, *The Wild Kingdom* (died 1986).

1908 An explosion and cave-in at the Union Pacific Coal Co. mine at Hanna, Wyo. killed more than 60 persons.

1914 Edmund S. Muskie, legislator, was born in Rumford, Me.; served Maine as governor (1955-59) and represented it in the Senate (1959-79); Secretary of State (1980).

1924 President Coolidge asked for the resignation of Attorney General Harry Daugherty for his role in the Teapot Dome scandal; Daugherty was charged with malfeasance, acquitted.

1969 Former President Eisenhower died in Washington, D.C. at 78.

1979 A major nuclear accident occurred near Harrisburg, Pa., when the cooling system of the No. 2 reactor at the Three Mile Island nuclear power plant malfunctioned; no deaths or injuries occurred.

1989 The New York Supreme Court ruled that the America's Cup, yachting's major prize, belonged to New Zealand, disqualifying the American boat, *Stars and Stripes*, for violating the spirit of the race; the ruling will be appealed.

MARCH 29

1630 Puritans sailed from Southampton for New England in 11 ships.

1638 Ft. Christina (now Wilmington) was established by Peter Minuit and Swedish settlers in what became the first permanent white settlement in Delaware.

1790 John Tyler, 10th president (1841-45), was born in Charles City County, Va.; represented Virginia in the House (1817-21) and Senate (1827-36) and served as governor (1825-27); elected vice president and became the first to succeed to the presidency on the death of the president (W.H. Harrison) (died 1862).

1799 New York legislature enacted a law providing a gradual freeing of slaves.

1812 The first wedding was held in the White House when Mrs. Lucy Payne Washington, widowed sister of First Lady Dolley Madison, married Supreme Court Justice Thomas Todd.

1813 John Tyler and Letitia Christian were married in New Kent County, Va.; Mrs. Tyler died during his presidency.

1819 Isaac M. Wise, Jewish leader, was born in Steingrub, Bohemia; a founder of American Reformed Judaism; a founder, president, Hebrew Union College, Cincinnati (1875-1900) (died 1900).

1819 Former President Jefferson was named rector of the U. of Virginia.

1821 Frank Leslie, publisher, was born in Ipswich, England; published several magazines, including *Popular Monthly*, which became *The American Magazine* (died 1880).

1823 Leopold Eidlitz, architect, was born in Prague; led a Gothic revival, building many American homes and churches; redesigned state capitol in Albany (died 1908).

1847 Gen. Winfield Scott, with 12,000 soldiers and marines, occupied Veracruz, Mexico.

1853 Elihu Thomson, electrical engineer and inventor, was born in Manchester, England; received more than 700 patents for electrical inventions (three-phase AC generator, street arc lamp); co-founder of Thomson-Houston Co., which merged with Edison General Electric to form General Electric (1892) (died 1937).

1859 Oscar F. Mayer, meat packer, was born in Kaisinger, Germany; developed small Chicago meat market into Oscar Mayer & Co. (1888), president, board chairman (1919-55) (died 1955).

1865 Gen. U.S. Grant began Appomattox campaign.

1867 Cy (Denton T.) Young, baseball player, was born in Gilmore, Ohio; pitched in 906 games, completing 751 and winning an all-time high 511; named to Baseball Hall of Fame (died 1955).

1869 Ales Hrdlicka, anthropologist, was born in Humpolec, Czechoslovakia; helped establish American physical anthropology (died 1943).

1874 Lou Henry Hoover, wife of President Hoover, was born in Waterloo, Ia. (died 1944).

1878 Albert Von Tilzer, composer, was born in Detroit, brother of Harry Von Tilzer (7/8/1872); wrote numerous hits ("Take Me Out to the Ball Game," "Put Your Arms Around Me," "Apple Blossom Time") (died 1956).

1881 Raymond M. Hood, architect, was born in Pawtucket, R.I.; designed part of Rockefeller Center and New York Daily News and Chicago Tribune buildings (died 1934).

1889 Howard Lindsay, actor and playwright, was born in Waterford, N.Y.; played Father in *Life with Father*, which he co-authored with Russel Crouse, and other plays (*State of the Union, Anything Goes, Call Me Madam*) (died 1968).

1894 George W. Merck, chemist, was born in New York City; headed pharmaceutical company (1925-50) producing streptomycin, vitamins (died 1957).

1916 Eugene J. McCarthy, legislator, was born in Watkins, Minn.; represented Minnesota in the House (1945-59) and Senate (1959-71); independent presidential candidate (1976).

1918 Pearl Bailey, singer and actress, was born in Newport News, Va.; starred in *Hello Dolly*, several movies (*Porgy and Bess*).

1937 The Supreme Court upheld the constitutionality of a minimum wage law (Washington State) and the right of collective bargaining on the railroads.

1951 Julius Rosenberg, his wife Ethel, and Morton Sobell were found guilty of conspiracy to commit wartime espionage; Rosenbergs were executed June 19, 1953; Sobell was sentenced to 30 years.

1961 The 23rd Amendment went into effect, giving voters of Washington, D.C. the right to vote in presidential elections.

1988 A new American-Japanese agreement allows American construction companies to work with Japanese contractors in building large public works projects in Japan.

1988 The No. 2 Justice Department official, Deputy Attorney General Arnold I. Burns, and five other officials resigned because of concern over Attorney General Edwin Meese's legal problems and his leadership.

MARCH 30

1624 About 30 families, mostly Walloons, sailed from Amsterdam under the leadership of Cornelis Jacobsen May, who was the colony's first director; on arrival in New York Bay, several families were left on Governor's Island, several went to what is now Gloucester, N.J., the rest went to Ft. Nassau (present-day Albany).

1691 An assembly of New York communities was called, a date which marks the beginning of representative government in New York.

1775 Great Britain enacted the New England Restraining Act, which forbade Massachusetts from trading with any nation but Britian and the British West Indies; later widened to other colonies.

1814 A new American attack on Montreal was repulsed; Gen. James Wilkinson retreated to Plattsburgh, N.Y. and was relieved of his command.

1822 President Monroe signed an act creating the Territory of Florida.

1842 The first anesthesia was used in an American operation by Dr. Crawford W. Long; used sulphuric ether on a patient in Jefferson, Ga. to remove a tumor from the back of his neck.

1853 Abigail P. Fillmore, first wife of President Fillmore, died in Washington at 55, about three weeks after the presidential term ended.

1858 DeWolf Hopper, actor, was born in New York City; starred in many light operas, best remembered for his recital of *Casey at the Bat* (died 1935).

1865 Union troops won a decisive victory in three days of fighting at Five Forks, Va.

1867 The Alaska purchase from Russia for $7.2 million was signed by President Andrew Johnson; sale became final June 20.

1868 The trial of President Andrew Johnson began before the Senate with a speech by Benjamin F. Butler for the prosecution.

1870 The 15th Amendment, declaring that race is no bar to voting, became effective.

1870 Congress re-admitted Texas to the Union.

1876 Clifford W. Beers, public health pioneer, was born in New Haven; hospitalized with a mental breakdown, he studied his recovery; a founder, Connecticut Society for Mental Hygiene (1908), first group of its kind; the national (1928), international (1931) mental hygiene organizations (died 1943).

1880 Metropolitan Museum of Art in New York City opened.

1881 Boston Symphony Orchestra was founded, with George Henschel as the first conductor; principal backer was Henry L. Higginson (11/18/1834).

1883 Jo Davidson, sculptor and painter, was born in New York City; sculpted many famous persons (Wilson, Clemenceau, Anatole France, Marshal Foch) (died 1952).

1888 James R. Williams, cartoonist, was born in Halifax, Nova Scotia; noted for syndicated cartoon, *Out Our Way* (died 1957).

1891 Arthur W.S. Herrington, engineer, was born in England; developed military vehicles, including the World War II jeep (died 1970).

1893 Thomas F. Bayard, Delaware public official, was named the first American ambassador assigned to Great Britain.

1913 Frankie Laine, popular singer, was born in Chicago; remembered for "The Wild Goose," and "Mule Train."

1919 McGeorge Bundy, public official, was born in Boston; special presidential assistant involved in Cuban missile crisis and Vietnam policies; president, Ford Foundation (1966-79).

1938 Warren Beatty, screen actor, was born in Richmond, Va., brother of Shirley MacLaine (4/24/1934); starred in several films (*Bonnie and Clyde, Shampoo, Reds*, which he also directed).

1940 Jerry Lucas, basketball player (Ohio State, San Francisco, New York Knicks), was born in Middletown, Ohio.

1972 Gabriel Heatter, radio commentator, died at 82; national newscaster whose opening words: "Ah, there's good news tonight" became a catch phrase.

1981 The assassination of President Reagan was attempted in Washington, D.C.; he suffered a chest wound; Press Secretary James S. Brady and two others were wounded; 25-year-old John W. Hinckley was charged with the attempt.

MARCH 31

1774 British Parliament passed the Boston Port Act, effective June 1; designed to punish city for the Tea Party by closing the port until East India Co. was paid for its loss; seat of government was moved to Salem, Mass.

1808 James P. Henderson, Texas pioneer, was born in Lincolnton, N.C.; first governor of Texas (1846-48), represented it in the Senate (1857-58) (died 1858).

1810 James Alden, Union naval officer, was born in Portland, Me.; commanded the *Brooklyn* at Mobile Bay; was target of Farragut's classic order, "Damn the torpedoes! Go ahead!" (died 1877).

1817 New York adopted a law prohibiting slavery, effective in 1827.

1833 Treasury Building in Washington, D.C. and many records were destroyed by fire.

1835 John LaFarge, church muralist, was born in New York City; developed opalescent glass for church use; did murals in various New York City churches (died 1910).

1840 President Van Buren issued an executive order setting a ten-hour day for government employees without a reduction in pay.

1850 Charles D. Walcott, geologist, was born in New York Mills, N.Y.; director, Geological Survey (1894-1907); secretary, Smithsonian Institution (1907-27) (died 1927).

1850 Former Vice President John C. Calhoun (1825-32) died in Washington, D.C. at 68.

1854 Commodore Matthew C. Perry negotiated a treaty opening Japanese ports to American commerce.

1862 Claude A. Swanson, Navy Secretary (1933-39), was born in Swansonville, Va.; represented Virginia in the House (1893-1906) and Senate (1910-33) and served as governor (1906-10) (died 1939).

1863 Caleb H. Baumes, lawyer and political leader, was born in Bethlehem, N.Y.; New York state legislator who wrote statute calling for life imprisonment on fourth felony conviction (died 1927).

1870 James M. Cox, newspaper publisher (Springfield, Dayton), was born in Jacksonville, Ohio; represented Ohio in the House (1909-13) and served as governor (1913-15, 1917-21); Democratic presidential candidate (1920) (died 1957).

1882 President Arthur signed an act providing a $5000 annual pension to widows of presidents; the first eligibles were the wives of Presidents Polk, Tyler, and Garfield.

1895 Vardis Fisher, author, was born in Annis, Ida.; known for novels about Mormon life (died 1968).

1895 John J. McCloy, banker and diplomat, was born in Philadelphia; president, World Bank (1947-49); first American high commissioner of Western Germany (1949-52); board chairman, Chase Manhattan Bank (from 1953) (died 1989).

1917 General Munitions Board was created by the Council of National Defense, effective Apr 9, with Frank A. Scott chairman.

1917 United States took formal possession of the Danish West Indies (Virgin Islands).

1918 Daylight saving time went into effect.

1931 Knute Rockne, Notre Dame football coach, died in a plane crash.

1933 Civilian Conservation Corps (CCC) was created to promote 250,000 jobs for unemployed males (18-25) in reforestation, road construction, erosion control, park and flood control projects; paid $30 a week, of which $25 was sent home to their families.

1934 The Philippine Independence Act was signed, providing for independence in 1944, after formation of a transitional government with a Filipino head.

1935 Herb Alpert, trumpeter and orchestra leader, was born in Los Angeles; founder, leader of Tijuana Brass.

1935 Richard Chamberlain, screen and television actor, was born in Beverly Hills, Cal.; best known for various television roles (*Dr. Kildare, Shogun, Thorn Birds*).

1968 President Lyndon Johnson announced he would not seek re-election.

1972 Representatives of the Major Leagues Baseball Players Association voted to strike over a pension dispute; this, the first strike, lasted 13 days.

1988 The Senate approved a $47.9 million Contra aid package a day after House approval for food, clothing, medicine, and housing assistance.

APRIL 1

1742 Samuel Bard, physician, was born in Philadelphia, son of John Bard (2/1/1716); physician to George Washington after the Revolution; a founder, medical school at King's (later Columbia) College; led in founding New York Hospital; author of book on midwifery (died 1821).

1764 Henry Ware, divinity professor, was born in Sherborn, Mass.; from his courses at Harvard, the Divinity School was organized (1816) (died 1845).

1789 House of Representatives was organized; elected Frederick A.C. Muhlenberg of Pennsylvania as the first Speaker; began sessions Apr 8.

1811 James McCosh, educator and philosopher, was born in Ayrshire, Scotland; president, Princeton U. (1868-88) (died 1894).

1823 Simon B.Buckner; Confederate general, was born in Hart County, Ky.; served in Mexican War; surrendered to Grant at Ft. Donelson (1862); served Kentucky as governor (1887-91) (died 1914).

1827 Thomas S. Hall, inventor, was born in Upper Bartlett, N.H.; invented electric automatic signal devices for railroad and highway uses (died 1880).

1834 James Fisk, financier, was born in Bennington, Vt.; epitome of the "robber baron;" called the Barnum of Wall St.; helped raise price of gold, reaping a fortune but causing a depression (died 1872).

1852 Edwin A. Abbey, painter and illustrator, was born in Philadelphia; illustrated numerous books; did murals for Boston Public Library, Pennsylvania State Capitol (died 1911).

1865 Gen. Robert E. Lee led the last assault of Civil War, trying unsuccessfully against the Union left flank at Five Forks, near Petersburg, Va.

1883 Lon Chaney, screen actor, was born in Colorado Springs, Colo; called "the man of a thousand faces," starred in *The Hunchback of Notre Dame* and *The Phantom of the Opera* (died 1930).

1884 Laurette Taylor, screen actress, was born in New York City; numerous starring roles (*Peg o'My Heart, The Old Lady Shows Her Medals*, various Shakespeare plays) (died 1946).

1885 Eli Lilly, drug manufacturer, was born in Indianapolis, Ind.; headed family pharmaceutical firm (1932-66) (died 1977).

1886 Wallace Beery, screen actor, was born in Kansas City, Mo.; starred in many films (*The Champ, Min and Bill, Dinner at Eight*) (died 1949).

1888 Clarence D. Batchelor, editorial cartoonist, was born in Osage City, Kan.; with the *New York Daily News* (1930-69) (died 1977).

1900 William Benton, advertising agency head and public official, was born in Minneapolis, Minn.; co-founder, Benton & Bowles; founded Chicago Round Table and published Encyclopedia Brittanica as Chicago U. vice president (1937-45); organized Voice of America as Assistant Secretary of State (1945-47); represented Connecticut in the Senate (1949-52) (died 1973).

1908 Abraham Maslow, humanistic psychologist, was born in New York City; altered ways of thinking about human needs, motivations, neurosis and health (died 1970).

1917 Armed American steamer, *Aztec*, torpedoed off French coast with loss of 28 lives.

1920 The 14th Census reported a population of 105,710,620, excluding outlying possessions; population center was 8.3 miles southeast of Spencer, Ind.

1922 William Manchester, author, was born in Attleboro, Mass.; wrote several best sellers (*Portrait of a President, Death of a President, American Caesar*).

1922 Wage reductions led to strike of 500,000 coal miners; ended in September with union concessions.

1930 The 15th Census showed a population rise of 17,064,426 in ten years to a total of 122,775,046.

1932 Debbie Reynolds, screen actress, was born in El Paso; starred in several films (*The Unsinkable Molly Brown, Singin' in the Rain*).

1939 An embargo on the sale of arms and ammunition to Spain was lifted and the United States recognized the Franco regime.

1939 Phil(ip H.) Niekro, baseball pitcher (Braves, Yankees) who won more than 300 games, was born in Blaine, Ohio

1943 The rationing of meat, fats, and cheese began.

1945 The Marines invaded Okinawa, gained complete control by June.

1946 Strike of 400,000 bituminous coal miners began.

1948 Soviet Russia set up a land blockade of Allied sectors of Berlin; British and American planes airlifted 2.3 million tons of food and coal into city; blockade lifted Sept 30, 1949.

1953 President Eisenhower signed an act creating the Department of Health, Education and Welfare; nominated (Apr 11) Oveta Culp Hobby as Secretary.

1954 The Air Force Academy was created.

1960 The first weather satellite, *Tiros I*, was launched.

1965 Helena Rubinstein, Polish-born beauty expert and cosmetics manufacturer, died at 94.

1986 Supreme Court ruled 6-3 that police could not interrogate a defendant at his arraignment without his lawyer present, once the defendant had requested an attorney.

1988 A 60-day cease fire began in the Nicaraguan fighting.

1988 The Campeau Corp. of Canada won the right to take over Federated Stores for $6.6 billion.

APRIL 2

1513 Ponce de Leon anchored off the coast of Florida, which he named; the landfall probably was near present St. Augustine.

1683 The Great Charter and Frame of Government for the province of Pennsylvania was issued; province was taken from William Penn (1692) when he fell into disfavor, returned in 1694; new frame of government drafted and adopted in 1699.

1689 Arthur Dobbs, colonial governor, was born in County Antrim, Ireland; purchased a 400,000 acre estate in North Carolina (1745), named governor (1754-62) (died 1765).

1720 Joseph Dudley, colonial official, died at 73; served as governor of Massachusetts Bay Colony (1702-15).

1775 Boonesboro, on the south side of the Kentucky River in what is now Madison County, was founded by Daniel Boone.

1787 Thomas Gage, British general and colonial administrator, died at 66; served with Braddock and in conquest of Canada; headed British troops in colonies (1763-73); last royal governor of Massachusetts (1774-75), precipitated American Revolution.

1792 Mint of the United States was established; replaced (2/12/1873) by Bureau of the Mint.

1811 James Monroe was named Secretary of State, took office Apr 6.

1814 Erastus B. Bigelow, inventor, was born in West Boylston, Mass.; invented a loom for making lace, figured fabrics, carpets (1851); founded, Bigelow carpet mill (about 1850); a founder of MIT (1861) (died 1879).

1833 Thomas H. Ruger, Union general, was born in Lima, N.Y.; saw action at Gettysburg, suppressed draft riots in New York City (1863), served in Tennessee and North Carolina campaigns (died 1907).

1844 George H. Putnam, publisher, was born in London, son of George P. Putnam (2/7/1814); president, George P. Putnam & Sons (1872-1930) (died 1930).

1850 James L. Laughlin, economist, was born in Deersfield, Ohio; helped set up Federal Reserve Bank system (died 1933).

1862 William B. Wilson, labor leader, was born in Blantyre, Scotland; a founder (1890), secretary-treasurer (1900-08), United Mine Workers; first Secretary of Labor (1913-21); represented Pennsylvania in the House (1907-13) (died 1934).

1862 Nicholas Murray Butler; educator, was born in Elizabeth, N.J.; a founder, first president, New York Teachers College (later Columbia Teachers); president, Columbia U. (1902-45); president, Carnegie Endowment for International Peace (1925-45); shared 1931 Nobel Peace Prize; Republican vice presidential candidate (1912) (died 1947).

1865 Both Richmond and Petersburg, Va. were evacuated by Confederate troops, following battle before Petersburg in which Gen. A.P. Hill of the Confederacy was killed.

1866 President Andrew Johnson issued a proclamation of peace ending "insurrection."

1866 Francis Hodur, religious leader, was born in Zarki, Poland; founder (1897), prime bishop (1907-53), Polish National Church of America (died 1953).

1869 Clifford K. Berryman, editorial cartoonist, was born near Versailles, Ky.; originated the "Teddy Bear" in cartoons of President Theodore Roosevelt; with *Washington Post* (1896-1907), *Washington Star* (1907-49) (died 1949).

1873 Sergei Rachmaninoff, composer, pianist, and conductor, was born near Novgorod, Russia; gave concerts throughout world; composed many piano concertos, short operas (*Francesca da Rimini*), symphonies, cantatas (*The Bells*) (died 1943).

1875 Walter P. Chrysler, auto manufacturer, was born in Wamego, Kan.; president, Buick Motors (1916-20); reorganized Willys Overland and Maxwell into the Chrysler Corp. (1924), board chairman (1924-25) (died 1940).

1907 Luke (Lucius B.) Appling, baseball player (White Sox 1930-50), was born in High Point, N.C.; lifetime batting average of .310; named to Baseball Hall of Fame.

1908 Buddy (Christian R.) Ebsen, stage, screen, and television actor, was born in Belleville, Ill.; best remembered for television roles (*Beverly Hillbillies, Barnaby Jones*).

1914 Assemblies of God, one of the largest Pentecostal churches, was organized in a 10-day convention in Hot Springs, Ark.

1917 President Wilson, addressing a joint session of Congress, called for a declaration of war against Germany (which was done Apr 4); termed German submarine warfare as "warfare against mankind," said the United States was joining the fight for ultimate world peace and "the world must be made safe for democracy."

1927 President Coolidge issued an executive order returning the naval oil reserves to the Navy Department from the Interior Department, where they had been since 1921.

1945 Don Sutton, baseball player (with various teams), was born in Clio, Ala.; in June 1986 became one of the few pitchers to have 300 or more victories.

1958 President Eisenhower, in a special message to Congress, called for the creation of NASA (National Aeronautics & Space Administration).

1980 President Carter signed the Crude Oil Windfall Profit Tax, believed to be the largest single tax ever imposed on an industry; expected to bring in about $227 billion in ten years.

APRIL 3

1737 Arthur St. Clair, Revolutionary general, was born in Thurso, Scotland; took part in battles of Trenton, Princeton; a member of the Continental Congress (1785-87), president (1787); governor of the Northwest Territory (1787-1802) (died 1818).

1753 Simon Willard, clockmaker, was born in Grafton, Mass.; specialized in church, hall, and gallery clocks; developed the "banjo" clock (died 1848).

1755 Simon Kenton, frontiersman, was born in Fauquier County, Va.; served as a scout in Kentucky, Northwest Territory; associated with Daniel Boone (died 1836).

1782 Alexander Macomb, War of 1812 general, was born in Detroit; defended Plattsburgh against British (1814); commanding general, U.S. Army (1828-41) (died 1841).

1783 Washington Irving, author, was born in New York City; wrote several classic short stories ("Rip Van Winkle," "Legend of Sleepy Hollow"); first American writer to be admired abroad; minister to Spain (1842-46) (died 1859).

1798 Charles Wilkes, Navy officer, was born in New York City; commanded exploration of Antarctic islands (1838-42); Wilkes Land in Antarctica named for him (died 1877).

1814 Lorenzo Snow, church leader, was born in Mantua, Ohio; president, Mormon Church (1898-1901); after passage of Edmunds (Anti-Polygamy) Act, he was convicted, imprisoned (1886); decision reversed by Supreme Court (1887) (died 1901).

1822 Edward Everett Hale, Unitarian clergyman and author, was born in Boston, nephew of Edward Everett (4/11/1794); pastor, South Congregational Church, Boston (1856-1901); remembered for short story, "The Man Without a Country" (died 1909).

1822 Henry M. Field, clergyman and editor, was born in Stockbridge, Mass.; held pastorates in St. Louis and Springfield, Mass.; editor, *The Evangelist* (1854-90) (died 1907).

1823 William M. Tweed, political boss, was born in New York City; controlled Tammany, New York politics; he and his ring swindled New York City treasury out of about $30 million; drive for his ouster led by *Harper's Weekly, New York Times*, and Samuel J. Tilden; Tweed was convicted, imprisoned (1873) (died 1878).

1837 John Burroughs, naturalist and author, was born in Roxbury, N.Y.; developed nature essay into literary form (died 1921).

1848 Chicago Board of Trade was organized; incorporated by special act of the Illinois legislature Feb 18, 1959.

1859 Reginald DeKoven, composer, was born in Middletown, Conn.; composed light operas (*Robin Hood, Rob Roy*); also the classic, *Oh, Promise Me* (died 1920).

1860 The first pony express between St. Joseph, Mo. and Sacramento, Cal. began; ended Oct 24, 1861 with the completion of the first transcontinental telegraph line.

1870 Sara A.M. Conboy, labor leader, was born in Boston; first woman elected to a national labor post (secretary-treasurer, United Textile Workers (1915-28) (died 1928).

1882 Jesse James, notorious bandit and outlaw, was shot and killed by two members of his band at St. Joseph, Mo.

1884 Bud (Harry C.) Fisher, cartoonist, was born in Chicago; created first widely-syndicated comic strip, *Mutt and Jeff* (1908) (died 1954).

1888 Thomas C. Kinkaid, World War II admiral, was born in Hanover, N.H.; commander, 7th Fleet (1943-45), supported MacArthur invasion (died 1972).

1888 John H. Hammond, engineer and inventor, was born in San Francisco; invented radio-controlled torpedo for coastal defense, system of selective radio telegraphy carrying eight simultaneous messages on one carrier wave (died 1965).

1893 Leslie Howard, stage and screen actor, was born in London; numerous hit plays (*Petrified Forest, Berkeley Square*), movies (*Petrified Forest, Scarlet Pimpernel, Of Human Bondage, Gone With the Wind*) (died 1943).

1898 Henry R. Luce, publisher, was born in Tengchow, China of American parentage; co-founder, *Time* magazine (1923); founder, *Fortune* (1930), *Life* (1936), *Sports Illustrated* (1954) (died 1967).

1898 George Jessel, entertainer, was born in New York City; comedian and toastmaster, known as the toastmaster general of the United States (died 1981).

1924 Marlon Brando, screen actor, was born in Omaha, Neb.; starred in numerous movies (*A Streetcar Named Desire, On the Waterfront, The Godfather, Last Tango in Paris*).

1926 Virgil I. Grissom, astronaut, was born in Mitchell, Ind.; one of the original astronauts, the second to travel in space; killed in capsule fire with two others in 1967.

1935 Robert C. Marshall, a witness at a New York City hearing on relief administration, said he taught workers "boondoggling;" he said "boondoggles" were gadgets or useful articles of scrap material.

1940 Isle Royale (Mich.) National Park was established.

1948 A $6.1 billion foreign aid act under the Economic Cooperation Administration went into effect; Paul G. Hoffman was named administrator.

1972 President Nixon devalued the dollar by 8.57% and raised the price of gold from $35 to $38 an ounce.

1988 First class postage rates increased 3¢ to 25¢ for the first ounce.

APRIL 4

1748 William White, Episcopal prelate, was born in Philadelphia; rector, Christ Church, Philadelphia (1776-1836); led move to Americanize the Anglican Church, by creating the Protestant Episcopal Church of America; first bishop of Pennsylvania (1787), presiding bishop (1795-1836) (died 1836).

1778 William Bard, insurance executive, was born in New York City, son of John Bard (4/1/1742); founder, president, New York Life Insurance & Trust Co. (1830-47), first company to make life insurance its primary business (died 1853).

1782 Sir Guy Carleton was made general-in-chief of British forces in America, commissioned to negotiate peace.

1792 Thaddeus Stevens, legislator, was born in Danville, Vt.; represented Pennsylvania in the House (1849-53, 1859-68), led movement to impeach President Andrew Johnson, managed the trial (died 1868).

1800 The first federal bankrupcy law was enacted, making possible the release of Robert Morris from prison; law repealed Dec 19, 1803.

1802 Dorothea L. Dix, social reformer, was born in Hampden, Me.; improved care of the insane, disturbed; prompted the building of care institutions in the United States and abroad; superintendent of women nurses in Civil War (died 1887).

1809 Benjamin Peirce, mathematician and astronomer, was born in Salem, Mass.; superintendent, U.S. Coast Survey (1867-74), renowned for many astronomical computations; author of mathematical textbooks (died 1880).

1818 The American flag was established as 13 alternate red and white stripes, representing the original states, and one star for each state on a blue field.

1821 Linus Yale, lock manufacturer, was born in Salisbury, N.Y.; cylinder-type lock he developd is basically the lock used today (died 1868).

1841 President William Henry Harrison died of pneumonia at 68, a month after his inauguration, the first president to die in office; had ridden horseback to the Capitol without a hat or coat despite the cold rain, then delivered a speech lasting one hour and 45 minutes (8578 words); Vice President John Tyler became president.

1843 William H. Jackson, pioneer photographer, was born in Keeseville, N.Y.; one of the first to photograph the American West (died 1942).

1850 Los Angeles was incorporated as a city.

1859 "Dixie," written by Daniel Emmett for Bryant's Minstrels, was first sung in Mechanics Hall, New York City.

1861 President Lincoln ordered a supply expedition to Ft. Sumter in Charleston Harbor; notified the South Carolina governor of the expedition.

1863 Samuel S. Childs, restaurateur, was born in Basking Ridge, N.J.; founded nationwide Childs restaurant chain (1888), introduced use of waitresses, calorie counts on menus (died 1925).

1865 Jefferson Davis made final appeal to the Confederacy to continue the war; the appeal was not supported by Gen. Robert E. Lee.

1866 George P. Baker, educator, was born in Providence; drama teacher ("47 Workshop"), Harvard; among his students were Eugene O'Neill, Philip Barry, John Dos Passos, Thomas Wolfe (died 1935).

1870 George A. Smith, religious leader, was born in Salt Lake City; president, Mormon Church (1945-51) (died 1951).

1875 Pierre Monteux, conductor, was born in Paris; led the Boston (1919-24), Paris (1930-38), of which he was also founder, and San Francisco (1934-52) symphonies (died 1964).

1875 Louis K. Liggett, merchant, was born in Detroit; founder, president, United Drug Co.; board chairman, Liggett Drug Co. (died 1946).

1876 Claude W. Kress, merchant, was born in Slatington, Pa.; co-founder with brother, Samuel H. (7/23/1863), of S.H. Kress & Co., dime store chain (died 1940).

1876 The Senate began impeachment hearing of charges against William W. Belknap, accused of selling privileges at Indian trading posts while Secretary of War (1869-76); acquitted Aug 1.

1888 Tris(tram) Speaker, baseball player, was born in Hubbard, Texas; outfielder with Boston Red Sox (1907-15), Cleveland Indians (1916-26); lifetime batting average of .344; named to Baseball Hall of Fame (died 1958).

1896 Robert E. Sherwood, author and playwright, was born in New Rochelle, N.Y.; chief speech writer for President Franklin Roosevelt; author (Roosevelt and Hopkins); plays (*Reunion in Vienna, Petrified Forest, Idiot's Delight, Abe Lincoln in Illinois, There Shall be No Night*) (died 1955).

1917 Declaration of war against Germany was passed by the Senate 82-6 and by the House 373-50.

1924 Gil(bert R.) Hodges, baseball player (Dodgers 1943-61), was born in Princeton, Ind.; named to Baseball Hall of Fame.

1933 American dirigible, *Akron*, broke up in a violent storm off Barnegat Bay, N.J.; 73 died.

1949 The North Atlantic Treaty was signed in Washington by the United States, France, Belgium, Canada, Denmark, Iceland, Italy, Luxembourg, Netherlands, Norway, Portugal, and the United Kingdom; ratified by the Senate July 21.

1951 Gen. Dwight D. Eisenhower established Supreme Headquarters, Allied Powers in Europe (SHAPE) in Paris.

1968 Rev. Martin Luther King Jr., civil rights leader, was assassinated in Memphis by James Earl Ray, who was captured in London Jan 8, 1969; sentenced to 99 years imprisonment.

1969 The world's first totally artificial heart was implanted in a human being in Houston by Dr. Denton A. Cooley; patient died Apr 8.

1975 An Air Force plane carrying Vietnamese children crashed near Saigon killing 172.

1981 The first Mexican-American mayor of an American city, 33-year-old Henry G. Cisneros, was elected in San Antonio, Tex.

1988 Gov. Evan Mecham was convicted 21-9 by the Arizona Senate in the first impeachment trial of a governor in almost 60 years; former Secretary of State Mofford was sworn in as governor to succeed Mecham.

1989 A(ngelo) Bartlett Giamatti, Yale University president (1976-86), was born in Boston; president, National (baseball) League (1986-89), baseball commissioner (1989) (died 1989).

APRIL 5

1621 John A. Carver, colonial leader, died at about 45; arrived on the *Mayflower*, which he chartered; served as first governor of Plymouth (1620-21).

1649 Elihu Yale, philanthropist, was born in Boston; made fortune with East India Co. (1671-99); donated books, goods to Collegiate School, which was moved from Branford, Conn. to New Haven and renamed in his honor (died 1721).

1684 Oloff S. Van Cortlandt, Dutch leader in New Amsterdam, died at 84; burgomaster (1655-60, 1662-63), treated with British on surrender of city (1664); Van Cortlandt Park in New York City named for him.

1726 Benjamin Harrison, colonial leader, was born in Berkeley, Va.; member of Virginia legislature (1749-75), Continental Congress (1774-78); a signer of the Declaration of Independence; governor of Virginia (1782-84) (died 1791).

1764 Britain passed the Sugar Act, modifying the Molasses Act of 1733 by raising the duty on sugar, lowering it on molasses.

1792 President Washington vetoed a bill to apportion representatives according to the first enumeration; this was the first presidential veto.

1793 The District of Columbia commissioners accepted the design of the Capitol by William Thornton; President Washington approved it July 25.

1816 Samuel F. Miller, jurist, was born in Richmond, Ky.; associate justice, Supreme Court (1862-90) (died 1890).

1822 President Monroe appointed Gen. Andrew Jackson military governor of Florida.

1822 Theodore R. Timby, inventor, was born in Dutchess County, N.Y.; invented (1862) revolving turret for gun battery, first featured on the *Monitor*, Union ironclad vessel (died 1909).

1838 Alpheus Hyatt, zoologist and paleontologist, was born in Washington; a leading invertebrate paleontologist, played a major role in establishing Woods Hole (Mass.) Marine Biology Laboratory; a founder, editor, *American Naturalist* (1867-71) (died 1902).

1856 Booker T. Washington, educator, was born a slave in Franklin County, Va.; established, first principal, Tuskegee (Ala.) Institute (1881-1915); at his death, school had 100+ buildings, a faculty of 200, and 1500 students (died 1915).

1858 W. Atlee Burpee, plant seed merchant, was born in Sheffield, Canada; began seed business (1876), developed huge mail order business (died 1915).

1871 Pop (Glenn S.) Warner, football coach (1896-1942), was born in Springville, N.Y.; coached at Cornell, Carlisle, Pittsburgh, Stanford, Temple (died 1954).

1871 Winchell Smith, playwright (*Brewster's Millions, The Fortune Hunter*), was born in Hartford, Conn.; co-author of *Lightnin'* (died 1933).

1872 Samuel C. Prescott, bacteriologist, was born in South Hampton, N.H.; discovered definitive scientific method for making canned food entirely sanitary (died 1962).

1874 Jesse H. Jones, Texas banker and publisher (*Houston Chronicle*), was born in Robertson County, Tenn.; chairman, Reconstruction Finance Corp. (RFC) (1933-39); administrator, Federal Loan Agency (1939-45), Secretary of Commerce (1940-45) (died 1956).

1894 Lawrence D. Bell, aviation pioneer, was born in Mentone, Ind.; founder, president, Bell Aircraft Corp., which produced World War II fighters (P-39); built first commercially-licensed helicopter and the X-1a, first plane to break the sound barrier (died 1956).

1897 President McKinley appointed Theodore Roosevelt as Assistant Secretary of Navy, served until May 6, 1898.

1899 Alfred Blalock, surgeon, was born in Culloden, Ga.; chief surgeon, Johns Hopkins Hospital (1941-63), developed technique for saving "blue babies" (died 1964).

1900 Spencer Tracy, screen actor, was born in Milwaukee; starred in many films (*Captains Courageous, Boys Town, The Old Man and the Sea, Guess Who's Coming to Dinner*) (died 1967).

1901 Chester B. Bowles, advertising executive and public official, was born in Springfield, Mass.; co-founder of Benton & Bowles, ad agency; governor of Massachusetts (1949-51); ambassador to India (1951-53, 1963-69) (died 1986).

1901 Melvyn Douglas, stage and screen actor, was born in Macon, Ga.; leading roles in many films (*Hud, Ninotchka, Sea of Grass*) (died 1981).

1908 Bette Davis, screen actress, was born in Lowell, Mass; starred in many movies (*Jezebel, Of Human Bondage, The Petrified Forest*).

1915 Jess Willard knocked out Jack Johnson in the 26th round in Havana to win the world's heavyweight boxing championship.

1917 Gregory Peck, screen actor, was born in La Jolla, Cal.; numerous starring roles (*The Yearling, To Kill a Mockingbiard, MacArthur*).

1920 Arthur Hailey, author, was born in Luton, England; popular novelist (*Airport, Wheels, Hotel, The Money Changers*).

1929 Ivar Giaever, physicist, was born in Bergen, Norway; made basic discoveries in electronic "tunnelling" and superconductivity (1960); shared 1973 Nobel Physics Prize for the discoveries.

1933 President Franklin Roosevelt ordered all private gold holdings surrendered to the Federal Reserve Bank.

1936 Tornadoes ripped through five Southern states, killing 421.

1982 Supreme Court in 5-4 decision held that seniority systems outlawing discrimination based on race or sex are legal.

1987 An interstate highway bridge on the New York Thruway collapsed near Amsterdam, N.Y. sending at least three cars and a tractor trailer plunging into Schoharie Creek 80 feet below; about a half dozen persons died.

1989 Colin L. Powell, Army general who served as deputy and national security advisor, became first black chairman of Joint Chiefs of Staff (1989).

APRIL 6

1712 Slaves in New York revolted; ended with six committing suicide, 21 were executed.

1745 William Dawes, one of the men who rode with Paul Revere to alert the colonists, was born in Boston (died 1799).

1785 John Pierpont, Unitarian clergyman, was born in Litchfield, Conn.; remembered for his musical composition, "Jingle Bells" (died 1866).

1789 The Senate was organized with nine of its 22 members present, named John Langdon of New Hampshire as the first president pro tem; counted electoral votes which made George Washington president and John Adams vice president (Washington had received all 69 votes cast for president, Adams 34 of 69 for vice president).

1802 Thomas W. Gilmer, Virginia governor (1840-41), was born in Gilmerton, Va.; as Navy Secretary (1844), he was killed when a gun exploded aboard the *Princeton* when President Tyler and his cabinet took a trip on the Potomac.

1805 Alexander E. Hosack, surgeon, was born in New York City; one of the first to use ether in major surgery, a pioneer in urology (died 1871).

1810 Edmund H. Sears, Unitarian clergyman, was born in Sandisfield, Mass.; wrote the hymn, "It Came Upon a Midnight Clear" (died 1876).

1823 Joseph Medill, newspaper owner, was born in St. John, New Brunswick; part owner, *Chicago Tribune* (1855-74), owner (1874-99); an original member of the Civil Service Commission; a founder, Republican Party (died 1899).

1830 Joseph Smith organized the Church of Jesus Christ of Latter Day Saints (Mormons) in Fayette, N.Y.

1832 The Black Hawk War began when Sac and Fox Indians sought to reoccupy their ceded lands in Wisconsin Territory and Illinois; ended Aug 2.

1841 John Tyler was sworn in as president in the Indian Queen Hotel in Washington, the first vice president to succeed to the presidency because of the death of the chief executive.

1854 William Strickland, architect, died at about 67; outstanding exponent of the Greek revival in the United States; did marble sarcophagus of Washington at Mt. Vernon.

1858 A presidential proclamation declared the Mormon Government in Utah in rebellion; six days later, Col. Thomas L. Kane, a friend of the Mormons, arrived in Salt Lake City to mediate the disputes.

1862 Two-day battle of Shiloh (Tenn.) began; one of fiercest battles of the war; Confederate Gen. Albert S. Johnston was killed, Confederates retreated; Union lost 13,700 out of 63,000, Confederates 11,000 out of 40,000.

1864 A convention began in New Orleans to prepare the Louisiana constitution; adopted July 23, including a provision abolishng slavery.

1865 Confederate forces under Gen. R.E. Lee, en route to Farmville, Va., was attacked by Union troops at Sayler's Creek, losing 6000 men.

1866 Lincoln Steffens, reform journalist, was born in San Francisco; with *McClure's* and *American* magazines; wrote *The Shame of the Cities* (died 1936).

1866 The Grand Army of the Republic was organized in Decatur, Ill. by Dr. Benjamin F. Stephenson (10/3/1823).

1874 Harry Houdini, escape artist, was born in Appleton, Wis.; noted for escapes from shackles, ropes, handcuffs, and locked containers (died 1926).

1884 Walter Huston, actor, was born in Toronto; starred in movies (*Dodsworth, Treasure of Sierra Madre*); stage (*Knickerbocker Holiday*) (died 1950).

1890 Anthony H.G. Fokker, plane designer, was born to Dutch parents in Kediri, Indonesia; designed German World War I planes, later trimotor planes for American long distance flights (North Pole, Atlantic, Pacific) (died 1939).

1892 Donald W. Douglas, aircraft manufacturer, was born in Brooklyn; founder (1920), president, Douglas Aircraft Co. (died 1981).

1892 Lowell J. Thomas, radio news commentator and author, was born in Woodington, Ohio; wrote numerous books about travel (died 1981).

1893 The Mormon Tabernacle in Salt Lake City, 40 years in construction, was completed.

1896 Widowed former president, Benjamin Harrison, married a widow, Mary S.L. Dimmick, in New York City.

1903 Mickey (Gordon S.) Cochrane, baseball player, was born in Bridgewater, Mass.; one of greatest catchers, played with Philadelphia Athletics (1925-33), managed Detroit (1934-37); named to Baseball Hall of Fame (died 1962).

1903 Harold E. Edgerton, electrical engineer, was born in Fremont, Neb.; developd high speed stroboscopic photography, applied to various scientific uses.

1909 Robert E. Peary, on his fourth try, led his team to the North Pole; team included Matthew Henson and four Eskimos.

1917 The United States formally declared war on Germany.

1927 Gerry (Gerald J.) Mulligan, musician, was born in New York City; baritone saxophone player, band leader, arranger and composer.

1928 James D. Watson, biochemist, was born in Chicago; shared 1962 Nobel Physiology/Medicine Prize for determining the structure of deoxyribonucleic acid (DNA).

1929 André Previn, pianist, composer, and conductor, was born in Berlin; with Houston Symphony (1967-69), London (1968-76); musical director, Pittsburgh Symphony (1976-).

1931 The Scottsboro Case began in Scottsboro, Ark., in which nine black youths were tried for allegedly raping two white girls; eight were sentenced to death, one to life imprisonment; verdict overturned by Supreme Court; three subsequent trials resulted in convictions and ensuing reversals; none ever executed.

1965 *Early Bird I,* the first commercial satellite, was launched by NASA for the Comsat Corp.

1968 HemisFair 68 opened in San Antonio, Tex.; the world's fair marked the 200th birthday of the city.

1987 The Dow Jones industrial average passed another milestone when the average went over the 2400 mark for the first time, reaching 2405.54.

APRIL 7

1640 Louis Hennepin, Recollet friar and missionary, was born in Flanders; explored much of middle America with LaSalle (died 1705).

1666 Gurdon Saltonstall, colonial official and clergyman, was born in Haverhill, Mass.; governor of Connecticut (1707-24); influenced chartering of Yale College, locating it to New Haven (died 1724).

1775 Francis C. Lowell, industrialist, was born in Newburyport, Mass.; built first complete American cotton spinning, weaving mill at Waltham, Mass. (1812-14); Lowell, Mass. named after him (died 1817).

1780 William Ellery Channing, religious leader, was born in Newport, R.I.; Congregational cleryman (Federal St. Church 1803-42), champion of liberal wing which became the Unitarian Church; called the apostle of Unitarianism; founder, American Unitarian Assn. (1825) (died 1842).

1786 William R. deV. King, Vice President, was born in Sampson County, N.C.; elected in 1853 but died of tuberculosis (Apr 18, 1853) before serving; represented Alabama in the Senate (1819-44, 1848-53); minister to France (1844-46).

1788 Rufus Putnam and a party of settlers of the Ohio Company established the first settlement in the Northwest Territory at what is now Marietta, Ohio.

1798 President John Adams signed an act that established the Mississippi Territory, which included the present state of Alabama.

1818 Spanish fort at St. Marks, Fla. captured by troops under Gen. Andrew Jackson.

1859 Jacques Loeb, biophysiologist, was born in Mayen, Germany; with various American universities, developed tropism theory to account for certain instincts and behaviors, pioneered in artificial parthenogenesis and in analysis of egg fertilization (died 1924).

1860 Will K. Kellogg, manufacturer, was born in Battle Creek, Mich.; worked in sanitarium of brother, John (2/26/1852), and developed breakfast cereals; founder, W.K. Kellogg Co. (1906) (died 1951).

1862 Treaty signed by the United States and Great Britain to suppress slave trade.

1862 Island #10, an important Confederate port in the Mississippi River, fell to Union troops under Gen. John Pope and Flag Officer A.F. Foote; about 7000 prisoners and stores were taken.

1868 A convention adopted a new constitution for Virginia; ratified Apr 18.

1869 William H. Walker, industrial chemist, was born in Pittsburgh; known for producing art glass, stainless steel, research in cellulose and petroleum technology (died 1934).

1869 David G. Fairchild, botanist, was born in East Lansing, Mich.; explored the world for plants useful for introduction to the United States (died 1954).

1873 John J. McGraw, baseball player and manager, was born in Truxton, N.Y.; managed New York Giants (1902-32), winning ten pennants, three World Series; named to Baseball Hall of Fame (died 1934).

1893 Irene Castle, dancer, was born in New Rochelle, N.Y.; with husband, Vernon (5/2/1887), helped popularize the one-step, turkey trot, Castle walk; also popularized bobbed hair (died 1969).

1893 Allen W. Dulles, public official, was born in Watertown, N.Y., brother of John Foster Dulles (2/25/1888); chief, Office of Strategic Services (OSS) in Switzerland, Germany (1942-45); deputy director (1951-53), director (1953-61), Central Intelligence Agency (CIA) (died 1969).

1893 Colorado granted full suffrage to women.

1896 Benny (Benjamin) Leonard, world lightweight boxing champion (1917-25), was born in New York City (died 1947).

1897 Walter Winchell, columnist and radio commentator, was born in New York City; began gossip column (1922), did weekly radio show (1930-50) (died 1972).

1908 Frank E. Fitzsimmons, president, Teamsters Union (1966-81), was born in Jeannette, Pa. (died 1981).

1915 Billie Holiday, jazz singer, was born in Baltimore; gained international fame for jazz-blues style (died 1959).

1922 Naval (Oil) Reserve #3, Teapot Dome, was secretly leased to Harry F. Sinclair by Interior Secretary Albert B. Fall; Sinclair reassigned it to Mammoth Oil Co. for $160 million in stock; on April 25, Elk Hills naval reserve was secretly leased to Edward L. Doheny.

1927 Television was demonstrated successfully for the first time with a picture of Commerce Secretary Herbert Hoover in Washington being shown in New York.

1939 Francis F. Coppola, film director, was born in Detroit; wrote, directed, produced *The Godfather* and its sequel; also wrote and directed *Apocalypse Now*; wrote screenplays (*Patton, Finian's Rainbow, The Great Gatsby*).

1941 The USO (United Service Organizations) was formed by presidential order; included the Salvation Army, YMCA, YWCA, Catholic Community Service, Jewish Welfare Board, and Travelers Aid.

1978 President Carter announced that production of a neutron bomb would be deferred.

1980 United States broke diplomatic relations with Iran following the taking of American hostages in Teheran.

APRIL 8

1726 Lewis Morris, colonial leader, was born in Bronx County, N.Y., half brother of Gouverneur Morris (1/31/1752); a member of Continental Congress, a signer of the Declaration of Independence (died 1798).

1732 David Rittenhouse, pioneer astronomer and surveyor, was born near Germantown, Pa.; built observatory and transit telescope, the first in America; invented collimating telescope; first director, U.S. Mint (1792-95) (died 1796).

1826 Henry Clay and John Randolph fought a harmless duel over the latter's charge of a deal between Clay and John Quincy Adams over election in the House.

1830 Mexican Congress enacted a law prohibiting slavery and the further settlement of Texas by American citizens.

1832 Howell E. Jackson, legislator and jurist, was born in Paris, Tenn.; represented Tennessee in the Senate (1881-86); associate justice, Supreme Court (1893-95) (died 1895).

1850 William H. Welch, pathologist, was born in Norfolk, Conn.; developed first American pathological laboratory at Bellevue Hospital (1879); a founder, Johns Hopkins Hospital and Medical School, dean (1893-1916); director, Johns Hopkins School of Hygiene and Public Health (1918-26) (died 1934).

1857 The Saucona Iron Co., predecessor of Bethlehem Steel Co., was formed in Bethlehem, Pa.

1869 Harvey W. Cushing, surgeon and educator, was born in Cleveland; with Johns Hopkins, Brigham hospitals; specialist in brain surgery (died 1939)

1886 Margaret Ayer Barnes, author, was born in Chicago; co-author of several plays (*Age of Innocence, Jenny*); best remembered for novel, *Years of Grace* (died 1967).

1892 Richard J. Neutra, architect, was born in Vienna; architectural approach called "biorealism," introduced international style to American architecture (died 1970).

1893 Mary Pickford, screen actress, was born in Toronto; called America's sweetheart; starred in many early films (*Tess of the Storm Country, Daddy Long Legs, Rebecca of Sunnybrook Farm* (died 1979).

1897 Louis Skidmore, architect, was born in Laurenceburg, Mo.; partner in firm which pioneered in design and structure (Air Force Academy) (died 1962).

1898 E(dgar) Y. (Yip) Harburg, lyricist, was born in New York City; various hit shows (*Finian's Rainbow, The Wizard of Oz*) (died 1981).

1903 Andrew Carnegie gave $250,000 to Cleveland for branch libraries.

1911 Melvin Calvin, chemist, was born in St. Paul, Minn.; awarded 1961 Nobel Chemistry Prize for establishing chemical steps of the photosynthesis process.

1912 Sonja Henie, ice skater, was born in Oslo; world champion figure skater (1927-37), Olympic gold medalist (1928, 1932, 1936) (died 1969).

1913 President Wilson appeared before a special session of Congress to urge tariff reductions; personal appearance was first for a president since 1800.

1918 Betty (Elizabeth B.) Warren Ford, wife of President Ford, was born in Chicago.

1918 The National War Labor Board was established, with former President Taft and Frank P. Walsh as co-chairmen.

1935 The Works Progress (later Project) Administration (WPA) began, creating a national works program, headed by Harry L. Hopkins; eight-year program employed more than 8.5 million persons on 1.4 million projects costing about $11 billion; resulting in 650,000 miles of highways, 125,000 public buildings, 8000 parks, 850 airports, and construction and repair of 124,000 bridges.

1949 The United States, Great Britain, and France agreed to establish the West German Republic.

1952 President Truman ordered the seizure of the nation's steel mills to avert a strike; the seizure was ruled illegal by the Supreme Court June 2.

1974 Hank Aaron hit his 715th home run in Atlanta, beating Babe Ruth's long-standing lifetime mark of 714.

1988 The Executive Presbytery of the Assemblies of God Church in Springfield, Mo. defrocked television evangelist Jimmy Swaggart for admitted sins after he refused to stop preaching for a year; Swaggart resigned from the Assemblies saying that a year's absence would destroy his ministry.

APRIL 9

1585 Second expedition was sent out by Sir Walter Raleigh, under Sir Richard Grenville, leaving settlers at Roanoke Island, N.C.

1597 John Davenport, founder of the New Haven Colony (1638), was baptised; with Theophilus Eaton, he helped draw up a code of laws; pastor of First Church, New Haven (1638-68), First Church, Boston (1668-70) (died 1670).

1682 Sieur de LaSalle reached the mouth of the Mississippi River, took possession of the entire area for France, naming it Louisiana.

1738 Rufus Putnam, Revolutionary officer, was born in Sutton, Mass., cousin of Israel Putnam (1/7/1718); an organizer of Ohio settlement company, a founder of Marietta, Ohio, first organized settlement in Northwest Territory; a judge, Northwest Territory (1790-96), U.S. Surveyor General (1796-1803) (died 1824).

1823 Lorenzo S. Coffin, railroad safety promoter, was born in Alton, N.H.; led successful campaign to require automatic coupling and hand-braking (died 1915).

1830 Eadweard J. Muybridge, motion picture pioneer, was born in Kingston, England; invented zoopraxiscope, which took and reproduced pictures of animal locomotion (died 1904).

1855 New York enacted statewide prohibition; declared unconstitutional in 1856.

1862 Charles H. Brent, Episcopal prelate, was born in Newcastle, Canada; chief of chaplains, American Expeditionary Force in World War I (died 1929).

1865 Henry H. Kitson, sculptor, was born in Huddersfield, England; known for various historical figures, including *The Minute Man* in Lexington, Mass. (died 1947).

1865 Gen. Robert E. Lee surrendered to Gen. U.S. Grant at Appomattox Court House, Va., in the farmhouse of William McLean, ending the Civil War; Grant and Lee met at 11:00 a.m.; Grant received the surrender of about 28,000 men; Confederate soldiers were paroled to go home; officers were permitted to keep their sidearms, and were allowed to keep their private horses and mules.

1865 Charles P. Steinmetz, electrical inventor, was born in Breslau, Germany; helped make alternating current commercially feasible; developed lightning arrestors for high powered transmission lines; patented more than 100 inventions (died 1923).

1867 Senate approved the treaty purchasing Alaska from Russia for $7.2 million.

1868 Benjamin R. Curtis, a counsel for President Andrew Johnson, made opening defense speech in the Senate impeachment trial.

1883 Charles H. Bonesteel, World War II general, was born in Ft. Sidney, Neb.; commander, American forces in Iceland (1941-42); Allied commander, Iceland (1942) (died 1964).

1888 Sol Hurok, impressario, was born in Pogar, Russia; for 65 years he brought the greatest performing artists to United States (died 1974).

1893 Charles E. Burchfield, artist, was born in Ashtabula Harbor, Ohio; water colorist (*Black Iron, Edge of Town, Freight Cars Under a Bridge*) (died 1967).

1898 Curly (Earl L.) Lambeau, football coach, was born in Green Bay, Wis.; founder, coach, Green Bay Packers (1919-49) (died 1965).

1898 Paul Robeson, singer and actor, was born in Princeton, N.J.; starred on stage (*Emperor Jones, Porgy and Bess, All God's Chillun*); numerous concert tours; internationally known social activist, civil rights leader; film actor (of the 1930s and 1940s) (died 1976).

1899 James S. McDonnell Jr., aircraft designer, was born in Denver; founder (1939), chairman (1939-67), McDonnell Aircraft Co.; merged with Douglas Aircraft, chairman (1967-80) (died 1980).

1903 Gregory Pincus, biologist, was born in Woodbine, N.J.; developed (with John Rock 3/24/1890) oral contraceptive (the pill) (died 1967).

1905 J. William Fulbright, legislator, was born in Summer, Mo.; president, U. of Arkansas (1939-41); represented state in House (1943-45) and Senate (1945-74); was one of best-known Senate Foreign Relations Committee chairs; initiated the Fulbright scholarships.

1910 Abraham A. Ribicoff, legislator and public official, was born in New Britain, Conn.; represented Connecticut in the House (1949-53) and Senate (1963-81), and served as governor (1954-61); Secretary of Health, Education and Welfare (1961-62).

1912 Children's Bureau was created in Department of Commerce and Labor; Julia Lathrop was first director.

1914 Several American sailors from the USS *Dolphin* were arrested in Tampico by Mexican troops; Americans demanded an apology, which was refused.

1917 Eddystone ammunition plant at Chester, Pa. was destroyed by an explosion, killing 122 persons.

1919 John P. Eckert, co-inventor of the computer, was born in Philadelphia; with John Mauchly (8/30/1907) invented the electronic computer, of which the third model was the Univac.

1926 Hugh M. Hefner, publisher, was born in Chicago; founder, publisher, *Playboy* magazine (1953), head of related enterprises (1959).

1939 Marian Anderson gave a concert on the steps of the Lincoln Memorial after being denied use of Constitution Hall in Washington.

1942 American and Filipino troops began the abandonment of Bataan Peninsula to the Japanese, with 37,000 taken prisoner; some escaped to Corregidor.

1945 An American Liberty ship exploded in the Bari, Italy harbor; 360 were killed, 1730 injured.

1963 Winston Churchill was granted honorary American citizenship.

1965 The Houston Astrodome opened.

APRIL 10

1606 The first charter of Virginia was issued by King James, providing for incorporation of the London Company, which established the first permanent English colony at Jamestown, and the Plymouth Company.

1644 William Brewster, colonial leader, died at 77, arrived on the *Mayflower*, a leader in the church and public affairs management of Plymouth Colony.

1664 Delegates from all New Netherlands localities met in New Amsterdam to seek protection against the English.

1780 George Armistead, War of 1812 officer, was born in New Market, Va.; successfully defended Ft. McHenry in Baltimore Harbor against the British (died 1818).

1790 President Washington signed the first patent act.

1794 Matthew C. Perry, naval officer, was born in Newport, R.I., brother of Oliver Hazard Perry (8/20/1785); pioneer advocate of naval steamships, established the first naval engineer corps, gunnery school; led fleet to Japan and negotiated treaty (1854) opening country to Western trade (died 1858).

1806 Leonidas Polk, Episcopal prelate and educator, was born in Raleigh, N.C.; missionary bishop to the Southwest (1838), bishop of Louisiana (1841); a founder, U. of the South at Sewanee, Tenn.; Confederate general, killed at Pine Mountain (1864).

1806 Horatio Gates, Revolutionary officer, died at 78; credited with victory over Burgoyne at Saratoga, although Schuyler and Arnold were primarily responsible; severely defeated at Camden, S.C. (1780); friends sought unsuccessfully to put him in Washington's place (the Conway cabal).

1810 Benjamin H. Day, newspaper executive, was born in West Springfield, Mass.; founded first penny daily paper, *New York Sun* (1833) (died 1889).

1816 The Second Bank of the United States was chartered after the nation was without a central bank for five years.

1817 John C. Robinson, Union general, was born in Binghamton, N.Y.; saw action at Fredericksburg, Chancellorsville, Gettysburg (where his statue stands on the battlefield), and Spotsylvania, where he lost a leg (died 1897).

1827 Lew(is) Wallace, Union general, was born in Brookville, Ind.; served in Mexican and Civil wars and on military court which tried the Lincoln conspirators; governor of the New Mexico Territory (1878-81); minister to Turkey (1881-85); author of *Ben Hur* (died 1905).

1832 Mary A. Eastin, niece of President Jackson, was married in the White House to Lucien J. Polk.

1833 David M. Gregg, Union general, was born in Huntingdon, Pa.; commanded cavalry on Union right wing at Gettysburg, repulsed Confederate attempt to turn flank (died 1916).

1835 Henry Villard, industrialist and publisher, was born in Speyer, Germany; headed Northern Pacific Railroad (1881-84), board chairman (1888-93); organized, headed, Edison General Electric Co. (1888-91); bought controlling interest in *New York Post, Nation* (1881) (died 1900).

1838 Frank S. Baldwin, inventor, was born in New Hartford, Conn.; invented an adding, calculating machine called the arithmometer (1874), which was redesigned as the Monroe calculator (died 1925).

1841 The *New York Tribune* began publication under Horace Greeley.

1845 Pittsburgh was almost completely destroyed by fire.

1847 Joseph Pulitzer, publisher, was born in Mako, Hungary; often called the father of modern American journalism; owner, publisher, *St. Louis Post Dispatch* (1878), *New York World* (1883); represented New York in the House (1885-87); his will established Columbia School of Journalism (1912), Pulitzer prizes (1917) (died 1911).

1861 The Massachusetts Institute of Technology (MIT) was incorporated.

1866 The Society for the Prevention of Cruelty to Animals (SPCA) was organized by Henry Bergh.

1868 George Arliss, actor, was born in London; starred on stage and screen (*Disraeli, Green Goddess*) (died 1946).

1879 John D. Hertz, founder, head of rental car service (1924), was born in Ruttka, Czechoslovakia (formerly Hungary); also founder, head of Chicago Yellow Cabs (1915) (died 1961).

1882 Frances Perkins, first woman cabinet officer, was born in Boston; New York State Industrial Commissioner (1929-33); Secretary of Labor (1933-45); member, U.S. Civil Service Commissin (1946-53) (died 1965).

1885 Bernard F. Gimbel, merchant, was born in Vincennes, Ind.; with store which bore his name (1907-66), president (1927-53), board chairman (1953-66) (died 1966).

1897 Ross Youngs, baseball player (Giants) was born in Shiner, Texas; named to Baseball Hall of Fame (died 1927).

1903 Clare Boothe Luce, playwright and diplomat, was born in New York City; with *Vogue, Vanity Fair* (1930-34); playwright (*The Women, Kiss the Boys Goodbye*); represented Connecticut in the House (1943-47); ambassador to Italy (1953-56), to Brazil (1959) (died 1987).

1910 Eddy (Edwin F.) Duchin, pianist and orchestra leader, was born in Cambridge, Mass. (died 1951).

1917 Robert B. Woodward, chemist, was born in Boston; awarded 1965 Nobel Chemistry Prize for his work in chemical synthesis (died 1979).

1927 Marshall W. Nireberg, biochemist, was born in New York City; with National Institutes of Health; shared 1968 Nobel Physiology/Medicine Prize for studies of the genetic code.

1941 President Franklin Roosevelt announced agreement with Denmark for American military bases in Greenland.

1942 The "death march" of American and Filipino prisoners began from Bataan; at least 5200 Americans died.

1945 Allied troops liberated the Buchenwald concentration camp.

1963 The nuclear submarine, *Thresher*, was lost in the North Atlantic with 129 men aboard.

APRIL 11

1711 William Rudolph, a leading Virginia planter, died at about 60; attorney general for the Crown in Virginia (1674-98); a founder of College of William & Mary.

1713 Treaty of Utrecht was signed ending the Queen Anne War.

1780 British began siege of Charleston; city surrendered May 13.

1794 Edward Everett, Unitarian clergyman and public official, was born in Dorchester, Mass.; represented Massachusetts in the House (1825-35) and Senate (1853-54) and served state as governor (1835-39); minister to England (1841-45); Secretary of State (1852-53); president, Harvard U. (1846-49); delivered dedication oration (two hours) of Gettysburg National Cemetery at time of Lincoln's address (died 1865).

1851 Adrian C. Anson, baseball player and Manager (mostly with Cubs), was born in Marshalltown, Iowa; had .339 batting average with more than 3500 hits in 27 years; named to Baseball Hall of Fame (died 1922).

1859 Enoch H. Crowder, director of Selective Service in World War I, was born in Edinburg, Mo. (died 1932).

1861 Gen. P.G.T. Beauregard demanded surrender of Ft. Sumter; refused by Union Maj. Robert Anderson, fort commander; later, Anderson agreed to evacuate fort by the 15th; was notified at 3:30 a.m. Apr 12 that bombardment would begin in an hour.

1862 Ft. Pulaski, commanding approach to Savannah, was captured by Union troops.

1862 Charles Evans Hughes, jurist and public official, was born in Glens Falls, N.Y.; serv ed New York as governor (1906-10); associate justice, Supreme Court (1910-16) and chief justice (1930-41); 1916 Republican presidential candidate; Secretary of State (1921-25) (died 1948).

1865 President Lincoln spoke from the White House balcony to a crowd celebrating the end of the war; talked of reconciliation, reconstruction in what turned out to be his last public address.

1879 Frank T. Hines, Army general and public official, was born in Salt Lake City; supervised transporting two million American troops to and from Europe (1918-19); director, Veterans Bureau (1923-30), administrator, Veterans Administration (1930-45); ambassador to Panama (1945-48) (died 1960).

1893 Dean G. Acheson, public official, was born in Middletown, Conn.; Secretary of State (1949-53); author (*Present at the Creation*) (died 1971).

1893 The first ambassador to the United States, Sir Julian Pauncefote of Great Britain, presented his credentials to President Cleveland.

1898 President McKinley sent a message to Congress on the events in Cuba which justified intervention.

1899 Percy L. Julian, chemist, was born in Montgomery, Ala.; did much to promote the use of soy products (died 1975).

1900 The Navy purchased its first submarine, equipped with an internal combustion engine and an electric motor; designed by John P. Holland (2/29/1840).

1913 Oleg Cassini, fashion designer, was born in Rome; began career designing costumes for Paramount Pictures, then went on his own.

1921 Iowa enacted the first state tax on cigarettes.

1930 Nicholas Brady, Secretary of the Treasury (1988) and nominated to serve by President-elect Bush (1989), was born in New York City; represented New Jersey in the Senate (1982).

1941 Office of Price Administration (OPA) was created with Leon Henderson as the first administrator.

1947 Jackie Robinson of the Brooklyn Dodgers became the first black baseball player in the major leagues.

1951 President Truman relieved Gen. Douglas MacArthur from his post as UN commander and commander of American forces in Japan and the Far East for his constant public criticism of American war policy; succeeded by Gen. Matthew B. Ridgway.

1953 Department of Health, Education and Welfare began operations with Oveta Culp Hobby as first secretary; divided into separate departments, Education, and Health and Human Services, in 1979.

1965 Elementary and Secondary Education Act was passed, providing large scale direct federal aid to elementary and secondary education, a historic breakthrough in American education.

1965 Thirty-seven tornadoes ripped across six Midwestern states, leaving 242 persons dead, 2500 injured, and $250 million in damage.

1968 President Lyndon Johnson signed the Civil Rights Act, designed to end discrimination in the rental and sale of homes and apartments.

1988 A preliminary 164-page pastoral letter was distributed to American Catholic bishops discussing sexism in the church; the letter was the third of three letters, one on peace being issued in 1983 and on the economy in 1986; a final draft of the sexism letter will be voted.

APRIL 12

1724 Lyman Hall, physician and public official, was born in Wallingford, Conn.; practiced medicine in Georgia; a member of Continental Congress (1775-80), a signer of Declaration of Independence; governor of Georgia (1783) (died 1798).

1755 *Connecticut Gazette*, the first newspaper in the state, was published in New Haven by James Parker.

1770 The Townshend duties on various imports were altered to limit them to tea; at the same time; the Quartering Act, which required the colonists to pay for the quartering of British troops, was allowed to expire.

1776 A convention of North Carolina colonists authorized its delegates to the Continental Congress to vote for independence, the first colony to do so.

1777 Henry Clay, legislator, was born in Hanover County, Va.; represented Kentucky in the House (1811-14, 1815-21, 1823-25), serving as Speaker every year but 1821, and in the Senate (1806-07, 1810-11, 1831-42, 1849-52); Secretary of State (1825-29); sought presidential nomination in 1824, 1832, 1844; drafted the Missouri Compromise, laid groundwork for Pan-Americanism (died 1852).

1779 Spain by secret Treaty of Aranjuez joined France in the war against Great Britain, but did not recognize American independence.

1791 Francis P. Blair, newsman and politician, was born in Abingdon, Va.; published the *Congressional Globe*, predecessor of the *Congressional Record*; a founder, Republican Party (died 1876).

1804 George W. Jones, public official, was born in Vincennes, Ind.; led efforts to create Wisconsin and Iowa territories; a first Iowa senator (1848-59) (died 1896)

1811 A group of colonists under John Jacob Astor founded the first American settlement in the Pacific Northwest—Astoria.

1818 The American flag in its present form, designed by Samuel C. and Mary Reid, was flown over the Capitol for the first time.

1831 U. of Alabama was founded at Tuscaloosa.

1831 Grenville M. Dodge, railroad engineer, was born in Danvers, Mass.; chief engineer, Union Pacific Railroad (1866-70); supervised building more than 10,000 miles of railroad, including linkup at Promontory Point, Utah (died 1916).

1838 John S. Billings, physician and librarian, was born in Switzerland County, Ind.; while in Army, expanded library of Surgeon General; designed Johns Hopkins Hospital; chief librarian, New York Public Library (1896-1913) (died 1913).

1844 Secretary of State John C. Calhoun signed a treaty of annexation with Texas but the Senate refused (35 to 16) to ratify treaty on June 8.

1853 Charles S. Bradley, inventor, was born in Victor, N.Y.; invented a rotary converter, a process for producing aluminum, a process for fixation of atmospheric hydrogen (died 1929).

1857 John T. Underwood, industrialist, was born in London; developed Underwood Typewriter Co. (1895) (died 1935).

1859 Frank E. Miller, physician, was born in Hartford; a student of voice, he originated "vocal art-science," a method of voice production (died 1932).

1861 The Civil War began as South Carolina trops fired on Ft. Sumter beginning at 4:30 a.m.; Union forces surrendered the following day.

1862 The first official regiment of black trops was organized by Gen. David Hunter; the regiment, composed of former slaves, was disbanded a short time later.

1865 Both Mobile and Montgomery, Ala. surrendered to Union troops.

1869 Hugh Jennings, baseball player and manager (Tigers 14 years), was born in Pittston, Pa.; named to Baseball Hall of Fame (died 1928).

1874 William B. Bankhead, legislator, was born in Moscow, Ala.; represented Alabama in the House (1916-40), serving as majority leader (1934-36) and Speaker (1936-40) (died 1940).

1880 Addie (Adrian) Joss, baseball pitcher (Indians) who won 160 games, was born in Juneau, Wis.; named to Baseball Hall of Fame (died 1978).

1887 Joe (Joseph V.) McCarthy, baseball manager, was born in Philadelphia; managed Cubs, Yankees; named to Baseball Hall of Fame (died1978).

1900 President McKinley signed an act to establish civil government in Puerto Rico, effective May 1.

1904 Lily Pons, coloratura soprano, was born in Draguignan, France; appeared in many operas and on concert stage (died 1976).

1908 Chelsea, Mass. was destroyed by fire, leaving 10,000 homeless.

1913 Lionel Hampton, musician, was born in Birmingham, Ala.; drummer and vibraphone player, orchestra leader.

1933 President Franklin Roosevelt named Ruth Bryan Rohde minister to Denmark and Iceland, the first American woman minister to a foreign country.

1934 Thaddeus Cahill, aviator, died at 67; invented electric typewriter, devices for heat engines, composing machines, and wireless telephony.

1937 Supreme Court sanctioned the power of Congress to regulate labor relations of persons engaged in interstate commerce in the case of *NLRB v. Jones & Laughlin.*

1945 President Franklin Roosevelt died suddenly in Warm Springs, Ga. of a cerebral hemorrhage at 63; Vice President Truman took the oath of office as president in the Cabinet Room of the White House from Chief Justice Harlan F. Stone.

1947 David Letterman, television personality, was born in Indianapolis.

1980 Protesting the Soviet invasion of Afghanistan, the U.S. Olympic Committee voted not to participate in the Olympic Games scheduled for Moscow.

1981 The first manned space shuttle, *Columbia*, successfully took off with John W. Young and Robert L. Crippen aboard; orbited earth 36 times in 54 hours, 22 minutes, landing successfully at Edwards Air Force Base, Cal. on Apr 14.

1983 Chicago elected itsfirst black mayor, Harold Washington, a former representative in the House.

1984 Two astronauts—James Van Hoften and George Nelson—aboard the space shuttle *Challenger* repaired a damaged Solar Maximum Observatory satellite, which had been inoperative for four years; repairs came after it was pulled into the shuttle's cargo bay the day before.

1985 Senator Jake Garn of Utah became the first congressional observer to ride into space as a crew member of the shuttle *Discovery* launched from Cape Canaveral.

APRIL 13

1710 Jonathan Carver, traveler and author, was born in Weymouth, Mass.; wrote first popular American travel book (*Travels in Interior Parts of America*) (died 1780).

1721 John Hanson, first "president," was born in Charles County, Md.; presiding officer of the first Continental Congress (1781-82) under Articles of Confederation (died 1783).

1743 Thomas Jefferson, third president (1801-09), was born in what is now Albemarle County, Va.; member of Continental Congress (1775, 1776, 1783-85); author of the Declaration of Independence; served Virginia as governor (1779-81); minister to France (1785-89); first Secretary of State (1790-94); Vice President (1797-1801); instrumental in founding U. of Virginia (1819) (died 1826).

1772 Eli Terry, clockmaker, was born in South Windsor, Conn; established assembly line in first American clock factory; with Seth Thomas (8/19/1785) developed a perfected wooden clock, which dominated the industry for years (died 1852).

1795 James Harper, publisher, was born in Newtown, N.Y.; with brother John (1/22/1797), founded family publishing business (1825) (died 1869).

1823 Sabato Morais, rabbi, was born in Leghorn, Italy; served Philadelphia congregations (1851-97); a founder, Jewish Theological Seminary, New York City (1886-97) (died 1897).

1832 Shadrach Bond, public official, died at 59; served as the first delegate to Congress from the Territory of Illinois (1812-14), then as state's first governor (1818-22).

1846 Pennsylvania Railroad chartered.

1851 Robert Abbe, surgeon, was born in New York City, brother of Cleveland Abbe (12/2/1838); first American surgeon to use radium in cancer treatment (died 1928).

1852 F(rank) W. Woolworth, merchant, was born in Rodman, N.Y.; began five cents store in Utica, N.Y. (1879), failed; tried again in Lancaster, Pa., successful; by 1900, there were 59 stores; by 1919, more than 1000; built Woolworth Building, New York City (1913), which at 792 ft. high was then the world's tallest building (died 1919).

1859 Henry T. Allen, World War I general, was born in Sharpsburg, Ky.; commander, 90th Division in France, occupation forces in Germany (1919) (died 1930).

1861 Maj. Robert Anderson and his federal troops surrendered to South Carolina troops after a 34-hour bloodless bombardment on Ft. Sumter.

1865 Gen. William T. Sherman's troops took Raleigh, N.C. from Confederate control.

1866 Butch Cassidy, outlaw and bank robber, was born in Beaver, Utah as Robert L. Parker (died 1909).

1870 Metropolitan Museum of Art in New York City was incorporated.

1873 John W. Davis, lawyer, was born in Clarksburg, W.Va.; represented West Virginia in the House (1911-13); Solicitor General (1913-18); ambassador to Great Britain (1918-21); 1924 Democratic presidential candidate (died 1955).

1874 Anson P. Stokes, Episcopal clergyman who was canon residentiary, National Cathedral, Washington (1924-39), was born in New York City (Staten Island); secretary, Yale U. (1899-1921) (died 1958).

1875 Ray Lyman Wilbur, educator and public official, was born in Boonesboro, Iowa; president, Stanford U. (1916-43), chancellor (1943-49); Secretary of the Interior (1929-33) (died 1949).

1886 Albert W. Stevens, balloonist and Army officer, was born in Belfast, Md.; made first photo of earth's curvature (1930), moon's shadow on earth during a solar eclipse (died 1949).

1890 Frank Murphy, public official and jurist, was born in Harbor Beach, Mich.; mayor of Detroit (1930-33); governor-general, commissioner, Philippine Islands (1933-36); Michigan governor (1936-38); Attorney General (1939-40); associate justice, Supreme Court (1940-49) (died 1949).

1896 Ira C. Eaker, World War II Air Forces general, was born in Field Creek, Tex.; led first American heavy bomber attack on Germany (Aug 17, 1942); headed, 8th Air Force (1942-44),. Mediterranean Allied Air Force (1944-45) (died 1988).

1907 Harold E. Stassen, public official, was born in West St. Paul, Minn.; governor of Minnesota (1939-43), president, U. of Pennsylvania (1948-53); perennial candidate for Republican presidential nomination.

1909 Eudora Welty, author, was born in Jackson, Miss.; wrote several popular novels (*Delta Wedding, The Ponder Heart, The Golden Apples*).

1919 Madalyn O'Hair, atheist, was born in Pittsburgh; led successful campaign to ban prayer in the public schools.

1941 Michael S. Brown, U. of Texas scientist, was born in New York City; shared 1985 Nobel Physiology/Medicine Prize for work on receptors that trap, absorb bloodstream particles with cholesterol.

1943 President Franklin Roosevelt dedicated the Jefferson Memorial in Washington on the 200th anniversary of Jefferson's birth.

1970 Apollo 13 mission developed serious problems about 200,000 miles from the earth when oxygen tanks and service modules exploded; completed mission around the moon and returned in the lunar module; splashed down successfully Apr 17

APRIL 14

1528 Pamphilo de Narvaez, Spanish explorer, landed near Tampa with a group of 400 colonists, marched north to Apalachee (near present Tallahasee); unable to find gold, they set sail for Mexico.

1614 Pocahontas, legendary savior of Capt. John Smith, was married to John Rolfe, who was credited with introducing tobacco growing (1612); marriage brought peace to Jamestown colony.

1789 Charles Thomson, secretary of Congress, arrived at Mt. Vernon to notify George Washington of his election as first president.

1792 The first apportionment act increased the number of members in the House to 105, one for every 33,000 inhabitants.

1796 Benjamin L.E. de Bonneville, explorer, was born in Paris; explored much of northwestern United States; served in both Mexican and Civil wars (died 1878).

1802 Horace Bushnell, Congregational clergyman, was born in Bantam, Conn.; considered the father of American religious liberalism; served church in Hartford (1833-61) (died 1876).

1810 Justin S. Morrill, legislator, was born in Strafford, Vt., represented Vermont in the House (1855-67) and Senate (1867-98); author of a tariff act (1861) and the Land Grant College Act, which led to numerous state agricultural and mechanical colleges (died 1898).

1813 Junius Spencer Morgan, banker, was born in West Springfield, Mass.; founder of the Morgan financial family business; organized, headed J.P. Morgan & Co. (1864-90) (died 1890).

1818 The office of Surgeon General was created.

1820 Maturin M. Ballou, journalist, was born in Boston, son of Hosea Ballou (4/30/1771); a founder, first editor, *Boston Globe* (died 1895).

1842 Adna R.Chaffee, Army officer, was born in Orwell, Ohio; served in Civil War, Spanish-American War, and led American relief expedition in Boxer rebellion in China (died 1914).

1861 John J. Carty, electrical engineer, was born in Cambridge; chief engineer, New York Telephone Co. (1889-1907), ATT (1907-19); vice president, ATT (1919-30); a pioneer in developing the telephone and switchboard; had numerous related inventions (died 1932).

1865 President Lincoln was fatally wounded at 10:15 p.m. by John Wilkes Booth, a Shakespearean actor (the son of Junius Booth 5/1/1796); the president was seated in a box in Ford Theater watching the play, *Our American Cousin*, when he was shot from behind; he died at 7:22 a.m. the next morning in the home of William Peterson, across the street from the theater.

1865 The Union flag was raised over Ft. Sumter in Charleston Harbor, four years and one day after the Civil War began there.

1874 Josiah Warren, social reformer, died at about 76; member of Owen Socialist community at New Harmony, Ind.; set up new social community, "Modern Times," on Long Island (1850-62), considered founder of America philosophical anarchism; invented process for making stereotype plates easily, cheaply.

1878 George M. Holley, industrialist, was born in Port Jervis, N.Y.; headed Holley Motor Co., which produced first practical motorcycle (1899); also a major supplier of carburetors (died 1963).

1879 James Branch Cabell, author, was born in Richmond, Va.; popular novelist of 1920s, 1930s; best remembered for *Jurgen* (died 1958).

1910 President Taft threw out first ball in baseball season opener between Washington and Philadelphia, the first president to do so.

1912 Chauncey Starr, nuclear engineer, was born in Newark; pioneer in design, development of early nuclear reactors.

1917 Committee on Public Information was established by executive order, with George Creel as chairman; Creel had edited various newspapers (Kansas City, Denver); office disbanded after the war.

1939 President Franklin Roosevelt, in a letter to Adolf Hitler, appealed for peace; a similar message went to the King of Italy.

1941 Julie Christie, screen actress, was born in Chukua, Ind.; starred in many films (*Dr. Zhivago, Darling, Shampoo*).

1942 Pete Rose, baseball player and manager, was born in Cincinnati; played with Reds and Phillies; one of two players with 4000 or more hits; became all-time leader with 4256, surpassing Ty Cobb's record in 1985.

1959 The Taft Memorial Bell Tower in Washington was dedicated in honor of Sen. Robert A. Taft.

1966 President Lyndon Johnson in Mexico City dedicated a statue of Lincoln; reaffirmed support of the Alliance for Progress.

1988 The Dow Jones industrial average fell 101.46 points after the government announced a $13.8 billion monthly deficit in February, the largest since October.

1988 A blast outside a GI club in Naples killed at least five people, wounded 15, including several American soldiers.

APRIL 15

1632 George Calvert, the first Lord Baltimore, died at about 53, shortly before charter creating Maryland as part of Virginia territory was approved; grant transferred to his son, Cecelius.

1638 New Haven was founded by Theophilus Eaton and the Rev. John Davenport.

1715 Yemassee Indians, incited by Spaniards, attacked South Carolina settlers, killing 400.

1741 Charles Willson Peale, foremost American portrait painter, was born in Queen Anne County, Md.; best known for paintings of George Washington, who sat for him repeatedly; founded first art museum in Philadelphia (died 1827).

1775 British grenadiers and light infantrymen in Boston were assigned special training, arousing suspicion of coming events.

1782 Eleazar W. Ripley, War of 1812 general, was born in Hanover, N.H.; saw action at Ft. Erie, Lundy's Lane; represented Louisiana in the House (1835-39) (died 1839).

1783 Congress ratified preliminary articles of peace, officially ending the American Revolution; treaty signed in Paris Sept 3, formally ratified by Congress Jan 14, 1784.

1786 Walter Channing, physician and educator, was born in Newport, R.I.; first professor of obstetrics and medical jurisprudence, Harvard Medical School; dean (1819-47) (died 1876).

1789 *Gazette of the United States*, a pro-administration newspaper, was established with John Fenno as editor.

1791 Alexander Garden, Scottish-born naturalist, died at 61; collected botanical, mineral, and zoological specimens; gardenia named for him.

1813 Gen. James Wilkinson led American forces in taking Spanish fort at Mobile; occupied the Mobile District of West Florida to the Perdido River.

1814 John L. Motley, historian and diplomat, was born in Dorchester, Mass.; historian of the Dutch; minister to Austria (1861-67), to Great Britain (1869-70) (died 1877).

1817 New York State legislature authorized construction of the Erie Canal; created a Canal board.

1821 Catesby ap Roger Jones, Confederate naval officer, was born in Selma, Ala.; commanded the *Merrimac* in its duel with the *Monitor* (died 1877).

1843 Henry James, author, was born in New York City, brother of William James (1/11/1842); spent most of life abroad; author (*Daisy Miller, Portrait of a Lady, The American*) (died 1916.

1850 San Francisco was incorporated by California's first legislature.

1859 William B. Parsons, engineer, was born in New York City; designed, built first units of New York City's subway system (1899-1904); built East River Tunnel (1904); chief engineer, Cape Cod Canal (1905-14) (died 1932).

1861 President Lincoln issued a proclamation that declared an "insurrection" existed; called on the states for 75,000 three-months volunteers.

1865 Vice President Andrew Johnson was sworn in as president in his suite at the Kirkwood House in Washington, three hours after the death of President Lincoln.

1869 Deming Jarves, pioneer glass manufacturer, died at 79; manufactured pressed glass known as Sandwich Glass at his factory in Sandwich, Mass.

1881 Hugh H. Bennett, soil scientist, was born in Wadesboro, N.C.; known as the father of soil conservation, he served as first director, Soil Conservation Service (died 1960).

1884 John Henry (Pops) Lloyd, star shortstop in Negro baseball, was born in Florida; named to Baseball Hall of Fame.

1889 A. Philip Randolph, labor and civil rights leader, was born in Crescent City, Fla.; organizer, president, Brotherhood of Sleeping Car Porters (1925-68); an organizer, March on Washington (1963) (died 1979).

1889 Thomas Hart Benton, artist, was born in Neosho, Mo., grandson of Thomas Hart Benton (3/14/1782); painted vigorous, realistic portraits of ordinary Midwest people; did murals for Missouri State Capitol, Truman Library (died 1975).

1892 General Electric Co. was established by the merger of Edison General Electric Co. and the Thomas Houston Electric Co.

1894 Bessie Smith, singer, was born in Chattanooga; one of the greatest blues singers (died 1937).

1902 Samuel K. Hoffman, propulsion engineer, was born in Williamsport, Pa.; pioneer in developing rocket engines.

1910 The 13th census reported a population of 91,972,266.

1912 The steamer *Titanic* sank on its maiden voyage after hitting an iceberg in the North Atlantic; 1513 of its 2340 passengers perished, including John Jacob Astor, Isidor Straus and his wife, George D. Widener, Benjamin Guggenheim.

1920 Niccolo Sacco, 29, a shoe factory worker and Bartolomeo Vanzetti, 32, a fish peddler, both radicals, were accused of killing two men in a payroll holdup at the Slater & Morrill shoe factory in South Braintree, Mass.; they were found guilty in 1921; despite appeals and worldwide protests, they were executed Aug 23, 1927.

1922 Leonard Baskin, sculptor, was born in New Brunswick, N.J.; also a noted graphic artist.

1933 Roy Clark, entertainer, was born in Meherrin, Va.; country music singer, musician, and television personality (*Hee Haw*).

1940 The 16th census reported a population of 131,669,275 and the center of population two miles southeast of Carlisle, Ind.

1950 The 17th census reported a population of 150,697,361 (including Alaska and Hawaii); the center of population was three miles northeast of Louisville, Ill.

1952 President Truman signed a formal peace treaty with Japan ending officially World War II.

1959 Secretary of State John Foster Dulles resigned because of an incapacitating illness; died May 4; Christian A. Herter was named to the post Apr 18.

1964 The Chesapeake Bay Bridge Tunnel, 17.6 miles long between the Eastern Shore of Virginia and Norfolk, was opened.

1986 American naval planes and ships bombed "terrorist" targets in Libya.

APRIL 16

1568 French force under Dominique de Gourgé recaptured Ft. Carolina (San Mateo) at the mouth of the St. James River in Florida; slaughtered all captives in retaliation for Spanish massacre of French settlers in 1565.

1683 William Leete, colonial leader, died at 70; a founder and town clerk of Guilford, Conn. (1639-62); deputy governor, New Haven Colony (1669-76), governor (1676-83).

1787 The first American play (Royall Tyler's *Contrast*) produced by an American professional company was staged in the John St. Theater, New York City.

1787 George Washington, notified two days earlier of his election as president, set out from Mt. Vernon for New York, arriving Apr 23; writing in his diary, he states: "I bade adieu to Mt. Vernon, to private life, and to domestic felicity, and with a mind oppressed with more anxious and painful sensations than I have words to express, set out for New York...with the best disposition to render service to my country in obedience to its call, but with less hope of answering its expectations."

1806 Hugh H. Toland, surgeon, was born in Guilders Creek, S.C.; known for operations on clubfoot, strabismus; founder (1864) of a private medical college in San Francisco at his own expense, which became part of U. of California (1873) (died 1880).

1856 Albert B. Dick, inventor and businessman, was born in Bureau County, Ill.; invented mimeograph process machine (c 1887); founded, headed, A.B. Dick Co. (died 1934).

1857 Henry S. Pritchett, astronomer, was born in Fayette, Mo.; superintendent, Coast and Geodetic Survey (1897-1900); president, MIT (1900-06); president, Carnegie Foundation for Advancement of Teaching (1906-30) (died 1939).

1861 North Carolina state troops seized Forts Caswell and Johnston.

1862 Confederate Congress passed a bill for compulsory military service for all white men 18 to 35; amended Sept 1862 to 18 to 45, and in Feb 1864 to 17 to 50.

1862 President Lincoln signed an act abolishing slavery in the District of Columbia; average compensation to slave holders by government was $300.

1863 Adm. David D. Porter led Union fleet of seven ironclads, three steamers, and ten barges past the Vicksburg batteries during the night.

1867 New York legislature created free state public school system.

1867 Wilbur Wright, aviation pioneer, was born in Millville, Ind.; with brother, Orville (8/19/1871), made historic flights at Kitty Hawk, N.C., after first experimenting with kites and gliders (died 1912).

1868 South Carolina voters ratified a new constitution during a two-day vote.

1889 Charles Chaplin, screen actor and producer, was born in London; starred, produced many films (*The Kid, The Gold Rush, City Lights, Modern Times*) (died 1977).

1890 Billy DeBeck, cartoonist, was born in Chicago; created *Barney Google and Snuffy Smith* (died 1942).

1890 Donald F. Jones, agricultural researcher, was born in Hutchinson, Kan.; made hybrid corn commercially feasible (died 1963).

1903 Paul Waner, baseball player, was born in Harrah, Okla.; one of greatest hitters, fielders in baseball; played mostly with Pittsburgh; named to Baseball Hall of Fame (died 1965).

1924 Henry Mancini, pianist and composer, was born in Cleveland; wrote several hits ("Moon River," "Days of Wine and Roses," "Dear Hearts"); film scores (*The Pink Panther, Glenn Miller Story, Breakfast at Tiffany's*).

1929 Senate confirmed former Vice President Charles G. Dawes as ambassador to Great Britain.

1947 Most of Texas City, Tex. destroyed by explosion of French vessel *Grandcamp* in the harbor; 516 were killed.

1947 Karim Abdul-Jabbar, basketball player, was born in New York City as Lew Alcindor; starred at UCLA, Los Angeles Lakers; became all-time leading scorer in National Basketball Association.

1966 A gala concert marked the final performance at the Metropolitan Opera House before moving to its new home in Lincoln Center.

APRIL 17

1524 Giovanni de Verrazano, a Florentine navigator for the French, arrived in New York Bay and Hudson River; then proceeded to Narragansett Bay.

1741 Samuel Chase, jurist, was born in Princess Anne, Md.; member of Continental Congress (1774-78, 1784, 1785), signer of Declaration of Independence; associate justice Supreme Court (1796-1811); impeached (1804) becaue of trial conduct five years earlier, acquitted (1805) (died 1811).

1743 John Page, colonial leader, was born in Gloucester County, Va.; represented Virginia in the House (1789-97) and served as lieutenant governor (1776-79) and governor (1802-05) (died 1808).

1763 *Georgia Gazette*, first newspaper in state, published in Savannah by James Johnson.

1770 Mahlon Dickerson, public official and legislator, was born in Hanover Neck, N.J.; served New Jersey as governor (1815-17) and in the Senate (1817-33); Navy Secretary (1834-38) (died 1853).

1824 United States and Russia signed treaty agreeing to 54°40' line as the southernmost limit of its territorial claims, withdrew restrictions against Bering Sea fishing.

1826 New York granted charter to Mohawk & Hudson Railroad, which later became the New York Central.

1837 J(ohn) P. Morgan, financier, was born in Hartford, son of Junius S. Morgan (4/14/1813); helped form U.S. Steel, General Electric; founder, present-day J.P. Morgan & Co. (1895); generous philanthropist (died 1913).

1838 Massachusetts passed a law forbidding the retail sale of spirituous liquors.

1842 Charles H. Parkhurst, Presbyterian clergymen and reformer, was born in Framingham, Mass.; attacked political corruption, organized vice in sermon (Feb 14, 1892), which aroused New York City and led to Lexow investigation, defeat of Tammany, and election of a reform administration (died 1933).

1849 William R. Day, jurist, was born in Ravenna, Ohio; Secretary of State (1898), led American commission to arrange peace with Spain; associate justice, Supreme Court (1903-22) (died 1923).

1859 Willis Van Devanter, jurist, was born in Marion, Ind.; associate justice, Supreme Court (1910-37) (died 1941).

1859 Walter C. Camp, football coach and selector, was born in New Britain, Conn; originator of choosing "All-American" football teams (1889), influential in shaping football rules; devised "daily dozen," a series of simple calisthenics (died 1925).

1861 Virginia seceded from the Union by a secret legislative vote of 88 to 5, which was later ratified by popular vote (128,884 to 32,134); Gov. John Letcher immediately seized Harpers Ferry (W.Va.) arsenal and Norfolk Navy Yard.

1861 Lewis Nixon, naval architect, was born in Leesburg; Va.; designed various battleships, operated own shipbuilding firm in Elizabeth, N.J. (died 1940).

1868 Mark L. Bristol, naval officer, was born in Glassboro, N.J.; served in Spanish-American War and World War I; high commissioner to Turkey (1919-27); commander, Asiatic fleet (1927); chairman, Navy general board (1930-32) (died 1939).

1870 Ray Stannard Baker, author and editor, was born in Lansing, Mich.; magazine editor, authorized biographer of President Wilson; wrote philosophical essays under name of David Grayson (*Adventures in Contentment*) (died 1946).

1871 Texas legislature approved creation of Texas A & M College.

1874 Clarence H. Mackay, businessman, was born in San Francisco; owner, head, Commercial Cable Co. and Postal Telegraph; completed trans-Pacific cable (1903) (died 1938).

1879 Albert S. Howell, photographic equipment manufacturer, was born in West Branch, Minn.; a founder (1907), Bell & Howell Co. (died 1951).

1882 President Arthur asked Congress for a levee system for the Mississippi River, which had made 85,000 homeless in March.

1890 Harry Plotz, bacteriologist, was born in Paterson, N.J.; developed protective vaccine against typhus; investigated cause of measles, worked on developing serum; studied viral diseases (died 1947).

1897 Thornton N. Wilder, author and playwright, was born in Madison, Wis.; author (*The Bridge of San Luis Rey, Woman of Andros, Heaven's My Destination*); playwright (*Our Town, The Skin of Our Teeth, The Merchant of Yonkers*—which eventually became *Hello Dolly*) (died 1975).

1916 American Academy of Arts & Letters, founded in 1904, incorporated.

1919 Josiah C. Cady, architect, died at 82; designed the original Metropolitan Opera House, the American Museum of Natural History.

1961 The Bay of Pigs invasion of Cuba by 1200 anti-Castro exiles was crushed; they had been trained, armed, and directed by Americans.

1973 President Nixon authorized a new investigation into the growing Watergate case with the appointment of a special prosecutor, Archibald Cox.

1989 The House Ethics Committee unanimously charged Speaker James C. Wright with 69 violations of House rules, the first time a Speaker was charged; committee found him guilty of improperly accepting gifts and evading limits on outside income.

APRIL 18

1644 Opechancanough began two-year war against the Virginians.

1689 An armed uprising in Boston forced the unpopular governor, Sir Edmund Andros, to take refuge in fort; later arrested and jailed for a year, then returned to England.

1775 Paul Revere, William Dawes, and Samuel Prescott spread word of the coming of the British troops; Revere was captured near Lexington, later released; Dawes had to turn back; Prescott went on to Concord warning Samuel Adams, John Hancock.

1799 John Y. Mason, legislator and public official, was born in Greenville County, Va.; represented Virginia in the House (1831-37); Attorney General (1845-46), Navy Secretary (1844-45, 1846-49); minister to France (1854-59) (died 1859).

1803 James Madison was named minister plenipotentiary to England.

1806 Congress passed a non-importation act, excluding many British articles because of raids against American shipping, impressment of seamen.

1831 New York University was chartered.

1847 Gen. Winfield Scott led American troops to victory at Battle of Cerro Gordo.

1853 Vice President William R. King died at 67 at his home near Caluba, Ala.

1857 Clarence S. Darrow, defense lawyer, was born in Kinsman, Ohio; defense attorney for Eugene V. Debs in Pullman strike case, the Leopold-Loeb murder case in Chicago, the Scottsboro case; opposed William Jennings Bryan in the Scopes "monkey" trial in Tennessee (died 1938).

1862 Successful six-day campaign began to move naval forces up the Mississippi River to New Orleans; Union fleet under command of Adm. David D. Porter.

1863 Union Col. Benjamin Grierson began successful raids from LaGrange, Tenn. to Baton Rouge, destroying rail and telegraph lines and Confederate stores.

1864 Richard Harding Davis, journalist, was born in Philadelphia; best-known, most influential newsman of his day; correspondent in six wars; author (*Ranson's Folly, The Dictator*) (died 1916).

1865 Confederate troops under Gen. Joseph E. Johnston surrendered to Union troops led by Gen. William T. Sherman near Raleigh, N.C.

1880 Sam(uel E.) Crawford, baseball player (Tigers), was born in Wahoo, Neb.; named to Baseball Hall of Fame (died 1968).

1882 Leopold Stokowski, conductor, was born in London; conductor, Cincinnati Symphony (1909-12), Philadelphia (1914-36), New York (1944-45); formed American Symphony Orchestra (1962) (died 1977).

1892 Eugene J. Houdry, inventor of catalytic cracking process for making gasoline, was born in Domont, France (died 1962).

1902 Menachem M. Schneerson, rebbe (spiritual head) of Lubavitch Hasidim (1951-), was born in Nikolayev, Russia; one of the most important figures in American and world Jewry.

1905 George H. Hitchings, research scientist, was born in Hoquiam, Wash.; shared 1988 Nobel Physiology/Medicine Prize for helping to develop drugs to fight leukemia, malaria, gout, organ transplant rejection, herpes, and bacterial infections.

1906 An earthquake struck San Francisco at about 5:12 a.m., followed by fires which razed more than four miles of the city; nearly 500 died.

1916 President Wilson sent an ultimatum to Germany after an unarmed French channel vessel, *Sussex*, was torpedoed Mar 24, with four Americans injured; Wilson threatened to sever diplomatic relations unless submarine warfare changed.

1917 Woman's suffrage went into effect in Rhode Island and Michigan.

1938 President Franklin Roosevelt pardoned Dr. Francis E. Townsend, originator of an old age pension plan; Townsend had been found guilty of contempt of Congress and sentenced to a 30-day prison term.

1940 Joseph L. Goldstein, Texas U. scientist, was born in Sumter, S.C.; shared 1985 Nobel Physiology/Medicine Prize for work on receptors that trap and absorb bloodstream particles that contain cholesterol.

1942 Sixteen American B-25s, led by Col. James H. Doolittle, bombed Tokyo, the first Allied air attack on Japan.

1942 President Franklin Roosevelt issued an executive order creating the War Manpower Commission; terminated Sept 19, 1945.

1944 Ernie Pyle, war correspondent, was killed by enemy gunfire on the island of Ie Shima.

1946 Catfish (James A.) Hunter, baseball pitcher (Royals, A's, Yankees) who won 224 games, was born in Hertford, N.C.; named to Baseball Hall of Fame.

1950 Postmaster General Jesse M. Donaldson ordered a cut in residential mail deliveries to once a day.

1978 The Senate approved 68-32 legislation to turn over the Panama Canal to Panama by the year 2000.

1983 The American embassy in Beirut was bombed; 17 Americans were killed.

1986 A Titan-34D rocket carrying a secret military payload blew up shortly after liftoff from the Vandenberg Air Force Base in California.

1987 Richard Wilbur, 66, was named the second American poet laureate, succeeding Robert Penn Warren.

1988 A presidential panel on airline safety recommended making the Federal Aviation Administration an independent agency, headed by a new safety "czar."

APRIL 19

1720 William Burnet was appointed governor of New York and New Jersey, and then Massachusetts, serving until his death in 1729.

1721 Roger Sherman, colonial leader, was born in Newton, Mass.; a Connecticut legislator and jurist, he was the only person to sign all the important colonial documents—Articles of Confederation, Articles of Association, Declaration of Independence, Constitution; co-author of the Connecticut Compromise at the Constitutional Convention, which created the modern Congress; represented Connecticut in the House (1789-91) and Senate (1791-93) (died 1793).

1775 The battles of Lexington and Concord occurred, marking the start of the American Revolution; colonists had been alerted to the planned British attack on the Concord supply depot; the British, commanded by Maj. John Pitcairn, arrived at Lexington at dawn, were met by 70 Minute Men under Capt. John Parker; sporadic fighting went on all day along the entire Lexington-Concord-Boston road; casualties were 73 British killed, 174 wounded, 26 missing; 93 Americans were killed, wounding, or missing.

1782 Holland recognized the independence of America, received John Adams as minister; followed by a loan of $2 million (June 11) and a treaty of commerce (Oct 8).

1791 William O. Butler, Army general, was born in Jessamine County, Ky.; served in the Mexican War; Democratic vice presidential candidate (1848) (died 1880).

1832 Lucretia Rudolph Garfield, wife of President Garfield, was born in Hiram, Ohio (died 1918).

1836 Augustus D. Juilliard, merchant and philanthropist, was born at sea to French parents; bequeathed bulk of fortune to provide musical education for promising students (died 1919).

1850 The Clayton-Bulwer Treaty between the United States and Great Britain was ratified; designed to relieve tensions over Central America and to make it possible for private enterprise to build and operate an isthmian canal.

1861 A mob of Southern sympathizers attacked a Massachusetts militia regiment marching through Baltimore; four soldiers and 12 civilians were killed.

1861 President Lincoln proclaimed a blockade of Confederate ports in South Carolina, Georgia, Alabama, Florida, Mississippi, Louisiana, and Texas.

1861 John G. Hibben, educator, was born in Peoria, Ill.; logic and psychology professor (1887-1912), president, Princeton U. (1912-32) (died 1933).

1865 May Robson, stage and screen actress, was born in New South Wales, Australia; numerous stage and screen hits (*Strange Interlude, Lady for a Day*) (died 1942).

1865 Funeral services were held for President Lincoln in Washington; burial services were held in Springfield, Ill. May 4.

1868 Paul P. Harris, club founder, was born in Racine, Wis.; founder, Rotary International in Chicago (Feb. 23, 1905) (died 1947).

1892 A gasoline-driven autombile was demonstrated by its inventors, Charles A. and J. Frank Duryea.

1897 The first Boston Marathon, from Boston to Hopkinton, was run.

1912 Glenn T. Seaborg, chemist, was born in Ishpeming, Mich.; chairman, Atomic Energy Commission (1961-71); shared 1951 Nobel Chemistry Prize for discovery of plutonium.

1917 The first American shots in World War I were fired by the American steamer *Magnolia* when it repulsed a submarine attack.

1919 Merce Cunningham, dancer and choreographer, was born in Centralia, Wash.; developed new forms of abstract dance called "choreography by chance."

1932 Andrea Mead (Lawrence), champion skier who won numerous American and international titles, was born in Rutland, Vt.

1951 Gen. Douglas MacArthur, relieved of his command by President Truman, addressed a joint session of Congress.

1956 Grace Kelly, screen actress, married Prince Rainier III, ruler of Monaco, and retired from the screen.

1967 Nineteen Western Hemisphere nations signed a declaration in Uruguay for the formation of a Latin American common market; President Lyndon Johnson signed for the United States.

1988 Milwaukee Mayor Henry W. Maier left office after serving for 28 years, the longest tenure of any big city mayor.

1989 A 16-inch gun on the battleship *Iowa* exploded during a routine test firing north of Puerto Rico, killing 47 crewmen.

APRIL 20

1676 Bacon's Rebellion began when Nathaniel Bacon led the frontiersmen of Virginia against the Indians because the governor refused to act.

1735 Richard Henderson, frontiersman, was born in Hanover County, Va.; with Daniel Boone, he built Boonesboro, one of first permanent Kentucky settlements; later established Nashville (died 1785).

1777 A New York convention adopted a state constitution.

1812 Vice President George Clinton died in Washington at 73, the first vice president to die in office.

1836 Wisconsin Territory was created.

1842 John M. Farley, Catholic prelate. was born in County Armagh, Ireland; archbishop of New York (1902-18), named cardinal 1911 (died 1918).

1842 Daniel C. French, sculptor, was born in Exeter, N.H.; best known for seated Lincoln in Lincoln Memorial, Washington; also did Minute Man, Concord, Mass. and John Harvard in Harvard U. yard (died 1931).

1861 Robert E. Lee resigned his command in the U.S. Army; accepted command of the Virginia Confederate forces; named a general June 18.

1867 John M. Bozeman, pioneer, was killed by Indians at 32; blazed new trail (1863) through Rockies between Yellowstone and Gallatin rivers to Virginia City.

1868 Georgia electorate ratified a new state constitution adopted by convention.

1882 Holland M. ("Howlin' Mad") Smith, World War II Marine Corps general, was born in Seale, Ala. (died 1967).

1891 Dave (David J.) Bancroft, baseball player (Phillies, Giants, Dodgers), was born in Sioux City, Iowa; named to Baseball Hall of Fame (died 1972).

1894 Harold Lloyd, screen actor, was born in Burchard, Neb.; made almost 200 films, mostly comedies (*The Freshman, Kid Brother, Movie Crazy*) (died 1971).

1898 Congress adopted a joint resolution authorizing the use of the Army and Navy to bring about Cuban independence; helped start Spanish-American War.

1905 Harold S. Marcus, merchant, was born in Dallas; president, Nieman-Marcus stores (1950-72).

1914 The House (323-29) and Senate (72-13) authorized President Wilson to take necessary actions in the wake of the Tampico, Mexico incident when American sailors were jailed.

1920 John P. Stevens, jurist, was born in Chicago; associate justice, Supreme Court (1975-).

1933 An executive order by President Franklin Roosevelt put an end to the export of gold; formally the nation went off the gold standard; ratified by Congress June 5.

1943 President Franklin Roosevelt conferred with Mexican President Avila Camacho at Monterey, Mexico on cooperation during and after the war.

1961 President Kennedy said the United States would not "abandon" Cuba to the Communists.

1971 Supreme Court ruled that busing could be used to achieve desegregation in dual school systems in the South.

1983 President Reagan signed the Social Security amendments which placed new federal employees under the system beginning Jan 1, 1984, gradually increasing the age of eligibility from 65 to 66 by 2009 and to 67 by 2027.

1984 Mabel Mercer, jazz singer, died at 84; Leonard Bernstein called her "the eternal guardian of elegance in the world of popular song."

1988 Supreme Court ruled that Congress is free to tax all interest on state and local government bonds, overruling an 1895 precedent ruling.

1988 The Supreme Court ruled 4-3 that alcoholism is "willful misconduct" and that the Veterans Administration could deny disability and other benefits to veterans disabled by the condition.

APRIL 21

1649 Maryland enacted the Toleration Act, designed to remove the charge that the colony was intolerant of Protestants, declaring in part: "...noe person or persons whatsoever...professing to believe in Jesus Christ, shall from henceforth bee any waies troubled, molested or discountenanced, for or in respect of his or her religion nor in the free exercise thereof...not any way compelled to beleefe or exercise of any other religion against his or her consent;" repealed by the Assembly Oct 1654.

1775 Lord Dunmore, Virginia governor, ordered all gunpowder in the Williamsburg magazine removed; this was done to place it under greater security, he said, and it would be returned.

1775 Alexander Anderson, engraver and illustrator, was born in New York City; made the first American wood engravings (died 1870).

1778 Thomas McAuley, theologian, was born in Coleraine, Ireland; a founder (1835), first president (1836-40); Union Theological Seminary (died 1862).

1789 John Adams took office as the first vice president.

1801 Robert F.W. Allston, agriculturist, was born in All Saints Parish, S.C.; developed a system of embankments and drainage ditches, making it possible to cultivate rice on marshland; governor of South Carolina (1856-58) (died 1864).

1809 Robert M.T. Hunter, legislator, was born in Essex County, Va.; represented Virginia in the House (1837-43, 1845-47), serving as Speaker (1839-41), and in the Senate (1847-61); Confederate Secretary of State (1861-62) (died 1887).

1818 Henry W. Shaw, author, was born in Lanesboro, Mass.; better known as Josh Billings (died 1885).

1828 *Webster's Dictionary* (two volumes) was published.

1832 Abraham Lincoln enlisted to serve in the Black Hawk War; discharged July 10.

1836 Mexican forces led by Gen. Antonio Santa Anna, who was captured, were defeated at San Jacinto by Texans under Sam Houston; Texas thus won its independence.

1838 John Muir, naturalist, was born in Dunbar, Scotland; led efforts to enact federal conservation laws, to establish Sequoia and Yosemite national parks (died 1914).

1855 The first railroad train crossed the Mississippi River's first bridge, which connected Rock Island, Ill. and Davenport, Iowa.

1870 Edwin S. Porter, inventor, was born in Connellsville, Pa.; worked with Edison on developing the motion picture camera; made the first story film, *The Life of an American Fireman* (1899) for Edison (died 1941).

1882 Percy W. Bridgman, physicist, was born in Cambridge; awarded 1946 Nobel Physics Prize for development of high pressure chambers to study matter at extreme pressure (died 1961).

1898 Spain broke off diplomatic relations with the United States.

1915 Anthony Quinn, screen actor, was born in Chihuahua, Mexico; starred in many films (*Zorba the Greek, Viva Zapata*).

1917 The Nebraska legislature enacted woman suffrage and statewide prohibition laws.

1918 San Jacinto and Hemet in California were destroyed by an earthquake.

1930 A fire in the Ohio State Penitentiary at Columbus resulted in 320 deaths.

1945 Seventh Army captured Nuremberg, Germany.

1955 The American occupation of Germany ended; troops remained on a contractual basis.

1958 A midair collision near Las Vegas killed 49 persons.

1962 The first American world's fair in 22 years—the Century 21 Exposition—opened in Seattle.

1986 Supreme Court ruled 5-4 that a person suing a news organization for libel must prove the damaging statements were false "on matters of public concern;" overturned several statutes which put burden of proof on news organizations.

APRIL 22

1669 Richard Mather, colonial religious leader, died at 72; teacher of Dorchester, Mass. church; a leader of colonial Congregationalism; co-author, *Bay Psalm Book.*

1688 Jonathan Dickinson, Presbyterian clergyman, was born in Hatfield, Mass.; obtained charter for College of New Jersey (later Princeton), its first president (1746-47) (died 1747).

1711 Eleazar Wheelock, Congregational clergyman, was born in Windham, Conn.; founder of Hanover, N.H., Dartmouth College (1769) (died 1779).

1729 Michael Hillegas, first treasurer of the United States (1777-89), was born in Philadelphia (died 1804).

1759 James Freeman, first American Unitarian, was born in Charleston, Mass.; a lay reader in New York City's King Chapel, was refused ordination because of his revisions in *Book of Common Prayer*; ordained as a Unitarian (1787) making King's Chapel first American Unitarian church; Freeman served until 1826 (died 1835).

1774 When a private consignee tried to land a load of tea in New York City, Sons of Liberty disguised themselves as Indians, dumped the tea into harbor; similar incidents occurred in Boston, Annapolis, Greenwich, N.J.

1786 Amos Lawrence, merchant, was born in Groton, Mass., brother of Abbott Lawrence (12/16/1792) and William Lawrence (9/7/1783); with brothers, developed textile manufacturing (died 1852).

1793 President Washington issued a neutrality proclamation declaring that the United States was at peace with both Great Britain and France; warned citizens to abstain from any acts of hostility against any belligerents.

1801 Elijah C. Bridgman, Congregational clergyman, was born in Belchertown, Mass.; was the first American missionary to China (1830) (died 1861).

1818 Cadwallader C. Washburn, businessman and public official, was born in Livermore, Me., brother of Elihu B. Washburne (9/23/1816); represented Wisconsin in the House (1855-61, 1867-71) and served it as governor (1872-74); founder, Washburn Crosby & Co., flour millers; donated observatory to U. of Wisconsin (died 1882).

1831 Alexander M. McCook, Union general, was born in Columbiana County, Ohio; served at Shiloh, Murfreesboro, Chickamauga (died 1903).

1832 Julius Sterling Morton, public official, was born in Adams, N.Y.; secretary of Nebraska Territory (1858-61); Secretary of Agriculture (1893-97), originated Arbor Day, which now is observed on his birthday (died 1902).

1842 Alexander Kohut, Conservative Jewish leader, was born in Feligyhaza, Hungary; a founder, Jewish Theological Seminary, New York City (1887) (died 1894).

1854 The Senate ratified the Gadsden Purchase by which the United States acquired from Mexico 45,535 sq.mi. of territory in southern Arizona and New Mexico for $10 million.

1874 Ellen (A.G.) Glasgow, author, was born in Richmond, Va.; wrote several popular novels (*Barren Ground, Vein of Iron, The Desendant*) (died 1945).

1876 Ole Edvart Rölvaag, author and educator, was born in Dönne Island, Norway; taught at St. Olaf College (1905-31), gained fame for *Giants in the Earth*, an epic of immigrant life on the South Dakota plains (died 1931).

1884 Otto Rank, psychoanalyst, was born in Vienna; a disciple of Freud, he broke with him on the basic theory (died 1939).

1887 James Norman Hall, author, was born in Colfax, Iowa; co-author (with Charles Nordhoff) of several novels (*Mutiny on the Bounty, Pitcairn Island, Botany Bay, The Hurricane*) (died 1951).

1889 Unassigned land in Indian Territory (Oklahoma) was opened to white settlement by a run for homestead claims by more than 50,000 settlers.

1898 President McKinley ordered a blockade of Cuban ports.

1898 The first shots of the Spanish-American War were fired off Key West, Fla., when the American ship *Nashville* captured the Spanish ship *Buena Ventura*.

1904 J. Robert Oppenheimer, physicist, was born in New York City; instrumental in developing the atomic bomb; headed Los Alamos, N.M. atomic laboratory (1943-45); chairman; Atomic Energy Commission advisory board (1947-53); director, Institute for Advanced Study, Princeton U. (1947-66) (died 1967).

1909 Rita Levi-Montalcini, medical researcher at Washington U. in the 1950s, was born in Turin, Italy; shared 1986 Nobel Physiology/Medicine Prize for the discovery of key proteins that control body growth.

1914 American Marines landed at Veracruz, Mexico; seized customs house and prevented the landing of German munitions; brought nations to the brink of war, which was averted by mediation of Argentina, Brazil, and Chile.

1916 Yehudi Menuhin, violinist, was born in New York City; a child prodigy, he was on concert stage since 1937.

1922 Charles Mingus, musician, was born in Nogales, Ariz.; a major figure in jazz of the 1950s/60s, one of the first to exploit the bass as a solo instrument (died 1979).

1936 Glen Campbell, country music singer, was born in Billstown, Ark.; recorded many hits ("Wichita Lineman," "Galveston").

1937 Jack Nicholson, screen actor, was born in Neptune, N.J.; starred in many films (*One Flew Over the Cuckoo's Nest, Terms of Endearment, Prizzi's Honor*).

1944 Allied troops landed at Hollandia, New Guinea.

1954 Televised hearings into alleged Communist infiltration of the Army were begun by Sen. Joseph R. McCarthy of Wisconsin; ended June 17.

1964 President Lyndon Johnson dedicated the Federal Pavilion at the World's Fair in New York City.

1970 The first "Earth Day" was observed as millions of Americans participated in anti-pollution demonstrations.

APRIL 23

1541 Francisco Vasquez de Coronado and his men left the Southwest, traveled across the Texas Panhandle and Oklahoma into eastern Kansas, then returned.

1662 A charter was granted by Charles II to John Winthrop on behalf of the Colony of Connecticut .

1731 William Williams, merchant, was born in Lebanon, Conn; a member of the Continental Congress (1776-78, 1783, 1784), a signer of the Declaration of Independence (died 1811).

1775 Massachusetts Provincial Congress authorized raising 13,000 men, named Artemus Ward as commander-in-chief, and appealed to other colonies for aid; by May 20, Rhode Island, New Hampshire, and Connecticut agreed to send 9500 men.

1778 John Paul Jones raided British shipping in Whitehaven (England) harbor.

1784 Continental Congress enacted a plan introduced by Thomas Jefferson for the territory between the Ohio and Mississippi rivers; two proposals were not accepted, one of them stating: "That after the year 1800 there shall be neither slavery nor involuntary servitude in any of the states."

1789 George Washington arrived in New York City for his inauguration, escorted to the first presidential mansion at 1 Cherry St. (Cherry and Queen Sts.).

1791 James Buchanan, 13th president (1857-61), was born near Mercersburg, Pa.; represented Pennsylvania in the House (1821-31) and Senate (1835-45); minister to Russia (1832-34), to Great Britain (1853-56); Secretary of State (1845-49) (died 1868).

1803 Adin Ballou, religious leader and social reformer, was born in Cumberland, R.I.; formed splinter Universalist group, helped form the Hopedale Community, a self-contained religious society, near Milford, Mass. (1841-59) (died 1890).

1813 Stephen A. Douglas, legislator, was born in Brandon, Vt.; represented Illinois in the House (1843-47) and Senate (1847-60); debated with Lincoln during 1858 senatorial campaign, ran against him for the presidency (1860) (died 1861).

1834 Chauncey M. Depew, lawyer and legislator, was born in Peekskill, N.Y.; president, New York Central Railroad (1885-99); represented New York in the Senate (1899-1911); a renowned speaker and wit (died 1928).

1831 Elbert E. Farman, diplomat and Egyptologist, was born in New Haven, N.Y.; served in Egypt many years as consul general, made vast collection of antiquities, which he donated to the Metropolitan Museum of Art; given Cleopatra's Needle for New York City's Central Park (died 1911).

1838 The *Great Western,* the first steamboat built for trans-Atlantic service, arrived in New York from Bristol, which it had left Apr 8.

1839 James B. Hammond, inventor, was born in Boston; invented a new style of typewriter (1880) (died 1913).

1840 Henry A. House, inventor, was born in Brooklyn; invented the buttonhole machine (1862), other attachments to sewing machines; steam-engine driven horseless carriage (died 1930).

1844 Sanford G. Dole, Hawaiian leader, was born in Honolulu; president, Republic of Hawaii (1894-98); first governor, Hawaii Territory (1900-03) (died 1926).

1852 Edwin Markham, poet, was born in Oregon City, Ore.; achieved success with *The Man With the Hoe* (died 1940).

1853 Winthrop M. Crane, paper manufacturer and public official, was born in Dalton, Mass.; with family paper business (from 1870); served Massachusetts as governor (1900-03) and represented it in the Senate (1904-14) (died 1920).

1856 Arthur T. Hadley, economist and educator, was born in New Haven; expert on railroad economics; taught at Yale (1883-99), president (1899-1921), led unprecedented growth of the university (died 1930).

1859 The first Colorado newspaper, *Rocky Mountain News*, began publication in Denver, William N. Byers as publisher.

1862 Alexis F. Lange, educator, was born in Lafayette County, Mo.; a leader in junior high school, junior college movements (died 1924).

1868 Popular vote in North Carolina ratified a new state constitution, adopted by convention Mar 16.

1880 Carl L. Norden, inventor of the bombsight, was born in Semarang, Java (died 1965).

1893 Frank Borzage, film director and producer (*Farwell to Arms, Seventh Heaven, Humoresque*), was born in Salt Lake City (died 1962).

1896 The Edison Vitascope, projecting motion pictures on a large screen, had its world premier at Koster and Biel's music hall, 34th St. and Herald Square, New York City.

1897 Lucius D. Clay, World War II Army general, was born in Marietta, Ga.; administrator of American occupied zone in Germany (1945-49) (died 1978).

1898 President McKinley issued a call for 125,000 volunteers for war with Spain.

1899 Vladimir Nabokov, author, was born in Leningrad; best remembered for *Lolita* (died 1977).

1900 Jim (James L.) Botomley, baseball player (Cardinals), was born in Oglesby, Ill.; named to Baseball Hall of Fame (died 1959).

1921 Warren E. Spahn, baseball player, was born in Buffalo; all-time great left-handed pitcher (Braves); won 363 games; named to Baseball Hall of Fame.

1928 Shirley Temple (Black), screen actress, was born in Santa Monica, Cal.; most famous child screen star; delegate to UN General Assembly (1969-70); chief of protocol (1976-77).

1940 Fire in Natchez, Miss. dance hall resulted in 198 deaths.

1951 Former Vice President Charles G. Dawes (1925-29) died in Evanston, Ill. at 85.

1968 United Methodist Church was officially formed with the merger of the Methodist Church (10.3 million members) and the Evangelical United Brethren Church (750,000 members).

APRIL 24

1676 Simon Willard, colonial leader, died at 71; a founder of Concord (1635); member, Massachusetts General Court (1654-76); commanded colonial troops in King Philip's War (1675).

1704 The first issue of an American continuous news periodical, the *Boston News Letter*, was published by John Campbell, the Boston postmaster; continued until 1776.

1766 Robert B. Thomas, editor, was born in Grafton, Conn.; founder, editor, *Farmer's Almanac* (1792-1846) (died 1860).

1784 Peter V. Daniel, jurist, was born in Stafford County, Va.; associate justice, Supreme Court (1841-60) (died 1860).

1800 Congress passed an act moving the seat of government to Washington.

1800 The Library of Congress was founded by the purchase of $5000 worth of books (152 works in 740 volumes); the library was to be operated "as may be necessary for the use of Congress."

1820 Congress enacted the land law, ending the credit system of the 1800 law and reducing the price of public land from $2 to $1.25 an acre.

1846 A Mexican force ambushed 63 American troops near Matamoras; two days later, Gen. Zachary Taylor informed Washington that "hostilities may now be considered as commenced."

1856 Isaac Gimbel, merchant, was born in Vincennes, Ind.; co-founder, first president, Gimbel Bros. Inc. department store (died 1931).

1862 Adm. John D. Farragut successfully ran his fleet by the Confederate forts on the lower Mississippi River in the dark, cutting them off from New Orleans, which then was occupied by Union troops under Gen. Benjamin F. Butler.

1874 John R. Pope, architect, was born in New York City; designed Constitution Hall, National Gallery of Art buildings in Washington (died 1937).

1876 Charles M. Manly, mechanical engineer, was born in Staunton, Va.; designed light five-cylinder radial gasoline engine for planes; considered first modern aircraft engineer; held about 50 patents on power generation (died 1927).

1879 Oris P. Van Sweringen, railroad executive, was born in Wooster, Ohio; with brother, Mantis (7/8/1881), developed Shaker Heights, a Cleveland suburb; controlled, operated many railroads (died 1936).

1882 Tony (Anthony F.) Sarg, illustrator and marionette maker, was born in Coban, Guatemala; creator of marionette shows (died 1942).

1898 Spain declared war on the United States.

1898 Russell H. Varian, physicist, was born in Washington; known for work in microwaves, electronics; co-inventor of Klystron, UHF resonator (died 1959).

1904 Willem DeKooning, painter, was born in Rotterdam; central figure in developing abstract expressionism.

1905 Robert Penn Warren, author, was born in Todd

County, Ky.; poet (*Now and Then Promises*) and first American poet laureate (1986), novelist (*All the King's Men*) (died 1989).

1917 President Wilson signed the Liberty Loan Act, authorizing the sale of $2 billion in 3-1/2% convertible gold bonds by public subscription.

1934 Shirley MacLaine, screen actress, was born in Richmond. Va., sister of Warren Beatty (3/30/1938); starred in many films (*Sweet Charity, Irma la Douce, Terms of Endearment*).

1942 Barbra Streisand, singer and actress, was born in New York City; starred on stage (*Funny Girl*), screen (*The Way We Were, Funny Lady, Yentl*); recording star.

1945 The American Third Army liberated the Dachau concentration camp.

1956 Alaska voters approved a constitution for the Territory.

1980 A military mission to rescue American hostages in Itan was aborted because of equipment failure; eight men were killed, much equipment lost.

1981 President Reagan ended the ban on American grain sales to the Soviet Union, which had been in effect 15 months.

1983 Supreme Court held 8-1 that the Internal Revenue Service could deny tax exemptions to private schools that practiced racial discrimination.

1988 An explosion and fire aboard the submarine USS *Bonefish* left 18 sailors injured and three missing.

APRIL 25

1769 Sir Marc I. Brunel, engineer, was born in Hacqueville, France; won design competition for the Capitol, but another was used for economy; built Thames tunnel (died 1849).

1776 James Madison was elected to the Virginia State convention; served on committee which drafted state constitution, adopted June 29.

1777 British troops began a three-day raid on Connecticut towns; burning Danbury (Apr 27); stopped at Ridgefield by Benedict Arnold with 600 men.

1781 The battle of Hobkirk's Hill, near Camden, S.C., resulted in a virtual standoff; British retreated, burning Camden on the way.

1798 The patriotic song, "Hail Columbia," composed by Joseph Hopkinson, was first sung in a theater in Philadelphia.

1812 The General Land Office, designed to handle public lands, was created as a bureau in the Treasury Department; moved to Interior Department 1849.

1838 The steamer *Moselle* exploded on the Ohio River near Cincinnati, killing 100 persons.

1854 Charles S. Tainter, inventor, was born in Watertown, Mass.; invented various sound recording instruments, including the Gramophone and Dictaphone (died 1940).

1861 Edwin R.A. Seligman, economist, was born in New York City, son of Joseph Seligman (11/22/1819); helped formulate income tax base, banking system for Federal Reserve; a founder, American Economic Assn. (died 1939).

1873 Howard R. Garis, author, was born in Binghamton, N.Y.; known for *Uncle Wiggley* series of children's books (died 1962).

1880 Michael Fokine, dancer and choreographer, was born in Leningrad; directed Diaghilev's Russian ballet, own American company (died 1942).

1898 Congress declared war on Spain, saying the war had been in effect since Apr 21.

1900 Wolfgang Pauli, physicist, was born in Vienna; first to explain behavior of a class of atomic particles and postulate existence of neutrino; awarded 1945 Nobel Physics Prize for that work (died 1958).

1906 William J. Brennan, jurist, was born in Newark; associate justice, Supreme Court (1956-).

1908 Edward R. Murrow, newsman and public official, was born in Greensboro, N.C.; with CBS (1936-61), became famous with broadcasts from London during World War II; starred in own interview shows (*See It Now, Person to Person*); director, U.S. Information Service (1961-64) (died 1965).

1909 William L. Pereira, architect, was born in Chicago; among his designs are the Los Angeles Museum of Art, the Houston Center (died 1985).

1918 Ella Fitzgerald, jazz singer, was born in Newport News, Va.; one of the leading singers of her time.

1944 George Herriman, cartoonist, died at 64; remembered for his *Krazy Kat* cartoon (1910-44), the first written and drawn for adult appreciation.

1945 The organizational meeting of the United Nations began in San Francisco with 50 nations attending; ended June 26.

1946 A railroad collision near Chicago resulted in 45 deaths.

1953 James D. Watson, American biologist, and Francis C.H. Crick, British biologist, announced success in making three-dimension molecular model of DNA (deoxyribose nucleic), a scientific discovery comparable to Newton's law of motion, Darwin's evolution theory, and Einstein's theory of relativity; shared 1962 Nobel Physiology/Medicine Prize for their work.

1959 The St. Lawrence Seaway was opened.

1962 The United States resumed nuclear testing near Christmas Island, largest atoll in the Pacific, following Russian refusal to sign an atomic testing accord.

1988 John Demjanjuk, Cleveland auto worker who was found guilty of torturing and killing thousands of Jews as a Nazi death camp guard, was sentenced by an Israeli court to be hanged.

APRIL 26

1598 Expedition of Juan de Onate reached the Rio Grande River, and then (May 4) the site of El Paso.

1607 Three vessels of the London Company, under command of Christopher Newport, arrived in Chesapeake Bay off Cape Henry , enroute to settling in Virginia; erected a cross (Apr 29) at Cape Henry; elected Edward M. Wingfield (1586-1613) as first governor, deposed him in Sept.

1702 Proprietors of West and East Jersey surrendered govermental authority to the Crown and the colony became a royal colony, governed by the governor of New York until 1738.

1718 Esek Hopkins, sea captain, was born in Scituate, R.I.; commander-in-chief, Continental Navy (1775-78); had insuperable difficulties in equipping, manning few available ships; censured and dismissed (died 1802).

1727 Samuel Cranston, colonial governor, died at 68; served as governor of Rhode Island (1698-1727).

1783 Seven thousand Loyalists sailed from New York for Nova Scotia or England.

1785 John James Audubon, ornithologist and artist, was born in Haiti; while unsuccessful as a storekeeper, he began painting birds; his *Birds of America* hailed as a masterpiece (died 1851).

1822 Frederick Law Olmsted, pioneer landscape architect, was born in Hartford; designed Central and Prospect parks in New York City, South Park in Chicago, U.S. Capitol grounds, and Boston park system (died 1903).

1828 Martha F. Finley, author, was born in Chillicothe, Ohio; pseudonym for Martha Farquaharson, author of Elsie Dinsmore stories (died 1909).

1830 Benjamin F. Tracy, public official, was born in Oswego, N.Y.; Navy Secretary (1889-93); increased number of battleships, raised standards of the service; described as the father of the American Navy (died 1915).

1830 Senate began impeachment hearing of James Peck, U.S. district judge of Missouri, for holding in contempt of court one who criticized his opinion; acquitted Jan 31, 1831.

1831 New York State abolished imprisonment for debt, effective Mar 1, 1832.

1834 Charles F. Browne, humorist, was born near Waterford, Me.; wrote numerous articles in *Vanity Fair* under name of Artemus Ward (died 1867).

1854 Massachusetts Emigrant Aid Society (later known as the New England Emigrant Aid Co.) was organized by Eli Thayer to promote the settlement of antislavery groups in Kansas; founded Lawrence and other communities in three-year history.

1865 Thirty-seven thousand Confederate soldiers surrendered at Hillsboro, N.C.

1865 John Wilkes Booth, assassin of President Lincoln, was shot and killed in a tobacco barn between Port Royal and Bowling Green, Va.

1871 Hutchinson I. Cone, naval officer, was born in Brooklyn; served in Spanish-American War, commanded naval aviation forces (1917-18) (died 1941).

1889 Leonard T. Troland, engineer, was born in Norwich, Conn.; invented multi-color process for motion pictures; chief engineer, Technicolor Motion Picture Corp.; also physicist and psychologist, conducting important experiments in vision (died 1932).

1891 Paul G. Hoffman, automaker and public official, was born in Chicago; president, Studebaker Corp. (1935-53), board chairman (1953-56); director of Marshall Plan (1948-50); president, Ford Foundation (1951-55); administrator, UN Development Program (1966-72) (died 1974).

1893 Anita Loos, author, was born in Sisson, Cal.; best known for *Gentlemen Prefer Blondes* (died 1981).

1900 Charles F. Richter, geophysicist, was born in Butler County, Ohio; developed method of measuring severity of earthquakes (Richter scale) (died 1985).

1900 Hack (Lewis R.) Wilson, baseball player, was born in Elwood City, Pa.; outfielder with Chicago Cubs 12 years, hit 244 home runs (56 in 1930); named to Baseball Hall of Fame (died 1948).

1907 Tercentenary Exposition opened in Jamestown, Va.; with President Theodore Roosevelt on hand.

1908 Dave Tough, leading drummer of 1930s, 40s, was born in Oak Park, Ill. (died 1948).

1914 Bernard Malamud, author (*The Fixer, The Tenant, Dubin's Lives*) was born in New York City (died 1986).

1917 I(eoh) M. Pei, architect, was born in Canton, China; designed L'Enfant Plaza and National Art Gallery in Washington.

1933 Arno A. Penzies, astrophysicist, was born in Munich; shared 1978 Nobel Physics Prize for work in cosmic microwave radiation.

1936 Carol Burnett, entertainer, was born in San Antonio; starred in several films, television series.

1939 President Franklin Roosevelt issued an executive order for the purchase of 571 military aircraft; asked for immediate construction of new naval bases.

1944 Montgomery Ward & Co., defying National Labor Relations Board orders, was seized by federal troops.

1952 The destroyer, *Hobson,* sank after colliding with the aircraft carrier, *Wasp*, during Atlantic maneuvers; 176 men lost.

1983 The National Commission on Excellence in Education issued a report calling American elementary and secondary education "mediocre;" recommended a number of steps for improvement.

1984 President Reagan began a six-day visit to China.

APRIL 27

1584 An expedition organized by Sir Walter Raleigh sailed for the New World; the expedition, commanded by Sir Richard Grenville and Ralph Lane, landed on Roanoke Island in July.

1686 Gov. Thomas Dongan officially signed a charter for New York City.

1773 The British Parliament, in an effort to help the near-bankrupt East India Co., removed all duties on tea exported to the American colonies; however, the three-penny import tax in America was retained; the improved position enabled the company to undersell all competitors.

1791 Samuel F.B. Morse, telegraph inventor, was born in Charlestown, Mass., son of Jedidiah Morse (8/23/1761); portrait painter (1815-37); a founder, first president, National Academy of Design (1826-42); developed telegraph and code for it; Congress (1843) voted $30,000 for an experimental line from Washington to Baltimore, which was built by Ezra Cornell; Morse sent the first message May 24, 1844; involved in long litigation before he was recognized as rightful developer (died 1872).

1805 Small force led by Capt. William Eaton, American consul at Tunis, and Lieut. Presley O'Bannon, aided by shelling from three American brigs, captured Dorna in Tripoli; led Pasha of Tripoli to sue for peace.

1813 American troops burned York (now Toronto), including the governor's residence and the assembly house; the American commander and explorer, Gen. Zebulon Pike, was killed in an explosion of a magazine during the assault; city was abandoned May 2.

1822 Ulysses S. Grant, 18th president (1868-76), was born in Pt. Pleasant, Ohio; Union general, who led all Union forces toward the end of the war (died 1885).

1838 Fire in Charleston, S.C. destroyed $3 million in property.

1846 President Polk signed a joint resolution authorizing him to notify Great Britain that joint occupation of Oregon was to be terminated; a year's notice required.

1846 Charles J. Van Depoele, inventor, was born in Lichtervelde, Belgium; demonstrated feasibility of electric trolleys; had more than 250 patents on electrical items (died 1892).

1854 The river steamer *Sultana* exploded near Memphis and sank, 1450 persons died.

1854 Benjamin N. Duke, tobacco company founder, was born in Durham, N.C.; with brother, James Duke (12/23/1856), founded tobacco factory near Durham, which became the American Tobacco Co.; headed company (1890-1929); large benefactor of Trinity College, Durham, which became Duke U. (died 1929).

1861 Maryland legislature voted 53-13 against secession.

1861 President Lincoln extended the blockade of Confederate ports to include Virginia and North Carolina.

1865 Cornell U. in Ithaca, N.Y. was chartered.

1870 The collapse of a building in Richmond, Va. resulted in 61 deaths and injuries to 12 persons.

1878 Frank Gotch, probably the greatest American professional wrestler, was born in Humboldt, Neb.; lost only six of 196 matches (died 1917).

1893 Norman Bel Geddes, designer, was born in Adrian, Mich.; stage designer, producer, or director of 200 operas, plays, films; foremost proponent of streamlining; designed Futurama at New York's World Fair (1939) (died 1958).

1896 Rogers Hornsby, baseball player (Cardinals), was born in Winters, Texas; life-time batting average of .358, hit all-time high of .424 in 1924; named to Baseball Hall of Fame (died 1963).

1896 Wallace H. Carothers, research chemist, was born in Burlington, Iowa; director, DuPont Research Lab (1926-37), developed neoprene; did basic research on nylon (died 1937).

1897 Grant's Tomb in New York City was dedicated by President McKinley.

1898 Ludwig Bemelmans, illustrator and author, was born in Meran, Austria (now Italy); remembered for *Madeline* books (died 1962).

1898 American fleet bombarded fortifications at Matanzas, Cuba.

1904 Arthur F. Burns, economist and diplomat, was born in Stanislau, Austria; chairman, Federal Reserve Board (1970-78); ambassador to West Germany (1981-85) (died 1987).

1916 Enos (Country) Slaughter), baseball player (Cardinals, Yankees), was born in Roxboro, N.C.; named to Baseball Hall of Fame.

1930 Earl Anthony, professional bowling's first million-dollar prize winner, was born in Kent, Wash.; won the Professional Bowling Assn. national tournament six times, American Bowling Congress Master Champion (1977, 1984); named to Pro Bowler Hall of Fame.

1941 President Franklin Roosevelt outlined a drastic economic program designed to combat inflation.

1950 Calvin Simmons, first black conductor of a major orchestra (Oakland Symphony 1979), was born in San Francisco (died 1982).

1975 Saigon was shelled and imperiled by approaching Communist forces; President Ford ordered the helicopter evacuation of remaining Americans.

1978 Scaffolding inside a cooling tower at the site of a nuclear power plant at Willow Island, W.Va. collapsed, killing 51 workers, including 11 members of one family.

1981 The Gerald R. Ford Library at Ann Arbor, Mich. was dedicated.

1981 Former Vice President Spiro T. Agnew was ordered by a Maryland judge to pay $247,735 to the state to compensate for the bribes and kickbacks he received while governor and vice president.

APRIL 28

1758 James Monroe, fifth President (1817-25), was born in Westmoreland County, Va.; member of Continental Congress (1783-86); represented Virginia in the Senate (1790-94) and served as governor (1797-1802, 1810-11); minister to France (1794-96), Great Britain (1803-07); Secretary of State (1811-17); War Secretary (1814-15) (died 1831).

1788 Maryland legislature by 63-11 ratified Constitution to enter Union as seventh state.

1815 Andrew J. Smith, Union general, was born in Bucks County, Pa. (died 1897).

1817 United States and Great Britain signed the Rush-Bagot Treaty, limiting armaments on the Great Lakes, providing for an unfortified American-Canadian border; ratified by the Senate Apr 16, 1818.

1849 *Minnesota Pioneer*, first newspaper in state, published in St. Paul.

1865 Bertram G. Goodhue, architect, was born in Pomfret, Conn.; designed Nebraska State Capitol, West Point Chapel, National Academy of Science (died 1924).

1878 Lionel Barrymore, actor, was born in Philadelphia, brother of Ethel Barrymore (8/15/1879) and John Barrymore (2/15/1882); starred in films (*You Can't Take It With You, Rasputin*), television (*Dr. Kildare* series); portrayed Scrooge in annual radio Christmas Carol reading (died 1954).

1917 Robert Anderson, playwright was born in New York City; remembered for *Tea and Sympathy* and *I Never Sang for My Father*.

1930 James A. Baker III, nominated by President-elect Bush to be Secretary of State (1989), was born in Houston; Treasury Secretary (1985-88), White House chief of staff (1981-85).

1941 A dim-out, 15 miles deep along the Atlantic Coast, was put in effect to combat submarine attacks.

1945 President Truman addressed the opening session of the United Nations in San Francisco by telephone.

1980 Cyrus Vance resigned as Secretary of State in protest against the aborted attempt to free the American hostages in Iran.

1988 About 60 persons were injured, three critically, in a midair explosion of a plane flying from Hilo to Honolulu; the pilot landed the plane safely.

APRIL 29

1745 Oliver Ellsworth, jurist, was born in Windsor, Conn.; delegate to Continental Congress (1777-84); co-author of Connecticut Compromise at Constitutional Convention which resulted in present Congress structure; represented Connecticut in the Senate (1789-96); chief justice, Supreme Court (1796-99) (died 1807).

1759 John Adlum, grape grower, was born in York, Pa.; pioneer in American grape growing, developed Catawba grape (died 1836).

1792 Matthew Vassar, founder, endower of Vassar College (1861), was born in Norfolk, England (died 1868).

1795 Lorrin Andrews, Congregational missionary to Hawaii, was born in East Windsor, Conn.; translated Bible into Hawaiian, published first Hawaiian newspaper (1834) (died 1868).

1814 The American sloop *Peacock* captured British brig *Epervier* and $120,000 in specie off the Florida coast.

1815 Abram Duryée, Union general who headed regiment of Zouaves in Civil War, was born in New York City; police commissioner, New York City (1873-84) (died 1890).

1820 Henry W. Allen, Confederate general, was born in Prince Edward County, Va.; saw action at Shiloh, Vicksburg; governor of Louisiana (1861-64) (died 1866).

1860 Lorado Taft, sculptor, was born in Elmwood, Ill.; one of first Americans to work on large designs (*Fountain of Time,* Chicago; *Columbus Fountain*) (died 1936).

1862 New Orleans surrendered to a Union naval force under Adm. David D. Farragut and Union troops under Gen. Benjamin Butler.

1863 William Randolph Hearst, publisher, was born in San Francisco, son of George Hearst (9/3/1820); headed newspaper, magazine chain; represented New York in the House (1903-07) (died 1951).

1870 Harrison P. Eddy, sanitary engineer, was born in Millbury, Mass.; leader in developing American water purification and sewage treatment (died 1937).

1872 Forest R. Moulton, astronomer, was born in LeRoy, Mich.; with Thomas C. Chamberlin, he propounded the spiral nebulae hypothesis (died 1952).

1877 Thomas A. Dorgan (TAD), cartoonist, was born in San Francisco; sports cartoonist, commentator, *New York Journal* (1900-29) (died 1929).

1880 Jonas Lie, artist, was born in Moss, Norway; numerous well-known works (*Wind Swept, Brooklyn Bridge, A New York Canyon*) (died 1940).

1885 Frank J. Fletcher, World War I and II naval officer, was born in Marshalltown, Iowa; commander in battles of Coral Sea, Midway (died 1973).

1885 Wallingford Riegger, composer, was born in Albany, Ga.; a leader in avant garde 20th century music (died 1961).

1893 Harold C. Urey, chemist, was born in Walkerton, Ind.; awarded 1934 Nobel Chemistry Prize for discovery of heavy hydrogen, reseach on other isotopes and structures of atoms and molecules (died 1981).

1899 Duke (Edward K.) Ellington, pianist, conductor, and composer ("Mood Indigo," "Satin Doll," "Black, Brown & Beige") was born in Washington (died 1974).

1899 Labor wars in Idaho silver mines culminated in dynamiting the Bunker Hill and Sullivan concentrator in Wardner.

1904 Russ Morgan, trombonist and band leader, was born in Scranton, Pa. (died 1969).

1931 Robert A. Gottlieb, editor, *The New Yorker* (1987-), was born in New York City; editor-in-chief, Simon & Schuster, then Knopf; president, A.A. Knopf (1973-87).

1932 Radio serial, *One Man's Family,* written by Carlton E. Morse, began; ran through 3256 episodes, ending May 8, 1959.

1934 Luis Aparicio, baseball player (White Sox, Orioles), was born in Maracaibo, Venezuela; named to Baseball Hall of Fame.

1936 Zubin Mehta, conductor, was born in Bombay; conductor, New York Philharmonic (1978), with Los Angeles Philharmonic (1962-78).

1955 Gustav Egloff, chemist, died at 69; developed multiple-coil process for cracking crude oil to increase high octane gasoline yield, method of making rubber from butane gas.

1957 Congress enacted the first Civil Rights Act since Reconstruction.

1975 American civilians were evacuated from Saigon as Communist forces completed the takeover of South Vietnam.

1986 The Council of Bishops of the United Methodist Church unanimously voted for "clear and unconditional" opposition to the use of nuclear weapons.

1988 American warships in the Persian Gulf allowed to protect neutral shipping under attack, according to rules announced by President Reagan.

1988 The Senate by a vote of 87-4 approved a $1 billion anti-AIDS program.

APRIL 30

1492 Privileges and prerogatives were granted Columbus by the Spanish rulers, Ferdinand and Isabella, making possible his exploration.

1771 Hosea Ballou, Universalist clergyman and editor, was born in Richmond, N.H.; an early leader of Universalism; founder, editor, *Universalist Magazine* (1819-28), the first Universalist periodical; author (*Treatise on the Atonement*) (died 1852).

1789 George Washington was inaugurated as first president on the balcony of Federal Hall (Wall and Broad Sts.), New York City; oath was administered by Robert R. Livingston, chancellor of New York State; Washington delivered first inaugural address in the Senate chamber in Federal Hall.

1798 The Navy Department was created by Congress; Benjamin Stoddert was nominated to be the first secretary.

1803 Napoleon signed the sale of the Louisiana Territory to the United States for 60 million francs (approximately $15 million); doubled area of the United States by adding 828,000 sq. mi. of land.

1812 Louisiana was admitted to the Union as the 18th state.

1821 College of Detroit became the U. of Michigan.

1822 Hannibal W. Goodwin, Episcopal clergyman, was born in Taughannock, N.Y.; inventor of photographic film (1887), received patent after long litigation (1898) (died 1900).

1823 Henry O. Houghton, printer and publisher, was born in Sutton, Vt.; founder, Riverside Press (1852) and publishing company bearing his name, later becoming Houghton Mifflin (1880) (died 1895).

1832 William Becknell, fur trader and explorer, died at about 42; blazed the Santa Fe trail from Franklin, Mo. to Santa Fe, N.M., which became the main commercial route to the Southwest.

1858 Mary Scott L. Dimmick Harrison, second wife of President Benjamin Harrison, was born in Honesdale, Pa. (died 1948).

1871 Fielding H. Yost, football coach, was born in Fairview, W.Va.; known as "Hurry-Up Yost," he coached at Michigan U. (1901-27) (died 1946).

1879 Stanley B. Resor, president of J. Walter Thompson ad agency (1916-55), was born in Cincinnati; board chairman (1955-61) (died 1962).

1888 John Crowe Ransom, poet and editor, was born in Pulaski, Tenn.; taught at Vanderbilt U. (1914-37), Kenyon College (1937-58); editor, *Kenyon Review* (1939-58); poet (*Poems About God, Chills and Fever*) (died 1974).

1888 President Cleveland appointed Melville W. Fuller as chief justice of the Supreme Court; confirmed by Senate July 20.

1900 Territory of Hawaii was created.

1900 Casey (John L.) Jones, engineer of the Cannonball Express, crashed his train into a stopped freight train near Vaughn, Miss.; legendary hero of railroading.

1901 Simon Kuznets, economist, was born in Kharkov, Russia; devised the Gross National Product measure; awarded 1971 Nobel Economics Prize (died 1985).

1904 President Theodore Roosevelt opened the Louisiana Purchase Exposition in St. Louis.

1916 Claude E. Shannon, mathematician, was born in Gaylord, Mich.; founded information theory on computer development, communications, etc.

1933 Willie Nelson, country music singer and composer, was born in Abbott, Tex.

1939 New York World's Fair was opened by President Franklin Roosevelt.

1948 Organization of American States (OAS), composed of 21 republics of the Western Hemisphere, was formed at Bogota, Colombia; ratified by nations in Dec.

1956 Alben W. Barkley, former Vice President (1949-53), died in Lexington, Va. at 78.

1970 President Nixon announced that American troops were being sent into Cambodia to eliminate Communist staging and communications areas.

1973 Three top presidential aides—H.R. Haldeman, John D. Ehrlichmann, and John W. Dean—and Attorney

General Richard Kleindienst resigned amid charges of White House coverup efforts in the Watergate case.

1975 The last Americans were evacuated from the embassy in Saigon, virtually bringing the Vietnam war to an end.

1975 South Vietnam announced its unconditional surrender to the Vietcong.

1986 Supreme Court unanimously dismissed a case seeking to defend an Illinois law regulating and restricting abortions.

MAY 1

1528 Pamphilo de Narvaez with 300 men began march across Florida, reached Indian town near present Tallahassee; built boats, then sailed in September along the Gulf Coast past the Mississippi River; swept out to sea and lost.

1562 Huguenot colonists led by Jean de Ribaut entered the St. John's River (Fla.) and built Ft. Charles on present Parris Island.

1637 Towns of Hartford, Wethersfield, and Windsor united in a self-governing confederation under the name of Connecticut .

1691 Representatives from Massachusetts, Plymouth, Hartford, and New York met in New York City to plan attacks on Montreal and Quebec.

1737 Elias Dayton, Revolutionary general, was born in Elizabeth, N.J.; served throughout the war, including the winter at Valley Forge; represented New Jersey in the House (1787-88) (died 1807).

1759 Jacob Albright, religious leader, was born in Pottstown, Pa.; a convert to Methodism, he tried to form a new movement, which was not recognized; he named it the Evangelical Association (later Church); Albright College in Reading, Pa. named for him (died 1808).

1764 Benjamin H. Latrobe, architect and engineer, was born in Fulneck, England; designed many public buildings (Capitol south wing, Capitol rebuilding after British burning in 1814); designed first American municipal water system in Philadelphia (died 1820).

1780 John McKinley, legislator and jurist, was born in Culpeper County, Va.; represented Alabama in the House (1832-36) and Senate (1826-30, 1836-37); associate justice, Supreme Court (1837-52) (died 1852).

1784 State legislature created the U. of New York.

1796 Junius Brutus Booth, actor, was born in London; one of world's greatest tragedians, starred in numerous Shakespearean roles (died 1852).

1825 George Inness, painter, was born in Newburgh, N.Y.; one of last of the Hudson River School (*Delaware Water Gap, Peace and Plenty*) (died 1894).

1830 Mary H. Jones, labor leader, was born in Cork, Ireland; known as "Mother Jones," she was a prominent speaker and organizer (died 1930).

1832 Capt. Benjamin de Bonneville led a wagon train from Ft. Osage on the Missouri River to the Columbia, starting a three-year exploration of the West.

1841 The first emigrant train with 47 persons left Independence, Mo. for California.

1845 Fourteen conferences of the Methodist Church met in Louisville, organized the Methodist Episcopal Church, South, after a dispute over slavery.

1847 Cornerstone laid for the Smithsonian Institution in Washington.

1847 Henry Demarest Lloyd, journalist, was born in New York City; first journalistic "muckraker" (*Chicago Tribune, Atlantic Monthly*); wrote about the railroads, oil industry (died 1903).

1852 Calamity Jane, frontierswoman, was born as Martha Jane Burke in Princeton, Mo.; a companion of Wild Bill Hickok and a sharpshooter (died 1903).

1853 Jacob Gordin, playwright, was born in Mirgorod, Russia; a leading American Yiddish playwright, he produced more than 30 original plays (died 1909).

1863 Four-day battle of Chancellorsville (Va.) began, one of greatest battles of the war; Confederate Gen. Stonewall Jackson was fatally wounded accidentally by his own men, died May 10; battle inconclusive; South lost 1665 killed, 9000 wounded; Union losses about 17,000.

1863 Union troops under Gen. U.S. Grant launched a series of victories at Ft. Gibson, which put them outside Vicksburg, Miss.; other victories were at Grand Gulf, Raymond, Jackson, Champion Hill, Big Black River Bridge.

1865 President Andrew Johnson issued an executive order for the creation of a military commission to try the Lincoln assassins.

1871 Supreme Court, with two new members, reversed the ruling of Feb 7, 1870 and made legal tender of Treasury notes issued before enabling legislation was passed.

1873 The first American penny postal card was issued.

1880 Albert D. Lasker, advertising executive and philanthropist, was born in Freiburg, Germany; owner, Lord & Thomas agency (1908-42); chairman, U.S. Shipping Board (1921-23); helped endow Chicago U. medical research, public health (died 1952).

1884 Work began on the Home Insurance Building, Chicago, considered the first American skyscraper; completed in the Fall of 1885.

1888 John F. O'Hara, Catholic prelate, was born in Ann Arbor, Mich.; president, Notre Dame University (1934-39); Archbishop of Philadelphia (1951-60), elevated to cardinal 1958 (died 1960).

1892 Howard Barlow, conductor, was born in Plain City, Ohio; conductor of "Voice of Firestone" radio show (died 1972).

1893 Columbian Exposition in Chicago opened by President Cleveland.

1894 "Coxey's Army" of 500 arrived in Washington from Massillon, Ohio to plead for work programs for the unemployed; Leader Jacob S. Coxey was arrested for trespassing.

1895 Leo Sowerby, musician, was born in Grand Rapids, Mich.; composer (*Canticle of the Sun*); organist, St. James Episcopal Church, Chicago (1927-62) (died 1968).

1896 J. Lawton Collins, World War II Army general, was born in New Orleans; commanded on Guadalcanal and in Europe (died 1987).

1896 Mark W. Clark, World War II Army general, was born in Madison Barracks, N.Y.; commanded American ground forces in Europe (1942), in North Africa, Italy (1943-44), in Austria (1945-47); commanded UN Korean forces (1952-53) (died 1984).

1898 Spanish fleet of ten vessels was destroyed or captured by Americans in Manila Harbor.

1898 Eugene R. Black, banker, was born in Atlanta; president, World Bank (1949-53).

1900 An explosion of blasting powder in a coal mine at Scofield, Utah killed 200.

1901 The Pan American Exposition opened in Buffalo; ran until Nov 2.

1909 The Walter Reed General Hospital in Washington opened.

1909 Kate Smith, singer, was born in Greenville, Va.; known as the first lady of radio (died 1986).

1911 Supreme Court ordered the dissolution of the Standard Oil Co. and the American Tobacco Co., which were found to be monopolies.

1915 The American oil tanker *Gulflight* was torpedoed by a German submarine off the Scilly Islands during a battle between the submarine and a British patrol; two Americans died.

1918 Jack Paar, entertainer, was born in Canton, Ohio; host of *Tonight Show* (1957-62), then did own show.

1923 Joseph Heller, author, was born in Brooklyn; best known for the novel *Catch 22*.

1925 (Malcolm) Scott Carpenter, astronaut, was born in Boulder, Colo.; second astronaut to make orbital space flight.

1931 The Empire State Building in New York City opened.

1937 Congress by joint resolution recapitulated earlier neutrality legislation and strengthened it, giving larger discretionary power to the president.

1943 Federal Government took over all Eastern coal mines because of a strike by 530,000 miners; Union President John L. Lewis ended strike May 2.

1960 The 18th Census reported a population of 179,323,175.

1970 The American population climbed over the 200 million mark in the 19th Census with a total of 203,302,031 and the center of population had moved to five miles east of Mascoutah, Ill.

1971 Amtrak, a unified rail passenger system, began operations.

1972 The Eisenhower Center, including the library, in Abilene, Kans. was dedicated.

1982 World's Fair opened in Knoxville, Tenn. with President Reagan on hand.

MAY 2

1740 Elias Boudinot, legislator and public official, was born in Philadelphia; represented New Jersey in the Continental Congress (1777, 1778, 1781-84) and the House (1789-95); director, U.S. Mint (1795-1805) (died 1821).

1776 France and Spain agreed to provide funds for arms for the Americans; this was done through fictitious companies.

1806 Edwin B. Morgan, express business pioneer, was born in Aurora, N.Y.; first president, Wells Fargo & Co. (1852); a founder, U.S. Express Co. (1854); a major stockholder, *New York Times* (died 1881).

1837 Henry M. Robert, parliamentarian, was born in Robertville, S.C.; military engineer, built defenses of Washington (1861); chief of engineers (1901); author of *Robert's Rules of Order* (1876) (died 1923).

1847 Hugh J. Chisholm, paper manufacturer, was born in Niagara Falls, Ontario; helped form International Paper Co. (1898), president (1899-1910) (died 1912).

1865 Clyde Fitch, playwright was born in Elmira, N.Y.; wrote numerous popular plays (*Nathan Hale, The Climbers, Truth, Barbara Frietchie*) (died 1909).

1866 Jesse W. Lazear, medical researcher, was born in Baltimore County, Md.; member of Walter Reed

Commission, allowed himself to be bitten by an infected mosquito and died (1900), helping prove that yellow fever is transmitted by mosquitoes.

1868 John Moody, financial analyst, was born in Jersey City; founder, *Moody's Manual of Railroads & Corporation Securities* (1900), *Moody's Magazines* (1905), *Moody's Analyses of Investments* (1909) (died 1958).

1871 Francis P. Duffy, Catholic chaplain, was born in Cobourg, Canada; organized, served, Church of Our Saviour, New York City; chaplain, 69th Regiment, National Guard, later the 165th Infantry, which he accompanied to Mexico (1917), Europe (1917-18) (died 1932).

1875 Owen J. Roberts, jurist, was born in Philadelphia; a prosecutor in Teapot Dome scandal; associate justice, Supreme Court (1930-45); dean, U. of Pennsylvania Law School (1948-51) (died 1955).

1879 James F. Byrnes, legislator and jurist, was born in Charleston; represented South Carolina in the House (1911-25) and Senate (1931-41) and served as its governor (1951-5); director, Office of Economic Stabilization (1942-43); associate justice, Supreme Court (1941-42); director, Office of War Mobilization (1943-45); Secretary of State (1945-47) (died 1972).

1887 Vernon B. Castle, dancer, was born in Norwich, England; with wife, Irene (4/7/1893), originated one-step, turkey trot, Castle walk; killed in plane crash (1918).

1887 Eddie (Edward T.) Collins, baseball player, was born in Millerton, N.Y.; second baseman, manager (Athletics, White Sox) (1908-30); named to Baseball Hall of Fame (died 1951).

1890 President Benjamin Harrison signed an act creating Oklahoma Territory.

1895 Lorenz Hart, lyricist, was born in New York City; worked with Richard Rodgers (*Pal Joey, Babes in Arms, Boys from Syracuse, Present Arms*) (died 1943).

1897 Norma Talmadge, screen actress, was born in Brooklyn; starred in many films (*DuBarry, Camille, Graustark*) (died 1957).

1903 Dr. Benjamin M. Spock, pediatrician and author, was born in New Haven; active opponent of Vietnam War, nuclear weapons; author of best selling (50+ million) *Baby and Child Care.*

1904 Bing (Harry L.) Crosby, singer and screen actor, was born in Tacomá, Wash.; one of the most popular entertainers of his time, recording star; many films (*White Christmas, Going my Way, High Society,* several *Road* pictures (died 1977).

1923 First transcontinental nonstop airplane flight begun by two Air Corps lieutenants; took 26 hours, 50 minutes to complete 2516-mile New York-San Diego flight.

1948 Larry Gatlin, country music singer and composer, was born in Seminole, Tex.

1972 A fire in the Sunshine silver mine in Kellogg, Ida. killed 91 persons.

1974 Former Vice President Spiro Agnew was disbarred by Maryland Court of Appeals as a result of his *nolo contendere* plea in 1973 on tax evasion charges.

1985 E.F. Hutton, one of nation's largest brokerage companies, pleaded guilty to 2000 federal charges of checking account manipulations.

1988 The Supreme Court ruled by a 6-2 vote that manufacturers may agree with retailers to stop supplying discount stores so long as they do not agree on prices or price levels.

1988 The United Methodist Church general conference in St. Louis refused by a vote of 676-293 to allow the ordination of practicing homosexuals.

MAY 3

1765 The first medical school in the United States (College of Philadelphia) was organized by Drs. John Morgan and William Shippen Jr.; later became U. of Pennsylvania School of Medicine.

1802 Washington was incorporated as a city with a mayor to be named by the president.

1843 William L. Wilson, public official, was born in Middlebury, Va. (now W.Va.); Postmaster General (1895-97), inaugurated rural free delivery; represented West Virginia in the House (1883-95) (died 1900).

1844 Wilbur O. Atwater, agricultural educator, was born in Johnsburg, N.Y.; set up first state agricultural extension station (1875); founder, director, Department of Agriculture Experiment Stations Office (1888-1907); developed caloric content of foods table, still in use (died 1907).

1849 Jacob A. Riis, journalist and reformer, was born in Ribe, Denmark; with *New York Times, New York Sun* (1877-99); his exposés led to improvements in schools, housing, recreational facilities; author (*How the Other Half Lives, Children of the Poor, Children of the Tenements*) (died 1914).

1851 Fifth great fire in San Francisco resulted in $12 million property loss with the destruction of 1500 homes.

1871 Henry S. Graves, forester, was born in Marietta, Ohio; director, Yale Forestry School (1900-10), dean (1922-39); chief, U.S. Forest Service (1910-20) (died 1951).

1886 Railroad strikers and strike breakers fought at the McCormack Harvesting Machine Co., Chicago; six men were killed; a meeting the following day resulted in the Haymarket Square riot.

1890 Benjamin Fairless, industrialist, was born in Pigeon Run, Ohio; president, U.S. Steel Co. (1938-52) (died 1962).

1891 Eppa Rixey, baseball pitcher (Phillies, Cincinnati) who won 266 games in 21 years, was born in Culpeper, Va.; named to Baseball Hall of Fame (died 1963).

1904 Red (Charles H.) Ruffing, baseball player, was born in Granville, Ill.; pitched for 22 years (Yankees, Red Sox) winning 273, losing 225; named to Baseball Hall of Fame (died 1986).

1906 Mary Astor, screen actress, was born in Quincy, Ill.; starred in several films (*Dodsworth, Little Women, The Maltese Falcon*) (died 1987).

1913 William M. Inge, playwright, was born in Independence, Kan.; wrote several hit plays (*Come Back, Little Sheba, Bus Stop, Dark at the Top of the Stairs*) (died 1973).

1916 A treaty was signed by Haiti and the United States for American control of the island; American forces occupied Haiti until 1930.

1917 The first American squadron of destroyers, commanded by Adm. William S. Sims, arrived in Queenstown, Ireland.

1917 Alaska territorial legislature appropriated $60,000 to start the U. of Alaska in Fairbanks.

1919 Pete Seeger, folk singer and composer, was born in New York City; composer ("Where Have All the Flowers Gone," "If I Had a Hammer," "Kisses Sweeter Than Wine").

1920 "Sugar" Ray Robinson, boxing champion, was born in Detroit; welterweight champion (1946-51), middleweight champion five times between 1951 and 1960 (died 1989).

1933 Steven Weinberg, physicist, was born in New York City; shared 1979 Nobel Physics Prize for establishment of the analogy between electromagnetism and the "weak" interactions of subatomic particles.

1936 Joan Collins, television actress (*Dynasty*), was born in London.

1959 The Unitarian and Universalist churches voted to merge.

1968 President Lyndon Johnson announced that the United States and North Vietnam had agreed to meet in Paris May 10 for preliminary talks to end the war.

1983 The National Conference of Catholic Bishops, meeting in Chicago, approved a pastoral letter condemning the nuclear arms race, called for a halt in the development, production, and deployment of nuclear weapons.

1986 An unmanned Delta rocket lost power after liftoff at Cape Canaveral, was destroyed after it veered out of control.

1988 The General Conference of the United Methodist Church approved a new hymnal.

1988 A special Philadelphia grand jury cleared Mayor W. Wilson Goode and all others involved of criminal liability for the death and destruction resulting from the 1985 fire and deaths of radical group MOVE members.

MAY 4

1493 Pope Alexander VI issued a bill of demarcation (*Inter caetera*) following Columbus' discovery of America, setting a demarcation line between Spanish and Portuguese territories.

1626 Peter Minuit arrived on Manhattan Island to set up the Dutch colony of Nieuw Amsterdam; became director of the New Netherlands.

1776 Rhode Island legislature renounced allegiance to the Crown; declared independence.

1778 Continental Congress ratified a treaty of alliance with France, the first and only such treaty ever made by the United States; also a treaty of commerce, amity.

1796 William H. Prescott, historian, was born in Salem, Mass., grandson of William Prescott (2/20/1726); remembered for books on conquest of Mexico, Peru (died 1859).

1796 Horace Mann, educator, was born in Franklin, Mass.; first secretary, Massachusetts Board of Education (1837-47); revolutionized school organization, teaching; instrumental in creating first American normal school (1839); represented Massachusetts in the House (1849-52); president, Antioch College (1853-59) (died 1859).

1820 Julia Gardiner Tyler, second wife of President Tyler, was born in Gardiner's Island, N.Y. (died 1889).

1821 Gordon McKay, inventor and manufacturer, was born in Pittsfield, Mass.; invented shoemaking machinery, including a heeler and lasting nailer, which revolutionized the industry (died 1903).

1822 President Monroe signed an act providing diplomatic relations with independent Latin American nations.

1826 Frederick E. Church, artist, was born in Hartford, Conn.; one of most notable of Hudson River School (died 1900).

1851 A large part of St. Louis was burned with a loss of $15 million in property.

1852 William L. McLean, publisher, was born in Mt. Pleasant, Pa.; publisher, *Philadelphia Bulletin* (1895-1931) (died 1931).

1860 Abraham L. Erlanger, theater manager, was born in Buffalo; a founder, Theater Syndicate (1896), which monopolized American theater in early 1900s (died 1930).

1862 Yorktown, Va., evacuated by the Confederates, was occupied by Union troops under Gen. George McClellan after a month-long siege.

1864 Gen. William T. Sherman and his Union troops began their march to the sea.

1871 The first professional league baseball game was played at Ft. Wayne, Ind., with the home team beating Cleveland 2-0.

1872 Harold Bell Wright, author, was born in Rome, N.Y.; wrote several popular novels (*The Shepherd of the Hills, The Winning of Barbara Worth*) (died 1944).

1872 Alexander M. Palmer, public official, was born in Moosehead, Pa.; Attorney General (1919-21), led raids during the "red scare;" represented Pennsylvania in the House (1909-15); Alien Property Custodian (1915-19) (died 1936).

1874 Frank Conrad, engineer and inventor, was born in Pittsburgh; instrumental in developing radio station KDKA, Pittsburgh, where public broadcasting began in Nov 1920 (died 1941).

1886 A peaceful meeting of railroad strikers in Haymarket Square, Chicago, became violent when police marched in to disperse crowd; a bomb was thrown, killing seven policemen, four strikers, and wounding 60; eight anarchists were later found guilty.

1886 John A. Holabird, architect, was born in Evanston, Ill.; helped design several Chicago buildings (Palmolive, Daily News, Board of Trade) (died 1945).

1889 Francis J. Spellman, Catholic prelate, was born in Whitman, Mass.; Bishop of New York (1932-39), Archbishop of New York (1939-67); elevated to cardinal 1946 (died 1967).

1891 The first inter-racial hospital, Provident, opened in Chicago.

1916 In response to several protests, Germany promised not to sink ships without warning, but refused to abandon submarine attacks.

1928 Betsy (Elizabeth E.) Rawls, a leading golfer of the 1950s, 1960s, was born in Spartanburg, S.C.; won women's U.S. Open four times, LPGA championship twice; named to LPGA Hall of Fame.

1930 Roberta Peters, operatic soprano, was born in New York City; starred in *Rigoletto, The Magic Flute.*

1970 Four students at Kent State U. in Ohio were killed by Ohio National Guardsmen during an anti-Vietnam demonstration on campus.

1974 Expo '74 opened in Spokane.

1980 Department of Health, Education and Welfare became the Department of Health and Human Services; Education was spun off to become a separate department.

1987 The Supreme Court ruled 7-0 that states may force Rotary clubs to admit women to membership, opening the way to breaking down the barriers of male-only organizations.

1988 A chemical plant in Henderson, Nev. that manufactured fuel for the space shuttle program was leveled by four explosions; 25 of 200 people in the plant were missing.

1989 A federal jury found Oliver L. North guilty of shredding documents, accepting an illegal gratuity and helping obstruct Congress in the Iran-Contra affair; acquitted of nine other charges; conviction appealed.

1989 The space shuttle *Atlantis*, which blasted off from Cape Canaveral, launched the Magellan space probe to map the surface of Venus.

MAY 5

1682 The Frame of Government for Pennsylvania was drawn up by William Penn; provided for a governor, council, and assembly to be elected by the freeholders; a cumbersome mechanism, it was replaced by the Charter of Privileges (1701).

1749 George Washington received his license as a surveyor from the College of William and Mary.

1775 Benjamin Franklin returned to Philadelphia after ten years absence in England; elected to Continental Congress May 6.

1778 Baron Friedrich Wilhelm von Steuben, German officer who fought in the American Revolution, was named inspector general of the Continental Army.

1796 William Pennington, public official, was born in Newark; served New Jersey as governor (1837-43) and represented it in the House (1859-61), serving as Speaker (1859-61) (died 1862).

1809 Frederick A.P. Barnard, educator, was born in Sheffield, Mass.; with U. of Mississippi (1856-61), Columbia College (1864-69), where he organized a college for women (1883), now named for him (died 1889).

1811 John W. Draper, medical educator and scientist, was born in Liverpool, England; a founder (1850), president, New York U. Medical School; developed first successful daguerrotype (1840), made other scientific contributions (died 1882).

1814 George M. Mowbray, industrialist, was born in Brighton, England; produced first refined oil, Titusville, Pa. (1859); made many improvements in explosives, produced nitroglycerin for manufacturing (died 1891).

1827 Andrew Johnson and Eliza McCardle were married in Greeneville, Tenn.

1830 John B. Stetson, hat maker, was born in Orange, N.J.; opened hat factory in Philadelphia (1865); by 1900, it was the largest hat company in the world (died 1906).

1832 Hubert H. Bancroft, historian, was born in Granville, Ohio; historian of western America; edited 39-volume history; turned over 60,000-volume library to the U. of California (died 1918).

1838 George H. Hammond, meat packer, was born in Fitchburg, Mass.; pioneered in transporting meat in refrigerated cars; Hammond, Ind. named for him (died 1886).

1839 Felix Agnus, Union general and publisher, was born in Lyons, France; wounded at Gaines Mills and Port Hudson; business manager, *Baltimore American* (1869-83), publisher (1883-1920); founder, publisher, *Baltimore Star* (1908-20) (died 1925).

1843 Reginald H. Fitz, physician, was born in Chelsea, Mass.; named appendicitis, proposed cure by surgery (died 1913).

1847 American Medical Association was founded when 250 delegates from more than 40 medical societies and 28 colleges met in Philadelphia; named Nathaniel Chapman as the first president.

1861 Peter C. Hewitt, electrical engineer, was born in New York City, son of Abram S. Hewitt (7/31/1822); invented a mercury-vapor lamp rectifier, discovered basic principle of vacuum tube amplifier (died 1921).

1862 The Battle of Williamsburg (Va.) resulted in a Confederate retreat toward Richmond to prevent a Union takeover; Union forces occupied city May 6.

1864 The three-day indecisive Battle of the Wilderness in Virginia (near Chancellorsville) began; cost the Union about 18,000 casualties, including 2200 killed; Confederate casualties were about 11,000.

1883 Chief (Charles A.) Bender, baseball player, was born in Brainerd, Minn.; a Chippewa Indian, he pitched 212 winning games, lost 128; named to Baseball Hall of Fame (died 1954).

1890 Christopher D. Morley, author, was born in Haverford, Pa.; wrote numerous novels (*Parnassus on Wheels, Kitty Foyle, Thunder on the Left*); collections of essays (died 1957).

1899 Freeman F. Gosden, radio entertainer, was born in Richmond, Va.; played Amos in *Amos 'n Andy* radio program.

1903 James Beard, cooking expert, was born in Portland, Ore.; author of several cookbooks (died 1985).

1914 Tyrone Power, screen actor, was born in Cincinnati; starred in several films (*In Old Chicago, Alexander's Ragtime Band, The Razor's Edge*) (died 1958).

1915 The Marines landed in Santo Domingo; occupation continued until 1924.

1915 Alice Faye, screen actress, was born in New York City; starred in many films (*Alexander's Ragtime Band, In Old Chicago, Little Old New York*).

1921 Arthur Schawlow, physicist, was born in Mt. Vernon, N.Y.; shared 1981 Nobel Physics Prize for work in developing laser spectroscopy technique; an inventor of laser beams.

1925 John T. Scopes, high school teacher, was arrested in Dayton, Tenn. for violation of the state law forbidding the teaching of evolution; indicted May 25.

1941 President Franklin Roosevelt issued an executive order for the increased production of heavy bombers; set a goal of 50 per month by March 1943, compared with 1941 production of nine per month.

1942 Sugar rationing began.

1942 Tammy Wynette, country music singer, was born in Red Bay, Ala.

1951 United States and Iceland entered into a defense agreement under which the United States undertook the defense of Iceland and was permitted to build and maintain a major air base.

1960 An American U-2 spy plane, piloted by Francis Gary Powers, was shot down over Russia; Powers was jailed.

1961 The first American spaceman, Navy Commander Alan B. Shepard Jr., rocketed 116.5 miles up in a two-orbit trip which took 15 minutes and 27 seconds.

1961 Congress raised the minimum wage from $1 to $1.25 an hour over a two-year period.

1980 Rev. Robert Drinan, the only priest in Congress, was barred from seeking re-election to his Massachusetts House seat by the Superior General of the Society of Jesus (Jesuits), of which Drinan was a member.

1988 A fire and explosion rocked a Shell Oil refinery in Norco, La. injuring 42 persons and leaving six missing; 2500 residents of the area were evacuated.

MAY 6

1606 John Norton, Puritan clergyman, was born in Hertfordshire, England; served pastorates in Ipswich and Boston (1638-63), active in persecuting Quakers in Massachusetts; composed first Latin book in the colonies (on church government) (1648) (died 1663).

1626 Peter Minuit bought Manhattan Island from the Man-a-Hat-a Indians for $24 worth of trinkets.

1635 John Haynes (1594-1654) was chosen governor of Massachusetts; moved to Connecticut, became the first governor under the Fundamental Laws (1639 and alternate years until his death).

1710 Richard Bland, colonial leader, was born in Berkeley, Va.; delegate to Continental Congress (1774, 1775); wrote "An Inquiry Into the Rights of the British Colonies" (1766), the earliest published defense of the colonial attitude on taxation (died 1776).

1743 Seth Warner, Revolutionary general, was born in Roxbury, Conn.; with Arnold and Allen at capture of Ticonderoga, led Vermont troops at Crown Point and Bennington (died 1784).

1748 Peleg Wadsworth, colonial leader, was born in Hiram, Me.; laid out defenses of Roxbury and Dorchester Heights (1775); represented Massachusetts in the House (1793-1807) (died 1829).

1776 British reinforcements forced Americans to abandon the siege of Quebec; began retreat from Canada, which ended in Ticonderoga in July.

1789 A Georgia convention adopted a new state constitution, effective in Oct.

1806 Chapin A. Harris, dental educator, was born in Pompey, N.Y.; wrote standard dental surgery text; co-founder (1840), dean, Baltimore College of Dental Surgery, first such school in the world (died 1860).

1808 William Strong, jurist, was born in Somers, Conn.; represented Pennsylvania in the House (1847-51); associate justice, Supreme Court (1870-80); chief figure in Supreme Court's reversal of its decision declaring the Legal Tender Act of 1862 unconstitutional (1870); decision for which he wrote majority opinion was reversed May 1, 1871 (died 1895).

1814 British troops from Kingston, Canada attacked and destroyed fort at Oswego, N.Y.

1830 Abraham Jacobi, physician, was born in Hartum, Germany; specialist in children's diseases, founder of American pediatrics (died 1919).

1835 James Gordon Bennett issued the first number of a four-page penny newspaper, *New York Herald* (one cent per copy, $3 per year); its declared policy: "We shall support no party, be the agent of no faction or coterie, and care nothing for any election, or any candidate, from president down to constable."

1843 Stirling Yates, admiral, was born in Baltimore; commander, Philippine squadron (1903-04); commander-in-chief, U.S. Fleet (1904-05) (died 1929).

1849 Wyatt Eaton, portrait painter, was born in Philipsburg, Canada of American parentage; a founder, Society of American Artists (1877), president (died 1896).

1853 Philander C. Knox, public official and legislator, was born in Brownsville, Pa.; represented Pennsylvania in the Senate (1904-09, 1917-21); Attorney General (1901-04), Secretary of State (1909-13); initiated what is known as "dollar diplomacy" (died 1921).

1856 Robert E. Peary, discoverer of North Pole, was born in Cresson, Pa.; Navy rear admiral, began Arctic exploration (1886), discovered North Pole on fourth try (Apr 6, 1909) (died 1920).

1858 Samuel B. McCormick, educator, was born in Westmoreland County, Pa.; president, Coe College (1897-1904), Western U. of Pennsylvania (1904-20), which he moved to Pittsburgh and developed into a major university (died 1928).

1861 Arkansas legislature voted 69-1 to secede from the Union.

1870 A(madeo) P. Giannini, banker, was born in San Jose, Cal.; founder, Bank of Italy (1904), which later became the Bank of America, one of the nation's largest; founded, Transamerica Corp. (1928) (died 1949).

1870 John T. McCutcheon, editorial cartoonist, was born in Tippecanoe County, Ind.; with the *Chicago Tribune* (1903-45) (died 1949).

1871 Richard B. Moore, chemist, was born in Cincinnati; with Bureau of Mines (1912-23); surveyed Colorado radium deposits, supervised first American production of radium salts; pioneer in urging use of helium in balloons (died 1931).

1875 William D. Leahy, admiral and diplomat, was born in Hampton, Iowa; chief of naval operations (1937-39); ambassador to Vichy France (1940-42); White House chief of staff during World War II (died 1959).

1882 Chinese Exclusion Act was passed, prohibiting immigration of Chinese laborers for ten years; restriction extended, until it finally became permanent.

1895 Rudolph Valentino, silent screen star, was born in Castellaneta, Italy; romantic idol of early 1920s (*The Sheik, Blood and Sand*) (died 1926).

1896 Samuel P. Langley demonstrated his "aerodrome" over the Potomac River; each time the miniature steam engine with wings sustained itself for 1-1/2 minutes, traversing a distance of more than a mile.

1898 Assistant Navy Secretary Theodore Roosevelt resigned to become a lieutenant colonel in the cavalry (Rough Riders).

1898 Daniel F. Gerber, food executive, was born in Fremont, Mich.; president, Gerber Products Co. (1945-64), introduced strained baby foods (died 1974).

1902 Harry L. Golden, author and editor, was born in New York City; editor, publisher, *The Carolina Israelite*; author (*Only in America, For 2¢ Plain*) (died 1981).

1913 Carmen Cavallero, musician, was born in New York City; pianist and orchestra leader.

1914 Randall Jarrell, poet, was born in Nashville; also a critic, novelist (*The Lost World; Blood for a Stranger; Little Friend, Little Friend*) (died 1965).

1915 Orson Welles, actor, director, and producer, was born in Kenosha, Wis.; stage and screen actor, producer (*Citizen Kane*); founder, Mercury Theater, whose realistic radio broadcast of imaginary Martian invasion (1938) created panic (died 1985).

1915 Theodore H. White, author and foreign correspondent, was born in Boston; best known for his "making of a president" books (1960, 1964, 1968) (died 1986).

1931 Willie Mays, baseball player, was born in Fairfield, Ala.; starred with the Giants (1951-72); named to Baseball Hall of Fame.

1933 The Supreme Court invalidated the Railroad Retirement Act.

1933 Barbara Aronstein Black, the first woman to head a major private law school, was born in New York City; named dean of Columbia Law School in 1986.

1937 The German zeppelin *Hindenburg* was destroyed by fire at the tower mooring at Lakehurst, N.J.; 36 died in the blaze.

1942 The island fort of Corregidor fell to the Japanese after holding out for four months.

1984 William A. Egan, the first governor of Alaska (1959), died at 69; he had been one of the leaders of the Alaskan statehood movement.

MAY 7

1738 George Whitefield, Methodist evangelist, arrived at Savannah from England.

1774 William Bainbridge, naval officer, was born in Princeton, N.J.; commanded the *Constitution* (Old Ironsides) in War of 1812 (died 1833).

1784 Thomas Jefferson was named a minister plenipotentiary to join Benjamin Franklin and John Adams to negotiate treaties with foreign powers.

1789 First presidential inaugural ball was held in the Assembly Room on lower Broadway in New York City.

1794 Edward Delafield, physician, was born in New York City; specialized in eye diseases; founder, first president, American Ophthalmological Society (1864) (died 1875).

1800 Territory of Indiana was created by dividing the Northwest Territory.

1833 Abraham Lincoln was named postmaster of New Salem, Ill. at $55 a year, plus franking privileges, exemption from military and jury duty; served for three years.

1836 Joseph G. Cannon, legislator, was born in New Garden, N.C.; represented Illinois in the House (1873-91, 1893-1913), serving as Speaker (1903-11); Speaker's power reduced (1910) after he was accused of autocratic methods of control (died 1926).

1862 Tennessee legislature voted to secede from the Union; ratified June 8 by a popular vote of 104,019 to 47,238.

1862 Senate began impeachment proceedings against West H. Humphreys, U.S. District Court judge in Tennessee; charged with aiding the rebellion, found guilty, removed.

1870 Marcus Loew, movie industry pioneer, was born in New York City; theater owner and movie producer (died 1927).

1873 Supreme Court Chief Justice Salmon P. Chase died in New York City at 65.

1879 California voters ratified their new state constitution which had been adopted by a convention March 3.

1892 Archibald MacLeish, poet, was born in Glencoe, Ill.; Librarian of Congress (1939-44); poet (*New Found Land, Conquistador, The Fall of the City, JB*) (died 1982).

1894 Francis Brennan, Catholic prelate, was born in Shenandoah, Pa.; first American dean of the Sacred Rota in Rome (1959-67), church's highest court of appeals (died 1968).

1901 Gary Cooper, screen actor, was born in Helena, Mont.; starred in many films (*Sergeant York, High Noon, Farwell to Arms, Mr. Deeds Goes to Town*) (died 1961).

1906 Congress authorized Alaska to have a delegate in the House.

1909 Edwin H. Land, camera inventor, was born in Bridgeport, Conn.; inventor of Polaroid cameras, film; founder, president, Polaroid Corp. (1937-).

1913 Simon Ramo, electronics engineer, was born in Salt Lake City; chief scientist for American intercontinental ballistics program.

1914 Eleanor R. Wilson, daughter of President and Mrs. Wilson, was married in the White House to Secretary of the Treasury William G. McAdoo.

1915 The British steamer *Lusitania* was sunk off the Irish coast by a German submarine, with a loss of 1200 lives, including 128 Americans, among them Elbert Hubbard, author and publisher; Charles Frohman, producer, and Alfred G. Vanderbilt.

1933 John Unitas, football player, was born in Pittsburgh; starred at quarterback with the Baltimore Colts (1956-72).

1938 David Baltimore, microbiologist, was born in New York City; shared 1970 Nobel Physiology/Medicine Prize for demonstrating the existence of "reverse transcriptase," a vital enzyme that reverses the normal DNA-to-RNA process.

1942 The two-day Battle of the Coral Sea began; resulted in the American fleet diverting the Japanese invasion of Port Moresby on New Guinea.

1943 Bizerte in North Africa captured by American 2nd Corps.

1945 The Germans surrendered to the Allies at 2:41 a.m. in General Eisenhower's headquarters, the "little red schoolhouse" in Reims, France.

1957 John F. Kennedy was awarded the Pulitzer Prize for biography for his *Profiles in Courage*.

1984 American veterans of the Vietnam War reached an out-of-court settlement with seven chemical companies in their class action suit relating to herbicide Agent Orange.

MAY 8

1541 Expedition of Hernando de Soto reached the Mississippi River, probably at the lower Chickasaw Bluffs, becoming the first Europeans to do so.

1639 William Coddington, who split with Anne Hutchinson after they founded Pocasset (later Portsmouth), founded Newport; the two Rhode Island colonies joined in 1640.

1778 Sir Henry Clinton arrived to succeed Sir William Howe as British commander.

1779 Spain declared war against Great Britain.

1795 The Post Office Department was established by Congress.

1821 William H. Vanderbilt, financier, was born in New Brunswick, N.J.; inherited fortune from father, Cornelius (5/17/1794); became president of New York Central Railroad (1877-83); had large holdings in Nickel Plate, Northwestern railroads; donated $100,000 to erect Cleopatra's Needle in Central Park (died 1885).

1829 Lewis M. Gottschalk, composer and pianist, was born in New Orleans; composed numerous works (*Tremolo Etude, Bamboula, Last Hope*) (died 1889).

1845 The Virginia Baptist Foreign Missionary Society called for a consultative convention in Augusta, Ga., where 293 delegates from nine states organized the Southern Baptist Convention; Dr. W.B. Johnson of South Carolina was named president.

1846 Oscar Hammerstein I, inventor, was born in Stettin, Germany; made fortune with about 100 inventions, including a cigar maker; built Manhattan Opera House, which was bought out by the Metropolitan Opera House (died 1919).

1846 Gen. Zachary Taylor led American troops to victory over Mexicans in a two-day battle at Palo Alto, forcing the Mexicans to retreat to Matamoras.

1855 John W. Gates, financier, was born in West Chicago, Ill.; known as "Bet a Million Gates," he formed, headed, American Steel & Wire Co.; president, Illinois Steel Co. (died 1911).

1858 Dan (Dennis J.) Brouthers, baseball player who batted .343 in 19 years with various teams, was born in Sylvan Lake, N.Y.; named to Baseball Hall of Fame (died 1932).

1861 Confederate Congress authorized army enlistments for the war.

1864 Two engagements at Spotsylvania Court House (Battles of the Wilderness) raged over four days without decision, many casualties; Grant is reported to have said: "I propose to fight it out along this line if it takes all summer."

1867 A convention in Annapolis completed a new Maryland constitution; ratified Sept 18.

1869 James R. Angell, educator, was born in Burlington, Vt., son of James B. Angell (1/7/1829); a founder of functional psychology; president, Yale U. (1921-37) (died 1949).

1871 United States and Great Britain signed a treaty submitting the *Alabama* claims to international arbitration; United States was awarded $15.5 million for damages by the Confederate marauding vessel by arbitrators in 1872.

1882 Peter J. McGuire, founder of the Carpenter's Union, recommended to the New York City Central Labor Union the creation of a "Labor Day."

1884 Harry S Truman, 33rd president (1945-53), was born in Lamar, Mo.; represented Missouri in the Senate (1935-45), Vice President (1945), became president on the death of President Franklin Roosevelt (died 1972).

1893 Francis Ouimet, golfer, was born in Brookline, Mass.; did much to popularize golf in the United States (died 1967).

1893 Edd(ie) Roush, baseball player, was born in Oakland City, Ind.; named to Baseball Hall of Fame.

1895 Fulton J. Sheen, Catholic prelate, was born in El Paso, Ill.; auxiliary bishop of New York (1951-66), bishop of Rochester (1966-69); popular radio, television personality (died 1979).

1895 Edmund Wilson, author and critic, was born in Red Bank, N.J.; critic for *The New Yorker*; author (*I Thought of Daisy, Memoirs of Hecate County*) (died 1972).

1899 Friedrich A. von Hayek, economist, was born in Vienna; shared 1974 Nobel Economics Prize; author (*Pure Theory of Capital, The Road to Serfdom*).

1910 Mary Lou Williams, all-time great jazz pianist, composer, was born in Pittsburgh (died 1981).

1926 Rida Young, librettist, died at 51; wrote many musical comedies (*Naughty Marietta, Maytime*) words for "Mother Machree."

1940 Peter B. Benchley, author, was born in New York City; a grandson of Robert C. Benchley (9/15/1889); wrote several best sellers (*Jaws, The Deep*).

1944 The first eye bank was established at the New York Hospital in New York City.

1984 American Presbyterian minister Benjamin Weir was kidnapped in West Beirut, Lebanon; released Sept 9, 1985.

1987 Former Senator Gary Hart of Colorado dropped out of the race for the Democratic presidential nomination after revelations about his secret association with an actress-model; blamed the press and campaign excesses for his action.

MAY 9

1712 Carolina colony separated into North and South Carolina.

1746 Theodore Sedgwick, legislator and jurist, was born in West Hartford, Conn.; represented Massachusetts in the Continental Congress (1785-88), in the House (1789-96, 1799-1802), serving as Speaker (1799-1801), and in the U.S. Senate (1796-99); served on the State Supreme Court (1802-13) (died 1813).

1775 Jacob J. Brown, War of 1812 general, was born in Bucks County, Pa.; led troops to victory at Chippawa and Lundy Lane (died 1828).

1781 British surrendered Pensacola and all of West Florida to the Spanish.

1785 James P. Espy, meteorologist, was born in Westmoreland County, Pa.; developed theory of storms, called the "storm king;" with War and Navy Departments, laid groundwork for telegraphic weather bulletins (died 1860).

1800 John Brown, anti-slavery leader, was born in Torrington, Conn.; led raid on Harpers Ferry (W.Va.), intended as a signal for a general insurrection of slaves; held arsenal for a day, then his band was overpowered by federal troops commanded by Robert E. Lee; convicted of treason, hanged (1859); became martyr of the anti-slavery cause.

1813 American troops under Gen. William Henry Harrison withstood attacks of British at Ft. Meigs, opposite present Maumee, Ohio.

1828 Charles H. Cramp, shipbuilder, was born in Philadelphia, son of William Cramp (9/22/1807); developed family shipbuilding company into America's largest, best known; president (1879-1903) (died 1913).

1832 Fifteen Seminole chiefs ceded their Florida lands to the United States.

1846 American troops routed a Mexican force of 6000 at Resaca de la Palma.

1850 Edward Weston, electrical engineer, was born in London; developed, manufactured dynamo-electrical machinery; invented improved cell (Weston cadmium cell), which was adopted as official standard of electromotive force (died 1936).

1882 Henry J. Kaiser, shipbuilder and auto manufacturer, was born in Canajoharie, N.Y.; headed company which built large dams (Bonneville, Grand Coulee), housing, ships in record time in World War II; tried unsuccessfully to build, market an inexpensive automobile, the Henry J. (died 1967).

1892 Brehon B. Somervell, World War II Army general, was born in Little Rock, Ark.; chief of Army Service Forces (1942-46) (died 1955).

1895 Richard Barthelmess, screen actor, (*Only Angels Have Wings, The Spoilers*, was born in New York City (died 1963).

1909 Gordon Bunschaft, architect, was born in Buffalo, N.Y.; best known for design of Lever Building, New York City.

1916 Germany apologized for the *Sussex* incident (Apr 18), ending crisis.

1918 Mike Wallace, television personality, was born in Brookline, Mass.; with Columbia Broadcasting System (1963-); best known for *Sixty Minutes*.

1918 Orville L. Freeman, public official, was born in Minneapolis; governor of Minnesota (1955-61), Secretary of Agriculture (1961-69).

1926 The first polar flight was made by then Lt. Comm. Richard E. Byrd and Floyd Bennett over the North Pole, making the 1360-mile round trip from Spitzbergen in 15-1/2 hours.

1928 Pancho (Richard A.) Gonzales, tennis great, was born in Los Angeles; held world's professional singles, doubles titles for 12 years.

1974 The House Judiciary Committee began impeachment hearings against President Nixon.

1980 The freighter *Summit Venture* rammed the Sunshine Skyway Bridge over Tampa Bay, collapsing one of the twin highway spans, 35 persons were killed.

1982 President Reagan proposed a two-step plan to reduce nuclear weapons and a meeting with Leonid Brezhnev in June; meeting later set for June 29 in Geneva.

MAY 10

1730 George Ross, colonial leader, was born in New Castle, Del.; a member of the Continental Congress (1774-77), a signer of Declaration of Independence (died 1779).

1755 Robert Gray, explorer, was born in Tiverton, R.I.; discovered Gray's Harbor, Ore. and the Columbia River (1791), which were the foundation for American claims to Oregon (died 1806).

1755 George Washington was named an aide to British General Edward Braddock.

1773 The Tea Act went into effect, giving the nearly bankrupt East India Co. an advantage in selling tea to the colonies.

1775 A force of 83 men under Ethan Allen surprised the garrison of 42 British at Ft. Ticonderoga, N.Y.; surrendered to Allen upon his demand "in the name of the great Jehovah and the Continental Congress."

1775 The second Continental Congress met in Philadelphia, approved an appeal written by John Jay to Canada to join the American colonies; John Hancock was named president after Peyton Randolph resigned May 24.

1776 The Massachusetts House of Representatives resolved that each town should meet and instruct its representatives "whether if the honorable Congress should, for the Safety of said Colonies, declare them Independent of the Kingdom of Great Britain, they the said Inhabitants will solemly engage with their Lives and Fortunes to Support the Congress in the Measure."

1776 John Adams and Richard Henry Lee introduced a resolution to the Continental Congress calling on the colonies to adopt "such government as shall...best conduce to the happiness and safety of their constituents in particular and America in general."

1779 A British force of 2500, brought in by ship from New York, occupied, then destroyed, Portsmouth and Norfolk, Va.

1783 The Society of the Cincinnati, oldest hereditary military society in North America, was founded by American Revolutionary army officers; George Washington was the first president general.

1789 Jared Sparks, editor and Unitarian clergymen, was born in Willington, Conn.; owner, editor, *North American Review*; president, Harvard (1849-53); published diplomatic correspondence of the Revolution, writings of Washington and Franklin, and ten volumes of American biographies (died 1866).

1797 The first vessel of the new navy, the *United States*, was launched in Philadelphia.

1800 Congress passed a land act, hoping to stimulate sales of public lands by the use of credit; the system encouraged speculation, made collections difficult; abandoned in 1820.

1800 Charles Knowlton, physician, was born in Templeton, Mass.; a birth control advocate, he wrote *Fruits of Philosophy* (1832), for which he was jailed for three months in Cambridge (died 1850).

1802 Horatio Allen, civil engineer, was born in Schenectady; designed, supervised construction of and operated first American-made locomotive; president, Erie Railroad (1843); consulting engineer for the Brooklyn Bridge (died 1890).

1813 Montgomery Blair, public official, was born in Franklin County, Ky., son of Francis P. Blair (4/12/1791); Postmaster General (1861-64), he introduced free city delivery, postal money orders, and the railway postoffice (died 1883).

1823 John Sherman, legislator and public official, was born in Lancaster, Ohio, brother of William T. Sherman (2/8/1820); represented Ohio in the House (1855-61) and Senate (1861-77, 1881-97); Secretary of the Treasury (1877-81); Secretary of State (1897-98) (died 1900).

1832 William R. Grace, merchant and shipowner, was born in Queenstown, Ireland; founder, shipping company in South American trade; mayor of New York City (1880-82, 1884-86) (died 1904).

1837 Panic of 1837 began when New York banks suspended specie payments, an action followed by other banks, after cotton prices fell almost 50%; ensuing depression lasted six years, with the South and West most affected.

1841 James Gordon Bennett Jr., editor, was born in New York City, son of James Gordon Bennett (9/1/1795); succeeded father as editor of *New York Herald*; sent Stanley to find Livingstone in Africa (1869-71), financed several explorations, established Paris edition of the *Herald* (died 1918).

1849 The Astor Place riot in New York City occurred when a mob of partisans of American actor Edwin Forrest tried to seize English actor William Macready on his farewell appearance; riot ensued, resulting in 22 dead, 36 injured.

1862 Confederates evacuated Norfolk, Va.; Union troops occupied the city.

1865 Jefferson Davis, Confederate president, was captured by Union troops near Irwinville, Ga.; imprisoned for two years at Ft. Monroe, Va.

1865 Presidential proclamation announced that "armed resistance to the authority of the Government in the insurrectionary states may be regarded at an end."

1866 Henry M. Blossom, playwright, was born in St. Louis; wrote several hit plays (*Checkers, The Yankee Consul, The Red Mill*) (died 1919).

1866 American Equal Rights Society was formed in New York City.

1868 Ed(ward G.) Barrow, baseball manager and executive (Yankees), was born in Springfield, Ill.; named to Baseball Hall of Fame (died 1953).

1869 Central Pacific and Union Pacific railroads joined at Promontory Point, Utah, forming the first transcontinental railroad.

1872 Women who seceded from the National Woman's Suffrage Association while meeting in New York City nominated Victoria Claflin Woodhull for president, the first woman presidential candidate; group took name of Equal Rights Party.

1876 Alexander Graham Bell, speaking before the American Academy of Arts & Sciences in Boston, announced and demonstrated the newly-invented telephone.

1876 The first American major international exposition was opened in Fairmount Park, Philadelphia by President Grant; marked the American centennial.

1886 Francis P. Biddle, Attorney General (1941-45), was born in Paris (died 1968).

1888 Max Steiner, composer, was born in Vienna; wrote many hit movie scores (*Gone With the Wind, The Caine Mutiny, The Treasure of Sierra Madre*) (died 1971).

1899 Fred Astaire, screen actor and dancer, was born in Omaha; began career with sister, Adele (1906); numerous starring film roles (*Top Hat, Easter Parade, Roberta, Holiday Inn*) (died 1987).

1899 Dimitri Tiomkin, musician and composer, was born in Russia; best known for film musical scores (*Lost Horizon, Duel in the Sun, High Noon, Old Man and the Sea, The Great Waltz*) (died 1979).

1902 David O. Selznick, movie producer, was born in Pittsburgh; produced many hits (*Gone With the Wind, The Prisoner of Zenda, Tom Sawyer*) (died 1965).

1908 Carl B. Albert, legislator, was born in McAlester, Okla.; represented Oklahoma in the House (1946-79), serving as Speaker (1971-76).

1916 The first Mother's Day was observed in Philadelphia and Grafton, W.Va.

1916 Milton Babbitt, composer, was born in Philadelphia; a pioneer in the field of electronically-produced music (*Composition for Synthesizer, Vision and Prayer*).

1917 Gen. John J. Pershing was appointed commanding general of the American Expeditionary Force, effective May 26.

1925 Stephen Bechtel Jr., chief executive officer of Bechtel Group, international construction firm, was born in Oakland, Cal.

1930 Adler Planetarium, first American public planetarium, opened in Chicago.

1934 Dust storms began in the Midwest, the aftermath of wartime over-plowing.

1939 The Methodist Episcopal Church, the Methodist Church South, and the Methodist Protestant Church completed a merger in Kansas City into the Methodist Church.

1939 Museum of Modern Art in New York City was dedicated.

1943 Richard G. Darman, Budget Director (1989-) was born in Charlotte, N.C., a presidential assistant (1981-85).

1945 A point system for the discharge of enlisted men was announced.

1950 President Truman signed an act creating the National Science Foundation.

1957 Phil(ip) Mahre, world class skier who won the 1984 Olympic gold medal for slalom, was born in White Pass, Wash.; won seven World Cup medals for various events.

1968 Peace talks began in Paris between the United States and North Vietnam.

1987 IBM researchers announced they have produced a ceramic material able to handle much greater amounts of electric current, opening the way for a new generation of high-speed computers, new medical instruments, and efficient power generation and storage.

MAY 11

1647 Peter Stuyvesant arrived in New Amsterdam to take control of the Dutch colonial government from William Kiefer.

1682 The General Court of Massachusetts repealed laws against observing Christmas and capital punishment for returning Quakers.

1690 English colonists, led by Sir William Phips, captured Port Royal, Nova Scotia, headquarters for French privateers which raided colonial shipping; this was one of the major engagements of the King William's War.

1769 Thomas Jefferson was elected to the Virginia House of Burgesses; re-elected five times, serving until 1775.

1779 John Hart, a signer of the Declaration of Independence , died at about 68; a New Jersey farmer, he was at 65 the oldest signer.

1791 Capt. Robert Gray entered the Columbia River, which he named after his ship; discovery was the basis for American claims to Oregon.

1816 The American Bible Society was formed in New York City.

1835 A convention began in Detroit, which adopted a state constitution June 29; ratified Nov 2; included a provision prohibiting slavery.

1836 The first Iowa newspaper, the *DuBuque Visitor*, was published by John King.

1846 A message by President Polk to the Congress led to a declaration of war against Mexico two days later; he stated that "Mexico has...shed American blood upon American soil;" the House voted 174-14 with 20 abstentions in favor of war, the Senate 40-2 with three abstentions.

1852 Charles W. Fairbanks, Vice President (1905-09), was born near Unionville Center, Ohio; represented Indiana in the Senate (1897-1905) (died 1918).

1854 Ottmar Mergenthaler, inventor of the linotype, was born in Hachtel, Germany; his machine resulted in an upsurge of publishing (died 1899).

1854 Albion W. Small, sociologist, was born in Buckfield, Me.; preeminent in establishing sociology as an American academic subject (died 1926).

1858 Minnesota was admiteed into the Union as the 32nd state.

1862 The *Merrimac*, Confederate ironclad vessel, was blown up by her commander off the Virginia coast to prevent its capture by Union forces.

1864 Union cavalry, led by Gen. Philip Sheridan, was checked at Yellow Tavern, six miles north of Richmond, Va.; Confederate Gen. J.E.B. Stuart was killed.

1880 George E. Haynes, sociologist and civil rights leader, was born in Pine Bluff, Ark.; co-founder, first executive director, National Urban League (1910-16); organized social science department, Fisk U. (1910-12); first black to receive a Ph.D. at Columbia U. (1912) (died 1960).

1881 Theodore van Karman, physicist, was born in Budapest; director, Guggenheim Jet Propulsion Laboratory (1930); did research for Bell X-1, first plane to break sound barrier; founder, Aerojet General (1942) (died 1963).

1884 Alma Gluck, lyric soprano, was born in Bucharest; had a short opera career, sang many years on concert stage (died 1938).

1885 King (Joseph) Oliver, musician, was born in Abend, La.; pioneer jazz cornetist, band leader; led first black jazz group to make records (died 1938).

1888 Irving Berlin, composer, was born in Temun, Russia; wrote about 800 songs, many of the greatest popular hits ("White Christmas," "Easter Parade," "God Bless America," "Alexander's Ragtime Band," "Always," "All Alone") (died 1989).

1891 Henry Morgenthau Jr., public official, was born in New York City; editor, *American Agriculturist* (1922-33); Secretary of the Treasury (1934-45); author, Morgenthau Plan for disarming Germany (died 1967).

1893 Martha Graham, dance teacher and choreographer, was born in Pittsburgh; one of the most influential figures in the dance.

1894 Pullman Co. workers in Chicago went on strike for higher pay, with the cooperation of workers on the railroads which rented Pullman cars; all the railroads were shut down by June 30.

1894 Ellsworth Bunker, diplomat, was born in Yonkers; ambassador to India (1956-61), to South Vietnam (1967-73); helped negotiate Panama Canal treaty (1977-78) (died 1984).

1895 William G. Still, composer and conductor, was born in Woodville, Miss.; first black American to conduct a major American symphony (Los Angeles 1936); composed numerous orchestral works (died 1979).

1897 Robert E. Gross, aircraft manufacturer, was born in Boston; bought Lockheed Aircraft Corp. (1932) for $40,000, developed it into a major plane manufacturer; introduced jet power for commercial aviation, developed Polaris missile (died 1961).

1903 Charley Gehringer, baseball player (Tigers 1926-42), was born in Fowlerville, Mich.; named to Baseball Hall of Fame.

1905 A tornado hit Snyder, Okla., killing 100 persons.

1910 Glacier (Mont.) National Park was established.

1912 Phil Silvers, entertainer was born in New York City; starred on stage (*Top Banana, High Button Shoes*), television (*Phil Silvers Show*) (died 1985).

1918 Richard P. Feynman, physicist, was born in New York City; shared 1965 Nobel Physics Prize for development of relativistic theory of quantum electrodynamics (died 1988).

1935 An executive order created the Rural Electrification Administration (REA) to finance electricity production and distribution in rural areas not served by private utilities.

1943 American amphibious forces landed on Attu Island, off Alaska, and in 19 days of heavy fighting secured the island.

1946 Robert K. Jarvik, physician and medical scientist, was born in Midland, Mich.; developed the first complete artificial heart.

1950 President Truman dedicated the Grand Coulee Dam on the Columbia River in Washington.

1953 Tornadoes hit Waco and San Angelo, Tex.; 124 killed, more than 500 injured.

1973 Charges against Daniel Ellsberg, who leaked the Pentagon Papers to the *New York Times*, were dismissed because of "conduct of the government" in the case.

MAY 12

1621 Edward Winslow and Susanna Fuller White were married in the first Plymouth Colony wedding.

1775 A small American force under Lt. Col. Seth Warner seized Crown Point, N.Y.

1780 After a 45-day land and water siege, Charleston, S.C. surrendered to British troops under Sir Henry Clinton; lost 5000 troops and four vessels, the heaviest American defeat of the war.

1789 The Tammany Society was founded in New York City as a patriotic association; soon became a political organization.

1806 James Shields, Army officer and public official, was born in Altamore, Ireland; served as governor of Oregon Territory (1849); represented Illinois (1849-55), Minnesota (1858-59) and Missouri (1879) in the Senate (died 1879).

1809 Robert C. Winthrop, legislator, was born in Boston; represented Massachusetts in the House (1840-50), serving as Speaker (1847-49), and in the Senate (1850-51) (died 1894).

1822 James L. Orr, legislator and public official, was born in Craytonville, S.C.; represented South Carolina in the House (1849-59), serving as Speaker (1857-59); South Carolina governor (1865-68); minister to Russia (1872-73) (died 1873).

1850 Henry Cabot Lodge, legislator and biographer, was born in Boston; represented Massachusetts in the House (1887-93) and Senate (1893-1924); as chairman of the Foreign Affairs Committee, led the successful fight against American participation in the League of Nations (died 1924).

1859 Lillian Nordica, soprano, was born in Farmington, Me.; performed in various operas at the Met (1896-1907) and on concert stage (died 1914).

1864 A renewed Battle of Spotsylvania Court House (the third Battle of the Wilderness) resulted in some advances for Union troops.

1866 William T. Manning, Episcopal prelate, was born in Northampton, England; rector, Trinity Church, New York City (1908-21), bishop of New York (1921-46) (died 1949).

1868 Al Shean, entertainer was born in Dornum, Germany; half of comedy team of Gallagher & Shean (died 1949).

1879 Ben Lear, World War II general, was born in Hamilton, Canada; commander, 2nd Army (1940-43) (died 1966).

1880 Lincoln Ellsworth, explorer, was born in Chicago; flew over North Pole with Amundsen and Nobile in dirigible (1926), over South Pole (1935); made transatlantic submarine exploration (1931) (died 1951).

1895 William F. Giauque, chemist, was born in Niagara Falls, Ontario; awarded 1949 Nobel Chemistry Prize for research in thermodynamics (died 1982).

1898 Louisiana constitution adopted, effective Sept 1.

1900 Mildred H. McAfee, educator, was born in Parkville, Mo.; president, Wellesley College (1936-49); first director, WAVES (1942-46).

1906 (William) Maurice Ewing, oceanographer, was born in Lockney, Tex.; contributed major portion of our knowledge of submarine topography (died 1974).

1925 Yogi (Lawrence P.) Berra, baseball player (Yankees), was born in St. Louis, Mo.; manager (Yankees, Mets); named to Baseball Hall of Fame.

1929 Burt Bacharach, composer, was born in Kansas City, Mo.; wrote movies scores (*Alfie, What's New Pussycat?, Butch Cassidy and the Sundance Kid*); plays (*Promises, Promises*; songs ("Walk on By," "What the World Needs Now").

1933 Agriculture Adjustment Act was passed in effort to provide temporary relief for farmers, to rehabilitate agriculture; functions later taken over by Department of Agriculture.

1933 Federal Emergency Relief Act was signed, setting up $500 million national relief program, directed by Harry Hopkins.

1936 Frank P. Stella, artist, was born in Malden, Mass.; a leader in "minimal" art movement; exclusive interest in color, structure.

1943 President Franklin Roosevelt and Prime Minister Winston Churchill met for two weeks in the White House to discuss European war plans.

1949 Soviets abandoned their blockade of Berlin after 13 months.

1962 American naval and ground forces were ordered to Laos.

1982 Braniff Airways suspended all operations, filed for bankruptcy the next day, the first major airline to do so.

1987 Doctors in Baltimore successfully transplanted a human heart from a living donor into another human and then transplanted a heart and lungs from an accident victim to the original heart donor.

MAY 13

1729 Henry W. Stiegel, glassmaker, was born in Cologne, Germany; founder of Manheim, Pa.; established glass factory (1764), his glassware became collectors' items (died 1785).

1742 Manasseh Cutler, Congregational clergymen and botanist, was born in Killingly, Conn.; served Ipswich Hamlet (now Hamilton), Mass. (1771-1823); prepared account of New England flora; organized Ohio Co. to colonize Ohio River Valley; helped draft ordinance to govern area (died 1823).

1774 Gen. Thomas Gage arrived in Boston as governor of Massachusetts and commander-in-chief of the army; at the same time, a Boston town meeting called for new economic sanctions against Great Britain.

1813 John S. Dwight, music critic and educator, was born in Boston; publisher, editor, *Journal of Music* (1852-81), which influenced American musical education, taste; helped organize Boston Philharmonic Society (1865) (died 1893).

1846 President Polk signed the declaration of war against Mexico.

1851 A convention in Annapolis adopted a new Maryland state constitution; ratified by the people June 4.

1857 Arthur W. Savage, inventor and manufacturer, was born in Jamaica; founder, Savage Arms Co. (1895); inventor of a dirigible, torpedo, improvements in rifle magazine (died 1938).

1861 Great Britain declared its neutrality in the Civil War, but recognized the rights of the Confederacy as a belligerent.

1864 Union troops under Gen. William T. Sherman began a series of battles at Resaca, Ga. on their way to Atlanta.

1864 The first soldier (a Confederate prisoner) was buried in Arlington National Cemetery.

1883 George N. Papanicolau, clinical anatomist, was born in Comi, Greece; with Cornell U. Medical School (1937-49), developed pap smear test (1928), but it was ignored until 1940 (died 1962).

1889 Theodore Roosevelt was appointed to the Civil Service Commission by President Benjamin Harrison; reappointed by President Cleveland, serving until 1895.

1893 Alvin A. ("Shipwreck") Kelly, flagpole sitter, was born; spent 20,613 hours on high perches, with a record 1177 hours atop an Atlantic City Steel Pier flagpole in 1930 (died 1952).

1908 The White House Conservation Conference began at the call of President Theodore Roosevelt; a direct outgrowth was the National Conservation Commission, headed by Gifford Pinchot.

1908 The Navy Nurses Corps was created by Congress.

1914 Joe Louis, boxing champion, was born in Lexington, Ala.; world heavyweight champion (1937-49) (died 1981).

1954 The St. Lawrence Seaway Development Corporation was established to develop, operate, and maintain the Seaway between Montreal and Lake Erie within the United States.

1984 Stanislaw M. Ulam, Polish-born mathematician, died at 75; a key figure in development of the hydrogen and atomic bombs, releasing their destructive energy; developed the Monte Carlo analysis, the use of random numbers to predict the result of chain reactions.

1985 Philadelphia police bombed a house containing members of a radical group after they refused to come out; the bomb touched off a fire which resulted in 11 deaths and the destruction of 61 row houses.

MAY 14

1602 An exploration led by Bartholomew Gosnold landed at Cape Cod, which he named; attempt at settlement in the area failed.

1634 Massachusetts Bay Company established representative form of government.

1737 Samuel H. Parsons, Revolutionary general, was born in Lyme, Conn.; headed Connecticut divisions, fought at Long Island (died 1789).

1752 Timothy Dwight, Congregational clergymen and educator, was born in Northampton, Mass., grandson of Jonathan Edwards (10/5/1703); chaplain to Army at West Point (1777-79); president, Yale U. (1795-1817) (died 1817).

1769 A land expedition led by Capt. Rivera y Moncada and Father Juan Crespi arrived at San Diego; a second expedition under Gaspar de Portola and Father Junipero Serra arrived in July.

1785 John Adams was named minister to England, serving until 1788.

1787 The Constitutional Convention, scheduled to start in Philadelphia, was unable to organize until May 25 because of late-arriving delegates.

1801 The Pasha of Tripoli declared war on the United States because of its refusal to increase tribute payments; war lasted until June 4, 1805.

1804 The Lewis and Clark Expedition set out from St. Louis on a two-year transcontinental exploration, ending Sept 23, 1806.

1812 West Florida was incorporated into the Mississippi Territory by Congress.

1836 A treaty was signed by Texas and Mexico, following the Texan victory at San Jacinto; captured Gen. Santa Anna pledged to secure Texas recognition but this was repudiated by the Mexican government.

1843 Henry O. Walker, artist, was born in Boston; best known for his murals, such as those in the Library of Congress (died 1929).

1852 Louise C. Adams, widow of President John Quincy Adams, died in Washington at 77.

1852 Alton B. Parker, jurist, was born in Cortland, N.Y.; served New York state courts (1889-1904); Democratic presidential candidate (1904) (died 1926).

1863 Union troops under Gen. U.S. Grant captured Jackson, Miss. enroute to Vicksburg.

1867 Jefferson Davis, former Confederate president, was released on parole from Ft. Monroe, Va. after nearly two years imprisonment.

1880 Bertie C. Forbes, author and publisher, was born in New Deer, Scotland; founder, editor, *Forbes Magazine*; author of several books on business, finance (died 1954).

1881 Ed(ward A.) Walsh, baseball pitcher who won 195 games (White Sox 1904-16), was born in Plains, Pa.; named to Baseball Hall of Fame (died 1959).

1889 South Dakota voters adopted a state constitution.

1897 Sidney Bechet, jazz musician, was born in New Orleans; all-time great soprano saxophonist (died 1959).

1898 Zutty (Arthur J.) Singleton, musician, was born in Bunker, La.; pioneered New Orleans style of jazz drumming, played with most great bands (1920-60) (died 1975).

1899 Earle B. Combs, baseball player (Yankees), was born in Pebworth, Ky.; named to Baseball Hall of Fame (died 1976).

1900 Supreme Court ruled that the inheritance tax levied under the War Revenue Act of 1898 was constitutional.

1913 Rockefeller Foundation was chartered by the New York legislature "to promote the well-being of mankind throughout the world."

1930 Carlsbad (N.M.) National Park was established.

1942 Women's Army Auxiliary Corps (WAAC), later the Women's Army Corps (WAC), was created; more than 65,000 women enlisted in about a year.

1948 President Truman announced that the United States had accorded *de facto* recognition of the Israel government; Israel's creation as an independent nation was proclaimed the same day.

1975 President Ford ordered an all-out attack to recover the American cargo vessel *Mayaguez* seized in Cambodia; operation was successful but at the cost of 15 Marine lives.

MAY 15

1702 The Queen Anne War began when England declared war on France.

1775 The Continental Congress, meeting in Philadelphia, resolved to put the colonies in a state of defense against British; recommended the establishment of state governments.

1776 The Virginia Convention instructed its delegates to offer a resolution to the Continental Congress for colonial independence.

1780 The people of Kentucky and Illinois counties of Virginia petitioned the Continental Congress to form them into separate states.

1788 James Gadsden, diplomat, was born in Charleston, grandson of Christopher Gadsden (2/16/1724); minister to Mexico (1853-54), made the purchase of 45,535, sq. mi. for $10 million; included what is now the southern strip of Arizona and New Mexico (died 1858).

1796 David Austin, Congregational clergymen, predicted the Second Coming for this day; after waiting all day with his congregation in Elizabeth, N.J., he preached on the text, "My Lord delayeth His coming."

1802 Isaac R. Trimble, Confederate general, was born in Culpeper County, Va.; served in Shenandoah Valley campaign and Gettysburg, where he was captured (died 1888).

1820 President Monroe signed the Slave Trade Act, providing the death penalty for those convicted of such trade, which was declared piracy.

1820 Congress granted a new charter to Washington, providing for popular election of its mayor.

1855 Louis Bamberger, merchant, was born in Baltimore; founded Bamberger department stores (1892), now part of Macy's; founded Station WOR, New York City (1922), Institute for Advanced Study, Princeton U. (1933) (died 1944).

1856 Lyman F. Baum, author, was born in Chittenango, N.Y.; wrote many children's fantasies, especially *The Wizard of Oz* (died 1919).

1860 Ellen L. Axson Wilson, first wife of President Wilson, was born in Savannah (died 1914).

1862 Department of Agriculture was created by Congress, headed by a commissioner; elevated to Secretary and a Cabinet member, Feb 9, 1889.

1862 The *Alabama*, a British-built Confederate warship, was launched in Liverpool; sank, captured, or burned more than 60 Union vessels.

1864 Union troops under Franz Sigel were turned back at New Market, Va. by Confederates under J.D. Breckenridge; battle featured a gallant charge by four companies of cadets from Virginia Military Institute.

1864 Gen. William T. Sherman led Union troops to victory at Resaca, Ga., then went on to home Rome, Ga., a Confederate supply center.

1869 The National Woman Suffrage Association was formed by Lucy Blackwell Stone.

1870 Henry L. Doherty, oil and utilities magnate, was born in Columbus, Ohio; organized, headed, Cities Services Co. (1910-39) (died 1939).

1887 John H. Hoover, World War I naval officer, was born in Seville, Ohio; head of the Caribbean command (1942) (died 1970).

1890 Katherine Anne Porter, author, was born near San Antonio; wrote many short stories, novels (*Flowering Judas; Pale Horse, Pale Rider; The Leaning Tower*) (died 1980).

1902 Richard J. Daley, public official, was born in Chicago; mayor of Chicago (1955-76), Democratic political leader (died 1976).

1904 Clifton Fadiman, critic and radio personality, was born in Brooklyn; literary critic (*The New Yorker* 1933-43); master of ceremonies of radio's *Information Please* (1933-48).

1905 Robert S. Abbott published the first issue of the *Chicago Defender*, which soon became the leading black newspaper.

1911 The Supreme Court upheld the decree of the Circuit Court against the Standard Oil Co. of New Jersey, which was declared a monopoly and a combination in restraint of trade; ordered its dissolution.

1915 Paul A. Samuelson, economist, was born in Gary, Ind.; awarded 1970 Nobel Economics Prize for efforts to raise scientific analysis in economic theory; author (*Foundations of Economic Analysis*).

1918 Airmail service began between Washington and New York City.

1918 Eddy Arnold, country music singer, was born in Henderson, Tex.; popular concert and record performer.

1928 The Flood Control Act was signed, appropriating \$325 million for a ten-year flood control program in the Mississippi Valley.

1929 Poisonous fumes from burning x-ray films killed 125 persons in the Crile Hospital Clinic in Cleveland.

1941 Joe DiMaggio of the New York Yankees began his record streak of hitting safely in 56 games.

1942 Gas rationing began in 17 Eastern states.

1953 George Brett, baseball player (Chiefs), was born in Glendale, W. Va.

1966 More than 10,000 anti-war protestors demonstrated against the Vietnam War at the White House.

1969 Associate Justice Abe Fortas resigned from the Supreme Court amid criticism for accepting a fee from Louis E. Wolfson, who was jailed for stock manipulation.

1972 Gov. George E. Wallace of Alabama was shot at a Laurel, Md. political rally; he was paralyzed from the waist down, ending his bid for the Democratic presidential nomination; Arthur H. Bremer, 21, was sentenced to 63 years imprisonment Aug 4 for the shooting.

1972 The island of Okinawa was returned to Japan.

1980 Maxie Anderson and his son, Kris, completed the first nonstop trip across North America in a 75-ft. high helium-filled baloon; the trip took four days.

1988 Twenty-seven persons were killed in a head-on collision between a pickup truck and a church bus returning from an outing near Carrollton, Ky.

MAY 16

1631 A fur trading post was established by William Clayborne on Kent Island in the Chesapeake Bay (near Annapolis).

1769 The Virginia House of Burgesses passed a set of resolutions unanimously, asserting that the sole right of taxation of Virginians lay with the governor and provincial legislature, that the colony had the right to petition the Crown for redress of grievances, and that Virginians must be tried in Virginia.

1780 Loammi Baldwin, civil engineer, was born in North Woburn, Mass., son of Loammi Baldwin (1/10/1740); considered father of American civil engineering (79-mile Union Canal, Charleston, Mass.; Norfolk (Va.) Navy drydocks) (died 1838).

1797 President John Adams sent the first war message to Congress; did not ask for a declaration of war against France but recommended military preparations.

1801 William H. Seward, public official, was born in Florida, N.Y.; served as governor of New York (1838-42) and represented it in the Senate (1849-61); Secretary of State (1861-69), best remembered for purchase of Alaska from Russia, which was then called "Seward's Folly" (died 1872).

1804 Elizabeth P. Peabody, educator and writer, was born in Billerica, Mass.; opened the first American kindergarten in Boston (1860) (died 1894).

1812 American frigate *President* defeated British sloop off Sandy Hook.

1824 Levi P. Morton, Vice President (1889-93), was born in Shoreham, Vt.; represented New York in the House (1879-81) and served it as governor (1895-96); minister to France (1881-85) (died 1920).

1824 Edmund Kirby-Smith, Confederate general, was born in St. Augustine, Fla.; headed Trans-Mississippi Department; last Confederate leader to surrender (June 2, 1865) (died 1893).

1827 Norman J. Colman, first Secretary of Agriculture, was born near Richfield Springs, N.Y.; editor, *Colman's Rural World* (1865-1911); commissioner of agriculture (1885-89), then Secretary (died 1911).

1831 David E. Hughes, inventor, was born in London; invented microphone (1878), induction balance, electromagnet; developed improved printing telegraph (died 1900).

1832 Philip D. Armour, meat packer, was born in Stockbridge, N.Y.; developed Armour & Co. (1870), president (1875-1901); responsible for utilizing waste products, introduction of refrigeration, preparation of canned meats; founder (1893), Armour Institute of Technology (died 1901).

1859 Cyrus Hall McCormick, industrialist, was born in Washington, son of Cyrus Hall McCormick (2/15/1809); first president, International Harvester Co. (1902-19), board chairman (1919-35) (died 1936).

1861 Irving W. Colburn, inventor, was born in Fitchburg, Mass.; developed a process for fabricating continuous sheets of flat glass (died 1917).

1868 The Senate, sitting on the impeachment of President Andrew Johnson, voted 35-19 on Article XI, the first impeachment article to be considered; the vote was one short of the necessary two-thirds; the article dealt with the president's removal of Secretary Stanton, veto of reconstruction acts.

1874 The Ashfield Reservoir above Williamsburg, Mass. collapsed, inundating the Mill River Valley; more than 100 persons died.

1882 Ogden M. Reid, editor and publisher, *New York Tribune* (1913-47), was born in New York City, son of Whitelaw Reid (10/27/1837); added the *New York Herald* (1924) (died 1947).

1886 Douglas Southall Freeman, editor and historian, was born in Lynchburg, Va.; editor, *Richmond News Leader* (1915-49); author (*R.E. Lee, Lee's Lieutenants, George Washington*) (died 1953).

1886 Peter L. Jensen, whose pioneering work made fidelity communications possible, was born in Stubbekobing, Denmark (died 1961).

1892 Manton S. Eddy, World War II general, was born in Chicago (died 1962).

1902 Jan W. Kiepura, operatic tenor, was born in Sosnowiec, Poland; known as the "Polish Caruso" (died 1966).

1905 Henry Fonda, stage and screen star, was born in Grand Island, Neb.; starred in many films (*Grapes of Wrath, Mr. Roberts, On Golden Pond*) (died 1982).

1910 The Bureau of Mines was established, effective July 1.

1911 Margaret Sullavan, actress, was born in Norfolk, Va.; stage and screen star (*Dinner at Eight, Stage Door*) (died 1960).

1912 Studs L. Terkel, author, was born in New York City; wrote many books based on tape-recorded interviews (*Hard Times, Working, Division Street, America*).

1913 Woody (Woodrow) Herman, jazz musician, was born in Milwaukee; saxophone player and orchestra leader (from 1936) (died 1987).

1918 The Espionage Act was passed by Congress strengthening the June 1917 act; drastically enforced by Attorney General Alexander M. Palmer; freedom of speech and press disappeared temporarily.

1919 Liberace (Wladzin Valentino), pianist and entertainer, was born in West Allis, Wis.; noted for flamboyant dress, candelabra on the piano (died 1987).

1920 Former Vice President Levi Morton (1889-93) died in Rhinebeck, N.Y. on his 96th birthday.

1929 The first Oscars were presented by the American Academy of Motion Picture Arts and Sciences in Hollywood.

1957 Joan Benoit (Samuelson), America's foremost female distance runner, was born in Cape Elizabeth, Me.; won first women's marathon in 1984 Olympics and other major races.

1971 The cost of first class postage was increased to eight cents.

1988 The Supreme Court ruled 6-2 that police without warrants may search garbage bags and other refuse containers that people leave outside their homes.

MAY 17

1733 British Parliament enacted the Molasses Act, placing heavy duties on the importation of rum and molasses from the French West Indies to the colonies; effect never felt because law was not enforced.

1741 John Penn, colonial leader, was born in Caroline County, Va.; a North Carolina lawyer, he was a member of the Continental Congress (1775-80), a signer of the Declaration of Independence (died 1788).

1760 John Greenwood, pioneer dentist, was born in Boston; reputed inventor of foot-power drill, springs to hold artificial plates in place, the use of porcelain for artificial teeth (died 1819).

1792 The New York Stock Exchange was organized at Merchants Coffee House.

1829 John Jay, former Secretary of State and Supreme Court chief justice, died at 84 near Bedford, N.Y.

1837 The *Baltimore Sun* was founded by Arunah S. Abell.

1846 Mexican troops evacuated Matamoras on the Rio Grande; the Mexican city then became American headquarters.

1849 Fire in St. Louis destroyed 400 buildings and 27 ships; a serious cholera epidemic followed.

1864 Harry Chandler, publisher, was born in Landaff, N.H.; developd the *Los Angeles Times* to million-plus circulation (1885-1942) (died 1944).

1875 Former Vice President John C. Breckenbridge (1857-61) died in Lexington, Ky. at 54.

1875 Joel E. Spingarn, publisher and civil rights leader, was born in New York City, brother of Arthur B. Spingarn (3/28/1878); a founder, Harcourt Brace & Co. (1919); a founder, National Association for the Advancement of Colored People (NAACP), president (1930-39) (died 1939).

1875 The first Kentucky Derby was held at Churchill Downs in Louisville with Aristides the winner; Oliver Lewis was the jockey.

1877 Former President Grant sailed from Philadelphia on a round-the-world trip.

1884 The Territory of Alaska was created; while really a district, it was run as a territory, which it became Aug 24, 1912; the laws of Oregon were extended to Alaska.

1903 James T. (Cool Papa) Bell, star of Negro baseball leagues, was born in Starkville, Miss.; named to Baseball hall of Fame.

1912 Archibald Cox, lawyer and educator, was born in Plainfield, N.J.; original special prosecutor in the Watergate investigation; fired by President Nixon Oct 20, 1973; Solicitor General (1961-65).

1914 Stewart Alsop, writer, was born in Avon, Conn., brother of Joseph W. Alsop Jr. (10/11/1910); wrote a syndicated newspaper column (died 1974).

1928 Congress established an airmail rate of five cents per ounce.

1946 The government seized the railroads to avert a strike; threat ended May 25.

1954 Supreme Court handed down the historic *Brown v. Board of Education* decision, unanimously ruling that racial segregation in public schools is unconstitutional because it violates the 14th Amendment clause guaranteeing equal protection of the laws.

1973 The Senate Watergate Commission began nationally televisied hearings.

1982 President Reagan formally proposed a constitutional amendment permitting organized prayer in public schools.

1982 Supreme Court ruled 6-3 that a law barring sex discrimination in federally-aided education programs applies to employees as well as students.

1987 A memorial service was held in Mayport, Fla., the home port of the guided missile frigate *Stark*, which was hit by an Iraqui missile in the Persian Gulf, killing 37 American sailors.

MAY 18

1631 The General Court of Massachusetts decreed that "no man shall be admitted to the body politic but such as are members of some of the churches within the limits" of the Colony.

1653 Rhode Island enacted the first law against slavery.

1769 The Virginia House of Burgesses, dissolved by Governor Botetourt, met informally in the Raleigh Tavern, adopted the Virginia Association, a nonimportation agreement which was widely copied.

1815 James B. Francis, hydraulic engineer, was born in Southleigh, England; inventor of widely-used water turbine (died 1893).

1834 Sheldon Jackson, missionary, was born in Minaville, N.Y.; first superintendent of public instruction in Alaska, responsible for creating many schools (died 1909).

1842 The Dorr Rebellion began in Rhode Island when supporters of Thomas W. Dorr made an unsuccessful attempt to seize a state arsenal; Dorr and his followers had set up their own government in northwest Rhode Island; Dorr was tried, sentenced to life imprisonment (June 25, 1844), released in 1845.

1846 American troops under Gen. Zachary Taylor occupied Matamoras.

1862 Josephus Daniels, journalist and diplomat, was born in Washington, N.C.; editor, *Raleigh News and Observer* (1894-1933); Secretary of Navy (1913-21); ambassador to Mexico (1933-41) (died 1948).

1873 Sime Silverman, editor, was born in Cortland, N.Y.; editor, *Variety* (1905-33) (died 1933).

1881 Josiah Henson, Methodist clergyman, died at 92; born a slave, he was reputedly the prototype of Uncle Tom in Harriet Beecher Stowe's book.

1883 Walter A. Gropius, architect, was born in Berlin; founder, director, Bauhaus School of Architecture in Weimar, Germany; professor, chairman, Harvrd Graduate School of Design (1938-52) (died 1969).

1889 Thomas Midgely, chemist, was born in Beaver Falls, Pa.; discovered anti-knock properties of tetraethyl lead (1922); vice president, Ethyl Gasoline Corp. (1923-44) (died 1944).

1891 Arthur J. Altmeyer, public official, was born in DePere, Wis.; chairman, Social Security Board (1937-46); director, Social Security Administration (1946-53) (died 1972).

1892 Ezio Pinza, operatic basso and actor, was born in Rome; enjoyed outstanding 22-year opera career, then starred in musicals (*South Pacific, Fanny*) (died 1957).

1897 Frank Capra, movie director, was born in Palermo, Sicily; known for several screen classics (*It Happened One Night, Mr. Deeds Goes to Town, You Can't Take It With You, Lost Horizon*.

1901 Vincent Du Vigneaud, biochemist, was born in Chicago; awarded 1955 Nobel Chemistry Prize for work on pituitary hormones (died 1978).

1902 A tornado killed 114 and injured 250 people in Goliad, Tex.

1902 Meredith Willson, composer, was born in Mason City, Iowa; remembered for two musicals (*The Music Man, The Unsinkable Molly Brown*) (died 1984).

1904 Jacob K. Javits, legislator, was born in New York City; served New York as attorney general (1954-56) and represented it in the House (1947-52) and Senate (1957-80) (died 1986).

1906 Forest fires in two days devastated 200 square miles in northern Michigan, destroyed eight towns and villages; after being extinguished, they began again and destroyed another 200 square miles.

1908 The motto, "In God We Trust," was restored to American coins.

1912 Perry Como, popular singer, was born in Canonsburg, Pa.; starred on television, made numerous records.

1917 President Wilson signed the Selective Service Act, calling for the registration of 21- to 30-year-old men.

1917 President Wilson issued an executive order sending one division to France, which landed at St. Nazaire June 26.

1933 Tennessee Valley Authority was created, undertaking a broad program of economic and social reconstruction; Arthur E. Morgan, Antioch College president, was chairman.

1936 The Supreme Court held the Bituminous Coal Conservation Act of 1935 unconstitutional.

1937 Brooks Robinson, baseball player, was born in Little Rock, Ark.; third baseman for Baltimore (1955-77); named to Baseball Hall of Fame.

1943 United Nations Conference on Food and Agriculture began in Hot Springs, Va.; resulted in formation of UN Food & Agriculture Organization.

1944 Allied forces captured Cassino, Italy.

1946 Reggie Jackson, baseball player, was born in Wyncote, Pa.; best remembered for hitting three home runs on three consecutive pitches in one World Series game (1978) for the New York Yankees.

1980 Mt. St. Helens, a volcano in southwest Washington, dormant for 123 years, erupted violently, resulting in 26 known dead and 46 missing; erupted periodically after that but less violently.

1987 The Supreme Court unanimously ruled that Jews, Arabs and others who suffer discrimination based on their "ancestry" are protected under statutes barring racial discrimination; also ruled that military employees killed or injured while on duty as a result of a civilian employee's negligence may not sue the government.

MAY 19

1643 Delegates from Plymouth, Connecticut , New Haven, and the Massachusetts Bay colonies met in Boston, created the New England Confederation, which lasted until 1684; Rhode Island was excluded.

1749 The Ohio Company, formed by a group of Virginia planters, acquired 500,000 acres south of and along the Ohio River for the purpose of fur trading and settlement.

1774 About 1000 persons erected a pole 45 feet high in Farmington, Conn., "consecrated to the shrine of liberty" and a copy of the Boston Port Act was burned.

1777 Button Gwinnett, 42-year-old public official, died of wounds suffered in a duel; represented Georgia in the Continental Congress (1776-77), signer of the Declaration of Independence.

1795 Johns Hopkins, financier, was born in Anne Arundel County, Md.; left fortune to endow university and hospital bearing his name (died 1873).

1796 Congress passed the first national game law.

1813 Tompkins H. Matteson, historical painter, was born in Peterboro, N.Y.; best known for the *Spirit of '76, The First Sabbath of the Pilgrims* and *Washington's Inaugural* (died 1884).

1828 President John Quincy Adams signed a protective tariff act considered unjust, called the "tariff of abominations."

1828 William Henry Harrison was appointed first minister to Colombia by President John Quincy Adams; recalled March 8, 1829 by President Jackson.

1857 John J. Abel, pharmacologist and physiological chemist, was born in Cleveland; isolated insulin in crystalline form and adrenalin (died 1938).

1863 Two unsuccessful assults were begun at Vicksburg by Union troops under Gen. U.S. Grant; Union force then settled down for a siege.

1864 Carl E. Akeley, naturalist and sculptor, was born in Clarendon, N.Y.; led expeditions for Field Museum, American Museum of Natural History; developed large habitat animal groups, new taxidermy methods; invented naturalist's motion picture camera, cement gun for sculpting (died 1926).

1877 Tom M. Girdler, a founder (1929), chief executive officer, Republic Steel (1930-56), was born in Clark County, Ind.; president, Jones & Laughlin Steel (1928-30) (died 1965).

1886 Manley O. Hudson, international law specialist, was born in St. Peters, Mo.; with Harvard Law School (1923-54); member, Permanent Court of Arbitration (1933-45), Permanent Court of International Justice (1936-45) (died 1960).

1888 William H. Simpson, commanding general, Ninth Army (1944-46), was born in Weathersford, Tex. (died 1980).

1917 Herbert Hoover was appointed food controller by President Wilson; became food administrator Aug 10 when the food and fuel control legislation was signed.

1921 Supreme Court Justice Edward D. White died at 76 in Washington.

1921 President Harding signed the first immigration quota act, restricting immigration to a maximum three percent of any nationality in a year.

1924 A soldiers' bonus was enacted over President Coolidge's veto; the original bonus was a 20-year endowment policy against which veterans could borrow; cash bonus payments were authorized in 1936, based on $1.25 per day of overseas service, $1 for American service.

1925 Malcolm X, Muslim leader, was born in Omaha as Malcolm Little; first "national minister" of Black

Muslims (1963-64); suspended, formed own sect (Organization of Afro-American Unity); assassinated 1965.

1934 James Lehrer, television news reporter (*MacNeil-Lehrer Report*), was born in Wichita, Kan.

1935 David Hartman, television host, was born in Pawtucket, R.I.; host of ABC's *Good Morning America* show (1975-87).

1940 Frank (Francisco A.) Lorenzo, aviation executive, was born in New York City; head of Texas Airlines, which acquired Continental, Eastern and Peoples lines.

1986 President Reagan signed the Firearms Owner Protection Act, loosening firearms curbs of the 1968 Gun Control Act.

1988 Carlo Lehder Rivas, reputed Colombian leader of a huge drug ring, was convicted by a jury in Jacksonville, Fla.

MAY 20

1663 William Bradford, printer, was born in Barnwell, England; helped found first American paper mill (1690), crown printer (1693-1742), official printer of New Jersey (1703-33); printed first American legislative proceedings, first New York paper money (1709), first American Book of Common Prayer, first newspaper in New York (the *Gazette* 1725) (died 1752).

1690 Portland, Me. (then called Casco) destroyed by French and Indians.

1691 James Blair was sent to England to obtain a charter for the College of William & Mary in Charlottesville; became first president (1693-1743).

1750 Stephen Girard, banker, was born in Bordeaux, France; founded (1812) bank in Philadelphia, which took over the business of the Bank of the United States; helped finance War of 1812, created the second Bank of the United States (1816); bequeathed funds to found Girard College for "poor, white, male orphans" (died 1831).

1759 William Thornton, architect, was born in in what is now the Virgin Islands; designed (with some modification) the Capitol, Octagon House in Washington (died 1828).

1768 Dolley (Dorothea) Todd Madison, wife of President Madison, was born in what is now Guilford County, N.C.; a legendary Washington hostess (died 1849).

1774 The British Parliament passed the Massachusetts Government Act to take "the executive power from the hands of the democratic part of the government; town meetings to be held only with permission of government;" also passed the Administration of Justice Act which made it possible to move trials to England.

1808 Thomas D. Rice, entertainer, was born in New York City; pioneer minstrel showman, known as the father of American minstrelsy (died 1860).

1818 William G. Fargo, express company leader, was born in Pompey, N.Y.; helped form two companies which later became the American Express Co., president (1868-81); organized Wells Fargo (1852), president (1870-72) (died 1881).

1825 Antoinette L.B. Blackwell, reformer, was born in Henrietta, N.Y., sister-in-law of Elizabeth Blackwell (2/3/1821); active worker for abolition, temperance, women's rights; first ordained woman minister (Congregational) (died 1921).

1826 Potter Palmer, merchant, was born in Albany; with two partners opened dry goods store in Chicago which revolutionized merchandising; later became Marshall Field & Co. (1881); built the Palmer House (died 1902).

1843 Albert A. Pope,founder of American bicycle industry, was born in Boston; began producing automobiles (1890) (died 1909).

1851 Emile Berliner, inventor, was born in Hanover, Germany; invented a microphone, gramophone, acoustic tile, a rotating cylinder internal combustion engine, a flat "platter" phonograph record (died 1929).

1861 The Confederacy voted to move its capitol from Montgomery, Ala. to Richmond, Va.; moved in June.

1861 North Carolina seceded from the Union, but convention would not submit question for popular ratification.

1862 The Homestead Act went into effect, providing settlers farms of 160 acres of surveyed public land after five years of continuous residence and payment of $26-$34 fee, or $1.25 an acre after six months residence.

1883 Edwin G. Nourse, economist, was born in Lockport, N.Y.; first chairman, Council of Economic Advisors (1946-49) (died 1974).

1890 Allan Nevins, historian, was born in Camp Point, Ill.; with Columbia U. (1928-58); author (*Ordeal of the Union*, various biographies) (died 1971).

1891 Earl R. Browder, Communist leader, was born in Wichita, Kan.; secretary-general, American Communist Party (1930-45), expelled as a "right deviationist" (died 1973).

1899 John M. Harlan, jurist, was born in Chicago, grandson of John M. Harlan (6/1/1833); associate justice, Supreme Court (1955-71) (died 1971).

1908 James Stewart, screen actor, was born in Indiana, Pa.; made many films (*The Philadelphia Story, The Far Country, Harvey, Mr. Smith Goes to Washington*).

1914 Representatives of Argentina, Brazil, and Chile began month-long unsuccessful meeting to resolve American-Mexican differences.

1926 President Coolidge signed the Air Commerce Act, placing civil aviation under control of the Commerce Department.

1927 Charles A. Lindbergh began his successful nonstop solo flight from New York to Paris, taking 33 hours, 39 minutes in his plane, the Spirit of St. Louis.

1932 Amelia Earhart became the first woman to fly solo across the Atlantic from Newfoundland to Ireland in approximately 15 hours.

1939 Transatlantic airmail service from New York began.

1941 Office of Civilian Defense was created by executive order; terminated June 30, 1945.

1985 The FBI arrested John A. Walker Jr., retired Navy warrant officer, for passing secrets to Russia; two other family members and a friend also were arrested.

1988 A woman opened gunfire at a school in Winnetka, Ill. killing an eight-year-old pupil, wounding four others; police later found her dead in a nearby house, apparently a suicide.

MAY 21

1542 Hernando de Soto died after a voyage from Oklahoma down the Arkansas River to its mouth.

1690 John Eliot, English missionary to the Indians for 30 years, died at 86; known as the apostle of the Indians, he published an Indian language catechism (1653), the Bible (1661-63), the first Bible published in North America.

1755 Alfred Moore, jurist, was born in New Hanover County, N.C.; associate justice, Supreme Court (1799-1804) (died 1810).

1796 Reverdy Johnson, jurist and diplomat, was born in Annapolis; defense attorney in Dred Scott case; represented Maryland in the Senate (1845-49, 1863-68), Attorney General (1849-50); minister to Great Britain (1868-69); helped keep Maryland in the Union (1861) (died 1876).

1798 Benjamin Stoddert became the first Secretary of the Navy.

1832 The first national nominating convention of the Democratic Party opened in Baltimore; unanimously endorsed President Jackson for a second term.

1855 Massachusetts enacted a stringent personal liberty act, which virtually nullified the Fugitive Slave Act, arose from the capture and return of a slave in 1854.

1855 Edmund J. James, educator, was born in Jacksonville, Ill.; president, Northwestern U. (1902-04), U. of Illinois (1904-20); founder, first president, American Academy of Political and Social Science (1890-1901) (died 1925).

1856 Civil war broke out in Kansas between pro- and anti-slavery forces; Lawrence was sacked by proslavery group, which was answered three days later by the massacre at Pottawatomie, led by John Brown; temporary peace reached Sept 15.

1862 Edwin P. Christy, entertainer, died at 47; originated the Christy Minstrels (1842), which originally were called the Virginia Minstrels.

1862 Congress passed legislation providing for the education of black children in Washington.

1867 Frances Densmore, music authority, was born in Red Wing, Minn.; foremost authority on songs of the American Indians (died 1957).

1868 John L. Hines, World War I Army officer, was born in White Sulphur Springs, W.Va.; served in France and Philippines; Army chief of staff (1924); commander, Philippines Department (1930-32) (died 1968).

1872 Richard Bennett, actor and producer, was born in Cass County, Ind.; starred in many plays (*Charley's Aunt, The Royal Family, The Barker*) (died 1944).

1874 Nellie Grant, daugher of President and Mrs. Grant, was married in the White House to Algernon C.F. Sartoris of the British legation.

1878 Glenn H. Curtiss, aviation pioneer, was born in Hammondsport, N.Y.; invented aileron; won trophy for first one-mile public airplane flight in America (1908); won $10,000 prize for Albany-New York flight in two hours, 51 minutes (1910); developed hydroplane; supplied planes to Allies in World War

I; developed Navy flying boat, which made first Atlantic crossing (1919) (died 1930).

1881 American Red Cross was originated with Clara Barton as president.

1898 Armand Hammer, industrialist, was born in New York City; head of Occidental Petroleum (1957-); noted art collector; instrumental in U.S.-U.S.S.R. trade negotiations.

1901 Horace Heidt, bandleader of the 1930s, 1940s, was born in Alameda, Cal. (died 1986).

1902 Marcel Breuer, architect, was born in Pecs, Hungary; pioneer furniture designer; designed HUD, Health and Human Services buildings in Washington; Whitney Museum, New York City; UNESCO Headquarters in Paris (died 1981).

1902 Earl Averill, baseball player (Indians), was born in Snohomish, Wash.; named to Baseball Hall of Fame (died 1983).

1904 Fats (Thomas) Waller, pianist, was born in New York City; orchestra leader, composer ("Honeysuckle Rose," "Ain't Misbehavin'") (died 1943).

1916 Harold Robbins, author, was born in New York City; wrote many popular novels (*The Dream Merchants, The Carpetbaggers, The Betsy*).

1917 About 2000 buildings in Atlanta burned, with damage estimated at $5 million.

1917 Raymond Burr, television actor (*Perry Mason*), was born in New Westminster, British Columbia.

1941 The American merchant vessel *Robin Moor* was sunk by a German submarine without warning in the South Atlantic.

1968 The nuclear submarine *Scorpion* was lost near the Azores with 99 aboard.

1969 President Nixon nominated Warren E. Burger as chief justice of the Supreme Court; confirmed June 23.

1980 President Carter ordered the evacuation of 710 families from the Love Canal area in Niagara Falls, a former dump for toxic chemical wastes.

MAY 22

1620 Louis de Frontenac, colonial official, was born in St. Germain, France; governor of New France (Canada) (1672-82, 1689-98) (died 1698).

1786 Arthur Tappan, silk merchant, was born in Northampton, Mass., brother of Lewis Tappan (5/23/1788); founder, *New York Journal of Commerce* (1827); made numerous endowments to religious institutions, helped found American Missionary Association (died 1865).

1802 Martha Washington, widow of President Washington, died at 70 at Mt. Vernon.

1807 Trial of Aaron Burr on conspiracy charges began in Richmond, Va.; acquitted Oct 20.

1826 Christopher C. Langdell, educator, was born in New Boston, N.H.; dean, Harvard Law School (1870-95), introduced case system teaching (died 1906).

1843 One thousand Easterners left from Independence, Mo. to settle in the Oregon territory, marking the beginning of a large migration westward.

1844 Mary Cassatt, artist, was born in Allegheny City, Pa., sister of A.J. Cassatt (12/8/1839); member of impressionist school, excelled in domestic scenes (died 1926).

1848 Democratic National Committee was formed in Baltimore.

1849 Abraham Lincoln obtained a patent on inflated cylinders "for buoying vessels over shoals;" never put to practical use.

1854 Congress passed the Kansas-Nebraska Act, permitting states an option on slavery and nullifying the Missouri Compromise.

1856 Sen. Charles Sumner of Massachusetts was physically assaulted in Senate chamber by Rep. Preston S. Brooks of South Carolina for a critical speech about his uncle, Sen. Andrew P. Butler of South Carolina; Sumner never fully recovered; House censure of Brooks failed but he resigned July 14.

1872 The Amnesty Act was passed, restoring civil rights to Southern citizens, except for 500 Confederate leaders.

1891 Robert G. Sproul, educator, was born in San Francisco; President U. of California (1930-58) (died 1975).

1902 Crater Lake (Ore.) National Park was established.

1902 Al(oysius H.) Simmons, baseball player, was born in Milwaukee; outfielder, mostly with Athletics; lifetime batting average of .334; named to Baseball Hall of Fame (died 1956).

1914 Vance O. Packard, author, was born in Granville Summit, Pa.; wrote a number of popular nonfiction books (*The Hidden Persuaders, The Waste Makers, The Pyramid Climbers*).

1915 George Baker, cartoonist, was born in Lowell, Mass.; best remembered for World War II *Sad Sack* cartoon (died 1975).

1920 Civil Service Retirement Act was passed by Congress, with compulsory retirement at 70 and annuity after 15 years service.

1928 T. Boone Pickens, financier, was born in Holdenville, Okla.; known as a corporate raider.

1943 Helen H. Taft, widow of President Taft, died in Washington at 82.

1946 The government seized the soft coal mines; a wage increase was granted a week later on government orders.

1953 President Eisenhower signed the Submerged Lands Act, which gave the federal government the rights to offshore lands of the seaboard states.

1971 The Lyndon Baines Johnson Library at the U. of Texas was dedicated by the former president.

1972 President Nixon arrived in Moscow for a week of summit talks, the first visit by an American president; resulted in strategic arms pact.

1987 Saragosa, Tex., a town of 350 persons, was completely wiped out by a tornado, killing 30 residents and injuring 121.

1988 Television evangelist Jimmy Swaggart preached for the first time since he lost his credentials as an Assemblies of God Church minister for self-confessed sins.

MAY 23

1609 A new charter was granted to the Virginia settlement making the Jamestown colony independent of the Plymouth Company; the grant extended 200 miles north and south of Point Comfort and "from sea to sea."

1740 John Gibson, colonial leader, was born in Lancaster, Pa.; fur trader, colonel in the Continental Army; commander, Ft. Pitt (1781-82), secretary of Indiana Territory (1800-16) (died 1822).

1788 The South Carolina legislature ratified the Constitution by a vote of 149-73 becoming the eighth state in the Union.

1788 Lewis Tappan, businessman, was born in Northampton, Mass., brother of Arthur Tappan (5/22/1786); founder (1841) of first credit rating agency, which later became Dun & Bradstreet (died 1873).

1810 Margaret Fuller, feminist and author, was born in Cambridgeport, Mass.; often called the first American woman professional journalist and first foreign correspondent (died 1850).

1811 The first Alabama newspaper, the *Mobile Centinel*, was founded outside Mobile (Ft. Stoddert) by Samuel Miller and John B. Hood.

1820 James B. Eads, engineer, was born in Lawrenceburg, Ind.; invented the diving bell, built a fleet of armor-plated gunboats to control the Mississippi River (1861), built a bridge across the Mississippi at St. Louis (1867-74); designed deep water channel for the Mississippi delta (died 1887).

1824 Ambrose E. Burnside, Union general, was born in Liberty, Ind.; commanded, Army of the Potomac (1862-63); commander at Fredericksburg (Va.) (1864), but failed to follow up advantage after a mine explosion; served Rhode Island as governor (1866-69) and represented it in the Senate (1875-81); gave name to "sideburns" which he wore (died 1881).

1830 Henry M. Teller, legislator and public official, was born in Granger, N.Y.; a first Senator from Colorado (1876-82, 1885-1909); Secretary of the Interior (1882-85) (died 1914).

1840 John F. Appleby, inventor, was born in Westmoreland, N.Y.; invented binder for grain reapers (1878), an automatic feed device for rifles (1864) (died 1917).

1861 Virginia voters approved (96,750 to 32,134) secession from the Union.

1862 Gen. Stonewall Jackson with 18,000 men took Front Royal, Va. at the start of the Shenandoah Valley campaign; took Winchester two days later.

1875 Alfred P. Sloan, automobile manufacturer, was born in New Haven; President , General Motors (1923-37), board chairman (1937-56) (died 1966).

1883 Douglas Fairbanks, screen actor, was born in Denver; starred in many silent films (*The Three Musketeers, Robin Hood, The Thief of Bagdad*) (died 1939).

1888 Zach(ariah D.) Wheat, baseball player (Brooklyn) who batted .317 in 19 years, was born in Hamilton, Mo.; named to Baseball Hall of Fame (died 1972).

1903 The first automobile trip across the United States began in San Francisco; ended Aug 1 in New York City.

1903 Wisconsin set up the first direct primary election voting system.

1908 Max Abramowitz, architect, was born in Chicago; designed U.S. Embassy in Rio de Janeiro, Columbia U. Law School, Lincoln Center Philharmonic Hall.

1908 John Bardeen, physicist, was born in Madison, Wis.; first to win two Nobel Physics prizes—shared 1956 prize for discovery of the transistor and the 1972 prize for developing the theory of superconductivity.

1910 Artie Shaw, musician, was born in New York City; clarinetist and orchestra leader (from 1936).

1911 New York Public Library was dedicated by President Taft.

1920 Helen O'Connell, singer, was born in Lima, Ohio; vocalist with Jimmy Doresy band.

1922 *Abie's Irish Rose*, a three-act comedy, opened in Fulton Theater, New York City; ran for 2327 performances, then a record.

1925 Joshua Lederberg, microbiologist, was born in Montclair, N.J.; shared 1958 Nobel Physiology/Medicine Prize for work with genetic mechanisms.

1934 Clyde Barrow, public enemy #1 in the Southwest, and his partner, Bonnie Parker, were shot to death by Texas Rangers and sherriff's deputies after a two-year robbery spree during which they killed 12 people.

1935 Donald P. Hodel, public official, was born in Portland, Ore.; Energy Secretary (1982-85), Interior Secretary (1985-89).

1939 U.S. submarine *Squalus* sank off Portsmouth, N.H.; 33 of 59 aboard were rescued by a diving bell.

MAY 24

1607 Three vessels of the London Company arrived at Jamestown, Va., 32 miles from the mouth of the James River; the 105 settlers were led by Capt. John Smith; during the first seven months, famine and disease reduced the colony to 32, but it was saved by the arrival of supply ships and firmer administration.

1624 The charter of the London Company was revoked and Virginia became a royal colony.

1764 A Boston town meeting was held to protest Parliament's passage of the Sugar Act, denouncing taxation without representation, and proposed united action by the colonies.

1768 Thomas Bacon, Anglican clergyman, died at about 68; served churches in Maryland and Delaware (1744-68); compiled the laws of Maryland (1765).

1816 Emanuel Leutze, historical painter, was born in Gmund, Germany; among his best known works are *Washington Crossing the Delaware* and *Westward the Course of Empire* (died 1868).

1818 The Seminole War ended with the capture of Pensacola by forces under Andrew Jackson.

1819 The *Savannah*, a fully-rigged sailing vessel with auxiliary steam power, left Savannah, Ga. and arrived in Liverpool, England 29 days and four hours later, the first ship to use steam in an Atlantic crossing.

1844 Samuel F.B. Morse tapped out the first message on his telegraph, "What hath God wrought?" in the Supreme Court chamber in Washington and the message was received in Baltimore.

1850 Henry W. Grady, newspaper executive, was born in Athens, Ga.; co-owner, editor, *Atlanta Constitution* (died 1889).

1852 Maurice F. Egan, journalist and diplomat, was born in Philadelphia; minister to Denmark, negotiated purchase of Danish West Indies, now the Virgin Islands (died 1924).

1854 Richard Mansfield, actor, was born in Helgoland, Germany; starred in Shakespearean plays, *Peer Gynt, Cyrano de Bergerac* (died 1907).

1854 A fleeing slave, Anthony Burns, was arrested in Boston; protests against his return to Virginia resulted in riots, callout of troops; returned but bought out of slavery; studied at Oberlin College (Ohio), became pastor of a Baptist church in Canada.

1856 John Brown, anti-slavery leader, led a group of abolitionists against pro-slavery settlers at Pottawatomie, Kan., killing five; murders not prosecuted.

1860 George L. Heins, architect, was born in Philadelphia; co-designer of the Cathedral of St. John the Divine, New York City (died 1907).

1860 James McK. Cattell, editor and psychologist, was born in Easton, Pa.; did pioneer research in mental and psychological testing; founder, president, Psychological Corp. (1921), concerned with practical applications of psychology; edited many scientific journals (died 1944).

1870 Benjamin N. Cardozo, jurist, was born in New York City; served on New York Court of Appeals (1917-32), chief justice (1926-32); associate justice, Supreme Court (1932-38), a leading spokesman for sociological jurisprudence (died 1938).

1878 Harry Emerson Fosdick, clergyman and author, was born in Buffalo; professor of practical theology, Union Theological Seminary (1915-46); pastor, Riverside Church, New York City (1931-46); spokesman for modern liberal Christianity; preached on *National Vespers*, nationwide radio program (1926-46) (died 1969).

1883 Elsa Maxwell, noted hostess, was born in Keokuk, Iowa (died 1963).

1883 The Brooklyn Bridge over the East River was opened, with President Arthur present.

1893 The Anti-Saloon League was formed in Oberlin, Ohio by the Rev. H.H. Russell; the Ohio plan was copied elsewhere, served as the model for Anti-Saloon League of America, formed in 1895.

1895 Samuel I. Newhouse, newspaper publisher, was born in New York City; founder, headed, newspaper chain, syndicate which bears his name (died 1979).

1898 Helen B. Taussig, physician, was born in Cambridge, Mass.; worked with Dr. Alfred Blalock in developing operation to save "blue babies" (died 1986).

1905 Martin Dihigo, star of Negro baseball leagues, was born in Havana, Cuba; named to Baseball Hall of Fame.

1909 Wilbur D. Mills, legislator, was born in Kennett, Ark.; represented Arkansas in the House (1938-77); as Ways and Means Committee chairman, he was very influential in taxation matters.

1927 Jack (John B. Jr.) Kelly, one of the finest American oarsmen, was born in Philadelphia, son of John Kelly Sr. (10/4/1890); won the Diamond Sculls at Henley (1947, 1949) and the American single sculls title eight times (died 1985).

1935 The first night major league baseball game was played at Crosley Field with Cincinnati beating the Philadelphia Phillies 2-1.

1937 The Supreme Court upheld the constitutionality of the Social Security Act.

1941 Bob Dylan, musician and composer, was born in Duluth; composed several popular hits, anthems of the 1960s civil rights movement ("Blowin' in the Wind," "The Times They are a'Changin'").

1950 The Maritime Administration was established.

1954 The Supreme Court, in a series of decisions, outlawed segregation in tax-supported colleges, junior colleges, universities, graduate schools, public housing, and public park, recreational and entertainment facilities.

1983 The Supreme Court ruled 8-1 that the Internal Revenue Service could deny tax exemptions to private schools that practiced racial discrimination.

1983 The 100th anniversary of the Brooklyn Bridge was celebrated with two million people looking on.

1988 President Reagan vetoed the trade bill but the House voted 308-113 to override the veto; the Senate on June 8 upheld the veto.

MAY 25

1539 Hernando de Soto arrived with 600 troops at Tamps Bay from Havana to complete the exploration of Florida.

1783 Philip P. Barbour, jurist, was born in Barboursville, Va., brother of James Barbour (6/10/1775); represented Virginia in the House (1814-25, 1827-30), serving as Speaker (1821-23, 1827-29); associate justice, Supreme Court (1836-41) (died 1841).

1787 The Constitutional Convention opened in Philadelphia when a quorum of seven states had arrived; finally 55 delegates attended; George Washington, a delegate from Virginia, was named president; William Jackson, secretary; convention ended Sept 17.

1793 The first Catholic priest, Stephen T. Badin, was ordained in the United States by Bishop John Carroll of Baltimore.

1803 Ralph Waldo Emerson, essayist and poet, was born in Boston; considered a sage, spokesman for American transcendentalism; author, essayist (*Society and Solitude, The Conduct of Life*) (died 1882).

1825 Daniel B. Wesson, inventor and manufacturer, was born in Worcester, Mass.; developed new repeating action for pistol and rifle; founder, Smith & Wesson Co. (1857) (died 1906).

1835 Henry C. Potter, Episcopal prelate, was born in Schenectady, N.Y., son of Alonzo Potter (7/6/1800); rector, Grace Church, New York City (1868-83); assistant bishop of New York (1883-87), bishop (1887-1908); began building the Cathedral of St. John the Divine (died 1908).

1844 A gasoline engine was patented by Stuart Perry.

1845 William Muldoon, an outstanding athlete of the 19th century, was born in Belfast, N.Y.; helped organize the Police Athletic League, New York City; chairman, New York State Boxing Commission (1921-23) (died 1933).

1847 John A. Dowie, faith healer and founder of the Christian Catholic Apostolic Church, was born in Edinburgh; founder, Zion City, north of Chicago; proclaimed himself Elijah the Restorer, deposed by revolt of followers (died 1907).

1850 A state convention adopted the New Mexico constitution, excluding slavery.

1862 Confederate troops under Gen. Stonewall Jackson routed Union troops at Winchester, Va.

1864 Gen. William T. Sherman's drive toward Atlanta continued with the repulse of a Confederate attack at New Hope Church.

1865 John R. Mott, YMCA leader, was born in Livingston Manor, N.Y.; general secretary YMCA (1915-31); head of U.S. Council, world alliance (1926-37); founder, Foreign Missions Conference (1893), World Student Christian Federation (1895); shared 1946 Nobel Peace Prize (died 1955).

1866 Carl E. ("Bunny") Schultze, cartoonist, was born in Lexington, Ky.; originated *Foxy Grandpa* comic strip (died 1939).

1878 Bill ("Bojangles") Robinson, dancer and entertainer, was born in Richmond, Va.; starred in vaudeville, many revues and *The Hot Mikado* (died 1949).

1879 St. Patrick's Cathedral in New York City was dedicated.

1883 Lesley J. McNair, World War I and II general, was born in Verndale, Minn.; commander, Army Ground Forces, killed in bombing at St. Lo, France 1944.

1886 Philip Murray, labor leader, was born in Blantyre, Scotland; vice president, United Mine Workers (1920-42); president, CIO (1940-52), United Steelworkers (1942-52) (died 1952).

1889 Igor I. Sikorsky, aviation pioneer, was born in Kiev, Russia; built, flew first successful multimotor plane (1913); founder, aircraft manufacturing firm (1923), first transatlantic clipper, workable helicopter (died 1972).

1898 An American expeditionary force of nearly 2500 sailed from San Francisco to Manila.

1898 Bennett A. Cerf, editor and publisher, was born in New York City; president, Modern Library (1925-71); founder, president, Random House (1927-65); compiled numerous anthologies; panelist on TV's *What's My Line* (died 1971).

1905 The International Joint Commission, designed to regulate the use of water at the Canadian-American boundary, met for the first time.

1908 Theodore Roethke, author, was born in Saginaw, Mich.; noted for his poetry of childhood and old age (died 1963).

1915 The American steamer *Nebraskan* was torpeded by a German submarine off Scotland.

1917 Theodore M. Hesburgh, president, Notre Dame U. (1952-87), was born in Syracuse, N.Y.; chairman, U.S. Civil Rights Commission (1969-72).

1921 Hal David, lyricist, was born in New York City; numerous hit songs ("What the World Needs Now," "Alfie," "Raindrops Keep Falling on My Head").

1921 Jack Steinberger, physicist, was born in Bad Kissingen, Germany; shared 1988 Nobel Physics Prize for helping capture neutrinos in a high energy beam to examine the structure of atomic particles.

1926 Miles Davis Jr., a leading jazz musician since the early 1940s, was born in Alton, Ill.; ushered in "cool" jazz.

1929 Beverly Sills, opera and concert singer, was born in New York City; sang with the New York City Opera (1955-79), director (1979-).

1940 President Franklin Roosevelt created the Office of Emergency Management.

1950 The Brooklyn-Battery Tunnel, the longest in the United States, opened.

1961 President Kennedy called for a moon project—"I believe that this nation should commit itself to achieving the goal, before this decade is out, of landing a man on the moon and returning him safely to earth."

1968 The Gateway Arch in St. Louis was dedicated.

1979 An American Airlines DC-10 jetliner crashed on takeoff at Chicago's O'Hare Airport, killing all 272 persons aboard in the worst American air disaster.

1986 More than five million Americans joined hands in an attempt to form a human chain across the nation in Hands Across America, designed to raise money for the hungry.

1987 Former Labor Secretary Raymond J. Donovan was acquitted of grand larceny and fraud charges which forced him from office more than two years previously; he was the first sitting Cabinet member to be indicted.

1987 The Supreme Court ruled 6-3 that suspects accused of serious crimes may be held in "preventive detention" before trial if a judge determines that they are a danger to the public.

1988 The Reagan Administration abandoned talks with General Manuel Noriega in efforts to get him to leave Panama.

1988 President Reagan arrived in Helsinki for three days of rest on his way to the Moscow summit meeting.

MAY 26

1637 Massachusetts and Connecticut colonists destroyed the Pequot Indian fort at Mystic, Conn., where more than 600 Indians were killed; tribe was practically annihilated near Fairfield, Conn.

1780 Combined British and Indian attack on St. Louis was beaten back and the British plan to take the Spanish and Illinois posts was dropped.

1781 The Bank of North America was incorporated in Philadelphia after congressional approval.

1790 The territory southwest of the Ohio River was created.

1828 Samuel W. Allerton, financier, was born in Amenia, N.Y.; co-founder, Union Stock Yards, Chicago (1865), a leader in Chicago community affairs, a builder of modern Chicago (died 1914).

1835 Edward P. Alexander, Confederate general, was born in Washington, Ga.; directed artillery at Gettysburg (died 1910).

1836 The House voted the first "gag rules," which would automatically table any matter relating to slavery; repealed 1844.

1837 Washington A. Roebling, engineer and bridge builder, was born in Saxonburg, Pa.; succeeded his father (John A. Roebling, 6/12/1806) as engineer for the Brooklyn Bridge construction; completed bridge (1883) (died 1926).

1845 Samuel J. Barrows, Unitarian clergyman and prison reformer, was born in New York City; editor, *Christian Register* (1880-96); influenced passage of first New York probation law and federal parole law (died 1909).

1864 Montana became a territory, formed out of part of Idaho Territory.

1865 Civil War hostilities ended with the surrender of Gen. Edmund Kirby-Smith and his troops to Gen. E.S. Canby at New Orleans.

1868 The Senate, meeting again on President Andrew Johnson's impeachment, again voted 35-19 on two other articles of impeachment, one vote short of the reqired two-thirds; failure to impeach resulted in the resignation of Secretary of War Edwin M. Stanton.

1872 Joseph Urban, architect and designer, was born in Vienna; designed many sets for theaters, operas, the Ziegfeld Theater, New School for Social Research (died 1933).

1876 Robert M. Yerkes, comparative psychologist, was born in Bradysville, Pa.; developed intelligence tests during World War I for more than 1.7 million men (died 1956).

1886 Al Jolson, entertainer, was born in Srednick, Russia; appeared in vaudeville, stage, and screen plays (*The Jazz Singer*—the first talking picture; *The Singing Fool* (died 1950).

1893 Maxwell Bodenheim, poet, was born in Hermanville, Miss.; known as the Bard of Greenwich Village (*Blackguard, Replenishing Jessica*) (died 1954).

1907 John Wayne, screen actor, was born in Winterset, Iowa; starred in numerous films (*True Grit, Red River, Sands of Iwo Jima*) (died 1979).

1907 Ida S. McKinley, widow of President McKinley, died in Canton, Ohio at 59.

1909 Eugenie M. Anderson, first woman American ambassador, was born in Adair, Iowa; ambassador to Denmark (1949-53), minister to Bulgaria (1962-64).

1917 Maj. Gen. John J. Pershing, named to command the American Expeditionary Force, was ordered to France with his staff.

1920 Peggy Lee, singer and lyricist, was born in Jamestown, S.D.; sang with Benny Goodman band (1941-43), made several films, concert and club appearances.

1939 Brent Musberger, sportscarter (CBS 1974-), was born in Portland, Ore.

1951 Sally K. Ride, first American woman in space, was born in Los Angeles.

1954 An explosion aboard the aircraft carrier *Bennington* off the Rhode Island coast killed 103 crewmen.

1977 Securities & Exchange Commission announced that the Lockheed Corporation paid nearly $38 million in bribes and extortion abroad.

MAY 27

1586 An expedition to destroy New Spain was led by Sir Francis Drake; destroyed the Spanish fort at St. Augustine, Fla.

1774 Eighty-nine members of Virginia's House of Burgesses met in Raleigh Tavern in Williamsburg, recommended a meeting of all colonies in a congress; delegates, including Washington, Jefferson, and Patrick Henry, were asked to sound out their constituencies and meet again.

1787 The first number of the Federalist Papers appeared; written by Alexander Hamilton, James Madison, and John Jay, they were designed to get New York to ratify the Constitution.

1794 President Washington nominated James Monroe as minister to France; served two years; President Jefferson renamed him in 1803, when he signed the treaty for the purchase of Louisiana Territory.

1794 Cornelius Vanderbilt, financier and businessman, was born in Port Richmond, N.Y.; known as the "Commodore," he founded the wealthy railroad, shipping family; built Grand Central Station, New York City; made large gifts to Central U., Nashville, which became Vanderbilt U. (died 1877).

1813 Then Col. Winfield Scott, assisted by American naval forces, captured Ft. George, N.Y.; British abandoned entire NiagaraFrontier to Americans.

1818 Amelia Jenks Bloomer, feminist, was born in Homer, N.Y.; pioneer in social reform; founder, *Lily* (1849-55), a paper designed for reform; wore proposed new women's costume, full-cut trousers under a short skirt, soon called a "bloomer" (died 1894).

1819 Julia Ward Howe, author, was born in New York City; wife of Samuel G. Howe (11/10/1801); wrote lyrics for "Battle Hymn of the Republic" (died 1910).

1832 William R. Ware, architect and educator, was born in Cambridge; founder, head, Columbia U. Architectural School (1881-1903); considered the founder of American architectural education (died 1915).

1835 Charles Francis Adams, historian and railroad reformer, was born in Boston, the grandson of John Quincy Adams; exposed corruption of railroads, served with Massachusetts railroad commission; president, Union Pacific Railroad (1884-1900) (died 1915).

1836 Jay Gould, financier, was born in Roxbury, N.Y.; had vast railroad holdings, controlled Western Union, New York City elevated railroads (died 1892).

1837 Wild Bill (James B.) Hickok, frontiersman, was born in Troy Grove, Ill.; legendary sharpshooter, fighter; shot during a poker game in Deadwood, Dakota Territory (1876).

1849 Adolph Lewisohn, philanthropist, was born in Hamburg; donor of Lewisohn Stadium to City College of New York; benefactor of many other universities (died 1938).

1861 Newport News, Va. was occupied by Union troops.

1875 Fire destroyed the French Catholic church in South Holyoke, Mass.; 120 persons died.

1878 Isadora Duncan, dancer, was born in San Francisco; a founder of modern expressive dancing (died 1927).

1880 Joseph C. Grew, pioneer career diplomat, was born in Boston; supervised setting up foreign service in State Department (1924-27); ambassador to Turkey (1927-32), to Japan (1932-41) (died 1965).

1885 Richard K. Turner, World War II admiral, was born in Portland, Ore.; a leading expert in amphibious warfare (died 1961).

1888 Frederick C. Sherman, World War II admiral, was born in Port Huron, Mich. (died 1957).

1894 Dashiell Hammett, author, was born in St. Mary's County, Md.; set style of hard-boiled private eye (*The Maltese Falcon, The Thin Man*) (died 1961).

1896 A tornado struck St. Louis, killing 306 people.

1907 Rachel L. Carson, biologist and author, was born in Springdale, Pa.; her books aroused environmental concerns (*Silent Spring, The Sea Around Us, The Edge of the Sea*) (died 1964).

1908 Harold J. Rome, composer, was born in Hartford, Conn.; wrote several musicals (*Pins and Needles, Fanny*).

1911 Hubert H. Humphrey, Vice President (1965-69), was born in Wallace, S.D.; represented Minnesota in the Senate (1949-64, 1971-78), 1968 Democratic presidential candidate (died 1978).

1912 Sam Snead, golfer, was born in Hot Springs, Va.; began winning career in the 1940s.

1912 John Cheever, author of short stories and novels (*The Wapshot Chronicle, The Wapshot Scandal*), was born in Quincy, Mass. (died 1982).

1915 Herman Wouk, author (*The Caine Mutiny, Winds of War, War and Remembrance*), was born in New York City.

1918 The Germans launched an attack between Soissons and Reims in an effort to draw reserves away from the northern sector; reached the Marne, then repulsed.

1923 Henry A. Kissinger, public official, was born in Furth, Germany; foreign policy advisor to President Nixon (1969-73), Secretary of State (1973-77); shared 1973 Nobel Peace Prize.

1924 The Methodist General Conference lifted the ban on dancing, theater attendance.

1929 Supreme Court upheld the constitutionality of the presidential pocket veto.

1930 John S. Barth, author, was born in Cambridge, Md.; wrote several experimental allegorical novels (*The Sot Weed Factor, Giles Goat Boy*).

1930 William S. Sessions, FBI director (1987-), was born in Fort Smith, Ark.

1933 The Century of Progress Exposition opened in Chicago.

1933 The Securities Act was passed by Congress, requiring registration of all new issues of securities with the Federal Trade Commission, along with a statement of financial condition to be available to prospective purchasers.

1935 Supreme Court held the National Industrial Recovery Act of 1933 to be unconstitutional; also declared the Frazier-Lehmke Farm Bankruptcy Act to be unconstitutional.

1937 The Golden Gate Bridge opened; completed at a cost of $35 million.

1943 The Office of War Mobilization was established with James F. Byrnes as director.

1988 Senate voted 93-5 to approve the Intermediate Range Nuclear Forces Treaty between the United States and the Soviet Union, the first arms control agreement to eliminate an entire class of nuclear weapons.

MAY 28

1672 Richard Nicolls, colonial administrator, died at 48; first British governor of New York (1664-68), taking over from the Dutch.

1754 George Washington, with a small band of men, surprised French troops at Great Meadow (ten miles east of present Uniontown, Pa.); this was the first battle and engagement of the French and Indian War.

1764 Edward Livingston, public official and legislator, was born in Columbia County, N.Y.; after representing New York in the House (1795-1801), moved to New Orleans, later representing Louisiana in the House (1823-29) and Senate (1829-31); Secretary of State (1831-33), minister to France (1833-35) (died 1836).

1780 Nathaniel Chapman, physician, was born in Summer Hill, Va.; founder, Philadelphia Medical Institute (1817), first American postgraduate medical school; first president, American Medical Association (1848) (died 1853).

1786 Louis McLane, public official and diplomat, was born in Smyrna, Del.; minister to England (1829-31, 1845-47); Secretary of Treasury (1831-33), of State (1833-34); president, Baltimore & Ohio Railroad (1837-47) (died 1857).

1807 (Jean) Louis Agassiz, naturalist and geologist, was born in Motier-en-Vully, Switzerland; pioneer in glaciation studies, zoology; stimulated interest in natural history; professor of natural history, Harvard's Lawrence Scientific School (1848-73); founder, Harvard Museum of Comparative Zoology (died 1873).

1818 P(ierre) G.T. Beauregard, Confederate general, was born in New Orleans; superintendent, West Point, at outbreak of Civil War; resigned to join Confederacy; commanded bombardment of Ft. Sumter, was at Bull Run, Shiloh; manager, Louisiana lottery (1870-88) (died 1893).

1818 *Walk-in-the-Water*, the first steamboat to navigate the upper Great Lakes, was launched in Buffalo; built by Noah Brown; with Capt. Job Fish in command, began its first successful voyage Aug 23 between Buffalo and Detroit.

1826 Benjamin G. Brown, legislator, was born in Lexington, Ky.; served Missouri as governor (1870-73) and represented it in the Senate (1863-67); vice presidential candidate, Liberal Republican Party (1872) (died 1885).

1837 Tony (Antonio) Pastor, actor and manager, was born in New York City; operated several theaters, developed legitimate vaudeville (died 1908).

1888 Jim (James F.) Thorpe, considered the greatest athlete of the first half of the 20th century, was born in Prague, Okla.; won both the decathlon and pentathlon at the 1912 Olympics, but he was stripped of his medals for having played professional baseball (medals returned to family in 1982); played football and baseball (died 1953).

1896 Warren Giles, president, National League (1951-70), was born in Tiskilwa, Ill.; named to Baseball Hall of Fame (died 1979).

1918 The first American military success was gained when the First Division under Gen. Robert Bullard captured and held Cantigny.

1925 Federal Judge McCormick in Los Angeles declared the Elks Hill lease of oil reserve lands to private companies void because the contracts were secured by fraud.

1936 Congress chartered the Veterans of Foreign Wars (VFW).

1938 Jerry (Jerome A.) West, basketball player (1961-74) and coach (1976-79) with the Los Angeles Lakers, was born in Cheylan, W.Va.; named to Basketball Hall of Fame.

1958 The Presbyterian Church in the United States of America merged with the United States Presbyterian Church of North America in Pittsburgh to form the United Presbyterian Church in the USA.

1977 A fire in a Southgate, Ky. supper club killed 164 persons.

1985 David P. Jacobsen, American director of the American University Hospital, was kidnapped in Beirut; released Nov 2, 1986.

MAY 29

1647 Freeman from four Rhode Island towns (Providence, Portsmouth, Newport, Warwick) met in Portsmouth, drafted a constitution, which established freedom of conscience, separated church and state, provided rights to towns, and created the Providence Plantations, with John Coggeshall as president.

1721 South Carolina was formally incorporated as a royal colony.

1736 Patrick Henry , colonial leader, was born in Hanover County, Va.; a leader of Virginia's radical faction; a member of Continental Congress (1774-76); instrumental in causing adoption of the Bill of Rights (the first ten amendments to the Constitution); served Virginia as its first governor (1776-79, 1784-86) (died 1799).

1765 Patrick Henry introduced a series of resolutions challenging the Stamp Act in Virginia's House of Burgesses and made his treason speech ("Caesar had his Brutus, Charles the First his Cromwell, and George the Third may profit by their example ... If this be treason, make the most of it"); Burgesses passed only the resolutions objecting to taxation without representation.

1787 Edmund Randolph submitted the "Virginia Plan" to the Constitutional Convention, calling for a bicameral legislature, which would choose an executive, a judiciary, and a council of revision with a veto over legislation.

1790 Rhode Island, which did not participate in the Constitutional Convention, ratified the Constitution by a legislative vote of 34-32, entering the Union as the 13th state.

1794 John Quincy Adams was nominated as minister to the Netherlands; served until 1797.

1824 Cadmus M. Wilcox, Confederate general, was born in Wayne County, N.C.; involved in most major battles, present at Appomattox surrender (died 1890).

1825 David B. Birney, Union general, was born in Huntsville, Ala.; commanded troops at Gettysburg (died 1864).

1826 Ebenezer Butterick, tailor and pattern maker, was born in Sterling, Mass.; invented paper patterns for shirts, suits, dresses (died 1903).

1844 James K. Polk was nominated for president by the Democratic convention, the first "dark horse" candidate; received no votes until the eighth ballot, nominated unanimously on the ninth.

1848 Wisconsin entered the Union as the 30th state.

1859 James H. Rand, inventor and manufacturer, was born in Tonawanda, N.Y.; invented, manufactured visible system of file dividers; merged (1927) with Remington (died 1944).

1865 President Andrew Johnson issued an amnesty proclamation to all (except the leaders of the Confederacy) who took the oath to obey the Constitution.

1878 Winford L. Lewis, chemist, was born in Gridley, Cal.; captain, Army Chemical Warfare Service (1917-18); developed poison gas (lewisite) named for him (died 1943).

1884 Bureau of Animal Industry was created to conduct federal meat inspection.

1890 U. of Florida was founded at Tarpon Springs.

1892 Frederick S. Faust, author, was born in Seattle; wrote under several pseudonyms (including Max Brand), turning out more than 500 full-length "pulps;" also did Dr. Kildare movie scripts (died 1944).

1898 The Spanish fleet was bottled up in the harbor of Santiago de Cuba.

1903 Bob (Leslie T.) Hope, entertainer, was born in Eltham, England; star of screen (various *Road* pictures with Bing Crosby) and television; traveled extensively to entertain American troops overseas.

1911 The Supreme Court dissolved the American Tobacco Co. as an illegal combination in restraint of trade.

1917 John F. Kennedy, 35th president, was born in Brookline, Mass., son of Joseph P. Kennedy (9/6/1888) and brother of Robert (11/20/1925) and Edward M. Kennedy (2/22/1932); represented Massachusetts in the House (1947-53) and Senate (1953-60); assassinated in Dallas 1963.

1932 Veterans demanding their full bonus marched on Washington; Army troops under Gen. Douglas MacArthur broke up the march.

1968 "Truth in Lending" Act was signed by President Lyndon Johnson.

1969 A presidential executive order established the Council of Environmental Quality; legislation enacted, effective Jan 1, 1970.

1978 The cost of first class postage was increased to 15 cents.

1988 Pope John Paul II named 25 new cardinals, including Archbishop James A. Hickey of Washington, D.C. and Archbishop Edmund C. Szoka of Detroit.

MAY 30

1806 Andrew Jackson and Charles Dickinson met in a duel at Harrison's Mills, Ky. over some remarks about Mrs. Jackson; Dickinson was killed, Jackson wounded.

1812 John A. McClernand, Union general, was born near Hardinsburgh, Ky.; saw action at Ft. Donelson, Shiloh, and Vicksburg (died 1900).

1848 Treaty of Guadelupe Hidalgo officially ended war with Mexico when ratifications were exchanged.

1854 Kansas-Nebraska Act was signed by President Pierce, creating two new territories, recognized principle of "squatter sovereignity," led to formation of Republican Party, and made Lincoln a national figure; bill repealed Missouri Compromise.

1862 Confederate troops evacuated Corinth, Miss., retiring to Tupelo, 50 miles south.

1865 John Catron, associate justice, Supreme Court (1837-65), died at about 79.

1867 Arthur V. Davis, president, Alcoa (1910-28), board chairman (1928-57), was born in Sharon, Mass. (died 1962).

1868 The first Memorial (Decoration) Day was observed; Gen. John A. Logan, commander-in-chief, Grand Army of the Republic (GAR), called for decorating soldiers' graves.

1871 Amos Rusie, baseball pitcher (Giants) who won 243 games, was born in Mooresville, Ind.; named to Baseball Hall of Fame (died 1942).

1883 Ludwig Lewisohn, author and critic, was born in Berlin; wrote novels (*Don Juan, The Island Within*), autobiography (*Upstream, Midchannel*); made numerous translations from the German (died 1955).

1886 Dorothy L.H.W. Eustis, guide dog training pioneer, was born in Philadelphia; founder (1929), the Seeing Eye, first dog guide training school (died 1946).

1887 Alexander Archipenko, sculptor, was born in Kiev, Russia; one of the first to adapt cubism to sculpture (died 1964).

1888 James A. Farley, public official, was born in Grassy Point, N.Y., Postmaster General (1933-40), Democratic national chairman (1932-40); broke with Roosevelt over third term; chairman, New York Athletic Commission (1925-33) (died 1976).

1890 Lawrence Langner, theatrical producer, was born in Swansea, Wales; a leader in forming the Theatre Guild (1919) (died 1962).

1899 Irving Thalberg, movie executive, was born in Brooklyn; produced several hit films (*The Big Parade, The Good Earth, Grand Hotel, Mutiny on the Bounty*) (died 1936).

1901 Cornelia Otis Skinner, actress and author, was born in Chicago, daughter of Otis Skinner (6/28/1858); monologist, author (*Tiny Garments, Dithers and Jitters*) (died 1979).

1901 The Hall of Fame for Great Americans on the New York University campus was dedicated.

1903 Countee Cullen, author, was born in New York City; played prominent role in Harlem "renaissance" of 1920s (died 1946).

1908 Aldrich-Vreeland Emergency Currency Law was enacted following a "bankers panic" (1907); law gave currency greater elasticity, created the National Monetary Commission to study the banking system.

1909 The National Conference on the Negro convened, led to forming of the National Association for the Advancement of Colored People (NAACP).

1909 Benny (Benjamin D.) Goodman, clarinetist, was born in Chicago; known as the "king of swing," led own orchestra from 1933 on (died 1986).

1911 The first Indianapolis 500 automobile race was held; won by Ray Harroun.

1912 Julius Axelrod, biochemist, was born in New York City; shared 1970 Nobel Physiology/Medicine Prize for studies of how nerve impulses are transmitted in the body.

1918 The first American troops arrived in Italy.

1922 The Lincoln Memorial in Washington was dedicated.

1937 Steelworkers attempting to organize the Republic Steel plant in South Chicago were fired on by police, resulting in four deaths, 84 injured.

1966 The *Surveyor I* satellite was launched; made first American soft landing on the moon June 2.

MAY 31

1636 Rev. Thomas Hooker and his followers reached and settled Hartford, Conn.

1650 A charter was granted Harvard College.

1684 Timothy Cutler, Anglican clergyman and educator, was born in Charlestown, Mass.; rector, Yale College (1719-22); rector, Christ Church, Boston (1723-65) (died 1765).

1689 A rebellion led by Jacob Leisler, a German trader, began with the capture of Ft. James (on Manhattan Island); went on sporadically for a year until a new governor of New England arrived March 29, 1691; Leisler and seven others were sentenced to death (Apr 1691), two were hanged May 26, the others were later pardoned.

1775 Frontiersmen of Charlotte, N.C. adopted the Mecklenburg Resolves which reputedly declared null and void all royal laws and commissions.

1790 The first copyright law was passed and signed.

1810 Horatio Seymour, public official, was born in Pompey Hill, N.Y.; served New York as governor (1853-55, 1863-65); Democratic presidential candidate (1868) (died 1886).

1819 Walt(er) Whitman, poet, was born in West Hills, Long Island, N.Y.; a major American poet, best known for "Leaves of Grass;" wrote free verse (died 1892).

1822 The first American Catholic cathedral (Cathedral of the Assumption of the Blessed Virgin Mary) was dedicated in Baltimore by Archbishop Marechal.

1837 William H.F. Lee, Confederate cavalry general, was born in Arlington, Va., son of Robert E. Lee (1/19/1807); served in Peninsula Campaign, second Bull Run, Five Forks; represented Virginia in the House (1887-91) (died 1891).

1861 Emily P. Bissell, Christmas Seal founder, was born in Wilmington, Del.; headed first drive to aid tubercular children (1907); designed, printed and sold the seals (died 1948).

1862 The two-day Battle of Fair Oaks (Seven Pines), just outside Richmond, Va., began; Confederates, who withdrew to Richmond later, lost 5700 men, including Gen. Joseph Johnston; Union force under Gen. George McClellan lost 4400.

1866 A secret Irish brotherhood, the Fenians, led by John O'Neill, left Buffalo to raid Canada; captured Ft. Erie, but were driven back across the river two days later.

1872 Charles G. Abbot, astrophysicist, was born in Wilton, N.H.; director, Smithsonian Astrophysical Observatory (1907-44); secretary, Smithsonian Institution (1928-44) (died 1973).

1885 Herbert F. Leary, World War II admiral, was born in Washington; commander, Allied naval forces, Australia-New Zealand (1942), U.S. Pacific Fleet task force (1942) (died 1957).

1889 Johnstown, Pa. was covered by a flood when a dam broke, wiping out seven towns in 15 minutes and killing 2200 persons; destroyed property worth more than $10 million.

1894 Fred Allen, humorist and entertainer, was born in Cambridge; starred on radio (1932-49) (died 1956).

1898 Claude E. Hooper, market analyst, was born in Kingsville, Ohio; pioneer in radio broadcast audience analysis (Hooper ratings) (died 1954).

1898 Norman Vincent Peale, clergyman and author, was born in Bowersville, Ohio; pastor, Marble Collegiate Reformed Church, New York City (1932-84); author (*The Art of Living, The Power of Positive Thinking*).

1903 Floods of the Kansas, Missouri, and Des Moines rivers resulted in the death of 200 persons, property damage of $17 million.

1908 Don Ameche, screen actor, was born in Kenosha, Wis.; starred in several films (*The Three Musketeers, Heaven Can Wait*).

1912 Henry M. Jackson, legislator, was born in Everett, Wash.; known as "Scoop," he represented Washington in the House (1941-53) and Senate (1953-83) (died 1983).

1913 The 17th Amendment, which provided for direct popular election of U.S. Senators, became effective.

1920 Edward Bennett Williams, lawyer, was born in Hartford; one of the most prominent American attorneys (died 1988).

1921 The Sacco-Vanzetti trial began; both were found guilty (July 14) for the holdup slaying of two men in South Braintree, Mass.

1924 Patricia Roberts Harris, public official, was born in Mattoon, Ill.; ambassador to Luxembourg (1965-67), Secretary of Housing & Urban Develpment (1977-79), of Health, Education and Welfare (1979-81) (died 1985).

1926 Philadelphia Sesquicentennial Exposition opened; closed Nov 30.

1930 Clint Eastwood, screen actor, was born in San Francisco; star of police and Western stories (*Dirty Harry, Magnum Force, Coogan's Bluff*).

1931 John R. Schrieffer, physicist, was born in Oak Park, Ill.; shared 1972 Nobel Physics Prize for theory of superconductivity.

1943 Joe Namath, football player, was born in Beaver Falls, Pa.; starred with U. of Alabama and New York Jets (1965-77).

1955 The Supreme Court ordered "all deliberate speed" in integrating public schools.

1961 President Kennedy conferred in Paris with French President DeGaulle.

1988 Nine accords were signed in Moscow by American and Russian officials during the summit meeting; two involved arms, the rest were cultural.

JUNE 1

1637 Jacques Marquette, Jesuit missionary and explorer, was born in Laon, France; explored much of central North America with Joliet (died 1675).

1660 Mary Dyer, English-born Quaker, was hanged in Boston for sedition; she was banished in 1657 but returned twice illegally to visit jailed Quakers.

1745 James Tilton, physician, was born in Kent County, Del.; served as chief of hospitals in Revolution; physician and surgeon general, U.S. Army (1813-15), set up first clear definition of duties of medical and sanitary staff; member, Continental Congress (1783-85) (died 1822).

1774 The Boston Port Act went into effect in retribution for the Tea Party and the citizens' refusal to pay for the destroyed tea; observed as a day of fasting.

1779 Thomas Jefferson became the second governor of Virginia, serving until 1781; succeeded Patrick Henry who had served the legal maximum of three terms.

1781 Augusta, Ga., besieged by the Americans since Apr 16, capitulated.

1789 President Washington signed the first act of Congress, which prescribed the oaths of allegiance by Congress, federal and state officials.

1792 Kentucky ratified the Constitution, entered the Union as the 15th state.

1796 Tennessee ratified the Constitution and became the 16th state in the Union.

1801 Brigham Young, Mormon leader, was born in Whitingham, Vt.; led Mormon Church after Joseph Smith's death (1847-77); led migration to Utah; first governor, Territory of Utah (1849-57) (died 1877).

1812 President Madison sent a war message to Congress, outlining the reasons for going to war with Great Britain; House voted for war (79-49) on June 4, the Senate (19-13) on June 18; the grounds were impressment of American seamen, violation of American neutral rights and territorial waters, the blockade of American ports, and refusal to revoke the Orders in Council.

1813 The *Chesapeake,* commanded by Capt. James Lawrence, defeated and captured by the British frigate, *Shannon*; the dying appeal of Lawrence, "Don't give up the ship" became the American Navy motto.

1814 Philip Kearny, Union general, was born in New York City, nephew of Stephen Kearny (8/30/1794); killed on a scouting expedition Sept 1, 1862.

1825 John H. Morgan, Confederate general, was born in Huntsville, Ala.; famed for cavalry raids; killed in action near Greenville, Tenn. Sept 4, 1864.

1831 John B. Hood, Confederate general, was born in Owingsville, Ky.; lost right leg at Chickamauga; conducted unsuccessful defense of Atlanta against Sherman (died 1879).

1833 John M. Harlan, jurist, was born in Boyle County, Ky.; associate justice, Supreme Court (1877-1911) (died 1911).

1849 Francis E. and Freelan Stanley, twin automakers, were born in Kingfield, Me.; Francis developed process for making photographic dry plates, which he sold to Kodak (1905); helped Freeland develop Stanley Steamer (1902-17); Francis died in 1918, Freelan in 1940.

1849 Territorial government of Minnesota was formed.

1855 Edward H. Angle, dentist, was born in Herrick, Pa.; founder of modern orthodontia, first school of orthodontia (St. Louis 1895) (died 1930).

1862 Robert E. Lee assumed command of the Army of Northern Virginia.

1863 Hugo Münsterberg, psychologist, was born in Danzig, Poland (then Germany); pioneer in applied psychology, built experimental psychology laboratory at Harvard (died 1916).

1863 Gen. Ambrose E. Burnside ordered closure of the *Chicago Times*, an anti-Lincoln newspaper; President Lincoln rescinded order June 4.

1864 Unsuccessful three-day assault on Cold Harbor, Va. began; heavy casualties on both sides, with 7000 in one day (June 3).

1868 Former President Buchanan died in Wheatland, Pa. at 77.

1870 The ninth Census showed a 22.6% increase in population to a total of 38,558,371.

1880 Tenth Census showed an increase of more than 11 million to 50,155,783; the center of population was eight miles south of Cincinnati.

1890 The eleventh Census reported a population of 62,947,714; the center of population had moved west to 20 miles east of Columbus, Ind.

1898 Trans-Mississippi Exposition opened in Omaha; closed Oct 31.

1901 John W. Van Druten, playwright, was born in London; author of several hits (*The Voice of the Turtle; I Remember Mama; Bell, Book and Candle; I Am a Camera*) (died 1957).

1905 Lewis & Clark Exposition opened at Portland, Ore.; closed Oct 14.

1909 Alaska-Yukon-Pacific Exposition opened in Seattle; closed Oct 16.

1918 An executive order was issued exempting conscientious objectors from military service, assigning them to farm work or positions with the Quakers.

1921 Race riots in Tulsa resulted in the death of 25 white persons and 60 blacks.

1921 Nelson S. Riddle, composer and orchestra leader, was born in Hackensack, N.J.; wrote much music for movies and television (died 1985).

1925 Former Vice President Thomas Marshall (1913-21) died in Washington at 71.

1926 Marilyn Monroe, screen actress, was born in Los Angeles; starred in several movies (*Seven Year Itch, Some Like It Hot, Bus Stop, Misfits*) (died 1962).

1937 Hoover (originally Boulder) Dam went into operation, supplying electricity to Los Angeles and Southern California.

1980 The 20th Census showed the population had grown to 226,504,825 and the center of population had moved across the Mississippi River to 1/4 mile west of DeSoto, Mo.

1988 President Reagan and Soviet leader Mikhail S. Gorbachev ended their fourth summit session—the first in Moscow—by putting into force the first treaty to require the destruction of nuclear weapons.

JUNE 2

1732 Martha Dandridge Custis Washington, wife of President Washington, was born in New Kent County, Va. (died 1802).

1773 John Randolph, colonial leader, was born in Prince George County, Va.; represented Virginia in the House (1799-1813, 1815-17, 1819-25, 1827-29) and Senate (1825-27); fought a harmless duel with Henry Clay (Apr 8, 1826); minister to Russia (1830) (died 1833).

1784 New Hampshire adopted a new constitution.

1817 George H. Corliss, inventor, was born in Easton, N.Y.; developed an improved steam engine; founder, Corliss Steam Engine Co.; builder of largest engines (died 1888).

1845 Arthur McArthur, Army officer, was born in Springfield, Mass.; served in Mexican, Civil, and Spanish-American wars; assistant chief of staff (1906-09) (died 1912).

1863 Wilbert Robinson, baseball manager (Dodgers 18 years), was born in Bolton, Mass.; named to Baseball Hall of Fame (died 1934).

1886 President Cleveland was married to Frances Folsom of Buffalo in the White House.

1886 Grover Whalen, New York City's official greeter (1919-35), was born (died 1962).

1890 Hedda Hopper, columnist, was born in Holidaysburg, Pa.; famed movie gossip columnist, screen actress (died 1966).

1891 Thurman W. Arnold, lawyer, was born in Laramie, Wyo.; headed anti-trust division, Justice Department , instituting 230 suits (1938-43) (died 1969).

1903 Johnny Weissmueller, swimmer and screen actor, was born in Windber, Pa.; gold medalist (five) in 1924, 1928 Olympics; made many *Tarzan* pictures (died 1984).

1909 Michael Todd, stage and screen producer, was born in Minneapolis; remembered for movie, *Around the World in 80 Days*; killed in plane crash (1958).

1941 Charles Evans Hughes resigned as chief justice of the Supreme Court after serving 11 years.

1941 A lend-lease agreement was signed with China.

1966 White House Conference on Civil Rights, attended by 2400, ended.

1987 Paul A. Volcker, chairman of the Federal Reserve for eight years, resigned; President Reagan named Alan Greenspan to succeed him.

1989 Traditionalist Episcopalians upset by the consecretation of the first woman bishop in the church's history, formed the Episcopal Synod of America in a meeting in Ft. Worth, Tex.

JUNE 3

1621 The Dutch West India Co. was chartered by the Netherlands State General to create colonies in the New World and along the west coast of Africa.

1726 Philip William Otterbein, religious leader, was born in Dillenburg, Germany; held German Reformed pastorates in Pennsylvania and Maryland; with Martin Boehm and others formed (1789) simple organization and a profession of faith, which became the United Brethren in Christ Church (died 1813).

1781 Thomas Jefferson resigned as governor of Virginia; offered post of peace commissioner but declined the appointment.

1790 A convention in South Carolina completed a new state constitution.

1803 Valentine W.L. Knabe, manufacturer, was born in Kreuzberg, Germany (now Poland); founded piano manufacturing plant in Baltimore (died 1884).

1808 Jefferson Davis, Confederate president (1861-65), was born in what is now Todd County, Ky.; represented Mississippi in the House (1845-46) and Senate (1847-51, 1857-61); Secretary of War (1853-57) (died 1889).

1819 Thomas Ball, sculptor, was born in Charlestown, Mass.; did many portrait busts, life-size Daniel Webster, a group with Lincoln and a kneeling slave (*Emancipation*) (died 1911).

1844 Garret A. Hobart, Vice President (1897-99), was born in Long Branch, N.J.; served in state legislature, Republican leader (died 1899).

1864 Congress passed the National Bank Act, which created the national banking system that existed until the Federal Reserve System came into being in 1913.

1869 Aristides Agramonte, physician and bacteriologist, was born in Camaguey, Cuba; on Walter Reed Commission, which discovered that yellow fever was transmitted by mosquitoes; organized, headed, Louisiana State U. Medical School tropical diseases department (died 1931).

1873 Otto Loewi, pharmacologist, was born in Frankfurt, Germany; shared 1936 Nobel Physiology/Medicine Prize for discoveries on chemical transmission of nerve impulses; forced to turn over his prize to Germany (1938) as price for emigration (died 1961).

1874 Ransom E. Olds, automaker, was born in Geneva, Ohio; founder, Olds Motor Vehicle Co. (1899); founder, Reo Motor Co., president (1904-24), chairman (1924-36) (died 1950).

1879 Raymond Pearl, statistician, was born in Farmington, N.H.; a founder of biometry (use of statistics in biology, medicine) (died 1940).

1880 Alexander Graham Bell transmitted first wireless telephone message on his newly-invented photophone.

1899 Georg von Békésy, physiologist, was born in Budapest, Hungary; awarded 1961 Nobel Physiology/Medicine Prize for findings concerning the stimulation of the cochlea of the ear (died 1972).

1900 Abel Green, writer and editor with *Variety* (1921-73), was born in New York City (died 1973).

1904 Charles R. Drew, surgeon, was born in Washington; developed blood banks, directed blood plasma program in United States, Great Britain in World War II (died 1950).

1904 Jan Peerce, leading tenor at the Metropolitan Opera, was born in New York City; first American to sing with Bolshoi Opera (died 1984).

1906 Josephine Baker, internationally famous singer and dancer, was born in St. Louis (died 1975).

1916 National Defense Act was passed, expanding regular army to 175,000 (to 225,000 in five years); also authorized National Guard of 450,000.

1918 American Second Division helped block German advance at Chateau-Thierry.

1926 Allen Ginsberg, writer, was born in Newark, N.J.; playwright, poet (*Howl, Kaddish*); introduced "flower power" in demonstration clashes with police (1965).

1936 Larry McMurtry, author, was born in Wichita Falls, Tex.; wrote many popular books (*All My Friends, Last Picture Show*).

1940 Sale of surplus war material to Great Britain was authorized; President Franklin Roosevelt released surplus arms, ammunition, and planes.

1942 Three-day Battle of Midway resulted in the first Japanese defeat, with the loss of four aircraft carriers; Americans lost one.

1942 Japanese bombed Dutch Harbor in the Aleutians, occupied islands of Attu, Agattu, and Kiska.

1961 President Kennedy met with Russian Premier Khruschev in Paris.

1965 Edward H. White became the first American to "walk" in space during a nearly 98-hour 62-orbit flight which ended June 7.

1974 Supreme Court ruled 5-3 that women must receive equal pay for equal work.

JUNE 4

1752 John E. Howard, colonial leader, was born in Baltimore County, Md.; served in Continental Army; member, Continental Congress (1784-88); represented Maryland in the Senate (1796-1803) and served as its governor (1789-91) (died 1827).

1754 George Washington and his small force built Ft. Necessity, east of present Uniontown, Pa.; surrendered to a superior force of French troops July 3.

1805 Peace was concluded between Tripoli and the United States after nearly four years of fighting; tribute payments to other Barbary states continued until 1816.

1845 The first American grand opera, *Leonora* by William H. Fry, was presented at the Chestnut St. Theater in Philadelphia.

1864 Union troops under Gen. Grant sought unsuccessfully to dislodge Lee's Confederate force at Cold Harbor, Va.

1878 Frank N.D. Buchman, evangelist, was born in Pennsburg, Pa.; director of Christian work, Penn State U. (1909-15); founded "A First Century Christian Fellowship" at Penn State and the Moral Rearmament movement (the Oxford Group) in Great Britain (died 1961).

1878 Alla Nazimova, actress, was born in Yalta, Russia; starred in Ibsen roles (died 1945).

1884 Fontaine T. Fox Jr., cartoonist, was born in Louisville, Ky.; created *Toonerville Trolley*, which he drew from 1906 to 1955 (died 1964).

1887 William A. Wheeler, former Vice President (1877-81), died at Malone, N.Y. at 68.

1896 The first Ford automobile was assembled in a brick workshed in Detroit.

1898 Jerauld Wright, naval officer, was born in Amherst, Mass.; led various amphibious operations; first Allied supreme commander of NATO forces.

1910 Robert B. Anderson, public official, was born in Burleson, Tex.; Navy Secretary (1953-54), Secretary of the Treasury (1957-61) (died 1989).

1911 Rosalind Russell, screen actress, was born in Waterbury, Conn.; starred in many films (*Craig's Wife, Gypsy, My Sister Eileen, Auntie Mame*) (died 1976).

1918 Former Vice President Charles W. Fairbanks (1905-09) died in Indianapolis at 66.

1919 Robert Merrill, operatic baritone, was born in New York City; sang with Metropolitan Opera (1945-75).

1944 Rome was occupied by the American Fifth Army and the British Eighth Army.

1985 The Supreme Court struck down an Alabama law permitting one minute of prayer or meditation in the public schools.

JUNE 5

1542 Luis Moscosco, appointed by Hernando De Soto to succeed him, led the expedition across Arkansas and Texas; believed to have gone west as far as the Trinity River.

1762 Bushrod Washington, jurist, was born in Westmoreland County, Va., nephew of George Washington; associate justice, Supreme Court (1798-1829); Mt. Vernon bequeathed to him and he lived there after 1802 (died 1829).

1773 Boston Committee of Correspondence signed a "Solemn League and Covenant," to be effective Oct 1, for the suspension of commerce with Great Britain.

1775 Lyman Spalding, physician, was born in Cornish, N.H.; investigated yellow fever, vaccination, and hydrophobia; founded the U.S. Pharmacoepia (1820) (died 1821).

1823 George T. Angell, reformer, was born in Southbridge, Mass.; active in working on crime prevention, protection of animals (died 1909).

1825 Jabez L.M. Curry, Confederate leader, was born in Lincoln County, Ga.; member, Confederate Congress and Army; minister to Spain (1885-88, 1902); president, Howard College, Alabama, worked to promote southern education (died 1903).

1831 Marcus J. Wright, Confederate general, was born in Purdy, Tenn.; compiled 70-volume record of Civil War (died 1922).

1840 Edward Cary, journalist, was born in Albany, N.Y.; editor, *New York Times* (1871-1917) (died 1917).

1845 Gen. Stephen Kearny began march from Ft. Leavenworth to occupy New Mexico, California.

1851 *Uncle Tom's Cabin* by Harriet Beecher Stowe began appearing in serial form in the *Washington National Era*; ran until Apr 1, 1852.

1854 Canadian Reciprocity Treaty was signed; designed to end disputes over fishing rights in American and Canadian waters.

1874 Jack (John D.) Chesbro, baseball pitcher who won 197 games (Pirates, Yankees), was born in North Adams, Mass.; named to Baseball Hall of Fame (died 1931).

1887 Ruth F. Benedict, anthropologist, was born in New York City; major contibutor to cultural anthropology, demonstrating the role of culture in individual personality formation; author (*Patterns of Culture*) (died 1948).

1917 More than nine million men registered for military service in local draft boards.

1919 Congress by joint resolution approved the woman's suffrage amendment (19th), sent it to the states for ratification; earlier the House voted 304-89 in favor, the Senate 56-25.

1920 The Women's Bureau was created in the Department of Labor.

1933 A joint congressional resolution voided the gold clause in government obligations and private contracts; abandoning the gold standard had been announced Apr 20 by President Franklin Roosevelt.

1934 Bill (William D.) Moyers, journalist, was born in Hugo, Okla.; press secretary to President Lyndon Johnson (1965-67); publisher, *Newsday* (1967-70); television reporter, commentator (1970-).

1942 United States declared war on Bulgaria, Hungary, and Rumania.

1947 Secretary of State George C. Marshall offered a plan at the Harvard commencement to extend American aid to European countries; Congress authorized about $12 billion over the next four years.

1950 Congress enacted President Truman's Point Four program.

1968 Sen. Robert F. Kennedy was shot fatally in a Los Angeles hotel by Sirhan Sirhan; died the next morning; Sirhan was found guilty of first degree murder Apr 17, 1969; sentenced to death, later changed to life imprisonment.

JUNE 6

1622 Claude Jean Allouez, Jesuit missinary, was born in St. Didier, France; served Great Lakes area, explored with Marquette; said to have baptized 10,000 Indians and preached to 100,000 (died 1689).

1755 Nathan Hale, Revolution martyr, was born in Coventry, Conn.; captured behind British lines (Sept 21, 1776), executed as a spy; his final words were: "I only regret that I have but one life to lose for my country."

1756 John Trumbull, artist, was born in Lebanon, Conn., son of Jonathan Trumbull (10/12/1710); painter of historical scenes, including *The Declaration of Independence*, murals for Capitol Rotunda, later removed because of dampness of the walls (died 1843).

1764 The Massachusetts Assembly asked Great Britain to repeal the Sugar Act, seeking the cooperation of the other colonies in its request.

1804 Louis A. Godey, publisher, was born in New York City; published *Godey's Lady's Book*, the first women's periodical in the United States (died 1878).

1809 Timothy S. Arthur, author and editor, was born near Newburgh, N.Y.; editor, *Arthur's Home Magazine*; best remembered for *Ten Nights in a Barroom* (died 1885).

1842 Steele MacKaye, playwright, was born in Buffalo; wrote several successful plays (*Hazel Kirke*), established first American dramatic school at the Lyceum Theater, New York City (died 1894).

1846 John Davey, tree care specialist, was born in Somersetshire, England; specialized in care of ornamental trees (died 1923).

1849 Ft. Worth, Tex. was established when Maj. Ripley A. Arnold and an American cavalry troop set up an outpost.

1858 Samuel Untermyer, lawyer, was born in Lynchburg, Va.; instrumental in getting antitrust, Federal Reserve, and Federal Trade Commission legislation passed (died 1940).

1862 Commodore C.H. Davis' Union vessels destroyed a Confederate fleet and took over Memphis.

1874 Sanford L. Cluett, industrialist, was born in Troy, N.Y.; with Cluett, Peabody, shirt and collar makers; invented Sanforizing process, named for him (died 1968).

1902 Jimmie Lunceford, musician, was born in Fulton, Miss.; saxophonist and orchestra leader (1929-47) (died 1947).

1904 Oregon adopted direct primary for party nominations.

1904 National Tuberculosis Association organized in Atlantic City.

1907 Bill (William M.) Dickey, baseball player (Yankees 1929-42), was born in Bastrop, La.; named to Baseball Hall of Fame.

1912 Mt. Katmai in Alaska erupted, resulting in the formation of the Valley of the Ten Thousand Smokes.

1918 American Marines launched attack on German positions in Belleau Wood, near Chateau Thierry; took positions three weeks later.

1933 National Employment System Act went into effect creating the U.S. Employment Service.

1934 Securities and Exchange Commission established with power to regulate trading in securities.

1941 Louis Chevrolet, automobile designer and racer, died at 63; with General Motors, designed the first Chevrolet (1911); main interest was racing cars.

1944 Allied troops landed on the Cherbourg Peninsula; about 175,000 men landed along a 60-mile front in Normandy, with between 4500 ships and 9000 aircraft involved; Allied casualties were about 10,000.

1946 President Truman nominated former Treasury Secretary Frederick M. Vinson as chief justice of the Supreme Court; confirmed June 20.

1949 President Truman established the office of U.S. High Commissioner for Germany, naming John J. McCloy to the post.

1983 James E. Casey, founder of a delivery system, died at 95; founded United Parcel Service (UPS) in 1907.

1989 House Speaker James C. Wright resigned his post and Democrats named Majority Leader Thomas S. Foley of Washington to the post.

JUNE 7

1494 Spain and Portugal signed the Treaty of Tordesillas establishing a line of demarcation in the New World, 370 leagues west of Cape Verde.

1629 A charter of 31 articles of freedom and exemptions by the Dutch West India Co. established privileges and the patroon system of land ownership in the New Netherlands and New Amsterdam.

1652 The General Court of Massachusetts set up a mint in Boston with the first issue the "pine tree shilling;" John Hull was the first mintmaster.

1712 Pennsylvania passed a law forbidding the importation of Africans.

1740 Alexander Spotswood, Virginia leader, died at about 64; lieutenant governor (1710-22), ran colony because governor was not present; developed Williamsburg as capitol, built the Governor's Palace and Wren Building of College of William & Mary.

1745 Lindlay Murray, grammarian, was born in Dauphin County, Pa.; called the father of English grammar; author of *English Grammar* (1795), which sold almost two million copies (died 1826).

1776 Richard Henry Lee of Virginia made a motion to the Continental Congress that "these united colonies are, and of right ought to be, free and independent states; that they are absolved from all allegiance to the British crown, and that all political connection between them and the State of Great Britain is, and ought to be, totally dissolved;" also called for foreign alliances and creation of a confederation of the colonies.

1776 American troops under Gen. John Sullivan were defeated at Three Rivers, between Quebec and Montreal, by British under Gen. Guy Carleton.

1824 Alfred Pleasanton, Union general, was born in Washington; served at Antietam, Fredericksburg, Chancellorsville, and commanded Union cavalry at Gettysburg (died 1897).

1843 Susan E. Blow, educator, was born in St. Louis, Mo.; started first American public kindergarten (St. Louis, 1873) (died 1916).

1845 John F. Goucher, Methodist clergyman and educator, was born in Waynesburg, Pa.; benefactor of Baltimore Women's College (renamed Goucher 1919), president (1890-1908) (died 1922).

1854 First American YMCA began in Buffalo, N.Y.

1884 Harry (Edward Henry) Greb, middleweight (1923-26) and light heavyweight (1922-23) boxing champion, was born in Pittsburgh (died 1926).

1894 Alexander P. DeSeversky, aeronautical engineer, was born in Tiflis, Russia; president, Seversky Aircraft Corp. (1931-39); invented various aviation devices, including a bomb sight (died 1974).

1896 Robert S. Mulliken, chemist and physicist, was born in Newburyport, Mass.; awarded 1966 Nobel Chemistry Prize for research on bond holding atoms together in a molecule.

1896 Vivien Kellems, businesswoman, was born in Des Moines, Ia.; outspoken opponent of alleged unfair taxation (died 1975).

1897 George Szell, musician, was born in Budapest, Hungary; concert pianist and conductor (Berlin State Opera, Metropolitan Opera, Cleveland Symphony) (died 1970).

1909 Peter W. Rodino Jr., legislator, was born in Newark, N.J.; represented New Jersey in the House (1949-89); chairman, House Judiciary Committee, which conducted impeachment proceedings on President Nixon.

1909 Jessica Tandy, actress, was born in London, England; starred in various plays (*A Streetcar Named Desire, The Fourposter, The Gin Game, A Delicate Balance*).

1917 Gwendolyn Brooks, poet (*A Street in Bronzeville, Annie Allen*), was born in Topeka, Kan.; first black woman to receive a Pulitzer Prize.

1917 Twenty delegates, representing Lions Clubs from around the country, met in Chicago to form the Lions International.

1920 The Supreme Court upheld the constitutionality of both the Volstead Act and the 18th Amendment, declared state law authorizing light wines and beer were invalid, and held that Congress had authority to define intoxicating liquors.

1928 Charles Strouse, composer of stage musicals (*Bye Bye Birdie, Golden Boy, Applause, Annie*), was born in New York City.

1979 President Carter approved the development of the MX missile.

JUNE 8

1633 The Dutch bought land from the Indians and erected Ft. Good Hope where Hartford, Conn. now stands.

1748 William Few, colonial leader, was born near Baltimore; represented Georgia in the Continental Congress (1780-82, 1785-88), Constitutional Convention; one of the state's first senators (1789-93) (died 1828).

1765 The Massachusetts House of Representatives, which had approved a resolution by James Otis, sent a circular letter to the other colonies calling for a meeting in October in New York "to consult together on the present circumstances of the colonies...;" the principal topic was to be the Stamp Act, which was scheduled to go into effect Nov 1.

1780 Robert McCormick, inventor, was born in Rockbridge County, Va.; inventor of a gristmill, hydraulic machine (1830); experimented unsuccessfully with threshing, reaping machines (died 1846).

1781 Benjamin Franklin, John Jay, and John Adams were named commissioners to negotiate peace with Great Britain.

1783 Thomas Sully, artist, was born in Horncastle, England; known to have painted more than 2600 works, mostly portraits, some historical scenes (died 1872).

1786 Samuel R. Betts, jurist, was born in Richmond, Mass.; renowned for decisions in admiralty law, served 41 years in U.S. District Court, Southern New York (died 1868).

1806 George Wythe, colonial leader and lawyer, died at 80; served as Virginia judge, taught many lawyers, including Thomas Jefferson; America's first law professor (College of William & Mary); member of Continental Congress (1775-77), a signer of the Declaration of Independence.

1813 David D. Porter, Union naval officer, was born in Chester, Pa.; served in Civil War, commanding mortar fleet at New Orleans and Vicksburg; superintendent, Naval Academy (1865-69) (died 1891).

1838 George M. Sternberg, pioneer bacteriologist, was born in Otsego County, N.Y.; Surgeon General (1893-1902), began Army Medical School, the Nurses and Dental Corps (died 1915).

1845 Former President Jackson died at 78 in the Hermitage near Nashville.

1847 Ida Saxton McKinley, wife of President McKinley, was born in Canton, Ohio (died 1907).

1848 Franklin H. King, agricultural scientist, was born in Whitewater, Wis.; invented the cylindrical tower silo (died 1911).

1861 Tennessee voters approved secession from the Union 104,913 to 47,238.

1862 Battle of Cross Keys occurred near Harrisonburg, Va. when 6500 Confederates under Gen. R.S. Ewell turned back 12,000 Union troops under Gen. John C. Fremont.

1862 Richard M. Bissell, insurance executive, was born in Chicago; organized Aetna and Connecticut General insurance companies; president, Hartford Insurance Co. (1913-41); a founder, Chicago Symphony Orchestra (1891) (died 1941).

1869 Frank Lloyd Wright, architect, was born in Richland Center, Wis.; disciple of organic architecture; designed Tokyo's Imperial Hotel, only building to withstand 1923 earthquake, and Guggenheim Museum, New York City (died 1959).

1872 President Grant signed an act making Post Office an executive department.

1877 Robert F. Wagner, legislator, was born in Hesse-Nassau, Germany; represented New York in Senate (1927-49); introduced Social Security, National Labor Relations Act, Railway Pension Act, 1937 Housing Law (died 1953).

1905 President Theodore Roosevelt urged Japanese and Russians to end their war; invited them to a peace conference in Portsmouth, N.H., which they accepted.

1908 President Theodore Roosevelt created the National Conservation Commission, with Gifford Pinchot as chairman.

1913 (James) Walter Kennedy, commissioner, National Basketball Association (1963-75), was born in Stamford, Conn. (died 1977).

1915 William Jennings Bryan resigned as Secretary of State because of disagreement with presidential policy on *Lusitania* sinking; succeeded by Robert Lansing.

1917 Byron R. (Whizzer) White, jurist, was born in Ft. Collins, Colo.; an All-American football player at Colorado U.; associate justice, Supreme Court (1962-).

1918 Robert Preston, actor, was born in Newton Highlands, Mass.; starred on stage (*Music Man; I Do, I Do*); screen (*Victor / Victoria*) (died 1987).

1936 Kenneth G. Wilson, Cornell U. physicist, was born in Waltham, Mass.; awarded 1982 Nobel Physics Prize for describing how pressure and temperature change structure of matter.

1939 President Franklin Roosevelt greeted King George VI and Queen Mary on their visit to the United States, the first by a British sovereign.

1953 Tornadoes hit southern Michigan, northwestern Ohio, and Massachusetts over a two-day period, killing 229.

1956 President Eisenhower, fully recovered from a heart attack, suffered an attack of ileitis; operated on successfully June 9.

1972 Congress enacted a bill for federal aid to college and university students and a $2 billion allocation to help elementary and secondary schools desegregate.

JUNE 9

1768 Samuel Slater, textile manufacturer, was born in Derbyshire, England; launched American cotton industry, manufactured fine cotton thread (died 1835).

1772 Irate Rhode Islanders attacked and burned the customs schooner *Gaspee* when it ran aground while pursuing a vessel near Providence.

1785 Sylvanus Thayer, Army engineer, was born in Braintree, Mass.; called the father of the Military Academy; superintendent (1817-33) (died 1872).

1786 Alexander McDougall, Revolutionary general, died at 54; a founder of Sons of Liberty in New York; took part in battles at White Plains, Germantown; commanded West Point after Benedict Arnold's departure.

1791 John Howard Payne, actor and playwright, was born in New York City; wrote about 60 plays, best remembered for lyrics of "Home, Sweet Home" from his opera, *Clari* (died 1852).

1851 Charles J. Bonaparte, public official, was born in Baltimore, son of Elizabeth P. Bonaparte (*see* 2/6/1785); served as Secretary of the Navy (1905-06), Attorney General (1906-09), launching many antitrust suits, including the American Tobacco Co.; a founder, president, National Municipal League (1894) (died 1921).

1861 U.S. Sanitary Commission, forerunner of Red Cross, organized by War Secretary.

1863 Battle of Brandy Station (Va.), the greatest cavalry battle of the war, occurred when Gen. Joseph Hooker tried to determine whether Confederate forces were moving northward.

1868 Edward F. McGlachlin, Army officer, was born in Fond du Lac, Wis.; served in Spanish-American War and World War I; commander, 1st Division (1918-19), 7th Division (1919-21) (died 1946).

1893 Cole Porter, composer, was born in Peru, Ind.; a leading composer of musicals (*Fifty Million Frenchmen, Wake Up and Dream, Anything Goes, DuBarry was a Lady, Panama Hattie, Kiss Me Kate, Can Can*) (died 1964).

1893 S(amuel) N. Behrman, playwright, was born in Worcester, Mass.; wrote several hit plays (*Biography, Serena Blandish, No Time for Comedy, Fanny*) (died 1973).

1893 Three floors of the Ford Theater in Washington collapsed during reconstruction work, killing 22 persons, injuring 68.

1895 Robert F. DeGraff, publisher who founded Pocket Books (1939), was born in Plainfield, N.J. (died 1981).

1899 Jim Jeffries knocked out Bob Fitzsimmons in the 11th round in Coney Island for the world heavyweight boxing championship.

1900 Fred Waring, orchestra leader and choral director, was born in Tyrone, Pa.; his chorus, The Pennsylvanians, appeared regularly from 1923 on (died 1984).

1901 George Price, cartoonist, was born in Coylesville, N.J.; helped modernize the magazine cartoon.

1902 Woodrow Wilson was unanimously elected president of Princeton U. by the trustees; served until 1910, when he became the governor of New Jersey.

1902 The first automatic vending restaurant (Horn & Hardart) opened at 818 Chestnut St. in Philadelphia.

1916 Robert S. McNamara, public official, was born in San Francisco; executive with Ford Motor Co. (1946-60); Secretary of Defense (1961-68); president, World Bank (1969-81).

1916 Les Paul, guitarist with Mary Ford, was born in Waukesha, Wis.

1930 Ben Abruzzo, balloonist who crossed both the Atlantic and Pacific oceans, was born in Rockford, Ill. (died 1985).

1941 Federal troops took over North American Aviation Co. in Ingleside, Cal. because strike there was hurting defense production.

1959 First American ballistic missile submarine (*George Washington*) was launched at Groton, Conn.

1972 A flash flood at Rapid City, S.D. caused 237 deaths and $160 million in damage.

1978 Larry Holmes defeated Ken Norton in 15 rounds at Las Vegas to win the heavyweight boxing championship.

1986 Supreme Court ruled 5-3 to invalidate Reagan administration "Baby Doe" ruling requiring hospitals to treat, feed severely handicapped infants on the grounds that refusing treatment was a form of discrimination.

JUNE 10

1586 Starving colonists at Roanoke Island, N.C. were rescued by Sir Francis Drake and returned to England.

1661 Massachusetts Bay Colony issued a declaration of liberties which indicated that English laws were not binding on the colonies.

1735 John Morgan, pioneer physician, was born in Philadelphia; founder, Philadelphia College of Surgeons, U. of Pennsylvania Medical College (1765); chief medical officer during the Revolution (1775-77) (died 1789).

1753 William Eustis, public official and legislator, was born in Cambridge; represented Massachusetts in the House (1801-05, 1820-23) and served it as governor (1823-25); Secretary of War (1809-13), resigning under criticism of the war's conduct; minister to Holland (1814-18) (died 1825).

1775 James Barbour, legislator and public official, was born in Barboursville, Va., brother of Philip P. Barbour (5/25/1783); represented Virginia in the Senate (1815-25) and served it as governor (1812-15); Secretary of War (1825-28); minister to Great Britain (1828-29) (died 1842).

1775 Continental Congress accepted John Adams' proposal that forces besieging Boston be accepted as a Continental Army; four days later it voted to raise six companies of riflemen in Pennsylvania, Maryland and Virginia and named a five-man committee to draft rules of administration of the Army.

1776 Continental Congress named a committee to prepare the Declaration of Independence, consisting of Thomas Jefferson, John Adams, Benjamin Franklin, Roger Sherman, and Robert R. Livingston; brought in draft June 28.

1810 Benjamin S. Ewell, Confederate officer and educator, was born in Washington; after the Civil War, he rebuilt burned buildings of the College of William & Mary in Williamsburg; kept charter in force by ringing bell periodically; finally got government help and school reopened in 1888 (died 1894).

1814 James W. Nye, Nevada pioneer, was born in DeRuyter, N.Y.; first and only Nevada territorial governor (1861-64), one of first Nevada senators (1864-73) (died 1876).

1816 A convention opened in Corydon, Ind., which later adopted a state constitution; slavery was prohibited.

1835 Rebecca Fulton, first woman U.S. senator, was born near Decatur, Ga.; appointed by Georgia governor Oct 3, 1922, served until Nov 22 (died 1930).

1849 David Lubin, fruit grower who organized growers to work on fruit growing problems, was born in Poland; also organized an international institute of agriculture (died 1919).

1850 A convention of nine slave states in Nashville called for extending the Missouri Compromise line west to the Pacific; a second convention in Nov denounced the Compromise, asserted the right of secession.

1861 A small Union force from Ft. Monroe, Va. was defeated by Confederate troops as it tried to capture a battery; this was the first battle of the Civil War.

1862 Mrs. Leslie Carter, actress, sometimes called America's Sarah Bernhardt, was born in Lexington, Ky.; starred in many plays (*Zaza, LaTosca*) (died 1937).

1864 The Confederate Congress authorized the use of men between 17 and 18 and 45 to 50 for military service.

1865 Frederick A. Cook, physician and polar explorer, was born in Callicon Depot, N.Y.; with early Peary polar expeditions, claimed to have reached the North Pole Apr 21, 1908; claim rejected after investigation of his data (died 1940).

1887 Harry F. Byrd, public officials and legislator, was born in Winchester, Va., brother of Richard E. Byrd (10/25/1888); represented Virginia in the Senate (1933-65) and served as its governor (1926-30) (died 1966).

1891 Al Dubin, lyricist, was born in Zurich, Switzerland; wrote many hits ("Tip Toe Through the Tulips," "42nd Street," "Shuffle Off to Buffalo," "Anniversary Waltz," "Lullaby of Broadway") (died 1945).

1897 A new state convention in Delaware went into effect.

1898 Marines made their first landing on Cuba, coming ashore at Guantanamo Bay.

1901 Frederick Loewe, composer, was born in Berlin, Germany; wrote several hit musicals (*Brigadoon, Paint Your Wagon, Camelot, My Fair Lady*), the movie score for *Gigi* (died 1988).

1903 Clyde R. Beatty, wild animal trainer, was born in Chillicothe, Ohio (died 1965).

1906 The Christian Science Cathedral in Boston was dedicated.

1915 Saul Bellow, author, was born in Lachine, Canada; awarded 1976 Nobel Literature Prize; among works were *Adventures of Augie March, Herzog, Henderson, The Rain King*.

1920 Federal Power Commission established; terminated Oct 1, 1977; functions transferred to Department of Energy.

1921 Bureau of Budget created in Treasury Department; became part of Office of Management and Budget (1970).

1922 Judy Garland, singer and screen actress, was born in Grand Rapids, Minn.; numerous films (*Wizard of Oz, A Star is Born, Babes in Arms*) (died 1969).

1933 F. Lee Bailey, criminal lawyer, was born in Waltham, Mass.; represented Dr. Sam Shepard, Capt. Medina in My Lai trial, Boston Strangler, Patty Hearst.

1935 Alcoholics Anonymous founded by William G. Wilson and Dr. Robert Smith in New York City.

1940 President Franklin Roosevelt, speaking at U. of Virginia, called for speedy American defense and help for those opposing force.

1943 Pay-as-you-go income tax law signed; effective July 1; affected all workers.

1967 Joseph E. Ritter, Catholic prelate, died at 76; archbishop of Indianapolis (1944-46), of St. Louis (1946-61), named cardinal 1961).

1971 President Nixon lifted 21-year embargo on trade with Communist China.

1974 President Nixon began first Middle East tour by an incumbent president.

1980 Supreme Court ruled unanimously that a zoning ordinance which limits development in the name of conservation does not necessarily violate the constitutional rights of affected proprty owners.

1983 Presbyterian Church (USA) was formed in Atlanta by merger of the United Presbyterian Church in the U.S.A. and the Presbyterian Church in the U.S., after a split of 122 years over the question of slavery and the Civil War.

JUNE 11

1741 Joseph Warren, physician, was born in Roxbury, Mass., brother of John Warren (7/27/1753); rode with Paul Revere to warn colonists; killed at the Battle of Bunker Hill June 17, 1775.

1796 Nathaniel Gorham, colonial leader, died at 58; member, Massachusetts Board of War (1778-81), Continental Congress (1782, 1783, 1785-87), its president (1786); member of the Constitutional Convention (1787).

1805 All of Detroit leveled by fire, leaving only one building standing.

1823 James L. Kemper, Confederate general, was born in Madison County, Va.; led right wing of Pickett's charge at Gettysburg (died 1895).

1825 Vice President Daniel D. Tompkins died at Staten Island, N.Y. at 50.

1850 The people of Kentucky ratified their state constitution.

1859 The famous Comstock lode of silver was discovered in Six Mile Canyon, Nev.

1879 Ralph Pulitzer, publisher, was born in St. Louis, son of Joseph Pulitzer (4/10/1847); president, Press

Publishing Co., which published the *New York World* (1911-30) (died 1939).

1879 Roger Bresnahan, baseball player, was born in Toledo, Ohio; catcher for 17 years with the Giants, Cardinals and Cubs; named to Baseball Hall of Fame (died 1944).

1880 Jeannette Rankin, legislator, was born near Missoula, Mont.; first woman member of Congress, representing Montana in the House (1917-19, 1941-43); cast vote against war declaration both in 1917 and 1941 (the only dissenting vote) (died 1973).

1886 David B. Steinman, bridge engineer, was born in New York City; built more than 40 major bridges worldwide (George Washington and Triborough, New York City; Thousand Islands over the St. Lawrence) (died 1960).

1913 Vincent T. Lombardi, football coach, was born in Brooklyn; football player (Fordham, New York Giants), coach (Giants, Green Bay Packers (1959-67), Washington Redskins) (died 1970).

1913 Risë Stevens, opera and concert mezzo soprano, was born in New York City; sang at Metropolitan Opera (from 1938) in such roles as Mignon and Carmen.

1918 American planes made their first air raid, dropping bombs on a railroad station at Dommary-Barancourt, near Metz.

1938 Johnny Vander Meer, Cincinnati Reds left hander, pitched a 3-0 no-hit game against the Boston Braves; four days later, he repeated against the Brooklyn Dodgers 5-0; earned the nickname of "Double No-Hitter."

1942 Gen. Dwight D. Eisenhower was named commander of the European Theater of Operations.

1947 Sugar rationing ended.

1956 Joe Montana, football quarterback (San Francisco 49ers (1979-   ), was born in Monongahela, Pa.

1958 Clarence DeMar, marathoner who won the Boston Marathon seven times between 1911 and 1930, died at 70.

1985 Karen Ann Quinlan, 31, died after more than ten years in a state of being irreversibly comatose; parents received court permission years before to disconnect her respirator.

1989 Rev. Jerry Falwell, founder of Moral Majority, announced the official disbanding of the religious right's political lobbying group because it had achieved its goals of keeping the United States from moving farther to the left.

JUNE 12

1775 Gov. Thomas Gage of Massachusetts Bay Colony issued a proclamation offering to pardon all rebels except Samuel Adams and John Hancock if they would lay down their arms and "return to their duties of peaceable subjects."

1776 The Continental Congress named a committee to prepare Articles of Confederation and Perpetual Union; plan submitted July 12.

1776 The Virginia Convention adopted a bill of rights drafted by George Mason, which had wide influence in the United States and later in France.

1792 A convention at Newcastle adopted a state constitution and established the state name of Delaware.

1806 John A. Roebling, engineer, was born in Muhlhausen, Germany; developed machinery and process for manufacturing wire rope, which he used to build suspension bridges; most famous was the Brooklyn Bridge, for which he made preliminary plans, began construction (died 1869).

1820 Constitution of Missouri was adopted by convention in St. Louis; ratified by the people Jan 6, 1821; provided for legislation to prevent free blacks and mulattoes from settling in the state.

1833 James B. Weaver, legislator, was born in Dayton, Ohio; represented Iowa in the House (1879-81, 1885-89); presidential candidate, Greenback-Labor Party (1880), People's Party (1892), winning 22 electoral votes and more than one million popular votes (died 1912).

1837 Samuel W. Abbott, physician and statistician, was born in Woburn, Mass.; a pioneer in public health movement and use of demographic studies (died 1904).

1838 President Van Buren signed an act establishing the Territory of Iowa.

1859 Thomas J. Walsh, legislator, was born in Two Rivers, Wis.; represented Montana in the Senate (1912-33), chairman of the Teapot Dome investigation; nominated for Attorney General (1933), but died before confirmation.

1864 Frank M. Chapman, ornithologist, was born in Englewood, N.J.; founder, editor, *Bird-Lore*; chairman, Ornithology Department, American Museum of Natural History (1920-42) (died 1945).

1871 Victor D. Brenner, sculptor, was born in Shavli, Russia; designed the Lincoln penny, the first portrait coin (died 1924).

1874 Charles L. McNary, legislator, was born near Salem, Ore.; represented Oregon in the Senate (1917-44); minority leader (1933-44); Republican vice presidential candidate (1940) (died 1944).

1877 Thomas C. Hart, World War II admiral, was born in Davison, Mich.; commander, Asiatic Fleet (1939-42), combined Allied fleet (1942); superintendent, Naval Academy (1931-34); represented Connecticut in the Senate (1945-47) (died 1963).

1893 John R. Hodge, World War II general, was born in Golconda, Ill. (died 1963).

1899 Fritz A. Lipmann, biochemist, was born in Königsberg, Germany (now Russia); shared 1953 Nobel Physiology/Medicine Prize for studies of living cells; discovered coenzyme A, a basic catalyst in animal metabolism (died 1986).

1905 Arthur S. Flemming, educator and public official, was born in Kingston, N.Y.; director, Office of Defense Mobilization (1952-57), Secretary of Health, Education & Welfare (1958-61); president, U. of Oregon (1961-68); member, Commission on Civil Rights (1974-81).

1906 Meat packing companies (Armour, Swift, Cudahy, Nelson Morris) were found guilty of violating Elkins Act, fined $15,000 each for accepting rebates.

1915 David Rockefeller, banker, was born in New York City, son of John D. Rockefeller Jr. (1/29/1874); top executive, Chase Manhattan Bank (1955-).

1922 Ed Wynn staged the first radio broadcast of a Broadway production (*The Perfect Fool*); the first broadcast with a studio audience.

1924 George H.W. Bush, Vice President (1981-89) and elected President in 1988, was born in Milton, Mass.; represented Texas in the Senate (1967-71), UN ambassador (1971-72), China liaison officer (1974-75), CIA director (1976-77).

1937 Pan-American Exposition opened in Dallas; closed Oct 31.

1939 The National Baseball Hall of Fame was dedicated at Cooperstown, N.Y.

1941 President Franklin Roosevelt nominated Associate Justice Harlan F. Stone for Chief Justice of the Supreme Court; confirmed June 27.

1942 President Franklin Roosevelt made a radio appeal for the scrap rubber campaign; more than 300,000 tons were collected between June 15 and 30.

1944 Big Bend (Tex.) National Park was established.

1963 Medgar Evers, field secretary for the NAACP, was shot to death from ambush in front of his home in Jackson, Miss.

1968 President Lyndon Johnson addressed the UN General Assembly in New York City shortly after it approved (95-4) the Nuclear Nonproliferation Treaty.

1971 Tricia (Patricia) Nixon, daughter of President and Mrs. Nixon, was married in the White House Rose Garden to Edward R.F. Cox.

1981 Major league baseball players went on strike over the free agent policy; strike ended Aug 9.

1987 The PTL (Praise the Lord) television ministry filed for reorganization under the federal bankruptcy code, blaming the "chaotic mismanagement" of founder Jim Bakker for piling up $70 million in debts.

JUNE 13

1784 Henry Middleton, colonial leader, died at 67, son of Arthur Middleton (9/7/1737); member of Continental Congress (1774-76), its president (Oct 1774-May 1775).

1786 Winfield Scott, Army general, was born near Petersburg, Va.; leading military man between Revolution and Civil War; general-in-chief of Army (1841-61); commanded American troops in Mexican War; 1852 Whig presidential candidate (died 1866).

1792 William A. Burt, surveyor and inventor, was born in Worcester, Mass.; invented a typographer, forerunner of the typewriter; solar compass, equatorial sextant (died 1858).

1793 Commerce with France was suspended as relations worsened.

1854 Bradley A. Fiske, inventor, was born in Lyons, N.Y.; among his inventions were an electric range finder, electric ammunition hoist, torpedo plane (died 1942).

1858 An explosion aboard the steamship *Pennsylvania* in the Mississippi River near Memphis killed 160 persons.

1866 The 14th Amendment was enacted, forbidding any state from depriving any person of life, liberty, or property without due process of law.

1868 Wallace C.W. Sabine, physicist, was born in Richwood, Ohio; founder of architectural acoustics (died 1919).

1872 Daniel W. Adams, Confederate general, died at 52; saw action at Chickamauga.

1879 Robert E. Wood, merchant, was born in Kansas City, Mo.; with Montgomery Ward (1919-24), Sears (1924-54), president, board chairman (1928-54); founder, All State Insurance Co. (died 1969).

1880 Vincent Rose, bandleader of 1900-40s and composer, was born in Palmermo, Sicily; known for several hits ("Avalon," "Whispering," "Blueberry Hill") (died 1944).

1888 President Cleveland signed an act establishing the Department of Labor to be headed by a commissioner, effective June 30.

1894 Mark Van Doren, poet and critic, was born in Hope, Ill., brother of Carl Van Doren (9/10/1885); literary editor, *The Nation* (1924-28), film critic (1935-38); prolific poet (died 1972).

1903 Red (Harold) Grange, football player, was born in Folksville, Pa.; the "Galloping Ghost," starred with Illinois U. (1923-25), Chicago Bears (1925-35).

1911 Luis Walter Alvarez, physicist, was born in San Francisco; co-developer of ground-controlled radar, making possible all-weather plane landings; awarded 1968 Nobel Physics Prize for study and discovery of "resonance" particles (died 1988).

1913 Ralph Edwards, television performer and producer, was born in Merino, Colo.

1915 Don Budge, tennis player, was born in Oakland, Cal.; one of few to win "grand slam" (American, Australian, British, French singles) in one year (1938).

1917 First American division embarked for France; arrived June 25.

1924 Torsten N. Wiesel, medical researcher, was born in Upsala, Sweden; shared 1981 Nobel Physiology/ Medicine Prize for research on brain's function in vision.

1933 Home Owners Loan Corporation (HOLC) was established to refinance nonfarm mortgages; loans were made on about one million mortgages by June 1936.

1935 Jim Braddock defeated Max Baer in 15 rounds in New York City to become world's heavyweight boxing champion.

1942 Office of War Information (OWI) was created by consolidating the Office of Facts & Figures, Office of Governmental Reports, and Coordinator of Information; abolished Aug 31, 1945.

1943 Office of Strategic Services (OSS) was established with William J. Donovan as director; designed to engage in intelligence operations; terminated Oct 1, 1945; forerunner of Central Intelligence Agency (CIA).

1946 "Major" Edward Bowes, radio personality, died at 82; originated amateur hour.

1967 President Lyndon Johnson nominated Thurgood Marshall to the Supreme Court, the first black to be named to the court; confirmed Aug 30.

1968 Chief Justice Earl Warren submitted his resignation from the Supreme Court.

1971 *New York Times* began publishing what came to be known as the Pentagon Papers, classified information on American-Indochina involvement; other newspapers followed suit; Supreme Court upheld the right to publish by 6-3 vote on June 30.

1989 President Bush vetoed legislation to raise the hourly minimum wage to $4.55; had urged Congress to limit raise to $4.25 an hour.

JUNE 14

1639 Fundamental Articles of New Haven, Conn. were adopted; they had been prepared by Theophilus Eaton and Rev. John Davenport.

1665 Thomas Willett became the first mayor of New York City.

1716 Peter Harrison, the first American architect, was born in York, England; designed King's Chapel in Boston, Christ Church in Cambridge (died 1775).

1775 Continental Congress passed a resolution authorizing formation of a Continental Army of 20,000—ten companies of expert riflemen; marks the birthday of the present Army.

1777 Continental Congress resolved that the American flag be "thirteen stripes alternate red and white, that the Union be 13 stars white in a blue field...".

1801 Heber C. Kimball, Mormon leader, was born in Sheldon, Vt.; ordained as one of the 12 original Mormon apostles (1836); one of Brigham Young's chief advisors; lieutenant governor, State of Deseret (Utah) (1849-68) (died 1868).

1805 Robert Anderson, Union officer, was born near Louisville, Ky.; in command of Ft. Sumter at the time of Confederate attack, starting Civil War (died 1871).

1810 Ward Hunt, jurist, was born in Utica, N.Y.; associate justice, Supreme Court (1873-82) (died 1886).

1811 Harriet Beecher Stowe, author, was born in Litchfield, Conn., daughter of Lyman Beecher (10/12/ 1775) and sister of Henry Ward Beecher (6/24/ 1813); wrote the famed *Uncle Tom's Cabin* (died 1896).

1820 John Bartlett, author and publisher, was born in Plymouth, Mass.; compiled well-known *Familiar Quotations* (died 1905).

1846 Americans raised the flag of the California Republic at Sonoma, which they had captured from the Mexicans June 11.

1855 Robert M. LaFollette, legislator, was born in Primrose, Wis.; represented Wisconsin in the House (1885-91) and Senate (1906-25), where he launched the Teapot Dome investigation; governor of Wisconsin (1900-06); Progressive Party presidential candidate (1924) (died 1925).

1862 John U. Nef, pioneer chemist, was born in Herisan, Switzerland; investigated bivalent carbons, fulminates, mechanism of organic reactions (died 1915).

1862 John J. Glennon, Catholic prelate, was born in County Meath, Ireland; archbishop of St. Louis (1903-46) (died 1946).

1868 Karl Landsteiner., pathologist, was born in Vienna; with Rockefeller Institute, discovered four types of human blood (1900), helping make transfusions safe; awarded 1930 Nobel Physiology/ Medicine Prize for that work (died 1943).

1884 John McCormack, operatic tenor, was born in Athlone, Ireland; with Metropolitan, Chicago operas; noted for roles in *Faust, La Boheme, Madam Butterfly* (died 1945).

1889 Samoan Treaty signed in Berlin, placing islands under joint control of United States, Great Britain, and Germany, with a fueling station for the American fleet.

1895 Louis Finkelstein, educator, was born in Cincinnati; president/chancellor, Talmud Jewish Theological Seminary (1940-72).

1898 An American expeditionary force of 17,000 sailed from Tampa for Cuba.

1900 Territory of Hawaii was established.

1906 Margaret Bourke-White, photographer, was born in New York City; with *Life* magazine (1936-69) (died 1971).

1909 Burl Ives, folk singer and screen actor, was born in Hull, Ill.; recording artist, made several movies (*Cat on a Hot Tin Roof, The Big Country*).

1914 Former Vice President Adlai E. Stevenson (1893-97) died in Chicago at 78.

1934 Max Baer knocked out Primo Carnera in 11 rounds in Long Island City for the world's heavyweight boxing championship.

1941 President Franklin Roosevelt ordered the freezing of all German and Italian assets in the United States.

1943 The Supreme Court ruled that school children could not be compelled to salute the flag if the ceremony conflicted with their religion; the case was brought by Jehovah's Witnesses.

1947 President Truman formally signed peace treaties with Italy, Hungary, Rumania, and Bulgaria.

1958 Eric Heiden, ice skater who won five Olympic gold medals in 1980, was born in LaCrosse, Wis.

1972 Environmental Protection Agency announced a near-total ban on the use of DDT, effective Dec 31, 1972.

1985 Terrorists seized a TWA plane between Athens and Rome with 104 Americans aboard; one American was killed before all the passengers were released by June 30.

1988 Howard H. Baker Jr., former Tennessee senator, resigned as White House chief of staff after 16 months service; he was succeeded by Kenneth M. Duberstein.

1989 Rep. Richard A. Gephardt of Missouri was elected House majority leader and Rep. William H. Gray III of Pennsylvania majority whip.

1989 Queen Elizabeth II of Great Britain made former President Reagan an honorary knight.

JUNE 15

1649 The first trial for witchcraft was held in Charlestown, Mass.; Margaret Jones was found guilty and executed.

1752 Benjamin Franklin, flying a kite in a thunderstorm, proved that lightning is electricity.

1767 Rachel Donelson Jackson, wife of President Jackson, was born in Halifax County, Va. (died 1828).

1773 Asher Benjamin, pioneer architect, was born in Greenfield, Mass.; wrote number of guides which influenced American architecture (died 1845).

1775 George Washington was unanimously appointed commander-in-chief of the colonial armies by the Continental Congress; Washington accepted the next day, saying he would serve without salary, keeping track of his expenses.

1776 The New Hampshire legislature adopted a declaration of independence, instructing its delegates to the Continental Congress to vote for it.

1787 William Paterson submitted the "New Jersey Plan" to the Constitutional Convention, calling for retention of the Confederation but giving Congress the power to tax, to regulate foreign and interstate commerce, and to name a plural executive and Supreme Court.

1800 Nation's capital was moved from Philadelphia to the District of Columbia.

1804 The 12th Amendment was ratified; required separate electoral vote for president and vice president.

1805 William B. Ogden, railroad executive, was born in Walton, N.Y.; first mayor of Chicago (1837); president, Chicago & Northwestern Railroad (1859-68); first president, Union Pacific Railroad (1862-63) (died 1877).

1826 Charles B. Smith, humorist, was born in Lawrenceville, Ga.; wrote under the pseudonym of Bill Arp (died 1903).

1833 Edward M. McCook, Union general, was born in Steubenville, Ohio; cavalry commander in Civil War; minister to Hawaii (1866-69); governor of Colorado Territory (1869-75) (died 1909).

1834 N.J. Wyeth began construction of first Idaho settlement, Ft. Hall on Snake River.

1836 Arkansas entered the Union as the 25th state.

1836 George L. Shoup, merchant and public official, was born in Kittaning, Pa.; governor of Idaho Territory (1889), first governor of Idaho state (Oct-Dec 1890) and its first senator (1890-1901) (died 1904).

1845 President Polk ordered Gen. Zachary Taylor to the Rio Grande to protect Texas in case Mexico declared war.

1846 The Oregon Treaty was signed by President Polk after it was ratified by the Senate, fixing the boundary between the United States and British North America along the 49th parallel, ending 50 years of boundary dispute.

1849 Former President Polk died in Nashville at 53.

1850 Willard Richards published the first newspaper in Utah, the *Deseret News*, in Salt Lake City.

1861 Union troops occupied Harpers Ferry, W.Va. after Confederate troops retreated to Winchester, Va.

1861 Ernestine Schumann-Heink, contralto, was born in Lieben, Austria (now Czechoslovakia); regarded as one of the greatest opera singers (died 1936).

1863 A Confederate force defeated Union troops at Winchester, Va.

1863 Confederate cavalry raided Chambersburg, Pa.

1864 The Arlington National Cemetery was established.

1864 Gen. U.S. Grant led an unsuccessful four-day assault on Petersburg, Va., losing more than 7500 men; began a siege which lasted nine months.

1869 Massachusetts appointed a Board of Railroad Commissioners, the first state railroad law.

1879 Samuel C. Lind, chemist and inventor, was born in McMinnville, Tenn.; invented electroscope for radium measurement; originator of ionization theory of chemical effects of radium rays (died 1965).

1881 William McFee, author, was born in London, England; novelist (*Casuals of the Sea, The Harbourmaster, Derelicts*) (died 1966).

1887 Malvina Hoffman, sculptor, was born in New York City; executed bronzes of 101 racial types for the Field Museum (died 1966).

1894 Robert Russell Bennett, composer and arranger, was born in Kansas City, Mo.; orchestrated all Rogers and Hammerstein musicals (died 1981).

1902 Erik H. Erickson, psychoanalyst, was born in Frankfurt, Germany; introduced concept of "identity crisis."

1903 Barney Oldfield became the first man to drive an automobile at 60 miles per hour.

1904 The steamer *General Slocum* burned in New York's East River, 1021 died; passengers were on an excursion from St. Mark's German Lutheran Church.

1910 David Rose, bandleader and composer (*Holiday for Strings*), was born in London, England.

1914 Saul Steinberg, artist, was born in Rimnicu-Sarat, Rumania; cartoonist and illustrator, mostly in *The New Yorker*.

1915 Thomas H. Weller, biologist, was born in Ann Arbor, Mich.; shared 1954 Nobel Physiology/Medicine Prize for work on isolating polio virus.

1916 Herbert A. Simon, economist, was born in Milwaukee; awarded 1978 Nobel Economics Prize for pioneering research in decision-making process in economic organizations.

1916 Marshall Field IV, head of Field Enterprises, was born in New York City; editor, publisher, *Chicago Sun-Times* (1949-65), *Chicago Daily News* (1958-65) (died 1965).

1917 Espionage Act was signed by President Wilson; called for 20 years in prison and up to $10,000 fine for aiding the enemy, obstructing recruiting, or refusal of service.

1923 Erroll Garner, jazz pianist and composer ("Misty"), was born in Pittsburgh (died 1977).

1924 President Coolidge signed a bill making all American-born Indians citizens.

1929 Agricultural Marketing Act was enacted by Congress to aid farm price stability.

1934 The Great Smoky Mountains (N.C.) National Park was established.

1934 The National Guard Act was signed by President Franklin Roosevelt making the Guard part of the Army in wartime or national emergency

1937 Waylon Jennings, country music singer, was born in Littlefield, Tex.

1938 Billy Williams, baseball player (Cubs) was born in Whistler, Ala.; named to Baseball Hall of Fame.

1939 A Mixed Claims Commission found Germany guilty of two explosions in 1916 and 1917 (Black Tom Island and Kingsland, N.J.), but Germany never paid the $55 million damage award.

1944 American troops landed on Mariana Islands; Saipan was taken July 9, Guam on Aug 10, and Tinian Aug 11.

1944 The first superfortress raid on Japan hit Yawata on Kyushu Island.

1946 Congress received from President Truman a proposal to merge the Army and Navy departments into a single Department of Defense.

1982 The Supreme Court ruled 5-4 that illegal aliens must have access to free education.

JUNE 16

1775 George Washington accepted the commission as commanding general of the Continental Army, saying ".... yet I feel great distress from a consciousness that my abilities may not be equal to the extensive and important task...".

1775 The Continental Congress created the office of Engineer of the Continental Army.

1778 British troops under Gen. Henry Clinton began evacuating Philadelphia.

1779 Sir Francis Bernard, colonial governor, died at 67; served as governor of New Jersey (1758-60) and Massachusetts (1760-69), a term described as "among the most turbulent."

1804 Alvin Adams, express business pioneer, was born in Andover, Vt.; founder (1854), Adams Express Co., which absorbed several companies, concentrated on the Northeast (died 1877).

1834 Wesley Merritt, Spanish-American War Army general, was born in New York City; superintendent, West Point (1882-87); commander-in-chief, American forces in the Philippines (1898), helped capture Manila (died 1910).

1858 Abraham Lincoln, nominated by Illinois Republicans in Springfield for the Senate, made the famous speech in which he said: "A house divided against itself cannot stand. I believe this government cannot endure permanently half slave and half free. I do not expect the Union to be dissolved; I do not expect the house to fall; but I do expect it will cease to be divided. It will become all one thing, or all the other."

1868 The *Atlanta Constitution* began publication.

1890 Stan Laurel, comedian, was born in Ulverston, England; half of the first great movie comedy team, Laurel and Hardy (died 1965).

1892 Raymond Rubicam, advertising executive, was born in Brooklyn; co-founder, chief executive officer, Young & Rubicam agency (1923-44) (died 1978).

1902 George C. Simpson, paleontologist, was born in Chicago; with American Museum of Natural History (1928-59); one of world's foremost authorities on evolutionary theory.

1902 Barbara McClintock, geneticist, was born in Hartford; awarded 1981 Nobel Physiology/Medicine Prize for pioneering work in genetic mechanisms.

1903 Helen Traubel, operatic soprano, was born in St. Louis; principal Wagnerian soprano, Metropolitan Opera (1939-53) (died 1972).

1917 Katherine Graham, newspaper executive, was born in New York City; publisher (1968-78), board chairman (1973-   ), *Washington Post.*

1933 Emergency Railroad Transportation Act became effective; provided for the reorganization of the industry under a federal administrator.

1933 Congress enacted the National Industrial Recovery Act, providing for federal control of nation's entire industrial structure through codes; the NRA, directed by Gen. Hugh Johnson, affected 500 industrial fields, 22 million employees; act also created Public Works Administration under Interior Secretary Harold L. Ickes, which eventually spent more than $4 billion on 34,000 public works projects; act held unconstitutional, NRA terminated Jan 1, 1936.

1933 President Franklin Roosevelt signed the Banking Act of 1933 creating the Federal Deposit Insurance Corp., guaranteeing bank deposits up to $5000.

1933 The Farm Credit Act went into effect, reorganizing agricultural credit.

1933 Navy Department was allocated $238 million for 32 new vessels.

1938 Joyce Carol Oates, author, was born in Lockport, N.Y.; wrote several popular novels (*By the North Gate, With Shuddering Fall*).

1944 An American air offensive was begun against the Japanese by B-29s.

1976 The American ambassador to Lebanon, Francis E. Maloy Jr., and an aide were killed by unidentified gunmen.

1978 President Carter and Gen. Omar Herrera signed treaties in Panama City which would turn over the Panama Canal to Panama in the year 2000.

1980 The Supreme Court ruled 5-4 that biological organisms can be patented under federal law.

JUNE 17

1579 Sir Francis Drake, preying on Spanish shipping and settlements along the Pacific coast, anchored in San Francisco Bay; took possession of the area in the name of Queen Elizabeth I.

1673 Louis Joliet, Father Pere Marquette, and five others reached the Mississippi River at Prairie du Chien, Wis.

1745 Louisburg, French fortress on Cape Breton Island, fell to the American and English forces under William Pepperell after a six-week siege.

1746 Joseph Winston, Revolutionary officer and legislator, was born in Louisa County, Va.; served at King's Mountain; represented North Carolina in the House (1793-95, 1803-07); Winston (now Winston-Salem) named for him (died 1815).

1751 Joshua Humphreys, naval architect, was born in Haverford, Pa.; designed, supervised construction of vessels used in War of 1812 (died 1838).

1768 Isaac Parker, jurist and educator, was born in Boston; served on Massachusetts Supreme Court (1806-30), chief justice (1814-30); helped establish Harvard Law School, where he taught (1816-30) (died 1830).

1774 The Massachusetts House of Representatives, meeting in Salem, approved a resolution by Samuel Adams for "a meeting of committees from the several colonies...to consult upon the present state of the colonies...and to deliberate and determine upon wise and proper measures to be by them recommended...and for the recovery and establishment of just rights and liberties, civil and religious, and the restoration of union and haromony between Great Britain and the colonies...".

1775 Battle of Bunker Hill, which was mostly fought on adjoining Breed's Hill, took place, with 1600 Americans and six cannons, led by Col. William Prescott, holding off two charges by British troops; Prescott reportedly commanded "Don't fire till you see the whites of their eyes;" Americans then retreated toward Cambridge on the third charge because of dwindling ammunition; British won position at cost of 1054 casualties; Americans lost about 100 dead, 267 wounded, and 30 prisoners.

1777 Gen. John Burgoyne and 7700 British troops began move south from St. Johns; objective was to meet British troops moving east along the Mohawk River and north along the Hudson River.

1778 A clash occurred between French and British naval units, officially marking the start of hostilities between the two countries.

1778 Continental Congress, in response to a British request for a peace conference, said it would only negotiate for withdrawal of the British and American independence.

1791 Abel P. Upshur, public official, was born in Northampton County, Va.; Secretary of the Navy (1841-43), Secretary of State (1843-44); killed with several other cabinet members and legislators Feb 28, 1844 when a gun exploded on a Navy frigate during an inspection.

1824 Bureau of Indian Affairs was established as a subsidiary of War Department.

1825 Bunker Hill Monument cornerstone was laid by Marquis de Lafayette; ceremony was addressed by Daniel Webster.

1837 Charles Goodyear obtained a patent for the manufacture of rubber tires.

1843 Bunker Hill Monument was dedicated by President Tyler, with Daniel Webster giving the address; monument stands on adjoining Breed's Hill.

1855 Richard A. Canfield, gambler, was born in New Bedford, Mass.; operated foremost gambling house on 44th Street, New York City, called the Monte Carlo of America; forced to close (1902) (died 1914).

1856 The first Republican presidential nominating convention opened in Philadelphia; named John C. Fremont as its candidate.

1860 Charles Frohman, theater manager and producer, was born in Sandusky, Ohio; responsible for evolution of the star system; died in sinking of the *Lusitania* (1915).

1863 The Travelers Insurance Co., first accident insurance company, was chartered in Hartford.

1867 John R. Gregg, inventor, was born in Rockcorry, Ireland; devised the popular shorthand system (died 1948).

1871 James W. Johnson, civil rights leader, was born in Jacksonville, Fla.; a founder, first secretary, National Association for the Advancement of Colored People (NAACP) (1916-30) (died 1938).

1872 The World's Peace Jubilee and International Music Festival opened in Boston; one event included a chorus of 20,000 and an orchestra of 2000, including church bells, cannons, and the Boston Fire Department banging out the "Anvil Chorus" on anvils; Patrick S. Gilmore was the conductor.

1882 Igor Stravinsky, composer, was born in Oranienbaum, Russia; leader of futurist group in modern music (ballets—*Le Sacre du Printemps, Petrouchka*; opera—*LeRossignol*; much other music) (died 1971).

1902 Sammy Fain, composer, was born in Chicago; numerous popular songs ("Love is a Many Splendored Thing," "That Old Feelin'," "Dear Hearts and Gentle People") (died 1989).

1902 Congress passed the Newlands Reclamation Act, which provided for government construction of irrigation works from the sale of public lands in 16 western and southwestern states.

1904 Ralph Bellamy, actor, was born in Chicago; star of stage and screen (*Sunrise at Campobello, Detective Story, State of the Union).*

1907 Charles Eames, furniture designer, was born in St. Louis; co-designer of contour-molded chair (died 1978).

1914 John Hersey, author, was born in Tientsin, China; wrote several popular books (*Into the Valley, A Bell for Adano, Hiroshima, The Wall*).

1917 Dean Martin, screen actor and entertainer, was born in Steubenville, Ohio; numerous films, various television shows.

1919 Kingman Brewster, educator and diplomat, was born in Longmeadow, Mass.; president, Yale U. (1963-71); ambassador to Great Britain (1977-81).

1928 Amelia Earhart became the first woman to fly the Atlantic Ocean when she was a passenger on a 20-hour flight from Newfoundland to Burry Port, Wales.

1942 *Yank*, the Army magazine, was first issued.

1946 Barry Manilow, composer, was born in New York City; wrote many popular songs ("Mandy," "I Write the Songs," "Can't Smile Without You").

1963 The Supreme Court ruled 8-1 that laws requiring recitation of the Lord's Prayer or Bible verses in public schools were unconstitutional.

1971 The United States and Japan signed a treaty returning Okinawa Island to the Japanese; was captured by Americans during World War II.

1972 Five men were arrested by Washington police for breaking into the Democratic national headquarters in the Watergate Building, starting the entire Watergate scandal.

1986 President Reagan announced that Warren Burger, Supreme Court chief justice for 17 years, was retiring and Associate Justice William Rehnquist was being nominated to succeed him; Senate confirmed the Rehnquist nomination Sept 17.

1987 Bernhard H. Goetz was acquitted of attempted murder by a New York City jury in the subway shootings of four men he said were going to rob him; he was convicted of a felony for carrying an unlicensed revolver.

JUNE 18

1778 The British, feeling threatened by a French blockade, evacuated Philadelphia; 3000 Tories accompanied the troops to New York City.

1798 The Naturalization Act was amended to require 14 years residence (had been five) and notice of intention five years before application; repealed Apr 14, 1802, and original 1795 act was re-enacted.

1798 Rep. Robert G. Harper of South Carolina gave the historical toast of "millions for defense but not one cent for tribute" at a dinner for John Marshall, envoy to France, in Philadelphia.

1802 Henry Durant, Congregational clergyman and educator, was born in Acton, Mass.; instrumental in getting charter for College of California (1855), which became U. of California (1868), its first president (1870-72) (died 1875).

1812 Congress completed its declaration of war against Great Britain.

1850 Cyrus H.K. Curtis, publisher, was born in Portland, Me.; established the *Ladies Home Journal* (1876), headed Curtis Publishing Co., which issued the *Journal, The Country Gentleman, Saturday Evening Post*; also owned the *Philadelphia Public Ledger, New York Post* (died 1933).

1854 Edward W. Scripps, publisher, was born near Rushville, Ill.; co-founder, *Cleveland Penny Press* (1878), added others papers (St. Louis, Cincinnati) to form first newspaper chain; co-founder, Scripps-McRae League (now Scripps Howard) and United Press (died 1926).

1857 Henry C. Folger, industrialist and philanthropist, was born in New York City; president, Standard Oil Co. of New York (1911-23), board chairman (1923-28); donated major Shakespeare collection, building to Washington, D.C. (died 1930).

1877 James Montgomery Flagg, illustrator, was born in Pelham Manor, N.Y.; painter, illustrator, best known for Uncle Sam recruiting poster, "I want you" (died 1960).

1886 Alexander Wetmore, ornithologist, was born in North Freedom, Wis.; noted for work on American birds; secretary, Smithsonian Institution (1945-52) (died 1978).

1896 Philip Barry, playwright, was born in Rochester, N.Y.; wrote several hits (*The Animal Kingdom, Holiday, Here Come the Clowns, The Philadelphia Story*) (died 1949).

1906 Kay Kyser, orchestra leader, was born in Rocky Mount, N.C. (died 1985).

1907 Jeannette McDonald, singer and screen actress, was born in Philadelphia; starred with Nelson Eddy (*The Merry Widow, Naughty Marietta*) (died 1965).

1910 The Mann-Elkins Act was passed, placing telephone, telegraph, cable and wireless companies under the Interstate Commerce Commission.

1913 Sylvia Porter, syndicated financial columnist, was born in Patchogue, N.Y.

1918 Jerome Karle, chemist, was born in New York City; awarded 1985 Nobel Chemistry Prize for developing mathematical techniques for the use of x-ray crystallography in body chemistry.

1918 Franco Modigliano, economist at MIT, was born in Rome, Italy; awarded 1985 Nobel Economics Prize for work on effect of household savings on financial markets.

1924 George L. Mikan, basketball player, was born in Joliet, Ill.; first "big" man in professional basketball, considered greatest player of 1900-1950 era.

1926 Allan R. Sandage, astronomer, was born in Iowa City, Ia.; co-discoverer of quasar (quasi-stellar radio source).

1932 Dudley R. Herschbach, chemist, was born in San Jose, Cal.; shared 1986 Nobel Chemistry Prize for helping create first detailed understanding of chemical reactions.

1939 Lou Brock, baseball player, was born in El Dorado, Ark.; base-stealing champion, among select few with more than 3000 hits (Cubs, Cards); named to Baseball Hall of Fame.

1941 Los Angeles and other southern California cities began receiving water from the $200 million Colorado Aqueduct on the Colorado River.

1942 The Manhattan District was organized for production of the atomic bomb, with Gen. Leslie R. Groves in charge.

1953 An Air Force Globemaster crashed near Tokyo, killing 129 persons.

1979 The SALT II agreement, limiting nuclear weapons, was signed in Vienna by President Carter and Soviet leader Leonid Brezhnev; Senate failed to ratify pact.

1983 The space shuttle *Challenger,* with five crew members, was launched at Cape Canaveral, Fla.; made perfect landing in Mojave Desert June 24; crew included first American woman astronaut, 25-year-old Sally K. Ride.

1987 Charles Glass, an American journalist, was kidnapped in Beirut, Lebanon; set free several weeks later.

1989 During the U.S. Open golf tournament in Rochester, N.Y. four golfers shot holes-in-one on the sixth hole in a space of less than two hours; there had never been more than one ace on a single hole and only 21 in all since 1895.

JUNE 19

1619 An English Separatist group living in Holland received a patent in name of John Wyncop, an English clergyman, for a colony within the Virginia Company; later merged with another group.

1754 The intercolonial Albany Congress began at the call of the British Board of Trade to conciliate the Iroquois; meetings ended July 11.

1773 Patsy Custis, 17-year-old stepdaughter of George Washington, died from one of her recurring "fits."

1781 Gen. Nathanael Greene and his troops failed to dislodge British from Fort 96, S.C.

1793 Joseph E. Sheffield, merchant, was born in Southport, Conn.; endowed scientific school named for him at Yale (1854) (died 1882).

1812 President Madison issued a proclamation of declaration of war against Great Britain after Congress voted such a declaration.

1816 William H. Webb, shipbuilder, was born in New York City; endowed Webb Institute of Naval Architecture at Glen Cove, N.Y. (died 1899).

1826 Charles L. Brace, social worker, was born in Litchfield, Conn.; a founder, executive secretary, Children's Aid Society (1853-90) (died 1890).

1846 First recorded baseball game was played in Hoboken, N.J.; with New York Knickerbockers losing to New York Club 23-1.

1856 Elbert Hubbard, author, was born in Bloomington, Ill.; wrote *A Message to Garcia*; founder, Roycroft Shop, East Aurora, N.Y., which revived old handicrafts; publisher, *The Philistine* (1895-1915), *The Era* (1908-15) magazines (died 1915).

1862 Slavery was abolished in the territories of the United States.

1863 William A. Brady, actor and producer, was born in San Francisco; produced more than 250 plays (died 1950).

1864 The *Alabama*, a British-built Confederate cruiser which preyed on Union shipping, was destroyed by the USS *Kearsage*, a Union warship, off the French coast.

1876 Raymond L. Ditmars, naturalist, was born in Newark, N.J.; reptile curator, Bronx Zoo (1899-1942); made important contributions to study of snakes (died 1942).

1878 The niece of President Hayes, Emily Platt, was married in the White House to Col. Russell Hastings.

1881 Jimmy (James J.) Walker, public official, was born in New York City; internationally famous and popular mayor of New York City (1926-32) (died 1946).

1885 Bartholdi's Statute of Liberty, presented by the French people, arrived in New York City in crates.

1886 William Howard Taft was married to Helen Herron in Cincinnati.

1896 Wallis Warfield, socialite, was born in Blue Ridge Summit, Pa.; became wife of the Duke of Windsor, who had renounced the crown to marry her (died 1986).

1902 Guy Lombardo, orchestra leader, was born in London, Canada; leader of the Royal Canadian orchestra for 50 years (died 1977).

1903 Lou (Henry Louis) Gehrig, baseball player, was born in New York City; first baseman, New York Yankees (1923-39), played record 2130 consecutive games; named to Baseball Hall of Fame (died 1941).

1910 Paul J. Flory, physical chemist, was born in Sterling, Ill.; awarded 1974 Nobel Chemistry Prize for developing analytic methods to study properties, structure of long-chain molecules.

1910 Abe Fortas, jurist, was born in Memphis, Tenn.; associate justice, Supreme Court (1965-69); nominated for chief justice but accusations of bribery forced him to request withdrawal of nomination (died 1982).

1920 The AFL, meeting in Montreal, endorsed the League of Nations.

1934 The National Archives were created; placed under the General Services Administration June 30, 1949.

1934 The Federal Trade Commission was established, replacing the Federal Radio Commission; control of telegraph, cable, and radio shifted from Interstate Commerce Commission to FCC.

1934 The National Labor Relations Board was created by joint resolution, replacing the National Labor Board.

1944 The Battle of the Philippine Sea resulted in the Japanese loss of three aircraft carriers and about 200 planes.

1953 Julius and Ethel Rosenberg, convicted as spies, were electrocuted in Sing Sing Prison after President Eisenhower turned down a final clemency plea.

1972 Tropical Storm Agnes moved from Florida to New York over a nine-day period with heavy rains and floods; hitting Pennsylvania the hardest; 177 persons were killed and $3 billion in damage resulted from the storm.

1977 Catholic Bishop John Neumann of Philadelphia, known for his development of parochial schools, was canonized—the first American male to achieve sainthood.

1987 The Supreme Court by a 7-2 vote struck down as "establishment of religion" a 1981 Louisiana law that required any public school teaching the theory of evolution to give equal time to the view of divine creation as a science.

JUNE 20

1658 Thomas Brattle, merchant, was born in Boston, Mass.; Harvard U. treasurer (1693-1713); chief organizer, Brattle St. Church; at odds with Mather, condemned the Salem witchcraft trials (died 1713).

1675 King Philip of the Wampanoag Indians attacked Swansea, touching off King Philip War, which ended Aug 12, 1676.

1732 James Edward Oglethorpe received a charter to settle between the Savannah and Altamaha rivers, originally part of South Carolina; charter granted liberty of conscience to all except Catholics.

1756 William R. Davie, attorney, was born in Egremont, England; instrumental in codification of colonial laws; cession of Tennessee to the Union, founding of North Carolina U.; governor of North Carolina (1798-99) (died 1820).

1774 More than 8000 persons attended a meeting in Philadelphia to oppose closing of Boston's port; marked start of Philadelphia revolutionary movement.

1778 Pierre Laclède, fur trader, died at about 54; selected site and founded St. Louis (1764), heading it until civil government was created.

1782 Continental Congress established the first great seal of the United States, featuring an American eagle, which remained through other changes.

1807 President Thomas Jefferson refused to appear as a witness at Aaron Burr's treason trial.

1823 Jesse L. Reno, Union general, was born in Wheeling, W.Va.; saw action at Manassas and Chantilly, killed at South Mountain Sept 14, 1862.

1824 John T. Morgan, Confederate general and legislator, was born in Athens, Tenn.; represented Alabama in the Senate (1877-1907) (died 1907).

1832 Benjamin H. Bristow, Treasury Secretary (1874-76), was born in Elkton, Ky.; was the first Solicitor General (1870-72) (died 1896).

1837 David J. Brewer, jurist, was born in what is now Izmir, Turkey to American missionary parents; associate justice, Supreme Court (1889-1910) (died 1910).

1841 Samuel F.B. Morse received patent for the telegraph.

1844 Francis E. Warren, legislator, was born in Hinsdale, Mass.; governor of Wyoming territory (1885-86, 1889-90) and state (1890), represented state in Senate (1890-93, 1895-1929); known as the father of reclamation (died 1929).

1858 Charles F. Murphy, political leader, was born in New York City; head of Tammany Hall (1902-24) (died 1924).

1858 Charles W. Chesnutt, author, was born in Cleveland, Ohio; considered first American black novelist (*The Conjure Woman, The Colonel's Dream*) (died 1932).

1860 Alexander Winton, automaker, was born in Grangemouth, Scotland; builder of first big cars (1897) (died 1932).

1863 West Virginia entered the Union as the 35th state.

1868 Helen M. Shepard, philanthropist, was born in New York City; endowed American Hall of Fame at New York U. (died 1938).

1874 A territorial government for the District of Columbia was abolished by Congress, replaced by a commission form of government.

1878 Arthur E. Morgan, educator and public official, was born in Cincinnati, Ohio; president, Antioch College (1920-36); chairman, Tennessee Valley Authority (1933-38), dismissed by President Franklin Roosevelt after he refused to substantiate charges against other commission members (died 1975).

1883 Royal E. Ingersoll, World War II admiral, was born in Washington; commander-in-chief, Atlantic Fleet (1942-43); commander, Western Sea Frontier (1944) (died 1976).

1898 Guam was occupied by American forces, led by Capt. Henry Glass of the USS *Charleston*.

1903 Glenna C. Vare, golfer, was born in New Haven, Conn.; dominated women's golf in 1920s.

1905 Lillian Hellman, author and playwright, was born in New Orleans, La.; plays (*The Children's Hour,*

The Little Foxes, The Watch on the Rhine); screen scenarios (*The Dark Angel, Dead End*) (died 1984).

1909 Errol Flynn, screen actor, was born in Hobart, Tasmania; numerous starring roles (*Robin Hood, Virginia City, Elizabeth and Essex*) (died 1959).

1921 Rep. Alice Robertson of Okla. presided over the House of Representatives for 30 minutes, the first woman to do so.

1924 Chet (Chester B.) Atkins, country music guitarist, was born in Luttrell, Tenn.; one of the greats in country music; a record company executive.

1924 Audie Murphy, soldier and screen actor, was born near Kingston, Tenn.; most decorated World War II soldier, including Congressional Medal of Honor; killed in a plane crash (1971).

1926 Eucharistic Congress of the Catholic Church opened near Chicago; attracted about one million pilgrims.

1927 Geneva Naval Conference, involving the United States. Great Britain and Japan, opened; ended in a stalemate.

1941 Congress was notified of the sinking by a German submarine of the first American merchant ship, the *Robin Moor*.

1943 Race riots began in Detroit; 34 died before riot was put down by federal troops.

1945 Anne Murray, popular singer, was born in Springhill, Nova Scotia.

1947 Everglades (Fla.) National Park was established.

1950 Lionel Richie, composer and singer, was born in Tuskegee, Ala.

1972 Howard D. Johnson, businessman, died at about 76; developed restaurant, motor lodge chain, which was largest food distributor after the Army and Navy.

1984 Supreme Court ruled unanimously that the Federal Aviation Administration (and by implication all federal agencies) may not be sued for damages for mistakes that contribute to disasters.

JUNE 21

1639 Increase Mather, Congregational clergyman and educator, was born in Dorchester, Mass., son of Richard Mather (4/22/1669); pastor, Boston Second Church (1664-1723); president, Harvard (1685-1701); his *Cases of Conscience Concerning Evil Spirits* (1693) is credited with ending the executions for witchcraft (died 1723).

1774 Daniel D. Tompkins, Vice President (1817-25), was born in what is now Scarsdale, N.Y.; served New York as governor (1807-17) (died 1825).

1779 Spain formally declared war on Great Britain, but refused to recognize American independence or pledge to fight until such independence was attained, as the French had done.

1788 New Hampshire, by a legislative vote of 57-46, ratified the Constitution and entered the Union as the ninth state; its ratification made the Constitution operative.

1810 Zachary Taylor and Margaret M. Smith were married near Louisville, Ky.

1831 George W. Nichols, music and art promoter, was born in Tremont, Me.; largely responsible for Cincinnati's development as a musical center; founder, first president, Cincinnati College of Music (1879-85) (died 1885).

1832 Joseph H. Rainey, legislator, was born in Georgetown, S.C.; he was the first black to serve in the House, representing South Carolina (1870-79) (died 1887).

1834 A patent was granted Cyrus H. McCormack for a grain reaper, the first successful automatic cutting machine.

1850 Daniel C. Beard, Boy Scout founder, was born in Cincinnati, Ohio; established American branch of the movement; national scout commissioner (1910-41) (died 1941).

1860 Congress authorized the post of Signal Officer, marking the start of the Army Signal Corps; Maj. Albert J. Myer was the first Signal Officer.

1880 Arnold L. Gesell, psychologist and pediatrician, was born in Alma, Wis.; pioneer in child development studies; founder, director, Yale Clinic of Child Development (1911) (died 1961).

1882 Rockwell Kent, artist and author, was born in Tarrytown Heights, N.Y.; known for landscapes, wood engraving, and lithography; author (*Wilderness, Voyaging N by E*) (died 1971).

1887 Norman L. Bowen, petrologist, was born in Kingston, Canada; pioneer in experimental petrology; made valuable contributions to optical glass industry (died 1956).

1888 Ralph H. Upson, aeronautical engineer, was born in New York City; designed first successful metal-clad airship; made major contributions to wing design (died 1968).

1890 Lewis H. Brereton, pioneer Air Forces officer, was born in Pittsburgh, Pa.; held various World War II commands (9th Air Force, Allied airborne forces in Western Europe) (died 1967).

1892 Reinhold Niebuhr, theologian, was born in Wright City, Mo.; with Union Theological Seminary (1930-60); one of the most influential 20th century theologians, proposed a Christian realism that recognized the persistence of evil, and the egotism and pride of nations and other social groups (died 1971).

1894 The Democratic silver convention was held in Omaha, Neb.; 1000 delegates voted for a free coinage plank in the platform.

1898 Donald Culross Peattie, botanist and author, was born in Chicago, Ill.; known for his popular nature stories (died 1964).

1911 The Supreme Court ordered the dissolution of DuPont de Nemours Co. as a combination in restraint of trade.

1912 Mary T. McCarthy, author, was born in Seattle, Wash.; her books include*The Group, Vietnam, Memories of a Catholic Girlhood* (died 1989).

1918 American troops completed the capture of Belleau Woods, helping to stop the German advance toward Paris.

1923 Judy Holliday, screen actress, was born in New York City; best remembered for her role in *Born Yesterday* (died 1965).

1923 The first presidential radio broadcast was made by President Harding, whose speech dedicating the Francis Scott Key Memorial in Baltimore was broadcast over WEAR (now WFBR).

1927 Carl B. Stokes, public official, was born in Cleveland, Ohio; elected mayor of Cleveland (1967-71), the first black mayor of a major American city.

1932 Jack Sharkey defeated Max Schmelling in 15 rounds in New York City to win the world's heavyweight boxing championship.

1933 The Great Lakes-Gulf waterway opened with the arrival of barges in Chicago from New Orleans.

1934 National Mediation Board was established.

1940 Richard M. Nixon married Thelma C. (Pat) Ryan in Riverside, Cal.

1961 President Kennedy opened a plant in Freeport, Tex. for the conversion of salt water to fresh water.

1973 In five separate cases all decided by 5-4 votes, the Supreme Court set rules for the suppression of pornography.

1982 A federal jury after four days of deliberation found John W. Hinckley Jr. not guilty by reason of insanity in the shooting of President Reagan and three others.

1982 Supreme Court by a 7-2 decision ruled that the 1871 Civil Rights Act permits individuals to sue state and local officials and agencies directly in federal courts.

JUNE 22

1793 The first extensive canal in the United States, the Middlesex Canal, was started to connect the Merrimac River and Woburn; completed 1808.

1807 The American frigate *Chesapeake* was stopped by the British frigate *Leopard* off the Virginia coast, the British claiming four men aboard were British deserters; the American commander, James Barron, refused to permit a search of the vessel, the British fired and killed three, wounded 18, and removed the four men.

1837 Arthur Gilman, educator, was born in Alton, Ill.; instrumental in obtaining instruction for women at Harvard (1879), developed Radcliffe College (1893) (died 1909).

1854 Connecticut passed a prohibition law (with a few minor exceptions); repealed in 1872.

1870 Congress passed an act creating the Department of Justice, with the Attorney General at its head.

1888 Alan Seeger, poet, was born in New York City; best known for "I Have a Rendezvous with Death" (died 1916).

1888 Harold H. Burton, legislator and jurist, was born in Jamaica Plain, Mass.; reform mayor of Cleveland (1935-40); represented Ohio in the Senate (1941-45); associate justice, Supreme Court (1945-58) (died 1964).

1898 Erich Maria Remarque, author, was born in Osnabrück, Germany; best known for *All Quiet on the Western Front* (died 1970).

1903 Carl Hubbell, baseball player, was born in Carthage, Mo.; star left handed pitcher for New York Giants (1928-43), won 253 games; named to Baseball Hall of Fame (died 1988).

1906 Anne Morrow Lindbergh, author, was born in Englewood, N.J., daughter of Dwight W. Morrow (*see* 9/12/1925); the wife of Charles Lindbergh, she wrote several popular books (*North to the Orient; Listen, the Wind*).

1910 Katherine Dunham, dancer and choreographer, was born in Chicago, Ill.; made effective theater of primitive and urban black dances; first to organize black troupe of professional caliber.

1912 The Progressive Party was organized by disgruntled Republicans; at its Aug 5 convention it nominated former President Theodore Roosevelt for president, Hiram Johnson of California for vice president.

1918 An empty troop train crashed into a circus train near Ivanhoe, Ind.; 68 persons were killed.

1921 Joseph Papp, director and producer, was born in Brooklyn; founder, producer, New York Shakespeare Festival, the Public Theater.

1921 Gower Champion, dancer and choreographer, was born in Geneva, Ill.; directed musicals (*Bye, Bye Birdie; Hello Dolly; The Happy Time*) (died 1980).

1922 The Herrin (Ill.) massacre occurred when several hundred striking coal miners forced non-union workers operating the mine to surrender; ordered to run for their lives and more than 20 were killed.

1922 Bill Blass, fashion designer, was born in Ft. Wayne, Ind.; noted for designing clothes for the tailored woman; also does men's wear, accessories.

1937 Joe Louis knocked out Jim Braddock in the eighth round at Chicago to win the world's heavyweight boxing championship; he was the youngest (23) to win crown.

1943 The 8th Air Force made its first large-scale daylight raid on the Ruhr.

1944 The GI Bill of Rights (Servicemen's Readjustment Act) was signed, providing benefits for World War II veterans.

1949 Ezzard Charles, after the retirement of Joe Louis, defeated Joe Walcot in 15 rounds in Chicago to gain the world's heavyweight boxing championship.

1949 Meryl Streep, screen actress, was born in Summit, N.J.; starred in many films (*Kramer vs. Kramer, Out of Africa*).

1970 President Nixon signed an extension of the 1965 Voting Rights Act lowering the voting age to 18.

JUNE 23

1780 The advance of British troops was checked by Americans under Gen. Nathanael Greene at Springfield, N.J.; British crossed to Staten Island, thus ending warfare in New Jersey.

1791 John Jones, surgeon, died at 62; published first surgical textbook (1775) in the colonies; was personal physician to Benjamin Franklin, attended Washington.

1803 Jason Lee, Methodist missionary, was born in Stanstead, Canada; worked with Indians in Oregon, helped organize white settlement near Salem; influential in establishing Oregon provisional government (died 1845).

1845 The Texas Congress in special session voted for annexation by the United States.

1875 Carl Milles, sculptor, was born in Lagga, Sweden; noted for *The Meeting of the Waters* in St. Louis, sculptures in Rockefeller Center (died 1955).

1876 Irvin S. Cobb, journalist and author, was born in Paducah, Ky.; worked on various newspapers, magazines (*Saturday Evening Post, Cosmopolitan*); author of several *Judge Priest* books, screen plays (died 1944).

1894 Alfred C. Kinsey, zoologist, was born in Hoboken, N.J.; founder, Institute for Sex Research, Indiana U. (1942); made massive study of sexual behavior, which shattered many myths (died 1956).

1906 Congress authorized $25,000 a year for presidential travel expenses; increased to $40,000 in 1948.

1913 William P. Rogers, public official, was born in Norfolk, N.Y.; Attorney General (1958-61), Secretary of State (1969-73).

1927 Bob Fosse, producer and choreographer, was born in Chicago, Ill.; produced a number of hit shows (*Pippin, Damn Yankees, Sweet Charity, Dancin', Cabaret* (movie) (died 1987).

1931 Wiley Post and Harold Gatty began a successful round-the-world flight in the *Winnie Mae*; took eight days, 15 hours, 51 minutes.

1936 Richard D. Bach, author, was born in Oak Park, Ill.; best remembered for *Jonathan Livingston Seagull*.

1938 The Civil Aeronautics Act was signed, creating the Civil Aeronautics Authority to supervise all but military aviation.

1940 Wilma Rudolph, athlete, was born in St. Bethlehem, Tenn.; won three gold medals in 1960 Olympic track events.

1947 Congress passed over President Truman's veto the Taft-Hartley Act, which limited the conduct of unions in labor-management disputes, banned the closed shop, called for 60 days' notice before striking, forbade union contributions to political campaigns.

1967 The Senate voted 92-5 to censure Sen. Thomas J. Dodd of Connecticut for using political funds for personal benefit.

JUNE 24

1497 John Cabot, Italian-born English explorer, sighted land, probably in the vicinity of Cape Breton or Newfoundland; went on to sail southeast, possibly reaching Maine.

1564 Huguenot colonists from France, led by René de Laudonniére, arrived at the St. John's River (Fla.) and built Fort Caroline.

1700 Samuel Sewall published in Boston "The Selling of Joseph," a tract condemning slavery.

1729 Edward Taylor, Puritan clergyman and poet, died at about 87; considered the finest poet of colonial America.

1771 E(leuthére) I. duPont, industrialist, was born in Paris, France; established (1802) a gunpowder plant near Wilmington, Del. forming the beginings of the vast DuPont company (died 1834).

1788 Thomas Blanchard, inventor, was born in Sutton, Mass.; invented the lathe, which paved the way for machine tools (died 1864).

1797 John J. Hughes, Catholic prelate, was born in County Tyrone, Ireland; bishop of New York (1842-50), first archbishop of New York (1850-64); founded St. John's College (1841), which became Fordham; began construction of St. Patrick's Cathedral (1858) (died 1864).

1803 Matthew Thornton, Irish-born physician and colonial legislator, died at 89; member of Continental Congress (1776-1778), a signer of the Declaration of Independence.

1811 John A. Campbell, jurist, was born in Washington, Ga.; associate justice, Supreme Court (1853-61), resigned to become Assistant Secretary of War for the Confederacy (1862-65) (died 1889).

1813 Henry Ward Beecher, clergyman, was born in Litchfield, Conn., son of Lyman Beecher (10/12/1775); served Plymouth Congregational Church, Brooklyn (1847-87), influential speaker, opposing slavery and favoring woman's suffrage; charged with adultery (1874), sensational six months trial ended with hung jury, exonerated by two church bodies (died 1887).

1834 The Senate rejected the nomination of Roger B. Taney for Secretary of the Treasury, the first rejection of a cabinet appointee.

1839 Gustavus F. Swift, meat packer, was born near Sandwich, Mass.; founder, head of what became Swift & Co. (1875); helped develop refrigerated car (died 1903).

1842 Ambrose G. Bierce, author, was born in Meigs County, Ohio; wrote *The Devil's Dictionary*; disappeared while with Pancho Villa in Mexico (1914).

1858 George von L. Meyer, public official and diplomat, was born in Boston, Mass.; ambassador to Italy (1900-05), to Russia (1905-07); Postmaster General (1907-09); Navy Secretary (1909-13) (died 1918).

1863 Hiram Brundage published the first newspaper in Wyoming, the *Daily Telegraph*, at Ft. Bridger.

1872 Francis W. Crowninshield, editor, was born in Paris of American parents; served various magazines, including *Vanity Fair* (1914-35) (died 1947).

1883 Victor F. Hess, physicist, was born in Schloss Waldstein, Austria; shared 1936 Nobel Physics Prize for discovery of cosmic radiation (died 1964).

1885 Woodrow Wilson was married to Ellen Louise Axson in Savannah, Ga.

1895 Jack Dempsey, boxing champion, was born in Manassa, Colo.; boxing champion (1919-26) (died 1983).

1898 The first land battle in Cuba occurred at Las Guasimas.

1900 Gene Austin, singer, was born in Gainsville, Tex.; top recording artist of 1920s ("My Blue Heaven") (died 1972).

1908 Former President Cleveland died at Princeton, N.J. at 71.

1915 Norman Cousins, author and editor, was born in Union City, N.J.; editor, *Saturday Review* (1940-78).

1916 John Ciardi, poet and critic, was born in Boston, Mass.; poetry editor, *Saturday Review* (1956-75); author of verse translations of Dante's *Inferno* (died 1986).

1916 William B. Saxbe, Attorney General (1974-75), was born in Mechanicsburg, Ohio; represented Ohio in the Senate (1969-74); ambassador to India (1975-77).

1918 About 27,000 American troops began two-day attack on Belleau Wood; this first major action resulted in complete possession of area.

1941 President Franklin Roosevelt promised aid to Soviet Russia.

1947 Gen. Dwight D. Eisenhower was named president of Columbia U.; took over after retirement from the Army Feb 7, 1947; installed Oct 12.

1948 The Russians halted all land and water traffic between the Western zones of Germany and Berlin, touching off the Berlin Airlift, ordered June 26.

1949 President Truman, in a special message to Congress, urged a program of technical assistance to underdeveloped areas, in what became known as the "Truman Doctrine;" enacted June 5, 1950.

1950 Fifty-eight died as plane over Lake Michigan.

1975 A jet liner crashed near Kennedy Airport, New York City; 113 were killed.

1982 Supreme Court ruled 8-1 that federal and state officials are entitled only to "qualified immunity" from civil damage suits arising from their official acts, not "absolute immunity" enjoyed by the President.

1982 Supreme Court ruled 5-4 that no president may be sued for damages for any official action that he takes while in office.

JUNE 25

1773 Eliphalet Nott, Presbyterian clergyman and educator, was born in Ashford, Conn.; president, Union College (1804-66); invented a base-burning stove using anthracite coal (died 1866).

1788 Virginia's convention, with anti-constitution forces led by Patrick Henry and those in favor by James Madison, ratified the Constitution 89-79, becoming the tenth state to enter the Union.

1831 President Jackson named Martin Van Buren minister to Great Britain; the Senate (Jan 25, 1832) rejected the nomination by Vice President Calhoun's tie-breaking vote.

1837 Charles T. Yerkes, financier and philanthropist, was born in Philadelphia, Penn.; street railway owner, developer in Chicago; bequest to U. of Chicago (1892) made Yerkes Observatory possible (died 1905).

1842 Reapportionment Act passed; called for district election of congressmen.

1862 The "Seven Days Battles" around Richmond began; Confederate troops under Gen. R.E. Lee forced Gen. McClellan's Union forces to retreat to Harrison's Landing; considered one of the fiercest battles of the war; although considered a Union victory, McClellan was unable to capture Richmond.

1868 President Andrew Johnson signed an act that provided an eight-hour work day for laborers and workmen in government employ.

1874 Rose C. O'Neill, author and illustrator, was born in Wilkes-Barre, Pa.; best remembered as originator, designer of Kewpie dolls (died 1944).

1876 Gen. George Custer made his last stand at Little Bighorn River in the Black Hills, when he attacked a large Indian force under Sitting Bull, which annihilated him and his 266 men.

1886 Henry H. (Hap) Arnold, Air Forces commander, was born in Gladwyne, Pa.; awarded trophy for 30-mile flight (1912), commanded Army Alaskan flight (1934); chief, Army Air Corps (1938), Air Forces (1941-45), during which he built the world's largest air force (died 1950).

1886 James F. McIntyre, Catholic prelate, was born in New York City; archbishop of Los Angeles (1948-79), named cardinal 1953 (died 1979).

1887 George Abbott, playwright, was born in Forestville, N.Y.; wrote or co-authored numerous musicals (*Three Men on a Horse, The Boys from Syracuse, On Your Toes, Fiorello*); actor and producer for more than 60 years.

1889 Lucy W. Hayes, wife of President Hayes, died in Fremont, Ohio at 57.

1890 Edwin L. James, editor, was born in Irvington, Va.; with *New York Times* (1915-50), managing editor (1932-50) (died 1951).

1892 A strike began against Carnegie Steel in Homestead, Pa. by the Amalgamated Association of Steel and Iron Workers; mills closed June 30.

1906 Stanford White, prominent architect, was shot to death in New York City by Harry K. Thaw, wealthy playboy, who was jealous of White's earlier friendship with Mrs. Thaw.

1910 The Postal Savings Bank system was established, effective Jan 3, 1911; system closed Mar 28, 1966.

1911 William H. Stein, biochemist, was born in New York City; shared 1972 Nobel Chemistry Prize for pioneering studies of enzymes.

1917 The first American troops arrived in France.

1938 The Fair Labor Standards Act was signed, raising the minimum wage of those in interstate commerce from 25 to 40 cents an hour, limiting hours to 44 per week, plus time and a half for overtime; also prohibited use of children under 16.

1941 President Franklin Roosevelt issued an executive order established the first Fair Employment Practices Committee; this was the forerunner of state fair employment practice laws.

1950 A North Korean force of 100,000 invaded the Republic of Korea at several points.

1957 The United Church of Christ was formed by the union of the Evangelical and Reformed Church and the Congregational Christian Church; officially to be in effect July 4, 1961.

1982 Secretary of State Alexander M. Haig resigned; succeeded by George P. Schultz.

1985 An explosion in a fireworks plant in Hallett, Okla. killed 21 persons.

1986 Supreme Court ruled 6-3 that libel suits brought by public officials and public figures should be dismissed before trial in the absence of "clear and convincing" evidence of malice.

1987 The Supreme Court ruled 5-4 that military personnel cannot sue the government or superior officers for damages, even in cases of gross and deliberate violations of their constitutional rights; it also held that military personnel may be court martialed for crimes unrelated to their service.

JUNE 26

1703 Thomas Clap, Congregational clergyman and educator, was born in Scituate, Mass.; headed Yale for 26 years, first as rector (1740-45), president (1745-66) (died 1767).

1741 John Langdon, colonial legislator, was born in Portsmouth, N.H.; member, Continental Congress (1775-76, 1783), "president" of New Hampshire (1785), governor (1788, 1805-09, 1810-11); represented state in the Senate (1789-1801), serving as first president *pro tempore* (1789) (died 1819).

1742 Arthur Middleton, colonial leader, was born in Charleson, S.C., son of Henry Middleton (*see* 6/13/1784); member of Continental Congress (1776-78, 1781-83), a signer of the Declaration of Independence (died 1787).

1778 The Battle of Monmouth (now Freehold), N.J. began; Americans and British each suffered about 350 casualties; Americans repulsed British, who returned to New York City.

1784 Spain closed the Mississippi to navigation by Americans.

1819 Abner Doubleday, was born in Ballston Spa, N.Y.; an Army officer, he is credited with invention and naming of baseball while attending school in Cooperstown, N.Y. (died 1893).

1833 Harvard U. conferred an honorary LL.D. degree on President Jackson, which was strongly opposed by an alumnus and former president, John Quincy Adams, who considered it a disgrace to confer the honor "upon a barbarian who could not write a sentence of grammar and could hardly spell his name."

1844 President Tyler, widowed two years earlier, married Julia Gardiner, daughter of a New York senator, in New York City; the first President to be married while in office.

1845 John McTammany, inventor, was born in Glasgow, Scotland; invented the mechanical player piano, a voting machine (died 1915).

1858 Federal troops established a post in Cedar Valley on Utah Lake by arrangement with Brigham Young; the Mormon rebellion ended and Gov. Alfred Cumming took office June 30.

1862 Gen. Robert E. Lee struck at Union forces in Mechanicville, Va. during the Seven Days Battles; Confederate withdrew to Richmond July 2, ending the Peninsula Campaign.

1863 Confederate troops under Gen. Jubal Early arrived at Gettysburg, Pa.; took York, Pa. the next day.

1865 Bernard Berenson, art critic and historian, was born in Biturmansk, Lithuania; foremost authority on Renaissance art (died 1959).

1885 Edwin C. Ernst, radiologist, was born in St. Louis, Mo.; known for diagnosis and treatment by x-ray and radium applications (died 1969).

1888 Lee Simonson, set designer, was born in New York City; designed sets for many Broadway hits; a founder, director, Theater Guild (1919-40) (died 1967).

1891 Sidney C. Howard, playwright, was born in Oakland, Cal.; many plays for stage and screen (*The Silver Cord, Salvation, The Late Christopher Bean*) (died 1939).

1892 Pearl S. Buck, author, was born in Hillsboro, W. Va.; author (*The Good Earth, Sons, House of Earth*); awarded 1938 Nobel Literature Prize (died 1973).

1894 Jeanne Eagels, actress, was born in Kansas City, Mo.; numerous starring roles, notably Sadie Thompson in *Rain* (died 1929).

1900 Army commission headed by Dr. Walter Reed was named to investigate yellow fever in Cuba; experiments resulted in discovery that the disease is spread by mosquitoes.

1901 Stuart Symington, legislator and public official, was born in Amherst, Mass.; represented Missouri in the Senate (1953-76); first Secretary of the Air Force (1947-50) (died 1988).

1902 William P. Lear, aircraft maker, was born in Hannibal, Mo.; founder, president, Lear Aviation Co.; engineed navigation aids, lightweight automatic pilot (died 1978).

1911 Edward H. Levi, educator and public official, was born in Chicago, Ill.; Attorney General (1975-77); president, U. of Chicago (1968-75).

1914 Babe (Mildred E.) Didrikson Zaharias, one of greatest women athletes, was born in Port Arthur, Tex.; 1932 Olympic gold medalist; three times U.S. Open golf champion (1948, 1950, 1954) (died 1956).

1929 Jules Feiffer, syndicated political and social cartoonist, was born in New York City, with *Village Voice* (1956-).

1934 The Evangelical & Reformed Church was formed by the union of the Evangelical Synod of North America and the Reformed Church in the United States.

1935 President Franklin Roosevelt established the National Youth Administration, providing work relief and employment programs for those between 16 and 25; also part-time employment for needy students; program ended July 12, 1943.

1936 The Merchant Marine Act went into effect, creating the Maritime Commission; became the Maritime Administration in 1950.

1944 American forces captured Cherbourg, France.

1945 President Truman witnessed the signing of the charter of the United Nations in San Francisco.

1948 The Berlin Airlift began in an effort to get around the Russian blockade.

1952 The Immigration and Naturalization Act was passed, removing the last racial and ethnic barriers to naturalization.

1958 The Mackinac Straits Bridge in Michigan was dedicated.

1959 The St. Lawrence Seaway was dedicated at Montreal by President Eisenhower and Queen Elizabeth II.

1968 The island of Iwo Jima was returned to Japan after nearly 23 years occupation.

1980 The House passed legislation to create the Synthetic Fuels Corporation to speed the development of alternate energy sources; passed by the Senate June 19.

1986 House of Representatives, for the first time in three years, approved a request from President Reagan for military aid to the Contras in Nicaragua, effective Oct 1.

1987 The Supreme Court ruled 5-4 that government regulators have limited power to grant public access to private property; the government's authority was limited to restricting the use of private land without paying the owners.

1987 Supreme Court Justice Lewis F. Powell Jr. resigned after 15 years service on the court.

JUNE 27

1542 Juan Cabrillo (Rodriguez) sailed along the coast of California, discovered San Diego Bay (Sept 28), Catalina Island (Oct 7), Drake's Bay (Nov 16).

1691 The province of Maryland, following a great deal of unrest, became a royal province, with Sir Lionel Copley as the first royal governor; restored to the proprietor, Charles Calvert, the fourth Lord Baltimore, 1715.

1696 Sir William Pepperell, American merchant and soldier, was born in Kittery Point, Me.; chief justice, Massachusetts Superior Court (1730-59); became first colonist to receive a baronetcy for leading a successful attack on Louisburg on Cape Breton Island (died 1759).

1776 Thomas Hickey, an Army guard, was hanged in New York City for plotting to kidnap George Washington and turn him over to the British.

1777 Gen. John Burgoyne, advancing from Canada, reached Crown Point, N.Y.

1787 Thomas Say, naturalist, was born in Philadelphia, Pa.; called the father of descriptive entomology in the United States (died 1834).

1809 John Quincy Adams was named minister to Russia.

1820 Ignaz A. Pilat, landscape gardener, was born in St. Agatha, Austria; laid out Central Park in New York City from plans of Frederick Law Olmsted and Calvert Vaux (died 1870).

1823 Dorman B. Eaton, public official, was born in Hardwick, Vt.; chairman, National Civil Service Commission (1873-75), drafted Civil Service Act (1883); headed, Civil Service Commission (1883-86) (died 1899).

1832 Cholera epidemic began in New York City; took 400 lives before it ended in Oct.

1844 Mob of men with blackened faces stormed the jail in Carthage, Ill. and murdered Mormon Church founder, Joseph Smith, and his brother, Hyrum.

1846 Henry E. Abbey, producer, was born in Akron, Ohio; managed many stars, tours of Sarah Bernhardt and Adelina Patti; first manager, Metropolitan Opera House, New York City (1883-96) (died 1896).

1850 Lafcadio Hearn, journalist and author, was born on Santa Maura Island, Greece; best known for his writings about Japan (died 1904).

1862 Gen. George B. McClellan abandoned the siege of Richmond, began retreat.

1863 Confederate troops under Gen. Robert E. Lee encamped at Carlisle, Pa.

1864 Gen. William T. Sherman and his Union troops were beaten back at Kenesaw Mountain, Ga. by Confederates under Gen. J.E. Johnston; Union losses 3000.

1870 Frank R. Lillie, zoologist, was born in Toronto, Can.; director, Woods Hole (Mass.) Marine Laboratory (1908-26), president (1925-42) (died 1947).

1872 Paul L. Dunbar, author, was born in Dayton, Ohio; son of an escaped slave; known for poetical works (*Majors and Minors, Lyrics of Lowly Life*) (died 1906).

1874 John Golden, playwright, was born in New York City; plays (*Turn to the Right, Lightnin', Susan and God*); composer of "Poor Butterfly" (died 1955).

1880 Helen Keller, author and lecturer, was born in Tuscumbia, Ala.; lost sight and hearing in illness at 19 months; lectured on behalf of the blind (died 1968).

1884 President Arthur signed an act creating the Bureau of Labor in the Department of the Interior.

1893 The Panic of 1893 was touched off when the New York City stock market crashed in the wake of dwindling gold reserves, tariffs, and depletion of surplus.

1899 Juan T. Trippe, airline executive, was born in Seabright, N.J.; founder, first president, Pan American Airways (1927-68) (died 1981).

1901 Merle A. Tuve, geophysicist, was born in Canton, S.D.; developed radiowave exploration of the ionosphere.

1905 Industrial Workers of the World (IWW) was organized in Chicago.

1927 Robert J. Keeshan, television actor, was born in Lynbrook, N.Y.; played Clarabelle on *Howdy Doody Show*, became Captain Kangaroo.

1934 President Franklin Roosevelt signed the Railway Labor Act, which upheld the rights of workers to organize and bargain, created national railroad adjustment board.

1942 FBI Director J.Edgar Hoover announced the arrest of eight Nazi saboteurs who had landed from submarines on the Long Island and Florida coasts.

1950 President Truman announced that, in keeping with the UN resolution calling for an immediate halt to the North Korean invasion which began two days earlier, he had ordered American air and sea forces to give the Korean Republican Army support and cover.

1957 Louisiana and Texas were struck by Hurricane Audrey and a tidal wave, leaving 531 dead or missing.

1959 Vice President Nixon and Queen Elizabeth II of Great Britain dedicated the $650 million St. Lawrence Hydroelectric Power Project at Massena, N.Y.

1980 President Carter signed a bill calling for the draft registration by young men 19 and 20 years old.

1989 A federal appeals court overturned Lyn Nofziger's conviction for illegal lobbying because of ambiguities in the conflict of interest law; had been a presidential aide, then a private lobbyist.

JUNE 28

1742 William Hooper, colonial leader, was born in Boston, Mass.; a member of the Continental Congress (1774-77), a signer of the Declaration of Independence (died 1790).

1776 Troops under William Moultrie beat off a heavy British bombardment on a fort of sand and palmetto logs on Sullivan Island in Charleston Harbor; all British ships were damaged and suffered 200 casualties; fort later named in his honor.

1776 Convention in Maryland authorized its congressional delegation to unite in declaring independence of the colonies.

1778 The Battle of Monmouth (now Freehold), N.J. ended in a standoff; later the British slipped away enroute to New York.

1794 The National Capitol Commission, through a misunderstanding, dismissed French architect,

Stephen Hallett; his design for the Capitol was second, but he had been hired to revise the plans of William Thornton.

1814 American sloop *Wasp* destroyed a British sloop near the English Channel.

1836 Former President Madison died in Montpelier, Va. at 85.

1858 Otis Skinner, actor, was born in Cambridge; one of the greatest character actors (*Kismet, Sancho Panza*), many Shakespearean roles (died 1942).

1862 Adm. David Farragut's fleet sailed past Confederate batteries at Vicksburg during the night.

1863 Gen. George G. Meade was named commander of the Army of the Potomac.

1873 Alexia Carrel, surgeon, was born in Ste. Fay-les-Lyon, France; awarded 1912 Nobel Physiology/Medicine Prize for work on vascular ligature and grafting of blood vessels and organs; developed early "artificial heart" medicine (died 1944).

1876 Oley Speaks, musician, was born in Canal Winchester, Ohio; concert baritone, composer ("Sylvia," "On the Road to Mandalay," "When the Boys Come Home") (died 1948).

1891 Carl Spaatz, World War II Air Forces general, was born in Boyertown, Pa.; chief, strategic bombing force, Germany (1944), Japan (1945); first Air Forces chief of staff (1947) (died 1974).

1894 President Cleveland signed an act creating Labor Day—the first Monday in Sept—as a legal national holiday.

1902 Richard Rodgers, composer, was born in New York City; composed many hit musicals—with Lorenz Hart (*Connecticut Yankee, Present Arms, Jumbo, Babes in Arms, Boys from Syracuse, Pal Joey*), with Oscar Hammerstein II (*Oklahoma, Carousel, South Pacific, The King and I, Flower Drum Song, The Sound of Music*) (died 1979).

1906 Marie Goeppert-Mayer, physicist, was born in Kattowitz, Germany (now Poland); shared 1963 Nobel Physics Prize for research on structure of the atom (died 1972).

1918 Chemical Warfare Service created in the Army.

1919 Treaty of Versailles was signed by Germany and the Allies, formally ending the war with Germany and providing for creation of the League of Nations.

1919 Harry Truman and Bess (Elizabeth V.) Wallace were married in Independence, Mo.

1927 Two Army Air Corps pilots—Lts. Lester J. Maitland and Albert F. Hegenberger—made the first successful flight from San Francisco to Honolulu.

1934 The National Housing Act was signed, creating the Federal Housing Administration (FHA) to insure loans for construction and repair of homes.

1937 Civilian Conservation Corps (CCC) was created; liquidated June 30, 1943.

1939 Regular transatlantic passenger air service began, with 22 persons aboard a Pan-Am clipper which flew from Pt. Washington, N.Y. to Lisbon.

1940 Congress passed the Alien Registration Act, directed toward eliminating subversive activities, which were causing concern on the eve of war; about five million registered between Aug 27 and Dec 26.

1941 The Office of Scientific Research and Development created by executive order.

1962 The Lutheran Church in America was founded by the consolidation of the United Lutheran Church in America, the Augustana Evangelical Lutheran Church, and Finnish Evangelical Lutheran Church.

1978 The Supreme Court by a 5-4 vote refused to allow a firm quota system in affirmative action plans, ordered the admission of Alan P. Bakke to a U. of California medical school; Bakke, a 38-year-old white, contended he had been a victim of reverse discrimination.

1988 Navy Capt. William E. Nordeen, 51-year-old American military attache in Athens, was killed by a car bomb.

1988 The Justice Department filed suit to oust the senior leadership of the International Brotherhood of Teamsters, charging that the union had made a pact with organized crime; called for a court-appointed trustee to oversee new elections for 1.7 million member union.

JUNE 29

1541 Hernando de Soto crossed the Mississippi River into Arkansas near Sunflower Landing.

1565 Pedro Menéndes de Avilés sailed from Cadiz, Spain with royal orders to destroy the French colonies in Florida.

1721 Johann Kalb (Baron de Kalb), German officer, was born in Hüttendorf; fought with the Americans; mortally wounded in action at Camden, S.C. Aug 16, 1780.

1721 John Ettwein, Moravian leader, was born in Freudenstadt, Germany; his official correspondence for the Moravian Church of North America is a treasure of American historical information; presiding officer of the church (1784-1802) (died 1802).

1767 Townshend Acts were passed by the Parliament and King, imposing new taxes on the colonies, effective Nov. 1; import duties were to be levied on glass, lead, paints, paper, and tea; widespread nonimportation followed.

1776 Virginia adopted a state constitution for which Thomas Jefferson wrote the preamble.

1830 John Q.A. Ward, sculptor, was born near Urbana, Ohio; first American-trained sculptor, did many outdoor works, equestrian statues (died 1910).

1832 Luigi Palma de Cesnola, Union general and archaeologist, was born in Rivarolo, Italy; served in the Shenandoah Valley campaign; American consul in Cyprus (1865-76), launched vast archaeological project; his collection was purchased by the Metropolitan Museum of Art, of which he became director (1879-1904) (died 1904).

1852 John B. McMaster, historian, was born in Brooklyn; pioneered in showing the influence of social and economic forces on national evolution; wrote eight-volume history of the American people (died 1932).

1858 George W. Goethals, Army engineer, was born in Brooklyn; in charge of the construction of the Panama Canal; governor, Canal Zone (1914-17) (died 1928).

1861 William J. Mayo, physician, was born in Leseur, Minn.; co-founder, with brother, Charles H. Mayo (7/19/1865), of Mayo Clinic (1915) (died 1939).

1863 James Harvey Robinson, historian and educator, was born in Bloomington, Ind.; pioneered in new methods and content of history teaching (Columbia 1892-1919); organizer, New School of Social Research, New York City (1919-21) (died 1936).

1865 William E. Borah, legislator, was born in Fairfield, Ill.; represented Idaho in the Senate (1907-40); chairman, Foreign Relations Committee (1924-40); opposed League of Nations, World Court (died 1940).

1868 George E. Hale, astronomer, was born in Chicago, Ill.; organized, directed, Yerkes Observatory (1895-1905), Mt. Wilson Observatory (1905-23); invented the spectroheliograph (1889) (died 1938).

1890 Robert Laurent, sculptor, was born in Concarneau, France; influenced the development of modern sculpture in the United States (died 1970).

1901 Nelson Eddy, singer and screen actor, was born in Providence; starred with Jeannette McDonald (*Rose Marie, Maytime, Naughty Marietta*) (died 1967).

1906 The Mesa Verde (Colo.) National Park was established.

1906 President Theodore Roosevelt signed the act creating the Bureau of Immigration and Naturalization.

1906 Congress authorized the preparation of plans for a lock canal in Panama.

1908 Leroy Anderson, composer, was born in Cambridge; among his works were "Syncopated Clock" and "Fiddle Faddle" (died 1975).

1910 Frank H. Loesser, composer, was born in New York City; a number of musicals (*Guys and Dolls, Most Happy Fella*; the hit song, "Praise the Lord and Pass the Ammunition") (died 1969).

1925 An earthquake destroyed downtown Santa Barbara, Cal. with a $20 million loss.

1933 Primo Carnera knocked out Jack Sharkey in the sixth round in New York City to win the world heavyweight boxing championship.

1936 Harmon Killebrew, baseball player (Senators, Twins), was born in Payette, Ida.; named to Baseball Hall of Fame.

1938 Olympic (Wash.) National Park was established.

1949 United States removed the last of its troops from Korea.

1954 Oprah Winfrey, talk show hostess, was born in Kosciusko, Miss.

1956 The Federal Aid Highway Act was signed, inaugurating the $33 billion inter-state highway system.

1966 American planes began bombing Hanoi area of Vietnam.

1972 The Supreme Court ruled that the death penalty is unconstitutional.

1972 The Supreme Court ruled that journalists have no right to withhold confidential information from grand juries.

1982 President Reagan signed an extension of the Voting Rights Act of 1965 with stronger provisions against discrimination.

1982 Arms control talks between the United States and Soviet Russia began in Geneva.

1988 The Supreme Court ruled 7-1 upholding the power of independent counsels to prosecute illegal acts by high-ranking government officials.

1988 The Supreme Court ruled that children testifying in sexual abuse cases must confront their alleged abusers "face to face;" put in doubt laws in 26 states which shield children from possible trauma in such confrontations.

JUNE 30

1632 A charter for Maryland (lands north of the Potomac River) was granted to George Calvert, the first Lord Baltimore; the charter was not issued until after his death and his son, Cecil Calvert, became the first proprietor; the charter set out the area between the Potomac River and 40° north.

1768 Elizabeth Kortright Monroe, wife of President Monroe, was born in New York City (died 1830).

1812 The first interest bearing Treasury notes were authorized.

1815 The Dey of Algiers signed a treaty agreeing to release all American prisoners and halting the molestation of American commerce; this occurred after the American fleet destroyed several Algerian raiding parties, sailed into Algiers harbor.

1819 William A. Wheeler, Vice President (1877-81), was born in Malone, N.Y.; represented New York in the House (1861-63, 1869-77) (died 1887).

1841 President Tyler signed an act for the relief of the widow of former President William Henry Harrison; the $25,000 was the first presidential widow pension.

1855 William B. Caperton, naval officer, was born in Spring Hill, Tenn.; involved in Vera Cruz and Caribbean operations (1915-16); commander-in-chief, Pacific Fleet (1916-19) (died 1941).

1859 Charles Blondin, French tightrope walker, crossed the Niagara River below the Falls on a tightrope.

1864 President Lincoln signed the Internal Revenue Act, which increased the income tax to 5% on incomes of $601 to $4999, to 10% on incomes over $10,000.

1865 The trial of eight persons involved in the Lincoln assassination began before a military commission; all were found guilty (John Wilkes Booth was killed earlier during his escape attempt).

1879 Walter Hampden, actor, was born in Brooklyn; best remembered for his role of Cyrano de Bergerac, which he played about 1000 times, and "The Admirable Crichton" (died 1955).

1882 Charles J. Guiteau, convicted murderer of President Garfield, was executed in Washington.

1900 A pier fire in Hoboken, N.J. killed more than 300 persons, did property damage of $4.6 million.

1905 William Zeckendorf, real estate developer, was born in Paris, Ill.; headed, Webb & Knapp, international realtors (1942-65) (died 1976).

1906 The Pure Food and Drug Act and Meat Inspection Act were signed by President Theodore Roosevelt.

1911 Czeslaw Milosz, author, was born in Sateiniai, Poland (now Lithuania); awarded 1980 Nobel Literature Prize; wrote among others, *The Captive Mind.*

1917 Lena Horne, entertainer, was born in New York City; singer and actress (*Cabin in the Sky, Stormy Weather*).

1918 Eugene V. Debs, Socialist leader, was arrested in Cleveland for interfering with military recruiting; sentenced to ten years.

1921 Former President Taft was appointed chief justice of the Supreme Court by President Harding; resigned because of ill health Feb 3, 1930.

1924 A federal grand jury in Washington indicted Albert B. Fall, Harry F. Sinclair, Edward L. Doheny, an oil executive, and his son for bribery and conspiracy to defraud the government in connection with the Teapot Dome oil leases.

1926 Paul Berg, biochemist, was born in New York City; shared 1980 Nobel Physiology/Medicine Prize for pioneering research in genetic engineering.

1938 President Franklin Roosevelt laid the cornerstone for the Federal Building at New York World's Fair.

1942 Robert D. Ballard, oceanographer, was born in Wichita, Kan.; headed Deep Sea Submergence Laboratory of Woods Hole (Mass.) Oceanographic Institution which found and explored the wreck of the *Titanic* in 1985 and 1986.

1943 An executive order officially ended the Works Project Administration (WPA), which in eight years employed more than 8.5 million persons on more than 1.4 million projects costing $11 billion.

1950 President Truman authorized Gen. Douglas MacArthur to use American ground forces to assist in halting North Korean aggression.

1951 Fifty persons were lost in a crash of an airliner north of Denver.

JUNE 30

1956 A midair collision of two airliners over the Grand Canyon killed 128 persons.

1971 Supreme Court by a 6-3 vote refused to bar newspapers from publishing the Pentagon Papers.

1982 Equal Rights Amendment (ERA) failed when three legislatures refused to approve the amendment before the midnight deadline; 38 states were needed to ratify.

1989 The Energy Department acknowledged for the first time that a weapons production plant could harm its neighbors, promised to pay $73 million to settle claims of up to 24,000 neighbors of the Feeds Materials Production Center in Fernald, Ohio.

JULY 1

1725 Comte de Rochambeau, French general in the American Revolution, was born in Vendome; commanded French troops at Yorktown (1781) (died 1807).

1769 Gaspar de Portola arrived in present-day San Diego, where he established a presidio; considered San Diego's founder.

1795 President Washington nominated John Rutledge as chief justice of the Supreme Court; presided until Dec 15, but not confirmed by the Senate; had served as associate justice (1789-91).

1802 Gideon Welles, editor and public official, was born in Glastonbury, Conn.; a founder, *Hartford Press*, the Republican Party; Secretary of the Navy (1861-69) (died 1878).

1805 Michigan Territory was established.

1817 Samuel L. Mather, financier, was born in Middletown, Conn.; developed iron ore deposits at Lake Superior; president, treasurer, Cleveland Iron Mining Co. (1869-90) (died 1890).

1818 Josiah Gorgas, Confederate general, was born in Dauphin County, Pa.; served in Mexican War; chief of ordnance, Confederate Army, and despite difficulties maintained steady flow of arms and ammunition (died 1883).

1819 John M. Brannan, Union general, was born in Washington; served in Mexican War and saw action at Chickamauga, Missionary Ridge (died 1892).

1833 Alfred T.A. Torbert, Union general, was born in Georgetown, Del.; served Sherman's army as cavalry commander (died 1880).

1840 The sixth census reported the American population had grown to 17,069,453, with the center of population south of Clarksburg, W.Va.

1847 The first adhesive American postage stamps went on sale (5¢ Benjamin Franklin, 10¢ George Washington).

1854 Albert B. Hart, historian and educator, was born in Clarksville, Pa.; edited several series of American histories (*Epochs of America, American Nation*) (died 1943).

1857 Roger Connor, baseball player (Giants), was born in Waterbury, Conn.; named to Baseball Hall of Fame (died 1931).

1858 Willard L. Metcalf, artist, was born in Lowell, Mass.; painter of New England scenes (*Family of Birches, Icebound, Twin Birches*) (died 1925).

1861 John Clarkson, baseball pitcher who won 326 games for various teams, was born in Cambridge, Mass.; named to Baseball Hall of Fame (died 1909).

1862 Pacific Railway Act was passed, providing assistance for a northern route transcontinental railroad (became the Union Pacific); about 45 million acres were provided and $60 million loaned.

1862 President Lincoln signed an act establishing the office of Commissioner of Internal Revenue.

1862 Congress passed an anti-polygamy act.

1862 David White, paleobotanist and geologist, was born in Palmyra, N.Y.; with U.S. Geological Survey (1886-1935), developed theory of carbon ratio, thereby helping found the petroleum industry (died 1935).

1862 Confederate troops under Gen. Robert E. Lee were defeated at Malvern Hill, Va. by Union troops under Gen. George McClellan; Confederates lost about 5500.

1863 The three-day battle of Gettysburg began; the battle was touched off when small detached forces met accidentally outside Gettysburg; a decisive victory for the Union, considered a turning point of the war; Union losses were 23,000, Confederates about 28,000.

1863 A Missouri convention adopted an ordinance that slavery should cease in the state July 4, 1870.

1877 Benjamin O. Davis, first black general in the Army, was born in Washington; his son, Benjamin O. Davis Jr., became the first black general in the Air Forces (died 1970).

1880 Abraham Levitt, founder of construction firm which built much post-World War II housing, was born in Brooklyn (died 1962).

1882 Susan Glaspell, author, was born in Davenport, Iowa; novelist, playwright (*Alison's House*) (died 1948).

1892 James M. Cain, author, was born in Annapolis, Md.; writer of suspense fiction (*The Postman Always Rings Twice, Double Indemnity*) (died 1977).

1893 President Cleveland was secretly operated on for cancer of the upper jaw aboard a yacht anchored in Long Island Sound; remained secret until 1917, when the doctor who performed the operation revealed the story.

1893 Walter F. White, civil rights leader, was born in Atlanta, Ga.; with NAACP (1918-55) as assistant secretary (1918-29), secretary (1931-55) (died 1955).

1898 Americans took the fortified ridge village of El Caney and San Juan Hill, commanding the heights overlooking Santiago, Cuba; Theodore Roosevelt commanded the dismounted Rough Riders at San Juan Hill.

1899 Gideons International was organized by three traveling men to distribute Bibles in hotels, motels, hospitals, and penal institutions.

1899 The world's first juvenile court opened in Chicago.

1899 Charles Laughton, actor, was born in Scarborough, England; many notable screen roles (*Henry VIII, Mutiny on the Bounty, Ruggles of Red Gap*) (died 1962).

1902 A territorial government was created for the Philippine Islands, with Filipinos becoming Philippine citizens and the start of partial self-government.

1902 William Wyler, movie director, was born in Mulhouse, France; directed many hit films (*Mrs. Miniver, Ben Hur, The Best Years of Our Lives*) (died 1981).

1902 A permanent census office was created.

1914 Prohibition went into effect in West Virginia.

1915 Statewide prohibition went into effect in Alabama.

1916 Olivia DeHaviland, screen actress, was born in Tokyo, Japan, sister of Joan Fontaine (10/22/1917); starred in several films (*Gone With the Wind, The Heiress*).

1916 Dwight D. Eisenhower and Mamie G. Doud were married in Denver.

1918 Sugar rationing went into effect, allowing two pounds per person a month.

1921 President Harding appointed Gen. John J. Pershing as chief of staff.

1929 Robert M. Hutchins, dean of Yale Law School, became the fifth president of the U. of Chicago; at 30, he was the youngest major university head.

1929 Gerald M. Edelman, biochemist, was born in New York City; shared 1972 Nobel Physiology/Medicine Prize for research on chemical structure and nature of antibodies.

1939 President Franklin Roosevelt by executive order consolidated 24 units and established the Federal Security Agency, the Federal Works Agency, and the Federal Loan Agency; the Security Agency was abolished Apr 11, 1953, the Works Agency June 30, 1949, and the Loan Agency June 30, 1947.

1940 Ben Turpin, actor, died at 71; star comedian of silent screen (1907-40), noted for cross-eyed expressions.

1941 The Mammoth Cave (Ky.) National park was established.

1943 Pay-as-you-go income tax plan went into effect.

1946 First peacetime atomic bomb test was conducted on Bikini Atoll in the Pacific.

1949 General Services Administration (GSA) was established to manage government property and records.

1961 Hawaii Volcanoes and Haleakala (Hawaii) national parks were established.

1961 Carl Lewis, 1984 Olympic track gold medalist, was born in Birmingham, Ala.

1964 Michigan's fourth constitution went into effect.

1966 Medicare, a government program designed to pay part of the medical expenses of those over 65, went into effect as part of the Social Security Administration.

1970 Office of Management and Budget was created.

1971 U.S. Postal Service, the reorganized Post Office Department, began operations.

1971 The 26th Amendment lowering the voting age to 18 went into effect.

1971 ACTION was created as an independent agency for administering volunteer service programs (Peace Corps, VISTA, Foster Grandparents, Retired Senior Volunteer Program, Senior Companion Program, National Center for Service Learning).

1973 Centersfor Disease Control was established in Atlanta, Ga.

1981 United Auto Workers rejoined the AFL-CIO after a 13-year split over policy.

1986 Four-day program of concerts, tall ships, ethnic festivals, and fireworks began to commemorate the 100th anniversary of the Statute of Liberty; statue underwent two years of restoration.

1987 President Reagan nominated 60-year-old Robert H. Bork, a judge on the U.S. Circuit Court of Appeals, to succeed Lewis F. Powell Jr. on the Supreme Court.

1988 President Reagan signed legislation expanding Medicare to help remove the threat of catastrophic illness.

1988 The Pentagon halted payments on nine military programs costing more than $1.2 billion because they may have been tainted by Defense Department fraud and bribery scandal.

JULY 2

1759 Nathan Read, inventor and engineer, was born in Warren, Mass.; designed multitubular steam boiler, double-acting steam engine, chain wheel device to propel boats, machine for cutting and heading nails; represented Massachusetts in the House (1800-03) (died 1849).

1776 Gen. William Howe and about 10,000 men landed unopposed on Staten Island; joined by a strong fleet and 150 transports under Lord Richard Howe; the garrison grew to 32,000 by August.

1776 The Continental Congress voted for independence by a vote of 12-0, with New York abstaining because it lacked instructions; then discussed Declaration of Independence and approved it without dissent two days later.

1776 New Jersey adopted its state constitution.

1777 Gen. John Burgoyne and his British troops began siege of Ft. Ticonderoga; Americans abandoned it July 6.

1777 Week-long convention at Windsor adopted the name of Vermont and a state constitution which forbade slavery; applied for admission to union of colonies.

1798 Former President Washington was nominated as lieutenant colonel and commander-in-chief of American armies by President John Adams; confirmed by Senate.

1807 President Jefferson issued a proclamation ordering British warships to leave American territorial waters.

1810 Robert A. Toombs, Confederate official and legislator, was born in Wilkes County, Ga.; represented Georgia in the House (1845-53) and Senate (1853-61); Confederate Secretary of State (1861), general; fled to England to escape arrest (1865-67) (died 1885).

1812 Peter Gansevoort, Revolutionary officer, died at 63; commander of Ft. George (1776) and Ft. Schuyler (1777), during siege by British-Indians.

1819 Lucius J. Knowles, inventor, was born in Hardwick, Mass.; invented a steam pump, improved and manufactured a loom (died 1884).

1840 Francis A. Walker, economist and educator, was born in Boston, Mass.; Union general (rising from private); chief, U.S. Bureau of Statistics (1869-71), supervised 1870 and 1880 census; Yale professor (1873-81), president, MIT (1881-97); studies on wage and profits influenced economic theory (died 1897).

1850 Robert Ridgway, ornithologist, was born in Mt. Carmel, Ill.; in charge of Smithsonian bird collection (1869-80); bird curator, U.S. National Museum (1880-1929) (died 1929).

1853 Frederick T. Gates, religious leader, was born in Maine, N.Y.; instrumental in getting John D. Rockefeller to endow U. of Chicago; became philanthropy advisor to Rockefeller, helped establish Rockefeller Foundation (died 1929).

1855 Clarence W. Barron, editor and publisher, was born in Boston, Mass.; perfected financial news reporting; bought Dow Jones, including *Wall St. Journal* (1901); founder, editor, *Barron's Weekly* (died 1928).

1862 Morrill Act, one of the most important pieces of legislation to aid education, was passed by Congress and signed by President Lincoln; granted public land to states for industrial, agricultural education; amounted to about 13 million acres.

1862 President Lincoln issued a proclamation calling for 300,000 volunteers for three years service.

1864 Gen. Jubal Early led his Confederate troops into Winchester, Va., enroute to Washington; occupied Martinsburg, W. Va.

1872 George W. Mundelein, Catholic prelate, was born in New York City; archbishop of Chicago (1915-39); named cardinal 1924 (died 1939).

1881 President Garfield was shot and fatally wounded by Charles J. Guiteau in a Washington railroad station; died Sept 19; the mentally unstable Guiteau was a disappointed office-seeker.

1890 The Sherman Anti-Trust Act was signed by President Benjamin Harrison, the first federal act passed which attempted to regulate trusts; the law was so general and ambiguous that the courts had to decide many points.

1894 Lewis W. Douglas, public official and diplomat, was born in Bisbee, Ariz., grandson of James Douglas (11/4/1837); represented Ariz. in the House (1927-33); Budget Director (1933-34); deputy administrator, War Shipping Board (1942-44), ambassador to Great Britain (1947-50) (died 1974).

1894 The Attorney General got an injunction against the American Railway Union, whose strike against the Pullman Co. affected all railroads; the union defied the injunction and federal troops were sent to help operate the trains.

1898 Anthony C. McAuliffe, World War II general, was born in Washington; commanding general at Bastogne, remembered for his answer to German surrender demand—"Nuts!" (died 1975).

1906 Hans A. Bethe, physicist, was born in Strasbourg, then in Germany; awarded 1967 Nobel Physics Prize for contributions to knowledge concerning the energy production of stars.

1908 Thurgood Marshall, jurist, was born in Baltimore, Md.; NAACP legal services director (1938-61); judge, U.S. Court of Appeals (1961-65); Solicitor General (1965-67); associate justice, Supreme Court (1967-), the first black to serve on the court.

1912 The first American dirigible, the *Akron*, exploded 2000 feet over Atlantic City, N.J., five were killed.

1915 A bomb exploded in the Senate reception room; had been placed by Eric Muenter, alias Frank Holt, a German instructor at Cornell U.

1917 The first regular convoy of merchant ships sailed for Europe from Hampton Roads (Norfolk), Va.; German submarine attack two days later was beaten off.

1917 More than 100 blacks were killed or wounded in a two-day riot in East St. Louis, Ill.; touched off by importation of blacks as strikebreakers.

1918 Robert W. Sarnoff, communications executive, was born in New York City, son of David Sarnoff (2/27/1891); president, RCA Corp. (1955-75).

1926 The Army Air Corps was created.

1932 Franklin D. Roosevelt set a precedent by appearing at the Democratic National Convention in Chicago to accept the presidential nomination—"I pledge myself to a new deal for the American people."

1937 Amelia Earhart Putnam and co-pilot, Fred Noonan, disappeared while on a flight near Howland Island in the Pacific.

1937 Richard Petty, auto racer, was born in Randleman, N.C.; won Daytona 500 six times; NASCAR champion five times.

1939 John H. Sununu, New Hampshire governor (1983-87), was born in Havana; nominated by President-elect Bush to be White House chief of staff (1989).

1955 Sen. Lyndon B. Johnson, majority leader, suffered a heart attack; did not return to Senate until December.

1964 President Lyndon B. Johnson signed the Civil Rights Act, which included provisions for public accommodations and equal employment opportunities.

1965 The Equal Employment Opportunity Commission became operational.

1982 The Supreme Court ruled 8-0 that the NAACP cannot be held liable financially for losses of white merchants during the seven-year boycott in Claiborne County, Miss.

1985 An announcement was issued of an agreement to hold an American-Russian summit meeting in Geneva Nov 19 and 20.

JULY 3

1731 Samuel Huntington, colonial leader, was born in Windham, Conn.; member of Continental Congress (1776-84), its president (1779-81, 1783); signer of Declaration of Independence; governor of Connecticut (1786-96) (died 1796).

1738 John S. Copley, artist, was born in Boston; the first great American portrait painter (died 1815).

1754 George Washington and 400 men were defeated at Ft. Necessity (Great Meadows, Pa.) by a French force of 900; formally surrendered July 4.

1775 George Washington took formal command of the Continental Army of 14,500 men at Cambridge, Mass.

1778 Settlers in the Wyoming Valley of Pennsylvania were attacked by British, aided by Tories and Indians; many were massacred; event was called "the surpassing horror of the Revolution."

1814 American troops under Gen. Jacob Brown captured Ft. Erie, Canada and pushed on to the Chippewa River.

1819 The first American savings bank (Bank for Savings) opened in New York City.

1844 Treaty of Wanghia was signed with China, the first treaty of peace, amity, and commerce with China.

1844 Dankmar Adler, architect, was born in Langfeld, Germany; partner of Louis Sullivan, did many buildings in Chicago, St. Louis (died 1900).

1878 George M. Cohan, actor and playwright, was born in Providence; acted in many plays which he wrote and produced (*Little Johny Jones, 45 Minutes from Broadway, Get-Rich-Quick Wallingford*); popular song writer ("Mary's a Grand Old Name," "I'm a

Yankee Doodle Dandy," "You're a Grand Old Flag," "Give My Regards to Broadway," "Over There") (died 1942).

1879 Alfred Korzybski, semanticist, was born in Warsaw, Poland; founder of general semantics; author of "Science and Sanity" (died 1950).

1890 Idaho was admitted to the Union as the 43rd state.

1898 The Spanish fleet was destroyed and 600 men killed when the fleet tried to run the American blockade of Santiago de Cuba harbor.

1900 John Mason Brown, critic and author, was born in Louisville, Ky.; drama critic, *Saturday Review*; author (*To All Hands, Daniel Boone*) (died 1969).

1902 President Theodore Roosevelt issued a proclamation of peace and amnesty for the Philippines.

1915 J.P. Morgan, acting as agent for the British Government on war contracts, was slightly wounded by Eric Muenter at Glen Cove, Long Island; Muenter, who had bombed the Senate reception room the previous day, committed suicide in jail three days later.

1930 Pete Fountain, Dixieland clarinetist and orchestra leader, was born in New Orleans, La.

1935 Harrison H. (Jack) Schmitt, astronaut and legislator, was born in Santa Rita, N.M.; astronaut (1965-75), piloted Apollo 17 lunar module on 1972 mission; represented New Mexico in the Senate (1977-83).

1974 President Nixon signed the limited nuclear agreements in Moscow.

1988 The American vessel *Vincennes* in the Persian Gulf mistakenly shot down an Iranian passenger plane, thinking it was a hostile attack plane, killing all 290 persons aboard.

1989 The Supreme Court by a 5-4 vote left intact the *Roe v. Wade* 1973 ruling establishing the constitutional right to abortion, but encouraged states to cut back sharply on that right; court ruled that states may require doctors to determine whether a fetus at least 20 weeks old is "viable" or capable of surviving outside the womb.

JULY 4

1584 The expedition sent out by Sir Walter Raleigh arrived off the coast of North Carolina, landing at Roanoke Island.

1752 The proprietary colony of Georgia became a royal colony as the original 21-year charter expired.

1776 The Continental Congress unanimously adopted the Declaration of Independence in Philadelphia; publicly proclaimed July 8 (New York did not vote approval until July 9 when instructions arrived.)

1778 George Rogers Clark led Americans to victory at the British post of Kaskaskia, Ill.; followed up victory with others over other Illinois posts, resulting in the Virginia legislature organizing the area as Illinois County in Oct.

1789 The first tariff law was enacted, imposing import duties "for the encouragement and protection of manufacturers."

1802 The U.S. Military Academy at West Point was formally opened.

1804 Nathaniel Hawthorne, author, was born in Salem, Mass.; wrote several classics (*The Scarlet Letter, Twice Told Tales, House of Seven Gables*) (died 1864).

1816 Fort Dearborn, at what is now Chicago, was rebuilt to replace the fort destroyed four years earlier.

1817 Work was begun on the Erie Canal with the groundbreaking at Rome, N.Y.; completed 1825.

1819 Edward R. Squibb, pharmaceutical manufacturer, was born in Wilmington, Del.; founder of chemical, pharmaceutical laboratory in Brooklyn (1858), became E.R. Squibb & Sons (1892) (died 1900).

1819 The territorial government of Arkansas was created.

1825 Groundbreaking ceremonies were held in Newark, Ohio for the 308-mile Ohio Canal between Cleveland and Portsmouth on the Ohio River; completed 1828.

1826 Two former presidents died the same day—Thomas Jefferson at Monticello at 83 and John Adams in Quincy, Mass. at 90; shortly before he died, Adams said: "Thomas Jefferson still survives;" actually, he had died a few hours earlier.

1826 Stephen C. Foster, composer, was born near Pittsburgh; composed numerous classic songs ("My Old Kentucky Home," "Massa's in the Cold, Cold Ground," "O Susanna," "Old Black Joe," "Old Folks at Home," "Camptown Races") (died 1864).

1827 Slavery was abolished in New York State under provisions of an 1817 law.

1828 The Baltimore & Ohio Railroad was begun with the cornerstone laying near Baltimore, with the last surviving signer of the Declaration of Independence, Charles Carroll, laying the first stone; this was the first American public railroad.

1828 President John Quincy Adams broke ground for the Chesapeake & Ohio Canal in Georgetown (Washington).

1828 James J. Pettigrew, Confederate general, was born in Lake Scuppernong, N.C.; led left wing in Pickett's charge at Gettysburg; mortally wounded in retreat from Gettysburg (1863).

1831 Former President Monroe died in New York City at 73.

1831 A treaty was concluded with France settling claims for depredations of American shipping during the Napoleonic wars; the French paid 25 million francs, the Americans 1.5 million francs.

1832 "America" was first sung publicly at Park St. Church in Boston.

1836 The territorial government of Wisconsin was established.

1836 The state of Illinois began building a canal to connect the Mississippi River and Lake Michigan; panic of 1837 temporarily halted work; opened Apr 23, 1848.

1840 An independent federal Treasury system was created with subtreasuries in New York City, Boston, Charleston, and St. Louis.

1845 Texas voters in convention in Austin approved annexation by the United States; action ratified by referendum Oct 13.

1846 Rebellious Californians, the so-called Bear Flaggers, held a victory celebration in Sonoma and declared California independent; the next day they created a military organization, with Col. John C. Fremont as commander.

1847 James A. Bailey, circus owner, was born in Detroit, Mich.; merged with P.T. Barnum in 1882 (died 1906).

1848 President Polk laid the cornerstone of the Washington Monument.

1850 The Clayton-Bulwer Treaty was ratified; called for the United States and Great Britain to refrain from occupying any part of Central America; replaced by the Hays-Paunceforte Treaty in 1902.

1851 President Fillmore laid the cornerstone for the south House extension of the Capitol; completed in Nov 1867.

1859 Mickey (Michael F.) Welch, baseball pitcher who won 311 games (Giants), was born in Brooklyn; named to Baseball Hall of Fame (died 1941).

1861 Francis B. Crocker, electrical engineer, was born in New York City; instrumental in establishing American electrical standards (died 1921).

1861 Congress met in special session at the call of President Lincoln, who described the steps taken in the war, asked for additional powers.

1862 Confederate cavalry under Gen. J.H. Morgan began three weeks of raiding along the Louisville & Nashville Railroad in Tennessee and Kentucky.

1863 Gen. John C. Pemberton led 30,000 Confederate troops in surrendering besieged Vicksburg to Gen. U.S. Grant; gave the Union control of the Mississippi River.

1863 Gen. Robert E. Lee and his Confederate troops began retreat from Gettysburg, retiring to a position west of Hagerstown, Md. before returning to Virginia.

1866 Fire in Portland, Me. destroyed 1500 buildings.

1867 Stephen T. Mather, public official, was born in San Francisco, Cal.; first director, National Park Service (1917-29); established coordinated national parks system and principles for their preservation and use (died 1930).

1872 Calvin Coolidge, 30th president (1923-29), was born in Plymouth, Vt.; assumed office Aug 2, 1923 on the death of President Harding; mayor of Northampton, Mass. (1910-11), governor of Mass. (1916-19) (died 1933).

1874 Steel bridge over the Mississippi River at St. Louis was opened.

1881 Tuskegee Institute opened with 30 students with Booker T. Washington as principal.

1883 Rube (Reuben L.) Goldberg, cartoonist, was born in San Francisco, Cal.; drew *Boob McNutt*, but best remembered for complicated machine cartoons (died 1970).

1884 The United States received the Statue of Liberty as a gift from the French people.

1885 Louis B. Mayer, movie executive, was born in Minsk, Russia; began with small New England movie chain; went into production, developed Metro Goldwyn Mayer, serving as production first vice president (died 1957).

1889 Five constitutional conventions began—North Dakota, South Dakota, Montana, Washington, and Idaho.

1891 Former Vice President Hannibal Hamlin (1861-65) died in Bangor, Me. at 81.

1894 The Republic of Hawaii was established.

1895 Irving Caesar, lyricist, was born in New York City; one of the great lyricists, remembered for "Tea for Two," "I Want to be Happy," "Crazy Rhythm."

1898 Gertrude Lawrence, actress, was born in London, England; starred in many hit plays (*Pygmalion, The King and I, Private Lives, Lady in the Dark*) (died 1952).

1898 Wake Island was captured by the Americans.

1900 Louis Armstrong, musician, was born in New Orleans, La.; "Satchmo" was a noted trumpeter, singer, orchestra leader (died 1971).

1902 William Howard Taft was appointed governor-general of the Philippine Islands by President McKinley as military rule of the islands ended.

1903 President Theodore Roosevelt sent the first message on the Pacific cable to the Philippines.

1910 Supreme Court Chief Justice Melville W. Fuller died in Sorrento, Me. at 77.

1911 The first workmen's compensation act went into effect in New Jersey.

1911 Mitch(ell) Miller, popular choral director, was born in Rochester, N.Y.; recording company executive.

1917 The first government aviation training field was opened in Rantoul, Ill.

1918 American shipyards launched 95 ships on this day.

1918 Twin columnist sisters—Ann Landers and Abigail Van Buren (Dear Abbie)—were born in Sioux City, Iowa as Esther P. (Landers) and Pauline E. (Abbie) Friedman.

1919 Jack Dempsey defeated Jess Willard in four rounds in Toledo to win the world's heavyweight boxing championship.

1921 Gerard Debreau, economist, was born in Calais, France; with U. of California; awarded 1983 Nobel Economics Prize for his work on how prices operate to balance production and consumption.

1927 Neil Simon, playwright, was born in New York City; wrote many successes (*Come, Blow Your Horn; Barefoot in the Park; The Odd Couple; Sweet Charity; Promises, Promises; The Sunshine Boys; Prisoner of Second Avenue; The Last of the Red Hot Lovers*).

1940 The Franklin D. Roosevelt Library in Hyde Park, N.Y. was dedicated by him.

1942 American Air Force crews participated in a British raid on the Netherlands, the first American air operation in Europe.

1946 The United States gave independence to the Philippine Islands by executive proclamation, recognizing the Republic of Philippines.

1950 President Eisenhower issued a proclamation making Hawaii the 50th state.

1966 President Lyndon Johnson signed an act creating the American Revolution Bicentennial Commission.

1967 The Freedom of Information Act went into effect, to make government information more readily available; withholding of information required the government to prove its sensitivity.

1976 Americans celebrated 200th anniversary of independence with events of all kinds; President Ford visited Independence Hall in Philadelphia, the site of the Declaration signing, and New York City, with its "tall ships" parade.

JULY 5

1756 William Rush, sculptor, was born in Philadelphia; first American-born sculptor; also known for carved ship figureheads; a founder, Pennsylvania Academy of Fine Arts (died 1833).

1776 Patrick Henry became Virginia's first governor.

1779 British troops ravaged the Connecticut coast, taking New Haven, Fairfield, and Norwalk.

1794 Sylvanus Graham, food reformer, was born in West Suffield, Conn.; advocated use of whole wheat, coarsely-ground flour (graham flour) (died 1851).

1801 David G. Farragut, Union naval officer, was born near Knoxville, Tenn.; captured the Mississippi River and Mobile Bay for the Union; reputedly said, at Mobile: "Damn the torpedoes, full speed ahead!"; Congress created for him special ranks of vice admiral (1864), admiral (1866) (died 1870).

1810 P(hineas) T. Barnum, showman, was born in Bethel, Conn.; opened American Museum of curios, exhibited Gen. Tom Thumb, brought Jenny Lind to America for concert tour; joined (1882) with James A. Bailey to form world's largest circus (died 1891).

1814 The Battle of Chippewa Falls, near Niagara Falls, took place, resulting in British withdrawal; however, failure of American naval forces at Sacketts Harbor, N.Y. to cooperate with land forces made American withdrawal necessary.

1841 William C. Whitney, financier and public official, was born in Conway, Mass.; a leader in New York City street railway system; Secretary of Navy (1885-89); prominent in horse racing (died 1904).

1843 Oregon settlers, meeting in Champoeg, adopted a constitution for a provisional government to serve until the United States could take over.

1860 Robert Bacon, financier and diplomat, was born in Jamaica Plain, Mass.; partner in J.P. Morgan & Co. (1894-1903), helped establish U.S. Steel, Northern Securities; Secretary of State (1909), ambassador to France (1909-12) (died 1919).

1865 Secret Service was established.

1867 James M. Wayne, jurist, died at 87, the last surviving associate of Chief Justice John Marshall; associate justice (1835-67).

1879 Dwight F. Davis, public official, was born in St. Louis, Mo.; Secretary of War (1925-29); governor-general, Philippines (1929-32); donor of cup for international tennis competition (died 1945).

1879 Wanda Landowska, pianist and harpsichordist, was born in Warsaw, Poland; noted teacher and composer (died 1959).

1888 Herbert S. Gasser, physiologist, was born in Platteville, Wis.; shared 1944 Nobel Physiology/Medicine Prize for work on functions of nerve fibers (died 1963).

1890 Frederick L. Allen, editor and author, was born in Boston, Mass.; editor, *Harpers* (1941-54); author (*Only Yesterday, Since Yesterday*) (died 1954).

1891 John H. Northrop, biologist and chemist, was born in Yonkers; shared 1946 Nobel Chemistry Prize for preparing enzyme, virus proteins in pure form.

1894 Gov. John P. Altgeld of Illinois protested the sending of federal troops on July 3 by President Cleveland to the Pullman strike in Chicago; he argued that state and local authorities could handle the situation; arrival of troops broke the strike.

1902 Henry Cabot Lodge, legislator and diplomat, was born in Nahant, Mass.; grandson of Henry Cabot Lodge (5/12/1850); represented Massachusetts in the Senate (1937-44, 1947-53); chief, UN mission (1953-60); Republican vice presidential candidate (1960); ambassador to South Vietnam (1963-64, 1965-67) (died 1985).

1918 The excursion steamer, *Columbia*, sank in the Illinois River near Peoria with the loss of 200 lives.

1935 Congress passed the National Labor Relations Act—the Wagner Act—for the peaceful settlement of labor disputes.

1945 Gen. Douglas MacArthur announced the recapture of the Philippine Islands.

1971 President Nixon certified the 26th Amendment lowering the voting age from 21 to 18.

1988 The 69th General Convention of the Episcopal Church meeting in Detroit unanimously approved an anti-discrimination resolution to protect AIDS sufferers.

1989 Federal Judge Gerhard A. Gesell fined Oliver L. North $150,000 for his crimes in the Iran-Contra affair; placed him on probation for two years and ordered him to perform 1200 hours of community service; had been convicted of destroying official documents, giving false statements and accepting an illegal gift.

JULY 6

1699 Capt. Kidd, pirate, was seized in Boston; sent to England where he was hanged in 1701.

1736 Daniel Morgan, Revolutionary general, was born in Hunterdon County, N.J.; served with Benedict Arnold at Quebec, commanded troops in North Carolina, defeating the British at Cowpens (died 1802).

1747 John Paul Jones, Revolutionary naval officer, was born in Kirkubride, Scotland; commanded the *Bonhomme Richard* in the fierce battle with the British *Serapis* (Sept 21, 1779); credited with quote, "I have not yet begun to fight!"; scored many victories over British (died 1792).

1759 Joshua Barney, naval officer, was born in Baltimore County, Md.; served gallantly in Revolution, commanded flotilla of barges which tried to stop British march on Washington, then joined land force at Bladensburg, Md., wounded and captured (died 1818).

1766 Alexander Wilson, ornithologist, was born in Paisley, Scotland; his seven-volume *American Ornithology* regarded as a classic (died 1813).

1768 Johann C. Beissel, German-born founder of the Dunkers, died at 78; organized (about 1730) the "Solitary Brethren of the Community of Seventh-day Baptists" (Dunkers) at Ephrata, Pa.; author of many hymns, which influenced American hymnology.

1775 The second Continental Congress adopted a declaration of the causes and necessity of taking up arms, drafted by John Dickinson and Thomas Jefferson, which said, in part: "We are reduced to the alternative of choosing an unconditional submission to the tyranny of irritated ministers, or resistance by force. The latter is our choice. We have counted the cost of this contest, and find nothing so dreadful as voluntary slavery... Our cause is just. Our union is perfect...".

1777 Gen. John Burgoyne with 8000 British troops captured Ft. Ticonderoga, which had been abandoned by American troops under Gen. Arthur St. Clair.

1785 Congress created a currency system devised by Robert Morris and Gouverneur Morris, with the dollar as its unit and a decimal ratio.

1790 Congress passed an act for a federal city in a ten-mile square on the Potomac River after 1800; until then Philadelphia would be the capital.

1798 Philo P. Stewart, educator and inventor, was born in Sherman, Conn.; co-founder, Oberlin (Ohio) College (1833); invented the Oberlin cookstove (died 1868).

1800 Alonzo Potter, Episcopal prelate, was born in Dutchess County, N.Y., brother of Horatio Potter (2/9/1802); bishop of Pennsylvania (1860-65), established hospital (1860), divinity school (1863) in Philadelphia (died 1865).

1831 Daniel C. Gilman, educator, was born in Norwich, Conn.; president, U. of California (1872-75), first president, Johns Hopkins (1875-1901) and Carnegie Foundation (1901-04); president, National Civil Service Reform League (1901-07) (died 1908).

1832 John B. Gordon, Confederate general, was born in Upson County, Ga.; saw action at Antietam, Chancellorsville, Spotsylvania; served Georgia as governor (1886-90) and represented it in the Senate (1873-80, 1891-97) (died 1904).

1835 Supreme Court Chief Justice John Marshall died in Philadelphia at 80.

1854 A meeting in Jackson, Mich., attended by former Whigs, Democrats, and Free Soilers, resulted in formation of the Republican Party.

1869 Agoston Haraszthy de Mokesa, pioneer grape grower, died at about 57; Hungarian grower, introduced Tokay, Zinfandel, and Shiras grapes to California (1849).

1869 Virginia ratified its new constitution, which recognized equal civil rights.

1875 Roger W. Babson, economist, was born in Gloucester, Mass.; pioneered in the use of charts to forecast business trends; founder of statistical organization, Babson Institute, and Webber College (for women) for sound business training (died 1967).

1876 Harry F. Sinclair, oil industry leader, was born in Wheeling, W. Va.; founder, president, Sinclair Oil Co. (1916-49); involved in Teapot Dome scandals, indicted but acquitted of conspiracy to defraud (1928); guilty of contempt of court and of Congress, served three months (1929) (died 1956).

1884 Harold S. Vanderbilt, businessman and sportsman, was born in Oakdale, Long Island, N.Y., grandson of William H. Vanderbilt (5/8/1821); in family's railroad empire; interested in sports, winning the America Cup (yaching) three times, developed contract bridge (died 1970).

1890 Leo Friedlander, sculptor, was born in New York City; did equestrian groups at Memorial Bridge, Washington; RCA Building entrance (died 1966).

1892 Jack Yellen, lyricist, was born in Razcki, Poland; wrote lyrics for several hits ("Ain't She Sweet?" "I Wonder What's Become of Sally," "Happy Days Are Here Again").

1892 The strike at the Carnegie Steel plant in Homestead, Pa. erupted into violence; seven guards and 11 strikers and spectators were shot to death; violence began with arrival of Pinkerton detectives; National Guard arrived July 2.

1894 Federal troops, ordered July 3 by President Cleveland, arrived in Chicago to protect the mails and interstate commerce affected by the Pullman strike; strike was broken in a week.

1896 James S. Love, textile manufacturer, was born in Cambridge; developed small family cotton mill into Burlington Industries Inc. (1923), first manufacturer of rayon (died 1962).

1920 Franklin D. Roosevelt, Assistant Secretary of the Navy, was nominated for the vice presidency by the Democratic National Convention.

1921 Nancy Davis Reagan, wife of President Reagan, was born in New York City.

1925 Merv Griffin, singer and television emcee, was born in San Mateo, Cal.; host of own talk show.

1932 The cost of first class postage was increased to three cents.

1933 The first major league All-Star game was held in Chicago, with the American League winning 4-2.

1944 Stampede at circus fire in Hartford, Conn. resulted in 168 killed and 193 injured.

1944 Part of a train plunged into a gorge near High Bluff, Tenn., 35 died.

1946 Sylvester Stallone, screen star and writer, was born in New York City; best known for his *Rocky* and *Rambo* films.

1948 President Truman announced the start of the Berlin Airlift to circumvent the Russian blockade of the city.

1953 (Irene) Temple Bailey, author, died; popular novelist (*Glory of Youth, Trumpeter Swan, Enchanted Ground*).

1957 The Harry S Truman Library was dedicated in Independence, Mo.

1960 President Eisenhower issued a proclamation reducing import quotas of Cuban sugar by 95% in answer to Castro's "deliberate policy of hostility toward the United States."

JULY 7

1540 Francisco Vasquez de Coronado, who had led a large force into New Mexico to capture the "Seven Cities of Cibola," captured the first city (Hawikuh, which became Granada-Cibola); explored areas north and east before turning back to Mexico.

1586 Thomas Hooker, liberal Puritan leader, was born in Leicestershire, England; helped found Hartford and frame the Fundamental Orders, which long served Connecticut as a constitution (died 1647).

1742 Gen. James Oglethorpe led a force to victory over the Spanish in the Battle of Bloody Marsh on St. Simon's Island, Ga.

1768 Philip S. Physick, pioneer surgeon, was born in Philadelphia; known as the father of American surgery; one of first to use animal ligature in surgery, leaving them in the tissues to be absorbed; devised a number of useful surgical instruments (died 1837).

1798 Congress repealed the treaties with France, terminating the alliance, and for the next two years an undeclared naval war followed.

1846 Naval forces under Commodore John D. Sloat went ashore at Monterey, raised the American flag, and proclaimed California a part of the United States.

1849 T(heophil) Mitchell Prudden, pathologist, was born in Middlebury, Conn.; first to make diphtheria antitoxin in the United States (died 1924).

1860 Abraham Cahan, editor and author, was born in Vilna, Poland; founder, editor, *Jewish Daily Forward* (1902-51); author (*Rise of David Levinsky, Yekl*) (died 1951).

1864 The first North Dakotan newspaper, *Frontier Scout*, was published by S.C. Winegar at Ft. Union.

1865 Four persons were hanged for participation in the conspiracy to kill President Lincoln—David E. Herold, Lewis Paine, George A. Atzerodt, Mrs. Mary E.J. Surrat; four others were imprisoned.

1890 Harry A. Noyes, chemist, was born in Marlboro, Mass.; developed freezing process for food (died 1970).

1898 Congress by joint resolution annexed the Hawaiian Islands.

1899 George Cukor, movie director, was born in New York City; directed many hits (*Little Women, My Fair Lady, A Star is Born, The Philadelphia Story*) (died 1983).

1906 Satchel (Leroy R.) Paige, baseball player, was born in Mobile, Ala.; legendary pitcher, who may have pitched in more than 2000 games in 20+ years; named to Baseball Hall of Fame (died 1982).

1907 Robert A. Heinlein, author, was born in Butler, Mo.; foremost American science fiction writer (*Farmer in the Sky, Stranger in a Strange Land*) (died 1988).

1909 Billy (William J.) Herman, baseball player (Cubs, Dodgers), was born in New Albany, Ind.; named to Baseball Hall of Fame.

1911 Gian-Carlo Menotti, composer, was born in Cadegliano, Italy; wrote various operas (*Amahl and the Night Visitors, The Medium, The Consul, The Telephone*).

1917 Lawrence F. O'Brien, public official, was born in Springfield, Mass.; Postmaster General (1965-68); chairman, National Democratic Party (1968-72); commissioner, National Basketball Assn. (1975-84).

1917 Emma Goldman and Alexander Berkman were sentenced to two years imprisonment and fined $10,000 for impeding registration in the military draft; Supreme Court upheld sentence Jan 14, 1918.

1927 Doc (Carl H.) Severinsen, musician, was born in Arlington, Ore.; trumpeter and orchestra leader, musical director of *Tonight Show* (1967-).

1941 American forces occupied Iceland at invitation of Icelandic government.

1946 Jimmy Carter and Rosalynn Smith were married in Plains, Ga.

1946 Pope Pius XII announced the canonization of Frances Xavier Cabrini (Mother Cabrini), the first American citizen to become a Catholic saint.

1947 Commission on Organization of the Executive Branch of the Government—the Hoover Commission—was created; recommendations (Apr 1, 1949) led to Reorganization Act of 1949.

1978 The Solomon Islands became an independent nation after having been a protectorate of the United States since World War II.

1987 Kiwanis International ended a 72-year men-only tradition by an overwhelming vote to let its 8200 clubs admit women to membership.

JULY 8

1657 Abraham DePeyster, colonial merchant and public official, was born in New Amsterdam (New York City); held virtually every city, colony post (died 1728).

1758 A British force was defeated at Ticonderoga by the French under Montcalm.

1776 The Declaration of Independence, adopted four days earlier, was published and proclaimed publicly in Philadelphia; (John Adams wrote: "...the bells rung all day and almost all night").

1778 The French fleet, commanded by Comte d'Estaing, arrived off the Delaware Capes, later off Sandy Hook, blockading the British for nearly two weeks; then sailed for Rhode Island.

1779 Spain authorized her subjects in Louisiana to capture English posts on the Mississippi River.

1779 Fairfield, Conn. was burned by the British and Hessians.

1826 Benjamin H. Grierson, Union officer, was born in Pittsburgh; led cavalry raid through the South, helped to capture Vicksburg; later, as general, fought the Indians (died 1911).

1839 John D. Rockefeller, oil industry leader, was born in Richford, N.Y.; founder, president, Standard Oil Co. (1870-1911); endowed four charitable corporations—Rockefeller Foundation, General Education Board, Laura Spellman Rockefeller Memorial, Rockefeller Institute for Medical Research (died 1937).

1862 Ella Reeve Bloor, a founder of American Communist Party, was born in Staten Island, N.Y.; known as "Mother Bloor" (died 1951).

1868 *Daily New Mexico* was published, the first newspaper in the state.

1869 William Vaughn Moody, poet and playwright, was born in Spencer, Ind.; wrote several hit plays (*The Great Divide, The Faith Healer*) (died 1910).

1872 Joseph M. Flint, surgeon and educator, was born in Chicago; professor, California (1901-07) and Yale (1907-21); organized first mobile hospital for troops in France (died 1944).

1872 Harry Von Tilzer, composer, was born in Detroit, brother of Albert Von Tilzer (3/29/1878); wrote many hits ("Bird in a Gilded Cage;" "Wait Till the Sun Shines, Nellie;" "I Want a Girl Just Like the Girl;" "In the Evening by the Moonlight") (died 1946).

1881 Mantis J. Van Sweringen, railroad executive, was born in Wooster, Ohio; with his brother, Otis (4/24/1879), developed Shaker Heights, a Cleveland suburb, and built street railway to it; bought Nickel Plate Railroad (1916), later bought others, at one time controlling 21,000 miles of railroad (died 1935).

1882 Percy A. Grainger, pianist and composer, was born in Melbourne, Australia; wrote many popular numbers ("Country Garden") (died 1961).

1889 John L. Sullivan won the heavyweight boxing championship from Jake Kilrain in Richburg, Miss., the last bare knuckles bout.

1891 Warren G. Harding was married to Florence K. DeWolfe in Marion, Ohio.

1896 William Jennings Bryan delivered his "Cross of Gold" speech in favor of silver coinage at the Democratic National Convention in Chicago, saying in part: "You shall not press down upon the brow of labor, this crown of thorns; you shall not crucify mankind upon a cross of gold;" nominated for president.

1899 David E. Lilienthal, public official, was born in Morton, Ill.; with Tennessee Valley Authority (1933-46), chairman (1941-46); chairman, Atomic Energy Commission (1946-50) (died 1981).

1900 George Antheil, composer, was born in Trenton, N.J.; concert pianist, ultra-modern composer (*Ballet Mecanique, Transatlantic, Archipelago*) (died 1959).

1906 Philip C. Johnson, architect, was born in Cleveland; best known for functionalist glass and steel buildings (Seagram Building, New York City; New York State Theater, Lincoln Center).

1907 George W. Romney, public official and auto manufacturer, was born in Chihuahua, Mexico to American parents; president, American Motors (1954-62);

governor of Michigan (1963-69); Secretary of Housing & Urban Development (1969-73).

1908 Nelson A. Rockefeller, public official, was born in Bar Harbor, Me., son of John D. Rockefeller Jr. (1/29/1874); Assistant Secretary of State (1944-45); Undersecretary of HEW (1952-56); governor of New York (1958-73); Vice President (1974-77) (died 1979).

1914 Billy Eckstine, a leading singer of 1940s-50s, was born in Pittsburgh.

1931 Roone Arledge, radio/television executive, was born in Forest Hills, N.Y.; head of ABC sports, news operations.

1937 Roald Hoffman, chemist, was born in Zloezow, Poland; shared 1981 Nobel Chemistry Prize for work in developing quantum mechanics rules which allow chemists to predict outcome of chemical reactions.

1950 Gen. Douglas MacArthur was named commander-in-chief of UN troops in Korea.

1957 Grace A. Coolidge, widow of President Coolidge, died in Northampton, Mass. at 78.

1976 Former President Nixon was disbarred by the Appellate Division, New York State Supreme Court, on charges of obstruction of justice in the Watergate investigation.

JULY 9

1577 Thomas W. De La Warr, colonial administrator, was born in England; named first governor and captain general of the Virginia colony (1610-11); returned to England to seek aid for the colony, died while returning to Virginia (1618).

1677 Sir William Berkeley, colonial governor, died at 71; had served as governor of Virginia (1642-76).

1750 Thomas Posey, Revolutionary officer and legislator, was born in Fairfax County, Va.; saw action at Saratoga, Stony Point; represented Louisiana in the Senate (1812-13) and served Indiana Territory as governor (1813-16) (died 1818).

1755 Gen. Edward Braddock, who arrived with 1450 men from England, was defeated by the French and Indians in the Battle of the Wilderness, on the Monongahela River; Braddock was mortally wounded, retreat was led by George Washington, who was in command of 450 colonial troops; British lost nearly 1000 men.

1766 Jacob Perkins, inventor, was born in Newburyport, Mass.; invented machine that cut and headed nails and tacks in one operation (c 1790); developed steel plates for printing bank notes, postage stamps (died 1849).

1793 Five-day constitutional convention ended in Windsor, completing Vermont's constitution; adopted by the legislature Nov 2, 1796.

1802 Thomas Davenport, inventor, was born in Williamsport, Vt.; developed first commercially-successful electric motor (1834) (died 1851).

1819 Elias Howe, inventor, was born in Spencer, Mass.; invented first practical sewing machine (1846) (died 1867).

1828 Claus Spreckels, sugar refiner, was born in Lamstedt, Germany; known as the "sugar king;" founder, Bay Sugar Refining Co. (1863), later became California Sugar; developed sugar plantations in Hawaii (died 1908).

1832 President Jackson named the first Commissioner of Indian Affairs; part of the War Department until 1849.

1846 American troops under Commodore John B. Montgomery occupied San Francisco.

1847 Edwin J. Houston, electrical engineer, was born in Alexandria, Va.; co-inventor of arc lighting system (1881) (died 1914).

1850 President Taylor died of coronary thrombosis at 66 in the White House after serving little more than a year.

1856 Daniel Guggenheim, industrialist and philanthropist, was born in Philadelphia, son of Meyer Guggenheim (2/1/1828); headed, American Refining & Smelting Co. (1905-19); founder, Guggenheim Foundation (died 1930).

1856 Nikola Tesla, electrician and inventor, was born in Smiljan, Yugoslavia (then Austria); inventor of motors, generators, transformers, Tesla coil, a system of arc lighting, wireless system of communication and power transmission, devices which made alternating current practical (died 1943).

1858 Franz Boas, anthropologist, was born in Minden, Germany; with Columbia U. (1896-1942); established modern structure of anthropology (died 1942).

1858 Richard A. Ballinger, public official, was born in Boonesboro, Iowa; Interior Secretary (1909-11), target of criticism and investigation of Alaska coal land claims; cleared, then resigned (died 1922).

1863 Port Hudson, Miss., untenable after fall of Vicksburg, fell to Union troops after six-week siege.

1864 Confederate troops under Gen. Jubal A. Early crossed the Potomac River into Maryland, met Union force at Monocacy, near Frederick, and held in check.

1870 Charles Hayden, banker, was born in Boston; founder, Hayden, Stone & Co., gave $150,000 for equipment for New York City planetarium named for him (died 1937).

1877 Bell Telephone Co. was formed, succeeding Bell Patent Association, the first telephone company.

1878 Hans V. Kaltenborn, newspaper and radio correspondent, was born in Milwaukee; on air 102 times in 18 days during Munich crisis (died 1965).

1881 Samuel L. Rothafel, theater operator, was born in Stillwater, Minn.; known as "Roxy," best remembered for Radio City Music Hall and development of precision dancers (Rockettes) (died 1936).

1887 Samuel Eliot Morison, historian, was born in Boston; author (*Admiral of the Ocean Sea, John Paul Jones*); as official American naval historian, he prepared 15-volume history of the Navy in World War II (died 1976).

1894 Dorothy Thompson, journalist and author, was born in Lancaster, N.Y.; syndicated columnist, foreign correspondent; wife of Sinclair Lewis (1928-42) (died 1961).

1897 Albert C. Wedemeyer, World War II general, was born in Omaha; commander, American forces in China (1944-46) (died 1989).

1908 Paul Brown, football coach, was born in Norwalk, Ohio; led Cleveland Browns (1946-62), Cincinnati Bengals (1968-76).

1911 John A. Wheeler, physicist, was born in Jacksonville, Fla.; received 1968 Enrico Fermi Award for his work in nuclear fission.

1947 O(renthal) J. Simpson, football player, was born in San Francisco; starred with U. of Southern California, Buffalo Bills (1969-77).

1974 Former Supreme Court Chief Justice Earl Warren died in Washington at 83.

1982 A Pan American Boeing 727 crashed after takeoff from Kenner, La.; killed 145 persons in the plane, eight on the ground.

JULY 10

1754 Delegates from New England, New York, Pennsylvania, and Maryland, meeting in Albany, approved a "Plan of Union" (mostly written by Benjamin Franklin), which called for a union of all colonies, except Georgia and Nova Scotia, under a president-general, appointed and paid by the Crown, and a council; the plan was rejected by the colonies and Great Britain.

1761 George Clinton, colonial governor, died at 75; governor of New York (1743-53).

1792 George M. Dallas, Vice-President (1845-49), was born in Philadelphia; represented Pennsylvania in the Senate (1831-33); minister to Russia (1837-39), to Great Britain (1856-61); Dallas, Tex. named for him (died 1864).

1795 President Washington issued the first presidential amnesty, or pardon, to all people involved in the Whiskey Rebellion on their signing an oath of allegiance to the United States.

1821 Christopher C. Augur, Union general, was born in Kendall, N.Y.; served in Mexican War, commanded defense of Washington (1863), various other commands (died 1898).

1825 Richard King, rancher, was born in Orange County, N.Y.; developed world's largest ranch, in Texas (600,000 acres at the time of his death, eventually more than one million acres) (died 1885).

1832 President Jackson vetoed a bill to re-charter the Second Bank of the United States, which became a major issue in his re-election campaign; bank had been in existence 20 years; federal funds were withdrawn in Sept and placed in state banks.

1834 James A.M. Whistler, artist, was born in Lowell, Mass.; noted painter, best known for his *Portrait of My Mother*; spent most of life in Europe (died 1903).

1839 Adolphus Busch, brewer, was born in Mainz, Germany; founder, head, Anheuser Busch Co. in St. Louis (1861); pioneered in pasteurization of beer, making long-distance unrefrigerated shipping possible (died 1913).

1850 Vice President Millard Fillmore was sworn in as president on the death of President Taylor.

1867 Finley Peter Dunne, journalist, was born in Chicago; remembered for his sketches of an Irish bartender, Mr. Dooley (died 1936).

1875 Mary M. Bethune, educator, was born in Mayesville, S.C.; founded school for black girls in Daytona, Fla. (1904); merged (1923) with Cookman

Institute to form Bethune-Cookman College, of which she was president (1923-42, 1946-47); founder, National Council of Negro Women (1937) (died 1955).

1888 Graham McNamee, radio announcer, was born in Washington; most popular announcer and master of ceremonies in 1930s (died 1942).

1889 Julia G. Tyler, widow of President Tyler, died in Richmond, Va. at 69.

1890 Wyoming became the 44th state.

1891 Rexford G. Tugwell, economist, was born in Sinclairville, N.Y.; member of the Roosevelt "brain trust;" governor, Puerto Rico (1941-46) (died 1979).

1894 Jimmy McHugh, composer, was born in Boston; composer of many hits ("I Can't Give You Anything But Love," "I Feel a Song Coming On," "Coming in on a Wing and a Prayer") (died 1969).

1897 John Gilbert, silent screen actor, was born in Logan, Utah (died 1936).

1902 Maurice N. Eisendrath, religious leader, was born in Chicago; President, Union of American Hebrew Congregations (1946-73) (died 1973).

1907 Federal Government filed suit against 65 corporations and 27 persons of the American Tobacco Co. as a combination in restraint of trade.

1919 Senate began consideration of the Versailles Treaty and the League of Nations; voted down initially Nov 19, reconsidered Mar 19, 1920.

1920 David Brinkley, television newsman, was born in Wilmington, N.C.; served with NBC (1951-81); teaming with Chet Huntley (1956-70), John Chancellor (1970-81); then to ABC as host of weekly news talk show.

1920 Owen Chamberlain, physicist, was born in San Francisco; shared 1959 Nobel Physics Prize for demonstrating existence of anti-proton.

1925 Scopes Trial, which challenged the teaching of evolutionary theory in school, began in Dayton, Tenn., pitting Clarence S. Darrow for the defense against a prosecution team which included William Jennings Bryan, who died a day after the trial ended; trial ended July 25 with the conviction and fining ($100) of John Thomas Scopes, the teacher.

1932 Jerry Herman, composer and lyricist, was born in New York City; wrote several hit musicals (*Hello, Dolly; Mame*).

1943 Arthur Ashe, tennis player, was born in Richmond, Va.; first black star in men's tennis, captain of U.S. Davis Cup team; Wimbledon champion (1975).

1943 Combined American, British, and Canadian amphibious forces invaded Sicily; ended successfully Aug 17 at a cost of 7400 American casualities.

1947 Arlo Guthrie, folk singer and composer, was born in New York City, son of Woody Guthrie (7/14/1912).

1962 Telstar I relayed the first transmission of television signals between the United States and Europe.

1985 Gunmen in Beirut kidnapped Thomas Sutherland, a dean at American University.

JULY 11

1681 A concession to the province of Pennsylvania was issued by William Penn to regulate land sales and grants, and to deal with Indian relations.

1767 John Quincy Adams, sixth president (1825-29), was born in Braintree (now Quincy), Mass., son of President John Adams; represented Massachusetts in the Senate (1803-08) and House (1831-48); minister to Netherlands (1794-96), to Germany (1796-1801), to Russia (1809-11), to Great Britain (1815); chief peace negotiator after War of 1812; Secretary of State (1817-25) (died 1848).

1774 Sir William Johnson, British official, died at 59; superintendent of Indian Affairs (1755-74).

1782 The British evacuated Savannah, which they had held since Dec 29, 1778.

1792 British evacuated posts west of the Alleghenies and Detroit was occupied by Capt. Moses Porter and 65 American soldiers.

1798 Marine Corps was established.

1804 Aaron Burr fatally wounded Alexander Hamilton in a duel at Weehawken, N.J. brought on by derogatory remarks by Hamilton during Burr's campaign for New York governor; Hamilton reportedly said Burr was "a dangerous man, and one who ought not to be trusted with the reins of government;" Hamilton died the next day.

1806 James Smith, Dublin-born lawyer, died at 87; a signer of the Declaration of Independence.

1813 Gen. Peter B. Porter led Americans in defeating the British in an attack on the Black Rock section of Buffalo.

1831 Henry C. Timken, inventor and manufacturer, was born near Hamburg, Germany; invented special type of carriage spring (1877) and a tapered roller bearing (1898); founder, Timken Roller Bearing Axle Co. (1898) (died 1909).

1836 Specie circular was issued by Treasury Secretary Levi Woodbury which stemmed violent speculation in public lands and revealed the unsoundness of many small Western banks.

1838 John Wanamaker, merchant, was born in Philadelphia; established one of first major department stores (1869), was the first to advertise, to offer full refunds; Postmaster General (1889-93) (died 1922).

1861 George W. Norris, legislator, was born in Sandusky County, Ohio; represented Nebraska in the House (1903-13) and Senate (1914-43); opposed American entry into World War II; leader in forming Tennessee Valley Authority, the 20th Amendment (died 1944).

1862 President Lincoln named Gen. Henry Halleck as general-in-chief of Union forces, replacing Gen. George McClellan.

1864 Confederate troops under Gen. Jubal A. Early reached within six miles of Washington, but retreated during the night.

1878 President Hayes removed Chester A. Arthur from post of Collector of the Port of New York.

1881 Clarence Budington Kelland, author, was born in Portland, Mich.; short story writer, created character of Scattergood Baines (died 1964).

1890 President Benjamin Harrison signed an act authorizing a bridge across the Hudson River, connecting New York and New Jersey.

1892 Armed union miners expelled nonunion miners and fought a pitched battle at the lead and silver mines at Coeur d'Alene, Ida.; trouble continued until 1905.

1899 E(lwyn) B. White, author, was born in Mt. Vernon, N.Y.; wrote many essays and items for *The New Yorker*; author (*Stuart Little, Charlotte's Web, Trumpet of the Swan*) (died 1985).

1915 Colin Kelly, first American World War II hero, was born in Madison, Fla.; piloted disabled bomber into a Japanese vessel after his crew bailed out (1941).

1920 Yul Brynner, actor, was born on Sakhalin Island, Japan; best remembered for *The King and I* (died 1985).

1927 Theodore H. Maiman, physicist, was born in Los Angeles; built first laser; founder, president, Laser Video Corp., Korad Corp.

1932 Nat(haniel W.) Niles, a pioneer in American figure skating, died in Boston at 45; won U.S. men's title in 1918, 1925, 1927 and with Theresa W. Blanchard won the pairs title nine times.

1936 President Franklin Roosevelt dedicated the Triborough Bridge in New York City.

1955 Air Force Academy accepted the first class of 306 cadets at an interim site at Lowery Air Force Base, Colorado.

1979 An orbiting unmanned space vehicle, *Skylab*, disintegrated over Australia and the Indian Ocean.

JULY 12

1808 The *Missouri Gazette* was published by Joseph Charles in St. Louis, the first newspaper west of the Mississippi; later became the *St. Louis Republican*.

1817 Henry David Thoreau, author and philosopher, was born in Concord, Mass.; one of the great figures in American literary and intellectual history; author (*Walden, A Week on the Concord and Merrimack Rivers*) (died 1862).

1821 Daniel H. Hill, Confederate general, was born in York District, S.C.; served in Peninsular Campaign, Antietam, Chickamauga (died 1889).

1840 Benjamin Altman, merchant, was born in New York City; opened small dry goods store (1865), developed into B. Altman & Co. department store; donated large art collection to Metropolitan Museum of Art (died 1913).

1843 Joseph Smith, Mormon leader, announced in Nauvoo, Ill. that a divine revelation had sanctioned the practice of polygamy; announcement caused bitter feelings among both Mormons and non-Mormons.

1849 Dolley Madison, widow of President Madison, died in Washington at 81.

1854 George Eastman, camera inventor, was born in Waterville, N.Y.; perfected method for making photographic dry plates (1880) and flexible film (1884); invented Kodak, first low-priced popularly-available camera (1888); founder, Eastman School of Music, Rochester, N.Y. (died 1932).

1871 A riot involving Irish Catholics and Protestants in New York City left 52 persons dead.

1895 R. Buckminster Fuller, builder and designer, was born in Milton, Mass.; known for his dymaxion inventions, developed the geodesic dome (died 1983).

1895 Oscar Hammerstein II, lyricist, was born in New York City, nephew of Oscar Hammerstein I (5/8/1846); lyricist of popular songs ("Rose Marie," "Sunny," "Who," "My Blue Heaven") and musicals (*Show Boat, New Moon, Oklahoma, Carousel, South*

Pacific, The King and I, The Flower Drum Song, The Sound of Music) (died 1960).

1895 Kirsten Flagstad, opera soprano, was born in Evanger, Norway; specialized in Wagnerian roles (died 1962).

1908 Milton Berle, entertainer, was born in New York City; starred on stage and television; the first television superstar (Uncle Miltie) (1948-67).

1913 Willis E. Lamb Jr., physicist, was born in Los Angeles; shared 1955 Nobel Physics Prize for work on the hydrogen spectrum.

1917 Andrew N. Wyeth, artist, was born in Chadds Ford, Pa., son of Newell C. Wyeth (*see* 10/22/1822); one of most popular painters of his time.

1925 Roger B. Smith, automaker, was born in Columbus, Ohio; chairman/chief executive officer, General Motors (1981-).

1934 Van (H. Levan) Cliburn, concert pianist, was born in Shreveport, La.; winner of International Tschaikowsky Piano Competition (1958).

1937 Bill Cosby, entertainer, was born in Philadelphia; comedian, first black with a starring role in a television series (*I Spy*).

1967 Black riots in Newark began, lasting five days during which 26 were killed, 1500 injured, and 1000 arrested; considerable property damage.

1974 John D. Erlichman, presidential aide, and three others were found guilty of conspiring to violate the civil rights of Dr. Lewis Fielding, psychiatrist to the man who leaked the Pentagon Papers, by breaking into his office.

1980 Richard Queen, an American hostage held at the embassy in Teheran, was released because of poor health.

1989 President Bush addressed the Hungarian Parliament in Budapest, the first president to do so.

JULY 13

1729 John Parker, colonial soldier, was born in Lexington, Mass.; commanded the Minutemen at Lexington on Apr 19, 1775; reputedly told his men: "Stand your ground. Don't fire unless fired upon. But if they mean to have a war, let it begin here." (died 1775).

1753 William Penn Academy in Philadelphia was chartered; later became the U. of Pennsylvania.

1787 The Continental Congress adopted the Northwest Ordinance, setting up a government for the area north of the Ohio River and west of New York, guaranteeing freedom of religion, support for schools, no slavery; the ordinance stated: "Religion, morality, and knowledge, being necessary to good government and the happiness of mankind, schools and the means of education shall forever be encouraged."

1814 José S. Alemany, Catholic prelate, was born in Vich, Spain; missionary bishop to the Southwest, first archbishop of San Francisco (1853-84) (died 1888).

1815 James A. Seddon, Confederate leader, was born in Fredericksburg, Va.; served as Secretary of War (1862-65) (died 1880).

1821 Nathan Bedford Forrest, Confederate general, was born in Bedford County, Tenn.; headed cavalry raiding force (died 1877).

1824 James I. Waddell, Confederate naval officer, was born in Pittsboro, N.C.; commanded the *Shenandoah*, which raided American whaling ships in the Pacific (died 1886).

1857 Franklin H. Martin, surgeon, was born in Jefferson County, Wis.; founder, American College of Surgeons; founder, editor, *Surgery, Gynecology and Obstetrics* (died 1935).

1862 Gen. Nathan Bedford Forrest led 2000 Confederate troops in capture of Murfreesboro, Tenn.

1863 Union troops captured Yazoo City, Miss.

1863 Four days of draft riots began in New York City, resulting in about 75 deaths; rioters protested provision allowing money payments in place of military service; payments ended in 1864.

1864 John Jacob Astor IV, businessman, was born in Rhinebeck, N.Y., great grandson of John Jacob Astor (7/17/1763); increased family fortune with vast New York City real estate holdings; died in sinking of the *Titanic* in 1912.

1865 An editorial by Horace Greeley in the *New York Tribune* used the expression, "Go west, young man, go west!;" he later gave credit for the phrase to J.L.B. Soule, who had used it in 1851 in the *Terre Haute* (Ind.) *Express*.

1886 Edward J. Flanagan, founder of Boys Town, was born in Roscommon, Ireland; founded Home for Boys near Omaha (1917), which later became Boys Town (died 1948).

1889 Stan(ley) Coveleski, baseball pitcher (Indians) who won 214 games, was born in Shamokin, Pa.; named to Baseball Hall of Fame (died 1984).

1890 A tornado caused the drowning deaths of 100 persons at Lake Pepin, Minn.

1901 Mickey (Edward P.) Walker, welterweight (1922-26) and middleweight (1926-31) boxing champion, was born in Elizabeth, N.J. (died 1981).

1912 The Senate declared the seat of William L. Lorimer of Illinois vacant after a two-year investigation of bribery charges.

1913 Dave Garroway, television personality, was born in Schenectady; popular in 1950s with own show and the *Today Show*, which he began (died 1983).

1917 An executive order called 678,000 men into military service from among those who had registered earlier.

1977 A 25-hour power failure struck the New York City area, leading to extensive looting; 3776 looters were arrested, property damages estimated at $135 million.

1985 President Reagan underwent successful surgery on the abdomen at the Bethesda Naval Medical Center; returned to the White House July 20.

JULY 14

1782 Jesse D. Elliott, War of 1812 naval officer, was born in Hagerstown, Md.; captured two British brigs on Lake Erie, the first American success of the war; second in command to Perry (died 1845).

1832 President Jackson signed a tariff act amending the 1828 act, but it was still unsatisfactory to the South.

1839 John C. Gray, lawyer, was born in Brighton, Mass.; a leading authority on real property law; co-founder, *American Law Review* (1866) (died 1915).

1853 Commodore Matthew C. Perry was received by Japanese Lord of Toda and negotiated a treaty opening Japan to American commerce.

1853 The first American world's fair—Exhibition of Industry of All Nations—opened in the new Crystal Palace in New York City with President Pierce on hand.

1855 New Hampshire enacted a prohibition law.

1857 Frederick L. Maytag, appliance manufacturer, was born in Elgin, Ill.; founder, Maytag Co. (1909) (died 1937).

1860 Owen Wister, author, was born in Philadelphia; remembered for *The Virginian*, which helped establish the cowboy as an American hero (died 1938).

1865 Arthur Capper, editor and public official, was born in Garnett, Kan.; editor, publisher, *Topeka Daily Capital*, several agricultural magazines; served as governor (1915-19) and represented Kansas in the Senate (1919-49) (died 1951).

1870 Congress approved an annual pension of $3000 to Mary Todd Lincoln, widow of President Lincoln; increased to $5000 in 1882.

1883 The first class of rabbis was ordained in the United States after graduating from Hebrew Union College in Cincinnati.

1898 Albert D. Chandler, public official, was born in Corydon, Ky.; known as "Happy," he served Kentucky as governor (1935-39, 1955-59) and represented it in the Senate (1939-45); commissioner of baseball (1945-51), named to Baseball Hall of Fame.

1903 Irving Stone, author, was born in San Francisco; wrote numerous popular books (*Lust for Life, The Agony and the Ecstasy, The President's Lady, Sailor on Horseback*) (died 1989).

1904 Isaac B. Singer, Yiddish author, was born in Radzymin, Poland; awarded 1978 Nobel Literature Prize (*The Family Moskat, The Magician of Lublin, The Manor*).

1906 William H. Tunner, Air Forces general who directed the Berlin Airlift, was born in Elizabeth, N.J. (died 1983).

1912 Woody (Woodrow W.) Guthrie, folk singer and composer, was born in Okemah, Okla.; wrote more than 1000 songs about American life (died 1967).

1913 Gerald R. Ford, 38th president (1974-77), was born in Omaha as Lesie L. King Jr. and assumed the name of his stepfather after he was formally adopted; represented Michigan in the House (1949-73); appointed Vice President (1973) on the resignation of Spiro T. Agnew, became president on the resignation of President Nixon.

1927 John Chancellor, television newsman and commentator, was born in Chicago; with NBC (1960-); director, Voice of America (1966-67).

1938 Howard Hughes completed record around-the-world flight in three days, 19 hours, 14 minutes and 28 seconds.

1986 One hundred sixty American soldiers arrived in Bolivia to help fight against production of cocaine.

JULY 15

1704 August G. Spangenberg, religious leader, was born in Klettenburg, Germany; founder, Moravian Church in North America, bishop (1735-62); returned to Germany (died 1792).

1779 Clement Clark Moore, lexicographer and author, was born in New York City, son of Benjamin Moore (10/5/1748); best known for the ballad: "'Twas the night before Christmas...;" helped found General Theological Seminary, New York City (1819) (died 1863).

1779 Gen. Anthony Wayne led 1200 men in a night bayonet attack on Stony Point, N.Y., a fort along the Hudson River western shore; captured all 700 British troops, dismantled the fort.

1796 Thomas Bulfinch, author, was born in Newton, Mass., son of Charles Bulfinch (8/8/1763); remembered for *Mythology* and *The Age of Fable* (died 1867).

1802 Robert Aitken, Scottish-born printer and engraver, died at 68; his major accomplishment, according to a Library of Congress catalog, was "the Aitken Bible, the first complete English Bible printed in America, and bearing an American imprint, and the only one authorized and approved by Congress to this day (June 1902)" (1781).

1813 The British fleet arrived in the Potomac River.

1850 Maria Frances Xavier Cabrini, first American saint, was born in Lodigiano, Italy; founder, Missionary Sisters of the Sacred Heart (1880), came to the United States (1889), naturalized; canonized 1946 (died 1917).

1900 Thomas Francis Jr., physician, was born in Gas City, Ind.; conducted an evaluation program of the Salk polio vaccine test (died 1969).

1901 Truman B. Douglass, clergyman, was born in Grinnell, Iowa; a moving spirit in unification of the Congregational and the Evangelical and Reformed denominations into the United Church of Christ (1957) (died 1969).

1903 Walter D. Edmonds, author, was born in Boonville, N.Y.; wrote several popular novels (*Rome Haul, Drums Along the Mohawk*).

1913 Augustus O. Bacon of Georgia became the first senator elected by popular vote.

1918 A three-day German attack began in the fourth battle of Champagne; turned back by 85,000 American and French troops.

1921 R. Bruce Merrifield, chemist, was born in Ft. Worth, Tex.; 1984 Nobel Chemistry Prize for synthesizing peptide and protein molecules.

1922 Leon M. Lederman, physicist, was born in New York City; shared 1988 Nobel Prize in Physics for helping capture neutrinos in a high-energy beam to examine the structure of atomic particles.

1933 Wiley Post began his round-the-world solo flight of 15,596 miles, which took seven days, 18 hours and 49-1/2 minutes.

1946 Linda Ronstadt, popular singer, was born in Tucson, Ariz.

1952 The first successful transatlantic helicopter flight started at Westover Air Force Base in Massachusetts; ended July 31 at Prestwick, Scotland.

1975 The United States and Soviet Russia began the Apollo-Soyuz space mission; the two spacecraft linked up in space two days later and orbited together for two days.

1988 The 17-man General Executive Board of the Teamsters Union elected William J. McCarthy as the new president to succeed the late Jackie Presser; the board by one vote rejected Presser's handpicked candidate, Secretary-Treasurer Weldon Mathis.

JULY 16

1661 Sieur d'Pierre Iberville, French explorer, was born in Montreal, Canada; established first French settlement in Louisiana, at what is now Biloxi, later at Mobile (1698) (died 1706).

1741 Vitus Bering, a Danish sea captain in the service of Russia, sighted the volcano of St. Elias in what is now Alaska; later landed at Kodiak.

1769 The Spanish Franciscan missionary, Junipero Serra, founded a mission at San Diego, the first European settlement in California.

1769 Edmund Fanning, sea captain and explorer, was born in Stonington, Conn.; called the Pathfinder of the Pacific, he discovered islands named for him (died 1841).

1782 A treaty was signed with France setting the amount owed by the United States ($7,037,037) to be repaid at 1.5 million livres a year beginning in 1785, continuing for 12 years.

1787 The Continental Convention accepted the Connecticut Compromise, which created the present congressional structure—equal representation in the Senate, the lower house based on population.

1790 President Washington signed an act setting Philadelphia as the seat of government from 1790 to 1800, during which a federal city was to be created along the Potomac River.

1798 The Public Health Service began with legislation authorizing Marine Hospitals to care for American merchant seamen.

1821 Mary Baker Eddy, founder of Christian Science Church, was born in Bow, N.H.; as an invalid, she sought many types of healing, founded the spiritual and metaphysical system known as Christian Science; wrote *Science and Health*, explaining the system; founded *Christian Science Monitor* (1883) (died 1910).

1829 Robert B. Potter, Union general, was born in Schenectady, N.Y., son of Alonzo Potter (7/6/1800); saw action at Fredericksburg, Vicksburg (died 1887).

1845 Theodore N. Vail, industrialist, was born near Minerva, Ohio, cousin of Alfred L. Vail (9/25/1807); general superintendent, railway mails; general manager, Bell Telephone Co. (1878-87); first president, American Telephone & Telegraph Co. (1885-89, 1907-19) (died 1920).

1863 After a one-week siege, Jackson, Miss. was evacuated by Confederate troops.

1874 Joseph L. Goldberger, public health physician, was born in Austria; with Public Health Service, discovered nature of and cure for pellagra (died 1929).

1874 Henry S. Tucker, Episcopal presiding bishop (1937-46), was born in Warsaw, Va.; Bishop of Virginia (1927-46) (died 1959).

1877 Ivy L. Lee, pioneer publicist, was born in Cedartown, Ga.; developed public relations as a profession; served Democratic National Committee, Pennsylvania Railroad, John D. Rockefeller (died 1934).

1877 Bela Schick, pediatrician, was born in Boglar, Hungary; developed test for susceptibility to diptheria; chief pediatrician, Mt. Sinai Hospital, New York City (died 1967).

1880 Kathleen Norris, author, was born in San Francisco; author of several popular novels (*The Rich Mrs. Burgoyne, Mother, Saturday's Child, The Sea Gull*) (died 1966).

1881 Louis F. Bachrach, photographer, was born in Baltimore; headed, Bachrach, Inc. (1915-55) (died 1963).

1882 Mary Todd Lincoln, widow of President Lincoln, died in Springfield, Ill. at 63.

1898 Santiago, with a garrison of 24,000, surrendered, virtually ending the Spanish-American War.

1903 Carmen Lombardo, vocalist with Guy Lombardo band, was born in London, Canada (died 1971).

1907 Barbara Stanwyck, screen actress, was born in Brooklyn; starred in many films, television series (*Big Valley*) (died 1990).

1911 Ginger (Virginia) Rogers, screen actress, was born in Independence, Mo.; starred with Fred Astaire in many musicals (*Roberta, Top Hat, Shall We Dance?*).

1935 The first automatic parking meter was installed in Oklahoma City.

1945 The first atomic bomb, produced in Los Alamos, N.M., was successfully exploded at Alamagordo, N.M.

1946 Bureau of Land Management was created in the Interior Department by consolidating the General Land Office and Grazing Service.

JULY 17

1744 Elbridge Gerry, Vice President (1813-14), was born in Marblehead, Mass.; member of Continental Congress (1776-81, 1782-85) and a signer of the Declaration of Independence; represented Massachusetts in the House (1789-93) and served it as governor (1810, 1811); his name is associated with politicized boundary lines (gerrymandering) (died 1814).

1745 Timothy Pickering, legislator and public official, was born in Salem, Mass.; adjutant general (1777-78), quartermaster general (1781-83), Continental Army; Postmaster General (1791-95), Secretary of War (1795), Secretary of State (1795-1800); represented Massachusetts in the Senate (1803-11) and House (1813-17) (died 1829).

1752 Gabriel Johnston, colonial governor, died at 53; served as governor of North Carolina (1734-52).

1754 King's (later Columbia) College opened in New York City.

1763 John Jacob Astor, fur trader and financier, was born in Waldorf, Germany; entered fur trade (1784), founded Astoria (1811) as a trading post, lost it to the British (1813); monopolized Mississippi and upper Missouri valleys fur trade; invested heavily in New York City real estate (died 1848).

1768 Stephen T. Badin, Catholic missionary, was born in Orleans, France; first Catholic priest ordained in the United States (1793); spent 26 years riding among settlements in Kentucky; about 1832, obtained the land on which Notre Dame U. was founded ten years later (died 1853).

1812 Combined British and Indian force took the garrison at Mackinac, where Lakes Huron and Michigan join.

1856 A railroad wreck near Philadelphia killed 66 children on an outing.

1864 Union troops under Gen. William T. Sherman crossed the Chattahoochee River, eight miles from Atlanta.

1864 James R. Gilmore, unofficial representative of President Lincoln, met with Confederate president, Jefferson Davis, in Richmond to discuss terms for ending war; conference failed because Union would not recognize Confederacy independence.

1889 Erle Stanley Gardner, lawyer and author, was born in Malden, Mass.; wrote the popular Perry Mason mystery series (died 1970).

1899 James Cagney, screen actor, was born in New York City; numerous starring roles (*Yankee Doodle Dandy, Mr. Roberts*) (died 1986).

1916 Federal Farm Loan Act went into effect, providing long-term credit, set up 12 farm loan banks; members of Loan Board named July 27.

1917 Lou(is) Boudreau, baseball player/manager (Indians, Red Sox), was born in Harvey, Ill.; named to Baseball Hall of Fame.

1938 Douglas ("Wrong Way") Corrigan flew the Atlantic from Brooklyn to Dublin despite lack of permission; claimed he thought he was flying to Los Angeles.

1944 An explosion of ammunition dumps in Port Chicago, Cal. killed more than 300 persons.

1945 President Truman, Prime Minister Winston Churchill (later Clement Atlee), and Premier Stalin met until Aug 2 in Potsdam, Germany to discuss postwar European problems.

1948 Delegates from 13 Southern states formed the Dixiecrats in Birmingham and nominated J. Strom Thurmond for president.

1955 Disneyland opened in Anaheim, Cal.

1975 Three American astronauts (Tom Stafford, Donald K. Slayton, Vance Brand) in an Apollo spacecraft linked up with a Soviet Soyuz spacecraft 140 miles above the earth and exchanged visits with the two Soviet cosmonauts.

1981 Two skywalks in the Hyatt Regency Hotel in Kansas City, Mo. collapsed, killing 113 people.

1984 George M. Low, Austrian-born educator and space scientist, died at 58; with NASA and predecessor agency (1949-76), directed planning for first manned moon landing and walk; president, Rensselaer Polytechnic Institute.

1986 LTV Corporation, second largest steel company, filed for bankruptcy, the largest industrial company ever to file for bankruptcy in United States.

1987 The Dow Jones industrial average closed above 2500 (2510.04) for the first time as the bull market continued.

JULY 18

1543 Survivors of the DeSoto expedition, led by Luis Moscosco, arrived at Tampa Bay, more than four years after it left there.

1663 The charter granted to Rhode Island guaranteed religious freedom regardless of "differences of opinions in matters of religion."

1670 Spain and England signed the Treaty of Madrid in which Spain recognized the right of England to her colonies in the Caribbean and in America.

1757 Royall Tyler, jurist and playwright, was born in Boston; chief justice, Vermont Supreme Court (1807-13); wrote *The Contrast,* the first professionally-produced comedy written by an American (died 1826).

1768 John Dickinson's patriotic ballad, "Song for American Freedom," was printed in the *Boston Gazette.*

1775 The second Continental Congress recommended the establishment of Committees of Safety in all the colonies to carry on the functions of government.

1854 Tom L. Johnson, inventor and street railway operator, was born near Georgetown, Ky.; invented coin farebox for street cars; represented Ohio in the House (1891-95), mayor of Cleveland (1901-09); acquired street railway interests in Indianapolis and Cleveland (died 1911).

1861 Samuel W. Stratton, physicist, was born in Litchfield, Ill.; prepared specifications for creation of Bureau of Standards, served as first director (1901-23); president, MIT (1923-30) (died 1931).

1864 President Lincoln sent Horace Greeley to meet with Confederate peace commissioners in Niagara Falls, Ontario; effort unsuccessful.

1886 Simon B. Buckner Jr., World War II general, was born in Munfordville, Ky., son of Simon B. Buckner (4/1/1823); commandant, West Point (1933-36); commanding general, Alaska (1940-44); headed Okinawa invasion, killed in action (1945).

1890 Charles Erwin Wilson, auto manufacturer, was born in Minerva, Ohio; vice president (1929-40), president (1941-52), General Motors; Secretary of Defense (1953-57) (died 1961).

1896 Patrick A. O'Boyle, Catholic prelate, was born in Scranton, Pa.; archbishop of Washington (1948-73), named cardinal 1967.

1906 Clifford Odets, playwright, was born in Philadelphia; wrote several hit plays (*Waiting for Lefty, Golden Boy*) (died 1963).

1911 Hume Cronyn, actor, was born in London, Canada; starred in various plays (*High Tor, The Fourposter, The Gin Game*).

1913 Red (Richard) Skelton, entertainer, was born in Vincennes, Ind.; starred on television and the screen.

1918 The second Battle of the Marne began, with about 85,000 American troops taking part in a battle that was the war's turning point; battle and major German offensive ended Aug 6.

1921 John H. Glenn Jr., astronaut and legislator, was born in Cambridge, Ohio; first American to orbit the earth (1962); represented Ohio in the Senate (1974-).

1929 Dick Button, figure skater, was born in Englewood, N.J.; gold medalist at 1948 and 1952 Olympics; world figure skating champion (1948-52).

1935 Tenley Albright, the first American woman to win the Olympic medal in figure skating (1956), was born in Newton Centre, Mass.; won American title (1951-56) and world championship (1953, 1955).

1944 American troops captured St. Lo, the French road center connecting Normandy and Brittany.

1947 The Presidential Succession Act was signed, providing that the House Speaker and the Senate President Pro Tem succeed the President before Cabinet members.

1951 Joe Walcott knocked out Ezzard Charles in the seventh round in Pittsburgh to win the world's heavyweight boxing championship.

1955 President Eisenhower attended the five-day Geneva Conference, conferring with British Prime Minister Anthony Eden, French Premier Edgar Faure and Russian Premier Nikolai Bulganin.

1969 A car driven by Sen. Edward M. Kennedy of Massachusetts plunged off a bridge on Chappaquidick Island, Mass.; a 28-year-old secretary, Mary Jo Kopechne, was found drowned in the car.

1984 A gunman killed 21 persons in and near a McDonald's restaurant in San Ysidro, Cal.; the gunman was shot and killed by police.

1988 James C. McKay, independent prosecutor, reported that Attorney General Edwin Meese III had probably broken the law in his personal finances management, but he largely exonerated him of wrongdoing in two major government scandals; McKay said he would not bring criminal charges.

JULY 19

1782 New York proposed a convention of states to amend the Articles of Confederation; Congress did not act on the proposal.

1806 Alexander D. Bache, physicist, was born in Philadelphia; superintendent, U.S. Coast Survey (1843-67); first president, National Academy of Sciences (1863) and Girard College (1836), an incorporator of Smithsonian Institution (died 1867).

1808 John Paterson, Revolutionary general, died at 64; served throughout the war (Bunker Hill, Trenton, Princeton, Valley Forge); represented New York in the House (1803-05).

1814 Samuel Colt, inventor, was born in Hartford; inventor, manufacturer of revolving breech pistol (1835), plant made extensive use of assembly line techniques (died 1862).

1823 George H. Gordon, Union general, was born in Charlestown, Mass.; raised regiment at start of war, serving as brigadier general through the war (died 1886).

1845 A fire in New York City resulted in property loss of $6 million.

1846 Edward C. Pickering, astronomer, was born in Boston, great grandson of Timothy Pickering (7/17/1745); pioneered in using photometric and spectroscopic techniques; director, Harvard Observatory (1876-1919) (died 1919).

1848 The first women's rights convention was held in Seneca Falls, N.Y., involving such persons as Sarah and Angelina Grimké, Lucretia Mott, and Elizabeth Cady Stanton; issued a declaration of sentiments and resolutions.

1860 Lizzie A. Bordon, charged with ax murder of her parents (Aug 4, 1892), was born in Fall River,

Mass.; acquitted after a sensational trial; gave rise to a popular chant of the day: "Lizzie Borden took an ax/And gave her mother 40 whacks,/When she saw what she had done,/She gave her father 41" (died 1927).

1865 Charles H. Mayo, physician, was born in Rochester, Minn.; with brother, William J. Mayo (6/29/1861), formed staff of St. Mary's Hospital, Rochester, which later became the Mayo Clinic on the strength of their $2.8 million gift (died 1939).

1876 Joseph Fielding Smith, Mormon leader, was born in Salt Lake City; president, Council of Twelve of the Church (1951-72) (died 1972).

1885 Malcolm Muir, editor and publisher, was born in Glen Ridge, N.J.; president, McGraw-Hill Inc. (1928-37), created *Business Week* (1929); president, publisher, editor-in-chief, *Newsweek* (1937-61) (died 1979).

1891 Paul V. McNutt, public official, was born in Franklin, Ind.; governor of Indiana (1933-37); high commissioner, Philippines (1937-39, 1945-46), then ambassador (1946-47); chairman, War Manpower Commission (1942-45) (died 1955).

1921 Rosalyn Yalow, medical physicist, was born in New York City; shared 1977 Nobel Physiology/Medicine Prize for research on role of hormones in the chemistry of the body.

1922 George S. McGovern, legislator, was born in Avon, S.D.; represent South Dakota in the House (1957-60) and Senate (1963-77); 1972 Democratic presidential candidate.

1944 American 5th Army captured Leghorn, Italy.

1967 Midair collision of Piedmont Boeing 727 and Cessna 310 near Hendersvonville, N.C. killed 82 persons.

1977 Two days of flooding in Johnstown, Pa. resulted in 68 deaths.

1984 Democratic National convention in San Francisco nominated New York Representative Geraldine A. Ferraro as its vice presidential candidate, the first woman to be named a candidate by a major party.

1989 A United Airlines DC-10 crashed while making an emergency landing at the Sioux City, Iowa airport; 111 died, 187 survived.

JULY 20

1591 Anne Hutchinson, religious liberal, was baptized in Alford, England; preached salvation by individual intuition of God without regard for church; banished from Massachusetts (1637), settled in Rhode Island.; family massacred by Indians (1643).

1605 Samuel de Champlain, on his second of 11 trips to eastern Canada, landed at Nanset Sound on Cape Cod.

1629 Samuel Skelton named pastor of the first church in Massachusetts at Salem; church constituted Aug 6 by an association of 30 persons.

1663 Samuel Stone, Puritan clergyman, died at 61; purchased site of Hartford from the Indians (1636), settled there, serving as minister (1636-63).

1749 George Washington was named official surveyor of Culpeper County, Va.

1789 The first federal navigation act was passed, imposing a duty on ship tonnage.

1832 Alexander L. Holley, builder and designer of steel plants, was born in Lakeville, Conn.; brought Bessemer process to the United States and improved it; began first American Bessemer operation in Troy, N.Y. (1865); built many steel plants (died 1882).

1838 (John) Augustin Daly, producer and playwright, was born in Plymouth, N.C.; drama critic, then adapted plays from French and German; wrote many original plays (*Under the Gaslight, The Red Scarf, Divorce*) (died 1899).

1864 Fighting began around Atlanta (Peach Tree Creek) and ended with Confederate evacuation of the city Sept 1.

1869 Joseph W. Byrns, legislator, was born in Cedar Hill, Tenn.; represented Tennessee in the House (1909-36), serving as majority leader (1932-35) and Speaker (1935-36) (died 1936).

1880 The Egyptian obelisk "Cleopatra's Needle," was placed in Central Park, New York City.

1890 Theda Bara, screen actress, was born in Cincinnati; starred as a "vamp" in silent films (died 1955).

1894 Wiley B. Rutledge Jr., jurist, was born in Cloverport, Ky.; justice, Court of Appeals (1939-43); associate justice, Supreme Court (1943-49) (died 1949).

1901 Heinie (Henry E.) Manush, baseball player, was born in Tuscumbia, Ala.; outfielder, various American League teams (1923-40); lifetime batting average of .330; named to Baseball Hall of Fame (died 1971).

1917 The drawing for the first military draft was held to determine the order of service.

1920 Elliot L. Richardson, public official, was born in Boston; Secretary of HEW (1970-73), Attorney General (1973), Secretary of Defense (1973).

1922 Alan S. Boyd, public official, was born in Jacksonville, Fla.; chairman, Civil Aeronautics Board (1961-65); first Secretary of Transportation (1966-69); chief executive officer, Amtrak (1971-).

1933 Gen. Hugh S. Johnson proclaimed the Blue Eagle as the emblem of the NRA (National Recovery Administration) and industrial recovery; discontinued Sept 5, 1935 following invalidation of the compulsory code system.

1969 Neil A. Armstrong, in flight of Apollo XI, became the first man to set foot on the moon at 4:17:40 EDT, quickly followed by Edwin E. (Buzz) Aldrin.

1976 An unmanned Viking I spacecraft was successfully landed for the first time on Mars.

JULY 21

1667 The Peace of Breda was signed, ending the second Anglo-Dutch War (1664-67) and confirmed British possession of New Netherlands (New York).

1742 John C. Symmes, Revolutionary officer, was born in Southhold, Long Island; served at Monmouth and Short Hills; member, Continental Congress (1785-86); founded colony centered around present Cincinnati (died 1814).

1802 David Hunter, Union general, was born in Washington; president of the commission which tried the Lincoln assassination collaborators; commander, Department of the South (1862), issued order (May 9, 1862) freeing the slaves in his department; order annulled ten days later by President Lincoln (died 1886).

1817 Joseph K. Barnes, physician, was born in Philadelphia; served as surgeon general (1864-82), attended two presidents on their death beds (Lincoln and Garfield) (died 1883).

1824 Stanley Matthews, jurist, was born in Cincinnati; represented Ohio in the Senate (1877-79); associate justice, Supreme Court (1881-89) (died 1889).

1826 Mahon Loomis, inventor, was born in Oppenheim, N.Y.; inventor of numerous electrical devices, pioneer in wireless telegraphy experiments, developed kaolin process to make artificial teeth (died 1886).

1838 John R. Brooke, Union general, was born in Montgomery County, Pa.; served at Fredericksburg, Chancellorville, Gettysburg, and Cold Harbor, where he was severely wounded; served in Spanish-American War, military governor of Puerto Rico and Cuba (1899) (died 1926).

1860 Chauncey Olcott, singer and actor, was born in Buffalo; wrote and sang, "My Wild Irish Rose;" introduced "Mother Macree" (died 1932).

1860 Edward J. Hanna, Catholic prelate, was born in Rochester; archbishop of San Francisco (1915-35) (died 1944).

1861 The first battle of Bull Run (near Manassas, Va.) occurred, with the Union army, led by Gen. Irvin McDowell, routed in several hours by Confederate force under Gens. Joseph E. Johnston and Stonewall Jackson; Union losses were 2900, Confederates 2000.

1864 Francis Folsom Cleveland, wife of President, was born in Buffalo (died 1947).

1867 The vanguard of westward-bound Mormons reached Salt Lake City; the rest of the migration arrived two days later, now celebrated by Mormons as the Day of Deliverance.

1881 George F. Dick, physician, was born in Ft. Wayne, Ind.; with wife, Gladys (12/1/1881); isolated the germ of scarlet fever, developed serum (died 1967).

1881 John Evers, baseball player, was born in Troy, N.Y.; with Cubs (1902-13), was middleman of Tinkers-Evers-Chance double play combination; named to Baseball Hall of Fame (died 1947).

1885 Francis Parkinson Keyes, author, was born in Charlottesville, Va.; wrote many popular novels (*Crescent Carnival, Fielding's Folly*) (died 1970).

1899 Ernest Hemingway, author, was born in Oak Park, Ill.; novelist (*Farewell to Arms, Death in the Afternoon, For Whom the Bell Tolls, The Old Man and the Sea*); awarded 1954 Nobel Literature Prize (died 1961).

1899 Hart Crane, poet, was born in Garrettsville, Ohio; remembered for "White Buidings" and "The Bridge" (died 1932).

1920 Isaac Stern, violinist, was born in Kreminiecz, Russia; considered one of world's greatest.

1930 Congress, in special session, ratified the London Naval Treaty, which had been signed Apr 22 by the United States, Great Britain, France, Italy, and Japan; became effective Jan 1, 1931; expired Dec 31, 1936.

1930 Veterans Administration was established as an independent agency.

1945 The Senate approved American membership in the United Nations Food & Agriculture Organization.

1956 President Eisenhower participated in three-day conference of 18 American republics in Panama City; conference issued declaration calling for solution of economic problems.

1959 The world's first atomic-powered merchant ship, the *Savannah*, was launched in Camden, N.J.

1976 A mysterious ailment, "Legionnaire's disease," killed 29 persons who attended a four-day convention in Philadelphia.

1987 Two Kuwaiti oil tankers were re-registered as American ships, the first of 11, as part of an administration plan to provide naval escorts for Kuwaiti oil shipments through the Persian Gulf.

JULY 22

1585 The first attempt to colonize Roanoke Island, N.C. was made with the arrival of 117 colonists; the attempt ended 1586, but another was made in 1587; the colony was left unprovided because of the Spanish war; colony was never found and became the legendary "lost colony;" the first child to be born in the United States to English parents, Virginia Dare, was born there Aug 18, 1587.

1620 Thirty Pilgrims from Scrooby, England, who had taken refuge in Holland, left Leyden for England to emigrate to America under the leadership of William Brewster.

1686 Gov. Thomas Dongan granted a city charter to Albany by which the city obtained all vacant and unappropriated lands within its limits; Peter Schuyler was named the first mayor.

1796 Moses Cleaveland, leading a party of 46 from the Connecticut Land Co., arrived at the mouth of the Cuyahoga River; laid out a plan for what later became the city of Cleveland.

1849 Emma Lazarus, poet, was born in New York City; best remembered for her lines (from "The New Colossus") inscribed on the pedestal of the Statue of Liberty ("Give me your tired, your poor...") (died 1887).

1861 Gen. George B. McClellan assumed command of the Department of Washington and Northeast Virginia.

1861 Congress enacted a law calling for the enlistment of 500,000 volunteers for a period of six months to not more than three years; three days later, the period of enlistment was changed to service "during the war."

1862 President Lincoln informed his cabinet that he planned to free the slaves on New Year's Day 1863; gave them a draft of the Emancipation Proclamation.

1882 Edward Hopper, artist, was born in Nyack, N.Y.; painter of realistic scenes of contemporary life (*Early Sunday Morning, Nighthawks*) (died 1967).

1888 Selman A. Waksman, microbiologist, was born in Priluki, Russia; awarded 1953 Nobel Physiology/Medicine Prize for co-discovery (1952) of streptomycin (died 1973).

1889 Morris Fishbein, physician and editor, was born in St. Louis; assistant editor (1913-24), editor (1924-49), *AMA Journal* (died 1976).

1891 Ely Culbertson, bridge expert, was born in Poiana de Verbilao, Rumania of American parents; invented a bridge system; editor, *Bridge World Magazine* (1929-55) (died 1955).

1893 Karl A. Menninger, psychologist who was co-founder of the Menninger Clinic in Topeka, Kan., was born in Topeka; co-founders were his father, Charles F., and brother, William C. (10/15/1899).

1893 Jesse Haines, baseball pitcher who won 210 games (Cardinals), was born in Clayton, Ohio; named to Baseball Hall of Fame (died 1978).

1898 Stephen Vincent Benet, poet and author, was born in Bethlehem, Pa., brother of William Rose Benet (2/2/1886); several popular works (*John Brown's Body, Western Star, The Devil and Daniel Webster*) (died 1943).

1898 Alexander Calder, sculptor and painter, was born in Philadelphia; developer of mobiles and stabiles (died 1976).

1905 A severe yellow fever epidemic began in New Orleans; ended in October with about 3000 cases and about 400 deaths.

1911 Prohibition in Texas was defeated by 6000 votes out of a total 462,000 cast.

1913 Tex (Charles B.) Thornton, president (1953-61), chairman (1953-81), Litton Industries, was born in Haskell, Tex. (died 1981).

1916 A bomb exploded in San Francisco during the Preparedness Day parade killing nine persons and injuring 40; Thomas Mooney and Warren K. Billings were eventually found guilty and sentenced; pardoned in 1939.

1918 President Wilson issued a proclamation placing the telephone and telegraph systems under government control; placed under Postmaster Aug 1.

1922 Jason Robards Jr., actor, was born in Chicago; starred in numerous Eugene O'Neill plays (*The Iceman Cometh, A Moon for the Misbegotten, A Thousand Clowns*).

1923 Robert J. Dole, legislator, was born in Russell, Kan.; represented Kansas in the House (1961-69) and Senate (1969-); chairman, Republican National Committee (1971-73); Republican vice presidential candidate (1976).

1932 Federal Home Loan Bank Act went into effect, creating a five-man Home Loan Bank Board and discount banks, designed to reduce foreclosures, stimulate residential construction.

1934 John Dillinger, gangster, was gunned down by law officers in front of the Biograph Theater in Chicago, ending a string of robberies and 16 murders.

1943 The American 7th Army took Palermo, Sicily.

1944 A monetary and financial conference ended three weeks of meetings in Bretton Woods, N.H.; attended by 44 nations and resulted in creation of the International Monetary Fund and the International Bank for Reconstruction and Development.

1963 President Kennedy signed an act to help states provide capital improvements for research in agricultural experiment stations.

JULY 23

1764 James Otis' pamphlet, "The Rights of the British Colonies Asserted and Proved" was published in Boston.

1816 Charlotte S. Cushman, actress, was born in Boston; starred on American (1835-58) and English (1845-49) stages (died 1876).

1834 James Gibbons, Catholic prelate, was born in Baltimore; Bishop of Richmond (1872-77), Archbishop of Baltimore (1877-1921); founder, first chancellor, Catholic U., Washington (1889) (died 1921).

1848 Richard F. Pettigrew, South Dakota pioneer, was born in Ludlow, Vt.; served South Dakota as one of its first senators (1889-1901) (died 1926).

1863 Samuel H. Kress, merchant, was born in Cherryville, Pa.; co-founder with brother, Claude W. Kress (4/4/1876), of S.H. Kress & Co., dime store chain; established foundation to purchase great art works for museums (died 1955).

1865 Edward T. Sanford, associate justice, Supreme Court (1923-30), was born in Knoxville, Tenn.; was a justice, U.S. Distrist Court (1908-23) (died 1930).

1874 James E. (Sunny Jim) Fitzsimmons, horse trainer, was born in Brooklyn; he saddled 2275 winners between 1907 and 1963 (died 1966).

1877 Colby M. Chester, first president, General Foods (1929-35), was born in Annapolis, Md. (died 1965).

1885 Former President Grant died in Mt. McGregor, near Saratoga, N.Y. at 63.

1888 Raymond T. Chandler, author, was born in Chicago; famed for hard-boiled detective novels (*The Big Sleep, Farewell My Lovely, The Lady in the Lake*) (died 1959).

1888 Gluyas Williams, cartoonist, was born in San Francisco; work appeared in various magazines and newspapers; illustrated works of Robert Benchley (died 1982).

1901 Ben Hibbs, editor, *Saturday Evening Post* (1942-61), was born in Fontana, Kan. (died 1975).

1906 Vladimir Prelog, chemist, was born in Sarajevo, Yugoslavia; shared 1975 Nobel Chemistry Prize for research on structure of biological molecules (antibiotics, cholesterol).

1918 Peewee (Harold H.) Reese, baseball player (Dodgers), was born in Ekron, Ky.; named to Baseball Hall of Fame.

1926 Robert M. Adams, archaeologist and anthropologist, was born in Chicago; director, Chicago U. Oriental Institute (1981-82); U. of Chicago provost (1982-84); secretary, Smithsonian Institution (1984-).

1936 Don Drysdale, baseball pitcher who won 209 games (Dodgers), was born in Van Nuys, Cal.; named to Baseball Hall of Fame.

1947 The Amvets, founded in Kansas City, Mo. in 1944, was chartered by Congress.

1967 Week-long riots began in Detroit, resulting in more than 40 deaths, 1000 injuries, destruction of 5000 homes; 4700 paratroopers and 8000 National Guardsmen were sent in to quell the rioting.

JULY 24

1608 Capt. John Smith began a six-week exploration of the Chesapeake Bay.

1679 New Hampshire was made a royal colony.

1696 Benning Wentworth, colonial governor, was born in Portsmouth, N.H.; first royal governor of New Hampshire (1741-64) (died 1770).

1701 Antoine Cadillac, French colonial governor, founded Ft. Pontchartrain du Detroit, which later became the city of Detroit; Cadillac became governor of Louisiana (1713-16).

1758 George Washington was elected to the Virginia House of Burgesses from Frederick County; marked his entry into politics; away at the time of election campaign, it cost him 39 pounds, six shillings for 130 gallons of rum, wine, beer, and cider.

1766 Pontiac, chief of the Ottawa Indians and leader of the war against the colonial outposts, signed a peace treaty in Oswego, N.Y.

1796 John M. Clayton, legislator, was born in Dagsborough, Del; represented Delaware in the Senate (1829-36, 1845-49, 1853-56); Secretary of State (1849-50), negotiating the treaty for a neutralized canal across Panama (died 1856).

1798 John A. Dix, Army officer and public official, was born in Boscawen, N.H.; served in War of 1812 and as a major general in Civil War; represented New York in the Senate (1845-49) and served it as governor (1873-75); Secretary of the Treasury (1861), minister to France (1866-69) (died 1879).

1803 Alexander J. Davis, architect, was born in New York City; one of the most successful exponents of Greek revival style (U. of North Carolina Assembly Hall, VMI buildings) (died 1892).

1822 Benn Pitman, shorthand expert, was born in Trowbridge, England; came to America to teach shorthand system developed by his brother, altered it; founded Photographic Institute, Cincinnati; invented electromechanical process of relief engraving (died 1910).

1829 Lewis Miller, inventor, was born in Greentown, Ohio; improved agricultural machinery (reapers, binders); co-founder, Chautauqua movement (1874) (died 1899).

1847 Brigham Young led the Mormons into the Great Salt Lake valley.

1855 William H. Gillette, actor and playwright, was born in Hartford; noted for his role as Sherlock Holmes (died 1937).

1858 Abraham Lincoln challenged Stephen A. Douglas to a series of debates in their race for the Senate; Lincoln lost when Illinois legislature selected Douglas by a vote of 54-46.

1862 Former President Van Buren died in Kinderhook, N.Y. at 79.

1864 Thomas McCarthy, baseball player with various teams, was born in Boston; named to Baseball Hall of Fame (died 1922).

1866 Tennessee was readmitted to the Union by joint resolution of Congress.

1876 Jean Webster, author, was born in Fredonia, N.Y.; wrote *Patty* series, *Daddy Long Legs* and *Dear Enemy* (died 1916).

1880 Ernest Bloch, composer and educator, was born in Geneva, Switzerland; composer (*Macbeth, A Lyric Drama; America, A Symphony*); founder, director Cleveland Music Institute (1920-25), San Francisco Music Conservatory (1925-30) (died 1959).

1892 Thomas H. Jones, sculptor, was born in Buffalo; best known for the *Tomb of the Unknown Soldier* in Arlington Cemetery (died 1969).

1898 Amelia Earhart, aviatrix, was born in Atchison, Kan.; first woman to cross the Atlantic in a plane as a passenger, Newfoundland to Wales (6/17/1928); flew own plane across (5/20-21/1932); lost on around-the-world flight in 1937.

1905 The remains of Adm. John Paul Jones, which had been found buried in France, were placed in a tomb at the Naval Academy, Annapolis.

1913 Britton Chance, biophysicist and physical biochemist, was born in Wilkes-Barre, Pa.; pioneered in study of rapid biologic reactions.

1914 Kenneth B. Clark, psychologist, was born in Panama Canal Zone; his work on race relations helped bring about Supreme Court school desegreation ruling.

1915 Excursion steamer *Eastland* capsized at its dock in the Chicago River as it was starting on a trip with about 2000 persons; 812, mostly women and children, were drowned.

1916 John D. MacDonald, author, was born in Sharon, Pa.; prolific short story, novel writer (*The Executioners, Key to the Suite, Condominium*) (died 1986).

1929 The Kellogg-Briand pact, renouncing war as an instrument of national policy, was formally proclaimed; later ratified by 63 nations.

1935 Pat(rick) Oliphant, editorial cartoonist, was born in Adelaide, Australia.

1953 Former President Hoover was named chairman of the Commission of Government Operations (the second Hoover Commission) by President Eisenhower; commission functioned until June 30, 1955.

1974 Supreme Court, by a vote of 8-0, ruled that President Nixon had to turn over 64 White House tapes to the Watergate special prosecutor.

JULY 25

1729 After more than 35 years as a proprietary colony, torn by unrest and dissension, North Carolina became a royal colony.

1750 Henry Knox, Revolutionary general, was born in Boston; served in many engagements during the war; first Secretary of War (1785-94) (died 1806).

1759 British troops took Ft. Niagara from the French.

1775 Anna Symmes Harrison, wife of President William Henry Harrison, was born in Morristown, N.J. (died 1864).

1814 The Battle of Lundy's Lane, near Niagara Falls, Ontario, was claimed as a victory by both the Americans and British.

1817 The first newspaper in Michigan, *Detroit Gazette*, was founded by John F. Sheldon and Ebenezer Reed.

1823 Benjamin T. Roberts, Methodist clergyman, was born in Gowanda, N.Y.; expelled from the church because of his criticism; became first general superintendent, Free Methodist Church (1860-93), which he organized after his expulsion (died 1893).

1824 Richard J. Oglesby, Union general and public official, was born in Oldham County, Ky.; served Illinois as governor (1865-73, 1885-89) and represented it in the Senate (1873-79) (died 1899).

1830 John Jacob Bausch, industrialist, was born in Suessen, Germany; co-founder, president, Bausch & Lomb Optical Co. (1853) (died 1926).

1840 Carroll D. Wright, educator and statistician, was born in Dumbarton, N.H.; first commissioner, Bureau of Labor (1885-1905); first president, Clark U. (1902-09); president, American Statistical Association (1897-1909) (died 1909).

1840 Flora A. Darling, patriotic society leader, was born in Lancaster, N.H.; co-founder, Daughters of the American Revolution (DAR) (died 1910).

1844 Thomas Eakins, artist, was born in Philadelphia; considered one of the greatest American realistic painters, featuring very detailed activities (*The Gross Clinic, The Chess Players*) (died 1916).

1854 David Belasco, playwright and producer, was born in San Francisco; author or co-author of many hits (*Girl of the Golden West, May Blossom; Laugh, Clown, Laugh*) (died 1931).

1856 Charles Major, author who wrote under the name of Sir Edwin Cuskoden, was born in Indianapolis; best known for *When Knighthood was in Flower* and *Dorothy Vernon of Haddon Hall* (died 1913).

1857 Frank J. Sprague, "father of electrical traction," was born in Milford, Conn.; invented train control systems, various motors; co-inventor, third rail system; founder, Sprague Electric Railway & Motor Co. (1884); constructed first modern trolley system (Richmond, Va.); founder, Sprague Electric Elevator Co., designed, installed high speed automatic elevators, making tall buildings practical (died 1934).

1868 The Territory of Wyoming was created out of parts of the Dakotas, Utah, and Idaho.

1870 Maxwell F. Parrish, painter and illustrator, was born in Philadelphia; best known for illustrations of *Mother Goose in Prose, Knickerbocker History of New York* (died 1966).

1894 Walter Brennan, actor, was born in Lynn, Mass.; character actor in about 100 films (*Come and Get It, Kentucky*); on television (*Real McCoys*) (died 1974).

1898 American occupation of Puerto Rico began; forces led by Gen. Nelson A. Miles.

1915 The American steamship, *Leelanaw*, was sunk by a German submarine off Scotland.

1927 Stanley Dancer, a leading harness racing driver, was born in New Egypt, N.J.; won the Hambletonian (1968, 1972, 1975, 1983) and was the first driver to top the $1 million mark in winnings.

1952 Puerto Rico became the first overseas American commonwealth; President Truman signed Puerto Rican Constitution Act.

1954 Walter Payton, football player, was born in Columbia, Miss.; starred with the Chicago Bears (1975-88) and is the all-time leading ground gainer.

1956 The Italian liner, *Andrea Doria*, sank off Nantucket Island after a collision; 52 died or were missing, 1600 persons were rescued.

1963 The United States, Great Britain, and Soviet Russia agreed on a limited nuclear test ban treaty, barring all but underground testing; ratified by the Senate Sept 24.

1987 Commerce Secretary Malcolm Baldridge was killed in a horse riding accident while practicing for a rodeo in northern California.

JULY 26

1739 George Clinton, Vice President (1805-12), was born in Little Britain, N.Y., brother of James Clinton (8/9/1733); member of Continental Congress (1775-76); governor of New York (1777-95, 1801-04) (died 1812).

1774 Freeholders of Albemarle County, Va. adopted resolutions drafted by Thomas Jefferson, urging the non-importation of British goods, with certain philosophical principles of the relations of colonies to Parliament.

1775 The Post Office Department was created by the Continental Congress, which named Benjamin Franklin as Postmaster General.

1777 British troops under Gen. Barry St. Leger began the siege of Ft. Stanwix, now part of Rome, N.Y.

1784 Charles Morris, naval officer, was born in Woodstock, Conn.; with Board of Navy Commissioners about 13 years, sometimes called the statesman of the American Navy, because of his administrative skills (died 1856).

1788 The New York legislature, by a vote of 30-27, ratified the Constitution, with Alexander Hamilton leading the pro-ratification forces; entered the Union as the 11th state.

1790 The House voted 34-28 (with three abstentions) to assume the debts of the states up to $21,500,000.

1796 George Catlin, artist, was born in Wilkes-Barre, Pa.; devoted to the study of American Indians and doing Indian portraits (died 1872).

1797 John Quicy Adams and Louise Catherine Johnson were married in London.

1799 Isaac Babbitt, inventor, was born in Taunton, Mass.; invented a journal box (1839), suggested that it be lined with an alloy now known as Babbitt metal; cast the first brass cannon in the United States (died 1862).

1805 Constantino Brumidi, painter, was born in Rome; best known for his frescoes in the Capitol (died 1880).

1822 Orange Judd, agricultural editor, was born near Niagara Falls, N.Y.; editor, publisher, *American Agriculturist* (1856-83); responsible for establishing first state agricultural experiment station (Wesleyan U.); editor, *Prairie Farmer* (1884-88) (died 1892).

1848 John D. Archbold, businessman, was born in Leesburg, Ohio; prominent in Standard Oil development (1882-1911); president, Standard Oil of New Jersey (1911-16) (died 1916).

1856 William Rainey Harper, educator, was born in New Concord, Ohio; professor of religion; first president, U. of Chicago (1891-1906) (died 1906).

1858 Ella Boole, prohibitionist, was born in Van Wert, Ohio; president, National Women's Christian Temperance Union (1925-33), international WCTU (1931-47) (died 1952).

1858 Edward M. House, presidential advisor, was born in Houston; "Colonel House" was a close advisor to President Wilson (died 1938).

1862 George B. Cortelyou, public official, was born in New York City; first secretary, Department of Commerce & Labor (1903-04), Postmaster General (1905-07), Secretary of Treasury (1907-09); president, New York Consolidated Gas Co., which became Con Edison (1909-35) (died 1940).

1874 Serge Koussevitsky, conductor, was born in Vyshni Vdochek, Russia; conductor, Boston Symphony (1924-49), founder of Berkshire Festival (1937) (died 1951).

1887 Reuben L. Kahn, immunologist, was born in Kovno, Lithuania (now Russia); developed blood serum test for diagnosis of syphilis (died 1979).

1893 George Grosz, expressionist painter, was born in Berlin; paintings attacked corruption, decadence of German society; condemned by Nazis (died 1959).

1898 Spanish Government, through the French, asked for American peace terms, which were communicated two days later.

1903 Estes Kefauver, legislator, was born near Madisonville, Tenn.; represented Tennessee in the House (1937-49) and Senate (1949-63), where he conducted televised hearings on crime; Democratic vice presidential candidate (1956) (died 1963).

1906 Gracie Allen, comedienne, was born in San Francisco; teamed with husband, George Burns (1/20/1896) on radio and in movies (died 1964).

1941 Philippine armed forces were nationalized by executive order, with Gen Douglas MacArthur named commander-in-chief of American Far East forces.

1947 Congress passed the National Security Act which unified the armed forces under a Secretary of Defense; created the National Security Council.

1989 President Bush signed legislation ending a half century of federal price controls on natural gas.

JULY 27

1690 The Protestant Association under John Goode seized St. Mary's, capital of Maryland, in revolt against the proprietary government.

1752 Samuel Smith, Revolutionary officer and legislator, was born in Carlisle, Pa., brother of Robert Smith (11/3/1757); served at Long Island and Monmouth, commanded defense of Baltimore in War of 1812; represented Maryland in the House (1793-1803, 1816-22) and Senate (1803-15, 1835-38), serving as president *pro tem* (1805-08) (died 1839).

1753 John Warren, physician and educator, was born in Roxbury, Mass., brother of Joseph Warren (6/11/1741); co-founder, Harvard Medical School (1782), its first professor of anatomy and surgery; a founder, president, Massachusetts Humane Society (died 1815).

1770 Robert Dinwiddie, colonial governor, died at 77; lieutenant governor of Virginia (1751-58), sent George Washington to protect the Ohio region from the French, sought unsuccessfully to get colonial cooperation for this protection.

1777 Two of the best known foreign officers to serve in the American Revolution arrived in Philadelphia—20-year-old Marquis de Lafayette and "Baron" Johann de Kalb; both were commissioned as major generals.

1789 The Department of Foreign Affairs was created by Congress and President Washington; changed to Department of State Sept 15, 1789.

1818 Eben N. Horsford, industrial chemist, was born in Moscow, N.Y.; developd process for making condensed milk, baking powder (died 1893).

1852 George F. Peabody, banker and educator, was born in Columbus, Ga.; director, General Education Board; treasurer, Southern Education Board—both Rockefeller philanthropies; Peabody Award for broadcasting excellence named in his honor (died 1938).

1853 Cyrus L.W. Eidlitz, architect, was born in New York City, son of Leopold Eidlitz (3/29/1823); designed Dearborn Station, Chicago; Buffalo Public Library; New York Times Building, New York City (died 1921).

1866 The Atlantic cable was brought to Newfoundland by Cyrus W. Field, opening telegraphic communication with Great Britain.

1867 Walter A. Sheaffer, fountain pen manufacturer, was born in Bloomfield, Iowa; founder, president, Sheaffer Pen Co. (1913-38) (died 1946).

1868 Alaska was organized as a territory.

1870 Bertram B. Boltwood, scientist, was born in Amherst, Mass.; made important contributions to knowledge of radioactivity; discovered element ionium (died 1927).

1880 Joe Tinker, baseball player (Cubs), was born in Muscotah, Iowa; part of famed Tinker-Evers-Chance double play combination; named to Baseball Hall of Fame (died 1948).

1882 Congress passed an act awarding a pension of $50,000 to Lucretia Garfield, widow of President Garfield.

1889 Bruce Bliven, magazine editor, was born in Emmettsburg, Iowa; editor, *New Republic* (1923-55) (died 1977).

1906 Leo Durocher, baseball player and manager, was born in West Springfield, Mass.; played with Yankees, Cardinals; managed Dodgers, Giants, and Cubs.

1922 Norman Lear, television producer and director, was born in New Haven; had many hit shows (*All in the Family, The Jeffersons, Maude, Sanford and Son*).

1947 The Housing & Home Finance Agency, predecessor of the Department of Housing and Urban Development, was created; ended with start of HUD Sept 5, 1965.

1948 Peggy Fleming, 1968 world and Olympic figure skating champion, was born in San Jose, Cal.

1953 An armistice was signed at Panmunjon, ending hostilities in Korea.

1974 House Judiciary Committee voted in favor of the first of three articles of impeachment of President Nixon; voted for the second July 29, third July 30; the full House by a vote of 412-3 accepted the committee report without debate.

JULY 28

1746 Thomas Hayward, jurist, was born in St. Luke's Parish, S.C.; a member of the Continental Congress (1776-78), a signer of the Declaration of Independence (died 1809).

1751 Joseph Habersham, colonial legislator, was born in Savannah; member of the Continental Congress (1785-86); Postmaster General (1795-1801) (died 1815).

1767 James A. Bayard, legislator, was born in Philadelphia; represented Delaware in the House (1797-1803) and Senate (1805-13); while in House, he was the intermediary who secured understanding with Thomas Jefferson which resulted in Jefferson's election as president by the House; one of three negotiators of Treaty of Ghent ending the War of 1812 (died 1815).

1778 Charles Stewart, naval officer, was born in Philadelphia; commanded the *Constitution* in War of 1812; senior flag officer (1859-62) (died 1869).

1795 Edwin A. Stevens, businessman and philanthropist, was born in Hoboken, N.J., brother of Robert L. Stevens (10/10/1787); inventor of a plow; manager, Camden & Amboy Railroad (1830-65); endowed Stevens Institute of Technology (died 1868).

1809 Ormsby M. Mitchel, astronomer, was born in Morganfield, Ky.; did much to popularize astronomy; with Cincinnati College (1836-59); Union general, died of yellow fever in 1862.

1840 Edward D. Cope, paleontologist, was born in Philadelphia; owner, editor, *American Naturalist* (1878-97); discovered about 1000 species of extinct vertebrates in the United States (died 1897).

1859 A convention approved Nevada's constitution; popular vote ratified action Sept 7.

1859 Ballington Booth, social worker, was born in Yorkshire, England, brother of Evangeline Booth (12/25/1865); founder, Volunteers of America (1896), after disagreement with his father, William Booth, Salvation Army founder, over Army operations in America, which Ballington headed (1887-96) (died 1940).

1868 The 14th Amendment went into effect, guaranteeing that a citizen's rights would not be abridged.

1868 Burlingame Treaty between the United States and China was signed, provided for free immigration between the two nations.

1881 John G. Machen, Presbyterian leader, was born in Baltimore; a leader of Presbyterian fundamentalists; founder (1936) of Presbyterian Church of America (died 1937).

1887 Marcel Duchamp, painter, was born in Blainville, France; his work stimulated major 20th century art trends (died 1968).

1901 Harry Bridges, labor leader, was born in Melbourne, Australia; long-time president, International Longshoreman's Union.

1901 Rudy (Hubert P.) Vallee, singer and orchestra leader, was born in Island Pond, Vt.; the original crooner (died 1986).

1901 Freddie (Frederick L.) Fitzsimmons, baseball pitcher who won 217 games (Giants, Dodgers), was born in Mishawaka, Ind. (died 1979).

1907 Earl S. Tupper, developer of Tupperware, was born in Berlin, N.H.; developed party approach to merchandising product (died 1983).

1907 William D. Haywood was acquitted of the 1905 murder of former Idaho Governor Stuenenerg for lack of corroborative evidence.

1915 Charles H. Townes, physicist, was born in Greenville, S.C.; shared 1964 Nobel Physics Prize for developing maser and principles of producing high-intensity radiation.

1915 President Wilson ordered military occupation of Haiti; order restored by Aug 1, puppet government set up; Haiti became semiprotectorate for ten years.

1929 Jacqueline Kennedy Onassis, widow of President Kennedy and Aristotle Onassis, was born in Southampton, N.Y.

1932 President Hoover ordered the Army to remove bonus marchers who refused to leave after the Senate (June 17) defeated the bonus bill; two marchers were killed in skirmishes with Washington police; Gen. Douglas MacArthur led troops.

1945 Jim (James R.) Davis, cartoonist (*Garfield*), was born in Marion, Ind.

1945 An Army B-25 bomber crashed into the Empire State Building, 13 were killed.

1945 The Senate approved the United Nations charter 89-2.

1965 President Lyndon Johnson announced a troop buildup in Vietnam, sending an additional 50,000 troops to bring total to 125,000.

1977 First Alaskan oil moved by 800-mile pipeline from Prudhoe Bay to Valdez.

1984 The Olympic Games began in Los Angeles.

JULY 29

1786 The first newspaper west of the mountains, *Pittsburgh Gazette*, was established by John Scull and Joseph Hull, two young Philadelphia printers.

1796 Walter Hunt, inventor, was born in Martinsburg, N.Y.; invented numerous items including a restaurant steam stable, knife sharpener, sewing machine (did not apply for a patent), fountain pen, safety pin (sold it for $400), disposable paper collar (died 1859).

1797 Daniel Drew, speculator and stock manipulator, was born in Carmel, N.Y.; as a cattleman was said to have watered cattle on way to slaughter, giving rise to term of stock watering; his benefactions made possible the founding of Drew Theological Seminary, Madison, N.J. (1866) (died 1879).

1805 Hiram Powers, sculptor, was born near Woodstock, Vt.; did busts of notables and other works (*Greek Slave, Daniel Webster, Fisher Boy*) (died 1873).

1806 Horace Abbott, iron manufacturer, was born in Sudbury, Mass.; specialized in iron manufacture for railroads, ships, including armor plate for the *Monitor* and other ironclads (died 1887).

1825 George H. Pendleton, legislator, was born in Cincinnati; represented Ohio in the House (1857-65) and Senate (1879-85); a leader in creation of the civil service; minister to Germany (1885-89) (died 1889).

1859 A convention in Wyandotte approved the Kansas constitution, which forbade slavery but restricted suffrage to white males; ratified Oct 4.

1861 Alice H. Lee Roosevelt, first wife of President Theodore Roosevelt, was born in Chestnut Hill, Mass. (died 1884).

1869 Booth Tarkington, author, was born in Indianapolis; author (*Penrod, Seventeen, The Magnificent Ambersons, Alice Adams*) (died 1946).

1877 (Charles) William Beebe, naturalist and author, was born in Brooklyn; director of ornithology and scientific research, New York Zoological Society; headed various expeditions; descended to the then (1934) record depth (3028 ft) in a bathysphere which he invented (died 1962).

1878 Don(ald R.O.) Marquis, writer, was born in Walnut, Ill.; newspaper columnist, *New York Sun, New York Tribune* (1912-25); creator of "archy and mehitabel" (died 1937).

1887 Sigmund Romberg, operetta composer, was born in Szeged, Hungary; wrote many hit shows (*Blossom Time, The Student Prince, Desert Song, Maytime*) (died 1951).

1892 William Powell, screen actor, was born in Pittsburgh; starred in many films (*The Thin Man, Life with Father, Mr. Roberts*) (died 1984).

1898 Isidor I. Rabi, physicist, was born in Rymanow, Austria; invented atomic molecular beam magnetic resonance method for observing spectra in radio-frequency range; awarded 1944 Nobel Physics Prize for work on magnetic movement of atomic particles (died 1988).

1899 United States signed the Hague Peace Convention for pacific settlement of disputes and various other international matters.

1910 Heinz L. Fraenkel-Courat, biochemist, was born in Breslau, Germany; worked on relationship between protein structure and biological activity.

1914 Marcel Bich, manufacturer, was born in Turin, Italy; set up Bic Pen Co. in the United States to manufacture pens and lighters.

1918 Edwin G. O'Connor, author, was born in Providence; best known for *The Last Hurrah* (died 1968).

1920 The first transcontinental airmail service began (New York to San Francisco).

1926 Don Carter, bowling great, was born in Miami; the outstanding bowler of the 1950s.

1935 Thomas E. Dewey was appointed special prosecutor in New York State to lead a drive against crime.

1957 Ratification was completed for American participation in the International Atomic Energy Agency.

1958 National Aeronautics & Space Administration (NASA) was established.

1967 A fire and explosion aboard the carrier *Forrestal* off Vietnam killed 134.

1974 Former Treasury Secretary John Connally was indicated in a milk-support bribery scandal; acquitted Apr 17, 1975.

1986 A federal jury in New York City awarded only $1 in damages to the United States Football League, which had sued the National Football League.

JULY 30

1609 Samuel de Champlain, on his third trip to Canada, voyaged up the Richlieu River and entered the lake named for him.

1619 The House of Burgesses convened in Virginia, the first representative assembly in the New World; convened by Gov. George Yeardley; met until Aug 6.

1630 The first church in Boston was organized in Charlestown, with John Wilson as teacher; transferred to Boston 1632.

1777 Gen. John Burgoyne and his British troops occupied Ft. Edward, N.Y. in their drive to split New York state.

1822 William T. Adams, author, was born in Bellingham, Mass.; known as Oliver Optic, he wrote about 120 books, 1000 stories, for boys; a teacher in the Boston public schools (1846-65) (died 1897).

1831 Helena P.H. Blavatsky, co-founder of Theosophical Society, was born in Ekaterinoslav, Russia; with Henry Steele Olcott (8/2/1832), founded Society (1875); set up official journal, *The Theosophist*; many of her so-called miracles were demonstrated to be frauds (died 1891).

1855 James E. Kelly, sculptor, was born in New York City; became known as the sculptor of American history; did various historical figures (died 1933).

1857 Thorstein B. Veblen, economist, was born in Cato, Wis.; economist, U. of Chicago (1892-1906); a founder, editor, *Journal of Political Economy* (1892-1905); author (*The Theory of the Leisure Class, The Theory of Business Enterprise*) (died 1929).

1863 Henry Ford, pioneer automaker, was born in Greenfield, Mich.; founder, president, Ford Motor Co. (1903-19, 1943-45), introduced the Model T and became world's largest car maker; introduced profit sharing (1914); chartered *Peace Ship* to Europe in an effort to end World War I; built Henry Ford Hospital, Detroit (died 1947).

1864 Part of the Confederate defenses of Petersburg, Va. was blown up, but failure to follow up quickly cost the Union force the advantage and 3000 men; six-week siege continued for another seven and a half months.

1866 A riot broke out in New Orleans as a constitutional convention was assembling; police fired on the mob, killing or wounding more than 200.

1880 Robert R. McCormick, newspaper publisher, was born in Chicago; editor, publisher *Chicago Tribune* (1920-55) (died 1955).

1880 Max(imilian J.) Hirsch, dean of American thoroughbred trainers, was born in Fredericksburg, Tex.; trained many winners, including triple-crown winner, Assault (died 1969).

1889 Vladimir Zworykin, electronics engineer, was born in Murom, Russia; television pioneer with RCA (1929-45), developed first practical television system (1938); his inventions made practical the electron microscope (1939) (died 1951).

1889 Emanuel Haldeman-Julius, author and publisher, was born in Philadelphia; author, publisher of Little Blue Books (biographies, "how-to" books) (died 1951).

1891 Casey (Charles D.) Stengel, baseball player and manager, was born in Kansas City, Mo.; player (Giants)/manager (Yankees with whom he won ten pennants and seven World Series); first manager (Mets); named to Baseball Hall of Fame (died 1975).

1907 The first elections were held in the Philippines; legislature convened Oct 16 for the first time.

1916 An explosion and fire in a munitions plant at Black Tom Island, N.J. destroyed $22 million worth of property; sabotage was suspected but no evidence was found.

1932 The Olympic Games opened in Los Angeles.

1940 The Act of Havana was approved unanimously by 21 republics of the Pan American Union, permitting the takeover of European colonies in the Western Hemisphere endangered by aggression; signed by President Franklin Roosevelt Oct 10.

1941 Paul Anka, singer and composer, was born in Ottawa, Canada; wrote many hits ("My Way," "She's a Lady," "You're Having My Baby").

1942 President Franklin Roosevelt signed an act establishing the Women Appointed for Voluntary Emergency Service (WAVES), the women's branch of the Navy.

1942 Commerce Secretary Harry L. Hopkins was married to Mrs. Louise Gill Macy in the White House.

1952 The 4.4 mile Chesapeake Bay Bridge near Annapolis was opened.

1965 The Medicare Act was signed by President Lyndon Johnson in Independence, Mo.; former President Truman, who first recommended it in 1954, was on hand.

1974 The House Judiciary Committee in a week-long session recommended adoption of three articles of impeachment of President Nixon for obstructing justice (27-11), abuse of power (28-10), and contempt of Congress (27-11).

JULY 31

1653 Thomas Dudley, colonial official, died at 77; served as Massachusetts governor (1634, 1640, 1645, 1650) and deputy governor 13 times; helped found Cambridge and as governor signed the charter of Harvard College.

1763 James Kent, jurist, was born in Putnam County, N.Y.; first law professor, Columbia U. (1793); justice, New York Supreme Court (1798-1804), chief justice (1804-23); chancellor, Court of Chancery (1814-23); his decisions helped create American system of equity (died 1847).

1771 Anthony Kohlman, Jesuit priest, was born in Kaiserberg, Germany; as administrator of New York diocese (1808-14), he won lawsuit to keep confessional information confidential; led to state legislation (1828) protecting the confessional (died 1836).

1775 The Continental Congress rejected Lord North's plan for reconciliation.

1789 The Customs Service was established.

1793 Thomas Jefferson submitted his resignation as Secretary of State, effective Dec 31, over policy differences with Alexander Hamilton and President Washington.

1803 John Ericsson, engineer, was born in Värmland Province, Sweden; developed screw propeller for ships; built *Monitor* for the Union Navy; made many improvements in steam machinery, launched new era in naval engineering (died 1889).

1804 The first newspaper in the Indiana territory, the *Indiana Gazette*, was founded in Vincennes by a Kentucky printer, Elihu Stout.

1813 British troops captured Plattsburgh, N.Y.; swept American shipping off Lake Champlain.

1813 American troops recaptured York (Toronto); again abandoned city.

1816 George H. Thomas, Union general, was born in Southampton County, Va.; known as the Rock of Chickamauga, commanded Army of the Cumberland; served at Chattanooga and Nashville (died 1870).

1822 Abram S. Hewitt, industrialist, was born in Haverstraw, N.Y.; co-founder, Cooper & Hewitt, developer of first American open hearth furnaces (1862), made first American steel; helped oust Tweed Ring; represented New York in the House (1874-79, 1881-86); mayor of New York City (1887-88) (died 1903).

1856 Harold C. Ernst, bacteriologist, was born in Cincinnati; with Harvard Medical School (1885-1922), established first diphtheria antitoxin laboratory (died 1922).

1859 Theobald Smith, pathologist, was born in Albany; worked on cause and nature of infections, parasitic diseases; developed a theory of immunization (died 1934).

1864 Edward N. Hurley, industrialist, was born in Galesburg, Ill.; originated, developed, pneumatic tool industry; chairman, Federal Trade Commission (1913-17); chairman, U.S. Shipping Board (1917-19) (died 1933).

1867 S(ebastian) S. Kresge, merchant, was born in Bald Mount, Pa.; headed dime store chain (1907-66) (died 1966).

1875 Former President Andrew Johnson died near Jonesborough, Tenn. at 66.

1882 Herbert E. Ives, inventor, was born in Philadelphia; pioneered in television and wire transmission of pictures; invented first practical artificial daylight lamp (died 1953).

1899 Robert T. Stevens, industrialist, was born; with J.P. Stevens & Co., president (1929-42, 1955-69); Army Secretary (1953-55) (died 1983).

1912 Milton Friedman, economist, was born in New York City; awarded 1976 Nobel Economics Prize for work in consumption analysis and monetary history and theory.

1917 American oil steamer *Montano* was torpedoed by a German submarine off the Irish coast; 24 men lost.

1919 Curt(is) Gowdy, sports broadcaster (NBC), was born in Green River, Wyo.

1919 Telephone and telegraph lines were returned to private ownership; had been under government control for a year.

1921 Whitney M. Young Jr., civil rights leader, was born in Lincoln Ridge, Ky.; executive director, National Urban League (1961-71) (died 1971).

1948 Idlewild International Airport was dedicated by President Truman; renamed Kennedy Airport in 1963.

1973 A Delta jetliner crashed in the fog while landing at Boston's Logan Airport; 89 persons were killed.

1975 Turkey refused to allow the United States to reopen bases there.

1989 Islamic militants announced in Beirut that they had hanged Marine Corps Lt. Col. William R. Higgins, an American hostage since Feb 1988.

AUGUST 1

1539 Hernando de Soto began march from Tampa into Florida and wintered near Pensacola Bay.

1768 Boston merchants agreed not to import British goods as a protest against the Townshend measures; within a few weeks, the example was followed by other Massachusetts communities and New York.

1769 A Spanish expedition under Gaspar de Portola and Father Juan Crespi reached what is now Los Angeles, calling it Our Lady Queen of Angels.

1770 William Clark, explorer, was born in Caroline County, Va., brother of George Rogers Clark (11/19/1752); co-leader of the Lewis and Clark Expedition (1804-06); governor, Missouri Territory (1813-21) (died 1838).

1774 The Virginia House of Burgesses adopted a series of resolutions drafted by Thomas Jefferson calling for non-importation of British goods and "to oppose by all just and proper means every injury to American rights;" this led to the dissolution of the House and delegates met in Raleigh Tavern.

1778 John C. Warren, physician and educator, was born in Boston, son of John Warren (7/27/1753); dean, Harvard Medical School (1816-19); co-founder, Massachusetts General Hospital (1821), its first surgeon (died 1856).

1779 Francis Scott Key, lawyer and poet, was born in what is now Carroll County, Md.; wrote the poem which later became "The Star Spangled Banner" put to the tune of a popular British drinking song ("To Anacreon in Heaven"); wrote it after watching British bombardment of Ft. McHenry in Baltimore Harbor and seeing the American flag still flying (died 1843).

1781 Lord Charles Cornwallis, with about 7500 troops, set up headquarters at Yorktown, Va., from which to campaign against the Americans.

1791 George Ticknor, educator, was born in Boston; popularized modern language studies at Harvard (1819-35); a founder, Boston Public Library (1852) (died 1871).

1793 A yellow fever epidemic struck Philadelphia, lasting until Nov 9; killed about 4000 persons.

1794 Federal Society of Journeymen Cordwainers (Shoemakers), the nation's first labor union, was organized in Philadelphia.

1800 The second Census reported the American population to be 5,308,483.

1815 Richard Henry Dana, author and admiralty lawyer, was born in Cambridge; wrote standard manual of maritime law; best remembered for *Two Years Before the Mast* (died 1882).

1818 Maria Mitchell, astronomer, was born in Nantucket, Mass.; first American woman astronomer (Vassar College 1865-89) (died 1889).

1819 Herman Melville, author, was born in New York City; wrote several popular books (*Moby Dick, Omoo, Typee*) (died 1891).

1830 The fifth Census reported a population of 12,866,020.

1843 Robert Todd Lincoln, public official, was born in Springfield, Ill., son of President Lincoln; Secretary of War (1881-85), minister to Great Britain (1889-93); president, Pullman Co. (1897-1911) (died 1926).

1873 First cable car put into service on Clay St. hill in San Francisco.

1875 Ernest T. Weir, steel manufacturer, was born in Pittsburgh; a founder, president, Weirton Steel Co. (1909); a founder, National Steel Co. (died 1957).

1876 Colorado was admitted to the Union as the 38th state.

1878 Eva Tanguay, entertainer, was born in Marbleton, Canada; star of musical comedy, vaudeville; remembered for theme, "I Don't Care" (died 1947).

1887 John C.H. Lee, World War II general who headed supply services in European Theater, was born in Junction City, Kas. (died 1958).

1894 Benjamin Mays, educator, was born in Epworth, S.C.; president, Morehouse College (1940-67) (died 1984).

1907 Army organized an aeronautical division in the Signal Corps, with one officer (Capt. Charles D. Chandler) and two enlisted men.

1916 Prohibition law was signed by Utah governor.

1921 Jack Kramer, tennis player, was born in Las Vegas; American singles champion (1946-47), Wimbledon champion (1947); profesional players tour organizer (1948).

1933 Dom DeLuise, comedian and screen actor, was born in New York City.

1943 A low-level American air raid was made on the oil refineries of Ploesti, Rumania.

1946 President Truman signed a law creating the five-member Atomic Energy Commission (now Nuclear Regulatory Commission) and providing assistance to private research in atomic energy.

1946 Congress enacted the Fulbright Act, which provided for the use of money received from the sale of war surplus to Allied governments for financing cultural and educational interchange.

1950 American citizenship and limited self-government was granted to Guam, which the United States received from Spain in 1898.

1958 First class postage was increased to four cents an ounce.

1966 25-year-old Charles Starkweather barricaded himself in a tower at the U. of Texas in Austin and shot and killed 13 persons and wounded 31 before being killed by police; earlier he had killed his wife and mother.

1976 A flash flood in the Colorado River canyon killed 139 persons and did extensive damage.

AUGUST 2

1567 Dominique de Gourges set sail from Bordeaux, France, to avenge the destruction of French colonies in Florida; in May 1568, he burned the Spanish forts and killed the settlers.

1754 Pierre C. L'Enfant, city planner, was born in Paris; after serving with the Continental Army, he renovated New York City Hall for the Congress as Federal Hall (1787); designed the layout of Washington; the expense of his work led to his dismissal (1792), but the excellence of the design was recognized and the work was carried out (1801) (died 1825).

1776 The Declaration of Independence was formally signed by 54 delegates to the Continental Congress.

1790 The results of the first Census were announced–3,929,214 persons, including 697,697 slaves and 59,557 free blacks.

1819 A convention in Huntsville adopted the Alabama constitution.

1832 The Sauk and Fox Indians were defeated at the Battle of Red Axe, midway between Prairie du Chien and LaCrosse, Wis.; Black Hawk War virtually ended.

1832 Henry S. Olcott, theosophist, was born in Orange, N.J.; co-founder, first president, Theosophical Society (1875-1907); editor, *Theosophist* (1888-1907) (died 1907).

1835 Elisha Gray, inventor, was born near Barnesville, Ohio; invented numerous telephone, telegraph devices; co-founder, Gray & Barton, which became Western Electric Co.; claimed invention of the telephone but a long patent battle was settled by the Supreme Court in favor of Alexander Graham Bell (died 1901).

1845 American troops under Gen. Zachary Taylor arrived in Corpus Christi.

1865 Irving Babbitt, educator, was born in Dayton, Ohio; with Harvard U. (1894-1933); co-founder of modern humanistic movement (died 1933).

1871 John Sloan, artist, was born in Lock Haven, Pa.; specialized in landscapes and portraits, magazine illustrations (died 1951).

1876 Wild Bill Hickok was killed in a Deadwood, S.D. saloon by Jack McCall, while playing poker; Hickok was holding two pairs (Aces and 8s), now known as a "dead man's hand."

1880 Arthur G. Dove, artist, was born in Canandaigua, N.Y.; generally held to be the first American abstract artist (died 1946).

1892 Jack L. Warner, movie executive, was born in London, Canada; with brothers (Harry, Sam, and Albert) formed a leading film company (1923); introduced the first talking picture (died 1978).

1894 Westbrook Pegler, journalist, was born in Minneapolis; sports writer, syndicated columnist (died 1969).

1905 Myrna Loy, screen actress, was born in Helena, Mont.; starred in several films (*The Thin Man, The Best Years of Our Lives, Broadway Bill).*

1909 The Army purchased its first heavier-than-air machine from the Wright brothers.

1909 The Lincoln penny was issued by the Philadelphia mint, replacing the Indian head.

1911 Harriet Quimby was licensed as the first American woman pilot.

1912 The Senate, by a vote of 51-4, extended the principle of the Monroe Doctrine to Asiatic powers by blocking the sale of 400,000 acres in Lower California to a Japanese syndicate; action was based on feeling the land had a potential military value.

1918 A state of war began between the United States and Russia; American affairs in Russia were put in the hands of a Swedish consul general.

1923 U.S. Steel Co. adopted an eight-hour day; had been 12 hours.

1923 President Harding, 55, died in San Francisco enroute from Alaska; succeeded by Vice President Calvin Coolidge.

1924 James A. Baldwin, author, was born in New York City; best known for several books (*Go Tell It on the Mountain; Nobody Knows My Name*) (died 1987).

1924 Carroll O'Connor, actor, was born in New York City; starred as Archie Bunker in television series, *All in the Family.*

1927 President Coolidge announced his non-candidacy for re-election: "I do not choose to run for president in 1928."

1939 Albert Einstein, in a letter to President Franklin Roosevelt, alerted him to the opportunity for developing an atomic bomb.

1939 The Hatch Act was passed, forbidding "pernicious" political activities by federal workers and office holders.

1985 A Delta Air Lines jumbo jet crashed during landing at Dallas-Ft. Worth Airport during a storm killing 132 persons.

AUGUST 3

1492 Christopher Columbus and his three ships (*Nina, Pinta* and *Santa Maria*) set sail from Palos, Spain for "China."

1777 British Gen. Barry St. Leger led his troops to victory at Ft. Stanwix on the Mohawk River, but vacated the fort (Aug 22) on hearing of colonial reinforcements; moved to Oswego.

1780 Benedict Arnold, at his own request, took command of the West Point fort.

1785 The first Episcopal ordination held in the United States, that of the Rev. Ashbel Baldwin at Middletown, Conn.

1795 The Treaty of Greenville was signed by Gen. Anthony Wayne and 90 Indian leaders, ending the fighting in Ohio; Indians ceded 25,000 sq.mi. of what is now southeast Indiana and southern Ohio.

1808 Hamilton Fish, legislator and public official, was born in New York City; represented New York in the House (1843-45) and Senate (1851-57) and served it as governor (1849-50); Secretary of State (1869-77), successfully negotiated the "Alabama claims" and northwest boundary dispute (died 1893).

1811 Elisha G. Otis, elevator developer, was born in Halifax, Vt.; devised automatic safety appliance for elevators; patented a steam elevator (1861), the foundation for the Otis elevator business (died 1861).

1814 The British advance across the Niagara River to Buffalo was checked at Black Rock by Morgan's Rifles.

1821 Uriah S. Stephens, labor leader, was born in Cape May, N.J.; an organizer, Garment Cutters Union (1862); a founder, Knights of Labor (1869) (died 1882).

1824 William B. Woods, jurist, was born in Newark, Ohio; associate justice, Supreme Court (1880-87) (died 1887).

1836 Greene V. Black, dentist, was born near Winchester, Ill.; his method for filling teeth is still used; developed silver amalgam (1895) for fillings (died 1915).

1841 Francis Delafield, pathologist, was born in New York City, son of Edward Delafield (5/7/1794); founder, first president, Association of American Physicians (1886); co-author of pathology textbook (1911) (died 1915).

1846 The Iowa state constitution, approved by a convention in May, was ratified; included a clause prohibiting slavery.

1846 Samuel M. Jones, manufacturer, was born in Beddgelert, Wales; developed oil extraction device; known as "Golden Rule" Jones for his enlightened employee practices; mayor of Toledo (1897-1904) (died 1904).

1855 Henry C. Bunner, writer and editor, was born in Oswego, N.Y.; first editor, *Puck Magazine* (died 1896).

1884 Louis Gruenberg, musician, was born in Brest-Litovsk, Russia; pianist, composer (score of operas—*Green Mansions, Emperor Jones; Jazz Suite* (died 1964).

1886 Russell C. Westover, cartoonist, was born in Los Angeles; creator of *Tillie the Toiler* (died 1966).

1894 Harry Heilmann, baseball player, was born in San Francisco; first baseman, batting champion with Detroit Tigers (1914-29); lifetime batting average of .342; named to Baseball Hall of Fame (died 1951).

1900 Ernie Pyle, journalist, was born in Dana, Ind.; prominent World War II correspondent; killed by sniper fire in the Pacific (died 1945).

1904 Albert Halper, author, was born in Chicago; wrote several popular novels (*Union Square, The Foundry, The Chute, Sons of the Fathers*).

1909 Walter Van Tilburg Clark, author, was born in East Oreland, Me.; wrote short stories, novels (*The Oxbow Incident, Track of the Cat*) (died 1971).

1918 Japan and the United States announced plans for joint intervention in Siberia; American troops landed at Vladivostok Aug 4.

1921 Richard Adler, composer, was born in New York City; wrote several hit musicals (*Pajama Game, Damn Yankees*).

1923 Vice President Calvin Coolidge was sworn in as president by his father, a justice of the peace, in Plymouth Notch, Vt., following the death of President Harding.

1924 Leon M. Uris, author, was born in Baltimore; wrote several popular books (*Exodus, Battle Cry, Mila 18, QB VIII, Trinity*).

1926 Tony Bennett, singer, was born in New York City; popular singer in concerts, clubs and television.

1949 The National Basketball League and the Basketball Association of America merged to form the National Basketball Association.

1958 The *Nautilus*, nuclear-powered submarine under command of William R. Anderson, became the first to cross under the Arctic ice of the North Pole.

1981 The federal air traffic controllers (Professional Air Traffic Controllers Organization) began a nationwide strike after rejecting the government's final offer; most of the 12,000 were fired and replaced.

1984 The stock market staged an unprecedented rally as more than 236 million shares changed hands on the New York Stock Exchange (rising 36 points), beating the previous day's record 172.8 million shares; more than 696 million shares were traded during the week.

AUGUST 4

1735 Trial of New York editor, Peter Zanger, ended in acquittal; he was arrested Nov 17, 1734 on a charge of libel; Philadelphia lawyer Andrew Hamilton established the principle of freedom of the press for which the New York Council gave him franchises of the city for "his learned and generous defense of the rights of mankind and the liberty of the press."

1789 Congress authorized the first federal bond issue to fund domestic, state debt.

1790 Congress authorized creation of the Revenue Cutter Service and Coast Guard, with ten vessels for the collection of revenue.

1816 Russell Sage, financier, was born in Oneida County, N.Y.; made fortune in wholesale groceries and stock market; represented New York in the House (1853-57); his widow endowed Russell Sage Foundation with $10 million (died 1906).

1817 Frederick T. Frelinghuysen, Secretary of State (1881-85), was born in Millstone, N.J.; represented New Jersey in the Senate (1866-69, 1871-77) (died 1885).

1823 Oliver P. Morton, legislator and public official, was born in Salisbury, Ind.; served Indiana as governor (1861-67) and as senator (1867-77) (died 1877).

1837 Texas petitioned Congress for annexation to the United States; refused Aug 25.

1858 Charles S. Palmer, chemist, was born in Danville, Ill.; invented basic process for cracking oil to get gasoline (1900); sold rights to Standard Oil (1916) (died 1939).

1860 Obed Hussey, inventor, died at 68; invented, manufactured a grain reaper (1834-58).

1861 Jesse W. Reno, engineer, was born in Ft. Leavenworth, Kas., son of Jesse L. Reno (6/20/1823); invented moving stairway (1892) (died 1947).

1865 John Flanagan, sculptor, was born in Newark; best known for the monumental clock in the Library of Congress.

1867 Jake (Jacob P.) Beckley, baseball player (Pirates, Cards, Reds) was born in Hannibal, Mo.; named to Baseball Hall of Fame (died 1918).

1874 The Chautauqua Movement began at Lake Chautauqua, near Jamestown, N.Y., with a two-week instructional course in Sunday School management by John H. Vincent, a Methodist clergyman, and Lewis Miller of Akron, Ohio; started popular programs which spread widely and rapidly.

1914 President Wilson declared American neutrality in World War I; offered American mediation to the warring nations.

1916 The United States bought the Danish West Indies (now Virgin Islands) from Denmark for $25 million; ratified by the Senate Sept 7.

1919 Walter B. Wriston, banker, was born in Middletown, Conn; executive vice president, First National City Bank (now Citibank), New York City (1960-67), president (1967-70), board chairman (1970-85).

1945 President Truman signed the Bretton Woods Act, which authorized the United States to participate in the UN Food and Agricultural Organization.

1947 Puerto Rico was given the right to elect its own governor by popular vote.

1963 Representatives of the United States, Soviet Russia, and Great Britain signed the Nuclear Test Ban Treaty, prohibiting the testing of nuclear weapons in space, above ground, or under water.

1964 Three white civil rights workers were found murdered and buried in an earthen dam on a farm near Philadelphia, Miss.

1964 President Lyndon Johnson announced American air attacks on North Vietnam oil storage and PT boat bases in retaliation for attacks on American destroyers in the Gulf of Tonkin.

1977 President Carter signed legislation creating the Department of Energy, effective Oct 1, with James R. Schlesinger as the first secretary.

AUGUST 5

1749 Thomas Lynch Jr., planter, was born in Winyah, S.C.; a member of Continental Congress (1776-77) and a signer of the Declaration of Independence; lost at sea (1779).

1774 George Washington was elected a delegate to the Continental Congress.

1819 John Bidwell, frontiersman, was born in Chautauqua County, N.Y.; led first party of settlers overland from the Missouri River to California (1841) (died 1900).

1858 The first successful Atlantic cable was laid; Queen Victoria and Secretary of State James Buchanan exchanged congratulations on Aug 16; broke down Sept 1; not restored to proper functioning until 1866.

1859 Thomas B. Osborne, biochemist, was born in New Haven; known especially for his investigations of vegetable proteins, discovery of the vitamin in cod-liver oil (died 1929).

1861 President Lincoln signed an income tax act—3% on incomes in excess of $800.

1864 Adm. David Farragut began the Union takeover of Mobile Bay from Confederate forces; Farragut during this engagement reputedly said: "Damn the torpedoes, full steam ahead."

1867 President Andrew Johnson asked for the resignation of Secretary of War Edwin M. Stanton; he refused and was suspended (Aug 12), removed Feb 12, 1868).

1867 Jacob Ruppert, brewer, was born in New York City; owner, Ruppert Brewery, New York Yankees (1914-39) (died 1939).

1875 Clare A. Briggs, cartoonist, was born in Reedsburg, Wis.; creator of *When a Feller Needs a Friend* and *Mr. and Mrs* (died 1930).

1875 Malin Craig, Army officer, was born in St. Joseph, Mo.; served in Spanish-American War and World War I; chief of staff (1935-39) (died 1945).

1879 Thomas Holcomb, Marine officer, was born in New Castle, Del.; served in World War I; Marine Corps commandant (1936-43); minister to Union of South Africa (1944-48) (died 1965).

1882 Hugh S. Johnson, general and public official, was born in Ft. Scott, Kas.; originated, supervised, Selective Service, World War I; director, National Recovery Act (NRA) (1933-34) (died 1942).

1886 Bruce Barton, advertising executive and author, was born in Robbins, Tenn.; head of advertising firm (Batton, Barton, Durstine, Osborne) (1918-67); represented New York in the House (1937-41); author (*The Man Nobody Knows, The Book Nobody Knows*) (died 1967).

1889 Conrad P. Aiken, author, was born in Savannah; wrote volumes of poetry (*Earth Triumphant, Brownstone Ecologues*); novels (*The Voyage, Great Circle, Conversation*) (died 1973).

1905 President Theodore Roosevelt met with Russian and Japanese peace commissioners in Oyster Bay, N.Y.; conference began Aug 9 in Portsmouth, N.H.

1906 Wasily Leontief, economist, was born in Leningrad; with Harvard U. (1931-75); awarded 1973 Nobel Economics Prize for developing input-output analysis used in economic planning.

1906 John Huston, movie director, was born in Nevada, Mo., son of Walter Huston (4/6/1884); directed several hit movies (*The Maltese Falcon, Treasure of Sierra Madre, Key Largo, Moby Dick, The African Queen*) (died 1987).

1914 Bryan-Chamoco Treaty was signed, granting the United States exclusive right to build an interoceanic canal in Nicaragua.

1917 The National Guard was transferred into the U.S. Army.

1926 The first talking picture, a series of short features, was shown at the Warner Theater in New York.

1930 Neil A. Armstrong, astronaut, was born in Wapakoneta, Ohio; first man to land on the moon (1969), saying as he stepped on it: "That's one small step for man, one giant step for mankind."

1933 The National Labor Board was established; with Sen. Robert F. Wagner of New York chairman, to decide collective bargaining disagreements.

1962 Marilyn Monroe, screen actress, died in Hollywood after an overdose of sleeping pills.

1982 The House of Representatives by a vote of 204-202 rejected an immediate freeze in American and Russian nuclear arsenals, accepted a call for cuts to be followed by a freeze.

1988 James A. Baker III resigned as Treasury Secretary to take over the Republican presidential campaign of Vice President George Bush, effective Aug 17; he was succeeded by Nicholas F. Brady, Wall St. investment banker.

AUGUST 6

1736 The *Virginia Gazette*, first newspaper in Virginia, was published in Williamsburg by William Parks.

1774 Ann Lee, founder of the American Shakers, landed in New York from England with eight followers.

1777 The bloody battle of Oriskany, N.Y., near Ft. Stanwix, occurred when 860 American troops were ambushed; both sides claimed victory; Gen. Nicholas Herkimer, 49, was mortally wounded in the battle.

1788 The draft of a proposed constitution was submitted to the Constitutional Convention by a five-man committee; debate went on until Sept 15.

1810 William D. Ticknor, publisher, was born in Lebanon, N.H.; founder of a leading American publishing house, published *Atlantic Monthly* and major American and English authors (died 1864).

1811 Judah P. Benjamin, public official, was born in St. Thomas, West Indies; represented Louisiana in the Senate (1852-61); Confederate Secretary of War, of State; went to England after the Civil War, served as Queen's Counsel (1872-83) (died 1884).

1819 Samuel P. Carter, officer, was born in Elizabethton, Tenn.; had distinction of being both a general (Union 1861-63) and an admiral with various commands, including commandant, Naval Academy (1870-73) (died 1891).

1828 Andrew T. Still, osteopath, was born in Jonesboro, Va.; founder of osteopathy, American School of Osteopathy, Kirksville, Mo. (1894) (died 1917).

1861 Edith K. Carow Roosevelt, second wife of President Theodore Roosevelt, was born in Norwich, Conn. (died 1948).

1864 Union naval forces captured all positions around Mobile Bay, occupied Ft. Gaines.

1867 James M. Loeb, banker, was born in New York City; banker, philanthropist; founder, publisher, Loeb Classical Library (died 1933).

1874 James T. Shotwell, international relations expert, was born in Strathroy, Canada; helped set up the United Nations (died 1965).

1889 George C. Kenney, Air Forces general, was born in Yarmouth, Nova Scotia; commander, Allied air forces in South Pacific (1942-45), Strategic Air Command (1945-48) (died 1977).

1893 Louella O. Parsons, columnist, was born in Freeport, Ill., wrote first American movies gossip column, widely syndicated (died 1972).

1895 Francis W. Reichelderfer, chief of U.S. Weather Bureau (1938-63), was born in Harlan, Ind. (died 1983).

1899 Ezra Taft Benson, president of Mormon Church (1985-), was born in Whitney, Ida.; Secretary of Agriculture (1953-61).

1905 Clara Bow, screen actress, was born in New York City; the "It" girl (flapper) of the 1920s (died 1965).

1908 Helen H. Jacobs, tennis player, was born in Globe, Ariz.; a star of 1920s, 30s; women's singles champion (1932-35), Wimbledon (1936).

1911 Lucille Ball, actress, was born in Jamestown, N.Y.; starred on screen and television (*I Love Lucy, The Lucy Show*) (died 1989).

1914 Ellen L. Wilson, first wife of President Wilson, died in the White House at 54.

1917 Robert Mitchum, actor, was born in Bridgeport, Conn.; numerous films (*The Longest Day, Ryan's Daughter*), television (*Winds of War*).

1926 Gertrude Ederle, 20, became the first woman to swim the English Channel, going from Cap Gris-Nez, France to Dover, England in 14 hours, 31 minutes.

1928 Andy Warhol, painter, was born in Pittsburgh; leader of pop art movement of 1960s; film director (*The Chelsea Girls, Mr. Hustler*) (died 1987).

1930 Joseph F. Crater, a New York Supreme Court judge, disappeared in New York City and no trace was ever found of him.

1945 An atomic bomb was dropped on Hiroshima, Japan, by an American plane, killing thousands; this was the first use of atomic energy in wartime.

1965 President Lyndon Johnson signed the Voting Rights Act.

AUGUST 7

1726 James Bowdoin, colonial leader and merchant, was born in Boston; a delegate to the Constitutional Convention, governor of Massachusetts (1785-87); Bowdoin U. named for him (died 1907).

1742 Nathanael Greene, Revolutionary general, was born in what is now Warwick, R.I.; Quartermaster General of Army (1778-80), resigned after congressional criticism; headed successful Army of the South (1780-82) (died 1786).

1789 The War Department was created, with Gen. Henry Knox as the first secretary; took office Sept 12.

1794 President Washington issued a proclamation ordering an end of the Whiskey Rebellion, riots in western Pennsylvania against the excise tax on whiskey; called on governors of Pennsylvania, Maryland, New Jersey, and Virginia for 15,000 militia to quell riots; created first presidential commission to study the problem; riots ended late in September.

1826 Robert G. Dun, businessman, was born in Chillicothe, Ohio; entered mercantile agency (1850), rose to head and organized it as R.G. Dun & Co. (1859); merged with Bradstreet Co. (1933) to form Dun & Bradstreet; publisher, *Dun's Review*, a business weekly (from 1893) (died 1900).

1839 John F. Dryden, insurance executive, was born in Farmington, Me.; established (1875), headed (1881-1912), Prudential Friendly Society, which became Prudential Insurance Co. (1878); represented New Jersey in the Senate (1902-07) (died 1911).

1846 Commodore John Sloat raised the American flag at the capital, Monterey, thus gaining California; a later rebellion was put down Jan 8, 1847.

1856 Lew Dockstader, entertainer, was born in Hartford; black-faced minstrel, one of the leading comedians of his time (died 1924).

1858 Charles R. Crane, industrialist and diplomat, was born in Chicago; president, Crane Co., valves and fittings maker (1912-14); on special mission to Russia (1917), minister to China (1920-21) (died 1939).

1861 Hampton, Va. was burned by Confederate troops.

1861 James B. Eads, St. Louis engineer, received a federal contract to build seven ironclad boats.

1886 Billie Burke, stage and screen actress, was born in Washington, D.C.; featured in many films (*Father of the Bride, Dinner at Eight, The Wizard of Oz*) (died 1970).

1886 Bill (William B.) McKechnie, baseball manager (various teams), was born in Wilkinsburg, Pa.; named to Baseball Hall of Fame (died 1965).

1887 Carl E. Wickman, transportation executive, was born in Varnhus, Sweden; formed company which became the Greyhound Corp. (1930), president (1930-46), chairman (1946-51) (died 1954).

1890 Elizabeth G. Flynn, American Communist leader, was born in Concord, N.H.; with Communist Party (1937-64), imprisoned (1951-53); died in Moscow (1964).

1900 The first Davis Cup matches began at the Longview Cricket Club in Boston, with the United States team defeating an English team 5-0.

1904 Ralph J. Bunche, United Nations official, was born in Detroit; awarded 1950 Nobel Peace Prize for mediating the Palestone war (1948-49) (died 1971).

1904 A train wreck at Eden, Colo. killed 96 persons.

1912 Former President Theodore Roosevelt, denied the Republican presidential nomination, accepted the nomination of the Progressive (Bull Moose) Party.

1918 Alice Wilson, niece of President Wilson, was married to the Rev. Isaac S. McElroy Jr. in the White House with the groom's father officiating.

1927 The International Peace Bridge at Buffalo was dedicated by Vice President Dawes and the Prince of Wales.

1942 Garrison (Gary E.) Keillor, author and story teller (*Lake Wobegone*), was born in Anoka, Minn.

1942 The Marines landed on Guadalcanal, where fighting went on for six months.

1944 The American Third Army reached Brest, France.

1953 The Refugee Relief Act was passed, admitting escapees from Communist aggression into the United States on an emergency basis outside regular quotas.

1964 Congress passed the Tonkin Resolution, authorizing presidential action in Vietnam after North Vietnamese boats reportedly attack American destroyers.

1982 New Jersey Governor Kean signed a bill reinstating the death penalty in that state.

1985 An agreement was reached ending the two-day strike of professional basketball players.

1989 Rep. Michael Leland of Texas and 15 others died when their plane crashed into a mountain in Western Ethiopia enroute to a refugee camp; Leland was chairman of the House Select Committee on Hunger.

AUGUST 8

1672 The Dutch fleet shelled New York, starting the third Anglo-Dutch War, and the English settlers quickly capitulated; Esopus and Albany were also occupied (Aug 15).

1763 Charles Bulfinch, architect, was born in Boston; designed state capitols of Massachusetts, Connecticut, and Maine; architect of National Capitol (1817-30) (died 1844).

1779 Benjamin Silliman, scientist, was born in Trumbull, Conn.; Yale's first chemistry professor, a founder of Yale Medical School (died 1864).

1799 Nathaniel B. Palmer, sea captain and explorer, was born in Stonington, Conn.; first person to sight Antarctica (Nov 18, 1820), but did not land; Palmer Peninsula named for him (died 1877).

1814 American and British peace commissioners met without reaching a solution in Ghent, Belgium; Americans were Henry Clay, John Quincy Adams, Albert Gallatin, James A. Bayard, and Jonathan Russell.

1814 Esther H. Morris, suffragette, was born in Tioga County, N.Y.; instrumnental in winning women's vote in Wyoming, the first state to provide the vote; first American woman justice of the peace (South Pass City, Wyo. 1870-74) (died 1902).

1819 Charles A. Dana, editor and publisher, was born in Hinsdale, N.H.; editor, *New York Tribune* (1847-62), owner and editor, *New York Sun* (1868-97); co-editor, 16-volume *New American Cyclopedia* (died 1897).

1822 George Stoneman, Union general, was born in Busti, N.Y.; led cavalry, Peninsular Campaign; served at Fredericksburg, Atlanta, and throughout south; governor of California (1883-87) (died 1894).

1839 Nelson A. Miles, Army officer, was born in Westminster, Mass.; served in Civil War, led campaigns against the Indians, and served in Spanish-American War; commander, U.S. Army (1895) (died 1925).

1857 Henry Fairfield Osborn, paleontologist, was born in Fairfield, Conn.; curator of vertebrate paleontology, head of American Museum of Natural History (1908-33) (died 1935).

1866 Matthew A. Henson, polar explorer, was born in Charles County, Md.; accompanied Peary on all his North Pole explorations; planted flag there (1909) (died 1955).

1879 Robert H. Smith, reformer, was born in St. Johnsbury, Vt.; co-founder, Alcoholics Anonymous, a self-help organization (1935) (died 1950).

1884 Sara Teasdale, author, was born in St. Louis; poetry ("Rivers to the Sea," "Love Song," "Dark of the Moon," "Strange Victory") (died 1933).

1887 Oliver E. Buckley, director of research, Bell Laboratories (1933-40), president (1940-52), was born in Sloan, Ia. (died 1959).

1890 Daughters of the American Revolution (DAR) was organized in Washington, D.C..

1890 Pauline Lord, actress, was born in Hanford, Cal.; starred in many plays, films (*Anna Christie, Ethan Frome*) (died 1950).

1896 Marjorie Kinnan Rawlings, author of *The Yearling*, was born in Washington, D.C. (died 1959).

1900 A hurricane smashed into Puerto Rico, killing about 2000 persons.

1900 Victor Young, band leader, was born in Chicago; composer ("Sweet Sue," "Street of Dreams," "My Foolish Heart") (died 1956).

1900 The United States won the first David Cup tennis matches; held in Brookline, Mass.

1901 Ernest O. Lawrence, physicist, was born in Canton, S.D.; awarded 1939 Nobel Physics Prize for his invention of the cyclotron, which accelerated advances in nuclear physics (died 1958).

1902 Welton D. Becket, architect, was born in Seattle; designed the Los Angeles Music Center (died 1969).

1908 Arthur J. Goldberg, public official, was born in Chicago; general counsel, CIO; Labor Secretary (1961-62); associate justice, Supreme Court (1962-65); United Nations ambassador (1965-68) (died 1990).

1937 Dustin Hoffman, actor, was born in Los Angeles; numerous starring roles in movies (*Kramer vs. Kramer, The Graduate, Tootsie*).

1942 Four heavy cruisers, three American, were lost in the Battle of Savo Island.

1945 President Truman signed the United Nations charter; ratified by the Senate.

1945 The Allies signed an agreement creating the International War Crimes Tribunal.

AUGUST 9

1619 Sir Thomas Dale, colonial administrator, died at about 40; marshal of Virginia, issued rigorous code to cope with colonists' "laziness and insubordination;" his tenure (1611-16) called "the five years of slavery."

1673 Anthony Colve became governor of New York City, which had been captured by a Dutch squadron; governed until Feb 19, 1674, when news arrived of the end of hostilities between England and Holland; New York was returned to the British.

1680 An Indian revolt drove Spanish settlers out of New Mexico for ten years; 400 colonists were killed, Santa Fe was sacked (Aug 15).

1733 James Clinton, Revolutionary general, was born in Orange County, N.Y., brother of George Clinton (7/26/1739); served at Montreal, Yorktown (died 1812).

1757 Settlers surrendered Ft. William Henry at the southern end of Lake George, N.Y.; the British garrison was massacred by Indians, the fort burned Aug 10.

1793 Solomon L. Juneau, fur trader, was born near Montreal; founder, first mayor of Milwaukee (1846) (died 1856).

1809 William B. Travis, lawyer and soldier, was born near Red Banks, S.C.; commanded the 188 Americans in the Alamo siege and died with them (1836).

1812 Egbert P. Judson, inventor, was born in Syracuse; invented first blasting explosives suitable for railroad construction (died 1893).

1813 The first American blackout occurred when St. Michaels, Md. received a report of an impending British shelling; women, children, and old people were evacuated; British overshot darkened town.

1814 Gen. Andrew Jackson concluded a treaty with the Creek Indians, ending a year-long war; Creeks gave up two-thirds of their territory to the United States.

1818 Capt. James Biddle, representing President Monroe, claimed the northwest Oregon trading post of Astoria as American territory; had been founded in 1811, taken by the British in 1813; restored to the United States Oct 6, 1818.

1819 William T.G. Morton, dentist, was born in Charlton, Mass.; first to use ether in teeth extraction (1846) (died 1868).

1827 William M. Stewart, lawyer and legislator, was born in Galen, N.Y.; while representing Nevada in the Senate (1864-75, 1887-1905), he wrote the 15th Amendment, which holds that race is no bar to voting rights (died 1909).

1829 The first American-made locomotive pulled a train on a new railroad at Honesdale, Pa.; driven by Horatio Allen, Delaware & Hudson Railroad engineer and designer of the locomotive.

1842 Webster-Ashburton Treaty was signed, fixing the American-Canadian border in Maine and Minnesota.

1848 Former President Van Buren was nominated for president by the Free Soil Party meeting in Buffalo; received 191,263 popular votes, no electoral votes.

1862 Confederate forces defeated Union troops at Cedar Mountain, Ga.

1896 Leonide Massine, dancer and choreographer, was born in Moscow; danced and choreographed with many companies (Ballet Russe, New York City Ballet) (died 1979).

1898 Spanish accepted peace terms ending the Spanish-American War; the treaty called for Spain to relinquish Cuba; cede Puerto Rico and a Ladrone island to the United States, and for the United States to occupy Manila until the Philippines decision was made in a treaty.

1905 The Russian-Japanese peace conference began in Portsmouth, N.H.

1910 Mayor William J. Gaynor of New York City was severely wounded by a discharged city employee; never fully recovered, died 1913.

1911 William A. Fowler, astrophysicist, was born in Pittsburgh; shared 1983 Nobel Physics Prize for "a complete theory of the formation of the chemical elements in our universe."

1916 Lassen (Cal.) National Park was established.

1919 Ralph Houk, baseball player (Yankees) and manager (Yankees, Tigers, Red Sox), was born in Lawrence, Kan.

1921 The Veterans Bureau was established to administer all veterans affairs; Col. Charles R. Forbes was named director.

1928 Robert J. Cousy, basketball player, was born in New York City; starred with Holy Cross U. and Boston Celtics (1951-63).

1945 The second atomic bomb was dropped by American planes, this time on Nagasaki, Japan.

1965 The explosion of a missile silo killed 53 at Searcy, Ark.

1974 President Nixon resigned, the first president to do so; was succeeded by Vice President Gerald R. Ford.

1988 The first baseball game under the lights was played in Wrigley Field, Chicago, the first time in 74 years; the game was scheduled for Aug 8 but was rained out.

1989 President Bush signed a $159 billion rescue package for the savings and loan industry; designed to clean up the most heavily indebted savings and loans; created the Resolution Trust Corp.

AUGUST 10

1622 The Council for New England granted John Mason and Sir Ferdinando Gorges a patent for all land lying between the Merrimack and Kennebec rivers in Maine.

1674 William Vesey, Anglican clergyman, was born in Braintree, Mass.; rector of Trinity Church, New York City (1697-1746); Vesey Street in New York City named for him (died 1746).

1753 Edmund J. Randolph, public official, was born in Williamsburg, Va.; a member of the Continental Congress (1779-82) and Constitutional Convention (1787); served Virginia as governor (1786-88); Attorney General (1789-94); Secretary of State (1794-95); chief counsel for Aaron Burr in his treason trial (1807) (died 1813).

1781 Robert R. Livingston of New York was named the first Secretary of Foreign Affairs, serving until Dec 1783.

1790 The *Columbia*, commanded by Capt. Robert Gray, arrived in Boston; completing the first round-the-world voyage by an American vessel; began Oct 1, 1787.

1806 Arunah S. Abell, newspaper publisher, was born in East Providence, R.I.; founder, *Philadelphia Public Ledger* (1836); founder, editor, publisher *Baltimore Sun* (1837-87) (died 1888).

1814 John C. Pemberton, Confederate general, was born in Philadelphia; in command of Vicksburg when it fell to Union troops under Gen. U.S. Grant (died 1881).

1815 William H. Fry, composer, was born in Philadelphia; wrote the first publicly-performed American-written grand opera (*Lenora*) (died 1964).

1821 Jay Cooke, banker, was born in Sandusky, Ohio; financed the Northern Pacific Railroad; when it failed, it precipitated the 1873 panic; had successful mining operations in Utah (died 1905).

1821 Missouri entered the Union as the 24th state.

1843 Joseph McKenna, legislator and jurist, was born in Philadelphia; represented California in the House (1885-1902); Attorney General (1897-98); associate justice, Supreme Court (1898-1925) (died 1926).

1846 Smithsonian Institution was established by Congress after a ten-year fight led by former President John Quincy Adams to accept an endowment from a Britisher, James Smithson, "to found at Washington under the name of Smithsonian Institution, an establishment for the increase and diffusion of knowledge among men."

1849 Horace Fletcher, nutritionist, was born in Lawrence, Mass.; began research, writing, and lecturing on nutrition; Fletcherism and fletcherize became part of the American language (died 1919).

1861 Confederate troops defeated a Union force at Wilson's Creek, Mo., as part of the internal battle over secession; Union Gen. Nathaniel Lyon was killed.

1868 Paul M. Warburg, banker, was born in Hamburg, Germany, brother of Felix W. Warburg (1/14/1871); with Kuhn, Loeb; helped plan national banking reorganization (1907-14), member of first Federal Reserve Board (1914-18); gained prominence by warning of 1929 stock market crash seven months in advance (died 1932).

1874 Herbert C. Hoover, 31st president (1929-33), was born in West Branch, Ia.; chairman, Belgian relief campaign (1915-19); American food administrator (1917-18); Secretary of Commerce (1921-28) (died 1964).

1887 In Chatsworth, Ill., 100 people were killed and hundreds more injured when a burning bridge collapsed under the weight of a crossing train.

1900 Philip Levine, immunologist, was born in Russia; was the first to recognize the Rh factor in blood.

1900 Norma Shearer, screen actress, was born in Montreal; starred in numerous films (*Smilin' Through, Strange Interlude, The Women, The Barretts of Wimpole Street*) (died 1983).

1914 The first members of the Federal Reserve Board were sworn in; Charles A. Hamlin of Boston was chairman.

1917 The Food and Fuel Control Act went into effect, empowering the president to set food and fuel prices and license producers and distributors.

1965 President Lyndon Johnson signed a $7.5 billion housing bill with a rent subsidy provision.

1972 The Herbert Hoover Library in West Branch, Ia. was dedicated.

1977 American and Panamanian negotiators reached an agreement in principle to turn over the Panama Canal to Panama by the year 2000.

1987 The Dow Jones industrial average climbed nearly 44 points to close above 2600 (2635.84) for the first time.

1988 President Reagan signed a bill providing reparation payments of $20,000 to each Japanese-American interned during World War II; the tax-free payments will be made to 60,000 survivors of the internment.

1988 The space shuttle *Discovery* main engines were successfully test fired after a series of delays; plans went ahead for the first space flight since the Jan 28, 1986 explosion of the shuttle *Challenger*.

1989 President Bush announced that he would name Gen. Colin L. Powell, former national security advisor, as chairman of the Joint Chiefs of Staff, the first black in that post.

AUGUST 11

1760 Philip Embury (1789-1835), the first Methodist clergyman in the United States, arrived in New York City; founded the Wesley Chapel (the first John St. Church) in 1768.

1766 Several persons were bayoneted by troops in New York City while trying to rebuild a Liberty Pole; probably the first blood shed for American liberty.

1777 Gen. John Burgoyne, in need of supplies, sent 700 men to Bennington, Vt.; they were routed by Americans led by Gen. John Stark on Aug 16.

1787 The *Kentucky Gazette* was founded in Lexington by the Kentucky surveyor, John Bradford; this was the first newspaper in the state.

1807 David R. Atchison, legislator, was born in Frogtown, Ky.; represented Missouri in the Senate (1843-55), serving as president pro tem 16 times; some felt he was president for one day (Mar 4, 1849), which would have been inauguration day for Zachary Taylor, who waited to be sworn in on Monday, Mar 5; a city in Kansas and county in Missouri named for him (died 1886).

1833 Robert G. Ingersoll, lawyer and orator, was born in Dresden, N.Y.; served as Illinois attorney general (1867-69); became popular speaker on agnosticism, attacking popular Christian beliefs (died 1899).

1841 Burt G. Wilder, zoologist and neurologist, was born in Boston; with Cornell U. (1867-1910), noted for studies of animal brains (died 1925).

1847 Benjamin R. Tillman, legislator, was born in Edgefield County, S.C.; served South Carolina as governor (1890-94) and represented it in the Senate (1895-1918); a leading southern spokesman, popularly known as "Pitchfork Ben" (died 1918).

1862 Carrie Jacobs Bond, composer, was born in Janesville, Wis.; wrote many popular songs ("A Perfect Day," "Just a-Wearyin' for You," "I Love You Truly") (died 1946).

1865 Gifford Pinchot, conservationist, was born in Simsbury, Conn.; first professional American forester; director, Forest Service (1898-1910); a founder, Yale School of Forestry, professor (1903-36); served Pennsylvania as governor (1923-27, 1931-35) (died 1946).

1867 Joseph M. Weber, entertainer was born in New York City; part of Weber and Fields vaudeville comedy team; theater manager (died 1942).

1881 Caroline C. Fillmore, second wife and widow of President Fillmore, died in Buffalo at 67.

1905 Erwin Chagaff, biochemist, was born in Vienna; his work ushered in the modern era of biochemical genetics.

1921 President Harding formally invited Great Britain, France, Italy, and Japan to discuss arms reduction and limitations.

1921 Alex P. Haley, author, was born in Ithaca, N.Y.; wrote popular *Roots* which also became a television series.

1925 Carl T. Rowan, syndicated columnist, was born in Ravenscroft, Tenn.; ambassador to Finland (1963); head, U.S. Information Agency (1964).

1925 Mike Douglas, television host, was born in Chicago; at one time, a singer in the big band era; host of a talk show.

1933 Jerry Falwell, religious leader, was born in Lynchburg, Va.; founder, head, Moral Majority.

1955 Two Flying Boxcars collided in midair over Germany; 66 killed.

1964 Congress approved the War on Poverty (Office of Economic Opportunity); all programs were taken over in 1973 by existing departments.

1965 Six days of rioting in the Watts section of Los Angeles began; resulted in 34 deaths, more than 1000 injuries, and fire damage of $175 million.

1975 The United States vetoed the admission into the United Nations of North and South Vietnam.

1988 Senate unanimously confirmed Richard L. Thornburgh, former Pennsylvania governor, as Attorney General, succeeding Edwin Meese; Thornburgh was sworn in Aug 13; nominated by President-elect Bush to continue in post (1989).

1988 President Reagan signed a $3.9 billion drought relief measure to aid stricken farmers hit by the worst drought in 50 years.

AUGUST 12

1658 A "rattle-watch" of eight men, the first police force, was established in New Amsterdam.

1676 King Philip of Narragansett Indians was killed by an Indian friend of the colonists and the war against the New England colonists ended.

1778 A storm prevented an engagement of French and British fleets off Newport, R.I.; the French fleet and 4000 troops sailed (Aug 22) for Boston for repairs.

1781 Robert Mills, architect, was born in Charleston; the first American-born architect, he served as architect of public buildings, designing the Treasury, Post Office, and Washington Monument (died 1855).

1791 Timothy Pickering was named first Postmaster General, taking office Aug 19.

1846 Richard K. Fox, publisher, was born in Belfast; publisher, *Police Gazette* (1877-1922) (died 1922).

1852 Michael J. McGivney, Catholic priest, was born in Waterbury, Conn.; principal founder of Knights of Columbus (1882) (died 1890).

1856 James B. Brady, financier, was born in New York City; salesman for railroad supply house (1879), became successful financier; known as "Diamond Jim," because of his jewelry (died 1917).

1859 Katherine L. Bates, author and educator, was born in Falmouth, Mass.; English professor, Wellesley College (1891-1925); wrote lyrics for patriotic hymn, "America, the Beautiful" (died 1929).

1862 Julius Rosenwald, merchant and philanthropist, was born in Springfield, Ill.; with Sears Roebuck as vice president (1895-1910), president (1910-25), board chairman (1925-32); set up $40 million fund for welfare of mankind; presented Chicago with Museum of Science and Industry (1929) (died 1932).

1867 President Andrew Johnson suspended Edward M. Stanton as Secretary of War.

1867 Edith Hamilton, classicist, was born in Dresden, Germany; popularized classical literature in the United States (died 1963).

1876 Mary Roberts Rinehart, author, was born in Pittsburgh; novels (*The Circular Staircase, Tish, The Breaking Point*); plays (*Tish, The Bat*) (died 1958).

1877 James W. Wadsworth, legislator, was born in Geneseo, N.Y., grandson of James S. Wadsworth (10/30/1807); represented New York in the Senate (1915-25) and House (1933-51) (died 1952).

1880 Christy (Christopher) Mathewson, baseball pitcher who won 372 games (Giants), was born in Factoryville, Pa.; one of first five to be named to Baseball Hall of Fame (died 1925).

1881 Cecil B. DeMille, movie director and producer, was born in Ashfield, Mass.; produced first full length movie (*The Squaw Man*) and many hits (*Ten Commandments, The King of Kings, Cleopatra, The Crusades*) (died 1959).

1882 George W. Bellows, painter and lithographer, was born in Columbus, Ohio; a leader among realists, did sports, war scenes (*Stag at Sharkeys, Up the Hudson, Polo Game at Lakewood*) (died 1925).

1882 Vincent Bendix, inventor, was born in Moline, Ill.; invented automobile starter, first mass producer of four-wheel brakes (died 1945).

1892 Ray Schalk, baseball player (White Sox), was born in Harvel, Ill.; named to Baseball Hall of Fame (died 1970).

1895 Lynde D. McCormick, World War II admiral, was born in Annapolis; involved in Coral Sea, Midway battles; commander, Atlantic Fleet (1951-52); Allied Atlantic commander, NATO (1952-54); president, Naval War College (1954-56) (died 1956).

1897 Otto Struve, astronomer, was born in Kharkov, Russia; discovered interstellar matter (died 1963).

1898 A protocol was signed ending the Spanish-American War.

1902 International Harvester Co. was incorporated in New Jersey with $120 million capitalization.

1919 Michael Kidd, dancer and choreographer, was born in New York City; choreographed numerous musicals (*Finian's Rainbow, Guys and Dolls, Can-Can*).

1927 Mstislav Rostropovich, cellist and conductor, was born in Baku, Russia; conductor, Washington National Symphony (1977-).

1960 *Echo I*, the first passive communications satellite, was launched.

1970 The postal reform measure was signed, creating an independent U.S. Postal Service, thus relinquishing government control after almost 200 years.

1988 Outgoing Attorney General Edwin Meese III announced the establishment of a new system of "special counsels" to investigate wrongdoings by members of Congress.

AUGUST 13

1751 Academy and College of Philadelphia, founded by Benjamin Franklin, opened; later merged into U. of Pennsylvania.

1788 James McGready (1758?-1817), Presbyterian clergyman, licensed to preach; inspired revivalist movement in Logan County, Ky. (1797-99), which swept through South and West.

1812 The *Essex*, commanded by Capt. David Porter, captured the British sloop, *Alert*.

1818 Lucy Blackwell Stone, women's rights leader, was born near West Brookfield, Mass.; helped organize national women's rights convention in Worcester, Mass. (1850); founder, American Woman's Suffrage Association (1869); founder, co-editor, *Woman's Journal* (1872-93) (died 1893).

1839 Michael A. Corrigan, Catholic prelate, was born in Newark; bishop of Newark, third archbishop of New York (1885-1902) (died 1902).

1844 A constitution framed by a New Jersey convention, restricting the ballot to "white male citizens," was ratified by the people.

1846 American troops under Commodore Robert F. Stockton and Capt. John C. Fremont defeated the Mexican defenders of Los Angeles; Mexicans retook the city later, holding it until Jan 10, 1847.

1849 Lenora M.K. Barry, labor leader, was born in Ireland; headed women's department, Knights of Labor; active in temperance, women's rights movements (died 1930).

1851 Felix Adler, educator and reformer, was born in Alzey, Germany; founder, Society of Ethical Culture (1876), a non-religious association for ethical improvement (died 1933).

1860 Annie Oakley, frontierswoman, was born in Darke County, Ohio; sharpshooter, starred in Buffalo Bill's Wild West Show (died 1926).

1867 George B. Luks, artist, was born in Williamsport, Pa.; painted many notable canvasses (*The Wrestlers, Little Madonna, Woman and Black Cat*); also created the comic strip *The Yellow Kid* (died 1933).

1895 Bert Lahr, actor, was born in New York City; starred in numerous Broadway musicals, movies (*The Wizard of Oz*) (died 1967).

1897 Detlev W. Bronk, physiologist and educator, was born in New York City; founder of biophysics; head of Rockefeller Institute (1953-68) (died 1975).

1898 American troops occupied Manila after nearly a year's siege and a one-day assault.

1899 Alfred J. Hitchcock, movie director and producer, was born in London; master of suspense films, radio and television shows (*The 39 Steps, The Lady Vanishes, Rear Window, Suspicion, Vertigo, The Birds, Dial M for Murder*) (died 1980).

1906 Racial violence in Brownsville, Tex. resulted in the death of one white man; 167 black soldiers from nearby Ft. Brown were dishonorably discharged on circumstantial evidence without a trial; action reversed in 1972, clearing men of the guilty verdict.

1912 Ben (William B.) Hogan, golfer, was born in Dublin, Tex.; considered one of three greatest golfers in the 1900-1950 era.

1912 Salvador E. Luria, biologist, was born in Turin, Italy; shared 1969 Nobel Physiology/Medicine Prize for work on the genetic structure of viruses.

1920 George Shearing, musician, was born in London; popular blind jazz pianist and composer.

1958 Malcolm Lockheed, aircraft manufacturer, died at about 71; founded forerunner of Lockheed Aircraft; designed hydraulic and auto braking systems.

1986 The Senate voted 53-47 to approve President Reagan's request for $100 million in aid to the Nicaraguan Contras; approved by House in June.

AUGUST 14

1607 Two ships of the Plymouth Company arrived at Popham Beach on the Sagadahoc (lower Kennebec) River in Maine; settlers built a fort, other buildings, but venture was abandoned Sept 1608 when the colony failed because of idleness and factionalism.

1734 Thomas Sumter, Revolutionary officer and legislator, was born near Charlottesville, Va.; served in South Carolina campaigns; represented state in the House (1789-93, 1797-1801) and Senate (1801-10) (died 1832).

1755 The Virginia legislature appointed George Washington a colonel in the Virginia regiment and commander-in-chief of Virginia forces protecting the frontier against the French and Indians.

1756 After a four-day siege, Oswego, N.Y. surrendered to French troops under Gen. Louis J. de Montcalm; fort was destroyed.

1773 Peter B. Porter, War of 1812 general and legislator, was born in Salisbury, Conn.; served at Chippawa, Lundy's Lane, and Ft. Erie; represented New York in the House (1809-13, 1815-16); Secretary of War (1828-29) (died 1844).

1776 A convention opened in Annapolis to prepare Maryland's constitution, which was proclaimed Nov 8.

1819 The first Texas newspaper, the *Texas Republican*, was published in Nacogdoches.

1848 The Territory of Oregon was established.

1860 Ernest Thompson Seton, naturalist and author, was born in South Shields, England; author (*Wild Animals I Have Known, Biography of a Grizzly*); chief scout, Boy Scouts of America (1910-15) (died 1946).

1863 Ernest L. Thayer, author, was born in Lawrence, Mass.; remembered for the ballad, "Casey at the Bat" (died 1940).

1869 Daniel C. Jackling, mining engineer, was born in Appleton City, Mo.; developed method of removing low-grade copper ore, revolutionized copper mining (died 1956).

1886 Arthur J. Dempster, physicist, was born in Toronto; built first mass spectrometer (died 1950).

1891 Sarah C. Polk, widow of President Polk, died in Nashville at 87.

1892 C. Bromley Oxnam, Methodist bishop, was born in Sonora, Cal.; a founder, National Council of Churches (1950); president, World Council of Churches (1948-54) (died 1963).

1899 Whit Burnett, anthologist, was born in Salt Lake City; co-founder, editor, *Story Magazine* (1931) (died 1973).

1900 Siege of foreign legations, including American, in Peking was raised by 5000 troops, ending Boxer Rebellion, an anti-foreign Chinese uprising; siege began June 17 and 231 foreigners and many Chinese Christians were killed.

1918 Anna Held, stage and vaudeville comedienne, died at 45.

1925 Russell W. Baker, journalist, was born in Loudon County, Va.; writer of syndicated column for *The New York Times*.

1935 Social Security Act was signed by President Franklin Roosevelt.

1941 Atlantic Charter was issued by President Franklin Roosevelt and Prime Minister Winston Churchill following a three-day meeting at sea off Newfoundland declaring their joint peace aims.

1945 The Japanese government surrendered, bringing World War II to a close.

1947 Danielle Steel, author (*Crossings, Changes, Secrets*), was born in New York City.

1947 Domestic airmail rate was reduced to five cents per ounce, effective Oct 1.

1959 Magic (Earvin) Johnson, basketball player (Los Angeles Lakers), was born in Lansing, Mich.

1964 Federal Employees Salary Act raised the salary of the vice president from $35,000 to $43,000.

1967 Floods damaged most buildings in Fairbanks, Alaska, with a loss of $200 million.

1969 World's largest mint opened in Philadelphia.

1974 The 40-year ban on private gold transactions was lifted.

AUGUST 15

1675 Nicholas Eaton, colonial administrator, died at 82; "president" of Rhode Island (1650-51, 1654), deputy governor (1666-69, 1670-71), governor (1672-74).

1694 A treaty was signed at Albany by representatives of Massachusetts, Connecticut , New York, and New Jersey and the Iroquois tribe.

1765 Andrew Oliver, the Boston Stamp Act agent, resigned; before the effective date of the Act (Nov 1), all agents had resigned.

1790 John Carroll was consecrated as the first American Catholic bishop at Lulworth Castle, England; served the Baltimore diocese.

1812 The garrison at Ft. Dearborn (site of Chicago) was massacred by Indians after it evacuated the post, which was burned the next day.

1814 Gen. Andrew Jackson assumed command of American troops at New Orleans.

1817 A Mississippi convention adopted a state constitution; later ratified by the legislature.

1824 John S. Chisum, frontiersman, was born in Hardeman County, Tenn.; at one time, he was the cattle "king," having the world's largest cattle herd (100,000) (died 1884).

1846 The *Californian*, published by Robert Semple and Walton Colton in Monterey, was the first newspaper in the state.

1855 Walter Hines Page, writer and diplomat, was born in Cary, N.C.; founder, editor, *The World's Work* (1900-13); editor, *Atlantic Monthly* (1895-98); ambassador to Great Britain (1913-18) (died 1918).

1859 Charles A. Comiskey, baseball player and owner, was born in Chicago; player for about 11 years, owner of Chicago White Sox (1900-31); named to Baseball Hall of Fame (died 1931).

1860 Florence K. DeWolfe Harding, wife of President Harding, was born in Marion, Ohio (died 1924).

1879 Ethel Barrymore, actress, was born in Philadelphia, daughter of Maurice Barrymore (3/26/1905) and sister of Lionel (4/28/1878) and John (2/15/1882); starred in numerous plays (*A Doll's House, Alice-Sit-by-the-Fire, The Constant Wife*) (died 1959).

1880 J(acob) J. Shubert, theater producer, was born in Syracuse; with brothers, Lee (3/15/1875) and Abe, were important figures in the theater (died 1963).

1881 Richard S. Reynolds, manufacturer, was born in Bristol, Tenn.; founder (1919), Reynolds Aluminum (originally U.S. Foil Co.) (died 1955).

1887 Edna Ferber, author and playwright, was born in Kalamazoo, Mich.; author (*So Big, Show Boat, Cimarron, Giant*); co-author of several plays (*The Royal Family, Dinner at Eight, Stage Door*) (died 1968).

1888 Albert Spaling, musician, was born in Chicago; a leading violinist of his day (died 1953).

1896 Sheldon Glueck, criminologist, was born in Warsaw; with wife, Eleanor, made pioneering studies of criminal character and behavior (died 1980).

1896 Gerty Theresa Cori, biochemist, was born in Prague; shared 1947 Nobel Physiology/Medicine Prize with husband, Carl F. (12/5/1896), for work on animal starch metabolism (died 1957).

1904 Bill Baird, puppeteer, was born in Grand Island, Neb.; led the 20th century revival of the puppet theater (died 1987).

1912 Julia Child, cooking expert and author, was born in Pasadena, Cal.; popular television performer, columnist; author of several cookbooks.

1914 The Panama Canal was formally opened to traffic; took seven years to build at a cost of $336,500,000; the Panama Railroad steamer, *Ancon*, took nine hours to pass through.

1919 President Wilson vetoed an act repealing daylight savings time; veto was overriden Aug 20.

1922 Lukas Foss, composer and conductor, was born in Berlin; led several symphonies (Buffalo 1963-71, Brooklyn 1971-81, Milwaukee 1981-).

1924 Phyllis S. Schlafly, women's leader, was born in St. Louis; a staunch opponent of the ERA (Equal Rights Amendment).

1935 Flier Wiley Post and entertainer Will Rogers died in a crash of Post's plane in Alaska.

1935 Vernon E. Jordan Jr., civil rights leader, was born in Atlanta; president, National Urban League (1972-81).

1944 The American 7th Army invaded southern France and drove up the Rhone Valley.

1945 Gasoline and fuel oil rationing ended.

1971 The Cost of Living Council was created by executive order; abolished July 1, 1974; President Nixon began a sweeping new economic program, imposing wage and price controls and a rent freeze; also devalued dollar by cutting its tie with gold.

1988 The Republican National Convention opened in New Orleans; nominated Vice President Bush for president, Indiana senator Daniel Quayle for vice president.

AUGUST 16

1777 Gen. John Stark led 1600 New Hampshire and Vermont troops to an important victory near Bennington, Vt., routing the British who sought supplies for Burgoyne's army.

1780 British troops under Lord Charles Cornwallis withstood an American attack on Camden, S.C., inflicting heavy losses on the Americans (800-900 dead, 1000 captured); Baron Johann de Kalb was mortally wounded.

1782 John Adams was named minister plenipotentiary to Holland.

1784 Nathan Hale, editor and publisher, was born in Westhampton, Mass., nephew of Nathan Hale (6/6/1755); owner, editor, *Boston Advertiser* (1814-54); a founder, *North American Review* (1815), *Christian Examiner* (1824) (died 1863).

1789 Amos Kendall, public official, was born in Dunstable, Mass.; Postmaster General (1835-40); business manager for Samuel F.B. Morse and the telegraph; a founder, Gallaudet College (died 1869).

1798 Mirabeau B. Lamar, public official, was born in Warren County, Ga.; vice president; Republic of Texas (1836); president (1838-41); minister to Nicaragua, Costa Rica (1857-59) (died 1859).

1802 Isaac Adams, inventor, was born in Rochester, N.H.; invented power printing press, used primarily for book printing in the 19th century (died 1883).

1811 George Jones, newspaper founder, was born in Poultney, Vt.; a founder, *New York Times* (1851); directed fight against Tweed Ring (died 1891).

1812 An American force of 2500 surrendered Detroit to a combined British-Indian force of 1300; Gen. William Hull surrendered the fort without firing a shot, fearing an Indian massacre of the women and children (including his daughter and grandchildren); British force led by Gen. Isaac Brock.

1824 Marquis de Lafayette, at the invitation of President Monroe, visited the United States staying nearly 16 months.

1828 Joseph B. Carr, Union general, was born in Albany; served at second Bull Run, Richmond, Petersburg, and Gettysburg, where he held the center of the Union line (died 1895).

1851 William H. Harvey, economist, was born in Buffalo, W.Va.; advocate of bimetallism; 1932 Liberal candidate for president (died 1936).

1854 Duncan Phyfe, Scottish-born cabinetmaker, died at 76; his first furniture shop on what is now Fulton St., New York City, turned out his neoclassical-style furniture.

1862 Amos Alonzo Stagg, football coach, was born in West Orange, N.J.; coached at U. of Chicago (1892-1933), U. of the Pacific (1933-46); introduced the huddle, man-in-motion, end-around play (died 1965).

1865 Dennis J. Dougherty, Catholic prelate, was born in Girardville, Pa.; Archbishop of Philadelphia (1918-51) (died 1951).

1868 Bernarr Macfadden, publisher and physical culturist, was born near Mill Spring, Mo.; publisher of several newspapers, magazines (*True Confessions, True Story, Photoplay*) (died 1955).

1879 James F. Bell, first president, General Mills (1928-34), was born in Philadelphia; board chairman (1934-47) (died 1961).

1882 The Harvard Annex, which later became Radcliffe College, was chartered.

1884 Hugo Gernsback, inventor and publisher, was born in Luxembourg; inventor of improved dry battery; helped establish science fiction (died 1967).

1892 Hal (Harold R.) Foster, cartoonist, was born in Halifax; known for his *Prince Valiant* strip (died 1982).

1894 George Meany, labor leader, was born in New York City; president, New York State Federation of Labor (1934-39); secretary-treasurer, AFL (1940-52), president (1952-55); president, AFL-CIO (1955-79) (died 1980).

1896 Gold was discovered on Bonanza Creek and the Klondike River in the Canadian Northwest Territory; gold rush followed (1897-99), when about 100,000 headed for the area.

1904 Wendell M. Stanley, biochemist, was born in Ridgeville, Ind.; virologist, Rockefeller Institute (1931-48); shared 1946 Nobel Chemistry Prize for preparing enzymes, virus proteins in pure form (died 1971).

1930 Frank Gifford, football player and television sportscaster, was born in Santa Monica, Cal.; starred with Southern California, Giants.

1987 The Great Basin National Park near Baker, Nev. was dedicated, the first new national park in 15 years in the 48 contiguous states.

1987 A Northwest Airlines jetliner crashed after taking off from the Detroit airport, killing 154 people.

AUGUST 17

1590 Sir John White arrived at Roanoke Island, N.C. and found no trace of the colonists he had left there July 22, 1585; fate of "Lost Colony" has never been determined.

1786 Davy Crockett, frontiersman, was born in Greene County, Tenn.; represented Tennessee in the House (1827-31, 1833-35); killed at the Alamo (1836).

1799 A convention in Frankfort adopted the Kentucky state constitution.

1803 Capt. John Whistler and a company of soldiers arrived in the Chicago area to build Ft. Dearborn; fort was destroyed in 1812, rebuilt 1816.

1804 Barbara Heck, Irish-born Methodist leader, died at 70; known as Mother of (American) Methodism, she helped organize the first Methodist church in the United States (New York City, 1765).

1807 Robert Fulton's steamboat, the *Clermont*, began its trip on the Hudson River; completed round trip from New York to Albany in 62 hours.

1859 John F. Queeny, chemical manufacturer, was born in Chicago; founder, Monsanto Chemical Co. (1901) (died 1933).

1864 Charles H. Cooley, educator, was born in Ann Arbor, Mich.; a founder of sociology in the United States (died 1929).

1864 Edward W. Eberle, naval officer, was born in Denton, Tex.; commanded the *Oregon* on dash around Cape Horn to participate in battle of Santiago in Spanish-American War; chief of naval operations (1923-27) (died 1929).

1866 Julia Marlowe, actress, was born in Caldbeck, England; starred in Shakespearean and other dramatic roles, many with her husband, Edward H. Sothern (12/6/1859) (died 1950).

1868 Gene Stratton Porter, author, was born in Wabash County, Ind.; popular novelist (*Freckles, Girl of the Limberlost, The Harvester*) (died 1924).

1887 Marcus Garvey, black nationalist leader, was born in Jamaica; founder, Universal Negro Improvement Association, the first important black movement (died 1940).

1887 Samuel A. Stritch, Catholic prelate, was born in Nashville; bishop of Toledo (1921-30); archbishop of Milwaukee (1930-39), of Chicago (1939-46); first American named to the Roman curia (1958), elevated to cardinal (1946) (died 1958).

1890 Harry L. Hopkins, public official, was born in Sioux City, Ia.; administrator, Federal Emergency Relief Administration (1933-38); Secretary of Commerce (1938-40); director, Lend Lease Administration (1941); special assistant to President Franklin Roosevelt (1942-45) (died 1946).

1892 Mae West, stage and screen actress, was born in Brooklyn; a sex symbol of the early 1930s (*Diamond Lil*) (died 1980).

1896 Leslie R. Groves, World War II general, was born in Albany; headed Manhattan Project, which developed the atomic bomb (1942-47) (died 1970).

1903 Joseph Pulitzer gave $1 million to establish the School of Journalism at Columbia U.

1918 Judge Kenesaw M. Landis in Chicago found 100 leaders of the IWW (Industrial Workers of the World) guilty of conspiracy against prosecution of the war.

1943 Week-long conference between President Franklin Roosevelt and Prime Minister Winston Churchill began in Quebec.

1961 The United States and 19 Latin American nations, meeting in Uruguay, signed the Alliance for Progress put forth by President Kennedy Mar 13.

1969 The two-day Hurricane Camille hit the Gulf Coast, leaving at least 300 dead and damage exceeding $300 million; resulted in torrential rains in West Virginia and Virginia, causing floods and killing about 50.

1978 Three Albuquerque, N.M. men (Ben Abruzzo, Max Anderson, Larry Newman) began the first successful crossing of the Atlantic Ocean in a balloon, flying the 3107 miles from Presque Isle, Me. to Paris in 137 hours, six minutes.

1988 The United States exploded a nuclear device under the Nevada desert with Soviet Russian scientists monitoring an American test for the first time.

1988 A Pakistan C-130 exploded shortly after takeoff from Islamabad, killing Pakistan President Zia, American Ambassador Arnold L. Raphel, Brig. Gen. Herbert M. Wasson, chief American defense representative to Pakistan, and 34 others.

AUGUST 18

1587 Virginia Dare was born, the first English child born in the United States; she was a part of the colony on Roanoke Island, N.C. which disappeared.

1774 Meriwether Lewis, explorer, was born in Albemarle County, Va.; named by President Jefferson, whom he served as private secretary, to explore the lands of the Louisiana Purchase; selected William Clark as co-leader; expedition successful (1804-06) (died 1809).

1795 President Washington signed the Jay Treaty with Great Britain.

1803 Nathan Clifford, jurist, was born in Rumney, N.H.; represented Maine in the House (1839-43), Attorney General (1846-48); associate justice, Supreme Court (1858-81) (died 1881).

1807 Charles Francis Adams, diplomat, was born in Boston, son of President John Quincy Adams; represented Massachusetts in the House (1858-61); minister to Great Britain (1861-68), keeping the British neutral during the Civil War; edited the works and memoirs of his father and grandfather (President John Adams) (died 1886).

1818 William F. Barry, artillery officer, was born in New York City; commander of artillery in Sherman's march to the sea; organized, headed, Artillery School, Ft. Monroe, Va. (1867-77) (died 1879).

1834 Marshall Field, merchant, was born near Conway, Mass.; became partner in dry goods store which became Marshall Field & Co., of which he was president (1881-1906); became world's largest wholesale and retail dry goods firm; donated land for U. of Chicago site; gave funds for Columbian Museum at Chicago's Worlds Fair (1893), now the Field Museum of Natural History (died 1906).

1846 Col. Stephen Kearny and an American force occupied Santa Fe and declared New Mexico annexed to the United States.

1847 Robley D. Evans, Spanish-American War admiral, was born in Floyd, Va.; perfected long distance signal light; commanded American fleet in round-the-world trip (1907) (died 1912).

1852 Margaret S. Taylor, widow of President Taylor, died near Pascagoula, Miss. at 63.

1871 Gus Edwards, composer and entertainer, was born in Hohensaliza, Germany; remembered for "School Days" and "By the Light of the Silvery Moon" (died 1945).

1873 Otto A. Harbach, librettist, was born in Salt Lake City; many hit librettos (*The Firefly; Kid Boots; Sunny; No, No, Nanette; Roberta; Rose Marie; The Desert Song*) (died 1963).

1893 Burleigh Grimes, baseball pitcher (Dodgers), was born in Clear Lake, Wis.; won 270 games; named to Baseball Hall of Fame (died 1985).

1917 Caspar W. Weinberger, Defense Secretary (1981-88), was born in San Francisco; Secretary of Health, Education & Welfare (1973-75), publisher, *Fortune* (1988-).

1920 The 19th Amendment, giving women the right to vote, was ratified with the approval of Tennessee, which later rescinded the action; considered ratified by Aug 26.

1927 Rosalynn Smith Carter, wife of President Carter, was born in Plains, Ga.

1934 Roberto Clemente, baseball player (Pirates), was born in Carolina, Puerto Rico; named to Baseball Hall of Fame (died 1972).

1935 Rafer Johnson, athlete, was born in Hillsboro, Tex.; won 1960 Olympic decathlon.

1937 Robert Redford, screen actor, was born in Santa Monica, Ca.; several hit films (*All the President's Men, Butch Cassidy and the Sundance Kid, The Natural, The Sting*).

1938 President Franklin Roosevelt and Canadian Prime Minister Mackenzie King dedicated the Thousand Islands Bridge over the St. Lawrence River.

1940 President Franklin Roosevelt and Canadian Prime Minister Mackenzie King agreed to set up a permanent joint defense board to defend the northern half of continent.

1941 President Franklin Roosevelt signed legislation extending military service to 18 months; House voted for it 203-202, Senate 45-30.

1955 Hurricane Diane ravaged six northeastern states, causing 180 deaths and $457 million in property damage.

1956 Alexander Graham Bell Museum opened in Baddeck, Nova Scotia, where he spent his summers for 35 years.

1969 A three-day music concert took place near Bethel, N.Y. and the affair, known as Woodstock, attracted about 300,000 young people.

1987 The Dow Jones industrial average rose 15.14 points to top the 2700 (2700.57) mark for the first time.

AUGUST 19

1751 Samuel Prescott, colonial leader, was born in Concord, Mass.; accompanied Paul Revere and William Dawes on the ride to alert the colonists (1775); captured by the British (1777), died in Halifax (1777).

1779 American troops under Capt. Henry ("Light Horse Harry") Lee made a successful surprise raid on the fort at Paulus Hook (now part of Jersey City).

1785 Seth Thomas, clock maker, was born in Wolcott, Conn.; associated with Eli Terry and Silas Hoadley; later formed own company (1812) (died 1859).

1793 Samuel G. Goodrich, author, was born in Ridgefield, Conn.; wrote under the name of Peter Parley, producing more than 100 children's stories (some done by staff members); founder, editor, Robert Merry's Museum (1841-50) (died 1860).

1800 James Lennox, bibliophile and philanthropist, was born in New York City; gave land and books to found the Lenox Library, New York City (1870) (died 1880).

1812 The *Constitution* (Old Ironsides), under the command of Capt. Isaac Hull, destroyed the British frigate, *Guerriere*, off Nova Scotia; bested the *Java* on Dec 29.

1814 Gen. Robert Ross led a landing of British troops at Benedict, Md., about 50 miles southeast of Washington.

1848 A letter was published in the *New York Herald* announcing the discovery of gold in California.

1851 Charles E. Hires, businessman, was born near Bridgeton, N.J.; developed root beer (died 1937).

1856 Gail Borden received a patent for "the concentration of milk;" condensed milk was the beginning of various instant foods.

1859 Henry I. Cobb, architect, was born in Brookline, Mass.; among his designs are the Newberry Library, Chicago; the Pennsylvania State Capitol; American U. buildings, Washington (died 1931).

1862 The *New York Tribune* published a letter by Horace Greeley, the "Prayer of 20 Million," in which he said that "all attempts to put down the rebellion and at the same time uphold its inciting cause are preposterous and futile."

1870 Bernard M. Baruch, financier, was born in Camden, S.C.; successful banker; chairman, War Industries Board (1918-19), various other boards in both World Wars; developed plan for development, control of atomic energy (died 1965).

1871 Orville Wright, aviation pioneer, was born in Dayton, Ohio; with brother, Wilbur (4/16/1867), made first successful flights in a motor-powered plane at Kitty Hawk, N.C. Dec 17, 1903 (died 1948).

1873 Fred Stone, actor, was born near Longmont, Colo.; one of the most popular comedians of his day (*The Wizard of Oz, Lightnin'*) (died 1959).

1877 Tom (Thomas T.) Connolly, legislator, was born in McLennan County, Tex.; served Texas in the House (1916-28) and Senate (1928-53) (died 1963).

1878 Manuel L. Quezon, Philippines leader, was born in Luzon; was first president, Commonwealth of the Philippines (1935-41) (died 1944).

1893 Alfred Lunt, actor, was born in Milwaukee; co-starred with wife, Lynn Fontanne (12/6/1887), in 27 plays (*The Guardsman, Design for Living, Taming of the Shrew*) (died 1977).

1902 Ogden Nash, poet, was born in Rye, N.Y.; produced humorous poetry collections (*Hard Lines, I'm a Stranger Here Myself, Good Intentions, The Face is Familiar*) (died 1971).

1903 James G. Cozzen, author, was born in Chicago; novelist (*Guard of Honor, By Love Possessed*) (died 1978).

1906 Philo T. Farnsworth, engineer, was born in Beaver, Wash.; developed early television system; held more than 300 patents in electronics (died 1971).

1914 President Wilson, in a message to the Senate, appealed for neutrality in World War I, had proclaimed such neutrality Aug 4.

1919 Malcolm S. Forbes, magazine publisher, was born in New York City; son of Bertie Forbes (5/14/1880); publisher, *Forbes*; noted balloonist (died 1990).

1931 Willie Shoemaker, jockey, was born in Fabens, Tex.; rode in more than 24,000 races, winning more than 7000.

1960 Francis Gary Powers, pilot of an American U-2 spy plane shot down over Russia (May 5, 1960), was convicted of espionage and sentenced to ten years imprisonment.

1974 Rodger P. Davies, ambassador to Cyprus, was killed by a sniper in Nicosia.

1988 Eight insolvent Texas savings and loan associations were merged into one institution by the Federal Home Loan Bank Board; the $2.5 billion bailout was the largest in the thrift industry.

AUGUST 20

1764 Samuel L. Mitchill, physician and legislator, was born in North Hempstead, Long Island; professor, Columbia U. (1792-1801); an organizer, vice president, Rutgers Medical College (1826-30); a founder, editor, *Medical Repository* (1797-1820); represented New York in the House (1801-04, 1810-13) and Senate (1804-09) (died 1831).

1765 Francis Asbury, Methodist leader, was born near Birmingham, England; missionary to the American colonies (1771); prominent in formation of American Methodist Episcopal Church (1779-84); consecrated as superintendent (1784), assumed title of bishop (1785), ruling this new church until his death (1816).

1781 American and French armies set out from Hudson River to capture the British under Cornwallis in Virginia.

1785 Oliver Hazard Perry, naval leader, was born in South Kingston, R.I., brother of Matthew C. Perry (4/10/1794); commanded naval forces in Lake Erie which defeated the British (1813); sent message; "We have met the enemy and they are ours" (died 1819).

1794 Gen. Anthony Wayne led American troops to victory over Indians in the Battle of Fallen Timbers at the Maumee Rapids (near present Toledo), ending 40 years warfare with the Indians in the Northwest Territory.

1832 Thaddeus S.C. Lowe, aeronaut and inventor, was born in what is now Riverton, N.H.; balloonist with meteorological interests, chief of aeronautics section, Army (1861-65); invented ice-making machine (1865), coke oven (died 1913).

1833 Benjamin Harrison, 23rd president (1889-93), was born in North Bend, Ohio, grandson of President William Henry Harrison; represented Indiana in the Senate (1881-87) (died 1901).

1834 Francis R.T. Nicholls, Confederate general, was born in Donaldsonville, La.; lost left arm at Winchester, left foot at Chancellorsville; first Louisiana governor after Reconstruction (1877); Louisiana chief justice (1892-1912) (died 1912).

1842 Senate ratified the Webster-Ashburton Treaty settling the Canadian-American boundary.

1847 Gen. Winfield Scott and his troops defeated Gen. Antonio Santa Ana and his Mexican army at Churubusco, four miles south of Mexico City; earlier in the day they had taken the heights of Contreras.

1860 Henry T. Rainey, legislator, was born near Carrollton, Ill.; represented Illinois in the House (1902-34, except 1921-23), serving as Speaker (1933-34) (died 1934).

1861 A convention in Wheeling of pro-Union Virginians called for the creation of a new state to be called Kanawha; ratified by popular vote of 18,862 to 514.

1866 President Andrew Johnson issued a proclamation declaring the insurrection and civil war at an end.

1873 Eliel Saarinen, architect, was born in Rantasalmi, Finland; designed League of Nations, Geneva; planned development of Canberra, Australia (died 1950).

1879 Ralph Budd, railroad executive, was born in Waterloo, Ia.; president, Burlington and Great Northern railroads; introduced streamlined trains (died 1962).

1881 Edgar A. Guest, journalist, was born in Birmingham, England; wrote daily "Breakfast Table Chat" for *Detroit Free Press*, including poems that were collected in *A Heap o' Livin'* (died 1959).

1886 Paul (J.O.) Tillich, philosopher and theologian, was born in Starzeddel, Germany; the most influential theologian of his time in North America (died 1965).

1905 Jack (Weldon J.) Teagarden, musician, was born in Vernon, Tex.; noted jazz trombonist with Red Nichols, Paul Whiteman; band leader (died 1964).

1908 Al(fonso R.) Lopez, baseball player (Dodgers, Braves), manager (White Sox, Indians) was born in Tampa, Fla.; named to Baseball Hall of Fame.

1910 Eero Saarinen, architect, was born in Kirkkonummi, Finland, son of Eliel Saarinen (1873 above); designed TWA Terminal, Kennedy Airport; Dulles Airport Terminal, Washington; St. Louis Arch; Beaumont Theater, Lincoln Center (died 1961).

1913 Roger W. Sperry, psychobiologist, was born in Hartford; with Caltech; shared Nobel Physiology/Medicine Prize for work on determining the roles played by each side of the brain.

1924 The Dawes Plan, a method of German reparation payments, was adopted; plan was worked out by a group of experts led by Charles G. Dawes; replaced by the Young Plan May 17, 1930.

1974 The House, without debate, voted 412-3, to accept three articles of impeachment of President Nixon recommended by its Judiciary Committee.

1988 A federal jury in New York ruled that the Hunt brothers—Nelson Bunker, William H., and

Lamar—conspired in an attempt to corner the world silver market a decade ago; they were ordered to pay more than $130 million in damages to Minpeco SA; an appeal was planned.

AUGUST 21

1783 Thomas Garrett, wealthy abolitionist, was born in Upper Darby, Pa.; in 40 years he helped about 300 runaway slaves escape; blacks in Wilmington, where he lived, called him "our Moses" (died 1871).

1796 Asher B. Durand, painter and steel engraver, was born near Newark; co-founder of Hudson River School of landscape painting; co-founder, National Academy of Design (died 1886).

1796 James Lick, financier and philanthropist, was born in Fredericksburg, Pa.; gave $700,000 for "a powerful telescope, superior to and more powerful than any telescope ever yet made," which became basis for Lick Observatory on Mt. Hamilton, Cal. (died 1876).

1822 John Fritz, ironmaster, was born in Chester, Pa.; general superintendent, chief engineer, Bethlehem Steel Co.; helped revolutionize American steel industry (died 1913).

1831 A slave insurrection led by Nat Turner in Southampton County, Va. resulted in the massacre of 55 whites and eventually more stringent laws for slaves.

1843 William Pepper, physician and educator, was born in Philadelphia; with U. of Pennsylvania Medical School (1868-94), founder of first American teaching hospital (1874), nursing school; provost, U. of Pennsylvania (1880-94); a founder, Wharton School of Finance, Philadelphia Free Library (died 1898).

1854 Frank A. Munsey, publisher, was born in Mercer, Me.; founder, publisher, *Argosy Magazine* (1896), *Munsey's Magazine* (1899); at one time owned the *New York Sun, New York Telegram* (died 1925).

1858 Lincoln-Douglas debates began in Ottawa, Ill., with about 12,000 on hand; continued to Oct 15; held in seven Illinois cities—Ottawa, Freeport, Jonesboro, Charleston, Galesburg, Quincy, and Alton.

1863 The Civil War in Missouri and Kansas culminated in a raid on Lawrence, Kan., when a band led by Confederate guerilla captain, William C. Quantrill, killed 150 men and wounded 30 others in what has been called "the most atrocious act of the Civil War."

1865 A convention in Jackson, Miss. adopted an ordinance outlawing slavery, repealed the ordinance seceding from the Union.

1878 American Bar Association organized at Saratoga, N.Y.

1896 Roark Bradford, author, was born in Lauderdale County, Tenn.; wrote *Old Man Adam an' His Children*, which was adapted into *Green Pastures*; also wrote *John Henry* (1948).

1904 Count (William) Basie, pianist and orchestra leader, was born in Red Bank, N.J.; an orchestra leader for more than 40 years (died 1984).

1917 President Wilson fixed the price of bituminous coal; two days later, anthracite; named Harry A. Garfield fuel administrator.

1928 Commerce Secretary Herbert C. Hoover resigned to run for president.

1936 Wilt(on) Chamberlain, basketball player, was born in Philadelphia; starred with San Francisco, Philadelphia, and Los Angeles; scored 31,491 points, including an average 30.1 points per game during his career.

1938 Kenny Rogers, country music singer, was born in Houston; sang with several groups (New Christy Minstrels, First Edition), became star solo singer.

1944 Dumbarton Oaks Conference opened in Washington to draw up the basic proposals for a postwar organization to succeed the League of Nations.

1945 An executive order by President Truman terminated Lend-Lease, which in five years supplied $50.6 billion in aid to foreign nations.

1959 Hawaii becamethe 50th state.

1974 President Ford nominated Nelson Rockefeller for appointment to the vacant vice presidency.

AUGUST 22

1607 Batholomew Gosnold, explorer and colonizer, died of malaria in Jamestown, Va. at about 37; explored New England coast, naming Cape Cod, Martha's Vineyard (after his daughter); vice-admiral of fleet which settled Jamestown, a site he opposed.

1777 British Gen. Barry St. Leger, hearing that an American force under Benedict Arnold was on the way to relieve Ft. Stanwix, retreated to Oswego and eventually Montreal, leaving stores and weapons and Gen. Burgoyne without help.

1778 James K. Paulding, author and public official, was born in Putnam County, N.Y.; wrote humorous pieces, defense against English criticism, many others; Secretary of Navy (1838-41) (died 1860).

1787 John Fitch successfully launched his first steamboat on the Delaware River, with members of the Constitutional Convention looking on.

1802 John I. Blair, railroad executive, was born near Belvidere, N.J.; a founder, Delaware, Lackawanna and Western and Union Pacific railroads; at one time, president of 16 lines (died 1899).

1807 Aaron Burr was tried in Richmond on charges of having levied war against the United States and planning to invade Mexico; acquitted Sept 1.

1814 Joshua Barney's flotilla of boats on the Patuxent River was unable to stop the British fleet nearing Washington.

1834 Samuel P. Langley, scientist and aeronautical pioneer, was born in Roxbury, Mass.; secretary, Smithsonian Institution (1887-1906); experimented in theory, construction of heavier-than-air aircraft, built models which successfully flew 3000 and 4200 ft. (1896), the first flights of mechanically-propelled heavier-than-air machines (died 1906).

1848 Ulysses S. Grant and Julia Boggs were married in St. Louis.

1848 Melville E. Stone, newspaper executive, was born in Hudson, Ill.; founder, owner, *Chicago Daily News* (1875-88); general manager, Associated Press in Illinois (1893-1900), national AP (1900-23) (died 1929).

1851 The yacht *America* won the cup offered by the Royal Yacht Society of England in a race around the Isle of Wight; the cup was presented to the New York Yacht Club; this was the first of the America's Cup races.

1864 Robert L. Howze, Army officer, was born in Overton, Tex.; served in Spanish-American War and Mexico; commanded, 38th Division in France (1918) and in Army of Occupation in Germany (1918-19) (died 1926).

1867 Charles F. Jenkins, inventor, was born near Dayton, Ohio; invented motion picture projector (1895), conical paper cup, one of the first automobile starters, many other devices (died 1934).

1868 Ernest R. Graham, architect, was born in Lowell, Mich.; designed Equitable and Flatiron buildings, New York City; Union Station, Washington; Field Museum and Wrigley Building, Chicago (died 1936).

1868 Willis R. Whitney, chemist, was born in Jamestown, N.Y.; director, General Electric Research Laboratory (1900-28), vice president of research (1928-41) (died 1958).

1878 Edward Johnson, operatic tenor, was born in Guelph, Canada; director, Metropolitan Opera House (1935-50) (died 1959).

1893 Dorothy Parker, author and poet, was born in West End, N.J.; critic, short story writer, poet (*Enough Rope, Not So Deep as a Well, Here Lies, Sunset Guns*) (died 1967).

1893 A tropical storm began an eight-day move from the Caribbean up the East Coast, killing 1000 persons; Charleston, S.C. was ravaged.

1920 Denton A. Cooley, heart surgeon, was born in Houston; a founder, Texas Heart Institute .

1920 Ray D. Bradbury, author, was born in Waukegan; wrote many popular science fiction works (*The Martian Chronicles, The Illustrated Man, Fahrenheit 451*).

1939 Carl Yastrzemski, baseball player, was born in Southampton, N.Y.; starred with Boston Red Sox (1961-83).

1978 Congress passed an amendment to the Constitution giving the District of Columbia full voting rights in Congress; needs ratification by three-fourths of the state legislatures.

AUGUST 23

1751 John Fenno, editor, was born in Boston; founder, editor, *Gazette of the United States* (1789-98) (died 1798).

1761 Jedidiah Morse, clergyman and geographer, was born in Woodstock, Conn.; considered the father of American geography; pastor, First Congregational Church, Charlestown, Mass. (1789-1819); author (*Geography Made Easy*—the first American geography book, went into 25 editions; *Elements of Geography, American Gazeteer*) (died 1826).

1775 King George III issued a proclamation declaring the American colonies in rebellion and ordered suppression of the rebellion.

1826 Francis Wayland, educator, was born in Boston; dean, Yale Law School (1873-1903) (died 1904).

1843 Mexican President Santa Anna notified the United States that Mexico would "consider equivalent to a declaration of war against the Mexican Republic the passage of an act of the incorporation of Texas in the territory of the United States."

1869 Edgar Lee Masters, author, was born in Garnett, Kan.; best known for *The Spoon River Anthology* (died 1950).

1879 The Church of Christ, Scientist, was chartered by Mary Baker Eddy.

1883 Jonathan M. Wainwright, World War II general, was born in Walla Walla, Wash.; defender of Bataan, Corregidor; prisoner of Japan (1942-45) (died 1953).

1887 Alvin Hansen, economist, was born in Viborg, S.D.; considered greatest economist of New Deal (died 1975).

1888 Morris L. Ernst, lawyer, was born in Uniontown, Ala.; general counsel, American Civil Liberties Union (1929-54); successful in getting release of James Joyce's *Ulysses* for American publication (died 1976).

1890 Aubrey W. Williams, government official, was born in Springville, Ala.; executive director, National Youth Administration (NYA) (1935-43) (died 1965).

1905 Ernie Bushmiller, cartoonist, was born in New York City; creator of *Nancy* (died 1982).

1912 Gene Kelly, dancer and screen actor, was born in Pittsburgh; starred in many musicals (*Cover Girl, On the Town, Singing in the Rain*).

1921 Kenneth J. Arrow, economist, was born in New York City; shared 1972 Nobel Economics Prize for work on theory of general economic equilibrium, which helps assess business risks, government economy, and welfare policies.

1921 Charles Lee Brown, industrialist, was born in Richmond, Va.; president, American Telephone & Telegraph (1977-78), chairman (1979-); reorganized AT&T after court-ordered divestiture of the Bell companies.

1922 George Kell, baseball player (Tigers), was born in Swifton, Ark.; named to Baseball Hall of Fame (died 1988).

1924 Robert M. Solow, economist, was born in New York City; 1987 Nobel Economics Prize.

1926 Rudolf Valentino, silent screen idol, died in New York City at 31.

1927 Niccola Sacco and Bartolomeo Vanzetti were executed in Charlestown, Mass. for alleged killing of two men in a Massachusetts payroll holdup despite a six-year worldwide campaign for their release; vindicated July 19, 1977 by a proclamation of the Massachusetts governor.

1931 Hamilton O. Smith, microbiologist, was born in New York City; shared 1978 Nobel Physiology/Medicine Prize for studies of the specificity of restriction enzymes.

1944 French troops recaptured Marseilles.

1982 Environmental Protection Agency proposed new rules to reduce lead in gasoline at a faster rate than had been scheduled.

1988 President Reagan signed a landmark trade bill designed to battle the trade deficit by streamlining the machinery for imposing import curbs and expanding job training.

AUGUST 24

1624 Sir Francis Wyatt, who had been governor of Virginia colony under the London company, was named the first royal governor by James I, serving for two years, then again from 1639-41.

1706 Charleston withstood an attack by French and Spanish privateers.

1795 James W. Wallack, actor and theater manager, was born in London; a Shakespearian actor, he was co-founder of Wallack's Theater, New York City (died 1864).

1810 Theodore Parker, Unitarian clergyman, was born in Lexington, Mass.; grandson of John Parker (7/13/1729); his liberality led him to found a new Congregational Society; a leader in anti-slavery agitation, a member of the secret committee aiding John Brown's raid on Harper's Ferry (died 1860).

1814 Gen. Robert Ross led 4500 British troops to victory over 6000 American militia under Gen. William Winder at Bladensburg, Md.; British went on the next day to burn the Capitol, White House, and Library of Congress in Washington, in retaliation for the burning of York (Toronto) Apr 27, 1813.

1823 John Newton, Union general, was born in Norfolk, Va.; served in most major engagements; chief, Army Engineers (1884-86); public works commissioner, New York City (1886-88); president, Panama Railroad Co. (1888-95) (died 1895).

1835 Lyman R. Blake, inventor was born in South Abington, Mass.; invented a form of shoe that can be sewn and a machine to sew soles on uppers (1858) (died 1883).

1846 Henry Gannett, cartographer, was born in Bath, Me.; known as the father of American mapmaking, he headed U.S. Board of Geographical Names (1890-1910); a founder, National Geographical Society (died 1914).

1847 Charles F. McKim, architect, was born in Chester County, Pa.; principal designer, Boston Public Library, old Madison Square Garden, Penn Station, White House restoration (died 1909).

1848 Fire aboard the liner *Ocean Monarch* off the coast of Wales killed 200 Americans.

1852 Jim (James H.) O'Rourke, baseball player (Braves, Giants), was born in Bridgeport, Conn.; named to Baseball Hall of Fame (died 1919).

1857 The Panic of 1857 began when the New York City branch of the Ohio Life Insurance & Trust Co. of Cincinnati failed; over-speculation in wheat belt real estate and railroad construction triggered the 18-month depression.

1886 William F. Gibbs, naval architect, was born in Philadelphia; directed mass production of American cargo ships in World War II (died 1967).

1887 Harry Hooper, baseball player (Red Sox), was born in Bell Station, Calif.; named to Baseball Hall of Fame (died 1974).

1890 Duke Kahanamoku, the best swimmer in the world between 1912 and 1928, was born in Honolulu; in his time, he held every record in distances up to a half mile (died 1968).

1895 Richard J. Cushing, Catholic prelate, was born in Boston; Archbishop of Boston (1944-70), the world's youngest archbishop at the time of his elevation (died 1970).

1898 Albert Claude, microbiologist, was born in Luxembourg; made fundamental discoveries in anatomy of cells, developed certrifuge methods for separating parts of cells; shared 1974 Nobel Physiology/Medicine Prize for that (died 1983).

1898 Malcolm Cowley, author and editor, was born in Belsano, Pa.; one of the most distinguished critics of American literature; author (*Blue Juanita, Emile's Return*) (died 1989).

1912 Panama Canal Act was passed, exempting vessels of American coastwise trade from payment of canal tolls; protested by Great Britain; President Wilson asked for change in the law and the exemption was eliminated.

1912 Congress created a domestic parcel post system.

1921 Peace treaty with Austria was signed in Vienna, signaling war's end July 2.

1925 Shirley Hufstedler, public official, was born in Denver; a California jurist, she was the first Secretary of Education (1979-81).

1949 North Atlantic Treaty Organization (NATO) was established, agreeing that "an armed attack against one or more of them (United States, Canada, ten European nations) . . . shall be considered an attack against them all."

1954 Congress passed the Communist Control Act which outlawed the Communist Party; signed by President Eisenhower.

1989 The Dow Jones industrial average reached a record high of 2734.64.

1989 The *Voyager 2* spacecraft passed the planet Neptune 3048 miles above its north pole after a 12-year 4.4 billion-mile journey.

1989 Under an agreement between Pete Rose and the baseball commissioner, Rose was permanently banished from baseball, pending an appeal after one year; Rose had been accused of betting on baseball but the agreement stated Rose would not be found formally guilty of betting.

AUGUST 25

1540 Hernando de Alarcon, Spanish explorer who sailed up the Gulf of California, arrived in the Colorado River and proceeded to approximately the junction of the Gila, Williams, and Colorado rivers.

1783 Samuel C. Reid, War of 1812 naval officer, was born in Norwich, Conn.; designed present American flag; the first one, made by his wife, Mary, was flown over the Capitol Apr 12, 1818 (died 1861).

1799 Andrew J. Donelson, Army officer and diplomat, was born near Nashville; reared by Andrew Jackson at The Hermitage, served as Jackson's aide and secretary (1829-37); negotiated treaty of annexation with the Republic of Texas (1844-45), minister to Prussia (1846-49); vice presidential candidate (1856) (died 1871).

1819 Allan Pinkerton, law enforcement official, was born in Glasgow; established first American private detective agency in Chicago (1850); guarded President-elect Lincoln on trip to Washington for inauguration; organized Secret Service (1861-62); prominent in breaking up "Molly Maguires" in coal industry union disorders (died 1884).

1822 Gardiner G. Hubbard, lawyer, was born in Boston; principal backer of Alexander Graham Bell, developer of commercial telephone use; a founder, *Sci-*

ence (1883); founder, first president, National Geographic Society (1888-97) (died 1897).

1825 Henry W. Birge, Union general, was born in Hartford; saw action at Port Hudson, Red River campaign (died 1888).

1828 Robert Trimble, jurist, died at 51; associate justice, Supreme Court (1817-28)

1836 Bret (Francis Brett) Harte, author, was born in Albany; author (*The Luck of Roaring Camp, The Outcasts of Poker Flat*) (died 1902).

1837 Calvin M. Woodward, educator, was born in Fitchburg, Mass.; pioneer in manual training high school development (St. Louis 1880) (died 1914).

1850 Bill (Edgar W.) Nye, writer and lecturer, was born in Shirley, Me.; wrote popular humorous articles (*Laramie, Wyo. Boomerang, New York World*) (died 1896).

1862 William C. Proctor, soap manufacturer, was born in Glendale, Ohio; president, Proctor & Gamble (1907-34); one of first to give half day off on Saturday, provide profit-sharing (died 1934).

1867 James W. Gerard, diplomat, was born in Geneseo, N.Y.; ambassador to Germany (1913-17) (died 1951).

1880 Joshua L. Cowen, inventor, was born in New York City; invented toy electric train (1900); headed Lionel Corp. (1940-65) (died 1965).

1912 Ted Key, cartoonist, was born in Fresno; creator of *Hazel*.

1913 Walter C. Kelly, cartoonist, was born in Philadelphia; creator of *Pogo* (died 1973).

1916 Frederic C. Robbins, microbiologist, was born in Auburn, Ala.; shared 1954 Nobel Physiology/Medicine Prize for his work on polio virus.

1916 National Park Service was established in the Interior Department.

1918 Leonard Bernstein, composer and conductor, was born in Lawrence, Mass.; composed several hit shows (*Candide, On the Town, West Side Story*); also various symphonies, operas, ballets; conductor, New York Philharmonic (1958-69).

1919 George C. Wallace, public official, was born in Clio, Ala.; served Alabama as governor (1962-66, 1970-78, 1983-87); American Independent Party presidential candidate (1972); shot and paralyzed at rally near Washington, D.C..

1921 Peace treaty with Germany signed in Berlin formally ending World War I as of July 2.

1927 Althea Gibson, tennis player, was born in Silver, S.C.; first black woman to win singles, doubles at Wimbledon, Forest Hills (1957-58).

1930 Sean Connery, screen actor (*James Bond* movies), was born in Edinburg, Scotland.

1931 Cecil D. Andrus, Interior Secretary (1977-81), was born in Hood River, Ore.; governor of Idaho (1970-77).

1944 Allied troops entered Paris.

1954 Hurricane Carol swept the East Coast for six days, killing 68, causing $500 million in property damage.

1958 Congress provided pensions of $10,000 to presidential widows (increased to $20,000 in 1971), to presidents $25,000 and up to $50,000 for office space, help (raised to $69,630 and $96,000).

1967 George Lincoln Rockwell, leader of the American Nazi Party, was shot to death by another party member in Arlington, Va.

1981 *Voyager 2*, an unmanned spacecraft, transmitted pictures of Saturn as it passed within 63,000 miles of the planet.

AUGUST 26

1765 Agitation over the forthcoming Stamp Act resulted in a raid in Boston in which the records of the vice-admiralty court were burned, the home of the comptroller of the currency ransacked, and the home and library of Chief Justice Thomas Hutchinson was looted.

1784 Stephen McCormick, inventor, was born in Auburn, Va.; invented a cast-iron plow with detachable parts (died 1875).

1791 John Fitch received a patent for a steamboat on which he had been working since 1785, successfully launched in 1787.

1817 U. of Michigan was established in Detroit by the state legislature.

1818 Illinois adopted its state constitution at a convention in Kaskaskia; included a clause prohibiting slavery.

1835 An address formulated by a committee of the Democratic nominating convention in Baltimore was published in the *Washington Globe*, which was the equivalent of the party's first platform.

1842 The start of the federal fiscal year was changed from Jan 1 to July 1.

1844 John W. Burgess, educator, was born in Cornersville, Tenn.; called the father of American political science; with Columbia U. (1890-1912) (died 1931).

1857 National Teachers Association organized in Philadelphia; became National Education Association in 1870.

1867 Robert R. Moton, educator, was born in Amelia County, Va.; head, Hampton Institute, Va. (1890-1915); succeeded Booker T. Washington as principal at Tuskegee Normal & Industrial Institute (1915-35) (died 1940).

1872 James Couzens, businessman and public official, was born in Chatham, Canada; general manager, Ford Motor Co. (1903-15); mayor of Detroit (1919-22); represented Michigan in the Senate (1922-36); endowed the Children's Fund of Michigan with $12 million (died 1936).

1872 Joseph T. Robinson, legislator, was born in Lonoke, Ark.; served Arkansas as governor (1913) and represented it in the House (1903-13) and Senate (1913-37); Democratic vice presidential candidate (1928) (died 1937).

1873 Lee DeForest, electrical engineer, was born in Council Bluffs, Ia.; sometimes called the father of radio; had more than 300 inventions (triode electron tube), made many contributions to wireless communications; designed, installed first high powered Navy radio stations; exhibited sound movies (1923) (died 1961).

1874 Zona Gale, author, was born in Portage, Wis.; numerous best sellers (*Miss Lulu Bette, Faint Perfume*) (died 1938).

1882 James Franck, physicist and biochemist, was born in Hamburg, Germany; shared 1925 Nobel Physics Prize for discovery of laws governing the impact of electrons on atoms (died 1964).

1884 Earl Derr Biggers, author, was born in Warren, Ohio; remembered for *Seven Keys to Baldpate* and the Charlie Chan stories (died 1933).

1886 Jerome C. Hunsaker, aeronautical engineer, was born in Creston, Ia.; organized first American aeronautical college course (aircraft design at MIT, 1914); designed NC-4 flying boat which flew the Atlantic (1919) (died 1984).

1901 Maxwell D. Taylor, World War II general, was born in Keytesville, Mo.; commander, 101st Airborne Division (1944-45); chairman, Joint Chiefs of Staff (1962-64); ambassador to South Vietnam (1964-65) (died 1987).

1904 Christopher Isherwood, author, was born in Cheshire, England; best known for Berlin stories which formed basis for play, *Cabaret* (died 1986).

1906 Albert B. Sabin, immunologist, was born in Bialystok, Russia; developed vaccine for polio prevention, an attenuated virus vaccine (1959), used widely throughout the world.

1913 Keokuk Dam, the largest dam in the world, opened across the Mississippi River.

1926 Ben(jamin C.) Bradlee, newspaper executive, was born in Boston; executive editor, *Washington Post* (1968-).

1935 Geraldine A. Ferraro, legislator, was born in Newburgh, N.Y.; represented New York in the House; 1984 Democratic vice presidential candidate, the first woman candidate of a major party.

1935 United Auto Workers, meeting in its first convention in Detroit, was chartered by the AFL.

1942 Wendell Willkie began his round-the-world fact-finding tour as a presidential special envoy.

1988 A federal jury in Newark, N.J. acquitted 20 reputed mob figures of racketeering charges ending what is believed to be the nation's longest federal criminal trial—21 months.

AUGUST 27

1637 Charles Calvert, colonial leader, was born in London; governor of Maryland (1661-75), proprietor of colony (1675-1715) (died 1715).

1640 Henry Dunster was chosen first president of Harvard College just three weeks after his arrival from England, where he had been curate of Bury.

1640 A plantation agreement was drawn up by the inhabitants of Providence, in which they covenanted, among other things, "to hould forth liberty of conscience."

1741 Joseph Reed, colonial leader, was born in Trenton, N.J.; served George Washington as military secretary; member, Continental Congress (1777, 1778); president, Pennsylvania supreme executive council (1778-81) (died 1785).

1749 James Madison, educator and clergyman, was born near Staunton, Va., second cousin of President Madison; first Episcopal bishop of Virginia (1790); president, College of William & Mary (1777-1812) (died 1812).

1776 A convention in New Castle adopted the name of Delaware State, chose Dover as its capital, and adopted a constitution, effective Sept 21, 1776.

1776 In the Battle of Long Island, a large British force routed the Americans, inflicting 1500 casualties on the 5000-man force; Americans withdrew while the British were preparing for siege of Brooklyn Heights.

1796 Sophia Smith, philanthropist, was born in Hatfield, Mass.; bequeathed inherited fortune to found Smith College at Northampton, Mass. (opened 1875) (died 1870).

1805 Sallie Chapman Law, hospital manager, was born in Wilkes County, N.C.; known as the mother of the Confederacy; organized, managed hospitals in the South during the Civil War (died 1894).

1809 Hannibal Hamlin, Vice President (1861-65), was born in Paris Hill, Me.; represented Maine in the House (1843-47) and Senate (1848-57, 1857-61, 1869-81) and served the state as governor (1857); minister to Spain (1881-82) (died 1891).

1824 Hiram G. Berry, Union general, was born in Rockland, Me.; saw action in Williamsburg, Fair Oaks, and Chancellorsville, where he was killed May 3, 1863.

1832 Black Hawk was surrendered by the Winnebago Indians, with whom he had taken refuge, to the Indian agency at Prairie du Chien, Wis., ending the brief Black Hawk War.

1839 Emory Upton, Union general and writer, was born near Batavia, N.Y.; served in Tennessee, Alabama, and Georgia; wrote on military tactics and history (died 1881).

1845 A Texas convention approved a state constitution; ratified by voters Oct 13.

1857 James J. Keane, Catholic prelate, was born in Joliet, Ill.; archbishop of Dubuque, Ia. (1911-29) (died 1929).

1858 The second Lincoln-Douglas debate was held in Freeport, Ill. and featured a statement by Douglas that slavery could be introduced or excluded by the people of an area.

1859 The world's first commercially-productive oil well was drilled by Edwin L. Drake at Titusville, Pa.; struck oil at 69-1/2 ft., producing about 25 barrels a day.

1864 John Buchanan published the first newspaper in Montana, the *Montana Post*, in Virginia City.

1865 James H. Breasted, archaeologist and historian, was born in Rockford, Ill.; with U. of Chicago (1894-1935), led numerous expeditions to Egypt and Mesopotamia; a leading Orientalist (died 1935).

1865 Charles G. Dawes, Vice President (1925-29), was born in Marietta, Ohio; Comptroller of Currency (1897-1901); organized, headed, Central Union Trust Co., Chicago (1902-21), chairman (1921-25); first U.S. budget director (1921); developed plan for German reparation payments; ambassador to Great Britain (1929-32); chairman, Reconstruction Finance Corp. (RFC) (1932); shared 1925 Nobel Peace Prize (died 1951).

1871 Theodore Dreiser, author, was born in Terre Haute, Ind.; wrote several popular novels (*Sister Carrie, An American Tragedy, The Titan, The Genius*) (died 1945).

1876 Eugene G. Grace, industrialist, was born in Goshen, N.J.; president, Bethlehem Steel Co. (1913-46), chairman (1946-48) (died 1960).

1877 Lloyd C. Douglas, Lutheran clergyman and author, was born in Columbia City, Ind.; successful novelist (*The Magnificent Obsession, White Banners, The Robe*) (died 1951).

1882 Samuel Goldwyn, movie producer, was born in Warsaw; helped form Metro Goldwyn Mayer, then became independent producer (died 1974).

1890 Man Ray, painter and photographer, was born in Philadelphia as Emmanuel Radinski; co-founder of "dada" group; developed rayograph (objects placed on photographic paper, which is then exposed—"cameraless photography") (died 1976).

1908 Lyndon B. Johnson, 36th president (1963-69), was born near Stonewall, Tex.; represented Texas in the House (1937-49) and Senate (1949-61); Vice President (1961-63), succeeded to presidency on the death of President Kennedy (died 1973).

1913 Martin D. Kamen, biochemist, was born in Toronto; discovered carbon-14 isotope, a basic tool in biochemical and archaeological research.

1915 Walter Heller, economist, was born in Buffalo; chairman, Council of Economic Advisors (1961-64) (died 1987).

1915 N. Ramsey, Harvard U. physicist who shared 1989 Nobel Physics Prize, was born in Washington, D.C.

1917 President Wilson replied to Aug 1 note from the Pope, rejecting the peace overture because negotiations were worthless until a German people's government was created.

1929 Ira Levin, author, was born in New York City; novelist (*Rosemary's Baby, The Boys from Brazil*); playwright (*No Time for Sergeants*).

1935 Federal Theater Project was organized under the Works Project Administration to provide employment for theater artists.

1948 Charles Evans Hughes, former Secretary of State and Supreme Court Chief Justice, died in Osterville, Mass. at 86.

1950 President Truman ordered the Army to seize the railroads to prevent a general strike; roads were returned to private owners in 1952.

1975 Ohio Gov. James Rhodes and 27 Ohio National Guardsmen were exonerated of blame in the shooting of 13 Kent State students, four of whom died, in May 1970 during an anti-Vietnam demonstration.

1988 More than 50,000 marchers re-enacted the Rev. Martin Luther King Jr. march with 250,000 civil rights activists 25 years ago in Washington, D.C.

AUGUST 28

1565 Spanish settlers under Pedro Menéndes de Avilés landed at St. Augustine, Fla., the oldest European settlement still in existence; city founded Sept 8.

1609 Henry Hudson in the *Half Moon* searching for the Northwest Passage, anchored in Delaware Bay.

1728 John Stark, Revolutionary general, was born in Londonderry, N.H.; served at Bunker Hill, Canadian expedition, Trenton, Princeton; led troops to victory at Bennington (died 1822).

1774 Elizabeth Anne Seton, the first American-born Catholic saint, was born in New York City; founder, first superior, Sisters of Charity (1809-21); founder, St. Joseph's College, Emmettsburg, Md.; canonized 1975 (died 1821).

1818 Jean Baptiste Point duSable, Haitian-born pioneer, died at about 73; called the father of Chicago, where he built the first house, opened the first trading post in 1770s.

1823 James Oliver, inventor, was born in Liddesdale, Scotland; invented process to make hard-faced plows, headed plow works (1869-1908) (died 1908).

1830 The locomotive, *Tom Thumb*, built by Peter Cooper, was tested on the Baltimore & Ohio Railroad.

1831 Lucy W. Webb Hayes, wife of President Hayes, was born in Chillicothe, Ohio (died 1889).

1841 Bernhard Listemann, violinist and conductor, was born in Schlotheim, Germany; founded Boston Philharmonic Club (1875) out of which developd the Boston Philharmonic Orchestra; concertmaster, Boston Symphony Orchestra (1881-85) (died 1917).

1861 A combined Union land and sea attack on Forts Clark and Hatteras on the North Carolina coast resulted in a Union takeover.

1862 Irving Hale, World War I general, was born in North Bloomfield, N.Y.; founder, Veterans of Foreign Wars (died 1930).

1867 The Midway Islands were occupied in the name of the United States by Capt. William Reynolds of the USS *Lackawanna*.

1878 George H. Whipple, pathologist and educator, was born in Ashland, N.H.; first dean, U. of Rochester Medical School (1921-55); shared 1934 Nobel Physiology/Medicine Prize for discovery of liver therapy against anemia (died 1976).

1893 Joseph T. McNarney, World War II general, was born in Emporium, Pa.; deputy supreme commander, Mediterranean; commander, American forces in Europe, military governor of Germany (1945-47) (died 1972).

1897 Louis Wirth, sociologist, was born in Gemünden, Germany; pioneered in urban problems (died 1952).

1899 Charles Boyer, screen actor, was born inFigeac, France; starred in many films (*Algiers, Gaslight, Arch of Triumph*) (died 1978).

1908 Roger T. Peterson, ornithologist, was born in Jamestown, N.Y.; author, illustrator of *Field Guide to the Birds*.

1910 Tjalling C. Koopmans, Yale economist, was born in s'Graveland, The Netherlands; shared 1975 Nobel Economics Prize for work in mathematics as it bears on such problems as production efficiency (died 1985).

1914 Richard Tucker, operator tenor, was born in Brooklyn; with the Metropolitan Opera (1945-75), with roles in *Aida, Pagliacci, La Boheme*, etc. (died 1975).

1963 About 200,000 persons demonstrated peacefully in Washington to support blacks' demands for equal rights; highlight of the event was a speech by Dr. Martin Luther King Jr.—"I have a dream that this nation will rise up and live out the true meaning of its creed—'We hold these truths to be self-evident; that all men are created equal.' "

1964 Three days of race rioting broke out in Philadelphia; more than 500 persons were injured, 350 were arrested.

1988 Nearly 70 persons were killed or died later of injuries when three Italian Air Force jets collided during an air show at the Ramstein, West Germany, U.S. Air Force Base; one of the planes crashed and skidded in a huge explosion into a crowd of spectators; hundreds were injured.

AUGUST 29

1629 Administration of the Massachusetts Bay Co. was transferred from England to America; John Winthrop was chosen governor of the colony in Oct.

1776 Men of John Glover's "amphibious" force ferried 9000 men from Long Island, where they were under British fire, across the East River to New York City.

1779 An American expedition led by Gens. John Sullivan and James Clinton defeated a force of 1500 Tories and Indians at Newtown, N.Y. (near present Elmira), ending raids on western Pennsylvania and New York settlements.

1780 Richard Rush, public official and diplomat, was born in Philadelphia, son of Benjamin Rush (12/24/1745); Comptroller of Treasury (1811-14), Attorney General (1814-17); Secretary of State (1817), Secretary of Treasury (1825-29); minister to Great Britain (1817-25), to France (1847-49) (died 1859).

1803 Joseph Galloway, colonial statesman, died at 72; practiced law in Philadelphia; unsuccessful in first Continental Congress trying to create an imperial legislature, rather than independence; went to England, spokesman for Loyalists.

1809 Oliver Wendell Holmes, author and poet, was born in Cambridge; wrote *The Autocrat of the Breakfast Table* and several well-known poems (*The Chambered Nautilus, Old Ironsides, Last Leaf*) (died 1894).

1811 Henry Bergh, reformer, was born in New York City; founder, president, American Society for the Prevention of Cruelty to Animals (SPCA) (1866-88); a founder, American Society for the Prevention of Cruelty to Children (1875) (died 1888).

1814 Alexandria, Va. was saved from destruction by the British fleet by payment of more than $100,000 worth of tobacco, naval stores, and merchandise.

1829 Patrick A. Feehan, Catholic prelate, was born in County Tipperary, Ireland; bishop of Nashville (1865-80), first archbishop of Chicago (1880-1902) (died 1902).

1857 Charles J. Glidden, telephone pioneer, was born in Lowell, Mass.; developed world's first telephone exchange (Lowell 1877), developed system rapidly throughout the country, sold it to Bell; also interested in automobiles, aviation (died 1927).

1862 Second two-day Battle of Bull Run began and Union troops under Gen. John Pope withdrew to Washington with losses of 14,000; Confederates under Gen. Stonewall Jackson lost 9100; Union Gen. Philip Kearny was killed in the battle.

1876 Charles F. Kettering, automotive engineer, was born near Loudonville, Ohio; developed automobile self-starter, helped form what is now Delco; president, General Motors Research Corp. (1920-47) (died 1958).

1899 Lyman L. Lemnitzer, World War II general, was born in Honesdale, Pa.; headed American, UN forces in Far East (1955-57); chairman, Joint Chiefs of Staff (1960-63); supreme commander, NATO forces (1963-69).

1899 George V. Denny Jr., moderator, Town Meeting of the Air (1932-52), was born in Washington, N.C. (died 1959).

1915 Ingrid Bergman, screen actress, was born in Stockholm; numerous starring roles (*Casablanca, Intermezzo, Joan of Arc, Gaslight*) (died 1982).

1916 The Organic Act of the Philippine Islands was passed, greatly enlarging self-government, promised independence as soon as stable government was organized.

1920 Charlie Parker, jazz saxophonist and composer, was born in Kansas City, Kan.; a founder of "bop" music and its leading exponent (died 1955).

1921 A peace treaty was signed with Hungary in Budapest declaring that World War I ended July 2.

1924 Dinah Washington, jazz blues singer, was born in Tuscaloosa, Ala.; known as the queen of the blues (died 1963).

1935 The Railroad Retirement Board was created to administer the railroad retirement and unemployment insurance programs.

1935 The "Labor Day storm" in southern Florida began, lasting nearly two weeks, with 40 persons killed; winds were estimated at 150-200 mph over the Florida Keys.

1938 Peter Jennings, television news announcer, was born in Toronto; with ABC from 1964, evening news anchor (1983-).

1958 Michael Jackson, entertainer, was born in Gary, Ind.; one of most popular singers, entertainers of early 1980s.

1960 Hurricane Donna began, raking the entire Eastern Seaboard with 140 mph winds for nearly two weeks; caused 148 deaths.

1986 Three Lutheran bodies approved a plan to merge into one denomination—the Evangelical Lutheran Church in America—on Jan 1, 1988; the merger will involve the Lutheran Church in America, the American Lutheran Church, and the Association of Evangelical Lutheran Churches.

AUGUST 30

1781 The French fleet, commnded by Adm. Francois de Grasse, arrived in Yorktown, Va. with 3000 troops.

1794 Stephen W. Kearny, Mexican War Army officer, was born in Newark; conquered New Mexico and helped win California (died 1848).

1813 One of the bloodiest Indian massacres in American history occurred at Ft. Mims, Ala., about 35 miles north of Mobile, in which about 250 persons were killed; marked the beginning of the Creek War.

1817 John Williams, Episcopal prelate, was born in Old Deerfield, Mass.; president, Trinity College (1848-53); presiding bishop, Episcopal Church (1887-99); a founder, dean, Berkeley Divinity School, Middletown, Conn. (1854-99) (died 1899).

1820 George F. Root, composer and teacher, was born in Sheffield, Mass.; founder, New York Normal Institute, to train music teachers (1853); composer of hymns ("The Shining Shore"), battle hymns ("The Battle Cry of Freedom;" "Tramp, Tramp, Tramp, the Boys are Marching;" "Just Before the Battle, Mother") (died 1895).

1821 Cornelius H. Delamater, mechanical engineer, was born in Rhinebeck, N.Y.; built first iron boats and first steam engines used in the United States; built engines for the *Monitor* and the first successful submarine (1881) (died 1889).

1822 Rowland H. Macy, merchant, was born on Nantucket Island, Mass.; opened a dry goods store, which later became Macy's department store (1858) (died 1877).

1834 A convention in Nashville, adopted the Tennessee constitution; ratified by popular vote in Mar 1835.

1837 Ellen L. Herndon Arthur, wife of President Arthur, was born in Culpeper Court House, Va. (died 1880).

1869 The first journey down the Colorado River, through the Grand Canyon, was completed by Maj. John Wesley Powell and nine men; the 900-mile trip from Green River in Wyoming to the Grand Wash Cliffs began May 24.

1893 Huey P. Long, public official, was born in Winnfield, La.; known as the "Kingfish," he served Louisiana as governor (1928-32) and represented it in the Senate (1932-35); assassinated in Louisiana State Capitol (1935).

1896 Raymond Massey, actor, was born in Toronto; starred in several films (*Scarlet Pimpernel, Abe Lincoln, East of Eden*), plays (*Idiot's Delight, Abe Lincoln in Illinois*) (died 1983).

1899 Kiki (Hazen S.) Cuyler, baseball player (Pirates, Cubs), was born in Harrisville, Mich.; named to Baseball Hall of Fame (died 1950).

1900 Franklin C. Fry, Lutheran leader, was born in Bethlehem, Pa.; president, United Lutheran church (1944-62), Lutheran World Federation (1957-63), American Lutheran Church (1962-68) (died 1968).

1901 Roy Wilkins, civil rights leader, was born in St. Louis; with NAACP (1931-80), executive secretary (1955-64), executive director (1965-80) (died 1981).

1901 John Gunther, foreign correspondent, was born in Chicago; author of *Inside* books (died 1970).

1904 Charles E. (Chip) Bohlen, diplomat, was born in Clayton, N.Y.; ambassador to Russia (1953-57), to Philippines (1957-59), to France (1962-68) (died 1974).

1907 John W. Mauchly, physicist, was born in Cincinnati; co-inventor of electronic computer (died 1980).

1907 Shirley Booth, actress, was born in New York City; starred on screen (*Come Back, Little Sheba*), on television (*Hazel*).

1909 Joan Blondell, screen actress, was born in New York City; several starring roles (*A Tree Grows in Brooklyn, Footlight Parade*) (died 1979).

1912 Edward M. Purcell, physicist, was born in Taylorville, Ill.; shared 1952 Nobel Physics Prize for measurement of magnetic fields in atomic nuclei.

1918 William D. Haywood and 14 other IWW (Industrial Workers of the World) members were sentenced to 20 years in prison, $20,000 fines, for violating the Espionage Act; 80 others received lesser sentences.

1961 President Kennedy named Gen. Lucius D. Clay as his personal representative in West Berlin, with the rank of ambassador.

1962 A "hot line" was installed connecting Washington and Moscow, permitting quick exchanges by the heads of state.

1983 The eighth space shuttle flight took off from Cape Canaveral, Fla., returned safely Sept 5; featured first flight by an American black astronaut, Guion S. Bluford II.

AUGUST 31

1778 British fleet brought Gen. Clinton's army to Rhode Island; raided shipping and towns in area.

1800 John Blair, jurist, died at 68; represented Virginia in the Constitutional Convention (1787); one of the original associate justices of Supreme Court (1789-96).

1822 Galusha A. Grow, public official, was born in Ashford, Conn.; represented Pennsylvania in the House (1850-63, 1894-1903) and served as Speaker (1861-63) (died 1907).

1847 A convention approved the Illinois constitution; ratified by popular vote Mar 6, 1848.

1874 Edward Lee Thorndike, psychologist and educator, was born in Williamsburg, Mass.; leader in experimental psychology and measurement of learning, intelligence (died 1949).

1875 Ed(ward S.) Plank, baseball pitcher (Athletics), was born in Gettysburg, Pa.; won 327 games in 17 years; named to Baseball Hall of Fame (died 1926).

1885 Dubose Heyward, author and librettist, was born in Charleston; wrote *Porgy* and *Mamba's Daughters*, libretto for *Porgy and Bess* (died 1949).

1886 An earthquake was felt over a 1000-mile area in the southeast; 90 percent of Charleston was damaged, 57 killed and property worth $5 million was destroyed.

1893 Clifton B. Cates, Marine Corps commandant (1948-52), was born in Tiptonville, Tenn. (died 1970).

1897 Frederic March, actor, was born in Racine, Wis.; starred on stage (*The Skin of Our Teeth, Long Day's Journey Into Night*), on screen (*Dr. Jekyll and Mr. Hyde, Best Years of Our Lives, Inherit the Wind*) (died 1975).

1897 A patent was issued to Thomas A. Edison for a motion picture camera.

1903 Arthur Godfrey, entertainer, was born in New York City; starred on radio and television, where he was a leading figure of 1940s and 1950s (died 1983).

1903 The first automobile (Packard) crossed the country—San Francisco to New York—under its own power; took 52 days.

1908 William Saroyan, author, was born in Fresno, Cal.; playwright (*The Time of Your Life, My Heart's in the Highlands*); novelist (*My Name is Aram, The Human Comedy*) (died 1981).

1918 Ted (Theodore S.) Williams, baseball player (Red Sox) who was considered one of the greatest hitters of all time, was born in San Diego; named to Baseball Hall of Fame.

1918 Alan Jay Lerner, playwright and lyricist, was born in New York City; wrote several hit musicals (*Paint Your Wagon, Brigadoon, My Fair Lady, Camelot*) (died 1986).

1935 Frank Robinson, baseball player/manager, was born in Beaumont, Tex.; first to be named Most Valuable Player in both leagues; first black major league manager (Indians 1975); named to Baseball Hall of Fame.

1942 The Bethesda Naval Medical Center was dedicated by President Franklin Roosevelt, who helped draft plans for the center.

1945 Itzhak Perlman, concert violinist, was born in Tel Aviv.

1955 Edwin Moses, Olympic 400-meter hurdles gold medalist (1976, 1984), was born in Dayton, Ohio; won 122 consecutive races (1977-87).

1969 Rocky Marciano, retired world heavyweight boxing champion, died in a plane crash.

1983 Russian planes shot down a Korean Air Lines plane which had drifted over Soviet territory on the island of Sakhalin; all 269 persons aboard died, including 52 Americans (Sept 1, American time).

1988 A Delta Boeing 727 jetliner crashed on takeoff at Dallas-Fort Worth Airport killing 13 persons, but 94 miraculously survived.

SEPTEMBER 1

1646 A synod of Congregational churches met in Cambridge "to discuss, dispute, and cleare up . . . such questions of church government and discipline . . . as they shall thinke needfull and meete; ..." at the third session, Aug 1648, they adopted the Cambridge Platform, which formulated relations between church and state; ratified by the congregations in 1651.

1655 Gov. Peter Stuyvesant led a force to capture Ft. Trinity (New Castle) and Ft. Christina (Sept 15), putting the Swedish colony (Delaware) under the Dutch.

1774 British troops from Boston seized cannon and powder at Charlestown and Cambridge to use for fortifying the Boston Neck.

1779 A French fleet of 35 ships arrived off Georgia.

1785 Peter Cartwright, Methodist clergyman, was born in Amherst County, Va.; a major figure in the religious development of the west (died 1872).

1791 Lydia H.H. Sigourney, author, was born in Norwich, Conn.; most widely read poet of her time ("How to be Happy," "Pocahontas," "The Faded Hope") (died 1865).

1795 James Gordon Bennett, publisher and editor, was born in Keith, Scotland; editor, *New York Enquirer*; founder, editor, *New York Globe* (1832), *New York Herald* (1835-67); developed many new journalistic procedures (died 1872).

1807 Aaron Burr was acquitted after a month-long treason trial in Richmond; he then went into exile in Europe to avoid further prosecutions (for murder of Hamilton in New York and New Jersey, for treason in Ohio, Kentucky, Louisiana, and Mississippi).

1814 The British fleet entered Penobscot Bay and at the cost of one man took all of Maine east of the Penobscot River.

1815 Peace was made with the Indians of the Northwest at a council in Detroit.

1821 William Becknell led a wagon train from Independence, Mo. for Santa Fe, opening the Santa Fe Trail.

1822 Hiram R. Revels, legislator and educator, was born in Fayetteville, N.C.; first black elected to the Senate, representing Mississippi (1870-71); president, Alcorn A & M (1871-74, 1876-1901) (died 1901).

1826 Alfred E. Beach, inventor, was born in Springfield, Mass., brother of Moses S. Beach (10/5/1822); developed shield for tunneling under rivers, streets; built a tunnel in New York City (1869), launching underground transportation (died 1896).

1849 Elizabeth Harrison, educator, was born in Athens, Ky.; leader in kindergarten movement; founder, president, teachers' training school (1887-1920) (died 1927).

1850 A convention in Monterey began consideration of California state constitution; adopted Oct 13, ratified Nov 13; contained clause prohibiting slavery.

1854 Cornerstone laid for first railroad bridge across the Mississippi River, between Rock Island, Ill. and Davenport, Ia.

1864 Gen. John B. Hood and his Confederate troops evacuated Atlanta, moved to Lovejoy's Station, 30 miles southeast, to protect Andersonville and its 34,000 Union prisoners.

1869 Cleveland Abbe, director of Cincinnati Observatory, began issuing weather reports, preceding the start of U.S. Weather Bureau in 1871.

1875 Edgar Rice Burroughs, author, was born in Chicago; creator of *Tarzan*, about whom he wrote 23 books (died 1950).

1877 Rex E. Beach, author, was born in Atwood, Mich.; noted for his Alaskan adventure novels (*The Barrier, Flowing Gold* (died 1949).

1892 Leverett Saltonstall, Massachusetts governor (1939-44) and its representative in the Senate (1944-67), was born in Chestnut Hill, Mass. (died 1979).

1894 A forest fire near Hinckley, Minn. burned more than 160,000 acres, killing 418.

1898 Jimmy Hatlo, cartoonist, was born in Providence; creator of "They'll Do It Every Time" and "Little Iodine" (died 1963).

1897 Walter P. Reuther, labor leader, was born in Wheeling, W.Va.; president, United Auto Workers (1946-70), president, CIO (1952-55) (died 1970).

1904 Joe Venuti, first great jazz violinist, was born at sea near New York (died 1978).

1909 Dr. Frederick Cook announced he had reached the North Pole Apr 21, 1908 (Peary reached the Pole Apr 6, 1909); Cook's proof was considered insufficient.

1915 Germany accepted limitations on submarine warfare demanded by the United States.

1923 Rocky (Rocco) Marciano, boxer, was born in Brocton, Mass.; world heavyweight champion (1952-56), retiring undefeated in 49 fights; died in plane crash (1969).

1933 Conway Twitty, country music singer, was born in Friarspoint, Miss.; composer of several country hits.

1937 President Franklin Roosevelt signed the Wagner-Steagall Act establishing the U.S. Housing Authority in the Department of the Interior to make low interest 60-year loans to local agencies, providing 10% of the funds for slum clearance and housing projects.

1951 The United States, Australia, and New Zealand signed a mutual security pact.

1961 A TWA Constellation crashed near Hinsdale, Ill. shortly after takeoff in Chicago, killing 78 persons.

1965 The Economic Development Administration was established by the Commerce Secretary to help in economic development of areas with severe unemployment.

1972 Bobby Fischer became the first American to win the world chess championship, defeating Boris Spassky of Soviet Russia.

1985 The wreckage of the ocean liner *Titanic*, which sank in 1912 carrying 1500 to their death, was found by an American-French search team.

1988 The Federal Communications Commission announced guidelines to bring high definition television to the United States in the 1990s, providing pictures twice as clear as they are now and improved sound.

SEPTEMBER 2

1630 Massachusetts Bay Colony governor met for first time with with his assistants.

1765 Henry Bouquet, British officer, died at 46; served in expedition against Ft. Duquesne, became colonial citizen; instrumental in crushing Indian rebellion under Pontiac (1763).

1789 Treasury Department established, with Alexander Hamilton becoming the first secretary Sept 11.

1831 William P. Frye, legislator, was born in Lewiston, Me.; represented Maine in the House (1871-81) and Senate (1881-1911), where he was president pro tem (1896-1911) (died 1911).

1837 James H. Wilson, Union general, was born near Shawneetown, Ill.; led cavalry forces in Tennessee and Georgia; second in command of Americans at Boxer Rebellion in Peking (died 1925).

1839 Henry George, economist, was born in Philadelphia; advocated single-tax plan, placing entire burden on the land; author (*Progress and Poverty*) (died 1897).

1850 Eugene Field, newspaper columnist, was born in St. Louis; best remembered for children's verse ("Wynken, Blinken and Nod;" "Little Boy Blue") (died 1895).

1850 Albert G. Spalding, sports businessman, was born in Ogle County, Ill.; co-founder with brother, James, of sporting goods firm; named to Baseball Hall of Fame (died 1915).

1855 Hoke Smith, newspaper owner and public official, was born in Newton, N.C.; owner, *Atlanta Journal* (1887-1900); served Georgia as governor (1907-09, 1911) and in the Senate (1911-21); Secretary of Interior (1893-96) (died 1931).

1864 Union troops under Gen. William T. Sherman occupied Atlanta after its evacuation the previous day.

1866 Hiram W. Johnson, legislator, was born in Sacramento, Cal.; served California as governor (1911-17) and in the Senate (1917-45); 1912 Progressive Party vice presidential candidate (died 1945).

1869 Hiram P. Maxim, was born in Brooklyn, son of Sir Hiram S. Maxim (2/5/1840); invented electrical instruments, automobile improvements, firearm silencer (died 1936).

1885 Many of the 400 Chinese imported to work in the Union Pacific Railroad coal mines were killed during an attack by 200 American miners.

1901 Adolph F. Rupp, basketball coach, was born in Halstead, Kan.; coached U. of Kentucky to 879 wins, four national championships (1930-77) (died 1977).

1914 A convention was signed with Panama defining the boundaries of the Panama Canal Zone, giving the United States control over harbor waters at Colon and Ancon.

1916 The Adamson Act was passed by Congress at the request of President Wilson, providing for an eight-hour day for railroad workers (had been ten) without reducing their wages; effective Jan 1, 1917.

1917 Cleveland Amory, author, was born in Nahant, Mass.; social historian (*The Proper Bostonians*); active conservationist.

1919 Communist Party of America was organized in Chicago.

1937 Peter V. Ueberroth, baseball commissioner, was born in Chicago; president, Los Angeles Olympic Organizing Committee (1982-84); baseball commissioner (1984-89).

1945 The Japanese signed a surrender document aboard the USS *Missouri* in Tokyo Bay.

1947 The Treaty of Rio de Janiero, a defense pact, was signed by 19 American nations, with President Truman on hand for final session; conference began Aug 15.

1948 Terry Bradshaw, football player, was born in Shreveport, La.; quarterback with Pittsburgh Steelers in 1970s, early 1980s.

1952 Jimmy Connors, tennis player, was born in East St. Louis, Ill.; numerous championships (U.S. singles, Wimbledon) in 1970s, 1980s.

1974 Federal standards for private pension plans were adopted.

1988 PTL movement founder Jim Bakker submitted a $165 million plan to buy back the television ministry assets; he had been ousted in 1987 after a sex scandal; Bakker was unable to produce a $3 million letter of credit which would have secured the deal.

SEPTEMBER 3

1609 Henry Hudson aboard the *Half Moon* arrived in New York Harbor, sailed up the river named for him to Albany.

1783 The final peace treaty ending the American Revolution was signed in Paris by John Adams, John Jay, and Benjamin Franklin for the United States and representatives of Great Britain, France, Spain, and Holland.

1803 Prudence Crandall, educator, was born in Hopkinton, R.I.; opened school (1831) for black girls in Canterbury, Conn.; prosecuted (1833), intensifying racial conflict; moved to Illinois (died 1890).

1811 John H. Noyes, social reformer, was born in Brattleboro, Vt.; formed society of Bible communists (1836), established (1848) Oneida Community in central New York; community flourished, became known for silverware; fled to Canada to avoid prosecution for adultery (died 1886).

1820 George Hearst, mining executive and newspaper publisher, was born in Franklin County, Mo.; developed numerous successful mining oprations; publisher, *San Francisco Examiner* (1880-91); represented California in the Senate (1886-91) (died 1891).

1833 The first issue of the *New York Sun* was published, the first penny paper in New York, with Benjamin H. Day as publisher.

1855 The Battle of Ash Hollow (Neb.) occurred when 1200 troops under Gen. W.S. Harney defeated Little Thunder and his Sioux Indians; the attack was designed to punish the Sioux for the Grattan massacre on the California trail.

1856 Louis H. Sullivan, architect, was born in Boston, considered the father of modernist architecture; co-designer, Auditorium Theater, Chicago; designer, Wainwright Building, St. Louis; Transportation Building at 1893 Chicago World Fair (died 1924).

1860 Edward A. Filene, merchant, was born in Salem, Mass.; developed family dry goods and clothing store; applied scientific management principles, promoted employees' welfare, originated bargain basement; founder, Twentieth Century Fund (died 1937).

1861 James Hartness, mechanical engineer and inventor, was born in Schenectady; invented flat turret lathe, automatic die, turret equatorial telescope, screw thread comparator (died 1934).

1895 The first professional football game was played in Latrobe, Pa., with the Latrobe YMCA defeating the Jeannette (Pa.) Athletic Club 12-0.

1901 Ted (Edwin H.) Patrick, editor, *Holiday* (1946-64), was born in Rutherford, N.J. (died 1964).

1905 Carl D. Anderson, physicist, was born in New York City; shared 1963 Nobel Physics Prize for discovery of the positron and ability to produce it artificially.

1907 Loren C. Eiseley, author and anthropologist, was born in Lincoln, Neb.; leading anthropologist who headed U. of Pennsylvania department (1947-59), curator of Early Man Museum (died 1977).

1910 Dorothy Maynor, soprano, was born in Norfolk, Va.; starred in opera and on concert stage (from 1939).

1912 Ohio voters ratified their new constitution; an amendment proposing woman suffrage was defeated.

1913 Alan Ladd, screen actor, was born in Hot Springs, Ark.; starred in several films (*Shane, The Great Gatsby*) (died 1964).

1925 The Navy dirigible *Shenandoah* broke up over Akron; 14 died.

1926 Anne Jackson, actress, was born in Allegheny, Pa.; with husband, Eli Wallach (12/7/1915), formed one of the finest American acting teams.

1939 A German submarine sunk the British passenger liner *Athenia* off the northwest Irish coast with a loss of 112 lives, including 28 Americans.

1940 The United States transferred 50 over-age destroyers to Great Britain in exchange for naval and air bases in Newfoundland, Bermuda, the Bahamas, Jamaica, St. Lucia, Trinidad, Antigua, and British Guiana.

1942 Allied troops crossed the Straits of Messina from Sicily to invade Italy.

1944 Allied troops liberated Brussells.

1976 The spacecraft *Viking II* landed on Mars.

SEPTEMBER 4

1781 Los Angeles was founded by 12 families on instructions of the Spanish governor.

1802 Marcus Whitman, medical missionary, was born in Rushville, N.Y.; served Indians in the Pacific Northwest, instrumental in securing Oregon for the United States; he, his wife, and 12 others were killed by Cayuse Indians Nov 29, 1847.

1803 Sarah Childress Polk, wife of President Polk, was born in Murfressboro, Tenn. (died 1891).

1804 Thomas U. Walter, architect, was born in Philadelphia; appointed architect of the Capitol (1851), designed, supervised construction of wings and dome of the Capitol (1861-65) (died 1887).

1810 Donald McKay, shipbuilder, was born in Nova Scotia; developed, built clipper ships, which were the fastest in the early 1850s (died 1880).

1846 Daniel H. Burnham, architect, was born in Henderson, N.Y.; chief of construction Chicago World Fair (1893); active in city planning (Chicago, Washington, Cleveland, San Francisco, Manila); designed many buildings (Montauk, Chicago; Flatiron, New York City; Union Station, Washington) (died 1912).

1847 The *Santa Fe Republican* was issued, the first English newspaper in New Mexico.

1848 Richard R. Bowker, editor, was born in Salem, Mass.; founder, editor, *Library Journal* (1876-1926); founder, American Library Association; editor, *Publisher's Weekly* (1884-1926) (died 1933).

1863 Union troops occupied Knoxville, Tenn., which had been evacuated.

1864 Atlanta's civilian population was ordered to leave the city.

1866 Simon Lake, mechanical engineer and naval architect, was born in Pleasantville, N.J.; built first gas engine submarine (1897) to operate successfully in the open sea (died 1945).

1875 Rollin Kirby, editorial cartoonist, was born in Galva, Ill.; with *New York World* and *World-Telegram* (1913-39), *New York Post* (1939-42) (died 1952).

1876 George P. Day, founder/head, Yale U. Press (1908-59), was born in New York City; treasurer, Yale U. (1910-42) (died 1959).

1886 Geronimo, Apache Indian chief, surrendered.

1906 Max Delbrück, biologist, was born in Berlin; one of the innovators of molecular biology; shared 1969 Nobel Physiology/Medicine Prize for study of the mechanism of virus infection in living cells (died 1981).

1908 Richard Wright, author, was born near Natchez, Miss.; wrote first influential protest novel by a black writer (*Native Son, Black Boy, The Outsider*) (died 1960).

1913 Stanford Moore, biochemist, was born in Chicago; with Rockefeller U., shared 1972 Nobel Chemistry Prize for pioneering studies in enzymes (died 1982).

1917 The first American was killed in France by bombs dropped on Army Base Hospital #5 at Dannes-Camiers.

1917 Henry Ford II, auto manufacturer, was born in Detroit, son of Edsel Ford (11/6/1893); chief executive officer, Ford Motor Co. (1945-80) (died 1987).

1918 American troops landed in Archangel, Russia; along with other Allied troops were assigned to protect ports.

1918 Paul Harvey, news reporter and commentator, ABC network (1944-), was born in Tulsa.

1918 Billy Talbert, tennis player, was born in Cincinnati; won several championships in 1950s; captain, American Davis Cup team (1952-57).

1949 Tom Watson, golfer, was born in Kansas City, Mo.; one of the great golfers of his time.

1951 Transcontinental television was inaugurated when President Truman spoke at the Japanese Peace Treaty Conference in San Francisco.

1957 Arkansas National Guardsmen, called out by Gov. Orval Faubus, barred nine black students from entering an all-white high school in Little Rock; after a court order and arrival of federal troops, students entered Sept 24.

1961 President Kennedy signed the act creating the Agency for Internatioal Development.

1971 A jet airliner crashed into a mountain near Juneau, Alaska, killing 111.

SEPTEMBER 5

1774 The first Continental Congress assembled in Carpenter's Hall (Chestnut St., between 3d and 4th), Philadelphia, and drew up a declaration of rights and grievances; 12 colonies sent 56 delegates to the meeting; ten resolutions were adopted Oct 14 setting forth the rights of the colonists, among them to "life, liberty and property" and of the provincial legislatures to exclusive power of lawmaking "in all cases of taxation and internal polity"; 13 parliamentary acts since 1763 were declared to violate American rights; Georgia was the only colony not represented; Peyton Randolph of Virginia presided over the Congress, which met until Oct 26.

1781 British fleet of 19 ships under Adm. Thomas Graves engaged the French fleet at the entrance to Chesapeake Bay; British were beaten, disabled, and forced to return to New York, leaving the waters off Yorktown under French control.

1795 A peace treaty was signed with Algiers, costing a total of $992,463.25 and an agreed annual tribute of $27,500.

1804 William A. Graham, legislator and public official, was born in Lincoln County, N.C.; served North Carolina as governor (1845-49), Secretary of the Navy (1850-52); Whig candidate for vice president (1852) (died 1875).

1713 The American brig, *Enterprise*, defeated the English brig, *Boxer*, off Monhegan Island, Me.

1833 George H. Hartford, merchant, was born in Augusta, Me.; took over (1869) Great Atlantic & Pacific Tea Co., developd it into a successful food chain (died 1917).

1835 John G. Carlisle, legislator and public official, was born in what is now Kenton County, Ky.; represented Kentucky in the House (1877-90), serving as Speaker (1888-89), and the Senate (1890-93); Secretary of Treasury (1893-97) (died 1910).

1836 Frank Abbott, dentist, was born in Shapleigh, Me.; invented many dental operating devices, some of which are still used (died 1897).

1856 Thomas E. Watson, legislator, was born near Thomson, Ga.; represented Georgia in the House (1891-93) and Senate (1921-22); Populist nominee for vice president (1896), for president (1904) (died 1922).

1875 Nap(oleon) Lajoie, baseball player, was born in Woonsocket, R.I.; second baseman (1896-1916), mostly with the Cleveland Indians; lifetime batting average of .338; named to Baseball Hall of Fame (died 1959).

1877 Crazy Horse, about 28, Sioux Indian chief, was killed while resisting imprisonment; led Ogalala tribe in Battle of Little Big Horn in which Custer and his men were wiped out.

1879 Frank B. Jewett, electrical engineer, was born in Pasadena, Cal.; president, Bell Telephone Laboratories (1925-44) (died 1949).

1880 James W. Bryce, engineer, was born in New York City; with IBM (from 1917), a pioneer in applying elecronics to business machines; held more than 500 patents (died 1949).

1882 First Labor Day parade held in New York City.

1897 Arthur C. Nielsen, market researcher, was born in Chicago; pioneered in rating of television programs (died 1980).

1902 Darryl F. Zanuck, movie producer, was born in Wahoo, Neb.; produced many hits, beginning with *The Jazz Singer* with Al Jolson (died 1979).

1905 Russian and Japanese representatives signed a peace treaty in Portsmouth, N.H., ending their war; President Theodore Roosevelt was mediator.

1916 Frank G. Yerby, author, was born in Augusta, Ga.; novelist (*The Foxes of Harrow, The Vixens, Pride's Castle, Beaton Row*).

1921 Jack J. Valenti, film executive, was born in Houston; special assistant to President Lyndon Johnson (1963-66); president, Motion Picture Association of America (1966-).

1927 Paul Volcker, economist, was born in Cape May, N.J.; president, Federal Reserve Bank, New York (1975-79); chairman, Federal Reserve Board (1979-88).

1929 Bob Newhart, entertainer, was born in Oak Park, Ill.; popular comedian of 1960s, television personality (1972-).

1939 The United States declared its neutrality in World War II and a proclamation by President Franklin Roosevelt prohibited the export of arms to belligerents.

1975 President Ford was unharmed when a Secret Service agent grabbed a pistol aimed at him by Squeaky (Lynette) Frome.

SEPTEMBER 6

1513 Vasco Nunez de Balboa started from Antigua de Darien to find "the other sea" described by Indians; crossed the Isthmus and discovered the Pacific Sept 25.

1628 A company of colonists, with John Endecott as governor, arrived at Salem, beginning permanent settlement of the Massachusetts Bay Colony.

1711 Henry M. Muhlenberg, religious leader, was born in Einbeck, Germany; as missionary to America, he organized the United Lutheran Church (1748); called the father of Lutheranism in America (died 1787).

1757 Marquis de Lafayette, French general, was born; an intimate associate of George Washington; served at Brandywine, Valley Forge, Yorktown (died 1834).

1781 New London, Conn. plundered and burned by the British.

1782 Martha Jefferson, wife of President Jefferson, died at Monticello at 33.

1805 Horatio Greenough, sculptor, was born in Boston; theory of functionalism is considered his greatest contribution to American art; did statue of Washington (now in Smithsonian), The Rescue (in the Capitol) (died 1852).

1811 James M. Gilliss, naval officer and astronomer, was born in Washington; founder of the Naval Observatory (died 1865).

1819 William S. Rosecrans, Union general, was born in Kingston, Ohio; drove Confederates from West Virginia, making possible creation of that state; headed, Army of the Mississippi, Missouri; minister to Mexico (1868-69); represented California in the House (1881-85); Register of the Treasury (1885-93) (died 1898).

1821 Alvin P. Hovey, Union general and public official, was born near Mt. Vernon, Ind.; credited with winning key battle of Vicksburg campaign; represented Indiana in the House (1887-89) and served as its governor (1889-91); minister to Peru (1865-70) (died 1891).

1842 Melville E. Ingalls, railroad executive, was born in Harrison, Me.; founder, president, Cincinnati, Indianapolis, St. Louis & Chicago Railway (1880-89) and later the consolidated company, the Big Four (1889-1905); president, Chesapeake & Ohio Railroad (1888-1900) (died 1914).

1860 Jane Addams, social worker, was born in Cedarville, Ill.; with Ellen Gates Starr, opened social settlement, Hull House, in Chicago; resident head (1889-1935); president, International Congress of Women (1919); shared 1931 Nobel Peace Prize (died 1935).

1861 Gen. Grant led Union troops in occupying Paducah, Ky.

1864 A convention in Annapolis adopted the Maryland constitution, calling for abolition of slavery; ratified by popular vote Oct 12-13; effective Nov 1.

1869 A coal mine disaster at Avondale, Pa. resulted in 108 deaths.

1873 Howard E. Coffin, engineer and businessman, was born near West Milton, Ohio; co-founder, vice president, Hudson Motor Car Co. (1909-30), designed Hudson car; founder, president, National Air Transport Inc. (1925-28), which later became United Airlines (died 1937).

1875 Arthur Train, lawyer and author, was born in Boston; wrote legal stories, many of them featuring the fictional *Ephraim Tutt* (died 1945).

1876 Boardman Robinson, painter and illustrator, was born in Somerset, Nova Scotia; painted murals in Radio City, Justice Department; pioneer political cartoonist (died 1952).

1878 Henry Seidel Canby, editor and author, was born in Wilmington; editor, *Saturday Review of Literature* (1924-36); author (*The Age of Confidence, Alma Mater, American Estimates*) (died 1961).

1888 Red (Urban C.) Faber, baseball pitcher (White Sox) was born in Cascade, Ia.; won 254 games; named to Baseball Hall of Fame (died 1976).

1888 Joseph P. Kennedy, public official, was born in Boston; first chairman, Securities & Exchange Commission (1934-35); chairman, Maritime Commission (1937); ambassador to Great Britain (1937-40) (died 1969).

1890 Claire L. Chennault, World War II aviator, was born in Commerce, Tex.; commander, American Air Forces in China (1942-45); founder, Flying Tigers (died 1958).

1891 John Charles Thomas, operatic baritone, was born in Meyersdale, Pa.; starred in opera and various radio programs (died 1960).

1893 John W. Bricker, public official, was born in Madison County, Ohio; served Ohio as governor (1939-45) and represented it in the Senate (1947-59); Republican vice presidential candidate (1944) (died 1986).

1899 The "open door" policy in China was announced by Secretary of State John Hay.

1899 Billy Rose, producer and composer, was born in New York City; wrote several hits ("Barney Google," "That Old Gang of Mine," "Me and My Shadow," Without a Song," "Paper Moon"); producer (*Jumbo, Aquacade, Carmen Jones*) (died 1966).

1901 President McKinley was shot while at the Pan-American Exposition in Buffalo by a 28-year-old anarchist, Leon F. Czolgosz; president died eight days later.

1901 Ernst Weber, engineer, was born in Vienna; pioneer in developing microwave communications equipment; president, Microwave Research Institute (1957-69).

1943 Part of the Congressional Limited was derailed near Philadelphia, 79 persons were killed.

1954 President Eisenhower announced that the United States had joined with five other nations to form an agency to investigate peacetime uses of atomic energy; the nations were Great Britain, Canada, France, Australia, and South Africa.

1978 Talks began at Camp David between President Carter, Egyptian President Sadat and Israeli Prime Minister Begin to achieve a Mideast accord.

1985 A DC-9 jetliner crashed on takeoff at the Milwaukee Airport, killing all 31 persons aboard.

SEPTEMBER 7

1630 Court of assistants, sitting at Charlestown, Mass., ordained that the new settlement across the Charles River on the Shawmut Peninsula be known as Boston, after Boston in Litchfield.

1664 British troops captured New Amsterdam from the Dutch, renamed it New York; Dutch recaptured it in Aug 1673 but ceded it to the British in Nov 1674.

1727 William Smith, clergyman and educator, was born in Aberdeen, Scotland; teacher, Academy & Charitable School, Philadelphia, which became the U. of Pennsylvania (1754); served as first provost (1755-91) (1803).

1729 William Burnet, colonial governor, died at 41; served as governor of New York and New Jersey (1720-27) and Massachusetts (1727-29).

1737 Arthur Middleton, colonial administrator, died at 56; led South Carolina movement to overthrow proprietary control (1719), acting governor during absence of crown representative (1725-31).

1749 René Auguste Chouteau, fur trader, was born in New Orleans, brother of Jean Pierre Chouteau (10/10/1758); helped found St. Louis (died 1829).

1783 William Lawrence, merchant, was born in Groton, Mass., brother of Amos Lawrence (4/22/1786) and Abbott Lawrence (12/16/1792); organized first company to manufacture woolen goods in Lowell, Mass. (c 1825) (died 1848).

1815 Howell Cobb, legislator and public official, was born in Jefferson County, Ga.; represented Georgia in the House (1843-51, 1855-57), serving as Speaker (1849-50); served state as governor (1851-55); Secretary of Treasury (1857-60); urged secession of Georgia at Lincoln's election; served as a Confederate general (died 1868).

1819 Thomas A. Hendricks, vice president (1885), was born near Zanesville, Ohio; represented Indiana in the House (1851-55) and Senate (1863-69) and served the state as governor (1872); commissioner, U.S. General Land Office (1855-59); served as vice president only from Mar 4 to Nov 25, 1885, dying in office.

1829 Ferdinand V. Hayden, geologist, was born in Westfield, Mass.; with U.S. Geological Survey (1872-96), instrumental in establishing Yellowstone National Park (died 1887).

1840 Luther C. Crowell, inventor, was born in Cape Cod, Mass.; invented square-bottomed paper bag, machinery for its manufacture; improved printing press (died 1903).

1846 Regents of the Smithsonian Institution met for the first time and named Joseph Henry (12/17/1797) as first secretary; served until 1878.

1860 Grandma (Anna M.) Moses, painter, was born in Greenwich, N.Y.; well-known "primitive" painter (died 1961).

1862 Confederate troops under Gen. Robert E. Lee occupied Frederick, Md.; had expected Union force to evacuate Harpers Ferry, W. Va.; when they did not, Lee split his forces.

1863 Union troops captured Ft. Wagner in Charleston Harbor.

1867 J(ohn) P. Morgan II, banker, was born in Irvington, N.Y., son of J.P. Morgan (4/17/1837); headed family firm; acted as agent for Allied governments in floating large American loans during World War I; donated art collection to Metropolitan Museum of Art, New York City (died 1943).

1871 The U. of Nebraska opened.

1873 Carl L. Becker, historian, was born in Lincoln Township, Ia.; taught at Cornell (1917-45); author (*Our Great Experiment in Democracy, Progress and Power*) (died 1945).

1875 Edward F. Hutton, founder, E.F. Hutton & Co., was born in New York City; chairman, senior partner (1904-62); founder, Freedoms Foundation (1949) (died 1962).

1892 Jim Corbett beat John L. Sullivan in 21 rounds in New Orleans for the world's heavyweight boxing championship; it was the first title fight using padded gloves.

1900 Taylor Caldwell, author, was born in Manchester, England; wrote many novels (*Dynasty of Death, The Eagles Gather, This Side of Innocence*) (died 1985).

1908 Michael E. DeBakey, surgeon, was born in Lake Charles, La.; pioneer in developing procedures for heart surgery and transplants.

1909 Elia Kazan, stage and screen director and author, was born in Istanbul; stage plays (*The Skin of Our Teeth, Death of a Salesman, Cat on a Hot Tin Roof*), screen plays (*On the Waterfront, Gentleman's Agreement*); author (*The Arrangement*).

1914 James A. Van Allen, physicist, was born in Mt. Pleasant, Ia.; specialized in high altitude research; discovered magnetosphere or Van Allen radiation belts around the earth (1958).

1916 United States Shipping Board was created.

1917 The American transport *Minnehaha* was sunk by a submarine off the Irish coast; 48 persons were lost.

1918 John E. Swearingen Jr., president/chairman, Indiana Standard Oil (1958-83); was born in Columbia, S.C.; named chief executive officer, Continental Illinois Corp. by the Federal Deposit Insurance Corp.

1923 (Mae) Louise Suggs, golfer who had 50 career victories, was born in Atlanta; won Women's Open (1948, 1952) and LPGA (1957); named to LPGA Hall of Fame.

1924 Daniel K. Inouye, legislator, was born in Honolulu; first elected representative of Hawaii and the first American of Japanese ancestry in Congress; represented Hawaii in the Senate (1963-   ).

1936 Buddy (Charles) Holly, singer and guitarist, was born in Lubbock, Tex.; a major influence on early rock-and-roll music (died 1959).

1965 A three-day hurricane, Betsy, hit the Gulf Coast states, killing 80 (mostly in New Orleans) and causing an estimated $1.3 billion in damage.

1988 Securities & Exchange Commission accused Drexel Burnham Lambert Inc. of extensive fraud, with Michael Milken, head of its junk-bond financing division, as the principal target.

SEPTEMBER 8

1565 First American Catholic parish was organized in St. Augustine, Fla.

1685 Thomas Fleet, newspaper publisher, was born in Shropshire, England; founder, publisher, *Boston Evening Post* (1735-58) (died 1758).

1779 French naval forces with 6000 men led by Adm. Comte d'Estaing arrived off Savannah from the West Indies.

1781 American troops under Gen. Nathanael Greene and Frances Marion, the "Swamp Fox," inflicted heavy losses on the British at Eutaw Springs, S.C., forcing their withdrawal to Charleston.

1815 Alexander Ramsey, public official, was born near Harrisburg, Pa.; governor of Minnesota as a territory (1849-53) and state (1859-63) and represented it in the Senate (1863-75); Secretary of War (1879-81) (died 1903).

1828 Margaret Olivia Sage, philanthropist, was born in Syracuse; inherited $70 million fortune from her husband, Russell (8/4/1816); established Russell Sage Foundation to improve American social and living conditions; her vast philanthropies to many institutions were attributed to an effort to counteract her husband's reputation as a skinflint (died 1918).

1828 Joshua L. Chamberlain, Union general, was born in Brewer, Me.; won Congressional Medal of Honor for actions at Gettysburg defending Little Round Top; served Maine as governor (1866-70); president, Bowdoin College (1871-73) (died 1914).

1829 Seth M. Brown, Confederate general, was born in Fredericksburg, Va.; saw action at Vicksburg, Richmond (died 1900).

1860 A Lake Michigan excursion ship, *Lady Elgin*, collided with a lumber ship; 300 persons were killed.

1872 George H. Dern, mining executive and public official, was born in Dodge County, Neb.; served as governor of Utah (1925-32), Secretary of War (1933-36); co-inventor of Holt-Dern ore roaster (died 1936).

1873 David O. McKay, church leader, was born in Huntsville, Utah; president, Mormon Church (1951-70) (died 1970).

1887 Jacob L. Devers, World War II general, was born in York, Pa.; headed invsion of southern France; commander, Army ground forces (1945-49) (died 1979).

1889 Robert A. Taft, legislator, was born in Cincinnati, son of President Taft; called "Mr. Republican," he represented Ohio in the Senate (1939-53) (died 1953).

1892 The pledge of allegiance to the flag appeared in the juvenile periodical, *The Youth's Companion*; written by Assistant Editor Francis Bellamy.

1896 Howard Dietz, lyricist, was born in New York City; wrote lyrics for several hit shows (*Three's a Crowd, Little Show, Merry-Go-Round*) (died 1983).

1900 A flood and tidal wave hit Galveston, with a loss of 6000 lives and a property loss of $15 million; a storm with 100 mph winds raged for 14 days.

1907 Buck (Walter F.) Leonard, known as "the black Lou Gehrig," was born in Rocky Mount, N.C.; named to Baseball Hall of Fame.

1920 Transcontinental airmail service was established between New York and San Francisco.

1922 Sid Ceasar, entertainer, was born in Yonkers; an early television star (*Show of Shows*).

1934 A fire aboard the steamer *Morro Castle* off the New Jersey coast resulted in 137 deaths.

1935 Huey Long, Louisiana senator and former governor, was fatally wounded in Baton Rouge by Dr. Carl A. Weiss; died two days later.

1943 Italy surrendered to the Allies; on Oct 13, it declared war on Germany.

1951 The Japanese peace treaty was signed in San Francisco by the United States, Japan, and 47 other nations.

1954 The Southeast Asia Treaty Organization (SEATO) was formed in Manila by the United States, Great Britain, France, Australia, New Zealand, the Philippines, Pakistan, and Thailand.

1971 The John F. Kennedy Center opened in Washington, D.C.

1974 President Ford issued an unconditional pardon to former President Nixon for all crimes he "committed or may have committed" while president.

1982 Founder William S. Paley announced his resignation as chairman of Columbia Broadcasting System, effective Apr 20, 1983; returned in the fall of 1986 with major company reorganization.

1982 An agreement was announced for the merger of the American Lutheran Church, the Association of Evangelical Lutheran Churches, and the Lutheran Church in America to form a single church of 5.5 million members.

1988 Angelo B. Giamatti, former Yale U. president and president of the National (Baseball) League, was named baseball's seventh commissioner, effective Apr 1, 1989 (died 1989); he succeeded Peter Ueberroth, who did not seek to be renamed.

SEPTEMBER 9

1675 The New England Confederation declared war on the Wampanoag Indians (the King Philip War); fighting lasted until Aug 1676 (two years longer in Maine), with the death of one out of every 16 men of military age, a cost of £90,000, and the destruction of 12 towns.

1711 Thomas Hutchinson, colonial governor, was born in Boston; colonial chief justice when the Stamp Act was upheld, as a result of which his home was burned by a mob (1765); royal governor of Massachusetts (1771-74), his actions hastened the Revolution; went to England where he lived until his death in 1780.

1721 Edmund Pendleton, colonial leader, was born in Caroline County, Va.; headed Virginia Committee of Safety; helped revise state laws; first Speaker, Virginia House of Delegates; first president, Virginia Supreme Court of Appeals (1779-1803) (died 1803).

1741 Russian explorers landed on Adak Island in the Aleutians.

1747 Thomas Coke, religious leader, was born in Brecon, Wales; named first American Methodist superintendent by John Wesley (1784); returned to England soon thereafter, making frequent trips to America (died 1814).

1753 George Logan, physician, was born near Germantown, Pa.; went to France at own expense to improve relations (1798-99); American government disapproved; Congress passed Logan Act forbidding a private citizen from carrying on diplomatic relations; represented Pennsylvania in the House (1801-07) (died 1821).

1789 The House, at the urging of James Madison, decided to recommend to the states the adoption of 17 amendments to the Constitution suggested during the ratification process; this was reduced by the Senate to 12 and submitted for ratification on Sept 25.

1789 William C. Bond, astronomer, was born in Portland, Me.; directed construction of Harvard Observatory, its first director (1839-59) (died 1859).

1791 The commission in charge of setting up a new seat of government decided to call the area, Territory of Columbia, and the capital, Washington.

1814 Royal E. House, inventor, was born in Rockland, Vt.; inventor of teletype machine (1846), many electrical devices (died 1895).

1823 Joseph Leidy, naturalist, was born in Philadelphia; wrote standard text on anatomy, laid foundation for American vertebrate paleontology (died 1891).

1841 President Tyler on the grounds of unconstitutionality vetoed the Second Bank Bill, passed to replace the repealed sub-treasury system; the Senate failed to override the veto.

1850 Victor F. Lawson, newspaper publisher, was born in Chicago; owner, *Chicago Daily News* (1876-1925), first penny newspaper in the west; pioneer in developing foreign news service; published, *Chicago Record-Herald* (1881-1914) (died 1925).

1850 California was admitted to the Union as the 31st state.

1850 Congress created the Territory of New Mexico and the Territory of Utah.

1863 Gen. William Rosecrans' Union troops entered Chattanooga, which had been evacuated by the Confederates.

1874 William D. Mitchell, public official, was born in Winona, Minn.; Solicitor General (1925-29), Attorney General (1929-33); chief counsel for congressional investigation of Japanese attack on Pearl Harbor (1945) (died 1955).

1877 Frank Chance, baseball player, was born in Fresno; first baseman, manager, Chicago Cubs; part of famed double play combination (Tinkers to Evers to Chance); named to Baseball Hall of Fame (died 1924).

1884 The American Historical Association was organized in Saratoga, N.Y.

1887 Alf(red M.) Landon, public official, was born in West Middlesex, Pa.; served Kansas as governor (1932-36); Republican presidential candidate (1936) (died 1987).

1889 Preston Dickinson, artist, was born in New York City; pioneer in modern art in the United States (died 1930).

1890 Marriner S. Eccles, economist, was born in Logan, Utah; member, Federal Reserve Board (1934-36), chairman (1936-48) (died 1977).

1893 The first child of a president born in the White House was Esther, second child of President and Mrs. Cleveland.

1895 The American Bowling Congress was organized.

1898 Frankie Frisch, baseball player, was born in New York City; known as the "Fordham Flash," he played with the Giants (1919-26) and Cardinals (1927-37); named to Baseball Hall of Fame (died 1973).

1899 Waite C. Hoyt, baseball player (Yankees), was born in Brooklyn; won 237 games; named to Baseball Hall of Fame (died 1984).

1899 C(yrus) R. Smith, Commerce Secretary (1968-69), was born in Minerva, Tex.; head, American Airlines.

1918 French and American troops launched an attack in the Argonne.

1919 Boston police went on strike; the National Guard was sent in and the strike was broken.

1921 Floods in San Antonio caused 250 death and property damage of $3 million.

1957 Congress passed the Civil Rights Act, the first of its kind since Reconstruction days; created the Civil Rights Commission and provided for federal enforcement of constitutional civil rights.

1965 The Department of Housing and Urban Development was created, effective Nov 9; Robert C. Weaver became the first secretary (sworn in Jan 17, 1966).

1969 The collision of a passenger jet and a light plane near Indianapolis killed 86 persons.

1986 American educator Frank Herbert Reed was kidnapped in West Beirut.

SEPTEMBER 10

1608 John Smith assumed the presidency of the Jamestown council.

1736 Carter Braxton, Revolutionary leader, was born in Newington, Va.; member, Continental Congress (1775-76, 1777-83, 1785) and a signer of the Declaration of Independence (died 1797).

1787 John J. Crittenden, legislator and public official, was born near Versailles, Ky.; represented Kentucky in the Senate (1817-19, 1835-41, 1842-48, 1855-61) and served state as governor (1848-50); Attorney General (1841, 1850-53); offered a compromise in the Senate to resolve North-South differences over slavery (died 1863).

1794 Blount College, which became the U. of Tennessee, was chartered.

1806 William Crompton, textile manufacturer, was born in Lancashire, England; with son, George, invented the improved weaving loom (died 1891).

1813 Oliver Hazard Perry led American naval forces to victory over the British fleet off Put-in-Bay in the Battle of Lake Erie; Americans captured two ships, two brigs, one schooner, one sloop; the British abandoned Detroit; Perry sent his classic message: "We have met the enemy and they are ours."

1832 Randall L. Gibson, Confederate general and legislator, was born in Woodford County, Ky.; served throughout Civil War; represented Louisiana in the House (1875-83) and Senate (1883-92); instrumental in founding Tulane U. (died 1892).

1833 President Jackson announced that the government would not continue to use the Second Bank of the United States as a depository; funds would be deposited in 23 state banks.

1836 Joseph Wheeler, Confederate general, was born near Augusta, Ga.; cavalry commander, Army of the Mississippi; also commanded a cavalry unit in the Spanish-American War; represented Alabama in the House (1881-1900; widely known for his efforts at complete reconciliation of the north and south (died 1906).

1839 Isaac K. Funk, editor and publisher, was born in Clifton, Ohio; founded book business, I.K. Funk & Co. (1877), which became Funk & Wagnalls; editor, *Literary Digest* (1890-1912), *Standard Dictionary, Jewish Encyclopedia* (died 1912).

1839 C(harles) S. Peirce, philosopher, was born in Cambridge; originator of pragmatic philosophy in the United States (died 1914).

1842 Letitia Tyler, wife of President Tyler, died in the White House at 51, the first First Lady to die there.

1846 A patent was issued to Elias Howe for the first practical sewing machine.

1863 Little Rock was captured by Union troops.

1874 Mark Sullivan, journalist, was born in Avondale, Pa.; popular columnist and commentator, author (*Our Times, The Education of an American*) (died 1952).

1885 Carl Van Doren, educator and author, was born in Hope, Ill., brother of Mark Van Doren (6/13/1884); English professor, Columbia U. (1911-30); author (*Benjamin Franklin, Mutiny in January, The Great Rehearsal*) (died 1950).

1886 Hilda Doolittle, poet, was born in Bethlehem, Pa.; wrote under name of "HD" ("Sea Garden," "Hymen," "Red Shoes for Bronze") (died 1961).

1892 Arthur H. Compton, physicist, was born in Wooster, Ohio, brother of Karl T. Compton (9/14/1887); shared 1927 Nobel Physics Prize for discovery of change in wave length of scattered x-rays, discovered electrical nature of cosmic rays (died 1962).

1894 United (later National) Daughters of the Confederacy (known as the UDC in the south) was organized in Nashville.

1895 George Kelly, baseball player (Giants, Reds), was born in San Francisco; named to Baseball Hall of Fame (died 1984).

1895 Melville J. Herskovitz, anthropologist, was born in Bellefontaine, Ohio; made major contributions to role of individual in culture, and African and Afro-American ethnology (died 1963).

1908 John A. Barr, chairman, Montgomery Ward (1955-64), was born in Akron, Ind.; dean, Northwestern U. Graduate Business School (1964-75) (died 1979).

1919 Gen. Pershing led the First Division in parade on New York's Fifth Avenue.

1924 N.F. Leopold Jr. and R.A. Loeb were convicted of murder of Robert Franks in Chicago after a sensational trial in which they were defended by Clarence Darrow; sentenced to life imprisonment.

1929 Arnold Palmer, golfer, was born in Youngstown, Pa.; the first golfing millionaire, he won Masters Title four times.

1934 Roger Maris, baseball player, was born in Hibbing, Minn.; Yankee outfielder who hit record 61 homeruns in one season (162 games), topping Babe Ruth's 60 (in 154 games) (died 1985).

1963 President Kennedy federalized the Alabama National Guard to halt the delay of school integration by Gov. George C. Wallace.

1965 George Baker, better known as Father Divine, died at about 88; organized Peace Mission movement in New York and Philadelphia areas, calling for communal living with a strict moral code; movement died quickly after his death.

SEPTEMBER 11

1776 A fruitless peace conference was held between the Americans and British on Staten Island; Benjamin Franklin, John Adams, and Edmund Rutledge conferred with Lord Howe, but there was no progress when the British demanded revocation of the Declaration of Independence.

1777 The British defeated the Americans at Brandywine, giving them control of Philadelphia, which they occupied Sept 26; Americans lost about 1000 men; the Marquis de Lafayette was slightly wounded.

1786 Delegates from Virginia, Pennsylvania, New Jersey, Delaware, and New York met in Annapolis and adopted an invitation to other states for a meeting the next May to revise the Articles of Confederation; delegates from the other states failed to arrive in time for the meeting.

1789 The first Secretary of the Treasury, Alexander Hamilton, was named by President Washington.

1789 President Washington signed an act establishing federal salaries—president $25,000; vice president $5000; chief justice $4000; associate justices $3500; Secretaries of State and Treasury $3500, Secretary of War $3000.

1814 American naval forces in Plattsburgh Bay on Lake Champlain routed a larger British force, ending British efforts to invade New York; the American fleet was commanded by Capt. Thomas MacDonough; the British land force retreated to Canada.

1821 Erastus F. Beadle, publisher, was born in Pierstown, N.Y.; originated dime novels, including those about *Deadwood Dick, Nick Carter,* the forerunners of modern paper-backs (died 1894).

1833 William H. Hatch, legislator, was born near Georgetown, Ky.; represented Missouri in the House (1875-95); responsible for legislation that provided a foundation for agricultural research; also active in getting cabinet status for the Department of Agriculture (died 1896).

1838 John Ireland, Catholic prelate, was born in Burnchurch, Ireland; bishop of St. Paul (1884-88), archbishop (1888-1918); influential in establishing Catholic U., Washington (1889); considered the greatest American churchman of his time (died 1918).

1844 Nelson O. Nelson, industrialist, was born in Norway; successful manufacturer of plumbing, building supplies; introduced profit-sharing (1886), which he advocated to reconcile differences between capital and labor (died 1922).

1850 Jenny Lind, the "Swedish nightingale," began her American concert tour at Castle Garden, New York City; gave 91 concerts, the last on June 9, 1851.

1852 The first Washington newspaper, the *Columbian*, was published in Olympia by James W. Wiley and Thornton F. McElroy.

1854 William Holabird, architect, was born in Dutchess County, N.Y.; established skeleton method of skyscraper building (Cook County Building, the City, Congress, LaSalle, and Sherman hotels, all in Chicago) (died 1923).

1861 The Kentucky legislature demanded that Confederate forces, which had seized Columbus, Ky., withdraw; a week later, the legislature created a military force to ensure the withdrawal.

1862 O. Henry, short story writer and columnist, was born in Greensboro, N.C. as William S. Porter; columnist, *New York World*; author (*The Gift of the Magi, The Furnished Room*) (died 1910).

1877 Rosika Schwimmer, feminist and pacifist, was born in Budapest; pioneer advocate of world government; convinced Henry Ford to sponsor peace ship to end World War I (died 1948).

1884 Harvey Fletcher, physicist, was born in Provo, Utah; headed a group which developed binaural, stereophonic sound (died 1981).

1893 The World Parliament of Religions opened in conjunction with the Columbian Exposition in Chicago.

1896 Robert S. Kerr, oil producer and legislator, was born in Ada, Okla.; co-founder, Kerr-McGee Oil Co.; served Oklahoma as governor (1943-47) and represented it in the Senate (1949-63) (died 1963).

1902 Jimmie Davis, country music singer, was born in Quitman, La.; governor of Louisiana (1944-48).

1913 Paul "Bear" Bryant, football coach, was born in Kingsland, Ark.; his teams won more than 330 games in 39 years, 26 of them with U. of Alabama (died 1983).

1937 Robert L. Crippen, astronaut, was born in Beaumont, Tex.; on two-man team which made first successful space shuttle flight (1981); commanded 1983 space shuttle flight with five-man team, including the first woman, and the 1984 seven-man flight.

1941 "Shoot-on-sight" policy was announced by President Franklin Roosevelt after a torpedo attack on the American destroyer *Greer* near Iceland; warned that German and Italian vessels entering American defensive waters did so at their own risk.

1944 President Franklin Roosevelt and Prime Minister Winston Churchill met in Quebec to discuss postwar problems in Germany.

1944 First Army units crossed the German border north of Trier.

1951 A passenger train rammed a Pennsylvania National Guard train near Newcomerstown, Ohio, killing 33.

1972 The Bay Area Rapid Transit system (BART), linking Oakland and San Francisco, went into operation.

1982 An Army helicopter carrying five crewmen and 39 members of the international parachuting team crashed at Mannheim, West Germany killing all aboard.

1985 Pete Rose of the Cincinnati Reds set a new major league record of 4192 career base hits, surpassing Ty Cobb's record set in 1928.

1986 The Dow Jones industrial average plunged 86.61 points in the busiest session in New York Stock Exchange history when a record 237.6 million shares changed hands; stocks dropped another 34.17 points the next day, ending a week when the average fell 141.03 points.

SEPTEMBER 12

1687 John Alden, colonial leader, died at about 88; a founder of Duxbury, Mass., influential member of Plymouth Colony; the last surviving signer of the Mayflower Compact; best remembered for having proposed to Priscilla Mullens on behalf of the shy Miles Standish.

1775 The Continental Congress reconvened and for the first time all 13 colonies were represented; Georgia sent delegation for the first time.

1776 Gen. George Washington evacuated American troops from Manhattan to avoid being trapped; set up fortifications on Harlem Heights.

1788 Alexander Campbell, church leader, was born in County Antrim, Ireland, son of Thomas Campbell (2/1/1763); denied a Baptist license at Brush Run, Pa. (1813), he became an itinerant preacher and then a co-founder, Disciples of Christ Church (1827); founder, president, Bethany College, W. Va. (1840-66) (died 1866).

1789 Henry Knox was named the first Secretary of War by President Washington.

1806 Andrew H. Foote, Union naval officer, was born in New Haven; commanded operations in upper Mississippi River; ardent temperance advocate, responsible for ending daily liquor ration on American ships (1862) (died 1863).

1811 James Hall, geologist and paleobotanist, was born in Hingham, Mass.; began study of American stratigraphy; first president, Geological Society of America (died 1898).

1812 Richard M. Hoe, inventor, was born in New York City, son of Robert Hoe (10/29/1784); invented rotary printing press, web press, and many other developments which led to modern newspaper press (died 1886).

1814 The British began an unsuccessful attack on Baltimore, including the shelling of Ft. McHenry, which led Francis Scott Key to write poem which later became "The Star Spangled Banner."

1818 Richard J. Gatling, inventor, was born in Hartford County, N.C.; invented first practical machine gun (1862), also steam plow, sowing machine (died 1903).

1825 Ainsworth R. Spofford, librarian, was born in Gilmantown, N.H.; librarian, Library of Congress (1864-97) (died 1908).

1839 John J. Keane, Catholic prelate, was born in Ballyshannon, Ireland; bishop of Richmond, Va. (1878-89), first rector of Georgetown U., Washington (1889-97), archbishop of Dubuque, Ia. (1900-11) (died 1918).

1862 Confederate troops began siege, bombardment of Harpers Ferry, W.Va.; took city Sept 15.

1869 The National Prohibition Party was organized in Chicago.

1876 Harry C. Stutz, auto manufacturer, was born near Ansonia, Ohio; co-founder, Stutz Auto Parts Co., which became Stutz Car Co. (1913), president (1913-19), produced the Stutz Bearcat (died 1930).

1877 Frederick H. Koch, educator, was born in Covington, Ky.; with U. of North Carolina (1918-44); a central figure in American folk playwrighting, organized many theater groups (died 1944).

1880 Henry L. Mencken, author and editor, was born in Baltimore; journalist, *Baltimore Herald, Sun;* co-editor, *Smart Set, American Mercury* (1924-33); author (*Prejudices, The American Language, Treatise on the Gods*) (died 1956).

1888 Grover C. Loening, aircraft engineer and manufacturer, was born in Bremen, Germany of American parentage; chief aeronautical engineer, Army Air Corps (1914-15); headed two aircraft companies (1917-38); invented strut-braced monoplane, an amphibian plane (died 1976).

1891 Arthur Hays Sulzberger, newspaper publisher, was born in New York City; with *New York Times* (1919-68); publisher (1935-61) (died 1968).

1893 Lewis B. Hershey, Army general, was born in Steuben County, Ind.; director, Selective Service System (1941-70) (died 1977).

1898 Ben(jamin) Shahn, artist, was born in Kaunas, Lithuania; devoted art to social and political causes, did paintings and murals of urban life; worked with Diego Rivera on "Man at the Crossroads" in New York's Rockefeller Center (died 1969).

1913 Jesse (James C.) Owens, track star, was born in Danville, Ala.; won four gold medals in 1936 Olympics (died 1980).

1918 The Battle of St. Mihiel began, the first distinctly American operation; involved 550,000 American troops; victory gained Sept 16 at cost of 7000 casualties, removed a German threat of long standing.

1918 Eugene V. Debs was convicted in Cleveland of violation of the Espionage Act; sentenced Sept 14 to ten years imprisonment.

1922 The American Episcopal Church voted to delete the word obey from the marriage service.

1924 Tom Landry, football player and coach, was born in Mission, Tex.; player with Giants, coach of Dallas Cowboys (1960-89).

1925 President Coolidge named the National Aircraft Board, headed by Dwight W. Morrow, to investigate government's role in aviation.

1928 A five-day hurricane moved from the Caribbean to Florida, killing 4000 persons, including 1836 in Florida.

1944 American troops entered Germany, crossing between Eupen and Trier.

1953 John F. Kennedy and Jacqueline Lee Bouvier were married in Newport, R.I.

1959 *Luna 2*, an unmanned spacecraft, became the first to land on the moon.

1964 Canyonlands (Utah) National Park was established.

1986 Joseph Cicippio, an accountant at American U., was abducted from the West Beirut campus.

1988 An Environmental Protection Administration study recommended that every house in the United States should be tested for radon.

1989 David N. Dinkins, Manhattan borough president, defeated three-term Mayor Edward I. Koch in the Democratic mayoral primary; subsequently became the city's first black mayor.

SEPTEMBER 13

1635 The Massachusetts General Court banished Roger Williams from Salem but authorized him to stay over the winter; he fled (Jan 1636) for fear of deportation and founded Provincetown (June 1636).

1755 Oliver Evans, inventor, was born near Newport, Del.; built first American high pressure steam engine; called the Watt of America (died 1819).

1761 Caspar Wistar, physician, was born in Philadelphia; author of first American textbook on anatomy; flower genus *Wistaria* named for him (died 1818).

1777 Gen. John Burgoyne led his British toops to an encampment at Saratoga, N.Y.

1788 With nine states having ratified the Constitution, Congress established New York City as a capital, set Jan 7, 1789 as the date for the appointment of presidential electors, who would ballot on Feb 4, 1789, and scheduled the first meeting of the new Congress for Mar 4, 1789.

1789 The first loan to the United States government was negotiated by Alexander Hamilton with New York banks.

1803 John Barry, a naval hero of the Revolution, died at 58; was the nation's first commodore.

1813 John Sedgwick, Union general, was born in Cornwall, Conn.; saw action at Antietam, Chancellorsville, Gettysburg; killed by a sniper at Spotsylvania May 9, 1864.

1814 Francis Scott Key, an attorney detained aboard a ship in Baltimore Harbor because of the British shelling of Ft. McHenry, wrote a poem which later became "The Star Spangled Banner;" British abandoned effort to capture Baltimore and withdrew to Halifax.

1817 John M. Palmer, Union general, was born in Scott County, Ky.; served at Chickamauga, Atlanta; served Illinois as governor (1869-73); presidential candidate of National or Gold Democrats Party (1896) (died 1900).

1826 Anthony J. Drexel, banker and newspaper owner, was born in Philadelphia; co-owner, *Philadelphia Ledger*; donor, founder, Drexel Institute of Technology, Philadelphia (died 1893).

1841 The Cabinet, except the Secretary of State, resigned because of President Tyler's veto of the Second Bank bill, the so-called fiscal corporation act.

1847 Americans using scaling ladders captured Chapultepec, which commanded the western approaches to Mexico City.

1851 Walter Reed, military surgeon, was born in Belroi, Va.; headed study of causes of yellow fever, typhoid fever; Washington Army hospital named for him (died 1902).

1857 Milton S. Hershey, manufacturer, was born in Derry Township, Pa.; founder, chocolate company in Lancaster, Pa. (1893); later developed city of Hershey around his plant; founder, Hershey Industrial School for orphan boys (died 1945).

1860 John J. Pershing, World War I general, was born in Linn County, Mo.; served in the Philippines, commanded force sent into Mexico to capture Pancho Villa; commander-in-chief, American Expeditionary Force (1917-19); Army chief of staff (1921-24) (died 1948).

1863 Cyrus Adler, religious leader and educator, was born in Van Buren, Ark.; first president, Dropsie College for Hebrew & Cognate Learning, Philadelphia (1908-40); president, Jewish Theological Seminary, New York City (1915-40); organizer (1892), president (1898-1940); American Jewish Historical Society; editor, *Jewish Encyclopedia, American Jewish Yearbook* (died 1940).

1866 Adolf Mayer, psychiatrist, was born in Niederweningen, Switzerland; a foremost psychiatrist, headed Phipps Psychiatric Clinic, Johns Hopkins (1910-41) (died 1950).

1874 Arnold Schönberg, composer, was born in Vienna; to America (1934), taught at UCLA; one of the great figures of modern music (*Pelleas and Melisande, Pierrot Lunaire*) (died 1951).

1876 Sherwood Anderson, author, was born in Camden, Ohio; poet and novelist (*Winesburg, Ohio; The Triumph of the Egg, Poor White, Dark Laughter*) (died 1941).

1880 Jesse L. Lasky, pioneer movie maker, was born in San Jose, Cal.; helped make *The Squaw Man* (with DeMille and Goldwyn), the first American feature length film, the first to be made in Hollywood; made more than 1000 films (died 1958).

1883 Lewis E. Lawes, prison warden was born in Elmira, N.Y.; warden of Sing Sing (N.Y.) prison (1919-40) (died 1947).

1886 Alain L. Locke, first American black student to receive a Rhodes Scholarship, was born in Philadelphia; with Howard U. philosophy department (1912-53), chairman (1918-53) (died 1954).

1911 Bill Monroe, country music singer and instrumentalist, was born in Rosine, Ky.; developed blue grass style of music.

1926 Andrew F. Brimmer, economist, was born in Newellton, La.; the first black member of the Federal Reserve Board (1966).

1939 Larry Speaks, presidential spokesman (Reagan), was born in Cleveland, Miss.

1960 The Act of Bogota was announced to provide for social and economic reform in Latin America with American help.

1971 More than 1000 state troopers and police stormed the Attica (N.Y.) prison, ending a four-day rebellion; nine hostages and 28 convicts were killed in the assault.

1982 The ICC authorized the merger of the Missouri Pacific and Western Pacific railroads with the Union Pacific to create the third largest American railroad.

1989 Fay Vincent, deputy baseball commissioner, was named commissioner to succeed A. Bart Giamatti, who died suddenly Sept 1.

SEPTEMBER 14

1638 John Harvard, 31-year-old Congregational clergyman, at his death bequeathed his 260-volume library and half his $2000 estate for a college; Newton (Cambridge) was selected as the site (Mar 13, 1639); school named for him.

1741 Robert Eden, colonial governor, was born in Durham, England; served as governor of Maryland (1768-76) (died 1784).

1742 James Wilson, legislator and jurist, was born in Carskerdon, Scotland; member, Continental Congress (1775-76, 1782, 1783, 1785-87) and Constitutional Convention (1787); a signer of Declaration of Independence; associate justice, Supreme Court (1789-98); first law professor, U. of Pennsylvania (1790-98) (died 1798).

1778 Continental Congress named Benjamin Franklin minister to France.

1813 James R. Wood, surgeon, was born in Mamaroneck, N.Y.; one of the most renowned American surgeons; a founder, Bellevue Hospital, New York City (1847), its chief surgeon; later helped add medical school and nation's first nurses training school; introduced first hospital ambulance service (died 1882).

1819 Henry J. Hunt, Union general, was born in Detroit; chief of artillery at Gettysburg, Army of the Potomac; considered the most capable artilleryman of Civil War (died 1889).

1836 Aaron Burr, former vice president (1801-05), died in New York City at 80.

1846 George B. Selden, inventor, was born in Clarkson, N.Y.; sold rights to gasoline motor to auto manufacturers on a royalty basis; Ford challenged the payments, arguing his (Ford's) motor was different, won protracted litigation (died 1922).

1847 A force of 11,000 Americans occupied Mexico City after taking the city protected by 30,000 troops.

1860 Hamlin Garland, author, was born in West Salem, Mass.; best known for *A Son of the Middle Border, A Daughter of the Middle Border* (died 1940).

1867 Charles Dana Gibson, illustrator, was born in Roxbury, Mass.; creator of "Gibson Girl;" author (*The Education of Mr. Pipp, The Americans*) (died 1944).

1869 Kid (Charles A.) Nichols, baseball pitcher (Braves) who won 360 games, was born in Madison, Wis.; named to Baseball Hall of Fame (died 1953).

1872 The final decision of the Geneva Arbitration Tribunal awarded $15.5 million to the United States from Great Britain for damages by the Confederate raider *Alabama*, which was built in Britian.

1883 Margaret H. Sanger, family planner, was born in Corning, N.Y.; founder, National Birth Control League (1914), which became Planned Parenthood Foundation (1942); set up first birth control clinic in Brooklyn (1916) (died 1966).

1887 Karl T. Compton, physicist and educator, was born in Wooster, Ohio, brother of Arthur H. Compton (9/10/1892); physics professor, Princeton (1919-30); president, Massachusetts Institute of Technology (MIT) (1930-48) (died 1954).

1887 Stanley (Stanislaus) Ketchel, probably the best middleweight boxer of all time, was born in Grand Rapids, Mich.; won 46 of his 61 bouts by knockout; was shot and killed in Springfield, Ohio in 1910.

1892 Ben Morreel, commander of Seabees in World War II, was born in Salt Lake City; board chairman, Jones & Laughlin Steel (1947-58) (died 1978).

1898 Hal B. Wallis, movie producer, was born in Chicago; produced many hits (*Little Caesar, Green Pastures, Casablanca, True Grit, Rose Tattoo*) (died 1986).

1901 Vice President Theodore Roosevelt was sworn in as president on the death of President McKinley, eight days after he was shot; oath was administered by U.S. District Judge John R. Hazel in the Ansley Wilcox home in Buffalo.

1910 Bernard A. Schriever, Air Forces general, was born in Berlin; headed the American intercontinental ballistics missile program (1954-66).

1915 Statewide prohibition was adopted by popular vote in South Carolina.

1920 Lawrence Klein, economist, was born in Omaha; awarded 1980 Nobel Economics Prize for development of economic models.

1940 Congress approved the first peacetime draft for military service.

1944 American forces invaded the Palau Islands, taking Peleliu and Augaur.

1959 Congress passed the Griffin-Landrum Act, which was designed to protect the rights of individual union members against "dictatorial, iron fisted" union officials' actions and to ensure free and democratic secret ballot elections.

1975 Elizabeth Ann Seton, first native-born American to be beatified (1962), was canonized.

1984 The first successful transatlantic solo balloon flight began at Caribou, Me. with Joe W. Kittinger the pilot; landed near Savona, Italy Sept 17.

SEPTEMBER 15

1655 Indians attacked New Amsterdam, Pavonia, and Staten Island, killing 100 Dutch settlers in three days and taking 150 prisoners.

1752 An English troupe, including Lewis Hallam, presented *The Merchant of Venice* in Williamsburg, Va., the first professional theatrical production in the colonies, marked the beginning of American theater.

1776 British troops under Gen. William Howe occupied New York City.

1789 James Fenimore Cooper, author, was born in Burlington, N.J.; the first important American novelist (*Last of the Mohicans, The Deerslayer, The Spy, The Pathfinder*) (died 1851).

1794 James Madison and Dolley Danbridge Payne Todd were married at Harewood in Jefferson County, Va.

1795 Zachariah Allen, inventor, was born in Providence; invented the first hot-air house heating system (1821) and an automatic steam-engine cutoff (1834) (died 1882).

1835 Richard Olney, public official, was born in Oxford, Mass.; Attorney General (1893-95); Secretary of State (1895-97), directed policy for settling Venezuela boundary dispute with Great Britain (died 1917).

1835 The first newspaper in Kansas, the *Kansas Weekly Herald*, was published in Leavenworth by William H. Adams.

1857 William Howard Taft, 27th president (1909-13), was born in Cincinnati; Solicitor General (1890-92), U.S. Circuit Court judge (1892-1900); first civil governor, Philippines (1901-04); Secretary of War (1904-08); professor of constitutional law, Yale (1913-21); chief justice, Supreme Court (1921-30) (died 1930).

1857 Brigham Young ordered Utah troops to repel the "invasion" of troops sent by the president to replace him as governor.

1862 Confederate troops under Gen. Stonewall Jackson captured Harpers Ferry, W.Va. and 10,700 Union troops and much equipment; the surrender included the garrisons at Winchester, Va. and Martinsburg, W.Va.

1865 A convention in Charleston, S.C. repealed the secession ordinance; abolished slavery four days later.

1876 Frank E. Gannett, founder, head of newspaper chain named for him, was born in Bristol, N.Y. (died 1957).

1876 Bruno Walter, conductor (Vienna, Los Angeles, New York, Minneapolis), was born in Berlin; conducted Salzburg Festival (1925-38) (died 1962).

1882 Arthur D. Whiteside, president, Dun & Bradstreet (1930-52), was born in East Orange, N.J..

1883 U. of Texas opened in Austin.

1887 U.S. Constitution centennial celebration began in Philadelphia.

1889 Robert C. Benchley, author and screen actor, was born in Worcester, Mass.; critic, author (*From Bed to Worse, My Ten Years in a Quandary*), screen actor (*The Treasurer's Report*) (died 1945).

1903 Roy Acuff, country music singer, was born in Maynardsville, Tenn.

1906 Rosey (Emmett) O'Donnell, World War II general, was born in New York City; commander-in-chief, Pacific Air Forces (died 1971).

1914 Creighton Abrams, Army general, was born in Springfield, Mass.; commanding general, Vietnam (1968-72); Army chief of staff (1972-74) (died 1974).

1918 Austro-Hungarian government suggested an "unofficial" peace conference; idea rejected by President Wilson.

1928 Cannonball (Julian) Adderley, jazz saxophonist, was born in Tampa, Fla. (died 1975).

1928 Bryce Canyon (Utah) National Park was established.

1929 Murray Gell-Mann, physicist, was born in New York City; awarded 1969 Nobel Physics Prize for contributions and discoveries concerning the classification of elementary particles and their interactions.

1938 Gaylord Perry, baseball pitcher who won 314 games (Giants, Indians, Rangers), was born in Williamston, N.C.

1950 American Marines made an amphibious landing on Womi Island, which dominates Inchon Harbor in Korea; Inchon later was taken.

1958 A train plunged into the bay near Bayonne, N.J.; 48 persons died.

1959 Soviet Premier Khruschev began 12-day visit to the United States.

1963 A Negro church in Birmingham was bombed; four black girls were killed, 20 were injured; racial rioting followed.

1969 Congress raised the salary of the vice president from $43,000 to $62,500.

1982 The Senate by a vote of 47-46 killed a proposal which would impose severe restrictions on a woman's right to have an abortion.

1988 Hurricane Gilbert, after raking Jamaica, the Caymans and the Yucatan Peninsula, struck Texas and adjoining Mexico, leaving about 20 dead and more than 500,000 homeless, mostly in Mexico; flooding affected the Mexican area resulting in the drowning of about 100 persons.

SEPTEMBER 16

1620 The *Mayflower* set sail from Plymouth, England with 101 persons (56 adults, 31 children, 14 indentured servants) and a crew of 48; voyage took 65 days, during which one passenger died, two children were born.

1671 Capt. Thomas Batts crossed the Blue Ridge Mountains, starting from the present Petersburg, Va., discovered the falls of the Great Kanawha River.

1672 Anne D. Bradstreet, poet, died at about 60; the first important woman writer in the United States (*The Tenth Muse*).

1766 Samuel Wilson, meat packer, was born in Arlington, Mass.; inspector of meat sold to the Army in the War of 1812; he stamped "U.S." on it for the "United States," but it was said to stand for "Uncle Sam," which he was called; the name came to symbolize the government itself (died 1854).

1776 The Continental Army under Gen. Washington repulsed the British in the Battle of Harlem.

1803 Orestes A. Brownson, author and editor, was born in Stockbridge, Vt.; editor of the influential *Brownson's Quarterly Review* (died 1876).

1804 Squire Whipple, civil engineer, was born in Hardwick, Mass.; invented a trapezoidal-shaped truss (the Whipple truss) used in bridge building (died 1888).

1822 Charles Crocker, financier, was born in Troy, N.Y.; helped form the Central Pacific Railroad, which joined the Union Pacific at Promontory Point, Utah; merged Central Pacific into the Southern Pacific, became president (1871-88) (died 1888).

1823 Francis Parkman, historian, was born in Boston; foremost historian of his time (*The Oregon Trail, France and England in North America*) (died 1893).

1832 George W.C. Lee, educator, was born in Ft. Monroe, Va., son of Robert E. Lee (1/19/1807); on staff of Jefferson Davis; president, Washington & Lee U. (1871-97) (died 1913).

1838 James J. Hill, financier and railroad head, was born in Rockwood, Canada; president, Great Northern Railway (1882-1907), board chairman (1907-12); helped develop iron ore deposits at Mesabi Range, Minn. (died 1916).

1852 Clarence Lexow, legislator, was born in Brooklyn; headed New York legislative investigation which uncovered corruption in New York City (died 1910).

1875 James C. Penney, merchant, was born in Hamilton, Mo.; began as store clerk at $2.27 a month (1895), developed 1500-store chain, board chairman (1916-46) (died 1971).

1877 Jacob Schick, razor manufacturer, was born in Des Moines; invented, manufactured magazine razor (1923), first successful electric razor (1924) (died 1937).

1883 Francis B. Davis Jr., president (1929-42), chairman (1929-49), U.S. Rubber Co., was born in Fort Edward, N.Y. (died 1962).

1893 Albert Szent-György, biochemist, was born in Budapest; awarded 1937 Nobel Physiology/Medicine Prize for work on biological combustion; isolated Vitamin C (died 1986).

1893 The Cherokee Strip, more than six million acres between Kansas and Oklahoma, was opened to settlers; about 90,000 persons took part in the wild scramble for land; eight were killed, many injured.

1893 Earl Carroll, theatrical producer, was born in Pittsburgh; wrote and produced several musicals, his annual *Varieties* (died 1948).

1899 Samuel Spewack, playwright, was born in Russia; with his wife, Bella, wrote many hit plays (*Spring Song; Boy Meets Girl; Kiss Me, Kate*) (died 1971).

1914 Allen Funt, television personality, was born in New York City; creator, host of *Candid Camera* program from early1950s.

1919 Congress granted a national charter to the American Legion.

1920 A bomb exploded in Wall St. at noon, killing 35 and injuring 100.

1924 Lauren Bacall, actress, was born in New York City; several starring film roles (*The Big Sleep, Key Largo*), on stage (*Applause*).

1926 Robert Schuller, television evangelist and clergyman, was born in Alton, Ia.

1927 Peter Falk, actor, was born in New York City; starred in several films, plays (*Prisoner on Second Avenue*), and television (*Colombo*).

1934 Elgin Baylor, basketball player, was born in Washington; starred with Los Angeles Lakers, coached New Orleans (1974-79).

1940 President Franklin Roosevelt signed the Selective Training and Service Act, the first peacetime military draft; all men 21 to 36 were required to register.

1943 Lae in New Guinea captured by American and Australian troops.

1966 The new Metropolitan Opera House in Lincoln Center opened with an American opera especially commissioned for the occasion—Samuel Barber's *Antony and Cleopatra*.

SEPTEMBER 17

1607 The first American jury trial was held in Jamestown, Va., when the deposed governor, Edward M. Wingfield, was found guilty of slandering Capt. John Smith, who was awarded £200, and John Robinson, awarded £100.

1656 Massachusetts enacted a severe law against Quakers, calling for their imprisonment at hard labor until shipped out; later (Oct 14) set a fine of 40 shillings per hour for harboring Quakers; every Quaker coming into the jurisdiction after punishment to suffer the loss of one ear, for the second offense the loss of the other, for the third offense having the tongue "bored through with a hot iron."

1730 Friedrich von Steuben, Revolutionary general, was born in Magdeburg, Germany; inspector general, given task of training the Army; served at Monmouth, Yorktown (died 1794).

1776 The Presidio, around which San Francisco grew, was founded by Jose Moraga, a lieutenant of Juan deAnza, Spanish officer and explorer.

1776 Langdon Cheves, legislator and banker, was born in Abbeville District, S.C.; represented South Carolina in the House (1810-15), serving as Speaker (1814-15); helped save and headed the United States Bank (1819-22) (died 1857).

1787 The Constitutional Convention, with 39 in favor and three abstentions, approved the final draft of the Constitution to be submitted to the states for ratification; the three abstainers (Gerry of Massachusetts, Randolph and Mason of Virginia) wanted another convention for amendments.

1796 President Washington issued his farewell address after completing two terms; he deplored the dangers of a party system, counseled that the public credit be cherished, advised steering clear of permanent foreign alliances; was not delivered as a speech but published Sept 19 in the *Philadelphia Daily American Advertiser*.

1800 Franklin Buchanan, naval officer, was born in Baltimore, planned the Naval Academy, its first superintendent (1845-47); commanded Confederate fleet in Mobile Bay, captured (1864) (died 1874).

1825 Lucius Q.C. Lamar, legislator and jurist, was born in Putnam County, Ga., nephew of Mirabeau Lamar (8/16/1798); represented Mississippi in the House (1857-60, 1873-77) and Senate (1877-85); Secretary of Interior (1885-88); associate justice, Supreme Court (1888-93) (died 1893).

1854 David D. Buick, auto manufacturer, was born in Arbroth, Scotland; founder, head, Buick Manufacturing Co. (1902-06) (died 1929).

1855 Cornerstone was laid for the Boston Public Library.

1862 The Battle of Antietam (or Sharpsburg) (Md.) occurred with no decisive result; Confederates under Gen. R.E. Lee withdrew on the 18th; considered significant because it stopped one of the greatest threats to Washington, caused Great Britain and France to postpone their decision to intervene, and was "the bloodiest single day" of the war, with nearly 5000 killed, 19,000 wounded.

1869 Ben Turpin, screen actor, was born in New Orleans; best known for his cross-eyed expression in films (1907-40) (died 1940).

1883 William Carlos Williams, poet, was born in Rutherford, N.J.; one of the leading literary figures of the 20th century (died 1963).

1900 J(ohn) Willard Marriott, businessman, was born in Marriott, Utah; founder, president, of restaurant and hotel chain bearing his name (1928-64), board chairman (1964-1985) (died 1986).

1900 Martha Ostenso, author, was born in Bergen, Norway; best known work was *Wild Geese* (died 1963).

1907 Warren E. Burger, jurist, was born in St. Paul, Minn.; chief justice, Supreme Court (1969-86).

1907 The state constitution was adopted by voters of Oklahoma, including prohibition.

1908 The first aviation casualty occurred at Ft. Meyer, Va., when a plane went out of control when its propeller blade broke; Lt. Thomas Selfridge was killed, Orville Wright was seriously injured.

1909 Edward N. Cole, president of General Motors (1967-74), was born in Marne, Mich. (died 1977).

1911 The first transcontinental flight (New York to Pasadena) began; Calbraith B. Rogers made 68 hops in 49 days to cover the 3,390 miles; flying time 82 hours.

1923 Hank Williams, singer and composer, was born in Georgiana, Ala.; composed many country western standards (*Your Cheatin' Heart, Jambalaya*) (died 1953).

1926 A hurricane near Miami caused 370 deaths, thousands of injuries, made about 50,000 people homeless, and caused $100 million in property damage.

1927 George Blanda, football player, was born in Youngwood, Pa.; scored 2022 points in 26-year career as quarterback, place kicker (Bears, Oilers, Raiders).

1930 Hoover Dam (originally Boulder Dam) was dedicated at Las Vegas, Nev.

1931 Anne Bancroft, actress, was born in New York City; starred in several plays (*Two for the Seesaw, The Miracle Worker*).

1934 Maureen Connolly, tennis player, was born in San Diego; star of early 1950s, but career ended when she suffered a crushed leg in a horseback riding accident (1954) (died 1969).

1947 The Freedom Train was dedicated in Philadelphia before 33,000-mile tour.

1959 Great Lakes steamer *Notonic* caught fire at Toronto pier, killing about 130.

1951 Jimmy Yancey, musician, died at 57; credited with originating boogie-woogie piano style.

1983 Humberto S. Medeiros, Catholic prelate, died at 67; archbishop of Boston (1970-83), named cardinal 1973.

1984 First solo balloon crossing of the Atlantic Ocean was completed by 56-year-old Joseph W. Kittinger of Orlando, Fla.

SEPTEMBER 18

1679 New Hampshire was set up as a separate province with a government vested in a president and council appointed by the King and an assembly chosen by the people.

1726 Nathaniel Folsom, colonial leader, was born in Exeter, N.H.; member, Continental Congress (1774-75, 1777-80); led New Hampshire state militia (1775); president, New Hampshire Constitutional Convention (1783) (died 1790).

1733 George Read, lawyer and colonial leader, was born near North East, Md.; member, Continental Congress (1774-77) and Constitutional Convention (1787); a signer of the Declaration of Independence; represented Delaware in the Senate (1789-93) and served as its chief justice (1793-98) (died 1798).

1777 As British troops moved on the city, the Liberty Bell was moved from Philadelphia to the Zion Reformed Church in Allentown, Pa.; returned a year later.

1779 Joseph Story, legislator and jurist, was born in Marblehead, Mass.; represented Massachusetts in the House (1808-09); associate justice, Supreme Court (1811-45); a pioneer in organizing, directing teaching at Harvard Law School, author of a famous series of commentaries (1832-45) (died 1845).

1793 President Washington laid the southeast cornerstone of the Capitol.

1796 Hosea Ballou, Universalist clergyman, was born in Guilford, Vt., nephew of Hosea Ballou (4/30/1771); held various pastorates; a founder, first president, Tufts College (1854-61) (died 1861).

1804 Walter L. Newberry, banker and philanthropist, was born in South Windsor, Conn.; endowed reference library (Newberry) in Chicago (died 1868).

1812 Herschel V. Johnson, public official, was born in Burke County, Ga.; served Georgia as governor (1853-57); Democratic vice presidential candidate (1860) (died 1880).

1848 Lucien Howe, ophthalmologist, was born in Standish, Me.; author of New York law requiring prophylactic drops in the eyes of newborn babies (1890); founder, ophthalmology laboratory, Harvard (1926); founder, Buffalo Eye & Ear Infirmary (1896) (died 1928).

1850 Congress passed the Fugitive Slave Act, which supplemented and amended an earlier (1793) act for handling fugitives from justice and runaway slaves.

1851 Henry J. Raymond and George Jones founded *The New York Times*.

1857 John H. Clarke, jurist, was born in Lisbon, Ohio; associate justice, Supreme Court (1916-22) (died 1945).

1859 Gilbert M. Hitchcock, newspaper publisher and legislator, was born in Omaha; founder, publisher, *Omaha World-Herald* (1885-89); represented Nebraska in the House (1903-05, 1907-11) and Senate (1911-23) (died 1934).

1870 Clark Wissler, anthropologist, was born in Wayne County, Ind.; curator, American Museum of Natural History (1906-41); author of ethnology classic, *The American Indian* (died 1947).

1873 The firm of Jay Cooke & Co. failed; many other investment firms went under the next day, touching off the panic of 1873; New York Stock Exchange closed for ten days; depression lasted until 1878.

1886 Powel Crosley, industrialist, was born in Cincinnati; founder, Crosley Radio Corp. (1921); president, Crosley Corp. (1921-45); owner, Cincinnati Reds baseball team (1934-61) (died 1961).

1895 Cotton States & International Exposition opened in Atlanta; closed Dec 31.

1905 Claudette Colbert, screen actress, was born in Paris; starred in many films (*It Happened One Night*).

1905 Greta Garbo, screen actress, was born in Stockholm; star of many movies (*Anna Christie, Anna Karenina, Camille, Ninotchka*).

1905 Agnes DeMille, dance director and choreographer, was born in New York City.

1907 Edwin M. McMillan, physicist, was born in Redondo Beach, Cal.; shared 1951 Nobel Chemistry Prize for co-discovery of transuranium elements; devised improvements in cyclotron.

1947 Department of Defense was created, consolidating the Navy, War, and Air Forces departments into one agency.

1986 The Transportation Department announced the approval of the purchase of Eastern Airlines for $676 million by Texas Air, which earlier had agreed to purchase People Express.

SEPTEMBER 19

1650 The Treaty of Hartford settled the boundary between New Netherland (New York) and Connecticut.

1676 Jamestown, Va. was burned by Nathaniel Bacon and planters in their war with Gov. William Berkeley, who refused to act against marauding Indians; the rebellion ended when 30-year-old Bacon died of fever Oct 26.

1727 *Maryland Gazette*, first newspaper in state, began publication in Annapolis.

1737 Charles Carroll, colonial leader, was born in Annapolis; member, Continental Congress (1776-78) and a signer of Declaration of Independence; one of the first Maryland senators (1789-92); an original director, Baltimore & Ohio Railroad (died 1832).

1739 Andrew Pickens, Revolutionary general, was born near Paxtang, Pa.; served with distinction at Cowpens, captured Augusta, Ga.; represented South Carolina in the House (1793-95) (died 1817).

1775 An American force under Col. Benedict Arnold left Newburyport, Mass. on an expedition to capture Canada; followed the Kennebec and Chaudiére rivers, reached the St. Lawrence Nov 9; another American force under Gen. Richard Montgomery followed the Lakes George-Champlain and Richelieu River route; met Arnold at Quebec Dec 2; joint American assault Dec 31 failed.

1777 The first battle of Bemis Heights (or Freeman's Farm) resulted in Gen. John Burgoyne's return to camp to await reinforcements which never showed up; technically Bemis Heights was a British victory.

1780 John H. Cocke, colonial leader, was born in Surry County, Va.; worked with Thomas Jefferson in planning, founding U. of Virginia; served on its Board of Visitors for 33 years; active opponent of slavery, dueling, intemperance (died 1866).

1782 British and American peace negotiators began talks in Paris.

1792 William B. Astor, businessman, was born in New York City, son of John Jacob Astor (7/17/1763); known as the landlord of New York because of vast holdings; built Astor Library, addition (died 1875).

1804 Elling Eielsen, religious leader, was born in Voss, Norway; founder of Evangelical Lutheran Church of America (1846) (died 1883).

1824 William Sellers, industrialist, was born in Delaware County, Pa.; founder, head, machine tool works (1848); proposed standard system of screw threads, adopted (1868) by federal government (died 1905).

1829 Gustav Schirmer, music publisher, was born in Königsee, Germany; formed, headed, music publishing company (1866-93) (died 1893).

1835 Ethan A. Hitchcock, public official, was born in Mobile; first American ambassador to Russia (1898); Secretary of Interior (1898-1907), did much to enlarge forest reserves and withdraw mineral lands from exploitation (died 1909).

1859 John F. Jameson, historian, was born in Somerville, Mass.; led successful drive for creation of National Archives; a founder, *American Historical Review*, editor (1895-1901, 1905-28) (died 1937).

1862 Confederate troops under Gen. Sterling Price were defeated by Union troops under Gen. William S. Rosecrans at Iuka, Miss.; prevented two Confederate forces from joining.

1863 A two-day battle of Chickamauga Valley, Ga., outside Chattanooga, began; Confederate troops under Gen. Braxton Bragg drove Union troops under Gen. William S. Rosecrans into Chattanooga, which was virtually besieged until reinforcements arrived; Confederates lost 18,450 men, the Union 16,170.

1864 Gen. Philip Sheridan and his Union troops defeated Confederates at Winchester, Va.; three days later, Union troops won again at Fisher's Hill and Cedar Creek, driving the Confederates from the Shenandoah Valley.

1872 Key Pittman, legislator, was born in Vicksburg, Miss.; represented Nevada in the Senate (1913-40), an effective spokesman for silver interests (died 1940).

1876 Vera C.S. Cushman, social worker, was born in Ottawa, Ill.; organized, Young Women's Christian Association (YWCA) (1906) (died 1946).

1881 President Garfield died in Elberon, N.J. at 49 as a result of the July 2nd shooting.

1899 Royal B. Lord, World War II general, was born in Worcester, Mass.; invented portable steel emplacement, portable cableway (died 1963).

1905 Leon Jaworski, attorney, was born in Waco, Tex.; special prosecutor in the Watergate case (1973-74) (died 1982).

1906 President Theodore Roosevelt issued a proclamation extending the eight-hour day to all government workers.

1907 Lewis F. Powell Jr., jurist, was born in Suffolk, Va.; associate justice, Supreme Court (1972-87).

1926 Duke (Edwin D.) Snider, baseball player (Dodgers), was born in Los Angeles; named to Baseball Hall of Fame.

1927 Harold Brown, educator and public official, was born in New York City; Secretary of Air Force (1965-69); Secretary of Defense (1977-81); president, California Institute of Technology (1969-77).

1940 Paul Williams, composer, was born in Omaha; wrote several popular hits (*We've Only Just Begun, Rainy Days and Mondays*).

1957 The first underground nuclear explosion occurred at the Nevada testing grounds.

1967 Martin Block, most important disc jockey of 1930s and 1940s, died in New York City.

1988 The Senate approved a free trade agreement with Canada, which the president signed, clearing the way for America's part in phasing out tariffs on $131 billion in goods crossing the border; Canadian Parliament still must act.

1989 The Appellate Division of the New York State Supreme Court returned the America's Cup to the United States, overturning an earlier lower court decision awarding it to New Zealand; an appeal is planned.

SEPTEMBER 20

1565 Spanish forces under Pedro Menéndes de Avilés destroyed the Huguenot settlement in Ft. Caroline at the mouth of the St. Johns River (Fla.), putting to death almost the entire garrison, "not as Frenchmen, but as Lutherans;" Spanish renamed the fort San Mateo.

1676 Edward Randolph, a special agent of the Crown, submitted the first of two reports in which he found that Massachusetts was not enforcing the Navigation Acts, was putting English citizens to death for their religious views, denying the right of appeal to the Privy Council, and refusing the oath of allegiance; his report resulted in forfeiture of the colony's charter (1684).

1809 Sterling Price, Confederate general and public official, was born in Prince Edward County, Va.; governor of Missouri (1853-57); saw action in Missouri, Arkansas, and Texas (died 1867).

1810 Joseph Harrison, mechanical engineer, was born in Philadelphia; devised a new principle in locomotive boiler construction, manufactured locomotive boilers (died 1874).

1820 George W. Morgan, Union general and legislator, was born in Washington County, Pa.; minister to Portugal (1858-61); served with Gens. Buell and Sherman; represented Ohio in the House (1867-68, 1869-73) (died 1893).

1820 John F. Reynolds, Union general, was born in Lancaster, Pa.; saw action at Fredericksburg, Chancellorsville; killed in first-day action at Gettysburg (7/1/1863).

1829 Albert J. Myer, Army officer, was born in Newburgh, N.Y.; organized, commanded a signal corps for the Army (1861); founder, supervised, U.S. Weather

Service as part of the corps (1870-80); Ft. Myer, Va. named for him (died 1880).

1833 David R. Locke, newspaper, was born in Vestal, N.Y.; gained fame for satirical anti-slavery campaign, written under name of Petroleum V. Nasby (died 1888).

1849 George B. Grinnell, naturalist, was born in Brooklyn; founder, Audubon Society (1886); original promoter, Glacier National Park; an expert in Plains Indians folklore; editor, *Forest and Stream* (1876-1911) (died 1938).

1850 Congress passed an act abolishng slave trade in Washington, effective Jan 1, 1851.

1850 Congress abolished flogging in the Navy.

1853 Elisha G. Otis installed the first safety elevator in New York City.

1861 Herbert Putnam, librarian, was born in New York City, son of George Putnam (2/7/1814); headed Library of Congress (1899-1939) (died 1955).

1865 A constitutional convention in Alabama repealed secession ordinance; abolished slavery two days later.

1878 Upton B. Sinclair, author, was born in Baltimore; wrote muckraking novels (*The Jungle, Oil, Coal*), 11-volume Lanny Budd series; Socialist candidate several times for Congress, president (died 1968).

1881 Vice President Arthur took the oath of office as president in his New York City home (123 Lexington Ave.) at 2:00 a.m., following President Garfield's death.

1884 Maxwell E. Perkins, editor, was born in New York City; with Scribner's, developed authors such as F. Scott Fitzgerald, Ernest Hemingway, Thomas Wolfe (died 1947).

1885 Jelly Roll (Ferdinand) Morton, musician, was born in New Orleans; considered one of the inventors of jazz; composer ("King Porter Stomp," "Jelly Roll Blues") (died 1941).

1902 A church fire in Birmingham killed 115 persons.

1913 S. Dillon Ripley, museum director, was born in New York City; secretary, Smithsonian Institution (1964-84).

1917 Red (Arnold J.) Auerbach, basketball coach (Boston Celtics 1950-66), was born in New York City; Celtics general manager (1967-).

1946 President Truman requested resignation of Commerce Secretary Henry A. Wallace because of his speech a week earlier criticizing American policy toward Russia.

1963 President Kennedy, speaking to the United Nations General Assembly, called for better American-Soviet cooperation and a joint expedition to the moon.

1977 United States and Canada agreed to build 2700-mile natural gas pipeline from Alaska to the lower 48 states.

1984 American Embassy annex in Beirut was bombed by an explosives-filled truck, killing 23 persons.

1988 Lauro F.M. Cavazos, president of Texas Tech University, was confirmed and sworn in as Secretary of Education, the first Spanish-American cabinet member; succeeded William J. Bennett who resigned.

SEPTEMBER 21

1595 Juan de Onate was appointed Spanish governor of New Mexico; commissioned to explore and settle the area.

1645 Louis Joliet, explorer, was born in Beaupre, Canada; explored much of the Great Lakes and Mississippi Valley; first sighted the Mississippi River in 1673 (died 1700).

1737 Francis Hopkinson, political leader and writer, was born in Philadelphia; published political satires against the British; member, Continental Congress (1776) and a signer of the Declaration of Independence (died 1791).

1776 Fire, either an accident or set by design, burned much of New York City's business district.

1776 Delaware adopted its state constitution and became a political unit; had been known as the "three lower countries" of Pennsylvania.

1776 Nathan Hale was captured by the British and hanged as a spy the next day; Hale at the hanging said: "I only regret that I have but one life to lose for my country."

1779 Spanish troops overpowered a British garrison at Baton Rouge and controlled the area for the next 20 years.

1780 Benedict Arnold, commander of the West Point garrison, met with British Major John André at Joshua Hett Smith's house on the west bank of the Hudson near Haverstraw to deliver plans of the fort; André was captured near Tarrytown by American troops two days later and Arnold fled to the British Sept 25.

1784 The first successful American daily newspaper, the *Pennsylvania Packet and General Advertiser*, was published by John Dunlap; later merged into the *North American*.

1788 Margaret Smith Taylor, wife of President Taylor, was born in Calvert County, Md. (died 1852).

1855 Samuel Rea, railroad president, was born in Hollidaysburg, Pa.; with Pennsylvania Railroad (1871-1925), rising from rodman to president (1912-25) (died 1929).

1856 Illinois Central Railroad from Chicago to Cairo was completed.

1867 Henry L. Stimson, public official, was born in New York City; Secretary of War (1911-13, 1940-45); Governor General, Philippines (1927-29); Secretary of State (1929-33) (died 1950).

1885 H(arold) T. Webster, cartoonist, was born in Parkersburg, W.Va.; noted for "The Timid Soul" (Casper Milquetoast), "Life's Darkest Moments" (died 1952).

1893 The first American gasoline-powered automobile was built by Charles E. and J. Frank Duryea.

1893 Frank Willard, cartoonist, was born in Anna, Ill.; creator of "Moon Mullins" (died 1958).

1926 Donald A. Glaser, physicist, was born in Cleveland; awarded 1960 Nobel Physics Prize for the invention of the "bubble chamber" to study subatomic particles.

1931 Larry Hagman, television actor, was born in Ft. Worth, son of Mary Martin (12/1/1913); starred in popular series, *I Dream of Jeannie* and *Dallas*.

1938 A New England hurricane resulted in 680 deaths, $400 million damage.

1965 The Water Quality Act was passed by Congress to meet problems of water pollution and shortages.

1981 The Senate by vote of 99-0 confirmed the appointment of Sandra Day O'Connor as the first woman Supreme Court justice; took her seat Sept 25.

1982 Football players went on strike against the National Football League, the first in-season strike in 61 years; ended Nov. 16.

1982 President Reagan signed a bill freeing intercity bus industry from many regulations governing routes and fares.

1989 A school bus with 83 students was rammed by a truck and plunged 40 feet into a water-filled pit near Alton, Tex.; 19 students were killed, one died later.

SEPTEMBER 22

1711 The Tuscarora Indian War began with the massacre of settlers along the Chowan and Roanoke rivers in North Carolina.

1768 Delegates from 26 Massachusetts towns met in Boston to draw up a statement of grievances.

1788 A group of New Jersey colonists reached their Ohio lands and founded Losantiville, later renamed Cincinnati.

1789 An act was passed to provide compensation for members of Congress—$6 for every day of the session and mileage.

1789 The Office of Postmaster General was created as a branch of the Treasury Department and Samuel Osgood was named Sept 26; Postmaster General became a member of the Cabinet Mar 9, 1829 and the Post Office became an executive department June 8, 1872.

1807 William Cramp, shipbuilder, was born in Philadelphia; established the ship-building company named for him (1830), president (1830-79) (died 1879).

1827 John G. Parke, Union general, was born near Coatesville, Pa.; served at Antietam, Fredericksburg, Vicksburg, Petersburg (died 1900).

1846 Gen. Stephen W. Kearny announced the creation of a temporary civil government in New Mexico, a month after his forces occupied Santa Fe.

1853 Hugh L. Scott, Army officer, was born in Danville, Ky.; served in Indian campaigns, became a negotiator with various tribes; Army chief of staff (1914-17) (died 1934).

1862 President Lincoln issued the preliminary Emancipation Proclamation; the formal document was issued Jan 1, 1863.

1870 Arthur Pryor, bandmaster, was born in St. Joseph, Mo.; played with John Philip Sousa, then formed own band (died 1942).

1895 Paul Muni, screen actor, was born in Lemberg, Austria; starred in many films (*Louis Pasteur, The Good Earth, Emile Zola*) (died 1967).

1901 Charles B. Huggins, physician, was born in Halifax, Nova Scotia; shared 1966 Nobel Physiology/Medicine Prize for discovery of role of hormones in treating cancer of the prostate.

1906 Race riots in Atlanta left 21 persons dead; city was placed under martial law.

1914 Prohibition law enacted in Virginia, effective Nov 1, 1916.

1918 American troops took over the Argonne Forest.

1919 A steel strike for union recognition began at the Gary (Ind.) U.S. Steel plant; ended in failure Jan 8, 1920.

1920 Bob (Robert G.) Lemon, baseball pitcher who won 207 games (Indians) and manager (Yankees), was born in San Bernardino, Cal.; named to Baseball Hall of Fame.

1922 Chen Ning Yang, physicist, was born in Hopei, China; with Institute for Advanced Study, Princeton (1944-65); shared 1957 Nobel Physics Prize for disproving principle of conservation of parity.

1927 Tommy LaSorda, baseball manager (Dodgers), was born in Norristown, Pa.

1966 United States offered to stop bombing North Vietnam if Hanoi would match the de-escalation; offer made to General Assembly of the United Nations.

1973 Dallas-Ft. Worth Airport was dedicated.

1975 A second assassination attempt on President Ford was made in San Francisco; Sara Jane Moore, a police and FBI informer, was apprehended.

1987 National Football League players went on strike but the team owners said they would continue playing with non-strikers after a one-week halt; strike was abandoned after four weeks.

1989 Hurricane Hugo, with 135 mph winds struck Charleston, S.C. and the adjoining coastline after midnight after wreaking havoc on the Virgin Islands and Puerto Rico; approximately 12 persons were killed in South Carolina, more than 20 in the Caribbean; damage was estimated in the billions.

SEPTEMBER 23

1728 Mercy Otis Warren, colonial writer, was born in Barnstable, Mass., sister of James Otis (2/5/1725); called the mother of the American Revolution; held a political salon during pre-Revolutionary days; wrote three-volume history of the Revolution, two anti-Tory plays (died 1814).

1745 John Sevier, frontiersman, was born near New Market, Va.; governor of temporary state of Franklin (1785-88), then first governor of Tennessee (1796-1801, 1803-09) and represented it in the House (1789-91, 1811-15) (died 1815).

1777 John Paul Jones, commander of the *Providence*, captured or burned ten prize vessels.

1779 American troops, with the help of the French fleet, made an unsuccessful siege of Savannah; French fleet left for Europe Oct 9.

1779 John Paul Jones in the *Bonhomme Richard* led an American squadron of six ships into battle with a British convoy, led by the *Serapis*, off the coast of England; in a fierce battle, the *Bonhomme Richard* bested the *Serapis*; during the battle, Jones reputedly said: "I have not yet begun to fight!"

1780 Major John André, adjutant general of the British Army, was captured while trying to make his way back to the British lines after having met Benedict Arnold two days earlier; had incriminating West Point plans on him.

1786 John England, Catholic prelate, was born in Cork, Ireland; bishop of Charleston, S.C. (1820-42); founded schools and *U.S. Catholic Miscellany*, the first American Catholic newspaper (died 1842).

1800 William H. McGuffey, educator and author, was born in Washington County, Pa.; author of the famed McGuffey *Readers*, standard texts in 19th century American schools (died 1873).

1806 The Lewis and Clark Expedition ended with the return to St. Louis; had started out May 14, 1804.

1816 Elihu B. Washburne, public official, was born in Livermore, Me., brother of Cadwallader C. Washburn (4/22/1818) who changed spelling of his surname; represented Illinois in the House (1853-69); Secretary of State (1869); minister to France (1869-77) (died 1887).

1823 James Black, prohibitionist, was born in Lewisburg, Pa.; first presidential candidate of National Prohibition Party (1872) (died 1893).

1830 Elizabeth K. Monroe, wife of President Monroe, died at Oak Hill, Va. at 62.

1833 President Jackson removed William J. Duane as Treasury Secretary for refusing to withdraw federal funds from the National Bank; withdrawn Oct 1 by his successor.

1838 Victoria Claflin Woodhull, social reformer, was born in Homer, Ohio; founder, Equal Rights Party (1872), its nominee for president (1872) (died 1927).

1845 The Knickerbocker Club, the first baseball team, was organized in New York City by Alexander J. Cartwright.

1852 William S. Halsted, surgeon, was born in New York City; developed local anesthesia (1885); performed first successful blood transfusion (1881), set up first school of surgery, Johns Hopkins Hospital (1890) (died 1922).

1867 John A. Lomax, folk song collector, was born in Goodman, Miss.; collected, recorded folk ballads; first curator, Archives of American Folk Songs, Library of Congress (1932-48) (died 1948).

1884 Adna R. Chaffee Jr., Army officer, was born in Junction City, Kas., son of Adna R. Chaffee (4/14/1842); organized Army's first mechanized brigade; assigned to develop armored forces (1938) (died 1941).

1884 Eugene Talmadge, public official, was born in Forsyth, Ga.; noted for flamboyant tactics; served Georgia as governor (1932-36, 1940-42, 1946) (died 1946).

1889 Walter Lippmann, columnist and author, was born in New York City; author (*A Preface to Politics, A Preface to Morals, The Good Society*) (died 1974).

1892 The first Christian Science church was organized in Boston by Mary Baker Eddy and 12 followers.

1897 Walter Pidgeon, screen actor, was born in East St. John, Canada; starred in many films (*Mrs. Miniver, Madame Curie*) (died 1984).

1899 Tom C. Clark, jurist, was born in Dallas; Attorney General (1945-49); associate justice, Supreme Court (1949-67) (died 1977).

1899 Louise Nevelson, sculptor, was born in Kiev, Russia; famed for large abstract wood sculptures (*Sky Cathedral*) (died 1988).

1901 The trial of Leon F. Czolgosz, assassin of President McKinley, began in Buffalo; lasted only eight hours and 26 minutes; in 34 minutes, the jury returned a verdict of guilty.

1920 Mickey Rooney, actor and entertainer, was born in Brooklyn; starred in movies (*Andy Hardy* series), on stage (*Sugar Babies*), and television.

1926 Gene Tunney beat Jack Dempsey in ten rounds in Philadelphia for the world heavyweight boxing championship.

1930 Ray Charles, musician, was born in Albany, Ga.; blind pianist and composer of jazz and pop music.

1949 Bruce Springsteen, singer and entertainer, was born in Freehold, N.J.

1952 Rocky Marciano knocked out Jersey Joe Walcott in 13 rounds in Philadelphia for the world heavyweight boxing title.

1966 Congress passed legislation raising the minimum wage to $1.40 an hour, effective Feb 1, 1967, and to $1.60 an hour Feb 1, 1968.

1987 Stock prices rose 75.23 points, a record-breaking one-day gain.

1988 The House approved and sent to President Reagan tightened curbs on textile, apparel and shoe imports; President Reagan vetoed the bill Sept 28, calling it "protectionism at its worst;" the House failed to override the veto.

1988 Former Presidential Adviser Michael K. Deaver was given a suspended three-year prison term and fined $100,000 for lying to a congressional committee and a grand jury about his lobbying after leaving the White House.

SEPTEMBER 24

1664 With the surrender of Ft. Orange (now Albany) by the Dutch to the British, the village of Beverwyck was renamed Albany.

1755 John Marshall, jurist, was born near Germantown, Va.; represented Virginia in the House (1799-1800); Secretary of State (1800-01); chief justice, Supreme Court (1801-35), exerted profound influence on legal, judicial history (died 1835).

1789 John Jay was named first chief justice of Supreme Court; confirmed Sept 26; continued to act as Secretary of State until Thomas Jefferson returned from France (Mar 22, 1790; first associate justices were James Wilson, Pa; John Rutledge, S.C.; William Cushing, Mass.; John Blair, Va. and Robert H. Harrison, Md.

1789 Federal Judiciary Act was passed, creating American judicial system much as it is today; established Supreme Court, Office of Attorney General (Edmund Randolph).

1827 Henry W. Slocum, Union general, was born in Delphi, N.Y.; commanded extreme right at Gettysburg; represented New York in the House (1869-73, 1883-85) (died 1894).

1837 Mark (Marcus A.) Hanna, businessman and political leader, was born in New Lisbon, Ohio; headed McKinley presidential campaign; chairman, Republican National Committee; represented Ohio in the Senate (1897-1904) (died 1904).

1843 Adam W. Wagnalls, publisher, was born in Lithopolis, Ohio; a founder, president, Funk & Wagnalls Co. (died 1924).

1862 Governors of 16 states met in Altoona, Pa. and approved President Lincoln's Emancipation Proclamation.

1869 "Black Friday" panic in securities market occurred when gold price fell from 163-1/2 to 133 when James Fisk, Daniel Drew, and Jay Gould tried to corner market.

1890 Mormon Church ended polygamy with a manifesto which called on Mormons to "refrain from contracting any marriage forbidden by the law of the land."

1890 Allen J. Ellender, legislator, was born in Montegut, La.; represented Louisiana in the Senate (1937-72) (died 1972).

1891 William F. Friedman, cryptologist, was born in Kishinev, Russia; considered world's greatest cryptologist, devised first solution for the rotor cipher machine (died 1969).

1895 André F. Cournand, physiologist, was born in Paris; at Columbia U., shared 1956 Nobel Physiology/Medicine Prize for discoveries concerning heart catheterization and pathological changes in the circulatory system.

1896 F. Scott Fitzgerald, author, was born in St. Paul, Minn.; spokesman for the lost generation, The Jazz Age (*The Great Gatsby, This Side of Paradise, Tender is the Night*) (died 1940).

1896 Tommy Armour, golfer, was born in Edinburgh; a golf leader of the 1920s, 1930s; won American and British Opens, the PGA title (died 1968).

1899 George F. Doriot, educator, was born in Paris; industrial management professor, Harvard (1926-66), credited with creating American professional business management corps.

1900 Ham(mond E.) Fisher, cartoonist, was born in Wilkes-Barre, Pa.; creator of "Joe Palooka" (died 1955).

1905 Severo Ochoa, biochemist, was born in Luarca, Spain; with NYU Medical School, shared 1959 Nobel Physiology/Medicine Prize for discoveries related to compounds within chromosomes.

1907 John R. Dunning, research scientist, was born in Shelby, Neb.; a pioneer experimenter in neutrons; with Naval Research Office (1946-75); first to demonstrate fission of uranium-235 (1940) (died 1975).

1910 Dixie (Fred) Walker, baseball player (Dodgers), was born in Villa Rica, Ga.; named to Baseball Hall of Fame (died 1982).

1930 John W. Young, astronaut, was born in San Francisco; made six space flights, taking part in first two-man flight (1952), pilot of first space shuttle (1981).

1936 Jim Henson, puppeteer, was born in Greenville, Miss.; creator of the Muppets for *Sesame Street*, own program.

1955 President Eisenhower suffered a "moderate" heart attack in Denver.

1957 President Eisenhower sent federal troops to Little Rock to preserve order and to allow black students to enter an all-white high school.

1962 The Fifth Circuit Court of Appeals ordered the U. of Mississippi to admit James H. Meredith, a black student.

1988 The Episcopal Diocese of Massachusetts elected the first female bishop in the 450-year history of the Anglican Church; the election of Rev. Barbara C. Harris of Philadelphia could result in some splits in the church.

SEPTEMBER 25

1493 Christopher Columbus sailed from Cadiz, Spain on his second voyage with a fleet of 17 ships and 1500 men; arrived in the Lesser Antilles Nov 3; named the island on which he landed Dominica.

1513 Vasco Nunez de Balboa discovered the Pacific Ocean after crossing the Isthmus of Panama.

1690 The first American newspaper, *Publick Occurrences Both Foreign and Domestick*, was issued in Boston by Benjamin Harris, with the announcement that it would be published once a month or oftener "if any glut of occurrences happen;" it was suppressed four days later.

1758 Christopher Sower, printer and publisher, died at 65; published a German edition of the Bible, one of the first in America.

1775 Ethan Allen, hero of Ticonderoga, and 38 men were captured by the British in the campaign against Montreal; not released until 1778.

1789 The first amendments to the Constitution, the Bill of Rights, were submitted to the states for ratification; 12 were submitted, ten ratified.

1807 Alfred L. Vail, telegraph pioneer, was born in Morristown, N.J., cousin of Theodore N. Vail (7/16/1845); partner of Samuel F.B. Morse in telegraph production; worked with Ezra Cornell in building first telegraph line (Baltimore to Washington) (died 1859).

1823 Thomas J. Wood, Union general, was born in Munfordville, Ky.; saw action at Chickamauga, Missionary Ridge (died 1906).

1832 William L. Jenney, architect, was born in Fairhaven, Mass.; designed first tall building to use steel as building material (Home Insurance Bldg., Chicago 1884), often considered the first skyscraper (died 1907).

1841 James M. Bailey, journalist, was born in Albany; sometimes called the first newspaper columnist (*Danbury* (Conn.) *News*) (died 1894).

1843 Melville R. Bissell, inventor, was born in Hartwick, N.Y.; invented, manufactured the carpet sweeper (died 1889).

1843 Thomas C. Chamberlin, geologist, was born in Mattoon, Ill.; specialized in study of glacial deposits and their evidence as to past climatic conditions; with F.R. Moulton (*see* 4/29/1872), developd the planetesimal or spiral nebulae theory of the earth's origin; founder, editor, *Journal of Geology* (1893-1922).

1846 The Mexicans surrendered Monterey to American troops led by Gen. Zachary Taylor.

1847 Vinnie Hoxie, sculptor, was born in Madison, Wis.; her full-length marble statue of President Lincoln is in the Capitol Rotunda (died 1914).

1855 William S. Benson, Navy officer, was born in Macon, Ga.; first chief of naval operations (1915-19) (died 1932).

1866 Thomas H. Morgan, zoologist and biologist, was born in Lexington, Ky.; awarded 1933 Nobel Physiology/Medicine Prize for discoveries on hereditary function of chromosomes; first native-born American, first non-physician to win this prize (died 1945).

1890 Sequoia (Cal.) National Park was established.

1897 William C. Faulkner, author, was born in New Albany, Miss.; wrote several popular novels (*A Fable, The Reivers*, the Snopes family series, *Sanctuary; Absalom, Absalom*); awarded 1949 Nobel Literature Prize (died 1962).

1899 James M. Landis, lawyer and educator, was born in Tokyo of American parentage; Federal Trade Commission (1933-34), Securities & Exchange Commission (1934-37); director, Civil Defense (1942-43); minister to Middle East (1943-44); dean, Harvard Law School (1937-46) (died 1964).

1903 Mark Rothko, painter, was born in Dvinsk, Russia; surrealistic pioneer in abstract expressionism (died 1970).

1905 Red (Walter W.) Smith, journalist, was born in Green Bay, Wis.; syndicated sports columnist (died 1982).

1925 The submarine *S-51* sank after colliding with a steamer off Block Island, 37 crewmen perished.

1926 Ford Motor Co. introduced eight-hour day, five-day work week.

1931 Barbara Walters, radio and television personality, was born in Boston; with *Today* show, then became first woman to anchor a national television news program (ABC 1976).

1956 The first transatlantic telephone cable went into operation.

1961 President Kennedy proposed to the UN General Assembly a series of steps leading to eventual nuclear disarmanent.

1962 Sonny Liston knocked out Floyd Patterson in the first round in Chicago to win the world's heavyweight boxing championship.

1978 Two planes collided over San Diego, killing 144 persons.

1988 Rev. Juniperro Serra, founder of California missions, was beatified by Pope John Paul II in the Vatican.

1988 The Supreme Court refused to stop a Flint, Mich. woman from having an abortion that her estranged husband had sought to prevent.

SEPTEMBER 26

1651 Francis D. Pastorius, colonial leader, was born in Sommerhausen, Germany; led a party of German Friends to Pennsylvania, settled and laid out Germantown (died 1720).

1774 John Chapman, better known as Johnny Appleseed, was born in Leominster, Mass.; ranged over the Ohio River Valley planting and pruning apple trees (1800-10) (died 1825).

1776 The Continental Congress named Silas Deane, Benjamin Franklin, and Thomas Jefferson to negotiate treaties of commerce and amity with European countries; Jefferson declined and was replaced by Arthur Lee.

1777 British under Gens. William Howe and Charles Cornwallis occupied Philadelphia and Germantown; Congress fled to Lancaster and later to York.

1781 Andrew Lewis, colonial leader, died at 61; led British to victory over Indians at Pt. Pleasant (1774), resulting in peace with Indians early in the Revolution; general in Continental Army.

1787 Protestors led by Daniel Shay confronted Massachusetts militia at Springfield and began sporadic fighting until the insurgents were routed in 1788; rebellion kept Massachusetts legislature from imposing direct tax, to lower court fees, and to exempt clothing and tools of one's trade, and household goods from the debt process.

1789 President Washington named Thomas Jefferson as the first Secretary of State; John Jay, who had been named the first Supreme Court chief justice, handled the State duties until Jefferson returned from France Mar 22, 1790; president also named Edmund Randolph of Virginia as Attorney General, Samuel Osgood of Massachusetts as Postmaster General.

1810 Southern expansionists captured Baton Rouge, proclaimed the independent state of the Republic of South Florida.

1813 Gen. Wade Hampton led American troops from Plattsburgh to Montreal; another force under Gen. James Wilkinson sailed Lake Ontario to the St. Lawrence River.

1831 First American third party, Anti-Masonic Party, held its first convention in Baltimore, nominating William Wirt for president.

1841 Stephen B. Elkins, legislator and industrialist, was born in Perry County, Ohio; represented New Mexico in the House (1872-77) and West Virginia in the Senate (1895-1011); War Secretary (1891-93); founded Elkins, W.Va. (died 1911).

1844 The first newspaper in Oklahoma, *Cherokee Advocate* (printed in English and Cherokee), was published in Tahlequa by William P. Ross.

1862 Arthur B. Davies, painter and printmaker, was born in Utica, N.Y.; organized (1908) the "Ashcan School" exhibit, a revolt of young American artists, and its follow-up, the Armory Show (1913) (died 1928).

1874 Oakes Ames, botanist, was born in North Easton, Mass., grandson of Oakes Ames (1/10/1804); with Harvard Botanical Garden (1899-1922), director (1910-22); donated his 57,000-specimen orchid herbarium to Harvard (died 1950).

1874 Lewis W. Hine, photographer, was born in Oshkosh, Wis.; originated the photo story (died 1940).

1888 T(homas) S. Eliot, author and poet, was born in St. Louis; lived in England, was a major figure in 20th century literature (*The Waste Land, Prufrock and Other Observations*); awarded 1948 Nobel Literature Prize (died 1965).

1888 James Frank Dobie, Texas folklorist, was born in Live Oak County, Tex.; wrote about 30 books (*Coronado's Children, Apache Gold and Yanqui Silver*) (died 1964).

1891 Charles Munch, musician, was born in Strasbourg, France; conducted several symphony orchestras (Paris, Boston 1949-62) (died 1968).

1898 George Gershwin, composer, was born in Brooklyn, brother of Ira Gershwin (*see* 12/6/1896); wrote many classics, hit shows ("Rhapsody in Blue," *Porgy and Bess,* "An American in Paris," *Girl Crazy, Of Thee I Sing*) (died 1937).

1901 Ted Weems, bandleader of 1920s, 1930s, was born in Pitcairn, Pa. (died 1963).

1914 Federal Trade Commission Act went into effect, which, according to President Wilson, was "to make men in a small way of business as free to succeed as men in a big way, and to kill monopoly in the seed."

1918 The Meuse-Argonne offensive began, designed to cut the main supply lines of the German army; involved 1.2 million American troops, suffered 120,000 casualties; ended Nov 11.

1919 President Wilson suffered a paralytic stroke in Pueblo, Colo., while on a speaking tour to promote the League of Nations and Versailles Treaty; he was left virtually incapacitated for the remainder of his term.

1925 Marty Robbins, country music composer and singer, was born in Glendale, Ariz.; wrote numerous hit songs (died 1983).

1940 A presidential proclamation banned the export of scrap iron and steel to any nation outside the Western Hemisphere, except Great Britain.

1947 Lynn Anderson, country music singer, was born in Grand Forks, N.D.

1950 American troops recaptured Seoul from the North Koreans.

1972 Americam Museum of Immigration opened at the base of the Statue of Liberty.

1983 An Australian yacht, *Australia II*, beat an American boat, *Liberty*, off Newport, R.I. to win the America Cup, which had not been lost by Americans in 132 years.

1986 President Reagan vetoed a bill applying economic sanctions against South Africa; the House overrude the veto Sept 29, the Senate on Oct 2.

SEPTEMBER 27

1514 Ponce de Leon received a patent from the Spanish crown to settle "the islands of Bimini and Florida," but on arriving the following February was attacked by the natives and mortally wounded.

1722 Samuel Adams, colonial leader, was born in Boston; tax collector of Boston (1756-64); member of Massachusetts legislature (1765-74); leader in agitation that led to the Boston Tea Party; member, Continental Congress (1774-81) and a signer of the Declaration of Independence; lieutenant governor, Massachusetts (1789-93), governor (1794-97) (died 1803).

1732 James Franklin, brother of Benjamin Franklin, published the first Rhode Island newspaper, the *Rhode Island Gazette*, in Newport.

1774 The Continental Congress voted non-intercourse (non-importation, export, or consumption) with Great Britain, set up a committee to carry out this resolution; adopted and signed Oct 20.

1777 The fifth Continental Congress met for one day at Lancaster, Pa.

1779 John Adams was named minister plenipotentiary to negotiate treaties of peace and commerce with Great Britain.

1809 Raphael Semmes, Confederate naval officer, was born in Charles County, Md.; commanded the British-built cruiser, *Alabama*, which destroyed 64 ships before being sunk off the English coast by the Union warship, *Kearsage* (died 1877).

1830 The Treaty of Dancing Rabbit Creek ended all Choctaw Indian claims to land in Mississippi and provided for their removal west of the Mississippi.

1840 Thomas Nast, editorial cartoonist, was born in Landau; Germany; with *Harper's Weekly* (1862-86); campaigned against the Tweed Ring, invented political symbols of the donkey and elephant (died 1902).

1840 Alfred T. Mahan, naval historian, was born in West Point, N.Y.; president, Naval War College (1886-89, 1892-93) (died 1914).

1846 Edward N. Westcott, banker and author, was born in Syracuse; best remembered as author of *David Harum*, which also became a play and movie (died 1898).

1855 Joy Morton, merchant, was born in Detroit; founder, president, Morton Salt Co. (1885-1934); founder, Morton Arboretum, Lisle, Ill. (died 1934).

1861 Edwin H. Anderson, librarian, was born in Zionsville, Ind.; served libraries in Pittsburgh, New York City (New York Public Library 1913-34); helped found Columbia U. library school (died 1947).

1887 James D. Dole, industrialist, was born in Jamaica Plain, Mass.; founder, Hawaiian Pineapple Co. (1901) and the Hawaiian pineapple industry (died 1958).

1896 Sam(uel J.) Erwin Jr., legislator, was born in Morgantown, N.C.; represented North Carolina in the House (1946-47) and Senate (1954-75); chairman, Senate Watergate Committee (1973-74) (died 1985).

1898 Vincent M. Youmans, composer, was born in New York City; wrote several light operas, hit songs ("Tea for Two," "Sometimes I'm Happy," "Without a Song," "Rise 'n Shine") (died 1946).

1919 Charles H. Percy, industrialist and legislator, was born in Pensacola, Fla.; president, Bell & Howell Co. (1948-64); represented Illinois in the Senate (1966-84).

1939 Kathy (Kathrynne A.) Whitworth, winner of more women's golf tournaments (88) than any other player, was born in Monahans, Tex.; named to LPGA Hall of Fame.

1964 The Warren Commission released a report concluding that Lee Harvey Oswald was solely responsible for the assassination of President Kennedy.

1979 The Department of Health, Education and Welfare was divided into two departments—Health and Human Services, headed by Patricia R. Harris, and Education, with Shirley Hufstedler named secretary on Dec 6.

1985 The General Synod of the United Church of Christ declared its ecumenical partnership with the Christian Church (Disciples of Christ).

1986 The Senate approved 74-23 the most comprehensive changes in the federal tax income system since World War II; House approved the measure 292-136.

1988 Reports circulated that laboratory carbon-testing of the material in the Shroud of Turin proved it was made in the 14th century and could not be the burial cloth of Christ as claimed.

1988 New York State health officials declared that it is safe for hundreds of former residents to return to Love Canal in Niagara Falls, N.Y.; had been declared a disaster area ten years earlier because of chemical contamination.

SEPTEMBER 28

1542 Spanish explorers, Juan Rodriguez Cabrillo and Bartolomé Ferrelo, searching for a direct route to the East Indies through Spanish waters, arrived at a Pacific coast port which they named San Miguel; they were in fact at what is now San Diego and were the discoverers of California.

1765 The ship *Diligence* arrived in the Cape Fear River with stamped paper for North Carolina, but was prevented from landing by armed colonists.

1774 The Continental Congress turned down by one vote a plan of Joseph Galloway of Pennsylvania to give the American colonists something approaching dominion status as a solution for home rule.

1776 A convention adopted the Pennsylvania state constitution.

1781 Yorktown, Va. was encircled by 9000 American and 7800 French troops, who began a siege of three weeks.

1788 The Continental Congress voted to transmit the draft of a new constitution to the states for ratification; would become operative when nine states had ratified.

1813 The British evacuated Detroit after the American victory (Sept 10) in the Battle of Lake Erie made their position untenable.

1839 Frances E.C. Willard, temperance crusader, was born in Churchville, N.Y.; president, Women's Christian Temperance Union (1879-98) and World WCTU (1891) (died 1898).

1840 George W. Peck, journalist, was born in Henderson, N.Y.; publisher, *Milwaukee Sun*, where his *Peck's Bad Boy* stories appeared (died 1916).

1850 President Fillmore appointed Brigham Young governor of the Territory of Utah.

1856 Kate Douglas Wiggin, author, was born in Philadelphia; remembered for *Rebecca of Sunnybrook Farm* and *Mother Carey's Chickens* (died 1923).

1863 Frederick W. MacMonnies, sculptor, was born in Brooklyn; many notable works (*Nathan Hale* in New York City, Columbian Fountain in Chicago) (died 1937).

1887 Avery Brundage, businessman and sports official, was born in Detroit; active in national, international amateur athletics; president, U.S. Olympic Association (1929-53), International Olympic Committee (1952-72) (died 1975).

1892 Thomas Parran Jr., physician, was born in St. Leonard, Md.; with Public Health Service (1917-30), surgeon general (1936-48); leader in efforts to control, eradicate venereal diseases (died 1968).

1893 Marshall Field III, publisher and philanthropist, was born in Chicago, grandson of Marshall Field (*see* 8/18/1834); founder, publisher, *Chicago Sun* (now *Sun-Times*) (1941); organized philanthropic Field Foundation (died 1956).

1895 Wallace K. Harrison, architect, was born in Worcester, Mass.; led design of United Nations Building, Rockefeller Center, Trylon and Perisphere at 1939 World Fair, Metropolitan Opera House in Lincoln Center (died 1981).

1901 William S. Paley, radio and television executive, was born in Chicago; president, Columbia Broadcasting System (1928-46), board chairman (1946-83).

1902 Ed(ward V.) Sullivan, journalist and television host, was born to New York City; columnist, *New York Daily News;* host of popular variety show (died 1974).

1902 Al(fred G.) Capp, cartoonist, was born in New Haven; creator of "Lil Abner" (died 1979).

1913 Alice Marble, tennis player, was born in Plumas County, Ca.; won American, Wimbledon singles in 1930s.

1918 The fifth Liberty Loan drive opened; closed Oct 19 with subscriptions of nearly $7 billion.

1920 A grand jury in Chicago indicted eight White Sox baseball players for "throwing" the 1919 World Series.

1924 Two of four Army Air Service planes reached Seattle, completing an around-the-world flight; made 57 stops in 175 days.

1937 President Franklin Roosevelt dedicated the Bonneville Dam on the Columbia River.

1940 National Airport in Washington was dedicated by President Franklin Roosevelt.

1987 Earthquakes struck southern California doing considerable damage, which was increased by a major aftershock on Sept 30.

SEPTEMBER 29

1780 Major John André, British officer, was found guilty by a court martial, headed by Gen. Nathanael Greene; hanged Oct 2; an aide to Sir Henry Clinton, he negotiated with Benedict Arnold for betrayal of West Point; captured in civilian clothes while returning to New York with papers in his boot.

1789 Congress established a 1000-man U.S. Army.

1789 President Washington signed the first federal appropriations act—$639,000 to defray expenses in 1789.

1829 Giles A. Smith, Union general, was born in Jefferson County, N.Y., brother of Morgan L. Smith (3/8/1821); served at Vicksburg, with Sherman on march through the Carolinas (died 1876).

1831 John M. Schofield, Union general, was born in Gerry, N.Y.; Secretary of War (1868-69); superintendent, West Point (1876-81); commanding general of the Army (1888-95) (died 1906).

1838 Henry H. Richardson, architect, was born in St. James Parish, La.; designed Lever and Austin Halls, Harvard; Marshall Field Building, Chicago (died 1886).

1859 Hermann M. Biggs, physician, was born in Trumansburg, N.Y.; pioneer in preventive medicine, introduced diphtheria toxin in America (1894) (died 1923).

1892 Elmer L. Rice, playwright, was born in New York City; wrote several hit plays (*Street Scene, Counsellor-at-Law, The Adding Machine*) (died 1967).

1895 Joseph B. Rhine, parapsychologist, was born in Waterloo, Pa.; with Duke U. (1927-65), Institute of Parapsychology, Durham, N.C. (1964-68); author (*Extra Sensory Perception*) (died 1980).

1901 Enrico Fermi, physicist, was born in Rome; helped build first sustained nuclear chain reaction (Dec 2, 1942, Chicago); awarded 1938 Nobel Physics Prize for production of neutron bombardment and for discovery of effectiveness of slow neutrons in producing radioactivity.

1906 Greer Garson, screen actress, was born in County Down, Ireland; starred in several movies (*Mrs. Miniver*).

1908 Gene Autry, western singer and screen actor, was born in Tioga, Tex.; made 82 pictures, wrote more than 250 songs; owner, California Angels baseball team.

1913 Stanley Kramer, screen director and producer, was born in New York City; many screen successes (*High Noon, Caine Mutiny, Death of a Salesman, Ship of Fools, Guess Who's Coming to Dinner*).

1915 Oscar Handlin, historian, was born in New York City; influential in field of social history; noted for work on American immigration (*The Uprooted*).

1927 A tornado struck St. Louis, killing 90 persons and injuring 1500; destroyed 5000 buildings and caused $50 million damage.

1931 James W. Cronin, physicist, was born in Chicago; shared 1980 Nobel Physics Prize for groundbreaking research on the "big bang" theory of the origin of the universe.

1941 American and British officials met in Moscow with Russians and agreed to send Russia large amounts of war material.

1948 Bryant Gumbel, television personality, was born in New Orleans; co-host of *Today* show (1982-).

1982 Cyanide placed in Tylenol capsules caused the death of seven persons in the Chicago area; killer was not found.

1986 The Soviets freed American journalist Nicholas Daniloff, who had been held in Moscow for allegedly spying; a day later, Gennadi Zakharov, a Soviet UN employee, pleaded no contest to a spying charge in New York City and was freed to return to the Soviet Union.

1987 Rev. Pat (M.G.) Robertson announced he would resign his Southern Baptist ordination and give up leadership of the multimillion dollar religious broadcasting empire to pursue his campaign for the Republican presidential nomination.

1988 The space shuttle *Discovery* lifted off successfully at Cape Canaveral, Fla. in the first American space shot since the tragic *Challenger* disaster in Jan 1986, when the capsule blew up after liftoff killing all seven aboard; landed successfully Oct 3 at Edwards Air Force Base, Cal.

SEPTEMBER 30

1762 Nathan Smith, pioneer surgeon, was born in Rehoboth, Mass.; founder, Yale Medical School and similar schools at Bowdoin, U. of Vermont (died 1829).

1774 The Continental Congress resolved to recommend that no American products be exported after Sept 10, 1775 unless the grievances of the colonies were taken care of before then.

1777 The sixth Continental Congress met in York, Pa.; adjourned June 27, 1778.

1800 The Treaty of Morfontaine, commonly known as the Convention of 1800, was agreed on, superseding the 1778 treaties with France; released the United States from its defensive alliance with France.

1803 Sylvester Marsh, inventor, was born in Compton, N.H.; built inclined railway to the top of Mt. Washington (1866-69); invented special engine design, cog rail, atmospheric brake for the railway (died 1884).

1809 William Henry Harrison, then governor of Indiana Territory, concluded a treaty with several Indian tribes in Ft. Wayne, Ind., by which the United States bought three million acres on the Wabash and White rivers; condemned by Tecumseh, Shawnee chief, who demanded return of the land.

1819 Thomas Jordan, Confederate general, was born in Luray, Va.; chief of staff to Gen. Beauregard; founder, editor, *Financial and Mining Record* (1870-92) (died 1895).

1861 William Wrigley Jr., chewing gum manufacturer, was born in Philadelphia; founder, president, gum company (1891-1932); owner, Chicago Cubs baseball team (died 1932).

1864 Percy L. Howe, dentist, was born in North Providence, R.I.; pioneer in dental research, demonstrated relationshp of oral and bodily health (died 1950).

1870 Thomas W. Lamont, banker, was born in Claverack, N.Y.; with J.P. Morgan & Co. (1911-48), board chairman (1943-48) (died 1948).

1875 Fred Fisher, composer, was born in Cologne, Germany of American parentage; wrote several popular hits ("Come, Josephine, in My Flying Machine;' "Peg o' My Heart;" "Dardanella;" "Chicago") (died 1942).

1882 The world's first hydroelectric plant began operations on the Fox River at Appleton, Wis.

1882 Charles L. Lawrance, aeronautical engineer, was born in Lenox, Mass.; designed first air-cooled aeronautical engine (died 1950).

1886 William Langer, legislator and public official, was born near Everest, N.D.; served North Dakota as governor (1932-40) withstanding a court fight; represented state in the Senate (1940-59) (died 1959).

1892 Leaders of the Amalgamated Association of Iron and Steel Workers on strike against the Carnegie Homestead plant were arrested on charges of treason against Pennsylvania.

1895 Lewis Milestone, film director (*The Front Page, All Quiet on the Western Front, Mutiny on the Bounty*), was born in Chisinau, Russia (died 1980).

1924 Truman Capote, author, was born in New Orleans; wrote several popular books (*In Cold Blood; Breakfast at Tiffany's; Other Voices, Other Rooms*) (died 1984).

1926 Robin Roberts, baseball pitcher who won 286 games (Phillies), was born in Springfield, Ill.; named to Baseball Hall of Fame.

1928 Elie Wiesel, author (*Night, Dawn, The Accident*), was born in Sughet, Rumania; awarded 1986 Nobel Peace Prize.

1930 Dad (C.M.) Joiner tapped the great East Texas oil field for the first time, making Dallas the oil center of the area.

1935 The first American opera, *Porgy and Bess*, written by George Gershwin, opened in Boston.

1943 Merchant Marine Academy in Kings Point, N.Y. was dedicated.

1948 Edith K.C. Roosevelt, widow of President Theodore Roosevelt, died in Oyster Bay, N.Y. at 87.

1952 Cinerama, a three-film strip process, opened in New York City; stimulated interest in wide screens.

1953 President Eisenhower nominated Earl Warren as chief justice of the Supreme Court; confirmed Oct 5.

1976 Congress overrode a presidential veto on a $50 billion appropriations bill for social services, including manpower, education, and health projects.

OCTOBER 1

1730 Richard Stockton, jurist, was born near Princeton, N.J.; member, Continental Congress (1776) and a signer of the Declaration of Independence (died 1781).

1732 Library Company began operations in Philadelphia with the arrival of books from England; the subscription library had been founded by Benjamin Franklin in Nov 1731.

1746 John P.G. Muhlenberg, Revolutionary general and legislator, was born in Trappe, Pa., the son of Henry M. Muhlenberg (9/6/1711); served at Stony Point, stormed British redoubts at Yorktown; represented Pennsylvania in the House (1789-91, 1793-94, 1799-1801) and in the Senate (1801) (died 1807).

1768 Two regiments of British soldiers arrived in Boston from Halifax to enforce customs laws.

1781 James Lawrence, War of 1812 naval officer, was born in Burlington, N.J.; commander of the *Chesapeake* in engagement with British ship *Shannon* on June 1, 1813; though mortally wounded, he rallied his men saying, "Don't give up the ship!", a phrase which became the Naval slogan.

1799 Rufus Choate, lawyer and legislator, was born in Essex, Mass.; eminent trial lawyer, who was described as one "who made it safe to murder," and orator; represented Massachusetts in the House (1831-34) and Senate (1841-45) (died 1859).

1800 The secret treaty of San Ildefonso was signed, whereby Spain returned Louisiana to France.

1804 William C.C. Clairborne was formally installed as territorial governor of Louisiana.

1812 The Territory of Missouri was created.

1813 Caroline C. McIntosh Fillmore, second wife of President Fillmore, was born in Morristown, N.J. (died 1881).

1820 The fourth Census reported the American population to be 9,638,453.

1826 Benjamin B. Hotchkiss, inventor, was born in Watertown, Conn.; invented a machine gun, magazine rifle (died 1885).

1832 Caroline L. Scott Harrison, first wife of Benjamin Harrison, was born in Oxford, Ohio (died 1892).

1832 Henry C. Work, composer, was born in Middletown, Conn.; wrote several popular songs ("Come Home, Father" (a temperance song); "Grandfather's Clock," "Marching Through Georgia") (died 1884).

1849 A convention in Frankfort adopted a new Kentucky state constitution.

1849 Michael H. DeYoung, newspaper executive, was born in St. Louis; co-founder (1865), editor (1880-1925), *San Francisco Chronicle* (died 1925).

1850 David R. Francis, public official, was born in Richmond, Ky.; served Missouri as governor (1889-93); Interior Secretary (1896-97); ambassador to Russia (1916-18) (died 1927).

1860 The eighth Census reported a population of 31,443,321 and the population center had moved to 20 miles south of Chillicothe, Ohio.

1881 William E. Boeing, airplane manufacturer, was born in Detroit; founder, Boeing Airplane Co. (1916) (died 1956).

1889 North Dakotans voted to adopt their constitution, including prohibition.

1890 President Benjamin Harrison signed an act transferring the Weather Bureau to the Department of Agriculture.

1890 Yosemite (Cal.) National Park was established.

1891 Stanford U. opened in Palo Alto, Cal.

1893 Faith C. Baldwin, author, was born in New Rochelle, N.Y.; wrote more than 60 novels (*Face Toward the Spring, Many Windows, New Girl in Town*) (died 1978).

1899 William A. Patterson, airline executive, was born in Honolulu; president (1934-63), chief executive officer (1963-80), United Air Lines (died 1980).

1903 The first World Series was played between the Boston Red Sox and Pittsburgh Pirates who won the first three games; however, Boston won the series.

1904 Vladimir Horowitz, concert pianist, was born in Kiev, Russia.

1908 Henry Ford introduced the Model T priced at $850.

1910 The *Los Angeles Times* offices were bombed, 21 employees were killed and the building was demolished; three union men were found guilty.

1914 Daniel J. Boorstin, historian, was born in Atlanta; had of the Library of Congress (1975-87); author (*The Americans*).

1917 A second Liberty Bond issue of $3.8 billion in 4% convertible gold bonds was authorized.

1920 Walter Matthau, actor, was born in New York City; starred in many films (*The Odd Couple, Fortune Cookie, Sunshine Boys*).

1920 Charles Ponzi, Boston speculator, was indicted on 86 counts of using the mails to defraud.

1924 Jimmy (James E.) Carter, 39th president (1977-81), was born in Plains, Ga.; served Georgia as governor (1970-74).

1924 William Rehnquist, jurist, was born in Milwaukee; associate justice, Supreme Court (1972-86), chief justice (1986-).

1935 Julie Andrews, actress, was born in Walton, England; starred on stage (*My Fair Lady*), screen (*Mary Poppins, Sound of Music*).

1942 The first American jet flight took place when a Bell XP-59A, powered by two I-16 General Electric turbojet engines, flew at Edwards Air Force Base, Cal.

1945 Rod(ney C.) Carew, baseball player (Twins, Angels), was born in Gaton, Panama; considered one of the great hitters of all times.

1955 The *Forrestal*, first of a new class of aircraft carriers, was commissioned; has a displacement of about 60,000 tons, a flight deck of more than 600 feet.

1960 The Connecticut General Assembly abolished county governments; necessary county functions were transferred to the state.

1961 Roger Maris of the New York Yankees hit his record-breaking 61st homerun of the year, breaking the old record of 60 set by Babe Ruth nearly 40 years earlier.

1962 James Meredith became the first black student at the U. of Mississippi after 3000 troops put down riots.

1965 The Administration on Aging was created; functions later transferred to the Human Development Office.

1979 Panama took control of the Panama Canal Zone.

1983 The Job Training Partnership Act of 1984 went into effect, replacing the Comprehensive Employment & Training Act (CETA), with training programs focusing primarily on the private sector.

1984 Labor Secretary Raymond J. Donovan was indicted in New York City on charges of participation in a scheme to defraud the New York Transit Authority; took leave of absence from cabinet; acquitted in 1987.

1986 President Carter Memorial Library was dedicated in Atlanta.

OCTOBER 2

1656 Connecticut passed a law to fine and banish Quakers.

1755 Hannah Adams, author, was born in Medfield, Mass.; the first American woman to make her living writing (*Truth and Excellence of the Christian Religion, History of the Jews*) (died 1831).

1780 British Major John André was hanged as a spy in Tappan, N.Y. for dealing with Benedict Arnold.

1782 Charles Lee, Revolutionary general, died at 51; critical of Washington, he was captured by British; during captivity he gave British plans for defeating the Americans; exchanged, put in charge of attack on Monmouth; began retreat instead; court martialed, dismissed from Army (1780).

1788 The Continental Congress was moved unceremoniously from its rooms in New York's City Hall so that the building could be renovated for the incoming new federal government.

1819 George W. Getty, Union general, was born in Washington; distinguished for defense of Suffolk (1863), with Army of the Shenandoah (1864), of the Potomac (1865) (died 1901).

1830 Charles Pratt, oil executive, was born in Watertown, Mass.; co-founder of company to refine crude oil; became Standard Oil executive after his company was sold; benefactor, founder, Pratt Institute, Brooklyn, for training artisans, draftsmen (died 1891).

1831 E(dwin) L. Godkin, editor, was born in Mayne, Ireland; founder, editor, *The Nation* (1865-81); editor, *New York Post* (1883-1900) into which *The Nation* had been merged (died 1902).

1835 The first battle of the Texas Revolution occurred in Gonzales, when Texans successfully refused to surrender a cannon to 100 Mexican soldiers.

1865 Connecticut voted against Negro suffrage.

1867 Theodore F. Green, legislator, was born in Providence; served Rhode Island as governor (1932-36) and represented it in the Senate (1936-60); was the oldest man to serve in the Congress (died 1966).

1871 Cordell Hull, public official and legislator, was born in Byrdstown, Tenn.; represented Tennessee in the House (1907-21, 1923-31) and Senate (1931-33); author of federal income tax laws (1913, 1916); Secretary of State (1933-44), called the father of the United Nations; awarded 1945 Nobel Peace Prize (died 1955).

1874 Edwin H. Crump, political leader, was born in Holly Springs, Miss.; political boss of Memphis area, Memphis mayor (1910-16, 1940) (died 1954).

1877 Carl T. Hayden, legislator, was born in what is now Tempe, Ariz.; represented Arizona in the House (1912-27) and Senate (1927-69), serving as president pro tem (1957-69) (died 1972).

1879 Wallace Stevens, insurance executive and poet, was born in Reading, Pa.; wrote much poetry (*Harmonium, Ideas of Order, Man with the Blue Guitar*) (died 1955).

1885 Ruth Bryan Rohde, diplomat, was born in Jacksonville, Ill., daughter of William Jennings Bryan (3/19/1860); first woman appointed to head an American diplomatic post (minister to Denmark 1933-36); represented Florida in the House (1919-23) (died 1954).

1889 First Pan-American Conference opened in Washington.

1891 Arizona territorial legislature adopted a constitution.

1895 Groucho (Julius H.) Marx, entertainer, was born in New York City; screen actor with brothers, television entertainer (died 1977).

1896 Bud (William) Abbott, comedian, was born in Asbury Park, N.J.; half of the Abbott and Costello comedy team (died 1974).

1901 Charles S. Draper, aeronautical engineer, was born in Windsor, Mo.; pioneered in navigational guidance systems for ships, planes, rockets (died 1988).

1909 Alex(ander G.) Raymond, cartoonist, was born in New Rochelle, N.Y.; creator of *Flash Gordon* and *Rip Kirby* (died 1956).

1919 James M. Buchanan, economist, was born in Murfreesboro, Tenn.; awarded 1986 Nobel Economics Prize for pioneering development of new methods for analyzing economic and political decision-making.

1932 Maury (Maurice) Wills, baseball player (Dodgers), was born in Washington.

1942 Office of Economic Stabilization was created; James F. Byrnes was named first director.

1967 Thurgood Marshall was sworn in as the first black Supreme Court justice.

1968 The North Cascades (Wash.) and Redwood (Cal.) National Parks were established.

1970 A plane carrying the Wichita State U. football team crashed at Silver Plume, Colo., 29 died.

1985 Screen actor Rock Hudson died at 59 in Los Angeles; his death from AIDS gave publicity to the disease and a strong impetus to efforts for fund raising to find a cure.

1988 The Catholic Archdiocese of Detroit announced recommendations to close 43 of Detroit's 112 churches serving 10,000 parishioners because of low membership and high operating costs; closings scheduled for June 1989.

OCTOBER 3

1656 Miles Standish, colonial leader, died at about 72; arrived on the *Mayflower*, served as military defender of the colony, treasurer for nine years and on the governor's council for 29 years.

1724 Hermon Husbands, agitator and revolutionist, was born probably in Cecil County, Md.; leader of the Whiskey Rebellion in western Pennsylvania; tried, condemned to death, but later pardoned (died 1793).

1777 James Jackson, physician, was born in Newburyport, Mass.; one of the first to introduce vaccination against smallpox (1800) (died 1867).

1784 Ithiel Town, architect, was born in Thompson, Conn.; designed state capitols in Indiana, North Carolina; the New Haven Center and Trinity churches, Customs House in New York City (died 1844).

1789 President Washington issued a proclamation establishing Thanksgiving Day; the first one was observed Nov 26.

1790 John Ross, half-breed Cherokee leader, was born near Lookout Mountain, Tenn.; son of a Scottish father and Cherokee mother, he was chief of the United Cherokee Nation (1839-66) (died 1866).

1800 George Bancroft, historian and public official, was born in Worcester, Mass.; Secretary of Navy (1845-46), established the Naval Academy; minister to Great Britain (1846-49), to Germany (1867-74); author of ten-volume American history (died 1891).

1802 George Ripley, Unitarian theologian, was born in Greenfield, Mass.; helped organize experimental Brook Farm community in Mass.; literary critic, *New York Tribune* (1849-80) (died 1880).

1803 John Gorrie, physician, was born in Charleston; devised method of treating malaria, other fever victims, in a cool room; eventually built machine (c

1842) to cool room, probably the first mechanical refrigerating device (died 1855).

1804 Townsend Harris, diplomat, was born in Sandy Hill, N.Y.; first American consul general to Japan after its opening (1855-59), minister (1859); negotiated commercial treaty with Japan; leading founder, City College of New York (died 1878).

1823 Benjamin F. Stephenson, physician, was born in Wayne County, Ill.; Union regimental surgeon (1861-64); founder (1866), Grand Army of the Republic (GAR) (died 1871).

1854 William C. Gorgas, Army physician, was born near Mobile, Ala., son of Josiah Gorgas (7/1/1818); chief sanitary officer, Havana (1898-1902), Panama Canal Commission (1904-13); did much to control yellow fever, assure canal's completion; Army Surgeon General (1914-18) (died 1920).

1862 Gen. William S. Rosecrans led his Union troops to victory over Confederates under Gen. Earl Van Dorn at Corinth, Miss.

1872 Fred Clarke, baseball player/manager (Pirates), was born in Winterset, Ia.; named to Baseball Hall of Fame (died 1960).

1892 U. of Idaho, chartered in 1889, opened.

1899 Gertrude Berg, radio and television actress, was born in New York City; wrote, starred in the Goldberg series (died 1966).

1900 Thomas C. Wolfe, author, was born in Asheville, N.C.; novelist (*Look Homeward, Angel; The Web and the Rock; You Can't Go Home Again*) (died 1938).

1910 A convention began in Santa Fe to adopt the New Mexico constitution.

1922 The first woman to serve in the Senate, Mrs. Rebecca L. Felton, was appointed by the Georgia governor to fill a vacancy; served until Nov 22.

1925 Gore Vidal, author, was born in West Point, N.Y.; wrote several novels, historical fiction (*Myra Breckenridge, Burr, 1876, Kalki*).

1941 Chubby Checker, entertainer, was born as Ernest Evans in Philadelphia; helped popularize the twist dance craze of early 1960s.

1951 Bobby Thomson, New York Giants third baseman, hit a homerun with two men on base in the bottom of the ninth inning to beat the Brooklyn Dodgers 5-4 and give the Giants the pennant; the Giants were 13-1/2 games behind on Aug 11 and wound up the season tied, then won two of three playoff games.

1965 The national origins quota system of immigration was abolished.

1970 The National Oceanic and Atmospheric Administration (NOAA) was formed by combining the Weather Service, Ocean Survey, and Marine Fisheries services.

1987 A sweeping new free trade agreement between the United States and Canada was announced; the pact would eliminate all tariffs between the two countries by 1999; must be approved by the Canadian Parliament and American Congress.

OCTOBER 4

1777 About 1000 Americans were lost in an audacious attack on British headquarters in Germantown, Pa. in an effort to free Philadelphia; attack was abandoned.

1809 Robert C. Schenck, Union general and public official, was born in Franklin, Ohio; saw action in both battles of Bull Run; represented Ohio in the House (1843-51, 1863-71); minister to Brazil (1851-53), to Great Britain (1871-76) (died 1890).

1810 Eliza McCardle Johnson, wife of President Andrew Johnson, was born in Leesburg, Tenn. (died 1876).

1812 American troops defeated the British at Ogdensburg, N.Y.

1822 Rutherford B. Hayes, 19th president (1877-81), was born in Delaware, Ohio; represented Ohio in the House (1865-67) and served it as governor (1867-71, 1875-76); became president in disputed election with Samuel J. Tilden, resolved by a 15-member electoral commission (died 1893).

1858 Michael I. Pupin, physicist, was born in Idvor, Hungary (now Yugoslavia); professor of electromechanics, Columbia (1901-31); invented multiplex telegraphy; improved coil for long distance telephony (died 1935).

1861 Frederic Remington, painter and sculptor, was born in Canton, N.Y.; known primarily as painter of animals, illustrator of American West scenes (died 1909).

1861 Walter Rauschenbusch, Baptist theologian, was born in Rochester, N.Y.; with Rochester Theological Seminary (1897-1918), founded Society of Jesus, which became the Brotherhood of the Kingdom; a leader in social interpretation and application of Christianity (died 1918).

1862 Edward Stratemeyer, author and publisher, was born in Elizabeth, N.J.; in his own name and pseudonyms (Carolyn Keene, Arthur M. Winfield, Ralph Bonehill, Franklin W. Dixon) turned out several series of youth books (*The Rover Boys, Tom Swift, The Hardy Boys, The Bobbsey Twins*) (died 1930).

1871 U. of Alabama at Tuscaloosa was reorganized and opened.

1879 Edward M. East, geneticist, was born in DuQuoin, Ill.; work led to development of hybrid corn (died 1938).

1884 Damon Runyon, journalist and author, was born in Manhattan, Kan.; screen plays (*Lady for a Day, Little Miss Marker*); author (*Blue Plate Special, Guys and Dolls*) (died 1946).

1890 John Kelly Sr., winner of the Olympic single (1920) and double sculls (1920, 1924), was born in Philadelphia (died 1960).

1893 Walter A. Maier, religious leader, was born in Boston; regular speaker, Lutheran Hour, popular weekly radio program (1930-50) (died 1950).

1895 Buster (Joseph F.) Keaton, screen actor, was born in Piqua, Kan.; silent screen comedian, master of deadpan (died 1966).

1905 Calvin Coolidge and Grace Anna Goodhue were married in Burlington, Vt.

1918 A shell loading plant in Morgan, N.J. exploded, leveling several nearby villages and killing 90 persons.

1918 Germany and Austria asked President Wilson to "take steps for restoration of peace" and to notify other belligerents of the request.

1922 Malcolm Baldrige, Secretary of Commerce (1981-87); was born in Omaha; died in a horse riding accident (1987).

1924 Charlton Heston, screen actor, was born in Evansville, Ill.; starred in many films (*Ben Hur, Julius Caesar)*.

1945 Gen. Douglas MacArthur, directing military occupation of Japan, issued orders restoring civil liberties, freeing political prisoners and abolishing the secret police.

1959 *Luna 3*, an unnamed satellite, was the first to circle the moon and send back pictures of the far side.

1965 Pope Pius VI arrived in New York City to deliver a peace message to the United Nations; later conferred with President Lyndon Johnson.

1974 The Joseph H. Hirschhorn Museum and Sculpture Garden opened in Washington.

OCTOBER 5

1609 John Smith, burned in a powder explosion, was deposed from the presidency of the Jamestown council and sent back to England.

1703 Jonathan Edwards, Congregational clergyman and educator, was born in East Windsor, Conn.; a powerful preacher, he was pastor of the Northampton Church (1729-50); dismissed over argument on church admission standards; regarded as the greatest theologian of American Puritanism; led a revival (1734-35) that spread through parts of Connecticut and paved the way for later tours of George Whitefield; president, College of New Jersey (later Princeton) (1757-58) (died 1758).

1748 Benjamin Moore, Episcopal prelate, was born in Newtown, Long Island, N.Y.; bishop of New York (1801-16); president, Columbia U. (1801-11) (died 1816).

1751 James Iredell, jurist, was born in Lewes, England; attorney general, North Carolina (1779-81); one of the original associate justices, Supreme Court (1790-99) (died 1799).

1774 The Assembly of Massachusetts met in Salem despite the ban on such meetings; named a Committee of Safety empowered to call out the militia and promote military organization.

1784 The Dutch Reformed Church Synod established the first American theological seminary in New York City; later became the New Brunswick Theological Seminary.

1787 Thomas Stone, colonial leader, died at 44; member, Continental Congress (1775-78) and a signer of the Declaration of Independence.

1804 Robert P. Parrott, ordnance expert and inventor, was born in Lee, N.H.; invented a rifle, the first American rifled cannon; his guns were used by the Union forces in the Civil War (died 1877).

1813 American troops under Gen. William Henry Harrison overtook and defeated retreating British-Indian forces near Thamesville, Ontario; Tecumseh was killed in the battle, resulting in the collapse of the Indian confederacy and its alliance with the British.

1818 A Connecticut convention adopted a state constitution; ratified by popular vote.

1822 Moses Sperry Beach, editor and inventor, was born in Springfield, Mass., brother of Alfred E. Beach (9/1/1826); owner, *New York Sun* (1852-68); invented device for feeding newsprint into presses from a roller; first to print on both sides of the paper at one time (died 1892).

1824 Henry Chadwick, sports writer, was born in Exeter, England; did much to promote professional baseball as writer on *New York Times, Brooklyn Eagle, New York Clipper*; edited, published annual official baseball guide; named to Baseball Hall of Fame (died 1908).

1829 Chester Alan Arthur, 21st president (1881-85), was born in Fairfield, Vt.; collector of Port of New York (1871-78); elected Vice President, serving from Mar 4 to Sept 19, 1881 when he became president at the death of Garfield (died 1886).

1848 Edward L. Trudeau, physician, was born in New York City; a specialist in tuberculosis; founder, Trudeau Sanitarium in the Adirondacks (1884), the Saranac Laboratory (1894), the first American laboratory devoted to the study of tuberculosis (died 1915).

1860 Gov. William H. Gist of South Carolina wrote a confidential letter to each cotton state governor informing him that if Abraham Lincoln were elected, South Carolina would call a secession convention.

1869 Frank H. Hitchcock, public official, was born in Amherst, Ohio; as Postmaster General (1909-13), he initiated parcel post, airmail, and postal savings (died 1935).

1877 The three-day battle of Bear Paws Mountains in Idaho ended when Chief Joseph surrendered to Col. Nelson A. Miles, ending the Nez Percé War.

1879 (Francis) Peyton Rous, physiologist, was born in Baltimore; with Rockefeller Institute (1910-45); shared 1966 Nobel Physiology/Medicine Prize for discovery of tumor-producing viruses; first to isolate cancer-causing virus (died 1970).

1882 Robert H. Goddard, physicist, was born in Worcester, Mass.; with Clark U. (1914-43), he engaged in rocket research for reaching high altitudes; known as the father of modern rocketry (died 1945).

1892 Two of the notorious Dalton brothers were killed in an attempted bank robbery in Coffeyville, Kan.; another was captured.

1895 Walter Bedell Smith, World War II and public official, was born in Indianapolis; chief of staff to Gen. Eisenhower (1942-46); ambassador to Russia (1946-49); director, CIA (1950-53); Undersecretary of State (1953-54) (died 1961).

1902 Ray A. Kroc, businessman, was born in Chicago; founder, president, McDonald's fast food chain (1955-68), board chairman (1968-84) (died 1984).

1908 Joshua Logan, director and producer, was born in Texarkana, Tex.; involved in numerous hit plays (*Mr. Roberts, South Pacific, Fanny*) and films (*Picnic, Bus Stop*) (died 1988).

1910 St. Patrick's Cathedral in New York City was dedicated by Archbishop John M. Farley of New York.

1931 Clyde Pangborn and Hugh Herndon Jr. arrived at Wenatchee, Wash. from near Tokyo, becoming the first to fly nonstop across the Pacific.

1986 A C-123K cargo plane carrying supplies to the Contras was shot down by Nicaraguan soldiers; two Americans died in the crash, a third, Eugene Hasenfus of Marinette, Wis., was captured; he was later convicted and sentenced to 30 years imprisonment but was pardoned by Nicaraguan President Daniel Ortega.

OCTOBER 6

1622 Piscataqua, N.H., at mouth of Piscataqua River, settled by three Plymouth merchants.

1767 (Johann Christian) Gottlieb Graupner, musician, was born in Verden, Germany; organized Boston Philharmonic Society (c 1810), first regular American concert orchestra (died 1836).

1777 Sir Henry Clinton began advance up the Hudson River to help Burgoyne at Saratoga; captured Forts Clinton and Montgomery, seven miles below West Point.

1779 Nathan Appleton, industrialist, was born in New Ipswich, N.H.; made significant contributions to American textile industry (died 1861).

1809 John W. Griffiths, naval architect, was born in New York City; designed the "clipper ship" (died 1882).

1846 George Westinghouse, inventor, was born in Central Bridge, N.Y.; most notable inventions were air brake and automatic signalling system; also developed system for wide distribution of electric power; founder (1886), Westinghouse Electric Co. to produce dynamos, transformers (died 1914).

1848 Allan McL. Hamilton, physician, was born in Brooklyn, grandson of Alexander Hamilton (1/11/1755); pioneer American neurologist (died 1919).

1857 Joseph T. Dickman, World War I general, was born in Dayton, Ohio; led Third Division, Fourth and Third Corps (1917-18); commanded Third Army in Germany (1918-19) (died 1927).

1859 Frank A. Seiberling, manufacturer, was born in Summit County, Ohio; founder (1898), Goodyear Tire & Rubber Co.; lost control (1921), then founded Seiberling Rubber Co. (died 1955).

1862 Albert J. Beveridge, legislator and author, was born in Highland County, Ohio; represented Indiana in the Senate (1899-1911); wrote four-volume biography of John Marshall (died 1927).

1866 Reginald A. Fessenden, inventor, was born in Milton, Canada of American parents; worked with Edison, invented high frequency alternator which led to first radio broadcast of voice and music (died 1932).

1868 George H. Lorimer, magazine editor, was born in Louisville; editor, *Saturday Evening Post* (1899-1937), raised circulation from 1800 to three million (died 1937).

1876 The American Library Association was organized in Philadelphia.

1884 The Naval War College was established by the Navy Department in Newport, R.I., the first institution of its kind, with Commodore Stephen B. Luce as the first president.

1888 Clarence C. Little, biologist, was born in Brookline, Mass.; head, Jackson Laboratory and managing director, American Society for Control of Cancer (1929-56); conducted research on cancer inheritance (died 1971).

1905 Helen Wills (Roark), tennis player, was born in Centerville, Cal.; American singles champion seven times, Wimbledon eight times in the 1920s, 1930s.

1906 Janet Gaynor, screen actress, was born in Philadelphia; starred in several films (*Seventh Heaven, A Star Is Born*) (died 1984).

1927 *The Jazz Singer* with Al Jolson opened in New York City, the first part-talking picture.

1938 The United States sent a strong protest to Japan following the 1937 invasion of China, violating the Open Door policy.

1955 An airliner crashed near Laramie, Wyo., killing 46 persons.

1978 Congress extended the deadline for ratification of the Equal Rights Amendment by 39 months.

1979 Pope John Paul II was the first pope ever received in the White House.

1987 The Senate Judiciary Committee voted to recommend to the full Senate that the nomination of Robert H. Bork to the Supreme Court be rejected; Senate turned down the nomination 58-42.

1987 Stock prices plunged 91.55 points on the Dow Jones industrial average to 2548.63, the largest one-day decline.

OCTOBER 7

1727 William S. Johnson, legislator and educator, was born in Stratford, Conn., son of Samuel Johnson (10/14/1696); member, Continental Congress (1784-87); represented Connecticut in the Senate (1789-91); president, Columbia College (1787-1800) (died 1819).

1728 Caesar Rodney, colonial leader, was born in Dover, Del.; member, Continental Congress (1774-76, 1777, 1778), and a signer of the Declaration of Independence; "president" of Delaware (1778-82) (died 1784).

1746 William Billings, composer, was born in Boston; the first professional American composer; published first of six collections (1770) (died 1800).

1756 The *New Hampshire Gazette*, the first newspaper in that state, was published in Portsmouth by Daniel Fowle.

1763 Great Britain issued a proclamation forbidding colonial settlement beyond the Allegheny Mountains in an effort to appease the Indians.

1765 The Stamp Act Congress, with 28 delegates, began more than two weeks of deliberations in New York City, passing resolutions opposing the tax on Oct 19; attending were delegates from all colonies except Virginia, New Hampshire, North Carolina, and Georgia.

1777 The second battle of Bemis Heights near Saratoga, N.Y. resulted in the defeat of Gen. John Burgoyne and his British troops by Americans under Benedict Arnold, who was severely wounded; Burgoyne retreated to Saratoga.

1777 Francis Nash, Revolutionary general, was killed in action at 35; Nash County, N.C. and Nashville, Tenn. were named for him.

1780 A British force of 1100 led by Maj. Patrick Ferguson was trapped and defeated atop King's Mountain on the Carolinas border by a force of 900 frontiersmen.

1792 George Mason, colonial statesman, died at 67; drew up the non-importation resolution following the enactment of the Stamp Tax Act and Townshend duties; also wrote most of Virginia's constitution; opposed the U.S. Constitution, refused to become one of Virginia's first senators.

1821 Richard H. Anderson, Confederate general, was born in Statesburg, S.C.; served at Antietam, Gettysburg (died 1879).

1826 The Quincy tramway, the first American railway, was completed, running three miles from Quincy to tidewater on the Neponset River.

1826 William B. Bate, Confederate general and public official, was born in Sumner County, Tenn.; saw action at Shiloh, Murfreesboro; served Tennessee as governor (1882-86) and represented it in the Senate (1886-1905) (died 1905).

1833 Margaret Fox, spiritualist, was born in Bath, Canada; with sister, Katherine, encouraged stories that spirits were responsible for knocking at their home in Wayne County, N.Y.; made public appearances throughout the United States and Europe, fostered spiritualism and an investigation of it (died 1893).

1842 Bronson C. Howard, playwright, was born in Detroit; author of several hit plays (*Saratoga, Shenandoah, Aristocracy*) (died 1908).

1848 Candy (William A.) Cummings, baseball player, was born in Ware, Mass.; named to Baseball Hall of Fame (died 1924).

1849 James Whitcomb Riley, poet, was born in Greenfield, Ind.; poems used a Hoosier dialect (*When the Frost is on the Punkin', The Old Swimmin' Hole*) (died 1916).

1856 John W. Alexander, artist, was born in Allegheny, Pa.; portrait painter, did murals for Library of Congress (*Evolution of the Book*) (died 1915).

1858 Charles F. Marvin, meteorologist, was born in Putnam, Ohio; chief, U.S. Weather Bureau (1913-34) (died 1943).

1865 A constitutional convention in Raleigh, N.C. repealed secession ordinance; two days later it abolished slavery.

1866 Martha M. Berry, educator, was born near Rome, Ga.; founder of schools for the underprivileged children of back country Georgia districts; considered one of 12 greatest American women (1931) (died 1942).

1888 Henry A. Wallace, Vice President (1941-45), was born in Adair County, Ia.; edited farm magazines (1910-33); Secretary of Agriculture (1933-40); Secretary of Commerce (1945-46); Progressive Party presidential candidate (1948) (died 1965).

1898 Alfred F. Wallenstein, conductor, was born in Chicago; first cellist, Chicago Symphony (1922-29), New York Philharmonic (1929-36); conductor, Los Angeles Symphony (1943-56) (died 1983).

1904 Chuck (Charles H.) Klein, baseball player who hit 300 home runs in career, was born in Indianapolis; named to Baseball Hall of Fame (died 1958).

1907 Helen C. MacInnes, author, was born in Glasgow; writer of suspense novels (*Assignment in Brittany, North from Rome, Decision at Delphi, Prelude to Terror*) (died 1985).

1911 Vaughn Monroe, orchestra leader and singer, was born in Akron; remembered for his theme song, "Racing with the Moon" (died 1973).

1916 German submarine *U-53* entered Newport, R.I. harbor, sank six merchant vessels off Nantucket Island on the next day and three more on the following day.

1970 President Nixon asked for a cease fire in Southeast Asia; turned down.

OCTOBER 8

1609 John Clarke, a founder of Rhode Island, was born in Westhorpe, England; he was a pioneer in American religious liberty (died 1676).

1720 Jonathan Mayhew, Congregational clergyman, was born in Chilmark, Mass.; his preaching at West Church, Boston (1747-66) began movement to Unitarianism (died 1766).

1810 James W. Marshall, co-discoverer of gold, was born in Hunterdon County, N.J.; a California pioneer, discovered gold Jan 24, 1848 while building a sawmill for John Sutter; launched gold rush (died 1885).

1838 John M. Hay, public official and biographer, was born in Salem, Ind.; ambassador to Great Britain (1897-98), Secretary of State (1898-1905); co-author with John Nicolay of ten-volume biography of Abraham Lincoln for whom he was private secretary (1860-65) (died 1905).

1840 Hawaii's first written constitution was promulgated, including such innovations as a popularly-elected legislature.

1846 Elbert H. Gary, steel executive, was born in Wheaton, Ill.; president, Federated Steel Co. (1898-1901); a leading organizer, U.S. Steel Co. (1901), board chairman (1903-27); Gary, Ind. named for him (died 1927).

1851 Hudson River Railroad opened between New York City and Albany.

1862 Confederate troops attacked Perryville, Ky.; although it was not a clear-cut victory for either side, the Confederates abandoned Kentucky.

1869 J. Frank Duryea, auto manufacturer, was born in Canton, Ill.; co-founder with brother, Charles (12/15/1861), of Duryea Motor Wagon Co.; won first automobile race (Chicago 1895) (died 1967).

1869 Former President Pierce died in Concord, N.H. at 64.

1871 The great Chicago fire, which burned 17,450 buildings and killed 250 persons, started in a barn at 137 DeKoven St. and lasted 27 hours; the loss was estimated at $196 million, left 100,000 homeless.

1871 A week-long forest fire began in Michigan and Wisconsin, destroyed a wide area, killed about 1200 persons, 600 of them in Peshtigo, Wis.

1890 Eddie (Edward V.) Rickenbacker, aviator, was born in Columbus, Ohio; World War I ace (credited with shooting down 26 planes); general manager, Eastern Air Lines (1935-38), president (1938-63); rescued after three weeks on a raft (1942) in the Pacific Ocean after a crash on a special flight for the government (died 1973).

1912 John W. Gardner, public official, was born in Los Angeles; president, Carnegie Corporation, Carnegie Foundation for Advancement of Teaching (1955-64); Secretary of Health, Education & Welfare (1965-68); director, National Urban Coalition; helped organize, headed, Common Cause (1970).

1914 Dr. Simon Flexner (3/25/1863) announced that he had succeeded in isolating and transmitting the germ of infantile paralysis.

1918 President Wilson, replying to a German-Austrian request for peace talks, demanded the evacuation of occupied territory as the first condition for an armistice; agreed (Oct 23) to submit matter to other governments.

1941 Jesse L. Jackson, civil rights leader, was born in Greenville, N.C.; founder, national director, Operation Breadbasket (1966-71); founder, executive director, Operation PUSH (1971-).

1941 The Office of Lend-Lease Administration was created by executive order.

1956 Don Larsen of the New York Yankees pitched the only perfect World Series game, allowing no one to reach first base and facing only 27 batters, beating Brooklyn 2-0.

1965 President Lyndon Johnson underwent a gall bladder operation in Bethesda Naval Center.

1974 The Franklin National Bank of New York City failed, the largest bank failure in American history.

1988 Five-day "siege of Atlanta" ended with 450 arrests of persons trying to block entrance to abortion clinics; periodic picketing began in July, more than 1100 protestors were jailed.

OCTOBER 9

1700 Yale College, founded in 1700, was chartered by the General Court and established in Saybrook, Conn.

1779 American and French troops were unsuccessful in trying to capture Savannah; Count Casimir Pulaski was wounded in the battle and died two days later.

1782 Lewis Cass, legislator and diplomat, was born in Exeter, N.H.; governor, Michigan Territory (1813-31), Secretary of War (1831-36), of State (1857-60); represented Michigan in the Senate (1849-57); Democratic presidential nominee (1848) (died 1866).

1822 George Sykes, Union general, was born in Dover, Del.; corps commander defending Little Round Top and Big Round Top at Gettysburg (died 1880).

1830 Harriet G. Hosmer, sculptor, was born in Watertown, Mass.; most successful sculptress of her day (died 1908).

1837 Francis W. Parker, educator, was born in Bedford, N.H.; a founder of progressive elementary education; founder, director, U. of Chicago School of Education (1901) (died 1902).

1839 Winfield S. Schley, Spanish-American War admiral, was born in Frederick County, Md.; directed destruction of Spanish fleet as it tried to run out of Santiago, Cuba; involved in controversy over who was credited with the naval victory (he or his commander, Adm. William T. Sampson, who was not present when the fleet emerged) (died 1911).

1858 The first overland mail stage from San Francisco reached St. Louis after 23 days and four hours; opposite stage, which left at the same time, reached San Francisco Oct 10 after 24 days, 20 hours and 35 minutes.

1860 Leonard Wood, Spanish-American War general, was born in Winchester, N.H.; organized the Rough

Riders (1898); governor of Cuba (1900-03), governor-general, Philippines (1921-27); Army chief of staff (1910-14) (died 1927).

1863 Gamaliel Bradford, author, was born in Boston; wrote many biographies (Lee, Civil War generals, Darwin) (died 1932).

1863 Edward W. Bok, editor and author, was born in Den Helder, Netherlands; editor-in-chief, *Ladies Home Journal* (1889-1919); author (*The Americanization of Edward Bok*) (died 1930).

1871 Elizabeth S. Kingsley, inventor of the double crostic puzzle, was born in Brooklyn (died 1957).

1873 Charles R. Walgreen, merchant, was born near Galesburg, Ill.; founder, developer of drug store chain named for him (died 1939).

1884 Martin E. Johnson, photographer, was born in Rockford, Ill.; with wife, Osa, photographed African wildlife (died 1937).

1888 The Washington Monument was opened to the public.

1890 Aimee Semple McPherson, evangelist, was born in Ingersoll, Canada; best known woman evangelist of her day; founder, Church of the Foursquare Gospel, Los Angeles, serving as its minister (1923-44) (died 1944).

1898 Joe Sewell, baseball player (Indians, Yankees), was born in Titus, Ala.; named to Baseball Hall of Fame.

1899 Rube (Richard W.) Marquard, baseball pitcher who won 201 games, was born in Cleveland; named to Baseball Hall of Fame (died 1980).

1899 (Charles) Bruce Catton, historian, was born in Petoskey, Mich.; author (*Mr. Lincoln's Army, Glory Road, A Stillness at Appomattox*); editor, *American Heritage* (1954-59) (died 1978).

1903 Walter F. O'Malley, president (1950-70)/owner (1957-79), Dodgers baseball team, was born in New York City (died 1979).

1910 Forest fires in northern Minnesota destroyed six towns, killing 400 persons, and causing about $100 million in property losses.

1940 John Lennon, singer and composer, was born in Liverpool, England; one of the Beatles, he was shot to death near his New York City apartment (1980).

1982 President Reagan suspended Poland's 22-year most favored nation trade status in response to Poland's outlawing of the Solidarity trade union.

1984 President Reagan signed law providing that Social Security Administration may not terminate disability benefits on the basis that disability no longer exists unless the beneficiary has medically improved and is able to work.

1985 Cruise ship *Achille Lauro* was highjacked in the Mediterranean; one American was killed before the ship was retaken.

1986 The Senate by a vote of 87-10 found U.S. District Judge Harry Claiborne guilty on three impeachment charges; he had been found guilty by a court but continued to draw his judicial salary until impeached.

1989 Two cancer researchers at the U. of California Medical School in San Francisco, Dr. J. Michael Bishop and Dr. Harold E. Varmus, were awarded the 1989 Nobel Prize in Physiology/Medicine; other awards went to Yale professor Sidney Altman and Thomas Cech of Colorado U. for chemistry; Norman F. Ramsay of Harvard and Hans Dehmelt of U. of Washington for physics.

OCTOBER 10

1615 An unsuccessful six-day siege was begun of an Iroquois stronghold, probably on Lake Onondaga, by the Hurons aided by Samuel de Champlain.

1738 Benjamin West, painter, was born near Springfield, Pa.; a leading American and English painter; charter member of Royal Academy (1768), president (1792-1820); historical painter to George III (died 1820).

1758 Jean Pierre Chouteau, fur trader and settler, was born in New Orleans, brother of Rene A. Chouteau (9/7/1749); established first permanent white settlement in Oklahoma (1796), near present Salina (died 1849).

1770 Benjamin Wright, engineer, was born in Wethersfield, Conn.; chief engineer, Erie Canal construction; called the father of American engineering (died 1842).

1775 Sir William Howe succeeded Gen. Thomas Gage as commander-in-chief of the British Army in America.

1777 Hezekiah Niles, newspaper editor, was born in Chester County, Pa.; editor, *Baltimore Post* (1805-11), *Niles Weekly Register* (1811-36), a very influential paper of the time (died 1839).

1780 Continental Congress adopted a policy on western lands ceded to the central government by any state.

1790 American troops led by Gen. Josiah Harmar were defeated by a force of Ohio Indians near Ft. Wayne, touching off a five-year war in the Northwest Territory.

1795 Samuel Fraunces, restaurateur, died at about 73; kept the famous Fraunces Tavern (1770-89) in New York City, where Washington said farewell to his officers; household steward to Washington (1789-94).

1828 Samuel J. Randall, legislator, was born in Philadelphia; represented Pennsylvania in the House (1863-90) and served as Speaker (1876-81); codified House rules and strengthened the Speaker's power (died 1890).

1831 Henry Mason, piano manufacturer, was born in Brookline, Mass., son of Lowell Mason (1/8/1792); with Emmons Hamlin founded Mason & Hamlin Organ Co. (1854), later included piano (died 1890).

1845 U.S. Naval Academy at Annapolis was formally opened as the Naval School; became known as the Academy in 1850; founded by Navy Secretary George Bancroft.

1861 Maurice B. Prendergast, painter, was born in Roxbury, Mass.; known for Boston street scenes, life in Venice; a leader of art radicals (died 1924).

1862 Confederate Gen. J.E.B. Stuart led his troops to capture of Chambersburg, Pa., destroyed stocks and took usable stores; returned to Virginia.

1863 Alanson B. Houghton, industrialist and diplomat, was born in Cambridge; president, Corning Glass Works (1910-18), board chairman (1918-41); represented New York in the House (1919-22); ambassador to Germany (1922-25), to Great Britain (1925-29) (died 1941).

1892 Earle E. Dickson, adhesive bandage inventor, was born in Grandview, Tenn. (died 1961).

1897 Elijah Muhammad, Black Muslim leader, was born near Sandersonville, Ga. as Elijah Poole; headed Black Muslims (1934-75) (died 1975).

1900 Helen Hayes, actress, was born in Washington; star of stage and screen (*Victoria Regina, Harriet,* on stage; *Airport, Sin of Madelon Claudet, Arrowsmith,* on screen).

1903 Vernon Duke, composer, was born in Pskov, Russia; composed several musicals (*Cabin in the Sky*), ballets for Serge Diaghilev (died 1969).

1908 Johnny Green, composer, was born in New York City; wrote many popular songs, best remembered for "Body and Soul."

1911 California adopted woman suffrage.

1920 Thelonius S. Monk, jazz composer and pianist, was born in Rocky Mount, N.C.; a founder of "bop."

1924 James D. Clavell, author, was born in England; wrote popular novels (*Taipan, Shogun*).

1934 An antiwar treaty of non-aggression and conciliation was signed by Argentina, Chile, Brazil, Mexico, Paraguay, Uruguay, and the United States in Rio de Janeiro.

1951 Congress passed the Mutual Security Act, which continued military and economic aid programs, marking new emphasis on military rather than economic aid.

1956 Martina Navratilova, tennis player, was born in Prague; considered world's greatest woman player of 1980s.

1960 *Courier 1-B*, first successful active communications satellite, was launched.

1973 Vice President Spiro T. Agnew resigned; pleaded *nolo contendere* (no contest) to charges of tax evasion, given three years probation, $10,000 fine.

OCTOBER 11

1614 The United Netherland Company was formed by Amsterdam merchants to settle "New Netherland" between 40° and 45° N; charter expired Jan 1, 1618.

1759 Mason L. Weems, Anglican priest, author, and publisher, was born in Anne Arundel County, Md.; known as "Parson Weems," who wrote the life of George Washington, including the apocryphal account of the cherry tree (died 1825).

1776 The battle of Valcour Island began when the American 83-gun fleet took up a position between Valcour Island and the western shore of Lake Champlain to halt the British 87-gun fleet; the British defeated the American force in a two-day battle but had to withdraw (Nov 3) to Canada because of the delay and the lateness of the season.

1779 Gen. (Count) Casimir Pulaski died of the wounds he received two days earlier in the siege of Savannah; a distinguished Polish officer serving with the Americans.

1835 Theodore Thomas, orchestra conductor, was born in Esens, Germany; conductor in New York and Chicago when there were few orchestras; conductor, Chicago Symphony (1891-1905) (died 1905).

1841 Louis Kempff, admiral, was born in Belleville, Ill.; in charge of American naval forces in Chinese waters during the Boxer Rebellion (died 1920).

1844 Henry J. Heinz, food company founder, was born in Pittsburgh; a founder, F & J Heinz Co. (1876), which became H.J. Heinz Co., president (1905-19); coined slogan of "57 varieties" (died 1919).

1855 James Gayley, metallurgist and inventor, was born in Lock Haven, Pa.; official with Carnegie and U.S. Steel, invented a bronze cooling plate for walls of blast furnace (1891), dry air blast and other steelmaking improvements (died 1920).

1863 Harry A. Garfield, public official and educator, was born in Hiram, Ohio, son of President Garfield; president, Williams College (1908-34); U.S. fuel administrator (1917-19) (died 1942).

1872 Harlan F. Stone, jurist, was born in Chesterfield, N.H.; dean, Columbia Law School (1910-24); Attorney General (1924-25); associate justice, Supreme Court (1925-41), chief justice (1941-46) (died 1946).

1881 Stark Young, critic and author, was born in Como, Miss.; drama critic (*New Republic, Theatre Arts*); author (*So Red the Rose, Heaven Trees*) (died 1963).

1882 Robert N. Dett, composer and conductor, was born in Drummondville, Canada; directed Hampton Institute choir (1913-43); one of the first to use Negro folk tunes for classical development (died 1943).

1884 Eleanor Roosevelt Roosevelt, wife of President Franklin Roosevelt, was born in New York City; set many precedents as First Lady; became magazine columnist; chairman, UN Commission on Human Rights (1946-53) (died 1962).

1890 The Daughters of the American Revolution was organized in Washington.

1897 Willie (William F.) Hoppe, billiards player, was born in Cornwall-on-the-Hudson, N.Y.; probably greatest billiards player of all time; won 51 titles between 1906 and 1952 (died 1959).

1897 Nathan F. Twining, World War II general, was born in Monroe, Wis.; directed air war against Japan; chairman, Joint Chiefs of Staff (1957-60) (died 1982).

1897 Joseph Auslander, author, was born in Philadelphia; poetry (*The Unconquerables*); translator (*Fables of La Fontaine, Sonnets of Petrarch*) (died 1965).

1906 Charles H. Revson, businessman, was born in Boston; a founder, president (1932-62), board chairman (1962-75), Revlon Inc., world's largest cosmetics and fragrance firm (died 1975).

1910 Joseph W. Alsop Jr., journalist, was born in Avon, Conn., brother of Stewart Alsop (5/17/1914); syndicated newspaper columnist (died 1989).

1918 Jerome Robbins, dancer and choreographer, was born in New York City; staged many ballets, films, plays (*West Side Story, Fiddler on the Roof*).

1928 The *Graf Zeppelin*, commanded by Dr. Hugo Eckener, began flight from Friedrichhafen, Germany to Baltimore, New York, and Lakehurst, N.J., with 20 passengers and a crew of 40; took approximately 111 hours for the 6300-mile trip.

1939 President Franklin Roosevelt named an advisory committee on uranium after learning about the possibility of an atomic bomb.

1942 The battle of Cape Esperance in the Solomon Islands began; Japanese lost an aircraft carrier and four destroyers.

1968 George White, stage producer and director, died in Hollywood at about 80; staged *George White's Scandals* from 1919 to 1939.

1984 Astronaut Kathryn D. Sullivan became the first American woman to walk in space.

1986 President Reagan and Mikhail Gorbachov, Soviet general secretary, began meetings in Reykjavik, Iceland; virtually reached agreement on missiles limitation but failed because of disagreement over SDI (Star Wars).

1988 The world's largest private bank, nine of its officers and 75 others were indicted in Washington on charges of laundering more than $32 million in cocaine proceeds for the Colombia Medellin cartel; Bank of Credit & Commerce International of Luxembourg was indicted for helping launder about $14 million through money transfers in branches in the United States, Europe, Central and South America.

OCTOBER 12

1492 Land was sighted from the *Pinta*, one of three vessels in Christopher Columbus' fleet seeking China; the land sighted was probably Watling's Island in the Bahamas, later renamed San Salvador.

1710 Jonathan Trumbull, colonial official, was born in Lebanon, Conn.; held various Connecticut state posts, including governor (1769-84); one of the first to foresee possible independence from Great Britain; Washington is said to have referred to him as Brother Jonathan, which became the phrase to describe the typical American (died 1785).

1769 Horace H. Hayden, dentist, was born in Windsor, Conn.; co-founder of first dental school in the world (Baltimore 1840) (died 1844).

1775 Lyman Beecher, Presbyterian clergyman, was born in New Haven; a fiery preacher, he served pastorates in Boston (1826-32), Cincinnati (1832-42); president, Lane Theological Seminary, Cincinnati (1832-52); accused of heresy by conservative foes, acquitted by the synod (died 1863).

1776 Gen. William Howe moved his main British force from New York City to Westchester, sought unsuccessfully to cut off American retreat to New Jersey.

1803 Alexander T. Stewart, merchant, was born in Lisburn, Ireland; founded (1823) what became New York's largest dry goods store, later acquired by John Wanamaker (died 1876).

1813 Lyman Trumbull, legislator, was born in Colchester, Conn.; served Illinois in the Senate (1855-73); introduced the resolution which became the 13th Amendment abolishing slavery (died 1896).

1815 William J. Hardee, Confederate general, was born in Camden County, Ga.; served at Shiloh, Missionary Ridge; wrote popular tactics manual (*Hardee's Tactics*) (died 1873).

1837 Treasury notes totaling $10 million were authorized to relieve economic distress brought on by the panic of 1837.

1840 Helena Modjeska, actress, was born in Cracow, Poland; on American stage (from 1877), specialized in serious dramatic and Shakespearean roles (died 1909).

1841 Joseph O'Dwyer, physician, was born in Cleveland; pioneer in successful use of intubation (to prevent asphyxiation) and serum in diphtheria (died 1898).

1846 Louis E. Levy, photoengraver, was born in Stenowitz, Austria (now Czechoslovakia); made photoengraving possible by inventing a photochemical etching process and co-inventing an etched glass screen for making half tones (died 1919).

1858 Isaac N. Lewis, inventor and Army officer, was born in New Salem, Pa.; invented an artillery position finder, a machine gun; originated modern artillery corps organization, adopted by Army (1902) (died 1931).

1860 Elmer A. Sperry, inventor and manufacturer, was born in Cortland, N.Y.; inventor of more than 400 items, best known for the gyrocompass, various gyrocontrols, high intensity arc searchlight; founder, Sperry Electric Co. (1880), Sperry Gyroscope Co. (1910), president (1910-29) (died 1930).

1860 William L. Sibert, Army engineer, was born in Gadsden, Ala.; engineer in Panama Canal construction; organized, directed, Army Chemical Warfare Service (1918-20) (died 1935).

1864 Supreme Court Chief Justice Roger B. Taney died in Washington at 87.

1874 Abraham A. Brill, psychiatrist, was born in Kanczuga, Austria (now Poland); known as the father of American psychoanalysis, translated works of Jung and Freud (died 1948).

1875 Rutherford B. Hayes elected governor of Ohio.

1876 A new constitution for North Carolina was ratified by popular vote.

1889 Perle Mesta, diplomat and hostess, was born in Sturgis, Mich.; foremost unofficial hostess in Washington in 1940s; envoy to Luxembourg (1949-53), serving as model for Irving Berlin's musical, *Call Me Madam* (died 1975).

1905 Rick (Richard B.) Ferrell, baseball player (Browns, Senators, Red Sox), was born in Durham, N.C.; named to Baseball Hall of Fame.

1906 Joe (Joseph E.) Cronin, baseball player and manager, was born in San Francisco; player/manager, Senators and Red Sox; president, American League (1959-73); named to Baseball Hall of Fame (died 1984).

1932 Dick Gregory, entertainer and civil rights activist, was born in St. Louis; leader in various civil rights activities.

1935 Luciano Pavarotti, operatic tenor, was born in Modena, Italy.

1954 The four-day hurricane, Hazel, killed 99 persons in the United States, 594 in Haiti, and 85 in Canada.

1973 Rep. Gerald R. Ford of Michigan became the first appointed vice president under the 25th Amendment governing succession; he succeeded Spiro T. Agnew who resigned; Ford was sworn in Dec 6.

1988 Developer Donald Trump agreed to buy the Eastern Airlines Northeast shuttle for about $350 million; renamed Trump Shuttle.

OCTOBER 13

1754 Mary L.H. McCauley, Revolutionary heroine, was born near Trenton, N.J.; better known as Molly Pitcher, she brought water to artillerymen at the battle of Monmouth; when her husband was overcome by heat, she took over his gun (died 1832).

1775 The U.S. Navy was founded when Congress created the Continental Navy of the American Revolution by authorizing the fitting out of two ships of ten guns each; increased to four ships Oct 30.

1792 The cornerstone of the original White House was laid; President John Adams became the first occupant in 1800.

1812 An American force making a premature attack on Queenston Heights in Canada was defeated with a loss of 1000 men; British Gen. Isaac Brock was killed.

1826 LaFayette C. Baker, detective, was born in Stafford, N.Y.; chief, U.S. Secret Service (1862-68), led in capture of John Wilkes Booth after the Lincoln assassination (died 1868).

1843 B'nai Brith, Jewish fraternal society, was founded.

1857 Minnesotans ratified their state constitution; slavery was prohibited.

1862 John R. Commons, economist, was born in Hollandsburg, Ohio; with U. of Wisconsin (1904-32); helped developed unemployment insurance system (died 1945).

1864 Union troops surrendered Dalton, Ga. to Confederates led by Gen. John B. Hood.

1876 Rube (George E.) Waddell, baseball player, was born in Bradford, Pa.; pitcher for Philadelphia Athletics for 13 years, won 193, lost 142; named to Baseball Hall of Fame (died 1914).

1886 Two-day storm along the Gulf of Mexico and floods in Texas took 247 lives.

1890 Conrad Richter, author, was born in Pine Grove, Pa.; writer of books on frontier life, westward expansion (*The Trees, The Town, The Fields*) (died 1968).

1892 Pennsylvania National Guardsmen were withdrawn from Homestead after 95 days; had guarded the Carnegie steel mill against strikers; violence was renewed Oct 20, strike ended Nov 20.

1908 Church of Nazarene was organized by merging a group of small religious bodies at a meeting in Pilot Point, Tex.

1909 Herbert L. Block, editorial cartoonist, was born in Chicago; better known as Herblock, with *Washington Post* (1946-), widely syndicated.

1910 Art Tatum, musician, was born in Toledo; nearly blind, became an internationally-famed jazz pianist (died 1956).

1917 Burr Tillstrom, puppeteer, was born in Chicago; gained fame with the *Kukla, Fran and Ollie* show on television (died 1985).

1918 Three days of forest fires in Minnesota and Wisconsin killed about 1000 persons, did $100 million in damage.

1931 Eddie (Edwin L.) Mathews, baseball player, manager (Braves), was born in Texarkana, Tex.; named to Baseball Hall of Fame.

1932 President Hoover laid the cornerstone for the new Supreme Court Building.

1938 Elzie C. Segar, cartoonist, died at 43; creator of *Popeye* (died 1929).

1942 Art Garfunkel, musician, was born in New York City; singer, composer ("Mrs. Robinson," "Scarborough Fair," "Bridge Over Troubled Waters"); teamed with Paul Simon in 1960s.

1970 The Senate voted 60-5 to reject the findings and recommendations of the Commission to Study Obscenity and Pornography; publicly rejected by President Nixon on Oct 24.

1978 President Carter signed the Civil Service Reform Act, the first major revision in the federal employment code since 1883.

1988 President Reagan signed a welfare reform bill which calls for the government to provide additional training and support while welfare recipients must find jobs.

1989 The Dow Jones industrial average fell 190.58 points to 2569.26, the second largest daily loss; market recovered much of loss in several days.

OCTOBER 14

1644 William Penn, founder of American Quakerism and Pennsylvania, was born in London; served as a trustee to manage the West Jersey colony in America, had an important role in framing its charter (1677); inherited from his father a large financial claim against Charles II for which he received a grant of what became Pennsylvania (1681); prepared frame of government, laid out Philadelphia, made treaties with the Indians (died 1718).

1696 Samuel Johnson, Anglican clergyman, was born in Guilford, Conn.; leader of Church of England in the colonies; first president, King's (later Columbia) College (1754-63) (died 1772).

1734 Francis Lightfoot Lee, colonial leader, was born in Westmoreland County, Va.; member, Virginia House of Burgesses (1758-76); member, Continental Congress (1775-79) and a signer of the Declaration of Independence (died 1797).

1765 The Town of Braintree, Mass. adopted instructions against the Stamp Act which were written by John Adams in his first venture into Massachusetts politics; widely copied throughout the state.

1773 Thomas Jefferson was appointed surveyor of Albemarle County by the College of William and Mary.

1774 The Continental Congress adopted a declaration of the rights of the colonies.

1814 Jean Baptiste Lamy, Catholic prelate, was born in Lempdes, France; missionary to the Southwest, bishop of Santa Fe (1853-75), archbishop (1875-85); commemorated in Willa Cather's *Death Comes for the Archbishop* (died 1888).

1842 The Croton Aqueduct, providing water for New York City, was opened.

1857 Joseph R. Lamar, jurist, was born in Elbert County, Ga.; associate justice, Supreme Court (1911-16) (died 1916).

1857 Elwood Haynes, inventor and pioneer auto manufacturer, was born in Portland, Ind.; with Apperson brothers, completed (July 4, 1894) a one-cylinder car (now in the Smithsonian); manufactured cars until 1920; discovered various alloys (tungsten chrome steel, chromium and nickel, cobalt and chromium; cobalt, chromium and molybdenum); patented stainless steel (1919) (died 1925).

1863 Union troops under Gen. George Meade repulsed a Confederate attack led by Gen. A.P. Hill at Bristoe Station, Va., ending another threat to Washington.

1866 Charles F. Hughes, naval officer, was born in Bath, Me.; served with British in North Sea (1917-18); commander-in-chief, operations chief, U.S. battle fleet (died 1934).

1873 Ray C. Ewry, athlete, was born in Lafayette, Ind.; won eight gold medals in Olympics (1900, 1904, 1908) (died 1937).

1876 Henry A. Ironside, evangelist, was born in Toronto; known as the archbishop of fundamentalism; pastor, Moody Memorial Church, Chicago (1930-48) (died 1951).

1890 Dwight D. Eisenhower, 34th president (1952-60), was born in Denison, Tex.; Allied commander in Europe, World War II; Army chief of staff (1954-58); president, Columbia U. (1948-50); commander, NATO forces (1950-52) (died 1969).

1892 Sumner Welles, public official, was born in New York City; Under Secretary of State, laid foundation for American good neighbor policy (died 1961).

1894 Maurice Pate, first executive director of UNICEF (1947-65), was born in Pender, Neb. (died 1965).

1894 E(dward) E. Cummings, poet, was born in Cambridge; his work featured unorthodox typography, highly experimental approaches (died 1962).

1896 Lillian Gish, screen actress, was born in Springfield, Ohio, sister of Dorothy Gish (3/11/1898); starred in early films (*Birth of a Nation, Orphans in the Storm*).

1906 Hannah Arendt, political scientist, was born in Hanover, Germany; author (*On Revolution, Eichmann in Israel*) (died 1975).

1910 John R. Wooden, basketball coach, was born in Martinsville, Ind.; coached UCLA (1948-78) to ten national championships.

1912 Former President Theodore Roosevelt was shot in the chest by a fanatic (John N. Scrank) in Milwaukee; bullet lodged near right lung fracturing a rib; Roosevelt went on to speaking engagement; assailant adjudged insane.

1916 First Professional Golfers Association (PGA) tournament was held in Mt. Vernon, N.Y.; won by Jim Barnes.

1916 C(harles) Everett Koop, Surgeon General (1982-89), was born in New York City.

1941 The Lanham Act was signed, authorizing $150 million for defense housing.

1943 The Eighth Air Force raided Schweinfurt, Germany ball-bearing plants.

1947 Air Forces Maj. Charles E. Yeager broke the sound barrier in a Bell X-1, a rocket plane, at Muroc, Cal.

1949 Eleven American Communist Party leaders were convicted after a nine-month trial for conspiracy to overthrow the government; ten were sentenced to five years, one to three years; Supreme Court upheld the convictions June 4, 1951.

1953 Clarence Saunders, merchant, died at 72; founder (1916) of Piggly Wiggly grocery chain, prototype of modern supermarkets.

1973 President Nixon was ordered by the Court of Appeals to turn over tapes to U.S. District Court Judge John J. Sirica in the Watergate situation; President Nixon unsuccessfully offered a summary of the tapes.

1983 A new translation of Bible readings to eliminate references to God as solely male was announced by the National Council of Churches.

1987 The Dow Jones industrial average took a record-breaking drop of 85.46 points for a loss of 3.81% of the market's value.

1988 Court documents discussed at a congressional hearing revealed that the government knew for decades that a nuclear weapons plants near Fernald, Ohio, near Cincinnati, was releasing thousands of tons of radioactive waste into the atmosphere endangering thousands of workers and area residents.

OCTOBER 15

1770 Baron de Botetourt (Norbonne B.), colonial governor of Virginia (1768-70), died at 52.

1818 Irvin McDowell, Union general, was born in Columbus, Ohio; commander, Department of Northeastern Virginia, defeated in first battle of Bull Run; corps commander at second Bull Run (died 1885).

1829 Asaph Hall, astronomer, was born in Goshen, Conn.; with Naval Observatory (1862-91); discovered (1877) the two satellites of Mars (died 1907).

1830 Helen Hunt Jackson, author, was born in Amherst, Mass.; wrote poetry, best remembered for novel, *Ramona* (died 1885).

1858 William S. Sims, World War I admiral, was born in Port Hope, Canada; headed World War I naval operations; considered most influential officer in naval history; promoted convoy system (died 1936).

1872 Edith B. Galt Wilson, second wife of President Wilson, was born in Wytheville, Va. (died 1961).

1873 Henry F. Ward, Methodist clergyman, was born in London; with Union Theological Seminary (from 1918); chairman, American Civil Liberties Union (1920-40); chairman, American League for Peace & Democracy (1930-40) (died 1966).

1878 Edison Electric Light Co., first electric company, was incorporated in New York City; began supplying power in 1882.

1881 Lena M. Phillips, organizer, was born in Nicholasville, Ky.; founder (1919), National Federation of Business & Professional Women's Clubs; executive secretary (1919-23), president (1926-29); founder of International Federation of Business & Professional Women (1930) (died 1955).

1881 P(elham) G. Wodehouse, author, was born in Guildford, England; wrote more than 90 novels, mostly farces about English gentry; creator of *Jeeves* (died 1975).

1883 Robert L. Ghormley, World War II naval officer, was born in Portland, Ore.; with naval planning and operations (1939-42); commander, Allied naval forces in South Pacific (1942) (died 1958).

1886 Jonas W. Ingram, World War II admiral, was born in Jeffersonville, Ind.; commander, South Atlantic Force (1942-44), Atlantic Fleet (1944-45) (died 1952).

1899 William C. Menninger, psychiatrist, was born in Topeka, Kan.; with brother, Karl Menninger (7/22/1893) and father, founded Menninger Clinic, neuropsychiatric center in Topeka (died 1966).

1900 Mervyn Leroy, film director, was born in San Francisco; best known for *The Wizard of Oz* (died 1987).

1906 Alicia Patterson, founder, editor/publisher, *Newsday* (1940-63), was born in Chicago (died 1963).

1908 John K. Galbraith, economist, was born in Iona Station, Canada; editor, *Fortune* (1943-48); ambassador to India (1961-63); chairman, Americans for Democratic Action (1967-69); author (*The Great Crash, The Affluent Society*).

1914 Clayton Anti-trust Act was signed, replacing the Sherman Act and strengthening federal antimonopoly laws.

1917 Arthur M. Schlesinger Jr., historian, was born in Columbus, Ohio, son of Arthur M. Schlesinger (2/27/1888); speechwriter for President Kennedy; cofounder, Americans for Democratic Action (1947); author (*The Age of Jackson, Robert Kennedy and His Times*).

1917 The American destroyer *Cassin* was torpedoed off the south Irish coast.

1920 Mario Puzo, author, was born in New York City; best known for *The Godfather*.

1924 Lee A. Iacocca, auto manufacturer, was born in Allentown, Pa.; with Ford Motor Co. (1960-78), president (1970-78); chief executive officer, Chrysler Motors (1979-).

1945 Jim Palmer, baseball pitcher who won nearly 300 games (Orioles), was born in New York City.

1948 Gerald R. Ford and Elizabeth B. Warren were married in Grand Rapids, Mich.

1966 Department of Transportation was created by combining eight elements from other departments; began operations Apr 1, 1967, with Alan S. Boyd as secretary.

1966 Guadalupe Mountains (Tex.) National Park was established.

OCTOBER 16

1649 The Maine government passed an act granting all Christians the right to form churches provided "they be orthodox in judgment and not scandalous in life."

1701 Yale U. was founded in Killingworth, Conn. as the Collegiate School by Congregationalists dissatisfied with the growing liberalism at Harvard.

1754 Morgan Lewis, Army officer and jurist, was born in New York City, son of Francis Lewis (3/21/1713); served in Revolution at Ticonderoga and Saratoga, and in War of 1812; served New York as chief justice (1801-04) and governor (1804-07) (died 1844).

1758 Noah Webster, lexicographer, was born in West Hartford, Conn.; writer of spellers (*American Spelling Book*), which helped standardize American spelling, grammar; worked 20 years on the *American Dictionary of the English Language*; a founder, Amherst College (died 1843).

1760 Jonathan Dayton, legislator, was born in what is now Elizabeth, N.J.; member, Continental Congress (1787-89), represented New Jersey in the House (1791-99), serving as Speaker (1795-99), and in the Senate (1799-1805); a founder of Dayton, Ohio (died 1824).

1775 Falmouth (now Portland), Me. was burned by the British, reacting to American privateer raids on British shipping.

1777 British troops under Gen. Henry Clinton burned Esopus (now Kingston), N.Y. but felt too insecure to push farther north to meet Burgoyne's forces near Saratoga; returned to New York City for reinforcements.

1835 William R. Shafter, Civil and Spanish-American wars general, was born in Kalamazoo County, Mich.; commanded expeditionary force to Cuba (1898) (died 1906).

1851 Frederick H. Gillett, legislator, was born in Westfield, Mass.; represented Massachusetts in the House (1893-1925), serving as Speaker (1919-25), and in the Senate (1925-31) (died 1935).

1855 Abraham Lincoln, speaking in Peoria, made his first public denunciation of slavery.

1859 John Brown and 17 men (including three of his sons) raided the Harpers Ferry (W.Va.) federal arsenal, further arousing national slavery passions; arsenal retaken by federal troops under (then) Col. Robert E. Lee two days later; Brown was tried, executed Dec 2.

1861 Charles A. Platt, artist, was born in New York City; painter of New England scenes; helped design Freer Art Gallery, U. of Illinois buildings (died 1933).

1875 U. of Provo was founded by Brigham Young in Utah; later became Brigham Young U.

1880 Frank Aydelotte, educator, was born in Sullivan, Ind.; introduced Oxford Plan of teaching while president of Swarthmore (1921-40); director, Institute of Advanced Study, Princeton (1940-47) (died 1956).

1885 Will(iam) Harridge, American League president (1931-58), was born in Chicago; named to Baseball Hall of Fame (died 1971).

1888 Eugene O'Neill, playwright, was born in New York City; wrote many hit plays (*Beyond the Horizon, Emperor Jones, Anna Christie, Desire Under the Elms, Strange Interlude, Mourning Becomes Electra, The Iceman Cometh*); awarded 1936 Nobel Literature Prize (died 1953).

1891 A mob in Valparaiso, Chile attacked American sailors from the cruiser, USS *Baltimore*; two were killed, several wounded.

1893 Carl L. Carmer, author, was born in Cortland, N.Y.; wrote several popular novels (*Stars Fell on Alabama, Listen for a Lonesome Drum, Genesee Fever*) (died 1976).

1898 William O. Douglas, associate justice, Supreme Court (1939-76), was born in Maine, Minn.; chairman, Securities & Exchange Commission (1936-39); outdoorsman, author (*Of Men and Mountains, A Living Bill of Rights*) (died 1980).

1899 Dismal Swamp Canal opened; original survey made by George Washington.

1900 Goose (Leon A.) Goslin, baseball player (Washington, Tigers), was born in Salem, N.J.; named to Baseball Hall of Fame (died 1971).

1916 The first birth control clinic opened at 46 Amboy St., Brooklyn by Margaret Sanger and others.

1940 More than 16 million men 21 to 36 registered for military training and service.

1946 Price controls on meat were lifted.

1973 The first black mayor of a major southern city, Maynard Jackson, was elected in Atlanta.

1987 Stocks plummeted 108.36 points on the Dow Jones industrial average when a record-breaking 338.4 million shares were traded.

1987 First Lady Nancy Reagan underwent a successful modified radical mastectomy.

1987 Eighteen-month-old Jessica McClure was successfully removed from an abandoned well shaft in Midland, Tex. after 57-1/2 hours of mass effort to get her out of shaft into which she tumbled while playing.

1988 The Pakistani government said sabotage was the cause of the crash Aug 17 near Islamabad which took the life of Pakistan President Zia, American Ambassador Arnold Raphel and ten top Pakistani generals.

OCTOBER 17

1691 New royal charter issued to Massachusetts, including Maine and Plymouth in the colony; called for a crown-appointed governor, a council elected by the General Court, subject to governor's veto, the substitution of a property requirement for voting instead of religion, royal review of legislation, appeals to the King.

1760 Anne Parrish, philanthropist, was born in Philadelphia; founder of industry house to employ needy women (1795), the first American charitable organization for women (died 1800).

1777 Gen. John Burgoyne and 5700 British troops surrendered at Saratoga after being surrounded by American forces and left without British reinforcements.

1780 Richard M. Johnson, vice president (1837-41), was born near Louisville; represented Kentucky in the House (1807-19, 1829-37) and Senate (1819-29); elected vice president by Senate when no candidate received majority of electoral votes (died 1850).

1781 Lord Charles Cornwallis, commanding an encircled British force at Yorktown, began negotiations for surrender.

1803 John Quincy Adams took his seat in the Senate, serving there until 1808.

1829 Delaware River-Chesapeake Bay Canal was opened.

1851 Thomas Fortune Ryan, financier, was born in Nelson County, Va.; an organizer, American Tobacco Co.; also involved in New York transportation, banks, and railroads (died 1928).

1859 Childe Hassam, painter, was born in Boston; leading American exponent of impressionism; known for scenes of New York City life (died 1935).

1859 Buck (William) Ewing, baseball player (Giants) and manager (Reds), was born in Hoaglands, Ohio; named to Baseball Hall of Fame (died 1906).

1864 Robert Lansing, public official, was born in Watertown, N.Y.; American representative in international negotiations; Secretary of State (1915-20), resigned at request of President Wilson, who accused him of holding unauthorized cabinet meetings during his (Wilson's) illness (died 1928).

1880 Charles H. Kraft, food manufacturer, was born in Ft. Erie, Canada; co-founder of cheese (now foods) company (1909); a pioneer in developing blended and pasteurized cheese (died 1952).

1886 Ernest W. Goodpasture, virologist and pathologist, was born in Montgomery County, Tenn.; made notable contributions to understanding infectious diseases (died 1960).

1895 Doris Humphrey, dancer and choreographer, was born in Oak Park, Ill.; a pioneer of American modern dance (died 1958).

1902 Nathanael West, author, was born in New York City; writer of surrealistic satires, remembered for *Miss Lonelyhearts* and *The Day of the Locust* (died 1940).

1909 Cozy (William R.) Cole, musician, was born in East Orange, N.J.; one of the greatest jazz percussionists (died 1981).

1915 Arthur Miller, playwright, was born in New York City; wrote many hit plays (*Death of a Salesman, The Crucible, A View from the Bridge*).

1917 The transport *Antilles* was torpedoed and sunk with a loss of 70 persons.

1918 Rita Hayworth, screen actress, was born in New York City; starred in several films (*Cover Girl, Pal Joey, My Gal Sal*) (died 1987).

1930 Jimmy Breslin, journalist and author, was born in New York City; columnist, author (*The Gang Who Couldn't Shoot Straight*).

1931 Al Capone was found guilty in Chicago Federal Court of income tax evasion, sentenced to 11 years.

1933 Albert Einstein arrived to make his home in Princeton, N.J.

1933 Commodity Credit Corporation organized to stabilize and protect farm income and prices, to help maintain balanced and adequate agricultural supplies.

1941 U.S. destroyer *Kearny* was torpedoed off Iceland by German submarine; 11 died.

1977 Supreme Court ruled that Concorde, a supersonic plane, could land at New York City's Kennedy Airport, ending 19-month legal battle.

1979 President Carter approved legislation creating the Department of Education; the Department of Health, Education and Welfare was renamed the Department of Health and Human Services.

1986 Congress approved a measure which virtually eliminated mandatory retirement at age 70; President Reagan later signed the bill.

1988 The United States and the Philippines concluded an agreement to guarantee American military use of strategic air and naval bases in the islands through 1991 in exchange for $962 million in American aid.

1989 An earthquake measuring 6.9 on the Richter scale hit the San Francisco Bay area at 5:04 p.m. Pacific time; at least 60 persons were killed, most of them by the collapse of upper deck of two-tier Interstate 880 in Oakland; 1,000 were injured, sustained billion dollars in damages; scheduled World Series game in San Francisco's Candlestick Park was cancelled, none of the 60,000 in the park at the time were injured.

OCTOBER 18

1595 Edward Winslow, colonial leader, was born in Droitwich, England; arrived on the *Mayflower* and served Plymouth Colony in various posts, including governor (1633, 1636, 1644) (died 1655).

1631 Michael Wigglesworth, clergyman and poet, was born in Yorkshire, England; his poem, *The Day of Doom* (1662) was first American best seller (died 1705).

1748 The Treaty of Aix-la-Chappelle (Aachen, Germany) ended the War of the Succession (King George's War); Louisbourg on Cape Breton Island was returned to France.

1774 Delegates to the first Continental Congress adopted a Continental Association pledging that their colonies would (1) cease all importation from Great Britain, (2) totally discontinue the slave trade, (3) institute non-consumption of British products and various foreign luxury products, and (4) embargo all exports to British, Ireland, and the West Indies; this is sometimes considered the first true American union.

1776 Thaddeus Kosciusko, Polish officer, was commissioned a colonel of engineers in the Continental Army; distinguished himself at Ticonderoga and Saratoga.

1787 Robert L. Stevens, inventor and shipbuilder, was born in Hoboken, N.J., brother of Edwin A. Stevens (7/28/1795); built the *Maria* (1844), the fastest sailing ship for 20 years; invented the T-rail for railroads, still in use (died 1856).

1812 Francis H. Smith, educator, was born in Norfolk, Va.; Confederate Army officer; first president, Virginia Military Institute (1839-89) (died 1890).

1818 Edward O.C. Ord, Union general, was born in Cumberland, Md.; saw action at Corinth and Vicksburg; held various postwar commands (died 1883).

1824 Allen B. Wilson, inventor and manufacturer, was born in Willet, N.Y.; patented a sewing machine (1850), Nathaniel Wheeler manufactured it (died 1888).

1831 Thomas Hunter, educator, was born in Ardglass, Ireland; organized the first evening high school, New York City (1866); organized, headed, Normal College, New York City (1870-1906); named for him (1914) (died 1915).

1839 Thomas B. Reed, legislator, was born in Portland, Me.; represented Maine in the House (1877-99), serving as Speaker (1889-90, 1895-99); responsible for rules which enhanced Speaker's power to speed legislation of majority (died 1902).

1844 Harvey W. Wiley, food chemist, was born in Kent, Ind.; established methods and philosophy of food analysis; called the father of the Food & Drug Administration; chief chemist, Agriculture Department (1883-1912) (died 1930).

1847 Henry O. Havemeyer, industrialist and art collector, was born in New York City; helped establish, headed, American Sugar Refining Co. (1891), which produced half of America's sugar; vast art collection given to Metropolitan Museum of Art (died 1907).

1867 Control of Alaska was transferred from Russia to the United States in ceremonies at Sitka.

1875 Harry E. Yarnell, Navy admiral, was born near Independence; Ia.; held various commands, including that of the Atlantic Fleet (1936-39) (died 1959).

1876 U. of Oregon was opened in Eugene.

1878 James Truslow Adams, historian, was born in Brooklyn; author (*The Founding of New England, Epic of America, The March of Democracy*) (died 1949).

1882 Charles M.A. Stine, chemist, was born in Norwich, Conn.; with duPont (from 1907), held numerous patents in propellant powder, high explosives, dyes, artificial leather, paint (died 1954).

1889 Fannie Hurst, author, was born in Hamilton, Ohio; novelist (*Imitation of Life, Humoresque, Anitra's Dance, Stardust, Lummox*) (died 1968).

1921 The Senate ratified separate treaties concluding peace with Germany, Austria, and Hungary.

1927 George C. Scott, screen actor, was born in Wise, Va.; starred in many films (*Patton, Dr. Strangelove, Hindenburg*).

1931 Rev. Herbert W. Chilstrom, first bishop of the Evangelical Lutheran Church, was born in Litchfield, Minn.; the church was formed by the merger of Lutheran denominations.

1935 An earthquake occurred near Helena, Mont., doing considerable damage.

1982 Bess Truman, widow of President Truman, died in Independence, Mo. at 98.

1988 Congress passed a bill changing the Veterans Administration into the 14th Cabinet department, effective in the spring of 1989; President Reagan signed the measure Oct 26.

1988 Most cigars sold in the United States and possibly some pipe and loose tobacco will carry cancer warning labels as result of an agreement reached by manufacturers to end a California law suit; action expected within five months.

1989 Space shuttle *Atlantis* lifted off from Cape Canaveral, Fla. and hours later released the nuclear-powered Galileo probe to Jupiter.

OCTOBER 19

1630 A general court, the first in New England, met in Boston.

1748 Martha W. Skelton Jefferson, wife of President Jefferson, was born in Charles City County, Va. (died 1782).

1765 A Stamp Act Congress, meeting in New York City, issued resolutions opposing the tax.

1774 The counterpart of the Boston Tea Party occurred in Annapolis harbor when a tea ship, *Peggy Stewart*, was burned by the colonists.

1779 Thomas C. Brownell, Episcopal prelate and educator, was born in Westport, Mass.; bishop of Connecticut (1819-65), presiding bishop (1852-65); first president, Trinity (then Washington) College (1823-31) (died 1865).

1781 A British force of 8000 men under Lord Charles Cornwallis, surrounded by American and French troops at Yorktown, surrendered; the defeated force marched out from Yorktown at 2 p.m. with their colors cased and the bands playing an old British march, *The World Turned Upside Down*; the British fleet, enroute from New York, learning of the surrender, returned to New York.

1834 Francis C. Barlow, Union general, was born in Brooklyn; served as New York attorney general, launched prosecution of the Tweed Ring (died 1896).

1848 Samuel Guthrie, chemist, died at 66; invented percussion priming powder, with a punch lock to explode it, replacing flintlock muskets; discovered chloroform; devised process for fast conversion of potato starch into sugar.

1861 William J. Burns, detective, was born in Baltimore; formed own agency (1909), with branches throughout the country; director, Bureau of Investigation (now the FBI) (1921-24) (died 1931).

1863 John H. Finley, educator and editor, was born in Grand Ridge, Ill.; president, Knox College (1892-99), City College of New York (1903-13); New York state education commissioner (1921-37); editor-in-chief, *New York Times* (1937-38) (died 1940).

1864 The battle of Cedar Creek, 60 miles west of Washington, was won by Union troops, ending Confederate control of the Shenandoah Valley.

1871 Walter B. Cannon, physiologist, was born in Prairie du Chien, Wis.; professor, Harvard Medical School (1900-42); pioneer in x-ray observation, discovered a substance (sympathin) which causes stimulation of certain organs (died 1945).

1876 Mordecai ("Three-fingered") Brown, baseball player, was born in Nyesville, Ind.; pitcher, mostly with Chicago Cubs; won 239 games, lost 130 in 14 seasons; named to Baseball Hall of Fame (died 1948).

1885 Charles E. Merrill, broker and businessman, was born in Green Cove Springs, Fla.; a founder, partner, Merrill Lynch (1914); founder, Safeway Stores, *Family Circle* magazine (died 1926).

1895 Lewis Mumford, architectural critic, was born in Flushing, N.Y.; writer on urban planning, conservation; author (*The Culture of Cities, The Urban Prospect, The City in History*) (died 1990).

1901 Arleigh A. Burke, World War II admiral, was born near Boulder, Colo.; known as "31-knot Burke," chief of naval operations (1955-59).

1910 Subrahmanyan Chandrasekhar, astrophysicist, was born in Lahore, India; with U. of Chicago, shared 1983 Nobel Physics Prize for work on evolution of stars.

1922 Jack Anderson, syndicated newspaper columnist, was born in Long Beach, Cal.; took over column, *Washington Merry Go Round*, from Drew Pearson on his death (1969).

1943 Secretary of State Cordell Hull, British Foreign Secretary Anthony Eden, and Soviet Foreign Commissar Vyacheslaw Molotov met in Moscow to discuss political and military matters, including opening of a second front.

1973 Arab oil-producing nations imposed a ban on oil exports to the United States after the outbreak of the Arab-Israeli war; lifted Mar 18, 1974.

1982 John Z. DeLorean, prominent automaker, was arrested in Los Angeles, charged with drug possession; accused of scheme to sell enough drugs to shore up his ailing auto company; eventually acquitted.

1987 Selling panic pushed the Dow Jones industrial average down a record 508 points, draining more than $500 billion from the value of stocks, a 22.6% loss of value.

OCTOBER 20

1629 John Winthrop was elected the first governor of the Massachusetts Bay Colony as the settlers were getting ready to sail from England.

1674 James Logan, pioneer and jurist, was born in County Armagh, Ireland; came to America as secretary to William Penn (1699); held various provincial posts, including chief justice, Pennsylvania Supreme Court (1731-39) (died 1751).

1783 The Continental Congress voted to meet alternately in Annapolis and Trenton until a permanent site was selected.

1803 The Senate by a 24-7 vote ratified the treaty with France transferring Louisiana to the United States; President Jefferson authorized the takeover Oct 30.

1812 Austin Flint, physician, was born in Petersham, Mass.; founder, professor, Buffalo (N.Y.) Medical College (1847-61); founder, Bellevue Hospital Medical College (1861); a pioneer in heart research (died 1886).

1816 James W. Grimes, legislator, was born in Deering, N.H.; served Iowa as governor (1854-58) and represented it in the Senate (1859-69); stricken by apoplexy during the President Andrew Johnson impeachment trial, he was carried into the Senate to vote for acquittal when his vote was needed to prevent impeachment (died 1872).

1818 The Convention of 1818, sequel to the Treaty of Ghent, was signed in London, agreeing on American fishing rights and the American-Canadian boundary.

1825 Daniel E. Sickles, Union general, was born in New York City; saw action at Chancellorsville and Gettysburg, where he lost his right leg; military governor of the Carolinas (1865-67); minister to Spain (1869-75); represented New York in the House (1857-61, 1893-95) (died 1914).

1853 Benjamin Harrison was married to Caroline L. Scott in Oxford, Ohio.

1859 John Dewey, philosopher and educator, was born in Burlington, Vt.; pioneer in progressive education; author (*School in Society, How We Think, Democracy and Education*) (died 1952).

1874 Charles Edward Ives, composer, was born in Danbury, Conn.; known for polytonal harmonies, unusual rhythms (died 1954).

1884 Bela Lugosi, stage and screen actor, was born in Lugos, Hungary; remembered for horror films (*Dracula, Frankenstein*) (died 1956).

1889 Benjamin T. Babbitt, inventor, died at 80; held more than 100 patents, including soap processes, an ordnance projector, steam boilers, and pumps.

1890 Sherman Minton, legislator and jurist, was born in Georgetown, Ind.; represented Indiana in the Senate (1935-41); judge, U.S. Circuit Court of Appeals (1941-49); associate justice, Supreme Court (1949-56) (died 1965).

1891 Samuel F. Bemis, historian, was born in Worcester, Mass.; historian of American diplomacy; author of two-volume study of John Quincy Adams (died 1973).

1895 William W. Wurster, architect, was born in Stockton, Ca.; designed Ghiardelli Square and Golden Gate Project, both in San Francisco (died 1973).

1900 Wayne L. Morse, legislator, was born in Madison, Wis.; dean, U. of Oregon law school; represented Oregon in the Senate (1945-69) (died 1974).

1905 Manfred B. Lee, author, was born in Brooklyn; with cousin, Frederic Dannay (1/11/1905), formed team which was Ellery Queen, mystery writer (died 1971).

1913 Grandpa (Marshall L.) Jones, country music personality and singer, was born in Niagara, Ky.

1925 Art Buchwald, syndicated humorous columnist, was born in Mt. Vernon, N.Y.

1931 Mickey Mantle, baseball player, was born in Spavinaw, Okla.; hit 536 homeruns as outfielder with Yankees; named to Baseball Hall of Fame.

1944 An explosion of huge liquid gas tanks in Cleveland resulted in a fire which raged through a 50-block area, killing 135, injuring 215.

1947 House Committee on Un-American Activities began hearings on alleged Communism in Hollywood; resulted in ten indictments for contempt of Congress.

1964 Former President Hoover died in New York City at 90.

1973 Watergate Special Prosecutor Archibald Cox was fired by President Nixon when Cox threatened to seek judicial ruling that the president was violating a court order to turn over tapes; Attorney General Elliot Richardson resigned rather than fire Cox, Deputy Attorney General Donald Ruckelshaus was fired for refusing to carry out the firing order.

1976 A ferry and tanker collided in the Mississippi River near Luling, La.; 77 persons died.

1979 John F. Kennedy Library in Boston was dedicated.

OCTOBER 21

1692 Gov. Benjamin Fletcher of New York also was commissioned as governor of Pennsylvania.

1736 William Shippen, physician, was born in Philadelphia; chief of medical department, Continental Army (1777-81); founder, president, College of Physicians, Philadelphia (1805-08) (died 1808).

1776 Town of Concord, Mass. called for a convention to prepare state constitution.

1776 George Washington withdrew his troops from New York City to White Plains.

1776 George Izard, War of 1812 general, was born in Richmond, England; served on Canadian front on Niagara River; criticized for failing to push advantage over British; resigned (1815); governor, Arkansas Territory (1825-28) (died 1828).

1785 Henry M. Shreve, riverboat captain, was born in Burlington County, N.J.; established practicability of steam navigation on the Mississippi River; Shreveport, La. named for him (died 1851).

1797 The *Constitution* (Old Ironsides) was launched in Boston; active in war with Tripoli and the War of 1812.

1808 Samuel F. Smith, Baptist clergyman, was born in Boston; wrote hymns ("The Morning Light is Breaking"), music for "America" (died 1895).

1855 Howard H. Russell, Congregational clergyman, was born in Stillwater, Minn.; a founder, first general superintendent, Anti-Saloon League of America (1895-1903) (died 1946).

1861 Battle of Ball's Bluff (near Leesburg, Va.) resulted in a Confederate victory.

1868 An earthquake struck San Francisco causing $3 million in damage.

1876 Ding (Jay N.) Darling, editorial cartoonist, was born in Norwood, Mich.; with *Des Moines Register, New York Tribune* (died 1962).

1877 Oswald T. Avery, genetic researcher, was born in Halifax, Nova Scotia; paved the way for genetic engineering with studies of cell structures (died 1955).

1879 After many fruitless experiments, Thomas A. Edison succeeded in making an incandescent lamp wherein a loop of carbonized cotton thread glowed in a vacuum for more than 40 hours.

1891 Ted (Edwin M.) Shawn, dancer, was born in Kansas City, Mo.; with wife, Ruth St. Denis (1/20/1877), formed Denishawn Dancers; founder, Jacob's Pillow Dance Festival (died 1972).

1892 The Columbian Exposition in Chicago was dedicated; opened to the public May 1, 1893.

1897 The Yerkes Observatory at Williams Bay near Lake Geneva, Wis. was opened and dedicated; built for the U. of Chicago by Charles T. Yerkes (6/25/1837).

1917 Dizzy (John B.) Gillespie, jazz trumpeter and arranger, was born in Cheraw, N.C.; known as the creator and king of bop.

1944 Aachen was captured, the first sizable German city taken by the Allies.

1928 Whitey (Edward C.) Ford, baseball pitcher, was born in New York City; with New York Yankees (1950-62); named to Baseball Hall of Fame.

1976 Congress repealed the Homestead Act of 1962 for all states except Alaska because there was no longer any public land suitable for cultivation.

1986 The American writer Edward Austin Tracy was kidnapped in Beirut.

1987 Confidence returned to Wall St. as the Dow Jones industrial average rose 186.84 points.

1988 Deposed President Ferdinand Marcos of the Philippines and his wife were indicted by a federal grand jury in New York City on racketeering charges for buying Manhattan real estate with hundreds of millions of dollars allegedly embezzled from their government; also charged with defrauding American financial institutions of more than $165 million.

OCTOBER 22

1693 Thomas Fairfax, colonial leader, was born in Kent, England; owned 5.2 million acres between the Potomac and Rappahannock rivers, living there from 1745 until his death in 1781; George Washington surveyed his holdings in the Shenandoah Valley.

1738 James Manning, Baptist clergyman and educator, was born in Piscataway, N.J.; founder, first president, Brown U. (1765-91) (died 1791).

1746 A charter was granted for the College of New Jersey (later Princeton) to Jonathan Dickinson, leading Presbyterian of his time and the first president of the college, which opened in Newark in May 1747.

1775 Peyton Randolph, colonial leader, died at about 54; president of the first two Continental Congress sessions (1774, 1775).

1780 John Forsyth, legislator and public official, was born in Fredericksburg, Va.; represented Georgia in the House (1813-18, 1823-27) and Senate (1818-19, 1829-34) and served it as governor (1827-29); minister to Spain (1829-33), gained Spanish approval of cession of Florida; Secretary of State (1834-41) (died 1841).

1813 Charles Scott, Revolutionary general and public official, died at about 74; served with Washington in Braddock's campaign against French and Indians (1755); commanded Virginia troops in Revolution; served in fighting against Indians; governor of Kentucky (1808-12).

1821 Collis P. Huntington, railroad builder, was born in Harwinton, Conn.; joined Central Pacific with Union Pacific at Promontory Point, Utah; president, Southern Pacific (1890-1900) (died 1900).

1832 Leopold Damrosch, composer and conductor, was born in Posen, Poland; founded New York Oratorio Society (1873), New York Symphony Society (1878); conducted first American performance of Wagner's major operas at the Met (died 1885).

1836 Sam Houston, who received 80% of the vote, took the oath of office as president of the independent Republic of Texas.

1843 Stephen M. Babcock, agricultural chemist, was born in Bridgewater, N.Y.; scientific dairying pioneer, developed test for milk's butterfat content (1890) (died 1931).

1854 James A. Bland, minstrel musician, was born in Flushing, N.Y.; composed many popular songs ("Carry Me Back to Old Virginny," "Oh Dem Golden Slippers," "In the Evening by the Moonlight") (died 1911).

1875 The Sons of the American Revolution (SAR) was organized in San Francisco.

1879 David H. Knott, hotel owner, was born in Orange, N.J.; formed Knott Hotels Corp. (1927), had 35 hotels and restaurants (died 1954).

1881 Clinton J. Davisson, physicist, was born in Bloomington, Ill.; shared 1937 Nobel Physics Prize for discovery of diffraction of electrons by crystals (died 1958).

1882 Newell C. Wyeth, artist, was born in Needham, Mass.; painter and illustrator of children's books (died 1945).

1883 First national horse show was held in Madison Square Garden, New York City.

1883 The Metropolitan Opera House, costing about $1,732,000, opened with a performance of Gounod's *Faust*.

1884 George W. Hill, tobacco company head, was born in Philadelphia; with American Tobacco Co., vice president, president (1925-46); devised unique Lucky Strike cigarette promotions (died 1946).

1887 John Reed, journalist and radical, was born in Portland, Ore.; with Pancho Villa in Mexico; remembered for his participation in the Russian October revolution (1917) and his book, *Ten Days That Shook the World*; indicted for sedition but escaped to Russia where he died (1920); buried in the Kremlin.

1889 John L. Balderston, playwright, was born in Philadelphia; remembered for *Berkeley Square*; screen writer (died 1954).

1890 Joseph N. Welch, attorney, was born in Primghar, Ia.; gained fame as special Army counsel in McCarthy televised hearings (1954) (died 1960).

1896 Charles G. King, chemist, was born in Entiat, Wash.; known for isolation, synthesis of Vitamin C, work on enzymes and synthetic fats.

1900 Edward R. Stettinius Jr., businessman and public official, was born in Chicago; president, U.S. Steel (1939); Lend-Lease administrator (1941-43); Undersecretary of State (1943-44); Secretary of State (1944-45); chairman of American delegation to UN conference (1945); first American UN delegate (1945-46) (died 1949).

1903 George W. Beadle, geneticist and educator, was born in Wahoo, Neb.; shared 1958 Nobel Physiology/Medicine Prize for discovering how genes transmit hereditary characteristics; president, U. of Chicago (1960-68).

1905 Karl G. Jansky, engineer, was born in Norman, Okla.; research led to radio astronomy; worked with Bell Research on static (died 1950).

1907 The panic of 1907 was begun by the failure of the Knickerbocker Trust Co. copper market actions; Westinghouse Electric went into receivership, Pittsburgh Stock Exchange closed, several banks failed; loans by J.P. Morgan & Co. and the Treasury Department checked the panic; crisis ended in Dec.

1907 Jimmy (James E.) Foxx, baseball player, was born in Sudlersville, Md.; starred with Philadelphia Athletics, Boston Red Sox (1925-42); career batting average of .325 and 534 homeruns; named to Baseball Hall of Fame (died 1957).

1913 A mine explosion in Dawson, N.M. killed 263 persons.

1913 Robert Capa, photographer, was born in Budapest; with *Life*, Magnum Photo covering various battle fronts (died 1954).

1914 Constance Bennett, screen actress, was born in New York City, daughter of Richard Bennett (5/21/1872) and sister of Joan Bennett (2/27/1910); a leading lady of the 1940s (*Lady With a Past, Topper*) (died 1965).

1917 The Alien Property Custodian was established to handle American assets of an enemy or an ally of an enemy; functions moved (1934) to Justice Department.

1922 Joan Fontaine, screen actress, was born in Tokyo; sister of Olivia DeHavilland (7/1/1916); starred in several films (*Rebecca, Suspicion*).

1925 Robert Rauschenberg, artist, was born in Port Arthur, Tex.; his "combine paintings" founded the pop art and neo-Dada movements of the 1950s.

1938 Chester F. Carlson discovered xerography, producing a dry image without a chemical reaction, in Rochester, N.Y.; his Haloid Co. was founded in 1957, later became Xerox Corp.

1962 The Soviet missile buildup in Cuba was revealed by President Kennedy; a naval and air quarantine of Cuba was begun; crisis ended Oct 28, quarantine ended Nov 20.

1965 The Highway Beautification Act was signed, providing for reduced federal highway assistance to states that do not control billboards and junkyards along the highways.

1979 The Shah of Iran flew to New York City for cancer treatments.

OCTOBER 23

1750 Thomas Pinckney, colonial leader, was born in Charleston, S.C., brother of Charles C. Pinckney (2/25/1746) and cousin of Charles Pinckney (10/26/1757); fought at Charleston and Camden; served South Carolina as governor (1787-89) and represented it in the House (1797-1801); minister to Great Britain (1792-95), to Spain (1795-96); unsuccessful Federalist vice presidential candidate (1796) (died 1828).

1817 James W. Denver, Union general and public official, was born in St. Louis County, Mo.; represented California in the House (1855-57); governor of Kansas Territory (1857-58); Denver, Colo. named for him (died 1892).

1827 Orville J. Victor, author and publisher, was born in Sandusky, Ohio; originated "dime novel" (c 1860); organized, trained, directed stable of writers to grind out such books (died 1910).

1831 Basil L. Gildersleeve, educator, was born in Charleston, S.C.; promoted classical studies in America; founder, editor, *American Journal of Philology* (1880-1920) (died 1924).

1835 Adlai E. Stevenson, Vice President (1893-97), was born in Christian County, Ky.; represented Illinois in the House (1875-77, 1879-81), Assistant Postmaster General (1885-89) (died 1914).

1838 Francis H. Smith, artist and engineer, was born in Baltimore; also successful author (*Col. Carter of Cartersville; Caleb West, Master Diver*) (died 1915).

1850 First national women's rights convention was held in Worcester, Mass.

1871 Edgar J. Goodspeed, biblical scholar, was born in Quincy, Ill.; chairman, New Testament Department , U. of Chicago (1923-37); helped prepared *Revised Standard Version of the New Testament* (died 1962).

1873 William D. Coolidge, physical chemist, was born in Hudson, Mass.; with General Electric, invented and made applications of ductile tungsten, invented tube for production of x-rays (died 1975).

1875 Gilbert N. Lewis, chemist, was born in Weymouth, Mass.; first to isolate heavy hydrogen isotope; developed various theories (atomic, valence, photon) (died 1946).

1876 Paul P. Cret, architect, was born in Lyon, France; designed numerous buildings (Folger Library, Federal Reserve, both in Washington) (died 1945).

1895 Clinton P. Anderson, public official and legislator, was born in Centerville, S.D.; Agriculture Secretary (1945-48); represented New Mexico in the Senate (1949-73) (died 1975).

1899 Bernt Balchen, aviator, was born in Tveit, Norway; pilot for numerous polar flights, including first flight over the South Pole (1929) (died 1973).

1905 Felix Bloch, physicist, was born in Zurich; shared 1952 Nobel Physics Prize for work in measurement of magnetic fields in atomic nuclei (died 1938).

1906 Gertrude Ederle, swimmer, was born in New York City; first woman to swim the English Channel (Aug 6, 1926), did it in 14 hours and 31 minutes.

1917 American troops saw their first action on the Western Front in the Toul sector.

1925 Johnny Carson, entertainer, was born in Corning, Ia.; star of the *Tonight Show* (1962-).

1934 Jean Piccard and his wife, Jeannette, flew from Michigan to Ohio in a balloon which reached an altitude of more than 57,000 ft.

1944 The three-day Battle of Leyte Gulf resulted in a major defeat for the Japanese navy, which lost two battleships, four aircraft carriers, nine cruisers, and nine destroyers.

1946 The opening session of the UN General Assembly in Flushing Meadows, Long Island, was addressed by President Truman.

1966 President Lyndon Johnson attended the seven-nation Manila Conference, which ended Oct 25; he pledged to "continue our military and other efforts...as long as may be necessary...until aggression is ended" in South Vietnam.

1983 A bomb-filled truck smashed through barriers at the Marine compound at the Beirut Airport, killing 241 Americans.

OCTOBER 24

1776 The Presbytery of Hanover petitioned the Virginia Assembly for religious liberty and removal of taxes to support the Anglican Church.

1781 George Washington's report of victory at Yorktown was read to the Continental Congress, whose members went in procession to a nearby Dutch Lutheran Church to give thanks.

1788 Sarah J. Buell Hale, editor, was born in Newport, N.H.; editor, *Ladies Magazine* (1828-37), which became *Godey's Lady's Book*, which she edited (1837-77) (died 1879).

1808 John Sartain, engraver, was born in London; introduced pictoral illustration to American periodicals (died 1897).

1830 Belva A.B. Lockwood, feminist, was born in Royalton, N.Y.; fought for right of women to practice before the Supreme Court, became the first admitted to do so; presidential nominee, National Equal Rights Party (1884, 1888) (died 1917).

1855 James S. Sherman, Vice President (1909-12), was born in Utica, N.Y.; represented New York in the House (1887-91, 1893-1909) (died 1912).

1861 The first transcontinental telegraph line was completed; the first telegram was received by President Lincoln from Sacramento, Cal.

1871 A riot in Los Angeles against Chinese by a mob resulted in the hanging of 15 and shooting of six.

1887 George W. Borg, manufacturer, was born in West Burlington, Ia.; helped develop disc auto/truck clutch; a founder, auto parts firm (Borg Warner) (1928) (died 1960).

1889 Arde Bulova, watch manufacturer, was born in New York City; developed family watch business, standardized many watchmaking procedures (died 1958).

1899 Gilda Gray, dancer known as the "Queen of the Shimmy," was born in Cracow, Poland (died 1959).

1904 Moss Hart, playwright and director, was born in New York City; co-author (with George S. Kaufman) *Once in a Lifetime, You Can't Take it With You, The Man Who Came to Dinner*; (with Kurt Weill and Ira Gershwin) *Lady in the Dark*; (with Irving Berlin) *Face the Music*; librettist (*As Thousands Cheer, Jubilee*); director (*My Fair Lady, Camelot*) (died 1961).

1931 The George Washington Bridge over the Hudson River opened.

1933 The Wages and Hours Act went into effect, setting up a minimum wage and maximum weekly hours.

1937 Juan Marichal, baseball pitcher who won 243 games (Giants), was born in Laguna Verde, Dominican Republic; named to Baseball Hall of Fame.

1945 United Nations came into formal existence when the Soviet Union deposited its ratification, bringing the total to 29 nations.

1949 The cornerstone was laid for the United Nations headquarters in New York City.

1962 President Kennedy issued a proclamation demanding that Russia dismantle its military bases in Cuba and withdraw its armaments; Russia agreed to do so a few days later.

1985 President Reagan, addressing the United Nations General Assembly on its 40th anniversary, asked the Soviet Union to join the United States in seeking settlements of five regional disputes involving Soviet-supported regimes.

OCTOBER 25

1741 Russian explorers, led by Vitus Bering, discovered Kiska Island in the Aleutians.

1764 John Adams and Abigail Smith were married in Weymouth, Mass., with the father of the bride, Rev. William Smith, performing the ceremony.

1811 Carl F.W. Walther, Lutheran leader, was born in Langenchursdorff, Germany; co-founder, Concordia Theological Seminary, president (1854-87); president, Missouri Synod (1846-50, 1864-78) (died 1887).

1812 U.S. frigate *United States* captured the British frigate *Macedonian* off Madeira Islands.

1850 The Southern Rights Association was formed in South Carolina to resist the anti-slavery states.

1859 Chester A. Arthur and Ellen L. Herndon were married in New York City.

1866 Gilbert Patten, author, was born in Corinna, Me.; better known as Burt L. Standish, who wrote adventure stories for boys (*Frank Merriwell* series) (died 1945).

1873 John N. Willys, auto manufacturer, was born in Canandaigua, N.Y.; originally manufactured bicycles; bought Overland Co., which became Willys-Overland Auto Co., president (1907-25); ambassador to Poland (1930-32) (died 1935).

1887 The Supreme Court, in the Wabash Railroad case, ruled that states do not have the power to regulate interstate traffic.

1888 Richard E. Byrd, aviator and explorer, was born in Winchester, Va., brother of Harry F. Byrd (6/10/1886); with Floyd Bennett (see below) became the first to fly over the North Pole (1926); made 42-hour transatlantic flight, New York to France (1927); flew over the South Pole (1929); made several Antarctic expeditions (1928-30, 1933-35) (died 1957).

1890 Floyd Bennett, aviator, was born near Warrensburg, N.Y.; pilot for first flight over the North Pole (1926) (see Byrd above) (died 1928).

1891 Charles E. Coughlin, Catholic priest, was born in Hamilton, Canada; his weekly radio program promoted radical economies, opposed New Deal; publisher, *Social Justice*, which was banned from the mails; church imposed silence on him (1942) (died 1979).

1892 Caroline L. Harrison, wife of President Benjamin Harrison, died in the White House at 60.

1902 Woodrow Wilson was inaugurated as president of Princeton U.

1902 Henry Steele Commager, historian, was born in Pittsburgh; with New York U., Columbia; author (*The Blue and the Gray, Era of Reform*); co-author (*The Growth of the American Republic*).

1904 Arshile Gorky, artist, was born in Khorkum Vari, Turkey; one of the leading expressionists in the United States (died 1948).

1912 Minnie Pearl (Sarah O.C. Cannon), entertainer, was born in Centerville, Tenn.

1914 John Berryman, poet, was born in McAlester, Okla; a major American poet of his era (*Homage to Mistress Bradstreet*) (died 1972).

1924 Bobby (Robert W.) Brown, baseball player (Yankees), was born in Seattle; president, American League (1984-).

1926 U. of California at Los Angeles (UCLA) was dedicated.

1929 Albert B. Fall was found guilty of accepting a bribe in the Teapot Dome scandal while Interior Secretary; sentenced Nov 1 to one year, $100,000 fine.

1930 Hannah H. Gray, educator, was born in Heidelberg, Germany; first woman president of a major American university (U. of Chicago 1978-).

1941 Helen Reddy, singer and screen actress, was born in Melbourne, Australia.

1946 A forest fire destroyed most of Bar Harbor, Me., damaged Acadia National Park.

1948 Dan Gable, champion wrestler and coach (Iowa U.), was born in Waterloo, Ia.; won 1972 Olympic gold medal in the 149-1/2 lb. class; his Iowa wrestlers have won 11 Big Ten titles (1977-87) without losing a match; named to Wrestling Hall of Fame.

1983 American troops landed on the island of Grenada in the West Indies in an effort to halt a Cuban buildup and to protect American students on the island; the island was secured within a few days.

OCTOBER 26

1757 Charles Pinckney, colonial leader, was born in Charleston, S.C.; a most important individual contributor to the Constitutional Convention; served South Carolina as governor (1789-92, 1796-98, 1806-10), represented it in the Senate (1798-1801) and House (1818-20); minister to Spain (1801-06) (died 1824).

1774 Massachusetts Committee of Safety was created with John Hancock as chairman.

1825 The 363-mile long Erie Canal opened; the canal boat *Seneca Chief* left Buffalo with Gov. DeWitt Clinton aboard; arrived in New York Nov 4; canal cost $7 million and cut travel time by a third, shipping costs by 90%.

1831 John W. Noble, Union general and Interior Secretary (1889-93), was born in Lancaster, Ohio (died 1912).

1832 A convention adopted the Mississippi constitution; ratified by general election.

1854 Charles W. Post, cereal maker, was born in Springfield, Ill.; developed Postum, then went into various breakfast cereals (died 1914).

1861 Richard D. Sears, tennis champion, was born in Boston; won national amateur singles (1881-87) and doubles (1882-87); president, U.S. Lawn Tennis Assn. (1887-88); one of first seven to be named to Tennis Hall of Fame (died 1943).

1863 Ellsworth M. Statler, hotel chain founder, was born in Somerset County, Pa.; began chain (1905), which later was taken over by Hilton Hotels (died 1928).

1876 H(enry) B. Warner, actor and director, was born in London; starred in several films (*King of Kings, Lost Horizon, Sorrell and Son*) (died 1958).

1877 Max Mason, mathematical physicist, was born in Madison, Wis.; invented several submarine detection devices; president, U. of Chicago (1925-28); Rockefeller Foundation (1929-36) (died 1961).

1881 A big shootout at the OK Corral occurred as the Earp brothers and Doc Holliday had a showdown with the Clanton gang; shootout actually occurred in alley near corral.

1894 John S. Knight, founder/head of newspaper chain bearing his name, was born in Bluefield, W.Va. (died 1981).

1899 Judy (William J.) Johnson, outstanding third baseman in Negro leagues, was born in Snow Hill, Md.; named to Baseball Hall of Fame.

1910 John J. Krol, Catholic Archbishop of Philadelphia (1961-), was born in Cleveland; elevated to cardinal 1967.

1911 Mahalia Jackson, gospel singer, was born in New Orleans; singing linked religious and secular music (died 1972).

1932 Charles E. Ashburner, America's first city manager, died at 62; an independent consultant and contractor, he completed repairs to a Staunton, Va. dam at a fifth of the local contractor's estimate; city council created new position of city manager; in three years (1908-11), he defined and set standards for the position.

1942 The first battle of Solomon Islands; Japanese fleet suffered heavy losses, American aircraft carrier *Hornet* was sunk.

1949 Minimum wage legislation raised the wage from 40 cents an hour to 75 cents.

OCTOBER 27

1659 In keeping with the Massachusetts law making it a capital offense for a Quaker to return after banishment, two Quakers—William Robinson and

Marmaduke Stevenson—were hanged on the Boston Common.

1749 Jared Ingersoll, legislator, was born in New Haven; a member of Continental Congress (1780, 1781) and the Constitutional Convention (1787); Pennsylvania attorney general (1790-99, 1811-17); Federalist vice presidential candidate (1812) (died 1822).

1763 William Maclure, geologist, was born in Ayr, Scotland; considered the father of American geology (died 1840).

1787 The first of 77 essays signed by "Publius," supporting the proposed Constitution, appeared in New York newspapers; later (with additional essays) they were collected as *The Federalist Papers*; most (about 51) were written by Alexander Hamilton, 28 by James Madison, five by John Jay.

1793 Eliphalet Remington, firearms manufacturer, was born in Suffield, Conn.; began manufacturing in Ilion, N.Y., then Springfield, Mass.; expanded into manufacture of implements (c 1856) (died 1861).

1795 Thomas Pinckney of South Carolina, minister to Spain, negotiated the Treaty of San Lorenzo with Spain, establishing the boundaries of Florida and Louisiana, and gave Americans right of free navigation on the Mississippi River.

1795 Samuel R. Hall, Congregational clergyman, was born in Croydon, N.H.; set up teachers' training school (1823), the first American normal school, in Concord, Vt. (died 1877).

1800 Benjamin F. Wade, legislator, was born in Feeding Hills, Mass.; represented Ohio in the Senate (1851-69), serving as president pro tem; would have become president if President Andrew Johnson had been impeached (died 1878).

1810 President Madison issued a proclamation taking possession of West Florida, from the Mississippi to the Perdido River, as part of the Louisiana Purchase.

1811 Isaac M. Singer, sewing machine manufacturer, was born in Pittstown, N.Y.; improved and patented an existing sewing machine (1851); by 1860, was world's foremost sewing machine manufacturer (died 1875).

1811 Stevens T. Mason, first governor of Michigan, was born in Loudon County, Va., grandson of Thomson Mason (2/26/1785); served from 1835 to 1840 (died 1843).

1822 George B. Armstrong, postal expert, was born in County Armagh, Ireland; credited with developing the railway mail service (died 1871).

1827 Albert Fisk, engineer, was born in Lauterbach, Germany; invented special form of truss and built some of America's longer railroad bridges; standardized freight rates, virtually founding railroad economics as a science (died 1897).

1828 Jacob D. Cox, lawyer and public official, was born in Montreal of American parentage; served Ohio as governor (1866-68), Secretary of Interior (1869-70); dean, Cincinnati Law School (1881-97); president, U. of Cincinnati (1885-89) (died 1900).

1837 Whitelaw Reid, newspaper editor and diplomat, was born near Xenia, Ohio; editor, *New York Tribune* (1872-1905); minister of France (1889-92); ambassador to Great Britain (1905-12) (died 1912).

1838 John D. Long, legislator and public official, was born in Buckfield, Me.; served Massachusetts as governor (1880-82) and represented it in the House (1883-89); Secretary of Navy (1897-1902) (died 1915).

1841 An American brig, *Creole*, carrying a cargo of slaves, sailed from Hampton Roads for New Orleans; slaves mutinied, killing one white crew member and forcing the mate to take the ship to the Bahamas; the British freed all the slaves except the actual revolt participants.

1858 Theodore Roosevelt, 26th president (1901-09), was born in New York City; led the Rough Riders in Cuba during the Spanish-American War; member, U.S. Civil Service Commission (1889-95); Assistant Secretary of Navy (1897-98); elected Vice President (1900), succeeding to the presidency after President McKinley was assassinated; awarded 1906 Nobel Peace Prize (died 1919).

1864 The ironclad Confederate ram *Albemarle* was sunk in the Plymouth (N.C.) harbor by a Union raiding party led by Lt. William B. Cushing.

1870 Roscoe Pound, legal educator, was born in Lincoln, Neb.; dean, U. of Nebraska Law School (1903-07); dean, Harvard Law School (1916-36); also a botanist of note (died 1964).

1873 James J. Davis, legislator and public official, was born in Tredegar, Wales; director-general, Loyal Order of Moose (1906-21), building membership to more than 600,000; Secretary of Labor (1921-30); represented Pennsylvania in the Senate (1930-44) (died 1947).

1874 Owen D. Young, industrialist, was born in Van Hornesville, N.Y.; counsel, General Electric (1913-22), board chairman (1922-39, 1942-44); a leader in developing German reparations plan (died 1962).

1880 Theodore Roosevelt and Alice H. Lee were married in Brookline, Mass.

1882 Mary Josephine Rogers, religious leader, was born in Roxbury, Mass.; founder of the Maryknoll Sisters (died 1955).

1904 The first New York City subway opened, running from City Hall to 145th St. on the West Side.

1919 President Wilson vetoed the Volstead prohibition enforcement bill; veto was overriden the same day by the House and on Oct 28 by the Senate.

1922 Ralph Kiner, baseball player, was born in Santa Rita, N.M.; outfielder (1946-56), mostly with Pittsburgh; homerun leader seven successive seasons, hit .369; named to Baseball Hall of Fame.

1923 Roy Lichtenstein, artist, was born in New York City; pioneered in "comic strip" paintings and the "pop" painting style.

1972 The Consumer Product Safety Commission was created.

OCTOBER 28

1586 Francis West, colonial governor, was born in England; commander at Jamestown (1612), governor of Virginia (1627-29) (died 1634).

1636 Harvard College was founded by an act of the Massachusetts General Court, which granted £400 toward a school or college to be built at Newtown (Cambridge).

1766 Leading New York City citizens signed an agreement banning the purchase of English goods until the Stamp Act was repealed; they were followed (Oct 31) by 200 New York City merchants, 400 Philadelphia merchants in Nov, 250 Boston merchants Dec 6.

1767 In the wake of the Townshend Acts, imposing import duties, a Boston town meeting drew up a list of British goods not to be purchased after Dec 31; similar action followed in Providence, Newport, and New York City.

1776 British troops under Gen. William Howe attacked Americans led by Gen. George Washington at White Plains, N.Y.; the British captured key hill positions but the Americans slipped away while the British awaited reinforcements.

1786 Isaac Sears, colonial merchant, died at about 56; a New York merchant, he seized the arsenal and customhouse on hearing of Lexington and Concord; held city until the army arrived; moved to Boston, from where he sent out privateers to prey on British commerce.

1798 Levi Coffin, anti-slavery leader, was born in New Garden City, N.C.; known as the president of the underground railway (died 1877).

1801 Henry Inman, artist, was born in Utica, N.Y.; one of the most prominent, versatile of first-generation American-trained artists (died 1846).

1808 Horace Smith, revolver developer and manufacturer, was born in Cheshire, Mass.; with Daniel B. Wesson invented and manufactured Smith & Wesson revolvers (1857) (died 1893).

1818 Abigail Adams, wife of President John Adams, died in Quincy, Mass. at 73.

1836 Homer D. Martin, landscape artist, was born in Albany; one of the first Americans to use impressionism in his work (died 1897).

1847 J. Walter Thompson, advertising pioneer, was born in Pittsfield, Mass.; founder, head (1878-1916) of one of nation's leading agencies (died 1928).

1858 Henry Koplik, pediatrician, was born in New York City; paved the way for diagnosis of measles; established first American milk depot to provide milk for poor infants (died 1927).

1865 A convention in Tallahassee repealed Florida's secession ordinance; abolished slavery Nov 6.

1869 Joseph B. DeLee, obstetrician, was born in Cold Spring, N.Y.; founder, Chicago Lying-In Hospital (1895), Chicago Maternity Center (1932) (died 1942).

1875 Gilbert H. Grosvenor, geographer and editor, was born in Istanbul of American parents; editor, *National Geographic Magazine* (1899-1954); president, National Geographic Society (1920-66) (died 1966).

1886 Statue of Liberty, which arrived dismantled in 214 packing cases from France and then erected on Bedloe (now Liberty) Island, was dedicated by President Cleveland.

1893 Carter H. Harrison, five-term Chicago mayor, was assassinated by P.E. Prendergast, a disappointed office seeker.

1896 Howard H. Hanson, composer and educator, was born in Wahoo, Neb.; director, Eastman School of Music (1924-64) (died 1981).

1907 Edith Head, fashion designer for the movies, was born in Los Angeles (died 1981).

1914 Jonas E. Salk, physician, was born in New York City; developed polio vaccine (1954); director, Salk Institute of Biological Studies (1963-).

1916 The American steamship *Lanso* was sunk by a German submarine off Portugal.

1919 The Volstead Act, implementing the 18th Amendment (Prohibition), was passed over President Wilson's veto by the Senate; House had acted the previous day.

1925 The court martial of Col. Billy Mitchell of the Air Service began; an outspoken critic of Army policies, he was found guilty (Dec 17), sentenced to suspension from rank, command, and duty; resigned Feb 1, 1926.

1926 Bowie Kuhn, baseball commissioner (1969-83), was born in Takoma Park, Md.

1941 Office of Lend-Lease Administration was created with Edward R. Stettinius as director.

1946 Atomic Energy Commission was established with David E. Lilienthal as the first chairman; later became the Nuclear Regulatory Commission.

1949 Bruce Jenner, 1976 Olympic decathlon winner, was born in Mt. Kisco, N.Y.

1986 The formal 100th birthday observance of the Statue of Liberty was held.

OCTOBER 29

1652 The Massachusetts Bay Colony, in defiance of Parliament, declared itself an independent commonwealth.

1784 Robert Hoe, printing press manufacturer, was born in Leicestershire, England; founder, R. Hoe & Co. (1823), press manufacturers (died 1833).

1796 Charles Lynch, colonial judge, died at 60; name associated with "lynching," although as a judge in Bedford County, Va. he never sentenced anyone to death.

1819 A convention in Portland adopted the Maine constitution; ratified by the people in town meetings Dec 6.

1828 Thomas F. Bayard, legislator and public official, was born in Wilmington, Del., grandson of James A. Bayard (7/28/1767); represented Delaware in the Senate (1869-84); Secretary of State (1885-89); first ambassador to Great Britain (1893-97) (died 1898).

1831 Othniel C. Marsh, paleontologist, was born in Lockport, N.Y.; first American paleontology professor; his many discoveries of fossils of extinct horses and pterodactyl contributed to the evolutionary theory (died 1899).

1832 James Gordon Bennett published the first issue of the *New York Globe*, a two-cents morning newspaper.

1860 Gen. Winfield Scott advised President Buchanan that certain national forts in the south be garrisoned to avoid their seizure by "insurgents;" advice was turned down lest it further excite the south.

1865 Charles H. Ingersoll, watchmaker, was born in Delta, Mich.; with brother, Robert H. Ingersoll (12/26/1859), founded company which made and sold inexpensive watches (1892) (died 1948).

1870 Robert B. Owens, electrical engineer, was born in Anne Arundel County, Md.; credited with discovery of alpha rays; invented an electromagnetic system for guiding ships and planes (died 1940).

1884 Several hundred Protestant clergymen met with presidential candidate, James G. Blaine, in Fifth Avenue Hotel, New York City, to assure him of their support; Rev. Samuel D. Burchard of the Hudson St. Presbyterian Church said: "We are Republicans and don't propose to leave our party and identify ourselves with the party whose antecedents are rum, Romanism, and rebellion;" remark later attributed to Blaine and was said to have cost him the election.

1891 Fanny Brice, entertainer, was born in New York City; comedienne in Ziegfield Follies, singer (*My Man*); played Baby Snooks on radio (1936-51) (died 1951).

1901 Leon F. Czolgosz, convicted slayer of President McKinley, was electrocuted in Auburn (N.Y.) State Prison.

1919 International Labor Organization (ILO) held its first meeting in Washington; Albert Thomas was named director general.

1920 Benjamin Benacerraf, pathologist, was born in Caracas, Venezuela; chairman, Harvard Medical Pathology Department; shared 1980 Nobel Physiology/Medicine Prize for discoveries of how genetic makeup determines body's response to infection and cancer.

1921 William H. Mauldin, cartoonist, was born in Mountain Park, N.M.; created World War II characters, Willie & Joe, in *Stars & Stripes*; editorial cartoonist.

1925 Zoot (John H.) Sims, saxophonist and clarinetist, was born in Inglewood, Cal. (died 1985).

1929 Stock market crash began, bringing on worst American depression; stock losses in the ensuing two years were estimated at $50 billion.

1940 First draft numbers were selected in Washington following the registration of over 16 million men.

1947 Frances F. Cleveland, widow of President Cleveland, died in Baltimore at 83.

1966 National Organization of Women (NOW) formed.

1969 Supreme Court ruled unanimously that school districts must end segregation "at once" and operate integrated systems "now and hereafter."

1974 Former President Nixon underwent surgery to prevent blood clot in leg from entering his lungs.

OCTOBER 30

1683 A Charter of Liberties was enacted by delegates from New York City, Albany, Schenectady, Esopus (Kingston, N.Y.), Martha's Vineyard, Nantucket, and Pemaquid (eastern Maine) which called for a meeting at least once in three years and its approval would be required for imposing taxes; approved by the Duke of York but later (1687) disapproved.

1735 John Adams, second president (1797-1801), was born in Quincy, Mass.; defended the British soldiers accused of murder in the Boston Massacre; member, Continental Congress (1774-78) and a signer of the Declaration of Independence; commissioner to France (1778-79), minister to the Netherlands (1780-85), first minister to Great Britain (1785-88); helped negotiate the peace treaty ending the Revolution; became first elected vice president (1789) (died 1826).

1768 First American Methodist chapel (42 John St., New York City) dedicated.

1807 James S. Wadsworth, Union officer, was born in Geneseo, N.Y.; commanded divisions at Fredericksburg, Gettysburg; mortally wounded at the Battle of the Wilderness (1864); founder, Free Soil Party.

1829 John Rogers, sculptor, was born in Salem, Mass.; noted for folk sculpture, groups (*The Slave Auction*, Civil War scenes) (died 1904).

1840 William G. Sumner, economist and sociologist, was born in Paterson, N.J.; one of the first, most influential American sociology teachers (Yale 1872-1910); advocated free trade, sound currency, development of big business; author (*Folkways*) (died 1910).

1857 Gertrude Atherton, author, was born in San Francisco; wrote many popular novels (*The Conqueror, Black Oxen*) (died 1948).

1862 Gen. William S. Rosecrans was named commander of Army of the Ohio, replacing Gen. D.C. Buell; renamed Army of the Cumberland.

1865 A convention in Milledgeville repealed Georgia's secession ordinance; abolished slavery Nov 4.

1873 Emily Post, author and columnist, was born in Baltimore; wrote novels, books on design; wrote book on etiquette (1922), syndicated newspaper column (died 1960).

1875 Missouri's state constitution was ratified by popular vote; effective Nov 30.

1877 Herbert W. Hoover, manufacturer, was born in North Canton, Ohio; a founder (1910), Hoover Suction Sweeper Co., president (1922-48), board chairman (1948-54) (died 1954).

1882 William F. Halsey, World War II admiral, was born in Elizabeth, N.J.; commander, Allied naval forces, South Pacific (1942-44), Third Fleet (1944-45); helped turn Battle of Leyte Gulf into a most overwhelming Allied victory (died 1959).

1883 Bob Jones, evangelist, was born in Dale County, Ala.; founder of Bob Jones U., Greenville, S.C.; toured world as evangelist, radio evangelist (died 1968).

1885 Ezra L. Pound, poet, was born in Hailey, Ida.; a major influence in American and English literature; lived in Italy as an expatriate; produced many works (*Cantos, Personae, Exultations*) (died 1972).

1886 Zoe Akins, poet and playwright, was born in Humansville, Mo.; best remembered for play, *The Old Maid* (died 1958).

1888 Alan G. Kirk, World War II admiral, was born in Philadelphia; commanded amphibious invasion force at Sicily, naval forces in Normandy landing; ambassador to Belgium (1946-49), to Soviet Russia (1949-52) (died 1963).

1894 Charles Atlas, physical culturist, was born in Italy; developed self into a physical model, built successful mail order physical fitness program (died 1972).

1895 Dickinson W. Richards, physician, was born in Orange, N.J.; helped develop technique of cardiac catheterization, opening a new era in heart research; shared 1956 Nobel Physiology/Medicine Prize for the development.

1898 Bill Terry, baseball player, was born in Atlanta; first baseman, manager, New York Giants (1922-41); named to Baseball Hall of Fame (died 1989).

1912 Vice President James S. Sherman died in Utica, N.Y. at 57.

1914 Marion Ladewig, considered the best woman bowler of all time, was born in Grand Rapids, Mich.; won seven women's national all-star titles and named woman bowler of the year (1950-54, 1957-59, 1963).

1918 Allied representativs met in Paris, drew up conditions for an armistice.

1928 Daniel Nathans, biologist, was born in Wilmington, Del.; shared 1978 Nobel Physiology/Medicine Prize for discovery of the application of restriction enzymes to problems of molecular genetics.

1938 Radio dramatization by Orson Welles and his Mercury Theater of *War of the Worlds* created a nationwide scare.

1941 U.S. destroyer *Reuben James* was torpedoed and sunk off Ireland; 100 of crew lost.

1972 President Nixon signed an amendment to the Social Security Act to provide an additional $5.3 billion for the elderly.

1988 Kraft Inc. agreed to a $13.1 billion buy-out by Philip Morris Companies Inc. in the biggest merger ever between two non-oil American companies.

OCTOBER 31

1740 William Paca, colonial leader, was born near Abingdon, Md.; member, Continental Congress (1774-79) and a signer of the Declaration of Independence; governor of Maryland (1782-85) (died 1799).

1754 The charter of the College of the Province of New York was signed by Gov. James DeLancey of New York; school later became King's College, then Columbia.

1783 A fourth convention in New Hampshire framed a constitution acceptable to the people, effective June 2, 1784; contained a clause forbidding slavery.

1791 The *National Gazette*, an anti-administration newspaper, was established with Philip Freneau as editor.

1800 *National Intelligencer*, a most quoted newspaper, began publication in Washington.

1801 Theodore D. Woolsey, educator, was born in New York City; president, Yale U. (1846-71) (died 1889).

1803 The *Philadelphia*, while participating in a blockade of the port of Tripoli, ran aground on a reef and was captured.

1816 Philo Remington, firearms manufacturer, was born in Litchfield, N.Y., son of Eliphalet Remington (10/27/1793); headed Remington Co. (1861-89), branched into agricultural equipment and typewriters (died 1889).

1826 Joseph R. Hawley, Union general and legislator, was born in Stewartville, N.C.; served throughout Civil War; served Connecticut as governor (1866) and represented it in the House (1872-75) and Senate (1881-1905) (died 1905).

1827 Richard M. Hunt, architect, was born in Brattleboro, Vt.; designed many mansions, main part of the Metropolitan Museum of Art, the National Observatory in Washington, Fogg Museum at Harvard; a founder, American Institute of Architects (died 1895).

1830 Andrew J. Aikens, newspaper publisher and editor, was born in Barnard, Vt.; developed ready-to-print newspaper page (1864), ultimately became the Western Newspaper Union (died 1909).

1831 Rudolf Eickemeyer, inventor, was born in Altenbamberger, Germany; held about 150 patents, including a hat-making machine that revolutionized the industry, a differential gear for mowing/reaping machine, many electrical machines and devices (died 1895).

1831 Daniel Butterfield, Union general, was born in Utica, N.Y.; with Meade at Gettysburg, Sherman on the march to the sea; composed bugle call, *Taps* (died 1901).

1860 Juliette G. Low, founder and president (1915-20) of the Girl Scouts, was born in Savannah; originally known as the Girl Guides (1912), became Girl Scouts (1913) (died 1927).

1863 William G. McAdoo, businessman and public official, was born near Marietta, Ga.; president, Hudson & Manhattan Railroad, which completed first tube under the Hudson River (Mar 8, 1904); Secretary of Treasury (1913-18); first chairman, Federal Reserve Board; represented California in the Senate (1933-38) (died 1941).

1864 Nevada was admitted to the Union as the 36th state.

1867 Ed(ward) J. Delahanty, baseball player, was born in Cleveland; first to win batting championship in both leagues; named to Baseball Hall of Fame (died 1903).

1869 William A. Moffett, naval officer, was born in Charleston; served at battles of Manila Bay (1898) and Vera Cruz (1914); headed Bureau of Aeronautics (1921-33) (died 1933).

1873 The International Peace Bridge across the Niagara River between Buffalo and Ft. Erie, Canada was completed.

1875 Eugene I. Meyer, banker and publisher, was born in Los Angeles; a successful investment banker; first president, organizer, World Bank (1946); purchased *Washington Post* at auction (1933) (died 1959).

1900 Ethel Waters, singer and actress, was born in Chester, Pa.; a star of *A Member of the Wedding*; popular blues singer (died 1977).

1930 Michael Collins, astronaut, was born in Rome; took part in first manned lunar mission (1969), piloting the command module.

1931 Dan(iel) Rather, television newsman, was born in Wharton, Tex.; CBS White House correspondent, anchor for *CBS Evening News* (1981-).

1940 National Institutes of Health in Bethesda, Md. were dedicated.

1950 Jane Pauley, co-host of the *Today* show (1976-89), was born in Indianapolis.

1963 A fire in the State Fairgrounds Coliseum in Indianapolis resulted in 74 deaths.

1986 The Beirut magazine, *Al Shiras*, published a story disclosing the visit of former National Security Adviser Robert McFarlane on a plane delivering arms to Iran.

NOVEMBER 1

1642 Jean Nicolet, French explorer, died at 44; he was the first European to reach Lake Michigan and the Wisconsin area (1634).

1678 William Coddington, colonial governor, died at 77; protested Massachusetts persecution of Anne Hutchinson, withdrew to Aquidneck (R.I.), where he was governor (1674, 1675, 1678).

1757 (Johann) George Rapp, religious leader, was born in Iptinger, Germany; founder of the Harmonites sect, towns of Harmony in Pennsylvania and Indiana; colony successful until 1903 (died 1847).

1764 Stephen Van Rensselaer, public official and legislator, was born in New York City; president, Erie Canal Commission (1825-39); founder, Rensselaer Polytechnical Institute (1824); represented New York in the House (1822-29), where he cast the deciding vote for John Quincy Adams in the presidential election of 1824 which was decided by the House; served state as lieutenant governor (1795-1801) (died 1839).

1765 The Stamp Act went into effect.

1767 Great Britain modified the trade laws, reducing the three-penny duty on foreign molasses imported by the colonists to one penny on all molasses; export duties on British West Indies sugar were removed, thus reducing its price.

1776 The Continental Congress authorized a lottery to raise $5000 for military purposes.

1784 The Continental Congress began its session in Trenton, N.J., continued for a year.

1800 President John Adams took up residence in the White House, the first president to do so; in a letter to his wife, he wrote: "I pray Heaven bestow the best of blessings on this house and all that shall hereafter inhabit it. May none but wise and honest men ever rule under this roof."

1808 John Taylor, religious leader, was born in Milnthorpe, England; president, Mormon Church (1880-87), forced into exile because of his polygamy (1884-87) (died 1887).

1815 Crawford W. Long, surgeon, was born in Danielsville, Ga.; reputedly the first to use ether in surgery (died 1878).

1818 James Renwick, architect, was born in New York City; revived Gothic designs (Grace Church, St. Patrick's Cathedral, CCNY, all in New York City; Smithsonian Institution, Corcoran Art Gallery, both in Washington) (died 1895).

1830 Former President John Quincy Adams was elected to the House of Representatives from the Plymouth, Mass. district, serving until his death in 1848.

1835 The second Seminole War began; continued intermittently for seven years.

1844 A convention at Iowa City approved the Iowa constitution.

1852 Louisiana residents ratified their state constitution, which had been adopted by a convention in Baton Rouge in July.

1860 Boies Penrose, legislator, was born in Philadelphia; represented Pennsylvania in the Senate (1897-1921); Republican boss of Pennsylvania (1904-21) (died 1921).

1861 Gen. George B. McClellan was named commander-in-chief of the Union Army; also became general-in-chief of the Army with the retirement of Gen. Winfield Scott.

1871 Stephen Crane, author, was born in Newark; best known for *The Red Badge of Courage* (died 1900)

1880 Grantland Rice, sportswriter, was born in Murfreesboro, Tenn.; wrote for the *New York Herald Tribune*, widely syndicated (died 1954).

1880 Sholem Asch, author, was born in Kutno, Poland; noted for biblical novels (*The Nazarene, The Apostle, Moses, Mary*) (died 1957).

1890 The Mississippi constitution was adopted by convention, effective Jan 1, 1891.

1897 The new Library of Congress opened.

1900 The 12th Census reported a gain of more than 13 million people in a decade to 75,994,575.

1918 A railroad wreck in the Malbone St. tunnel in Brooklyn killed 92 persons.

1941 The Rainbow Bridge over the Niagara River at Niagara Falls was opened.

1949 Helen Hokinson, cartoonist, died in an airplane crash at 56; her cartoons, usually in *The New Yorker*, featured the middle-aged matron and club member.

1949 Two planes collided over Washington, 55 persons died.

1950 An assassination attempt was made on President Truman in Washington by two Puerto Rican nationalists; one was killed, as was a White House guard, Leslie Coffelt.

1952 The first hydrogen device was exploded at Eniwetok Atoll in the Pacific.

1955 A United Air Lines DC-6 exploded, crashed at Longmont, Colo., killing 44; the explosion was caused by a bomb planted on the plane.

1960 Fernando Valenzuela, baseball pitcher (Dodgers), was born in Navajoa, Mexico.

1973 Leon Jaworski of Texas was named special Watergate prosecutor; succeeding Archibald Cox who had been fired by President Nixon.

1977 American membership in the International Labor Organization (ILO) was terminated at the direction of the president; the United States had been a member since 1934.

1979 Mamie Eisenhower, widow of President Eisenhower, died in Washington at 82.

1981 The cost of first class postage rose to 20 cents.

1982 Bowie Kuhn was deposed as baseball commissioner when five National League teams voted not to renew his contract.

NOVEMBER 2

1734 Daniel Boone, legendary frontiersman, was born near Reading, Pa.; made numerous trips to Kentucky, guiding settlers there (1775), erected fort on site of what is now Boonesboro (died 1820).

1760 Lewis B. Morris, legislator, was born in Scarsdale, N.Y.; represented Vermont in the House (1797-1803); he withheld vote on the 36th ballot in the Jefferson-Burr contest for the presidency, turning the election to Jefferson (died 1825).

1772 At the call of Samuel Adams, a Boston town meeting created a 21-man standing Committee of Correspondence to communicate Boston's position to other communities and "to the World;" James Otis was chairman; other colonies formed similar committees and by Feb 1774 only North Carolina and Pennsylvania were without such committees.

1790 Jacob R. Hardenbergh, Dutch Reformed clergyman and educator, died at 54; a founder of Queens (later Rutgers) College (1766), president (1786-90).

1791 The U. of Vermont was chartered; opened in Burlington 1800.

1795 James K. Polk, 11th president (1845-49), was born in Mecklenburg County, N.C.; represented Tennessee in the House (1825-39), serving as Speaker (1835-39); also served his state as governor (1839-41) (died 1849).

1802 John Thompson, banker, was born in Peru, Mass.; founder, president, First National Bank, New York City (1863-73); founder, Chase National Bank (1877) (died 1891).

1810 Andrew A. Humphreys, Army officer, was born in Philadelphia; led survey of Mississippi delta (1850-51, 1857-61); Union general through Civil War; chief, Army Engineers (1866-79) (died 1883).

1865 Warren G. Harding, 29th president (1921-23), was born in Morrow County, Ohio; a newspaper editor (*Marion* (Ohio) *Star*); represented Ohio in the Senate (1915-21); died in San Francisco (1923) while enroute to Washington from a speaking tour.

1869 Voters in New York ratified a new constitution, but refused to waive property qualification of black men.

1880 Thomas A. Edison demonstrated the first direct current underground power transmission system.

1885 Harlow Shapley, astronomer, was born in Nashville, Mo.; astronomer, Mt. Wilson Observatory (1914-21); director, Harvard Observatory (1921-52) (died 1972).

1885 Winthrop W. Aldrich, banker and diplomat, was born in Providence; president, board chairman, Chase National Bank (1933-53); ambassador to Great Britain (1953-57) (died 1974).

1886 Florida ratified its new constitution.

1889 North Dakota entered the Union as the 39th state and South Dakota as the 40th.

1897 Dennis King, actor, was born in Coventry, England; star of musicals (*Rose Marie, Vagabond King, Three Musketeers*) (died 1983).

1897 Richard B. Russell, legislator, was born in Winder, Ga.; represented Georgia in the Senate (1933-71) and served state as governor (1931-33) (died 1971).

1903 Travis Jackson, baseball player (Giants), was born in Waldo, Ark.; named to Baseball Hall of Fame (died 1987).

1908 Bunny (Roland B.) Berigan, trumpeter, was born in Hilbert, Wis.; a leader in the 1930s swing era (died 1942).

1913 Burt Lancaster, screen actor, was born in New York City; starred in several films (*Elmer Gantry, The Bird Man of Alcatraz, The Killers*).

1917 Postage rates went from two to three cents for first class mail; postcards from one to two cents.

1920 Public radio broadcasting began at Station KDKA in Pittsburgh, providing the first election results; first regular evening broadcasts began Nov 30.

1922 Barber B. Conable Jr., president, World Bank (1985-), was born in Warsaw, N.Y.; represented New York in the House (1965-85).

1923 Billy (William) Haughton, a leading harness race driver, was born in Gloversville, N.Y.; won the Hambletonian four times and ranks fourth in races won (4910) and purses earned ($40.2 million); named to Harness Racing Hall of Fame (died 1986).

1932 Melvin Schwartz, physicist, was born in New York City; shared 1988 Nobel Physics Prize for helping capture neutrinos in a high energy beam to examine the structure of atomic particles.

1939 Congress enacted and President Franklin Roosevelt signed an amended neutrality law to permit belligerents to purchase and remove, at their own risk, war materials.

1962 President Kennedy announced that Soviet missile bases in Cuba were being dismantled and "progress is now being made toward restoration of peace in the Caribbean."

1972 The Bureau of Indian Affairs Building in Washington was invaded by 500 American Indians who were protesting Bureau policies.

1983 President Reagan signed a bill designating the third Monday in January as a national holiday honoring Rev. Martin Luther King Jr.

1986 David P. Jacobsen, an American hostage in Beirut, was released.

NOVEMBER 3

1620 The Council of New England was incorporated in Plymouth, England "for the planting, ruling, ordering, and governing New England in America."

1623 The Dutch West India Co. authorized sending five to six families to start a settlement in New Netherland.

1723 Samuel Davies, Presbyterian clergyman, was born in New Castle County, Del.; a founder, Hanover Presbytery, the first in Virginia (1755); raised funds in England for the College of New Jersey (later Princeton), president (1759-61) (died 1761).

1741 William Irvine, Revolutionary general, was born in Enniskillen, Ireland; captured in Canadian expedition (June 1776), exchanged (1778); commander, Ft. Pitt, Pittsburgh (1781-83) (died 1804).

1757 Robert Smith, public official, was born in Lancaster, Pa., brother of Samuel Smith (7/27/1752); served as Secretary of Navy (1801-09) and Secretary of State (1809-11) (died 1842).

1762 A secret Treaty of Ildefonso between Spain and France called for the transfer to Spain of the Louisiana Territory west of the Mississippi River.

1775 St. John's, Canada, under siege since Sept 6 by 1000 American troops, surrendered to Gen. Richard Montgomery; the Canadian expedition was designed to prevent a British invasion from the north.

1793 Stephen F. Austin, Texas colonizer, was born in Wythe County, Va.; carried out the colonization plans of his father, Moses; directed the colony's government, maintained peace and order; imprisoned in Mexico City (1833-34) for advocating Texas independence (died 1836).

1794 William Cullen Bryant, editor and poet, was born in Cummington, Mass.; co-owner and co-editor, *New York Evening Post* (1829-78); poet (*Thanatopsis, To a Waterfowl*) (died 1878).

1816 Jubal A. Early, Confederate general, was born in Franklin County, Va.; led raid in the Shenandoah Valley (1864); remained an unreconstructed rebel, never taking the oath of allegiance to the United States after the war (died 1894).

1834 Charles L. Fleischmann, industrialist, was born in Budapest; founder of yeast manufacturing firm (died 1897).

1841 Isabella M. Alden, author, was born in Rochester, N.Y.; wrote books for juveniles (the *Pansy* books) (died 1930).

1845 Edward D. White, jurist, was born in LaFourche Parish, La.; associate justice, Supreme Court (1894-1910), chief justice (1910-21); known for "the rule of reason" in anti-trust cases (died 1921).

1854 Jokichi Takamine, chemist, was born in Takaoa, Japan; developed a starch-digesting enzyme for distilling industry; isolated adrenalin from supra-adrenal gland (died 1922).

1879 Vihjalmur Stefansson, Arctic explorer, was born in Arnes, Canada; learned and taught how man can live in cold regions (died 1962).

1884 Joseph W. Martin, legislator, was born in North Attleboro, Mass.; represented Massachusetts in the House (1925-67), serving as Speaker (1947-49, 1953-55) (died 1968).

1887 Nat Fleischer, writer and editor, was born in New York City; outstanding boxing authority; founder, editor, *Ring Magazine* (1922-72); author of many books on boxing (died 1972).

1891 William McKinley was elected governor of Ohio.

1897 Idaho amended its constitution to permit woman suffrage.

1900 The first auto show opened in New York City's Madison Square Garden.

1903 Julian P. Boyd, historian, was born in Converse, S.C.; at Princeton U., best known as editor of Jefferson papers (died 1980).

1903 Walker Evans, editor and photographer, was born in St. Louis; first photographer to have an exhibition in Museum of Modern Art (1938); associate editor, *Fortune* (1945-65) (died 1975).

1908 Bronco (Bronislaw) Nagurski, football player, was born in Rainy River, Canada; starred with U. of Minnesota, Chicago Bears (1930-37) (died 1990).

1909 James Reston, journalist, was born in Clydebank, Scotland; reporter and columnist, *New York Times* (1939-).

1918 Bob Feller, baseball pitcher (Indians) who won 266 games, was born in Van Meter, Ia.; led American League in strikeouts seven times; named to Baseball Hall of Fame.

1933 Michael S. Dukakis, governor of Massachusetts (1975-79, 1983-), was born in Brookline, Mass.; 1988 Democratic presidential nominee.

1949 Larry Holmes, world heavyweight boxing champion (1978-85), was born in Cuthbert, Ga.

1979 Ku Klux Klan members killed five demonstrators at an anti-Klan rally in Greensboro, N.C.

NOVEMBER 4

1493 Christopher Columbus, on his second voyage, arrived at the Leeward Islands in the West Indies and explored Puerto Rico.

1732 Thomas Jefferson, colonial leader and jurist, was born in Calvert Country, Md.; a member of the Continental Congress (1774-77), where he nominated George Washington as Army commander-in-chief; first governor of Maryland (1777-79); associate justice, Supreme Court (1791-93) (died 1819).

1791 An American force led by Gen. Arthur St. Clair was virtually wiped out by Indians at Ft. Wayne, Ind.; two-thirds of the 900 men were killed or wounded; St. Clair resigned from Army command (1792).

1794 James Monroe, minister to France, effected the release of Thomas Paine from a Paris prison, where he had been held for about a year on a technicality.

1796 A treaty of peace, friendship, and navigation was signed with Tripoli.

1809 Benjamin R. Curtis, jurist, was born in Watertown, Mass.; associate justice, Supreme Court (1851-57), who wrote one of two dissenting opinions in the Dred Scott case; served as counsel for President Andrew Johnson during the impeachment trial (died 1874).

1810 John Allen, dentist, was born in Broome County, N.Y.; perfected type of denture still in use (1851); founder, Ohio College of Dental Surgery, second such school in the world; also founded New York College of Dentistry (died 1892).

1813 The British offered to negotiate for peace directly with the United States.

1816 Stephen J. Field, jurist, was born in Haddam, Conn.; associate justice, Supreme Court (1863-97), his decisions were important in developing constitutional law (died 1899).

1833 William P. Hepburn, legislator, was born in Wellsville, Ohio; represented Iowa in the House (1881-87, 1893-1909), instrumental in enactment of Pure Food & Drug Act (1906); Solicitor of the Treasury (1889-93) (died 1916).

1837 James Douglas, metallurgist and mining engineer, was born in Quebec; president, Copper Queen Consolidated Mining Co. in Arizona, where he brought about reforms in mining, metal industries; Douglas, Ariz. named for him (died 1918).

1841 Benjamin F. Goodrich, tire manufacturer, was born in Ripley, N.Y.; founded company which bears his name (1876) (died 1888).

1841 The first migrant wagon train from Missouri reached California.

1842 Abraham Lincoln and Mary Todd were married in Springfield, Ill.

1862 Richard J. Gatling received a patent for his multiple-barreled rapid-fire gun.

1873 Bobby (Roderick J.) Wallace, baseball player (Indians, Cards), player/manager (Browns), was born in Pittsburgh; named to Baseball Hall of Fame (died 1960).

1874 Sewell L. Avery, merchant, was born in Saginaw, Mich.; president, Montgomery Ward (1931-55); resisted federal attempts to take Ward property (1944), was carried bodily from his office (died 1960).

1876 James E. Fraser, sculptor, was born in Winona, Min.; did numerous busts, monuments; designed the Indian head nickel, Victory medal (1919) (died 1953).

1879 Will Rogers, author and entertainer, was born in Oologaw, Okla.; starred in numerous films, stage revues, Wild West shows; syndicated columnist (died 1935).

1881 Denver was made the permanent capital of Colorado.

1884 A new constitution for Montana was ratified by popular vote.

1906 Bob Considine, journalist, was born in Washington; was correspondent, syndicated columnist with Hearst papers for nearly 40 years (died 1975).

1916 Walter L. Cronkite, television newsman, was born in St. Joseph, Mo.; anchor for *CBS Evening News* (1962-81).

1918 Art Carney, actor, was born in Mt. Vernon, N.Y.; starred in films (*Harry and Tonto, The Odd Couple*), television (*The Honeymooners*).

1931 Buddy (Charles) Bolden, musician, died at about 63; legendary creator of jazz in New Orleans at the turn of the century.

1979 Iranian militants seized the American Embassy in Teheran and took more than 66 hostages, demanding that the Shan be returned to Iran; most Americans were held until Jan 20, 1981.

1982 Secretary Richard S. Schweiker of the Department of Health & Human Services approved regulations requiring tamper-proof packaging on almost all non-prescription drugs.

1988 President Reagan signed a bill ratifying an international treaty banning genocide which was drafted 40 years ago; signing marked success of efforts of Wisconsin Senator William Proxmire who made 3300 daily speeches over 19 years urging American ratification.

NOVEMBER 5

1639 The Massachusetts General Court named Richard Fairfield of Boston as postmaster to care for letters "brought from beyond the seas or to be sent thither" and to receive a penny for each.

1732 John Glover, leader of "amphibious" forces, was born in Salem, Mass.; led Americans in ferrying Gen. Washington and his men across the Delaware River and 9000 men across the East River from Long Island to escape the British.

1733 (John) Peter Zenger began publication of the *New York Weekly Journal*, which eventually became the object of a precedent-setting trial.

1742 Sir John Johnson, British official, was born in Johnstown, N.Y., son of Sir William Johnson (*see* 7/11/1774); organized Tories and Indians for raids on Americans in the Mohawk and Schoharie valleys during the Revolution (died 1830).

1757 Joseph Anderson, public official, was born in White Marsh, Pa.; represented Tennessee in the Senate (1797-1815), serving as president pro tem (1804-05); first Comptroller of the Treasury (1815-36) (died 1837).

1779 Washington Allston, painter, was born in Waccamaw, S.C.; considered the first important romantic landscape painter (died 1843).

1781 John Hanson, Maryland delegate to the Continental Congress, was elected "President of the United States in Congress Assembled," in effect the presiding officer of the Congress, but sometimes considered the first president.

1791 The *Knoxville Gazette* was founded nearly a year before the city at what is now Rogersville, Tenn. by George Roulstone and Robert Ferguson; this was the first newspaper in Tennessee.

1792 Isaac Toucey, legislator and public official, was born in Newtown, Conn.; represented Connecticut in the House (1835-39) and Senate (1852-57) and served the state as governor (1846-47); Attorney General (1848-49), Secretary of the Navy (1857-61) (died 1869).

1814 Ft. Erie, Canada was abandoned and blown up by Americans, ending American attempts to capture Canada; Americans withdrew across the river to Buffalo.

1818 Ben(jamin F.) Butler, Union general, was born in Deerfield, N.H.; commanded land forces in capturing New Orleans (1862); represented Massachusetts in the House (1867-75, 1877-79), leading the impeachment movement against President Andrew Johnson; governor of Massachusetts (1882-84) (died 1893).

1832 William W. Averell, Union general, was born in Cameron, N.Y.; distinguished cavalry raider; invented a system of asphalt paving, insulating conduits for electrical wires (died 1900).

1850 Michigan voters ratified their state constitution; a proposal for Negro suffrage was defeated.

1850 Ella Wheeler Wilcox, author, was born near Madison, Wis.; wrote syndicated daily poem, collected in more than 20 volumes (*Drops of Water, Poems of Passion, Sweet Danger*) (died 1919).

1855 Eugene V. Debs, labor and political leader, was born in Terre Haute, Ind.; national secretary, Brotherhood of Locomotive Firemen (1880-97), leader of the Pullman strike, Chicago (1894) for which he was arrested, imprisoned for six months for contempt; organized Social Democratic Party of America (1897), its presidential candidate five times (1900-20); indicted for violation of 1918 Espionage Act, sentenced to ten years, released 1921 (died 1926).

1857 Ida M. Tarbell, author, was born in Erie County, Pa.; editor, *McClure's Magazine* (1896-1906); associate editor, *American Magazine* (1906-15); author of history of Standard Oil Co., which led to federal investigation and eventual dissolution of company (died 1944).

1862 George A. Ball, glass manufacturer, was born near Greensburg, Ohio; developed glass canning jar (1884) (died 1955).

1863 James W. Packard, auto manufacturer, was born in Warren, Ohio; founder with brother, William D., of Packard Electric Co. (1890); designed motor car (1899), president, Packard Motor Car Co. (1902-15) (died 1928).

1869 Nicholas Longworth, legislator, was born in Cincinnati, great grandson of Nicholas Longworth (1/16/1782); represented Ohio in the House (1903-13, 1915-31), serving as Speaker (1925-31); married daughter of President Theodore Roosevelt (Alice) in the White House (1906) (died 1931).

1872 Boss (William M.) Tweed, who controlled New York City and plundered its treasury, was convicted and sent to jail.

1879 Will R. Hays, movie "czar," was born in Sullivan, Ind.; chairman, Republican National Committee (1918-21), Postmaster General (1921-22); president, Motion Pictures Producers & Distributors (1922-45) (died 1954).

1885 Will(iam J.) Durant, author, was born in North Adams, Mass.; author of 11-volume *Story of Civilization* (with wife, Ariel) and others (*The Story of Philosophy, The Mansions of Philosophy*) (died 1981).

1893 Raymond F. Loewy, industrial designer, was born in Paris; specialized in product design, packaging, transportation, and buildings (died 1986).

1894 Beardsley Ruml, economist, was born in Cedar Rapids, Ia.; author of federal income tax withholding system (1943) (died 1960).

1895 Charles MacArthur, playwright, was born in Scranton, Pa.; co-author of many plays (*The Front Page, Twentieth Century* (with Ben Hecht); *Lulu Belle, Salvation*) (died 1956).

1895 George B. Selden was granted a patent for a 'road engine,' the first American patent for a gasoline-driven car.

1912 Roy Rogers, television and screen actor, was born in Cincinnati; formed musical group, "Sons of the Pioneers;" made numerous films, television shows; former owner of chain of fast food restaurants named for him.

1918 The Allies agreed to accept President Wilson's 14 points as the basis for peace discussions.

1921 A proclamation was issued creating Nov 11 as Armistice Day.

1943 The Senate, by a vote of 85-5, approved the idea of a postwar international organization.

1946 New Jersey adopted new constitution, first change since 1844.

1953 President Eisenhower empowered the New York State Power Authority to develop with Canada a St. Lawrence River hydroelectric project.

1982 Women became full-fledged firefighters in New York City with the graduation of 11 women and 103 men from the Fire Academy.

1987 President Reagan's second nominee to the Supreme Court, Douglas H. Ginsburg, admitted that he smoked marijuana in the 1960s and 1970s; a few days later, he asked that his nomination be withdrawn.

NOVEMBER 6

1643 A general court composed of two deputies each from four Connecticut towns (New Haven, Stamford, Guilford, Milford) adopted a Frame of Government, established the Mosaic law as the basis of its legal system.

1752 George Washington was appointed district adjutant with the rank of major of Virginia by Gov. Robert Dinwiddie; his first military appointment.

1758 John Adams was admitted to practice law before the Supreme Court in Boston.

1789 See of Baltimore created, with John Carroll as first bishop.

1822 Gordon Granger, Union general, was born in Jay, N.Y.; served throughout Civil War, with special distinction at Chickamauga (died 1876).

1832 Joseph Smith, Mormon leader, was born in Kirtland, Ohio, son of Joseph Smith (12/23/1805); accepted presidency of an offshoot of the original Mormon Church—the Reorganized Latter Day Saints Church (1860-1914)—which opposed polygamy (died 1914).

1841 Nelson W. Aldrich, legislator, was born in Foster, R.I.; represented Rhode Island in the House (1878-81) and Senate (1881-1911); chairman, National Monetary Commission, which led to the formation of the Federal Reserve System (died 1915).

1851 Charles H. Dow, editor and economist, was born in Sterling, Conn.; with Edward D. Jones, founded *Wall Street Journal* (1882), inaugurated publication of an average calculated from the daily market price of selected representative securities (the Dow Jones) (died 1902).

1854 John Philip Sousa, composer and bandmaster, was born in Washington; known as the "march king," he directed the U.S. Marine Band (1880-92), then his own band; wrote 140 marches ("Stars and Stripes Forever," "Semper Fidelis"), ten comic operas (*El Capitan, The Bride-Elect*) (died 1932).

1861 James Naismith, basketball originator, was born in Almonte, Canada; developed game while he was a physical education instructor at Springfield (Mass.) YMCA (1891) (died 1939).

1869 The first intercollegiate football game was played at New Brunswick, N.J. with Rutgers defeating Princeton 6-4.

1886 Gus(tav G.) Kahn, lyricist, was born in Coblenz, Germany; wrote many hit lyrics ("Ain't We Got Fun;" "My Buddy;" "Toot, Toot, Tootsie;" "I'll See You in My Dreams;" "Chloe") (died 1941).

1887 Walter Johnson, baseball pitcher who won 414 games (Senators, 1907-27), was born in Humboldt, Kan.; one of first five to be named to Baseball Hall of Fame (died 1946).

1888 Taylor Spink, editor (*Sporting News* 1914-62), was born in St. Louis (died 1962).

1890 Henry K. Sherrill, presiding bishop, American Episcopal Church (1946-58), was born in Brooklyn (died 1980).

1892 Harold W. Ross, editor, was born in Aspen, Colo.; founder, editor, *The New Yorker* (1925-51) (died 1951).

1893 Edsel B. Ford, auto manufacturer, was born in Detroit, son of Henry Ford (7/30/1863); president, Ford Motor Co. (1919-43) (died 1943).

1896 Fibber McGee, radio entertainer, was born in Peoria, Ill. as Jim Jordan; with wife, Molly, had popular radio show in the 1930s (died 1988).

1903 The United States recognized Panama's independence from Colombia.

1916 Ray Conniff, musician, was born in Attleboro, Mass.; leader of choral group.

1917 New York voters adopted woman suffrage constitutional amendment; Ohio voters turned it down.

1921 James Jones, author, was born in Robinson, Ill.; remembered for *From Here to Eternity* (died 1977).

1928 Franklin D. Roosevelt was elected governor of New York; re-elected in 1930.

1931 Mike Nichols, entertainer and director, was born in Berlin; television comedian (with Elaine May); director (stage—*The Odd Couple, Plaza Suite, The Gin Game*; screen—*Who's Afraid of Virginia Woolf?, The Graduate*).

1934 Nebraska adopted a unicameral legislature.

NOVEMBER 7

1637 Anne Hutchinson was sentenced to banishment from the colony by the Massachusetts General Court for her religious opinions; allowed to remain until Mar.

1731 Robert Rogers, frontiersman, was born in Methuen, Mass.; headed Rogers Rangers, raiders during the French & Indian War; later imprisoned on charges of espionage, escaped and organized the Queens Rangers; defeated at White Plains, fled (1780) to England (died 1795).

1763 Benedict J. Flaget, Catholic prelate, was born in Contournat, France; called the Bishop of the Wilderness, serving area between the Alleghenies and the Mississippi River (1810-50) (died 1850).

1785 The Continental Congress began new session in New York; ended Nov 3, 1786; reopened three days later in the final session under the confederation.

1800 Platt R. Spencer, calligrapher, was born in East Fishkill, N.Y.; originator, teacher of Spencerian style of penmanship; author of penmanship books (died 1864).

1811 The Battle of Tippecanoe occurred after unsuccessful negotiations with Shawnee chief, Tecumseh; Americans suffered heavy losses but battle was considered a great victory for repulsing Indian attackers; Americans were led by William Henry Harrison.

1814 American troops under Gen. Andrew Jackson captured Pensacola, Fla. from the British.

1832 Andrew D. White, educator, was born in Homer, N.Y.; a founder, first president, Cornell U. (1868-85); minister to Germany (1879-81), to Russia (1892-94), ambassador to Germany (1897-1902) (died 1918).

1835 A Texas convention made a provisional declaration of independence from Mexico, demanding self-rule; organized provisional government Nov 13.

1837 Elijah P. Lovejoy, abolitionist editor, was shot and killed by a mob at Alton, Ill. while trying to protect his paper, *The Alton Observer*; known as "the martyr abolitionist."

1860 Gov. Joseph E. Brown of Georgia recommended to the legislature that a convention be called to consider secession; Jan 16 set for the convention.

1861 The Battle of Belmont, Mo., Gen. Grant's first Civil War battle and first defeat, occurred; attack on Belmont was designed to keep Gen. Leonidas Polk and his troops from aiding the Confederates in Missouri.

1862 President Lincoln relieved Gen. George B. McClellan of his command of the Army of the Potomac, replacing him with Gen. Ambrose E. Burnside.

1864 George L. Hartford, merchant, was born in Brooklyn, son of George H. Hartford (9/5/1833); helped develop Atlantic & Pacific grocery chain (died 1957).

1864 Eleanor M. (Cissie) Patterson, newspaper publisher, was born in Chicago, granddaughter of Joseph Medill (4/6/1823) and sister of Joseph M. Patterson (1/6/1879); had interest in *Chicago Times, New York Daily News*; owner, publisher, *Washington Herald, Washington Times* (died 1948).

1868 Royal S. Copeland, physician and legislator, was born in Dexter, Mich.; president, New York City Board of Health (1918-23); represented New York in the Senate (1923-38), sponsor of much pure food and drug legislation (died 1938).

1876 Presidential election resulted in the Democratic candidate, Samuel J. Tilden, getting a popular vote margin of 250,000; however, returns were in dispute in Florida, Louisiana, South Carolina, and Oregon; without these, Tilden was one electoral vote short of election; resolved by an electoral commission in favor of Rutherford B. Hayes by one vote.

1882 Grover Cleveland was elected governor of New York.

1886 Chester Barnard, telephone executive, was born in Malden, Mass.; president, USO (United Service Organizations) (1942-45), which provided entertainment for military personnel (died 1961).

1893 Colorado adopted woman suffrage by popular vote.

1906 Eugene Carson Blake, Presbyterian clergyman, was born in St. Louis; president, National Council of Churches (1954-57); general secretary, World Council of Churches (1966-72) (died 1985).

1908 New York Circuit Court ruled against the American Tobacco Co., holding it was a trust and combination in restraint of trade.

1915 Italian liner *Ancona* was sunk without warning by an Austrian submarine; 27 Americans were among the 272 victims.

1916 The American steamship *Columbian* was sunk by a German submarine off Spain.

1918 Billy (William F.) Graham, evangelist, was born in Charlotte, N.C.; conducted evangelistic missions throughout the world.

1920 Max Kampelman, chief arms control negotiator (1983-90), was born in New York City.

1922 Al Hirt, musician, was born in New Orleans; jazz trumpeter and orchestra leader.

1950 Hawaii voters ratified their state constitution.

1962 Eleanor Roosevelt, widow of President Franklin Roosevelt, died in New York City at 78.

1967 John Nance Garner, former vice president (1933-41) died in Uvalde, Tex. at 98.

1967 The first two black mayors were elected in major cities—Carl B. Stokes in Cleveland and Richard G. Hatcher in Gary, Ind.

1967 Corporation for Public Broadcasting was created.

NOVEMBER 8

1701 The Charter of Liberties, prepared by William Penn, was adopted; remained Pennsylvania's constitution until the Revolution; called for a unicameral legislature, with laws being prepared by the governor with the consent of the Assembly.

1725 The *New York Gazette*, first newspaper in New York province, was published by William Bradford.

1731 The Library Company of Philadelphia was founded by Benjamin Franklin; a subscription library, it opened with the arrival of books from England in 1732.

1732 John Dickinson, "penman" of the Revolution, was born in Talbot County, Md.; wrote the declaration of rights and grievances of the Stamp Act Congress; active in early Congresses (1774-80) and the Constitutional Convention; sought conciliation with England; voted against the Declaration of Independence (died 1808).

1772 William Wirt, lawyer, was born in Bladensburg, Md.; as Attorney General (1817-29), he was involved in many precedent-setting cases (*McCulloch v. Maryland, Gibbons v. Ogden,* the *Dartmouth College* case); presidential candidate, Anti-Masonic Party (1831) (died 1834).

1813 Gen. Andrew Jackson led Americans to victory in the Battle of Talladega (Ala.) against Creek Indians.

1821 George H. Bissell, oil industry pioneer, was born in Hanover, N.H.; founder, head, Pennsylvania Rock Oil Co. (1854), which drilled the world's first successful oil well (1859) in Titusville, Pa. (died 1884).

1830 Oliver O. Howard, Union general, was born in Leeds, Me.; commanded Sherman's right wing on the march to the sea; headed Freedmen's Bureau (1865-72); a founder, president, Howard U., Washington (1869-73) (died 1909).

1836 Milton Bradley, lithographer and game manufacturer, was born in Vienna, Me.; invented successful game (Checkered Game of Life), formed company for games, kindergarten materials (died 1911).

1837 Mt. Holyoke College was founded by Mary Lyon at South Hadley, Mass.

1838 Rufus W. Peckham, jurist, was born in Rensselaerville, N.Y.; associate justice, Supreme Court (1895-1909) (died 1909).

1848 George W. Gould, ophthalmologist, was born in Auburn, Me.; invented bifocal lens glasses; compiled several medical dictionaries (died 1922).

1861 The USS *San Jacinto*, commanded by Capt. Charles Wilkes, stopped the British steamer *Trent* and removed James H. Mason and John Slidell, Confederate diplomats on their way to England; imprisoned in Ft. Warren, Mass. until Dec 26.

1864 Gen. George B. McClellan, Lincoln's unsuccessful opponent for the presidency, resigned from the Army.

1869 Joseph F. Rutherford, religious leader, was born in Booneville, Mo.; president, Jehovah's Witnesses (1916-42) (called Russellites until 1925), imprisoned (1917-19) for counseling people to be conscientious objectors (died 1942).

1871 Robert W. Bingham, newspaper executive and diplomat, was born in Orange County, N.C.; publisher, *Louisville Courier-Journal, Times*; ambassador to Great Britain (1933-37) (died 1937).

1883 Charles Demuth, painter, was born in Lancaster, Pa.; a key figure in introducing cubist technique to the United States (died 1935).

1889 Montana was admitted to the Union as the 41st state.

1896 Bucky (Stanley R.) Harris, baseball player and manager, was born in Port Jervis, N.Y.; second baseman, Washington Senators (1919-28); manager 29 years (Washington, Detroit, Red Sox, Yankees); named to Baseball Hall of Fame (died 1977).

1897 Dorothy Day, welfare worker and author, was born in New York City; religious journalist, publisher, *Catholic Worker*; organized hospitality houses for the urban poor (died 1980).

1898 Theodore Roosevelt was elected governor of New York.

1900 Margaret Mitchell, author of *Gone With the Wind*, her only book, was born in Atlanta (died 1949).

1909 Katherine Hepburn, actress, was born in Hartford, Conn.; starred on stage, screen and television (*The Philadelphia Story, The African Queen, Morning Glory, Guess Who's Coming to Dinner, The Lion in Winter, On Golden Pond*).

1910 A Washington state constitutional amendment provided woman suffrage.

1910 Franklin D. Roosevelt was elected to the New York Senate.

1933 Harry L. Hopkins was named head of the Civil Works Administration, created to place four million unemployed on public works projects; agency spent $933 million on 190,000 projects; terminated March 1934.

1942 Angel Cordero, a leading jockey, was born in San Juan, Puerto Rico; by 1987, he was third in career purses and fourth in wins, including the Kentucky Derby three times, Preakness twice and Belmont Stakes once.

1942 American and British forces landed in French North Africa, under command of Gen. Dwight D. Eisenhower; took Casablanca, Oran and Algiers.

1966 Edward W. Brook, Republican from Massachusetts, became the first black to be popularly elected to the Senate, the first to serve there in 85 years.

1984 The space shuttle *Discovery* was launched at Cape Canaveral, Fla.; during the eight-day mission it captured two stray communications satellites.

1988 Vice President George Bush was elected president, defeating Massachusetts Governor Michael S. Dukakis and becoming the first sitting vice president since Martin Van Buren (1836) to be elected president.

NOVEMBER 9

1724 John Thomas, Revolutionary general, was born in Marshfield, Mass.; was in command at Roxbury, captured Dorchester Heights, forcing British evacuation of Boston; commanded operations against Quebec; died of smallpox June 2, 1776.

1731 Benjamin Banneker, mathematician and publisher, was born in Ellicott, Md.; published annual almanac (1791-1802); finished planning of Washington after Pierre L'Enfant was dismissed (died 1806).

1793 William Maxwell, a Kentucky printer, established the *Centinel of the North-Western Territory* in Cincinnati.

1795 Josiah Tattnall, naval officer, was born near Savannah; served in War of 1812 and Mexican War; in Confederate navy, commander of the *Virginia* (the former *Merrimac*), which he sank to prevent its capture, and the coastal defenses of Virginia, Georgia, and South Carolina (died 1871).

1801 Gail Borden, inventor, was born in Norwich, N.Y.; developed method of condensing milk (1856), formed what later became Borden Co.; invented a meat biscuit, a variety of juice concentrates; considered the father of the instant food industry (died 1874).

1802 Elijah P. Lovejoy, abolitionist editor, was born in Albion, Me.; he was killed by a mob as he tried to protect his paper *Alton* (Ill.) *Observer*, Nov. 7, 1837.

1824 The first presidential election in which the popular vote was tabulated gave Andrew Jackson 152,901 votes, John Quincy Adams 114,023, Henry Clay 47,217, and William H. Crawford 46,979.

1825 A(mbrose) P. Hill, Confederate general, was born in Culpeper, Va.; initiated attack that began Battle of Gettysburg; killed in action at Petersburg, Va. in 1865.

1833 Sally Louisa Tompkins, Confederate officer, was born in Matthews County, Va.; known as Captain Sally, she was the only woman commissioned by the Confederate Army; turned her Richmond home into a hospital (died 1916).

1853 Stanford White, architect, was born in New York City; helped design old Madison Square Garden, Washington Arch, both in New York City (died 1906).

1857 The Oregon constitution was ratified by popular vote.

1858 John M. Carrère, architect, was born in Rio de Janeiro of American parentage; designed numerous buildings including Carnegie Institution, Senate and House office buildings, the New York Public Library (died 1911).

1865 Frederick Funston, Spanish-American War general, was born in New Carlisle, Ohio; captured Filipino guerilla, Emilio Aguinaldo; commanded force which captured Vera Cruz (1914) (died 1917).

1872 The richest quarter of Boston was burned in a three-day fire, destroying 767 buildings, with an estimated value of $75 million, and killing 14 persons.

1873 Marie Dressler, actress, was born in Coburg, Canada; after a stage career, starred in movies (*Min and Bill, Tugboat Annie, The Late Christopher Bean*) (died 1934).

1874 Albert F. Blakeslee, botanist, was born in Geneseo, N.Y.; demonstrated that chemicals could interfere with genetic mechanism (died 1954).

1881 Herbert T. Kalmus, engineer, was born in Chelsea, Mass.; a developer of the Technicolor process of movie-making; president, Technicolor Inc. (1922-63) (died 1963).

1886 Ed Wynn, comedian and entertainer, was born in Philadelphia; starred on stage (*The Perfect Fool*) radio (*Texaco Fire Chief*) (died 1966).

1898 Leonard Carmichael, museum official, was born in Germantown, Pa.; secretary, Smithsonian Institution (1953-64), credited with modernizing institution (died 1973).

1906 President Theodore Roosevelt left for an inspection trip of Panama, the first president to leave the country while in office; also visited Puerto Rico Nov 21.

1906 Muggsy (Francis J.) Spanier, musician, was born in Chicago; cornetist and major figure in Dixieland jazz scene (died 1967).

1908 Bernard Kilgore, newspaper executive, was born in Albany, Ind.; with *Wall St. Journal* (1929-67), president (1945-67) (died 1967).

1911 Lincoln Memorial National Park at Hodgenville, Ky. was dedicated by President Taft.

1915 R. Sargent Shriver, public official and diplomat, was born in Westminster, Md.; first director, Peace Corps (1960-65); first director, Office of Economic Opportunity (War on Poverty) (1964-68); ambassador to France (1968-70); Democratic vice presidential candidate (1972).

1918 Spiro T. Agnew, Vice President (1969-73), was born in Baltimore; governor of Maryland (1966-68); resigned vice presidency amid charges of illegal financial dealings; pleaded no contest to federal income tax evasion charges.

1918 President Wilson named Herbert Hoover to represent the United States in organization of European food relief, which distributed about 46 million tons (1918-20).

1918 Kaiser Wilhelm of Germany abdicated.

1918 German delegates were given terms of armistice by Gen. Ferdinand Foch in Compiegne Forest near Rethonde.

1918 Florence Chadwick, long distance swimmer, was born in San Diego; first woman to swim English Channel both ways (Aug 8, 1950); swam Catalina Channel, the Bosporus, Straits of Gibraltar.

1934 Carl Sagan, astronomer, was born in New York City; provided valuable insight into origin of life in earth's primeval environment; a science popularizer in his books (*The Dragons of Eden, Brocam's Brain*) and on television.

1935 The CIO (Congress of Industrial Organizations) was established.

1935 Bob (Robert) Gibson, baseball pitcher who won 251 games (Cards), was born in Omaha; named to Baseball Hall of Fame.

1943 An agreement was signed in the White House by 44 nations to create the United Nations Relief & Rehabilitation Administration (UNRRA).

1965 A power failure lasting 13-1/2 hours blacked out the northeast United States and southeastern Canada; New York City was hardest hit.

1965 Department of Housing and Urban Development began operations; Robert C. Weaver was named first Secretary Jan 18, 1966.

NOVEMBER 10

1674 The Dutch occupation of New York City, which began in August 1673, ended after the signing of the Treaty of Westminster.

1766 Queens College (which later became Rutgers) at New Brunswick, N.J. was chartered.

1775 The Continental Congress created the Marine Corps by authorizing two battalions of Marines.

1776 John Paul Jones, commanding two ships (*Providence* and *Alfred*) captured many British prizes in a three-week foray off Nova Scotia.

1792 Samuel Nelson, jurist, was born in Hebron, N.Y.; with New York Supreme Court (1831-45), chief justice (1837-45); associate justice, Supreme Court (1845-72) (died 1873).

1801 Samuel G. Howe, physician, was born in Boston; husband of Julia Ward Howe, he worked for education of the blind; founder, director of what became the Perkins School for the Blind, Boston (1832-76); founded first school for the mentally retarded (died 1876).

1808 The Osage Treaty was signed, with Indians ceding nearly all of present Missouri and Arkansas, north of the Arkansas River.

1821 A New York State convention adopted a new constitution which abolished the requirement of property ownership for voting.

1827 Alfred H. Terry, Union general, was born in Hartford; saw action at first Bull Run, Port Royal, Ft. Fisher, Richmond, and Petersburg (died 1890).

1843 Former President John Quincy Adams delivered the oration at the cornerstone laying of Mt. Adams Astronomical Observatory near Cincinnati, the first American observatory.

1860 The South Carolina legislature called for a convention in Columbia Dec 17 to consider secession.

1865 Capt. Henry Winz, a commander of the Andersonville (Ga.) Confederate prison, was hanged following a trial by a military commission; subsequent investigations questioned the legality of the action.

1867 Alexander P. Moore, newspaper executive, was born in Pittsburgh; editor, *Pittsburgh Leader* (1904-28); owner, *New York Daily Mirror, Boston Advertiser* (1928-30); ambassador to Spain (1923-25), to Peru (1928-30) (died 1930).

1869 Wayne B. Wheeler, prohibitionist, was born in Trumbull County, Ohio; general superintendent (1898-1915), national superintendent, Anti-Saloon League; claimed authorship of 18th Amendment (died 1927).

1871 Henry M. Stanley, *New York Herald* correspondent, found the missionary, Dr. David Livingstone, at Lake Tanganyika, and offered the famous greeting, "Dr. Livingstone, I presume?"

1871 Winston Churchill, author, was born in St. Louis; known for historical novels (*Richard Carvel, The Crisis, The Crossing*) (died 1947).

1874 Donald B. MacMillan, explorer, was born in Provincetown, Mass.; was with Peary (1908-09), led many other expeditions (1913-37) (died 1970).

1879 Vachel Lindsay, author, was born in Springfield, Ill.; poet (*General William Booth Enters Heaven, Congo, Abraham Lincoln Walks*) (died 1931).

1893 John P. Marquand, author, was born in Wilmington, Del.; wrote short stories (*Mr. Moto* series), novels (*The Late George Apley, Wickford Point, H.M. Pulham, Esq.*) (died 1960).

1896 John K. Northrop, aviation engineer, was born in Newark; co-founder, chief engineer, Lockheed Aircraft Corp. (1927), formed Avion Corp. (1927), Northrop Corp. (1938) (died 1981).

1896 Jimmy Dykes, baseball player (Athletics), player/manager (White Sox), was born in Philadelphia (died 1976).

1909 Johnny Marks, composer, was born in Mt. Vernon, N.Y.; best known for "Rudolph the Red-Nosed Reindeer" (died 1985).

1913 Karl J. Shapiro, author, was born in Baltimore; critic, poet ("Person, Place, Thing;" "The Place of Love"); poetry consultant, Library of Congress (1946-47).

1914 The port of Houston was symbolically opened to international commerce when President Wilson pushed a button in the White House.

1988 Energy Department announced that Texas had been selected as the site of the $4.4 billion superconducting super-collider over six other states; site, 35 miles south of Dallas, will—if constructed—be the largest scientific instrument ever built—a 53-mile long racetrack-shaped tunnel.

NOVEMBER 11

1647 Massachusetts enacted a law requiring a community with 50 householders to maintain a school and every town with 100 householders to maintain a grammar school.

1771 Ephraim McDowell, surgeon, was born in Rockbridge County, Va.; pioneer in abdominal surgery, performed first recorded American operation in ovarian surgery (1809) (died 1830).

1776 A Maryland convention adopted a state constitution.

1778 The Cherry Valley Massacre occurred at an outpost 46 miles west of Albany when Butler's Rangers and Indians under Joseph Brant attacked, killing 30 and taking 71 prisoners, burning all the buildings, killing all cattle.

1781 Cyrus Alger, manufacturer and inventor, was born in West Bridgewater, Mass.; produced ammunition in the War of 1812; designed first cylinder stove, the first gun with a rifled barrel (died 1856).

1799 Charles S. Bent, fur trader, was born in Charleston, W.Va. (then Virginia); with his brothers, he built Bent's Fort in Colorado, served as civil governor of New Mexico (1846-47) (died 1847).

1811 Ben McCulloch, scout and Confederate general, was born in Rutherford County, Tenn.; served as scout in the Mexican War, killed by a sharpshooter at the Battle of Pea Ridge, Ark. (1862).

1813 An American force was defeated by Canadian troops 90 miles north of Montreal; the campaign against Montreal was abandoned.

1831 Nat Turner, insurrectionist, was hanged; he led a rebellion of slaves in Virginia, which resulted in the deaths of 55 whites.

1836 Henry M. Alden, editor, was born near Darby, Vt.; editor, *Harper's Magazine* (1863-1919) (died 1919).

1858 James A. Garfield and Lucretia Rudolph were married in Hiram, Ohio.

1859 Samuel Insull, utility head and financier, was born in London; private secretary to Thomas A. Edison; vice president, Edison General Electric (1889-92); president, Chicago Edison Co., later Consolidated Edison; tried for fraud on holding companies, stock transactions; acquitted (died 1938).

1864 George W. Crile, surgeon, was born in Chilo, Ohio; contributed much to the study of shock from surgery; a founder, director, Cleveland Clinic Hospital (1921) (died 1943).

1872 Maude Adams, actress, was born in Salt Lake City; starred in many stage plays (*Little Minister, L'Aiglon, Peter Pan*—which she performed about 1500 times) (died 1953).

1872 Frederick A. Stock, conductor, was born near Cologne, Germany; conductor, Chicago Symphony (from 1905), general music director, Chicago World's Fair (1933) (died 1942).

1874 James L. Kraft, food manufacturer, was born in Ft. Erie, Canada, brother of Charles H. Kraft (10/17/1880); principal founder, J.L. Kraft Brothers & Co. (1909) (died 1953).

1875 Vesto M. Slipher, astronomer, was born near Mulberry, Ind.; with Lowell Observatory (1901-52), director (1916-52); directed research which led to the discovery of the planet Pluto (died 1969).

1885 Stanford University was founded in California; opened 1891.

1885 George S. Patton, World War II general, was born in San Gabriel, Cal.; served in Mexico and World War I; first man detailed to tank corps (1917); commander, 2nd Army Corps, North Africa; 7th Army in Sicily, 3rd Army in Western Europe (died 1945).

1889 Washington was admitted to the Union as the 42nd state.

1891 Rabbit (Walter J.V.) Maranville, baseball player, was born in Springfield, Mass.; shortstop (1912-35), mostly with Boston Braves; named to Baseball Hall of Fame (died 1954).

1893 Clarence D. Chamberlin, aviator, was born in Denison, Ia.; pilot of monoplane in record 3911-mile nonstop flight from Roosevelt Field, N.Y. to Germany in 42 hours, 31 minutes (1927) (died 1976).

1897 Gordon W. Allport, psychologist, was born in Montezuma, Ind.; with Harvard (1930-67), developed a concept of personality which dealt with real, present problems rather than searching for childhood trauma (died 1967).

1899 Pat O'Brien, screen actor, was born in Milwaukee; starred in many films (*The Front Page, The Last Hurrah, Knute Rockne*) (died 1983).

1899 Pie (Harold J.) Traynor, baseball player (Pirates), was born in Framingham, Mass.; named to Baseball Hall of Fame (died 1972).

1900 Hugh D. Scott Jr., Pennsylvania legislator, was born in Fredericksburg, Va.; served in the House (1941-45, 1947-59) and Senate (1959-76), Republican leader (1969-76); Republican national chairman (1948-49).

1901 A new Alabama constitution was adopted by popular vote.

1918 The armistice was signed at 5:00 am bringing World War I to a close as the Germans agreed to terms; firing ended at 11:00 am at the fronts.

1921 A burial ceremony was held at the site of the Tomb of the Unknown Soldier in Arlington Cemetery with President Harding on hand.

1922 Kurt Vonnegut Jr., author (*Player Piano, Slaughterhouse Five, The Sirens of Titan*), was born in Indianapolis.

1932 The Tomb of the Unknown Soldier in Arlington National Cemetery was dedicated by War Secretary Patrick J. Hurley.

1966 The vote to merge the Methodist Church and the Evangelical United Brethren Church was ratified; the new United Methodist Church, the largest American Protestant church, will combine ten million Methodists and 750,000 Evangelical UB members.

1984 President Reagan dedicated the Vietnam Veterans Memorial in Washington.

1985 The Mormon Church elected Ezra Taft Benson, 80, as president, succeeding Spencer Kimball.

1987 President Reagan nominated Federal Appeals Judge Anthony M. Kennedy to fill the Supreme Court vacancy; this was the third nominee for the post; confirmed by the Senate Feb 3, 1988.

NOVEMBER 12

1655 Sir Francis Nicholson, colonial administrator, was born near Richmond, England; served as lieutenant governor of the New England Dominion (1688) and Virginia (1690-92); governor of Maryland (1694-98), of Virginia (1698-1705), of South Carolina (1720-25) (died 1728).

1751 Margaret Corbin, Revolutionary heroine, was born in Franklin County, Pa.; took over husband's gun position at Ft. Washington after he was killed (1776) and was completely disabled; granted a lifetime pension (died 1800).

1770 Joseph Hopkinson, jurist, was born in Philadelphia, son of Francis Hopkinson (9/21/1737); represented Pennsylvania in the House (1815-19), U.S. district judge (1828-42); wrote patriotic song, "Hail Columbia" (died 1842).

1790 Letitia Christian Tyler, first wife of President Tyler, was born in New Kent County, Va. (died 1842).

1815 Elizabeth Cady Stanton, women's rights leader, was born in Johnstown, N.Y.; organized women's rights convention in Seneca Falls, N.Y. (1848), worked for 40 years with Susan B. Anthony; first president, National Woman's Suffrage Association (1869-90), also American Woman's Suffrage Association (died 1902).

1825 George Munro, publisher, was born in West River, N.C.; one of the leading publishers of "dime" novels (1863-93), publisher of weekly *Fireside Companion* (1866-96) (died 1896).

1831 Eli H. Janney, inventor, was born in Loudon County, Va.; invented automatic railway car coupler (1868) (died 1912).

1846 Samuel Theobald, ophthalmologist, was born in Baltimore; a founder of Baltimore Eye, Ear & Throat Dispensary, hospital; introduced use of boric acid for eye diseases (died 1930).

1864 Gen. William T. Sherman sent his last message before starting the next day on the 32-day "march to the sea," during which he would be out of touch.

1877 Warren R. Austin, legislator and diplomat, was born in Highgate, Vt.; represented Vermont in the House (1931-46); delegate to UN (1947-53) (died 1962).

1880 Harold R. Stark, World War II admiral, was born in Wilkes-Barre, Pa., chief of naval operations (1939-42); European waters commander (1942-45) (died 1972).

1886 Joseph N. Pew Jr., board chairman, Sun Oil Co. (1947-63), was born in Pittsburgh; Pennsylvania Republican leader (died 1963).

1889 DeWitt Wallace, publisher, was born in St. Paul, Minn.; co-founder with wife, Lila B. Wallace (12/25/1889), publisher, *Readers Digest* (died 1981).

1908 Harry A. Blackmun, associate justice Supreme Court (1970-), was born in Nashville, Ill.

1920 Jo Stafford, singer (with Tommy Dorsey band), was born in Coalinga, Cal.

1921 An armaments conference began in Washington, continued to Feb 6, 1922; major powers agreed to curtail naval construction, outlaw poison gas, restrict submarine attacks on shipping, and respect integrity of China.

1927 Holland Tunnel under the Hudson River between New York City and Jersey City was opened to traffic.

1929 Grace Kelly, screen actress, was born in Philadelphia; starred in several films (*Country Girl, High Society*); married Prince Ranier of Monaco (1956) (died 1982).

1936 The San Francisco-Oakland Bridge opened.

1942 A three-day naval battle of Guadalcanal assured American success in land fighting on the island; Japanese lost two battleships, a cruiser, two destroyers, ten transports; Americans lost two cruisers, seven destroyers.

1942 The Kaiser Shipyards, which built 1460 ships during World War II, set a construction record with the ship *Robert E. Peary*, which was launched four and a half days after the keel was laid.

1980 An unmanned spacecraft, *Voyager I*, came within 77,000 miles of Saturn, transmitting valuable data back to earth.

1981 The first successful nonstop balloon crossing of the Pacific Ocean was completed; left Japan Nov 10; the four-man crew was composed of Ben Abruzzo, Larry Newman, Rocky Aoki, and Ron Clark.

1987 The Ethics Committee of the American Medical Association told the nation's doctors that they cannot refuse to treat people infected with the AIDS virus.

NOVEMBER 13

1644 Massachusetts Bay General Court banished all Baptists from the colony.

1775 Americans under Gen. Richard Montgomery occupied Montreal, which had been abandoned by the British; occupation lasted until June 15, 1776.

1807 Lt. Zebulon B. Pike sighted a peak in Colorado, which was later named for him.

1809 John A.B. Dahlgren, naval officer, was born in Philadelphia; developed naval ordnance, including an 11-inch (Dahlgren) gun; reorganized, equipped the naval ordnance yard in Washington (died 1870).

1813 Allen G. Thurman, legislator, was born in Lynchburg, Va.; represented Ohio in the House (1845-47) and Senate (1869-81); Democratic vice presidential candidate (1888) (died 1895).

1814 Joseph Hooker, Union general, was born in Hadley, Mass.; wounded at Antietam; commnander, Army of the Potomac (Jan-May 1863), relieved at his own request; served with Gens. George Thomas and William T. Sherman (died 1879).

1833 Edwin T. Booth, actor, was born near Bel Air, Md., son of Junius Brutus Booth (*see* 5/1/1796) and brother of John Wilkes Booth (*see* 4/14/1865); a foremost actor of his day, noted for his Hamlet (died 1893).

1834 Peter A.B. Widener, businessman and philanthropist, was born in Philadelphia; active in meat, street railway industries; left large art collection to Philadelphia; founder, Crippled Children's Training School (died 1915).

1838 Joseph Fielding Smith, religious leader, was born in Far West, Mo., nephew of Joseph Smith (12/23/1805); president, Mormon Church (1901-18), did much to strengthen church organizatin and to foster friendly relations with non-Mormons (died 1918).

1843 Mt. Rainier in Washington erupted.

1850 California voters ratified their constitution, which had been adopted a month earlier by a convention.

1853 John Drew, actor, was born in Dublin; starred in numerous plays with Maude Adams and Ada Rehan (died 1927).

1856 Louis D. Brandeis, attorney and jurist, was born in Louisville; special counsel for the people in numerous wage-hour cases; associate justice, Supreme Court (1916-34), first to use economic and sociological data to buttress legal arguments (died 1941).

1864 James Cannon Jr., prohibitionist, was born in Salisbury, Md.; a Methodist bishop (1918-44); a leader of Anti-Saloon League of America; active opponent of Alfred E. Smith's candidacy for president (1928) (died 1944).

1864 Arthur Fairbanks, educator, was born in Hanover, N.H.; director, Museum of Fine Arts, Boston (1907-25); fine arts professor, Dartmouth U. (1928-33) (died 1944).

1866 Abraham Flexner, medical educator, was born in Louisville, brother of Simon Flexner (3/25/1863); made major study of American medical education (1910), which became basis for modern American medical education; organizer, director, Institute for Advanced Study, Princeton (1930-39) (died 1959).

1872 Louis G. Hupp, automotive pioneer who with his brother produced the Hupmobile in the 1920s, was born. (died 1961).

1893 Edward A. Doisy, biochemist, was born in Hume, Ill.; shared 1943 Nobel Physiology/Medicine Prize for analysis of Vitamin K.

1898 Earl Sande, jockey, was born in Groton, S.D.; premier jockey of the 1920s; his mounts included Man O' War (died 1968).

1900 Samuel K. Allen, physicist who developed the first nuclear physics laboratory (U. of Chicago (1935-41), was born in Chicago; was part of a group which developed first successful chain reaction (died 1965).

1909 A fire in a Cherry, Ill. mine killed 259 miners.

1938 Francis Xavier (Mother) Cabrini was beatified; she later became the first American citizen proclaimed a Catholic saint.

1942 The draft age was lowered to 18, with deferments limited to war industries, agriculture, hardship cases, and the clergy.

1982 The Vietnam War Memorial was dedicated in Washington; two black granite walls listed the names of all 57,939 Americans who died in the war.

1986 President Reagan, on national television, acknowledged an 18-month "secret diplomatic initiative" involving the shipment of "small amounts of defensive weapons and spare parts" to Iran, but denied any trade of arms for hostages.

NOVEMBER 14

1765 Robert Fulton, inventor and engineer, was born in Lancaster County, Pa.; invented practical submarine (1800), with torpedoes (1805); developed steamboat *Clermont* (1807), which made New York to Albany round trip in 62 hours; invented machine for sawing marble, for spinning flax, for weaving hemp into rope (died 1815).

1784 Samuel Seabury (1729-1798) was consecrated by the non-juring Jacobite bishops of the Episcopal Church in Scotland as the first American Episcopal bishop; English bishops had refused his application.

1785 A convention of the State of Frankland (later Tennessee) met in Greenville and adopted its constitution; John Sevier was named governor.

1803 Jacob Abbott, educator and author, was born in Hallowell, Me.; founder, Mt. Vernon School for Girls, Boston (1829); successful writer of juvenile stories (28 volumes of *Rollo* books, 36 volumes of *Harper's Story* books) (died 1879).

1819 Christopher Rodgers, Union naval officer, was born in Brooklyn; headed South Atlantic blockading squadron (1862-63); superintendent, Naval

Academy (1874-78); commander-in-chief, Pacific Squadron (1878-80) (died 1892).

1820 Anson Burlingame, legislator and diplomat, was born in New Berlin, N.Y.; represented Massachusetts in the House (1855-61); minister to China (1861-67); responsible for treaty (1868) establishing reciprocal rights of citizens of both countries (died 1870).

1828 James B. McPherson, Union general, was born near Clyde, Ohio; chief engineer on Grant's staff; commanded Army of the Tennessee; killed by skirmishers near Atlanta 1864.

1850 Jesse W. Fewkes, ethnologist, was born in Newton, Mass.; worked with Hopi Indians, collecting thousands of artifacts and assuring preservation of Hopi pueblos, cliff dwellings; with Bureau of American Ethnology (1895-1928), chief (1918-28) (died 1930).

1861 Frederick J. Turner, historian, was born in Portage, Wis.; developed theory that American civilization was an outgrowth of political and environmental forces, that frontier had a large influence on development (*Rise of the New West, The Frontier in American History*) (died 1932).

1863 Leo H. Baekeland, chemist and inventor, was born in Ghent, Belgium; invented, manufactured photographic paper and synthetic resin named Bakelite, one of the first plastics with widespread application (died 1944).

1864 Gen. William T. Sherman set out with 60,000 men from Atlanta on his march to the sea, cutting a 60-mile swath along 300 miles, destroying virtually everything in his path.

1871 Ernest K. Coulter, lawyer and humanitarian, was born in Columbus, Ohio; an organizer, New York Children's Court (1902-12); founder of Big Brother movement (1900); general manager, Society for the Prevention of Cruelty to Children (1914-36) (died 1952).

1881 The trial of Charles Jules Guiteau, accused of assassinating President Garfield began in Washington; found guilty Nov 25.

1889 Nellie Bly, newspaper reporter, began her record-breaking, round-the-world trip; finished in 72 days, 6 hours, 11 minutes, 14 seconds.

1896 Mamie G. Doud Eisenhower, wife of President Eisenhower, was born in Boone, Ia. (died 1979).

1897 John Steuart Curry, painter, was born in Dunavant, Kan.; painted murals for Interior, Justice departments buildings, Kansas Capitol (died 1946).

1900 Aaron Copland, composer, was born in Brooklyn; composed several ballets (*Billy the Kid, Appalachian Spring*), movie scores (*Of Mice and Men, Our Town, The Red Pony, The Heiress*).

1904 Dick Powell, screen actor, was born in Mt. View, Ark.; starred in many musical films, television series (died 1963).

1908 Joseph R. McCarthy, legislator, was born in Grand Chute, Wis.; represented Wisconsin in the Senate (1947-57); his investigative methods gave rise to the term "McCarthyism;" censured by Senate (1954) (died 1957).

1930 Edward H. White II, astronaut, was born in San Antonio; the first astronaut to walk in space; killed with two others in capsule fire (1967).

1937 The Congress of Industrial Organizations (CIO) was established in Pittsburgh by delegates to the convention of the Committee for Industrial Organizations; John L. Lewis was named president.

1955 Daniel J. Tobin, union leader, died at 80; president of the Teamsters Union (1907-52).

1970 Seventy-five persons died as a plane carrying the Marshall University football team and staff crashed near Kenova, W.Va.

1988 The Transportation Department ordered a wide range of drug testing for more than four million transportation workers, including random testing; most transportation companies were ordered to have comprehensive testing programs in place by Dec 1989.

NOVEMBER 15

1637 The Massachusetts General Court ordered that Harvard College was "to bee at Newtowne" (later renamed Cambridge).

1753 George Washington and a small party left for Ft. LeBoeuf, about 12 miles south of Erie, Pa., to maintain friendly relations with the Indians of Six Nations, locate sites for forts, and carry a message to the French asking them to leave what was considered British territory; message delivered Dec 12 but the French refused to leave.

1777 Small American forces holding two New Jersey forts along the Hudson River (Mifflin and Mercer) evacuated the positions after three weeks of British shelling.

1777 The Continental Congress adopted the "Articles of Confederation and Perpetual Union" after a year of intermittent debates; states did not complete ratification until Mar 1, 1781.

1797 Thurlow Weed, journalist and political leader, was born in Greene County, N.Y.; political leader of New York; editor, *Albany Evening Journal* (1830-62) (died 1882).

1805 The Lewis and Clark Expedition reached the mouth of the Columbia River.

1807 Peter H. Burnett, public official, was born in Nashville; a California pioneer and its first governor (1849-51) (died 1895).

1807 James H. Hammond, legislator, was born in Newberry District, S.C.; served South Carolina as governor (1842-44) and represented it in the House (1835-36) and Senate (1857-60); remembered for his Mar 4, 1858 taunt of northern sympathizers—"You dare not make war on cotton . . . Cotton is king!" (died 1864).

1846 Tampico, Mexico was captured by American troops.

1854 The first Nebraska newspaper, the *Nebraska Palladium*, was published in Belleview by Thomas Morton.

1863 Four Union divisions under Gen. William T. Sherman arrived in Chattanooga.

1873 Sara Josephine Baker, pediatrician, was born in Poughkeepsie, N.Y.; organized, directed first government child hygiene bureau (1908-23), bringing New York City's child death rate to lowest of any large city (died 1945).

1880 Ralph C. Browne, inventor, was born in Salem, Mass.; invented electrical system, mechanism for North Sea mine barrage in World War I, a portble x-ray apparatus, an airlift mine pump (died 1960).

1881 Franklin P. Adams, columnist, was born in Chicago; known as FPA, he wrote *The Conning Tower* column (1922-41); regular panelist on Information Please radio program (died 1960).

1881 A conference of labor organizations began in Pittsburgh; ended with formation of the Federation of Organized Trades and Labor Unions of the United States and Canada; merged with American Federation of Labor (1896).

1882 Felix Frankfurter, jurist, was born in Vienna; Harvard law professor (1914-39); associate justice, Supreme Court (1939-62) (died 1965).

1887 Marianne C. Moore, poet, was born in St. Louis; several poetry collections (*What Are Years, Observations, Nevertheless*) (died 1972).

1887 Georgia O'Keeffe, painter, was born in Sun Prairie, Wis.; known especially for New Mexico desert scenes and symbolic abstractions (died 1986).

1891 W. Averell Harriman, public official, was born in New York City, son of Edward H. Harriman (2/25/1848); in family railroad, shipping businesses; Lend-Lease coordinator (1941-43); ambassador to Russia (1943-46), to Great Britain (1946); Secretary of Commerce (1946-48); governor of New York (1954-58); ambassador-at-large (1961, 1965-75) (died 1986).

1891 (W.) Vincent Astor, financier, was born in New York City, son of John Jacob Astor (7/13/1864); headed corporation publishing *Newsweek*; a social reformer (died 1959).

1892 James F. Stevens, author, was born in Albia, Ia.; wrote the *Paul Bunyan* stories (died 1971).

1896 The street lights in Buffalo were switched on by power from Niagara Falls, 20 miles away; the first long distance electric transmission.

1900 The Carnegie Institute of Technology was founded by Andrew Carnegie in Pittsburgh; opened 1905.

1906 Curtis E. LeMay, World War II general, was born in Columbus, Ohio; headed bomber groups in Europe, China; commander, Strategic Air Command (1957-61); chief of staff, Air Forces (1961-65).

1906 The United States brought suit in St. Louis against the Standard Oil Co. of New Jersey and 70 other corporations and partnerships, and seven persons, including John D. Rockefeller, under the Sherman Anti-Trust Act.

1929 Edward Asner, actor, was born in Kansas City, Mo.; starred on television in the *Mary Tyler Moore Show* and the *Lou Grant* series.

1935 Commonwealth of the Philippines inaugurated under the presidency of Manuel Quezon.

1969 About 250,000 persons took part in an anti-Vietnam demonstration march in Washington.

1987 A Continental DC-9 crashed on takeoff from the Denver airport killing 28 people aboard and injuring 54 persons.

NOVEMBER 16

1753 James McHenry, colonial leader, was born in County Antrim, Ireland; private secretary to Washington (1778-80), to Lafayette (1780-81); member, Continental Congress (1783-86), Constitutional Convention (1787); War Secretary (1796-1800); fort in Baltimore Harbor named for him (died 1816).

1764 Return J. Meigs, jurist and legislator, was born in Winchester, Ky.; served Ohio as its first chief justice (1803-04) and governor (1810-14), represented the state in the Senate (1808-10); Postmaster General (1814-23) (died 1824).

1776 British under Gen. William Howe captured Ft. Washington, N.Y., taking nearly 3000 prisoners.

1821 Emmons Hamlin, manufacturer, was born in Rome, N.Y.; with Henry Mason, developed, manufactured pianos, organs (died 1885).

1823 Henry G. Davis, businessman, was born in Baltimore; 1904 Democratic vice presidential candidate (died 1916).

1873 W(illiam) C. Handy, composer, was born in Florence Ala.; wrote down, published "blues" (St. Louis, Beale St., Memphis blues) (died 1958).

1876 The Alabama constitution was ratified by popular vote.

1889 George S. Kaufman, playwright, was born in Pittsburgh; co-author of numerous hits (*The Man Who Came to Dinner, You Can't Take it With You, Once in a Lifetime, Dulcy, Beggar on Horseback, Dinner at Eight*) (died 1961).

1896 Lawrence M. Tibbett, operatic baritone, was born in Bakersfield, Cal.; sang with Metropolitan Opera from 1923, appeared in several movies (died 1960).

1899 Mary Margaret McBride, popular radio commentator, was born in Paris, Mo.; conducted daytime radio talk show (1934-54) (died 1976).

1905 Eddie (Albert Edwin) Condon, guitarist and band leader, was born in Goodland, Ind.; a leading promoter of Dixieland music (died 1973).

1907 Oklahoma entered the Union as the 46th state.

1909 Burgess Meredith, actor, was born in Cleveland; starred on stage (*High Tor, Winterset*), screen (*Of Mice and Men, Advise and Consent*).

1914 The Federal Reserve System was inaugurated with the opening of 12 Federal Reserve banks.

1917 President Wilson issued a proclamation requiring the registration of enemy aliens, forbidding them in the District of Columbia, the Panama Canal Zone, and waterfront areas.

1933 The United States recognized Soviet Russia and established diplomatic relations.

1946 The Evangelical United Bretheran Church was organized by the union of the Evangelical Church and the Church of the United Brethren in Christ.

1982 The strike of National Football League players ended after eight weeks.

NOVEMBER 17

1734 Peter Zenger, editor of the *New York Weekly Journal* was arrested for criticizing the administration.

1764 The Indian war led by Chief Pontiac ended with their surrender on the Muskingum River in the Ohio Territory.

1788 Seth Boyden, inventor and manufacturer, was born in Foxborough, Mass.; developed a process for making patent leather (1819), malleable cast iron (1826), sheet iron, a hat-shaping machine; manufactured locomotives, steam and stationary engines (died 1870).

1790 Solyman Brown, Congregational clergyman and dentist, was born in Litchfield, Conn.; founder of American dentistry as an organized profession (died 1876).

1800 Congress convened in Washington for the first time.

1835 Frederick Leypoldt, publisher and bibliographer, was born in Stuttgart, Germany; editor, publisher, *Literary Bulletin* (1868-73), which became *Publishers Weekly* (1873); a founder, publisher, *Library Journal* (died 1884).

1863 A two-week siege of Knoxville, Tenn. was begun by Confederate troops; ended when Confederates retreated before approaching Union troops.

1865 William M. Burton, chemist and industrialist, was born in Cleveland; introduced process for getting gasoline by cracking petroleum (1913) (died 1954).

1877 Frank P. Lehm, aviation pioneer, was born in Mansfield, Ohio; first Army airship, balloon pilot; headed air service of 2nd Army (1918-19); organized, commanded, Air Corps Training Center (1926-30) (died 1963).

1878 Hans Zinsser, bacteriologist, was born in New York City; at Harvard Medical School, an expert in infectious diseases, helped develop immunization against some typhus fevers (died 1940).

1878 Grace Abbott, social worker, was born in Grand Island, Neb.; chief, Child Labor Division, Children's Bureau (1921-34); leading advocate of child labor laws (died 1939).

1881 Samuel Gompers led in the formation of the Federation of Organized Trades and Labor Unions, forerunner of American Federation of Labor.

1888 Donald M. Nelson, merchant and public official, was born in Hannibal, Mo.; with Sears Roebuck (1912-42); executive vice president (1939-42); chairman, War Production Board (1942-44) (died 1959).

1902 Eugene P. Wigner, physicist, was born in Budapest; shared 1963 Nobel Physics Prize for research on structure of atom and its nucleus; helped construct first atomic reactor (1942).

1904 Paul Cadmus, artist, was born in New York City; known for several popular works (*The Fleet's In, Greenwich Village Cafeteria, Coney Island*).

1904 Isamu Noguchi, sculptor and designer, was born in Los Angeles; among his best known works is "Kouros;" furniture designs (died 1989).

1904 William H. Hastie, first black federal judge (1937), was born in Knoxville, Tenn.; governor of Virgin Islands (1946-49) (died 1976).

1930 Robert B. Mathias, athlete and legislator, was born in Tulare, Cal.; Olympic decathlon champion (1948, 1952); represented California in the House (1967-75).

1934 Lyndon B. Johnson and Claudia Alta (Ladybird) Taylor were married in San Antonio.

1944 Tom (G. Thomas) Seaver, baseball pitcher who won more than 300 games (with several teams), was born in Fresno, Cal.

1982 Marie L. Garibaldi was sworn in as the first woman judge on the New York State Supreme Court.

NOVEMBER 18

1618 A charter of privileges, orders, and laws was granted Virginia settlers, giving them a voice in their own government.

1787 King's Chapel in Boston, the first Anglican church in New England, became the first American Unitarian church with the ordination of James Freeman, who had been refused Anglican ordination because of his revisions of the Book of Common Prayer.

1799 Joseph Dixon, inventor, was born in Marblehead, Mass.; pioneered in the industrial use of graphite (died 1869).

1801 John Butterfield, businessman, was born in Berne, N.Y.; owner of street car and express companies in Utica, N.Y.; merged with two other companies to form American Express Co. (1850); organized Wells, Fargo & Co. to carry overland mail west of St. Louis (1852) (died 1869).

1810 Asa Gray, botanist, was born in Sauquoit, N.Y.; foremost American botanist of mid-1800s; professor of natural history, Harvard (1842-73); a major early American supporter of Charles Darwin (died 1888).

1820 Nathaniel B. Palmer in the sloop *Hero* discovered the peninsula extending from the Antarctic continent; peninsula later named for him.

1824 Franz Sigel, Union general, was born in Sinsheim, Germany; saw action at Pea Ridge, the second Bull Run (died 1902).

1828 John A.J. Creswell, public official, was born in Port Deposit, Md.; as Postmaster General (1869-74), instituted great improvements in postal service (died 1891).

1834 Henry L. Higginson, banker, was born in New York City; founder (1881), Boston Symphony Orchestra, which he financed (1881-1918) (died 1919).

1841 Paul J. Pelz, architect, was born in Seitendorf, Germany; co-winner of design competition for Library of Congress (1873); designed buildings for Georgetown University of Virginia (died 1918).

1847 The revised constitution of New York was adopted and ratified.

1857 Rose M. Knox, manufacturer, was born in Mansfield, Ohio; co-founder of gelatin company (1890), president (1908-47) (died 1950).

1861 Josiah K. Lilly, pharmaceutical manufacturer, was born in Greencastle, Ind., son of Eli Lilly (4/1/1885); president, Eli Lilly & Co. (1898-1932), board chairman (1932-48) (died 1948).

1867 William J. Flynn, detective, was born in New York City; chief, U.S. Secret Service (1912-17); director, bureau of investigation, Justice Department (1919-21), a predecessor of the FBI (died 1928).

1870 Dorothy Dix, columnist, was born in Montgomery County, Tenn. as Elizabeth Gilmer; wrote popular advice-to-lovelorn column, beginning in New Orleans (1896), widely syndicated from 1901 (died 1951).

1874 The National Women's Temperance Union was organized in Cleveland, with Mrs. Anna Wittenmeyer of Philadelphia as president, Miss Frances E. Willard of Chicago, corresponding secretary.

1874 Clarence S. Day Jr., author, was born in New York City, grandson of Benjamin H. Day (4/10/1810); wrote several autobiographical books which formed the basis for the play, *Life With Father* (died 1935).

1880 Actress Sarah Bernhardt made her first American appearance at the Booth Theater in New York City.

1883 Four standard time zones were established by the railroads.

1886 Former President Arthur died in New York City at 57.

1886 Charles Edward Wilson, industrialist, was born in New York City; with General Electric (1899-1950), president (1940-42, 1944-50); vice chairman, War Production Board (1942-44) (died 1972).

1886 James S. Kemper, insurance executive, was born in Van Wert, Ohio; founder, Lumbermen's Mutual Casualty Co. (1912), Kemper Group (died 1980).

1889 Amelita Galli-Curci, coloratura soprano, was born in Milan, Italy; with the Metropolitan Opera from 1920 (died 1963).

1899 Eugene Ormandy, musician, was born in Budapest; concert violinist and conductor (Minneapolis Symphony 1931-36, Philadelphia, from 1936) (died 1985).

1901 The second Hay-Pauncefort Treaty between the United States and Great Britain was signed, recognizing the exclusive right of the United States to construct, regulate, and manage any isthmian canal; ratified Dec 16.

1901 George H. Gallup, pollster, was born in Jefferson, Ia.; founder, American Institute of Public Opinion (1935) to conduct polls (died 1984).

1903 United States concluded a treaty with Panama for the construction of a canal; provided for a lease of a ten-mile strip across the isthmus in perpetuity for $10 million and an annual fee of $250,000 beginning nine years after ratification; Senate ratified treaty Feb 23, 1904.

1906 George Wald, biologist, was born in New York City; noted for work on Vitamin A and the eye, for which he shared the 1967 Nobel Physiology/Medicine Prize.

1909 Johnny Mercer, lyricist, was born in Savannah; wrote many hit lyrics ("Blues in the Night," "Accentuate the Positive," "Laura," "Lazy Bones," "Autumn Leaves," "Moon River," "Days of Wine and Roses," "Satin Doll," "Black Magic") (died 1976).

1922 Stanley Cohen, researcher at Vanderbilt Medical School, was born in New York City; shared 1986 Nobel Physiology/Medicine Prize for discovery of key proteins that control body growth.

1923 Alan B. Shepard Jr., astronaut, was born in East Derry, N.H.; first American in space, suborbital flight (May 5, 1961); fifth man on moon (1971) and first to hit a lunar golf ball.

1942 Linda Evans, television actress (*Dynasty*), was born in Hartford, Conn.

1965 Henry A. Wallace, former Vice President (1941-45), died in Danbury, Conn. at 77.

1978 Rep. Leo J. Ryan of California and four other Americans were shot to death as they prepared to leave Guyana by members of the Peoples Temple; soon after more than 900 members of the Temple were murdered or committed suicide.

1987 The Iran-Contra House-Senate Committee in its final report stated that President Reagan bears the "ultimate responsibility" for the Iran-Contra affair because he allowed "a cabal of zealots" to seize control of policy and bypass the law. "The Iran initiative succeeded only in replacing three American hostages with another three, arming Iran with 2004 TOWs and more than 200 vital spare parts for Hawk missile batteries, improperly generating funds for the Contras and other covert actions . . . damaging relations between the executive and Congress and engulfing the president in one of the worst credibility crises of any administration in U.S. history."

NOVEMBER 19

1493 Puerto Rico was discovered by Christopher Columbus on his second voyage.

1752 George Rogers Clark, frontiersman, was born near Charlottesville, Va., brother of William Clark (8/1/1770); governor of Illinois Territory, which he conquered (1779-83) (died 1818).

1794 Jay's Treaty, a treaty of commerce, navigation, and amity was signed in London by Lord Grenville, British foreign minister, and John Jay, acting Secretary of State; resolved question of control of the northwest posts.

1811 John A. Winslow, Union naval officer, was born in Wilmington, N.C.; commanded the *Kearsage* when it destroyed the Confederate raider *Alabama* (1864) (died 1873).

1831 James A. Garfield, 20th president (1880-81), was born in Cuyahoga County, Ohio; represented Ohio in the House (1863-80); fatally wounded in a Washington railroad station July 2, 1881, died Sept 19.

1832 South Carolina legislature protested the 1828 and 1832 national tariffs.

1834 Franklin Pierce and Jane M. Appleton were married in Amherst, Mass.

1835 Fitzhugh Lee, one of ablest Confederate cavalry officers, was born in Fairfax County, Va., nephew of Robert E. Lee (1/19/1807); also commanded a corps in Spanish-American War (died 1905).

1850 Richard M. Johnson, former vice president (1837-41), died in Frankfort, Ky. at 70.

1862 Billy (William A.) Sunday, evangelist, was born in Ames, Ia.; professional baseball player (1883-90), became successful evangelist, revivalist (1896) (died 1935).

1863 President Lincoln delivered the immortal two-minute speech dedicating the Gettysburg, Pa. battlefield as a national cemetery; principal address by Edward Everett lasted two hours.

1875 Hiram Bingham, explorer who discovered Inca ruins, Machu Picchu, was born in Honolulu; served Connecticut as governor (1924-25) and in the Senate (1925-33) (died 1956).

1887 James B. Sumner, biochemist, was born in Canton, Mass.; shared 1946 Nobel Chemistry Prize for preparing enzymes, virus proteins in pure form (died 1955).

1899 Allen Tate, author, was born in Clarke County, Ky.; biographer (Robert E. Lee, Stonewall Jackson, Jefferson Davis); poet (*Ode to the Confederate Dead, Winter Sea*) (died 1979).

1905 Tommy Dorsey, musician, was born in Shenandoah, Pa., brother of Jimmy Dorsey (2/29/1904); trombonist and orchestra leader (died 1956).

1912 George E. Palade, biologist, was born in Jassy, Rumania; shared 1974 Nobel Physiology/Medicine Prize for contributions to understanding the inner workings of living cells.

1915 Earl W. Sutherland Jr., biochemist, was born in Burlingame, Kan.; shared 1971 Nobel Physiology/Medicine Prize for research on how hormones work (died 1974).

1919 The Senate rejected the Versailles Treaty and League of Nations after a debate which began July 10.

1919 Zion (Utah) National Park was established.

1921 Roy Campanella, baseball player, was born in Philadelphia; catcher with Brooklyn Dodgers (1948-57), career cut short by paralyzing auto accident; named to Baseball Hall of Fame.

1936 Dick Cavett, television talk show host and interviewer, was born in Gibbon, Neb.

1938 Ted (Robert E.) Turner, sportsman and television executive, was born in Cincinnati; owner, Atlanta baseball and basketball teams, cable broadcasting network; won America's Cup (1977) yacht races.

1942 Calvin Klein, fashion designer, was born in New York City.

1963 Former President Eisenhower rededicated the national cemetery at Gettysburg 100 years after its dedication by President Lincoln.

1974 President Ford conferred in Tokyo with the Japanese Prime Minister and the Emperor of Japan, the first incumbent president to visit Japan.

1979 Iran released 13 black and women hostages who were being held in the American Embassy.

1985 President Reagan and Soviet General Secretary Mikhail Gorbachev met in Geneva for five hours on this and the next day; no substantative agreements were reached.

1985 The largest civil judgment in American history ($10.53 billion) was assessed against Texaco Inc. by a state court jury in Houston; recipient of the judgment would be the Pennzoil Co.

NOVEMBER 20

1726 Oliver Wolcott, colonial leader, was born in Windsor, Conn., son of Roger Wolcott (1/4/1679); member, Continental Congress (1775-78, 1780-84), signer of Declaration of Independence; led Connecticut troops during Revolution; served state as lieutenant governor (1787-96), governor (1796-97) (died 1797).

1733 Philip J. Schuyler, colonial leader, was born in Albany; member, Continental Congress (1775, 1778-81); represented New York in the Senate (1789-91, 1797-98); a founder, Union College (died 1804).

1776 British under Lord Charles Cornwallis captured Ft. Lee, N.J. but Americans under Gen. Nathanael Greene escaped.

1776 Gen. Washington began a successful retreat across the Hudson to New Jersey.

1811 Construction began on the Cumberland Road, connecting Cumberland, Md. and Wheeling, W.Va.; road later was extended and became the main route for settlers of the West.

1817 The first Seminole War began; ended May 24, 1818 with capture of Pensacola, Fla.

1819 The first Arkansas newspaper, the *Arkansas Gazette*, was published in Arkansas Post by William E. Woodruff.

1837 Lewis E. Waterman, businessman, was born in Decatur, N.Y.; developed, manufactured an improved fountain pen (1884) (died 1901).

1855 Josiah Royce, philosopher, was born in Grass Valley, Cal.; most important American exponent of absolute idealism; author (*The Religious Aspect of Philosophy*) (died 1916).

1866 Kenesaw M. Landis, jurist, was born in Millsville, Ohio; U.S. district judge (1905-21); first baseball commissioner (1921-44); named to Baseball Hall of Fame (died 1944).

1867 Patrick J. Hayes, Catholic prelate, was born in New York City; archbishop of New York (1919-38); named cardinal (1924) (died 1938).

1869 Clark C. Griffith, baseball pitcher who won 240 games; manager (White Sox, Yankees); co-owner, president, Senators (1920-55); named to Baseball Hall of Fame (died 1955).

1873 William W. Coblentz, physicist, was born in North Lima, Ohio; pioneer in infra-red spectrophotometry; founder, radiometry section, National Bureau of Standards; a major figure in setting international radiation standards (died 1962).

1874 James M. Curley, public official, was born in Boston; served Boston as mayor 16 years between 1914 and 1950 and Massachusetts as governor (1934-36); represented state in the House (1911-14, 1942-46); was the model for the hero of *The Last Hurrah* (died 1958).

1878 Claude G. Bowers, author and diplomat, was born in Hamilton County, Ind.; historian (*Jefferson and Hamilton, The Tragic Era*); ambassador to Spain (1933-39), to Chile (1939-53) (died 1958).

1884 Norman M. Thomas, Socialist leader, was born in Marion, Ohio; a founder, American Civil Liberties Union (1920); presidential candidate five times of Socialist Party (1928-48) (died 1968).

1887 Earnest A. Hooton, anthropologist, was born in Clemansville, Wis.; laid foundation for American physical anthropology; author (*Up From the Ape, Why Men Behave Like Apes*) (died 1954).

1889 Edwin P. Hubble, astronomer, was born in Marshfield, Mo.; served at Mt. Wilson Observatory (1919-53), studied nebulae (died 1953).

1900 Chester Gould, cartoonist, was born in Pawnee, Okla.; creator of *Dick Tracy* (died 1985).

1909 U.S. Circuit Court of Appeals held Standard Oil Co. of New Jersey to be an illegal corporation and ordered its dissolution.

1917 American troops participated in an allied offensive which broke through the Hindenburg Line.

1925 Robert F. Kennedy, public official was born in Brookline, Mass., son of Joseph P. Kennedy (9/6/1888) and brother of President Kennedy; Attorney General (1961-64); represented New York in the Senate (1965-68); assassinated in Los Angeles while campaigning for the presidential nomination (1968).

1932 Richard Dawson, television personality, was born in Hampshire, England; played in *Hogan's Heroes*, master of ceremonies of *Family Feud*.

1945 President Truman appointed Gen. Dwight D. Eisenhower as Army chief of staff, Fleet Admiral Chester W. Nimitz as chief of naval operations.

1945 International War Crimes Tribunal began trial of 24 top Nazi leaders in Nuremberg; 18 were convicted.

1967 National Commission on Product Safety was created.

1968 An explosion and fire in a Mannington, W.Va. coal mine killed 78 miners.

1974 The Justice Department filed a civil anti-trust suit against American Telephone & Telegraph Co.

1988 Mother Katherine Drexel, a Philadelphia nun, was beatified by Pope John Paul II; born to wealth, she took a vow of poverty and founded (1891) the Sisters of the Blessed Sacrament for Indians and Colored People.

NOVEMBER 21

1620 Pilgrim leaders aboard the *Mayflower* anchored off what is now Provincetown, Mass., drafted a compact signed by 41 adults which set up "a civil body politic" to frame "just and equal laws;" named John Carver as governor.

1729 Josiah Bartlett, colonial leader, was born in Amesbury, Mass.; a signer of Declaration of Independence; New Hampshire Superior Court associate justice (1782-88), chief justice (1788-90); "president" of New Hampshire (1790-92) and its first governor (1793-94) (died 1795).

1785 William Beaumont, surgeon, was born in Lebanon, Conn.; studied digestive process by exhaustive experiments with a patient whose stomach was exposed by a gunshot wound; his study (1833) considered greatest contribution to knowledge of gastric digestion (died 1853).

1789 North Carolina's legislature ratified the Constitution by a vote of 194-77, making it the 12th state in the Union.

1806 Charles Merriam, publisher, was born in West Brookfield, Mass.; founder, head, G & C Merriam Co. (1832), publisher of textbooks, dictionaries (died 1887).

1812 Ft. Niagara, N.Y. was fired on by the British from Forts George and Newark.

1818 Lewis H. Morgan, anthropologist, was born near Aurora, N.Y.; studied American Indian culture, called the father of American anthropology (died 1881).

1834 Frederick Weyerhaeuser, lumberman, was born in Niedersaulheim, Germany; acquired vast timber holdings, called the "lumber king" (died 1914).

1835 Hetty (Henrietta H.) Green, financier, was born in New Bedford, Mass.; inherited fortune from father, Edward M. Robinson (1/8/1800); became feared Wall St. operator; reputed to be the richest American woman in early 1900s (died 1916).

1847 The *Phoenix* sank off Sheboygan, Wis., taking 148 lives, 127 of them immigrants arriving from the Netherlands.

1867 Vladimir N. Ipatieff, chemist, was born in Moscow; determined structure of isoprene, the basic rubber molecule; developed process for making low-grade gasoline into high octane (died 1952).

1883 William F. Lamb, architect, was born in Brooklyn; remembered for his work on the Empire State Building (died 1952).

1887 Thomas A. Edison announced the invention of the phonograph; exhibited the device on Nov 28.

1891 Edward Ellsberg, engineer and inventor, was born in New Haven; invented underwater torch for cutting steel, improved methods for dehydrating and dewaxing lubricating oil, and of cracking crude oil for the manufacture of anti-knock gasoline.

1899 Vice President Garrett A. Hobart died in Paterson, N.J. at 55.

1904 Coleman Hawkins, musician, was born in St. Joseph, Mo.; creator of tenor saxophone for jazz (died 1969).

1905 Freddie (Fred C.) Lindstrom, baseball player (Giants), was born in Chicago; named to Baseball Hall of Fame (died 1981).

1907 Jim Bishop, author, was born in Jersey City; best remembered for hour-by-hour accounts of notable events (*The Day Lincoln Was Shot, The Day Christ Died, The Day Kennedy Was Shot*) (died 1987).

1916 Sid Luckman, football player, was born in New York City; quarterback with Chicago Bears (1939-50), first T-formation quarterback.

1920 Stan(ley F.) Musial, baseball player (Cards 1941-63), was born in Donora, Pa.; batting champion seven times, Most Valuable Player three times; named to Baseball Hall of Fame.

1924 Florence K. Harding, widow of President Harding, died in Marion, Ohio at 64.

1942 The Alcan Highway to Alaska opened.

1943 Larry Mahan, an outstanding rodeo performer, was born in Brooke, Ore.; won World Champion All-Around Cowboy title (1966-71, 1973) and twice was bullriding world champion.

1964 The Verrazano Narrows Bridge over New York Harbor opened.

1979 A mob attacked the American Embassy in Islamabad, Pakistan killing four persons.

1980 A fire in the MGM Grand Hotel in Las Vegas killed 87 persons.

NOVEMBER 22

1643 Sieur de La Salle, explorer, was born in Rouen, France; traversed the Mississippi River, claiming the territory for France (died 1687).

1704 First independent assembly of Delaware met in New Castle, ceasing to be the "lower counties of Pennsylvania."

1744 Abigail Smith Adams, wife of President John Adams, was born in Weymouth, Mass.; a noted writer of letters, which were published posthumously (died 1818).

1754 Abraham Baldwin, legislator, was born in Guilford, Conn.; represented Georgia in Continental Congress (1789) and in House (1789-98) and Senate

(1799-1807); a founder, first president, U. of Georgia (1798) (died 1807).

1791 John W. Jones, legislator, was born near Amelia Court House, Va.; represented Virginia in the House (1835-45), serving as Speaker (1843-45) (died 1848).

1795 William Henry Harrison and Anna T. Symmes were married in North Bend, Ohio.

1800 Linn Boyd, legislator, was born in Nashville; represented Kentucky in the House (1835-37, 1839-55), serving as Speaker (1851-55); elected Kentucky lieutenant governor (1859), but died before taking office.

1819 Joseph Seligman, financier, was born in Baiersdorf, Germany; founder of international banking house; aided Union cause by marketing bonds abroad; member of Committee of 70 which exposed Tweed Ring (died 1880).

1837 Adelbert R. Buffington, inventor, was born in Wheeling, W.Va.; co-inventor of Buffington-Crozier disappearing gun carriage (died 1922).

1840 William Robinson, inventor, was born in County Tyrone, Ireland; invented system of automatic electric signaling, the basis for all modern automatic block signaling systems (died 1921).

1842 Mt. St. Helens in Washington erupted.

1847 Mexican government notified the United States it had appointed commissioners to negotiate peace.

1856 Heber J. Grant, church leader, was born in Salt Lake City; president of Mormon Church (1918-45) (died 1945).

1858 William Stanley, electrical engineer and inventor, was born in Brooklyn; invented transformer, two-phase motors, generators (died 1916).

1868 John Nance Garner, Vice President (1933-41), was born in Red River County, Tex.; represented Texas in the House (1903-33), Speaker (1931-33) (died 1967).

1875 Vice President Henry Wilson died in Washington at 63.

1898 Sarah G. Blanding, educator, was born in Lexington, Ky.; president, Vassar College (1946-64) (died 1984).

1899 Hoagy (Hoagland H.) Carmichael, pianist and composer, was born in Bloomington, Ind.; wrote several popular classics ("Stardust," "Rockin' Chair," "Georgia on My Mind," "Lazy River") (died 1981).

1900 Wiley Post, aviator, was born in Grand Saline, Tex.; twice flew around the world; plane crash in Alaska (1935) killed him and passenger, Will Rogers.

1902 David J. McDonald, president of Steelworkers Union (1952-65), was born in Pittsburgh (died 1979).

1917 The National Hockey League was formed.

1935 The *China Clipper* left Alameda, Cal. in first trans-Pacific airmail flight; arrived in Manila seven days later.

1943 President Franklin Roosevelt, Prime Minister Winston Churchill, and Chinese President Chiang Kai-shek met in Cairo to discuss war in Asia and the Pacific; meeting lasted four days.

1943 Billie Jean King, tennis player, was born in Long Beach, Cal.; won American, Wimbledon singles titles five times in 1960s, 1970s.

1950 A standing commuter train was struck by another train at Richmond Hill, N.Y., killing 79 persons.

1963 President Kennedy was shot and killed by a sniper in Dallas, Tex., Gov. John B. Connally was wounded; Lee Harvey Oswald was charged with the shooting; Vice President Lyndon B. Johnson was sworn in as president aboard Air Force One at Love Field, Dallas, by U.S. District Judge Sarah T. Hughes.

NOVEMBER 23

1726 Edward Bass, Episcopal prelate, was born in Dorchester, Mass.; rector at Newburyport, Mass. church (1752-97); first bishop of Massachusetts (1797-1803), at a time when the bishopric included Rhode Island and New Hampshire (died 1803).

1749 Edward Rutledge, colonial leader, was born in Charleston, S.C., brother of John Rutledge (*see* 7/1/1795); member of Continental Congress (1774-77) and a a signer of the Declaration of Independence; served South Carolina as governor (1798-1800) (died 1800).

1765 Twelve county judges of Frederick, Md. became the first American jurists to repudiate the British Stamp Act.

1804 Franklin Pierce, 14th president (1853-57), was born in Hillsboro, N.H.; represented New Hampshire in the House (1833-37) and Senate (1837-42) (died 1869).

1814 Vice President Elbridge Gerry died in Washington at 70.

1817 William C.C. Claiborne, frontier governor, died at 52; served as governor of Mississippi Territory (1801-03) and Territory of Orleans (1804-12); first governor of Louisiana (1812-16) and one of its senators (1817).

1818 James Vick, horticulturist, was born in Chichester, England; developed largest American mail order seed business; his experiments in cross-breeding, gardening exerted wide influence (died 1882).

1852 Vermont enacted a prohibition law.

1855 Frank F. Fletcher, World War I admiral, was born in Oskaloosa, Ia.; chief of the Atlantic Fleet; inventor of Fletcher breach mechanism and gun mounts (died 1928).

1859 Joseph A. Holmes, geologist, was born in Laurens, S.C.; with U.S. Geological Survey (1904-10); first director, U.S. Bureau of Mines (1910-15); popularized slogan "Safety first" (died 1915).

1859 Billy the Kid, outlaw, was born in New York City as William H. Bonney; most notorious outlaw of the American Southwest (died 1881).

1863 Three-day Battle of Missionary Ridge (or Lookout Mountain), near Chattanooga, began; the Union victory led by Gen. U.S. Grant made possible the drive through Georgia to the sea and division of the south; Confederate losses were 8684, Union about 6000.

1878 Ernest J. King, World War II admiral, was born in Lorain, Ohio; headed combined American fleet; chief of naval operations (1942-45), principal architect of Allied victory at sea (died 1956).

1887 Boris Karloff, actor, was born in London; starred in various monster screen roles, also as villainous brother in *Arsenic and Old Lace* (died 1969).

1889 Alexander M. Patch, World War II general, was born in Ft. Huachuca, Ariz.; commanded 7th Army in invasion of southern France (died 1945).

1927 Otis Chandler, newspaper publisher, was born in Los Angeles, grandson of Harry Chandler (5/17/1864); publisher (*Los Angeles Times* (1960-).

1928 Jerry (Jerold L.) Bock, composer, was born in New Haven; composer of several musicals (*Fiorello, Fiddler on the Roof*).

1942 SPARS (Semper Paratus Service), the women's branch of the Coast Guard, was created.

1945 Food rationing, except sugar, was ended.

1963 A fire in the Golden Age Nursing Home in Fitchville, Ohio killed 63 persons.

1974 President Ford and Soviet leader Leonid Brezhnev conferred in Vladivostok on offensive nuclear weapons.

NOVEMBER 24

1713 Juniperro Serra, Franciscan missionary, was born in Mallorca, Spain; set up first European settlement in San Diego (1769), called the apostle of California (died 1784).

1726 Pelatiah Webster, publicist, was born in Lebanon, Conn.; wrote the first proposal (1783) for a United States— "A Dissertation on the Political Union of the Thirteen United States of North America" (died 1795).

1784 Zachary Taylor, 12th president (1849-50), was born in Orange County, Va.; commanded the Army of the Rio Grande in the Mexican War; captured Monterey, defeated Santa Anna at Buena Vista (1846), ending the war (died 1850).

1807 Joseph Brant, Mohawk Indian chief, died at 65; commanded Indian forces cooperating with the British during the Revolution; responsible for Cherry Valley massacre (1778), ravaged Mohawk Valley; settled in Canada after the war.

1818 David H. Agnew, surgeon and educator, was born in Lancaster County, Pa.; a brilliant medical lecturer and surgeon, U. of Pennsylvania (1870-89); subject of Thomas Eakins' painting, *The Agnew Clinic*; chief medical consultant when President Garfield was mortally wounded (1881) (died 1892).

1832 A South Carolina convention passed an ordinance to nullify the federal tariff act, which placed duties on foreign imports; called for refusal to make payments after Feb 1, 1833; legislature ratified act three days later.

1841 Richard Croker, political boss, was born in County Cork, Ireland; with Tammany Hall from 1862; headed New York City politics (1886-1902); moved to Ireland to live (1903) (died 1922).

1844 Charles V. Gridley, Spanish-American War admiral, was born in Logansport, Ind.; immortalized in famous command by Adm. George Dewey—"You may fire when ready, Gridley!" (died 1898).

1849 Frances H. Burnett, author, was born in Manchester, England; wrote children's books (*Little Lord Fauntleroy*) (died 1924).

1853 Bat (William B.) Masterson, frontier sheriff, was born in Iroquois County, Ill.; sheriff in Ford County, Kan., assisted Wyatt Earp in Tombstone, Ariz.

(1880-1902); sports writer, *New York Morning Telegraph* (1902-21) (died 1921).

1859 Cass Gilbert, architect, was born in Zanesville, Ohio; designed Minnesota Capitol, St. Louis Library; Woolworth Building, New York City; Supreme Court (died 1934).

1868 Scott Joplin, musician, was born in Texarkana, Tex.; ragtime pianist, composer ("Maple Leaf Rag," the opera *Tremonisha*) (died 1917).

1869 National woman's suffrage convention was held in Cleveland; organized Woman's Suffrage Association.

1871 National Rifle Association was organized in New York City.

1876 Hideyo Noguchi, bacteriologist, was born in Inawashiron, Japan; made significant findings in etiology of syphillis, paresis, and other diseases (died 1928).

1876 Walter B. Griffin, architect, was born in Maywood, Ill.; won international design competition for Canberra, Australia; supervised construction (1913-21) (died 1937).

1877 Alben W. Barkley, Vice President (1949-53), was born in Graves County, Ky.; represented Kentucky in the House (1913-27) and Senate (1927-49, 1955-56) (died 1956).

1888 Dale Carnegie, public speaking teacher, was born in Maryville, Mo.; set up Institute for Effective Speaking & Human Relations; author (*How to Win Friends and Influence People*) (died 1955).

1890 George E. Stratemeyer, Air Forces general, was born in Cincinnati; held various commands, including China-Burma-India (1943-45) (died 1969).

1911 Joe (Joseph M.) Medwick, baseball player (Cardinals), was born in Carteret, N.J.; had lifetime batting average of .324; named to Baseball Hall of Fame (died 1975).

1912 Garson Kanin, author, was born in Rochester, N.Y.; playwright (*Born Yesterday*); screen director (*Diary of Anne Frank, Funny Girl*).

1922 Colorado River compact was signed by representatives of seven states to control use of river water.

1925 William F. Buckley Jr., editor and author, was born in New York City; founder, editor, *National Review* (1955-); columnist, author (*God and Man at Yale, Serving the Queen, Stained Glass*).

1926 Tsung-Dao Lee, physicist, was born in Shanghai; with Columbia U. (1953-); shared 1957 Nobel Physics Prize for work concerning the parity laws of physics.

1938 Oscar Robertson, basketball player, was born in Charlotte, Tenn.; starred with Cincinnati U. (1958-60), Cincinnati professional team (1960-70) and Milwaukee (1970-74).

1942 Marlin Fitzwater, White House press spokesman (1987-89) and nominated by President-elect Bush to be press secretary, was born in Salina, Kan.

1963 Lee Harvey Oswald, accused assassin of President Kennedy, was shot and killed in the Dallas city jail by Jack Ruby, a Dallas nightclub owner; Ruby was sentenced to death Mar 14, 1964 but a new trial was ordered after appeal; Ruby died before the new trial in 1967.

1987 The United States and Soviet Russia resolved their remaining differences over a new treaty banning medium and shorter-range missiles; the U.S. will dismantle 364 cruise and *Pershing 2* missiles deployed in Europe and the Soviet Union will dismantle 553 *SS-20* and *SS-4* missiles over a three-year period.

1988 President Reagan announced he would veto a comprehensive ethics bill because it was "flawed, excessive and discriminatory;" had passed the House 347-7 and by a voice vote in the Senate.

NOVEMBER 25

1757 Henry B. Livingston, jurist, was born in New York City; son of William Livingston (11/30/1723); associate justice, Supreme Court (1806-23) (died 1823).

1758 John Forbes led British troops to victory over the French at Ft. Duquesne, later renamed Pittsburgh.

1758 John Armstrong, legislator and public official, was born in Carlisle, Pa.; represented New York in the Senate (1800-02, 1803-04); minster to France (1804-10); Secretary of War (1813-14), held largely responsible for failures in War of 1812 (died 1843).

1783 The last of the British troops left New York City.

1816 Lewis M. Rutherford, astrophysicist, was born in Morrisania, N.Y.; made first telescopes designed for celestial photography (died 1892).

1817 John Bigelow, diplomat, was born in Malden, N.Y.; co-editor, co-owner, *New York Post* (1848-61); consul general in Paris, then minister to France (1861-66); whild there, he discovered original manuscript of Benjamin Franklin's autobiography (died 1911).

1835 Andrew Carnegie, steel industry leader and philanthropist, was born in Dunfermline, Scotland; chief owner, Homestead Steel Works (1888), controlled seven other companies, then consolidated them into Carnegie Steel Co. (1899); merged with U.S. Steel (1901) and retired; devoted rest of life to distributing wealth to libraries, education, international pece (died 1919).

1835 Arthur Sewall, shipbuilder and banker, was born in Bath, Me.; built full-rigged ships, steel sailing vessels; Democratic vice presidential nominee (1896) (died 1900).

1846 Carry A. Nation, temperance leader, was born in Garrard County, Ky.; maintained that since Kansas was a prohibition state, any citizen could destroy anything in a place selling intoxicants; armed with a hatchet (an imposing figure at six feet and 175 pounds), she went on wrecking sprees (died 1911).

1862 Ethelbert W. Nevin, composer, was born in Edgeworth, Pa.; known for *The Rosary* and *Mighty Lak a Rose* (died 1901).

1855 Paul Starrett, builder, was born in Lawrence, Kan.; with two brothers, founded Starrett Bros. Inc., construction firm which built the Flatiron and Empire State buildings in New York City (died 1957).

1867 Senate Judiciary Committee resolved that President Andrew Johnson "be impeached for high crimes and misdemeanors."

1869 Ben(jamin B.) Lindsey, jurist, was born in Jackson, Tenn.; set up, headed, first American juvenile court (Denver 1900-27); created new conciliation court (Los Angeles 1939); advocated family court, companionate marriages (died 1943).

1874 Joe Gans, boxing champion, was born in Baltimore; considered greatest lightweight boxer, champion (1902-08) (died 1910).

1885 Vice President Thomas A. Hendricks died in Indianapolis at 66.

1893 Joseph Wood Krutch, editor and essayist, was born in Knoxville, Tenn.; editor, *The Nation* (1924-52); professor, Columbia U. (1936-52) (died 1970).

1896 Virgil G. Thomson, composer and critic, was born in Kansas City, Mo.; music critic, *New York Herald Tribune* (1940-54); composer of scores for film documentaries (*The Plow That Broke the Plains, The River, Louisiana Story*).

1899 William R. Burnett, author, was born in Springfield, Ohio; novelist (*Little Caesar, The Asphalt Jungle*) (died 1982).

1913 Jessie W. Wilson, daughter of President and Mrs. Wilson, was married in the White House to Francis B. Sayre.

1914 Joe (Joseph P.) DiMaggio, baseball player, was born in Martinez, Cal.; with Yankees (1936-51), set record of hitting safely in 56 consecutive games; named to Baseball Hall of Fame.

1915 Ku Klux Klan was revived by William J. Simmons of Atlanta.

1926 The National Broadcasting Co. went on the air with 24 radio stations.

1939 Martin Feldstein, economist, was born in New York City; chairman, Council of Economic Advisors (1981-84); with Harvard U. (1967-).

1950 Eighteen Communist Chinese divisions launched a surprise attack on Korea.

1957 President Eisenhower suffered a stroke; made a speedy recovery, returning to duty on Dec 9.

1986 President Reagan announced the resignation of National Security Advisor John M. Poindexter and the dismissal of his aide, Lt. Col. Oliver North; it was announced that an inquiry disclosed that some proceeds of arms sales to Iran had gone into a Swiss bank account to finance military aid to the Nicaraguan Contras.

NOVEMBER 26

1727 Artemas Ward, Revolutionary general, was born in Shrewsbury, Mass.; assumed command of colonial troops after Lexington and directed siege of Boston until Gen. Washington arrived; member, Continental Congress (1780-81) and represented Massachusetts in the House (1791-95) (died 1800).

1783 The Continental Congress began holding its sessions in the Maryland State House in Annapolis; continued until June 3, 1784.

1789 Thanksgiving celebrated as national holiday for first time.

1791 The first cabinet meeting was held as President Washington met with the secretaries of war, state, and treasury, and the attorney general.

1792 Sarah Moore Grimké, social reformer, was born in Charleston, S.C.; with her sister, Angelina E. Grimké (2/20/1805), became Quakers and took an active role in abolitionist and women's rights movements (died 1873).

1807 Oliver Ellsworth, former Supreme Court chief justice (1796-99), died in Windsor, Conn. at 62.

1807 William S. Mount, artist, was born in Setauket, N.Y.; first native-born painter to make a career of genre painting (scenes of common every-day life) (died 1868).

1828 William H. Sylvis, labor leader, was born in Indiana County, Pa.; a founder, president, National Labor Union (1868-69) (died 1869).

1832 Mary E. Walker, physician and women's rights activist, was born in Oswego, N.Y.; served as a nurse with the Union Army (1861-64); wore men's clothes to attract attention to women's rights (died 1919).

1857 Edward C. Potter, sculptor, was born in New London, Conn.; best known for animals; especially the lions at entrance to New York Public Library (died 1923).

1861 A convention in Wheeling adopted the West Virginia state constitution.

1866 Hugh Duffy, baseball player, was born in Cranston, R.I.; outfielder with Chicago, Boston National League teams (1890-1901); player-manager, Philadelphia Phillies (1904-06); named to Baseball Hall of Fame (died 1954).

1876 Willis H. Carrier, inventor and manufacturer, was born in Angola, N.Y.; founder, president, Carrier Corp. (1915-31), board chairman (1931-43) (died 1950).

1883 President Arthur attended the unveiling of the statue of Washington on the steps of the Sub-Treasury Building in New York City.

1894 Norbert Wiener, mathematician, was born in Columbia, Mo.; taught mathematics at MIT for 42 years, developed science of cybernetics, on which much modern automation is based (died 1964).

1895 William G. Wilson, reformer, was born in East Dorset, Vt.; co-founder of Alcoholics Anonymous, a self-help organization (1935); with wife, Lois, founded Al-Anon for spouses of alcoholics, Alateen for chidren (died 1971).

1909 Lefty (Vernon) Gomez, baseball player, was born in Rodeo, Cal.; pitched for New York Yankees (1930-42), won 189, lost 102; named to Baseball Hall of Fame (died 1989).

1912 Eric Sevareid, journalist and commentator, was born in Velva, N.D.; newspaper, television reporter.

1922 Charles M. Schulz, cartoonist, was born in Minneapolis; creator of syndicated cartoon, *Peanuts* (1950).

1924 George Segal, sculptor, was born in New York City; known for life-size tableaux.

1975 President Ford announced that the federal government would help New York City meet its financial obligations and avoid defaulting on its loans.

NOVEMBER 27

1703 James DeLancey, colonial jurist, was born in New York City; chief justice, New York Supreme Court (1733-60), heard Peter Zenger case (died 1760).

1746 Robert R. Livingston, colonial leader and legislator, was born in New York City; member, Continental Congress (1775-78, 1779-81, 1784-85); administered oath of office to President Washington as New York State Chancellor (1777-1801); first American secretary of foreign affairs (1781-83); minister to France (1801-04); aided Robert Fulton in building steamboat (died 1813).

1806 President Jefferson issued a proclamation warning citizens of the Aaron Burr conspiracy to set up a separate nation west of the Alleghenies.

1843 Cornelius Vanderbilt, businessman and philanthropist, was born in Staten Island, N.Y., son of William H. Vanderbilt (5/8/1821); headed various railroad companies; bequeathed $1.5 million to Yale, with brothers endowed Vanderbilt Clinic at Columbia U. (died 1899).

1848 Henry A. Rowland, physicist, was born in Honesdale, Pa.; first physics professor, Johns Hopkins U. (1875-1901); invented concave grating for spectroscope, determined mechanical equivalent of heat (died 1901).

1857 Alfred Cumming was named Utah governor by President Buchanan, who proclaimed the territory in rebellion.

1857 S. Adolphus Knopf, physician, was born in Halle, Germany; specialist in treating tuberculosis; founder, New York City, national tuberculosis associations (died 1940).

1870 Joseph S. Mack, truck manufacturer, was born in Mt. Cobb, Pa.; with brothers, founded a wagon company (1889), built first successful gas-powered truck, bus (1900) (died 1953).

1874 Charles A. Beard, historian, was born in Knightstown, Ind.; professor of history, politics, at Columbia U.; noted for economic interpretation of American institutional development; a founder, New School for Social Research; with wife, Mary, wrote *The Rise of American Civilization* (died 1948).

1881 Thomas I. Parkinson, president, Equitable Life Assurance Society (1927-53), was born in Philadelphia (died 1959).

1893 Richard K. Sutherland, World War II officer, was born in Hancock, Md.; chief of staff, Philippine military missions (1938-41), American Far East forces (1941-45) (died 1966).

1901 The Army War College was established in Washington as an officers' postgraduate school; Gen. Tasker H. Bliss was named president.

1901 Ted (Edward B.) Hùsing, pioneer radio announcer of 1920s, was born in New York City (died 1962).

1903 Lars Onsager, physical chemist, was born in Oslo, Norway; awarded 1968 Nobel Chemistry Prize for development of equations in thermodynamics (died 1976).

1909 James Agee, critic and author, was born in Knoxville, Tenn.; screenwriter (*The Quiet One, The African Queen, Mr. Lincoln*); author (*A Death in the Family*) (died 1955).

1912 David Merrick, theatrical producer, was born in New York City; produced many hits (*Fanny; Gypsy; Becket; Carnival; Oliver; Hello, Dolly; I Do, I Do; Promises, Promises*).

1917 Bob Smith, entertainer, was born in Buffalo; created, starred in *Howdy Doody*, popular children's show.

1963 President Lyndon Johnson, in an address to the Congress, pledged to continue the late President Kennedy's policies and urged action on civil rights and tax cuts.

NOVEMBER 28

1773 The first ships carrying tea arrived in Boston Harbor.

1777 John Adams was named commissioner to France.

1777 British troops occupied Rhode Island.

1792 Nathan Lord, Congregational clergyman and educator, was born in South Berwick, Me.; president, Dartmouth College (1828-63) (died 1870).

1795 The United States bought peace from Algiers and Tunis by paying $800,000, supplying a frigate, and paying an annual tribute of $25,000.

1831 John W. Mackay, miner and financier, was born in Dublin; began as miner, then gained control of richest part of Comstock lode; co-founder, Commercial Cable Co. (1883), which laid two submarine cables to Europe; founder, Postal Telegraph Cable Co. (1886), in unsuccessful effort to break Western Union monopoly (died 1902).

1837 John W. Hyatt, inventor, was born in Starkey, N.Y.; discovered fundamental principles in making celluloid, a process for solidifying hard woods, a water filter and purifier (died 1920).

1857 Benjamin K. Rachford, physician, was born in Alexandria, Ky.; conducted important research in digestion; started Babies Milk Fund in Cincinnati (1909) (died 1929).

1866 David Warfield, actor, was born in San Francisco; a star in the early 1900s (*The Auctioneer, Music Master*) (died 1951).

1866 Henry Bacon, architect, was born in Watseka, Ill.; involved in various memorials to famous Americans, best known for the Lincoln Memorial in Washington (died 1924).

1866 John Barrett, diplomat, was born in Grafton, Vt.; served in several Latin American countries; director-general, Pan American Union (1907-20) (died 1938).

1868 Robert S. Abbott, newspaper editor and publisher, was born on St. Simons Island, Ga.; founder, editor, publisher, *Chicago Defender* (died 1940).

1873 Frank Phillips, oil industry executive, was born in Scotia, Neb.; co-founder, Phillips Petroleum (1917), president (1917-47) (died 1950).

1894 Brooks Atkinson, journalist, was born in Melrose, Mass.; with *New York Times* 31 years as drama critic, war correspondent during World War II (died 1984).

1895 Jose Iturbi, concert pianist and conductor, was born in Valencia, Spain; conductor for several musicals, films (died 1980).

1895 The first automobile race was held in Chicago, with J. Frank Duryea winning the 54-mile race driving at 7-1/2 miles an hour.

1903 J. Howard McGrath, public official and legislator, was born in Woonsocket, R.I.; Attorney General (1949-52); served Rhode Island as governor (1940-45) and represented it in the Senate (1945-49) (died 1966).

1908 Explosion, cave-in at Marianna Mine, Monongahela, Pa. killed more than 100 persons.

1909 Rose Bampton, operatic soprano, was born in Cleveland; made debut with Metropolitan Opera in 1932.

1919 American-born Lady Nancy Astor was elected to the House of Commons from Plymouth, the first woman ever elected to Parliament.

1942 Coffee rationing began.

1942 A Boston nightclub, Cocoanut Grove, burned, killing 498 persons.

1943 The Teheran Conference between President Franklin Roosevelt, Prime Minister Winston Churchill, and Premier Joseph Stalin began, ending four days later with agreement for the invasion of France.

1964 *Mariner 4*, an unmanned satellite, photographed the surface of Mars and studied the Martian atmosphere.

1982 The space shuttle, with a crew of six, including western European scientists for the first time, took off from Cape Canaveral; made numerous scientific experiments; landed at Edwards Air Force Base, Cal. Dec 8.

NOVEMBER 29

1727 Ezra Stiles, Congregational clergyman and educator, was born in North Haven, Conn.; pastor, Second Congregational Church, New Haven (1755-76); president, Yale (1778-95), considered most learned man of his time in New England (died 1795).

1729 Charles Thomson, colonial leader, was born in County Derry, Ireland; leader of Philadelphia business opposition to British policies; called the Sam Adams of Philadelphia, secretary of Continental Congress (1774-89) (died 1824).

1760 The French surrendered Detroit to English troops under Maj. Robert Rogers.

1773 The New York Sons of Liberty adopted resolutions against the tax on tea and the exclusive right of the East India Co.; warned that anyone selling, buying, or transporting such tea "shall be deemed an enemy to the liberties of America."

1802 A convention in Chillicothe ratified the Ohio constitution, which included a clause prohibiting slavery.

1811 Wendell Phillips, reformer, was born in Boston; an abolitionist; president, Anti-Slavery Society (1865-70); later advocated other causes (penal reform, prohibition, woman suffrage) (died 1884).

1816 Morrison R. Waite, jurist, was born in Lyme, Conn.; chief justice, Supreme Court (1874-88) (died 1888).

1832 Louisa May Alcott, author, was born in Germantown, Pa.; best remembered for *Little Women* (died 1888).

1864 The Sand Creek massacre occurred in Kiowa County, Colo., when more than 100 Indians were killed by American cavalrymen led by Col. John M. Chivington.

1876 Joseph E. Davies, diplomat, was born in Watertown, Wis.; U.S. commissioner of corporations (1913-15); chairman, Federal Trade Commission (1915-16), vice chairman (1916-18); ambassador to Russia (1936-38); author (*Mission to Moscow*) (died 1958).

1890 First Army-Navy game played at West Point; Navy won 20-0.

1895 Busby Berkeley, choreographer, was born in Los Angeles; staged large scale, spectacular dances for stage, numerous films (died 1976).

1908 Adam Clayton Powell Jr., legislator, was born in New Haven; pastor, Abyssinian Baptist Church, Harlem (1936-71); first black city councilman, New York (1941-44); represented New York in the House (1945-67, 1969-71) (died 1972).

1923 Frank Reynolds, television newsman, was born in East Chicago, Ind.; with ABC (1963-83); anchor of evening news (1978-82) (died 1983).

1929 Richard E. Byrd, with Bernt Balchen as pilot, became the first to fly over the South Pole.

1950 National Council of Churches was formed by 29 major American Protestant, four Eastern Orthodox churches.

1963 President Lyndon Johnson named an investigating commission into assassination of President Kennedy; Supreme Court Chief Justice Earl Warren chairman.

1988 George Mitchell, senator from Maine (1984-), was elected Senate Majority Leader to succeed Sen. Robert Byrd of W.Va.

NOVEMBER 30

1723 William Livingston, legislator and public official, was born in Albany, brother of Philip Livingston (1/15/1716); member, Continental Congress (1774-76) and delegate to Constitutional Convention (1787); first governor of New Jersey (1776-90) (died 1790).

1725 Martin Boehm, religious leader, was born in Lancaster County, Pa.; co-founder, United Brethren

Church; consecrated bishop of Mennonite Church (1759) but excluded from Mennonite communion because of his liberal views; joined with Philip William Otterbein and others to form UB Church (1789) (died 1812).

1729 Samuel Seabury, Episcopal prelate, was born in Groton, Conn.; consecrated as first American Episcopal bishop (Conn. 1784) (died 1796).

1782 The provisional treaty of peace was signed by the American colonies and Great Britain in Paris.

1810 Oliver F. Winchester, firearms manufacturer, was born in Boston; developed Winchester rifle (c 1866) (died 1880).

1819 Cyrus W. Field, businessman, was born in Stockbridge, Mass.; amassed fortune in paper business; built, promoted first American submarine transatlantic cable, which worked briefly (1858), then achieved success (1866) (died 1892).

1829 The first Welland Canal, connecting Lakes Erie and Ontario, was opened.

1835 Mark Twain, author, was born in Florida, Mo. as Samuel M. Clemens; wrote many classics (*Tom Sawyer, Huckleberry Finn, The Innocents Abroad, A Connecticut Yankee in King Arthur's Court, Life on the Mississippi*) (died 1910).

1858 Charles A. Coolidge, architect, was born in Boston; among his designs were the Harvard Medical School, Chicago Public Library and Art Institute , Rockefeller Institute in New York City (died 1936).

1864 Union troops under Gen. George H. Thomas turned back Confederate troops under Gen. John Hood at Franklin, Tenn.; Confederate Gen. Patrick R. Cleburne was killed.

1869 Mississippi ratified its new constitution, which had been rejected in 1868.

1869 Texas voters ratified their new constitution.

1908 The Root-Takahira agreement was reached in an exchange of notes between Secretary of State Elihu Root and Japanese Ambassador Takahira; called for Japanese confirmation of the Open Door policy in China.

1911 Standard Oil Co. of New Jersey went out of existence as each subsidiary company assumed control of its own affairs in keeping with court-ordered dissolution.

1915 Henry Taube, chemist, was born in Saskatchewan, Canada; became America's foremost inorganic chemist; awarded 1983 Nobel Chemistry Prize for "work in the mechanism of electron transfer reactions, especially in metal complexes."

1915 An explosion at a Dupont plant near Wilmington, Del. killed 31 persons; believed to have been caused by sabotage.

1917 The Rainbow Division, representing every state, arrived in France.

1924 Shirley A. Chisholm, legislator, was born in Brooklyn; first black woman popularly elected to Congress; represented New York in the House (1969-82).

1926 Andrew V. Schally, medical researcher, was born in Wilno, Poland; shared 1977 Nobel Physiology/Medicine Prize for research in the role of hormones in the chemistry of the body.

1929 Dick Clark, television personality and producer, was born in Mt. Vernon, N.Y.

1942 First war loan drive began, resulting in the sale of nearly $13 billion in bonds between Nov 30 and Dec 23.

1957 Floyd Patterson knocked out Archie Moore in the fifth round in Chicago to become world heavyweight boxing champion.

1984 The basis for merger of nine Protestant denominations was reached by the Consultation of Church Union after 22 years of effort; the denominations are: African Methodist Episcopal, African Methodist Episcopal Zion, Disciples of Christ, Christian Methodist, Episcopal, International Council of Community Churches, Presbyterian, United Methodist, and United Church of Christ.

DECEMBER 1

1741 Samuel Kirkland, missionary, was born in Norwich, Conn.; worked with Iroquois, instrumental in keeping Six Nations neutral during Revolution; founded Hamilton Oneida Academy (1793), which became Hamilton College (1812) (died 1808).

1763 Patrick Henry, arguing Parson's Cause case, challenged the authority of the Crown to disallow colonial statutes.

1777 Baron Friedrich von Steuben, a Prussian military officer, arrived in Portsmouth, N.H., offered his services to the American Army.

1810 The Census reported the American population to be 7,239,881 and the center of population was 40 miles northwest of Washington.

1814 Gen. Andrew Jackson and his troops arrived in New Orleans to defend it against the British.

1824 The Electoral College met to cast its presidential votes with the following result: Andrew Jackson 99, John Quincy Adams 84, William H. Crawford 41, Henry Clay 37; no candidates having received a majority of the 261 electoral votes from the 24 states, the election was sent to the House of Representatives, which elected Adams president, John C. Calhoun vice president.

1826 William Mahone, Confederate general, was born in Southampton County, Va.; saw action at Malvern Hill, the second Bull Run; represented Virginia in the Senate (1881-87) (died 1895).

1834 President Jackson in his annual message to Congress reported that the national debt had been eliminated.

1845 President Polk in his message to Congress claimed Oregon for the United States.

1850 The Seventh Census reported a rise of 36% in the United States population to 23,191,876.

1872 Gerard Swope, industrialist, was born in St. Louis, brother of Herbert B. Swope (*see* 1/5/1882); first president, International General Electric (1919); president, General Electric (1922-40, 1942-44) (died 1957).

1879 Lane Bryant, merchant, was born in Lithuania as Lena Himmelstein; pioneered in merchandising maternity and stout women's ready-made clothes; founded chain bearing her name.

1886 Jefferson Caffery, diplomat, was born in Lafayette, La.; ambassador to Cuba (1934-37), to Brazil (1937-44), to France (1944-49), to Egypt (1949-55) (died 1974).

1886 Rex Stout, author, was born in Noblesville, Ind.; wrote Nero Wolfe mysteries (died 1975).

1896 Ray Henderson, composer, was born in Buffalo; wrote many hits ("That Old Gang of Mine," "Alabamy Bound," "Bye, Bye, Blackbird," "Five Foot Two, Eyes of Blue") (died 1970).

1899 Robert H.W. Welch Jr., reformer, was born in Chowan County, N.C.; with family candy business until 1957; founder, John Birch Society (1958) (died 1985).

1909 First Christmas savings club was opened by Carlisle (Pa.) Trust Co.

1911 Walter Alston, baseball manager (Dodgers 1954-75), was born in Butler County, Ohio; named to Baseball Hall of Fame (died 1984).

1912 Minoru Yamasaki, architect, was born in Seattle; designed New York City's World Trade Center (died 1986).

1913 First drive-in gas station was opened by Gulf Refining Co. in Pittsburgh.

1913 Mary Martin, singer and actress, was born in Weatherford, Tex.; several starring roles (*South Pacific; Peter Pan; I Do, I Do*).

1918 First American troops returned from Europe, landed in New York City.

1935 Woody (Heywood) Allen, director and writer, was born in Brooklyn; several hit films (*What's New, Pussycat?; Sleeper, The Front, Annie Hall, Zelig*).

1936 President Franklin Roosevelt addressed the opening session of the Inter-American Conference for Maintenance of Peace in Buenos Aires.

1939 Lee Trevino, golfer, was born in Dallas; first to win American, Canadian, and British opens in one year (1971).

1942 Nationwide gasoline rationing went into effect.

1945 Bette Midler, screen actress and singer, was born in Paterson, N.J.

1955 Rosa Parks refused to give her seat on a bus to a white man in Montgomery, Ala; touched off a major boycott led by the Rev. Martin Luther King Jr. and an eventual Supreme Court decision outlawing segregation on buses.

1956 Virgin Islands National Park was established.

1958 A parochial school in Chicago burned, killing 90 children and three teachers.

1969 The first draft lottery since World War II was held in New York City.

1988 President Reagan vowed not to pardon former aide Oliver L. North but he ruled out releasing sensitive documents for North's defense; the action could force dismissal of the major charges against North, former National Security Advisor John M. Poindexter and two other defendants in the Iran-Contra affair.

DECEMBER 2

1738 Richard Montgomery, Revolutionary general, was born in Dublin; killed at the siege of Quebec Dec 31, 1775.

1823 The Monroe Doctrine was enunciated, opposing European intervention in the Western Hemisphere; the doctrine was contained in President Monroe's seventh annual message to Congress, stating in part: "The American continents, by the free and independent conditions which they have assumed and maintained, are henceforth not to be considered a subject for future colonization by any European powers."

1832 A convention in Dover adopted a revised Delaware constitution.

1832 John Carbutt, photographer, was born in Sheffield, England; devised new gelatin-covered dry plate, introduced the orthochromatic plate, giving correct color value in photography (died 1905).

1844 The gag rules, which were adopted by the House between 1836 and 1840, were repealed; the rules were designed to forbid considering any petitions relating to slavery.

1863 Jane M.A. Pierce, wife of President Pierce, died in Andover, Mass. at 57.

1863 Charles Ringling, circus owner, was born in McGregor, Iowa; began first circus (1884) with four brothers, bought others out and by 1907 had the leading circus in America (died 1926).

1863 Thomas Crawford's bronze sculpture, *Freedom,* was placed atop the Capitol dome.

1864 Carl Van Anda, journalist, was born in Georgetown, Ohio; managing editor, *New York Times* (1904-32) (died 1945).

1866 Harry T. Burleigh, singer and composer, was born in Erie, Pa.; soloist, St. George's Episcopal Church, New York City, 52 years; with choir of Temple Emanu-el, New York City, 25 years; first to arrange about 100 Negro spirituals (died 1949).

1884 Ruth Draper, world renowned monologist, was born in New York City (died 1956).

1885 George R. Minot, medical researcher, was born in Boston; shared 1934 Nobel Physiology/Medicine Prize for discovery of liver therapy for anemia (died 1950).

1886 The widowed Theodore Roosevelt was married to Edith K. Carow in London.

1893 William Gaxton, stage and screen actor (*A Connecticut Yankee, 50 Million Frenchmen*), was born in San Francisco (died 1963).

1895 Jesse Crawford, organist, was born in Woodland, Cal.; featured at Paramount Theater, New York City (died 1962).

1895 Daughters of the American Revolution (DAR) was chartered by Congress.

1906 Peter C. Goldmark, inventor, was born in Budapest; developed color television (1940), first commercially-successful long-playing record (1948) (died 1977).

1912 Supreme Court ruled that the merger of the Union Pacific and Southern Pacific railroads constituted a combination in restraint of trade; merger dissolved.

1924 Alexander M. Haig Jr., Army general and public official, was born in Philadelphia; aide to President Nixon (1969-74); commander, NATO forces (1974-79); Secretary of State (1981-82).

1925 Julie Harris, actress, was born in Grosse Pointe Park, Mich.; starred in several plays (*Member of the Wedding, Forty Carats, I Am a Camera, The Belle of Amherst*).

1932 Bob (Robert E. L.) Pettit, basketball player (Louisiana State U., St. Louis Hawks), was born in Baton Rouge, La.

1942 Enrico Fermi, Arthur Compton, and their colleagues succeeded in achieving a controlled chain reaction of uranium under the Stagg Field stands at the University of Chicago, marking the beginning of the atomic age.

1954 The Senate, by a vote of 67-22, cited Wisconsin Senator Joseph R. McCarthy for contempt of the Senate elections subcommittee, for the abuse of its members, and insults to the Senate during the Army televised hearings.

1970 Environmental Protection Agency came into being as 13 administrative units from other agencies were combined.

1980 Three Alaska national parks were created– Katmai, Kenai Fjords, and Lake Clark across the Cook

Inlet from Anchorage; also Mt. McKinley National Park was renamed Denali National Park.

1982 The first permanent artificial heart was implanted in a human being—61-year-old retired dentist Barney Clark—at the University of Utah Medical Center; Clark was kept alive about three months.

1988 The United Nations General Assembly voted overwhelmingly to move its session from New York City to Geneva after Secretary of State George Shultz denied a visa for PLO Chairman Yasser Arafat to speak at the UN's New York meeting.

DECEMBER 3

1677 About 4000 tobacco farmers in Albemarle colony of Carolina issued a manifesto justifying the rebellion against selling tobacco through New England; the rebellion, led by John Culpeper and George Durant, ended two years later without settlement.

1755 Gilbert C. Stuart, painter, was born in North Kingston, R.I.; renowned portrait painter, best known for various portraits and unfinished Athenaeum head of George Washington (died 1828).

1789 Virginia ceded ten square miles of land to Congress for a seat of government.

1807 David Alter, physicist, was born in Westmoreland County, Pa.; his discoveries made possible the spectroscopic determination of the chemical nature of gases (died 1881).

1807 Gamaliel Bailey, anti-slavery editor, was born in Mt. Holly, N.J.; editor, *Cincinnati Philanthropist* (1835-47), the first anti-slavery journal in the West, and *National Era*, Washington (1847-59), in which he serialized *Uncle Tom's Cabin* (died 1859).

1809 Samuel Adler, rabbi who helped lay foundation for Reformed Judaism, was born in Worms, Germany; rabbi, Emanu-El Congregation, New York City; helped revise the prayer book (died 1891).

1818 Illinois was admitted to the Union as the 21st state.

1826 George B. McClellan, Union general, was born in Philadelphia; commander, Army of the Potomac, replaced (1862) because of his over-cautiousness; Democratic presidential nominee (1864); governor of New Jersey (1878-81) (died 1885).

1833 Oberlin Collegiate Institute in Oberlin, Ohio opened as the first American coeducational college.

1838 Cleveland Abbe, meteorologist, was born in New York City; director, Cincinnati Observatory (1868), began issuing weather reports (1869); joined Weather Bureau on its organization (1871), retired in 1916 (died 1916).

1838 A convention in St. Joseph adopted Florida's constitution.

1842 Ellen H. Richards, chemist, was born in Dunstable, Mass.; instructor, MIT (1884-1911); an organizer, first president, American Home Economics Association (1908) (died 1911).

1842 Charles A. Pillsbury, flour miller, was born in Warner, N.H.; bought share of small flour mill (1869), introduced new methods; became world's largest flour miller by 1889 (died 1889).

1857 Carl Koller, ophthalmologist, was born in what is now Susice, Czechoslovakia; introduced cocaine as a local anesthetic in eye operations (New York 1884), launching use of local anesthesia in other operations (died 1944).

1863 Confederate Gen. James Longstreet began retreat from Knoxville, Tenn., ending siege, as Union forces under Gen. William T. Sherman approached.

1868 The treason trial of Jefferson Davis, Confederate president, began in Richmond; following unconditional amnesty proclamation, the charges were dropped Feb 25, 1869.

1870 George H. Denny, educator, was born in Hanover County, Va.; president, Washington & Lee U. (1902-11); president, chancellor, U. of Alabama (1912-55) (died 1955).

1871 Newton D. Baker, public official, was born in Martinsburg, W. Va., mayor of Cleveland (1912-16), Secretary of War (1916-21) , member, Permanent Court of Arbitration at The Hague (1928-36) (died 1937).

1873 Atwater Kent, manufacturer, was born near Burlington, Vt.; founder, head, leading radio manufacturing company of 1920s (died 1949).

1892 Julius Ochs Adler, newspaper executive, was born in Chattanooga; executive vice president, general manager, *New York Times* (1935-55) (died 1955).

1903 John von Neumann, mathematician, was born in Budapest; with Institute for Advanced Study, Princeton (1933-57); built mathematical analyzer which speeded development of hydrogen bomb (died 1957).

1910 Mary Baker Eddy, founder of Christian Science Church, died in Newton, Mass. at 89.

1912 Senate began impeachment hearings of Robert W. Archibald, associate judge, Commerce Court;

charged with collusion with coal mine owners and railroad officials; found guilty Jan 13, 1913 on five of 13 counts, removed from bench.

1930 Andy Williams, singer, was born in Wall Lake, Ia.; popular recording star, television performer.

1974 The spacecraft *Pioneer II* passed the planet Jupiter on its course for Saturn.

DECEMBER 4

1584 John Cotton, religious leader, was born in Derby, England; teacher, First Church , Boston; headed Congregationalism in United States; opposed democratic institutions, responsible for expulsion of Anne Hutchinson, Roger Williams (died 1652).

1674 Jacques Marquette and two companions, caught by onset of winter, built a cabin on site of Chicago, becoming the first white men to live there.

1682 First Pennsylvania assembly met at Upland (now Chester); incorporated Delaware settlements into Pennsylvania, adopted a code, naturalized settlers already there.

1730 William Moultrie, Revolutionary general, was born in Charleston, S.C.; repulsed British attack on Sullivan's Island (now Ft. Moultrie) in Charleston harbor; defended Charleston (1779); served South Carolina as governor (1785-87, 1794-96); a British prisoner (1780-82) (died 1805).

1736 Thomas Godfrey, playwright, was born in Philadelphia; wrote first American full-length play (*The Prince of Parthia*) produced on a professional stage (died 1763).

1777 Lord William Howe led 14,000 British troops to attack Americans; returned Dec 8 without attacking.

1783 Gen. George Washington took leave of his officers at Fraunces Tavern, New York City, saying: "With a heart full of love and gratitude, I now take leave of you. I most devoutly wish that your latter days may be as prosperous and happy as your former ones have been glorious and honorable."

1833 American Anti-Slavery Assn. was organized in Philadelphia and a constitution written, primarily by William Lloyd Garrison.

1860 George A. Hormel, meat packer, was born in Buffalo; founder, president, Hormel & Co. (1892-1928); produced first American canned hams (died 1946).

1861 Lillian Russell, actress and singer, was born in Clinton, Iowa; feminine ideal of her age (died 1922).

1865 Luther H. Gulick, co-founder of Camp Fire Girls, was born in Honolulu; director, Springfield (Mass.) YWCA, cooperated with James Naismith in developing basketball (died 1918).

1867 The Grange (formally the Patrons of Husbandry) was organized to protect the farmers' interests.

1867 Charles A. Herty, chemist, was born in Milledgeville, Ga.; invented method of turpentine orcharding, method of determining oil in cottonseed products, process of making white paper from young Southern pines (died 1938).

1868 Jesse C. Burkett, baseball player (Indians, Reds, Cards), was born in Wheeling, W. Va.; named to Baseball Hall of Fame (died 1953).

1875 William "Boss" Tweed, convicted of swindling New York City of about $200 million, was helped to escape from jail and flee to Cuba.

1880 Gar(field) Wood, racing boat builder and racer, was born Mapleton, Iowa; credited with developing the Navy PT boat (died 1971).

1882 A nine-man congressional tariff commission, after six months study, recommended substantial tariff reductions.

1895 Arthur Murray, dancing teacher, was born in New York City; with his wife, Kathryn, organized chain of 450 dance schools in the United States.

1895 A new constitution was adopted by a South Carolina convention, effective Jan 1, 1896.

1897 Robert Redfield, anthropologist, was born in Chicago; with Chicago U. (1927-58), author (*Tepotzlan, Peasant Society and Culture, The Little Community*) (died 1958).

1903 Frank D. Merrill, World War II Army officer, was born in Hopkinton, Mass.; headed Merrill's Marauders against the Japanese in Burma.

1905 Munro Leaf, writer and illustrator, was born in Hamilton, Md.; author (*Grammar Can Be Fun, Manners Can Be Fun, The Story of Ferdinand, Wee Gillis*) (died 1976).

1908 Alfred D. Hershey, geneticist and virologist, was born in Owosso, Mich.; shared 1969 Nobel Physiology/Medicine Prize for discoveries on the genetic structure of viruses.

1915 Henry Ford and a delegation of peace advocates sailed from New York on the *Oscar II*, chartered by Ford, "to try to get the boys out of the trenches and back to their homes by Christmas" and to end the war; Ford left the delegation Dec 22 in Christiana and returned home.

1922 Deanna Durbin, singer and screen actress, was born in Winnipeg, Canada; popular star of 1930s, 1940s (*Three Smart Girls, Mad About Music*).

1923 Maria Callas, soprano, was born in New York City; sang 43 leading roles in more than 500 performances in the world's opera houses (died 1977).

1924 John C. Portman Jr., architect, was born in Walhalla, S.C.; designed Peachtree Center in Atlanta, several Hyatt-Regency House hotels.

1928 Senate ratified the Kellogg-Briand peace pact with only one dissenting vote (Blaine of Wisconsin).

1943 The second Cairo conference began with President Franklin Roosevelt, Prime Minister Winston Churchill, and President Ismet Inonu of Turkey present; ended Dec 6.

1963 The use of English in the United States in place of Latin for parts of the Catholic mass and for the sacraments was approved by the Ecumenical Council.

1980 A fire in the Stouffer Inn in Harrison, N.Y. killed 26 persons.

1984 Four hijackers seized a Kuwaiti plane enroute to Pakistan and held 161 hostages on the ground at Teheran Airport until Iranian security men stormed the plane Dec 9; two Americans were shot to death before the rescue.

DECEMBER 5

1775 The siege of Quebec was begun by American troops under Benedict Arnold and Gen. Richard Montgomery.

1776 Phi Beta Kappa, the first American fraternity, was founded at the College of William & Mary in Williamsburg, Va.

1777 The first New Jersey newspaper, the *New Jersey Gazette*, was published in Burlington by Isaac Collins.

1779 John Sergeant, legislator, was born in Philadelphia; represented Pennsylvania in the House (1815-23, 1827-29, 1837-41); National Republican vice presidential candidate (1832) (died 1852).

1782 Martin Van Buren, eighth president (1837-41), was born in Kinderhook, N.Y.; represented New York in the Senate (1821-28) and served the state as governor (1828); Secretary of State (1829-41), Vice President (1833-37) (died 1862).

1786 George Washington was appointed as one of seven Virginia delegates to a proposed convention of states in Philadelphia.

1792 Electors selected by the states re-elected President Washington and Vice President John Adams; Washington received 132 votes (one from Vermont, two from Maryland did not vote); Adams received 77 votes to 50 for George Clinton.

1796 Andrew Jackson took his seat in the House of Representatives, the first member from Tennessee; served until 1797, when he was elected to the Senate, serving Nov 1797 to Apr 1798 and again in 1823-25.

1803 Thomas J. Rusk, Texas leader, was born in Pendleton District, S.C.; a leader in Texas' fight for independence; first chief justice, Texas Supreme Court (1840), represented state in the Senate (1846-57) (died 1857).

1805 Michael B. Menard, fur trader, was born in La-Prairie, Canada; operated in Texas and Arkansas; developed city of Galveston (1836); Menard County, Tex. named for him (died 1856).

1831 Former President John Quincy Adams took his seat in the House as a representative from Massachusetts, serving until 1848.

1839 George A. Custer, Army general, was born in New Rumley, Ohio; with his men, he was slain by Indians at the Battle of Little Big Horn (6/25/1876) in what has become known as "Custer's last stand."

1841 Marcus Daly, mine owner, was born in Ireland; developed Anaconda Copper Co. at Butte, Mont. (died 1900).

1848 President Polk's annual message confirmed the news of the discovery of gold in California and gave impetus to the gold rush.

1876 The Conway Theater in Brooklyn burned; about 295 persons died.

1879 Clyde V. Cessna, airplane builder, was born in Hawthorne, Ia; built first cantilever plane (1927); founder, head of Cessna Co. (died 1954).

1896 Carl F. Cori, biochemist, was born in Prague; shared 1947 Nobel Physiology/Medicine Prize with his wife (Gerty T. Cori 8/15/1896) and B.A. Houssey; the Coris discovered the course of catalytic conversion of glycogen (died 1984).

1901 Walt(er E.) Disney, movie producer, was born in Chicago; developed animated movie cartoons, creator of Mickey Mouse, Donald Duck; produced many hit films (*Snow White, Fantasia, Mary Poppins*); created theme parks (Disney World, Disneyland) (died 1966).

1901 Grace Moore, soprano, was born in Slabtown, Tenn.; starred in opera, on stage and screen; killed in plane crash in Copenhagen Jan 26, 1947.

1902 J. Strom Thurmond, legislator, was born in Edgefield, S.C.; served South Carolina as governor (1946-48) and represented it in the Senate (1955-) as the only successful write-in candidate; "Dixiecrat" presidential nominee (1948), receiving 39 electoral votes.

1904 Arnold Gingrich, publisher, was born in Grand Rapids, Mich.; founder, publisher, *Esquire* magazine (died 1976).

1906 Otto Preminger, movie director, was born in Vienna; directed numerous films (*Forever Amber, Exodus, Anatomy of a Murder, Advise and Consent*) (died 1986).

1933 The 21st Amendment, repealing the 18th (Prohibition) Amendment, went into effect.

1946 President Truman appointed a Committee on Civil Rights to recommend "more adequate and effective means and procedures for the protection of the civil rights of the people of the United States;" asked for legislation Feb 2, 1948 on its recommendations; a law was enacted Sept 9, 1957.

1955 The American Federation of Labor and the Congress of Industrial Organizations merged to form the AFL-CIO with 15 million members.

1974 Hazel Wightman, early tennis star, died at 88; won numerous titles between 1910 and 1930.

1984 The American Medical Association called for an end to both professional and amateur boxing because of its danger to health.

1988 Jim Bakker, former president of the PTL television ministry, was indicted on 24 federal charges of fraud and conspiracy, as were several of his associates; the TV evangelist resigned in 1987 amid a sex and hush money scandal.

DECEMBER 6

1637 Sir Edmund Andros, colonial governor, was born on Guernsey Island, off England; governor, New York Province (1674), of the Dominion of New England (1686) but his rule was resented and ignored; colonists rebelled (1688), jailed him, and finally sent him back to England; governor of Virginia (1692-97) (died 1714).

1683 Gov. Thomas Dongan granted a charter to New York City, which set up a government consisting of a mayor, six aldermen, six common councillors; charter officially signed Apr 27, 1686.

1752 Gabriel Duval, public official and jurist, was born in Prince Georges Co., Md.; first Comptroller of the Treasury (1802-11); associate justice, Supreme Court (1811-36) (died 1844).

1776 Kentucky was established as a county of Virginia.

1790 James Monroe took his seat as a senator from Virginia, serving until 1794.

1823 (John) Eberhard Faber, pencil manufacturer, was born in Stein, Germany; set up first American pencil factory (1861); first to put eraser on pencil (died 1879).

1830 The Naval Observatory was established in Washington.

1833 John S. Mosby, Confederate officer, was born in Edgemont, Va.; commanded independent cavalry unit (Mosby's Rangers) raiding Union positions (died 1916).

1836 Charles F. Chandler, chemist, was born in Lancaster, Mass.; president, New York City Board of Health (1867-84), invented flushing toilet water closet, refused to patent it in the public interest (died 1925).

1840 Richard H. Pratt, Army officer and educator, was born in Rushford, N.Y.; served in Civil War and on frontier; organized first non-reservation Indian school, which became Carlisle (Pa.) Indian Industrial School; principal (1879-1904) (died 1924).

1847 Abraham Lincoln took his seat in the House of Representatives.

1859 Edward H. Sothern, actor, was born in New Orleans; toured in Shakespearean repertoire with wife, Julia Marlowe (8/17/1866) (died 1933).

1859 Herbert M. Lord, Army officer and public official, was born in Rockland, Me.; Army finance director (1918-22), U.S. budget director (1922-29) (died 1930).

1863 Atlee Pomerene, legislator and attorney, was born in Berlin, Ohio; represented Ohio in the Senate (1911-23); special prosecutor in Teapot Dome investigation (1924) (died 1937).

1863 Charles M. Hall, inventor and industrialist, was born in Thompson, Ohio; invented method of producing pure aluminum by electrolysis (1886); his company later became Alcoa (died 1914).

1864 President Lincoln appointed Salmon P. Chase as chief justice, Supreme Court; confirmed the same day; served until 1873.

1867 Karl T. F. Bitter, sculptor, was born in Vienna; directed sculpture at various world fairs; his four figures (*Architecture, Sculpture, Painting, Music*) are at the front entrance of the Metropolitan Museum of Art (died 1915).

1867 A convention in Alabama framed a new constitution.

1872 William S. Hart, silent screen actor, was born in Newburgh, N.Y.; the leading cowboy movie star of his day (died 1946).

1883 Thomas E. Braniff, airline executive, was born in Salina, Kan.; founder of airline named for him (1930) (died 1954).

1884 The Washington Monument was completed; dedicated Feb 1885.

1886 (Alfred) Joyce Kilmer, poet, was born in New Brunswick, N.J.; best remembered for the poem "Trees" (died 1918).

1887 Lynn Fontanne, actress, was born in London; with husband, Alfred Lunt (*see* 8/19/1892), formed most famous American theater couple (*The Guardsman, Design for Living, The Taming of the Shrew*) (died 1983).

1889 Jefferson Davis, president of the Confederacy, died in New Orleans at 81.

1889 Robert W. Woodruff, who made Coca-Cola a household word, was born in Columbus, Ga.; Coca-Cola president (1923-39), board chairman (1939-55) (died 1985).

1891 Lou Little, football coach, was born in Leominster, Mass.; at Georgetown (1924-30), Columbia (1930-56) (died 1979).

1896 Ira Gershwin, lyricist, was born in New York City, brother of George Gershwin (*see* 9/26/1898), for whom he wrote lyrics; other hits (*Lady in the Dark*; stage; *Cover Girl, A Star is Born*; screen) (died 1983).

1898 Alfred Eisenstadt, photojournalist, was born in Dinschau, Germany; developed technique of candid camera news reporting the picture story.

1899 Jocko (John B.) Conlon, baseball umpire, was born in Chicago; named to Baseball Hall of Fame (died 1989).

1904 President Theodore Roosevelt in annual message to Congress developed corollary to the Monroe Doctrine—inasmuch as we do not permit European intervention in Latin American affairs, America must preserve order and protect life and property in those countries; later led to intervention in some countries.

1907 A coal mine explosion at Monogah, W. Va. resulted in 361 deaths.

1916 American aviation volunteers formed the Lafayette Escadrille to help the Allies; with American entry into the war, it became the 103rd Pursuit Squadron.

1917 American destroyer *Jacob Jones* was torpedoed and sunk by a German submarine off the English coast.

1920 Dave Brubeck, pianist and composer, was born in Concord, Cal.; a leading force in contemporary jazz.

1921 Otto Graham, football player and coach, was born in Waukegan, Ill.; starred at Northwestern U., Cleveland Browns (1946-55); coach (Redskins, Coast Guard Academy).

1941 A project was begun by the Office of Scientific Research and Development to study the feasibility of building an atomic bomb.

1949 Leadbelly (Huddie Ledbetter), legendary folk singer and 12-string guitar player, died at about 64.

1977 The longest coal strike in American history began; ended Mar 25, 1978.

1979 Shirley M. Hufstedler, California jurist, was named the first Secretary of Education; served until 1981.

1988 Soviet leader Mikhail S. Gorbachev arrived in New York City to address the United Nations General Assembly on Dec 7; lunched with President Reagan and Vice President (and President-elect) Bush.

1988 President-elect Bush announced he would nominate Robert A. Mosbacher as Commerce Secretary, Carla A. Hills as U.S. trade representative; Michael J. Boskin as chairman of the Council of Economic Advisors, and Thomas R. Pickering as ambassador to the United Nations; he also announced he would keep Lauro F. Cavazos on as Education Secretary.

DECEMBER 7

1672 Richard Bellingham, colonial governor, died at about 80; had been Massachusetts lieutenant governor (1635, 1640, 1653, 1655-65) and governor (1641, 1654, 1665-72).

1787 Delaware legislators unanimously ratified the Constitution, becoming the first state in the Union.

1804 Noah H. Swayne, jurist, was born in Frederick County, Va.; associate justice, Supreme Court (1862-81) (died 1884).

1818 Henry Peterson, editor, was born in Philadelphia; editor, *Saturday Evening Post* (1846-74) (died 1891).

1835 James K. Polk, a member of the House from Tennessee for ten years, was elected Speaker, serving until 1839.

1841 Michael Cudahy, meat packer, was born in County Kilkenny, Ireland; a partner in Armour & Co. (1875-90); formed, headed own company (1890-1910) (died 1910).

1842 The New York Philharmonic Orchestra presented its first concert.

1850 Solomon Schechter, religious leader, was born in Focsani, Rumania; president, Jewish Theological Seminary (1902-15); founder, United Synagogue of America (1913) (died 1915).

1862 Union troops victorious at Prairie Grove, Ark.

1863 Richard W. Sears, merchant, was born in Stewartville, Minn.; acquired shipment of abandoned watches, sold them by mail; hired Alvah C. Roebuck to repair them; organized Sears Roebuck (1893), president (1893-1909) (died 1914).

1866 Edwin H. Hughes, Methodist prelate, was born in Moundville, W. Va.; bishop (1908-50); senior bishop of Methodist Church (1932-50) (died 1950).

1867 The House by a vote of 108-57 turned down a Judiciary Committee 5-4 recommendation to impeach President Andrew Johnson.

1873 Willa S. Cather, author, was born in Winchester, Va.; an editor, *McClure's Magazine* (1905-12); author (*O Pioneers, My Antonia, Death Comes for the Archbishop*) (died 1947).

1874 Blacks in Vicksburg, Miss. attacked the courthouse in an attempt to prevent the ouster of a sheriff; 75 blacks were killed before attack ended.

1879 Rudolf Friml, composer and pianist, was born in Prague; composed hit operettas (*The Firefly, Rose Marie, The Vagabond King*) (died 1972).

1883 Edmund E. Day, educator, was born in Manchester, N.H.; founder, dean of first business administration school (Michigan U. 1924-27); president, Cornell U. (1937-51) (died 1951).

1888 Heywood Broun, journalist, was born in Brooklyn; wrote for several New York newspapers, syndicated columnist (*It Seems to Me*); a founder, American Newspaper Guild (died 1939).

1905 Gerard F. Kuiper, astronomer, was born in Haren Karspell, Netherlands; known for discoveries and theories of the solar system (died 1973).

1915 Eli Wallach, actor, was born in New York City; starred on stage (*The Rose Tattoo, Teahouse of the August Moon*), on screen (*The Magnificent Seven, The Misfits*).

1917 Congress passed a joint resolution declaring war on Austria-Hungary.

1941 The Japanese launched a surprise attack on Pearl Harbor in Hawaii and on other Pacific islands, destroying or damaging 19 warships, 150 planes, and killing 2400 persons; attacks also were launched on the Philippines, Guam, Midway, Hong Kong, and the Malay Peninsula.

1946 A fire in the Winecoff Hotel in Atlanta killed 120 persons, injured 100.

1947 Johnny Bench, baseball player (Reds) was born in Oklahoma City.

1956 Larry Bird, basketball player (Boston Celtics), was born in French Lick, Ind.

1987 A Pacific Southwest Airlines commuter jet crashed near Harmony, Cal., killing all 44 persons aboard.

1987 Soviet leader Mikhail S. Gorbachev arrived in Washington to sign the treaty scrapping some medium and short range missiles; signing occurred Dec 9.

DECEMBER 8

1765 Eli Whitney, cotton gin inventor, was born in Westboro, Mass.; invented the gin (1793), operated a factory to manufacture muskets (1801), using interchangeable parts (died 1825).

1801 President Jefferson's first annual message to Congress was sent in written form, breaking the precedent of personal appearance; written messages continued until 1913.

1812 Henry V. Poor, economist, was born in Andover, Me.; editor, *American Railroad Journal* (1849-62); published railroad manuals, handbook of investment securities (died 1905).

1816 August Belmont, banker and sportsman, was born in Alzei, Germany; developed own banking firm; consul general for Austria in America (1844-50); minister to the Netherlands (1853-57); noted art collector, race horse owner (Man o' War) (died 1890).

1828 Clinton B. Fisk, Union general, was born in western New York; founded Fisk University for blacks, chartered 1867 (died 1890).

1831 James Hoban, architect, died at 69; designed and supervised construction of original White House (1792-1800) and its replacement (1815-29).

1839 Alexander J. Cassatt, railroad executive, was born in Pittsburgh, brother of Mary Cassatt (*see* 5/22/1844); president, Pennsylvania Railroad (1899-1906), built Penn Station, New York City (died 1906).

1841 James H. Logan, jurist and horticulturist, was born in Rockville, Ind.; served California Superior Court (1880-92); produced new variety of berry, the loganberry (died 1928).

1856 Henry T. Mayo, World War I admiral, was born in Burlington, Vt.; commander-in-chief, Atlantic Fleet (1916-19) (died 1937).

1858 Harry P. Huse, admiral, was born in West Point, N.Y.; served during World War I; commander, American naval forces in Europe (1920-22) (died 1942).

1858 Alfred H. Cowles, engineer, was born in Cleveland; a pioneer in electric smelting; founder (1885), president, Electric Smelting & Aluminum Co. (died 1929).

1859 William H. O'Connell, Catholic prelate, was born in Lowell, Mass.; bishop of Portland, Me. (1901-06), archbishop of Boston (1907-44), named cardinal 1911 (died 1944).

1861 William C. Durant, auto manufacturer, was born in Boston; organized, headed, Durant Dort Carriage Co., world's largest buggy maker; organized Buick Motor Co. (1905), General Motors (1908), president (1916-20); founder, Durant Motor Co. (1921) (died 1947).

1863 President Lincoln issued a proclamation of amnesty and reconstruction of the seceding states; no state was actually restored under this plan.

1879 Louisiana's new constitution, adopted in April, was ratified by popular vote; the capital was moved from New Orleans to Baton Rouge.

1885 Kenneth Roberts, author, was born in Kennebunk, Me.; writer of historical novels (*Rabble in Arms, Arundel, Oliver Wiswell, Northwest Passage*) (died 1957).

1886 The American Federation of Labor (AFL) was organized in Columbus, Ohio by 25 labor groups representing 150,000 members.

1888 Fiske Kimball, architect, was born in Newton, Mass.; known for work on restoration of historical houses (Monticello); member of board which planned reconstruction of Colonial Williamsburg, construction of the Rockefeller Center (died 1955).

1889 Hervey Allen, author, was born in Pittsburgh; best known for *Anthony Adverse* (died 1949).

1891 Percy L. Crosby, cartoonist (*Skippy*), was born in Brooklyn (died 1964).

1894 James Thurber, author and cartoonist, was born in Columbus, Ohio; cartoonist for *The New Yorker*; author (*The Secret Life of Walter Mitty, My Life and Hard Times, 13 Clocks, Fables of Our Time*) (died 1961).

1913 Delmore Schwartz, author, was born in Brooklyn; poet and short story writer (*In Dreams Begin Responsibilities, The World is a Wedding, Summer Knowledge*) (died 1966).

1925 Sammy Davis Jr., entertainer and screen actor, was born in New York City; starred on stage (*Mr. Wonderful, Golden Boy*) and screen (*Porgy and Bess, Sweet Charity*).

1941 Congress declared war on Japan in 33 minutes in the wake of the Pearl Harbor attack; Jeannette Rankin, Montana representative, cast lone vote against the declaration; she also voted against war in 1917.

1947 Thomas Cech, Colorado U. chemist who shared 1989 Nobel Chemistry Prize, was born in Chicago, Ill.

1953 President Eisenhower, speaking to the UN General Assembly, proposed the launching of an international "atoms for peace" program through an international atomic energy agency.

1980 Former Beatle John Lennon was shot and killed outside his New York City apartment by a former psychiatric patient.

1988 It was a bad day for American fliers — five were killed when a helicopter crashed in northern Honduras during a training exercise, five others when a DC-7 from the U.S. Agency for International Development was shot down over Mauritania, and an American pilot and at least three others when an Air Force plane crashed in Ramscheid, West Germany during a training flight.

DECEMBER 9

1561 Sir Edwin Sandys, founder of the Virginia colony, was born in England; assisted in obtaining charter for the Mayflower (died 1629).

1776 A British force under Gen. Henry Clinton captured Newport, R.I.

1848 Joel Chandler Harris, author, was born in Putnam County, Ga.; remembered for his *Uncle Remus* stories (died 1908).

1871 Joe (Joseph J.) Kelley, baseball player (Orioles, Dodgers, Reds), was born in Cambridge, Mass.; named to Baseball Hall of Fame (died 1943).

1879 Benjamin D. Foulois, pioneer aviator, was born in Washington, Conn.; established the Air Force (1910); chief, Army Air Corps (1931-35) (died 1967).

1886 Clarence Birdseye, inventor, was born in Brooklyn; invented a process for freezing food, also an infrared heat lamp; founder of what later became General Foods Corp. (died 1956).

1898 Emmett Kelly, circus clown, was born in Sedan, Kan.; known as Weary Willie (died 1979).

1902 Lucius M. Beebe, journalist, was born in Wakefield, Mass.; syndicated columnist on cafe society; publisher, *Territorial Enterprise*, Virginia City, Nev. (1950-60) (died 1966).

1906 Freddy Martin, bandleader from 1930s on, was born in Cleveland.

1907 The first Christmas seals went on sale in Wilmington, Del.

1911 Lee J. Cobb, actor, was born in New York City; best remembered for role of Willy Loman in *Death of a Salesman* (died 1976).

1912 Thomas P. (Tip) O'Neill, legislator, was born in Cambridge; represented Massachusetts in the House (1953-87); served as Speaker (1977-87).

1917 L. James Rainwater, physicist, was born in Council, Idaho; shared 1975 Nobel Physics Prize for theory that some atomic nuclei are asymmetrical, not spherical (died 1986).

1918 Kirk Douglas, screen actor, was born in Amsterdam, N. Y.; starred in many films (*Spartacus, The Glass Menagerie, Seven Days in May*).

1919 William N. Lipscomb, physical chemist, was born in Cleveland; awarded 1976 Nobel Chemistry Prize for work on structure bonding mechanisms of boranes.

1932 Bill Hartack, jockey, was born in Colver, Pa.; rode record five Kentucky Derby winners.

1958 The John Birch Society, an anti-Communist organization, was formed by Robert H.W. Welch Jr., a retired candy manufacturer; named for an American captain killed by Chinese Communists in 1945.

1962 The Petrified Forest (Ariz.) National Park was established.

1967 Lynda Bird Johnson, daughter of President and Mrs. Lyndon Johnson, was married in the White House to Charles S. Robb.

DECEMBER 10

1607 Capt. John Smith left Jamestown, Va. and ascended the Chickahominy River to get provisions; he was captured by the Indians and according to legend was saved by Pocahontas, daughter of the Indian chief, Powhatan.

1741 John Murray, Universalist clergyman, was born in Alton, England; called the father of American Universalism, he set up his pastorate in the Independent Church of Christ in Gloucester, Mass. (1779-93), the Universalist Society, Boston (1793-1809) (died 1815).

1783 Henry Leavenworth, Army general, was born in New Haven; Army commander in the southwest; fort and city named for him (died 1834).

1785 Daniel Appleton, publisher, was born in Haverhill, Mass.; co-founder of family publishing house (1838) (died 1849).

1787 Thomas H. Gallaudet, Congregational clergyman, was born in Philadelphia; founded first free American school for deaf in Hartford (1817), principal (1817-30); Gallaudet College in Washington named for him (died 1851).

1795 Matthias W. Baldwin, industrialist, was born in Elizabethtown, N.J.; manufactured steam engines, locomotives (1832), firm later became the Baldwin Locomotive Works (died 1866).

1813 Zachariah Chandler, public official and legislator, was born in Bedford, N.H.; Interior Secretary (1875-77), represented Michigan in the Senate (1857-75, 1879); a founder of the Republican Party (died 1879).

1817 Mississippi was admitted to the Union as the 20th state.

1830 Emily Dickinson, writer, was born in Amherst, Mass.; one of America's foremost poets; her work was published posthumously (died 1886).

1832 President Jackson issued a proclamation to the people of South Carolina, saying that their acts nullifying the 1828 and 1832 tariffs were "incompatible with the existence of the Union" and "an impractical absurdity."

1851 Melvil Dewey, librarian, was born in Adams Center, N.Y., director, New York State Library (1889-1906); founder, director, New York State Library School (1887-1906); originated decimal classification system; founder, American Library Association (died 1931).

1859 Frederick U. Adams, inventor, was born in Boston; invented many street-lighting devices (electric lamp supports, posts) and railroad rolling-stock designs;

founder (1893), editor, *The New Time*, a reform magazine (died 1921).

1864 Gen. William T. Sherman and his Union troops arrived in Savannah, after a 300 mile march to the sea; took Ft. McAllister three days later.

1869 The Territory of Wyoming passed a women's suffrage law.

1883 Alfred Kreymborg, poet and editor, was born in New York City; poet ("Mushrooms," "Less Lonely," "Manhattan Men"); co-editor, *American Caravan*, a literary miscellany (1927-31) (died 1966).

1886 Horace B. Liveright, publisher, was born in Osceola Mills, Pa.; co-founder, president, Boni and Liveright (1918-30) (died 1933).

1890 Edward J. H. O'Brien, writer and editor, was born in Boston; edited *The Best Short Stories* annually (1915-40), *The Best British Short Stories* annually (1921-40) (died 1941).

1896 The first intercollegiate basketball game was played in New Haven, with Wesleyan defeating Yale 4 to 3.

1898 The Treaty of Paris was concluded with Spain, formally ending the Spanish-American War; Spain ceded Puerto Rico, Guam, and the Philippines to the United States for $20 million, relinquished all claim and title to Cuba, and assumed $400 million Cuban debt; ratified by the Senate Feb 6, 1899.

1906 Walter H. Zinn, physicist, was born in Kitchener, Canada; developed the first breeder reactor (1951).

1906 President Theodore Roosevelt was awarded the 1906 Nobel Peace Prize for his role in ending the Russo-Japanese War; the first American to win the Peace Prize.

1911 Chet (Chester R.) Huntley, newsman, was born in Cardwell, Mont.; teamed with David Brinkley (1956-70) on the NBC Evening News (died 1974).

1913 Morton Gould, composer and conductor, was born in Philadelphia; guest conductor of major symphonies; composer of musicals (*Billion Dollar Baby*), ballets (*Fall River Legend*).

1917 Boys' Town, 11 miles west of Omaha, was founded by Rev. Edward J. Flanagan.

1920 President Wilson was awarded the 1919 Nobel Peace Prize.

1926 Vice President Charles G. Dawes shared the 1925 Nobel Peace Prize.

1934 Howard M. Temin, molecular biologist, was born in Philadelphia; shared the 1975 Nobel Physiology/Medicine Prize for research on a process by which a virus can change the genetic makeup of a cell.

1941 The Japanese landed on Luzon in the Philippines.

1948 The UN General Assembly adopted the Universal Declaration of Human Rights, drafted by its Commission on Human Rights, headed by Mrs. Eleanor Roosevelt.

1971 The Farm Credit Administration was established.

1985 The Supreme Court ruled 5-4 against the use in court of self-incriminating evidence against a defendant that was obtained by stealth without counsel being present for the defendant.

DECEMBER 11

1586 John Mason, a founder of New Hampshire, was born in King's Lynn, England; co-founder of company which settled on Piscataqua River (died 1635).

1620 Pilgrims sighted what is now Plymouth and created a settlement there Dec 25, calling it New Plymouth.

1750 Isaac Shelby, Revolutionary general, was born in Washington County, Md.; defeated British at King's Mountain; served Kentucky as its first governor (1792-96, 1812-16) (died 1826).

1775 Governor Dunmore of Virginia, who placed the colony under martial law and began to raise an army, was decisively defeated by a mixed force of 900 Virginians and North Carolinians at Great Bridge, Va.

1816 Indiana was admitted to the Union as the 19th state.

1818 Jerome I. Case, inventor, was born in Williamstown, N.Y.; invented a threshing machine (1844), manufactured agricultural machinery (died 1891).

1824 Jonathan Letterman, Army surgeon, was born in Canonsburg, Pa.; reorganized field medical service, introduced ambulance service for battlefield casualties (died 1872).

1833 Albert G. Ellis and John V. Suydam published the first newspaper in Wisconsin, the *Green Bay Intelligencer*.

1854 Charles G. Radbourn, baseball pitcher who won 308 games (Braves, Providence), was born in Rochester, N.Y.; named to Baseball Hall of Fame (died 1897).

1876 Ada Louise Comstock, educator, was born in Moorehead, Minn.; dean, Smith College (1912-23); president, Radcliffe College (1923-43) (died 1973).

1882 Fiorello H. LaGuardia, public official, was born in New York City; represented New York in the House (1917-19, 1923-33); New York City mayor (1933-45); director, Office of Civilian Defense (1941-42); director general, UNRRA (United Nations Relief & Rehabilitation Administration) (1946) (died 1947).

1882 The Bijou Theater in Boston became the first theater lighted by Edison's incandescent lights for a performance of Gilbert & Sullivan's *Iolanthe*.

1886 Victor McLaglen, screen actor, was born in London; starred in many films (*The Informer, What Price Glory?, The Quiet Man*) (died 1959).

1890 Mark Tobey, painter, was born in Centerville, Wis.; work described as "white-line" or "white writing," a synthesis of Oriental brushwork and American abstractionism (died 1976).

1892 John A. Larson, psychiatrist, was born in Shelbourne, Nova Scotia; invented the polygraph (lie detector) (1921).

1896 Woman's suffrage became effective in Idaho.

1903 Marine Corps formally occupied Guantanamo, naval station ceded by Cuba to the United States.

1905 Pare Lorentz, documentary film maker, was born in Clarksburg, W. Va.; among his works are *The Plow That Broke the Plains* and *The River*.

1922 A second agreement was made by which Interior Secretary Albert Fall leased the Elk Hills Naval Oil Reserve in California to E.M. Doheny, an oil executive.

1941 Germany and Italy declared war on the United States, which in turn declared war on Germany.

1941 The Japanese captured Guam.

1982 A chemical storage tank exploded at the Union Carbide plant near Destrehan, La.; 20,000 people were evacuated as a safety measure.

1982 The seven largest black denominations representing 65,000 churches and 20 million Christians established the Congress of National Black Churches.

1985 General Electric Co. agreed to buy RCA Corp. for $6.28 billion, the biggest corporate merger outside the oil industry.

DECEMBER 12

1745 John Jay, jurist and public official, was born in New York City; member, Continental Congress (1774-79); drafted New York's first constitution (1777), was New York's first chief justice (1777-78) and served it as governor (1795-1801); Secretary of Foreign Affairs (1784-89); chief justice, Supreme Court (1789-94) (died 1829).

1776 The Continental Congress, fearing a British attack on Philadelphia, moved its deliberations to Baltimore.

1786 William L. Marcy, legislator, was born in Sturbridge, Mass.; represented New York in the Senate (1831-33) and served it as governor (1833-39); Secretary of War (1845-49), of State (1853-57); coined phrase "spoils system" ("To the victor belong the spoils of the enemy") (1832) (died 1857).

1787 Pennsylvania legislators ratified the Constitution by a vote of 46-23, making it the second state of the Union.

1791 The Bank of the United States, created Feb 25, 1791, opened its doors for business in Philadelphia.

1805 William Lloyd Garrison, editor, was born in Newburyport, Mass.; founder, editor, *The Liberator* (1831-66), an anti-slavery journal; a founder, American Anti-Slavery Society, president (1843-65) (died 1879).

1805 Henry Wells, businessman, was born in Thetford, Vt.; co-founder of an express company which merged into American Express Co. (1850), president (1850-68); organized Wells Fargo (1852) to operate in the West (died 1878).

1806 Isaac Leeser, rabbi and editor, was born in Westphalia, Germany; rabbi of two Philadelphia synagogues (1829-68); founder, editor, *The Occident and American Jewish Advocate* (1843-68); founder, Maimonides College (1868) (died 1868).

1830 Joseph O. Shelby, Confederate general, was born in Lexington, Ky.; served as cavalry commander, mostly in Western theaters (died 1897).

1843 William P. Dillingham, legislator, was born in Waterbury, Vt.; represented Vermont in the Senate (1900-23), wrote bill which set immigration quotas for more than 40 years; served state as governor (1888-90) (died 1923).

1846 The Treaty of New Granada (Colombia) was signed, conveying the right of way to the United States to cross the Isthmus of Panama and guaranteeing neutrality of the isthmus and sovereignty of New Granada.

1849 Peter F. Collier, publisher, was born in County Carlow, Ireland; in publishing business (1877), founder and publisher, *Colliers Weekly* (1896-1909) (died 1909).

1864 Arthur Brisbane, columnist, was born in Buffalo; editor, *New York Evening Journal* (1897-1921); daily editorial columnist (from 1918), syndicated to about 1000 weekly, daily newspapers (died 1936).

1864 Paul E. More, essayist and literary critic, was born in St. Louis; worked on various publications, wrote 11 volumes of essays; co-founder of modern humanism (died 1937).

1866 Edward A. Ross, sociologist, was born in Virden, Ill.; with U. of Wisconsin (1906-37); a founder of American sociology (died 1951).

1876 First prohibition amendment to the Constitution proposed in House by Henry W. Blair of New Hampshire.

1878 Rachel Crothers, writer, was born in Bloomington, Ill.; playwright (*The Three of Us, Susan and God, Nice People*); an organizer, American Theater Wing, which operated the stage door canteens (died 1958).

1881 Arthur Garfield Hays, civil liberties leader, was born in Rochester, N.Y.; general counsel, national director, American Civil Liberties Union (1912-54) (died 1954).

1881 Harry M. Warner, president, Warner Bros. (1923-56), was born in Krasnosielce, Poland (died 1958).

1893 Edward G. Robinson, screen actor, was born in Bucharest; starred in many films (*Little Caesar, Brother Orchid, Five-Star Final*) (died 1973).

1910 President Taft nominated Associate Justice Edward D. White as chief justice of the Supreme Court; confirmed by Senate the same day.

1912 Henry Armstrong, boxing champion, was born in Columbus, Miss.; held three titles simultaneously (featherweight, welterweight, lightweight) (1937-38) (died 1988).

1913 First crossword puzzle, by Arthur Wynne, was published in the *New York World*.

1915 Frank Sinatra, singer and screen actor, was born in Hoboken, N.J.; made many concert, record appearances; movies (*From Here to Eternity, Pal Joey*).

1923 Bob Barker, television personality (*The Price is Right*), was born in Darrington, Wash.

1927 Robert Noyce, technologist and manufacturer, was born in Burlington, Iowa; invented the integrated circuit, founder of several Silicon Valley (Cal.) high-tech companies.

1928 Helen Frankenthaler, artist, was born in New York City; work was transitional between abstract expressionism and color field painting.

1937 Japanese bombers, while on a bombing attack on China, sank the American gunboat *Panay* and three Standard Oil supply ships, 27 miles above Nanking on the Yangtze River; Japan accepted responsibility, made formal apology, and paid indemnities.

1985 A DC-8 jetliner carrying 284 homebound American soldiers and eight crew members crashed on takeoff after refueling at Gander, Newfoundland; all killed.

1985 President Reagan signed the Gramm-Rudman balanced-budget law which set progressively lower federal deficit targets for FY 1986 through 1991; called for automatic federal spending cuts if targets are not met.

1987 A. Bartlett Giamatti, 48-year-old president of Yale University (1977-86), became president of the National (Baseball) League.

DECEMBER 13

1810 Clark Mills, sculptor, was born in Onandaga County, N.Y.; did first American equestrian statue (Gen. Jackson facing the White House), which also was the first large bronze statue cast in the United States; did many busts (died 1883).

1816 The first American savings bank, the Provident Institution for Savings, in Boston, was incorporated; opened Feb 25, 1819.

1818 Mary Todd Lincoln, wife of President Lincoln, was born in Lexington, Ky. (died 1882).

1835 Phillips Brooks, Episcopal prelate, was born in Boston; rector, Trinity Church, Boston (1869-91); bishop of Massachusetts (1891-93); wrote "O Little Town of Bethlehem" (died 1893).

1837 William Lyon McKenzie, Canadian insurgent leader who led an unsuccessful raid on Toronto, set up a provisional government on Navy Island; surrendered Jan 13, 1838, imprisoned for 18 months for violating American neutrality.

1844 John H. Patterson, industrialist, was born in Dayton, Ohio; bought National Manufacturing Co. (1884), developed it into the successful National Cash Register Co. (died 1922).

1856 A(bbot) Lawrence Lowell, educator, was born in Boston; president, Harvard(1909-33); had great impact on higher education (died 1943).

1857 Lucius W. Nieman, newspaper editor, was born in Bear Creek, Wis.; editor, part owner, *Milwaukee Journal*; endowed Nieman Fellowships for journalism at Harvard (died 1935).

1862 The Battle of Fredericksburg (Va.) occurred between 122,000 Union troops under Gen. A.E. Burnside and 78,000 Confederates under Gen. Robert E. Lee; massed attack failed, Union forces withdrew; Union losses were 1,284 dead and 9,600 wounded; Confederates about 600 dead, 4,700 wounded; Burnside was replaced by Gen. Joseph Hooker.

1863 Mason M. Patrick, Army officer, was born in Lewisburg, W. Va.; chief of air service, AEF (1918-19), chief of Army Air Service (1921-27) (died 1942).

1886 Roy S. Durstine, partner in BBDO (Batton, Barton, Durstine and Osborn), advertising agency (1918-39), was born in Jamestown, N.D. (died 1962).

1887 Alvin C. York, most decorated World War I American soldier, was born in Pall Mall, Tenn.; awarded Congressional Medal of Honor for capturing German machine gun nest and 90 men (died 1964).

1890 Marc(us C.) Connelly, playwright, was born in McKeesport, Pa.; co-author (*Dulcy, Merton of the Movies, Beggar on Horseback*); author (*Green Pastures*) (died 1980).

1897 Drew Pearson, columnist, was born in Evanston, Ill.; syndicated columnist with Robert Allen (1932-42)(Washington Merry-Go-Round); alone (1942-69) (died 1969).

1899 Harold K. Guinzburg, co-founder, Viking Press (1925), was born in New York City; founder of Literary Guild (1926) (died 1961).

1915 Ross MacDonald, author, was born in Las Gatos, Cal. as Kenneth Millar; wrote many mystery novels, created Lew Archer, detective (died 1983).

1920 George Shultz, public official, was born in New York City; Secretary of Labor (1969-70); director, Office of Management & Budget (1970-72); Secretary of Treasury (1972-74), of State (1982-89)

1921 A four-power treaty involving Pacific possessions was signed by the United States, Great Britain, France, and Japan; became effective Aug 17, 1923.

1923 Philip W. Anderson, physicist, was born in Indianapolis; shared 1977 Nobel Physics Prize for work underlying computer memories, electronic devices.

1925 Dick Van Dyke, actor, was born in West Plains, Mo.; starred on stage (*Bye Bye Birdie*), screen (*Mary Poppins*) and on television.

1979 The Supreme Court ordered the dismissal of a suit by 24 congressmen challenging the president's termination of a defense treaty with Taiwan.

1988 The Quadrennial Commission on Executive, Legislative and Judicial Salaries recommended a 50% pay increase for Congress, federal judges and other top federal officials; congressmen and federal judges would be raised from $99,500 to $135,000, cabinet members from $89,500 to $155,000, the vice president and chief justice from $115,000 to $175,000; proposal was approved by the president but disapproved by the House and the Senate; compromise pay increases were subsequently passed.

DECEMBER 14

1715 Thomas Dongan, colonial administrator, died at 81; governor of New York (1682-88).

1773 A large number of Bostonians met to discuss the arrival of a ship loaded with tea; voted to ask the owner to send the ship and tea back to England.

1774 Ft. William and Mary in Portsmouth (N.H.) harbor was captured by 400 men, probably the first blow for independence.

1775 Philander Chase, Episcopal prelate, was born in Cornish, N.H.; frontier bishop (Ohio 1819-31, Illinois 1835); presiding bishop (1843-52); founder, Kenyon College (1824) (died 1852).

1777 Thomas Conway was appointed a major general against General Washington's recommendation; Conway led conspiracy (Conway Cabal) to supplant Washington with Horatio Gates; plot discovered, Conway resigned.

1779 James Madison was elected to the Continental Congress, the youngest delegate; served until 1786.

1780 Judah P. Spooner and Timothy Green IV published the first newspaper in Vermont, the *Vermont Gazette and Green Mountain Post-Boy*, in Westminster.

1782 The British evacuated Charleston, S.C. after more than two years occupation.

1790 Alexander Hamilton proposed the creation of a national bank; approved by the Senate (Dec 23, 1790) and House (Feb 8, 1791) and signed by President Washington (Feb 25, 1791).

1794 Erastus Corning, merchant and industrialist, was born in Norwich, Conn.; a founder, first president, New York Central Railroad; mayor of Albany (died 1872).

1799 George Washington, after a ride in snow and rain around his estate, developed acute laryngitis; after being bled, he died at Mt. Vernon at 67; President John Adams asked Americans to wear crepe on their left arm for 30 days in his memory; eulogized in Congress by Henry Lee as "first in war, first in peace, first in the hearts of his countrymen."

1801 Joseph Lane, Oregon pioneer and Mexican War general, was born in Buncombe County, N.C.; governor of Oregon Territory (1848-50), one of its first senators (1859-61) (died 1881).

1814 The Battle of Lake Borgne preceded the battle for New Orleans, with the British clearing the western approach to the city and skirting its fortifications; British delayed attack on New Orleans because of their heavy losses, thus providing time for an organized defense.

1819 Alabama was admitted to the Union as the 22nd state.

1829 John M. Langston, diplomat and educator, was born in Louisa, Va.; minister to Haiti (1877-85); president, Virginia Normal and Collegiate Institute (1885-97) (died 1897).

1856 Louis Marshall, lawyer and Jewish leader, was born in Syracuse; involved in numerous civil rights and labor cases; a founder, Jewish Welfare Board; chairman, American Jewish Relief Committee during World War I (died 1929).

1884 Jane Cowl, actress, was born in Boston; many starring roles (*Lilac Time, Smilin' Through, Within the Law, Common Clay*) (died 1950).

1885 Brock Pemberton, theatrical director and producer, was born in Leavenworth, Kan.; produced many hits (*Miss Lulu Bett, Strictly Dishonorable, Kiss the Boys Goodbye, Harvey*) (died 1950).

1894 Eugene V. Debs was sentenced to six months in prison for contempt of court during the Pullman strike; other leaders were given three months.

1896 James H. Doolittle, Air Forces general, was born in Alameda, Cal.; pioneer aviator, led B-25 raid on Tokyo (1942); commanded Air Forces in North African invasion; commander, 8th Air Force in Europe (1944).

1902 Julia D. Grant, widow of President Grant, died in Washington at 76.

1904 The Chicago Orchestra Hall opened with a concert conducted by Theodore Thomas.

1904 The Senate began impeachment hearings against District Judge Charles Swayne of Florida for incompetence and corruption; acquitted Feb 27,1905.

1909 Edward L. Tatum, geneticist, was born in Boulder, Colo.; shared 1958 Nobel Physiology/Medicine Prize for discovering how genes transmit hereditary characteristics (died 1975).

1911 Spike (Lindley A.) Jones, musician, was born in Long Beach, Cal.; leader of orchestra which featured unusual arrangements and sound effects (died 1965).

1919 Shirley Jackson, author, was born in San Francisco; short story writer ("The Lottery," "Life Among the Savages") (died 1965).

1920 Congress, as part of its naval appropriations bill, asked the president to call an international naval conference.

1934 Charlie Rich, country and Western singer, was born in Forrest City, Ark.; known as "the Silver Fox," he made many hit records.

1946 John D. Rockefeller Jr. gave $8.5 million toward the purchase of New York City property for the United Nations headquarters.

1965 Connecticut voters ratified their new state constitution by a vote of 178,432 to 84,129.

1988 President Reagan, in a surprising reversal, authorized "a substantive dialogue" with the PLO (Palestine Liberation Organization); three weeks earlier a visa was denied PLO leader Yasser Arafat to come to the United States because the PLO was involved in terrorism.

1988 President-elect Bush announced he would nominate Clayton Yeutter to be Secretary of Agriculture; had served as U. S. trade representative (1986-89).

DECEMBER 15

1689 James Blair was appointed ecclesiastical representative of the Bishop of London in Virginia; founded the College of William & Mary (1693), its first president (1693-1743).

1770 Thomas Jefferson was commissioned lieutenant of Albemarle County and "Chief Commander of all His Majesty's Militia, Horse and Foote" in that county.

1778 Maryland refused to ratify the Articles of Confederation until the rights to Western territories were clarified.

1791 The Bill of Rights—the first ten amendments to the Constitution— went into effect after ratification by the states.

1795 The Senate, by a vote of 14-10, rejected the nomination of John Rutledge as chief justice of the Supreme Court because of his speech opposing the Jay Treaty before his nomination.

1814 The Hartford Convention began to consider revisions in the Constitution; ended Jan 5, 1815 with a statement declaring that states had a right to protect their own best interests; set up a committee to negotiate with the Federal Government but disbanded after the victory at New Orleans and the Treaty of Ghent.

1831 Franklin B. Sanborn, newspaper editor and abolitionist, was born in Hampton Falls, N.H.; arranged financing for John Brown's raid on Harpers Ferry; narrowly avoided prosecution (died 1917).

1835 The Mexican Government abolished all local rights in Texas.

1836 A fire in Washington destroyed the Post Office and Patent Office buildings.

1837 George B. Post, architect, was born in New York City; pioneered in introducing elevators in buildings, using iron floor beams, supplying steam heat in business buildings; among his buildings were those at City College of New York, New York Stock Exchange, the Wisconsin Capitol (died 1913).

1846 John E. Pillsbury, naval officer, was born in Lowell, Mass.; with U.S. Coast Survey (1875-91), made study of Gulf Stream; engaged in Santiago blockade (1898) (died 1919).

1848 Edwin H. Blashfield, artist, was born in New York City; did murals (Evolution of Civilization) in dome of Library of Congress (died 1936).

1855 Kansas ratified its state constitution; prohibited slavery.

1861 Charles E. Duryea, auto manufacturer, was born near Canton, Ill.; reputed to be the father of the automobile; with brother, J. Frank Duryea (*see* 10/8/1869), organized Duryea Motor Wagon Co. (1895), sold first car (1896); inventor of spray carburetor (1892), first to use pneumatic tires on cars (1893) (died 1938).

1863 Arthur D. Little, chemical engineer, was born in Boston; invented processes for chrome tanning, electrolytic manufacture of chlorates, artificial silk, gas; superintendent of first American mill producing sulphite wood pulp (died 1935).

1864 Union troops under Gen. George Thomas and Gen. John M. Schofield routed Confederates under Gen. John B. Hood in two-day battle before Nashville.

1877 John T. McNicholas, Catholic prelate, was born in County Mayo, Ireland; archbishop of Cincinnati (1925-50) (died 1950).

1888 Maxwell Anderson, author, was born in Atlantic, Pa.; many hit plays (*Elizabeth the Queen, Mary of Scotland, High Tor, Key Largo, Winterset, Anne of the Thousand Days, Bad Seed*); co-author of *What Price Glory?* (died 1959).

1890 Sitting Bull, 56-year-old Sioux chief, who led his tribe against Americans, died after being shot in a scuffle with Indian police at Standing Rock (S.D.) reservation.

1892 J. Paul Getty, oil industry leader, was born in Minneapolis; developed family business into a vast company (1956); considered one of world's wealthiest men, leaving over $1 billion when he died in 1976.

1908 The U.S. Circuit Court issued a final decree against the tobacco trust, American Tobacco Co. et al, and restrained the combined companies from interstate and foreign trade.

1913 Muriel Rukeyser, poet, was born in New York City; wrote poetry on social and political themes (*Orpheus, Walter Lily Fire, Elegies*) (died 1980).

1938 President Franklin Roosevelt spoke at the groundbreaking ceremonies for the Jefferson Memorial in Washington.

1944 The plane in which Glenn Miller, orchestra leader, was a passenger disappeared on a flight from England to France.

1965 Walter M. Schirra Jr. and Thomas P. Stafford completed the first space rendezvous when their Gemini capsule joined with that of Frank Borman and James A. Lovell Jr.

1967 The Silver Bridge over the Ohio River, connecting Pt. Pleasant, W. Va. and Kanauga, Ohio, collapsed; 46 persons were killed.

1976 The *Argo Merchant* ran aground off Nantucket Island, resulting in a 7.7 million gallon oil spill.

DECEMBER 16

1773 Boston Tea Party took place as 50 to 60 colonists disguised as Mohawk Indians dumped 342 chests of tea from the vessel, *Dartmouth,* into the harbor to protest the import duty on tea.

1792 Abbott Lawrence, textile manufacturer, was born in Groton, Mass.; with brothers (Amos 4/22/1786 and William 9/7/1783), he founded textile industry in Lawrence, Mass.; represented Massachusetts in the House (1835-40); minister to Great Britain (1849-52) (died 1855).

1811 An earthquake centered near New Madrid, Mo. resulted in an area of 30,000 square miles sinking from 5 to 15 ft.; listed among the greatest known earthquakes in history.

1817 John S. Carlile, legislator, was born in Winchester, Va.; represented Virginia in the House (1855-57), a leader in creation of state of West Virginia, which he represented in the Senate (1861-65) (died 1878).

1828 John Beatty, Union general and legislator, was born near Sandusky, Ohio; saw action at Murfreesboro, Lookout Mountain, and Knoxville; represented Ohio in the House (1868-73) (died 1914).

1830 John F. Hartranft, Union general and public official, was born near Pottstown, Pa.; served through Civil War; governor of Pennsylvania (1873-79) (died 1889).

1833 Seaman A. Knapp, agriculturist, was born in Schroon Lake, N.Y.; developed rice growing in Louisiana (died 1911).

1835 The "great fire" in New York City destroyed 700 buildings in the heart of the city, causing $20 million in property damage.

1844 Helen F. G. Villard, social activist, was born in Boston, wife of Henry Villard (*see* 4/10/1835) and daughter of William Lloyd Garrison (*see* 12/12/1805); head of Women's Peace Society (1919-28); a founder, NAACP (died 1928).

1846 The Mormon Battalion, enroute from New Mexico to California, captured Tucson.

1846 A convention in Madison framed a Wisconsin state constitution; rejected by a referendum in Apr 1847.

1854 Joseph Fels, manufacturer and social reformer, was born in Halifax Court House, Va.; founder, Fels-Naphtha (Soap) Co.; championed single-tax program (died 1914).

1854 Austin M. Knight, World War I admiral, was born in Ware, Mass.; had various assignments, including president, Naval War College (1913-17); commander, Asiatic Fleet (1917-18) (died 1927).

1857 Edward E. Barnard, astronomer, was born in Nashville; with Lick and Yerkes observatories; using wide-angle cameras he photographed Milky Way, opened new astronomical field of study; discovered first new satellite of Jupiter since Galileo (died 1923).

1857 The new chamber for the House of Representatives in the Capitol was completed.

1863 George Santayana, philosopher and author, was born in Madrid; professor, Harvard (1889-1912); author (*The Life of Reason, The Sense of Beauty, The Last Puritan*) (died 1952).

1863 Ralph A. Cram, architect, was born in Hampton Falls, N.H.; supervising architect for Princeton U. (1907-29); helped plan buildings for West Point, Rice Institute, Cathedral of St. John the Divine (died 1942).

1868 Benevolent and Protective Order of Elks was organized in New York City.

1877 Artur Bodanzky, conductor and composer, was born in Vienna; conductor, Metropolitan Opera Company (1915-39) (died 1939).

1901 Margaret Mead, anthropologist and author, was born in Philadelphia; with American Museum of Natural History (1926-69); author (*Coming of Age in Samoa, Sex and Temperament, And Keep Your Powder Dry*) (died 1978).

1907 A fleet of 16 American battleships began a world cruise to demonstrate American naval strength; returned Feb 21, 1909.

1918 The Colorado governor signed a statewide prohibition law; prohibition went into effect in Nevada.

1941 The French liner *Normandie* in New York Harbor was taken over by the Navy.

1943 The collision of two railroad streamliners near Lamberton, N. C. resulted in the death of 73 persons.

1944 The Battle of the Bulge began as Germans tried to sever American lines in the Belgium-Luxembourg area; turned back by Christmas Day.

1951 A plane plunged into the Elizabeth River after takeoff from the Elizabeth (N.J.) Airport; 56 were killed.

1960 A midair collision of two airliners over New York City resulted in 134 dead.

1963 President Lyndon Johnson signed a bill setting up a $1.2 billion construction program for college classrooms, laboratories, and libraries.

1974 President Ford and French President d'Estaing completed two days of meetings on energy and gold policies on the island of Martinique.

1988 Lyndon H. LaRouche Jr., political maverick, was convicted of 13 counts of tax- and mail-fraud conspiracy for cheating the IRS and his supporters; a perennial presidential candidate, LaRouche faces a maximum penalty of 65 years in prison and fines totaling $3.25 million.

1988 President-elect Bush announced he would nominate John G. Tower to be his Secretary of Defense; Tower, 63, served Texas in the Senate (1962-84).

1988 Ambassador Robert H. Pelletreau Jr. and four representatives of the Palestine Liberation Organization met in Tunis for 90 minutes in a historic meeting of the two sides.

DECEMBER 17

1540 Hernando DeSoto reached the Mississippi River; remained until Apr 25,1541.

1623 Plymouth Colony established trial by jury.

1734 William Floyd, colonial leader, was born in Brookhaven, N.Y.; member, Continental Congress (1774-77, 1778-83) and a signer of the Declaration of Independence; represented New York in the House (1789-91) (died 1821).

1748 James M. Varnum, Revolutionary general and legislator, was born in Dracut, Mass.; commanded Forts Mercer and Mifflin on the Delaware; member, Continental Congress (1780-82, 1786, 1787) (died 1789).

1754 George Washington leased Mt. Vernon from his half-brother's widow at an annual rent of 15,000 lbs. of tobacco; inherited estate in 1761.

1758 Nathaniel Macon, legislator, was born in what is now Warren County, N.C.; represented North Carolina in the House (1791-1815), serving as Speaker (1801-07), and in the Senate (1815-28), serving as president pro tem (1826-27) (died 1837).

1762 Pliny Earle, inventor and manufacturer, was born in Leicester, Mass.; invented wool- and cotton-carding machinery (died 1832).

1777 France recognized the independence of the 13 American colonies.

1792 South Carolina enacted a law prohibiting the importation of slaves; amended Dec 18, 1817, repealed Dec 16, 1818.

1797 Joseph Henry, physicist, was born in Albany; first developed the electro-magnet, primitive versions of the telegraph, electric motor; first secretary, director, Smithsonian Institution (1846-78); unit of induction, "henry," named for him (died 1878).

1807 John Greenleaf Whittier, writer and editor, was born in Haverhill, Mass.; poet (Ichabod, Barbara Frietchie); a founder, editor, *Atlantic Monthly* (died 1892).

1815 John Bapst, educator, was born in LaRoche, Switzerland; founder, Boston College (1858) (died 1887).

1817 Henry R. Worthington, inventor and manufacturer, was born in New York City; developed direct steam pump (1859), invented duplex steam feed pump (died 1880).

1824 Thomas S. King, Unitarian clergyman, was born in New York City; served pastorates in Boston (1848-60), San Francisco (1860-64); helped save California for the Union cause (died 1864).

1835 Alexander Agassiz, zoologist, was born in Neuchatel, Switzerland, son of Louis Agassiz (5/28/1807); developed, headed, Calumet, Hecla copper mines; curator, Harvard's Museum of Comparative Zoology (1874-85), director (1902-10) (died 1910).

1860 James H. McGraw, publisher, was born in Panama, N.Y.; publisher of technical magazines (McGraw-Hill 1916-48) (died 1948).

1861 Arthur E. Kennelly, electrical engineer, was born in Bombay,,India; established units, standards adopted internationally (died 1939).

1866 Supreme Court in Milligan case held that no branch of the government has the power to suspend writ of habeas corpus where the courts are open.

1892 Edwin J. Cohn, chemist, was born in New York City; with Harvard (1912-53), did much work on fractionating blood (died 1953).

1894 Arthur Fiedler, conductor, was born in Boston; founder, leader, Boston Pops orchestra (1930-79) (died 1979).

1903 Wilbur and Orville Wright demonstrated the first motor driven airplane at Kitty Hawk, N.C., with Orville first flying 120 feet in 12 second; Wilbur then went 852 feet in 59 seconds.

1903 Erskine Caldwell, author, was born in White Oak, Ga.; best known for *Tobacco Road* and *God's Little Acre*; collaborated with photographer- wife, Margaret Bourke-White (6/14/1906) on several pictorial books.

1906 William McM. Martin Jr., economist, was born in St. Louis; first salaried president, New York Stock Exchange (1938-41); director, Export-Import Bank (1945-50); chairman, Federal Reserve Board (1951-70).

1908 Willard F. Libby, physicist, was born in Grand Valley, Colo.; awarded 1960 Nobel Chemistry Prize for using carbon-14 to measure time in archaeology and geology (died 1980).

1927 Submarine S-4 sank after colliding with a Coast Guard destroyer off Provincetown, Mass.; all 40 men aboard were lost.

1941 Rear Admiral Chester Nimitz replaced Admiral Husband Kimmel as commander-in-chief of the American Pacific Fleet.

1985 President Reagan vetoed a bill which would have limited American imports of textiles.

DECEMBER 18

1680 Josiah Winslow, colonial governor, died at about 51; governor of Plymouth Colony (1673-80), the first native-born colonial governor.

1776 A North Carolina convention adopted the state constitution, named Richard Caswell governor.

1787 A New Jersey convention unanimously ratified the Constitution, becoming the third state in the Union.

1789 Virginia consented to separation of Kentucky counties from its jurisdiction.

1813 The British captured Ft. Niagara in a surprise attack.

1819 Isaac T. Hecker, Catholic priest, was born in New York City; principal founder, Paulist Fathers, superior (1858-88); founder, *Catholic World* (1865), *Young Catholic* (1870); organized Catholic Publication Society (1870) (died 1888).

1820 The Alabama legislature chartered a state university at Tuscaloosa.

1835 Lyman Abbott, Congregational clergyman and editor, was born in Roxbury, Mass., son of Jacob Abbott (11/14/1803); editor, *Illustrated Christian Weekly* (1876), became co-editor, *Christian Union* (1876-81), editor in chief (1881-99), and continued when they became *The Outlook*; pastor, Plymouth Congregational Church (1890-99); author (*Theology of an Evolutionist, The Spirit of Democracy*) (died 1922).

1858 The *Territorial Enterprise*, the first newspaper in Nevada, was published by William L. Jernegan and Alfred James.

1860 A South Carolina convention in Charleston adopted an ordinance of secession from the Union and declared itself an independent commonwealth; formally adopted by the legislature Dec 20.

1861 Edward A. MacDowell, musician, was born in New York City; composer (*Indian Suite, Woodland Sketches, Sea Pieces*) (died 1908).

1864 Samuel F. Cadman, Congregational clergyman, was born in Wellington, England; served churches in New York City; president (1924-28) and its radio minister (1928-36), Federal Council of Churches of Christ, the first radio minister (died 1936).

1865 The 13th Amendment, which prohibited slavery, was ratified.

1872 William H. Standley, diplomat and naval officer, was born in Ukiah, Cal.; chief of naval operations (1933-37); ambassador to Russia (1942-43) (died 1963).

1881 Gladys Dick, physician, was born in Pawnee City, Neb.; with husband, George F. Dick (7/21/1881), made important discoveries about scarlet fever (died 1963).

1886 Ty(rus R.) Cobb, baseball player, was born in Narrows, Ga.; probably greatest offensive baseball player of all time; lifetime batting average .367 with 4191 hits in 33 years, mostly with Detroit; among first five to be named to Baseball Hall of Fame (died 1961).

1888 Robert Moses, public official, was born in New Haven; headed New York State and New York City park commissions (1924-64); president, New York World Fair (1964-65) (died 1981).

1890 Edwin H. Armstrong, radio pioneer, was born in New York City; best known for development of FM (frequency modulation) radio transmission; also invented superheterodyne circuit, basic to modern radio, television, radar (died 1954).

1895 The Anti-Saloon League was founded in Washington.

1898 Fletcher Henderson, musician, was born in Cuthbert, Ga.; a most influential jazz arranger, orchestra leader (died 1952).

1904 George Stevens, film director, was born in Oakland, Cal.; directed many hit movies (*Gunga Din, A Place in the Sun, Shane, Giant, Diary of Anne Frank*) (died 1975).

1913 Ray Meyer, basketball coach (DePaul 1942-85), was born in Chicago.

1915 The widowed President Wilson married a widow, Mrs. Edith B. Galt, in Washington.

1916 Betty Grable, screen actress, was born in St. Louis; she was the pin-up girl of World War II (died 1973).

1916 President Wilson suggested peace negotiations to World War I belligerents, asked for a statement of terms; Central Powers and Turkey suggested no terms but asked for a meeting in a neutral country; the Allies asked for reparations, the return of conquered areas, and freedom for Czechs and Slavs.

1939 Dr. Harold E. Varmus, who shared the 1989 Nobel Physiology/Medicine Prize for his cancer research, was born in Oceanside, N.Y.

1941 Office of Defense Transportation was created by executive order.

1947 Steven Spielberg, movie producer, was born in Cincinnati; produced a number of hit movies (*ET, Raiders of the Lost Ark*).

1958 The Score satellite was launched, becoming the first to transmit voice messages from space.

1964 President Lyndon Johnson announced a new sea-level canal would be constructed in Central America or Colombia and a new treaty had been proposed to Panama to replace the 1903 pact.

1972 President Nixon ordered the resumption of bombing over North Vietnam.

DECEMBER 19

1675 During the "Great Swamp Fight," New England troops led by Gen. Josiah Winslow captured the Narragansett fort, with more than 1000 Indians killed or captured.

1714 John Winthrop, astronomer and physicist, was born in Boston; did important astronomy research at Harvard (1738-79); established first American experimental physics laboratory (1746) (died 1779).

1732 *Poor Richard's Almanack* was published in Philadelphia for the first time by Benjamin Franklin.

1753 John Taylor, legislator and agriculturist, was born in Caroline County, Va.; represented Virginia in the Senate (1792-94, 1803, 1822-24); pioneered in crop rotation (died 1824).

1776 Thomas Paine published first issue of "American Crisis," in which he stated: "These are the times that try men's souls..."

1777 Gen. Washington and his troops established their headquarters in Valley Forge, Pa. for the winter.

1779 The Council of Pennsylvania conducted a courtmartial of Benedict Arnold on two trivial charges brought by Philadelphia permitting the entry of unauthorized vessels into the port and using state wagons to transport private property; court directed a reprimand by the commander-in-chief.

1813 After the British captured Ft. Niagara, they burned the villages of Youngstown, Lewiston, and Manchester.

1814 Edwin M. Stanton, public official, was born in Steubenville, Ohio; Attorney General (1860-41); Secretary of War (1862-67), dismissed by President Andrew Johnson for opposing his policies, touching off an impeachment effort by his enemies; resigned (May 1868) when impeachment effort failed, named to Supreme Court (1869) but died before he could take his seat.

1817 James J. Archer, Confederate general, was born in Harford County, Md.; served at Manassas, Antietam, Gettysburg, where he was captured; died soon after his release in 1864.

1846 Ambrose Swasey, inventor and manufacturer, was born in Exeter, N.H.; co-founder, Warner & Swasey (1881), makers of machine tools, astronomical instruments; invented a range and position finder (died 1937).

1849 Henry C. Frick, steel industry leader, was born in West Overton, Pa.; built, operated coke ovens; chairman, Carnegie Steel Co. (1889-1900), a leader in the consolidation which resulted in the U.S. Steel Co. (1901); endowed the Frick Museum of Art, New York City (which once was his home) (died 1919).

1852 Albert A. Michelson, physicist, was born in Strelno, Germany; head of physics department, U. of Chicago (1892-1931); established speed of light; first American to be awarded the Nobel Physics Prize (1907) for his spectroscopic and metrologic investigations (died 1931).

1865 Minnie Maddern Fiske, actress, was born in New Orleans; starred in many plays, popularized Ibsen's plays in the United States (died 1932).

1869 George H. Doran, publisher, was born in Toronto; founded publishing company (1907), merged with F. N. Doubleday (1927) to form Doubleday, Doran & Co. (died 1956).

1888 Fritz Reiner, conductor, was born in Budapest; led orchestras in Cincinnati (1922-31), Pittsburgh (1938-48), and Chicago (1953-62) (died 1963).

1890 The State University of Oklahoma was founded in Norman; opened 1892.

1894 Ford Frick, journalist and baseball executive, was born in Wawaka Ind.; a New York sports writer; baseball commissioner (1951-65); named to Baseball Hall of Fame (died 1978).

1901 Oliver H. P. LaFarge, writer and anthropologist, was born in New York City; president, American Association of Indian Affairs (1933-42, 1948-63); best remembered book is *Laughing Boy* (died 1963).

1903 George Snell, laboratory scientist, was born in Bradford, Mass.; shared 1980 Nobel Physiology/Medicine Prize for discoveries of how genetic makeup determines the body's response to infection and cancer development.

1907 A mine explosion at Jacob's Creek, Pa. killed 239 miners.

1920 David H. Susskind, producer and television host, was born in New York City; host of syndicated talk show (died 1987).

1934 Al(bert W.) Kaline, baseball player (Tigers 1953-74), was born in Baltimore; named to Baseball Hall of Fame.

1941 The Office of Censorship, headed by Byron Price, was created by executive order.

1943 William C. DeVries, who headed the team which placed the first Jarvik-7 heart into a human being (1982), was born in New York City.

1945 President Truman named Eleanor Roosevelt, widow of President Franklin Roosevelt, to the American UN delegation; she later became head of the UN Human Rights Commission.

1946 Laffit Pincay, leading jockey in career purse earnings ($116.1 million) and second in career victories, was born in Panama City, Panama; outstanding jockey five times and named to Racing Hall of Fame.

1950 Gen. Dwight D. Eisenhower was appointed supreme commander of European defense by the NATO ministers; resigned May 30, 1952 to accept the Republican presidential nomination.

1960 Fire aboard the aircraft carrier *Constellation*, under construction in the Brooklyn Navy Yard, killed 50 and injured 150, doing $50 million damage.

1967 President Lyndon Johnson began a week-long round-the-world trip, including stops in Australia, Thailand, South Vietnam, Pakistan, Italy, and the Azores.

1974 Nelson A. Rockefeller was confirmed and sworn in as Vice President.

1984 The United States withdrew from UNESCO (United Nations Educational, Scientific & Cultural Organization) because of the agency's mismanagement and politicization.

1987 Texaco Inc. and Pennzoil Co. signed a final settlement designed to end their $10.3 billion lawsuit and close the most costly legal battle in American history.

1988 President-elect Bush announced he would nominate veteran New York congressman Jack Kemp to be Secretary of Housing and Urban Development.

DECEMBER 20

1606 Colonists set sail from England to Virginia in three ships.

1686 Sir Edmund Andros arrived in Boston to assume the leadership of the New England government and to organize a Dominion of New England (to include New York, New Jersey, and Pennsylvania) for more effective military operations in the event of war with France and for better enforcement of the Navigation Acts.

1744 Joshua Clayton, colonial leader, was born in Cecil County, Md.; served as "president" of Delaware (1789-92) and its first governor (1792-96) (died 1798).

1776 The 3rd Continental Congress opened in Baltimore.

1783 Virginia ceded western lands to the central government; this opened the way for Maryland to ratify the Articles of Confederation.

1803 The United States took formal possession of Louisiana after its purchase, with William C.C. Claiborne, governor of the Mississippi Territory, representing the United States and Pierre Clement de Laussat the French.

1812 Sacagawea, Indian interpreter, died at about 25; she was the only woman to accompany the Lewis and Clark Expedition.

1813 Samuel J. Kirkwood, Interior Secretary (1881-82), was born in Harford County, Md.; served Iowa as governor (1860-64, 1876-77) and represented it in the Senate (1866-67, 1877-81) (died 1894).

1832 Robert Y. Hayne, South Carolina governor, issued a counter-proclamation to President Jackson's nullification proclamation; called for a general convention of states to consider federal-state relations.

1860 South Carolina seceded from the Union, stating that "the union now subsisting between South Carolina and other states, under the name of the 'United States of America' is hereby dissolved."

1862 Confederate troops captured the Union supply base at Holly Springs, Miss., destroying a large quantity of supplies.

1864 Gen. William T. Sherman's Union troops took over Savannah, completing an eight- month march to the sea; Confederate troops retreated to Charleston.

1867 William W. ("Pudge") Heffelfinger, legendary football player, was born in Minneapolis; starred for Yale (1888-91), on all-time football team (died 1954).

1868 Harvey S. Firestone, tire manufacturer, was born in Columbiana, Ohio; organized Firestone Tire & Rubber Co. (1900), president (1903-32), chairman (1932-38); promoted rubber growing in the Philippines and South America (died 1938).

1876 Walter S. Adams, astronomer, was born in Antioch, Syria to American missionary parents; director, Mt. Wilson Observatory (1923-46), developed method of determining distance of a star from earth by comparing its luminosity to its apparent brightness (died 1956).

1879 Earle Ovington, aeronautical engineer, was born in Chicago; first American airmail pilot (1911); invented various electrical appliances, including high frequency apparatus (died 1936).

1881 Branch W. Rickey, baseball executive, was born in Stockdale, Ohio; manager, club president (Dodgers, Cardinals, Pirates); instituted "farm" system; brought first black player (Jackie Robinson) into major leagues; named to Baseball Hall of Fame (died 1965).

1884 William G. Mennen, toiletries manufacturer, was born in Newark; president, Mennen & Co. (1916-65) (died 1968).

1899 John J. Sparkman, legislator, was born in Hartselle, Ala.; represented Alabama in the House (1936-46) and Senate (1946-78); 1952 Democratic vice presidential candidate (died 1985).

1900 Gabby (Charles L.) Hartnett, baseball player, was born in Woonsocket, R.I.; catcher Cubs (1922-40); named to Baseball Hall of Fame (died 1972).

1900 Ted Fio Rito, bandleader, was born in Newark; composer (*King for a Day; Laugh, Clown, Laugh*) (died 1971).

1901 Robert J. Van de Graaff, physicist, was born in Tuscaloosa, Ala.; known for development of high voltage electrostatic generator, nuclear physicist (died 1967).

1904 Irene Dunne, screen actress, was born in Louisville; starred in several films (*The Awful Truth, Life With Father*).

1930 President Hoover signed the $116 million emergency construction act to aid the unemployed and the $45 million drought relief act.

1941 Admiral Ernest King was named commander-in-chief of American naval forces.

1945 The Senate by a vote of 65-7 and the House by a 344-15 passed the United Nations Participation Act, making the United States a member.

1952 An Air Force plane crashed on takeoff at Larson Air Force Base, Moses Lake, Wash.; 87 were killed.

1989 An invasion force of about 20,000 American troops overthrew the regime of Gen. Manuel A. Noriega in Panama; Noriega went into hiding for several days, then sought refuge in the Vatican mission in Panama City; surrendered to American drug agents Jan 3, 1990 and was flown to Miami to stand trial on drug charges; Panama Canal traffic was halted for one day by the invasion, the first closing in 75 years.

DECEMBER 21

1624 The charter of a Swedish West India Co. was granted to William Usselinx under which a colony was established on the Delaware River.

1719 The *Boston Gazette*, the third American newspaper, began publication under William Brocker; lasted until 1798.

1740 Arthur Lee, diplomat, was born in Westmoreland County, Va., brother of Richard H. Lee (1/20/1732) and Francis L. Lee (10/14/1734); arranged for French help for the Continental Army, several other foreign missions (died 1792).

1790 Samuel Slater began production in Pawtucket, R.I. in the first American cotton mill using new cotton cording and spindle mill machinery.

1837 Joseph G. McCoy, pioneer cattleman, was born in Sangamon County, Ill.; began driving cattle from Texas to Abilene, Kan.; later helped open the Chisholm Trail (died 1915).

1860 Henrietta Szold, Jewish leader, was born in Baltimore; founder, president, Hadassah, the American women's Zionist organization (1916-26) (died 1945).

1866 The Fetterman Massacre occurred near Ft. Kearny, Wyo., when 90 American soldiers under Capt. William J. Fetterman were massacred by Sioux Indians.

1876 Irénée DuPont, president, DuPont Co. (1919-26), was born in Wilmington, Del. (died 1963).

1890 Herman J. Muller, geneticist, was born in New York City; with Indiana U. (1945-67); awarded 1946 Nobel Physiology/Medicine Prize for work on hereditary effects of x-rays on genes (died 1967).

1891 John W. McCormack, legislator, was born in Boston; represented Massachusetts in the House (1928-71), majority leader (1940-41), Speaker (1962-71) (died 1980).

1892 Walter Hagen, one of three best golfers of 1900-50 era, was born in Rochester, N.Y.; won British (four times), American (two) and French Opens in 1920s (died 1969).

1895 Eric Johnston, executive, was born in Washington; national director, U.S. Chamber of Commerce (1934-41), president (1942-45); president, Motion Picture Producers & Distributors (1945-52) (died 1963).

1911 Josh Gibson, legendary Negro League baseball player, was born in Buena Vista, Ga.; named to Baseball Hall of Fame.

1918 Donald T. Regan, financier and public official, was born in Cambridge, Mass.; Treasury Secretary (1981-85), White House chief of staff (1985-); had been chairman, Merrill Lynch & Co.

1928 President Coolidge signed legislation for construction of the Boulder Dam; construction began Sept 17, 1930, completed 1936; renamed Hoover Dam.

1935 Phil Donahue, television personality, was born in Cleveland; host of daily talk show.

1937 Jane Fonda, screen actress, was born in New York City, daughter of Henry Fonda (5/16/1905); numerous starring roles (*Klute, Coming Home, On Golden Pond*); social activist, physical fitness authority.

1944 Bastogne was besieged by the Germans; siege lifted Dec 26.

1951 An explosion and fire in a West Frankfort, Ill. coal mine took 119 lives.

1954 Chris Evert (Lloyd), tennis player, was born in Ft. Lauderdale, Fla.; won many championships in 1970s, 1980s.

1979 Congress approved $1.5 billion in federal loan guarantees to the financially-strapped Chrysler Corp.

1988 Drexel Burnham Lambert Inc. agreed to plead guilty to six federal felony counts and pay a record $650 million fine to settle the biggest securities fraud case in history.

1988 A Pan-Am 747 enroute from Frankfurt, Germany to New York City exploded in mid-air over Lockerbie, Scotland, killing all 259 aboard and 11 on the ground; a week later investigators determined that a bomb in a suitcase was the cause.

DECEMBER 22

1696 James E. Oglethorpe, British general, was born in London; received charter (1732) to establish a colony of unemployed persons in Georgia; accompanied first group of immigrants (1733-34); founded Savannah; came again in 1735-36 and 1738-43 (died 1785).

1719 The first Pennsylvania newspaper, *American Weekly Mercury*, was published in Philadelphia by Andrew Bradford and John Copson.

1727 William Ellery, colonial leader, was born in Newport, R.I.; member, Continental Congress (1776-81, 1783-85) and a signer of the Declaration of Independence; chief justice, Rhode Island (1785) (died 1820).

1775 Esek Hopkins was named commander-in-chief of the colonial fleet and captains were named (John Paul Jones was then a first lieutenant); Hopkins faced insuperable difficulties, relieved of command 1778.

1789 Levi Woodbury, public official and jurist, was born in Francestown, N.H.; served New Hampshire as governor (1823-25) and represented it in the Senate (1825-31, 1841-45); Secretary of Navy (1831-34), of Treasury (1834-41); associate justice, Supreme Court (1845-51) (died 1851).

1807 Congress passed an Embargo Act, the first, designed to bring warring powers (Great Britain and France) to terms and end severe effects on American commerce; proved unenforceable and withdrawn Mar 1, 1809.

1821 Josiah B. Grinnell, Congregational clergyman and legislator, was born in New Haven; founded Grinnell, Iowa (1854); instrumental in planning Grinnell College; represented Iowa in the House (1863-67) (died 1891).

1823 Thomas W.S. Higginson, Unitarian clergyman and author, was born in Cambridge; active in anti-slavery movement; colonel of first black regiment (1862-64); biographer (Longfellow, Whittier) (died 1911).

1826 James S. Negly, Union general, was born in East Liberty, Pa.; saw action at Murfreesboro (died 1901).

1828 Rachel Jackson, wife of President Jackson, died in Nashville at 61.

1843 Prentiss Ingraham, author, was born in Adams County, Miss.; wrote about 700 adventure ("dime") novels, many of them about his friend, Buffalo Bill (died 1904).

1852 Opie Read, author, was born in Nashville; founder, editor, humorous journal, *Arkansas Traveler* (1883-91); author of adventure stories (died 1939).

1856 Frank B. Kellogg, attorney and public official, was born in Potsdam, N.Y.; successful federal prosecutor of anti-trust cases (Standard Oil, Union Pacific); Secretary of State (1925-29), co-author of Kellogg-Briand peace pact; awarded 1929 Nobel Peace Prize (died 1937).

1869 Edwin Arlington Robinson, author, was born in Head Tide, Me.; poet (*The Town Down the River, Merlin, Lancelot, Tristram*) (died 1935).

1869 Bainbridge Colby, public official, was born in St. Louis; Secretary of State (1920-21) (died 1950).

1883 Edgard Varese, composer, was born in Paris; one of the leading experimenters of 20th Century music (died 1965).

1885 Deems Taylor, composer and music critic, was born in New York City; wrote many compositions (*Peter Ibbetson, The King's Henchman, Jurgen*); radio commentator, New York Philharmonic broadcasts (died 1966).

1901 Andre Kostelanetz, conductor, was born in Leningrad; conductor of Boston Symphony, gained fame from radio broadcasts which began 1928 (died 1980).

1903 Haldan K. Hartline, biophysicist, was born in Bloomsburg, Pa.; shared 1967 Nobel Physiology/Medicine Prize for work on the human eye (died 1983).

1911 Grote Reber, astronomer and radio engineer, was born in Wheaton, Ill.; built first radio telescope (1937), pioneer in radio astronomy, mapped sources of light and low frequency.

1912 Claudia Alta Taylor (Ladybird) Johnson, wife of President Lyndon Johnson, was born in Karnack, Tex.

1919 About 250 alien radicals were deported.

1922 James C. Wright Jr., legislator, was born in Ft. Worth, Tex.; represented Texas in the House (1955-89), serving as Speaker (1987-89).

1941 The amended Selective Service Act was signed, extending military service to those between 20 and 44, with registration for all men between 18 and 64.

1944 Steve (Stephen N.) Carlton, baseball pitcher who won more than 300 games, was born in Miami; played with several teams (Cards, Phils) and was a leader in strikeouts with more than 4000.

1984 Bernhard Goetz, a New Yorker, shot and wounded four teen-age boys on a subway train after one of them asked for $5 and, according to him, threatened him.

1988 President-elect Bush announced five nominees for top federal posts—Louis Sullivan for Secretary of Health and Human Services; Samuel Skinner, a Chicago transit official, for Secretary of Transportation; New Mexico congressman Manuel Lujan for Interior Secretary; former Illinois congressman Edwin Derwinski to head the newly-created Veterans Affairs Department; William Reilly, head of the World Wildlife Fund, to head the Environmental Protection Agency.

DECEMBER 23

1770 Demetrius A. Gallitzin, Catholic priest, was born in The Hague, Netherlands; first Catholic priest to be ordained and wholly trained in the United States; served as a missionary in western Pennsylvania (died 1840).

1775 A royal proclamation was issued closing the American colonies to all commerce, effective Mar 1, 1776.

1778 Col. Archibald Campbell led 3500 British troops to the mouth of the Savannah River; six days later they dispersed a small American force holding the city.

1783 Gen. George Washington appeared before Congress in Annapolis to resign his commission and to "take leave of all the employments of public life."

1784 The Continental Congress, which had been meeting in Trenton, N.J., voted to move to New York City until a permanent capital was ready; the Congress named a commission to lay out a federal district on the banks of the Delaware.

1788 The Maryland legislature ceded ten square miles of land to Congress for a seat of government.

1805 Joseph Smith, Mormon Church founder, was born in Sharon, Vt.; began to have visions (1820) telling him that the church of Christ had been withdrawn from earth and he was to restore it; received golden plates (1827) which he translated into *The Book of Mormon*; founded church Apr 6, 1830 at Fayette, N.Y.; moved church successively to Ohio, Missouri, and Illinois; arrested and jailed; pulled from Illinois jail by a non-Mormon mob, killed June 27, 1844.

1814 An advance guard of 2400 British troops landed seven miles below New Orleans; they were turned back by an American attack.

1823 The traditional Christmas story written by Clement C. Moore ("'Twas the night before Christmas...") appeared anonymously in the *Troy* (N.Y.) *Sentinel*.

1833 Charles B. Richards, mechanical engineer, was born in Brooklyn; invented first steam-engine indicator suitable for high-speed engines, machine for testing the strength of metals; professor, Sheffield Scientific School, Yale U. (1884-1909) (died 1919).

1850 Oscar S. Straus, diplomat and public official, was born in Otterberg, Germany, brother of Isidor Straus (*see* 2/6/1845) and Nathan Straus (*see* 1/31/1848); minister to Turkey (1887-89, 1898-1900, 1906-10); member, Permanent Court of Arbitration (1902-06); Secretary of Commerce & Labor (1906-09) (died 1926).

1853 William H. Moody, legislator and jurist, was born in Newbury, Mass.; special prosecutor in Lizzie Borden case; represented Massachusetts in the House (1895-1902); Secretary of Navy (1902-04), Attorney General (1904-06); associate justice, Supreme Court (1906-10) (died 1917).

1856 James B. Duke, tobacco industry leader, was born in Durham, N.C.; with brother, Benjamin (4/27/1855), became industry leaders; headed American Tobacco Co. (1890-1911), which was dissolved by the Supreme Court (1911); large donor to Trinity College, which became Duke U. (died 1925).

1860 Harriet Monroe, poet and editor, was born in Chicago; founder, editor, *Poetry Magazine* (1912-36) (died 1936).

1861 The British presented a note demanding the release of James M. Mason and John Slidell, Confederate diplomats who were seized aboard a British ship; the British called the seizure an "affront to the British flag and a violation of international law;" the United States agreed, released them Dec 26.

1862 Connie Mack, baseball manager, was born in East Brookfield, Mass., as Cornelius McGillicuddy; owned, managed, Philadelphia Athletics (1901-51), winning nine pennants, five world championships; named to Baseball Hall of Fame (died 1956).

1864 George H. Parker, zoologist, was born in Philadelphia; one of the first American experimental zoologists (died 1955).

1867 Sarah B. Walker, businesswoman, was born in Delta, La.; known as "Madam C.J. Walker," she developed a formula for straightening tightly-curled hair; became one of the first women millionaires (died 1919).

1872 John C. Marin, artist, was born in Rutherford, N.J.; painter (Sunset Casco Bay, Lower Manhattan from the River) (died 1953).

1873 (Robert) Burns Mantle, drama critic and editor, was born in Watertown, N.Y.; critic, *New York Daily News* (1922-45); edited annual collection of "Best Plays" (1919-47) (died 1948).

1876 Edwin T. Meredith, publisher, was born in Avoca, Iowa; published various farm magazines; founder, publisher, *Successful Farming, Better Homes & Gardens*; Secretary of Agriculture (1920-21) (died 1928).

1900 Otto Soglow, cartoonist who created "The Little King," was born in New York City (died 1973).

1909 Barney Ross, lightweight (1933-35) and welterweight (1934-38) boxing champion, was born in New York City (died 1967).

1913 President Wilson signed the Owens-Glass Federal Reserve Act, which established the Federal Reserve System, the first comprehensive reorganization of the national banking system since 1863.

1918 José Greco, dancer and choreographer, was born in Montorio nei Frentani, Italy; one of the greatest Spanish-type dancers.

1935 Paul Hornung, football player, was born in Louisville; starred at Notre Dame, Green Bay Packers (1957-66); named to Football Hall of Fame.

1939 Myron C. Taylor, industrialist, was named personal representative of President Franklin Roosevelt to the Vatican and Pope Pius XII.

1941 Wake Island fell to the Japanese.

1947 Bill (William H.) Rodgers, one of the best marathoners, was born in Hartford, Conn.; won the Boston (four times), New York (four times), set records in the ten-mile and 25- kilometer distances.

1970 The north tower of the World Trade Center in New York City was topped out, making it the tallest (1350 ft.) building in the world.

1982 The Senate broke a filibuster and approved a five cents a gallon gas tax and a truck user fee increase to finance highway repairs and transit projects; the House approved Dec 7.

1985 President Reagan notified Congress of his decision to observe the unratified SALT II treaty, which was due to expire Dec 31.

1986 Voyager, piloted by Dick Rutan and Jeana Yeager, completed a nonstop, around-the-world flight without refueling, landing at Edwards Air Force Base, Cal. after a flight of nearly 26,000 miles in nine days, three minutes and 44 seconds.

DECEMBER 24

1737 Silas Deane, colonial diplomat, was born in Groton, Conn.; member, Continental Congress (1774-76); sent to France to secure supplies and aid; enlisted the services of Lafayette, Pulaski, and Steuben (died 1789).

1745 William Paterson, legislator and jurist, was born in County Antrim, Ireland; member, Constitutional Convention (1787); one of the first Senators from New Jersey (1789-90) and served the state as attorney general (1776-83) and governor (1790-92); associate justice, Supreme Court (1793-1806) (died 1806).

1745 Benjamin Rush, colonial leader, was born near Philadelphia; member, Continental Congress (1776-77) and a signer of the Declaration of Independence; set up first free dispensary (1786), helped organize Pennsylvania Medical School; wrote first American chemistry textbook; Treasurer of the Mint (1797-1813) (died 1813).

1772 Barton W. Stone, religious leader, was born near Port Tobacco, Md.; a founder of Disciples of Christ Church (died 1844).

1782 The French army, which had been fighting for the American cause for nearly two and a half years, sailed for home from Boston.

1802 Horace Green, laryngologist, was born in Chittenden, Vt.; the first American physician to specialize in diseases of throat, air passages (died 1866).

1809 Kit (Christopher) Carson, frontier guide and explorer, was born in Madison County, Ky.; guide for expeditions of Fremont (1840s); a scout in the Mexican War (died 1868).

1814 The Treaty of Ghent was signed by negotiators in London, bringing the War of 1812 to a close; included return of captured territory and creation of commissions to decide on disputed boundaries.

1821 William F. Poole, librarian, was born in Salem, Mass.; librarian in Boston (1852-69), Cincinnati (1871-73), Chicago (1874-94); launched the *Index to Periodical Literature* (died 1894).

1851 Fire in the Library of Congress did extensive damage, destroying 35,000 of the 55,000 books (including two thirds of the 6500 purchased from Thomas Jefferson in 1814).

1863 James H. McRae, World War I general, was born in Lumber City, Ga.; commander, 78th Division (1918-19), Philippine Department (1924-26), 2d Corps area (1926-27) (died 1940).

1865 The Ku Klux Klan was formed as a social club by six young Confederate veterans in Pulaski, Tenn.

1873 The American temperance movement began when Eliza Trimble Thompson of Hillsboro, Ohio led 70 women from a prayer meeting to the outside of a saloon, sang and pleaded for the owner to close it; visited 12 others on succeeding days; the movement spread elsewhere.

1877 Thomas A. Edison applied for a patent for his newly-invented phonograph.

1881 Charles W. Cadman, composer, was born in Johnstown, Pa.; made a study of North American Indian songs and composed several popular numbers (*The Land of the Misty Water, The Garden of Death*); also wrote a cantata (*The Vision of Sir Launfall*), operettas, operas (died 1946).

1885 Paul Manship, sculptor, was born in St. Paul, Minn.; best known work is the Prometheus fountain in Rockefeller Center, New York City (died 1966).

1887 Lucrezia Bori, lyric soprano, was born in Valencia, Spain; sang with the Metropolitan Opera (1912-36) (died 1960).

1893 Harry Warren, musician, was born in Brooklyn; composed many hit songs (*I Found a Million Dollar Baby, 42nd Street, Lullaby of Broadway, Shuffle Off to Buffalo, Chattanooga Choo-Choo, September in the Rain; Atchison, Topeka and Santa Fe*) (died 1981).

1905 Howard R. Hughes, businessman, was born in Houston; owner, Hughes Tool Co., branched into aviation, movies (producing *Hells Angels, The Outlaw*); owned much of the Las Vegas "strip;" became a recluse (died 1976).

1906 Reginald A. Fessenden, developer of the high frequency alternator, made the first radio broadcast of voice and music from his station in Brant Rock, Mass.

1907 John F. Cody, Catholic prelate, was born in St. Louis; archbishop of New Orleans (1964-65), of Chicago (1965-82); named cardinal 1967 (died 1982).

1914 Robert E. Cushman Jr., Marine Corps commandant (1972-75), was born in St. Paul, Minn. (died 1985).

1921 President Harding pardoned Eugene V. Debs and 23 others convicted under wartime espionage and other laws; effective Dec 25,1921.

1929 A fire in the White House destroyed the interior and contents of the executive offices; official papers were saved; President Hoover operated out of the Executive Office Building next door until Apr 25, 1930.

1930 Robert Joffrey, dancer and choreographer, was born in Seattle; founder, faculty director, American Ballet Center (1953-65); founder, Joffrey Ballet (1956) (died 1988).

1943 Gen. Dwight D. Eisenhower was designated as supreme commander, Allied Expeditionary Forces.

1951 *Amahl and the Night Visitors* by Gian-Carlo Menotti was broadcast for the first time; repeated on television annually.

1965 Holiday truce began in Vietnam along with a 37-day suspension of American bombing.

1988 The lower house of the Canadian Parliament voted final approval to the US-Canadian free trade agreement which over a ten-year period will create a largely free market of 270 million people; the Canadian Senate approved Dec 30; the U.S. Congress had approved earlier; went into effect Jan 1, 1989.

1988 President-elect Bush selected Elizabeth H. Dole, former Transportation Secretary (1983-87), to become Labor Secretary.

DECEMBER 25

1709 John Peter Miller, Dutch Reformed clergyman, was born in Zweikirchen, Germany; became head of German Seven-Day Baptists (Dunkers) in Ephrata, Pa. (1768-96); engaged by Continental Congress to translate Declaration of Independence into several languages (1776) (died 1796).

1724 The first building of the Church of England opened in the American colonies in Stratford, Conn. by the Rev. Samuel Johnson.

1756 Simeon DeWitt, cartographer, was born in Wawarsing, N.Y.; cartographer for the Continental Army; New York State surveyor general (1784-1834) (died 1834).

1776 Gen. George Washington led the famed crossing of the ice-clogged Delaware River to surprise the British in Trenton, N.J.

1784 Sixty clergymen met in Baltimore to form the American Methodist Church; Francis Asbury and Thomas Coke were unanimously elected as superintendents; the group adopted the English discipline, liturgy, prayer book, hymns, and 24 articles of religion prepared by John Wesley.

1793 Edward T. Taylor, religious leader, was born in Richmond, Va.; known as "Father Taylor," he served as chaplain of Boston's Seamen's Bethel (1829-71) (died 1871).

1810 Lorenzo L. Langstroth, apiarist, was born in Philadelphia; invented movable frame beehive which revolutionized the bee industry; developed methods for large-scale honey production (died 1895).

1813 John Roach, ironmaster and shipbuilder, was born in County Cork, Ireland; built marine engines and iron steamships; sometimes called the "father of American iron shipbuilding" (died 1887).

1817 Samuel Sloan, railroad executive, was born in Lisburn, Ireland; president, Delaware, Lackawanna & Western Railroad (1867-99), board chairman (1899-1907) (died 1907).

1821 Clara Barton, American Red Cross founder, was born in Oxford, Mass.; worked with International Red Cross, succeeded after five years to have United States sign the Geneva agreement; first president, American Red Cross (1882-1904) (died 1912).

1829 Patrick S. Gilmore, band leader and composer, was born in Dublin; remembered for *When Johnny Comes Marching Home Again* (died 1892).

1830 South Carolina Canal and Railroad Co. (now part of Southern Railway) initiated scheduled service on first six miles of line from Charleston; its steam locomotive, Best Friend, was the first to pull a string of cars in the United States.

1837 Zachary Taylor led Americans to victory over the Seminoles near Lake Okechobee, Fla. in the second Seminole War.

1851 Herman Frasch, chemist, was born in Gaildorf, Germany; devised method of desulphurizing crude oils and hot water smelting process for extracting sulphur, thus founding American sulphur mining industry (died 1914).

1855 Pud (James F.) Galvin, baseball pitcher, was born in St. Louis; won 361 games in career; named to Baseball Hall of Fame (died 1902).

1865 Evangeline C. Booth, Salvation Army leader, was born in London, seventh child of William Booth, who founded the Army; commanded American Salvation Army (1904-34), the world organization (1934-50) (died 1950).

1868 President Andrew Johnson issued a proclamation of unconditional pardon and amnesty to all concerned in the "insurrection."

1870 Helena Rubinstein, cosmetics manufacturer, was born in Cracow, Poland (died 1965).

1886 Kid (Edward) Ory, musician, was born in LaPlace, La.; leading exponent of New Orleans jazz; composer (*Muskrat Ramble*) (died 1973).

1887 Conrad Hilton, hotel chain founder, was born in San Antonio, N.M.; began buying hotels in 1918, formed Hilton Hotel Corp. (1946); owned 125 hotels worldwide at his death in 1979.

1888 David Lawrence, journalist and publisher, was born in Philadelphia; syndicated columnist, founder and editor, *U.S. News & World Report* (1933) (died 1973).

1889 Lila Bell Wallace, publisher, was born in Vinden, Canada; co-founder with husband, DeWitt (11/12/1889), of *Readers Digest* (1921) (died 1984).

1893 Robert L. Ripley, cartoonist, was born in Santa Rosa, Cal.; developed widely-syndicated *Believe It or Not* feature (1918) (died 1949).

1899 Humphrey Bogart, screen actor, was born in New York City; starred in many movies (*The Maltese Falcon, Casablanca, Treasure of the Sierra Madre, The African Queen*) (died 1957).

1904 Gladys Swarthout, mezzosoprano and actress, was born in Deepwater, Mo.; sang with the Met (1929-45), made several movies (died 1969).

1907 Cab(ell) Calloway, entertainer, was born in Rochester, N.Y.; orchestra leader and "hi-di-ho" singer; stage and screen actor.

1924 Rod Serling, television playwright, was born in Syracuse; remembered for *Twilight Zone* series, *Patterns, Requiem for a Heavyweight* (died 1975).

1948 Barbara Mandrell, entertainer, was born in Houston; country singer, featured television performer.

DECEMBER 26

1738 Thomas Nelson, colonial leader, was born in Yorktown, Va.; a signer of the Declaration of Independence; governor of Virginia (1781) (died 1789).

1776 The Battle of Trenton was fought after 2400 American troops crossed the icy Delaware River at night and surprised about 1400 Hessians, capturing 918 and killing 30, while suffering only five casualties.

1812 The British began a blockade of the Chesapeake and Delaware bays; later extended to the mouth of the Mississippi and the ports of New York, Charleston, Port Royal, and Savannah; eventually included New England.

1817 President Monroe assigned Gen. Andrew Jackson to command the troops against the Seminole Indians.

1820 Dion Boucicault, actor, playwright and theater manager, was born in Dublin; a great influence on the 19th Century American theater (*The Octoroon, The Colleen Bawn*) (died 1890).

1825 President John Quincy Adams accepted an invitation to send delegates to a congress of American nations in Panama, provoking long arguments in Congress, which finally approved; the action was too late because one delegate had died, the other arrived after the congress had adjourned.

1837 George Dewey, Spanish-American War admiral, was born in Montpelier, Vt.; led American naval forces to victory in Manila Bay (May 1, 1898) (died 1917).

1837 Morgan G. Bulkeley, insurance executive, was born in East Haddam, Conn.; first president, Aetna Life (1879-1922), first president, National (Baseball) League (1876), named to Baseball Hall of Fame; served Connecticut as governor (1889-93) and represented it in the Senate (1905-11) (died 1922).

1844 James L. Reid, agriculturist, was born near Russellville, Ohio; bred "Reid's yellow dent" corn, which became leading American variety; organized seed business (died 1910).

1859 Robert H. Ingersoll, watchmaker, was born in Delta, Mich., brother of Charles H. Ingersoll (10/29/1865); developed mail order business in rubber stamps, switched to $1 watches (1892); sold more than 70 million by 1919 (died 1928).

1860 Federal troops, sufficient to man only one of three forts in Charleston Harbor, were moved from Ft. Moultrie to Ft. Sumter to avoid a clash; South Carolina troops occupied Ft. Moultrie Dec. 27.

1891 Henry V. Miller, author, was born in New York City; remembered for *Tropic of Cancer* and *Tropic of Capricorn* (died 1980).

1908 Jack Johnson knocked out Tommy Burns in the 14th round at Sydney, Australia to gain the world heavyweight boxing championship.

1917 A proclamation by President Wilson placed all railroads under government control; Treasury Secretary William G. McAdoo was appointed director general of the railroad administration; roads returned to owners Mar 1, 1920.

1921 Steve Allen, entertainer, was born in New York City; originated the *Tonight* show (1950); had other shows; composed about 2000 songs, wrote several books.

1924 Glenn Davis, outstanding football player (Army 1944-46), was born in Claremont, Cal.; known as "Mr. Outside."

1935 Shenandoah (Va.) National Park was established.

1972 Former President Truman died in Independence, Mo. at 88.

DECEMBER 27

1771 William Johnson, jurist, was born in Charleston, S.C.; associate justice, Supreme Court (1804-34) (died 1834).

1797 Charles Hodge, Presbyterian clergyman, was born in Philadelphia; one of the most important American religious figures of the 19th century; author (*Systematic Theology*) (died 1878).

1798 William W. Corcoran, banker and art patron, was born in Washington; founder of Corcoran Art Gallery, Washington, to which he gave his own collection, large sums of money for maintenance (died 1888).

1829 Hinton R. Helper, writer, was born in what is now Davie County, N.C.; published (1857) *The Impending Crisis of the South, and How to Meet It,* an antislavery book of which 100,000 were distributed in the North, contributing to the start of the Civil War (died 1909).

1864 Peyton C. March, World War I general, was born in Easton, Pa.; reorganized the War Department as chief of staff (1918-21) (died 1955).

1881 Donald C. Brace, publisher, was born in West Winfield, N.Y.; president, Harcourt Brace (1942-48) (died 1955).

1883 Cyrus S. Eaton, financier and industrialist, was born in Pugwash, Nova Scotia; once clerk to John D. Rockefeller; active in Cleveland utilities, Cleveland Cliffs Co.; helped found Republic Steel Co. (1930) (died 1979).

1892 The cornerstone was laid for the Cathedral of St. John the Divine in New York City; still incomplete, but work has been resumed.

1896 Louis Bromfield, author, was born in Mansfield, Ohio; novelist (*The Green Bay Tree, Early Autumn*); scientific agriculturist (Malabar Farm) (died 1956).

1904 Marlene Dietrich, screen actress and entertainer, was born in Berlin; starred in many films (*The Blue Angel, Algiers*).

1906 Oscar Levant, pianist and composer, was born in Pittsburgh; composed music for *The American Way* and various other musicals; panelist on *Information Please* radio show, had several movie roles (died 1972).

1915 William H. Masters, physician, was born in Cleveland; with his physician-wife, Virginia E. Johnson, specialized in human sexuality problems; wrote a number of popular books.

1941 Rationing began, starting with tires; ended late 1945, except for sugar; at its peak, there were 13 programs in effect.

1943 The Army took over all American railroads to prevent a strike; returned to private management Jan 18, 1944.

1968 Frank Borman, James A. Lovell Jr. and William A. Anders completed the first flight to the moon, sending back pictures of the moon's surface.

DECEMBER 28

1714 George Whitefield, evangelist, was born in Gloucester, England; preached throughout the colonies (1740, 1744-48, 1769), sparking religious revival; founder of Calvinistic Methodists after he broke with the Wesleys over predestination (died 1770).

1789 Thomas Ewing, public official, was born near what is now West Liberty, W.Va.; represented Ohio in the Senate (1831-37, 1850-51); Secretary of Treasury (1841), first Secretary of the Interior (1849-50) (died 1871).

1825 James Wilkinson, Army officer, died at 68; served at Montreal, Trenton, and Princeton; involved in Conway Cabal, forced to resign Army commission; implicated in Aaron Burr's conspiracy, acquitted; commanded American forces on Canadian frontier (1813).

1832 Vice President Calhoun resigned over the nullification dispute and tariffs; returned by South Carolina to the Senate the next year.

1832 St. Louis U., first university west of the Mississippi, chartered.

1835 President Jackson nominated Roger B. Taney as chief justice, Supreme Court, after the death of John Marshall; confirmed by Senate Mar 15, 1836.

1835 An American force of 112 was wiped out (four survived) when Indians ambushed them at the start of the Florida War near Tampa Bay; known as the Dade Massacre, after the troop leader, Major Francis L. Dade.

1846 Iowa was admitted to the Union as the 29th state.

1856 Woodrow Wilson, 28th president (1913-21), was born in Staunton, Va.; professor, president, Princeton U. (1902-10), governor of New Jersey (1910-12); a leader in the formation of the League of Nations; awarded 1919 Nobel Peace Prize (died 1924).

1873 William D. Harkins, nuclear chemist, was born in Titusville, Pa.; predicted existence of the neutron and deuterium; his research was basic to the nuclear fission process.

1890 Russell L. Maxwell, World War II general, was born in Oakdale, Ill.; commander, American troops in North Africa (1942) (died 1968).

1896 Roger H. Sessions, composer, was born in Brooklyn; composed operas (*Trial of Lucullus, Montezuma*), chamber music, concertos (died 1985).

1900 Ted (Theodore A.) Lyons, baseball pitcher (White Sox) who won 260 games in 21 years, was born in Lake Charles, La.; named to Baseball Hall of Fame (died 1986).

1902 Mortimer J. Adler, educator and editor, was born in New York City; organized Great Books Program at U. of Chicago; founder, Institute of Philosophical Research; editor, *Encyclopaedia Britannica, Annals of America.*

1905 Earl ("Fathah") Hines, pianist and orchestra leader, was born in Duquesne, Pa.; a leading influence in the development of swing (died 1983).

1905 Charlie Weaver, entertainer, was born in Toledo as Cliff Arquette; a popular television performer (died 1974).

1929 Owen Bieber, president, United Auto Workers (1983-), was born in North Dorr, Mich.

1958 The Baltimore Colts beat the New York Giants in the first overtime game for the National Football League championship in New York City; Alan Ameche scored after eight and a quarter minutes of overtime play to give the Colts a 23-17 win.

1961 Edith B. Wilson, widow of President Wilson, died in Washington at 89.

1981 President Reagan imposed sanctions on the Soviet Union for its role in the Polish crackdown on independent labor unions.

DECEMBER 29

1778 Savannah was captured by 3500 British troops.

1780 John Adams was named minister to Holland.

1800 Charles Goodyear, rubber company founder, was born in New Haven; bought patent rights to a sulphur treatment process from N.M. Haywood (*see* 1/19/1808), then developed vulcanization process basic to rubber manufacturing (died 1879).

1805 Asa Packer, railroad executive, was born in Groton, Conn.; developed, headed, Lehigh Valley Railroad; endowed Lehigh U. (died 1879).

1808 Andrew Johnson, 17th president (1865-69), was born in Raleigh, N.C.; represented Tennessee in the House (1845-53) and Senate (1857-62, 1875); served the state as governor (1853-57) and as its military governor (1862-64); elected Vice President and became president on the death of Lincoln; impeachment sought in 1868 but lost by one vote (died 1875).

1812 USS *Constitution* captured the British frigate Java off Brazil.

1813 A combined British and Indian force crossed the Niagara River and burned Black Rock and Buffalo in reprisal for the American burning of Newark in Canada (Dec 10).

1835 A treaty was approved which provided for the removal of the Cherokees and other tribes of the South to a reservation west of the Mississippi River in return for land, the expense of the move, and $5 million.

1837 A party of Canadian militia crossed the Niagara River, boarded the small American steamboat, *Caroline,* which was suspected of carrying supplies to Canadian insurgents; vessel was set afire, cast adrift; one American died.

1845 Texas admitted to the Union as the 28th state.

1862 Union troops were defeated at Chickasaw Bluffs, Miss., in an unsuccessful effort to get to Vicksburg.

1871 Meyer London, legislator, was born in Suwalki Province, Poland; a founder, American Socialist Party (1899-1901); represented New York in the House (1915-19, 1921-23) (died 1926).

1876 A railroad bridge collapsed in a snowstorm at Ashtabula, Ohio; 92 died.

1879 Gen. Billy (William) Mitchell, air power advocate, was born in Nice, France of American parentage; court martialled for his outspoken views; convicted, sentenced to five years suspension, resigned (1926) (died 1936).

1891 Joyce C. Hall, greeting card manufacturer, was born in David City, Neb.; opened wholesale card business with brother in Kansas City, Mo. (1910); bought engraving plant (1916); by 1968 the company (Hallmark) was world's largest greeting card business; president, Hallmark Cards Inc. (1913-66) (died 1982).

1902 Argentine Foreign Minister Luis M. Drago enunciated a policy which said that collection of financial claims in the Western Hemisphere by force would violate the Monroe Doctrine; the policy arose out of a dispute over unpaid Venezuelan debts, which later went to arbitration.

1907 Robert C. Weaver, public official, was born in Washington; first Secretary of Housing and Urban Development (1966-69) and the first black to serve in the cabinet.

1937 Mary Tyler Moore, actress, was born in Brooklyn; starred in several television series (*Dick Van Dyke Show,* her own shows) and movies.

1970 President Nixon signed the Occupational Safety & Health Act, authorizing the setting of federal standards.

DECEMBER 30

1784 Stephen H. Long, explorer, was born in Hopkinton, N. H.; explored the upper Mississippi Valley and Rocky Mountains (died 1864).

1794 Christian Metz, religious leader, was born in Neuwied, Germany; led 800 settlers in forming the Community of True Inspiration in Ebenezer, N.Y. (1842-54), then moved to Iowa, where it became the Amana Community (died 1867).

1819 John W. Geary, soldier and public official, was born in Westmoreland County, Pa.; fought in Mexican and Civil wars (Chancellorsville, Gettysburg, military governor of Savannah); served as first mayor of San Francisco (1851-52) and as governor of Pennsylvania (1867-73) (died 1873).

1844 Charles A. Coffin, electrical industry leader, was born in Somerset County, Me.; merged two firms to create General Electric Co. (1892), president (1892-1913), board chairman (1913-22) (died 1926).

1847 John P. Altgeld, public official, was born in Nieder Selters, Germany; controversial governor of Illinois (1890-96); pardoned agitators involved in Haymarket riot (1886), protested President Cleveland's sending federal troops to control Pullman strike (died 1902).

1851 Asa G. Candler, manufacturer, was born in Carroll County, Ga.; developer, manufacturer of Coca Cola, president (1887-1916); mayor of Atlanta (1917-18) (died 1929).

1852 Rutherford B. Hayes and Lucy Ware Webb were married in Cincinnati.

1853 The Gadsden Purchase was signed, calling for the United States to pay $10 million to Mexico for 29,640 square miles of land in southern New Mexico and Arizona to straighten out the American-Mexican border; the purchase was negotiated by James Gadsden, minister to Mexico.

1860 President Buchanan refused to meet commissioners from South Carolina, which had voted to secede Dec 20; advised them by letter that Ft. Sumter, S.C. would be defended.

1860 South Carolina troops seized the federal arsenal in Charleston.

1862 During the night of Dec 30-31, the Union ironclad vessel, *Monitor*, went down in a gale off Cape Hatteras, N.C.; four officers and 12 men drowned.

1863 Willlam H. Park, physician and bacteriologist, was born in New York City; authority on public health aspects of diphtheria, pneumonia, tuberculosis, and poliomyelitis (died 1939).

1867 Simon Guggenheim, capitalist and philanthropist, was born in Philadelphia; served Colorado in the Senate (1907-13); founder, John Simon Guggenheim Memorial Foundation (died 1941).

1869 The Noble Order of Knights of Labor was organized in Philadelphia by the garment cutters union.

1873 Alfred E. Smith, legislator and public official, was born in New York City; served as governor of New York (1918-20, 1922-28); Democratic presidential candidate (1928) (died 1944).

1880 Alfred Einstein, musicologist, was born in Munich, Germany, a second cousin of Albert Einstein (3/14/1879); a world authority on musicology (died 1952).

1898 Vincent Lopez, musician, was born in Brooklyn; pianist and orchestra leader for many years (died 1975).

1899 The American Telephone & Telegraph Co. was formed.

1900 Clarence L. Barnhart, lexicographer, was born in Plattsburgh, Mo.; co-editor of several dictionaries (*Thorndike-Barnhart*).

1903 Fire in the Iroquois Theater in Chicago's Loop took 602 lives, mostly from smoke, suffocation, and panic.

1905 Former Idaho Governor Frank Steunenberg was killed; a former miner, found guilty of the murder, claimed the killing was ordered by the union (Western Federation of Miners); "Big Bill" Hayward, secretary, and other officers of the Federation were tried, acquitted.

1935 Sandy (Sanford) Koufax, baseball player, was born in Brooklyn; one of the greatest left handers; won 111 with the Brooklyn Dodgers, lost 34 (1962-66); pitched four no-hit games; named to Baseball Hall of Fame.

1935 Marian Anderson, one of world's great contraltos, made her New York debut.

1969 President Nixon signed into law the most far-reaching tax reform bill in American history; was expected to lower taxes by five percent and remove nine million low income Americans from the tax rolls.

1988 President Reagan and President-elect Bush were subpoenaed as defense witnesses in the criminal trial of retired Lt. Col. Oliver L. North in the Iran-Contra affair.

DECEMBER 31

1775 About 1000 American troops led by Benedict Arnold and Gen. Richard Montgomery, besieging Quebec since Jan 5, were defeated in an attack on the city; Gen. Montgomery was killed; the siege continued through the winter; Americans finally evacuated area June 15.

1781 Thc Bank of North America, the first national bank, was founded by Robert Morris and chartered by Congress; had been approved May 26, 1781.

1783 Thomas Macdbnough, War of 1812 naval officer, was born in New Castle County, Del.; defeated British in the Battle of Lake Champlain (1814) (died 1825).

1808 John Nixon, colonial leader, died at 75; led Philadelphia guard in battles at Amboy and Princeton; an organizer of Bank of Pennsylvania (1780); president, Bank of North America (1792-1808).

1815 George G. Meade, Union general, was born in Cadiz, Spain; commander, Army of the Potomac (1863-65), led Union troops at Gettysburg (died 1872).

1851 Henry C. Adams, economist, was born in Davenport, Iowa; pioneer in public finance, relation of government and industry; Michigan U. (1886-1921) (died 1921).

1853 Tasker H. Bliss, World War I general and diplomat, was born in Lewisburg, Pa.; helped negotiate various treaties after Spanish-American War and World War I; first commandant, Army War College (1903-05); chief of staff during World War I, transforming small peacetime army into huge war machine (died 1930).

1857 King (Michael J.) Kelly, baseball player (Chicago, Boston); legendary player who was subject of fans' chants, "Slide, Kelly, slide;" named to Baseball Hall of Fame (died 1894).

1860 John T. Thompson, Army officer, was born in Newport, Ky.; co-inventor of the Thompson submachine gun (died 1940).

1862 Four-day Battle of Stone River (near Murfreesboro, Tenn.) began as a Confederate victory; unable to hold gains retreated; sometimes considered a turning point in war; each army had 1200 casualties.

1864 George M. Dallas, former Vice President (1845-49), died in Philadelphia at 72.

1864 George W. Ritchey, astronomer, was born in Tuppers Plains, Ohio; inventor of fixed vertical universal type of reflecting telescope, cellular type of optical mirrors; designed, built 40-inch reflecting telescope at Naval Observatory (died 1945).

1867 Valcour Aime, pioneer Louisiana sugar planter and refiner, died at 69; built first American sugar refinery.

1870 Thomas H. Connally, baseball umpire, was born in Manchester, England; chief of American League umpires (1931-54); named to Baseball Hall of Fame (died 1961).

1880 George C. Marshall, World War II general and diplomat, was born in Uniontown, Pa.; an aide to Gen. John J. Pershing (1919-24), Army chief of staff (1939-45), with major responsibility for American troops in World War II; unsuccessful mediator in Chinese war; Secretary of State (1947-50), Secretary of Defense (1950-51); awarded 1953 Nobel Peace Prize for promoting the Marshall Plan (died 1959).

1884 Stanley F. Reed, jurist, was born in Mason County, Ky.; Solicitor General (1935-38); associate justice, Supreme Court (1938-57) (died 1980).

1884 Elizabeth Arden, cosmetics leader, was born in Ontario, Canada; founder, owner of company bearing her name; operated 100 beauty salons in Canada, United States, and Europe (died 1966).

1904 Nathan Milstein, violinist, was born in Odessa, Russia; regarded as the leading interpreter of concertos.

1905 Jule Styne, composer, was born in London; known for his musical comedies (*High Button Shoes, Gentlemen Prefer Blondes, Gypsy, Funny Girl*).

1918 Statewide prohibition went into effect in Montana.

1943 John Denver, musician and entertainer, was born in Roswell, N.M.; singer, composer ("Leaving on a Jet Plane," "Rocky Mountain High"); screen actor (*Oh, God*).

1944 A crash of two sections of the Pacific Limited near Ogden, Utah resulted in 50 deaths.

1972 Roberto Clemente, baseball player with the Pittsburgh Pirates (1955-72), died in a plane crash at 38.

1975 The cost of first class postage rose to 13 cents.

1986 A fire in the Dupont Plaza Hotel in San Juan, Puerto Rico killed 96 persons.

1988 The Federal Home Loan Bank Board expected to have sold 222 insolvent savings and loan associations at year's end at an estimated bail-out cost of $38.6 billion; the 1988 total compared with 48 in 1987 and 277 in the depression year 1938.

BIBLIOGRAPHY

Almanac of American History, edited by Arthur M. Schlesinger Jr.; G.P. Putnam's Sons, New York 1983

American Authors 1600-1900, edited by Stanley J. Kunitz and Howard Haycraft; H.W. Wilson Co., New York 1938

Baseball Encyclopedia, edited by Joseph Reichler; Macmillan Publishing Co., New York; various editions

Biographical Encyclopedia of Science and Technology, edited by Isaac Asimov; Doubleday & Co. 1972

Book of Presidents, Tim Taylor; Arno Press, New York 1972

Congressional Directory, Government Printing Office, Washington, D.C.; various years

Country Music Encyclopedia, edited by Melvin Shestack; Thomas Y. Crowell Co., New York 1974

Current Biography yearbooks (1960-); H.W. Wilson Co., New York

Dictionary of American Biography, Charles Scribner's Sons, New York, 26 volumes

Dictionary of American History, Charles Scribner's Sons, New York, 1976

Dictionary of Dates by Helen Rex Keller; Macmillan Co., 1936 (2 volumes)

Encyclopedia Americana, several editions

Encyclopedia Britannica, several editions

Encyclopedia of American Facts and Dates, edited by Gorton Carruth; Harper & Row, New York, 1987

Encyclopedia of Popular Music and Jazz, 1900-1950, edited by Roger D. Kinkle; Arlington House Publishers 1974

Encyclopedia of World Biography, McGraw Hill Book Co., New York 1973 (12 volumes)

Facts About the Presidents by Joseph N. Kane; H.W. Wilson Co., New York 1982

Grove's Dictionary of Music and Musicians, St. Martin's Press, New York 1973

Guide to Congress, Congressional Quarterly, Washington, D.C. 1976, 1982

Peter's Almanac, Dr. Lawrence J. Peter; William Morrow & Co., New York 1982

Webster's American Biographies, edited by Charles Van Doren; G & C Merriam Co. 1974

Webster's Biographical Dictionary, G & C Merriam Co. 1976

Who Was Who in America, Marquis Who's Who Inc., Chicago (8 volumes)

Who Was Who on the Screen, edited by Evelyn Mack Truitt; R.R. Bowker, New York 1977

Who's Who in American Politics, R.R. Bowker Co., New York; various editions

World Almanac, various years

World Almanac Book of Who, 1980

World Authors 1950-1970, edited by John Wakeman; H.W. Wilson., New York 1975

INDEX

Aaron, Hank (Henry L.) .... Feb 5, 1934, Apr 8, 1974
Abbe, Cleveland .... Dec 3, 1838, Sept 1, 1869
Abbe, Robert .... Apr 13, 1851
Abbey, Edwin A. .... Apr 1, 1852
Abbey, Henry E. .... June 27, 1846
Abbot, Charles G. .... May 31, 1872
Abbott, Bud (William G.) ...... Oct 2, 1896
Abbott, Frank .... Sept 5, 1836
Abbott, George .... June 25, 1887
Abbott, Grace .... Nov 17, 1878
Abbott, Horace .... July 29, 1806
Abbott, Jacob .... Nov 14, 1803
Abbott, Lyman .... Dec 18, 1835
Abbott, Robert S. .... Nov 28, 1868, May 15, 1905
Abbott, Samuel W. .... June 12, 1837
Abdul-Jabbar, Karin .... April 16, 1947
Abel, John J. .... May 19, 1857
Abell, Arunah S. .... Aug 10, 1806, May 17, 1837
Abernathy, Ralph D. .... Mar 11, 1926
Abortion .... Sept 26, 1988, Oct 8, 1988
Abramowitz, Max .... May 23, 1908
Abruzzo, Ben .... June 9, 1930, Aug 17, 1978, Nov 12, 1981
Abrams, Creighton .... Sept 15, 1914
Acheson, Dean G. .... Apr 11, 1893
Acheson, Edward G. .... Mar 9, 1856
ACTION .... July 1, 1971
Acuff, Roy .... Sept 15, 1903
Adamic, Louis .... Mar 23, 1899
Adams, Abigail .... Nov 22, 1744, Oct 25, 1764, Oct 28, 1818
Adams, Alvin .... June 16, 1804
Adams, Ansel .... Feb 20, 1902
Adams, Charles Francis .... Aug 18, 1807
Adams, Charles Francis .... May 27, 1835
Adams, Charles K. .... Jan 24, 1835
Adams, Daniel W. .... June 13, 1872
Adams, Edwin .... Feb 3, 1834
Adams, Franklin P. .... Nov 15, 1881
Adams, Frederick U. .... Dec 10, 1859
Adams, Hannah .... Oct 2, 1755
Adams, Henry Brooks .... Feb 16, 1838
Adams, Henry C. .... Dec 31, 1851
Adams, Isaac .... Aug 16, 1802
Adams, James Truslow .... Oct 18, 1878
Adams, John .... Oct 30, 1735, Nov 6, 1758, Oct 25, 1764, Oct 14, 1765, May 10, 1776, June 10, 1776, Nov 28, 1779, Sept 27, 1779, Dec 29, 1780, Feb 25, 1781, June 8, 1781, Apr 19, 1782, Aug 16, 1782, Apr 3, 1783, Sept 3, 1783, Feb 24, 1785, May 24, 1785; *1789* Feb 4, Apr 6, Apr 21; Dec 5, 1792, May 16, 1797, Nov 1, 1800, July 4, 1826
Adams, John Quincy .... July 11, 1767, May 29, 1794, July 26, 1797, Oct 17, 1803, Mar 6, 1809, June 27, 1809, Aug 8, 1814, Mar 5, 1817, Nov 9, 1824, Dec 1, 1824, Feb 9, 1825, Feb 25, 1828, Nov 1, 1830, Dec 5, 1831, June 26, 1833, Jan 21, 1842, Nov 10, 1843, Aug 10, 1846, Feb 21, 1848
Adams, Louise C. .... Feb 12, 1775, July 27, 1797, May 14, 1852
Adams, Maude .... Nov 11, 1872
Adams, Robert M. .... July 23, 1926
Adams, Roger .... Jan 2, 1889
Adams, Samuel .... Sept 27, 1722, Feb 11, 1768, Nov 2, 1772, June 17, 1774, June 12, 1775
Adams, Samuel Hopkins ...... Jan 26, 1871
Adams, Walter S. .... Dec 20, 1876
Adams, William .... Jan 25, 1807
Adams, William T. .... July 30, 1822
Adams, William W. .... Mar 22, 1819
Addams, Charles S. .... Jan 7, 1912
Addams, Jane .... Sept 6, 1860
Adderley, Cannonball (Julian) .... Sept 15, 1928
Ade, George .... Feb 9, 1866
Adler, Cyrus .... Sept 13, 1863
Adler, Dankmar .... July 3, 1844
Adler, Felix .... Aug 13, 1851
Adler, Julius Ochs .... Dec 3, 1892
Adler, Mortimer J. .... Dec 28, 1902
Adler, Richard .... Aug 3, 1921
Adler, Samuel .... Nov 13, 1900
Adlum, John .... Apr 29, 1759
Agassiz, Alexander .... Dec 17, 1835
Agassiz, (Jean) Louis .... May 28, 1807
Agee, James .... Nov 27, 1909
Agency for International Development .... Sept 4, 1961
Aging, Administration .... Oct 1, 1965
Agnew, David H. .... Nov 24, 1818
Agnew, Spiro T. .... Nov 9, 1918, Oct 10, 1973, May 2, 1974, Apr 27, 1981
Agnus, Felix .... May 5, 1839
Agramonte, Aristides .... June 3, 1869
Agriculture .... May 15, 1862, Dec 4, 1867, Mar 2, 1887, Feb 9, 1889, July 17, 1916, June 15, 1929; *1933* May 12, June 16, Oct 17; Jan 31, 1934, May 27, 1935, Jan 6, 1936, Feb 16, 1938, July 22, 1963, Dec 10, 1971, Jan 5, 1979, Aug 11, 1988
Aguinaldo, Emilio .... Feb 4, 1899, Mar 23, 1901
AIDS .... Oct 2, 1985; *1988* Jan 4, Feb 24, Mar 25, Apr 29, July 5
Aiken, Conrad P. .... Aug 5, 1889
Aiken, Howard H. .... Mar 9, 1900
Aikens, Andrew J. .... Oct 31, 1830
Ailey, Alvin .... Jan 5, 1931
Aime, Valcour .... Dec 31, 1867
Air Forces .... Aug 1, 1907, July 2, 1926, Sept 18, 1947
Air Force Academy *see* Military Academies
Aitken, Robert .... July 15, 1802
Akeley, Carl E. .... May 19, 1864
Akins, Zoe .... Oct 30, 1886
Alabama .... Jan 6, 1702, Mar 20, 1702, May 23, 1811, Aug 30, 1813, Mar 3, 1817, Aug 2, 1819,

Dec 14, 1819, Dec 18, 1820, Apr 12, 1831, Feb 24, 1860, Jan 11, 1861, Sept 20, 1865, Dec 6, 1867, Oct 4, 1871, Nov 16, 1876, Nov 11, 1901, Sept 20, 1902, July 1, 1915, Dec 1, 1955, Sept 10, 1963, Sept 15, 1963, Mar 4, 1987
Alabama Claims .... May 15, 1862, June 19, 1864, May 8, 1871, Sept 14, 1872
Alamo .... Feb 23, 1836, Mar 6, 1836
Alarcon, Hernando de .... Aug 25, 1540
Alaska .... *1741* July 16, Sept 9, Oct 25; *1867* Mar 30, Apr 9, Oct 18; July 27, 1868, May 17, 1884, Aug 16, 1896, Jan 24, 1903, May 7, 1906, June 6, 1912, May 3, 1917, Feb 2, 1925, June 3, 1943, Nov 21, 1942, May 11, 1943, Apr 24, 1956, Jan 3, 1959, Mar 27, 1964, Aug 14, 1967, Sept 4, 1971, Mar 9, 1975, July 5, 1977, July 28, 1977, Mar 27, 1986
Albany, N.Y. .... Sept 3, 1609, Mar 30, 1624, Sept 24, 1664, July 22, 1686, June 19, 1754, July 10, 1754
Albee, Edward F. .... Mar 12, 1928
Albert, Carl B. .... May 10, 1908
Albright, Jacob .... May 1, 1759
Albright, Tenley .... July 18, 1935, Feb 15, 1953
Alcoholics Anonymous .... June 10, 1935
Alcoholism .... Feb 11, 1988, Apr 20, 1988
Alcott, Louisa May .... Nov 29, 1832
Alda, Alan .... Jan 28, 1936
Alden, Henry M. .... Nov 11, 1836
Alden, Isabella M. .... Nov 3, 1841
Alden, James .... Mar 31, 1810
Alden, John .... Sept 12, 1687
Aldrich, Nelson W. .... Nov 6, 1841, Jan 8, 1912
Aldrich, Winthrop W. .... Nov 2, 1885
Aldrin, Edwin E. Jr. .... July 20, 1969
Alemany, José S. .... July 13, 1814
Alexander, Edward P. .... May 26, 1835
Alexander, Franz (G.) .... Jan 22, 1891
Alexander, Grover C. .... Feb 26, 1887
Alexander, John W. .... Oct 7, 1856
Alexander, William .... Jan 15, 1783
Alexanderson, Ernst F.W. .... Jan 25, 1878
Alger, Cyrus .... Nov 11, 1781
Alger, Horatio .... Jan 13, 1832
Alger, Russell A. .... Feb 27, 1836
Algiers ....(*see also* Tripoli) Sept 5, 1795, Nov 28, 1795, June 30, 1815
Ali, Muhamnad .... Jan 18, 1942, Feb 25, 1964, Feb 15, 1978
Alien Property Custodian .... Oct 22, 1917
Alien Registration Act .... June 28, 1940
Alinsky, Saul D. .... Jan 30, 1909
Allen, Ethan .... Jan 21, 1738, May 10, 1775, Sept 25, 1775
Allen, Florence E. .... Mar 23, 1884
Allen, Fred .... May 31, 1894
Allen, Frederick L. .... July 5, 1890
Allen, Gracie .... July 26, 1906
Allen, Henry T. .... Apr 13, 1859
Allen, Henry W. .... Apr 29, 1820
Allen, Harvey .... Dec 8, 1889
Allen, Horatio .... May 10, 1802, Aug 9, 1829
Allen, John .... Nov 4, 1810
Allen, Richard .... Feb 14, 1760
Allen, Samuel K. .... Nov 13, 1900
Allen, Steve .... Dec 26, 1921
Allen, Woody (Heywood) .... Dec 1, 1935
Allen, Zachariah .... Sept 15, 1795
Allerton, Samuel W. .... May 26, 1828
Allison, William B. .... Mar 2, 1829
Allouez, Claude Jean .... June 6, 1622
Allport, Gordon W. .... Nov 11, 1897
Allston, Robert F.W. .... Apr 21, 1801
Allston, Washington .... Nov 5, 1779
Alpert, Herb .... Mar 31, 1935
Alsop, Joseph W. Jr. .... Oct 11, 1910
Alsop, Stewart .... May 17, 1914
Alston, Walter .... Dec 1, 1911
Alter, David .... Dec 3, 1807
Altgeld, John P. .... Dec 30, 1847, July 5, 1897
Altman, Benjamin .... July 12, 1840
Altmeyer, Arthur J. .... May 18, 1891
Alvarez, Luis Walter .... June 13, 1911
Amateur Athletic Union .... Jan 21, 1888
Ameche, Don .... May 31, 1908
Amendments, Constitutional .... Sept 9, 1789, Sept 25, 1789, Dec 15, 1791, Feb 7, 1795, Jan 8, 1798, June 15, 1804, Feb 1, 1865, Dec 18, 1865, June 13, 1866, July 28, 1868, Feb 26, 1869, Mar 30, 1870, Feb 25, 1913, May 31, 1913, Jan 29, 1919, June 5, 1919, Jan 16, 1920, Aug 18, 1920, Jan 23, 1933, Dec 5, 1933, Feb 27, 1951, Mar 29, 1961, Jan 23, 1964, Feb 10, 1967; *1971* Mar 10, July 1, July 5; Mar 22, 1972, Aug 22, 1978, Oct 6, 1978
American Academy of Arts & Letters .... Apr 17, 1916
American Anti-Slavery Assn. .... Dec 4, 1833
American Automobile Assn. .... Mar 4, 1902
American Ballet Theater .... Jan 11, 1940
American Bar Assn. .... Aug 21, 1878
American Bible Society .... May 11, 1816
American Federation of Labor .... Dec 8, 1886, June 19, 1920, Feb 9, 1955, Dec 5, 1955
American Historical Assn. .... Sept 9, 1884
American Legion .... Mar 15, 1919, Sept 16, 1919
American Library Assn. .... Oct 6, 1876
American Medical Assn. .... May 5, 1847, Jan 18, 1943, Mar 23, 1982, Dec 5, 1984, Nov 12, 1987
American Red Cross .... May 21, 1881
American Telephone & Telegraph Corp. .... Dec 30, 1899, Jan 14, 1949, Nov 20, 1974, Jan 8, 1982, Jan 1, 1984
American Tobacco Co. .... July 10, 1907, Nov 7, 1908, Dec 15, 1908, May 1, 1911, May 29, 1911
Ames, Oakes .... Jan 10, 1804, Feb 27, 1873
Ames, Oakes .... Sept 26, 1874

Ammann, Othmar H. .... Mar 26, 1879
Amory, Cleveland................. Sept 2, 1917
Amtrak .... May 1, 1971
Amvets .... July 23, 1947
Anders, William A................ Dec 27, 1968
Anderson, Alexander .... Apr 21, 1775
Anderson, Carl D. .... Sept 3, 1905
Anderson, Carl T.................. Feb 14, 1865
Anderson, Clinton P. .... Oct 23, 1895
Anderson, Edwin H............... Sept 27, 1861
Anderson, Eugenie M. .... May 26, 1909
Anderson, George T. .... Mar 3, 1824
Anderson, Jack .... Oct 19, 1922
Anderson, James P. .... Feb 12, 1822
Anderson, Joseph .... Nov 5, 1757
Anderson, Joseph R. .... Feb 6, 1813
Anderson, Judith .... Feb 10, 1898
Anderson, Leroy .... June 29, 1908
Anderson, Lynn .... Sept 26, 1947
Anderson, Marian .... Feb 17, 1902, Dec 30, 1935, Apr 9, 1939, Jan 7, 1955
Anderson, Martin B. .... Feb 12, 1815
Anderson, Max .... Aug 17, 1978, May 15, 1980
Anderson, Maxwell .... Dec 15, 1888
Anderson, Philip W............... Dec 13, 1923
Anderson, Rasmus B. .... Jan 12, 1846
Anderson, Richard H. .... Oct 7, 1821
Anderson, Robert .... June 14, 1805
Anderson, Robert .... Apr 28, 1917
Anderson, Robert B............... June 4, 1910
Anderson, Sherwood .... Sept 13, 1876
Anderson, Terry .... Mar 16, 1985
André, John .... *1780* Sept 21, Sept 23, Sept 29, Oct 2
Andretti, Mario G. .... Feb 28, 1940
Andrew, Samuel .... Jan 29, 1656
Andrews, Frank M. .... Feb 3, 1884
Andrews, Julie .... Oct 1, 1935
Andrews, Lorrin .... Apr 29, 1795, Feb 14, 1834
Andrews, Roy ChapmanJan 26, 1884
Andros, Sir Edmund .... Dec 6, 1637, Dec 20, 1686, Jan 12, 1687, Apr 18, 1689
Andrus, Cecil D. .... Aug 25, 1931
Anfinsen, Christian B. .... Mar 26, 1916
Angell, George T. .... June 5, 1823
Angell, James B. .... Jan 7, 1829
Angell, James R. .... May 8, 1869
Angle, Edward H.................. June 1, 1855
Anglican Church*see* Church of England
Animal Industry, Bureau of *see* Meat
Anka, Paul .... July 30, 1941
Annenberg, Walter H............ Mar 13, 1908
Anson, Adrian C................... Apr 11, 1851
Antheil, George .... July 8, 1900
Anthony, Earl .... Apr 27, 1930
Anthony, Susan B. .... Feb 15, 1820, Jan 23, 1869, Feb 12, 1974
Anti-Saloon League .... Dec 18, 1895
Anti-trust .... July 2, 1890, Mar 10, 1902, Jan 30, 1905, Nov 15, 1906, July 10, 1907, Nov 7, 1908, Dec 15, 1908, Nov 20, 1909; *1911*—May 1, May 15, May 29, June 21; Dec 2, 1912, Oct 15, 1914, Jan 14, 1949, Nov 20, 1974, Jan 8, 1982
Aparicio, Luis .... Apr 29, 1934
Appleby, John F. .... May 23, 1840
Appleseed, Johnny .... Sept 26, 1774
Appleton, Daniel .... Dec 10, 1785
Appleton, Nathan.................. Oct 6, 1779
Appleton, William H. .... Jan 27, 1814
Appling, Luke (Lucius B.).......................... Apr 2, 1907
Arcaro, Eddie (George E.) .... Feb 19, 1916
Archbold, John D. .... July 26, 1848
Archer, James J. .... Dec 19, 1817
Archibald, Robert W. .... Dec 3, 1912
Archipenko, Alexander .... May 30, 1887
Arden, Elizabeth .... Dec 31, 1884
Arendt, Hannah .... Oct 14, 1906
Arizona .... Apr 22, 1854, Mar 3, 1859, Feb 24, 1863, Mar 12, 1885, Oct 2, 1891, Feb 9, 1911, Mar 18, 1911, Feb 14, 1912, Jan 1, 1915, Mar 4, 1930
Arkansas .... *1819*— Mar 2, July 4, Nov 20; Jan 4, 1836, June 15, 1836; *1861*— Feb 8, Mar 18, May 6; Feb 6, 1915, Jan 24, 1917, Apr 6, 1931, Jan 12, 1932, Sept 4, 1957, Sept 24, 1957, Aug 9, 1965
Arledge, Roone .... July 8, 1931
Arlen, Harold .... Feb 15, 1905
Arlington National Cemetery........................... May 13, 1864, June 15, 1864, Nov 11, 1921, Nov 11, 1932
Arliss, George .... Apr 10, 1868
Armistead, George .... Apr 10, 1780
Armistead, Lewis A. .... Feb 18, 1817
Armour, Philip D. .... May 16, 1832
Armour, Tommy .... Sept 24, 1896
Armstrong, Edwin H. .... Dec 18, 1890, Jan 5, 1940
Armstrong, George B. .... Oct 27, 1822
Armstrong, Henry .... Dec 12, 1912
Armstrong, John .... Nov 25, 1758
Armstrong, Louis .... July 4, 1900
Armstrong, Neil A................. Aug 5, 1930, July 20, 1969
Army .... June 10, 1775, June 14, 1775, Jan 6, 1776, Mar 11, 1779, Sept 29, 1789, Mar 16, 1802, June 21, 1860, Nov 27, 1901, June 3, 1916, Aug 5, 1917, June 28, 1918, July 2, 1926, June 15, 1934, May 14, 1942, Sept 18, 1947, Feb 1, 1988, Feb 10, 1988
Arnaz, Desi(derio) .... Feb 2, 1917
Arno, Peter .... Jan 8, 1904
Arnold, Benedict .... Jan 14, 1741, Dec 5, 1775, Dec 31, 1775, Dec 19, 1779; *1780* Jan 26, Aug 3, Sept 21; Jan 5, 1781
Arnold, Eddy .... May 15, 1918
Arnold, Henry H. .... June 25, 1886
Arnold, Thurman W............. June 2, 1891
Aroostock "War" *see* Maine
Arp, Bill *see* Smith, Charles H.
Arquette, Cliff *see* Weaver, Charlie
Arrow, Kenneth J. .... Aug 23, 1921
Arthur, Chester Alan .... Oct 5, 1829, Oct 25, 1859, July 11, 1878, Sept 20, 1881, Nov 18, 1886
Arthur, Ellen L. .... Aug 30, 1837, Oct 25, 1859, Jan 12, 1880
Arthur, Timothy S. .... June 6, 1809

Articles of Confederation ...... June 12, 1776, Nov 15, 1777, Jan 2, 1781, Mar 1, 1781, July 19, 1782, Sept 11, 1786, Feb 21, 1787
Asbury, Francis .... Aug 20, 1745, Dec 25, 1784
Asch, Sholem .... Nov 1, 1880
Ashburner, Charles E. .... Oct 26, 1932
Ashe, Arthur .... July 10, 1943
Asimov, Isaac .... Jan 2, 1920
Asner, Edward .... Nov 15, 1929
Assemblies of God .... Apr 2, 1914
Astaire, Fred .... May 10, 1899
Astor, John Jacob .... July 17, 1763, Apr 12, 1811
Astor, John Jacob IV .... July 13, 1864
Astor, Mary .... May 3, 1906
Astor, Lady Nancy .... Nov 28, 1919
Astor, Vincent .... Nov 15, 1891
Astor, William B. .... Sept 19, 1792
Astrodome .... Apr 9, 1965
Atchison, David R. .... Aug 11, 1807
Atherton, Gertrude .... Oct 30, 1857
Atkins, Chet (Chester B.) .... June 20, 1924
Atkinson, Brooks .... Nov 28, 1894
Atlanta, Ga. .... *1864* May 25, July 20, Sept 1, Sept 2, Sept 4; June 16, 1868, Sept 22, 1906, May 21, 1917, Dec 7, 1946, Oct 16, 1973, Mar 13, 1981
Atantic Charter .... Aug 14, 1941
Atlas, Charles .... Oct 30, 1894
Atomic Energy .... *1939* Jan 25, Aug 2, Oct 11; Dec 6, 1941, June 18, 1942, Dec 2, 1942; *1945* July 16, Aug 6, Aug 9; *1946* Jan 24, July 1, Aug 1, Oct 28; Jan 1, 1947, Jan 31, 1950, Nov 1, 1952, Dec 8, 1953, Sept 6, 1954, July 29, 1957, Sept 19, 1957, July 21, 1959, Sept 25, 1961, Apr 25, 1962, July 25, 1963, Aug 4, 1963, June 12, 1968, July 3, 1974, Jan 19, 1975, Apr 7, 1978, Mar 28, 1979, June 18, 1979, Aug 5, 1982, May 3, 1983, Oct 14, 1988
Atterbury, William W. .... Jan 31, 1866
Atwater, Wilbur O.. .... May 3, 1844
Auden, W(ystan) H. .... Feb 21, 1907
Audobon, John James .... Apr 26, 1785
Auerbach, Red (Arnold J.) .... Sept 20, 1917
Augur, Christopher C. .... July 10, 1821
Auslander, Joseph .... Oct 11, 1897
Austin, David .... May 15, 1796
Austin, Gene .... June 24, 1900
Austin, Stephen F. .... Nov 3, 1793, Jan 17, 1821, Jan 3, 1834
Austin, Warren R. .... Nov 12, 1877
Australia .... Sept 1, 1951
Auto Racing .... May 30, 1911
Automobile .... Apr 19, 1892, Sept 21, 1893, Nov 28, 1895, Nov 3, 1900; *1903* May 23, June 15, Aug 31; Oct 1, 1908, May 30, 1911, Dec 1, 1913, Jan 5, 1914, Jan 14, 1914, Jan 2, 1974, Dec 21, 1979, Mar 9, 1987
Autry, Gene .... Sept 29, 1907
Averill, William W. .... Nov 5, 1832
Averill, Earl .... May 21, 1902
Avery, Oswald T. .... Oct 21, 1877
Avery, Sewell L. .... Nov 4, 1874
Aviation .... Jan 9, 1793, Dec 17, 1903, Aug 1, 1907, Sept 17, 1908, Aug 2, 1909; *1911* Jan 6, Jan 18, Aug 2, Sept 17; July 2, 1912, Dec 6, 1916, July 4, 1917, Jan 8, 1919, Feb 21, 1922, May 2, 1923, Sept 28, 1924; *1926* May 9, May 20, July 2; *1927* May 20, June 28; *1928* July 17, Oct 1; Nov 29, 1929; *1931* June 23, Oct 5; May 20, 1932; *1933* Apr 4, July 15; Oct 23, 1934, Nov 22, 1935, May 6, 1937; *1938* June 23, July 14, July 17; June 28, 1939, Sept 28, 1940; *1942* Jan 6, Oct 1; July 28, 1945, Oct 14, 1947, July 31, 1948, Mar 2, 1949, June 24, 1950; *1952* Jan 22, Feb 11, July 15; *1955* Mar 22, Aug 11, Oct 6, Nov 1; Apr 21, 1958, Dec 3, 1959, Mar 17, 1960, Sept 1, 1961, Mar 1, 1962, July 19, 1967, Sept 9, 1969, July 31, 1973; *1975* Apr 4, June 24; Oct 17, 1977, Aug 17, 1978, May 25, 1979, May 15, 1980; *1981* Aug 3, Nov 12; *1982* Jan 13, May 12, July 9, Sept 11; *1983* Aug 31, Sept 1, 1983; *1984* Sept 14, Sept 17; *1985* Jan 21, Aug 2, Sept 6, Dec 12; *1986* Sept 18, Dec 23; *1987* Mar 9, Aug 16, Nov 15, Dec 7; *1988* Mar 23, Apr 18, Apr 28, Aug 17, Aug 28, Aug 31, Oct 12, Dec 8, Dec 21
Aviles, Pedro Menendez de *see* Menendez de Aviles, Pedro
Axelrod, Julius .... May 30, 1912
Aydelotte, Frank .... Oct 16, 1880
Ayer, Frances W. .... Feb 4, 1848

Baade, Walter .... Mar 24, 1893
Babbitt, Benjamin T. .... Oct 20, 1889
Babbitt, Irving .... Aug 2, 1865
Babbitt, Isaac .... July 26, 1799
Babbitt, Milton .... May 10, 1916
Babcock, George H. .... Jan 17, 1832
Babcock, James F. .... Feb 23, 1844
Babcock, Stephen M. .... Oct 22, 1843
Babson, Roger W. .... July 6, 1875
Bacall, Lauren .... Sept 16, 1924
Bach, Richard D. .... June 23, 1936
Bache, Alexander D. .... July 19, 1806
Bachrach, Burt .... May 12, 1929
Bacharach, Louis F. .... July 16, 1881
Backus, Isaac .... Jan 20, 1724
Bacon, Augustus O. .... July 15, 1913
Bacon, Frank .... Jan 16, 1864
Bacon, Henry .... Nov 28, 1866
Bacon, Leonard .... Feb 19, 1802
Bacon, Nathaniel .... Apr 20, 1676, Sept 19, 1676
Bacon, Robert .... July 5, 1860
Bacon, Thomas .... May 24, 1768
Badin, Stephen T. .... July 17, 1768, May 25, 1793
Baekeland, Leo H. .... Nov 14, 1863
Baez, Joan .... Jan 9, 1941
Bailey, F. Lee .... June 10, 1933
Bailey, Gamaliel .... Dec 3, 1807
Bailey, James A. .... July 4, 1847
Bailey, James M. .... Sept 25, 1841
Bailey, Liberty H. .... Mar 15, 1858
Bailey, Mildred .... Feb 27, 1907
Bailey, Pearl .... Mar 29, 1918
Bailey, Temple .... July 6, 1953
Bainbridge, William .... May 7, 1774
Baird, Bill .... Aug 15, 1904
Baird, Spencer F. .... Feb 3, 1823

Baker, Frank .... Mar 13, 1886
Baker, George .... May 22, 1915
Baker, George .... Sept 10, 1965
Baker, George F. .... Mar 27, 1840
Baker, George P. .... Apr 4, 1866
Baker, Howard H. Jr. .... Feb 28, 1987, June 14, 1988
Baker, James A. III .... Apr 28, 1930, Aug 5, 1988
Baker, Josephine .... June 3, 1906
Baker, Lafayette C. .... Oct 13, 1826
Baker, Newton D. .... Dec 3, 1871
Baker, Ray Stannard .... Apr 17, 1870
Baker, Richard .... Jan 7, 1949
Baker, Russell W. .... Aug 14, 1925
Baker, Saea Josephine .... Nov 15, 1873
Bakker, Jim .... June 12, 1987, Dec 5, 1988
Balanchine, George .... Jan 9, 1904
Balboa, Vasco Nunez de .... Sept 6, 1513, Sept 25, 1513
Balch, Emily G. .... Jan 8, 1867
Balchen, Bernt .... Oct 23, 1889, Nov 29, 1929
Balderston, John L. .... Oct 22, 1889
Baldrige, Malcolm .... Oct 4, 1922, July 25, 1987
Baldwin, Abraham .... Nov 22, 1754
Baldwin, Faith C. .... Oct 1, 1893
Baldwin, Frank S. .... Apr 10, 1838
Baldwin, Henry .... Jan 14, 1780
Baldwin, James A. .... Aug 2, 1924
Baldwin, Loammi .... Jan 10, 1740
Baldwin, Loammi .... May 16, 1780
Baldwin, Matthias W. .... Dec 10, 1795
Baldwin, Roger N. .... Jan 21, 1884
Ball, George A. .... Nov 5, 1862
Ball, Lucille .... Aug 6, 1911
Ball, Thomas .... June 3, 1819
Ballantine, Ian K. .... Feb 15, 1916
Ballard, Robert D. .... June 30, 1942
Ballinger, Richard A. .... July 9, 1858
Ballou, Adin .... Apr 23, 1803
Ballou, Hosea .... Apr 30, 1771
Ballou, Hosea .... Sept 18, 1796
Ballou, Maturin M. .... Apr 14, 1820
Baltimore, Md. .... Nov 6, 1789, Sept 12, 1814, Feb 5, 1817,May 31, 1822, May 17, 1837, Feb 1, 1840, Apr 19, 1861, Feb 7, 1904
Baltimore, David .... May 7, 1938
Bamberger, Louis .... May 15, 1855
Bampton, Rose .... Nov 28, 1909
Bancroft, Anne .... Sept 17, 1931
Bancroft, Dave (David J.) ..... Apr 20, 1891
Bancroft, George .... Oct 3, 1800, Oct 10, 1845
Bancroft, Hubert H. .... May 5, 1832
Bankhead, Tallulah .... Jan 31, 1903
Bankhead, William B. .... Apr 12, 1874
Banking .... May 26, 1781, Dec 31, 1781, Jan 7, 1782, Feb 7, 1784, Sept 13, 1789, Dec 14, 1790; *1791* Feb 8, Feb 25, Dec 12; Feb 20, 1811, June 30, 1812, Apr 10, 1816, Dec 13, 1816, Jan 1, 1817, Jan 7, 1817, Mar 6, 1819, July 3, 1819, Jan 3, 1831, July 10, 1832, Sept 10, 1833, July 11, 1836, Sept 9, 1841, Sept 13, 1841, Feb 25, 1863, June 3, 1864, May 30, 1908, Dec 1, 1909, June 25, 1910, Jan 3, 1911, Jan 8, 1912, Dec 23, 1913, Aug 10, 1914, Nov 16, 1914, July 22, 1932; *1933* Mar 6, Mar 9, Mar 12, June 13, June 16; *1934* Jan 30, Feb 12, June 6; May 29, 1968, Oct 8, 1974; *1988* Mar 17, Aug 19, Oct 11
Banks, Ernie .... Jan 31, 1931
Banks, Nathaniel P. .... Jan 30, 1816
Banneker, Benjamin .... Nov 9, 1731
Bapst, John .... Dec 17, 1815
Baptist Church .... Nov 13, 1644, July 6, 1768, May 8, 1845
Bara, Theda .... July 20, 1890
Barber, Samuel .... Mar 9, 1910, Sept 16, 1966
Barbour, James .... June 10, 1775
Barbour, Philip P. .... May 25, 1783
Bard, John .... Feb 1, 1716
Bard, Samuel .... Apr 1, 1742
Bard, William .... Apr 4, 1778
Bardeen, John .... May 23, 1908
Barker, Bob .... Dec 12, 1923
Barker, Ma .... Jan 16, 1935
Barkley, Alben W. .... Nov 24, 1877, Apr 30, 1956
Barlow, Francis C. .... Oct 19, 1834
Barlow, Howard .... May 1, 1892
Barlow, Joel .... Mar 24, 1754
Barnard, Chester .... Nov 7, 1886
Barnard, Edward E. .... Dec 16, 1857
Barnard, Frederick A.P. .... May 5, 1809
Barnard, Henry .... Jan 24, 1811
Barnes, Albert C. .... Jan 2, 1872
Barnes, Joseph K. .... July 21, 1817
Barnes, Margaret Ayer .... Apr 8, 1886
Barney, Joshua .... July 6, 1759
Barnhart, Clarence L. .... Dec 30, 1900
Barnum, P(hineas) T. .... July 5, 1810
Barr, Alfred H. Jr. .... Jan 28, 1902
Barr, John A. .... Sept 10, 1908
Barr, Stringfellow .... Jan 15, 1897
Barrett, Charles S. .... Jan 28, 1866
Barrett, John .... Nov 28, 1866
Barron, Clarence W. .... July 2, 1855
Barron, James .... Mar 22, 1820
Barrow, Clyde .... May 23, 1934
Barrow, Edward G. .... May 10, 1868
Barrows, Samuel J. .... May 26, 1845
Barry, John .... Sept 13, 1803
Barry, Lenora M.K. .... Aug 13, 1849
Barry, Philip .... June 18, 1896
Barry, William F. .... Aug 18, 1818
Barryymore, Ethel .... Aug 15, 1879
Barrymore, John .... Feb 15, 1882
Barrymore, Lionel .... Apr 28, 1878
Barrymore, Maurice .... Mar 26, 1905
Barth, Carl G.L. .... Feb 28, 1860
Barth, John S. .... May 27, 1930
Barthelmess, Richard .... May 9, 1895
Bartlett, John .... June 14, 1820
Bartlett, Josiah .... Nov 21, 1729
Bartók, Béla .... Mar 25, 1881
Barton, Benjamin S. .... Feb 10, 1766
Barton, Bruce .... Aug 5, 1886
Barton, Clara .... Dec 25, 1821, Mar 21, 1881
Barton, Seth M. .... Sept 8, 1829
Bartram, John .... Mar 21, 1699
Baruch, Bernard M. .... Aug 19, 1870, Mar 4, 1918
Baryshnikov, Mikhail .... Jan 28, 1948
Baseball .... Sept 23, 1845, June 19, 1846,

May 4, 1871, Feb 2, 1876, Jan 29, 1900, Oct 1, 1903, Apr 14, 1910, Sept 28, 1920, Nov 12, 1920, July 6, 1933, May 24, 1935, Jan 29, 1936, June 11, 1938, June 12, 1939, May 15, 1941, Oct 3, 1951, Oct 8, 1956, Oct 1, 1961, Mar 31, 1972, Apr 8, 1974, June 21, 1981, Aug 7, 1985, Dec 12, 1986, Aug 9, 1988
Baseball Hall of Fame .... June 12, 1939
Basie, Count (William) .... Aug 21, 1904
Basketball .... Jan 20, 1892, Dec 10, 1896
Baskin, Leonard .... Apr 15, 1922
Bass, Edward .... Nov 23, 1726
Batchelor, Clarence D. .... Apr 1, 1888
Bate, William B. .... Oct 7, 1826
Bates, Katherine L. .... Aug 12, 1859
Baton Rouge, La .... Feb 1, 1949
Batterson, James G. .... Feb 23, 1823
Batts, Thomas .... Sept 16, 1671
Baugh, Sammy .... Mar 17, 1914
Baum, Lyman F. .... May 15, 1856
Baumes, Caleb H. .... Mar 31, 1863
Bausch, John Jacob .... July 25, 1830
Bayard, James A. .... July 28, 1767, Aug 8, 1814
Bayard, Thomas F. .... Oct 29, 1828, Mar 30, 1893
Baylor, Elgin .... Sept 16, 1934
Beach, Alfred E. .... Sept 1, 1826
Beach, Frederick C. .... Mar 27, 1848
Beach, Moses Sperry .... Oct 5, 1822
Beach, Moses Yale .... Jan 15, 1800
Beach, Rex E. .... Sept 1, 1877
Beadle, Erastus F. .... Sept 11, 1821
Beadler, George W. .... Oct 22, 1903
Bean, Judge Roy .... Mar 16, 1903
Beard, Charles A. .... Nov 27, 1874
Beard, Daniel C. .... June 21, 1850
Beard, James .... May 5, 1903
Beatles .... Feb 7, 1964
Beatty, Clyde R. .... June 10, 1903
Beatty, John .... Dec 16, 1828
Beatty, Warren .... Mar 30, 1938
Beaumont, William .... Nov 21, 1785
Beauregard, P.G.T. .... May 28, 1818, Apr 11, 1861
Bechet, Sidney .... May 14, 1897
Bechtel, Stephen Jr. .... May 10, 1925
Becker, Carl L. .... Sept 7, 1873
Becker, George F. .... Jan 5, 1847
Becket, Welton D. .... Aug 8, 1902
Beckley, Jake (Jacob P.) .... Aug 4, 1867
Beckley, John .... Jan 29, 1801
Becknell, William .... Sept 1, 1821, Apr 30, 1832
Beebe, Lucius M. .... Dec 9, 1902
Beebe, (Charles) William .... July 29, 1877
Beech, Walter H. .... Jan 30, 1891
Beech Nut Co. .... Feb 17, 1988
Beecher, Henry Ward .... June 24, 1813
Beecher, Lyman .... Oct 12, 1775
Beers, Clifford W. .... Mar 30, 1876
Beecher, Lyman .... Oct 12, 1775
Beers, Clifford W. .... Mar 30, 1876
Beery, Wallace .... Apr 1, 1886
Begin, Menachem .... Sept 6, 1978
Behn, Sosthenes .... Jan 30, 1882
Behrman, S(amuel) N. .... June 9, 1893
Beiderbecke, Bix (Leon B.) .. Mar 10, 1903
Beirut *see* Lebanon
Beissel, Johann C. .... July 6, 1768
Békésy, Georg von .... June 3, 1899
Belafonte, Harry .... Mar 1, 1927
Belasco, David .... July 25, 1854
Belcher, Jonathan .... Jan 8, 1682
Bel Geddes, Norman *see* Geddes, Norman Bel
Belknap, William W. .... Apr 4, 1876
Bell, Alexander Graham .... Mar 3, 1846; *1876* Mar 7, Mar 10, May 10; June 3, 1880, Jan 25, 1915, Aug 18, 1956
Bell, Bert .... Feb 25, 1894
Bell, James F. .... Jan 9, 1856
Bell, James F. .... Aug 16, 1879
Bell, John .... Feb 18, 1797
Bell, Lawrence D. .... Apr 5, 1894
Bell Telephone Co. .... July 9, 1877
Bellamy, Edward .... Mar 26, 1850
Bellamy, Ralph .... June 17, 1904
Bellingham, Richard .... Dec 7, 1672
Bellow, Saul .... June 10, 1915
Bellows, George W. .... Aug 12, 1882
Belmont, Alva E.S. .... Jan 17, 1853
Belmont, August .... Dec 8, 1816
Bemelmans, Ludwig .... Apr 27, 1891
Bemis, Samuel F. .... Oct 20, 1891
Benacerraf, Benjamin .... Oct 29, 1920
Bench, Johnny .... Dec 7, 1947
Benchley, Peter B. .... May 8, 1940
Benchley, Robert C. .... Sept 15, 1889
Bender, Chief (Charles A.) ... May 5, 1883
Bendix, Vincent .... Aug 12, 1882
Benedict, Ruth F. .... June 5, 1887
Beneke, Tex (Gordon) .... Feb 12, 1914
Benet, Stephen Vincent .... July 22, 1898
Benet, William Rose .... Feb 2, 1886
Benjamin, Asher .... June 15, 1773
Benjamin, Judah P. .... Aug 6, 1811
Bennett, Constance .... Oct 22, 1914
Bennett, Floyd .... Oct 25, 1890, May 9, 1926
Bennett, Hugh H. .... Apr 15, 1881
Bennett, James Gordon .... Sept 1, 1795, Oct 29, 1832, May 6, 1835
Bennett, James Gordon Jr. . May 10, 1841
Bennett, Joan .... Feb 27, 1910
Bennett, Richard .... May 21, 1872
Bennett, Robert Russell .... June 15, 1894
Bennett, Tony .... Aug 3, 1926
Benny, Jack .... Feb 14, 1894
Benoit, Joan .... May 16, 1957
Benson, Ezra Taft .... Aug 6, 1899
Benson, William S. .... Sept 25, 1855
Bent, Charles S. .... Nov 11, 1799
Benton, Thomas Hart .... Mar 14, 1782
Benton, William .... Apr 1, 1900
Bentsen, Lloyd .... Feb 11, 1921
Berenson, Bernard .... June 26, 1865
Berg, Gertrude .... Oct 3, 1899
Berg, Patty .... Feb 13, 1918
Berg, Paul .... June 30, 1926
Bergen, Edgar .... Feb 16, 1903
Berger, Victor L. .... Feb 28, 1860

Bergh, Henry .... Aug 29, 1811, Apr 10, 1866
Bergman, Ingrid .... Aug 29, 1915
Berigan, Bunny (Roland B.) .... Nov 2, 1908
Bering, Vitus .... July 16, 1741, Oct 25, 1741
Berkeley, Busby .... Nov 29, 1895
Berkeley, Sir William .... July 9, 1677
Berkowitz, Henry .... Mar 18, 1857
Berle, Adolf A. Jr. .... Jan 29, 1895
Berle, Milton .... July 12, 1908
Berlin, Airlift .... *1948* Apr 1, June 24, June 26, July 6; May 12, 1949
Berlin, Irving .... May 11, 1888
Berliner, Emile .... May 20, 1851
Bernard, Sir Francis .... June 16, 1779
Bernard, Henry .... Jan 24, 1811
Bernhardt, Sarah .... Nov 18, 1880
Bernstein, Leonard .... Aug 25, 1918
Berra, Yogi (Lawrence P.) .... May 12, 1925
Berry, Chuck (Charles E.) .... Jan 15, 1926
Berry, Hiram G. .... Aug 27, 1824
Berry, Martha M. .... Oct 7, 1866
Berryman, Clifford K. .... Apr 2, 1869
Berryman, John .... Oct 25, 1914
Bethe, Hans A. .... July 2, 1906
Bethlehem Steel Co. .... Apr 8, 1857
Bethune, Mary M. .... July 10, 1875
Betts, Samuel R. .... June 8, 1786
Beveridge, Albert J. .... Oct 6, 1862
Bich, Marcel .... July 29, 1914
Biddle, Francis B. .... May 10, 1886
Biddle, James .... Feb 18, 1783, Aug 9, 1818
Biddle, Nicholas .... Jan 8, 1786
Bidwell, John .... Aug 5, 1819
Bieber, Owen .... Dec 28, 1819
Bienville, Jean Baptiste .... Feb 23, 1680, Jan 6, 1702
Bierce, Ambrose G. .... June 24, 1842
Bierstadt, Albert .... Jan 7, 1830
Bigelow, Erastus B. .... Apr 2, 1814
Bigelow, Henry Jacob .... Mar 11, 1818
Bigelow, John .... Nov 25, 1817
Biggers, Earl Derr .... Aug 26, 1884
Biggs, Hermann M. .... Sept 29, 1859
Bill of Rights *see* Amendments, Constitutional
Billings, John S. .... Apr 12, 1838
Billings, Josh *see* Shaw, Henry M.
Billings, William .... Oct 7, 1746
Billy the Kid .... Nov 23, 1859
Bing, Rudolf .... Jan 9, 1902
Bingham, Hiram .... Nov 19, 1875
Bingham, Robert W. .... Nov 8, 1871
Bingham, William .... Mar 8, 1752
Birch, John, Society *see* John Birch Society
Bird, Larry .... Dec 7, 1956
Birdseye, Clarence .... Dec 9, 1886
Birge, Henry W. .... Aug 25, 1825
Birkhoff, Garrett .... Jan 10, 1911
Birney, David B. .... May 29, 1825
Birney, James G. .... Feb 4, 1792
Bishop, Jim .... Nov 21, 1907
Bissell, Emily P. .... May 31, 1861
Bissell, George H. .... Nov 8, 1821, Jan 1, 1855
Bissell, Melville R. .... Sept 25, 1843
Bissell, Richard M. .... June 8, 1862
Bitter, Karl T.F. .... Dec 6, 1867
Bittner, John J. .... Feb 25, 1904
Black, Barbara A. .... May 6, 1933
Black, Eugene R. .... May 1, 1898
Black, Greene V. .... Aug 3, 1836
Black, Hugo L. .... Feb 27, 1886
Black, James .... Sept 23, 1823
Black, Jeremiah S. .... Jan 10, 1810
Black Hawk War .... *1832* Apr 6, Apr 21, Aug 2, Aug 27
Blackmun, Harry A. .... Nov 12, 1908
Blackout .... Aug 8, 1813
Blackwell, Antoinette L.B. .... May 20, 1825
Blackwell, Elizabeth .... Feb 3, 1821, Jan 23, 1849
Blaik, Earl (Red) .... Feb 15, 1897
Blaine, James G. .... Jan 31, 1830, Oct 29, 1884
Blair, Francis P. .... Apr 12, 1791
Blair, Francis P. Jr. .... Feb 19, 1821
Blair, James .... Feb 8, 1689, Dec 15, 1689, May 20, 1691
Blair, John .... Sept 24, 1789, Aug 31, 1800
Blair, John I. .... Aug 22, 1802
Blair, Montgomery .... May 10, 1813
Blake, Eli W. .... Jan 27, 1795
Blake, Eubie .... Feb 7, 1883
Blake, Eugene Carson .... Nov 7, 1906
Blake, Lyman R. .... Aug 24, 1835
Blakeslee, Albert F. .... Nov 9, 1874
Blalock, Alfred .... Apr 5, 1899
Blanchard, Jean Pierre .... Jan 9, 1793
Blanchard, Theresa W. .... Mar 12, 1978
Blanchard, Thomas .... June 24, 1788
Bland, James A. .... Oct 22, 1854
Bland, Richard .... May 6, 1710
Blanda, George .... Sept 17, 1927
Blanding, Sarah G. .... Nov 22, 1898
Blashfield, Edwin H. .... Dec 15, 1848
Blass, Bill .... June 22, 1922
Blatchford, Samuel .... Mar 9, 1820
Blavatsky, Helena P.H. .... July 30, 1831
Blind .... Mar 2, 1829
Bliss, Tasker H. .... Dec 31, 1853, Nov 27, 1901
Blitzstein, Marc .... Mar 2, 1905
Bliven, Bruce .... July 27, 1889
Bloch, Ernest .... July 24, 1880
Bloch, Felix .... Oct 23, 1905
Bloch, Konrad Emil .... Jan 21, 1912
Block, Herbert L. (Herblock) .... Oct 13, 1909
Block, Martin .... Sept 19, 1967
Blodgett, Katherine B. .... Jan 10, 1898
Bloembergen, Nicolaas .... Mar 11, 1920
Blondell, Joan .... Aug 30, 1909
Blondin, Charles .... June 30, 1859
Blood Bank .... Mar 15, 1937
Bloomer, Amelia Jenks .... May 27, 1818
Bloor, Ella Reeve .... July 8, 1862
Blossom, Henry M. .... May 10, 1866

Blount, William .... Mar 26, 1749, Jan 14, 1799
Blow, Susan E. .... June 7, 1843
Bly, Nellie .... Nov 14, 1889, Jan 25, 1890
B'nai B'rith .... Oct 13, 1843
Boas, Franz .... July 9, 1858
Bobbs, William C. .... Jan 25, 1861
Bock, Jerry (Jerrold L.) .... Nov 23, 1928
Bodanzky, Artur .... Dec 16, 1877
Bodenheim, Maxwell .... May 26, 1893
Boehm, Martin .... Nov 30, 1725
Boeing, William E. .... Oct 1, 1881
Boesky, Ivan .... Mar 6, 1937
Bogardus, James .... Mar 14, 1800
Bogart, Humphrey .... Dec 25, 1899
Bohlen, Charles E. .... Aug 30, 1904
Bok, Edward W. .... Oct 9, 1863, Feb 1, 1929
Bolden, Buddy (Charles) .... Nov 4, 1931
Bolger, Ray .... Jan 10, 1904
Bolivia .... July 14, 1986
Boltwood, Bertram B. .... July 27, 1870
Bombeck, Erma .... Feb 21, 1927
Bonaparte, Charles J. .... June 9, 1851
Bonaparte, Elizabeth P. .... Feb 6, 1785
Bond, Carrie Jacobs .... Aug 11, 1862
Bond, Julian .... Jan 14, 1940, Jan 10, 1966
Bond, Shadrach .... Apr 13, 1832
Bond, William C. .... Sept 9, 1789
Bonesteel, Charles H. .... Apr 9, 1885
Bonneville, Benjamin L.E. de .... Apr 14, 1796, May 1, 1832
Bonneville Dam .... Sept 28, 1937
Bonney, William H. *see* Billy the Kid
Bonus/Bonus March .... May 19, 1924, May 29, 1932, July 28, 1932
Books .... Jan 22, 1789, Apr 21, 1828, Mar 20, 1852
Boole, Ella .... July 26, 1858
Boone, Daniel .... Nov 2, 1734, Mar 10, 1775, Apr 2, 1775
Boorstin, Daniel J. .... Oct 1, 1914
Booth, Ballington .... July 28, 1859, Mar 21, 1896
Booth, Edwin T. .... Nov 13, 1833
Booth, Evangeline .... Dec 25, 1865
Booth, John Wilkes .... Apr 14, 1865, Apr 26, 1865
Booth, Junius Brutus .... May 1, 1796
Booth, Shirley .... Aug 30, 1907
Borah, William E. .... June 29, 1865
Borden, Gail .... Nov 9, 1801, Aug 19, 1856
Borden, Lizzie A. .... July 19, 1860
Borg, George W. .... Oct 24, 1887
Borge, Victor .... Jan 3, 1909
Borglum, Gutzon .... Mar 25, 1871
Bori, Lucrezia .... Dec 24, 1887
Bork, Robert H. .... July 1, 1987, Oct 6, 1987
Borlaug, Norman E. .... Mar 25, 1914
Borman, Frank .... Mar 14, 1928, Dec 15, 1965, Dec 27, 1968
Borzage, Frank .... Apr 23, 1893
Boston .... *1630* July 30, Sept 7, Oct 19; June 7, 1652, Oct 27, 1659, Jan 1, 1673; *1687* Mar 22, Mar 25; Apr 18, 1689, Sept 25, 1690, Apr 24, 1704, Dec 21, 1719, Mar 17, 1737, Mar 20, 1760, May 24, 1764; *1765* Aug 15, Aug 26; Oct 28, 1767; *1768* Aug 1, Oct 1; Mar 5, 1770, Nov 2, 1772; *1773* June 5, Nov 28, Dec 14, Dec 16; *1774* Mar 31, June 1; Jan 20, 1775; *1776* Mar 4, Mar 17; Feb 6, 1784, Nov 18, 1787, Jan 22, 1789; *1816* Dec 12, Dec 13; June 17, 1825, Mar 2, 1829, June 17, 1843, May 24, 1854, Sept 17, 1855; *1872* June 17, Nov 9; Mar 30, 1881, Dec 11, 1882, Apr 19, 1897, June 10, 1906, Sept 9, 1919, Sept 30, 1935, Nov 28, 1942, Oct 20, 1979
Boston Tea Party .... *1773* Nov 28, Dec 14, Dec 16
Botetourt, Baron de .... Oct 15, 1770
Bottomley, Jim (James L.) .... Apr 23, 1900
Boucicault, Dion .... Dec 26, 1820
Boudinot, Eias .... may 2, 1740
Boudreau, Lou .... July 17, 1917
Boulder Dam .... Dec 21, 1928, Sept 17, 1930, June 1, 1937
Bouquet, Henry .... Sept 2, 1765
Bourke-White, Margaret .... June 14, 1906
Boutwell, George S. .... Jan 28, 1818
Bow, Clara .... Aug 6, 1905
Bowditch, Nathaniel .... Mar 26, 1773
Bowdoin, James .... Aug 7, 1726
Bowen, Catherine Drinker .... Jan 1, 1897
Bowen, Norman L. .... June 21, 1887
Bowers, Claude G. .... Nov 20, 1878
Bowes, "Major" Edward .... June 13, 1946
Bowie, David .... Jan 8, 1947
Bowie, James .... Mar 6, 1836
Bowker, Richard R. .... Sept 4, 1848
Bowles, Chester B. .... Apr 5, 1901
Bowling .... Sept 9, 1895
Boxer Rebellion .... Aug 14, 1900
Boxing .... Feb 7, 1882, Sept 8, 1889, Sept 7, 1892, June 9, 1899, Feb 23, 1906, Dec 28, 1908, May 5, 1915, July 4, 1919, Sept 23, 1926, June 21, 1932, June 29, 1933, June 14, 1934, June 13, 1935, June 22, 1937, June 22, 1949, July 18, 1951, Sept 23, 1952, Nov 30, 1957, Sept 25, 1962, Feb 25, 1964, Feb 16, 1970, Feb 23, 1973, Feb 15, 1978, June 9, 1978, Dec 5, 1984
Boyd, Alan S. .... July 20, 1922, Jan 10, 1967
Boyd, Julian P. .... Nov 3, 1903
Boyd, Linn .... Nov 22, 1800
Boyden, Seth .... Nov 17, 1788
Boyer, Charles .... Aug 28, 1899
Boylston, Zabdiel .... Mar 9, 1679
Boy Scouts of America .... Feb 8, 1910
Boys Town .... Dec 10, 1917
Bozeman, John M. .... Apr 20, 1867
Brace, Charles L. .... June 19, 1826
Brace, Donald C. .... Dec 27, 1881
Bradbury, Ray D. .... Aug 22, 1920
Bradford, Gamaliel .... Oct 9, 1863
Bradford, Roark .... Aug 21, 1896
Bradford, William .... Mar 19, 1590
Bradford, William .... May 20, 1663
Bradlee, Ben(jamin C.) .... Aug 26, 1921
Bradley, Charles S. .... Apr 12, 1853
Bradley, Joseph P. .... Mar 14, 1813
Bradley, Milton .... Nov 8, 1836
Bradley, Omar N. .... Feb 12, 1893

Bradshaw, Terry .... Sept 2, 1948
Bradstreet, Anne D. .... Sept 16, 1672
Brady, James B. .... Aug 12, 1856
Brady, James S. .... Mar 30, 1981
Brady, Matthew B. .... Jan 16, 1896
Brady, Nicholas .... Apr 11, 1930
Brady, William A. .... June 19, 1863
Bragg, Braxton .... Mar 22, 1817
Brand, Max *see* Faust, Frederick S.
Brandeis, Louis D. .... Nov 13, 1856, Jan 28, 1916
Brando, Marlon .... Apr 3, 1924
Braniff, Thomas E. .... Dec 6, 1883
Braniff Airways .... May 12, 1982
Brannan, John M. .... July 1, 1819
Brant, Joseph .... Nov 11, 1778, Nov 24, 1807
Brattain, Walter H. .... Feb 10, 1902
Brattle, Thomas .... June 20, 1658
Braun, Werner von .... Mar 23, 1912
Braxton, Carter .... Sept 10, 1736
Bray, Thomas .... Feb 15, 1730
Brazil .... Mar 11, 1977
Breasted, James H. .... Aug 27, 1865
Breckenridge, John C. .... Jan 21, 1821, May 17, 1875
Bremer, Arthur H. .... May 15, 1972
Brennan, Francis .... May 7, 1894
Brennan, Walter .... July 25, 1894
Brennan, William M.J. .... Apr 25, 1906
Brenner, Victor D. .... June 12, 1871
Brent, Charles H. .... Apr 9, 1862
Brereton, Lewis H. .... June 21, 1890
Breslin, Jimmy .... Oct 17, 1930
Bresnahan, Roger .... June 11, 1879
Brett, George .... May 15, 1953
Brett, George H. .... Feb 7, 1886
Bretton Woods
Conference .... July 22, 1944
Breuer, Marcel .... May 21, 1902
Brewer, David J. .... June 20, 1837
Brewster, Kingman .... June 17, 1919
Brewster, William .... July 22, 1620, Apr 10, 1644
Brice, Fanny .... Oct 29, 1891
Bricker, John W. .... Sept 6, 1893
Bridger, James .... Mar 17, 1804
Bridges .... May 24, 1833, Sept 1, 1854, Apr 21, 1855, Jan 2, 1871, Oct 31, 1873, July 4, 1874, May 24, 1883, July 11, 1890, Aug 7, 1927, Oct 24, 1931, Jan 5, 1933, July 11, 1936, Nov 12, 1936, May 27, 1937, Jan 27, 1938, Aug 18, 1938, Nov 1, 1941, July 30, 1952, June 26, 1958, Apr 15, 1964, Nov 21, 1964, May 9, 1980, May 24, 1983
Bridges, Calvin B. .... Jan 11, 1889
Bridges, Harry R. .... July 28, 1901
Bridgman, Elijah C. .... Apr 22, 1801
Bridgman, Percy W. .... Apr 21, 1882
Briggs, Charles A. .... Jan 15, 1841
Briggs, Clare A. .... Aug 5, 1875
Brill, Abraham A. .... Oct 12, 1874
Brimmer, Andrew F. .... Sept 13, 1926
Brinkley, David .... July 10, 1920
Brisbane, Arthur .... Dec 12, 1864
Bristol, Mark L. .... Apr 17, 1868
Bristow, Benjamin H. .... June 20, 1832
British/Britain *see* Great Britain
Brock, Lou .... June 18, 1939
Brock, William .... Mar 15, 1985
Brokaw, Tom .... Feb 6, 1940
Bromfield, Louis .... Dec 27, 1896
Bronk, Detlev N. .... Aug 13, 1897
Brooke, Edward W. .... Nov 8, 1966
Brooke, John R. .... July 21, 1838
Brookings, Robert S. .... Jan 22, 1850
Brooklyn . *see* New York City
Brooksm Gwendolyn E. .... June 7, 1917
Brooks, James .... Feb 27, 1873
Brooks, Phillips .... Dec 13, 1835
Brooks, Preston S. .... May 22, 1857
Brooks, Van Wyck .... Feb 16, 1886
Brooks, William T.H. .... Jan 28, 1821
Brough, Louise .... Mar 11, 1923
Broun, Heywood .... Dec 7, 1888
Brouthers, Dan (Dennis J.) . May 8, 1858
Browder, Earl R. .... May 20, 1891
Brown, Benjamin G. .... May 28, 1826
Brown, Bobby (Robert W.) ... Oct 25, 1924
Brown, Charles F. .... Jan 17, 1771
Brown, Charles Lee .... Aug 23, 1921
Brown, Harold .... Sept 19, 1927
Brown, Helen Gurley .... Feb 18, 1922
Brown, Henry B. .... Mar 2, 1836
Brown, Jacob J. .... May 9, 1775
Brown, Jim .... Feb 17, 1936
Brown, John .... May 9, 1800, May 24, 1856, Oct 16, 1859
Brown, John Mason .... July 3, 1900
Brown, Joseph R. .... Jan 26, 1810
Brown, Michael S. .... Apr 13, 1941
Brown, Mordecai .... Oct 19, 1876
Brown, Nacio Herb .... Feb 22, 1896
Brown, Olympia .... Jan 5, 1835
Brown, Paul .... July 9, 1908
Brown, Seth M. .... Sept 8, 1829
Brown, Solyman .... Nov 17, 1790
Browne, Charles F. .... Apr 26, 1834
Browne, Ralph C. .... Nov 15, 1880
Brownell, Thomas C. .... Oct 19, 1779
Browning, John M. .... Jan 21, 1855
Brownson, Orestes A. .... Sept 16, 1803
Brubeck, Dave .... Dec 6, 1920
Bruce, Blanche Kelso .... Mar 1, 1841
Bruce, David K.E. .... Feb 12, 1898
Brumidi, Constantino .... July 26, 1805
Brundage, Avery .... Sept 28, 1887
Brunel, Marc I. .... Apr 25, 1769
Brush, Charles F. .... Mar 17, 1849
Bryan, Charles W. .... Feb 10, 1867
Bryan, William Jennings ..... Mar 19, 1860, July 8, 1896, June 8, 1915, July 10, 1925
Bryant, Lane .... Dec 1, 1879
Bryant, Paul (Bear) .... Sept 11, 1913
Bryant, William Cullen .... Nov 3, 1794
Bryce, James W. .... Sept 5, 1880
Brynner, Yul .... July 11, 1920
Buchanan, Franklin .... Sept 17, 1800
Buchanan, James .... Apr 23, 1791, June 1, 1868
Buchanan, James M. .... Oct 2, 1919
Buchman, Frank N.D. .... June 4, 1878

Buchwald, Art .... Oct 20, 1925
Buck, Frank .... Mar 17, 1884
Buck, Pearl S. .... June 26, 1892
Buckley, Oliver E. .... Aug 8, 1887
Buckley, William .... Mar 7, 1984
Buckley, William F. Jr. .... Nov 24, 1925
Buckner, Simon B. .... Apr 1, 1823
Buckner, Simon B. Jr. .... July 18, 1886
Budd, Ralph .... Aug 20, 1879
Budge, Don .... June 13, 1915
Budget, Bureau of the .... June 10, 1921
Buffalo Bill *see* Cody, William F.
Buffington, Adelbert R. .... Nov 22, 1837
Buford, John .... Mar 4, 1826
Buick, David D. .... Sept 17, 1854
Bulfinch, Charles .... Aug 8, 1763
Bulfinch, Thomas .... July 15, 1796
Bulkeley, Morgan G. .... Dec 26, 1837
Bulkeley, Peter .... Jan 31, 1583
Bull, Ephraim W. .... Mar 4, 1806
Bullard, Robert L. .... Jan 15, 1861
Bulova, Arde .... Oct 24, 1889
Bunche, Ralph J. .... Aug 7, 1904
Bundy, McGeorge .... Mar 30, 1919
Bunker, Ellsworth .... May 11, 1894
Bunner, Henry C. .... Aug 3, 1855
Bunshaft, Gordon .... May 9, 1909
Buntline, Ned *see* Judson, Edward Z.C.
Burbank, Luther .... Mar 7, 1849
Burchard, Samuel D. .... Oct 29, 1884
Burchfield, Charles E. .... Apr 9, 1893
Bureau of Animal Industry .. May 29, 1884
Bureau of Indian Affairs .... Mar 11, 1824, Feb 27, 1973
Bureau of Land Management .... July 16, 1946
Burger, Warren E. .... Sept 17, 1907, May 21, 1969, June 17, 1986
Burgess, Charles F. .... Jan 5, 1873
Burgess, Gelett .... Jan 30, 1866
Burgess, John W. .... Aug 26, 1844
Burgess, Thornton W. .... Jan 4, 1874
Burke, Arleigh A. .... Oct 19, 1901
Burke, Billie .... Aug 7, 1886
Burke, Martha Jane *see* Calamity Jane
Burkett, Jesse C. .... Dec 4, 1868
Burleigh, Harry T. .... Dec 2, 1866
Burlingame, Anson .... Nov 14, 1820
Burnet, William .... Apr 19, 1720, Sept 7, 1729
Burnett, Carol .... Apr 26, 1936
Burnett, Frances H. .... Nov 24, 1849
Burnett, Peter H. .... Nov 15, 1807
Burnett, Whit .... Aug 14, 1899
Burnett, William R. .... Nov 25, 1899
Burnham, Daniel H. .... Sept 4, 1846
Burns, Anthony .... May 24, 1854
Burns, Arnold I. .... Mar 29, 1988
Burns, Arthur F. .... Apr 27, 1904
Burns, George .... Jan 20, 1896
Burns, William J. .... Oct 19, 1861
Burnside, Ambrose E. .... May 23, 1824, Nov 7, 1862, Jan 25, 1863, June 1, 1863
Burpee, W. Atlee .... Apr 5, 1858
Burr, Aaron .... Feb 6, 1756, Feb 11, 1801, Feb 17, 1801, July 11, 1804, Nov 27, 1806; *1807* Jan 22, Feb 19, May 22, June 20, Aug 22, Sept 1; Sept 14, 1836
Burr, Raymond .... May 21, 1917
Burroughs, Edgar Rice .... Sept 1, 1875
Burroughs, John .... Apr 3, 1837
Burroughs, William S. .... Jan 28, 1855
Burt, William A. .... June 13, 1792
Burton, Harold H. .... June 22, 1888
Burton, William M. .... Nov 17, 1865
Busch, Adolphus .... July 10, 1839
Bush, George H.W. .... June 12, 1924; *1988* Nov 8, Dec 6, Dec 19, Dec 22, Dec 24
Bush, Vannevar .... Mar 11, 1890
Bushman, Francis X. .... Jan 10, 1883
Bushmiller, Ernie .... Aug 23, 1905
Bushnell, Horace .... Apr 14, 1802
Butler, Ben(jamin F.) .... Nov 5, 1818
Butler, Nicholas Murray .... Apr 2, 1862
Butler, Pierce .... Mar 17, 1866
Butler, William O. .... Apr 19, 1791
Butterfield, Daniel .... Oct 31, 1831
Butterfield, John .... Nov 18, 1801
Butterick, Ebanezer .... May 29, 1826
Button, Dick .... July 18, 1929
Byers, William N. .... Feb 22, 1831
Byrd, Harry F. .... June 10, 1887
Byrd, Richard E. .... Oct 25, 1888, May 9, 1926, Nov 29, 1929
Byrd, Robert C. .... Jan 15, 1918
Byrd, William III .... Mar 28, 1674
Byrnes, James F. .... May 2, 1879, Oct 2, 1942, May 27, 1943
Byrns, Joseph W. .... July 20, 1869

Cabell, James Branch .... Apr 14, 1879
Cabell, William C. .... Jan 1, 1827
Cabet, Etienne .... Jan 1, 1788
Cable, transoceanic .... Aug 5, 1858, July 27, 1866, Jan 1, 1903, July 4, 1903, Sept 25, 1956
Cabot, John .... June 24, 1497
Cabrillo, Juan .... June 27, 1542, Sept 28, 1542, Mar 1, 1543
Cabrini, Maria Frances Xavier .... July 15, 1850, Nov 13, 1938, July 7, 1946
Cadillac, Antoine .... July 24, 1701
Cadman, Charles W. .... Dec 24, 1881
Cadman, Samuel P. .... Dec 18, 1864
Cadmus, Paul .... Nov 17, 1904
Cadwallader, John .... Feb 10, 1786
Cady, Josiah C. .... Apr 17, 1919
Caesar, Irving .... July 4, 1895
Caesar, Sid .... Sept 8, 1922
Caffery, Jefferson .... Dec 1, 1886
Cagney, James .... July 17, 1899
Cahan, Abraham .... July 7, 1860
Cahill, Holger .... Jan 13, 1887
Cahill, Thaddeus .... Apr 12, 1934

Cain, James M. .... July 1, 1892
Calamity Jane .... May 1, 1852
Calder, Alexander .... July 22, 1898
Caldwell, Erskine .... Dec 17, 1903
Caldwell, Philip .... Jan 27, 1920
Caldwell, Sarah .... Mar 6, 1924
Caldwell, Taylor .... Sept 7, 1900
Calendar, Gregorian .... Jan 1, 1752
Calhoun, John C. .... Mar 18, 1782, Dec 28, 1832, Apr 12, 1844, Mar 31, 1850
California .... June 27, 1542, Sept 18, 1542; *1769* May 14, July 1, July 16; Feb 3, 1777, May 1, 1841, Nov 4, 1841; *1846* June 14, July 4, July 7, July 9, Aug 7, Aug 13, Aug 15; Jan 24, 1848, Aug 19, 1848, Feb 12, 1849, Feb 28, 1849; *1850* Apr 15, Sept 1, Sept 9, Nov 13; Mar 23, 1867, Mar 23, 1868, May 7, 1879, Nov 11, 1885, Jan 1, 1886, Oct 1, 1891, Jan 1, 1902, Oct 10, 1911, Aug 2, 1912, Jan 1, 1914, Apr 21, 1918, June 29, 1925, Oct 25, 1926, Mar 13, 1928, July 17, 1944, Feb 9, 1971, July 18, 1984
Callas, Maria .... Dec 4, 1923
Calloway, Cab(ell) .... Dec 25, 1907
Calvert, Charles .... Aug 27, 1637
Calvert, George .... Apr 15, 1632, June 30, 1632
Calvert, Leonard .... Mar 25, 1634
Calvin, Melvin .... Apr 8, 1911
Cameron, Simon .... Mar 8, 1799
Camp, Walter C. .... Apr 17, 1859
Camp David Accord .... Mar 26, 1979
Campanella, Roy .... Nov 19, 1921
Campbell, Alexander .... Sept 12, 1788
Campbell, Glen .... Apr 22, 1936
Campbell, John A. .... June 24, 1811
Campbell, Thomas .... Feb 1, 1763
Campeau Corp. .... Apr 1, 1988
Canada .... May 1, 1691, Dec 5, 1775, Apr 28, 1817, Oct 20, 1818, Dec 13, 1837, Dec 29, 1837, Jan 5, 1838, Feb 8, 1839, Aug 9, 1842, Aug 20, 1842, June 5, 1854, May 31, 1866, Aug 16, 1896, Jan 24, 1903, May 25, 1905, Jan 11, 1909, Jan 2, 1929, Aug 18, 1940, Feb 27, 1950, Jan 17, 1961, Sept 20, 1977, Mar 17, 1985, Mar 18, 1986, Oct 3, 1987, Jan 2, 1988, Dec 24, 1988
Canals .... June 22, 1793, Apr 15, 1817, July 4, 1817, July 4, 1825, Oct 26, 1825, July 4, 1828, Oct 17, 1829, Nov 30, 1829, July 4, 1836, Oct 16, 1899, Jan 2, 1900, Dec 18, 1964
Canby, Henry Seidel .... Sept 6, 1878
Candler, Asa G. .... Dec 30, 1851
Canfield, Richard A. .... June 17, 1855
Canham, Erwin D. .... Feb 13, 1904
Caniff, Milton A. .... Feb 28, 1907
Cannon, James Jr.. .... Nov 13, 1864
Cannon, Joseph G. .... May 7, 1836
Cannon, Walter B. .... Oct 19, 1871
Cantor, Eddie .... Jan 31, 1892
Capa, Robert .... Oct 22, 1913
Caperton, William B. .... June 30, 1855
Capitol .... Apr 5, 1793, Sept 18, 1793, June 28, 1794, Aug 24, 1814, July 4, 1851, Dec 16, 1857, Jan 4, 1859, Dec 2, 1863, Mar 1, 1971
Capone, Al .... Jan 17, 1899, Oct 17, 1931
Capote, Truman .... Sept 30, 1924
Capp, Al(fred G.) .... Sept 28, 1909
Capper, Arthur .... July 14, 1865
Capra, Frank .... May 18, 1897
Caraway, Hattie W. .... Jan 12, 1932
Carbutt, John .... Dec 2, 1832
Cardozo, Benjamin N. .... May 24, 1870
Carew, Rod .... Oct 1, 1945
Carey, Mathew .... Jan 28, 1760
Carey, Max .... Jan 11, 1890
Carle, Frankie .... Mar 25, 1903
Carleton, Mark A. .... Mar 7, 1866
Carlile, John S. .... Dec 16, 1817
Carlisle, John G. .... Sept 5, 1835
Carlson, Anton J. .... Jan 29, 1875
Carlson, Chester F. .... Feb 8, 1906, Oct 22, 1938
Carlson, Evans F. .... Feb 26, 1896
Carlton, Steve .... Dec 22, 1944
Carmer, Carl L. .... Oct 16, 1893
Carmichael, Hoagy (Hoagland H.) .... Nov 22, 1899
Carmichael, Leonard .... Nov 9, 1898
Carnegie, Andrew .... Nov 25, 1835, Nov 15, 1900, Mar 12, 1901, Jan 28, 1902, Apr 8, 1903
Carnegie, Dale .... Nov 24, 1888
Carnegie, Hattie .... Mar 14, 1886
Carnegie Hall .... Feb 20, 1982
Carnegie Institution .... Jan 28, 1902
Carney, Art .... Nov 4, 1918
Carolina .... Dec 3, 1677, Jan 12, 1682
Carothers, Wallace H. .... Apr 27, 1896
Carpenter, Scott .... May 1, 1925
Carr, Eugene A. .... Mar 20, 1830
Carr, Gene .... Jan 7, 1881
Carr, Joseph B. .... Aug 16, 1828
Carrel, Alexis .... June 28, 1873
Carrére, John M. .... Nov 9, 1858
Carrier, Willis H. .... Nov 26, 1876
Carrington, Henry B. .... Mar 2, 1824
Carroll, Charles .... Sept 19, 1737, July 4, 1828
Carroll, Earl .... Sept 16, 1893
Carroll, John .... Jan 8, 1735, Feb 15, 1776, Nov 6, 1789, Aug 15, 1790
Carson, Johnny .... Oct 23, 1925
Carson, Kit (Christopher) .... Dec 24, 1809
Carson, Rachel .... May 27, 1907
Carter, Don .... July 29, 1926
Carter, Hodding .... Feb 3, 1907
Carter, Jimmy .... Oct 1, 1924, July 7, 1946, Jan 21, 1977, Jan 24, 1977; *1978* Apr 7, June 16, Sept 6, Oct 13; *1979* Jan 1, Mar 26, June 7; *1980* Jan 24, May 21, June 27; Oct 2, 1986
Carter, Mrs. Leslie .... June 10, 1862
Carter, Rosalynn S. .... Aug 18, 1927, July 7, 1946
Carter, Samuel P. .... Aug 6, 1819
Cartwright, Peter .... Sept 1, 1785
Carty, John J. .... Apr 14, 1861
Caruso, Enrico .... Feb 25, 1873
Carver, George Washngton .... Jan 5, 1943
Carver, John A. .... Nov 21, 1620, Apr 5, 1621
Carver, Jonathan .... Apr 13, 1710
Cary, Edward .... June 5, 1840

Case, Jerome I. .... Dec 11, 1818
Casey, James E. .... June 6, 1983
Cash, Johnny .... Feb 26, 1932
Cass, Lewis .... Oct 9, 1782
Cassatt, Alexander J. .... Dec 8, 1839
Cassatt, Mary S. .... May 22, 1844
Cassidy, Butch .... Apr 13, 1866
Cassini, Oleg .... Apr 11, 1913
Castle, Irene .... Apr 7, 1893
Castle, Vernon B. .... May 2, 1887
Cates, Clifton B. .... Aug 31, 1893
Cather, Willia S. .... Dec 7, 1873
Catholicism .... Sept 8, 1565, Feb 26, 1732, Jan 31, 1752, Jan 23, 1789, Nov 6, 1789, Aug 15, 1790, May 25, 1793, Mar 10, 1810, Mar 28, 1811, May 31, 1822, Mar 15, 1875, May 25, 1879, Feb 2, 1882, Jan 14, 1893, May 3, 1893, Mar 14 1897, Oct 5, 1910, Mar 24, 1924, June 20, 1926, Dec 4, 1963, May 5, 1980; *1988* Mar 15, Mar 25, Apr 11, Oct 2
Catlett, Sidney .... Jan 17, 1910
Catlin, George .... July 26, 1796
Catron, John .... May 30, 1865
Catt, Carrie Chapman .... Jan 9, 1859
Cattell, James McK. .... May 24, 1860
Catton, Bruce .... Oct 9, 1899
Cavallaro, Carmen .... May 6, 1913
Cavazos, Lauro F. .... Sept 20, 1988, Dec 6, 1988
Cavett, Dick .... Nov 19, 1936
Census .... Mar 1, 1790, Aug 2, 1790, Aug 1, 1800, Dec 1, 1810, Oct 1, 1820, Aug 1, 1830, July 1, 1840, Dec 1, 1850, Oct 1, 1860, June 1, 1870, June 1, 1880, Jan 8, 1889, June 1, 1890, Nov 1, 1900, Mar 6, 1902, July 1, 1902, Aug 15, 1910, Apr 1, 1920, Apr 1, 1930, Apr 15, 1940, Apr 15, 1950, May 1, 1960, May 1, 1970, June 1, 1980
Center for Disease Control .... July 1, 1973
Central Intelligence Agency .... Jan 20, 1946
Cerf, Bennet .... May 25, 1898
Carmak, Anton J. .... Feb 15, 1933, Mar 6, 1933
Cesnola, Luigi Palma di .... June 29, 1832
Cessna, Clyde V. .... Dec 5, 1879
Chadwick, Florence .... Nov 9, 1918
Chadwick, Henry .... Oct 5, 1824
Chaffee, Adna R. .... Apr 14, 1842
Chaffee, Adna R. Jr. .... Sept 23, 1884
Chaffee, Roger B. .... Jan 27, 1967
Chamberlin, Joshua L. .... Sept 8, 1828
Chamberlain, Owen .... July 10, 1920
Chamberlin, Richard .... Mar 31, 1935
Chamberlain, Wilt(on) .... Aug 21, 1936
Chamberlin, Clarence D. .... Nov 11, 1893
Chamberlin, Thomas C. .... Sept 25, 1843
Champion, Gower .... June 22, 1921
Champlain, Samuel de .... July 20, 1605, July 30, 1609
Chance, Britton .... July 24, 1913
Chance, Frank .... Sept 9, 1877
Chancellor, John .... July 14, 1927
Chandler, Albert D. .... July 14, 1898
Chandler, Charles F. .... Dec 6, 1836
Chandler, Harry .... May 17, 1864
Chandler, Otis .... Nov 23, 1927
Chandler, Raymond T. .... July 23, 1888
Chandler, Zachariah .... Dec 10, 1813
Chandrasekhar, Subrahmanyan .... Oct 19, 1910
Chaney, Lon .... Apr 1, 1883
Channing, Carol .... Jan 31, 1923
Channing, Walter .... Apr 15, 1786
Channing, William Ellery .... Apr 7, 1780
Channing, William F. .... Feb 22, 1820
Chanute, Octave .... Feb 18, 1832
Chapin, Charles V. .... Jan 17, 1856
Chapin, Roy D. .... Feb 23, 1880
Chaplin, Charles .... Apr 16, 1889
Chapman, Frank M. .... June 12, 1864
Chapman, John *see* Appleseed, Johnny
Chapman, Nathaniel .... May 28, 1780, May 5, 1847
Chargaff, Erwin .... Aug 11, 1905
Charles, Ray .... Sept 23, 1930
Charleston, S.C. .... Aug 24, 1706, Jan 13, 1733, Jan 1, 1735, Feb 18, 1735, Jan 12, 1773, June 28, 1776, Apr 11, 1780, May 12, 1780, Dec 14, 1782, Dec 25, 1830, Aug 27, 1838, Dec 26, 1860, Dec 30, 1860, Jan 9, 1861, Feb 18, 1865, Aug 31, 1886, Aug 22, 1893
Charter of Liberties .... Oct 30, 1683
Chase, Edna W. .... Mar 14, 1877
Chase, Lucia .... Mar 24, 1907
Chase, Mary C. .... Feb 25, 1907
Chase, Mary Ellen .... Feb 24, 1887
Chase, Philander .... Dec 14, 1775
Chase, Salmon P. .... Jan 13, 1808, Dec 6, 1864, May 7, 1873
Chase, Samuel .... Apr 17, 1741, Feb 15, 1776, Mar 1, 1805
Chauncy, Isaac .... Feb 20, 1772
Chauncy, Charles .... Jan 1, 1705
Chautauqua Assembly .... Aug 4, 1874
Chayafsky, Paddy .... Jan 29, 1923
Checker, Chubby .... Oct 3, 1941
Cheever, Ezekiel .... Jan 25, 1615
Cheever, John .... May 27, 1912
Chemical Warfare Service .... June 28, 1918
Cheney, Charles E. .... Feb 18, 1869
Chennault, Claire L. .... Sept 6, 1890
Chesbro, Jack (John D.) .... June 5, 1874
Chesnutt, Charles W. .... June 20, 1858
Chester, Colby M. .... Feb 29, 1844
Chester, Colby M. .... July 23, 1877
Cheves, Langdon .... Sept 17, 1776
Chevrolet, Louis .... June 6, 1941
Chiang Kai-shek .... Nov 22, 1943
Chicago .... Dec 4, 1674, Aug 17, 1803, Aug 15, 1812, July 4, 1816, Mar 4, 1837, Apr 3, 1848, Oct 8, 1871, May 1, 1884, May 3/May 4, 1886, May 4, 1891, Oct 21, 1892, May 1, 1893, Oct 28, 1893, May 11, 1894, July 1, 1899, Jan 2, 1900, Dec 30, 1903,. Dec 14, 1904, May 15, 1905, July 24, 1915, June 7, 1917, Sept 10, 1924, Feb 14, 1929, May 10, 1930; *1933* May 27, June 21, July 6; Mar 15, 1937, May 30, 1937, Apr 25, 1946, Dec 1, 1958, Sept 29, 1982, Apr 12, 1983, Aug 9, 1988
Child, Julia .... Aug 15, 1912
Child, Lydia M. .... Feb 11, 1802
Children's Bureau .... Apr 9, 1912
Childs, Samuel S. .... Apr 4, 1863

Chile .... Oct 16, 1891
Chilstrom, Herbert W. .... Oct 18, 1931
China .... Feb 22, 1784, July 3, 1844, July 28, 1868, May 6, 1882, Sept 6, 1899, Aug 14, 1900, Jan 13, 1905, Nov 30, 1908, Dec 12, 1937, Oct 6, 1938, June 2, 1941, Jan 28, 1945, June 10, 1971, Feb 21, 1972, Feb 22, 1973, Jan 1, 1979, Apr 26, 1984
Chisholm, Hugh J. .... May 2, 1847
Chisholm, Shirley A. .... Nov 30, 1924
Chisum, John S. .... Aug 15, 1824
Chittenden, Thomas .... Jan 6, 1730
Choate, Joseph H. .... Jan 24, 1832
Choate, Rufus .... Oct 1, 1799
Chouteau, Jean Pierre .... Oct 10, 1758
Chouteau, Pierre .... Jan 19, 1789
Chouteau, René A. .... Sept 7, 1749
Christ Church .... Feb 27, 1773
Christian Endeavor Society . Feb 2, 1881
Christian Science Church .... Aug 23, 1879, Sept 23, 1892, June 10, 1906
Christie, Julie .... Apr 14, 1941
Christmas Seals .... Dec 9, 1907
Christy, Edwin P. .... May 21, 1862
Christy, Howard C. .... Jan 10, 1873
Chrysler, Walter P. .... Apr 2, 1875
Chrysler Corp. .... Dec 21, 1979
Church, Frederick E. .... May 4, 1826
Church of England .... Mar 22, 1687, Dec 25, 1724
Church of Jesus Christ of Latter Day Saints *see* Mormons
Church of the Nazarene .... Oct 13, 1908
Church/school separation .... June 4, 1985
Churchill, Thomas J. .... Mar 10, 1824
Churchill, Winston .... Nov 10, 1871
Churchill, Winston S. .... Aug 14, 1941; *1943* Jan 14, May 12, Aug 17, Nov 22, Nov 28, Dec 4; Sept 11, 1944, Feb 3, 1945, July 17, 1945, Mar 5, 1946, Apr 9, 1963
Ciardi, John .... June 24, 1916
Cicippio, Joseph .... Sept 12, 1986
Cigarettes *see* Smoking
Cincinnati, Society of .... May 10, 1783
Cisneros, Henry G. .... Apr 4, 1981
Citizenship .... Feb 10, 1855, June 15, 1924
Civil Aeronautics Authority .... June 23, 1938
Civil Rights .... Oct 2, 1865, Mar 27, 1866, June 13, 1866, Feb 13, 1867, July 28, 1868, July 6, 1869, May 22, 1872, Mar 1, 1875, Feb 12, 1909, Dec 5, 1946, May 17, 1954, May 31, 1955; *1957* Apr 29, Sept 4, Sept 9; Feb 1, 1960, Oct 1, 1963; *1963* Mar 3, June 12, Aug 28, Sept 10, Sept 15; July 2, 1964, Aug 4, 1964, Mar 7, 1965, Mar 21, 1965, June 2, 1966, Apr 11, 1968, Apr 5, 1982, May 18, 1987, Jan 27, 1988, Mar 16, 1988
Civil Service/Civil Service Commission .... June 25, 1868, Mar 3, 1871, Jan 16, 1883, May 22, 1920, Aug 2, 1939, Oct 13, 1978
Civil War
1860 .... Oct 5, Oct 29, Dec 18, Dec 20, Dec 26, Dec 30
1861 .... Jan 3, Jan 4, Jan 6, Jan 9, Jan 10, Jan 11, Jan 12, Jan 17, Jan 19, Jan 24, Jan 26, Feb 1, Feb 4, Feb 8, Feb 9, Feb 16, Feb 28, Mar 2, Mar 4, Mar 6, Mar 11, Mar 16, Mar 18, Apr 4, Apr 11, Apr 12, Apr 13, Apr 15, Apr 16, Apr 17, Apr 19, Apr 27, May 6, May 7, May 8, May 13, May 20, May 23, May 27, June 8, June 9, June 10, June 15, July 4, July 21, July 22, Aug 7, Aug 10, Aug 28, Sept 6, Sept 11, Oct 21, Nov 1, Nov 7, Nov 8, Dec 23
1862 .... Jan 19, Jan 27, Jan 30, Jan 31, Feb 6, Feb 8, Feb 12, Feb 16, Feb 25, Mar 3, Mar 6, Mar 9, Mar 11, Mar 14, Apr 6, Apr 7, Apr 11, Apr 12, Apr 16, Apr 18, Apr 24, Apr 29, May 4, May 5, May 10, May 11, May 15, May 23, May 25, May 30, May 31, June 1, June 6, June 8, June 25, June 26, June 27, June 28, July 1, July 2, July 4, July 11, July 13, Aug 9, Aug 19, Aug 29, Sept 7, Sept 12, Sept 15, Sept 17, Sept 19, Oct 3, Oct 8, Oct 10, Oct 30, Nov 7, Dec 7, Dec 13, Dec 20, Dec 29, Dec 30, Dec 31
1863 .... Jan 2, Jan 11, Jan 25, Jan 30, Mar 3, Mar 9, Apr 16, Apr 18, May 1, May 14, May 19, June 9, June 15, June 26, June 27, June 28, July 1, July 4, July 9, July 13, July 16, Aug 21, Sept 4, Sept 7, Sept 9, Sept 10, Sept 19, Oct 14, Nov 15, Nov 17, Nov 23, Dec 3, Dec 8
1864 .... Feb 7, Feb 14, Feb 17, Mar 9, Mar 12, May 4, May 5, May 8, May 11, May 12, May 13, May 15, May 25, June 1, June 4, June 10, June 15, June 19, June 27, July 2, July 9, July 11, July 17, July 18, July 20, July 30, Aug 5, Aug 6, Sept 1, Sept 2, Sept 4, Sept 19, Oct 13, Oct 19, Oct 27, Nov 8, Nov 12, Nov 14, Nov 30, Dec 10, Dec 15, Dec 20
1865 .... Jan 13, Jan 28, Feb 3, Feb 6, Feb 17, Feb 18, Feb 22, Mar 2, Mar 10, Mar 27, Mar 29, Mar 30, Apr 1, Apr 2, Apr 4, Apr 6, Apr 9, Apr 12, Apr 13, Apr 14, Apr 18, Apr 26, May 10, May 26, May 29, Nov 10 *Also* Apr 2, 1866, Aug 20, 1866, Mar 2, 1867, Dec 25, 1868, May 22, 1872

Civil Works Emergency Relief Act ... Feb 15, 1934
Civilian Conservation Corps (CCC) ... Mar 31, 1933, June 28, 1937
Claflin, Victoria ... Sept 23, 1838, May 10, 1872
Claiborne, Harry ... Oct 9, 1986
Claiborne, William C.C. ... Dec 20, 1803, Oct 1, 1804, Nov 23, 1817
Clap, Thomas ... June 26, 1703
Clark, Abraham ... Feb 15, 1726
Clark, Alvan ... Mar 8, 1804
Clark, Barney ... Dec 2, 1982
Clark, Champ (James Beauchamp) ... Mar 7, 1850
Clark, Dick ... Nov 30, 1929
Clark, Francis E. ... Feb 2, 1881
Clark, George Rogers ... Nov 19, 1752, July 4, 1778, Feb 25, 1779
Clark, John B. ... Jan 26, 1847
Clark, Kenneth B. ... July 24, 1914
Clark, Mark W. ... May 1, 1896
Clark, Roy ... Apr 15, 1933
Clark, Tom C. ... Sept 23, 1899
Clark, Walter van Tilburg ... Aug 3, 1909
Clark, William ... Aug 1, 1770
Clarke, Fred ... Oct 3, 1872
Clarke, John ... Oct 8, 1609
Clarke, John H. ... Sept 18, 1857
Clarkson, John ... July 1, 1861
Claude, Albert ... Aug 24, 1898
Clausen, A(lden) W. ... Feb 17, 1923
Clavell, James D. ... Oct 10, 1924
Clay, Cassius *see* Ali, Muhammad
Clay, Henry ... Apr 12, 1777, Aug 8, 1814, Nov 9, 1824, Dec 1, 1824, Apr 8, 1926, Jan 29, 1850
Clay, Lucius D. ... Apr 23, 1897, Aug 30, 1961
Clayton, Henry DeL. ... Feb 10, 1857
Clayton, John M. ... July 24, 1796
Clayton, Joshua ... Dec 20, 1744
Cleaveland, Moses ... Jan 29, 1754, July 22, 1796
Cleburne, Patrick R. ... Mar 17, 1828, Nov 30, 1864
Clemens, Samuel *see* Twain, Mark
Clemente, Roberto ... Aug 18, 1934, Dec 31, 1972
Cleveland, Ohio ... July 22, 1796, Apr 8, 1903, May 15, 1929, Oct 20, 1944, Nov 7, 1967
Cleveland, Frances F. ... July 21, 1864, June 2, 1886, Oct 29, 1947
Cleveland, (Stephen) Grover ... Mar 18, 1837, Nov 7, 1882, June 2, 1886, Oct 28, 1886, July 1, 1893, Sept 9, 1893, July 5, 1894, June 24, 1908
Cliburn, Van (H. Levan) ... July 12, 1934
Clifford, Nathan ... Aug 18, 1803
Clinton, DeWitt ... Mar 2, 1769
Clinton, George ... July 10, 1761
Clinton, George ... July 26, 1739, Apr 20, 1812
Clinton, Sir Henry ... May 8, 1778
Clinton, James ... Aug 9, 1733
Cluett, Sanford L. ... June 6, 1874
Clymer, George ... Mar 16, 1739
Coast and Geodetic Survey ... Feb 10, 1807
Coast Guard ... Aug 4, 1790, Jan 28, 1915, Nov 23, 1942
Cobb, Henry I. ... Aug 19, 1859
Cobb, Howell ... Sept 7, 1815
Cobb, Irwin S. ... June 23, 1876
Cobb, Lee J. ... Dec 9, 1911
Cobb, Ty(rus) ... Dec 18, 1886, Jan 29, 1936
Coblentz, William W. ... Nov 20, 1873
Cochrane, Mickey (Gordon S.) ... Apr 6, 1903
Cocke, John H. ... Sept 19, 1780
Coddington, William ... May 8, 1639, Nov 1, 1678
Cody, John P. ... Dec 24, 1907
Cody, William F. ... Feb 26, 1946
Coffin, Charles A. ... Dec 30, 1844
Coffin, Henry Sloane ... Jan 5, 1877
Coffin, Howard E. ... Sept 6, 1873
Coffin, Levi ... Oct 28, 1798
Coffin, Lorenzo S. ... Apr 9, 1823
Coffin, (Robert Peter) Tristrum ... Mar 18, 1892
Coggeshall, John ... May 29, 1647
Cohan, George M. ... July 3, 1878
Cohen, Stanley ... Nov 18, 1922
Cohn, Edwin J. ... Dec 17, 1892
Coke, Thomas ... Sept 9, 1747, Dec 25, 1784
Colbert, Claudette ... Sept 18, 1905
Colburn, Irving W. ... May 16, 1861
Colby, Bainbridge ... Dec 22, 1869
Colby, Frank M. ... Feb 10, 1865
Colden, Cadwallader ... Feb 7, 1688
Cole, Cozy (William R.) ... Oct 17, 1909
Cole, Edward N. ... Sept 17, 1909
Cole, Nat "King" ... Mar 17, 1919
Cole, Thomas ... Feb 1, 1801
Colfax, Schuyler ... Mar 23, 1823, Jan 13, 1885
Colgate, William ... Jan 25, 1783
Collamer, Jacob ... Jan 8, 1791
Colleges *see* Education
Collier, Peter F. ... Dec 12, 1849
Collins, Eddie (Edward T.) ... May 2, 1887
Collins, J. Lawton ... May 1, 1896
Collins, James J. ... Jan 16, 1870
Collins, Joan ... May 3, 1936
Collins, Michael ... Oct 31, 1930
Colman, Norman J. ... May 16, 1827, Feb 9, 1889
Colman, Ronald ... Feb 9, 1891
Colorado ... Aug 26, 1540, Apr 23, 1859, Feb 28, 1861, Aug 1, 1876, Nov 4, 1881, Apr 7, 1893, Nov 7, 1893, Mar 3, 1915, Dec 16, 1918, June 30, 1951
Colorado River Compact ... Nov 24, 1922
Colt, Samuel ... July 19, 1814, Feb 25, 1836
Columbia University ... Oct 31, 1754
Columbus, Christopher ... *1492* Apr 30, Aug 3, Oct 12; *1493* May 4, Sept 25, Nov 4, Nov 19
Colve, Anthony ... Aug 9, 1673
Combs, Earle B. ... May 14, 1899

Comiskey, Charles A. .... Aug 15, 1859
Commager, Henry Steele ..... Oct 25, 1902
Commerce, Department of ... Feb 14, 1903, Mar 4, 1913
Committee on Public Information .... Apr 14, 1917
Commodity Credit Corp. .... Oct 17, 1933
Commons, John R. .... Oct 13, 1862
Communications .... Mar 3, 1843, May 24, 1844, Oct 24, 1861, July 27, 1866, July 9, 1877, Jan 28, 1878, Dec 30, 1899, June 18, 1910, Jan 25, 1915, July 22, 1918, July 31, 1919, Nov 2, 1920, Jan 7, 1927, June 19, 1934, Jan 5, 1940, Nov 7, 1967
Communist Party .... Sept 2, 1919, Jan 2, 1920, Jan 17, 1949, Oct 14, 1949, Aug 24, 1954
Como, Perry .... May 18, 1912
Compton, Arthur B. .... Sept 10, 1892, Dec 2, 1942
Compton, Karl T. .... Sept 14, 1887
Comtroller of the Currency .. Feb 25, 1863
Compulsory testing .... Feb 11, 1988
Comstock, Ada Louise .... Dec 11, 1876
Comstock, Anthony .... Mar 7, 1844
Conable, Barber B. Jr. .... Nov 2, 1922, Mar 13, 1986
Conant, James B. .... Mar 26, 1893
Conboy, Sara A.M. .... Apr 3, 1870
Condon, Eddie (Albert E.) .... Nov 16, 1905
Condon, Edward .... Mar 2, 1902
Cone, Hutchinson I. .... Apr 26, 1871
Confederacy *see* Civil War
Congregational Church .... Dec 4, 1584, Sept 1, 1646, May 15, 1796, Feb 2, 1881, June 25, 1957
Congress .... *1789* Mar 4, Apr 1, Apr 6, June 1, Aug 4, Sept 22, Sept 29; July 26, 1790, Apr 14, 1792, Feb 20, 1794, May 19, 1796, Nov 17, 1800, Feb 17, 1801, Dec 8, 1801, Mar 19, 1816, Jan 27, 1818, Mar 3, 1823, Feb 9, 1825, May 26, 1836, Jan 8, 1840, Feb 20, 1840, June 25, 1842, Dec 2, 1844, Mar 3, 1845, May 22, 1854, May 30, 1854, Jan 4, 1859, Mar 2, 1867, Mar 4, 1873, Jan 20, 1874, Jan 25, 1900, Jan 26, 1907, Feb 20, 1907, July 13, 1912, May 31, 1913, July 2, 1915, Jan 10, 1918, Dec 14, 1920, June 20, 1921, Oct 3, 1922, Jan 12, 1932, Jan 23, 1933, May 1, 1937, Oct 20, 1947, Oct 10, 1951, Mar 1, 1954, Oct 13, 1970, Sept 30, 1976, Jan 3, 1980, Jan 24, 1980, Dec 23, 1982, Dec 12, 1985; *1986* Feb 7, June 26, Oct 9
Congress of Industrial Organizations (CIO) .... Nov 9, 1935, Nov 14, 1937, Feb 9, 1955, Dec 5, 1955
Conlon, Jocko (John B.) .... Dec 6, 1899
Connally, John .... Nov 22, 1963, July 29, 1974
Connally, Thomas H. .... Dec 31, 1870
Connally, Tom .... Aug 19, 1877
Connecticut .... June 8, 1633, May 31, 1636, May 1, 1637, Jan 14, 1638, Apr 15, 1638, Jan 24, 1639, June 14, 1639, Nov 6, 1643, Sept 19, 1650, Oct 2, 1656, Jan 7, 1658, Apr 23, 1662, Jan 5, 1665, May 1, 1691, Oct 9, 1700, Dec 25, 1754, Apr 12, 1755, May 19, 1774, Jan 9, 1788, Dec 15, 1814, Oct 5, 1818, June 22, 1854, Oct 2, 1865, Oct 1, 1960, Dec 14, 1965
Connelly, Marc(us) .... Dec 13, 1890
Conner, David .... Mar 20, 1856
Connery, Sean .... Aug 25, 1930
Conniff, Ray .... Nov 6, 1916
Connolly, Maureen .... Sept 17, 1934
Connor, Roger .... July 1, 1857
Connors, Jimmy .... Sept 2, 1952
Conrad, Frank .... May 4, 1874
Conscription *see* Selective Service
Conservation .... May 19, 1796, Mar 3, 1891, May 13, 1908, June 8, 1908, Jan 11, 1909, June 10, 1980
Considine, Bob .... Nov 4, 1906
Constitutional Convention .... Jan 21, 1786; *1787* May 14, May 25, May 29, June 15, July 16, Sept 17; *1788* Mar 24, Aug 6, Sept 28
Consumer Product Safety/Commission .... Oct 27, 1972
Continental Congress .... *1774* Sept 5, Sept 27, Sept 28, Sept 30, Oct 14, Oct 18; *1775* May 10, May 15, June 10, June 14, June 15, July 6, July 18, July 31, Sept 12; *1776* Feb 15, Mar 3, May 10, May 15, June 7, June 10, June 12, July 2, July 4, Sept 26, Nov 1, Dec 12, Dec 20; *1777* Mar 4, June 14, Sept 27, Sept 30, Nov 15; May 4, 1778, Mar 1, 1799, Oct 10, 1780, Oct 24, 1781, June 20, 1782; *1783* Apr 15, Oct 20, Nov 26; *1784* Jan 14, Mar 1, Apr 23, Nov 1, Dec 23; Jan 11, 1785, Nov 7, 1785, Feb 21, 1787, July 13, 1787; *1788* Sept 13, Sept 28, Oct 2
Converse, Frederick S. .... Jan 5, 1871
Conway, Thomas .... Dec 14, 1777
Conwell, Russell H. .... Feb 15, 1843
Cook, Frederick A. .... June 10, 1865, Sept 1, 1909
Cook, Capt. James .... Jan 20, 1778
Cooke, Jay .... Aug 10, 1821, Sept 18, 1873
Cooke, Terence J. .... Mar 1, 1921
Cooley, Charles H. .... Aug 17, 1864
Cooley, Denton A. .... Aug 22, 1920, Apr 4, 1969
Coolidge, Calvin .... July 4, 1872, Oct 4, 1905, Aug 3, 1923, Jan 10, 1927, Aug 2, 1927, Feb 4, 1928, Jan 5, 1933
Coolidge, Charles A. .... Nov 30, 1858
Coolidge, Grace A. .... Jan 3, 1879, Oct 4, 1905, July 8, 1957
Coolidge, William D. .... Oct 23, 1873
Coolidge Dam .... Mar 4, 1930
Cooper, Gary .... May 7, 1901
Cooper, Hugh L. .... Apr 28, 1865
Cooper, James Fenimore .... Sept 15, 1789
Cooper, Kent .... Mar 22, 1880
Cooper, Leon N. .... Feb 28, 1930
Cooper, Peter .... Feb 12, 1791
Cope, Edward D. .... July 28, 1840
Copeland, Royal S. .... Nov 7, 1868
Copland, Aaron .... Nov 14, 1900
Copley, John S. .... July 3, 1738
Coppola, Francis F. .... Apr 7, 1939
Copyright .... May 31, 1790, Mar 3, 1865
Corbett, Harvey W. .... Jan 8, 1873
Corbin, Margaret .... Nov 12, 1751
Corcoran, William W. .... Dec 27, 1798
Cordero, Angel .... Nov 8, 1942

Cori, Carl F. .... Dec 5, 1896
Cori, Gerty Theresa .... Aug 15, 1896
Corliss, George H. .... June 2, 1817
Cornell, Ezra .... Jan 11, 1807
Cornell, Katherine .... Feb 16, 1893
Corning, Erastus .... Dec 14, 1794
Cornish, John .... Mar 16, 1827
Coronado, Francisco Vasquez de .... July 7, 1540, Apr 23, 1541
Corporation for Public Broadcasting .... Nov 7, 1967
Correll, Charles J. .... Feb 2, 1890
Corrigan, Douglas .... July 17, 1938
Corrigan, Michael A. .... Aug 13, 1839
Cortelyou, George B. .... July 26, 1862, Feb 14, 1903
Cosby, Bill .... July 12, 1937
Cosell, Howard .... Mar 25, 1920
Cost of Living Council .... Aug 15, 1971
Costello, Lou .... Mar 6, 1908
Cotton, John .... Dec 4, 1584
Cottrell, Frederick G. .... Jan 10, 1877
Coughlin, Charles E. .... Oct 25, 1891
Coulter, Ernest K. .... Nov 14, 1871
Council of Economic Advisors .... Feb 20, 1946
Council of Environmental Quality .... May 29, 1969, Jan 1, 1970
Cournand, André F. .... Sept 24, 1895
Court of Appeals .... Jan 15, 1780
Court of Claims .... Feb 24, 1855
Cousins, Norman .... June 24, 1915
Cousy, Robert J. .... Aug 9, 1928
Couzens, James .... Aug 26, 1872
Coveleski, Stan(ley) .... July 13, 1889
Cowen, Joshua .... Aug 25, 1880
Cowl, Jane .... Dec 14, 1884
Cowles, Alfred H. .... Dec 8, 1858
Cowles, Gardner .... Jan 31, 1903
Cowley, Malcolm .... Aug 24, 1898
Cox, Archibald .... May 17, 1912, Apr 17, 1973, Oct 20, 1973
Cox, Jacob D. .... Oct 27, 1828
Cox, James M. .... Mar 31, 1870
Coxey's Army .... May 1, 1894
Cozzens, James G. .... Aug 19, 1903
Crafts, James M. .... Mar 8, 1839
Craig, Malin .... Aug 5, 1875
Craik, James .... Feb 6, 1814
Cram, Donald J. .... Apr 22, 1919
Cram, Ralph A. .... Dec 16, 1863
Cramp, Charles H. .... May 9, 1828
Cramp, William .... Sept 22, 1807
Crandall, Prudence .... Sept 3, 1803
Crane, Charles R. .... Aug 7, 1858
Crane, Hart .... July 21, 1899
Crane, Stephen .... Nov 1, 1871
Crane, Winthrop H. .... Apr 23, 1853
Cranston, Samuel .... Apr 26, 1727
Crater, Joseph F. .... Aug 6, 1930
Crawford, Jesse .... Dec 2, 1895
Crawford, Joan .... Mar 23, 1908
Crawford, Thomas .... Mar 22, 1813, Dec 2, 1863
Crawford, William H. .... Feb 24, 1772, Nov 9, 1824, Dec 1, 1824, Feb 9, 1825
Crazy Horse .... Sept 5, 1877
Creationism .... Mar 4, 1987
Creek War .... Aug 30, 1813, Mar 27, 1814
Creel, George E. .... Apr 14, 1917
Crespi, Juan .... May 14, 1769, Aug 1, 1769, Jan 1, 1782
Creswell, John A.J. .... Nov 18, 1828
Cret, Paul P. .... Oct 23, 1876
Crick, Francis C.H. .... Apr 25, 1943
Crile, George W. .... Nov 11, 1864
Crippen, Robert L. .... Sept 11, 1937, Apr 12, 1981
Crisp, Charles F. .... Jan 29, 1845
Crittenden, John J. .... Sept 10, 1787
Crocker, Charles .... Sept 16, 1822
Crocker, Francis B. .... July 4, 1861
Crockett, Davy .... Aug 17, 1786, Mar 6, 1836
Croker, Richard .... Nov 24, 1841
Croly, Herbert D. .... Jan 23, 1869
Crompton, William .... Sept 10, 1806
Cronin, James W. .... Sept 29, 1931
Cronin, Joe .... Oct 12, 1906
Cronkite, Walter .... Nov 4, 1916
Cronyn, Hume .... July 18, 1911
Crosby, Bing (Harry L.) .... May 2, 1904
Crosby, Fanny .... Mar 24, 1820
Crosby, Percy L. .... Dec 8, 1891
Crosley, Powel .... Sept 18, 1886
Cross, Roy .... Jan 13, 1884
Crossword puzzles .... Dec 12, 1913
Crothers, Rachel .... Dec 12, 1878
Crouse, Russel .... Feb 20, 1893
Crowder, Enoch H. .... Apr 11, 1859
Crowell, Luther C. .... Sept 7, 1840
Crowninshield, Francis W. .... June 24, 1782
Crozier, William .... Feb 19, 1855
Crump, Edward H. .... Oct 2, 1874
Cuba .... *1898* Feb 15, Apr 11, Apr 20, Apr 22, June 24; Dec 11, 1903, July 6, 1960; *1961* Jan 3, Apr 17, Apr 20; *1962* Oct 22, Oct 24, Nov 2
Cudahy, Michael .... Dec 7, 1841
Cugat, Xavier .... Jan 1, 1900
Cukor, George .... July 7, 1899
Culbertson, Ely .... July 22, 1891
Cullen, Countee .... May 30, 1903
Cullum, George W. .... Feb 25, 1809
Cumming, Alfred .... Nov 27, 1857
Cummings, Candy (William A.) .... Oct 7, 1848
Cummings, E(dward) E. .... Oct 14, 1894
Cummins, Albert B. .... Feb 15, 1850
Cunningham, Merce .... Apr 19, 1919
Curley, James M. .... Nov 20, 1874
Currier, Nathaniel .... Mar 27, 1813
Curry, Jabez L.M. .... June 5, 1825
Curry, John Steuart .... Nov 14, 1897
Curtis, Benjamin R. .... Nov 4, 1809, Apr 9, 1868
Curtis, Charles .... Jan 25, 1860, Feb 8, 1936
Curtis, Cyrus H.K. .... June 18, 1850
Curtis, George W. .... Feb 24, 1824
Curtiss, Glenn H. .... May 21, 1878, Jan 6, 1911
Cushing, Caleb .... Jan 17, 1800

Cushing, Harvey W. .... Apr 8, 1869
Cushing, Richard J. .... Aug 24, 1895
Cushing, William .... Mar 1, 1732
Cushing, William B. .... Oct 27, 1864
Cushman, Charlotte S. .... July 23, 1816
Cushman, Robert E. Jr. .... Dec 24, 1914
Cushman, Vera C.S. .... Sept 19, 1876
Custer, George A. .... Dec 5, 1839
Custis, Patsy .... June 19, 1773
Customs Service .... July 31, 1789
Cutler, Manasseh .... May 13, 1742
Cutler, Timothy .... May 31, 1684
Cutter, Charles A. .... Mar 14, 1837
Cuyler, Kiki (Hazen S.) .... Aug 30, 1899
Czolgosz, Leon F. .... Sept 6, 1901, Sept 23, 1901, Oct 29, 1901

Dahlgren, John A.B. .... Nov 13, 1809
Dakota Territory .... Mar 2, 1861
Dale, Sir Thomas .... Aug 9, 1619
Daley, Richard J. .... May 15, 1902
Dallas, George M. .... July 10, 1792, Dec 31, 1864
Dalton Brothers .... Oct 5, 1892
Daly, Augustin .... July 20, 1838
Daly, Marcus .... Dec 5, 1841
Damien, Father .... Jan 30, 1840
Damrosch, Leopold .... Oct 22, 1832
Damrosch, Walter J. .... Jan 30, 1862
Dams .... Aug 26, 1913, May 11, 1915; *see also* specific dams
Dana, Charles A. .... Aug 8, 1819
Dana, James D. .... Feb 12, 1813
Dana, Richard Henry .... Aug 1, 1815
Dancer, Stanley .... July 25, 1927
Daniel, Peter V. .... Apr 24, 1784
Daniels, Josephus .... May 18, 1862
Daniloff, Nicholas .... Sept 29, 1986
Dannay, Frederic .... Jan 11, 1905
Dare, Virginia .... Aug 18, 1587
Darling, Ding (Jay N.) .... Oct 21, 1876
Darling, Flora A. .... July 25, 1840
Darman, Richard G. .... May 10, 1943
Darrow, Clarence S. .... Apr 18, 1857, Sept 10, 1924, July 10, 1925
Daugherty, Harry M. .... Mar 28, 1824
Daughters of the American Revolution (DAR) .... Aug 8, 1890, Oct 11, 1890, Dec 2, 1895
Daughters of the Confederacy, United (National) (UDC) .... Sept 10, 1894
Davenport, John .... Apr 9, 1597, Apr 15, 1638, June 14, 1639
Davenport, Thomas .... July 9, 1802
Davey, John .... June 6, 1846
David, Hal .... May 25, 1921
Davidson, Jo .... Mar 30, 1883
Davidson, William L. .... Feb 1, 1781
Davie, William R. .... June 20, 1756
Davies, Arthur B. .... Sept 26, 1862
Davies, Joseph E. .... Nov 29, 1876
Davies, Rodger P. .... Aug 19, 1974
Davies, Samuel .... Nov 3, 1723
Davis, Alexander J. .... July 24, 1803
Davis, Arthur V. .... May 30, 1867
Davis, Benjamin O. .... July 1, 1877
Davis, Bette .... Apr 5, 1908
Davis Cup .... Aug 7, 1900
Davis, David .... Mar 9, 1815
Davis, Dwight F. .... July 5, 1879
Davis, Elmer H. .... Jan 13, 1890
Davis, Francis B. Jr. .... Sept 16, 1883
Davis, Glenn .... Dec 26, 1924
Davis, Henry G. .... Nov 16, 1823
Davis, James J. .... Oct 27, 1873
Davis, Jefferson .... June 3, 1808, Feb 8, 1861, Feb 18, 1861; *1865* Jan 28, Apr 4, May 10; May 14, 1867, Dec 3, 1868, Dec 6, 1889
Davis, Jim (James R.) .... July 28, 1945
Davis, Jimmie .... Sept 11, 1902
Davis, John W. .... Apr 13, 1873
Davis, Miles D. Jr. .... May 25, 1926
Davis, Nathan S. .... Jan 9, 1817
Davis, Owen .... Jan 29, 1874
Davis, Richard Harding .... Apr 18, 1864
Davis, Sammy Jr. .... Dec 8, 1925
Davis, William H. .... Jan 12, 1942
Davisson, Clinton J. .... Oct 22, 1881
Dawes, Charles G. .... Aug 27, 1865, Aug 20, 1924, Dec 10, 1926, Apr 16, 1929, Jan 22, 1932, Apr 23, 1951
Dawes, Samuel .... Nov 3, 1723
Dawes, William .... Apr 6, 1745, Apr 18, 1775
Dawson, Richard .... Nov 20, 1932
Day, Benjamin H. .... Apr 10, 1810, Sept 3, 1833, Jan 1, 1842
Day, Clarence S. Jr. .... Nov 18, 1874
Day, Dorothy .... Nov 8, 1897
Day, Edmund E. .... Dec 7, 1883
Day, George P. .... Sept 4, 1876
Day, William R. .... Apr 17, 1849
Daylight Saving Time .... Mar 19, 1918, Mar 31, 1918, Aug 15, 1919
Dayton, Elias .... May 1, 1737
Dayton, Jonathan .... Oct 16, 1760
Dayton, Ohio .... Jan 1, 1914
Dayton, William L. .... Feb 17, 1807
Dean, Dizzy (Jerome) .... Jan 16, 1911
Dean, James .... Feb 8, 1931
Dean, John W. .... Apr 30, 1973
Deane, Silas .... Dec 24, 1737, Mar 3, 1776, Sept 26, 1776
Dearborn, Henry .... Feb 23, 1751
Deaver, Michael K. .... Sept 23, 1988
DeBakey, Michael E. .... Sept 7, 1908, Apr 21, 1966
DeBeck, Billy .... Apr 15, 1890
Debreau, Gerard .... July 4, 1921
Debs, Eugene .... Nov 5, 1885, Dec 14, 1894, Jan 24, 1895, Jan 27, 1900; *1918* June 30, Sept 12; Mar 10, 1919, Dec 24, 1921
Debt, Public .... Jan 1, 1783
Debye, Peter J.W. .... Mar 24, 1884
Decatur, Stephen .... Jan 5, 1779, Feb 16, 1804, Mar 22, 1820

Declaration of
Independence .... *1776* June 10, July 2, July 4, July 8, Aug 2; July 4, 1976
Deere, John .... Feb 7, 1804
Deerfield Massacre .... Feb 29, 1704
Defense, Department of .... Jan 15, 1943, June 15, 1946; *1947* July 26, Sept 18; *1988* July 1, Dec 29
DeForest, Lee .... Aug 26, 1873
DeGraff, Robert F. .... June 9, 1895
DeHavilland, Olivia .... July 1, 1916
DeKalb, Baron Johann *see* Kalb, Baron Johann de
DeKooning, Willem .... Apr 24, 1904
DeKoven, Reginald .... Apr 3, 1859
DeKruif, Paul H. .... Mar 2, 1890
Delafield, Edward .... May 7, 1794
Delafield, Francis .... Aug 3, 1841
Delahanty, Ed(ward J.) .... Oct 31, 1887
Delamater, Cornelius H. Aug 30, 1821
DeLancey, James .... Nov 27, 1703
Delano, Jane A. .... Mar 12, 1862
Delaware .... Dec 21, 1624, Mar 29, 1638, Feb 15, 1643, Sept 1, 1655, Dec 4, 1682, Nov 20, 1704, Aug 27, 1776, Sept 21, 1776, Dec 7, 1787, June 12, 1792, Dec 2, 1832, Jan 3, 1861, Sept 3, 1861, June 10, 1897
De La Warr, Thomas W. ...... July 9, 1571, Feb 28, 1610
Delbrück, Max .... Sept 4, 1906
DeLee, Joseph B. .... Oct 28, 1869
Dello Joio, Norman .... Jan 24, 1913
Delmonico, Lorenzo .... Mar 13, 1813
DeLorean, John Z. .... Oct 19, 1982
DeLuise, Dom .... Aug 1, 1933
DeMar, Clarence .... June 11, 1958
DeMille, Agnes .... Sept 18, 1905
DeMille, Cecil B. .... Aug 21, 1881
Demjanjuk, John .... Apr 25, 1988
Democratic Party *see* Political Parties
Dempsey, Jack .... June 24, 1895, July 4, 1919, Sept 23, 1926
Dempster, Arthur J. .... Aug 14, 1886
Demuth, Charles .... Nov 8, 1883
Denby, Edwin .... Apr 7, 1922; *1924* Feb 8, Feb 18; Feb 28, 1927
Denmark .... Feb 25, 1783, Aug 4, 1916, Jan 17, 1917, Apr 10, 1941
Dennison, Aaron L. .... Mar 6, 1812
Denny, George H. .... Dec 3, 1870
Denny, George V. .... Aug 29, 1899
Densmore, Frances .... May 21, 1867
Dentistry .... Feb 1, 1840
Denver, James W. .... Oct 23, 1817
Denver, John .... Dec 31, 1943
DePalma, Ralph .... Jan 23, 1884
Depew, Chauncey W. .... Apr 23, 1834
DePayster, Abraham .... July 8, 1657
DePortola, Gaspar *see* Portola, Gaspar de
Dern, George H. .... Sept 8, 1872
DeRose, Peter .... Mar 10, 1900
Derwinski, Edwin .... Dec 22, 1988
Deseret, State of *see* Utah
DeSeversky, Alexander P. .... June 7, 1894
DeSmet, Pierre Jean .... Jan 30, 1801
DeSoto, Hernando .... *1539* May 25, Aug 1; *1540* Mar 3, Dec 17; *1541* May 8, June 29; *1542* May 21, June 5; July 18, 1543
DeSylva, Buddy
(George G.) .... Jan 27, 1896
Detroit .... July 24, 1701, Nov 29, 1760, July 11, 1796, June 11, 1805, Aug 16, 1812, Sept 10, 1813, Sept 28, 1813, Aug 26, 1817, June 20, 1943, July 23, 1967
Dett, Robert N. .... Oct 11, 1882
Devers, Jacob L. .... Sept 8, 1887
DeVoto, Bernard A. .... Jan 11, 1897
DeVries, Peter .... Feb 27, 1910
DeVries, William C. .... Dec 19, 1943
Dewey, George .... Dec 26, 1837
Dewey, John .... Oct 20, 1859
Dewey, Melvil .... Dec 10, 1851, Jan 5, 1887
Dewey, Thomas E. .... Mar 24, 1902, July 29, 1935
DeWitt, Simeon .... Dec 25, 1756
DeYoung, Michael H. .... Oct 1, 1849
Diamond, Neil .... Jan 24, 1941
Dick, Albert B. .... Apr 16, 1856
Dick, George F. .... July 21, 1881
Dick, Gladys .... Dec 18, 1881
Dickerson, Mahlon .... Apr 17, 1770
Dickey, Bill .... June 6, 1907
Dickey, James .... Feb 2, 1923
Dicksinson, Emily .... Dec 10, 1830
Dickinson, John .... Nov 8, 1732, July 18, 1768, July 5, 1775
Dicksinson, Jonathan .... Apr 22, 1688, Oct 22, 1746
Dickinson, Preston .... Sept 9, 1889
Dickman, Joseph T. .... Oct 6, 1857
Dickson, Earle E. .... Oct 10, 1892
Dietrich, Marlene .... Dec 27, 1904
Dietz, Howard .... Sept 8, 1896
Dillinger, John .... July 22, 1934
Dillingham, William P. .... Dec 12, 1843
DiMaggio, Joe .... Nov 25, 1914, May 15, 1941
Dinwiddie, Robert .... July 27, 1770
Dirks, Rudolph .... Feb 26, 1877
Dirksen, Everett M. .... Jan 4, 1896
Disasters .... Mar 20, 1760, Sept 21, 1776, Aug 1, 1793
1805 .... June 11, 1805, Dec 16, 1811, June 27, 1832, Dec 16, 1835, Dec 15, 1836; *1838* Apr 25, ap 27; Jan 13, 1840; *1845* Apr 10, July 19; Nov 21, 1847, Aug 24, 1848, May 17, 1849;
1851 .... May 3, May 4, Dec 24; Apr 27, 1854, July 17, 1856, June 13, 1858, Sept 8, 1860, July 4, 1866, Oct 21, 1868, Sept 6, 1869, Apr 27, 1870, Oct 8, 1871, Nov 9, 1872, May 16, 1874,
1875 .... May 27, 1875; *1876* Dec 5, Dec 29; Jan 10, 1883, Feb 19, 1884; *1886* Apr 31, Oct 13; Aug 10, 1887; *1888* Mar 11, Mar 12; *1889* Jan 6, May

31; July 13, 1890; *1893* June 9, Apr 22; Sept 1, 1894, May 27, 1896;
1900 .... May 1, June 30, Aug 8, Sept 8; *1902* May 18, Sept 20; *1903* May 31, Dec 30; *1904* Feb 7, June 15, Aug 7; *1905* Feb 20, May 11, July 22; *1906* Apr 18, May 18; *1907* Dec 6, Dec 19; *1908* Jan 13, Mar 4, Mar 28, Apr 12, Nov 28; Nov 13, 1909; *1910* Oct 1, Oct 9; Mar 25, 1911; *1912* Apr 15, July 2; *1913* Mar 21, Oct 22; *1915* July 24, Nov 30; *1916* Mar 21, July 22, July 30; *1917* Apr 9, May 21; *1918* Apr 21, June 22, July 5, Oct 4, Oct 13, Nov 1; Sept 16, 1920, Sept 9, 1921; Jan 27, Feb 21;
1925 .... Mar 18, June 29, Sept 3, Sept 25; Sept 17, 1926; *1927* Sept 29, Dec 17; *1928* Mar 13, Sept 12; May 15, 1929, Apr 21, 1930, Apr 4, 1933; *1934* May 10, Sept 8; *1935* Aug 29, Oct 18; Apr 5, 1936; *1937* Mar 18, May 6; *1938* Jan 27, Sept 21; May 23, 1939, Apr 23, 1940; *1942* Jan 16, Nov 28; *1943* Sept 6, Dec 16; *1944* July 6, July 17, Oct 20, Dec 31; *1945* Apr 9, July 28, Sept 17; *1946* Apr 25, Oct 25, Dec 7; *1947* Mar 25, Apr 16; *1949* Sept 17, Nov 1;
1950 .... June 24, Nov 22; *1951* Feb 6, June 30, Sept 11, Dec 16, Dec 21; *1952* Jan 22, Feb 11, Mar 21, Apr 26, Dec 20; *1953* May 11, June 8, June 18; *1954* May 26, Aug 25, Oct 12; *1955* Mar 22, Aug 11, Aug 18, Oct 6; *1956* June 30, July 25; June 27, 1957; *1958* Apr 21, Sept 15, Dec 1; Feb 3, 1959;
1960 .... Mar 17, Aug 29, Dec 16, Dec 19; Sept 1, 1961, Mar 1, 1962; *1963* Apr 10, Oct 31, Nov 23; Mar 27, 1964; *1965* Apr 11, Aug 9, Sept 7; *1966* Aug 1, Oct 23; *1967* July 19, July 29, Aug 14, Dec 15; *1968* May 21, Nov 20; *1969* Aug 17, Sept 9;
1970 .... Oct 2, Nov 14; *1971* Feb 9, Sept 4; *1972* Feb 26, May 2, June 9, June 19; *1975* Apr 4, June 24; *1976* July 21, Aug 1, Oct 20, Dec 15; May 28, 1977; *1978* Apr 27, Sept 25; May 25, 1979;
1980 .... May 9, May 18, Nov 21, Dec 4; July 17, 1981; *1982* Jan 13, July 9, Sept 11, Dec 11; Apr 31;
1983 .... Sept 1, 1983, July 18, 1984; *1985* Jan 21, May 13, June 25, Aug 2, Sept 6, Dec 12; Dec 31, 1986; *1987* Jan 5, Apr 5, May 22, Aug 16, Sept 28, Nov 18; *1988* Jan 2, Apr 24, May 4, May 5, May 15, May 20, Aug 17, Aug 28, Aug 31, Sept 15, Dec 21; Oct 17, 1989
Disney, Walt(er) E. .... Dec 5, 1901
Disneyland .... July 17, 1955
District of Columbia .... Dec 23, 1788; *1789* Jan 23, Feb 12, Dec 3; July 6, 1790, July 16, 1790; *1791* Jan 24, Mar 3, Sept 9; June 28, 1794; *1800* Apr 24, June 15, Nov 17; Feb 27, 1801, Mar 4, 1801, May 3, 1802, Aug 24, 1814, May 15, 1820, Mar 31, 1833, Dec 15, 1836, Sept 20, 1850, Apr 16, 1862, May 21, 1862, Jan 8, 1867, June 20, 1874, Feb 21, 1885, June 9, 1893, May 1, 1909, Mar 27, 1912, Nov 12, 1921, Jan 27, 1922, May 30, 1922, July 21, 1932, Sept 28, 1940, Jan 15, 1943, Apr 14, 1959, Mar 29, 1961, Aug 28, 1963, May 15, 1966, Jan 8, 1968, Jan 21, 1968, Nov 15, 1969, Sept 9, 1971, Jan 16, 1975, Aug 1, 1976, Mar 9, 1977; *1982* Jan 13, Nov 8, Nov 13, Dec 8
Ditmars, Raymond L. .... June 19, 1876
Divine, Father *see* Baker, George (1965)
Dix, Dorothea L. .... Apr 4, 1802
Dix, Dorothy .... Nov 18, 1870
Dix, John A. .... July 24, 1798
Dixon, Joseph .... Nov 18, 1799
Dixon, Thomas .... Jan 11, 1864
Dobbs, Arthur .... Apr 2, 1689
Dobie, James Frank .... Sept 26, 1888
Dockstader, Lew .... Aug 7, 1856
Dodd, Thomas J. .... June 23, 1967
Dodge, Grenville M. .... Apr 12, 1831
Dodge, Mary E.M. .... Jan 26, 1831
Doheny, Edward L. .... Dec 11, 1922, Apr 7, 1922, June 30, 1924
Doherty, Henry L. .... May 15, 1870
Doisy, Edward A. .... Nov 13, 1893
Dole, Elizabeth H. .... Dec 24, 1988
Doles, James D. .... Sept 27, 1887
Dole, Robert J. .... July 22, 1923
Dole, Sanford B. .... Apr 23, 1844
Dollar, Robert .... Mar 20, 1844
Domingo, Placido .... Jan 21, 1941
Donahue, Phil .... Dec 21, 1935
Donaldson, Walter .... Feb 15, 1893
Donelson, Andrew J. .... Aug 25, 1799
Dongan, Thomas .... Dec 6, 1683; *1686* Apr 27, July 22; Dec 14, 1715
Donovan, Raymond .... Oct 1, 1984, Mar 15, 1985, May 25, 1987
Donovan, William J. .... Jan 1, 1883, June 13, 1943
Doolittle, Hilda (HD) .... Sept 10, 1886
Doolittle, James H. .... Dec 14, 1896, Apr 18, 1942
Doran, George H. .... Dec 19, 1869
Dorgan, Thomas A. .... Apr 29, 1877

Doriot, Georges F. .... Sept 24, 1899
Dorr Rebellion .... May 18, 1842
Dorsey, George A. .... Feb 6, 1868
Dorsey, Jimmy .... Feb 29, 1904
Dorsey, Tommy .... Nov 19, 1905
Dos Passos, John R. .... Jan 14, 1896
Doubleday, Abner .... June 26, 1819
Doubleday, Frank N. .... Jan 8, 1862
Dougherty, Dennis J. .... Aug 16, 1865
Douglas, Donald W. .... Apr 6, 1892
Douglas, James .... Nov 4, 1837
Douglas, Kirk .... Dec 9, 1918
Douglas, Lewis W. .... July 2, 1894
Douglas, Lloyd C. .... Aug 27, 1877
Douglas, Melvyn .... Apr 5, 1901
Douglas, Mike .... Aug 11, 1925
Douglas, Stephen A. .... Apr 23, 1813, May 30, 1854, Aug 21, 1858, Aug 27, 1858
Douglas, William O. .... Oct 16, 1898
Douglass, Frederick .... Feb 7, 1817
Douglass, Truman B. .... July 15, 1901
Dove, Arthur G. .... Aug 2, 1880
Dow, Charles H. .... Nov 6, 1851
Dow, Herbert H. .... Feb 26, 1866
Dow, Neal .... Mar 20, 1804
Dowie, John A. .... May 25, 1847
Downs, Hugh .... Feb 14, 1921
Dozier, James L. .... Jan 19, 1982
Drago, Luis M. .... Dec 29, 1902
Drake, Edwin L. .... Aug 27, 1859
Drake, Sir Francis .... June 17, 1579, May 27, 1586, June 10, 1586
Draper, Charles S. .... Oct 2, 1901
Draper, Henry .... Mar 7, 1837
Draper, John W. .... May 5, 1811
Draper, Ruth .... Dec 2, 1884
Dreiser, Theodore .... Aug 27, 1871
Dressler, Marie .... Nov 9, 1873
Drew, Charles R. .... June 3, 1904
Drew, Daniel .... July 29, 1797, Sept 24, 1869
Drew, John .... Nov 13, 1853
Drexel, Anthony J. .... Sept 13, 1826
Drexel Burnham Lambert .... Sept 7, 1988, Dec 21, 1988
Drexel, Mother Katherine .... Nov 20, 1988
Drinan, Rev. Robert .... May 5, 1980
Drugs .... *1988* Feb 11, May 19, Nov 14
Dryden, John F. .... Aug 7, 1839
Drysdale, Don .... July 23, 1936
Duane, James .... Feb 6, 1733
Duane,William .... Feb 17, 1872
Dubin, Al .... June 10, 1891
Dubinsky, David .... Feb 22, 1892
DuBois, William E.B. .... Feb 23, 1868
Dubos, René J. .... Feb 20, 1901
Dubs, Adolph .... Feb 14, 1979
Duchamp, Marcel .... July 28, 1887
Duché, Jacob .... Jan 31, 1737
Duchin, Eddy (Edwin F.) .... Apr 10, 1910
Dudley, Joseph .... Apr 2, 1720
Dudley, Thomas .... July 31, 1653
Duer, William .... Mar 18, 1747
Duffy, Edmund .... Mar 1, 1899
Duffy, Francis F. .... May 2, 1871
Duffy, Hugh .... Nov 26, 1866
Dukakis, Michael S. .... Nov 3, 1933
Duke, Benjamin N. .... Apr 27, 1855
Duke, James B. .... Dec 23, 1856
Duke, Vernon .... Oct 10, 1903
Dulbecco, Renato .... Feb 2, 1914
Dulles, Allen W. .... Apr 7, 1893
Dulles, John Foster .... Feb 25, 1888, Jan 12, 1955, Apr 15, 1959
Duluth, Daniel G. .... Feb 25, 1710
Dumbarton Oaks Conference .... Aug 21, 1944
Dumont, Allen B. .... Jan 29, 1901
Dun, Robert G. .... Aug 7, 1826
Dunbar, Paul L. .... June 27, 1872
Duncan, David Douglas .... Jan 23, 1916
Duncan, Isadore .... May 27, 1878
Dunham, Katherine .... June 22, 1920
Dunlap, William .... Feb 19, 1766
Dunne, Finley Peter .... July 10, 1867
Dunne, Irene .... Dec 20, 1904
Dunning, John R. .... Sept 24, 1907
Dunster, Henry .... Aug 27, 1640, Feb 27, 1659
DuPont Company .... June 21, 1911, Nov 30, 1915, Mar 24, 1988
DuPont, E(leuthere) I. .... June 24, 1771
DuPont, Irénée .... Dec 21, 1876
DuPont, Margaret Osborne .. Mar 4, 1918
DuPont, Pierre S. .... Jan 15, 1870
DuPont, Pierre S. IV .... June 22, 1935
Durand, Asher B. .... Aug 21, 1796
Durant, Henry .... June 18, 1802
Durant, Thomas C. .... Feb 6, 1820
Durant, Will(iam J.) .... Nov 5, 1885
Durant, William C. .... Dec 8, 1861
Durante, Jimmy .... Feb 10, 1893
Durbin, Deanna .... Dec 4, 1922
Durocher, Leo .... July 27, 1906
Durstine, Roy S. .... Dec 13, 1886
Duryea, Charles E. .... Dec 15, 1861, Apr 19, 1892, Sept 21, 1893
Duryea, J. Frank .... Oct 8, 1869, Apr 19, 1892, Sept 21, 1893, Nov 28, 1895
Duryée, Abram .... Apr 29, 1815
DuSable, Jean Baptiste Point .... Aug 28, 1818
Dutton, Edward P. .... Jan 4, 1831
Duval, Gabriel .... Dec 6, 1752
DuVigneaud, Vincent .... May 18, 1901
Dwight, John S. .... May 13, 1813
Dwight, Timothy .... May 14, 1752
Dyer, Mary .... June 1, 1660
Dykes, Jimmy .... Nov 10, 1896
Dykstra, Clarence A. .... Feb 25, 1883
Dylan, Bob .... May 24, 1941

Eads, James B. .... Mar 23, 1820, Aug 7, 1861
Eagels, Jeanne .... June 26, 1894
Eaker, Ira C. .... Apr 13, 1896
Eakins, Thomas .... July 25, 1844
Eames, Charles .... June 17, 1907
Earhart, Amelia .... July 24, 1898, June 17, 1928, May 20, 1932, July 2, 1937

Earle, Pliny .... Dec 17, 1762
Early, Jubal A. .... Nov 2, 1816
Earp, Wyatt .... Mar 19, 1848, Oct 26, 1881
Earth Day .... Apr 22, 1970
Earthquakes *see* Disasters
East, Edward M. .... Oct 4, 1879
Eastern Airlines .... Sept 18, 1986
Eastman, George .... July 12, 1854
Eastman, Max .... Jan 4, 1833
Easton, Nicholas .... Aug 15, 1675
Eastwood, Clint .... May 31, 1930
Eaton, Cyrus S. .... Dec 27, 1883
Eaton, Dorman B. .... June 27, 1823, Jan 16, 1883
Eaton, Theophilus .... Apr 15, 1638, June 14, 1639, Jan 7, 1658
Eaton, Wyatt .... May 6, 1849
Eberle, Edward W. .... Aug 17, 1864
Ebsen, Buddy (Christian R.) .... Apr 2, 1908
Eccles, Marriner S. .... Sept 9, 1890
Eckert, John P. .... Apr 9, 1919
Eckstine, Billy .... July 8, 1914
Economic Cooperation Administration .... Apr 3, 1948
Economic Development Administration .... Sept 1, 1965
Economy .... Dec 21, 1790, Apr 4, 1800, Dec 22, 1807, Mar 2, 1824; *1837* May 10, Oct 12; Aug 19, 1856, Aug 24, 1857, Sept 24, 1869, Sept 18, 1873, Feb 4, 1887, June 27, 1893, Jan 22, 1895, Oct 22, 1907; *1914* Jan 5, Sept 26; Oct 29, 1929, Dec 20, 1930, Jan 22, 1932; *1933* Mar 6, Mar 9, Apr 5, May 12, June 13, June 16, July 20, Nov 8; Feb 15, 1934; *1935* Apr 8, May 27, June 26, Aug 27; Jan 1, 1936; *1941* Jan 7, Apr 11, *1942* Jan 16, Apr 18, Oct 2; June 30, 1943, Feb 20, 1946, Apr 3, 1948, Sept 1, 1965, Aug 15, 1971, Oct 19, 1973, Aug 3, 1984; *1985* Dec 11, Dec 17; *1987* Jan 9, Jan 23, Mar 20, Apr 6, July 17, Aug 10, Aug 18, Sept 23, Oct 3, Oct 6, Oct 14, Oct 16, Oct 19, Oct 21; *1988* Jan 2, Jan 8, Feb 18, Mar 17, Apr 1, Apr 14, May 24, Aug 19, Aug 20, Aug 23, Sept 19, Sept 23, Oct 30
Eddy, Harrison P. .... Apr 29, 1870
Eddy, Manton S. .... May 16, 1892
Eddy, Mary Baker .... July 16, 1821, Aug 23, 1879, Sept 23, 1892, Dec 3, 1910
Eddy, Nelson .... June 29, 1901
Edelman, Gerald M. .... July 1, 1929
Eden, Robert .... Sept 14, 1741
Ederle, Gertrude .... Oct 23, 1906, Aug 6, 1926
Edgerton, Harold E. .... Apr 6, 1903
Edison, Thomas A. .... Feb 11, 1847, Dec 24, 1877, Oct 21, 1879; *1880* Jan 1, Jan 27, Nov 2; Dec 11, 1882, Nov 21, 1887, Jan 7, 1894, Apr 23, 1896, Aug 31, 1897
Edmonds, Walter D. .... July 15, 1903
Edmunds, George F. .... Feb 1, 1828
Education .... Nov 11, 1647, Aug 13, 1751, July 13, 1753, July 17, 1754, July 13, 1787, Dec 3, 1833, Jan 7, 1839, May 21, 1862, July 2, 1862, Mar 2, 1867, Apr 16, 1867, Mar 10, 1869, Aug 16, 1882, Dec 3, 1883, Jan 12, 1903, Aug 1, 1946, Mar 8, 1948, May 17, 1954, May 31, 1955, Sept 4, 1957, Sept 24, 1957, Apr 24, 1962, Oct 1, 1962; *1963* June 17, Sept 10, Dec 16; Apr 11, 1965, Oct 29, 1969, Apr 20, 1971, June 8, 1972, Sept 27, 1979, Oct 17, 1979, May 17, 1982, June 15, 1982, Apr 26, 1983, May 24, 1983
Education, Department of .... Mar 2, 1867, Sept 27, 1969
Edwards, Clarence R. .... Jan 1, 1860
Edwards, Gus .... Aug 18, 1871
Edwards, Jonathan .... Oct 5, 1703
Edwards, Ralph .... June 13, 1913
Edwards, Richard S. .... Feb 18, 1882
Egan, Maurice F. .... May 24, 1852
Egan, William A. .... May 6, 1984
Egloff, Gustav .... Apr 29, 1955
Ehrlichman, John D. .... Apr 30, 1973, Jan 1, 1974, July 12, 1974
Eickemeyer, Rudolf .... Oct 31, 1831
Eidlitz, Cyrus L.W. .... July 27, 1853
Eidlitz, Leopold .... Mar 29, 1823
Eielsen, Elling .... Sept 19, 1804
Einstein, Albert .... Mar 14, 1879, Oct 17, 1933, Aug 2, 1939
Einstein, Alfred .... Dec 30, 1880
Eiseley, Loren C. .... Sept 3, 1907
Eisendrath, Maurice N. .... July 10, 1902
Eisenhower, Dwight D. .... Oct 14, 1890, July 1, 1916, June 11, 1942, Dec 24, 1943, Jan 16, 1944, Nov 20, 1945, June 24, 1947, Feb 11, 1949, Dec 19, 1950, Apr 4, 1951, Dec 8, 1953; *1955* Jan 19, Feb 22, July 18, Sept 24; June 8, 1956, July 21, 1956; *1957* Jan 5, Mar 9, Sept 24, Nov 25; Jan 3, 1961, Mar 28, 1969, May 1, 1972
Eisenhower, Mamie .... Nov 14, 1896, July 1, 1916, Nov 1, 1979
Eisenstadt, Alfred .... Dec 6, 1898
Elections .... Jan 7, 1789, Feb 11, 1801, Feb 17, 1801, Nov 9, 1824, Feb 9, 1825, June 25, 1842, Jan 23, 1845, Mar 30, 1870, Nov 7, 1876, Jan 29, 1877, Feb 3, 1887, May 23, 1903, June 6, 1904, Jan 26, 1907, May 31, 1913, Apr 3, 1963
Electoral College .... Feb 4, 1789, Feb 17, 1801, Dec 1, 1824, Feb 9, 1825
Elion, Gertrude B. .... Jan 23, 1918
Eliot, Charles W. .... Mar 20, 1834, Mar 10, 1869
Eliot, John .... May 21, 1690
Eliot, T(homas) S. .... Sept 26, 1888
Elkins, Stephen B. .... Sept 26, 1841
Elks .... Dec 16, 1868
Ellender, Allen J. .... Sept 24, 1890
Ellery, William .... Dec 22, 1727
Ellet, Charles .... Jan 1, 1810
Ellicott, Andrew .... Jan 24, 1754
Ellington, Duke (Edward K.) .... Apr 29, 1899
Elliott, Jesse D. .... July 14, 1782
Elliott, Maxine .... Feb 5, 1871
Ellis Island .... Jan 1, 1892
Ellison, Ralph W. .... Mar 1, 1914
Ellsberg, Daniel .... May 11, 1973
Ellsberg, Edward .... Nov 21, 1891
Ellsworth, Lincoln .... May 12, 1880
Ellsworth, Oliver .... Apr 29, 1745, Nov 26, 1807
Elman, Mischa .... Jan 20, 1891
Emancipation Proclamation .... *1862* July 22, Sept 22, Sept 24; Jan 1, 1863
Embury, Philip .... Aug 11, 1760

Emerson, Ralph Waldo .... May 25, 1803
Emmett, Daniel D. .... Jan 31, 1843
Employment *see* Labor
Endecott, John .... Sept 6, 1628, Mar 15, 1665
Enders, John F. .... Feb 10, 1897
Energy/Energy,
Department of .... Sept 30, 1882, June 10, 1920, Aug 4, 1977, June 26, 1980, Nov 10, 1988
Engineers, Corps of .... June 16, 1775, Mar 11, 1779, Mar 16, 1802
England, John .... Sept 23, 1786
Environment .... May 13, 1908, Jan 11, 1909, Nov 24, 1922, Jan 2, 1929, Sept 21, 1965, May 29, 1969, Jan 1, 1970, Aug 22, 1970, Dec 2, 1970, June 14, 1972, Feb 18, 1976, May 21, 1980, June 10, 1980, Apr 24, 1981, Mar 23, 1982, Feb 22, 1983, Dec 23, 1985; *1986* Mar 18, July 17, Sept 11; Feb 1, 1988, Sept 12, 1988
Environmental
Protection Agency .... Dec 2, 1970, June 14, 1972, Aug 23, 1982
Episcopal Church .... Mar 25, 1687, Apr 4, 1748, Nov 14, 1784, Aug 3, 1785, Feb 18, 1869, Sept 12, 1922, July 5, 1988, Sept 24, 1988
Equal Employment Opportunity Commission .... July 2, 1965
Equal Rights .... May 10, 1866, Jan 19, 1869
Equal Rights
Amendment .... Mar 22, 1972, June 30, 1982
Ericsson, John .... July 31, 1803
Erie Canal .... Apr 15, 1817, July 4, 1817, Oct 26, 1825
Erikson, Erik H. .... June 15, 1902
Erlanger, Abraham .... May 4, 1860
Erlanger, Joseph .... Jan 5, 1874
Ernst, Edwin C. .... June 26, 1885
Ernst, Harold C. .... July 31, 1856
Ernst, Morris L. .... Aug 23, 1888
Ervin, Sam(uel J. Jr.) .... Sept 27, 1896, Feb 7, 1973
Erving, Julius .... Feb 22, 1950
Espionage Act .... June 15, 1917, May 16, 1918
Esposito, Phil .... Feb 20, 1942
Espy, James P. .... May 9, 1785
Ettwein, John .... June 29, 1721
Eustis, Dorothy L.H.W. .... May 30, 1886
Eustis, William .... June 10, 1753
Evan, Ernest *see* Checker, Chubby
Evangelical and
Reformed Church .... June 26, 1934, June 25, 1957
Evangelical United
Brethren Church .... Nov 6, 1946
Evans, George H. .... Mar 25, 1805
Evans, John .... Mar 9, 1814
Evans, Linda .... Nov 18, 1942
Evans, Oliver .... Sept 13, 1755
Evans, Robley D. .... Aug 18, 1846
Evans, Walker .... Nov 3, 1903
Evarts, William M. .... Feb 6, 1818
Eveleth, Jonathan J. .... Jan 1, 1855
Everett, Edward .... Apr 11, 1794, Nov 19, 1863
Evers, John .... July 21, 1881
Evers, Medgar .... June 12, 1963
Evert, Chris .... Dec 21, 1954
Ewell, Benjamin S. .... June 10, 1810
Ewell, Richard S. .... Feb 8, 1817
Ewing, Buck (William) .... Oct 17, 1859
Ewing, (William)
Maurice .... May 12, 1906
Ewing, Thomas .... Dec 28, 1789, Mar 3, 1849
Ewry, Ray C. .... Oct 14, 1873
Export-Import Bank .... Feb 12, 1934, July 31, 1945
Expositions, fairs *see* World Fairs
Eye bank .... May 8, 1944

Faber, (John) Eberhard .... Dec 6, 1833
Faber, Red (Urban .... Sept 6, 1888
Fadiman, Clifton .... May 15, 1904
Fain, Sammy .... June 17, 1902
Fair Employment
Practices Commission .... June 25, 1941
Fair Labor Standards
Act .... June 25, 1938
Fairbanks, Arthur .... Nov 13, 1864
Fairbanks, Charles W. .... May 11, 1852, June 4, 1918
Fairbanks, Douglas .... May 23, 1883
Fairbanks, Thaddeus .... Jan 17, 1796
Fairchild, David G. .... Apr 7, 1869
Fairfax, Thomas .... Oct 22, 1693
Fairless, Benjamin .... May 3, 1890
Falk, Peter .... Sept 16, 1927
Fall, Albert B. .... Apr 7, 1922, Dec 11, 1922, Mar 4, 1923, Feb 8, 1924, June 30, 1924, Feb 28, 1927, Oct 25, 1929
Falwell, Jerry .... Aug 11, 1933, Feb 24, 1988
Fanning, Edmund .... July 16, 1769
Fargo, William G. .... May 20, 1818
Farish, William S. .... Feb 23, 1881
Farley, James A. .... May 30, 1888
Farley, John M. .... Apr 20, 1842
Farm Credit
Administration .... Dec 10, 1971
Farman, Elbert E. .... Apr 23, 1831
Farmer, Fannie M. .... Mar 23, 1857
Farmer, James L. .... Jan 12, 1920
Farmer, Moses G. .... Feb 9, 1820
Farnsworth, Philo T. .... Aug 19, 1906
Farragut, David G. .... July 5, 1801, Apr 24, 1862, Aug 5, 1864
Farrar, Geraldine .... Feb 28, 1882
Farrell, James A. .... Feb 15, 1863
Farrell, James T. .... Feb 27, 1904
Faubus, Orval .... Jan 7, 1910, Sept 4, 1957
Faulkner, William C. .... Sept 25, 1897
Fauquier, Francis .... Mar 3, 1768
Faust, Frederick S. .... May 29, 1892
Faye, Alice .... May 5, 1915
Fechner, Robert .... Mar 22, 1876
Federal Communications
Commission .... June 19, 1934
Federal Deposit
Insurance Corp. .... June 16, 1933
Federal Farm Mortgage
Corp. .... Jan 31, 1934
Federal Home Loan Bank .... July 22, 1932

Federal Housing Administration .... June 28, 1934
Federal Loan Agency .... July 1, 1939
Federal National Mortgage Assn. .... Feb 10, 1938
Federal Power Commission .. June 10, 1920
Federal Radio Commission .. Feb 23, 1927
Federal Reserve System ...... Jan 8, 1912, Dec 23, 1913, Aug 10, 1914, Nov 16, 1914
Federal Security Agency ...... July 1, 1939
Federal Theater Project .... Aug 27, 1935
Federal Trade Commission .. Sept 26, 1914, May 27, 1933
Federal Works Agency .... July 1, 1939
Federalist Papers .... May 27, 1787, Oct 27, 1787
Feehan, Patrick A. .... Aug 29, 1829
Feiffer, Jules .... June 26, 1929
Feldstein, Martin .... Nov 25, 1939
Feller, Bob .... Nov 3, 1918
Fels, Joseph .... Dec 16, 1854
Fels, Samuel S. .... Feb 16, 1860
Felt, Dorr E. .... Mar 18, 1862
Felton, Rebecca .... Oct 3, 1922
Fenians .... May 31, 1866
Fenno, John .... Aug 23, 1751, Apr 15, 1789
Ferber, Edna .... Aug 15, 1887
Ferguson, Tom .... Dec 20, 1950
Ferlinghetti, Lawrence .... Mar 24, 1919
Fermi, Enrico .... Sept 29, 1901, Dec 2, 1942
Fernald, Ohio .... Oct 14, 1938
Fernow, Bernhard E. .... Jan 7, 1851
Ferraro, Geraldine A. .... Aug 26, 1935, July 19, 1984
Ferrelo, Bertolomé .... Sept 28, 1542
Ferrer, Jose .... Jan 8, 1912
Ferris, George W.G. .... Jan 8, 1912
Fessenden, Reginald A. .... Oct 6, 1866, Dec 24, 1906
Few, William .... June 8, 1748
Few, William P. .... Dec 29, 1867
Fewkes, Jesse W. .... Nov 14, 1850
Feynman, Richard P. .... May 11, 1918
Fiedler, Arthur .... Dec 17, 1894
Field, Cyrus W. .... Nov 30, 1819, July 27, 1866
Field, David Dudley .... Feb 13, 1805, Jan 7, 1872
Field, Eugene .... Sept 2, 1850
Field, Henry M. .... Apr 3, 1822
Field, Marshall .... Aug 18, 1834
Field, Marshall III .... Sept 28, 1893
Field, Marshall IV .... June 15, 1916
Field, Stephen D. .... Jan 31, 1846
Field, Stephen J. .... Nov 4, 1816
Fields, Lew(is M.) .... Jan 1, 1867
Fields, W(illiam) C. .... Jan 29, 1880
Filene, Edward A. .... Sept 3, 1860
Filion, Hervé .... Feb 1, 1940
Fillmore, Abigail P. .... Mar 13, 1798, Feb 5, 1826, Mar 30, 1853
Fillmore, Caroline C. .... Oct 1, 1813, Feb 10, 1858, Apr 11, 1881
Fillmore, Millard .... Jan 7, 1800, Feb 5, 1826, July 10, 1850, Feb 10, 1858, Mar 8, 1874
Fink, Albert .... Oct 27, 1827
Finkelstein, Louis .... June 14, 1895
Finley, John H. .... Oct 19, 1863
Finley, Martha F. .... Apr 26, 1828
Fio Rito, Ted .... Dec 20, 1900
Fire *see* Disasters
Firestone, Harvey S. .... Dec 20, 1868
Firestone Tire & Rubber Co. .... Feb 16, 1988
Fiscal year .... Aug 26, 1842
Fischer, Bobby .... Sept 1, 1972
Fish, Hamilton .... Aug 3, 1808
Fishbein, Morris .... July 22, 1889
Fisher, Bud (Harry C.) .... Apr 3, 1884
Fisher, Charles T. .... Feb 16, 1880
Fisher, Dorothy Canfield .... Feb 17, 1879
Fisher, Fred .... Sept 30, 1875
Fisher, Frederic J. .... Jan 2, 1878
Fisher, Ham(mond) .... Sept 24, 1900
Fisher, Irving .... Feb 27, 1867
Fisher, John D. .... Mar 27, 1797
Fisher, Vardis .... Mar 31, 1895
Fisk, Clinton B. .... Dec 8, 1828
Fisk, James .... Apr 1, 1834, Sept 24, 1869
Fiske, Bradley A. .... June 13, 1854
Fiske, Minnie Maddern .... Dec 19, 1865
Fitch, Clyde .... May 2, 1865
Fitch, John .... Jan 21, 1743, Aug 22, 1787, Aug 26, 1791
Fitch, Val L. .... Mar 10, 1923
Fitz, Reginald H. .... May 5, 1843
Fitzgerald, Ella .... Apr 25, 1918
Fitzgerald, F. Scott .... Sept 24, 1896
Fitzpatrick, Daniel R. .... Mar 5, 1891
Fitzpatrick, Thomas .... Feb 7, 1854
Fitzsimmons, Frank E. .... Apr 7, 1908
Fitzsimmons, Freddie (Frederick L.) .... July 28, 1901
Fitzsimmons, James E. .... July 23, 1874
Fitzwater, Marlin .... Nov 24, 1942
Flag, American .... Jan 1, 1776, June 14, 1777, Apr 4, 1818, Apr 12, 1818, Sept 8, 1892
Flaget, Benedict J. .... Nov 7, 1763
Flagg, Ernest .... Feb 6, 1857
Flagg, James Montgomery .... June 18, 1877
Flagler, Henry M. .... Jan 2, 1830, Jan 10, 1870
Flagstad, Kirsten .... July 12, 1895
Flaherty, Robert J. .... Feb 16, 1884
Flanagan, Edward J. .... July 13, 1886, Dec 10, 1917
Flanagan, John .... Aug 4, 1865
Fleet, Thomas .... Sept 8, 1685
Fleischer, Nat .... Nov 3, 1887
Fleischmann, Charles L. .... Nov 3, 1834
Flemming, Arthur S. .... June 12, 1905
Flemming, Peggy .... July 27, 1948
Fletcher, Alice C. .... Mar 15, 1838
Fletcher, Benjamin .... Oct 21, 1692
Fletcher, Frank F. .... Nov 23, 1855
Fletcher, Frank J. .... Apr 29, 1885
Fletcher, Harvey .... Sept 11, 1884
Fletcher, Horace .... Aug 10, 1849
Flexner, Abraham .... Nov 13, 1866
Flexner, Simon .... Mar 25, 1863, Oct 8, 1914
Flick, Elmer H. .... Jan 11, 1876

Flint, Austin .... Oct 20, 1812
Flint, Joseph M. .... July 8, 1872
Florida .... Mar 3, 1513, Apr 2, 1513, Feb 20, 1528, Apr 14, 1528, May 25, 1539, July 18, 1543, May 1, 1562, June 24, 1564; *1565* June 29, Aug 28, Sept 8, Sept 20; Aug 2, 1567, Apr 16, 1568, May 27, 1586, Mar 9, 1781, Sept 26, 1810, Oct 27, 1810, Jan 15, 1811, May 14, 1812, Nov 7, 1814, Apr 7, 1818, May 24, 1818, Feb 22, 1819, Mar 30, 1822, May 9, 1832, Dec 3, 1838, Mar 3, 1845, Jan 10, 1861, Oct 28, 1865, Nov 2, 1886, May 29, 1890, Jan 1, 1914, Feb 1, 1929, Aug 29, 1935, Jan 22, 1976
Flory, Paul J. .... June 19, 1910
Floyd, William .... Dec 17, 1734
Flynn, Elizabeth G. .... Aug 7, 1890
Flynn, Errol .... June 20, 1909
Flynn, Francis M. .... Jan 25, 1903
Flynn, William J. .... Nov 18, 1867
Fokine, Michel .... Apr 25, 1880
Fokker, Anthony H.G. .... Apr 6, 1890
Folger, Henry C. .... June 18, 1857
Folsom, Nathaniel .... Sept 18, 1726
Fonda, Henry .... May 16, 1905
Fonda, Jane .... Dec 21, 1937
Fontaine, Joan .... Oct 22, 1917
Fontanne, Lynn .... Dec 6, 1887
Food and Drug Administration .... June 30, 1906, Jan 1, 1907
Football .... Nov 6, 1869, Nov 29, 1890, Sept 3, 1895, Jan 1, 1902, Dec 28, 1958, Jan 15, 1967, Sept 21, 1982, Nov 16, 1982, July 29, 1986, Sept 22, 1987
Foote, Andrew H. .... Sept 12, 1806
Forbes, Bertie C. .... May 14, 1880
Forbes, Malcolm S. .... Aug 19, 1919
Ford, Betty (Elizabeth B.) .... Apr 8, 1918, Oct 15, 1948
Ford, (Tennessee) Ernie .... Feb 13, 1919
Ford Foundation .... Jan 15, 1916
Ford, Gerald R. .... July 14, 1913, Oct 15, 1948, Oct 12, 1973; *1974* Aug 9, Sept 8, Nov 19, Nov 23, Dec 16; May 14, 1975, Sept 5, 1975, Mar 24, 1976, Apr 27, 1981
Ford, Henry .... July 30, 1863, June 3, 1896, Oct 1, 1908, Jan 5, 1914, Jan 14, 1914, Dec 4, 1915, Sept 25, 1926
Ford, Henry II .... Sept 4, 1917
Ford, John .... Feb 1, 1895
Ford, Whitey (Edward C.) .... Oct 21, 1928
Foreign Policy .... Jan 10, 1781, Apr 20, 1793, Dec 21, 1807, May 4, 1822, Dec 1, 1823, Jan 5, 1838, July 29, 1899, Sept 6, 1899, Dec 29, 1902, Dec 6, 1904, Jan 13, 1905, Aug 2, 1912, Aug 11, 1921, Nov 12, 1921, Jan 10, 1927; *1929* Jan 2, Jan 15, July 24; Jan 2, 1933, Nov 16, 1933, Oct 10, 1934, May 1, 1937, Oct 6, 1938, Apr 1, 1939, July 30, 1940, Aug 18, 1940, Jan 6, 1941, Mar 11, 1941, Mar 12, 1947, June 5, 1947, May 14, 1948; *1949* Jan 20, Jan 31, Apr 4, Apr 8, June 24, Aug 24; June 5, 1950; *1951* May 5, Sept 1, Oct 20; *1954* Mar 8, Sept 6, Sept 8; Jan 12, 1955, July 21, 1956, Jan 5, 1957, Mar 9, 1957; *1961* Jan 3, Mar 13, Aug 17, Sept 4; Oct 23, 1966, Jan 27, 1967, Apr 19, 1967; *1974* Jan 6, Mar 18, Nov 19, Nov 23, Dec 16; July 31, 1975, Mar 9, 1977, Mar 11, 1977, Jan 1, 1979, Jan 12, 1980, Apr 7, 1980, Apr 24, 1981; *1982* May 9, June 29, Aug 5; Dec 19, 1984; *1985* Feb 4, Mar 12, Mar 17, July 2, Nov 19, Dec 23; *1986* Sept 26, Sept 29, Oct 11, Nov 13, Nov 25; *1988* Jan 2, May 27, May 31, June 1, Dec 14
Forestry .... Feb 25, 1799, Mar 3, 1891
Forrest, Edwin .... Mar 9, 1806, May 10, 1849
Forrest, Nathan B. .... July 13, 1821
Forrestal, James V. .... Feb 15, 1892
Forsyth, John .... Oct 22, 1780
Fortas, Abe .... June 19, 1910, May 15, 1969
Fosdick, Harry Emerson .... May 24, 1878
Foss, Lukas .... Aug 15, 1922
Fosse, Bob .... June 23, 1927
Foster, Abigail K. .... Jan 15, 1810
Foster, Hal (Harold R.) .... Aug 16, 1892
Foster, John W. .... Mar 2, 1836
Foster, Stephen C. .... July 4, 1826
Foster, Thomas J. .... Jan 1, 1843
Foster, William Z. .... Feb 25, 1881
Foulois, Benjamin D. .... Dec 9, 1879
Fountain, Pete .... July 3, 1930
Fowler, William A. .... Aug 9, 1911
Fox, Fontaine T. .... June 4, 1884
Fox, Margaret .... Oct 7, 1833
Fox, Richard K. .... Aug 12, 1846
Fox, William .... Jan 1, 1879
Foxx, Jimmy .... Oct 22, 1907
Foy, Eddie .... Mar 9, 1856
Foyt, A(nthony) J. Jr. .... Jan 16, 1935
Fraenkel-Courat, Heinz L. .. July 29, 1910
France .... Feb 10, 1763, May 2, 1776, Sept 26, 1776, Dec 17, 1777, Feb 6, 1778, May 4, 1778, July 15, 1782, June 13, 1793, May 16, 1797, July 7, 1798, Sept 30, 1800, Oct 1, 1800, Oct 20, 1803, Mar 23, 1810, July 4, 1831, July 4, 1884, Dec 13, 1921, Apr 8, 1949
Francis, David R. .... Oct 1, 1850
Francis, James B. .... May 18, 1815
Francis, Joseph .... Mar 12, 1801
Francis, Thomas Jr. .... July 15, 1900
Franck, James .... Aug 26, 1882
Frankenthaler, Helen .... Dec 12, 1928
Frankfurter, Felix .... Nov 15, 1882
Franklin, Benjamin .... Jan 17, 1706, Nov 8, 1731, Oct 1, 1732, Dec 19, 1732, June 15, 1752, July 10, 1754, Jan 31, 1774, May 5, 1775, July 26, 1775; *1776* Feb 15, June 10, Sept 26; Sept 14, 1778, June 8, 1781, Sept 3, 1783
Franklin, James .... Sept 27, 1732
Franklin, William B. .... Feb 27, 1832
Franklin National Bank .... Oct 8, 1974
Frasch, Herman .... Dec 25, 1851
Fraser, James E. .... Nov 4, 1876
Fraunces, Samuel .... Oct 10, 1795
Freedmen's Bureau .... Mar 3, 1865
Freedom of Information .... July 4, 1967
Freedom Train .... Sept 17, 1947
Freeman, Douglas Southall .. May 16, 1886
Freeman, James .... Apr 22, 1759, Nov 18, 1787
Freeman, Orville L. .... May 9, 1918
Freer, Charles L. .... Feb 25, 1856
Frelinghuysen, Frederick T. . Aug 4, 1817
Fremont, John C. .... Jan 21, 1813, July 4, 1846, Jan 31, 1848, June 17, 1856
French, Aaron .... Mar 23, 1823

French, Daniel C. .... Apr 20, 1850
French, Paul C. .... Mar 19, 1903
French & Indian War .... *1754* May 27, June 4, July 3; July 9, 1755, Aug 14, 1756, Aug 9, 1757, July 8, 1758, Nov 25, 1758, July 25, 1759, Nov 20, 1760, Feb 10, 1763
Freneau, Philip .... Jan 2, 1752, Oct 31, 1791
Frick, Ford .... Dec 19, 1894
Frick, Henry C. .... Dec 19, 1849
Frieden, Betty .... Feb 4, 1921
Friedlander, Leo .... July 6, 1890
Friedman, Esther P. *see* Landers, Ann
Friedman, Milton .... July 31, 1912
Friedman, Pauline E. *see* Van Buren, Abby
Friedman, William F. .... `Sept 24, 1891
Fries, John .... Jan 7, 1799
Friml, Rudolf .... Dec 7, 1879
Frisch, Frankie .... Sept 9, 1898
Fritz, John .... Aug 21, 1822
Frohman, Charles .... June 17, 1860
Fromm, Erich .... Mar 23, 1900
Fromme, Squeaky (Lynette) .... Sept 5, 1975
Frontenac, Louis de .... May 22, 1620
Frost, Arthur B. .... Jan 17, 1851
Frost, Robert .... Mar 26, 1874
Fry, Franklin C. .... Aug 30, 1900
Fry, William H. .... Aug 10, 1815
Frye, William P. .... Sept 2, 1831
Fuertes, Louis A. .... Feb 7, 1874
Fulbright, J. William .... Apr 9, 1905, Aug 1, 1946
Fuller, Alfred C. .... Jan 13, 1885
Fuller, Margaret .... May 23, 1810
Fuller, Melville W. .... Feb 11, 1833, Apr 30, 1888, July 4, 1910
Fuller, R. Buckminster .... July 12, 1895
Fulton, Rebecca .... June 10, 1835
Fulton, Robert .... Nov 14, 1765, Aug 17, 1807
Funk, Casimir .... Feb 23, 1884
Funk, Isaac K. .... Sept 10, 1839
Funk, Wilfred J. .... Mar 20, 1883
Funston, Frederick .... Nov 9, 1865
Funt, Allen .... Sept 15, 1914
Furuseth, Andrew .... Mar 12, 1854

Gable, Clark .... Feb 1, 1901
Gable, Dan .... Oct 25, 1948
Gadsden, Christopher .... Feb 16, 1724
Gadsden, James .... May 15, 1788, Dec 30, 1853, Apr 22, 1854
Gage, Thomas .... May 13, 1774, June 12, 1775, Apr 2, 1787
Gaines, Edmund P. .... Mar 20, 1777
Galbraaith, John K. .... Oct 15, 1908
Gale, Zona .... Aug 26, 1874
Gallatin, Albert .... Jan 29, 1761, Aug 8, 1814
Gallaudet, Thomas H. .... Dec 10, 1787, Apr 15, 1817
Gallaudet College .... Mar 13, 1988
Galli-Curci, Amelita .... Nov 18, 1889
Gallitzin, Demetrius A. .... Dec 23, 1770, Mar 18, 1795
Galloway, Joseph .... Sept 28, 1774, Aug 29, 1803
Galvin, Pud (James F.) .... Dec 25, 1855
Gamow, George .... Mar 4, 1904
Gannett, Frank E. .... Sept 15, 1876
Gannett, Henry .... Aug 24, 1846
Gans, Joe .... Nov 25, 1874
Gansewoort, Peter .... July 2, 1812
Garand, John C. .... Jan 1, 1888
Garbo, Greta .... Sept 18, 1905
Garden, Alexander .... Apr 15, 1791
Garden, Mary .... Feb 20, 1874
Gardener, Helen H. .... Jan 21, 1853
Gardner, Erle Stanley .... July 17, 1889
Gardner, John W. .... Oct 8, 1912
Garfield, Harry A. .... Oct 11, 1863, Aug 21, 1917
Garfield, Lucretia R. .... Apr 19, 1832, Nov 11, 1858, Mar 14, 1918
Garfunkel, Art .... Oct 13, 1942
Garibaldi, Marie L. .... Nov 17, 1982
Garis, Howard R. .... Apr 25, 1873
Garland, Hamlin .... Sept 14, 1860
Garland, Judy .... June 10, 1922
Garn, Jake .... Apr 12, 1985
Garner, Errol .... June 15, 1923
Garner, John Nance .... Nov 22, 1868, Nov 7, 1967
Garrett, Thomas .... Aug 21, 1783
Garrison, William Lloyd .... Dec 12, 1805, Jan 1, 1831, Dec 4, 1833
Garroway, Dave .... July 13, 1913
Garson, Greer .... Sept 29, 1906
Garvey, Marcus .... Aug 17, 1887
Gary, Elbert H. .... Oct 8, 1846
Gasser, Herbert S. .... July 5, 1888
Gates, Caleb F. .... Oct 18, 1857
Gates, Frederick T. .... July 2, 1853
Gates, Horatio .... Apr 10, 1806
Gates, John W. .... May 8, 1855
Gatlin, Larry .... May 2, 1948
Gatling, Richard J. .... Sept 12, 1818, Nov 4, 1862
Gatti-Casazza, Giulio .... Feb 3, 1869
Gaxton, William .... Dec 2, 1893
Gayle, Crystal .... Jan 9, 1951
Gayley, James .... Oct 11, 1855
Gaynor, Janet .... Oct 6, 1906
Gaynot, William J. .... Aug 9, 1910
Geary, John W. .... Dec 30, 1819
Geddes, Norman Bel .... Apr 27, 1893
Gehrig, Lou (Harry Louis) .... June 19, 1903
Gehringer, Charley .... May 11, 1903
Geiger, Roy S. .... Jan 25, 1885
Geisel, Theodore S. .... Mar 2, 1904
Gell-Mann, Muray .... Sept 15, 1929
General Education Board .... Jan 12, 1903
General Electric Co. .... Apr 15, 1892, Dec 11, 1985
General Land Office .... Apr 25, 1812
General Munition Board .... Mar 31, 1917
General Services Administration .... June 19, 1934, July 1, 1949
Genocide .... Nov 4, 1988
Geological Survey .... Mar 3, 1879
George, Henry .... Sept 2, 1839
George, Walter F. .... Jan 29, 1878
Georgia .... Jan 13, 1733, Jan 6, 1736, July 7, 1742, July 4, 1752, Apr 17, 1763, Feb 5, 1777, Jan 27, 1785, Jan 2, 1788, May 6, 1789, Jan 7, 1795, Nov 7,

1860, Jan 19, 1861, Oct 30, 1865, Mar 11, 1868, Apr 20, 1868, Jan 1, 1908, Jan 10, 1966
Gerard, James W. .... Aug 25, 1867
Gerber, Daniel F. .... May 6, 1898
Germany .... Feb 10, 1915, Sept 1, 1915, Apr 18, 1916, May 9, 1916; *1917* Feb 3, Apr 2, Apr 6; Nov 9, 1918, Aug 25, 1921, Jan 10, 1923, Aug 20, 1924, June 15, 1939, Dec 11, 1941, Mar 7, 1945, May 7, 1945, Apr 8, 1949, June 6, 1949, Apr 21, 1955
Gernsback, Hugo .... Aug 16, 1884
Geronimo .... Sept 4, 1886, Feb 17, 1909
Gerry, Elbridge .... July 17, 1744, Feb 11, 1812, Nov 23, 1814
Gershwin, George .... Sept 26, 1898, Sept 30, 1935
Gershwin, Ira .... Dec 6, 1896
Gesell, Arnold L. .... June 21, 1880
Getty, J. Paul .... Dec 15, 1892
Getty, George W. .... Oct 2, 1819
Gettysburg, Pa. .... *1863* June 26, July 1, July 4, Nov 19; Nov 19, 1963
Getz, Stan .... Feb 2, 1927
Ghormley, Robert L. .... Oct 15, 1883
Giaever, Ivar .... Apr 5, 1929
Giammati, A.Bartlett .... Dec 12, 1986, Sept 8, 1988
Giannini, A(madeo) P. .... May 6, 1870
Giauque, William F. .... May 12, 1895
Gibbons, James .... July 23, 1834
Gibbs, Josiah Willard .... Feb 11, 1839
Gibbs, Oliver W. .... Feb 21, 1822
Gibbs, William F. .... Aug 24, 1896
Gibran, Kahlil .... Jan 6, 1883
Gibson, Althea .... Aug 25, 1927
Gibson, Bob .... Nov 9, 1935
Gibson, Charles Dana .... Sept 14, 1867
Gibson, John .... May 23, 1740
Gibson, Randall L. .... Sept 10, 1832
Gideons International .... July 1, 1899
Gifford, Frank .... Aug 16, 1930
Gilbert, Alfred C. .... Feb 15, 1884
Gilbert, Cass .... Nov 24, 1859
Gilbert, John .... July 10, 1897
Gilbert, Rufus H. .... Jan 26, 1832
Gilbert, Walter .... Mar 21, 1932
Gildersleeve, Basil L. .... Oct 23, 1831
Giles, Warren .... May 28, 1896
Gillespie, Dizzy (John B.) .... Oct 21, 1917
Gillett, Frederick H. .... Oct 16, 1851
Gillette, King C. .... Jan 5, 1855
Gillette, William H. .... July 24, 1855
Gilliss, James M. .... Sept 6, 1811
Gillmore, Quincy A. .... Feb 28, 1825
Gilman, Arthur .... June 22, 1837
Gilman, Daniel C. .... July 6, 1831
Gilmer, Elizabeth *see* Dix, Dorothy
Gilmer, Thomas W. .... Apr 6, 1802
Gilmore, Gary M. .... Jan 17, 1977
Gilmore, James R. .... July 17, 1864
Gilmore, Patrick S. .... Dec 25, 1829, July 17, 1872
Gimbel, Bernard F. .... Apr 10, 1885
Gimbel, Isaac .... Apr 24, 1856
Gingrich, Arnold .... Dec 5, 1903
Ginn, Edwin .... Feb 14, 1838
Ginsberg, Allen .... June 3, 1926
Ginsburg, Douglas H. .... Nov 5, 1987
Girard, Stephen .... May 20, 1750
Girdler, Tom M. .... May 19, 1877
Girl Scouts .... Mar 12, 1912
Girty, Simon .... Feb 18, 1818
Gish, Dorothy .... Mar 11, 1898
Gish, Lillian .... Oct 14, 1896
Gist, William H. .... Oct 5, 1860
Givney, Rev. Joseph M. .... Feb 2, 1882
Gladden, Washington .... Feb 11, 1836
Glaser, Donald A. .... Sept 21, 1926
Glasgow, Ellen .... Apr 22, 1874
Glaspell, Susan .... July 1, 1882
Glass, Carter .... Jan 4, 1858
Glass, Charles .... June 18, 1987
Gleason, Jackie .... Feb 26, 1916
Gleaves, Albert .... Jan 1, 1858
Glenn, John H. Jr. .... July 18, 1921, Feb 20, 1962
Glennon, John J. .... June 14, 1862
Glidden, Charles J. .... Aug 29, 1857
Glidden, Joseph F. .... Jan 18, 1813, Feb 15, 1876
Glover, John .... Nov 5, 1732, Aug 29, 1776
Gluck, Alma .... May 11, 1884
Glueck, Sheldon .... Aug 15, 1896
Goddard, Robert H. .... Oct 5, 1882, Mar 16, 1926
Godey, Louis A. .... June 6, 1804
Godfrey, Arthur .... Aug 31, 1903
Godfrey, Thomas .... Dec 4, 1736
Godkin, E(dwin) L. .... Oct 2, 1831
Goeppert-Mayer, Maria *see* Mayer, Maria Goeppert
Goethals, George W. .... June 29, 1858, Feb 26, 1907
Goetz, Bernhard .... Dec 22, 1984, June 17, 1987
Gold/Silver .... *1848* Jan 24, Aug 19, Dec 5; Feb 28, 1849, June 11, 1859, Mar 18, 1869, Feb 12, 1873, Feb 28, 1878, June 21, 1894, July 8, 1896, Aug 16, 1896, Mar 14, 1900; *1933* Apr 5, Apr 20, June 5; Jan 30, 1934, Aug 14, 1974, Aug 20, 1988
Goldberg, Arthur J. .... Aug 8, 1908
Goldberg, Rube (Reuben L.) .... July 4, 1883
Goldberger, Joseph .... July 16, 1874
Golden, Harry L. .... May 6, 1902
Golden, John .... June 27, 1874
Goldman, Edwin Franko .... Jan 1, 1878
Goldman, Emma .... July 7, 1917
Goldmark, Peter C. .... Dec 2, 1906
Goldsborough, Louis M. .... Feb 18, 1805
Goldstein, Joseph L. .... Apr 18, 1940
Goldwater, Barry M. .... Jan 1, 1909
Goldwyn, Samuel .... Aug 27, 1882
Golf .... Oct 14, 1916
Gomberg, Moses .... Feb 8, 1866
Gomez, Lefty (Vernon) .... Nov 26, 1909
Gompers, Samuel .... Jan 27, 1850, Nov 17, 1881
Gonzalez, Pancho .... May 9, 1928
Goodhue, Bertram G. .... Apr 28, 1869
Goodman, Benny .... May 30, 1909
Goodpasture, Ernest W. .... Oct 17, 1886
Goodrich, Benjamin F. .... Nov 4, 1841
Goodrich, Samuel G. .... Aug 19, 1793
Goodspeed, Edgar J. .... Oct 23, 1871
Goodwin, Hannibal W. .... Apr 30, 1822
Goodwin, Nat .... Jan 31, 1919

Goodyear, Charles .... Dec 29, 1800, June 17, 1837
Gorbachev, Mikhail S. .... Dec 7, 1987, Dec 6, 1988
Gordin, Jacob .... May 1, 1853
Gordon, George H. .... July 19, 1823
Gordon, John B. .... July 6, 1832
Goren, Charles H. .... Mar 4, 1901
Gorgas, Josiah .... July 1, 1818
Gorgas, William C. .... Oct 3, 1854
Gorham, Jabez .... Feb 18, 1792
Gorham, Nathaniel .... June 11, 1796
Gorky, Arshile .... Oct 25, 1904
Gorrie, John .... Oct 3, 1803
Gorton, Samuel .... Mar 7, 1644
Gosden, Freeman F. .... May 5, 1899
Goslin, Goose (Leon A.) .... Oct 16, 1900
Gosnold, Bartholomew .... May 14, 1602, Aug 22, 1607
Gotch, Frank .... Apr 27, 1878
Gottlieb, Robert A. .... Apr 29, 1931
Gottschalk, Louis M. .... May 8, 1829
Goucher, John F. .... June 7, 1845
Goudy, Frederic W. .... Mar 8, 1865
Gould, Chester .... Nov 20, 1900
Gould, George .... Nov 8, 1848
Gould, Jay .... May 27, 1836, Sept 24, 1869
Gould, Morton .... Dec 10, 1913
Gowdy, Curt(is) .... July 31, 1919
Grable, Betty .... Dec 18, 1916
Grace, Eugene G. .... Aug 27, 1876
Grace, William R. .... May 10, 1832
Grady, Henry W. .... May 24, 1850
Graham, Billy (William F.) .. Nov 7, 1918
Graham, Clarence H. .... Jan 6, 1906
Graham, Ernest R. .... Aug 22, 1868
Graham, Katherine .... May 11, 1893
Graham, Otto .... Dec 6, 1921
Graham, Sylvester .... July 5, 1794
Graham, William A. .... Sept 5, 1804
Grainger, Percy A. .... July 8, 1882
Grand Army of the
Republic (GAR) .... Apr 6, 1866
Grange, The .... Dec 4, 1867
Grange, Red (Harold) .... June 13, 1903
Granger, Gordon .... Nov 6, 1822
Grant, Cary .... Jan 18, 1904
Grant, Heber J. .... Nov 22, 1856
Grant, Julia D. .... Jan 26, 1826, Apr 22, 1848, Dec 14, 1902
Grant, Ulysses S. .... Apr 27, 1822, Aug 22, 1848, Jan 30, 1863, Mar 9, 1864, Mar 12, 1864, Apr 9, 1865, May 21, 1874, May 17, 1877, July 23, 1885, Apr 27, 1897
Graupner, Gottlieb .... Oct 6, 1767
Graves, Henry S. .... May 3, 1871
Graves, William S. .... Mar 27, 1865
Gray, Asa .... Nov 18, 1810
Gray, Elisha .... Aug 2, 1835
Gray, Gilda .... Oct 24, 1899
Gray, Hannah H. .... Oct 25, 1930
Gray, Harold L. .... Jan 20, 1894
Gray, Horace .... Mar 24, 1848
Gray, John C. .... July 14, 1839
Gray, Robert .... May 10, 1755, Aug 10, 1790, May 11, 1791
Grayson, David *see* Baker, Roy Stannard
Grayson, William .... Mar 12, 1790
Great Britain .... July 21, 1667, July 18, 1670, May 17, 1733, June 19, 1754, Oct 7, 1763; *1764* Mar 9, Apr 5; *1765* Mar 8, Mar 24; *1766* Jan 17, Mar 7, Mar 17; *1767* June 29, Nov 1; Apr 12, 1770; *1773* Apr 27, May 10; *1774* Mar 31, May 13, May 20; *1775* Jan 20, Jan 23, Feb 9, Mar 30, May 25, Aug 23, Dec 23; June 21, 1779; *1782* Feb 27, Mar 20, Apr 4; July 11, 1792, Nov 19, 1794, June 8, 1802, Apr 18, 1806; *1807* June 22, July 2; Apr 28, 1817; *1850* Apr 19, July 4; Apr 7, 1862, Apr 11, 1893, Feb 10, 1915, Dec 13, 1921, June 20, 1927, June 8, 1939; *1940* June 3, Sept 3; Mar 11, 1941, Apr 8, 1949; *1963* July 25, Aug 4; Jan 27, 1967
Greb, Harry .... June 7, 1884
Greco, José .... Dec 23, 1918
Greeley, Horace .... Feb 3, 1811, Apr 10, 1841, Aug 19, 1862, July 18, 1864, July 13, 1865
Greeley, Adolphus W. .... Mar 27, 1844
Green, Abel .... June 3, 1900
Green, Hetty
(Henrietta H.) .... Nov 21, 1835
Green, Horace .... Dec 24, 1802
Green, Johnny .... Oct 10, 1908
Green, Joseph A. .... Jan 14, 1881
Green, Paul E. .... Mar 17, 1894
Green, Theodore F. .... Oct 2, 1867
Green, William .... Mar 3, 1873
Greenberg, Hank .... Jan 11, 1911
Greene, Harold H. .... Feb 6, 1923
Greene, Nathanael .... Aug 7, 1742, Sept 8, 1781
Greene, William .... Mar 16, 1696
Greenough, Horatio .... Sept 6, 1805
Greenslade, John W. .... Jan 11, 1880
Greenspan, Alan L. .... Mar 6, 1926, June 2, 1987
Greenwood, John .... May 17, 1760
Gregg, David M. .... Apr 10, 1833
Gregg, John R. .... June 17, 1867
Gregg, William .... Feb 2, 1800
Gregory, Dick .... Oct 12, 1932
Grenada .... Oct 25, 1983
Gresham, Walter Q. .... Mar 17, 1832
Gretzsky, Wayne .... Jan 26, 1961, Mar 25, 1982
Grew, Joseph C. .... May 27, 1880
Grey, Zane .... Jan 31, 1875
Gridley, Charles V. .... Nov 24, 1844
Gridley, Ricchard .... Jan 3, 1711
Grier, Robert C. .... Mar 5, 1794
Grierson, Benjamin H. .... July 8, 1826
Griffin, Merv .... July 6, 1925
Griffin, Walter B. .... Nov 24, 1876
Griffith, Clark C. .... Nov 20, 1869
Griffith, D(avid) W. .... Jan 22, 1875
Griffiths, John W. .... Oct 6, 1809
Grimes, Burleigh .... Aug 18, 1893
Grimes, James W. .... Oct 20, 1816
Grimké, Angelina E. .... Feb 20, 1805, July 19, 1848
Grimké, Sarah M. .... Nov 26, 1792, July 19, 1848
Grinnell, George B. .... Sept 20, 1849
Grinnell, Josiah B. .... Dec 22, 1821
Grissom, Virgil I. .... Apr 3, 1926, Jan 27, 1967
Grofe, Ferde .... Mar 27, 1892
Gropius, Walter A. .... May 18, 1883
Gross, Robert E. .... May 11, 1897

Grossett, Alexander .... Jan 17, 1875
Grosvenor, Gilbert H. .... Oct 28, 1875
Grosz, George .... July 26, 1893
Grove, Lefty (Robert M.) .... Mar 6, 1900
Groves, Leslie R. .... Aug 17, 1896, June 18, 1942
Grow, Galusha A. .... Aug 31, 1822
Gruenberg, Louis .... Aug 3, 1884
Gruening, Ernest .... Feb 6, 1887
Gruenther, Alfred M. .... Mar 3, 1899
Grumann, Leroy R. .... Jan 4, 1895
Guam .... June 20, 1898, Aug 1, 1950
Guest, Edgar A. .... Aug 20, 1881
Guggenheim, Daniel .... July 9, 1856
Guggenheim, Meyer .... Feb 1, 1828
Guggenheim, Simon .... Dec 30, 1867
Guillemin, Roger C.L. .... Jan 11, 1924
Guinan, Texas (Mary L.) .... Jan 12, 1884
Guinzburg, Harold K. .... Dec 13, 1899
Guiteau, Charles J. .... July 2, 1881, Nov 14, 1881, Jan 25, 1882, June 30, 1882
Gulick, Luther H. .... Dec 4, 1865
Gumbel, Bryant .... Sept 29, 1948
Guns .... May 19, 1986
Gunther, John .... Aug 30, 1901
Guthrie, Arlo .... July 10, 1947
Guthrie, Samuel .... Oct 19, 1848
Guthrie, Woody (Woodrow W.) .... July 14, 1912
Gwinnett, Button .... May 19, 1777

Habersham, Joseph .... July 28, 1751
Hackett, James H. .... Mar 15, 1800
Hadden, Britton .... Mar 3, 1923
Hadley, Arthur T. .... Apr 23, 1856
Hafey, Chick (Charles J.) .... Feb 12, 1903
Hagen, Walter .... Dec 21, 1892
Hagman, Larry .... Sept 21, 1931
Hague, Frank .... Jan 17, 1876
Haig, Alexander M. Jr. .... Dec 2, 1924, June 25, 1982
Hailey, Arthur .... Apr 5, 1920
Haines, Jesse .... July 22, 1893
Haiti .... July 28, 1915, May 3, 1916
Hakim, Albert .... Mar 16, 1988
Halas, George S. .... Feb 2, 1895
Haldeman, H.R. .... Apr 30, 1973, Jan 1, 1974
Haldeman-Julius, Emanuel .... July 30, 1889
Hale, Edward Everett .... Apr 3, 1822
Hale, George E. .... June 29, 1868
Hale, Irving .... Aug 28, 1862
Hale, Nathan .... June 6, 1755, Sept 21, 1776
Hale, Nathan .... Aug 16, 1784
Hale, Sarah J.B. .... Oct 24, 1788
Hale, William J. .... Jan 5, 1876
Haley, Alex P. .... Aug 11, 1921
Hall, Asaph .... Oct 15, 1829
Hall, Charles M. .... Dec 6, 1863, Feb 23, 1886
Hall, Granville Stanley .... Feb 1, 1844
Hall, James .... Sept 12, 1811
Hall, James Norman .... Apr 22, 1887
Hall, Joyce C. .... Dec 29, 1891
Hall, Lyman .... Apr 12, 1724
Hall, Samuel R. .... Oct 27, 1795
Hall, Thomas S. .... Apr 1, 1827
Hall of Fame .... May 30, 1901
Halleck, Henry W. .... Jan 16, 1815, July 11, 1862
Hallett, Stephen .... June 28, 1794
Halliburton, Richard .... Jan 9, 1900
Hallidie, Andrew S. .... Mar 16, 1836
Hallowell, Robert .... Mar 12, 1886
Halper, Albert .... Aug 3, 1904
Halsey, William F. .... Oct 30, 1882
Halsted, William S. .... Sept 23, 1852
Hamilton, Alexander .... Jan 11, 1755, May 27, 1787, Oct 27, 1787, July 26, 1788, Sept 11, 1789, Jan 14, 1790, July 11, 1804
Hamilton, Alice .... Feb 27, 1869
Hamilton, Allan M. .... Oct 6, 1848
Hamilton, Andrew .... Aug 4, 1735
Hamilton, Billy (William R.) Feb 16, 1866
Hamilton, Edith .... Aug 12, 1867
Hamlin, Charles S. .... Aug 10, 1914
Hamlin, Cyrus .... Jan 5, 1811
Hamlin, Emmons .... Nov 16, 1821
Hamlin, Hannibal .... Aug 27, 1809, July 4, 1891
Hammer, Armand .... May 21, 1898
Hammer, William J. .... Feb 26, 1858
Hammerstein, Oscar I .... May 8, 1846
Hammerstein, Oscar II .... July 12, 1895
Hammett, Dashiell .... May 27, 1894
Hammond, George H. .... May 5, 1838
Hammond, James B. .... Apr 23, 1839
Hammond, James H. .... Nov 15, 1807
Hammond, John H. .... Apr 3, 1888
Hammond, Laurens .... Jan 11, 1895
Hampden, Walter .... June 30, 1879
Hampton, Lionel .... Apr 12, 1913
Hampton, Wade .... Mar 28, 1818
Hancock, John .... Jan 12, 1737, Oct 26, 1774, May 10, 1775, June 12, 1775
Hancock, Winfield S. .... Feb 14, 1824
Hand, Learned .... Jan 27, 1872
Handlin, Oscar .... Sept 29, 1915
Hands Across America .... May 25, 1986
Handy, W(illiam) C. .... Nov 16, 1873
Hanna, Edward J. .... July 21, 1860
Hanna, Mark (Marcus A.) .... Sept 24, 1837
Hansen, Alvin .... Aug 23, 1887
Hansen, Niels E. .... Jan 4, 1866
Hanson, Howard H. .... Oct 28, 1896
Hanson, John .... Apr 13, 1721, Nov 5, 1781
Haraszthy de Mokesa, Agoston .... July 6, 1869
Harbach, Otto A. .... Aug 18, 1873
Harbor improvements .... Mar 3, 1823
Harbord, James G. .... Mar 21, 1866
Harburg, E.Y. (Yip) .... Apr 8, 1898
Harcourt, Alfred .... Jan 31, 1881
Hardee, William J. .... Oct 12, 1815
Hardenbergh, Henry J. .... Feb 6, 1847
Hardenbergh, Jacob R. .... Nov 2, 1790
Harding, Florence K. .... Aug 15, 1860, July 8, 1891, Nov 21, 1924
Harding, Warren G. .... Nov 2, 1865, July 8, 1891, Aug 11, 1921, June 21, 1923,

Aug 2, 1923
Hardy, Oliver .... Jan 18, 1892
Hare, Robert .... Jan 17, 1781
Harkins, William D. .... Dec 28, 1873
Harkness, Edward S. .... Jan 22, 1874
Harlan, John M. .... June 1, 1833
Harlan, John M. .... May 20, 1899
Harlow, Jean .... Mar 3, 1911
Harmon, Millard F. Jr. .... Jan 19, 1888
Harney, Benjamin R. .... Mar 6, 1871
Harper, James .... Apr 13, 1795
Harper, John .... Jan 22, 1797
Harper, Robert G. .... June 18, 1798, Jan 14, 1825
Harper, William
Rainey .... July 26, 1856
Harridge, Will(iam) .... Oct 16, 1885
Harriman, Edward H. .... Feb 25, 1848
Harriman, W. Averell .... Nov 15, 1891
Harris, Bucky
(Stanley R.) .... Nov 8, 1896
Harris, Chapin A. .... May 6, 1806
Harris, Jed .... Feb 25, 1900
Harris, Joel Chandler .... Dec 9, 1848
Harris, Julie .... Dec 2, 1925
Harris, Louis .... Jan 6, 1921
Harris, Patricia R. .... May 31, 1924, Sept 27, 1979
Harris, Paul P. .... Apr 19, 1868
Harris, Roy E. .... Feb 12, 1898
Harris, Sam H. .... Feb 3, 1872
Harris, Townsend .... Oct 3, 1804
Harrison, Anna S. .... July 25, 1775, Nov 22, 1795, Feb 25, 1864
Harrison, Benjamin .... Apr 5, 1726
Harrison, Benjamin .... Aug 20, 1833, Oct 20, 1853, Apr 6, 1896, Mar 13, 1901
Harrison, Caroline L. .... Oct 1, 1832, Oct 20, 1853, Oct 25, 1892
Harrison, Carter H. .... Oct 28, 1893
Harrison, Elizabeth .... Sept 1, 1849
Harrison, Joseph .... Sept 20, 1810
Harrison, Mary S.L. .... Apr 30, 1858, Apr 6, 1896, Jan 5, 1948
Harrison, Peter .... June 14, 1716
Harrison, Robert H. .... Sept 24, 1789
Harrison, Ross G. .... Jan 13, 1870
Harrison, Wallace K. .... Sept 28, 1895
Harrison, William Henry .... Feb 9, 1773, Nov 22, 1795, Sept 30, 1809, Nov 7, 1811, May 9, 1813, Oct 5, 1813, May 19, 1828, Apr 4, 1841
Hart, Albert B. .... July 1, 1854
Hart, Gary .... May 8, 1987
Hart, John .... May 11, 1779
Hart, Lorenz .... May 2, 1895
Hart, Moss .... Oct 24, 1904
Hart, Thomas C. .... June 12, 1877
Hart, William S. .... Dec 6, 1872
Hartack, Bill .... Dec 9, 1932
Harte, Bret .... Aug 25, 183
Hartford, Conn. .... June 8, 1633, May 31, 1636, Feb 8, 1794, Apr 15, 1817, July 6, 1944
Hartford, George H. .... Sept 5, 1833
Hartford, George L. .... Nov 7, 1864
Hartford, John A. .... Feb 10, 1872
Hartford Convention .... Dec 15, 1814
Hartline, Haldan K. .... Dec 22, 1903
Hartman, David .... May 19, 1935
Hartness, James .... Sept 3, 1861
Hartnett, Gabby
(Charles L.) .... Dec 20, 1900
Hartranft, John F. .... Dec 16, 1830
Harvard, John .... Sept 14, 1638
Harvard University/
College .... Oct 28, 1636, Nov 15, 1637, Sept 14, 1638, Mar 13, 1639, Aug 27, 1640, May 31, 1650, June 26, 1833, Mar 10, 1869, Aug 16, 1882
Harvey, Frederick H. .... Feb 9, 1901
Harvey, Paul .... Sept 4, 1918
Harvey, William H. .... Aug 16, 1851
Hasenfus, Eugene .... Oct 5, 1986
Hassam, Childe .... Oct 17, 1859
Hastie, William H. .... Nov 17, 1904
Hastings, Thomas .... Mar 11, 1860
Hatch, William H. .... Sept 11, 1833
Hatch Act .... Aug 2, 1939
Hatcher, Richard G. .... Nov 7, 1967
Hatlo, Jimmy .... Sept 1, 1898
Haughton, Billy .... Nov 2, 1923
Hauptmann, Bruno
Richard .... Jan 2, 1935
Havemeyer, Henry O. .... Oct 18, 1847
Hawaii .... Jan 20, 1778, Feb 14, 1834, Oct 8, 1840, Jan 30, 1875, Jan 20, 1887, Jan 17, 1893, Feb 14, 1893, July 4, 1894, July 7, 1898, Apr 30, 1900, June 14, 1900, Dec 7, 1941, July 4, 1950, Nov 7, 1950, Mar 22, 1955, Aug 21, 1959, Jan 3, 1985
Hawkins, Coleman .... Nov 21, 1904
Hawks, Frank M. .... Mar 28, 1897
Hawley, Joseph R. .... Oct 31, 1826
Hawley, Paul R. .... Jan 31, 1891
Hawthorne, Charles W. .... Jan 8, 1872
Hawthorne, Nathaniel .... July 4, 1804
Hay, John M. .... Oct 8, 1838
Hayden, Carl T. .... Oct 2, 1877
Hayden, Charles .... July 9, 1870
Hayden, Ferdinand V. .... Sept 7, 1829
Hayden, Horace H. .... Oct 2, 1769
Hayek, Friedrich A. von .... May 8, 1899
Hayes, Helen .... Oct 10, 1900
Hayes, Lucy W. .... Aug 28, 1831, Dec 30, 1852, June 25, 1889
Hayes, Patrick J. .... Nov 20, 1867, Mar 24, 1924
Hayes, Rutherford B. .... Oct 4, 1822, Dec 30, 1852, Oct 12, 1875, Nov 7, 1876, Jan 29, 1877, June 19, 1878, Jan 17, 1893
Hayne, Robert Y. .... Dec 20, 1832
Haynes, Elwood .... Oct 14, 1857
Haynes, George E. .... May 11, 1880
Haynes, John .... May 6, 1635
Hays, Arthur Garfield .... Dec 12, 1881
Hays, Will R. .... Nov 5, 1879
Hayward, George .... Mar 9, 1791
Hayward, Nathaniel M. .... Jan 19, 1808
Hayward, Thomas .... July 28, 1746
Haywood, William D. .... Feb 4, 1869, Dec 30, 1905, Feb 17, 1906, July 28, 1907,

Aug 30, 1918
Hayworth, Rita .... Oct 17, 1918
Head, Edith .... Oct 28, 1907
Health .... Feb 23, 1954, Mar 24, 1976
Health, Education and Welfare, Department of .... Apr 1, 1953, Apr 11, 1953, Sept 27, 1979, Oct 17, 1979, May 4, 1980
Health and Human Services, Department of .... Sept 27, 1979, Oct 17, 1979, May 4, 1980
Hearn, Lafcadio .... June 27, 1850
Hearst, George .... Sept 3, 1820
Hearst, Patricia .... Jan 1, 1979
Hearst, William Randolph .... Apr 29, 1863
Heatter, Gabriel .... Mar 30, 1972
Hecht, Ben .... Feb 28, 1894
Heck, Barbara .... Aug 17, 1804
Hecker, Isaac T. .... Dec 18, 1819
Heffelfinger, William W. (Pudge) .... Dec 20, 1867
Hefner, Hugh M. .... Apr 9, 1926
Heiden, Eric .... June 14, 1958
Heidt, Horace .... May 21, 1901
Heifetz, Jascha .... Feb 2, 1901
Heilmann, Harry .... Aug 3, 1894
Heimlich, Henry .... Feb 3, 1920
Heinlein, Robert A. .... July 7, 1907
Heinrich, Anthony P. .... Mar 11, 1781
Heins, George L. .... May 24, 1860
Heinz, Henry J. .... Oct 11, 1844
Heiss, Carol .... Jan 20, 1940
Held, Anna .... Aug 14, 1918
Held, John Jr. .... Jan 10, 1889
Heller, Joseph .... May 1, 1923
Heller, Walter .... Aug 27, 1915
Hellman, Lillian .... June 20, 1905
Helper, Hinton R. .... Dec 27, 1829
Hemingway, Ernest .... July 21, 1899
Hench, Philip S. .... Feb 28, 1896
Henderson, David B. .... Mar 14, 1840
Henderson, Fletcher .... Dec 18, 1898
Henderson, James P. .... Mar 31, 1808
Henderson, Leon .... Apr 11, 1941
Henderson, Ray .... Dec 1, 1896
Henderson, Richard .... Apr 20, 1735
Henderson, Skitch (Lyle) ...... Jan 27, 1918
Hendricks, Thomas A. .... Sept 7, 1819, Nov 25, 1885
Henie, Sonja .... Apr 8, 1912
Hennepin, Louis .... Apr 7, 1640
Henry, Joseph .... Dec 17, 1797, Sept 7, 1846
Henry, Patrick .... May 29, 1736, Dec 1, 1763, Mar 22, 1765, May 29, 1765, Mar 23, 1775, July 5, 1776
Henson, Jim .... Sept 24, 1936
Henson, Josiah .... May 18, 1881
Henson, Matthew A. .... Aug 8, 1866
Hepburn, James C. .... Mar 13, 1815
Hepburn, Katherine .... Nov 8, 1909
Hepburn, William P. .... Nov 4, 1833
Herbert, Victor .... Feb 1, 1859
Herblock *see* Block, Herbert L.
Hering, Constantine .... Jan 1, 1800
Herkimer, Nicholas .... Aug 6, 1777
Herman, Billy (William J.) ... July 7, 1909
Herman, Jerry .... July 10, 1932
Herman, Woody (Woodrow) .... May 16, 1913
Herne, James A. .... Feb 1, 1839
Herreshoff, James B. .... Mar 18, 1834
Herreshoff, Nathanael G. .... Mar 18, 1848
Herriman, George .... Apr 25, 1944
Herrington, Arthur W.S. ..... Mar 30, 1891
Herron, Francis J. .... Feb 17, 1837
Herschbach, Dudley R. .... June 18, 1932
Herschel, Clemens .... Mar 23, 1842
Hersey, John .... June 17, 1914
Hershey, Alfred D. .... Dec 4, 1908
Hershey, Lenore .... Mar 20, 1920
Hershey, Lewis B. .... Sept 12, 1893
Hershey, Milton S. .... Sept 13, 1857
Herskovitz, Melville J. .... Sept 10, 1895
Herter, Christian A. .... Mar 28, 1895
Herty, Charles A. .... Dec 4, 1867
Hertz, John D. .... Apr 4, 1879
Hertz Co. .... Jan 25, 1988
Hesburgh, Theodore M. .... May 25, 1917
Hess, Victor F. .... June 24, 1883
Heston, Charlton .... Oct 4, 1924
Hewes, Joseph .... Jan 23, 1730
Hewitt, Abram S. .... July 31, 1822
Hewitt, Henry K. .... Feb 11, 1887
Hewitt, Peter C. .... May 5, 1861
Heyward, DuBose .... Aug 31, 1885
Heyward, Thomas .... July 28, 1746
Hibben, John G. .... Apr 19, 1861
Hibbs, Ben .... July 23, 1901
Hickey, James A. .... May 29, 1988
Hickey, Thomas .... June 27, 1776
Hickok, (Wild) Bill .... May 27, 1837, Aug 2, 1876
Higgins, William R. .... Feb 17, 1988
Higginson, Henry L. .... Nov 18, 1834
Higginson, Thomas W.S. ...... Dec 22, 1823
Highways .... Nov 20, 1811, Nov 21, 1942, Feb 22, 1955, June 29, 1956, Oct 22, 1965, Jan 2, 1974, Dec 23, 1982
Hill, A(mbrose) P. .... Nov 9, 1825, Apr 2, 1865
Hill, Daniel H. .... July 12, 1821
Hill, George W. .... Oct 22, 1884
Hill, James J. .... Sept 16, 1838
Hillegus, Michael .... Apr 22, 1729
Hillman, Sidney .... Mar 23, 1887, Jan 7, 1941
Hilton, Conrad .... Dec 25, 1887
Hinckley, John W. Jr. .... Mar 30, 1981, June 21, 1982
Hine, Lewis W. .... Sept 26, 1874
Hines, Duncan .... Mar 26, 1880
Hines, Earl .... Dec 28, 1905
Hines, Frank T. .... Apr 11, 1879
Hines, John L. .... May 21, 1868
Hires, Charles E. .... Aug 19, 1851
Hirsch, Alcan .... Feb 1, 1885
Hirschhorn, Joseph H. .... Oct 4, 1974
Hirt, Al .... Nov 7, 1922
Hiss, Alger .... Jan 21, 1950
Hitchcock, Alfred J. .... Aug 13, 1899

Hitchcock, Ethan A. .... Sept 19, 1835
Hitchcock, Frank H. .... Oct 5, 1869
Hitchcock, Gilbert M. .... Sept 18, 1859
Hitchcock, Thomas Jr. .... Feb 11, 1900
Hitchings, George H. .... Apr 18, 1905
Hoban, James .... Dec 8, 1831
Hobart, Garrett A. .... June 3, 1844, Nov 21, 1899
Hobby, Oveta Culp .... Jan 19, 1905, Apr 11, 1953
Hobby, William P. .... Mar 26, 1878
Hockey .... Nov 22, 1917, Mar 25, 1982
Hodel, Donald P. .... May 23, 1935
Hodes, Henry I. .... Mar 19, 1899
Hodge, Charles .... Dec 27, 1797
Hodge, John R. .... June 12, 1893
Hodges, Courtney H. .... Jan 5, 1887
Hodges, Gil(bert R.) .... Apr 4, 1924
Hodur, Francis .... Apr 2, 1866
Hoe, Richard M. .... Sept 12, 1812
Hoe, Robert .... Oct 29, 1784
Hoffa, James R. .... Feb 14, 1913
Hoffman, Dustin .... Aug 8, 1937
Hoffman, Malvina .... June 15, 1887
Hoffman, Paul G. .... Apr 26, 1891, Apr 3, 1948
Hoffman, Samuel K. .... Apr 15, 1902
Hoffman, Roald .... July 8, 1937
Hoffman, Hans .... Mar 21, 1880
Hofstadter, Robert .... Feb 5, 1915
Hogan, Ben .... Aug 13, 1912
Hokinson, Helen .... Nov 1, 1949
Holabird, John A. .... May 4, 1886
Holabird, William .... Sept 11, 1854
Holbrook, Hal (Harold R.) ... Feb 17, 1925
Holcomb, Thomas .... Aug 5, 1879
Holiday, Billie .... Apr 7, 1915
Holidays .... May 11, 1682, Oct 3, 1789, Nov 26, 1789, May 30, 1868, May 8, 1882, Sept 5, 1882, Feb 19, 1887, June 28, 1894, Nov 5, 1921, Jan 1, 1971, Nov 2, 1983
Holland *see* Netherlands
Holland, Clifford M. .... Mar 13, 1883
Holland, John P. .... Feb 29, 1840, Apr 11, 1900
Hollerith, Herman .... Feb 29, 1860, Jan 8, 1889
Holley, Alexander L. .... July 20, 1832
Holley, George M. .... Apr 14, 1878
Holley, Robert W. .... Jan 28, 1922
Holliday, Judy .... June 21, 1923
Holly, Buddy (Charles) .... Sept 7, 1936
Holman, Nat .... Feb 1, 1896
Holmes, Burton .... Jan 8, 1870
Holmes, Joseph A. .... Nov 23, 1859
Holmes, Larry .... Nov 3, 1949
Holmes, Oliver Wendell .... Aug 29, 1809
Holmes, Oliver Wendell .... Mar 8, 1841
Holt, Henry .... Jan 3, 1840
Holt, Joseph .... Jan 6, 1807
Holt, Luther E. .... Mar 4, 1855
Home Owners Loan Corp. .... June 13, 1933
Homer, Winslow .... Feb 24, 1836
Homestead Act/
Homesteading .... May 20, 1862, Jan 1, 1863, Apr 22, 1889, Oct 21, 1976
Homosexuals .... Feb 10, 1988, May 2, 1988
Honduras .... Mar 17, 1988
Hood, John B. .... June 1, 1831
Hood, Raymond M. .... Mar 29, 1881
Hooner, Joseph .... Nov 13, 1814, Jan 26, 1863
Hooker, Thomas .... July 7, 1586, May 31, 1636
Hooks, Benjamin .... Jan 31, 1925
Hooper, Claude .... May 31, 1898
Hooper, Harry .... Aug 24, 1887
Hooper, William .... June 28, 1742
Hooton, Earnest A. .... Nov 20, 1887
Hoover, Herbert .... Aug 10, 1874, Feb 10, 1899, May 19, 1917, Nov 9, 1918, Jan 3, 1919, Mar 4, 1921, Aug 21, 1928, Jan 21, 1947, July 7, 1947, July 28, 1932, July 24, 1953, Oct 20, 1964, Aug 10, 1972
Hoover, Herbert W. .... Oct 30, 1877
Hoover, J. Edgar .... Jan 1, 1895
Hoover, John H. .... May 15, 1887
Hoover, Lou Henry .... Mar 29, 1874, Feb 10, 1899, Jan 7, 1944
Hoover Dam *see* Boulder Dam
Hope, Bob (Leslie T.) .... May 29, 1903
Hopkins, Esek .... Apr 26, 1718, Dec 22, 1775
Hopkins, Harry L. .... Aug 17, 1890, Nov 8, 1933, Apr 8, 1935, July 30, 1942
Hopkins, Johns .... May 19, 1795
Hopkins, Mark .... Feb 4, 1802
Hopkins, Stephen .... Mar 7, 1707
Hopkinson, Francis .... Sept 21, 1737
Hopkinson, Joseph .... Nov 12, 1770, Apr 25, 1798
Hoppe, Willie .... Oct 11, 1897
Hopper, DeWolf .... Mar 30, 1858
Hopper, Edward .... July 22, 1882
Hopper, Hedda .... June 2, 1890
Horgan, Stephen H. .... Feb 2, 1854
Horlick, William .... Feb 23, 1846
Hormel, George A. .... Dec 4, 1860
Horne, Lena .... June 30, 1917
Horne, Marilyn B. .... Jan 16, 1934
Hornsby, Rogers .... Apr 27, 1896
Hornung, Paul .... Dec 23, 1935
Horowitz, Vladimir .... Oct 1, 1904
Horse racing .... May 17, 1875
Horse show .... Oct 22, 1893
Horsford, Eben N. .... July 27, 1818
Hosack, Alexander E. .... Apr 6, 1805
Hosmer, Harriet G. .... Oct 9, 1830
Hostages .... Nov 4, 1979, Nov 19, 1979, Jan 29, 1980, Apr 24, 1980, Jan 20, 1981, Mar 7, 1984, Dec 4, 1984, Jan 8, 1985, Mar 16, 1985, Nov 2, 1986
Hotchkiss, Benjamin B. .... Oct 1, 1826
Houdini, Harry .... Apr 6, 1874
Houdry, Eugene J. .... Apr 18, 1892
Houghton, Alanson B. .... Oct 10, 1863
Houghton, Henry O. .... Apr 30, 1823
Houk, Ralph .... Aug 9, 1919
Hours, Minimum *see* Minimum Wage, Hours
House, Edward M. .... July 26, 1858
House, Henry A. .... Apr 23, 1840
House, Royal E. .... Sept 9, 1814
House of Representatives *see* Congress
Housing .... Jan 23, 1881, July 22, 1932, June 28, 1934, Sept 1, 1937, Feb 10, 1938, Oct 14, 1941,

Feb 24, 1942, July 27, 1947, Aug 10, 1965
Housing & Urban Development, Department of .... July 27, 1947, Sept 9, 1965, Nov 9, 1965, Jan 17, 1966
Houston, David F. .... Feb 17, 1866
Houston, Edwin J. .... July 9, 1847
Houston, Sam .... Mar 2, 1793, Mar 2, 1836, Oct 22, 1836, Mar 18, 1861
Hovey, Alvin P. .... Sept 6, 1821
Howard, Bronson, C. .... Oct 7, 1842
Howard, John E. .... June 4, 1752
Howard, Leslie .... Apr 3, 1893
Howard, Oliver O. .... Nov 8, 1830, Mar 3, 1865
Howard, Roy W. .... Jan 1, 1883
Howard, Sidney C. .... June 26, 1891
Howe, Elias .... July 9, 1819, Sept 10, 1846
Howe, Gordie .... Mar 21, 1928
Howe, Julia Ward .... May 27, 1819
Howe, Lucien .... Sept 18, 1848
Howe, Percy L. .... Sept 30, 1864
Howe, Samuel G. .... Nov 10, 1801
Howe, Sir William .... May 8, 1778
Howell, Albert S. .... Apr 17, 1879
Howell, John A. .... Mar 16, 1840
Howells, William Dean .... Mar 1, 1837
Howze, Robert L. .... Aug 22, 1864
Hoxie, Vinnie .... Sept 25, 1847
Hoyt, Waite C. .... Sept 9, 1899
Hrdlicka, Ales .... Mar 29, 1869
Hubbard, Elbert .... June 19, 1856
Hubbard, Gardiner G. .... Aug 25, 1822
Hubbard, Lafayette R. .... Mar 13, 1911
Hubbell, Carl .... June 22, 1903
Hubble, Edwin P. .... Nov 20, 1889
Hübel, David H. .... Feb 27, 1926
Hudson, Henry .... Aug 28, 1609, Sept 3, 1609
Hudson, Manley O. .... May 19, 1886
Hudson, Rock .... Oct 2, 1985
Hudson River .... July 11, 1890, Feb 25, 1907, Nov 12, 1927
Hufstedler, Shirley M. .... Aug 24, 1925, Dec 6, 1979
Huggins, Charles B. .... Sept 22, 1901
Huggins, Miller .... Mar 27, 1879
Hughes, Charles Evans .... Apr 11, 1862, Feb 3, 1930, June 2, 1941, Aug 27, 1948
Hughes, Charles F. .... Oct 14, 1866
Hughes, David E. .... May 16, 1831
Hughes, Edwin H. .... Dec 7, 1866
Hughes, Howard R. .... Dec 24, 1905, July 14, 1938
Hughes, John J. .... June 24, 1797
Hughes, Langston .... Feb 1, 1902
Hughes, Rupert .... Jan 31, 1872
Hull, Bobby .... Jan 3, 1939
Hull, Cordell .... Oct 2, 1871, Oct 19, 1943
Hull, Isaac .... Mar 9, 1773, Aug 19, 1812
Hull, William .... Aug 16, 1812, Jan 3, 1814, Mar 26, 1814
Humphrey, Doris .... Oct 17, 1895
Humphrey, Hubert H. .... May 27, 1911, Jan 13, 1978
Humphreys, Andrew A. .... Nov 2, 1810
Humphreys, Joshua .... June 17, 1751
Humphreys, West H. .... May 7, 1862
Hunger .... May 25, 1986
Hunsaker, Jerome C. .... Aug 26, 1886
Hunt, (Nelson) Bunker .... Feb 22, 1926
Hunt, H(aroldson) H. .... Feb 17, 1889
Hunt, Henry J. .... Sept 14, 1819
Hunt, Richard M. .... Oct 31, 1827
Hunt, Walter .... July 29, 1796
Hunt, Ward .... June 14, 1810
Hunter, David .... July 21, 1802
Hunter, Robert M.T. .... Apr 21, 1809
Hunter, Thomas .... Oct 18, 1831
Hunting *see* Conservation
Huntington, Collis P. .... Oct 22, 1821
Huntington, Henry E. .... Feb 27, 1850
Huntington, Samuel .... July 3, 1731
Huntley, Chet (Chester R.).. Dec 10, 1911
Hupp, Louis G. .... Nov 13, 1872
Hurd, Peter .... Feb 22, 1904
Hurley, Edward N. .... July 31, 1864
Hurley, Patrick J. .... Jan 8, 1883
Hurok, Sol .... Apr 9, 1888
Hurst, Fannie .... Oct 18, 1889
Husbands, Hermon .... Oct 3, 1724
Huse, Harry P. .... Dec 8, 1858
Husing, Ted (Edward B.) ..... Nov 27, 1901
Hussey, Obed .... Aug 4, 1860
Huston, John .... Aug 5, 1906
Huston, Walter .... Apr 6, 1884
Hutcheson, William L. .... Feb 7, 1874
Hutchins, Robert M. .... Jan 17, 1899, July 1, 1929
Hutchinson, Anne .... July 19, 1591, Nov 7, 1637, Mar 7, 1638
Hutchinson, Thomas .... Sept 9, 1711
Hutson, Don .... Jan 31, 1913
Hutton, E.F. .... Sept 7, 1875, May 2, 1985
Hyatt, Alpheus .... Apr 5, 1838
Hyatt, John W. .... Nov 28, 1837
Hyde, Henry B. .... Feb 15, 1834

Iacocca, Lee .... Oct 15, 1924
Iberville, Sieur Pierre L. d' ... July 16, 1661, Feb 9, 1690, Jan 17, 1700, Mar 20, 1702
Iceland .... July 7, 1941, May 5, 1951
Ickes, Harold L. .... Mar 15, 1874, June 16, 1933
Idaho .... June 15, 1834, Mar 3, 1863, July 4, 1889, July 3, 1890, July 11, 1892, Oct 3, 1892, Dec 11, 1896, Nov 3, 1897, Apr 29, 1899, Jan 1, 1915, Mar 1, 1915, May 2, 1972
Illinois .... May 15, 1780, Mar 1, 1809, Aug 26, 1818, Dec 3, 1818, July 4, 1836, Aug 31, 1847, Mar 6, 1848, Feb 28, 1867, Aug 10, 1887, July 5, 1894, July 6, 1894, Jan 2, 1900, Nov 13, 1909, July 2, 1917, July 4, 1917, July 5, 1918, June 22, 1922, Dec 21, 1951
Immigration .... May 6, 1882, Mar 3, 1891, Jan 1, 1892, June 29, 1906, May 19, 1921, June 28, 1940, June 26, 1952, Aug 7, 1953, Oct 3, 1965, Sept 26, 1972
Income tax .... Aug 5, 1861, Jan 1, 1862, July 1, 1862, June 30, 1864, Feb 25, 1913, Jan 11, 1916, Jan 24, 1916, June 10, 1943, July 1, 1943, Sept 27, 1986
Indiana .... May 7, 1800, July 31, 1804, June 10, 1816, Dec 11, 1816, Jan 3, 1825, Feb 10, 1851, May 30, 1911, Feb 9, 1917, Feb 28, 1917
Indians .... Oct 10, 1615, Mar 22, 1621, Mar 22, 1622, May 26, 1637, Feb 25, 1643, Apr 18, 1644,

Sept 15, 1655; *1675* June 20, Sept 9, Dec 19; Aug 12, 1676, Aug 9, 1680, Aug 15, 1694, Jan 7, 1699, Sept 22, 1711, Jan 28, 1712, Mar 23, 1713, Apr 15, 1715, June 19, 1754, Aug 9, 1757, Nov 17, 1764, July 24, 1766, Nov 11, 1778, Jan 21, 1785, Jan 9, 1789, Oct 10, 1790, Nov 4, 1791, Aug 20, 1794, Aug 3, 1795, Oct 10, 1808, Sept 30, 1809, Nov 7, 1811, Aug 15, 1812; *1813* Jan 22, Aug 30, Oct 5, Nov 8; Mar 27, 1814, Aug 9, 1814, Sept 1, 1815, Nov 20, 1817, May 24, 1818, Mar 11, 1824, June 17, 1824, Sept 27, 1830; *1832* Mar 24, May 9, July 9, Aug 2; *1835* Nov 1, Dec 28, Dec 29; Dec 25, 1837, Sept 3, 1855, Nov 29, 1864, Dec 21, 1866, Oct 5, 1877, Feb 8, 1887, June 15, 1924, Nov 2, 1972, Feb 27, 1973, Jan 22, 1976

Industrial Recovery Act .... June 16, 1933
Industrial Workers of the World (IWW) .... June 27, 1905, Jan 11, 1912, Aug 17, 1918, Aug 30, 1918, Jan 2, 1920
Ingalls, Melville E. .... Sept 6, 1842
Inge, William M. .... May 3, 1913
Ingersoll, Charles H. .... Oct 29, 1865
Ingersoll, Jared .... Oct 27, 1749
Ingersoll, Robert G. .... Aug 11, 1833
Ingersoll, Robert H. .... Dec 26, 1859
Ingersoll, Royal E. .... June 20, 1883
Ingraham, Prentiss .... Dec 22, 1843
Ingram, Jonas W. .... Oct 15, 1886
Inman, Henry .... Oct 28, 1801
Inness, George .... May 1, 1825
Inouye, Daniel K. .... Sept 7, 1924
Insull, Samuel .... Nov 11, 1859
Insurance .... Jan 1, 1735, Jan 11, 1759, Feb 8, 1794, Mar 9, 1830, Jan 1, 1860, June 17, 1863, Jan 1, 1927, Jan 28, 1932
Interior, Department of .... Mar 3, 1849
International Bank of Reconstruction & Development .... July 22, 1944
International Business Machine Corp. (IBM) .... Jan 8, 1982
International Development, Agency for .... Sept 4, 1961
International Harvester Co. . Aug 12, 1902
International Joint Commission .... May 25, 1905
International Labor Organization .... Oct 29, 1919, Nov 1, 1977
International Monetary Fund .... July 22, 1944
Interstate Commerce Act/Commission .... Feb 4, 1887, June 18, 1910
Iowa .... May 11, 1836, June 12, 1838, Nov 1, 1844, Aug 3, 1846, Dec 28, 1846, Jan 22, 1855, Mar 4, 1884, Apr 11, 1921
Ipatieff, Vladimir N. .... Nov 21, 1867
Iran .... *1979* Oct 22, Nov 4, Nov 19; *1980* Jan 29, Apr 7, Apr 24; Jan 20, 1981, Dec 4, 1984; *1986* Jan 17, Oct 31, Nov 13, Nov 25; July 3, 1988
Iran-Contra Affair .... *1987* Feb 27, Mar 4, Nov 18; Mar 16, 1988; Dec 30, 1988
Iredell, James .... Oct 5, 1751
Ireland, John .... Sept 11, 1838
Ironside, Henry A. .... Oct 14, 1876
Irvin, Monte (Montford M.) .... Feb 25, 1919
Irvine, William .... Nov 3, 1741
Irving, Washington .... Apr 3, 1783
Isaacs, Samuel M. .... Jan 4, 1804
Isherwood, Christopher .... Aug 26, 1904
Israel .... May 14, 1948, Jan 31, 1949
Italy .... Apr 14, 1988
Iturbi, José .... Nov 28, 1895
Ives, Burl .... June 14, 1909
Ives, Charles Edward .... Oct 20, 1874
Ives, Frederick E. .... Feb 17, 1856
Ives, Herbert E. .... July 31, 1882
Ives, James M. .... Mar 5, 1824
Iwo Jima .... June 26, 1968
Izard, George .... Oct 21, 1776

Jackling, Daniel C. .... Aug 14, 1869
Jackson, Andrew .... Mar 15, 1767, Jan 17, 1794, Dec 5, 1796, May 30, 1806, Nov 8, 1813; *1814* Mar 27, Aug 9, Aug 15, Dec 1; Jan 8, 1815, Dec 26, 1817, May 24, 1818, Apr 5, 1821; *1824* Nov 9, Dec 1; Feb 9, 1825; *1832* Apr 10, July 10, Dec 10; *1833* June 26, Sept 23; *1834* Jan 29, Mar 28, Dec 1; Jan 30, 1835, June 8, 1845
Jackson, Ann .... Sept 3, 1926
Jackson, Charles D. .... Mar 16, 1902
Jackson, Helen Hunt .... Oct 15, 1830
Jackson, Henry M. .... May 31, 1912
Jackson, Howell E. .... Apr 8, 1832
Jackson, James .... Oct 3, 1777
Jackson, Jesse L. .... Oct 8, 1941
Jackson, Mahalia .... Oct 26, 1911
Jackson, Maynard .... Oct 16, 1973
Jackson, Michael .... Aug 29, 1958
Jackson, Rachel D. .... June 15, 1767, Jan 17, 1794, Dec 22, 1828
Jackson, Reggie .... May 18, 1946
Jackson, Robert H. .... Feb 13, 1892
Jackson, Sheldon .... May 18, 1834
Jackson, Shirley .... Dec 14, 1919
Jackson, Stonewall (Thomas J.) .... Jan 21, 1824; *1862* May 23, May 25, Sept 15; May 1, 1863
Jackson, Travis .... Nov 2, 1903
Jackson, William H. .... Apr 4, 1843
Jacobi, Abraham .... May 6, 1830
Jacobs, Helen H. .... Aug 6, 1908
Jacobsen, David P. .... May 28, 1985, Nov 2, 1986
James, Edmund J. .... May 21, 1855
James, Edwin L. .... June 25, 1890
James, Harry .... Mar 15, 1916
James, Henry .... Apr 15, 1843
James, Jesse .... Apr 3, 1882
James, William .... Jan 11, 1842
Jameson, John F. .... Sept 19, 1859
Jamestown, Va. .... May 24, 1607, Sept 17, 1607; *1608* Jan 2, Jan 7, Sept 10; Mar 23, 1609, Oct 5, 1609, Feb 28, 1610, Sept 19, 1676, Apr 26, 1907
Janis, Elsie .... Mar 16, 1889
Janney, Eli H. .... Nov 12, 1831
Jansky, Karl G. .... Oct 22, 1905
Japan .... July 14, 1853, Mar 31, 1854, Aug 9, 1905, Sept 5, 1905, Nov 30, 1908, Dec 13, 1921,

June 20, 1927, Dec 12, 1937, Oct 6, 1938, Dec 7, 1941, Dec 8, 1941, Feb 19, 1942; *1945* Aug 6, Aug 9, Aug 14, Sept 2, Oct 4; Sept 8, 1851, Apr 15, 1952, Mar 8, 1954, Jan 15, 1960, June 17, 1971, May 15, 1972, June 26, 1980, Mar 29, 1988
Japanese internees .... Aug 10, 1988
Jarrell, Randall .... May 6, 1914
Jarves, Deming .... Apr 15, 1869
Jarvik, Robert K. .... May 11, 1946
Javits, Jacob K. .... May 18, 1904
Jaworski, Leon .... Sept 19, 1905, Nov 1, 1973
Jay, Charles T. .... Feb 17, 1895
Jay, John .... Dec 12, 1745, May 10, 1775, June 8, 1781, Sept 3, 1783, May 27, 1787, Oct 27, 1787, Sept 24, 1789, Nov 19, 1794, May 17, 1829
Jeffers, Robinson .... Jan 10, 1887
Jeffers, William M. .... Jan 2, 1876
Jefferson, Joseph .... Feb 20, 1829
Jefferson, Martha W.S. .... Oct 19, 1748, Jan 1, 1772, Sept 6, 1782
Jefferson, Thomas .... Apr 13, 1743, May 11, 1769, Dec 15, 1770, Jan 1, 1772, Oct 14, 1773, July 26, 1774, Aug 1, 1774, July 5, 1775, June 10, 1776, Sept 26, 1776, June 1, 1779, June 3, 1781; *1784* Mar 1, Apr 23, May 7; Mar 10, 1785, Jan 16, 1786, Sept 26, 1789, Feb 14, 1790, Mar 22, 1790, July 31, 1793; *1801* Feb 11, Feb 17, Feb 27, Mar 4, Dec 8; Jan 18, 1803, Jan 17, 1806, Nov 27, 1806; *1807* Jan 22, June 20, July 2; Jan 30, 1815, Mar 29, 1819, July 4, 1826, Dec 15, 1938, Apr 13, 1943
Jeffries, John .... Feb 5, 1745
Jenco, Lawrence .... Jan 8, 1985
Jenkins, Charles F. .... Aug 22, 1867
Jenner, Bruce .... Oct 28, 1949
Jenney, William L. .... Sept 25, 1832
Jennings, Hugh .... Apr 12, 1869
Jennings, Peter C. .... Aug 29, 1938
Jennings, Waylon .... June 15, 1937
Jensen, Peter L. .... May 16, 1886
Jessel, George .... Apr 3, 1898
Jewett, Frank B. .... Sept 5, 1879
Jews .... Jan 11, 1775, July 14, 1883, Jan 2, 1887, Jan 28, 1916, Mar 13, 1988
Jobs, Steven P. .... Feb 24, 1955
Joffrey, Robert .... Dec 24, 1930
John Birch Society .... Dec 9, 1958
John Paul II .... Oct 6, 1979, Feb 19, 1988, May 29, 1988
Johns, Jasper .... May 15, 1930
Johnson, Andrew .... Dec 29, 1808, May 5, 1827, Mar 4, 1862; *1865* Apr 15, May 1, May 29; Mar 27, 1866; *1867* Jan 7, Aug 5, Aug 12, Nov 25, Dec 7; *1868* Jan 13, Feb 21, Feb 24, Mar 3, Mar 13, Mar 23, Mar 30, Apr 9, May 16, May 26, Dec 25; Mar 5, 1875, July 31, 1875
Johnson, Ban (Byron B.) .... Jan 6, 1864
Johnson, Cave .... Jan 11, 1793
Johnson, Edward .... Aug 22, 1878
Johnson, Eldridge R. .... Feb 6, 1867
Johnson, Eliza M. .... Oct 4, 1810, May 5, 1827, Jan 15, 1876
Johnson, Guy .... Mar 5, 1788
Johnson, Herschel V. .... Sept 18, 1812
Johnson, Hiram W. .... Sept 2, 1866
Johnson, Howard D. .... June 20, 1972
Johnson, Hugh S. .... Aug 5, 1882, June 16, 1933, July 20, 1933
Johnson, James W. .... June 17, 1871
Johnson, Sir John .... Nov 5, 1742
Johnson, John H. .... Jan 19, 1918
Johnson, Ladybird (Claudia A.) .... Dec 22, 1912, Nov 17, 1934
Johnson, Lyndon B. .... Aug 27, 1908, Nov 17, 1934, Jan 3, 1953, Jan 5, 1955, July 2, 1955; *1963* Nov 22, Nov 27, Dec 16; Apr 22, 1964, Aug 10, 1965, Oct 8, 1965; *1966* Apr 14, Oct 23, Oct 26; Dec 9, 1967, Dec 19, 1967, Jan 8, 1968, May 31, 1968, May 22, 1971, Jan 22, 1973
Johnson, Magic (Earwin) .... Aug 14, 1959
Johnson, Martin E. .... Oct 9, 1884
Johnson, Philip C. .... July 8, 1906
Johnson, Rafer .... Aug 18, 1935
Johnson, Reverdy .... May 21, 1796
Johnson, Richard M. .... Oct 17, 1780, Nov 19, 1850
Johnson, Richard W. .... Feb 7, 1827
Johnson, Samuel .... Oct 14, 1696, Dec 25, 1724
Johnson, Thomas .... Nov 4, 1732
Johnson, Tom L. .... July 18, 1854
Johnson, Walter .... Nov 6, 1887, Jan 29, 1936
Johnson, William .... Dec 27, 1771
Johnson, Sir William .... July 11, 1774
Johnson, William S. .... Oct 7, 1727
Johnston, Albert S. .... Feb 2, 1803, Apr 6, 1862
Johnston, Eric .... Dec 21, 1895
Johnston, Gabriel .... July 17, 1752
Johnston, Joseph E. .... Feb 3, 1807
Johnstown, Pa. .... May 31, 1889
Joiner, Dad (C.M.) .... Sept 30, 1930
Joliet, Louis .... Sept 21, 1645, June 17, 1673
Jolson, Al .... May 26, 1886, Oct 6, 1927
Jones, Bob .... Oct 30, 1883
Jones, Bobby (Robert T.) .... Mar 17, 1902
Jones, Catesby ap Roger .... Apr 15, 1821
Jones, Casey (John L. .... Apr 30, 1900
Jones, Donald F. .... Apr 16, 1890
Jones, George .... Aug 16, 1811, Sept 18, 1851
Jones, George W. .... Apr 12, 1804
Jones, Grandpa (Marshall L.) .... Oct 20, 1913
Jones, Isham .... Jan 31, 1894
Jones, James .... Nov 6, 1921
Jones, Jesse H. .... Apr 5, 1874
Jones, John .... July 23, 1791
Jones, John Paul .... July 6, 1747, Nov 10, 1776, Sept 23, 1777, Apr 23, 1778, Sept 23, 1779, July 24, 1905
Jones, John W. .... Nov 22, 1791
Jones, Mary H. .... May 1, 1830
Jones, Melvin .... Jan 7, 1879
Jones, Quincy .... Mar 14, 1933
Jones, Rufus M. .... Jan 25, 1863
Jones, Samuel M. .... Aug 3, 1846
Jones, Spike (Lindley A.) .... Dec 14, 1911
Jones, Thomas H. .... July 24, 1892
Joplin, Scott .... Nov 24, 1868
Jordan, Barbara .... Feb 21, 1936
Jordan, David Starr .... Jan 19, 1851

Jordan, Thomas .... Sept 30, 1819
Jordan, Vernon E. Jr. .... Aug 15, 1935
Joss, Addie (Adrian).............. Apr 12, 1880
Judd, Orange .... July 26, 1822
Judson, Edward Z.C. .... Mar 20, 1823
Judson, Egbert P.................. Aug 9, 1812
Juilliard, Augustus D. .... Apr 19, 1836
Julian, Percy L. .... Apr 11, 1899
Juneau, Solomon L. .... Aug 9, 1793
Justice, Department of .... Sept 24, 1789, Feb 24, 1855, June 22, 1870, Mar 29, 1988
Juvenile Court....................... July 1, 1899

Kahanamoku, Duke .... Aug 24, 1890
Kahn, Albert......................... Mar 21, 1869
Kahn, Gus(tav G.) .... Nov 6, 1886
Kahn, Louis I. .... Feb 20, 1901
Kahn, Otto H......................... Feb 21, 1867
Kahn, Reuben L. .... July 26, 1887
Kaiser, Henry J. .... May 9, 1882, Nov 12, 1942
Kalb, Johann de .... June 29, 1721, July 27, 1777, Aug 16, 1780
Kaline, Al .... Dec 19, 1934
Kalmus, Herbert T. .... Nov 9, 1881
Kaltenborn, Hans V. .... July 9, 1878
Kamen, Martin D. .... Aug 27, 1913
Kampelman, Max................. Nov 7, 1920
Kanawha *see* West Virginia
Kander, John .... Mar 18, 1927
Kanin, Garson .... Nov 24, 1912
Kansas .... Sept 15, 1835, Mar 30, 1854, Dec 15, 1855, May 21, 1856, July 29, 1859, Jan 29, 1861, Feb 19, 1881, May 1, 1971
Kantor, MacKinlay .... Feb 4, 1904
Karle, Jerome .... June 18, 1918
Karloff, Boris .... Nov 23, 1887
Karman, Theodore von .... May 11, 1881
Kasdan, Lawrence E. .... Jan 14, 1949
Katzenbach, Nicholas deB.... Jan 17, 1922
Kaufman, George S. .... Nov 16, 1889
Kay, Ulysses S. .... Jan 7, 1917
Kaye, Danny .... Jan 18, 1913
Kaye, Sammy .... Mar 13, 1913
Kazan, Elia .... Sept 7, 1909
Keane, James J. .... Aug 27, 1857
Keane, John J........................ Sept 12, 1839
Kearney, Philip .... June 1, 1814, Aug 29, 1862
Kearny, Stephen .... Aug 30, 1794, June 5, 1845, Aug 18, 1846, Sept 22, 1846, Jan 8, 1847, Jan 10, 1847
Keaton, Buster (Joseph F.).. Oct 4, 1895
Keaton, Diane .... Jan 5, 1946
Keefe, Tim(othy J.) .... Jan 1, 1857
Keeler, Willie .... Mar 3, 1872
Keen, William W. .... Jan 19, 1837
Keeshan, Robert J. .... June 27, 1927
Kefauver, Estes .... July 26, 1903
Keifer, Joseph W. .... Jan 30, 1836
Keillor, Garrison .... Aug 7, 942
Keith, Benjamin F. .... Jan 26, 1846
Keith, Minor C. .... Jan 19, 1848
Kell, George .... Aug 23, 1922
Kelland, Clarence B. .... July 11, 1881
Kellems, Vivien .... June 7, 1896
Keller, Helen A...................... June 27, 1880
Kelley, Joe (Joseph J.) .... Dec 9, 1871
Kelley, Oliver H. .... Jan 7, 1826
Kellogg, Frank B. .... Dec 22, 1856, Aug 27, 1928, July 24, 1929
Kellogg, John H..................... Feb 26, 1852
Kellogg, Will K. .... Apr 7, 1860
Kelly, Alvin A. (Shipwreck)........................ May 13, 1893
Kelly, Colin .... July 11, 1915
Kelly, Emmett .... Dec 9, 1898
Kelly, Eric P. .... Mar 16, 1884
Kelly, Gene .... Aug 23, 1912
Kelly, George .... Sept 10, 1895
Kelly, Grace .... Nov 12, 1929, Apr 19, 1956
Kelly, James E. .... July 30, 1855
Kelly, John Sr. .... Oct 4, 1890
Kelly, John Jr. (Jack)........... May 24, 1927
Kelly, King (Michael J.)....... Dec 31, 1857
Kelly, Walter C. .... Aug 25, 1913
Kemp, Hal (James H.) .... Mar 27, 1905
Kemp, Jack .... Dec 19, 1988
Kemper, James L. .... June 11, 1823
Kemper, James S. .... Nov 18, 1886
Kempff, Louis .... Oct 11, 1841
Kendall, Amos .... Aug 16, 1789
Kendall, Edward C. .... Mar 8, 1886
Kennan, George F. .... Feb 16, 1904
Kennedy, Anthony M. .... Nov 11, 1987, Feb 3, 1988
Kennedy, Edward M. (Ted) .. Feb 22, 1932, July 18, 1969
Kennedy, John F. .... May 29, 1917, Sept 12, 1953, May 7, 1957; 1961 Mar 13, Mar 26, May 25, May 31, June 3, June 21, Sept 25; *1963* Sept 20, Nov 22, Nov 29; Sept 27, 1964, Oct 20, 1974
Kennedy, Joseph P. .... Sept 6, 1888
Kennedy, Robert F. .... Nov 20, 1925, June 5, 1968
Kennedy, Walter .... June 8, 1913
Kenney, George C. .... Aug 6, 1889
Kent, Atwater .... Dec 3, 1873
Kent, James .... July 31, 1763
Kent, Rockwell .... June 21, 1882
Kent State U. .... May 4, 1970, Aug 27, 1975
Kenton, Simon .... Apr 3, 1755
Kenton, Stan .... Feb 19, 1912
Kentucky .... Mar 16, 1750, Dec 6, 1776, May 15, 1780, Apr 11, 1787, Aug 11, 1787, Dec 18, 1789, May 26, 1790, June 1, 1792, Aug 17, 1799, Feb 13, 1844, Oct 1, 1849, June 11, 1850, May 20, 1861, Sept 11, 1861, May 17, 1875, May 28, 1977
Keppler, Joseph .... Feb 1, 1838
Kern, Jerome D. .... Jan 27, 1885
Kerouac, Jack (Jean-Louis) .. Mar 12, 1922
Kerr, Michael C. .... Mar 15, 1827
Kerr, Robert S. .... Sept 11, 1896
Ketcham, Hank (Henry K.) .... Mar 14, 1920
Ketchel, Stanley .... Sept 14, 1887
Kettering, Charles F. .... Aug 29, 1876
Key, Francis Scott .... Aug 1, 1779, Sept 12, 1814, Sept 13, 1814
Key, Ted................................. Aug 25, 1912
Keyes, Francis Parkinson.......................... July 21, 1885

Khorana, Har Gobind .... Jan 9, 1922
Khruschev, Nikita S. .... Sept 15, 1959
Kidd, Capt. .... July 6, 1699
Kidd, Michael .... Aug 12, 1919
Kiefer, Joseph W. .... Jan 30, 1836
Kieft, Willem .... Mar 28, 1638, Feb 25, 1643
Kiepura, Jan W. .... May 16, 1902
Kilgore, Bernard .... Nov 9, 1908
Killebrew, Harmon .... June 29, 1936
Kilmer, Joyce .... Dec 6, 1886
Kimball, Fiske .... Dec 8, 1888
Kimball, Heber C. .... June 14, 1801
Kimmel, Husband .... Dec 17, 1941
Kinealy, John H. .... Mar 18, 1864
Kiner, Ralph .... Oct 27, 1922
King, Billie Jean .... Nov 22, 1943
King, Charles G. .... Oct 22, 1896
King, Clarence .... Jan 6, 1842
King, Dennis .... Nov 2, 1897
King, Ernest J. .... Nov 23, 1878, Dec 20, 1941
King, Frank .... Apr 9, 1883
King, Franklin H. .... June 8, 1848
King, John .... Jan 1, 1813
King, Larry .... Jan 1, 1929
King, Martin Luther Jr. .... Jan 15, 1929, Dec 1, 1955, Aug 28, 1963, Mar 21, 1965, Apr 4, 1968, Nov 2, 1983, Aug 27, 1988
King, Richard .... July 10, 1825
King, Rufus .... Mar 24, 1755
King, Thomas S. .... Dec 17, 1824
King, Wayne .... Feb 16, 1901
King, William .... Feb 9, 1768
King, William R.D. .... Apr 7, 1786, Mar 24, 1853, Apr 18, 1853
King George's War .... June 16, 1745, Oct 18, 1748
King Philip's War .... June 20, 1675, Sept 9, 1675, Dec 19, 1675, Aug 12, 1676
King William's War .... May 11, 1690
Kingsley, Elizabeth S. .... Oct 9, 1871
Kinkaid, Thomas C. .... Apr 3, 1888
Kinsey, Alfred C. .... June 23, 1894
Kiplinger, Willard M. .... Jan 8, 1891
Kirby, Rollin .... Sept 4, 1875
Kirby-Smith, Edmund .... May 16, 1824
Kirk, Alan G. .... Oct 30, 1888
Kirkland, J. Lane .... Mar 12, 1922
Kirkland, Samuel .... Dec 1, 1741
Kirkwood, Samuel J. .... Dec 20, 1813
Kissinger, Henry A. .... May 27, 1923
Kitson, Henry H. .... Apr 9, 1865
Kittinger, Joe W. .... *1984* Sept 14, Sept 17
Kiwanis International .... Jan 21, 1915, July 7, 1987
Klein, Calvin .... Nov 19, 1942
Klein, Chuck (Charles H.) .... Oct 7, 1904
Klein, Lawrence .... Sept 14, 1920
Kleindienst, Richard .... Apr 30, 1973
Klem, William J. .... Feb 22, 1874
Knabe, Valentine W.L. .... June 3, 1803
Knapp, Seaman A. .... Dec 16, 1833
Knight, Austin M. .... Dec 16, 1854
Knight, John S. .... Oct 26, 1894
Knights of Columbus .... Feb 2, 1882
Knights of Labor .... Dec 30, 1869, Jan 1, 1879, Mar 6, 1889
Knipling, Edward F. .... Mar 20, 1909
Knopf, Alfred A. .... Sept 12, 1892
Knopf, S. Adolphus .... Nov 27, 1857
Knott, David H. .... Oct 22, 1879
Knowles, Lucius J. .... July 2, 1819
Knowlton, Charles .... May 10, 1800
Knox, Frank (William F.) .... Jan 1, 1874
Knox, Henry .... July 25, 1750, Sept 12, 1789
Knox, Philander C. .... May 6, 1853
Knox, Rose M. .... Nov 18, 1857
Knudsen, William S. .... Mar 25, 1879, Jan 7, 1941
Koch, Frederick H. .... Sept 12, 1877
Kohlmann, Anthony .... July 31, 1771
Kohut, Alexander .... Apr 22, 1842, Jan 2, 1887
Koller, Carl .... Dec 3, 1857
Kollsman, Paul .... Feb 22, 1900
Koop, C. Everett .... Oct 14, 1916
Koopmans, Tjalling C. .... Aug 28, 1910
Koplik, Henry .... Oct 28, 1858
Korea .... June 29, 1949; *1950* June 25, June 27, June 30, July 8, Sept 15, Sept 26, Nov 25; Jan 4, 1951, July 27, 1953, Jan 23, 1898, Sept 1, 1983
Kornberg, Arthur .... Mar 3, 1918
Korzybski, Alfred .... July 3, 1879
Kosciuszko, Thaddeus .... Feb 12, 1746, Oct 18, 1776
Kostelanetz, André .... Dec 22, 1901
Koufax, Sandy (Sanford) .... Dec 30, 1935
Koussevitsky, Serge .... July 25, 1874
Kovacs, Ernie .... Jan 23, 1919
Kraft, Charles H. .... Oct 17, 1880
Kraft, Christopher C. .... Feb 28, 1924
Kraft, James L. .... Nov 11, 1874
Kramer, Jack .... Aug 1, 1921
Kramer, Stanley .... Sept 29, 1913
Krantz, Judith .... Jan 9, 1928
Kreisler, Fritz .... Feb 2, 1875
Kresge, S(ebastian) S. .... July 31, 1867
Kress, Claude W. .... Apr 4, 1876
Kress, Samuel H. .... July 23, 1863
Kreymborg, Alfred .... Dec 10, 1883
Kroc, Ray A. .... Oct 5, 1902
Kroger, Bernard H. .... Jan 24, 1860
Krol, John J. .... Oct 26, 1910
Krueger, Walter .... Jan 26, 1881
Kruif, Paul de *see* DeKruif, Paul
Krupa, Gene .... Jan 15, 1909
Krutch, Joseph Wood .... Nov 25, 1893
Kuhn, Bowie .... Oct 28, 1926, Nov 1, 1982
Kuiper, Gerard P. .... Dec 7, 1905
Ku Klux Klan .... Dec 24, 1865, Nov 25, 1915, Nov 3, 1979
Kusch, Polycarp .... Jan 26, 1911
Kuznets, Simon .... Apr 30, 1901
Kyser, Kay .... June 18, 1906

Labor .... Aug 1, 1794, Jan 29, 1834, Mar 31, 1840, June 25, 1868, Dec 30, 1869, Jan 1, 1879, Nov 15, 1881, Nov 17, 1881, May 8, 1882, Sept 2, 1882; *1886* Mar 6, May 3, Dec 2; Jan 25, 1890; *1892* July 11,

Sept 30, Oct 13; June 28, 1894, Apr 29, 1899, June 27, 1905, July 7, 1905, Sept 19, 1906, Feb 3, 1908, Oct 1, 1910, July 4, 1911, Jan 11, 1912, Apr 8, 1918, Aug 17, 1918, Feb 6, 1919, Oct 29, 1919, Jan 2, 1920, May 22, 1920, June 22, 1922, Sept 25, 1926, Jan 28, 1932, Mar 23, 1932, Aug 5, 1933, Oct 24, 1933, June 19, 1934, June 27, 1934; *1935* July 5, Aug 29, Nov 9; *1937* Mar 2, Mar 29, Apr 12, May 30, Nov 14; June 25, 1938, Aug 2, 1939, Mar 19, 1941, June 25, 1941, Jan 12, 1942, Feb 9, 1943, May 1, 1943, June 23, 1947, Jan 3, 1949, Feb 9, 1955, Dec 5, 1955, Sept 14, 1959, Sept 23, 1966, Jan 5, 1970, Nov 1, 1977, July 1, 1981, Oct 1, 1983

Labor, Department of .... June 27, 1884, June 13, 1888, Feb 14, 1903, Apr 9, 1912, Mar 4, 1913, Jan 3, 1918, June 5, 1920, June 6, 1933

Lachaise, Gaston .... Mar 1, 1882
Laclede, Pierre .... Feb 15, 1764, June 20, 1778
Ladd, Alan .... Sept 3, 1913
Ladd, George T. .... Jan 19, 1842
Ladewig, Marion .... Oct 30, 1914
Laemmle, Carl .... Jan 17, 1867
LaFarge, John .... Mar 31, 1835
LaFarge, Oliver H.P. .... Dec 19, 1901
Lafayette, Marquis de .... Sept 6, 1757, July 27, 1777, Aug 16, 1824, June 17, 1825
LaFollette, Robert M. .... June 14, 1855, Jan 21, 1911
LaGuardia, Fiorello H. .... Dec 11, 1882, Jan 18, 1942
Lahm, Frank P. .... Nov 17, 1877
Lahr, Bert .... Aug 13, 1895
Laine, Frankie .... Mar 30, 1913
Lajoie, Nap(oleon) .... Sept 5, 1875
Lake, Simon .... Sept 4, 1866
Lamar, Joseph R. .... Oct 14, 1857
Lamar, Lucius Q. .... Sept 17, 1825
Lamar, Mirabeau B. .... Aug 16, 1798
Lamb, William F. .... Nov 21, 1883
Lamb, Willis E. Jr. .... July 12, 1913
Lambeau, Curly (Earl L.) .... Apr 9, 1898
Lamme, Benjamin G. .... Jan 12, 1864
Lamont, Thomas W. .... Sept 30, 1870
Lamy, Jean Baptiste .... Oct 14, 1814
Lancaster, Burt .... Nov 2, 1913
Land, Edwin H. .... May 7, 1909
Land, Emory S. .... Jan 9, 1879
Landers, Ann .... July 4, 1908
Landis, James M. .... Sept 25, 1899
Landis, Kenesaw M. .... Nov 20, 1866, Nov 12, 1920, Jan 12, 1921
Landon, Alf(red M.) .... Sept 9, 1887
Landowska, Wanda .... July 5, 1879
Landry, Tom .... Sept 12, 1924
Landsteiner, Kafr .... June 14, 1868
Lane, Burton .... Feb 2, 1912
Lane, Joseph .... Dec 14, 1801
Langdell, Christopher C. .... May 22, 1926
Langdon, John .... June 26, 1741, Apr 6, 1789
Lange, Alexis F. .... Apr 23, 1862
Langer, William .... Sept 30, 1886
Langley, Samuel P. .... Aug 22, 1834, May 6, 1896
Langmuir, Irving .... Jan 31, 1881
Langner, Lawrence .... May 30, 1890
Langston, John M. .... Dec 14, 1829
Langstroth, Lorenzo L. .... Dec 25, 1810
Lanier, Sidney .... Feb 3, 1842
Lansing, Robert .... Oct 17, 1864, Feb 13, 1920
Lanston, Tolbert .... Feb 3, 1844
Lardner, Ring(gold) .... Mar 6, 1885
LaRouche, Lyndon H. Jr. .... Dec 16, 1988
Larsen, Don .... Oct 8, 1956
Larson, John A. .... Dec 11, 1892
LaSalle, Sieur de .... Nov 22, 1643, Feb 6, 1682, Apr 9, 1682, Mar 19, 1687
Lasker, Albert D. .... May 1, 1880
Lasky, Jesse L. .... Sept 13, 1880
LaSorda, Tommy .... Sept 22, 1927
Lathrop, Julia .... Apr 9, 1912
Latin America .... May 4, 1822, Dec 26, 1825, Oct 2, 1889, Dec 29, 1902, Aug 5, 1914, May 5, 1915, July 28, 1915, May 3, 1916, Jan 10, 1927, Jan 2, 1933, Oct 10, 1934, Feb 15, 1936, Dec 1, 1936, July 30, 1940, Mar 6, 1945, Sept 2, 1947, Apr 30, 1948, July 21, 1956, Sept 13, 1960, Mar 13, 1961, Aug 17, 1961, Dec 18, 1964, Apr 19, 1967, Mar 11, 1977
Latrobe, Benjamin H. .... May 1, 1764
Laughlin, James L. .... Apr 2, 1850
Laughton, Charles .... July 1, 1899
Laurel, Stan .... June 16, 1890
Laurens, Henry .... Mar 6, 1724
Laurent, Robert .... June 29, 1890
Law, Bernard F. .... Mar 22, 1984
Law, Sallie Chapman .... Aug 27, 1805
Lawes, Lewis A. .... Sept 13, 1883
Lawrence, Abbott .... Dec 16, 1792
Lawrence, Amos .... Apr 22, 1786
Lawrence, Charles L. .... Sept 30, 1882
Lawrence, David .... Dec 25, 1888
Lawrence, Ernest O. .... Aug 8, 1901
Lawrence, Gertrude .... July 4, 1898
Lawrence, James .... Oct 1, 1781, June 1, 1813
Lawrence, William .... Sept 7, 1783
Laws, Samuel S. .... Mar 23, 1824
Lawson, Victor F. .... Sept 9, 1850
Lawton, Henry W. .... Mar 17, 1843
Lazarus, Emma .... July 22, 1849
Lazear, Jesse W. .... May 2, 1866
Leadbelly (Huddie Ledbetter) .... Dec 6, 1949
Leaf, Munro .... Dec 4, 1905
League of Nations .... Jan 8, 1918; *1919* Feb 14, July 10, Nov 19; *1920* Jan 10, Feb 11, Mar 19, June 19
Leahy, William D. .... May 6, 1875
Lear, Ben .... May 12, 1879
Lear, Norman .... July 27, 1922
Lear, William P. .... June 26, 1902
Leary, Herbert F. .... May 31, 1885
Leavenworth, Henry .... Dec 10, 1783
Lebanon .... June 16, 1976; *1983* Apr 18, Oct 23; *1984* Feb 26, Mar 7, Sept 20; Jan 8, 1985; *1986* Sept 9, Sept 12, Oct 21; Feb 7, 1988
Lederberg, Joshua .... May 23, 1925
Lederman, Leon M. .... July 15, 1922
Lee, Ann .... Feb 29, 1736, Aug 6, 1774
Lee, Arthur .... Dec 21, 1740, Sept 26, 1776
Lee, Charles .... Oct 2, 1782
Lee, Fitzhugh .... Nov 19, 1835

Lee, Francis L. .... Oct 14, 1734
Lee, George W.C. .... Sept 16, 1832
Lee, Gypsy Rose .... Jan 9, 1914
Lee, Henry .... Jan 29, 1756, Aug 19, 1779
Lee, Ivy L. .... July 16, 1877
Lee, Jason .... June 23, 1803
Lee, John C.H. .... Aug 1, 1887
Lee, Joseph .... Mar 8, 1862
Lee, Manfred B. .... Oct 20, 1905
Lee, Peggy .... May 26, 1920
Lee, Richard Henry .... Jan 31, 1732, May 10, 1776, June 7, 1776
Lee, Robert E. .... Jan 19, 1807, Apr 20, 1861, June 1, 1862, Feb 6, 1865, Apr 9, 1865
Lee, Samuel P. .... Feb 13, 1812
Lee, Tsung-Dao .... Nov 24, 1926
Lee, William H.F. .... May 31, 1837
Leeser, Isaac .... Dec 12, 1806
Leete, William .... Apr 16, 1683
LeGallienne, Eva .... Jan 11, 1899
Legionnaire's Disease .... July 21, 1976
Lehm, Frank P. .... Nov 17, 1877
Lehman, Herbert H. .... Mar 28, 1878
Lehmann, Lotte .... Feb 27, 1888
Lehrer, James .... May 19, 1934
Leidy, Joseph .... Sept 9, 1823
Leigh, Mitch (Irwin S.) .... Jan 30, 1928
Leinsdorf, Erich .... Feb 4, 1912
Leisler, Jacob .... May 31, 1689
Lejeune, John A. .... Jan 10, 1867
Leland, Henry M. .... Feb 16, 1843
LeMay, Curtis E. .... Nov 15, 1906
Lemmon, Jack .... Feb 8, 1925
Lemnitzer, Lyman L. .... Aug 29, 1899
Lemon, Bob .... Sept 22, 1920
LeMoyne, Jean Baptiste .... Feb 23, 1680
Lend Lease *see* World War II
L'Enfant, Pierre C. .... Aug 2, 1754
Lennon, John C. .... Oct 9, 1940, Dec 8, 1980
Lenox, James .... Aug 19, 1800
Leonard, Benny .... Apr 7, 1896
Leonard, Harry W. .... Feb 8, 1861
Leontieff, Wassily .... Aug 5, 1906
Leopold and Loeb .... Sept 10, 1924
Lerner, Alan Jay .... Aug 31, 1918
LeRoy, Mervyn .... Oct 15, 1900
Lescaze, William .... Mar 27, 1896
Leslie, Frank .... Mar 29, 1821
Letterman, David .... Apr 12, 1947
Letterman, Jonathan .... Dec 11, 1824
Leutze, Emmanuel .... Mar 24, 1816
Levant, Oscar .... Dec 27, 1906
Leverett, John .... May 16, 1679
Levi, Edward H. .... June 26, 1911
Levi-Montalcini, Rita .... Apr 22, 1909
Levin, Ira .... Aug 27, 1929
Levin, Jeremy .... Mar 7, 1984
Levine, Jack .... Jan 3, 1915
Levine, Philip .... Aug 20, 1900
Levit, Braham .... July 1, 1880
Levitt, Abraham .... July 1, 1880
Levitt, William J. .... Feb 11, 1907
Levy, Louis E. .... Oct 12, 1846
Lewis, Andrew .... Sept 26, 1784
Lewis, Carl .... July 1, 1961
Lewis, Francis .... Mar 21, 1713
Lewis, Gilbert N. .... Oct 23, 1875
Lewis, Isaac N. .... Oct 12, 1858
Lewis, Jerry (Joseph L.) .... Mar 16, 1926
Lewis, John L. .... Feb 12, 1880, Nov 14, 1937, May 1, 1943
Lewis, Meriwether .... Aug 18, 1774
Lewis, Morgan .... Oct 16, 1754
Lewis, Sinclair .... Feb 7, 1885
Lewis, Ted .... Jan 6, 1892
Lewis, Winford L. .... May 29, 1878
Lewis and Clark Expedition .... Jan 18, 1803, May 14, 1804, Nov 15, 1805, Sept 23, 1806
Lewisohn, Adolph .... May 27, 1849
Lewisohn, Ludwig .... May 30, 1883
Lexow, Clarence .... Sept 16, 1852, Jan 30, 1894
Leypoldt, Frederick .... Nov 17, 1835
Libby, Willard F. .... Dec 17, 1908
Liberace (Wladzin Valentino) .... May 16, 1919
Libraries .... Nov 8, 1731, Oct 1, 1732, Sept 17, 1855, Oct 6, 1876, Jan 5, 1887, Mar 12, 1901, May 23, 1911
Library of Congress .... Apr 24, 1800, Jan 29, 1801, Jan 30, 1815, Dec 24, 1851, Mar 3, 1865, Mar 2, 1867, May 23, 1911
Libya .... Apr 15, 1986
Lichtenstein, Roy .... Oct 27, 1923
Lick, James .... Aug 21, 1796
Lie, Jonas .... Apr 29, 1880
Lieber, Francis .... Mar 18, 1800
Liggett, Hunter .... Mar 21, 1857
Liggett, Louis K. .... Apr 4, 1875
Lilienthal, David E. .... July 8, 1899, Jan 1, 1947
Lillie, Frank R. .... June 27, 1870
Lilly, Eli .... Apr 1, 1885
Lilly, Josiah K. .... Nov 18, 1861
Limon, José .... Jan 12, 1908
Lincoln, Abraham .... Feb 12, 1809, Apr 21, 1832, Mar 6, 1833, May 7, 1833, Nov 4, 1842, Dec 6, 1847, May 22, 1849, Oct 16, 1855; *1858* June 16, July 24, Aug 21, Aug 27; Feb 27, 1860, Feb 11, 1861, Feb 23, 1861; *1862* Jan 27, Jan 31, Mar 6, Apr 16, July 22, Sept 22, Sept 24; *1863* Jan 1, Jan 25, June 1, Nov 19, Dec 8; *1865* Feb 1, Feb 3, Apr 11, Apr 14, Apr 19, May 1, June 30, July 7; May 30, 1922
Lincoln, Benjamin .... Jan 24, 1733
Lincoln, Joseph C. .... Feb 13, 1870
Lincoln, Mary Todd .... Dec 13, 1818, Nov 4, 1842, July 16, 1882
Lincoln, Robert Todd .... Aug 1, 1843
Lind, Jenny .... Sept 11, 1850
Lind, Samuel C. .... June 15, 1879
Lindbergh, Anne Morrow .... June 22, 1906, Mar 1, 1932
Lindbergh, Charles A. .... Feb 4, 1902, May 20, 1927, Mar 1, 1932, Jan 2, 1935
Lindenthal, Gustav .... May 21, 1850
Lindsay, Howard .... Mar 29, 1889

Lindsay, Vachel .... Nov 10, 1879
Lindsey, Ben(jamin B.) .... Nov 25, 1869
Lindstrom, Freddie
(Fred C.) .... Nov 21, 1905
Lions Club .... June 7, 1917
Lipman, Fritz A. .... June 12, 1899
Lippincott, Joshua B. .... Mar 18, 1813
Lippmann, Walter .... Sept 23, 1889
Lipscomb, William N. .... Dec 8, 1919
Listenmann, Bernhard .... Aug 28, 1841
Little, Arthur D. .... Dec 15, 1863
Little, Clarence C. .... Oct 6, 1888
Little, Lou .... Dec 6, 1891
Liverwright, Horace B. .... Dec 10, 1886
Livingston, Edward .... May 28, 1764
Livingston, Henry B. .... Nov 25, 1757
Livingston, Philip .... Jan 15, 1716
Livingston, Robert R. .... Nov 27, 1746, June 10, 1776, Aug 10, 1781, Apr 30, 1789
Livingston, William .... Nov 30, 1723
Lloyd, Harold .... Apr 20, 1894
Lloyd, Henry Demarest .... May 1, 1847
Locke, Alain L. .... Sept 13, 1886
Locke, David R. .... Sept 20, 1833
Locke, John .... Feb 19, 1792
Lockheed, Malcolm .... Aug 13, 1958
Lockheed Corp. .... May 26, 1977
Lockwood, Belva A.B. .... Oct 24, 1830
Lodge, Henry Cabot .... May 12, 1850
Lodge, Henry Cabot .... July 5, 1902
Loeb, Jacques .... Apr 7, 1859
Loeb, James M. .... Aug 6, 1867
Loeb, Robert F. .... Mar 14, 1895
Loening, Grover C. .... Sept 12, 1888
Loesser, Frank H. .... June 29, 1910
Loew, Marcus .... May 7, 1870
Loewe, Frederick .... June 10, 1901
Loewi, Otto .... June 3, 1873
Loewy, Raymond F. .... Nov 5, 1893
Lofting, Hugh .... Jan 14, 1886
Logan, George .... Sept 9, 1753
Logan, James .... Oct 20, 1674
Logan, James H. .... Dec 8, 1841
Logan, John A. .... Feb 9, 1826, May 30, 1868
Logan, Joshua .... Oct 5, 1908
Lomax, Alan .... Jan 15, 1915
Lomax, John A. .... Sept 23, 1867
Lombard, Carole .... Jan 16, 1942
Lombardi, Vincent T. .... June 11, 1913
Lombardo, Carmen .... July 16, 1903
Lombardo, Guy .... June 19, 1902
London, Jack (John G.) .... Jan 12, 1876
London, Meyer .... Dec 29, 1871
Long, Crawford W. .... Nov 1, 1815, Mar 30, 1842
Long, Huey P. .... Aug 20, 1893, Sept 3, 1935
Long, John D. .... Oct 27, 1838
Long, John L. .... Jan 1, 1861
Long, Stephen H. .... Dec 30, 1784
Longden, Johnny .... Feb 14, 1907
Longfellow, Henry
Wadsworth .... Feb 27, 1807
Longstreet, James .... Jan 8, 1821
Longworth, Nicholas .... Jan 16, 1782
Longworth, Nicholas .... Nov 5, 1869, Feb 17, 1906
Loomis, Mahlon .... July 21, 1826
Loos, Anita .... Apr 26, 1893
Lopez, Al(fonso R.) .... Aug 20, 1908
Lopez, Nancy .... Jan 6, 1957
Lopez, Vincent .... Dec 30, 1898
Lord, Herbert M. .... Dec 6, 1859
Lord, Nathan .... Nov 28, 1792
Lord, Pauline .... Aug 8, 1890
Lord, Royal B. .... Sept 19, 1899
Lorentz, Pare .... Dec 11, 1905
Lorenzo, Frank
(Francisco A.) .... May 19, 1940
Lorimer, George H. .... Oct 6, 1868
Lorimer, William L. .... July 13, 1912
Los Angeles .... Aug 1, 1769, Sept 4, 1781, Aug 13, 1846, Jan 10, 1847, Apr 4, 1850, Oct 24, 1871, Oct 1, 1910, July 30, 1932, June 18, 1941, Aug 11, 1965, May 17, 1974
"Lost Colony" *see* North Carolina
Louganis, Greg .... Jan 29, 1960
Louis, Joe .... May 13, 1914, June 22, 1937
Louisiana .... Apr 9, 1682, Jan 17, 1700, Jan 6, 1702, Mar 20, 1702, Nov 3, 1762, Sept 21, 1779, Oct 1, 1800; *1803* Apr 30, Oct 20, Dec 20; *1804* Mar 10, Mar 26, Oct 1, Mar 3, 1805, Sept 26, 1810, Jan 22, 1812, Apr 30, 1812, Nov 1, 1852, Jan 2, 1860, Jan 26, 1861, Apr 6, 1864, Mar 2, 1867, Dec 8, 1879, May 12, 1898, Feb 1, 1949, Jan 1, 1975, July 9, 1982
Love, James S. .... July 6, 1896
Lovejoy, Elijah P. .... Nov 9, 1802, Nov 7, 1837
Lovell, James A. Jr. .... Dec 15, 1965, Dec 27, 1968
Low, George M. .... July 19, 1984
Low, Juliette G. .... Oct 30, 1860, Mar 12, 1912
Low, Seth .... Jan 18, 1850
Lowe, Thaddeus S.C. .... Aug 20, 1832
Lowell, A(bott)
Lawrence .... Dec 13, 1856
Lowell, Amy .... Feb 9, 1874
Lowell, Francis C. .... Apr 7, 1775
Lowell, James Russell .... Feb 22, 1819
Lowell, Percival .... Mar 13, 1855
Lowell, Robert T.S. .... Mar 1, 1917
Loy, Myrna .... Aug 2, 1905
Lubin, David .... June 10, 1849
Lubitsch, Ernst .... Jan 29, 1892
Lucas, Jerry .... Mar 30, 1946
Luce, Clare Boothe .... Apr 10, 1903
Luce, Henry R. .... Apr 3, 1898, Mar 3, 1923
Luce, Stephen B. .... Mar 25, 1827, Oct 6, 1884
Luckman, Sid .... Nov 21, 1916
Ludlow, Roger .... Mar 7, 1590
Lufbery, Raoul V.G. .... Mar 21, 1885
Lugosi, Bela .... Oct 20, 1884
Lujan, Manuel .... Dec 22, 1988
Luks, George B. .... Aug 13, 1867
Lunceford, Jimmie .... June 6, 1902
Lundy, Benjamin .... Jan 4, 1789
Lunt, Alfred .... Aug 19, 1893
Luria, Salvador E. .... Aug 13, 1912
Lurton, Horace H. .... Feb 26, 1844
Lutheran Church .... Sept 6, 1711, Jan 1, 1961, June 28, 1962, Sept 8, 1982, Aug 29, 1986, Mar 20, 1987, Jan 1, 1988

Lynch, Charles .... Oct 29, 1796
Lynch, Thomas Jr. .... Aug 5, 1749
Lynn, Loretta .... Jan 14, 1932
Lyon, Mary M. .... Feb 28, 1797, Nov 8, 1837
Lyon, Nathaniel .... Aug 10, 1861
Lyons, Ted .... Dec 28, 1900

McAdoo, William G. .... Oct 31, 1863, May 7, 1914, Dec 26, 1917, Jan 1, 1918
McAfee, Mildred H. .... May 12, 1900
McAlexander, Ulysses G. ...... Aug 30, 1864
McAllister, Ward .... Jan 31, 1895
MacArthur, Arthur .... June 2, 1845
MacArthur, Charles .... Nov 5, 1895
MacArthur, Douglas .... Jan 26, 1880, May 29, 1932, July 28, 1932, July 26, 1941, Mar 17, 1942, Jan 9, 1945, Oct 4, 1945, July 8, 1950, Apr 11, 1951, Apr 19, 1951
McArthur, Duncan .... Jan 14, 1772
McArthur, John D. .... Mar 26, 1897
McAuley, Thomas .... Apr 21, 1778
McAuliffe, Anthony C. .... July 2, 1898
McBride, Mary Margaret .... Nov 16, 1899
McBurney, Charles .... Feb 17, 1845
McCallum, Daniel C. .... Jan 21, 1815
McCandless, Bruce II .... Feb 7, 1984
McCarthy, Eugene J. .... Mar 29, 1916
McCarthy, Joe (Joseph V.) .... Apr 12, 1887
McCarthy, Joseph R. .... Nov 14, 1908, Apr 22, 1954, Dec 2, 1954
McCarthy, Mary T. .... June 21, 1912
McCarthy, Thomas .... July 24, 1864
McCarthy, William J. .... July 15, 1988
McCauley, Mary L.H. .... Oct 13, 1754
McClellan, George B. .... Dec 3, 1826, July 22, 1861, Nov 1, 1861; *1862* Mar 11, Sept 2, Nov 7; Nov 8, 1864
McClellan, John L. .... Feb 25, 1896
McClernand, John A. .... May 30, 1812
McClintock, Barbara .... June 16, 1902
McCloskey, John .... Mar 10, 1810, Mar 15, 1875
McCloy, John J. .... Mar 31, 1895, June 6, 1949
McClure, Jessica .... Oct 16, 1987
McClure, Robert A. .... Mar 4, 1897
McClure, Samuel S. .... Feb 17, 1857
McCollum, Elmer V. .... Mar 3, 1879
McCook, Alexander M. .... Apr 22, 1831
McCook, Edward M. .... June 15, 1833
McCormack, John .... June 14, 1884
McCormack, John W. .... Dec 21, 1891
McCormick, Cyrus H. .... Feb 15, 1809, June 21, 1834
McCormick, Cyrus Hall .... May 16, 1859
McCormick, Lynde D. .... Aug 12, 1895
McCormick, Robert .... June 8, 1780
McCormick, Robert R. .... July 30, 1880
McCormick, Samuel B. .... May 6, 1858
McCormick, Stephen .... Aug 26, 1784
McCosh, James .... Apr 1, 1811
McCovey, Willie .... Jan 10, 1938
McCoy, Joseph G. .... Dec 21, 1837
McCullers, Carson .... Feb 19, 1917
McCulloch, Ben .... Nov 11, 1811
McCutcheon, John T. .... May 6, 1870
McDonald, David J. .... Nov 22, 1902
McDonald, Eugene F. Jr. ...... Mar 11, 1890
McDonald, Jeannette .... June 18, 1907
McDonald, John D. .... July 24, 1916
McDonald, Ross .... Dec 13, 1915
McDonnell, James S. Jr. ...... Apr 9, 1899
Macdonough, Thomas .... Dec 31, 1783
McDougall, Alexander .... June 9, 1786
McDougall, Alexander .... Mar 16, 1845
MacDowell, Edward A. .... Dec 18, 1861
McDowell, Ephraim .... Nov 11, 1771
McDowell, Irvin .... Oct 15, 1818
McEnroe, John .... Feb 16, 1959
Macfadden, Bernarr .... Aug 16, 1868
McFee, William .... June 15, 1881
McGee, Fibber .... Nov 6, 1896
McGillicuddy, Cornelius *see* Mack, Connie
McGinley, Phyllis .... Mar 21, 1905
McGinnity, Joe .... Mar 19, 1871
McGivney, Michael J. .... Aug 12, 1852
McGlachlin, Edward F. .... June 9, 1868
McGovern, George S. .... July 19, 1922
McGrath, J. Howard .... Nov 28, 1903
McGraw, James H. .... Dec 17, 1860
McGraw, John J. .... Apr 7, 1873
McGready, James .... Aug 13, 1788
McGuffey, William H. .... Sept 23, 1800
McGuire, Peter J. .... May 8, 1882
Machen, John G. .... July 28, 1881
McHenry, James .... Nov 16, 1753
McHugh, Jimmy .... July 10, 1894
MacInness, Helen C. .... Oct 7, 1907
McIntire, Samuel .... Feb 6, 1811
McIntosh, Lachlan .... Mar 17, 1725
McIntyre, James F. .... June 25, 1886
McIntyre, O(scar) O. .... Feb 18, 1884
Mack, Connie .... Dec 23, 1862
Mack, Joseph S. .... Nov 27, 1870
Mackey, Clarence H. .... Apr 17, 1874
McKay, David O. .... Sept 8, 1873
McKay, Donald .... Sept 4, 1810
McKay, Gordon .... May 4, 1821
Mackay, John W. .... Nov 28, 1831
Mackaye, Steele .... June 6, 1842
McKean, Thomas .... Mar 19, 1734
McKechnie, Bill (William B.) .... Aug 7, 1886
McKellar, Kenneth .... Jan 29, 1869
McKenna, Joseph .... Aug 10, 1843
McKenzie, William Lyon ...... Dec 13, 1837
McKim, Charles F. .... Aug 24, 1847
McKinley, Ida S. .... June 8, 1847, Jan 25, 1871, May 26, 1907
McKinley, John .... May 1, 1780
McKinley, William .... Jan 29, 1843, Jan 25, 1871, Nov 3, 1891, Sept 6, 1901, Sept 14, 1901
McLaglen, Victor .... Dec 11, 1886
MacLaine, Shirley .... Apr 24, 1934
McLane, Louis .... May 28, 1786
McLaws, Lafayette .... Jan 15, 1821
McLean, John .... Mar 11, 1785

McLean, William L. .... May 4, 1852
MacLeish, Archibald .... May 7, 1892
MacLeod, Gavin .... Feb 28, 1930
McLoughlin, Maurice E. .... Jan 7, 1890
Maclure, William .... Oct 27, 1763
McManus, George .... Jan 23, 1884
McMaster, John B. .... June 29, 1852
MacMillan, Donald B. .... Nov 10, 1874
McMillan, Edwin M. .... Sept 18, 1907
MacMonnies, Frederick W. .. Sept 28, 1863
McMurtry, Larry .... June 3, 1936
McNair, Lesley J. .... May 25, 1883
McNamara, Robert S. .... June 9, 1916
McNamee, Graham .... July 10, 1888
McNarney, Joseph T. .... Aug 28, 1893
McNary, Charles L. .... June 12, 1874
MacNeil, Robert .... Jan 19, 1931
McNichols, John T. .... Dec 15, 1877
McNutt, Paul V. .... July 19, 1891
Macomb, Alexander .... Apr 3, 1782
Macon, Nathaniel .... Dec 17, 1758
MacPhail, Larry
(Leland S.) .... Feb 3, 1890
McPherson, Aimee Semple ... Oct 9, 1890
McPherson, James B. .... Nov 14, 1828
McQueen, Steve .... Mar 24, 1930
McRae, James H. .... Dec 24, 1863
Macready, William .... May 10, 1849
McReynolds, James C. .... Feb 3, 1862
McTammany, John .... June 26, 1845
Macy, Rowland H. .... Aug 20, 1822
Madison, Dolley .... May 20, 1768, Sept 15, 1794, July 12, 1849
Madison, James .... Aug 27, 1749
Madison, James .... Mar 16, 1751, Apr 25, 1776, Jan 14, 1778, Feb 14, 1779, Dec 14, 1779, May 27, 1787, Oct 27, 1787, Sept 9, 1789, Sept 15, 1794, Apr 18, 1803, June 1, 1812, June 19, 1812, June 28, 1836
Magazines *see* Newspapers/Magazines
Mahan, Alfred T. .... Sept 27, 1840
Mahan, Larry .... Nov 21, 1943
Mahone, William .... Dec 1, 1826
Mahre, Phil(ip) .... May 10, 1957
Maier, Henry W. .... Apr 19, 1988
Maier, Walter A. .... Oct 4, 1893
Mail .... Nov 5, 1639, Jan 1, 1673, Mar 2, 1685, Feb 17, 1692, July 26, 1775, Sept 22, 1789, May 8, 1795, Mar 9, 1829, Feb 15, 1842, Mar 3, 1845, July 1, 1847, Mar 3, 1851, Jan 1, 1856, Oct 9, 1858, Apr 3, 1860, June 8, 1872, May 1, 1873, Mar 3, 1883, Mar 3, 1885, Mar 3, 1893, June 25, 1910, Jan 3, 1911, Aug 24, 1912, Jan 1, 1913, Nov 2, 1917, May 15, 1918, *1920* July 29, Sept 8; May 17, 1928, May 20, 1930, July 6, 1932, Nov 22, 1935, May 20, 1939, Aug 14, 1947, Apr 18, 1950, Aug 1, 1958, Jan 7, 1963, Jan 7, 1968; *1970* Mar 18, Aug 12; *1971* May 16, July 1; Mar 2, 1974, Dec 31, 1975, May 29, 1978; *1981* Mar 22, Nov 1; Apr 3, 1988
Mailer, Norman K. .... Jan 31, 1923
Maiman, Theodore H. .... July 11, 1927
Maine, ... Aug 14, 1607, Oct 16, 1649, May 20, 1690, Jan 1, 1785, Jan 3, 1787, Oct 29, 1819, Mar 3, 1820, Mar 15, 1820, Feb 8, 1839, Mar 3 1839, July 4, 1866, Oct 25, 1946
Major, Charles .... July 25, 1856
Malamud, Bernard .... Apr 26, 1914
Malcolm X .... May 19, 1925, Feb 21, 1965
Malone, Dumas .... Jan 10, 1892
Maloy, Francis E. Jr. .... June 16, 1976
Manchester, William .... Apr 1, 1922
Mancini, Henry .... Apr 16, 1924
Mandrell, Barbara .... Dec 25, 1948
Manilow, Barry .... June 17, 1946
Manly, Charles M. .... Apr 24, 1876
Mann, Horace .... May 4, 1796
Manning, James .... Oct 22, 1738
Manning, William T. .... May 12, 1866
Mansfield, Mike
(Michael J.) .... Mar 16, 1903
Mansfield, Richard .... May 24, 1854
Manship, Paul .... Dec 24, 1885
Mantle, Burns .... Dec 23, 1873
Mantle, Mickey .... Oct 20, 1931
Manush, Heinie (Henry E.) .. July 20, 1901
Maranville, Rabbit
(Walter J.V.) .... Nov 11, 1891
Marble, Alice .... Sept 28, 1913
March, Frederic .... Aug 31, 1897
March, Peyton C. .... Dec 27, 1864
Marciano, Rocky (Rocco) .... Sept 1, 1923, Sept 23, 1952, Aug 31, 1969
Marcos, Ferdinand .... Oct 21, 1988
Marcus, Harold S. .... Apr 20, 1905
Marcy, William L. .... Dec 12, 1786
Marichal, Juan .... Oct 24, 1937
Marin, John C. .... Dec 23, 1872
Marine Corps .... July 11, 1798, Nov 10, 1775, Dec 11, 1903
Marino, Eugene A. .... Mar 15, 1988
Marion, Francis .... Sept 8, 1781, Feb 26, 1795
Maris, Roger .... Sept 10, 1934, Oct 1, 1961
Maritime Commission/
Administration .... June 26, 1936, May 24, 1950
Markham, Edwin .... Apr 23, 1852, Jan 15, 1899
Marks, Johnny .... Nov 10, 1909
Marlowe, Julia .... Aug 17, 1866
Marquand, John P. .... Nov 10, 1893
Marquand, Rube
(Richard W.) .... Oct 9, 1889
Marquette, Jacques .... June 1, 1637, July 17, 1673, Dec 4, 1674
Marquis, Albert W. .... Jan 10, 1855
Marquis, Don .... July 29, 1878
Marriott, John Willard .... Sept 17, 1900
Marsh, Othniel C. .... Oct 29, 1831
Marsh, Reginald .... Mar 14, 1898
Marsh, Sylvester .... Sept 30, 1803
Marshall, George C. .... Dec 31, 1880, June 5, 1947
Marshall, James W. .... Oct 8, 1810, Jan 24, 1848
Marshall, John .... Sept 24, 1755, Jan 20, 1801, Jan 31, 1801, July 6, 1835
Marshall, Louis .... Dec 14, 1856
Marshall, Robert C. .... Apr 3, 1935
Marshall, Thomas R. .... Mar 14, 1854, June 1, 1925
Marshall, Thurgood .... July 2, 1908, June 13, 1967, Oct 2, 1967
Martha Turpin, Sister St. *see* Turpin, Sister St. Martha

Martin, Dean .... June 17, 1917
Martin, Edward S. .... Jan 2, 1856
Martin, Franklin H. .... July 13, 1857
Martin, Freddy .... Dec 8, 1906
Martin, Glenn L. .... Jan 17, 1886
Martin, Homer D. .... Oct 28, 1836
Martin, Joseph W. .... Nov 3, 1884
Martin, Luther .... Feb 9, 1748
Martin, Mary .... Dec 1, 1913
Martin, William McC. .... Dec 17, 1906
Marvin, Charles F. .... Oct 7, 1858
Marvin, Lee .... Feb 19, 1924
Marx, Groucho (Julius H.) ... Oct 2, 1895
Maryland .... May 16, 1631, Apr 15, 1632, June 30, 1632, Mar 25, 1634, Apr 21, 1649, July 27, 1690, June 27, 1691, Sept 19, 1727, Nov 23, 1765, Oct 19, 1774; *1776* June 28, Aug 14, Nov 11; Dec 15, 1778, Jan 2, 1781, Mar 1, 1781, Apr 28, 1788, Dec 23, 1788, May 13, 1851, Apr 27, 1861, Sept 6, 1864, May 8, 1867, July 30, 1952, Apr 27, 1981
Maslow, Abraham .... Apr 1, 1908
Mason, George .... June 12, 1776, Oct 7, 1792
Mason, Henry .... Oct 10, 1831
Mason, James H. .... Nov 8, 1861, Dec 23, 1861, Jan 1, 1862
Mason, John .... Dec 11, 1586
Mason, John .... Jan 30, 1672
Mason, John Y. .... Apr 18, 1799
Mason, Lowell .... Jan 8, 1792
Mason, Max .... Oct 26, 1877
Mason, Stevens T. .... Oct 27, 1811
Mason, Thomson .... Feb 26, 1785
Massachusetts .... May 14, 1602, Nov 21, 1620, Dec 11, 1620, Dec 17, 1623, Mar 19, 1628, Sept 6, 1628; *1629* Mar 4, Aug 29, Oct 20; Sept 2, 1630, Feb 5, 1631, May 18, 1631, May 14, 1634, Sept 13, 1635, Mar 3, 1636, Nov 7, 1637, Nov 5, 1639, Nov 13, 1644, Nov 11, 1647, June 15, 1649, May 31, 1650, June 7, 1652, Oct 29, 1652, Sept 17, 1656, Oct 27, 1659, June 10, 1661, Sept 20, 1676, May 11, 1682, Apr 18, 1689, May 1, 1691, Oct 17, 1691, Jan 7, 1699, Feb 29, 1704, Apr 24, 1704, June 6, 1764, June 8, 1765, Feb 11, 1768, Sept 22, 1768; *1774* May 13, May 20, June 17, Oct 5, Oct 26; *1775* Feb 1, Feb 9, Apr 23, June 12; May 10, 1776, Oct 21, 1776, Jan 1, 1779, Mar 2, 1780, Jan 3, 1787, Sept 26, 1787, Feb 6, 1788, Mar 26, 1788, June 22, 1793, Feb 11, 1812, Jan 31, 1817, Apr 17, 1838, Mar 3, 1842, May 21, 1855, Apr 10, 1861, June 15, 1869, Apr 12, 1908, Jan 1, 1927
Massey, Raymond .... Aug 30, 1896
Massine, Léonide .... Aug 9, 1896
Masters, Edgar Lee .... Aug 23, 1869
Masters, William H. .... Dec 27, 1915
Masterson, Bat (William B.) .... Nov 24, 1853
Mather, Cotton .... Feb 12, 1663
Mather, Increase .... June 21, 1639
Mather, Richard .... Apr 22, 1669
Mather, Samuel L. .... July 1, 1817
Mather, Stephen T. .... July 4, 1867
Mathews, Eddie (Edwin L.) .. Oct 13, 1931
Mathewson, Christy .... Aug 12, 1880, Jan 29, 1936
Mathias, Robert B. .... Nov 17, 1930
Matteson, Tompkins H. .... May 19, 1813
Matthau, Walter .... Oct 1, 1920
Mathews, Stanley .... June 21, 1824
Mauchly, John W. .... Aug 30, 1907
Mauldin, William H. .... Oct 29, 1921
Maury, Matthew F. .... Jan 14, 1806
Maxim, Hiram P. .... Sept 2, 1869
Maxim, Sir Hiram S. .... Feb 5, 1840
Maxim, Hudson .... Feb 3, 1853
Maxwell, Elsa .... May 24, 1883
Maxwell, Russell L. .... Dec 28, 1890
Mayer, Louis B. .... July 4, 1885
Mayer, Maria Goeppert .... June 28, 1906
Mayer, Oscar F. .... Mar 29, 1859
Mayer, Oscar G. .... Mar 10, 1888
Mayhew, Jonathan .... Oct 8, 1720
Maynor, Dorothy .... Sept 3, 1910
Mayo, Charles H. .... July 19, 1865
Mayo, Henry T. .... Dec 8, 1856
Mayo, William J. .... June 29, 1861
Mays, Benjamin .... Aug 1, 1894
Mays, Willie .... May 6, 1931
Maytag, Frederick L. .... July 14, 1857
Mead, Andrea .... Apr 19, 1932
Mead, Larkin G. .... Jan 3, 1835
Mead, Margaret .... Dec 16, 1901
Meade, George G. .... Dec 31, 1815, June 28, 1863
Meany, George .... Aug 16, 1894
Meat .... May 29, 1884, Jan 30, 1905, June 12, 1906, June 30, 1906
Mechan, Evan .... *1988* Jan 8, Feb 5, Apr 4
Medeiros, Humberto S. .... Sept 7, 1983
Medicare *see* Social Security
Medicine .... May 3, 1765, Jan 8, 1943, Apr 4, 1969; *1987* May 12, Nov 12
Medill, Joseph .... Apr 6, 1823
Medina, Harold R. .... Jan 17, 1949
Medwick, Joe .... Nov 24, 1911
Meese, Edwin III .... *1988* Mar 29, July 18, Aug 12
Mehta, Zubin .... Apr 29, 1936
Meigs, Return J. .... Nov 16, 1764
Melchoir, Lauritz .... Mar 20, 1890
Mellon, Andrew W. .... Mar 24, 1855, Mar 17, 1941
Melville, George W. .... Jan 10, 1841
Melville, Herman .... Aug 1, 1819
Memminger, Christopher G. .... Jan 9, 1803
Menard, Michel B. .... Dec 5, 1805
Mencken, Henry L. .... Sept 12, 1880
Mendel, Lafayette B. .... Feb 5, 1872
Menendez de Aviles, Pedro .. June 29, 1565, Aug 28, 1565, Sept 20, 1565
Menjou, Adolph .... Feb 18, 1890
Menen, William G. .... Dec 20, 1884
Menninger, Karl A. .... July 22, 1893
Menninger, William C. .... Oct 15, 1899
Mennonites .... Feb 18, 1688
Menotti, Gian-Carlo .... July 7, 1911, Dec 24, 1951
Menuhin, Yehudi .... Apr 22, 1916
Mercer, Hugh .... Jan 12, 1777
Mercer, Johnny .... Nov 18, 1909
Mercer, Mabel .... Apr 20, 1984

Merck, George W. .... Mar 29, 1894
Meredith, Burgess .... Nov 16, 1909
Meredith, Edwin T. .... Dec 23, 1876
Meredith, James H. .... Sept 24, 1962, Oct 1, 1962
Mergenthaler, Ottmar. .... May 11, 1854
Merman, Ethel .... Jan 16, 1909
Merriam, Charles .... Nov 21, 1806
Merrick, David .... Nov 27, 1912
Merrifield, R. Bruce .... July 15, 1921
Merrill, Charles E. .... Oct 19, 1885
Merrill, Frank D. .... Dec 4, 1903
Merrill, Robert .... June 4, 1919
Merritt, Leonidas .... Feb 20, 1844
Merritt, Wesley .... June 16, 1834
Merton, Thomas .... Jan 31, 1915
Mesta, Perle .... Oct 12, 1889
Metcalf, Willard L. .... July 1, 1858
Methodism .... May 7, 1738, Sept 9, 1747; *1760* Feb 14, Aug 11; Oct 30, 1768, Dec 25, 1784, May 1, 1845, May 27, 1924, May 10, 1939, Apr 23, 1968, Apr 29, 1986; *1988* May 2, May 3
Metropolitan Museum of Art .... Apr 13, 1870, Mar 30, 1880
Metropolitan Opera House .... Oct 22, 1883, Jan 7, 1955, Apr 16, 1966, Sept 16, 1966
Metz, Christian .... Dec 30, 1794
Mexican War
1846 .... Apr 24, May 8, May 9, May 11, May 13, May 17, May 18, June 14, July 4, July 7, July 9, Aug 7, Aug 13, Aug 18, Sept 25, Nov 15, Dec 16
1847 .... Jan 8, Jan 10, Jan 13, Feb 23, Feb 28, Mar 2, Mar 9, Mar 29, Apr 18, Aug 20, Sept 13, Sept 14, Nov 22
1848 .... Feb 2, Mar 10, May 30
Mexico .... Jan 12, 1828, Apr 8, 1830, Apr 21, 1836, May 14, 1836, Aug 23, 1843, Mar 6, 1844, Mar 28, 1845, Apr 22, 1854; *1914* Apr 9, Apr 20, Apr 22, May 20; *1916* Jan 11, Mar 10, Mar 15; Feb 5, 1917, Feb 3, 1944
Meyer, Adolf .... Sept 13, 1866
Meyer, Albert G. .... Mar 9, 1903
Meyer, Eugene I. .... Oct 31, 1875
Meyer, George von L. .... June 24, 1858
Meyer, Ray .... Dec 18, 1893
Michelson, Albert A. .... Dec 19, 1852
Michener, James A. .... Feb 3, 1907
Michigan .... Jan 11, 1805, July 1, 1805, July 25, 1817, Aug 26, 1817, Apr 30, 1821, May 11, 1835, Jan 26, 1837, Mar 18, 1837, Nov 5, 1850, Feb 3, 1855, May 18, 1906, Apr 18, 1917, June 26, 1958, July 1, 1964, Apr 27, 1981
Middleton, Arthur .... Sept 7, 1737
Middleton, Arthur .... June 26, 1742
Middleton, Henry .... June 13, 1784
Midgely, Thomas .... May 18, 1889
Midler, Bette .... Dec 1, 1945
Midway Islands .... Aug 28, 1867, June 3, 1942
Mielziner, Jo .... Mar 19, 1901
Mies van der Rohe, Ludwig .... Mar 27, 1886
Mifflin, Thomas .... Jan 10, 1744
Mikan, George L. .... June 18, 1924
Miles, Nelson A. .... Aug 8, 1839, Oct 5, 1877
Milestone, Lewis .... Sept 30, 1985
Military Academies .... Mar 16, 1802, July 4, 1802, Oct 10, 1845, Sept 30, 1943, Aug 1, 1954, July 11, 1955
Milland, Ray .... Jan 30, 1908
Millay, Edna St. Vincent ...... Feb 22, 1892
Milledge, John .... Feb 9, 1881
Miller, Arthur .... Oct 17, 1915
Miller, Charles R. .... Jan 17, 1849
Miller, David H. .... Jan 2, 1875
Miller, Frank E. .... Apr 12, 1859
Miller, Glenn .... Mar 1, 1904, Dec 15, 1944
Miller, Henry J. .... Feb 1, 1860
Miller, Henry V. .... Dec 26, 1891
Miller, John Peter .... Dec 25, 1709
Miller, Lewis .... July 24, 1829, Aug 4, 1874
Miller, Max .... Feb 9, 1899
Miller, Mitch .... July 4, 1911
Miller, Samuel F. .... Apr 5, 1816
Miller, Stanley .... Mar 7, 1930
Miller, William .... Feb 15, 1782, Mar 21, 1843
Miller, William E. .... Mar 22, 1914
Milles, Carl .... June 23, 1875
Millikan, Robert A. .... Mar 22, 1868
Mills, Clark .... Dec 13, 1810
Mills, Robert .... Aug 12, 1781
Mills, Wilbur D. .... May 24, 1909
Milosz, Czeslaw .... June 30, 1911
Milstein, Nathan .... Dec 31, 1904
Minelli, Liza .... Mar 12, 1946
Mines, Bureau of .... May 16, 1910
Mingus, Charles .... Apr 22, 1922
Minimum Wages, Hours ...... Mar 31, 1840, Sept 19, 1906, Mar 19, 1917, Aug 2, 1923, Oct 24, 1933, Mar 29, 1937, June 25, 1938, Feb 9, 1943, Oct 26, 1949, May 5, 1961, Sept 23, 1966, Jan 1, 1976, Jan 1, 1978
Minnesota .... Mar 3, 1848, Apr 28, 1849, June 1, 1849, Mar 4, 1851, Oct 13, 1857, May 11, 1858
Minot, George R. .... Dec 2, 1885
Mint *see* Money
Minton, Sherman .... Oct 20, 1890
Minuit, Peter .... May 4, 1626, May 6, 1626, Mar 29, 1638
Mississippi .... Apr 7, 1798, Aug 15, 1817, Dec 10, 1817, Oct 26, 1832, Jan 9, 1861, Aug 21, 1865, Feb 13, 1867, Nov 30, 1869, Feb 23, 1870, Nov 1, 1900, Feb 19, 1908, Oct 1, 1962, Aug 4, 1964
Mississippi River .... Dec 17, 1540, May 8, 1541, June 17, 1673, Apr 9, 1682, Jan 17, 1700, June 26, 1784, Sept 1, 1854, Apr 21, 1855, July 4, 1874, Apr 17, 1882, May 15, 1928
Missouri .... Feb 15, 1764, Mar 3, 1805, July 12, 1808, Oct 1, 1812, Mar 3, 1820, June 12, 1820, Aug 10, 1821, Feb 21, 1839, May 1, 1841, Feb 28, 1861, July 1, 1863, Oct 30, 1875, July 17, 1981, Feb 22, 1983
Mitchel, Ormsby M. .... July 28, 1809

Mitchell, Billy (William) .... Dec 29, 1879, Oct 28, 1925, Feb 1, 1926
Mitchell, George .... Nov 29, 1988
Mitchell, John .... Feb 4, 1870
Mitchell, John N. .... Jan 1, 1974
Mitchell, Margaret .... Nov 8, 1900
Mitchell, Maria .... Aug 1, 1818
Mitchell, S(ilas) Weir .... Feb 15, 1829
Mitchell, William D. .... Sept 9, 1874
Mitchill, Samuel L. .... Aug 20, 1764
Mitchum, Robert .... Aug 6, 1917
Mitropoulos, Dimitri .... Feb 18, 1896
Mitscher, Marc A. .... Jan 26, 1887
Mix, Tom .... Jan 6, 1880
Mize, Johnny .... Jan 7, 1913
Mizner, Addison .... Feb 5, 1933
Modigliano, Franco .... June 18, 1918
Modjeska, Helena .... Oct 12, 1840
Moffett, William A. .... Oct 31, 1869
Mokesa, Agostan Haraszthy de *see* Haraszthy de Mokesa, Agoston
Mondale, Walter F. .... Jan 5, 1928
Money .... June 7, 1652, July 6, 1785, Apr 2, 1792, Feb 12, 1873, Mar 14, 1900, May 18, 1908, Aug 2, 1909, Apr 20, 1933, June 5, 1933, Jan 30, 1934, July 22, 1944, Aug 14, 1969, Apr 3, 1972, Feb 12, 1974
Monk, Theolonius S. .... Oct 10, 1920
Monroe, Elizabeth K. .... June 30, 1768
Monroe, Bill .... Sept 13, 1911
Monroe, Harriet .... Dec 23, 1860
Monroe, James .... Apr 28, 1758, Feb 16, 1786, Dec 6, 1790, May 27, 1794, Nov 4, 1794; *1803* Jan 11, Mar 8, Apr 18; Apr 2, 1811, Mar 9, 1820, Dec 2, 1823, July 4, 1831
Monroe, Marilyn .... June 1, 1926, Aug 5, 1962
Monroe, Vaughn .... Oct 7, 1911
Montana .... May 26, 1864, Aug 27, 1864, Nov 4, 1884, July 4, 1889, Nov 8, 1889, Feb 17, 1893, Dec 31, 1918, Oct 18, 1935
Montana, Joe .... June 11, 1956
Monteux, Pierre .... Apr 4, 1875
Montgomery, Richard .... Dec 2, 1738; *1775* Nov 13, Dec 5, Dec 31
Montgomery Ward & Co. .... Apr 26, 1944
Moody, Dwight L. .... Feb 5, 1837
Moody, John .... May 2, 1868
Moody, William H. .... Dec 23, 1853
Moody, William Vaughn .... July 8, 1869
Moore, Alexander P. .... Nov 10, 1867
Moore, Alfred .... May 21, 1755
Moore, Benjamin .... Oct 5, 1748
Moore, Clement Clark .... July 15, 1779, Dec 23, 1823
Moore, George C. .... Mar 29, 1973
Moore, George T. .... Feb 23, 1871
Moore, Grace .... Dec 5, 1901
Moore, Hugh K. .... Jan 3, 1872
Moore, Marianne C. .... Nov 15, 1827
Moore, Mary Tyler .... Dec 29, 1937
Moore, Richard B. .... May 6, 1871
Moore, Stanford .... Sept 4, 1913
Moorer, Thomas H. .... Feb 9, 1912
Morais, Sabato .... Apr 13, 1823, Jan 2, 1887
Moran, Thomas .... Jan 12, 1837
More, Paul E. .... Dec 12, 1864
Morgan, Angela .... Jan 24, 1957
Morgan, Arthur E. .... June 20, 1878, May 18, 1933
Morgan, Charles H. .... Jan 8, 1831
Morgan, Daniel .... July 6, 1736
Morgan, Edwin B. .... May 2, 1806
Morgan, George W. .... Sept 20, 1820
Morgan, Harcourt A. .... Feb 8, 1867
Morgan, John .... June 10, 1735
Morgan, John H. .... June 1, 1825
Morgan, J(ohn) P. .... Apr 17, 1837
Morgan, J(ohn) P. II .... Sept 7, 1867, July 3, 1915
Morgan, John T. .... June 20, 1824
Morgan, Junius S. .... Apr 14, 1813
Morgan, Lewis H. .... Nov 21, 1818
Morgan, Russ .... Apr 29, 1904
Morgan, Thomas H. .... Sept 25, 1866
Morgenthau, Henry J. .... May 11, 1891
Morison, Samuel Eliot .... July 9, 1887
Morley, Christopher D. .... May 5, 1890
Morley, Edward W. .... Jan 29, 1838
Mormons .... Apr 26, 1830, July 12, 1843, June 27, 1844, July 24, 1847; *1858* Apr 6, June 26; July 1, 1862, July 21, 1867, Mar 22, 1882, Sept 24, 1890; *1893* Jan 4, Apr 6; Jan 25, 1900, Feb 20, 1907, Nov 11, 1985
Morreel, Ben .... Sept 13, 1892
Morrill, Justin S. .... Apr 14, 1810, July 2, 1862
Morris, Charles .... July 26, 1784
Morris, Esther H. .... Aug 8, 1814
Morris, Gouverneur .... Jan 31, 1752, July 6, 1785
Morris, Lewis .... Apr 8, 1726
Morris, Lewis B. .... Nov 2, 1760
Morris, Robert .... Jan 31, 1734; *1781* Feb 20, Dec 31; July 6, 1785, Apr 4, 1800
Morris, Dwight W. .... Sept 12, 1925
Morse, Carlton E. .... Apr 29, 1932
Morse, Jedidiah .... Aug 23, 1761
Morse, Samuel F.B. .... Apr 27, 1791, June 20, 1841, Mar 3, 1843, May 24, 1844
Morse, Sidney E. .... Feb 7, 1794
Morse, Wayne L. .... Oct 20, 1900
Morton, George A. .... Jan 2, 1936
Morton, Jelly Roll (Ferdinand) .... Sept 20, 1885
Morton, Joy .... Sept 27, 1855
Morton, Julius Sterling .... Apr 22, 1832
Morton, Levi P. .... May 6, 1824, May 16, 1920
Morton, Oliver P. .... Aug 4, 1823
Morton, William T.B. .... Aug 9, 1819
Mosby, John S. .... Dec 6, 1833
Moscosco, Luis .... June 5, 1542, July 18, 1543
Moses, Edwin .... Aug 31, 1955
Moses, George H. .... Feb 9, 1869
Moses, Grandma (Anna M.) .... Sept 7, 1860
Moses, Robert .... Dec 18, 1888
Moss, John C. .... Jan 5, 1838
Mostel, Zero (Sam) .... Feb 28, 1915
Mother's Day .... May 10, 1908
Motherwell, Robert .... Jan 24, 1915

Motion pictures .... Jan 7, 1894, Apr 23, 1896, Aug 31, 1897, Aug 5, 1926, Oct 6, 1927, May 16, 1929, Sept 30, 1952
Motley, John L. .... Apr 15, 1814
Moton, Robert R. .... Aug 26, 1867
Mott, John R. .... May 25, 1865
Mott, Lucretia C. .... Jan 3, 1793, July 19, 1848
Moulton, Forest R. .... Apr 29, 1872
Moultrie, William .... Dec 4, 1730, June 28, 1776
Mount, William S. .... Nov 26, 1807
Mt. St. Helen .... Nov 22, 1842, May 18, 1980
Mowatt, Anna C. .... Mar 5, 1819
Mowbray, George M. .... May 5, 1814
Moyers, Bill .... June 5, 1934
Mudd, Roger .... Feb 9, 1928
Muenter, Eric .... July 2, 1915, July 3, 1915
Muhammad, Elijah .... Oct 10, 1897
Muhlenberg, Frederick A.C. .... Jan 1, 1750, Apr 1, 1789
Muhlenberg, Henry M. .... Sept 6, 1711
Muhlenberg, John P.G. .... Oct 1, 1746
Muir, John .... Apr 21, 1838
Muir, Malcolm .... July 19, 1885
Muldoon, William .... May 25, 1845
Mulford, Clarence E. .... Feb 3, 1883
Muller, Herman J. .... Dec 21, 1890
Mulligan, Gerry (Gerald J.) .... Apr 6, 1927
Mulliken, Robert S. .... June 7, 1896
Mumford, Lewis .... Oct 19, 1895
Munch, Charles .... Sept 26, 1891
Mundelein, George W. .... July 2, 1872, Mar 24, 1924
Muni, Paul .... Sept 22, 1895
Munoz-Marin, Luis .... Feb 18, 1898, Jan 2, 1949
Munro, George .... Nov 12, 1825
Munsey, Frank A. .... Aug 21, 1854
Münsterberg, Hugo .... June 1, 1863
Murdoch, Rupert .... Mar 11, 1931
Murphy, Audie .... June 20, 1924
Murphy, Charles F. .... June 20, 1858
Murphy, Frank .... Apr 13, 1890
Murphy, Isaac .... Feb 12, 1896
Murphy, William P. .... Feb 6, 1892
Murray, Anne .... June 20, 1945
Murray, Arthur .... Dec 4, 1895
Murray, John .... Dec 10, 1741
Murray, Lindley .... June 7, 1745
Murray, Philip .... May 25, 1886
Murrow, Edward R. .... Apr 25, 1908
Musburger, Brent .... May 26, 1939
Museums .... Jan 12, 1773, Apr 13, 1870, Mar 30, 1880, May 10, 1939, June 12, 1939, May 17, 1941, Jan 8, 1968
Musial, Stan(ley F.) .... Nov 21, 1920
Muskie, Edmund S. .... Mar 28, 1914
Muybridge, Eadweard .... Apr 9, 1830
Myer, Albert J. .... Sept 20, 1829, June 21, 1860

Nabokov, Vladimir .... Apr 23, 1899
Nader, Ralph .... Feb 27, 1934
Nagurski, Bronco (Bronislaw) .... Nov 3, 1908
Naismith, James .... Nov 6, 1861, Jan 20, 1892
Namath, Joe .... May 31, 1943
Narvaez, Pamphillo de .... *1528* Feb 20, Apr 14, May 1
Nasby, Petroleum V. *see* Locke, David R.
Nash, Charles W. .... Jan 28, 1864
Nash, Francis .... Oct 7, 1777
Nash, Ogden .... Aug 19, 1902
Nashville, Tenn. .... Jan 1, 1780
Nast, Condé .... Mar 26, 1874
Nast, Thomas .... Sept 27, 1840, Jan 15, 1870
Nathan, George Jean .... Feb 14, 1882
Nathans, Daniel .... Oct 30, 1928
Nation, Carry A. .... Nov 25, 1846, Jan 21, 1901
National Academy of Sciences .... Mar 3, 1863
National Aeronautics & Space Administration (NASA) .... Mar 3, 1915, Apr 2, 1958, July 29, 1958
National Aircraft Board .... Sept 12, 1925
National anthem .... July 4, 1832, Mar 3, 1931
National Archives .... June 19, 1934
National Association for the Advancement of Colored People (NAACP) .... Feb 12, 1909, May 30, 1909, June 12, 1963
National Assotion of Manufacturers .... Jan 22, 1895
National Black Churches Council .... Dec 11, 1982
National Broadcasting Co. .... Nov 25, 1926
National Bureau of Standards .... Mar 3, 1901
National Commission of Product Safety .... Nov 20, 1967
National Commission on Civil Disorders .... Mar 2, 1968
National Conservation Commission .... Jan 11, 1909
National Council of Churches .... Nov 29, 1950
National Defense Mediation Board .... Mar 19, 1941
National Education Association .... Aug 26, 1857
National Gallery of Art .... Mar 17, 1941
National Geographic Society .... Jan 27, 1888
National Guard .... Aug 5, 1917, June 15, 1934
National Housing Agency .... Feb 24, 1942
National Institute of Arts & Letters .... Feb 4, 1913
National Institutes of Health .... Oct 31, 1946
National Labor Board .... Aug 5, 1933
National Labor

Relations Board/Act .... June 19, 1934, June 5, 1935
National Mediation Board .... June 21, 1934
National Monetary Commission .... May 30, 1908
National Oceanic & Atmospheric Administration .... Oct 3, 1970
National Organization of Women (NOW) .... Oct 29, 1966
National Parks .... Mar 1, 1872, Sept 25, 1890, Oct 1, 1890, Mar 2, 1899, May 22, 1902, Jan 9, 1903, June 29, 1906, May 11, 1910, Nov 9, 1911, Jan 26, 1915, Aug 9, 1916, Aug 25, 1916, Feb 26, 1917, Feb 26, 1919, Nov 19, 1919, Mar 4, 1921, Sept 15, 1928, Feb 26, 1929, May 14, 1930, June 15, 1934, Dec 26, 1935, June 29, 1938, Mar 4, 1940, Apr 3, 1940, July 1, 1941, June 12, 1944, June 20, 1947, Dec 1, 1956, July 1, 1961, Dec 9, 1962, Sept 12, 1964, Oct 15, 1966, Oct 2, 1968, Jan 8, 1971, Dec 2, 1980, Aug 16, 1987
National Press Club .... Feb 4, 1928
National Recovery Administration (NRA) .... June 16, 1933, Jan 1, 1936
National Rifle Assn. .... Nov 24, 1871
National Science Foundation .... May 10, 1950
National Security Council .... July 26, 1947
National Tuberculosis Assn. June 6, 1904
National War Labor Board ... Apr 8, 1918, Jan 12, 1942
National Women's Temperance Union (WCTU) .... Nov 18, 1874
National Youth Administration .... June 26, 1935
Naturalization .... Jan 29, 1795, June 18, 1798, Mar 3, 1891, June 29, 1906, June 26, 1952
Naval Academy *see* Military Academies
Naval Observatory .... Dec 6, 1830
Navratilova, Martina .... Oct 10, 1956
Navy .... Oct 13, 1775, Dec 22, 1775, May 10, 1797, Oct 21, 1797, Apr 30, 1798, June 22, 1807, Oct 10, 1845, Sept 20, 1850; *1862* Jan 30, May 9, May 11, Dec 30; Oct 6, 1884, Oct 16, 1891, Feb 15, 1898, Apr 11, 1900, Dec 16, 1907, May 13, 1908, Dec 14, 1920, Nov 12, 1921, Sept 3, 1925, Sept 25, 1925, June 20, 1927, Dec 17, 1927; *1930* Jan 21, May 15, July 21; Jan 25, 1933, June 16, 1933, May 17, 1938, Mar 23, 1939, Dec 16, 1941, July 30, 1942, Aug 31, 1942, June 15, 1946, Sept 18, 1947, Apr 26, 1952, Jan 21, 1954, May 26, 1954, Oct 1, 1955, Aug 3, 1958, June 9, 1959, Dec 19, 1960, Apr 10, 1963, July 29, 1967, Jan 23, 1968, May 21, 1968, May 17, 1987; *1988* Apr 14, Apr 24, Apr 29, July 3
Nazimova, Alla .... June 4, 1878
Neale, Thomas .... Feb 17, 1692
Nebraska .... May 30, 1854, Nov 15, 1854, Mar 16, 1855, Mar 1, 1867, Feb 15, 1869, Sept 7, 1871, June 1, 1898, Apr 21, 1917, Jan 6, 1919, Nov 6, 1934
Nef, John U. .... June 14, 1862
Negly, James S. .... Dec 22, 1826
Negroes (*see also* Slavery) ... Jan 12, 1869
Neihardt, John G. .... Jan 8, 1881
Nelson, Byron .... Feb 4, 1912
Nelson, Donald M. .... Nov 17, 1888, Jan 16, 1942
Nelson, Knute .... Feb 2, 1843
Nelson, Nelson O. .... Sept 11, 1844
Nelson, Samuel .... Nov 10, 1792
Nelson, Thomas .... Dec 26, 1738
Nelson, Willie .... Apr 30, 1933
Netherlands .... June 3, 1621, July 21, 1667, Aug 8, 1672, Apr 19, 1782
Neuharth, Allen H. .... Mar 22, 1924
Neumann, John N. .... Mar 28, 1811
Neumann, John von .... Dec 3, 1903
Neutra, Richard J. .... Apr 8, 1892
Nevada .... Dec 18, 1858, June 11, 1859, July 28, 1859, Mar 2, 1861, Oct 31, 1864, Dec 16, 1918, Apr 21, 1958
Neve, Felipe de .... Feb 3, 1777
Nevelson, Louise .... Sept 23, 1899
Nevin, Ethelbert W. .... Nov 25, 1862
Nevins, Allan .... May 20, 1890
New Amsterdam *see* New York City
New England Company .... Mar 19, 1628
New England Confederation/ Council .... Nov 3, 1620, Aug 10, 1622, Jan 13, 1630, May 19, 1643, Sept 9, 1675
New Hampshire .... Jan 31, 1583, Oct 6, 1622, July 24, 1679, Sept 18, 1679, Oct 7, 1756, Dec 14, 1774, Jan 5, 1776, June 15, 1776, Oct 31, 1783, June 2, 1784, June 21, 1788, July 14, 1855
New Jersey .... Feb 10, 1665, Feb 1, 1682, Apr 26, 1702, Oct 22, 1746, Nov 10, 1766, July 2, 1776, Dec 5, 1777, Dec 18, 1787, Feb 15, 1804, Aug 13, 1844, June 30, 1900, Feb 25, 1907, July 4, 1911, July 30, 1916, Oct 4, 1918, May 6, 1937, Nov 5, 1946, Feb 11, 1952, Sept 15, 1958, July 12, 1964, Aug 7, 1982, Feb 3, 1988
New Mexico .... Sept 21, 1595, Aug 9, 1680, Aug 18, 1846, Sept 22, 1846, Sept 4, 1847, May 25, 1850, Sept 9, 1850, Apr 22, 1854, July 8, 1868, Oct 3, 1910, Jan 6, 1912, Oct 22, 1913, Mar 9, 1916, July 16, 1945, Jan 2, 1980
New Netherlands *see* New York State
New Orleans .... Feb 17, 1805; *1814* Dec 1, Dec 14, Dec 23; Jan 8, 1815, Feb 1, 1861, Apr 29, 1862, July 30, 1866, Dec 8, 1879, Mar 14, 1891, July 22, 1905, June 21, 1933
New York City .... *1626* May 4, May 6; Mar 28, 1638, May 11, 1647, Feb 2, 1653, Sept 15, 1655, Aug 12, 1658, Sept 7, 1664, June 14, 1665, Aug 8, 1672; *1673* Jan 1, Aug 9; Nov 10, 1674, Dec 6, 1683, Apr 6, 1712; *1754* July 17, Oct 31; *1766* Jan 28, Aug 11; Oct 30, 1768, Jan 18, 1770, Apr 22, 1774; *1776* Sept 15, Sept 21; Nov 25, 1783, Oct 5, 1784, Jan 11, 1785, Apr 16, 1787; *1788* Sept 13, Oct 2; *1789* Mar 4, Apr 23, May 7, May 12; July 3, 1819, Feb 7, 1827, Apr 18, 1831; *1832* June 27, Oct 29; Sept 3, 1833; *1835* May 6, Dec 16; Apr 10, 1841; *1842* Oct 14, Dec 7; Jan 31, 1843, July 19, 1845, May 10, 1849, Sept 18, 1851, July 14, 1853, Apr 4, 1859, July 13, 1863, Apr 13, 1870; *1871* Jan 2, July 12; Jan 13, 1874, Dec 4, 1875, Oct 15, 1878, May 25, 1879; *1880* Mar 30, July 20; Sept 5, 1882; *1883* May 24, Dec 27, 1892, Jan 30, 1894, Apr 27, 1897, Jan 1, 1898; *1901* Mar 12, May 30; *1904* June 15, Oct 27; *1908* Jan 9, Jan 21; *1910* Aug 9, Oct

5; *1911* May 23, May 25; Sept 16, 1920, May 23, 1922; *1931* May 1, Oct 24; July 11, 1936, May 10, 1939, Jan 11, 1940, Feb 9, 1942, July 28, 1945, July 31, 1948, Oct 24, 1949, Dec 3, 1959, Nov 21, 1964, Nov 9, 1965; *1966* Jan 1, Apr 16, Sept 16; Dec 23, 1970, Nov 26, 1975, July 13, 1977, Nov 5, 1982, May 24, 1983, Dec 22, 1984
New York State .... Apr 17, 1524, Sept 13, 1609, Oct 11, 1614, Nov 3, 1623, Mar 30, 1624, June 7, 1629, Feb 25, 1643, Sept 19, 1650, Apr 10, 1664, Feb 23, 1665, July 21, 1667, Feb 19, 1674, Oct 30, 1683, May 31, 1689, Feb 9, 1690, Mar 30, 1691, May 1, 1691, Nov 8, 1725, Aug 9, 1757, Sept 21, 1776, Apr 20, 1777, Nov 1, 1778, July 19, 1782, May 1, 1784, Oct 27, 1787, July 26, 1788, Mar 29, 1799; *1817* Mar 31, Apr 15; Nov 10, 1821, July 4, 1827, Apr 26, 1831, Nov 18, 1847, Apr 9, 1855, Jan 1, 1860, Apr 27, 1865, Apr 16, 1867, Nov 2, 1869, Jan 23, 1881, Nov 15, 1896, Feb 25, 1907, Nov 6, 1917, June 12, 1939, Aug 18, 1969, Sept 13, 1971
New York Stock Exchange (*see also* Economy) .... May 17, 1792, Mar 8, 1817, Sept 11, 1986
New Zealand .... Sept 1, 1951, Feb 4, 1985
Newark, N.J. .... July 12, 1967
Newberry, Walter L. .... Sept 18, 1804
Newcomb, Simon .... Mar 12, 1835
Newhart, Bob .... Sept 5, 1929
Newhouse, Samuel I. .... May 24, 1895
Newman, Larry .... Aug 17, 1978, Nov 12, 1981
Newman, Paul .... Jan 26, 1925
Newport, Christopher .... Apr 26, 1607, Jan 2, 1608
Newspapers/Magazines .... Sept 25, 1690, Apr 24, 1704, Dec 21, 1719, Dec 22, 1719, Nov 8, 1725, Sept 19, 1727, Jan 8, 1732, Sept 27, 1732, Nov 5, 1733, Aug 6, 1736, Feb 13, 1741, Apr 12, 1755, Oct 7, 1756, Apr 17, 1763, Dec 5, 1777, Dec 14, 1780, Feb 12, 1781, Sept 21, 1784, Jan 1, 1785, July 29, 1786, Apr 11, 1787, Aug 11, 1787, Feb 12, 1789, Apr 15, 1789, Oct 31, 1791, Nov 5, 1791, Nov 9, 1793, Oct 31, 1800, July 31, 1804, Mar 25, 1805, July 12, 1808, May 23, 1811, July 25, 1817, Aug 14, 1819, Nov 20, 1819, Mar 16, 1827, Jan 1, 1831, Oct 29, 1832; *1833* Jan 1, Sept 3, Dec 11; Feb 14, 1834, May 6, 1835, Sept 15, 1835, May 11, 1836, Mar 25, 1837, May 17, 1837, Apr 10, 1841, Jan 1, 1842, Feb 13, 1844, Sept 26, 1844, Feb 5, 1846, Aug 15, 1846, Sept 4, 1847, Apr 28, 1849, June 15, 1850, Sept 18, 1851, Sept 11, 1852, Nov 15, 1854, Sept 18, 1858, Dec 18, 1858, Mar 3, 1859, Apr 23, 1859, June 1, 1863, June 24, 1863, July 7, 1864, Aug 27, 1864, Sept 19, 1867, June 16, 1868, July 8, 1868, Mar 30, 1880, May 15, 1905, Oct 1, 1910, Mar 15, 1913, Dec 12, 1913, Feb 8, 1918, Mar 3, 1923, Feb 4, 1928, June 17, 1942, Jan 25, 1961, June 13, 1971, Apr 21, 1986, Jan 13, 1988
Newton, John .... Aug 24, 1823
Niagara Falls .... June 30, 1859, Nov 15, 1896, May 25, 1905, Jan 11, 1909, Jan 2, 1929, Jan 27, 1938, Nov 1, 1941, Feb 27, 1950, May 21, 1980, Sept 27, 1988
Nicaragua (*see also* Latin America) .... *1986* June 26, Aug 13, Oct 5, Nov 25; Mar 31, 1988, Apr 1, 1988
Nichols, George W. .... June 21, 1831
Nichols, Kid (Charles A.) .... Sept 14, 1869
Nichols, Mike .... Nov 6, 1931
Nicholls, Francis R.T. .... Aug 20, 1834
Nicholson, Sir Francis .... Nov 12, 1655
Nicholson, Jack .... Apr 22, 1937
Nicklaus, Jack .... Jan 21, 1940
Nicolay, John G. .... Feb 26, 1832
Nicolet, Jean .... Nov 1, 1642
Nicolls, Richard .... Feb 23, 1665, May 28, 1672
Niebuhr, Reinhold .... June 21, 1892
Niehaus, Charles H. .... Jan 24, 1855
Niekro, Phil(ip H.) .... Apr 1, 1939
Nielsen, Arthur C. .... Sept 5, 1897
Nieman, Lucius W. .... Dec 13, 1857
Nieuwland, Julius A. .... Feb 14, 1878
Niles, Hezekiah .... Oct 10, 1777
Niles, Nat .... July 11, 1932
Nimitz, Chester W. .... Feb 24, 1885, Dec 17, 1941, Nov 20, 1945
Nirenberg, Marshall W. .... Apr 10, 1927
Nixon, John .... Dec 31, 1808
Nixon, Lewis .... Apr 17, 1861
Nixon, Pat (Thelma C.) .... Mar 16, 1912, June 21, 1940
Nixon, Richard M. .... Jan 9, 1913, June 21, 1940, Dec 30, 1969, June 22, 1970, Oct 7, 1970; *1971* Mar 4, June 10, June 12, July 5; *1972* Jan 5, Feb 7, Feb 21, Apr 3, May 22, Oct 30; Dec 18; *1973* Jan 15, Apr 17, Oct 14, Oct 30; *1974* Jan 2, Jan 4, Jan 6, May 9, June 10, July 3, July 24, July 27, July 30, Aug 9, Aug 20, Sept 8, Oct 29; July 8, 1976
Noble, John W. .... Oct 26, 1831
Noel, Cleo A. Jr. .... Mar 2, 1973
Nofziger, Lyn .... Feb 11, 1988
Noguchi, Hideyo .... Nov 24, 1876
Noguchi, Isamo .... Nov 17, 1904
Noll, Chuck .... Jan 5, 1931
Noll, John F. .... Jan 25, 1875
Norden, Carl L. .... Apr 23, 1880
Nordeen, William E. .... June 28, 1988
Nordhoff, Charles B. .... Feb 1, 1887
Nordica, Lillian .... May 12, 1859
Norfolk, Va. .... Jan 1, 1776, Apr 15, 1964
Noriega, Manuel .... *1988* Feb 5, Mar 19, May 25; Dec 20, 1989
Norris, Frank .... Mar 5, 1870
Norris, George W. .... July 11, 1861
Norris, Kathleen .... July 16, 1880
North, Elisha .... Jan 8, 1771
North, Oliver L. .... Mar 16, 1988, Mar 18, 1988; Dec 1, 1988, Dec 30, 1988
North Atlantic Treaty Organization (NATO) .... Apr 3, 1949, Aug 24, 1949
North Carolina .... *1584* Mar 25, Apr 27, July 4; Apr 9, 1585, July 22, 1585, June 10, 1586, Aug 18, 1587, Aug 17, 1594, Dec 3, 1677, Jan 12, 1682, Sept 22, 1711, Jan 28, 1712, May 9, 1712, July 25, 1729, Sept 18, 1765, May 31, 1775, Apr 12, 1776, Dec 18, 1776, Nov 21, 1789, May 20, 1861, Oct 7, 1865, Apr 23, 1868, Oct 12, 1876, Jan 31, 1908, Feb 1, 1960
North Dakota .... Mar 2, 1861, July 7, 1864, Feb 23, 1882, July 4, 1889, Oct 1, 1889, Nov 2, 1889, Jan 23, 1917
Northrop, John H. .... July 5, 1891
Northrop, John K. .... Nov 10, 1895
Norton, John .... May 6, 1606
Norworth, Jack .... Jan 5, 1879

Nott, Eliphant .... June 25, 1773
Nourse, Edwin G. .... May 20, 1883
Noyce, Robert .... Dec 12, 1927
Noyes, Crosby S. .... Feb 16, 1825
Noyes, Harry A. .... July 7, 1890
Noyes, John H. .... Sept 3, 1811
Noyes, LaVerne .... Jan 7, 1849
Nuclear Energy *see* Atomic Energy
Nuclear Regulatory
  Commission .... Jan 19, 1975
Nuclear war .... Apr 29, 1986
Nuclear weapons *see* Atomic energy
Nuttall, Thomas .... Jan 15, 1786
Nye, Bill (Edgar W.) .... Aug 25, 1850
Nye, James W. .... June 10, 1814

Oakley, Annie .... Aug 13, 1860
Oates, Joyce Carol .... June 16, 1938
Obata, Gyo .... Feb 28, 1923
Oberlin College .... Dec 3, 1833
Oberon, Merle .... Feb 19, 1911
O'Boyle, Patrick A. .... July 18, 1896
O'Brien, Edward J.H. .... Dec 10, 1890
O'Brien, Lawrence F. .... July 7, 1917
O'Brien, Pat .... Nov 11, 1899
Occupational Safety &
  Health Act .... Dec 29, 1970
Ochoa, Severo .... Sept 24, 1905
Ochs, Adolph S. .... Mar 12, 1858
O'Connell, Helen .... May 23, 1920
O'Connell, William H. .... Dec 8, 1859
O'Connor, Carroll .... Aug 2, 1924
O'Connor, Edwin G. .... July 29, 1918
O'Connor, Sandra Day .... Mar 26, 1930, Sept 21, 1981
O'Conor, Charles .... Jan 22, 1804
Odets, Clifford .... July 18, 1906
O'Donnell, Rosey
  (Emmett) .... Sept 15, 1906
O'Dwyer, Joseph .... Oct 12, 1841
Office of Censorship .... Dec 19, 1941
Office of Civilian Defense .... May 20, 1941, Jan 18, 1942
Office of Defense
  Transportation .... Dec 18, 1941
Office of Economic
  Opportunity .... Aug 11, 1964
Office of Economic
  Stabilization .... Oct 2, 1942
Office of Emergency
  Management .... May 25, 1940
Office of Lend Lease
  Administration .... Oct 28, 1941
Office of Management
  and Budget .... June 10, 1921, July 1, 1970
Office of Personnel Management *see* Civil Service
Office of Price
  Administration .... Apr 11, 1941, Jan 30, 1942
Office of Production
  Management .... Jan 7, 1941
Office of Scientific Research
  and Development .... Jan 28, 1941
Office of Strategic
  Services .... June 13, 1943
Office of War
  Information .... June 13, 1942
Office of War
  Mobilization .... May 27, 1943
Ogden, Rollo .... Jan 19, 1856
Ogden, William B. .... June 15, 1805, Mar 4, 1837
Oglesby, Richard J. .... July 25, 1824
Oglethorpe, James E. .... Dec 22, 1696, June 20, 1732, Jan 13, 1733, Feb 12, 1733, July 7, 1742
O'Hair, Madalyn .... Apr 13, 1919
O'Hara, John F. .... May 1, 1888
O'Hara, John H. .... Jan 31, 1905
O. Henry .... Sept 11, 1862
Ohio .... May 19, 1749, Jan 21, 1785, Apr 7, 1788, Sept 22, 1788, Nov 9, 1793, July 22, 1796, Nov 29, 1802, Mar 1, 1803, Mar 10, 1851, Dec 3, 1883, Mar 4, 1908, Sept 3, 1912, Jan 1, 1914, Feb 21, 1917, Nov 6, 1917, May 15, 1929, May 24, 1935, Sept 11, 1951
Oil *see* Petroleum
O'Keeffe, Georgia .... Nov 15, 1887
Oklahoma .... Sept 26, 1844, Apr 22, 1889, May 2, 1890, Dec 19, 1890, Sept 16, 1893; *1907* Mar 15, Sept 17, Nov 16; June 1, 1921
Olcott, Chauncey .... July 21, 1860
Olcott, Henry S. .... Aug 2, 1832
Oldenburg, Claes .... Jan 28, 1929
Oldfield, Barney .... Jan 29, 1878, June 15, 1903
Olds, Irving S. .... Jan 22, 1887
Olds, Ransom E. .... June 3, 1964
Oliphant, Pat(rick) .... June 24, 1935
Oliver, Andrew .... Mar 28, 1706, Aug 15, 1765
Oliver, James .... Aug 28, 1823
Oliver, King (Joseph) .... May 11, 1885
Olmsted, Frederick Law .... Apr 26, 1822
Olney, Richard .... Sept 15, 1835
Olympic Games .... *1932* Feb 4, July 30; *1980* Jan 24, Feb 12, Apr 12; July 28, 1984
O'Malley, Walter F. .... Oct 9, 1903
Onassis, Jacqueline
  Kennedy .... July 28, 1929, Sept 12, 1953
Onate, Juan de .... Sept 21, 1595, Apr 26, 1598
O'Neill, Eugene .... Oct 16, 1888
O'Neill, Rose C. .... June 25, 1874
O'Neill, Thomas P. (Tip) .... Dec 9, 1912
Onsager, Lars .... Nov 27, 1903
Opel, John R. .... Jan 5, 1925
Opera .... June 4, 1845
Oppenheimer, J. Robert .... Apr 22, 1904
Opper, Frederic B. .... Jan 2, 1857
Optic, Oliver *see* Adams, William T.
Ord, Edward O.C. .... Oct 18, 1818
Oregon .... Mar 1, 1543, May 11, 1791, Apr 12, 1811, Aug 9, 1818, Dec 1, 1834, May 22, 1843, July 5, 1843, Dec 1, 1845; *1846* Feb 5, Apr 27, June 15; Aug 14, 1848, Nov 9, 1857, Feb 14, 1859, Oct 18, 1876, May 17, 1884, Feb 19, 1887, June 6, 1904, Feb 18, 1915
Organization of
  American States .... Apr 30, 1948
Organization for
  Economic Cooperation
  & Development .... Mar 16, 1961

Ormandy, Eugene .... Nov 18, 1899
O'Rourke, Jim (James H.) ... Aug 24, 1852
Orr, Bobby .... Mar 20, 1948
Orr, James L. .... May 12, 1822
Ory, Kid (Edward) .... Dec 25, 1886
Osborn, Henry Fairfield .... Aug 8, 1857
Osborne, Thomas B.............. Aug 5, 1859
Osgood, Samuel..................... Feb 3, 1748, Sept 16, 1789
Ostenso, Martha .... Sept 17, 1900
Oswald, Lee Harvey............. Nov 22, 1963, Nov 24, 1963, Sept 27, 1964
Otis, Elisha G....................... Aug 3, 1811, Sept 20, 1853
Otis, Elwell S. .... Mar 25, 1838
Otis, Harrison G.................. Feb 10, 1837
Otis, James .... Feb 5, 1725, July 23, 1764, June 8, 1765, Nov 2, 1772
Ott, Mel .... Mar 2, 1909
Otterbein, Philip William .... June 3, 1726
Ouimet, Francis .... May 8, 1893
Outcault, Richard F. .... Jan 14, 1863
Ovington, Earle .... Dec 20, 1879
Owen, Robert .... Jan 3, 1825
Owens, Jesse (James C.) ...... Sept 12, 1913
Owens, Michael J. .... Jan 1, 1859
Owens, Robert B. .... Oct 29, 1870
Oxnam, G. Bromley .... Aug 14, 1891

Paar, Jack .... May 1, 1918
Paca, William .... Oct 31, 1740
Packaging .... Nov 4, 1982
Packard, James W. .... Nov 5, 1863
Packard, Vance O. .... May 22, 1914
Packer, Asa .... Dec 29, 1805
Page, Charles G. .... Jan 25, 1812
Page, John .... Apr 17, 1743
Page, Walter Hines .... Aug 15, 1855
Paige, Satchel (Leroy R.) ...... July 7, 1906
Paine, John K........................ Jan 9, 1839
Paine, Robert T. .... Mar 11, 1731
Paine, Thomas....................... Jan 29, 1737, Jan 10, 1776, Dec 19, 1776, Nov 4, 1794
Paine, Willis S....................... Jan 1, 1848
Pakistan .... Jan 6, 1974, Nov 21, 1979, Jan 12, 1980, Aug 17, 1988
Palade, George E................... Nov 19, 1912
Palestine Liberation Organization .... Dec 14, 1988, Dec 16, 1988
Paley, William S.................... Sept 28, 1901, Sept 8, 1982
Palma de Cessnola, Luigi *see* Cessnola, Luigi Palma de
Palmer, Alexander M. .... May 4, 1872, May 16, 1918
Palmer, Alice F...................... Feb 21, 1855
Palmer, Arnold .... Sept 10, 1929
Palmer, Charles S. .... Aug 4, 1858
Palmer, Daniel D. .... Mar 7, 1845
Palmer, Jim .... Oct 15, 1945
Palmer, John M..................... Sept 13, 1817
Palmer, Nathaniel B. .... Aug 8, 1799, Nov 18, 1820
Palmer, Potter .... May 20, 1826
Panama Canal/Zone .... Dec 12, 1846, Apr 19, 1850, Feb 5, 1900, Nov 18, 1901, Jan 20, 1902; *1903* Jan 22, Nov 6, Nov 18; Feb 26, 1905, June 29, 1906, Feb 26, 1907, Aug 24, 1912; *1914* Jan 7, Jan 27, Aug 15, Sept 2; Jan 23, 1955, Jan 9, 1964, Dec 18, 1964, Aug 10, 1977; *1978* Mar 16, Apr 18, June 16; Oct 1, 1979; Dec 20, 1989
Papanicolau, George N. .... May 13, 1883
Papp, Joseph .... June 22, 1921
Park, Maud............................ Jan 25, 1871
Park, Robert E. .... Feb 14, 1864
Park, William H. .... Dec 30, 1863
Parke, John G. .... Sept 22, 1827
Parker, Alton B. .... May 14, 1852
Parker, Bonnie .... May 23, 1934
Parker, Charlie .... Aug 29, 1920
Parker, Dorothy .... Aug 22, 1893
Parker, Francis W. .... Oct 9, 1837
Parker, George H. .... Dec 23, 1864
Parker, Isaac .... June 17, 1678
Parker, John .... July 13, 1729, Apr 19, 1775
Parker, Robert L. *see* Cassidy, Butch
Parker, Theodore .... Aug 24, 1810
Parkhurst, Charles H. .... Apr 17, 1842
Parking meters .... July 16, 1935
Parkinson, Thomas I. .... Nov 27, 1881
Parkman, Francis .... Sept 16, 1823
Parks, Rosa .... Dec 1, 1955
Parley, Peter *see* Goodrich, Samuel G.
Parran, Thomas Jr................ Sept 28, 1892
Parris, Samuel .... Feb 27, 1720
Parrish, Anne .... Oct 17, 1760
Parrish, Maxfield F............... July 25, 1870
Parrott, Robert P. .... Oct 5, 1804
Parsons, Louella .... Aug 6, 1893
Parsons, Samuel H. .... May 14, 1737
Parsons, Theophilus .... Feb 24, 1750
Parsons, William B. .... Apr 15, 1859
Parton, Dolly .... Jan 19, 1946
Partridge, Alden .... Feb 12, 1785
Pastor, Tony (Antonio).......... May 28, 1837
Pastorius, Francis D. .... Sept 26, 1651
Patch, Alexander M. .... Nov 23, 1889
Pate, Maurice .... Oct 14, 1894
Patents/Patent Office .... Apr 10, 1790, June 16, 1980
Paterson, John .... July 19, 1808
Paterson, William .... Dec 24, 1745, June 15, 1787
Patrick, Mason M.................. Dec 13, 1863
Patrick, Ted (Edwin H.)........ Sept 3, 1901
Patten, Gilbert .... Oct 25, 1866
Patterson, Alicia .... Oct 15, 1906
Patterson, Eleanor M. (Cissie) .... Nov 7, 1884
Patterson, John H................. Dec 13, 1844
Patterson, Joseph M. .... Jan 6, 1879
Patterson, William A. .... Oct 1, 1899
Patton, George S. .... Nov 11, 1885
Paul, Alice .... Jan 11, 1885
Paul, Les .... June 9, 1916
Paulding, James K. .... Aug 22, 1778
Pauley, Jane .... Oct 31, 1950
Pauli, Wolfgang .... Apr 25, 1900
Pauling, Linus C. .... Feb 28, 1901
Pavarotti, Luciano .... Oct 12, 1935
Payne, John Howard .... June 9, 1791
Payton, Walter .... July 25, 1954
Peabody, Elizabeth P. .... May 16, 1804

Peabody, George .... Feb 18, 1795
Peabody, George F. .... July 27, 1852
Peace Corps. .... Mar 1, 1961
Peale, Charles Willson .... Apr 15, 1741
Peale, Norman Vincent .... May 31, 1898
Peale, Rembrandt .... Feb 22, 1778
Pearl, Minnie .... Oct 25, 1912
Pearl, Raymond .... June 3, 1879
Pearson, Drew .... Dec 12, 1897
Peary, Robert E. .... May 6, 1856, Apr 6, 1909
Pease, Dr. Daniel .... Jan 7, 1949
Pease, Francis G. .... Jan 14, 1881
Peattie, Donald Culrose .... June 21, 1898
Peck, George W. .... Sept 28, 1840
Peck, Gregory .... Apr 5, 1916
Peck, James H. .... Apr 26, 1830
Peckham, Rufus W. .... Nov 8, 1838
Pecora, Ferdinand .... Jan 6, 1882
Peerce, Jan .... June 3, 1904
Pegler, Westbrook .... Aug 2, 1894
Pegram, George B. .... Jan 25, 1939
Pei, I(eoh) M. .... Apr 26, 1917
Peirce, Benjamin .... Apr 4, 1809
Peirce, C(harles) S. .... Sept 10, 1839
Peirce, John .... Feb 20, 1620
Pelz, Paul J. .... Nov 18, 1841
Pemberton, Brock .... Dec 14, 1885
Pemberton, John C. .... Aug 10, 1814
Pendleton, Edmund .... Sept 9, 1721
Pendleton, George H. .... July 29, 1825
Penn, John .... May 17, 1741
Penn, William .... Oct 14, 1644, Mar 4, 1681, Feb 1, 1682, May 5, 1682, Nov 8, 1701
Penney, James C. .... Sept 16, 1875
Pennington, William .... May 5, 1796
Pennock, Herb(ert) .... Feb 10, 1894
Pennsylvania .... Mar 4, 1681, July 11, 1681, May 5, 1682, Dec 4, 1682, Apr 2, 1683, Nov 8, 1701, June 7, 1712, Dec 22, 1719, Jan 7, 1751, July 13, 1753, June 20, 1774, Sept 28, 1776, Mar 1, 1780, Jan 1, 1784, Sept 21, 1784, July 29, 1786, Dec 12, 1787, Mar 24, 1828, Jan 3, 1831, Jan 1, 1855, Feb 22, 1855, Aug 27, 1859, May 31, 1889, July 6, 1892, Oct 13, 1892, Dec 19, 1907, Jan 13, 1908, Apr 9, 1917
Pennzoil Co. .... Dec 9, 1987
Penrose, Boies .... Nov 1, 1860
Pensions .... Sept 2, 1974
Pensions, presidential .... June 30, 1841, July 14, 1870, Mar 31, 1882, July 27, 1882, Aug 25, 1958, Jan 8, 1971
Pensions, soldiers *see* Veterans
Pentagon Papers .... June 13, 1971, May 11, 1973
Penzias, Arno A. .... Apr 26, 1933
Peoples Temple .... Nov 18, 1978
Pepper, William .... Aug 21, 1843
Pepperell, Sir William .... June 27, 1696, June 17, 1745
Percy, Charles H. .... Sept 27, 1919
Pereira, William L. .... Apr 25, 1909
Perelman, S(idney) J. .... Feb 1, 1904
Perkins, Frances .... Apr 10, 1882, Mar 3, 1933
Perkins, George W. .... Jan 31, 1862
Perkins, Jacob .... July 9, 1766
Perkins, Marlin .... Mar 28, 1905
Perkins, Maxwell E. .... Sept 20, 1884
Perlman, Itzhak .... Aug 31, 1945
Permanent Court of International Justice .... Jan 27, 1926
Perry, Gaylord .... Sept 15, 1938
Perry, Matthew C. .... Apr 10, 1794, July 14, 1853, Mar 31, 1854
Perry, Oliver Hazard .... Aug 20, 1785, Sept 10, 1813
Perry, Stuart .... May 25, 1844
Pershing, John J. .... Sept 13, 1860, Mar 10, 1916, Mar 15, 1916, May 10, 1917, May 26, 1917, Sept 10, 1919, July 1, 1921
Persian Gulf .... *1987* May 17, July 21; *1988* Apr 29, July 3
Peters, Roberta .... May 4, 1930
Peterson, Henry .... Dec 7, 1818
Peterson, Roger T. .... Aug 28, 1908
Petroleum .... Jan 1, 1855, Aug 27, 1859, Jan 10, 1870, Jan 10, 1901, Dec 1, 1913, Apr 7, 1922, Apr 2, 1927, Sept 30, 1930, May 22, 1953, Oct 19, 1973, Mar 18, 1974, Mar 9, 1975; *1977* Jan 24, July 28; Apr 2, 1980, Aug 23, 1982
Pettigrew, James J. .... July 4, 1828
Pettigrew, Richard F. .... July 23, 1848
Pettit, Bob .... Dec 2, 1932
Petty, Richard .... July 2, 1937
Pew, Joseph N. Jr. .... Nov 12, 1886
Phelps, Anson G. .... Mar 24, 1781
Phelps, William Lyon .... Jan 2, 1865
Phi Beta Kappa .... Dec 5, 1776
Philadelphia .... Nov 8, 1731; *1732* Feb 26, Oct 1; Aug 13, 1751, July 13, 1753, Jan 11, 1759, May 3, 1765, June 20, 1774, July 8, 1776; *1777* Mar 4, Sept 18, Sept 26; June 18, 1778, Jan 7, 1782, July 16, 1790, Aug 1, 1793, Aug 1, 1794, June 15, 1800, Jan 7, 1817, May 25, 1837, June 4, 1845; *1876* Jan 1, May 10; Sept 15, 1887, June 9, 1902, May 10, 1908, May 31, 1926, Aug 28, 1964, Aug 14, 1969, July 21, 1976, May 13, 1985, Mar 6, 1986, May 3, 1988
Philippine Islands .... Aug 13, 1898, Feb 4, 1899, Feb 6, 1900, Mar 23, 1901, July 4, 1901, July 1, 1902, July 3, 1902, July 30, 1907, Aug 29, 1916, Jan 13, 1933, Mar 31, 1934, Mar 24, 1935, Nov 15, 1935, July 26, 1941; *1942* Jan 2, Jan 7, Apr 9, Apr 10, May 6; *1945* Jan 9, Mar 10, July 5; July 4, 1946
Phillips, Frank .... Nov 28, 1873
Phillips, Lena M. .... Oct 15, 1881
Phillips, Thomas W. .... Feb 23, 1835
Phillips, Wendell .... Nov 29, 1811
Phips, Sir William .... Feb 2, 1651, May 11, 1690
Phyfe, Duncan .... Aug 16, 1854
Physick, Philip S. .... July 7, 1768
Piccard, Auguste .... Jan 28, 1884
Piccard, Jean .... Jan 28, 1884, Oct 23, 1934
Pickens, Andrew .... Sept 19, 1739
Pickens, T. Boone .... May 22, 1928
Pickering, Edward C. .... July 19, 1846
Pickering, John .... Mar 3, 1803
Pickering, Timothy .... July 17, 1745
Pickering, Timothy .... Aug 12, 1791
Pickering, William H. .... Feb 15, 1858
Pickett, George E. .... Jan 25, 1825

Pickford, Mary .... Apr 8, 1893
Pidgeon, Walter..................... Sept 23, 1897
Pierce, Franklin .... Nov 23, 1804, Nov 19, 1834, Feb 24, 1855, Oct 8, 1869
Pierce, Jane M.A. .... Mar 12, 1806, Nov 19, 1834, Dec 2, 1863
Pierce, John R. .... Mar 27, 1910
Pierpont, John .... Apr 6, 1785
Pierson, Abraham .... Mar 5, 1707
Pike, Zebulon M. .... Jan 5, 1779, Nov 13, 1806, Apr 27, 1813
Pilat, Ignaz A. .... June 27, 1820
Pilgrims .... Feb 2, 1619; *1620* July 22, Sept 16, Nov 21, Dec 11; *1621* Jan 21, Mar 22, May 12; Dec 17, 1623, Jan 13, 1630, Mar 29, 1630
Pillsbury, Charles A. .... Dec 3, 1842
Pillsbury, John E. .... Dec 15, 1846
Pincay, Lafitte .... Dec 19, 1946
Pinchot, Gifford .... Aug 11, 1865, Feb 1, 1905, May 13, 1908, June 8, 1908, Jan 11, 1909, Jan 7, 1910
Pinckney, Charles .... Oct 26, 1757
Pinckney, Charles C. .... Feb 25, 1746
Pinckney, Thomas .... Oct 23, 1750, Oct 27, 1795
Pincus, Gregory .... Apr 9, 1903
Pinkerton, Allan .... Aug 25, 1819
Pinkham, Lydia E. .... Feb 19, 1819
Pinkney, William .... Mar 17, 1764
Pinza, Ezio .... May 18, 1892
Piper, William T. .... Jan 8, 1881
Piston, Walter H. .... Jan 20, 1894
Pitcher, Molly *see* McCauley, Mary L.H.
Pitkin, Walter B. .... Feb 6, 1878
Pitman, Ben .... July 24, 1822
Pitney, Mahlon .... Feb 5, 1858
Pittman, Key .... Sept 19, 1872
Pittsburgh, Pa. .... July 29, 1786, Feb 28, 1787, Apr 10, 1845, May 6, 1858, Dec 1, 1913, Nov 2, 1920
Plank, Ed(ward S.) .... Aug 31, 1875
Platt, Charles A. .... Oct 16, 1861
Pleasanton, Alfred .... June 7, 1824
Pledge of allegiance .... Sept 8, 1892
Plotz, Harry .... Apr 17, 1890
Plymouth *see* Pilgrims
Pocahontas .... Dec 10, 1607, Apr 14, 1614
Poe, Edgar Allan .... Jan 19, 1809, Jan 29, 1845
Poe, Orlando M. .... Mar 7, 1832
Poindexter, John M. .... Mar 16, 1988, Dec 1, 1988
Poinsett, Joel R. .... Mar 2, 1779
Poitier, Sidney .... Feb 20, 1927
Poland .... Oct 9, 1982
Polar exploration .... Nov 18, 1820, Feb 7, 1821, Jan 19, 1840, Apr 6, 1909, Sept 1, 1909, May 9, 1926, Nov 29, 1929
Police .... Aug 12, 1658, Jan 13, 1874, Sept 9, 1919
Polish National Catholic Church .... Mar 14, 1897
Political parties .... May 12, 1789, Sept 26, 1831, May 21, 1832, Aug 26, 1835, Feb 3, 1836, Jan 19, 1840, May 29, 1844, May 22, 1848, Feb 28, 1854, July 6, 1854, June 17, 1856, Sept 12, 1869, Jan 15, 1870, June 21, 1894, Jan 27, 1900, Jan 21, 1911, June 22, 1912, July 17, 1948, Oct 14, 1949, Aug 24, 1954
Polk, James K. .... Nov 21, 1795, Jan 1, 1824, Dec 7, 1835, May 29, 1844, May 13, 1846, June 15, 1849
Polk, Leonidas .... Apr 10, 1806
Polk, Sarah C. .... Sept 4, 1903, Jan 1, 1824, Aug 14, 1891
Pollock, Channing .... Mar 4, 1880
Pollock, Jackson .... Jan 28, 1912
Pollution *see* Environment
Polygamy *see* Mormons
Pomerene, Atlee .... Dec 6, 1863
Ponce de Leon, Juan .... Mar 3, 1513, Apr 2, 1513, Sept 27, 1514
Pons, Lily .... Apr 12, 1904
Ponselle, Rosa .... Jan 22, 1897
Pontiac .... July 24, 1766
Pony Express *see* Mail
Ponzi, Charles .... Oct 1, 1920
Poole, William F. .... Dec 24, 1821
Poor, Henry V. .... Dec 8, 1812
Pope, Albert A. .... May 20, 1843
Pope, John .... Mar 16, 1822
Pope, John R. .... Apr 24, 1874
Porter, Cole .... June 9, 1893
Porter, David D. .... June 8, 1813
Porter, Edwin S. .... Apr 21, 1870
Porter, Gene Stratton .... Aug 17, 1868
Porter, James M. .... Jan 6, 1793
Porter, Katherine Anne .... May 15, 1890
Porter, Peter B. .... Aug 14, 1773, July 11, 1813
Porter, Sylvia .... June 18, 1913
Porter, William S. *see* O. Henry
Portman, John C. Jr. .... Dec 4, 1924
Portola, Gaspar de .... July 1, 1769, Aug 1, 1769
Portugal .... June 7, 1494
Posey, Thomas .... July 9, 1750
Post, Charles W. .... Oct 26, 1854
Post, Emily .... Oct 30, 1873
Post, George B. .... Dec 15, 1837
Post, Wiley .... Nov 22, 1900, June 23, 1931, July 15, 1933, Aug 15, 1935
Postage *see* Mail
Postmaster General/ Post Office Department ... July 26, 1775, Sept 22, 1789, Aug 12, 1791, May 8, 1795, Mar 9, 1829, June 8, 1872, Aug 12, 1970, July 1, 1971
Potter, Alonzo .... July 6, 1800
Potter, Edward C. .... Nov 26, 1857
Potter, Henry C. .... May 25, 1835
Potter, Horatio .... Feb 9, 1802
Potter, Robert B. .... July 16, 1829
Pound, Ezra .... Oct 30, 1885
Pound, Roscoe .... Oct 27, 1870
Powderly, Terence V. .... Jan 22, 1849
Powell, Adam Clayton Jr. ..... Nov 29, 1908, Mar 1, 1967
Powell, Dick .... Nov 14, 1904
Powell, John Wesley .... Mar 24, 1834, Aug 30, 1869
Powell, Lewis F. .... Sept 19, 1907, June 26, 1987
Powell, William .... July 29, 1892
Power, Frederick B. .... Mar 4, 1853
Power, Tyrone .... May 5, 1914

Powers, Francis Gary .... May 5, 1960, Aug 19, 1960
Powers, Hiram .... July 29, 1805
Pownall, Thomas .... Feb 25, 1805
Pratt, Charles .... Oct 2, 1830
Pratt, Francis A. .... Feb 15, 1827
Pratt, Richard H. .... Dec 6, 1840
Pratt, William V. .... Feb 28, 1869
Prelog, Vladimir .... July 23, 1906
Preminger, Otto L. .... Dec 5, 1906
Prendergast, Maurice B. .... Oct 10, 1861
Presbyterian Church .... Feb 5, 1723, Jan 15, 1841, May 28, 1958, June 10, 1983
Prescott, Samuel .... Aug 19, 1751, Apr 18, 1775
Prescott, Samuel C. .... Apr 5, 1872
Prescott, William .... Feb 20, 1726, July 17, 1775
Prescott, William H. .... May 4, 1796
Presidency .... *1789* Jan 7, Feb 4, May 7; Nov 26, 1791, Feb 21, 1792, Apr 15, 1792, July 10, 1795, Feb 17, 1801, June 15, 1804, Nov 9, 1824, Feb 9, 1825, Jan 30, 1835, Mar 3, 1845, Jan 29, 1877, Jan 19, 1886, June 23, 1906, Mar 4, 1909, Feb 1, 1913, Mar 15, 1913, May 27, 1929, Jan 23, 1933, Jan 20, 1937, May 1, 1937, July 18, 1947, Jan 19, 1949, Feb 27, 1951, Jan 19, 1955, Jan 25, 1961, Aug 30, 1963, Feb 10, 1967, Jan 17, 1969, Jan 8, 1971, Dec 13, 1979
Presley, Elvis .... Jan 8, 1935
Preston, Robert .... June 8, 1918
Previn, Andre .... Apr 6, 1929
Price, Byron .... Mar 25, 1891, Dec 19, 1941
Price, George .... June 9, 1901
Price, Leontyne .... Feb 10, 1927
Price, Sterling .... Sept 20, 1809
Price control .... Jan 8, 1777, Aug 21, 1917, Apr 11, 1941, Jan 30, 1942, Oct 16, 1946, Jan 24, 1977
Prince, Harold S. .... Jan 30, 1928
Princeton University .... Oct 22, 1746
Pritchett, Henry S. .... Apr 16, 1857
Pritzker, Abram N. .... Jan 6, 1896
Procter, William C. .... Aug 25, 1862
Prohibition .... Apr 17, 1838, Nov 23, 1852, Jan 22, 1854; *1855* Jan 22, Feb 3, Mar 16, Apr 9, July 14; Sept 12, 1869, Dec 24, 1873, Nov 18, 1874, Dec 12, 1876, Feb 19, 1881, Mar 4, 1884, Oct 1, 1889, May 24, 1893, Dec 18, 1895, Sept 17, 1907; *1908* Jan 1, Jan 31, Feb 19; Jan 21, 1909, July 22, 1911; *1914* Mar 1, July 1, Sept 22; *1915* Jan 1, Feb 6, Feb 18, Mar 1, Mar 3, July 1, Sept 14; Aug 1, 1916; *1917* Feb 9, Feb 15, Apr 21; *1918* Mar 22, Dec 16, Dec 31; *1919* Jan 29, Oct 27, Oct 28; Jan 16, 1919; *1920* Jan 5, Jan 16, June 7; Mar 22 1933, Dec 5, 1933
Protestant churches .... Nov 30, 1984
Proxmire, William .... Nov 4, 1988
Prudden, T. Mitchell .... July 7, 1849
Pryor, Arthur .... Sept 22, 1870
PTL (Praise the Lord) ministry .... June 12, 1987, Sept 2, 1988, Dec 5, 1988
Public Credit/Public Credit Act .... Jan 14, 1790, Mar 18, 1869
Public Health Service .... July 16, 1798
Public land .... Oct 10, 1780, May 10, 1800, Apr 25, 1812, Apr 24, 1820, July 11, 1836, May 20, 1862, July 2, 1862, Jan 1, 1863, Mar 3, 1877, Mar 3, 1891, June 17, 1902, May 22, 1953, Oct 21, 1976
Public Works Administration .... June 16, 1933, Apr 3, 1935
Puerto Rico .... Nov 19, 1493, July 25, 1898, Apr 12, 1900, Aug 8, 1900, Mar 2, 1917, Aug 4, 1947, Jan 2, 1949, July 25, 1952, Mar 1, 1954
Pulaski, Kazmierz (Casimir) .... Mar 4, 1747, Oct 11, 1779
Pulitzer, Joseph .... Apr 10, 1847, Aug 17, 1903
Pulitzer, Joseph .... Mar 21, 1885
Pulitzer, Ralph .... June 11, 1879
Pullman, George M. .... Mar 3, 1831
Pupin, Michael I. .... Oct 4, 1858
Purcell, Edward M. .... Aug 30, 1912
Pure Food & Drug Act .... June 30, 1906
Puritans *see* Pilgrims
Purnell, Benjamin .... Mar 27, 1861
Putnam, George H. .... Apr 2, 1844
Putnam, George P. .... Feb 7, 1814
Putnam, Herbert .... Sept 20, 1861
Putnam, Israel .... Jan 7, 1718
Putnam, Rufus .... Apr 9, 1738, Apr 7, 1788
Puzo, Mario .... Oct 15, 1920
Pyle, Ernie .... Aug 3, 1900, Apr 18, 1945
Pyle, Howard .... Mar 5, 1853

Quakers .... Oct 14, 1644, Sept 17, 1656, Oct 2, 1656, Oct 27, 1659, Mar 23, 1662, May 11, 1682
Quantrill, William C. .... Aug 21, 1863
Quayle, Daniel .... Feb 4, 1947
Queen, Ellery *see* Lee, Manfred and Dannay, Frederick
Queen, Richard .... July 12, 1980
Queen Anne War .... May 15, 1702, Apr 11, 1713
Queeny, John F. .... Aug 17, 1859
Quezon, Manuel L. .... Aug 19, 1878, Nov 15, 1935
Quimby, Harriet .... Aug 2, 1911
Quincy, Josiah .... Feb 23, 1744
Quinlan, Karen Ann .... June 11, 1985
Quinn, Anthony .... Apr 21, 1915

Rabi, Isidor I. .... July 29, 1898
Rachford, Benjamin K. .... Nov 28, 1857
Rachmaninoff, Sergei W. .... Apr 2, 1873
Racketeering .... Aug 26, 1988
Radbourn, Charles G. .... Dec 11, 1854
Radford, Arthur W. .... Feb 27, 1896
Radio .... Dec 24, 1906, Nov 2, 1920, June 12, 1922, June 21, 1923, Nov 25, 1926, Feb 23, 1927, Apr 29, 1932, June 19, 1934, Oct 30, 1938, Jan 5, 1940, Nov 7, 1967, Mar 18, 1985, Feb 3, 1988
Railroads .... *1826* Apr 17, Oct 7; Feb 28, 1827; *1828* May 24, July 4; Aug 9, 1829; *1830* Jan 7, Aug 28, Dec 25; Apr 13, 1846, Oct 8, 1851, Sept1, 1854, Apr 21, 1855, *1856* Jan 5, Sept21; July 1, 1862; *1869* May 10, June 15; Nov 18, 1883, Jan 5, 1886, Aug 10, 1887, Jan 5, 1893, May 11, 1894, Aug 7, 1904, Dec 2, 1912, Sept2, 1916, Dec 26, 1917, Jan 1, 1918, Mar 21, 1918; *1920* Feb 28, Mar 1; June 16, 1933, June 27, 1934, Aug 29, 1935; *1943* Sept 6, Dec 16, Dec 27; Apr 25, 1946, May 17, 1946, Aug 27, 1950; *1951* Feb 6, Sept11; May 1, 1971, Sept 13, 1982, Jan 5, 1987, Feb 11, 1988

Rainey, Henry T. .... Aug 20, 1860
Rainey, Joseph H. .... June 21, 1832
Rainwater, L. James .... Dec 9, 1917
Raleigh, Sir Walter .... *1584* Mar 25, Apr 27, July 4; Apr 9, 1585
Ramo, Simon .... May 7, 1913
Ramsey, Alexander .... Sept 8, 1815
Rand, Ayn .... Feb 2, 1905
Rand, James H. .... May 29, 1859
Rand, Sally .... Jan 2, 1904
Randall, Samuel J. .... Oct 10, 1828
Randall, Tony .... Feb 26, 1920
Randolph, A. Philip .... Apr 15, 1889
Randolph, Edmund J. .... Aug 10, 1753, May 29, 1787; *1789* July 24, Sept 26
Randolph, Edward .... Sept 20, 1676
Randolph, George W. .... Mar 10, 1818
Randolph, James Madison .... Jan 17, 1806
Randolph, John .... June 2, 1773, Apr 5, 1826
Randolph, Peyton .... Sept 9, 1774, Oct 22, 1775
Randolph, William .... Apr 11, 1711
Rank, Otto .... Apr 22, 1884
Rankin, Jeannette .... Jan 11, 1880, Dec 8, 1941
Ransom, John Crowe .... Apr 30, 1888
Raphel, Arnold L. .... *1988* Aug 17, Oct 11
Rapp, (Johann) George .... Nov 1, 1757
Rather, Dan(iel) .... Oct 31, 1931
Rationing .... *1918* Jan 26, July 1; Dec 27, 1941; *1942* May 5, May 15, Nov 28, Dec 1; Mar 1, 1943, Apr 1, 1943; *1945* Aug 15, Nov 23; June 11, 1947
Rauschenburg, Robert .... Oct 22, 1925
Rauschenbusch, Walter .... Oct 4, 1861
Rawlings, Marjorie Kinnan .... Aug 8, 1896
Rawls, Betsy .... May 4, 1928
Ray, Man .... Aug 27, 1890
Rayburn, Sam T. .... Jan 6, 1882
Raymond, Alex(ander G.) ..... Oct 2, 1909
Raymond, Henry J. .... Jan 24, 1820, Sept 18, 1851
Raymond, John H. .... Mar 7, 1814
RCA Corp. .... Dec 11, 1985
Rea, Samuel .... Sept 21, 1855
Read, George .... Sept 18, 1733
Read, Nathan .... July 2, 1759
Read, Opie .... Dec 22, 1852
Reagan, Nancy D. .... July 6, 1921, Mar 3, 1952, Oct 16, 1987
Reagan, Ronald .... Feb 6, 1911, Jan 24, 1940, Mar 3, 1952; *1981* Mar 13, Mar 30, Apr 24, Dec 28; *1982* Mar 23, May 9, May 17, June 29, Sept 21, Oct 9; *1984* Apr 26, Jan 14, Jan 17, Mar 18, May 19, June 17, Sept 26, Oct 11, Nov 13, Nov 25; Mar 4, 1987; *1988* May 25, Nov 24, Dec 1, Dec 14
Reber, Grote .... Dec 22, 1911
Reclamation .... June 17, 1902
Reconstruction .... Mar 2, 1867
Reconstruction Finance Corp. (RFC) .... Jan 22, 1932
Reddy, Helen .... Oct 25, 1941
Redfield, Robert .... Dec 4, 1897
Redfield, William C. .... Mar 26, 1789, Mar 4, 1913
Redford, Robert .... Aug 18, 1937
Reed, Frank H. .... Sept 9, 1986
Reed, John .... Oct 22, 1887
Reed, John S. .... Feb 7, 1939
Reed, Joseph .... Aug 27, 1741
Reed, Stanley F. .... Dec 31, 1884
Reed, Thomas B. .... Oct 18, 1839
Reed, Walter .... Sept 13, 1851, June 26, 1900, May 1, 1909
Reese, Peewee (Harold H.) .. July 23, 1918
Regan, Donald T. .... Dec 21, 1918
Rehnquist, William .... Oct 1, 1924, June 17, 1986
Reichelderfer, Francis W. ..... Aug 6, 1895
Reid, James L. .... Dec 26, 1844
Reid, Ogden M. .... May 16, 1882
Reid, Samuel C. .... Aug 25, 1783, Apr 12, 1818
Reid, Whitelaw .... Oct 27, 1837
Reilly, William .... Dec 22, 1988
Reiner, Fritz .... Dec 19, 1888
Religious freedom .... Nov 7, 1637, Mar 7, 1638, Aug 27, 1640, Mar 16, 1641, Apr 21, 1649, Oct 16, 1649, July 18, 1663, Oct 24, 1776, Jan 16, 1786, July 13, 1787, June 14, 1943, Mar 5, 1984
Remarque, Erich Maria .... June 22, 1898
Remington, Eliphant .... Oct 27, 1793
Remington, Frederic .... Oct 4, 1961
Remington, Philo .... Oct 31, 1816
Remsen, Ira .... Feb 10, 1846
Reno, Jesse W. .... Aug 4, 1861
Reno, Jesse L. .... June 20, 1823
Renwick, James .... Nov 1, 1818
Republican Party *see* Political Parties
Resor, Stanley B. .... Apr 30, 1879
Reston, James .... Nov 3, 1909
Retirement .... Oct 17, 1986
Retten, Mary Lou .... Jan 24, 1968
Reuther, Walter P. .... Sept 1, 1907
Revels, Hiram R. .... Sept 1, 1822
Revere, Paul .... Jan 1, 1735, Apr 18, 1775
Revolution, American .... Jan 18, 1770, Nov 29, 1773
1774 .... Apr 22, May 19, Sept 1, Dec 14
1775 .... Feb 1, Feb 9, Feb 26, Apr 15, Apr 18, Apr 19, Apr 21, Apr 23, May 10, May 12, May 25, May 30, June 10, June 12, June 14, June 15, June 17, July 3, Aug 23, Sept 19, Sept 25, Oct 10, Oct 16, Nov 3, Nov 13, Dec 5, Dec 11, Dec 22, Dec 23, Dec 31
1776 .... Jan 1, Feb 15, Feb 27, Mar 3, Mar 4, Mar 17, May 2, May 6, May 10, June 7, June 27, June 28, July 2, Aug 27, Aug 29, Sept 11, Sept 12, Sept 15, Sept 16, Sept 21, Sept 26, Oct 11, Oct 12, Oct 21, Oct 28, Nov 10, Nov 16, Nov 20, Dec 9, Dec 12, Dec 25, Dec 26
1777 .... Jan 3, Apr 25, June 17, June 27, July 2, July 6, July 26, July 27, July 30, Aug 3, Aug

6, Aug 11, Aug 16, Aug 22, Sept 11, Sept 13, Sept 18, Sept 19, Sept 23, Sept 26, Oct 4, Oct 6, Oct 7, Oct 16, Oct 17, Nov 15, Nov 28, Dec 4, Dec 17, Dec 19
1778 .... Feb 6, Feb 23, Apr 23, May 4, May 8, June 16, June 17, June 18, June 26, June 28, July 3, July 4, July 8, Aug 12, Aug 31, Nov 11, Dec 23, Dec 29
1779 .... Jan 6, Jan 29, Feb 25, Mar 3, Mar 11, Apr 12, May 8, May 10, June 21, July 5, July 8, July 15, Aug 19, Aug 29, Sept 1, Sept 8, Sept 21, Sept 23, Oct 9, Dec 19
1780 .... Feb 11, Apr 11, May 12, May 26, June 23, Aug 3, Aug 16, Sept 23, Oct 7
1781 .... Jan 1, Jan 5, Jan 17, Jan 20, Feb 1, Mar 9, Mar 15, Apr 25, May 9, June 1, June 8, June 19, Aug 1, Aug 20, Aug 30, Sept 5, Sept 6, Sept 8, Sept 28, Oct 17, Oct 19, Oct 24
1782 .... Feb 27, Mar 20, Apr 4, Apr 19, July 11, Sept 19, Nov 30, Dec 14, Dec 24
1783 .... Jan 20, Feb 5, Feb 25, Mar 10, Mar 24, Apr 15, Apr 26, May 10, Sept 3, Nov 25, Dec 4
Also Jan 14, 1784, Jan 8, 1802, June 17, 1843, July 4, 1966
Revson, Charles H. .... Oct 11, 1906
Reynolds, Burt .... Feb 11, 1936
Reynolds, Debbie .... Apr 1, 1932
Reynolds, Edwin .... Mar 23, 1831
Reynolds, Frank .... Nov 29, 1923
Reynolds, John F. .... Sept 20, 1820
Reynolds, Richard S. .... Aug 15, 1881
Rhine, Joseph B. .... Sept 29, 1895
Rhode Island .... Sept 29, 1635, Aug 27, 1640, Mar 16, 1641, May 29, 1647, May 18, 1653, July 18, 1663, Jan 12, 1687, Sept 27, 1732, June 9, 1772, May 4, 1776, Jan 8, 1777, Feb 23, 1784, Mar 24, 1788, May 29, 1790, May 18, 1842, Apr 18, 1917
Ribicoff, Abraham .... Apr 9, 1910
Rice, Alice Hegan .... Jan 11, 1870
Rice, Dan .... Jan 25, 1833
Rice, Elmer L. .... Sept 29, 1892
Rice, Grantland .... Nov 1, 1880
Rice, Sam (Edgar C.) .... Feb 20, 1890
Rice, Thomas D. .... May 20, 1808
Rich, Charlie .... Dec 14, 1934
Richards, Bob (Rev. Robert E.) .... Feb 20, 1926
Richards, Charles B. .... Dec 23, 1833
Richards, Dickinson W. .... Oct 30, 1895
Richards, Ellen H. .... Dec 3, 1842
Richards, Theodore W. .... Jan 31, 1868
Richards, Vinnie (Vincent) ... Mar 20, 1903
Richardson, Elliot L. .... July 20, 1920, Oct 20, 1973
Richardson, Henry H. .... Sept 29, 1838
Richie, Lionel .... June 20, 1950
Richter, Burton .... Mar 22, 1931
Richter, Charles F. .... Apr 26, 1900
Richter, Conrad .... Oct 13, 1890
Rickard, Tex (George L.) ...... Jan 2, 1871
Rickenbacker, Eddie (Edward V.) .... Oct 8, 1890
Ricketts, Howard T. .... Feb 9, 1871
Rickey, Branch W. .... Dec 20, 1881
Rickover, Hyman G. .... Jan 27, 1900
Riddle, Nelson S. .... June 1, 1921
Ride, Sally K. .... May 26, 1951, June 18, 1983
Ridgway, Matthew B. .... Mar 3, 1895, Apr 11, 1951
Ridgway, Robert .... July 2, 1850
Riegger, Wallingford .... Apr 29, 1885
Riis, Jacob A. .... May 3, 1849
Riley, James Whitcomb .... Oct 7, 1849
Rillieux, Norbert .... Mar 17, 1806
Rinehart, Mary Roberts .... Aug 12, 1876
Ringling, Charles .... Dec 2, 1863
Riots .... May 10, 1849, July 13, 1863, July 30, 1866; *1871* July 12, Oct 24; *1874* Jan 13, Dec 7; *1886* Feb 7, May 3-4; *1906* Aug 13, Sept 22; July 2, 1917, June 1, 1921, June 20, 1943, Sept 15, 1963; *1964* July 12, Aug 28; Aug 11, 1965; *1967* July 12, July 23, Mar 2, 1968, Sept 13, 1971, Jan 2, 1980
Ripley, Eleazar .... Apr 15, 1782
Ripley, George .... Oct 3, 1802
Ripley, Robert L. .... Dec 25, 1893
Ripley, S. Dillon .... Sept 20, 1913
Ritchey, George W. .... Dec 31, 1864
Rittenhouse, David .... Apr 8, 1732
Rittenhouse, William .... Feb 17, 1708
Ritter, Joseph E. .... June 10, 1967
Ritter, Tex (Woodward M.) .... Jan 12, 1907
Rixey, Eppa .... May 3, 1891
Roach, Hal .... Jan 14, 1892
Roach, John .... Dec 25, 1813
Roanoke Island *see* North Carolina
Robards, Jason Jr. .... July 22, 1922
Robbins, Frederic C. .... Aug 25, 1916
Robbins, Harold .... May 21, 1916
Robbins, Jerome .... Oct 11, 1918
Robbins, Marty .... Sept 26, 1925
Robert, Henry M. .... May 2, 1837
Roberts, Benjamin T. .... July 25, 1823
Roberts, Brigham A. .... Jan 25, 1900
Roberts, Kenneth .... Dec 8, 1885
Roberts, Oral .... Jan 24, 1918
Roberts, Owen J. .... May 2, 1875
Roberts, Robin .... Sept 30, 1926
Robertson, Alice .... June 20, 1921
Robertson, Oscar .... Nov 24, 1938
Robertson, Pat (M.G.) .... Mar 22, 1930, Sept 29, 1987
Robeson, Paul .... Apr 9, 1898
Robinson, Bill .... May 25, 1878
Robinson, Boardman .... Sept 6, 1876
Robinson, Brooks .... May 18, 1937
Robinson, Edward G. .... Dec 12, 1893

Robinson, Edward G. .... Feb 13, 1919
Robinson, Edward M. .... Jan 8, 1800
Robinson, Edwin Arlington .... Dec 22, 1869
Robinson, Frank .... Aug 31, 1935
Robinson, Jackie .... Jan 31, 1919, Apr 11, 1947
Robinson, James H. .... June 29, 1863
Robinson, John .... Mar 1, 1625
Robinson, John C. .... Apr 10, 1817
Robinson, Joseph T. .... Aug 26, 1872
Robinson, (Sugar) Ray .... May 3, 1920
Robinson, Wilbert .... June 2, 1863
Robinson, William .... Nov 22, 1840
Robson, May .... Apr 19, 1865
Rochambeau, Comte de .... July 1, 1725
Rock, John .... Mar 24, 1890
Rockefeller, David .... June 12, 1915
Rockefeller, John D. .... July 8, 1839, Jan 10, 1870, Jan 22, 1903, Nov 15, 1906, Mar 1, 1910
Rockefeller, John D. Jr. .... Jan 29, 1874, Dec 14, 1946
Rockefeller, Nelson A. .... July 8, 1908, Dec 19, 1974, Jan 26, 1979
Rockefeller Founation .... Mar 1, 1910, May 14, 1913
Rockne, Knute .... Mar 4, 1888, Mar 31, 1931
Rockwell, George L. .... Aug 25, 1967
Rockwell, Norman .... Feb 3, 1894
Rodgers, Bill .... Feb 23, 1947
Rodgers, Christopher .... Nov 14, 1819
Rodgers, Jimmie .... Sept 8, 1897
Roddgers, Richard .... June 28, 1902
Rodgers, William L. .... Feb 4, 1860
Rodino, Peter W. Jr. .... June 7, 1909
Rodman, Hugh S. .... Jan 6, 1839
Rodney, Caesar .... Oct 7, 1728
Rodzinski, Artur .... Jan 2, 1892
Roebling, John A. .... June 12, 1806
Roebling, Washington A. ...... May 26, 1837
Roethke, Theodore .... May 25, 1908
Rogers, Calbraith B. .... Sept 17, 1911
Rogers, Ginger (Virginia) .... July 16, 1911
Rogers, Henry H. .... Jan 29, 1840
Rogers, James G. .... Mar 3, 1867
Rogers, John .... Oct 30, 1829
Rogers, Kenny .... Aug 21, 1938
Rogers, Mary Josephine .... Oct 27, 1882
Rogers, Robert .... Nov 7, 1731
Rogers, Roy .... Nov 5, 1912
Rogers, Will .... Nov 4, 1879, Aug 15, 1935
Rogers, William P. .... June 23, 1913
Rohde, Ruth Bryan .... Oct 2, 1885, Apr 12, 1933
Rolfe, John .... Apr 14, 1614
Rölvaag, Ole Edvart .... Apr 22, 1876
Romberg, Sigmund .... July 29, 1887
Rome, Harold .... May 27, 1908
Romnes, H(aakon) I. .... Mar 2, 1907
Romney, George W. .... July 8, 1907
Ronstadt, Linda .... July 15, 1946
Rooney, Mickey .... Sept 23, 1920
Roosevelt, Alice H.L. .... July 29, 1861, Oct 27, 1880, Feb 15, 1884
Roosevelt, Edith K.C. .... Aug 6, 1861, Dec 2, 1886, Sept 30, 1948
Roosevelt, Eleanor .... Oct 11, 1884, Mar 17, 1905, Dec 19, 1945, Dec 10, 1948, Nov 7, 1962
Roosevelt, Franklin D. .... Jan 30, 1882, Mar 17, 1905, Nov 8, 1910, July 6, 1920, Nov 6, 1928, July 2, 1932; *1933* Feb 15, Mar 4, Mar 6, Mar 9, Mar 12, Mar 22; Jan 30, 1934, Feb 15, 1936, Dec 1, 1936; *1937* Jan 20, Feb 5, Sept 28; *1939* Apr 14, Apr 26, Jan 1; July 4, 1940; *1941* Jan 6, Mar 17, Apr 27, May 5, June 14, Aug 14; Feb 19, 1942, Aug 31, 1942; *1943* Jan 14, May 12, Aug 17, Nov 22, Nov 28, Dec 4; Sept 11, 1944, Feb 3, 1945, Apr 12, 1945
Roosevelt, Theodore .... Oct 27, 1858, Oct 27, 1880, Feb 15, 1884, Dec 2, 1886, May 13, 1889, Apr 5, 1897, May 6, 1898, Nov 8, 1898, Sept 14, 1901, Dec 6, 1904, June 8, 1905, Aug 5, 1905; *1906* Feb 17, Nov 9, Dec 10; June 8, 1908; *1912* June 22, Aug 7, Oct 14; Jan 6, 1919
Roosevelt Dam .... Mar 18, 1911
Root, Elihu .... Feb 15, 1845, Jan 7, 1872, Nov 30, 1908
Root, George F. .... Aug 30, 1820
Root, John W. .... Jan 10, 1850
Rose, Billy .... Sept 6, 1899
Rose, David .... June 15, 1910
Rose, Pete .... Apr 14, 1942, Sept 11, 1985
Rose, Vincent .... June 13, 1880
Rosecrans, William S. .... Sept 6, 1819, Oct 30, 1862
Rosenberg, Julius and Ethel .... Mar 29, 1951, June 19, 1953
Rosenwald, Julius .... Aug 12, 1862
Ross, Barney .... Dec 23, 1909
Ross, Betsy .... Jan 1, 1752
Ross, Diana .... Mar 26, 1944
Ross, Edward A. .... Dec 12, 1866
Ross, George .... May 10, 1730
Ross, Harold W. .... Nov 6, 1892
Ross, John .... Oct 3, 1790
Ross, Nellie Tayloe .... Jan 5, 1925
Rostropovich, Mstislav .... Aug 12, 1927
Rotary Club .... Feb 23, 1905, May 4, 1987
Roth, Philip .... Mar 19, 1933
Rothafel, Samuel I. (Roxy) .... July 9, 1881
Rothko, Mark .... Sept 25, 1903
Rous, Peyton .... Oct 5, 1879
Roush, Edd(ie) .... May 8, 1893
Rowan, Carl T. .... Aug 11, 1925
Rowland, Henry A. .... Nov 27, 1848
Roxy *see* Rothafel, Samuel L.
Royce, Josiah .... Nov 20, 1855
Rozelle, Pete (Alvin R.) .... Mar 1, 1826
Rubicam, Raymond .... June 16, 1892
Rubinstein, Arthur .... Jan 28, 1887
Rubinstein, Helena .... Dec 25, 1870
Ruby, Harry .... Jan 27, 1895
Ruby, Jack .... Nov 24, 1963, Mar 14, 1964, Jan 3, 1967
Ruckelshaus, Donald .... Oct 20, 1973
Rudolph, Wilma .... June 23, 1940
Ruffin, Edmund .... Jan 5, 1794
Ruffing, Red (Charles H.) .... May 3, 1904
Ruger, Thomas H. .... Apr 2, 1833
Rugg, Harold O. .... Jan 17, 1886

Rukeyser, Muriel .... Dec 15, 1913
Ruml, Beardsley .... Nov 5, 1894
Rumford, Count *see* Thompson, Benjamin
Runyon, Damon .... Oct 4, 1884
Rupp, Adolph F. .... Sept 2, 1901
Ruppert, Jacob .... Aug 5, 1867
Rural Electrification
Administration (REA) .... May 11, 1935
Rush, Benjamin .... Dec 24, 1745
Rush, Richard .... Aug 29, 1780
Rush, William .... July 5, 1756
Rusie, Amos .... May 30, 1871
Rusk, Dean .... Feb 9, 1909
Rusk, Thomas J. .... Dec 5, 1803
Russell, Bill (William F.) ..... Feb 12, 1934
Russell, Charles Taze .... Feb 16, 1852
Russell, Howard H. .... Oct 21, 1855
Russell, Jonathan .... Aug 8, 1814
Russell, Lillian .... Dec 4, 1861
Russell, Richard B. .... Nov 2, 1897
Russell, Rosalind .... June 4, 1911
Russell, William B. .... Jan 31, 1812
Russia .... Mar 8, 1813, Apr 17, 1824, Apr 9, 1867, Aug 9, 1905, Sept 5, 1905, Aug 2, 1918, Jan 12, 1920, Nov 16, 1933, June 24, 1941, Sept 29, 1941, Apr 1, 1948, June 24, 1948, May 12, 1949, May 5, 1960; *1962* Oct 22, Oct 24, Nov 2; *1963* July 25, Aug 4, Aug 30, Aug 31; Jan 27, 1967, Mar 26, 1972, May 22, 1972, Nov 23, 1974, Dec 28, 1981, Aug 31-Sept. 1, 1983, Nov 19, 1985, Oct 11, 1986; *1987* Nov 24, Dec 7; *1988* May 27, May 31, June 1
Russworm, John B. .... Mar 16, 1827
Rustin, Bayard .... Mar 17, 1910
Rutan, Dick .... Dec 23, 1986
Ruth, Babe (George H.) .... Feb 6, 1895, Jan 29, 1936
Rutherford, Joseph F. .... Nov 8, 1869
Rutherford, Lewis M. .... Nov 25, 1816
Rutledge, Edward .... Nov 23, 1749
Rutledge, John .... Jan 1, 1795, Dec 15, 1795, Sept 24, 1789
Rutledge, Wiley B. Jr. .... July 20, 1894
Ryan, Leo J. .... Nov 18, 1978
Ryan, Nolan .... Jan 31, 1947
Ryan, Patrick J. .... Feb 20, 1831
Ryan, Thomas Fortune .... Oct 17, 1851
Ryan, Albert P. .... Mar 19, 1847
Ryan, Charles W. .... Jan 16, 1892

Saarinen, Eero .... Aug 20, 1910
Saarinen, Eliel .... Aug 20, 1873
Sabin, Albert B. .... Aug 26, 1906
Sabine, Wallace C.W. .... June 13, 1868
Sacagawea .... Dec 20, 1812
Sacco, Nicola and
Vanzetti, Bartolomeo .... Apr 15, 1920, May 31, 1921, Aug 23, 1927
Sagan, Carl .... Nov 9, 1934
Sage, Margaret Olivia .... Sept 8, 1828, Mar 12, 1907
Sage, Russell .... Aug 4, 1816
St. Clair, Arthur .... Apr 3, 1737, Nov 4, 1791
St. Denis, Ruth .... Jan 20, 1879
St. Gaudens, Augustus .... Mar 1, 1848
St. John, John P. .... Feb 25, 1833
St. Lawrence Seaway .... Nov 5, 1953, Jan 20, 1954, May 13, 1954, Apr 25, 1959, June 26, 1959, June 27, 1959
St. Louis, Mo. .... Feb 15, 1768, June 20, 1778, Dec 28, 1832, May 17, 1849, May 4, 1851, July 4, 1874, May 27, 1896, Sept 29, 1927, May 25, 1968
St. Patrick's Day .... Mar 17, 1737
Salaries, Federal .... Sept 11, 1789, Sept 22, 1789, Jan 27, 1818, Mar 19, 1816, Mar 3, 1853, Mar 3, 1873, Mar 4, 1873, Jan 20, 1874, Mar 4, 1909, Mar 4, 1925, Mar 20, 1933, Jan 19, 1949, Mar 2, 1955, Aug 14, 1964, Jan 17, 1969, Sept 15, 1969, Dec 13, 1988
Salinger, J(erome) D. .... Jan 1, 1919
Salk, Jonas E. .... Oct 28, 1914
Saltonstall, Gurdon .... Apr 7, 1666
Saltonstall, Leverett .... Sept 1, 1892
Salvador, Francis .... Jan 11, 1775
Samoan Islands .... Jan 17, 1878, Mar 16, 1889, June 14, 1889
Sampson, William T. .... Feb 9, 1840
Samuelson, Paul A. .... May 15, 1915
San Francisco .... June 17, 1579, Sept 17, 1776, July 9, 1846, Feb 12, 1849, Feb 28, 1849, Apr 15, 1850, May 3, 1851, Oct 21, 1868, Aug 1, 1873, Apr 18, 1906, Feb 20, 1915, July 22, 1916, Jan 5, 1933, Nov 12, 1936, May 27, 1937, Feb 18, 1939, Sept 11, 1972, Oct 17, 1989
Sanborn, Franklin B. .... Dec 15, 1831
Sandage, Allan R. .... June 18, 1926
Sandburg, Carl .... Jan 6, 1878
Sande, Earl .... Nov 13, 1898
Sandys, Sir Edwin .... Dec 9, 1561
Sanford, Edward T. .... July 23, 1865
Sanger, Margaret H. .... Sept 14, 1883, Oct 16, 1916
Santayana, George .... Dec 16, 1863
Sapir, Edward .... Jan 26, 1884
Sarazen, Gene .... Feb 27, 1901
Sarg, Tony
(Anthony F.) .... Apr 24, 1882
Sargent, John S. .... Jan 12, 1856
Sarnoff, David .... Feb 27, 1891
Sarnoff, Robert W. .... July 2, 1918
Saroyan, William .... Aug 31, 1908
Sartain, John .... Oct 24, 1808
Satterlee, Henry Y. .... Jan 11, 1843
Saunders, Clarence .... Oct 14, 1953
Savage, Arthur W. .... May 13, 1857
Savannah, Ga. .... Feb 12, 1733, Dec 29, 1778, July 11, 1782, Dec 20, 1864
Saxbe, William B. .... June 24, 1916
Saxton, Joseph .... Mar 22, 1799
Say, Thomas .... June 27, 1787
Sayre, Lewis A. .... Feb 29, 1820
Schaefer, Rudolph J. .... Feb 21, 1863
Schalk, Ray .... Aug 12, 1892
Schally, Andrew V. .... Nov 30, 1926
Schawlow, Arthur .... May 5, 1921
Schechter, Solomon .... Dec 7, 1850
Schenck, Robert C. .... Oct 4, 1809
Scherman, Harry .... Jan 1, 1887
Schick, Bela .... July 16, 1877
Schick, Jacob .... Sept 16, 1877
Schiff, Dorothy .... Mar 11, 1903
Schiff, Jacob H. .... Jan 10, 1847

Schildkraut, Joseph .... Mar 22, 1896
Schipa, Tito .... Jan 2, 1890
Schirmer, Gustav .... Sept 19, 1829
Schirra, Walter M. Jr. .... Dec 15, 1965
Schlafly, Phyllis .... Aug 15, 1924
Schlesinger, Arthur M. .... Feb 27, 1888
Schlesinger, Arthur M. Jr. .. Oct 15, 1917
Schlesinger, James R. .... Feb 15, 1929, Aug 4, 1977
Schley, Winfield S. .... Oct 9, 1839
Schmitt, Harrison S. (Jack) .. July 3, 1935
Schmucker, Samuel S. .... Feb 28, 1799
Schneerson, Menachem M. .... Apr 18, 1902
Schofield, John M. .... Sept 29, 1831
Schönberg, Arnold .... Sept 13, 1874
School prayers .... June 19, 1987
Schrank, John N. .... Oct 14, 1912
Schrieffer, John R. .... May 31, 1931
Schriever, Bernard A. .... Sept 14, 1910
Schulberg, Budd .... Mar 27, 1914
Schuller, Robert .... Sept 16, 1926
Schultze, Carl E. .... May 25, 1866
Schulz, Charles M. .... Nov 26, 1922
Schumann-Heink, Ernestine .... June 15, 1861
Schurz, Carl .... Mar 2, 1829
Schuyler, Philip J. .... Nov 20, 1733
Schwab, Charles M. .... Feb 18, 1862
Schwartz, Delmore .... Dec 8, 1913
Schwartz, Melvin .... Nov 2, 1932
Schwimmer, Rosika .... Sept 11, 1877
Schwinger, Julian S. .... Feb 12, 1918
Science .... Mar 3, 1863, Jan 8, 1889, May 5, 1925, Mar 13, 1930, Jan 2, 1936, June 28, 1941, Jan 16, 1948, Jan 7, 1949, May 10, 1950, Apr 25, 1953, Dec 2, 1983, Jan 3, 1985, May 10, 1987
Scopes, John T. .... *1925* May 25, July 10
Scott, Charles .... Oct 22, 1813
Scott, Frank A. .... Mar 31, 1917
Scott, George C. .... Oct 18, 1927
Scott, Hugh D. Jr. .... Nov 11, 1900
Scott, Hugh L. .... Sept 22, 1853
Scott, Winfield .... June 13, 1786, May 27, 1813, Mar 3, 1849; *1847* Mar 29, Aug 20; Oct 29, 1860
Scottsboro Case .... Apr 6, 1931
Scowcroft, Brent .... Mar 19, 1925
Scribner, Charles .... Feb 21, 1821
Scripps, Edward W. .... June 18, 1854
Scripps, James E. .... Mar 19, 1835
Seaborg, Glenn T. .... Apr 19, 1912
Seabury, Samuel .... Nov 30, 1729, Nov 14, 1784
Seabury, Samuel .... Feb 22, 1873
Seal of the United States ...... June 20, 1782
Seaman, Elizabeth *see* Bly, Nellie
Sears, Edmund H. .... Apr 6, 1810
Sears, Isaac .... Oct 28, 1786
Sears, Richard D. .... Oct 26, 1861
Sears, Richard W. .... Dec 7, 1863
Seaton, William W. .... Jan 11, 1785
Seattle, Wash. .... Jan 28, 1861, Feb 7, 1886, Jan 6, 1889, Feb 6, 1919, Apr 21, 1962
Seaver, Tom (G. Thomas) ..... Nov 17, 1944
Secord, Richard W. .... Mar 16, 1988
Secret Service .... July 5, 1865
Securities/Securities & Exchange Commission ...... May 27, 1933, June 6, 1934, Jan 24, 1977, May 26, 1977, Sept 7, 1988
Sedaka, Neil .... Mar 13, 1939
Seddon, James A. .... July 13, 1815
Sedgwick, Ellery .... Feb 27, 1872
Sedgwick, John .... Sept 13, 1813
Sedgwick, Theodore .... May 9, 1746
See, Thomas J.J. .... Feb 19, 1866
Seed, Miles A. .... Feb 24, 1843
Seeger, Alan .... June 24, 1888
Seeger, Pete .... May 3, 1919
Segal, George .... Nov 26, 1924
Segar, Elzie C. .... Oct 13, 1958
Segré, Emilio G. .... Feb 1, 1905
Seiberling, Frank A. .... Oct 6, 1859
Seixas, Gershon M. .... Jan 14, 1745
Selden, George B. .... Sept 14, 1846, Nov 5, 1895
Selective Service .... Apr 16, 1862, Mar 3, 1863; *1917* May 18, June 5, July 13, July 20; *1918* Jan 7, June 1; *1940* Sept 14, Sept 16, Oct 16, Oct 29; *1941* Aug 18, Dec 22; Nov 13, 1942, Dec 1, 1969, Jan 27, 1973, June 27, 1980
Selfridge, Thomas .... Sept 17, 1908
Seligman, Edwin R.A. .... Apr 25, 1861
Seligman, Joseph .... Nov 22, 1819
Selleck, Tom .... Jan 29, 1945
Sellers, William .... Sept 19, 1824
Selznick, David O. .... May 10, 1902
Semmes, Raphael .... Sept 27, 1809
Senate *see* Congress
Sennett, Mack .... Jan 17, 1880
Sergeant, John .... Dec 5, 1779
Serkin, Rudolf .... Mar 28, 1903
Serling, Rod .... Dec 25, 1924
Serra, Juniperro .... Nov 24, 1713, July 16, 1769, Sept 25, 1988
Sessions, Roger H. .... Dec 28, 1896
Sessions, William S. .... May 27, 1930
Seton, Elizabeth Anne .... Aug 28, 1774, Sept 14, 1975
Seton, Ernest Thompson .... Aug 14, 1860
Seuss, Doctor *see* Geisel, Theodore S.
Sevareid, Eric .... Nov 26, 1912
Severinson, Doc (Carl H.) ..... July 7, 1927
Sevier, John .... Sept 23, 1745, Nov 14, 1785
Sewall, Arthur .... Nov 25, 1835
Sewall, Samuel .... Mar 28, 1652, June 24, 1700
Seward, William H. .... May 16, 1801
Sewell, Joe .... Oct 9, 1898
Sexual abuse .... June 29, 1988
Seymour, Horatio .... May 31, 1810
Shafter, William R. .... Oct 16, 1835
Shahn, Ben(jamin) .... Sept 12, 1828
Shakers, American .... Feb 29, 1736
Shannon, Claude E. .... Apr 30, 1916
Shapiro, Karl J. .... Nov 10, 1913
Shapley, Harlow .... Nov 2, 1885
Sharp, William G. .... Mar 14, 1859
Shaw, Anna Howard .... Feb 14, 1847

Shaw, Artie .... May 23, 1910
Shaw, Henry W. .... Apr 21, 1818
Shaw, Irwin .... Feb 27, 1913
Shaw, Lemuel .... Jan 9, 1781
Shaw, Wilbur .... Oct 31, 1902
Shawn, Ted .... Oct 21, 1891
Shay's Rebellion .... *1787* Jan 25, Sept 26
Sheaffer, Walter A. .... July 27, 1867
Shean, Al .... May 12, 1868
Shearer, Norma .... Aug 10, 1900
Shearing, George .... Aug 13, 1920
Sheeen, Fulton J. .... May 8, 1895
Sheffield, Joseph E. .... June 19, 1793
Shehan, Lawrence J. .... Mar 18, 1898
Shelby, Isaac .... Dec 11, 1750
Shelby, Joseph O. .... Dec 12, 1830
Sheldon, Charles M. .... Feb 26, 1857
Sheldon, Edward B. .... Feb 4, 1886
Sheldon, Sidney .... Feb 11, 1917
Shell Oil .... Feb 1, 1988
Shepard, Alan B. Jr. .... Nov 18, 1923, May 5, 1961
Shepard, Helen M. .... June 20, 1868
Sheridan, Philip H. .... Mar 6, 1831, May 11, 1864, Mar 27, 1865
Sherman, Frederick C. .... May 27, 1988
Sherman, James S. .... Oct 24, 1855
Sherman, John .... May 10, 1823
Sherman, Roger .... Apr 19, 1721, June 10, 1776
Sherman, William T. .... Feb 8, 1820; *1864* May 4, May 25, Nov 12, Nov 14, Dec 10, Dec 20
Sherrill, Henry K. .... Nov 6, 1890
Sherwood, Robert E. .... Apr 4, 1896
Shields, James .... May 12, 1806
Shippen, William .... Oct 21, 1736
Shipping .... Feb 22, 1784, July 20, 1789, Mar 23, 1810, Jan 4, 1818, May 27, 1818, May 24, 1819, Apr 23, 1838, Apr 15, 1912, July 4, 1917, June 26, 1936, Feb 9, 1942, Nov 12, 1942, July 25, 1956, July 21, 1959, Oct 9, 1985
Shiras, George .... Jan 26, 1832
Shirer, William L. .... Feb 23, 1904
Shirley, William .... Mar 24, 1771
Shockley, William B. .... Feb 13, 1910
Shoemaker, Willie .... Aug 19, 1931
Sholes, Christopher L. .... Feb 13, 1819
Shore, Dinah .... Mar 1, 1921
Shotwell, James T. .... Aug 6, 1874
Shoup, George L. .... June 15, 1836
Shreve, Henry M. .... Oct 21, 1785
Shriver, R. Sarent .... Nov 9, 1915, Mar 1, 1961
Shubert, J(acob) J. .... Aug 15, 1880
Shubert, Lee .... Mar 15, 1875
Shultz, George .... Dec 13, 1920, June 25, 1982
Shute, Samuel .... Jan 12, 1662
Sibert, William L. .... Oct 12, 1860
Sibley, Hiram .... Feb 6, 1807
Sickles, Daniel E. .... Oct 20, 1825
Sigel, Franz .... Nov 18, 1824
Signal Corps .... Sept 20, 1829, Jan 21, 1860
Sigourney, Lydia H.H. .... Sept 1, 1791
Sigsbee, Charles D. .... Jan 16, 1845
Sikorsky, Igor I. .... May 25, 1889
Silliman, Benjamin .... Aug 8, 1779
Sills, Beverly .... May 25, 1929
Silver *see* Gold/Silver
Silver, Abba Hillel .... Jan 28, 1893
Silverman, Sime .... May 18, 1873
Silvers, Phil .... May 11, 1912
Simmons, Al(oysius) .... May 22, 1902
Simmons, Calvin .... Apr 27, 1950
Simon, Herbert A. .... June 15, 1916
Simon, Neil .... July 4, 1927
Simon, Richard L. .... Mar 6, 1899
Simonson, Lee .... June 26, 1888
Simpson, George G. .... June 16, 1902
Simpson, O(renthal) J. .... July 9, 1947
Simpson, William H. .... May 19, 1888
Sims, James M. .... Jan 25, 1813
Sims, William S. .... Oct 15, 1858
Sims, Zoot (John H.) .... Oct 29, 1925
Sinatra, Frank .... Dec 12, 1915
Sinclair, Harry F. .... July 6, 1876, Apr 7, 1922, June 30, 1924
Sinclair, Upton B. .... Sept 20, 1878
Singer, Isaac B. .... July 14, 1904
Singer, Isaac M. .... Oct 27, 1811
Singleton, Zutty (Arthur J.) May 14, 1898
Sirica, John J. .... Mar 19, 1904
Sisler, George .... Mar 24, 1893
Sitting Bull .... Mar 24, 1893
Skelton, Red (Richard) .... July 18, 1913
Skelton, Samuel .... July 20, 1629
Skidmore, Louis .... Apr 8, 1897
Skinner, B(urrhus) F. .... Mar 20, 1904
Skinner, Cornelia Otis .... May 30, 1901
Skinner, Otis .... June 28, 1858
Skinner, Samuel .... Dec 22, 1988
Skouras, Spyros P. .... Mar 28, 1893
Slater, Samuel .... June 9, 1768, Dec 21, 1790
Slaughter, Enos (Country) ... Apr 27, 1916
Slavery .... May 18, 1653, Feb 18, 1688, June 24, 1700, Apr 6, 1712, June 7, 1712, July 2, 1777, Mar 1, 1780, Mar 2, 1780, Oct 31, 1783, Feb 23, 1784, Apr 23, 1784, July 13, 1787, Mar 26, 1788, Dec 17, 1792, Feb 12, 1793, Mar 22, 1794, Nov 29, 1802, Feb 15, 1804, Mar 2, 1807, Jan 1, 1808, June 10, 1816, Mar 31, 1817, Aug 26, 1818, Mar 3, 1819, Mar 3, 1820, May 15, 1820, June 4, 1827, Dec 4, 1833, May 11, 1835, May 26, 1836, Jan 8, 1840, Oct 27, 1841, Dec 2, 1844, Aug 3, 1846, Mar 13, 1848; *1850* May 25, June 10, Sept 1, Sept 18, Sept 20, Oct 21; *1854* Apr 26, May 22, May 24; Oct 16, 1855, Dec 15, 1855, Oct 13, 1857, July 29, 1859; *1862* Mar 6, Apr 7, Apr 16, June 19, July 22, Sept 22, Sept 24; *1863* Jan 1, Mar 26, July 1; *1864* Jan 19, Mar 18, Apr 6, Sept 6; *1865* Jan 9, Feb 1, Feb 22, Aug 21, Sept 15, Sept 20, Oct 7, Oct 28, Oct 30, Dec 18
Slidell, John .... Nov 8, 1861, Dec 23, 1861, Jan 1, 1862
Slipher, Vesto M. .... Nov 11, 1875
Sloan, Alfred P. .... May 23, 1875
Sloan, John .... Aug 2, 1871
Sloan, Samuel .... Dec 25, 1817
Slocum, Henry W. .... Sept 24, 1827
Slye, Maude .... Feb 8, 1879
Small, Albion W. .... May 11, 1854

Smallwood, William .... Feb 12, 1792
Smet, Pierre Jean de *see* DeSmet, Pierre Jean
Smith, Alfred E. .... Dec 30, 1873
Smith, Andrew J. .... Apr 28, 1815
Smith, Bessie .... Apr 15, 1894
Smith, Bob .... Nov 27, 1917
Smith, Charles H. .... June 15, 1826
Smith, C(yrus) R. .... Sept 9, 1899
Smith, Dean .... Feb 28, 1931
Smith, Francis H. .... Oct 18, 1812
Smith, Francis H. .... Oct 23, 1838
Smith, Francis M. .... Feb 2, 1846
Smith, Frederick M. .... Jan 21, 1874
Smith, George A. .... Apr 4, 1870
Smith, George O. .... Feb 22, 1871
Smith, Gerrit .... Mar 6, 1797
Smith, Giles A. .... Sept 29, 1829
Smith, Hamilton O. .... Aug 23, 1931
Smith, Hoke .... Sept 2, 1855
Smith, Holland M. .... Apr 20, 1882
Smith, Horace .... Oct 28, 1808
Smith, James .... July 11, 1806
Smith, Jedidiah S. .... Jan 6, 1799
Smith, Capt John .... *1607* May 24, Sept 17, Dec 10; July 24, 1608, Sept 10, 1608, Oct 5, 1609
Smith, Joseph .... Dec 23, 1805, Apr 6, 1830, July 23, 1843, June 27, 1844
Smith, Joseph .... Nov 6, 1832
Smith, Joseph Fielding .... Nov 13, 1838
Smith, Joseph Fielding .... July 19, 1876
Smith, Kate .... May 1, 1909
Smith, Morgan L. .... Mar 8, 1821
Smith, Nathan .... Sept 30, 1762
Smith, Red (Walter W.) .... Sept 25, 1905
Smith, Robert .... Nov 3, 1757
Smith, Robert H. .... Aug 8, 1879, June 10, 1935
Smith, Roger B. .... July 12, 1925
Smith, Samuel .... July 27, 1752
Smith, Samuel F. .... Oct 21, 1808
Smith, Sidney .... Feb 13, 1877
Smith, Sophie .... Aug 27, 1796
Smith, Theobald .... July 31, 1859
Smith, Walter Bedell .... Oct 5, 1895
Smith, William .... Sept 7, 1727
Smith, Winchell .... Apr 5, 1871
Smithsonian Institution .... Aug 10, 1846, Sept 7, 1846, May 1, 1847
Smoking .... Jan 21, 1908, Apr 11, 1921, Jan 11, 1964
Smoot, Reed .... Feb 20, 1907
Snead, Sam .... May 27, 1912
Snell, George .... Dec 19, 1903
Snider, Duke (Edwin D.) ..... Sept 19, 1926
Snow, Lorenzo .... Apr 3, 1814
Social Security .... Aug 14, 1935, May 24, 1937, July 30, 1965, July 1, 1966, Oct 30, 1972, Jan 1, 1974, Apr 20, 1983, Oct 9, 1984, July 1, 1988
Society for the Prevention of Cruelty to Animals (SPCA) .... Apr 10, 1866
Soglow, Otto .... Dec 23, 1900
Solomon Islands .... July 7, 1978
Solow, Robert M. .... Aug 23, 1924
Somervell, Brehon B. .... May 9, 1892
Sondheim, Stephen J. .... Mar 22, 1930
Sons of the American Revolution (SAR) .... Oct 22, 1875
Sorin, Edward F. .... Feb 6, 1814
Sorokin, Pitrim A. .... Jan 21, 1889
Sothern, Edward H. .... Dec 6, 1859
Sousa, John Philip .... Nov 6, 1854
South Carolina .... May 1, 1562, Jan 12, 1682, Aug 24, 1706, Jan 28, 1712, May 9, 1712, Mar 23, 1713, Apr 15, 1715, May 29, 1721, Jan 8, 1732, Jan 1, 1735, Jan 12, 1773, Mar 19, 1778, May 23, 1788, June 3, 1790, Dec 17, 1792, Jan 10, 1805, Dec 18, 1828; *1832* Nov 19, Nov 24, Dec 10, Dec 20; Oct 25, 1850; *1860* Oct 5, Nov 10, Dec 18, Dec 20, Dec 30; Sept 15, 1865, Apr 16, 1868, Dec 4, 1895, Feb 16, 1915, Sept 14, 1915
South Dakota .... Mar 2, 1861; *1889* May 14, July 4, Nov 2; June 9, 1972, Feb 27, 1973
Southeast Asia Treaty Organization (SEATO)..... Sept 8, 1954
Soviet Union *see* Russia
Sower, Christopher .... Sept 25, 1758
Sowerby, Leo .... May 1, 1895
Spaatz, Carl .... June 28, 1891
Space exploration .... Mar 3, 1915, Mar 16, 1926, Jan 10, 1946; *1958* Jan 31, Apr 2, July 29, Dec 18; Sept 12, 1959, Oct 4, 1959; *1960* Apr 1, Aug 12, Oct 10; May 5, 1961, May 25, 1961, Feb 20, 1962, July 10, 1962, Sept 20, 1963, Nov 28, 1964; *1965* Apr 6, June 3, Dec 15; May 30, 1966, Jan 27, 1967, Jan 9, 1968, Dec 27, 1968, July 20, 1969, Apr 13, 1970, Jan 5, 1972, Mar 2, 1972, Dec 3, 1974, July 15, 1975, July 17, 1975, July 20, 1976, Sept 30, 1976, Mar 5, 1979, July 11, 1979, Nov 12, 1980, Apr 12, 1981, Aug 25, 1981, Nov 28, 1982, June 18, 1983, Aug 30, 1983; *1984* Feb 7, Apr 12, Oct 11, Nov 8; Apr 12, 1985; *1986* Jan 28, Apr 18, May 3; Aug 10, 1988, Sept 29, 1988
Spahn, Warren E. .... Apr 23, 1921
Spain .... June 7, 1494, July 18, 1670, Nov 3, 1762, May 2, 1776; *1779* Apr 12, May 8, June 21, July 8; Mar 24, 1783, June 26, 1784, Oct 27, 1795, Oct 1, 1800, Feb 22, 1819, Apr 21, 1898, Apr 24, 1898, Apr 1, 1939
Spalding, Albert .... Aug 15, 1888
Spalding, Albert G. .... Sept 1, 1850
Spalding, Lyman .... June 5, 1775
Spangenberg, August G. .... July 15, 1704
Spanier, Muggsy (Francis J.) .... Nov 9, 1906
Spanish-American War .... *1898* Feb 15, Mar 21, Apr 11, Apr 20, Apr 22, Apr 23, Apr 24, Apr 25, Apr 27, May 1, May 25, May 29, June 10, June 14, June 20, June 24, July 1, July 3, July 4, July 16, July 25, July 26, Aug 9, Aug 12, Aug 13, Dec 10
Sparkman, John J. .... Dec 20, 1899
Sparks, Jared .... May 10, 1789
Spearker, Tris(tram) .... Apr 4, 1888
Speakes, Larry .... Sept 13, 1939
Speaks, Oley .... June 28, 1876
Spellman, Francis J. .... May 4, 1889
Spencer, Platt R. .... Nov 7, 1800
Sperry, Elmer A. .... Oct 12, 1860
Spewack, Samuel .... Sept 16, 1899

Spielberg, Steven .... Dec 18, 1947
Spillane, Mickey
(Frank M.) .... Mar 9, 1918
Spingarn, Arthur B. .... Mar 28, 1878
Spingarn, Joel E. .... May 17, 1875
Spink, (J.B.) Taylor .... Nov 6, 1888
Spitz, Mark .... Feb 10, 1950
Spock, Benjamin M. .... May 2, 1903
Spofford, Ainsworth R. .... Sept 12, 1825
Spotswood, Alexander .... June 7, 1640
Sprague, Frank J. .... July 25, 1857
Spreckels, Claus .... July 9, 1828
Springsteen, Bruce .... Sept 23, 1949
Sproul, Robert G. .... May 22, 1891
Spruance, Raymond A. .... Jan 3, 1886
Squibb, Edward R. .... July 4, 1819
Squier, George O. .... Mar 21, 1865
Stafford, Jo .... Nov 21, 1920
Stafford, Thomas P. .... Dec 15, 1965
Stagg, Amos Alonzo .... Aug 16, 1862
Stalin, Joseph .... Nov 28, 1943, Feb 4, 1945, July 17, 1945
Stallone, Sylvester .... July 6, 1946
Stamp Act .... *1765* Mar 8, Mar 22, June 8, Aug 15, Aug 26, Sept 28, Oct 7, Oct 14, Oct 19, Nov 1, Nov 23; *1766* Jan 17, Feb 11, Mar 17, Oct 28
Stamps *see* Mail
Stanberry, Henry .... Feb 20, 1803
Standard Oil Co. .... Jan 10, 1870, Nov 15, 1906, Nov 20, 1909; *1911* May 1, May 15, Nov 20
Standish, Burt L. *see* Patten, Gilbert
Standish, Miles .... Feb 17, 1621, Oct 3, 1656
Standley, William H. .... Dec 18, 1872
Stanford, Leland .... Mar 9, 1824
Stanley, Francis E. and
Freelan .... June 1, 1849
Stanley, Henry M. .... Jan 28, 1841, Nov 10, 1871
Stanley, Wendell M. .... Aug 16, 1904
Stanley, William .... Nov 22, 1858
Stanton, Edwin M. .... Dec 19, 1814, Aug 5, 1867, Aug 12, 1867; *1868* Jan 13, Feb 21, May 26
Stanton, Elizabeth Cady ...... Nov 12, 1815, July 19, 1848, Mar 19, 1860, Jan 23, 1869
Stanton, Frank L. .... Feb 22, 1857
Stanton, Frank N. .... Mar 20, 1908
Stanwyck, Barbara .... July 16, 1907
Stargell, Willie .... Mar 6, 1941
Stark, Harold R. .... Nov 12, 1880
Stark, John .... Aug 27, 1728, Aug 16, 1777
Starr, Chauncey .... Apr 14, 1912
Starrett, Paul .... Nov 25, 1866
Stassen, Harold E. .... Apr 13, 1907
State Department .... Jan 10, 1781, July 27, 1789, Feb 14, 1790, Mar 22, 1790
Statler, Ellsworth M. .... Oct 26, 1863
Statue of Liberty .... Feb 22, 1877, July 4, 1884, June 19, 1885, Oct 28, 1886, Sept 26, 1972, July 1, 1986, Oct 28, 1986
Staubach, Roger .... Feb 5, 1942
Steel .... Apr 8, 1857, Feb 25, 1901, Apr 8, 1952
Steel, Danielle .... Aug 14, 1947
Stefansson, Vihjalmur .... Nov 3, 1879
Steffens, Lincoln .... Apr 6, 1866
Steichen, Edward .... Mar 27, 1879
Stein, Gertrude .... Feb 3, 1874
Stein, William H. .... June 25, 1911
Steeinbeck, John E. .... Feb 27, 1902
Steinberg, Saul .... June 15, 1914
Steinberger, Jack .... May 25, 1921
Steinem, Gloria .... Mar 25, 1934
Steiner, Max .... May 10, 1888
Steinman, David B. .... June 11, 1886
Steinmetz, Charles P. .... Apr 9, 1865
Steinway, Henry E. .... Feb 15, 1797
Steinway, William .... Mar 5, 1835
Stella, Frank P. .... May 12, 1936
Stengel, Casey
(Charles D.) .... July 30, 1891
Stephens, Alexander H. .... Feb 11, 1812, Feb 4, 1861, Feb 8, 1861, Feb 3, 1865
Stephens, Uriah S. .... Aug 3, 1821
Stephenson, Benjamin F. ... Oct 3, 1823, Apr 6, 1866
Stern, Isaac .... July 21, 1920
Stern, Otto .... Feb 17, 1888
Sternberg, George M. .... June 8, 1838
Stetson, John B. .... May 5, 1830
Stettinius, Edward R. Jr. ..... Oct 22, 1900, Oct 28, 1941
Steuben, Baron
Friedrich von .... Sept 17, 1730, Dec 1, 1777, Feb 23, 1778, May 5, 1778
Steunenberg, Frank .... Dec 30, 1905
Stevens, Albert W. .... Apr 13, 1886
Stevens, Edwin A. .... July 28, 1795
Stevens, George .... Dec 18, 1904
Stevens, James F. .... Nov 15, 1892
Stevens, John .... Mar 6, 1838
Stevens, John P. .... Apr 20, 1920
Stevens, Risë .... June 11, 1913
Stevens, Robert L. .... Oct 18, 1787
Stevens, Robert T. .... July 31, 1899
Stevens, Thaddeus .... Apr 4, 1792
Stevens, Wallace .... Oct 2, 1879
Stevenson, Adlai E. .... Oct 23, 1835, June 14, 1914
Stevenson, Adlai E. .... Feb 5, 1900
Stevenson, Andrew .... Jan 21, 1784
Stewart, Alexander T. .... Oct 12, 1803
Stewart, Charles .... July 28, 1778
Stewart, Jimmy .... May 20, 1908
Stewart, Philo P. .... July 6, 1798
Stewart, Potter .... Jan 23, 1915
Stewart, William M. .... Aug 9, 1827
Stiegel, Henry W. .... May 13, 1729
Stieglitz, Alfred .... Jan 1, 1864
Stigler, George J. .... Jan 17, 1911
Stiles, Ezra .... Nov 29, 1727
Still, Andrew T. .... Aug 6, 1828
Still, William G. .... May 11, 1895
Stilwell, Joseph W. .... Mar 19, 1883, Mar 10, 1942
Stimson, Henry L. .... Sept 21, 1867
Stine, Charles M.A. .... Oct 18, 1882
Stirling, Lord see Alexander, William
Stirling, Yates .... May 6, 1843
Stock, Frederick A. .... Nov 11, 1872

Stock market *see* Economy
Stockton, Richard .... Oct 1, 1730
Stoddert, Benjamin .... Apr 30, 1798, May 21, 1798
Stokes, Anson P. .... Feb 22, 1838
Stokes, Anson P. .... Apr 13, 1874
Stokes, Carl B. .... June 21, 1927, Nov 7, 1967
Stokowski, Leopold .... Apr 18, 1882
Stone, Barton W. .... Dec 24, 1772
Stone, Edward Durrell .... Mar 9, 1902
Stone, Ellen .... Feb 23, 1902
Stone, Fred .... Aug 19, 1873
Stone, Harlan F. .... Oct 11, 1872, June 12, 1941
Stone, Irving .... July 14, 1903
Stone, Lucy Blackwell .... Aug 13, 1818, May 15, 1869
Stone, Melville E. .... Aug 22, 1848
Stone, Samuel .... July 20, 1663
Stone, Thomas .... Oct 5, 1787
Stoneman, George .... Aug 8, 1822
Storms *see* Disasters
Story, Joseph .... Sept 18, 1779
Stout, Rex .... Dec 1, 1886
Stout, William B. .... Mar 16, 1880
Stowe, Harriet Beecher .... June 14, 1811, June 5, 1851,Mar 20, 1852
Stratemeyer, Edward .... Oct 4, 1862
Stratemeyer, George E. .... Nov 24, 1890
Stratton, Charles S. *see* Tom Thumb, General
Stratton, Samuel W. .... July 18, 1861
Straus, Isidor .... Feb 6, 1845
Straus, Nathan .... Jan 31, 1848
Straus, Oscar S. .... Dec 23, 1850
Strauss, Joseph B. .... Jan 9, 1870
Stravinsky, Igor .... June 17, 1882
Streep, Meryl .... June 22, 1949
Streisand, Barbra .... Apr 24, 1942
Strickland, William .... Apr 6, 1854
Strikes .... *1886* Mar 6, May 3-4; *1892* June 25, July 6, Sept 30, Oct 13; *1894* May 11, July 2, July 5, July 6; Jan 11, 1912; *1919* Feb 6, Sept 9, Sept 22; Apr 1, 1922, June 22, 1922, May 30, 1937, June 9, 1941, May 1, 1943; *1946* Apr 1, May 22; Mar 15, 1948, Jan 1, 1966, Mar 18, 1970, Mar 31, 1972, Dec 6, 1977; *1981* June 12, Aug 3; *1982* Sept 21, Nov 14; Sept 22, 1987
Stritch, Samuel A. .... Aug 17, 1887
Strong, Caleb F. .... Jan 9, 1743
Strong, George V. .... Mar 14, 1880
Strong, William .... May 6, 1808
Strouse, Charles .... June 7, 1928
Strout, Richard L. .... Mar 14, 1898
Struve, Otto .... Aug 12, 1897
Stuart, Gilbert C. .... Dec 3, 1755
Stuart, J.E.B. (Jeb) .... Feb 6, 1833, May 11, 1864
Studebaker, Clement .... Mar 12, 1831
Stutz, Harry C. .... Sept 12, 1876
Stuyvesant, Peter .... May 11, 1647, Sept 1, 1655
Styne, Jule .... Dec 31, 1905
Suffrage .... Nov 10, 1821, July 29, 1859, Oct 2, 1865, Jan 8, 1867; *1869* Jan 23, Feb 26, May 15, Nov 24, Dec 10; *1870* Feb 12, Mar 30; Apr 7, 1893, Nov 3, 1897, May 23, 1903; *1917* Jan 10, Jan 23, Feb 21, Feb 28; *1918* Jan 10, Apr 18, Nov 6; Jan 5, 1919, Aug 18, 1920, Feb 27, 1922, Mar 29, 1961, Jan 23, 1964, Aug 6, 1965, June 22, 1970; *1971* Mar 10, July 1; Feb 7, 1972, Aug 22, 1978, June 29, 1982
Sugar Act .... *1764* Mar 9, Apr 5, June 6
Suggs, Louise .... Sept 7, 1923
Sullavan, Margaret .... May 16, 1911
Sullivan, Ed(ward V.) .... Sept 18, 1902
Sullivan, John .... Feb 17, 1740
Sullivan, John L. .... Feb 7, 1882, July 8, 1889, Sept 7, 1892
Sullivan, Kathryn D. .... Oct 11, 1984
Sullivan, Louis .... Dec 22, 1988
Sullivan, Louis H. .... Sept 3, 1856
Sullivan, Mark .... Sept 10, 1874
Sully, Thomas .... June 8, 1773
Sulzberger, Arthur Hays .... Sept 12, 1891
Sulzberger, Arthur O. .... Feb 5, 1926
Summerall, Charles P. .... Mar 4, 1867
Sumner, Charles .... Jan 6, 1811, May 22, 1856
Sumner, Edwin V. .... Jan 30, 1797
Sumner, James B. .... Nov 19, 1887
Sumner, William G. .... Oct 30, 1840
Sumter, Thomas .... Aug 14, 1734
Sunday, Billy (William A.) .... Nov 19, 1862
Sununu, John H. .... July 2, 1939
Supreme Court .... Sept 24, 1789, Feb 1, 1790, Feb 18, 1793, Dec 15, 1795, Mar 8, 1796
1800s .... Feb 24, 1803, Feb 20, 1809; *1818* Feb 1, Mar 16; Mar 2, 1824, Feb 2, 1827, Feb 26, 1833, Mar 1, 1837, Mar 6, 1857, Mar 3, 1863, Dec 17, 1866, Jan 14, 1867, Feb 7, 1870, May 1, 1871, Jan 14, 1878, Feb 15, 1879, Mar 1, 1880, Jan 24, 1881, Oct 25, 1887, Mar 22, 1894,
1900s .... May 14, 1900, Jan 4, 1904; Jan 30, Feb 20; *1908* Feb 3, Feb 24; *1911* May 1, May 15, May 29, Jan 21; Dec 2, 1912, Jan 5, 1915; *1916* Jan 24, Jan 28; *1917* Jan 8, Mar 19; Jan 17, 1918, Mar 10, 1919; *1920* Jan 5, June 7; Feb 27, 1922, Feb 28, 1927, May 27, 1929, Feb 24, 1931, Oct 13, 1932; *1933* Jan 7, May 6; *1935* May 24, May 27; *1936* Jan 1, Jan 6, May 18; *1937* Feb 5, Mar 29, Apr 12, May 24;
1930s-1970s .... Jan 30, Feb 27; Feb 3, 1941; *1943* Jan 18, June 14; Mar 8, 1948, Jan 3, 1949; May 17, 1954, May 31, 1955, Mar 26, 1962; *1963* Mar 18, June 17; *1964* Feb 17, Mar 9; June 13, 1968, Oct 29, 1969; *1971* Apr 20, June 30; June 29, 1972; *1973* Jan 22, June 21; July 24, 1974, Oct 17, 1977, June 29, 1978, Dec 13, 1979;

1980s .... June 10, June 16; Mar 8, 1981; *1982* Mar 23, Apr 5, May 17, June 15, June 21, June 24, July 2; *1983* Apr 24, May 24; *1984* Mar 5, June 20; *1985* June 4, Dec 10; *1986* Jan 4, Feb 7, Apr 1, Apr 21, Apr 30, June 9, June 17, June 25; *1987* Jan 14, Jan 15, Mar 3, May 4, May 18, May 25, June 19, June 25, June 26; *1988* Jan 13, Feb 3, Feb 24, Apr 20, May 2, May 16, June 29, Sept 26
Surgeon General .... Apr 14, 1818, Jan 11, 1964
Surrogate motherhood .... Feb 3, 1988
Susskind, David H. .... Dec 19, 1920
Sutherland, Earl W. Jr. .... Nov 19, 1915
Sutherland, George .... Mar 25, 1862
Sutherland, Richard K. .... Nov 27, 1893
Sutherland, Thomas .... July 10, 1985
Sutter, John A. .... Feb 15, 1803, Jan 24, 1848
Sutton, Don .... Apr 2, 1945
Swaggart, Jimmy .... *1988* Feb 21, Apr 8, May 22
Swanson, Claude A. .... Mar 31, 1862
Swanson, Gloria .... Mar 27, 1899
Swarthout, Gladys .... Dec 25, 1904
Swasey, Ambrose .... Dec 19, 1846
Swayne, Charles .... Dec 14, 1904
Swayne, Noah H. .... Dec 7, 1804
Swearingen, John E. Jr. ...... Sept 7, 1918
Sweden .... Feb 5, 1783
Swift, Gustavus F. .... June 24, 1839
Swingle, Walter T. .... Jan 8, 1871
Swope, Gerard .... Dec 1, 1872
Swope, Herbert Bayard .... Jan 5, 1882
Sykes, George .... Oct 9, 1822
Sylvia, William H. .... Nov 26, 1828
Symington, Stuart .... June 26, 1901
Symmes, John C. .... July 21, 1742
Symons, Thomas W. .... Feb 7, 1849
Synthetic Fuel Corp. .... June 26, 1980
Szell, George .... June 7, 1897
Szent-Györgyi, Albert .... Sept 16, 1893
Szilard, Leo .... Feb 11, 1898
Szoka, Edmund C. .... May 29, 1988
Szold, Henrietta .... Dec 21, 1860

Taft, Helen H. .... Jan 2, 1861, June 19, 1886, May 22, 1943
Taft, Lorado .... Apr 29, 1860
Taft, Robert A. .... Sept 8, 1889, Apr 14, 1959
Taft, William Howard .... Sept 15, 1857, June 19, 1886, Feb 14, 1890, Feb 6, 1900, July 4, 1901, Jan 11, 1904, Feb 1, 1904, Jan 7, 1910, Apr 14, 1910, Apr 8, 1918, June 30, 1921, Feb 3, 1930, Mar 8, 1930
Tainter, Charles S. .... Apr 25, 1854
Taiwan .... Jan 1, 1979
Takamine, Jokichi .... Nov 3, 1854
Talbert, Billy .... Sept 4, 1918
Talmadge, Eugene .... Sept 23, 1884
Talmadge, Norma .... May 2, 1897
Tammany Society .... May 12, 1789
Tandy, Jessica .... June 7, 1909
Taney, Roger B. .... Mar 17, 1777, June 24, 1834, Dec 28, 1835, Mar 28, 1836, Oct 12, 1864
Tanguay, Eva .... Aug 1, 1878
Tappan, Arthur .... May 22, 1786
Tappan, Lewis .... May 23, 1788
Tarbell, Ida M. .... Nov 5, 1857
Tariff .... July 4, 1789, May 19, 1828, Dec 18, 1828; *1832* July 14, Nov 19, Nov 24, Dec 10, Dec 20; Mar 2, 1833, Dec 4, 1882, Apr 8, 1913
Tarkenton, Fran .... Feb 3, 1940
Tarkington, Booth .... July 29, 1869
Tarski, Alfred .... Jan 14, 1902
Tate, Allen .... Nov 19, 1899
Tattnall, Josiah .... Nov 9, 1795
Tatum, Art .... Oct 13, 1910
Tatum, Edward L. .... Dec 14, 1909
Taube, Henry .... Nov 30, 1915
Taussig, Edward D. .... Jan 17, 1898
Taussig, Helen B. .... May 24, 1898
Taxes .... Dec 30, 1969
Taylor, Bayard .... Jan 11, 1825
Taylor, David W. .... Mar 4, 1864
Taylor, Deems .... Dec 22, 1885
Taylor, Edward .... June 24, 1729
Taylor, Edward T. .... Dec 25, 1793
Taylor, Elizabeth .... Feb 27, 1932
Taylor, Frederick W. .... Mar 20, 1856
Taylor, George .... Feb 23, 1781
Taylor, John .... Dec 19, 1753
Taylor, John .... Nov 1, 1808
Taylor, John W. .... Mar 26, 1784
Taylor, Laurette .... Apr 1, 1884
Taylor, Margaret S. .... Sept 21, 1788, Jan 21, 1810, Aug 18, 1852
Taylor, Maxwell D. .... Aug 26, 1901
Taylor, Moses .... Jan 11, 1806
Taylor, Myron C. .... Jan 18, 1874, Dec 23, 1939
Taylor, Richard .... Jan 27, 1826
Taylor, Zachary .... Nov 24, 1784, Jan 21, 1840, Dec 25, 1837, June 15, 1845, Apr 2, 1845; *1846* May 8, May 18; Feb 23, 1847, July 9, 1850
Teagarden, Jack .... Aug 20, 1905
Teamsters .... *1988* June 28, July 15
Teapot Dome .... *1922* Apr 4, Dec 11; *1924* Feb 8, Feb 18, Mar 13, Mar 28, June 30; May 28, 1925; *1927* Feb 28, Apr 2; Oct 25, 1929
Teasdale, Sara .... Aug 8, 1884
Telegraph .... June 20, 1841, May 3, 1843, May 24, 1844, Feb 17, 1855, Oct 24, 1861, July 27, 1866, Jan 19, 1881, Jan 1, 1903, July 4, 1903, June 18, 1910, July 22, 1918, July 31, 1919, June 19, 1934
Telephone .... Mar 10, 1876, July 9, 1877, Jan 28, 1878, Jan 25, 1915, July 22, 1918, July 31, 1919, Jan 7, 1927, Sept 25, 1956, Aug 30, 1963
Television .... Apr 7, 1927; *1951* Jan 14, Sept 4, Dec 24; Apr 22, 1954, Jan 25, 1961, July 10, 1962, Nov 7, 1967, Mar 18, 1985, Feb 3, 1988
Teller, Edward .... Jan 15, 1908
Teller, Henry M. .... May 23, 1830
Temin, Howard M. .... Dec 10, 1934
Temperance *see* Prohibition

Temple, Shirley .... Apr 23, 1928
Tennent, Gilbert .... Feb 5, 1703
Tennessee .... Jan 1, 1780, Nov 14, 1785, Nov 5, 1791, Sept 10, 1794, Feb 7, 1796, June 1, 1796, Aug 30, 1834, Apr 27, 1854; *1861* Feb 9, May 7, June 8; Mar 4, 1862; *1865* Jan 9, Feb 22; July 24, 1866, Jan 21, 1909, Mar 1, 1914, Feb 25, 1918, Apr 23, 1940, July 6, 1944, May 1, 1982
Tennessee Valley Authority (TVA) .... May 18, 1933, Jan 30, 1939
Tennis .... *1900* Aug 7, Aug 8
Terhune, Albert PaysonDec 21, 1872
Terkel, Studs .... May 16, 1912
Terman, Lewis M. .... Jan 15, 1877
Terrorism .... Nov 4, 1979, Apr 24, 1980, Jan 20, 1981; *1983* Apr 18, Oct 23, *1984* Sept 20, Dec 4; *1985* June 14, Oct 9
Terry, Alfred H. .... Nov 10, 1827
Terry, Bill .... Oct 30, 1898
Terry, Eli .... Apr 13, 1772
Terry, Luther L. .... Jan 11, 1964
Tesla, Nikola .... July 9, 1856
Texaco .... Nov 19, 1985, Dec 19, 1987, Feb 23, 1988
Texas .... Apr 26, 1598, Aug 14, 1819, Jan 17, 1821, May 24, 1825, Apr 8, 1830; *1835* Oct 2, Nov 7, Dec 15; *1836* Feb 23, Mar 2, Mar 6, Apr 21, May 14; *1837* Mar 1, Mar 17, Aug 4; Aug 23, 1843; *1844* Mar 6, Apr 12; *1845* Jan 25, Mar 1, Mar 28, June 15, June 23, July 4, Aug 2, Aug 27, Dec 29; June 6, 1849, Feb 1, 1861, Mar 18, 1861, Nov 30, 1869, Mar 30, 1870, Apr 17, 1871, Sept 15, 1883,
1900s .... Sept 8, 1900, Jan 10, 1901, Aug 13, 1906, July 22, 1911, Nov 10, 1914, Mar 21, 1916, Mar 26, 1917, Mar 22, 1918, Sept 9, 1921; *1937* June 12, Apr 16; May 11, 1953, Aug 1, 1966, Sept 2, 1973, Apr 4, 1981, Aug 2, 1985, Nov 10, 1988
Thalberg, Irving .... May 30, 1899
Thanksgiving .... Nov 26, 1789
Thayer, Ernest L. .... Aug 14, 1863
Thayer, James B. .... Jan 15, 1831
Thayer, John M. .... Jan 24, 1820
Thayer, Sylvanus .... June 9, 1785
Theiler, Max .... Jan 30, 1899
Theobald, Samuel .... Nov 12, 1864
Thomas, Augustus .... Jan 8, 1857
Thomas, George H. .... July 31, 1826, Jan 19, 1862
Thomas, Isaiah .... Jan 19, 1750
Thomas, John .... Nov 9, 1724
Thomas, John Charles .... Sept 6, 1891
Thomas, John J. .... Jan 8, 1810
Thomas, Lowell .... Apr 6, 1892
Thomas, Norman M. .... Nov 20, 1884
Thomas, Robert B. .... Apr 24, 1766
Thomas, Seth .... Aug 19, 1785
Thomas, Theodore .... Oct 11, 1835, Dec 14, 1904
Thompson, Benjamin .... Mar 26, 1753
Thompson, Dorothy .... July 9, 1894
Thompson, John .... Nov 2, 1802
Thompson, John T. .... Dec 31, 1860
Thompson, J. Walter .... Oct 28, 1847
Thompson, Sam(uel L.) .... Mar 5, 1860
Thompson, Smith .... Jan 17, 1768
Thompson, Charles .... Nov 29, 1729, Apr 14, 1789
Thomson, Elihu .... Mar 29, 1853
Thomson, Virgil G. .... Nov 25, 1896
Thoreau, Henry David .... July 12, 1817
Thorek, Max .... Mar 10, 1880
Thornburgh, Richard L. .... Aug 11, 1988
Thorndike, Edward .... Aug 31, 1874
Thornton, Matthew .... June 24, 1803
Thornton, Tex (Charles B.) .... July 22, 1913
Thornton, William .... May 20, 1759
Thorpe, Jim (James F.) .... May 28, 1888
Thurber, James .... Dec 8, 1894
Thurman, Allen G. .... Nov 13, 1813
Thurmond, J. Strom .... Dec 5, 1902, July 17, 1948
Tibbett, Lawrence M. .... Nov 16, 1896
Ticknor, George .... Aug 1, 1791
Ticknor, William D. .... Aug 6, 1810
Tiffany, Charles L. .... Feb 15, 1812
Tiffany, Louis C. .... Feb 18, 1848
Tilden, Samuel J. .... Feb 9, 1814, Jan 29, 1877
Tilden, William T. Jr. .... Feb 10, 1893
Tilghman, Matthew .... Feb 17, 1718
Tillich, Paul .... Aug 20, 1886
Tillman, Benjamin R. .... Aug 11, 1917
Tillstrom, Burr .... Oct 13, 1917
Tilton, James .... June 1, 1745
Tilyou, George C. .... Feb 3, 1862
Timby, Theodore R. .... Apr 5, 1822
Time zones .... Nov 18, 1883
Timken, Henry C. .... July 11, 1831
Ting, Samuel C.C. .... Jan 26, 1936
Tinker, Grant A. .... Jan 11, 1926
Tinker, Joe .... July 27, 1880
Tiomkin, Dimitri .... May 10, 1899
Titanic .... Apr 15, 1912, Sept 1, 1985
Tobacco .... Dec 3, 1677, Dec 15, 1908, Jan 11, 1964, Oct 18, 1988
Tobey, Mark .... Dec 11, 1890
Tobin, Daniel J. .... Nov 14, 1955
Tobin, James .... Mar 5, 1918
Todd, David .... Mar 19, 1855
Todd, Michael .... June 2, 1909
Todd, Thomas .... Jan 23, 1765
Toland, Hugh H. .... Apr 16, 1806
Tompkins, Daniel D. .... June 21, 1774, June 11, 1825
Tompkins, Sally Louisa .... Nov 9, 1833
Tom Thumb, General .... Jan 4, 1838
Toombs, Robert A. .... July 2, 1810
Torbert, Alfred T.A. .... July 1, 1833
Toscanini, Arturo .... Mar 25, 1867
Toucey, Isaac .... Nov 5, 1792
Tough, Dave .... Apr 26, 1908

Tournament of Roses *see* California
Tower, John G. .... Dec 16, 1988
Towers, John H. .... Jan 30, 1885
Town, Ithiel .... Oct 3, 1784
Townes, Charles H. .... July 28, 1915
Townsend, Anne .... Feb 3, 1984
Townsend, Dr. Francis E. .... Jan 13, 1867, Jan 1, 1934, Apr 18, 1938
Track and field .... Apr 19, 1897
Tracy, Benjamin F. .... Apr 26, 1830
Tracy, Edward A. .... Oct 21, 1986
Tracy, Spencer .... Apr 5, 1900
Train, Arthur .... Sept 6, 1875
Transportation, Department of .... Oct 15, 1966, Jan 10, 1967, Nov 14, 1988
Traubel, Helen .... June 16, 1903
Travis, William B. .... Aug 9, 1809, Feb 23, 1836, Mar 6, 1836
Travolta, John .... Feb 18, 1954
Traynor, Pie (Harold J.) .... Nov 11, 1899
Treasury, Department of .... Sept 2, 1789, Sept 11, 1789, Mar 31, 1833, July 4, 1840, Feb 25, 1863
Treaties .... June 7, 1494, Sept 19, 1650, July 18, 1670, Feb 19, 1674, Aug 15, 1694, Jan 7, 1699, Apr 11, 1713, Oct 18, 1748, Nov 3, 1762, Feb 10, 1763, July 24, 1766, Feb 6, 1778, May 4, 1778, Apr 12, 1779, July 15, 1782, Nov 30, 1782; *1783* Jan 20, Apr 15, Sept 3; Jan 14, 1784, Jan 9, 1789, Nov 19, 1794; *1795* Aug 3, Aug 18, Sept 5, Oct 27; Nov 4, 1796
  1800s .... Sept 3, 1800, Oct 20, 1803, Nov 10, 1808, Aug 9, 1814, Dec 24, 1814, Feb 17, 1815, June 30, 1815, Feb 17, 1817, Apr 28, 1817, Oct 20, 1818, Feb 22, 1819, Apr 17, 1824, Jan 12, 1828, Sept 27, 1830, July 4, 1831, Dec 29, 1835, May 14, 1836, Aug 20, 1842; *1844* Apr 12, July 3, Aug 9; June 15, 1846, Dec 12, 1846, Jan 13, 1847; *1848* Feb 2, Mar 10, May 30; Apr 19, 1850, July 4, 1850, July 14, 1853, June 5, 1854, Apr 7, 1862, Apr 9, 1867, July 28, 1868, May 8, 1871, Jan 30, 1875, Jan 17, 1878, Jan 20, 1887, July 14, 1889, Feb 14, 1893, Dec 10, 1898, July 29, 1899
  1900s .... Feb 5, 1900, Nov 18, 1901, Jan 22, 1903, Nov 18, 1903, Sept5, 1905, Nov 30, 1908, Jan 11, 1909, Aug 5, 1914, May 3, 1916, June 28, 1919, Jan 21, 1920; *1921* Aug 24, Aug 25, Aug 29, Oct 18, Dec 23; Aug 27, 1928, Dec 4, 1928; *1929* Jan 2, Jan 15, July 24; July 21, 1930, Oct 10, 1934, Feb 3, 1944, June 14, 1947, Sept 2, 1947, Apr 4, 1949, Aug 24, 1949, Feb 27, 1950; *1951* May 5, Sept 1, Sept 8; Apr 15, 1952, Mar 8, 1954, Sept 8, 1954, Jan 23, 1955, Jan 15, 1960, Jan 17, 1961, Mar 16, 1961, July 25, 1963, Aug 4, 1963, Jan 27, 1967, June 17, 1971, Mar 26, 1972, Mar 16, 1978, Mar 26, 1979, June 18, 1979, Dec 23, 1985; *1987* Oct 3, Nov 24, Dec 7; *1988* Jan 2, Mar 29, May 27, May 31, June 1, Nov 4, Dec 24
Trenholm, George A. .... Feb 25, 1807
Trevino, Lee .... Dec 1, 1939
Trimble, Isaac R. .... May 15, 1802
Trimble, Robert .... Aug 25, 1828
Tripoli (Algiers) .... Sept 5, 1795, Nov 28, 1795, Nov 4, 1796, May 14, 1801, Feb 6, 1802, Oct 31, 1803, Feb 16, 1804, Apr 27, 1805, June 4, 1805, June 30, 1815
Trippe, Juan T. .... June 27, 1899
Troland, Leonard T. .... Apr 26, 1889
Trudeau, Edward L. .... Oct 5, 1898
Truman, Bess (Elizabeth V.) .... Feb 13, 1885, June 28, 1919, Oct 18, 1982
Truman, Harry S. .... May 8, 1884, June 28, 1919; *1945* Apr 12, July 17; *1946* Jan 20, Sept 20; Mar 12, 1947, July 31, 1948; *1949* Jan 20, June 24; *1950* Jan 31, May 11, June 5, Aug 27, Nov 1; Apr 11, 1951, Apr 8, 1952, Apr 15, 1952, July 6, 1957, Dec 26, 1972
Trumbull, John .... June 6, 1756
Trumbull, Jonathan .... Oct 12, 1710
Trumbull, Jonathan .... Mar 26, 1740
Trumbull, Lyman .... Oct 12, 1813
Trump, Donald J. .... *1988* Mar 26, Oct 12
Tryon, William .... Jan 27, 1788
Tubman, Harriet .... Mar 10, 1913
Tucker, Henry S. .... July 16, 1874
Tucker, Richard .... Aug 28, 1914
Tucker, Sophie .... Jan 13, 1884
Tugwell, Rexford G. .... July 10, 1891
Tunnels .... Feb 25, 1907, Jan 9, 1908, Nov 12,1927, May 25, 1950, Apr 15, 1964
Tunney, Gene .... Sept 23, 1926
Tupper, Earl S. .... July 28, 1907
Turner, Frederick J. .... Nov 14, 1861
Turner, Nat .... *1831* Aug 21, Nov 11
Turner, Richard K. .... May 27, 1885
Turner, Roger F. .... Mar 3, 1909
Turner, Ted (Robert E.) .... Nov 19, 1938
Turner, William H. .... July 14, 1906
Turpin, Ben .... Sept 17, 1869
Turpin, Sister Martha .... Jan 31, 1752
Tuskegee Institute .... July 4, 1881

Tuttle, Daniel S. .... Jan 26, 1837
Tuve, Merle A. .... June 27, 1901
Twain, Mark .... Nov 30, 1835
Tweed, William M. .... Apr 3, 1820; *1872* Jan 7, Nov 5; Dec 4, 1875
Twining, Nathan F. .... Oct 11, 1897
Twitty, Conway .... Sept 1, 1933
Tylenol .... Sept 29, 1982
Tyler, John .... Mar 29, 1790, Mar 29, 1813; *1841* Apr 6, Sept 9, Sept 13; Jan 31, 1842, Jan 10, 1843, Feb 28, 1844, June 26, 1844, Mar 3, 1845; *1861* Jan 17, Feb 4, Mar 2; Jan 18, 1862
Tyler, Julia G. .... May 4, 1820, June 26, 1844, July 10, 1889
Tyler, Letitia C. .... Nov 12, 1790, Mar 29, 1813, Sept 10, 1842
Tyler, Royall .... July 18, 1757, Apr 16, 1787

Ueberroth, Peter V. .... Sept 2, 1937
Ulam, Stanislaw M. .... May 13, 1984
Underwood, John T. .... Apr 12, 1857
Unemployment Insurance .... Jan 28, 1932
Union of Socialist Soviet Republics(USSR) *see* Russia
Unitarian Church .... Oct 8, 1720, Apr 22, 1759, Nov 18, 1787, May 3, 1959
Unitas, John .... May 7, 1933
United Auto Workers .... Aug 26, 1935, July 1, 1981
United Church of Christ .... June 25, 1957, Sept 27, 1985
United Daughters of the Confederacy .... Sept 10, 1894
United Mine Workers .... Jan 25, 1890, Jan 25, 1946, Jan 5, 1970
United Nations .... Jan 1, 1942; *1943* May 18, Nov 5, Nov 9; Aug 21, 1944; *1945* Feb 28, Apr 25, Apr 28, June 26, July 21, July 28, Aug 4, Aug 8, Oct 24, Dec 20; *1946* Jan 10, Jan 24, Oct 23, Dec 14; Dec 10, 1948, Oct 24, 1949, Sept 20, 1963, Oct 4, 1965, June 12, 1968, Aug 11, 1975, Dec 19, 1984, Oct 24, 1985, Feb 19, 1986, Dec 2, 1988
United Service Organizations (USO) .... Apr 7, 1941
United States Employment Service .... Jan 2, 1918, June 6, 1933
United States Housing Authority .... Sept 1, 1937
United States Sanitary Commission .... June 9, 1861
United States Shipping Board .... Sept 7, 1916
United States Steel Co. .... Feb 25, 1901, Sept 22, 1919, Aug 2, 1923, Mar 2, 1937
Universalist Church .... Dec 10, 1741, Jan 1, 1779, Jan 5, 1835, May 3, 1959
Untermyer, Samuel .... June 6, 1858
Updike, Daniel B. .... Feb 24, 1860
Updike, John H. .... Mar 18, 1932
Upjohn, Richard .... Jan 22, 1802
Upshur, Abel P. .... June 17, 1791, Feb 28, 1844
Upson, Ralph H. .... June 21, 1888
Upton, Emory .... Aug 27, 1839
Urban, Joseph .... Aug 27, 1839
Urban, Joseph .... May 26, 1872
Urey, Harold C. .... Apr 29, 1893
Uris, Leon M. .... Aug 2, 1924
Utah .... Mar 4, 1849, June 15, 1850, Sept 9, 1850, Sept 15, 1857, Nov 27, 1857, June 26, 1858, May 10, 1869, Feb 12, 1870, Oct 16, 1875, Jan 4, 1896, May 1, 1900, Aug 1, 1916, Jan 17, 1977

Vail, Alfred L. .... Sept 25, 1807
Vail, Theodore N. .... July 16, 1845
Valenti, Jack J. .... Sept 5, 1921
Valentino, Rudolph .... May 6, 1895, Aug 23, 1926
Valenzuela, Fernando .... Nov 1, 1960
Vallee, Rudy (Hubert P.) ...... Sept 7, 1914
Van Allen, James A. .... Sept 7, 1914
Van Allstyne, Egbert .... Mar 5, 1882
Van Anda, Carl A. .... Dec 2, 1864
Van Buren, Abby .... July 4, 1908
Van Buren, Hannah H. .... Mar 8, 1783, Feb 21, 1807, Feb 5, 1819
Van Buren, Martin .... Dec 5, 1782, Feb 21, 1807, Mar 6, 1829, June 25, 1831, Jan 25, 1832, Mar 31, 1840, Aug 9, 1848, July 24, 1862
Van Cortlandt, Oloff S. .... Apr 5, 1684
Van de Graaff, Robert J. .... Dec 20, 1901
Van Depoele, Charles J. .... Apr 27, 1846
Van Devanter, Willis .... Apr 17, 1859
Van Doren, Carl .... Sept 10, 1885
Van Doren, Mark .... June 13, 1894
Van Druten, John W. .... June 1, 1901
Van Dyke, Dick .... Dec 13, 1925
Van Heusen, James .... Jan 26, 1913
Van Loon, Hendrik W. .... Jan 14, 1862
Van Renssalaer, Stephen ..... Nov 1, 1764
Van Slyke, Lucius L. .... Jan 6, 1859
Van Sweringen, Mantis .... July 8, 1881
Van Sweringen, Oris P. .... Apr 24, 1879
Van Vleck, John H. .... Mar 13, 1899
Vance, Cyrus R. .... Mar 27, 1917, Apr 28, 1980
Vance, Dazzy (Clarence A.) .... Mar 4, 1891
Vandegrift, Alexander A. ..... Mar 13, 1887
Vandenberg, Arthur H. .... Mar 22, 1884
Vandenberg, Hoyt S. .... Jan 24, 1899
Vanderbilt, Cornelius .... May 27, 1794
Vanderbilt, Cornelius .... Nov 27, 1843
Vanderbilt, Harold S. .... July 6, 1884
Vanderbilt, William H. .... May 8, 1821
VanderMeer, Johnny .... June 11, 1938
Vanzetti, Bartolomeo *see* Sacco and Vanzetti
Vare, Glenna C. .... June 20, 1903
Varese, Edgard .... Dec 22, 1883
Varian, Russell H. .... Apr 24, 1898
Varnum, James M. .... Dec 17, 1748
Varnum, Joseph B. .... Jan 29, 1751
Vasey, George .... Feb 28, 1822
Vassar, Matthew .... Apr 29, 1792
Vatican .... Jan 10, 1984
Vaughn, Sarah .... Mar 27, 1924
Veblen, Thorstein B. .... July 30, 1854
Veeck, William L. Jr. .... Feb 9, 1914
Venuti, Joe .... Sept 1, 1904
Vermont .... Jan 15, 1777, July 2, 1777,

Dec 14, 1780, Feb 12, 1781; *1791* Jan 10, Mar 4, Nov 2; July 9, 1793, Nov 23, 1852
Verrazano, Giovanni de .... Jan 17, 1524, Apr 17, 1524
Versailles Peace Conference. *1919* Jan 18, June 28, July 10, Nov 19; Feb 11, 1920, Mar 19, 1920
Very, Frank W. .... Feb 10, 1852
Vesey, William .... Aug 10, 1674
Vespucci, Amerigo .... Mar 9, 1454
Veterans .... Mar 18, 1818, Mar 14, 1903, Mar 15, 1919, May 19, 1924, May 29, 1932, July 28, 1932, Mar 20, 1933, June 22, 1944
Veterans Bureau/ Administration .... Aug 9, 1921, July 21, 1930, Oct 18, 1988
Veterans of Foreign Wars (VFW) .... May 28, 1936
Vick, James .... Nov 23, 1818
Victor, Orville J. .... Oct 23, 1827
Vidal, Gore .... Oct 3, 1925
Vidor, King .... Feb 8, 1895
Vietnam .... May 12, 1962; *1964* Aug 4, Aug 7; *1965* Feb 8, Mar 8, July 28, Dec 24; *1966* Jan 31, May 15, June 29, Sept 22, Oct 25, Oct 26; *1968* Jan 30, May 3, May 10; *1969* Jan 18, Nov 15; *1970* Apr 30, May 4, July 10, Oct 7; Mar 4, 1971, Dec 18, 1972, Jan 15, 1973; *1975* Apr 27, Apr 29, Apr 30, Aug 11; Jan 21, 1977, Nov 13, 1982, May 7, 1984, Nov 11, 1984
Villa, Pancho .... *1916* Jan 11, Mar 9, Mar 10, Mar 15
Villard, Helen F.G. .... Dec 16, 1844
Villard, Henry .... Apr 10, 1835
Villard, Oswald G. .... Mar 13, 1872
Vincent, John H. .... Feb 23, 1832, Aug 4, 1874
Vinson, Frederick M. .... Jan 22, 1890, June 6, 1946
Vinson, Maribel .... Feb 15, 1961
Virgin Islands .... Aug 4, 1916; *1917* Jan 17, Mar 31
Virginia .... *1606* Apr 10, Dec 20; *1607* Apr 25, May 24, Sept 17; May 23, 1609, Feb 28, 1610, Nov 18, 1618; *1619* June 19, July 30; Feb 20, 1620, Mar 22, 1622; *1624* May 24, Aug 24; Mar 2, 1643, Apr 18, 1644, Jan 30, 1649, Mar 23, 1662, Sept 16, 1671, Feb 25, 1673; *1676* Apr 20, Sept 19; Jan 29, 1677, Feb 8, 1689, Aug 6, 1736, Feb 27, 1737, Sept 15, 1752, Mar 22, 1765; *1769* May 16, May 18; Mar 12, 1773; *1774* May 27, July 26, Aug 1; *1775* Mar 23, Apr 21; *1776* Jan 1, May 15, June 12, June 29, July 5, Oct 24; Jan 2, 1781, Dec 20, 1783; *1786* Jan 16, Jan 21; June 25, 1788; *1789* Dec 3, Dec 18; Mar 25, 1825; *1861* Apr 17, May 23; Apr 7, 1868, July 6, 1869, Jan 26, 1870, Apr 26, 1907, Sept 22, 1914
Volcker, Paul .... Sept 5, 1927, June 2, 1987
Volstead Act *see* Prohibition
Volunteers of America .... Mar 21, 1896
Von Braun, Werner *see* Braun, Werner von
Von Hayek, Friedrich A. *see* Hayek, Friedrich von
Von Karman, Theodore *see* Karman, Theodore von
Von Steuben, Baron Friedrich *see* Steuben, Baron Friedrich von
Von Tilzer, Albert .... Mar 29, 1878
Von Tilzer, Harry .... July 8, 1872
Vonnegut, Kurt Jr. .... Nov 11, 1922
Voting *see* Suffrage
Vought, Chance M. .... Feb 26, 1890

Waddell, James I. .... July 13, 1824
Waddell, Rube (George E.) ... Oct 13, 1876
Wade, Benjamin F. .... Oct 27, 1800
Wadsworth, James S. .... Oct 30, 1807
Wadsworth, James W. .... Aug 12, 1877
Wadsworth, Peleg .... May 6, 1748
Waesche, Russell R. .... Jan 6, 1886
Wages *see* Minimum Wages/Hours
Wagnalls, Adam W. .... Sept 24, 1843
Wagner, Honus (John P.) ..... Feb 24, 1874, Jan 29, 1936
Wagner, Robert F. .... June 8, 1877, Aug 3, 1933, July 5, 1935
Wainwright, Jonathan M. .... Aug 23, 1883
Wait, ThomasB. .... Jan 1, 1785
Wait, William B. .... Mar 25, 1839
Waite, Morrison R. .... Nov 29, 1816, Jan 19, 1874, Mar23, 1888
Wake Island .... Jan 17, 1898, July 4, 1898
Waksman, Selman A. .... July 22, 1888
Walcott, Charles D. .... Mar 31, 1850
Wald, George .... Nov 18, 1906
Wald, Lillian D. .... Mar 9, 1867
Walgreen, Charles R. .... Oct 9, 1873
Walker, Francis A. .... July 2, 1840
Walker, Henry O. .... May 14, 1843
Walker, Herschel .... Mar 3, 1962
Walker, James J. .... June 19, 1881
Walker, John A. Jr. .... May 29, 1985
Walker, Mary E. .... Nov 26, 1832
Walker, Mickey .... July 13, 1901
Walker, Sarah B. .... Dec 23, 1867
Walker, Thomas .... Jan 25, 1715, Mar 16, 1750
Walker, William H. .... Apr 7, 1869
Wall Street *see* Economy
Wallace, Bobby (Roderick J.) Nov 4, 1873
Wallace, DeWitt .... Nov 12, 1889
Wallace, George C. .... Aug 25, 1919, Sept 10, 1963, May 15, 1972
Wallace, Henry A. .... Oct 7, 1888, Sept 20, 1946, Nov 18, 1965
Wallace, Lew(is) .... Apr 10, 1827
Wallace, Lila Bell .... Dec 25, 1889
Wallace, Mike .... May 9, 1918
Wallach, Eli .... Dec 7, 1915
Wallack, James W. .... Aug 24, 1795
Wallenstein, Alfred .... Oct 7, 1898
Waller, Fats (Thomas) .... May 21, 1904
Wallis, Hal B. .... Sept 14, 1899
Walsh, David I. .... Nov 11, 1872
Walsh, Ed .... May 14, 1881
Walsh, Frank P. .... Apr 8, 1918
Walsh, Thomas J. .... June 12, 1859
Walter, Bruno .... Sept 15, 1876
Walter, Thomas U. .... Sept 4, 1804
Walters, Barbara .... Sept 25, 1931
Walthall, Henry B. .... Mar 18, 1878
Walther, Carl F.W. .... Oct 25, 1811
Walton, George .... Feb 2, 1804
Wanamaker, John .... July 11, 1838

Waner, Lloyd J. .... Mar 16, 1906
Waner, Paul .... Apr 16, 1903
War Department .... Aug 7, 1789, Sept 12, 1789, June 15, 1946, Sept 18, 1947
War Manpower Commission .... Apr 18, 1942
War of 1812
1812 .... May 16, June 1, June 18, June 19, July 17, Aug 13, Aug 16, Aug 19, Oct 4, Oct 13, Oct 25, Nov 21, Dec 26, Dec 29
1813 .... Jan 22, Feb 24, Mar 8, Apr 15, Apr 27, May 9, May 27, June 1, July 11, July 15, July 31, Aug 9, Sept 5, Sept 10, Sept 26, Sept 28, Oct 5, Nov 4, Nov 11, Dec 18, Dec 19, Dec 29
1814 .... Jan 3, Mar 28, Mar 30, Apr 29, May 6, June 28, July 3, July 5, July 25, Aug 3, Aug 8, Aug 19, Aug 22, Aug 24, Aug 29, Sept 1, Sept 11, Sept 12, Nov 5, Nov 7, Dec 1, Dec 14, Dec 15, Dec 23, Dec 24
1815 .... Jan 8, Jan 15, Feb 20
Also Feb 27, 1817
War on Poverty *see* Office of Economic Opportunity
War Production Board .... Jan 16, 1942
War Shipping Administration .... Feb 7, 1942
Warburg, Felix M. .... Jan 14, 1871
Warburg, Paul M. .... Aug 10, 1868
Ward, Artemas .... Nov 26, 1727
Ward, Artemus *see* Browne, Charles F.
Ward, Henry A. .... Mar 9, 1834
Ward, Henry F. .... Oct 15, 1873
Ward, John Q.A. .... June 29, 1830
Ward, Montgomery .... Feb 17, 1843
Ward, Monty (John M.) .... Mar 3, 1860
Ware, Henry .... Apr 1, 1764
Ware, William R. .... May 27, 1832
Warfield, David .... Nov 28, 1866
Warfield, Wallis .... June 19, 1896
Warhol, Andy .... Aug 6, 1928
Waring, Fred .... June 9, 1900
Warner, Glenn S. (Pop) .... Apr 5, 1871
Warner, Harry M. .... Dec 12, 1881
Warner, H(enry) B. .... Oct 26, 1876
Warner, Jack L. .... Aug 2, 1892
Warner, Seth .... May 6, 1743
Warren, Earl .... Mar 19, 1891, Sept 30, 1953, Nov 29, 1963, Sept 27, 1964, June 13, 1968, July 9, 1974
Warren, Francis E. .... June 20, 1844
Warren, Gouverneur K. .... Jan 8, 1830
Warren, Harry .... Dec 24, 1893
Warren, John .... July 27, 1753
Warren, John C. .... Aug 1, 1778
Warren, Josph .... June 11, 1741
Warren, Josiah .... Apr 14, 1874
Warren, Mercy Otis .... Sept 23, 1728
Warren, Robert Penn .... Apr 24, 1905, Feb 26, 1986
Warren, Whitney .... Jan 29, 1864
Warren, William F. .... Mar 13, 1833
Washburn, Cadwallader C. .... Apr 22, 1818
Washburne, Elihu B. .... Sept 23, 1816
Washington, Booker T. .... Apr 5, 1856, July 4, 1881
Washington, Bushrod .... June 5, 1762
Washington, D.C. *see* District of Columbia
Washington, Dinah .... Aug 29, 1924
Washington, George .... Feb 22, 1732, May 5, 1749, July 20, 1749, Nov 5, 1753, Feb 1, 1753, Nov 15, 1753; *1754* Jan 16, May 27, June 4, July 3, Dec 17; *1755* May 10, July 9, Aug 14; July 24, 1758, Jan 6, 1759, Mar 14, 1761, Feb 27, 1773, June 19, 1773, Aug 5, 1774; *1775* Mar 25, June 15, June 16, July 3; *1776* Jan 1, June 27, Dec 25; *1783* May 10, Dec 4, Dec 23; Dec 5, 1786, May 25, 1787; *1789* Jan 7, Feb 4, Apr 6, Apr 14, Apr 16, Apr 23, Apr 30, June 1, Sept 29; Jan 8, 1790, Jan 24, 1791, Nov 26, 1791, Apr 5, 1792, Dec 5, 1792, Mar 4, 1793, Apr 22, 1793, Aug 7, 1794, July 10, 1795, Sept 17, 1796, July 2, 1798, Dec 14, 1799, July 4, 1848, Nov 26, 1883, Dec 6, 1884, Oct 16, 1899
Washington, Harold .... Apr 12, 1983
Washington, Martha .... June 2, 1732, Jan 6, 1759, May 22, 1802
Washington Monument .... July 4, 1848, Dec 6, 1884, Feb 21, 1885, Oct 9, 1888
Washington (State) .... Nov 22, 1842, Nov 13, 1843, Sept 11, 1852, Mar 2, 1853, Jan 28, 1861; *1889* Jan 6, July 4, Nov 11; Mar 28, 1890, Nov 8, 1910, Feb 6, 1919, Apr 21, 1962, May 4, 1974, May 18, 1980
Water *see* Environment
Watergate .... June 17, 1972; *1973* Feb 7, Apr 17, Apr 30, May 17, Oct 14, Oct 20, Nov 1; *1974* Jan 1, Jan 4, Jan 6, July 8, July 12, July 24, July 27, July 30, Aug 20, Sept 8
Waterhouse, Benjamin .... Mar 4, 1754
Waterman, Lewis E. .... Nov 20, 1837
Waters, Ethel .... Oct 31, 1900
Watson, Elkanah .... Jan 22, 1758
Watson, James D. .... Apr 6, 1928, Apr 25, 1953
Watson, John B. .... Jan 9, 1878
Watson, Thomas A. .... Jan 18, 1854, Mar 10, 1876, Jan 25, 1915
Watson, Thomas E. .... Sept 5, 1856
Watson, Thomas J. .... Feb 17, 1874
Watson, Thomas J. Jr. .... Jan 8, 1914
Watson, Tom .... Sept 4, 1949
Watterson, Henry .... Feb 16, 1840
Waugh, Sidney .... Jan 17, 1904
WAVES .... July 30, 1942
Wayland, Francis .... Aug 23, 1826
Wayne, Anthony .... Jan 1, 1745, July 15, 1779, Aug 20, 1794, Aug 3, 1795
Wayne, James M. .... July 5, 1867
Wayne, John .... May 26, 1907
Weather Bureau/Service .... Sept 20, 1829, Feb 9, 1870, Jan 3, 1871, Oct 1, 1890, Oct 3, 1970
Weaver, Charlie .... Dec 28, 1905
Weaver, James B. .... June 12, 1833
Weaver, Robert C. .... Dec 29, 1907, Jan 17, 1966

Webb, Alexander S. .... Feb 15, 1835
Webb, James H. Jr. .... Feb 22, 1988
Webb, James W. .... Feb 8, 1802
Webb, William H. .... June 19, 1816
Webbe, John .... Feb 13, 1741
Weber, Ernst .... Sept 6, 1901
Weber, Joseph M. .... Aug 11, 1867
Webster, Daniel .... Jan 18, 1782, June 17, 1825, June 17, 1843
Webster, H(arold) T. .... Sept 21, 1885
Webster, Jean .... July 24, 1876
Webster, Noah .... Oct 16, 1758, Apr 21, 1828
Webster, Pelatiah .... Nov 24, 1726, Feb 16, 1783
Webster, William H. .... Mar 3, 1987, Dec 6, 1988
Wedemeyer, Albert C. .... July 9, 1897
Weed, Thurlow .... Nov 15, 1797
Weems, Mason L. .... Oct 11, 1759
Weems, Ted .... Sept 26, 1901
Weill, Kurt .... Mar 2, 1900
Weinberg, Steven .... May 3, 1933
Weinberger, Caspar W. .... Aug 18, 1917
Weir, Benjamin .... May 8, 1984
Weir, Ernest T. .... Aug 1, 1875
Weissmuller, Johnny .... June 2, 1903
Welch, Joseph N. .... Oct 22, 1890
Welch, Mickey (Michael F.) ...... July 4, 1859
Welch, Robert H.W. Jr. .... Dec 1, 1899, Dec 9, 1958
Welch, William H. .... Apr 8, 1850
Welk, Lawrence .... Mar 11, 1903
Welfare .... Oct 13, 1988
Weller, Thomas H. .... June 15, 1915
Welles, Gideon .... July 1, 1802
Welles, Orson .... May 6, 1915, Oct 30, 1938
Welles, Sumner .... Oct 14, 1892
Wells, Henry .... Dec 12, 1805
Wells, Horace .... Jan 21, 1815
Welty, Eudora .... Apr 13, 1909
Wentworth, Benning .... July 24, 1696
Wesley, John and Charles .... Jan 6, 1736
Wesson, Daniel B. .... May 25, 1825
West, Benjamin .... Oct 10, 1738
West, Francis .... Oct 28, 1586
West, Jerry .... May 28, 1938
West, Mae .... Aug 17, 1892
West, Nathanael .... Oct 17, 1902
West Point se Military Academies
West Virginia .... Aug 20, 1861, Nov 26, 1861, Mar 26, 1863, June 20, 1863, Dec 6, 1907, July 1, 1914, Nov 20, 1968, Nov 14, 1970, Feb 26, 1972
Westcott, Edward N. .... Sept 27, 1846
Western Union .... Jan 19, 1881
Westinghouse, George .... Oct 6, 1846
Westmoreland, William C. .... Mar 26, 1914
Weston, Edward .... May 9, 1850
Weston, Edward .... Mar 24, 1886
Weston, Thomas .... Feb 20, 1620
Westover, Russell C. .... Aug 3, 1886
Wetmore, Alexander .... June 18, 1886
Weyerhaeuser, Frederick .... Nov 21, 1834
Whalen, Grover A. .... June 2, 1886
Wharton, Edith .... Jan 24, 1862
Wharton, Joseph .... Mar 3, 1826
Wheat, Zach(ariah) .... May 23, 1888
Wheeler, Burton K. .... Feb 27, 1882
Wheeler, Earle G. .... Jan 13, 1908
Wheeler, John A. .... July 9, 1911
Wheeler, Joseph .... Sept 10, 1836
Wheeler, Wayne B. .... Nov 10, 1869
Wheeler, William A. .... June 30, 1819, June 4, 1887
Wheelock, Eleazar .... Apr 22, 1711
Wheelock, John .... Jan 28, 1754
Whipple, George H. .... Aug 28, 1878
Whipple, Henry B. .... Feb 15, 1822
Whipple, Squier .... Sept 16, 1804
Whipple, William .... Jan 14, 1730
Whiskey Rebellion .... Aug 7, 1794, July 10, 1795
Whistler, James A.M. .... July 10, 1834
White, Andrew D. .... Nov 7, 1832
White, Byron R. .... June 8, 1917
White, David .... July 1, 1862
White, E(lwyn) B. .... July 11, 1899
White, Edward D. .... Nov 3, 1845, Dec 12, 1910, May 19, 1921
White, Edward H. II .... Nov 14, 1930, June 3, 1965, Jan 27, 1967
White, George .... Oct 11, 1968
White, Rev. John .... Mar 19, 1628
White, John .... Feb 14, 1802
White, Pearl .... Mar 4, 1889
White, Stanford .... Nov 9, 1853, June 25, 1906
White, Theodore H. .... May 6, 1915
White, Walter F. .... July 1, 1893
White, William .... Apr 4, 1748
White, William Allen .... Feb 10, 1868
Whitefield, George .... Dec 28, 1714, May 7, 1738
Whitehead, Alfred North .... Feb 15, 1861
White House .... Oct 13, 1792, Nov 1, 1800, Jan 17, 1806, Mar 29, 1812, Aug 24, 1814, Jan 1, 1818, Mar 9, 1820, Feb 25, 1828, Apr 10, 1832, Jan 31, 1842, May 21, 1874, June 19, 1878, Sept 9, 1893, Feb 17, 1906, Nov 25, 1913, May 7, 1914, Jan 10, 1917, Nov 10, 1917, Aug 7, 1918, Dec 24, 1929, July 30, 1942, Mar 27, 1952, Dec 9, 1967, June 12, 1971, Mar 26, 1979
Whiteman, Paul .... Mar 28, 1891
Whiteside, Arthur D. .... Sept 15, 1882
Whitlock, Brand .... Mar 4, 1869
Whitman, Marcus .... Sept 4, 1802
Whitman, Walt .... May 31, 1819
Whitney, Eli .... Dec 8, 1765, Mar 14, 1794
Whitney, William C. .... July 5, 1841
Whitney, Willis R. .... Aug 22, 1868
Whittaker, Charles E. .... Feb 22, 1901
Whittier, John Greenleaf .... Dec 17, 1807
Whitworth, Kathy .... Sept 27, 1939
Wickman, Carl E. .... Aug 7, 1887
Widener, Peter A.B. .... Nov 13, 1834
Wiener, Norbert .... Nov 26, 1894
Wiesel, Elie .... Sept 30, 1928
Wiesel, Torsten N. .... June 13, 1924
Wiggin, Kate Douglas .... Sept 28, 1856
Wigglesworth, Michael .... Oct 18, 1631
Wightman, Hazel .... Dec 5, 1974
Wigner, Eugene P. .... Nov 17, 1902

Wilbur, Ray Lyman .... Apr 13, 1875
Wilbur, Richard..................... Apr 18, 1987
Wilcox, Cadmus M. .... May 29, 1824
Wilcox, Ella Wheeler .... Nov 5, 1850
Wilcox, Stephen .... Feb 12, 1830
Wilder, Burt G. .... Aug 11, 1841
Wilder, Thornton .... Apr 17, 1897
Wiley, Harvey W. .... Oct 18, 1844
Wilkes, Charles .... Apr 3, 1798, Jan 19, 1840, Nov 8, 1861
Wilkins, Roy .... Aug 30, 1901
Wilkinson, James .... Dec 28, 1825
Willard, Emma .... Feb 23, 1787
Willard, Frances E.C. .... Sept 28, 1839
Willard, Frank .... Sept 21, 1893
Willard, Simon .... Apr 24, 1676
Willard, Simon .... Apr 3, 1753
Willett, Thomas..................... June 14, 1665
Williams, Andy .... Dec 3, 1930
Williams, Aubrey W. .... Aug 23, 1890
Williams, Bert .... Mar 4, 1922
Williams, Billy .... June 15, 1938
Williams, Daniel Hale .... Jan 18, 1858
Williams, Edward Bennett .... May 31, 1920
Williams, George H. .... Mar 26, 1820
Williams, Gluyas .... July 23, 1888
Williams, Hank .... Sept 17, 1923
Williams, Mary Lou .... May 8, 1910
Williams, James R. .... Mar 30, 1888
Williams, John .... Aug 30, 1817
Williams, Paul .... Sept 19, 1940
Williams, Roger...................... Feb 5, 1631, Sept 13, 1635
Williams, Ted .... Aug 31, 1918
Williams, Tennessee (Thomas L.)........................ Mar 26, 1911
Williams, William .... Apr 23, 1731
Williams, William C. .... Sept 17, 1883
Willis, Nathaniel P. .... Jan 20, 1806, Jan 1, 1842
Willkie, Wendell L. .... Feb 18, 1892, Aug 26, 1942
Wills, Helen .... Oct 6, 1905
Wills, Maury (Maurice) .... Oct 2, 1932
Willson, Meredith .... May 18, 1902
Willys, John N. .... Oct 25, 1873
Wilmot, David .... Jan 20, 1814
Wilson, Alexander .... July 6, 1766
Wilson, Allen B. .... Oct 18, 1824
Wilson, Charles EdwardNov 18, 1886
Wilson, Charles Erwin .... July 18, 1890
Wilson, Edith B. .... Oct 15, 1872, Dec 18, 1915, Dec 28, 1961
Wilson, Edmund .... May 8, 1895
Wilson, Ellen L. .... May 15, 1860, June 24, 1885, Aug 6, 1914
Wilson, Hack (Lewis R.) .... Apr 26, 1900
Wilson, Henry .... Feb 16, 1812, Nov 22, 1875
Wilson, Henry B. .... Feb 23, 1861
Wilson, James .... Sept 14, 1742, Sept 24, 1789
Wilson, James H. .... Sept 2, 1837
Wilson, Kemmons .... Jan 5, 1913
Wilson, Kenneth G. .... June 8, 1936
Wilson, Robert W. .... Jan 10, 1936
Wilson, Samuel .... Sept 16, 1766
Wilson, Thornton A. .... Feb 8, 1921
Wilson, William A. .... Mar 6, 1984
Wilson, William B. .... Apr 2, 1862, Jan 25, 1890, Mar 4, 1913
Wilson, William G. .... Nov 26, 1895, June 10, 1935
Wilson, William L. .... May 3, 1843
Wilson, Woodrow .... Dec 28, 1856, June 24, 1885, June 9, 1902, Oct 25, 1902, Jan 7, 1911, Apr 8, 1913, Nov 25, 1913, May 7, 1914, July 28, 1915, Dec 18, 1915, Apr 18, 1916; 1917 Jan 22, Feb 26, Apr 2; *1918* Jan 8, Jan 26, Aug 7, Nov 5; *1919* Jan 18, Feb 14, Sept 26; Feb 13, 1920, Dec 10, 1920, Feb 3, 1924
Winant, John G. .... Feb 23, 1889
Winchell, Walter .... Apr 7, 1897
Winchester, Oliver F. .... Nov 30, 1810
Winebrenner, John .... Mar 25, 1797
Winfrey, Oprah .... June 29, 1954
Winslow, Edward .... Oct 18, 1595
Winslow, John A. .... Nov 19, 1811
Winslow, Josiah .... Dec 19, 1675, Dec 18, 1680
Winston, Joseph .... June 17, 1746
Winthrop, John .... Jan 12, 1588, Aug 29, 1629, Oct 20, 1629
Winthrop, John .... Feb 12, 1606, Apr 23, 1662
Winthrop, John .... Dec 19, 1714
Winthrop, Robert C. .... May 12, 1809
Winton, Alexander .... June 20, 1860
Wirt, William .... Nov 8, 1772, Sept 26, 1831
Wirth, Louis .... Aug 28, 1897
Wirtz, W. Willard .... Mar 4, 1912
Wisconsin .... Dec 11, 1833, Apr 20, 1836, July 4, 1836, Dec 16, 1846, Mar 13, 1848, May 29, 1848, Sept 30, 1882, Mar 23, 1903, Jan 28, 1932
Wise, Isaac M. .... Mar 29, 1819
Wise, John .... Feb 24, 1808
Wisae, Stephen S. .... Mar 17, 1874
Wissler, Clark .... Sept 18, 1870
Wistar, Caspar .... Sept 13, 1761
Wister, Owen .... July 14, 1860
Witherspoon, John .... Feb 5, 1723
Witte, Edwin E. .... Jan 4, 1887
Wodehouse, P(elham) G. .... Oct 15, 1881
Wolcott, Oliver .... Nov 20, 1726
Wolcott, Oliver .... Jan 11, 1760
Wolcott, Roger .... Jan 4, 1679
Wolfe, Thomas C. .... Oct 3, 1900
Women's Army Corps (WAC) .... May 14, 1942
Women's Bureau .... June 5, 1920
Women's Rights .... July 19, 1848, Oct 23, 1850; *1869* Jan 19, Jan 23, May 15, Nov 24, Dec 10; Feb 12, 1870, Feb 17, 1879, Nov 7, 1893, Dec 11, 1896, Nov 3, 1897, Nov 8, 1910, Oct 10, 1911; *1917* Jan 10, Jan 23, Feb 21, Feb 28, Mar 26, Apr 18, Apr 21, Nov 6; Jan 10, 1918, June 5, 1919, Aug 18, 1920; *1922* Feb 27, Sept 12; Mar 22, 1972, Jan 22, 1973, June 3, 1974, Oct 6, 1978; *1982* June 30, Sept 15, Nov 5; *1987* Jan 14, May 4, July 7; *1988* Feb 2, Apr 11
Wood, Garfield .... Dec 4, 1880
Wood, Grant .... Feb 13, 1892
Wood, James R. .... Sept 14, 1813
Wood, Leonard .... Oct 9, 1860

Wood, Robert E. .... June 13, 1879
Wood, Thomas J. .... Sept 25, 1823
Woodbury, Levi .... Dec 22, 1789
Woodcock, Leonard F. .... Feb 15, 1911
Wooden, John R. .... Oct 14, 1910
Woodhull, Victoria Claflin *see* Claflin, Victoria
Woodruff, Robert W. .... Dec 6, 1889
Woodruff, Wilford .... Mar 1, 1807
Woods, William B. .... Aug 3, 1824
Woodward, Calvin M. .... Aug 25, 1837
Woodward, Joanne .... Feb 27, 1930
Woodward, Robert B. .... Apr 10, 1917
Wool, John E. .... Feb 29, 1784
Woollcott, Alexander .... Jan 19, 1887
Woolsey, Theodore D. .... Oct 31, 1801
Woolworth, F(rank) W. .... Apr 13, 1852, Feb 22, 1879
Worden, John L. .... Mar 12, 1818
Work, Henry C. .... Oct 1, 1832
Workmen's Compensation ... July 4, 1911
Works Progress
Administration (WPA) ..... Apr 8, 1935, Aug 27, 1935, June 30, 1943
World Fairs .... July 14, 1853, May 10, 1876, Oct 21, 1892, May 1, 1893, Sept 11, 1893, Sept 18, 1895, June 1, 1898, May 1, 1901, Apr 30, 1904, June 1, 1905, June 1, 1909, Jan 1, 1915, Feb 20, 1915, May 31, 1926, May 27, 1933, June 12, 1937, June 30, 1938, Feb 18, 1939, Apr 21, 1962, Apr 22, 1964, Apr 6, 1968, May 4, 1974, May 1, 1982
World War I
1914 .... Aug 4, Aug 19
1915 .... Jan 28, Feb 10, Feb 19, Feb 23, Mar 10, May 1, May 7, May 25, July 2, July 25, Sept 1, Nov 7, Dec 4
1916 .... Feb 10, Apr 18, May 4, May 9, June 3, July 30, Oct 7, Oct 28, Nov 7, Dec 6, Dec 18
1917 .... Jan 22, Feb 1, Feb 3, Feb 26, Mar 9, Mar 12, Mar 21, Mar 25, Mar 31, Apr 1, Apr 2, Apr 4, Apr 6, Apr 9, Apr 14, Apr 19, Apr 24, May 3, May 10, May 18, May 26, June 5, June 13, June 15, June 25, July 2, July 4, July 7, July 13, July 20, July 31, Aug 5, Aug 10, Aug 21, Aug 27, Sept 4, Sept 7, Sept 15, Oct 1, Oct 15, Oct 17, Oct 23, Nov 16, Nov 20, Nov 30, Dec 6, Dec 7, Dec 26
1918 .... Jan 1, Jan 8, Jan 26, Feb 5, Feb 8, Feb 25, Mar 25, Mar 26, May 16, May 27, May 28, May 30, June 1, June 3, June 6, June 11, June 21, June 24, July 1, July 4, July 15, July 18, July 22, Aug 2, Aug 3, Sept 4, Sept 9, Sept 12, Sept 15, Sept 22, Sept 26, Sept 28, Oct 4, Oct 8, Oct 30, Nov 5, Nov 9, Nov 11, Dec 1
1919 .... Feb 24, June 28, Sept 10, Dec 22
1920 .... Jan 12
1921 .... Aug 24, Aug 25, Aug 29, Oct 13
1923 .... Jan 10
World War II
1939 .... Apr 14, Apr 26, Sept 3, Sept 5, Nov 2
1940 .... May 25, June 3, June 10, June 28, July 30, Aug 18, Sept 3, Sept 26
1941 .... Jan 6, Mar 11, Apr 7, Apr 10, Apr 28, May 5, May 21, June 2, June 20, June 24, July 7, July 26, Aug 14, Aug 18, Sept 11, Sept 19, Oct 8, Oct 17, Oct 28, Oct 30, Dec 6, Dec 7, Dec 8, Dec 10, Dec 11, Dec 16, Dec 17, Dec 19, Dec 20, Dec 22, Dec 23, Dec 27
1942 .... Jan 2, Jan 7, Jan 14, Jan 24, Jan 26, Jan 28, Feb 1, Feb 7, Feb 9, Feb 19, Feb 27, Mar 10, Mar 12, Mar 17, Apr 9, Apr 10, Apr 18, May 5, May 6, May 7, May 15, June 3, June 5, June 11, June 12, June 17, June 27, July 4, July 30, Aug 7, Aug 8, Sept 3, Oct 2, Oct 11, Oct 26, Nov 8, Nov 12, Nov 13, Nov 28, Nov 30, Dec 1
1943 .... Jan 14, Jan 27, Feb 3, Feb 9, Mar 1, Mar 3, Mar 17, Apr 1, Apr 20, May 1, May 7, May 11, May 12, May 27, June 22, July 10, July 22, Aug 1, Aug 17, Sept 8, Sept 16, Oct 14, Oct 19, Nov 22, Nov 28, Dec 4, Dec 24, Dec 27
1944 .... Jan 11, Jan 16, Jan 22, Jan 23, Jan 31, Feb 1, Mar 4, Mar 6, Apr 22, Apr 26, May 18, June 4, June 6, June 15, June 16, June 19, June 22, June 26, July 18, July 19, Aug 7, Aug 15, Aug 21, Aug 23, Aug 25, Sept 3, Sept 11, Sept 12, Sept 14, Oct 21, Oct 23, Dec 16, Dec 21
1945 .... Jan 9, Jan 28, Feb 4, Feb 19, Feb 23, Mar 6, Mar 7, Mar 10, Apr 1, Apr 9, Apr 10, Apr 21, Apr 24, May 7, May 10, July 5, July 17, Aug 6, Aug 8, Aug 9, Aug 14, Aug 15, Aug 21, Sept 2, Nov 20, Nov 23
Worth, William J. .... Mar 1, 1794
Worthington, Henry R. .... Dec 17, 1817
Worthy, James .... Feb 27, 1961
Wouk, Herman .... May 27, 1915
Wright, Benjamin .... Oct 10, 1770

Wright, Carroll D. .... July 25, 1840
Wright, Elizur .... Feb 18, 1804
Wright, Frank Lloyd .... June 8, 1869
Wright, Harold Bell .... May 4, 1872
Wright, Henry (Harry) .... Jan 10, 1835
Wright, Horatio G. .... Mar 6, 1820
Wright, James C. Jr. .... Dec 22, 1922
Wright, Jerauld .... June 4, 1898
Wright, Marcus J. .... June 5, 1831
Wright, Mickey .... Feb 14, 1925
Wright, Orville .... Aug 19, 1871, Dec 17, 1903, Sept 17, 1908
Wright, Richard N. .... Sept 4, 1908
Wright, Wilbur .... Apr 16, 1867, Dec 17, 1903
Wrigley, William Jr. .... Sept 30, 1861
Wriston, Walter B. .... Aug 4, 1919
Wurlitzer, Rudolph .... Jan 31, 1831
Wurster, William W. .... Oct 20, 1895
Wyant, Alexander H. .... Jan 11, 1836
Wyatt, Sir Francis .... Aug 24, 1624
Wyeth, Andrew N. .... July 12, 1917
Wyeth, Newell C. .... Oct 22, 1862
Wyler, William .... July 1, 1902
Wyman, Jane .... Jan 14, 1914, Jan 24, 1940
Wynette, Tammy .... May 5, 1942
Wynn, Early .... Jan 6, 1920
Wynn, Ed .... Nov 9, 1886, June 12, 1922
Wyoming .... June 24, 1863, July 25, 1868, Dec 10, 1869, Mar 4, 1886, July 10, 1890, Feb 15, 1917, Jan 5, 1925, Oct 6, 1955
Wythe, George .... June 8, 1806

Yablonski, Joseph A. .... Jan 5, 1970
Yachting .... Aug 22, 1851, Sept 26, 1983
Yale, Elihu .... Apr 5, 1649
Yale, Linus .... Apr 4, 1821
Yale University .... Oct 9, 1700, Oct 16, 1701
Yalow, Rosalyn .... July 19, 1921
Yamasaki, Minoru .... Dec 1, 1912
Yancey, Jimmy .... Sept 17, 1951
Yang, Chen Ning .... Sept 22, 1922
Yarborough, Cale(b) .... Mar 27, 1939
Yarnell, Harry E. .... Oct 18, 1875
Yastrzemski, Carl .... Aug 22, 1939
Yates, Sterling .... May 6, 1843
Yawkey, Tom (Thomas A.) .... Jan 21, 1903
Yeager, Charles E. .... Feb 13, 1923, Oct 14, 1947
Yeager, Jeana .... Dec 23, 1986
Yellen, Jack .... July 6, 1892
Yerby, Frank G. .... Sept 5, 1916
Yerkes, Charles T. .... June 25, 1837
Yerkes, Robert M. .... May 26, 1876
Yeutter, Clayton .... Dec 14, 1988
York, Alvin C. .... Dec 13, 1887
Yost, Fielding H. .... Apr 30, 1871
Youmans, Vincent M. .... Sept 27, 1898
Young, Andrew .... Mar 12, 1932
Young, Brigham .... June 1, 1801, July 24, 1847, Sept 28, 1850, Sept 15, 1857, Oct 16, 1875
Young, Chic (Murat B.) .... Jan 9, 1901
Young, Cy (Denton T.) .... Mar 29, 1867
Young, Ella F. .... Jan 15, 1845
Young, John W. .... Sept 24, 1930, Apr 12, 1981
Young, Owen D. .... Oct 27, 1874
Young, Rida .... May 8, 1926
Young, Robert .... Feb 22, 1907
Young, Stark .... Oct 11, 1881
Young, Victor .... Aug 8, 1900
Young, Whitney M. Jr. .... July 31, 1921
Young Men's Christian Association (YMCA) .... June 7, 1854
Young Men's Hebrew Association (YMHA) .... Mar 22, 1874
Youngs, Ross .... Apr 10, 1897

Zaharias, Babe Didrikson .... Jan 26, 1914
Zangara, Giuseppe .... Feb 15, 1933
Zanuck, Darryl F. .... Sept 5, 1902
Zeckendorf, William .... June 30, 1905
Zellerbach, James D. .... Jan 17, 1892
Zenger, Peter .... Nov 5, 1733, Nov 17, 1734, Aug 4, 1735
Ziegfeld, Florenz .... Mar 21, 1869
Zinn, Walter H. .... Dec 10, 1906
Zinsser, Hans .... Nov 17, 1878
Zukor, Adolph .... Jan 7, 1873
Zwicky, Fritz .... Feb 15, 1898
Zworykin, Vladimir .... July 30, 1889, Jan 2, 1936